MW01621114

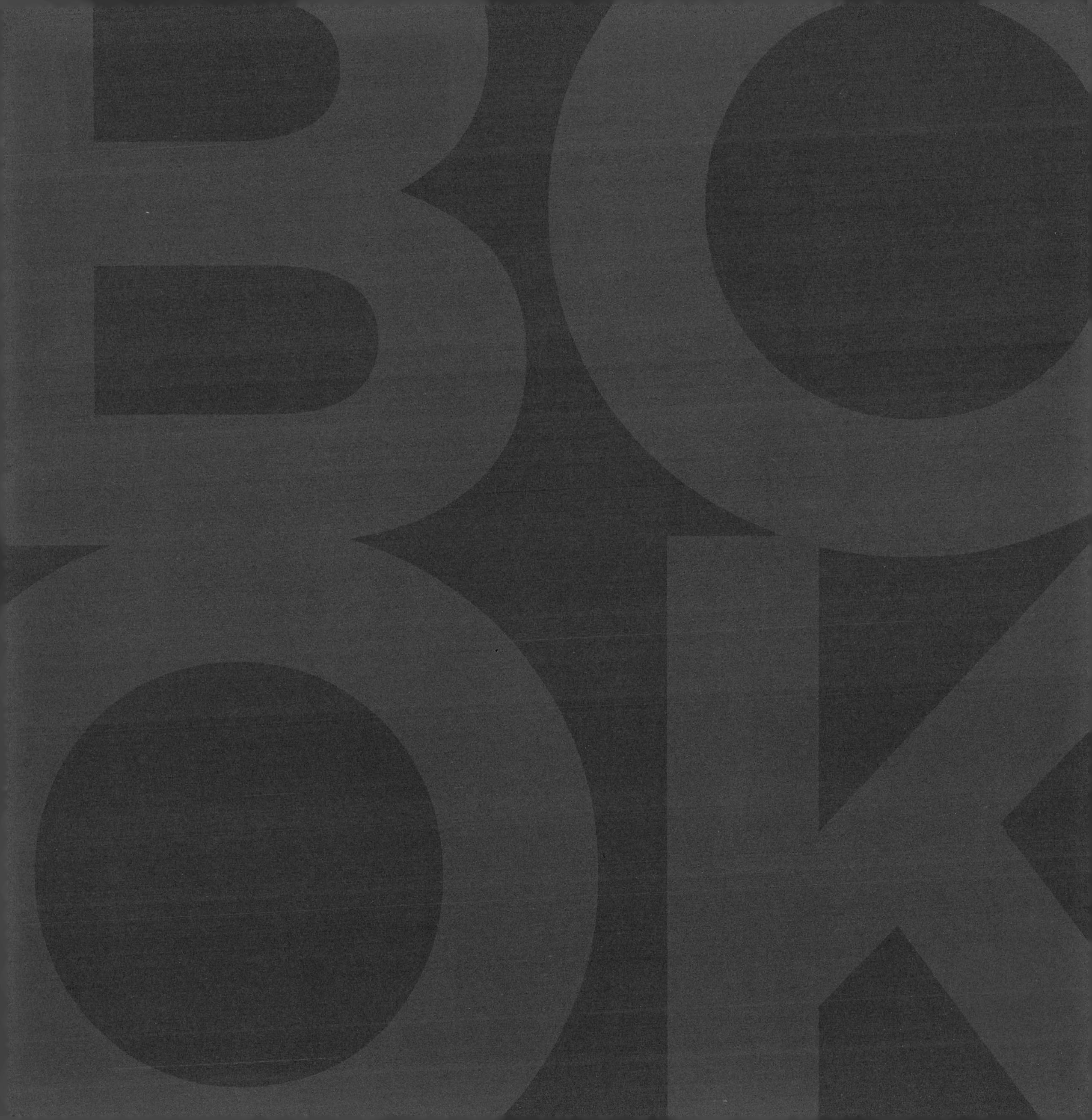
BO
OK

CHINA
ARTBOOK

中国当代艺术

中国当代艺术

UTA GROSENICK
CASPAR H. SCHÜBBE 出版人

咨询顾问 Amelie von Wedel

CHINA ARTBOOK

UTA GROSENICK
CASPAR H. SCHÜBBE Eds.

Amelie von Wedel worked as the art consultant
Beratung durch Amelie von Wedel

DUMONT

CONTENTS
INHALT
目录

PREFACE
VORWORT

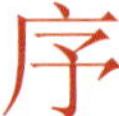

CHINA ART BOOK offers, for the first time, an independent selection of 80 of the most important contemporary Chinese artists. CHINA ART BOOK provides information on a wide range of those artists being currently in great demand, in China and all around the world, for exhibitions and publications, and so the book does not intend to present a certain collection of Chinese art or artists from one particular gallery.

Contemporary Chinese art has fascinated both art connoisseurs and the general public for some time. Thanks to the open-minded and liberal attitude of the Chinese government a vivid art scene could develop. The Chinese artists did not only clear the Western art beginning from Classical Modernity to most recent tendency in remarkable speed, but even soon created their own image spaces which oscillate between tradition and super-innovation in a fascinating way.

The Chinese art market is growing as rapidly as the Chinese economy and almost daily new commercial art galleries are established, especially in Beijing. Notwithstanding a row of the artists being presented by European and US galleries, the Chinese art trade follows its own rules. The demand of private collectors all over the world for works of contemporary artists is immense and the amounts paid for those works at auction are increasing steadily.

In the People's Republic of China the establishment of 1000 new museums is planned for the next ten years to come, exhibiting the art being created nowadays. On the international level a boom of exhibitions of current Chinese art is to be observed – there is no biennial without Chinese contemporary artists, and even the great museums between Seoul and Los Angeles have started, although inertly, to buy works of Chinese artists for their collections.

CHINA ART BOOK presents in three languages (English, German, and Chinese) the 80 most outstanding artists of the contemporary Chinese art scene, an informative text written by renowned writers about each artist's life and work together with comprehensive graphical material of

Mit CHINA ART BOOK liegt zum ersten Mal eine unabhängige Auswahl der 80 wichtigsten zeitgenössischen chinesischen Künstlerinnen und Künstler vor. Das Buch präsentiert dabei weder eine bestimmte Sammlung chinesischer Kunst noch den Fundus einzelner Galerien, sondern bietet eine breit angelegte Zusammenschau all derjenigen Künstler, die momentan in China selbst und weltweit in Ausstellungen und Publikationen sowie im Handel besonders gefragt sind.

Die aktuelle chinesische Kunst übt seit geraumer Zeit eine besondere Faszination auf alle aus, die sich beruflich oder privat mit Kunst befassen. Dank der Offenheit der chinesischen Regierung gegenüber der zeitgenössischen Kunst konnte im Reich der Mitte eine ungemein lebendige Kunstszene entstehen. Und in beachtlichem Tempo haben die chinesischen Künstler nicht nur die Kunst des Westens von der Klassischen Moderne bis zur jüngsten Avantgarde aufgearbeitet, sondern sich auch ihre eigenen Bildräume geschaffen, die faszinierend zwischen Tradition und Superinnovation oszillieren.

Ebenso rasant wie die chinesische Wirtschaft expandiert auch der chinesische Kunstmarkt, und fast täglich werden, vor allem in Peking, neue kommerzielle Galerien eröffnet. Obwohl inzwischen eine Reihe der Künstler auch von europäischen und US-amerikanischen Galerien vertreten wird, operiert der chinesische Kunsthandel doch nach seinen eigenen Gesetzen. Die Nachfrage von Privatsammlern aus aller Welt nach den Werken der zeitgenössischen Künstler Chinas ist immens, und die Summen, die in Auktionshäusern für sie gezahlt werden, wachsen stetig.

In der Volksrepublik werden in den nächsten zehn Jahren 1000 neue Museen gegründet, in denen dann vor allem jene Kunst zu sehen sein wird, die im Augenblick entsteht. Auf internationaler Ebene gibt es schon jetzt einen regelrechten Boom von Ausstellungen aktueller chinesischer Kunst – keine Biennale kommt mehr ohne sie aus, und mittlerweile kaufen die großen Museen zwischen Seoul und Los Angeles, wenn auch noch zögerlich, die ersten Arbeiten chinesischer Künstler für ihre Kollektionen.

CHINA ART BOOK 首次收录了80位最具影响力的中国当代艺术家。当前在中国和全球各地范围内展览和书籍的需求量非常大，因此 CHINA ART BOOK 提供这些艺术家的多方信息，也未打算提供某个画廊的某个中国艺术家或某个艺术的信息。

一定时间内，中国当代艺术既为专业艺术鉴赏家所痴迷，也受到一般公众的热衷。由于中国政府对艺术的开明和自由的态度，中国艺术界才欣欣向荣。中国艺术家们不但以非凡的速度掌握了古典现代到当前最新趋势的西方艺术，他们甚至用独特的方式创作了介于传统和超创新之间的形象空间。

伴随着中国经济的迅猛发展，中国艺术日新月异，每天几乎都有一个商业化画廊在中国成立，尤以北京为最。尽管本书收录了一些欧洲和美国画廊推荐的艺术家，但中国艺术交易仍遵循其自己的规则。全球私人收藏家对当代艺术家作品的需求里量巨大，而且拍卖会上的出价金额也不断稳步攀升。

在未来十年内，中华人民共和国境内预计将有1000多间新画廊成立，用来展示当代艺术家的作品。当今中国艺术已繁荣到国际水平-没有一个双年展上看不到中国当代艺术家的作品，甚至从韩国首尔到美国洛杉矶之间的许多著名博物馆也已开始购买中国艺术家的作品。

CHINA ART BOOK以英、德、中三种文字介绍中国当代艺术界中最杰出的80位艺术家。书中艺术家的生活及工作信息由著名作家撰文，并配有各个作品阶段翔实的图片资料以及重要展览和出版物的数据信息。在艺术家简介中，由艺术家肖像、艺术家的简短陈述以及艺术家姓名的发音标注组成。本书详细介绍性文章由Birgit Hopfener女士撰写，以深邃的眼光整体上介绍中国艺术界，同时对艾未未先生的访谈也是本书的重要内容。

我们在此向在CHINA ART BOOK项目中给我们提供策划和实施帮助的人士表示感谢：

all work stages, as well as data of main exhibitions and publications – a portrait of the artist and a short statement of the related artist as well as the phonetic writing of the name complete the description. The introductory detailed essay by Birgit Hopfener provides insight into the Chinese art scene in general, while the interview with the artist Ai Weiwei highlights the beginning thereof.

We want to thank those who supported us in the concept and realisation of this elaborate book project CHINA ART BOOK:

- *Firstly the artists, their managers and assistants, the galleries presenting them and their colleagues, followed by*

- *Amelie von Wedel and her team in London, Pei-fen Sung und Xiaolan Bi, providing the contact to the artists, supporting our request for graphical material, which could be done only in Chinese among many other tasks and who did their work with great enthusiasm,*

- *our authors Feng Boyi, Biljana Ciric, Birgit Hopfener, Wu Hung, Gregor Jansen, Carol Lu, Victoria Lu, Barbara Pollack, Karen Smith, David Spalding, Philip Tinari, and Qiu Zhijie, writing their texts with deep knowledge,*

- *the editor Ralph Henry Fischer, who being in charge of all texts did his work with utmost care coordinating all linguists and proofreaders,*

- *the designer Jonas Lundin, Stockholm, giving the book the unique layout as well as the graphic artists Birgit Haermeyer and Birgit Beyer realising this layout with utmost diligency,*

- *the team of the publisher DuMont at Cologne as Ina Bierwagen, Sabine Bleßmann, and Nora Karbach, contributing a lot of work to CHINA ART BOOK,*

and last but not least the publisher Marcel Hartges, who accompanied the project from the very beginning with great enthusiasm.

Uta Grosenick and Caspar H. Schübbe, Cologne and Verbier as of October 2007

CHINA ART BOOK präsentiert in drei Sprachen (Englisch, Deutsch und Chinesisch) die 80 renommiertesten Künstlerinnen und Künstler der zeitgenössischen chinesischen Kunstszene jeweils mit umfangreichem Bildmaterial aus allen Werkphasen, einem informativen Text von einem sachkundigen Autor zu Leben und Werk sowie den wichtigsten Ausstellungen und Publikationen – eine Porträtaufnahme und ein kurzes Statement des Künstlers sowie die phonetische Schreibung seines Namens runden den Eintrag ab. Ein ausführlicher einführender Bericht eröffnet zudem einen guten Einblick in die chinesische Kunstszene, während ein Interview mit dem wichtigen Pekinger Künstler Ai Weiwei ihre Anfänge beleuchtet.

Dank sagen möchten wir all denen, die uns bei der Konzeption und Umsetzung dieses aufwändigen Buchprojekts mit Rat und Tat unterstützt haben:

- Zunächst den Künstlerinnen und Künstlern, ihren Studiomanagern und Assistenten, den sie vertretenden Galerien und deren Mitarbeitern, sogleich gefolgt von

- Amelie von Wedel und ihrem Londoner Team, Pei-fen Sung und Xiaolan Bi, die uns die Kontakte zu den Künstlern vermittelten sowie sämtliche Anfragen nach Bildmaterial, die nur auf Chinesisch zu bewerkstelligen waren (und vieles andere mehr), mit großem Engagement erledigten,

- unseren Autoren Biljana Ciric, Feng Boyi, Birgit Hopfener, Gregor Jansen, Carol Lu, Victoria Lu, Barbara Pollack, Qiu Zhijie, Karen Smith, David Spalding, Philip Tinari und Wu Hung, die ihre Texte mit Begeisterung und profundem Wissen verfasst haben,

- dem Lektor Ralph Henry Fischer, der alle Texte mit höchster Sorgfalt betreut sowie alle Übersetzer und Redakteure koordiniert hat,

- dem Designer Jonas Lundin, der in Stockholm dem Buch sein unverwechselbares Layout gegeben hat, sowie den Grafikerinnen Birgit Haermeyer und Birgit Beyer, die es mit großer Genauigkeit umgesetzt haben,

- dem Team des Kölner DuMont Verlags Sabine Bleßmann, Ina Bierwagen und Nora Karbach, die tatkräftig an CHINA ART BOOK mitgearbeitet haben,

und last but not least dem Verleger Marcel Hartges, der das einzigartige Projekt von Anfang an mit großem Enthusiasmus begleitet hat.

Uta Grosenick und Caspar H. Schübbe,
Köln und Verbier im Oktober 2007

- 首先是艺术家，他们的经纪人和助手，推荐他们的画廊以及他们的同事，还有

- Amelie von Wedel 和其伦敦团队的 Pei-fen Sung 和 Xiaolan Bi，负责与艺术家的联系且协助我们搜集图片，他们在工作中付出了很大的热情。

- 本书作者冯博一，Biljana Ciric, Birgit Hopfener，巫鸿，Gregor Jansen，卢迎华（Carol Lu），Victoria Lu, Barbara Pollack, Karen Smith, 丁达韦（David Spalding），Philip Tinari 和邱志杰，以专业渊博的知识撰写了各自的文章，

- 编辑 Ralph Henry Fischer，负责全部文本的编辑工作，以最大的谨慎协调所有议员和校对。

- 设计 Jonas Lundin, Stockholm，为本书提供了独一无二的版面设计，绘图艺术家为完成版面尽职尽责。

- 科隆的DuMont 出版社团队如 Ina Bierwagen, Sabine Bleßmann和 Nora Karbach为本书的出版作出了大量工作。

最后但并非重要，我们感谢出版商 Marcel Hartges，他从项目开始就以极大的热情陪伴着我们。

Uta Grosenick 和Caspar H. Schübbe,
在科隆和维尔比耶
2007年10月

Uta Grosenick, Caspar H. Schübbe and DuMont Publisher thank the following persons, collections, and galleries for providing graphical material and information, without their generous support the realisation of this book could not have be done:

Gao Yuan, Ai Weiwei Studio
Alicia Lu, Cai Guo-Qiang Studio
Galerie Luis Campaña, Cologne
Maurizio Rigillo, Verusca Piazzesi
Galleria Continua, San Gimigniano/Beijing
Cui Xiuwen Studio
Liu Chang
Britta Färber, Julia Felshart, Sammlung Deutsche Bank
Isabelle Gay-Crosier
Bridget Donahue, Jessie Green, Barbara Gladstone Gallery, New York
Chang Tsong- Zung, Hanart TZ Gallery, Hong Kong
Grace Li Gallery, Zürich
Zsuzsa Cserhati, Livia Gnos, Galerie Urs Meile, Beijing/Luzern
Iris Scheffler, Keumhwa Kim, Alexander Ochs Galleries, Berlin/Beijing
Meg Maggio, Dang Rong, Pékin Fine Arts, Beijing
Nicolette Kwok, The Red Mansion Foundation, London
Philly Adams, Annabel Fallon, The Saatchi Gallery, London
Christa Schübbe
Chen Yan, Helen Zhu, Zhu Xiaozheng, ShanghART Gallery, Shanghai
Meng Fan, Shen Shaomin Studio
Marianne Heller, Rita Sager, Sigg Collection, Mauensee
Prof. Werner Spies
Ros Holmes, UniversalStudios, Beijing
Xiao Shen, Zhang Wei, Vitamin Creative Space, Guangzhou
Wang Junyi, Wang Guangyi Studio
Jesse Coffino-Greenberg, Xu Bing Studio
Astrid Gagnard, Yan Pei-Ming Studio
Liu Junming, Zeng Fanzhi Studio
Hu Jun Jun, Zhu Yun, Zhang Huan Studio, Zhao Hongyan

Uta Grosenick, Caspar H. Schübbe und der DuMont Verlag danken folgenden Personen, Sammlungen, Institutionen und Galerien für die großzügige Bereitstellung von Bildmaterial und Informationen, denn ohne ihre Unterstützung wäre es nicht möglich gewesen, dieses Buch in dieser Form und diesem Umfang zu realisieren:

Gao Yuan, Ai Weiwei Studio
Alicia Lu, Cai Guo-Qiang Studio
Galerie Luis Campaña, Köln
Maurizio Rigillo, Verusca Piazzesi
Galleria Continua, San Gimignano/Peking
Cui Xiuwen Studio
Liu Chang
Britta Färber, Julia Felshart, Sammlung Deutsche Bank
Isabelle Gay-Crosier
Bridget Donahue, Jessie Green, Barbara Gladstone Gallery, New York
Chang Tsong-Zung, Hanart TZ Gallery, Hongkong
Grace Li Gallery, Zürich
Zsuzsa Cserhati, Livia Gnos, Galerie Urs Meile, Peking/Luzern
Iris Scheffler, Keumhwa Kim, Alexander Ochs Galleries, Berlin/Peking
Meg Maggio, Dang Ron, Pékin Fine Arts, Peking
Nicolette Kwok, The Red Mansion Foundation, London
Philly Adams, Annabel Fallon, The Saatchi Gallery, London
Christa Schübbe
Chen Yan, Helen Zhu, Zhu Xiaozheng, ShanghART Gallery, Shanghai
Meng Fan, Shen Shaomin Studio
Marianne Heller, Rita Sager, Sigg Collection, Mauensee
Prof. Werner Spies
Ros Holmes, UniversalStudios, Peking
Xiao Shen, Zhang Wei, Vitamin Creative Space, Guangzhou
Wang Junyi, Wang Guangyi Studio
Jesse Coffino-Greenberg, Xu Bing Studio
Astrid Gagnard, Yan Pei-Ming Studio
Liu Junming, Zeng Fanzhi Studio
Hu Jun Jun, Zhu Yun, Zhang Huan Studio, Zhao Hongyan

Uta Grosenick 和Caspar H. Schübbe 及 DuMont出版社向为本书提供图片资料和信息的以下人士，收藏机构和画廊表示深深的谢意，没有他们慷慨的帮助，就不可能实现本书的出版：

艾未未工作室，Gao Yuan
蔡国强工作室，Alicia Lu
Luis Campaña画廊，科隆
常青画廊，圣吉米纳诺/北京，Maurizio Rigillo，Verusca Piazzesi
崔岫闻 工作室
刘畅
德意志银行艺术收藏，Britta Färber，Julia Felshart
Isabelle Gay-Crosier
巴巴拉. 格莱德斯通画廊, 纽约, Bridget Donahue, Jessie Green
汉雅轩，香港，Chang Tsong-Zung
Grace Li 画廊, 苏黎世
麦勒画廊, 卢塞恩，Zsuzsa Cserhati，Livia Gnos
Alexander Ochs Galleries, 柏林/北京，Iris Scheffler，Keumhwa Kim
Pékin Fine Arts，北京，Meg Maggio，Dang Rong
红楼基金会, 伦敦，Nicolette Kwok
Saatchi 画廊, 伦敦，Philly Adams，Annabel Fallon
Christa Schübbe
香格纳画廊, 上海, Chen Yan，Helen Zhu，Zhu Xiaozheng
沈少民工作室，孟凡，Sigg Collection，Mauensee，Marianne Heller；Rita Sager
Prof. Werner Spies
U空间，北京, Ros Holmes
Vitamin Creative Space，广州 Xiao Shen，Zhang Wei
王广义工作室, 王俊艺
徐冰工作室，Jesse Coffino-Greenberg
严培明工作室，Astrid Gagnard
曾梵志工作室, 刘华明
张洹工作室，胡军军, 赵鸿雁

（刘华明）

IN THE MIDDLE OF THE GOLDRUSH
MITTENDRIN IM GOLDRAUSCH
淘金热中期

BIRGIT HOPFENER

Chinese arts caught between commerce and ambition

It cannot be denied: Contemporary Chinese arts have left the backwaters and are now unanimously celebrated in the international art scene. You can also clearly see this on the world map for contemporary art. Following New York in the 1980s and Berlin in the 1990s Beijing is today one of the most exciting artistic centres in the world.
Starting with only five galleries for contemporary art at the beginning of the 1990s the number has risen to over 100 today and no end in sight. Everywhere in China institutions change and expand rapidly. For example, numerous private or publicly financed museums and project rooms opened in 2006, while at the same time the so called Residency-Programs were developed, which offers foreign artists the opportunity to work in China for some time. In Beijing, Shanghai and Guangzhou new art fairs attract more and more Chinese and international dealers, collectors and art lovers and even the world wide boom for biannual art festivals has reached the People's Republic. In short: The art scene is increasingly professional, internationally orientated and fascinates many people because of its thrillingly lively vibrancy.

Beijing and Shanghai are ideal to meet the crème de la crème of the international art crowd. Sooner or later Museum's directors, curators, critics and artists will become attracted by the positive and creative atmosphere, to see it with their own eyes and seek inspiration.

Once considered off-track and exotic, contemporary Chinese art has today gained the peak of attention and esteem. There are also financial reasons – at auctions of Sotheby's and Christie's in New York contemporary Chinese paintings in particular achieved top prices in 2006; and there is even a discussion as to whether these prices really reflect the quality of the works of art or whether this is just a case of a short-term boom caused by China's rapid economic growth.

Another point: While established art circles in western countries (still) work along quite fixed institutional structures which more or less clearly define the roles and scope of the

Der chinesische Kunstbetrieb zwischen Kommerz und Anspruch

Es ist unabweisbar: Die zeitgenössische chinesische Kunst hat ihre langjährige Außenseiterposition verlassen und wird nun von der internationalen Kunstwelt nahezu einhellig gefeiert. Dies macht sich auch auf der Weltkarte der Gegenwartskunst bemerkbar: Nach New York in den 1980er und Berlin in den 1990er Jahren gilt heute Peking als eine der spannendsten Kunstmetropolen überhaupt. Gab es dort zu Beginn der 1990er Jahre gerade einmal fünf Galerien mit zeitgenössischer Kunst, so sind es heute über 100, und landesweit expandiert und verändert sich die institutionelle Landschaft rapide. So eröffneten im Jahr 2006 zahlreiche privat oder öffentlich finanzierte Museen und Projekträume, gleichzeitig wurden viele sogenannte Residency-Programme entwickelt, die ausländischen Künstlern die Möglichkeit bieten, eine Zeit lang in China zu arbeiten. In Peking, Shanghai und Guangzhou ziehen junge Kunstmessen mehr und mehr chinesische und internationale Händler, Sammler und Interessierte an, und auch der weltweite Biennalenboom hat mittlerweile in der Volksrepublik Einzug gehalten. Kurz: Die Szene gewinnt zunehmend an Professionalität und Internationalität und zieht aufgrund ihrer erregend quirligen Lebendigkeit viele in ihren Bann. Will man die Crème de la crème der internationalen Artcrowd treffen, dann sind Peking und Shanghai ideale Reiseziele, denn magisch angezogen von der kreativen Atmosphäre kommen früher oder später alle hierher, um sich nachhaltig inspirieren zu lassen: Museumsdirektoren, Kuratoren, Galeristen, Kritiker und Künstler. Ehedem als peripher und exotisch abgetan, erfährt die zeitgenössische chinesische Kunst heute höchste Aufmerksamkeit und Wertschätzung. Dies hat nicht zuletzt ökonomische Gründe – auf den Auktionen der großen Auktionshäuser Sotheby's und Christie's in New York erzielte 2006 besonders die aktuelle chinesische Malerei Höchstpreise; und schon wird diskutiert, ob die hohen Preise der Qualität der Kunstwerke tatsächlich angemessen sind oder ob es sich nicht bloß um eine kurzlebige Hausse handelt, die sich schlicht aus dem rasanten chinesischen Wirtschaftswachstum erklärt. Hinzu kommt: Im Unterschied zur etablierten westlichen Kunstszene, wo man sich (noch)

中国艺术在商业利益和志向两者之间挣扎

不可否认：当代中国艺术已改往日的一潭死水，如今一致在国际艺术界上亮相。我们也可从当代艺术的世界地图上清楚地看到这点，继上世纪80年代的纽约和90年代的柏林之后，今天北京成为最具活力的全球艺术中心之一。当代艺术画廊的数量从上世纪90年代仅有的五个，现在上升到100多个，前景不可估量，中国各地的机构纷纷改变性质并迅速地扩大规模。例如，在2006年就有为数众多的私有或者公有博物馆和展馆成立，与此同时所谓的居民计划也开始实施，这个计划是为外籍艺术家在中国提供一定时期的工作机会。在北京，上海和广州，新艺术展会吸引越来越多的中外交易商，收藏家和艺术爱好者，甚至全球范围的双年艺术节也登陆中国。总而言之，当代中国艺术界不断向专业化，以国际为导向发展，其勃勃生机而强烈地吸引着许多人。

北京和上海是国际杰出艺术人士最理想的的城市。迟早博物馆的馆长，策展人，评论家和艺术家将会被这里的积极创造性的氛围所吸引，用他们自己的视角去审视并从中发掘灵感。当代中国艺术曾经被视为偏远的异国情调的艺术，而如今获得最大程度的关注和尊重。其中也有资金因素的存在--特别是在纽约苏士比，嘉士德　拍卖上，当代中国的绘画摘得　2006年最高价；甚至有人争论，如是否价格能真正地反映艺术作品的质量；是否这仅仅是因为中国快速经济增长而引起的昙花一现

另一种观点：西方国家建立艺术圈，并以一种相对固定的机构性结构运行着，或多或少明晰地定义了参与艺术人群的角色和范围，而在中国这种情况很令人困惑，中国才刚刚开始发展组织化结构。当然，可信的艺术评估工具的缺失是蔓延的艺术市场症结。另一方面，当代中国艺术界具有吸引力正是因为具有更大范围的发展和创造力的无结构的混乱形式：一种表面上繁荣舞台布景下几乎所有的东西都在流动，很多事情都有可能实现。

people involved, the situation in China is most confusing and is only beginning to develop organisational structures. Of course, the lack of reliable instruments for art evaluation can be problematic for this rampant art market. On the other hand China's contemporary art scene appeals because of this very situation of pre-structural chaos with lots of scope for development and creativity: a thriving and seemingly anarchic scenery where nearly everything is moving and many things are possible.

A short history of contemporary Chinese art

Because of the need for catching up with the modern and post-modern developments in western art, contemporary Chinese art has developed rapidly since its beginnings shortly after the country opened up in 1979 and the complex reception of western art and theory at the same time is characteristic for this development.

If the first avant-garde group of artists The Stars at the end of the 1970s and the beginning of the 1980s, which was closely connected to the democratic movement of the time, still worked with the traditional paintings and sculptures (where they mostly recapped 19th and 20th century art), the so-called 85th-movement in the middle of the 1980s already covered the whole range of modern and post-modern art and, leaving traditional genres behind, started to experiment with contemporary methods of artistic expression.

The 85th-movement reached its peak and also its end with the exhibition 'China-Avantgarde' which opened in February 1989 after many discussions and fights with officials in the sacred rooms of the National Gallery in Beijing. In the tense political situation, where freedom of expression was frowned upon, everybody was very nervous and the exhibition closed a few hours after opening. The official reason being a performance by the artist Xiao Lu who shot twice at her installation "Dialogue" which was interpreted as a subversive activity. And after the massacre of Tian'anmen in June the same year not only the student's democratic movement but also the idealistic 85th-movement broke off. Many artists emmigrated or sought safety by retiring from public life.

Before this incident, artists believed that society was changing and tried to win the public for their projects, the 1990s however are generally characterised by public withdrawal and a focus on personal and individual subjects. There were hardly any exhibitions in public places in the 1990s partly because of national censorship but also for financial reasons because renting large exhibition space was very expensive. So they organised small, often experimental shows in the western Open-Studio-Style in private flats or with the help of expats in China; sometimes even in embassy buildings. So while contemporary Chinese art was hardly noticed by people in China itself Chinese artists increasingly displayed their works at international exhibitions abroad since 1993, for example at the Biannuals in Venice and São Paulo or the Documenta in Kassel (Germany): here they were welcomed with open arms by the increasingly fascinated public.

in recht eindeutigen institutionellen Strukturen bewegt, die die Handlungsspielräume und Rollen der Akteure mehr oder weniger klar definieren, ist die chinesische Situation äußerst unübersichtlich und entwickelt erst in Ansätzen eine gewisse Ordnungsstruktur. Sicher ist für diesen wild wuchernden Kunstmarkt nicht unproblematisch, dass die Kunstproduktion noch verlässlicher Evaluierungsinstrumente entbehrt. Andererseits liegt der besondere Reiz in China heute gerade in diesem vorstrukturellen Chaos zahlloser Freiräume, die ein hohes Maß an Kreativität fördern: eine anarchisch anmutende Landschaft, in der beinahe alles offen und vieles möglich ist.

Die jüngste chinesische Kunst im Zeitraffer

Resultierend aus dem starken Bedürfnis, möglichst schnell nach- und aufzuholen, was westliche Moderne und Postmoderne vorgaben, ist die zeitgenössische chinesische Kunst seit ihren Anfängen kurz nach der Öffnung des Landes 1979 durch ein enormes Entwicklungstempo und eine komplexe Gleichzeitigkeit bei der Rezeption westlicher Kunst und Kunsttheorie geprägt. Arbeitete die erste Avantgarde-Künstlergruppe „Die Sterne", die im engen Zusammenhang mit der damaligen Demokratiebewegung stand, Ende der 1970er, Anfang der 1980er Jahre noch in den traditionellen Medien Malerei und Skulptur (wobei sie sich insbesondere mit der westlichen Kunst des 19. und frühen 20. Jahrhunderts auseinandersetzte), rezipierte die sogenannte 85er Bewegung Mitte der 1980er Jahre bereits die gesamte Entwicklung der modernen und postmodernen Kunst und löste sich dabei rasch von den traditionellen Gattungen, um mit zeitgenössischen Ausdrucksmitteln zu experimentieren. Ihren Höhe- und gleichzeitigen Endpunkt erreichte die 85er Bewegung in der Ausstellung „China-Avantgarde", die im Februar 1989, nach vielen Diskussionen mit den offiziellen Stellen, schwer erkämpft in den heiligen Hallen der staatlichen Nationalgalerie in Peking stattfand. Durch die angespannte politische Situation, die eine freie Meinungsäußerung nur sehr begrenzt zuließ, war die Stimmung äußerst nervös, und die Ausstellung wurde schon wenige Stunden nach der Eröffnung geschlossen – offiziell wegen eines als subversiv eingestuften performativen Aktes der Künstlerin Xiao Lu, die zwei Schüsse auf ihre Installation „Dialog" abfeuerte. Und nach der Auflösung der studentischen Demokratiebewegung im Juni desselben Jahres war auch das Ende der idealistischen 85er Bewegung gekommen. Viele Künstler emigrierten ins Ausland oder zogen sich in den Schutz des Privaten zurück. Hatte man bis zu dieser Zäsur an große gesellschaftliche Veränderungen geglaubt und die Öffentlichkeit gesucht, um die Gesellschaft für die eigenen Projekte zu begeistern, so waren die 1990er Jahre generell durch einen Rückzug ins Private und die Beschäftigung mit persönlichen und individuellen Fragen gekennzeichnet. Aufgrund der staatlichen Zensur, aber auch aus profanen finanziellen Gründen fanden Ausstellungen in öffentlichen Räumen in den 1990er Jahren kaum mehr statt, denn das Anmieten von großen Ausstellungsflächen war sehr teuer. Stattdessen organisierte man nun kleine, oft experimentelle Schauen in westlicher Open-Studio-Manier in Privatwohnungen oder mit Unterstützung in China ansässiger Ausländer auch in Botschaftsgebäuden. Während also die

当代中国艺术的短暂历史

由于追赶西方艺术现代和后现代发展的需要，自1979年改革开放不久以后开始，当代中国艺术已经迅速发展，这种发展是对西方艺术和理论的复杂接受发展为特征的。

如果中国第一个先锋派艺术家团体星星画会出现在上世纪70年末期80年代初期，（星星画会紧密地与同时期的民主运动相连，仍以传统绘画和雕塑方式创作。他们大多翻新19世纪和20世纪的艺术形式），那么所谓的80年代中期的85美术运动早就覆盖现代和后现代艺术所有范围，领先传统的艺术形式，而开始体验当代艺术表现手法了。

在与官方的争论和斗争之后，1989年二月，中国当代艺术展，　在北京全国美术馆一间庄重的展室里展出，85美术运动达到其顶峰同时也是其结局。在紧张的政治形势下言论自由不受官方欢迎，人人神情紧张，展出在开始后的数小时后被关闭。官方的理由是因为艺术家肖鲁　朝其装置《对话》射击两次，这一行为被认为是破坏性行为。在同年的天安门事件之后，不但学生民主运动而且连理想主义的85美术运动也被迫中止，许多艺术家移居海外或是退出公众生活以保人身安全

在天安门事件之前，艺术家相信社会正在改变，并努力以作品赢得社会的关注，然而90年代总体上是以社会退步为特征，集中于私人和个体主体上。在90年代，在公共场所几乎没有任何艺术展览举行，部分由于国家的审查制度，另外也由于资金因素因为承租大型展出场地费用非常昂贵。所以艺术家以西方开放工作室的形式策划小规模通常是试验性展出，这些展出在私人公寓内或是在移居中帮助下举行，有时甚至在大使馆的建筑里。在当代中国艺术很难被中国民众注意的时候，自1993年中国艺术家逐增地在海外的国际艺术展出中展示自己的作品，如在威尼斯双年展和圣保罗双年展和卡塞尔文献展，在那里他们受到越来越多的痴迷公众的欢迎。

在2000年，上海双年展尤其是由艾未未，冯博一策划的策划的展出《不合作的方式》很快出名，标志着发展的变化，有助于增长中国本土展出数量而且促使更多公众关注当代艺术。2002年第一次在广州举办的三年展是中国以及海外现代艺术发展之路又一个里程碑，展出由著名策展人和历史学家巫鸿　策划，回顾了1990到2000年的中国艺术发展历程。

从上世纪80年代初期，中国艺术家似乎才意识到他们的目标：通过他们的作品从公众甚至中国本土公众中发现不断增长的利益。然而许多艺术家，策展人评论家，以及观众批判这种积极的反映大多归结于艺术市场的繁荣和经济因素而非批评和学术上的观察。也许有人早已想到1989年由肖鲁　创作的装置《对话》（作品同时也引发一场激烈的政治事件）总有一天会卖到200，000美元，这在2006年秋天由中国嘉德拍卖行举行的的拍卖会上实现了。

In 2000, The Shanghai-Biannual and in particular the scandalous show 'Fuck Off' organised by Ai Weiwei and Feng Boyi shot to fame – marking a change in this development and helped to increase exhibitions in China itself and to draw more public attention to contemporary art. Taking place for the first time in 2002 the Guangzhou-Triannual was another milestone on the way of contemporary Chinese art in the People's Republic and abroad, it was organised by the famous curator and art historian Wu Hung and gave a review of Chinese art from 1990 to 2000.

The aim of Chinese artists since the beginning of the 1980's seems to have been realised, with their work finding increasing interest from the public even in China itself. However, many artists, curators, critics and observers complain that this positive reception is mostly due to the boom in the art market and economic factors and not because of critical and academic examination. Who would have thought in 1989 that the installation "Dialogue" by Xiao Lu which we have already mentioned – which turned into a hot political issue at the time – would one day sell for $200,000 as happened at the 2006 autumn action of the Chinese auction house 'Guardian' in Beijing.

Art as an investment – Decorating social advancement

Quite a lot of Chinese have profited immensly by the economic reforms of the last couple of years and by successful "socialistic market economy"; this even led to the development of middle and upper classes. And after buying houses and cars the members of these new wealthy social classes are quite ready to spend their money on art both for refinement and as a cultural boost to their social status – which has always been the custom in China. Until recently people mostly invested in traditional art, believing that this would prove to be a safe investment, but a shortage on the antique market because of the great demand and a growing number of forgeries made the Chinese nouveau-riche turn their interest towards modern art. This shift in interest was also motivated by the high prices which especially Chinese cynical realistic paintings 'Political Pop' achieved abroad – for example, the painting "Bloodline Series" by Zhang Xiaogang (1998) whose painting "Bloodline Series: Three Comrades" changed hands in March 2007 at Sotheby's in New York for 2,112,000 US dollars. This also attracts speculators as financially strong buyers of Chinese art deal with expensive works of art as they would deal with shares to raise the prices. They are hardly interested in playing the responsible part of a real collector who would also support the artist.

Mechanism of the art markets

The art market in China does not work in the way we are used to from here. Galleries only play a minor part compared to in the western hemisphere. Artists rarely grant galleries exclusive rights to their works. Hoping to make a fast buck artists often sell their own works in their studios or with the help of curators or agents. Artists are slow to understand and are just beginning to realise that selling directly can

zeitgenössische chinesische Kunst im eigenen Land von der Öffentlichkeit so gut wie gar nicht wahrgenommen wurde, nahmen chinesische Künstler seit 1993 vermehrt an internationalen Ausstellungen im Ausland teil, etwa an den Biennalen in Venedig und São Paulo oder an der Documenta in Kassel. Dort trafen sie auf ein zunehmend interessiertes Publikum. Die Shanghai-Biennale im Jahr 2000, vor allem aber die zahlreichen Satellitenshows – am berühmtesten wurde die von Ai Weiwei und Feng Boyi kuratierte Skandalschau „Fuck Off" – leiteten dann einen nachhaltigen Wandel ein und trugen dazu bei, dass Ausstellungsaktivitäten auch in China selbst wieder zunahmen und die zeitgenössische Kunst in der Öffentlichkeit stärkere Aufmerksamkeit erfuhr. Ein weiterer bedeutsamer Meilenstein zur Durchsetzung der zeitgenössischen chinesischen Kunst in der Volksrepublik selbst, aber auch über die Landesgrenzen hinaus, war die 2002 erstmals stattfindende Guangzhou-Triennale, die von dem renommierten Kurator und Kunsthistoriker Wu Hung betreut wurde und einen Überblick über die chinesische Kunst von 1990 bis 2000 bot. Was die chinesischen Künstler seit Beginn der 1980er Jahre anstrebten, scheint heute wahr geworden zu sein – ihre Kunst findet auch in China selbst eine ständig wachsende Öffentlichkeit. Viele Künstler, Kuratoren, Kritiker und Beobachter beklagen allerdings, dass diese zunächst erfreulich erscheinende Rezeption sich in erster Linie dem boomenden Kunstmarkt und ökonomischen Faktoren verdankt und weniger einer kritischen oder akademischen Auseinandersetzung. Wer hätte etwa 1989 schon vermutet, dass die erwähnte Installation „Dialog" der Künstlerin Xiao Lu – damals ein brisantes Politikum – einmal für 200.000 US-Dollar über den Tisch gehen würde? So geschehen bei der Herbstauktion des chinesischen Auktionshauses Guardian 2006 in Peking.

Kunst als Investition und Dekoration für den Aufstieg

Relativ viele Chinesen haben in den vergangenen Jahren von den wirtschaftlichen Reformen und der so erfolgreichen „sozialistischen Marktwirtschaft" profitiert; es entwickelte sich eine regelrechte Mittel- und Oberschicht. Und nach dem Erwerb von Häusern und Autos sind Angehörige dieser neuen Wohlstandsschichten heute zunehmend bereit, ihr Geld auch in Kunst anzulegen, gleichsam als Veredelung und kulturelle Erhöhung ihres gesellschaftlichen Status – ein in China seit jeher übliches Vorgehen. Investierte man bis vor kurzem hauptsächlich noch in traditionelle Kunst, weil man annahm, auf diese Weise eine sichere Anlage zu tätigen, führten die baldige Knappheit am Antiquitätenmarkt sowie das hohe Aufkommen an gefälschten Objekten bei neureichen Chinesen zu einem verstärkten Interesse für die moderne Kunst. Äußerst motivierend für solches Engagement sind natürlich die hohen Preise, die insbesondere die chinesische Malerei des Zynischen Realismus und des Political Pop im Ausland erzielt – beispielhaft sei hier Zhang Xiaogangs „Bloodline Series" genannt: Das Bild „Bloodline: Three Comrades" wechselte im März 2007 bei Sotheby's in New York für 2.112.000 US-Dollar den Besitzer. Unter den finanziell häufig sehr potenten Käufern chinesischer Kunst befinden sich viele Spekulanten, die teure Arbeiten wie Aktien handeln, um die Preise weiter in die Höhe zu treiben. Mit der verantwortungsvollen Rolle eines echten Sammlers,

艺术是一种投资---修饰社会的进步

非常多中国人从过去几年的经济改革和成功的社会主义市场经济中受益非浅，甚至导致了中产和上层阶级的发生了变化。在购房买车以后这些新贵阶层的确准备在购置艺术品，一方面是高雅的需要，另一方面在文化上提高他们的社会地位。这早已经是中国的一种习惯。直至最近，人们大多投资于传统艺术品，他们相信这是一种安全的投资方式。但是由于巨大需求以及大量的赝品导致古董市场的短缺。从而促使新贵阶层把兴趣投向现代艺术品。利益的转变也是受艺术品的高价格所驱动，特别是中国愤世嫉俗写实主义油画《政治波普》在海外所取得高价格。例如，《血脉系列：三人同志》张晓刚（1998）于2007年三月在纽约苏士比拍卖会以2,112,000美圆的价格转手交易，这也吸引投机商如财力雄厚的中国艺术品买家交易昂贵的艺术品，因为其可以从提高价格中获取收益。这些投机商人没有兴趣扮演真正收藏家的负责角色，真正的收藏家同时会资助艺术家。

艺术品市场的运行机制

中国的艺术品市场　　并非象我们这里模式运转，与西方世界相比，画廊起到很小的作用。艺术家很少授予画廊其作品的全部权利。为了快速赚钱，艺术家常常在他们的工作室里或是通过策展人，经纪人交易他们的作品。他们现在慢慢地领会到并刚刚开始意识到：在长期内直接交易会损害他们的艺术生涯；在长期内通过画廊的专业代理会获得资金和艺术上的双重利益。

由此在2006年我们看到中国本土画廊数量强劲上升，这可能受到中国新贵阶层对当代艺术品不断增长的利益的影响。与此同时，中国本土拍卖行也设立当代中国艺术品专门部门。例如，上文提到的中国嘉德拍卖行于2006年12月举办《中国当代艺术20年》专场拍卖会，特别是85美术运动的作品具有亮点。作品被海外富豪所购买，但更为重要的是被中国本土的买家所购买。

在中国艺术品市场里，拍卖行的作用超出其他形式的范围。因为在中国拍卖行没有可信的信息资源以及缺乏当代艺术质量和价值讨论平台，拍卖不仅在决定艺术品的货币价值起很大作用，同时在提升作品的艺术品位也扮演主要角色。这是与西方真正不同的地方，在西方收藏家常常通过画廊重视专家的建议，宁愿在一手市场购买艺术品而非二手市场。

新兴收藏家

除艺术品投机商之外，真正中国的当代艺术品收藏家的数量也在增长，最著名的当数北京的管毅。今天像他一样的许多收藏家在过去和与上世纪的学生运动紧密联系，他们有些人的朋友甚至在艺术界，这些收藏家与艺术家一起分享1989年天安门抗议运动终止的悲怆回忆。与那些把艺术品作为财产或是

harm their career in the long run and that professional representation through an art gallery has both financial and artistic advantages in the long run.
As a result 2006 – possibly in reaction of the increasing interest in contemporary Chinese art by China's nouveau-riche – saw a strong increase in local galleries. And local auction houses also set up sections specialising in contemporary Chinese art. For example the auction house 'Guardian' mentioned earlier in the text, held an auction in Beijing named '20 years of Contemporary Chinese Art' in November 2006 with several highlights of the 85th-movement in particular, which were bought by affluent buyers from abroad but above all by buyers from the People's Republic itself.

The power of auction houses on the Chinese art market is out of scale with everything else. Because there are still no reliable sources of information and platforms for discussion on subjects of quality and value of contemporary art in China, auctions play a major part not only in deciding the monetary value of a work of art but also in developing the general taste in art. This is the real difference to the west where collectors usually value expert advice through galleries and would rather buy art works on the so-called primary market than on the secondary market.

New Collectors

Apart from art seculators the number of serious collectors of contemporary art in China is also growing – the best known example is surely Guan Yi in Beijing. Like him many serious collectors today were at the time closely connected to the student movement of the 1980s, same of them even then had friends in the art scene and share their traumatic memories of the break down of the protests on Tian'anmen-Square in 1989. In contrast to collectors from the nouveau-riche who buy art as assets or to decorate their apartments, Guan Yi and other collectors like him are more interested in the „difficult" conceptional art, in installations and video works. Guan Yi's collection which contains numerous large installations by Huang Yongping, Ai Weiwei and Gu Dexin can be seen by appointment in a warehouse in Songzhuang, one of Beijing's artists' quarters in the east of the town. Guan Yi's support of contemporary art is on a large scale and strong – he presents western art theory and artists to the Chinese public in series, which he publishes together with the philosopher Wang Minan and with the help of Guangdong's museum of art. He is also planning a professionally operating museum for his collection which would exhibit both Chinese and foreign art.

Moving towards a fixed infrastructure

China is quite ready to develop an infrastructure for contemporary art. Building museums is of great cultural, educational and political interest in this regard, and by 2008, the year of the Olympic Games in Beijing, several thousand private and public museums shall be built all over the country. There is already a large demand for private and public exhibition rooms, however, the over-emphasis on the financial question, and defects in quality of exhibitions due to a

der auch interessiert ist, den Werdegang eines Künstlers zu fördern, haben sie nichts im Sinn.

Mechanismen des Kunstmarkts

Der Kunstmarkt in China funktioniert keineswegs so wie im Westen: Galerien spielen hier eine untergeordnete Rolle. Kaum ein Künstler übergibt einer Galerie die Exklusivrechte seiner Arbeiten. Verführt vom schnellen Geld, werden Verkäufe stattdessen häufig in den Ateliers durch die Künstler selbst oder mit Hilfe von Kuratoren oder Agenten getätigt. Erst langsam entwickelt sich bei den Künstlern das Bewusstsein, dass solcher Direktverkauf längerfristig karriereschädigend sein kann und die professionelle Vertretung durch eine Galerie sowohl finanziell als auch künstlerisch eine größere Nachhaltigkeit ermöglicht. So war im Jahr 2006 ein starker Zuwachs an Galerien zu beobachten. Und auch lokale Auktionshäuser haben Abteilungen eingerichtet, die sich auf zeitgenössische chinesische Kunst spezialisieren. Ein Beispiel ist das bereits erwähnte Haus Guardian, das im November 2006 in Peking eine Auktion unter dem Titel „20 Jahre Zeitgenössische Chinesische Kunst" durchführte und zahlreiche Highlights insbesondere der 85er Bewegung im Angebot hatte, die von zahlungskräftigen Käufern aus dem Ausland, vor allem aber aus der Volksrepublik selbst, ersteigert wurden. Die Macht der Auktionshäuser im Gefüge des Kunstmarkts ist in China unverhältnismäßig groß. Da es im Land selbst bisher kaum verlässliche Informationsquellen und Plattformen des Austauschs zu Qualität und Wert der zeitgenössischen Kunst gibt, spielen Auktionen nicht nur bei der Bestimmung pekuniärer Werte, sondern auch bei der Ausbildung des Kunstgeschmacks eine maßgebliche Rolle. Dies ist ein großer Unterschied zum Westen, wo der Sammler in der Regel die persönliche Beratung in einer Galerie schätzt und den Erwerb eines Kunstwerks auf dem Primärmarkt dem Zweitmarkt vorzieht.

Neue Sammler

Neben den Kunstspekulanten steigt in China aber auch die Zahl ernst zu nehmender Sammler von zeitgenössischer Kunst – der berühmteste ist wohl der in Peking ansässige Guan Yi. Viele dieser Sammler standen der Studentenbewegung der 1980er Jahre nahe, einige waren schon damals mit Akteuren aus der Kunstszene befreundet und teilen mit ihnen die traumatische Erinnerung an die Niederschlagung der Proteste auf dem Platz des Himmlischen Friedens 1989. Im Unterschied zu den neureichen Sammlern, die Kunst in erster Linie als Anlage erwerben oder um ihre Wohnungen zu dekorieren, interessieren sich Sammler wie Guan Yi für die „schwierigere" Konzeptkunst, für Installationen und Video-Arbeiten. Die Sammlung Guan Yis, die u. a. zahlreiche große Installationen der Künstler Huang Yongping, Ai Weiwei und Gu Dexin umfasst, ist in Songzhuang, einem Kunstviertel im Osten Pekings, in einem Lagerhaus untergebracht und kann dort nach Vereinbarung besichtigt werden. Guan Yis Engagement für die zeitgenössische Kunst ist groß und überzeugend – er macht nicht nur in einer Publikationsreihe, die er mit dem Philosophen Wang Minan und mit Unterstützung des Guangdonger Kunstmuseums herausgibt,

当作装饰品的新贵收藏家相比，管毅和与他相似的收藏家，对那些很难懂的观念性艺术品，装置作品和录相作品更感兴趣。管毅　的收藏中有大量的黄永砯，艾未未和　顾德新的装置作品，作品陈列在宋庄的一座仓库里，宋庄是位于北京东部的艺术家聚集区。管毅在很大程度并且强有力对当代艺术进行资助。他按系列把西方理论和艺术家呈现给中国公众。在广东博物馆的帮助下，与哲学家汪民安一起出版了这套作品。他还正计划为其收藏品筹建一个专业运作的博物馆，以展出其中外艺术品。

向固定的基础设施发展

中国的确在准备为当代艺术发展基础设施。兴建博物馆具有巨大的文化，教育和政治利益的考虑，到2008年北京奥运会，将会有数千个私有和公有博物馆在中国建立。虽然早有对私有和公有博物馆的大量需求，然而过于强调资金问题以及由于缺乏合格策展人，学者而忽视展出质量也是症结所在。因为预算紧张，许多机构被迫对外租借其展室，最典型的例子是2003年在上海开馆的第一个当代艺术博物馆上海多伦现代美术馆。许多公有或者半公有博物馆从资金角度而非策展人的角度去设计展出。

一座新建的当代艺术博物馆计划在2007年9月开馆，该馆更强调博物馆的教育性性质。博物馆位于798艺术园区，前址是位于北京大山子的一座工厂，国际媒体曾经报道过大山子艺术区。该馆由比利时尤伦斯基金会出资建造，尤伦斯基金会是欧洲拥有最多和最重要当代艺术品的基金会之一，紧次于瑞士的Ulli　Sigg。博物馆由中国艺术历史学家和策展人　费大为　担任馆长，被设计为不但具有展览功能而具有图书馆功能以及以机敏的观念呈现给北京市民。

仅仅在3年以前，地方当局还计划为新兴产业让步而推倒这片区域。危险避免了，如今许多国际性和本土画廊以及艺术家工作室落户在798艺术园区，自2004年起，一年一度的由黄锐和其合作人黎静策划的大山子国际艺术节也在此举行。由于官方管理机构认识到798艺术园区经济潜力，把它当作文化产业进行商业化运行，因此这片区域面临失去本身特征的危险。
在北京，798艺术园区并不是唯一艺术和文化集中的区域，其他艺术家聚集区也在北京各地成长壮大，例如位于草场地东北的艺术东区，在那里坐落着布尔思和皮力U空间，艾未未的中国艺术文件仓库　和瑞士卢塞恩Urs Meile画廊等。位于望京北湖渠酒厂艺术园的韩国阿拉里奥画廊也以其与博物馆同一水平的展出而著名。在上海的莫干山路，也称M50，性质与北京的798艺术园区类似，也是一个艺术文化中心。

双年展和三年展

艺术双年展在北京秋季和上海轮流展出，北京双年展更多的保守性，不接受如装置作品和录相作品等

lack of qualified curators and scholars can be problematic. Many institutions are forced to rent out their rooms because their budgets prove insufficient – a typical example being the first museum for contemporary art 'Duolun' which opened in 2003 in Shanghai. Many public or semi-public museums design their exhibitions from a financial point of view rather than from a curator's point of view.

A new museum for contemporary art is planned to open in September 2007 with greater emphasis on the museum's educational qualities in the Artist's Quarter 798, a former factory site in Beijing's district Dashanzi which is well published in the international media. This museum was initiated by the Belgian foundation Guy and Myriam Ullens which owns one of the largest and most important collections of contemporary art in Europe next to Ulli Sigg from Switzerland. With the Chinese art historian and curator Fei Dawei as director, this museum is designed to offer not only exhibitions but also a library and a clever concept of presentation to Beijing's citizens.
Only three years ago the local authorities planed to pull down the area to make way for new industries. The danger could be averted and the Artist's Quarter 798 is today home to many international and local galleries and artists' workshops and since 2004 to the annual Dashanzi's Art Festival under the direction of Huang Rui and his partner Berenice Angremy. The quarter now faces new danger of losing its identity as the official administration corporation has realised 798's economic potentials and is strongly pushing its commercialisation as cultural industry. But 798 is not the only area in Beijing with a concentration of art and culture, other artist quarters have grown up all over the city, for example the East End Art Zone in Caochangdi in the north-east which is home to Waling Boers and Pi Li's Universal Studios, Ai Weiwei's galleries China Art and Archive Warehouse, Urs Meile' art gallery and many others. The Korean gallery Arario in an old destillery in Wang Jing is also noted for its exhibitions on a par with museums.
In Shanghai the Moganshan Road, also refered to by its street number as 'M 50', which is very similar to '798 Space' in Beijing, is the centre of artistic interest.

Biannuals and Triennials

Art-biannuals take place in turn in Beijing in autumn and in Shanghai. While Beijing's biannual is more conservative and excludes such „new" genres as installations or video-art Shanghai's biannual which is organised by a team of international curators is more professional. In both cities however the inofficial exhibitions called satellite shows which are organised by independant exhibitors all over the city are far more exciting.
The most interesting large art event taking place regularly in China is the international Guangzhou-Triennial. 2005' theme under the direction of Hans Ulrich Obrist in cooperation with Hou Hanru was art from the Pearl River Delta in south China. The Curators Qiu Zhijie and Zuo Jing designed a second great Triennial for Chinese Art for Nanjing in 2005 with the theme 'Archaeology of the Future' presenting the positions of a younger generation of Chinese artists. This triennial has no fixed location and takes turns in different

westliche Kunsttheorien und Künstler dem chinesischen Publikum zugänglich, sondern plant für die Zukunft auch ein professionell geleitetes Museum für seine Sammlung, die neben Arbeiten aus China auch Kunst aus dem Ausland umfasst.

Auf dem Weg zu einer Infrastruktur

Allmählich beginnt sich in China eine Infrastruktur für zeitgenössische Kunst zu entwickeln. Die Etablierung von Museen hat dabei eine enorme kulturpolitische Bedeutung. Bis zum Jahr 2008, dem Jahr der Olympischen Spiele in Peking, sollen landesweit mehrere tausend private und öffentliche Museen entstehen. Tatsächlich gibt es derzeit einen Boom an privaten und öffentlichen Ausstellungsräumen. Problematisch sind allerdings die oft allzu starke ökonomische Ausrichtung und die qualitativen Defizite in der Ausstellungserarbeitung, weil es an gut ausgebildeten Kuratoren und Wissenschaftlern mangelt. Und da ihre Budgets oft zu klein sind, um handlungsfähig zu sein, sehen sich viele Einrichtungen gezwungen, ihre Räumlichkeiten zu vermieten. Selbst in vielen staatlichen oder halb-staatlichen Museen werden Ausstellungen in den seltensten Fällen nach kuratorischen, vielmehr nach finanziellen Gesichtspunkten konzipiert. Im durch die Medien international bekannten Kunstviertel 798, einem ehemaligen Fabrikgelände im Pekinger Distrikt Dashanzi, soll dagegen im Herbst 2007 ein Museum für zeitgenössische chinesische Kunst eröffnet werden, das auf kuratorische Qualität setzt. Initiiert durch die belgische Stiftung „Guy und Myriam Ullens", die in Europa neben dem Schweizer Ulli Sigg über eine der größten und wichtigsten Sammlungen zeitgenössischer chinesischer Kunst verfügt, ist unter der Leitung des Kunsthistorikers und Kurators Fei Dawei ein Museum geplant, das dem Pekinger Publikum neben Ausstellungen auch eine Bibliothek und ein Vermittlungsprogramm anbieten wird. Das Kunstviertel 798, in dem sich viele internationale und lokale Galerien sowie Künstler mit ihren Ateliers angesiedelt haben, stand vor drei Jahren noch vor dem drohenden Abriss durch die Stadtregierung. Diese Gefahr ist zwar abgewendet, doch nun fürchtet das Viertel um seine Identität, weil die offizielle Verwaltungsfirma sein ökonomisches Potenzial erkannt hat und die kulturindustrielle Kommerzialisierung vehement vorantreibt. Doch 798 ist nicht der einzige Ort in der Hauptstadt, an dem Kunst und Kultur verdichtet stattfinden, auch anderswo gibt es Kunstviertel, so die East End Art Zone im nordöstlichen Caochangdi, wo die Universal Studios von Waling Boers und Pi Li sowie das China Art & Archives Warehouse von Ai Weiwei und die Galerie Urs Meile angesiedelt sind. Auch die in einer ehemaligen Destillerie untergebrachte koreanische Galerie Arario im Viertel Wang Jing macht mit Ausstellungen auf Museumsniveau von sich reden. In Shanghai ist eine Adresse in der Moganshan Road, nach der Hausnummer auch kurz M 50 genannt und der 798 sehr ähnlich, das Hauptziel der Kunstinteressierten.

Biennalen und Triennalen

Im Herbst ungerader Jahre findet in Peking und in geraden Jahren in Shanghai eine Kunst-Biennale statt. Während die

新艺术形式，而由国际策展人团队策划的上海双年展更具专业性。在两地，然而被称作卫星展的非正式展出更另人兴奋，展出由来自全市的独立参展者策划参加。在中国最受关注的定期举行的大型艺术大事是国际广州艺术三年展。2005年的展出由Hans Ulrich Obrist，侯瀚如合作策划，主题是“别样---一个特殊的现代化实验空间”。

2005年策展人邱志杰，左靖策划了在南京举行第二届中国艺术三年展，以“未来考古学”为主题，表达了中国青年一代艺术家的位置。这一三年展没有固定的场址，在不同的城市间轮流进行。2008年第三届三年展的展出地至今仍未确定。

艺术展在中国

由于当代中国艺术的巨大国际和国家利益，艺术展才得以立足，特别是在上海和北京。在上海有秋季举行的上海艺术博览会和春季举行的上海艺术沙龙展。在北京现今也有两个艺术展，因董梦阳在2006年秋天也创建了竞争性展会“艺术北京”，董梦阳是中国国际画廊博览会的前总监，该展览在过去的三年春季举行。董梦阳 准确地运用时下的需求，他把展会的概念定位为不仅是销售展出，而且也是专业和观念的灵感。

国际性展出也开始进军中国市场，如2006年9月初全球最重要的艺术展Art Basel在北京的全国美术馆策划了以“中国:世界艺术舞台上的新机遇”为主题的小组讨论会，因此也产生了关于继在美国迈亚密之后，Art Basel有可能不久在中国设立办事处的的流言。如今，翘首所盼的首届上海艺术博览会国际当代艺术展将于2007年9月初在上海举行，该展由艺术经纪人Pierre Huber（日内瓦一家画廊老板）与巴塞尔艺术节前总监Lorenzo Rudolf等共同参与策划，将促进亚洲和西方艺术界之间的交流。

中国艺术界的主要特征

中国艺术界是由若干个有联合关系的艺术家占支配性地位。中国本土有几个独立的策展人如冯博一，顾振清，栗宪庭、冷林，朱其，皮力 和卢杰等。他们有些拥有自己的画廊或是半商业展室，有些作为博物馆的策展人，或是与画廊和财力雄厚的房地产商合作开展项目。对于房地产开发商对展览和艺术产品作出的贡献是特有的中国现象，因为当代艺术至今尚未有来自政府的资助也没有任何激励体制，正如我们所知，与私有房地产商合作关系提供了一条良好如果没有困难的融资渠道，即使是长期或是短期的大型的艺术项目。这意味着独立的策展人利用刚完工的建筑作为起临时展出场地，同时获取设备和展册的资金支持。
象北京今日美术馆或是广州的三年展，广州三年展是与广东美术博物馆合作举行，同时也是与房地产商合作。当代艺术来源于流行风尚因此代表了现代的生活方式。所以双方都可从中获益：艺术家和策展人得以实现其项目，而房地产商对艺术的贡献也

cities. The location for the third triennial event in 2008 has not yet been decided.

Art fairs in China

Thanks to the great international and national interest in contemporary Chinese art, art fairs could establish themselves, especially in Beijing and Shanghai. In Shanghai there is the Shanghai Art Fair in autumn and the Art Shanghai in spring. The Capital also has two art fairs now since Dong Mengyan, the former director of the 'China International Gallery Exposition' which has been in spring for the last three years, also created the rival event 'Art Beijing' in autumn 2006. Correctly assessing the current demand Dong aims at a concept for his fairs which offers not only sales exhibitions but also academic and conceptual inspiration.

International hosts of fairs are starting to enter the Chinese market too – for example the most important art fair in the world 'Art Basel' organised a panel discussion in Beijing's National Gallery at the beginning of September 2006 with the subject „China: New Opportunities in the Global Art Arena", thus lending credence to the rumour that after Miami in the USA 'Art Basel' might soon open a branch office in China. At present the highly anticipated first international fair 'ShContemporary' initiated by Pierre Huber, gallery owner in Geneva in cooperation with Lorenzo Rudolf, former director of 'Art Basel' will take place at the beginning of September in Shanghai, enforcing the exchange between Asian and Western art scene.

Leading Characters in the Chinese Art Scene

China's art scene is dominated by several actors with complex interactions. There are "independant" local curators like Feng Boyi, Gu Zhenqing, Li Xianting, Leng Lin, Zhu Qi, Pi Li,Lu Jie, Carol Lu or Li Zhenhua some of whom have their own galleries or semi-commercial show-rooms, some work as curators in museums or work on projects in cooperation with galleries or financially strong building developers. For building developers to contribute to the exhibition system and art production is a specific Chinese phenomenon. As there is as yet hardly any government aid for contemporary art and no endowment system – as we know it – a partnership with a private development company often offers a good if not unproblematic way of financing even large art projects in the long or short run. This means that independent curators use just finished building shells as temporary exhibition space and recieve financial support for equipment and catalogues. But museums like the Today Art Museum in Beijing or the Triennial in Guangzhou which is held in cooperation with the Guangdong Art Museum also cooperate with building developers.

Contemporary art happens to be en vogue and therefore suggests modern life-style which sells well – so both sides profit from this alliance: Artists and curators get to realise their projects and the building developer's contribution to art is good publicity for their often highly-priced apartments.

Pekinger Veranstaltung als die wesentlich konservativere gilt und „neue" Gattungen wie Installation oder Videokunst ausklammert, gibt sich die Shanghaier Biennale, von einem international besetzten Kuratorenteam ausgerichtet, professioneller. In beiden Metropolen sind aber ohnehin die begleitenden Satellitenshows, die von unabhängigen Ausstellungsmachern an verschiedenen Orten in den zwei Städten organisiert werden, weitaus spannender. Unter den regelmäßigen großen Kunstveranstaltungen in China ist die internationale Guangzhou-Triennale am interessantesten. 2005 richtete sie unter der Regie von Hans Ulrich Obrist und in Zusammenarbeit mit Hou Hanru den thematischen Fokus auf die Kunstproduktion im südchinesischen Pearl River Delta. Die Kuratoren Qiu Zhijie und Zuo Jing konzipierten 2005 für Nanjing die zweite „Triennial for Chinese Art" unter dem Thema „Archaeology of the Future" und stellten dort die Positionen einer jüngeren chinesischen Künstlergeneration vor. Diese Triennale ist an keinen festen Ort gebunden, sondern wandert von Stadt zu Stadt.

Kunstmessen in China

Dank des großen internationalen und nationalen Interesses an der zeitgenössischen chinesischen Kunst haben sich insbesondere in den Metropolen Peking und Shanghai auch Kunstmessen etabliert. In Shanghai findet im Herbst die Shanghai Art Fair und im Frühjahr die Art Shanghai statt. Auch in der Hauptstadt gibt es inzwischen zwei Kunstmessen, nachdem Dong Mengyan, der ehemalige Direktor der seit drei Jahren im Frühjahr stattfindenden Messe China International Gallery Exposition, im Herbst 2006 die Konkurrenzveranstaltung Art Beijing ins Leben rief. Die Bedürfnisse der Zeit richtig einschätzend, strebt Dong ein Messeprofil an, das neben der Verkaufsausstellung für das Publikum auch akademische und konzeptionelle Inspiration bieten soll. Internationale Messeveranstalter stehen ebenfalls schon für den chinesischen Markt bereit – so organisierte die weltweit wichtigste Kunstmesse Art Basel Anfang September 2006 in der Pekinger Nationalgalerie eine Podiumsdiskussion zum Thema „China: New Opportunities in the Global Art Arena" und nährte damit das Gerücht, dass es neben Miami in den USA vielleicht schon bald auch in China einen Ableger der Baseler Messe geben werde. Mit großer Spannung wird augenblicklich dem Auftakt der internationalen Messe ShContemporary in Shanghai entgegengesehen, die von dem Genfer Galeristen Pierre Huber zusammen mit dem ehemaligen Direktor der Art Basel Lorenzo Rudolf angeregt wurde, um den Austausch zwischen der asiatischen und westlichen Kunstszene zu intensivieren.

Protagonisten in der chinesischen Kunstarena

Wie in jeder anderen bestimmen auch in der chinesischen Kunstszene viele Akteure das vielschichtige Geschehen, und ihr Zusammenspiel ist äußerst komplex. Da gibt es zum einen die „unabhängigen" einheimischen Kuratoren, wie Feng Boyi, Gu Zhenqing, Li Xianting, Leng Lin, Zhu Qi, Pi Li, Lu Jie, Carol Lu oder Li Zhenhua, von denen einige inzwischen eigene Galerien oder halbkommerzielle

为其高价公寓作了良好的宣传。例如2005年的广州三年展是在一个居民区举行，居民区里一座由Rem Koolhaas设计的艺术博物馆正在建设中；在展出同时合作房地产商安排检验新公寓，并打出标语：您将在超市购物时碰到著名的艺术家。

政府贡献

虽然中国政府远远没有为当代中国的艺术提供资金资助，以及因为审查制度的原因有些展出仍然遭关闭（禁止主题依旧是　对毛泽东的轻蔑，文化大革命，性，和裸体），但中国政府确实在渐增地投资于国外举行的当代中国艺术展出。如在2001年在柏林汉堡火车站美术馆举办的《生活在此时》，2003年在法国巴黎蓬皮度艺术中心的《中国怎么样》，　2005年在与中国文化部的合作下，以官方的中国馆首次参加威尼斯双年展得以实现　到目前为止，中国政府对文化和艺术的长期资助无兴趣，当代艺术实际上被作为一种光耀的政治手段向世界展示积极，现代，国际化中国形象。

媒体和艺术评论家

中国媒体对当代艺术的报道数量毫无疑问地增加了，如今甚至生活时尚杂志也报道展出和成功艺术家。更多的综合性文章以描述性手法而非批评性手法出现在众多的中国艺术杂志上如《艺术世界》，《东方艺术》，《新艺术》。国际艺术杂志如Flash Art, Artforum 和Contemporary如今也定期地报道中国艺术界动态。
关于当代中国艺术的最佳英文杂志是在台北发行的季刊《艺术》，著名中国艺术鉴赏家为其撰稿。

紧次纸质媒体，互连网为当代中国艺术的争论提供了众多平台。最主要的是网页是arts.tom.com，其提供重大开幕，最新出版物和时下争论主题等可信信息。另一个重要信息资源是不同中国艺术家和策展人的博客论坛。与之相比，官方媒体仍然受审查制度的管制，因此官方媒体的讨论更具争议性。

中国依然缺乏有效的结构性艺术复查和艺术评估惯例，就这点而言可以可以作出更大的贡献。北京大学艺术历史学家朱青生写了＂年刊设计“尝试改善这种情况，书中总结在过去时期内当代中国艺术界的主要事件和争论观点。全球唯一机构亚洲艺术文献库已经承担了搜集所有关于亚洲现代艺术的材料。并公诸于世。在AAA网站上可能搜索到目录专题著作杂志和其他材料或查询到在全球事件标下与亚洲艺术相关的正在进行的全球性展出或者相关事件。

现今中国艺术家

为实现培训艺术家，评论家和策展人的国际标准，学者如今正在讨论大学和专业结构的过时的境况。在不久以前《长征计划》的倡议中，一群中国艺术

For example: The last Triennial of Guangzhou in 2005 took place in a residential area where an art museum designed by Rem Koolhaas was being built; the building developer involved arranged new apartment inspections for the same period and advertised with the slogan "You will meet famous artists while shopping at the supermarket".

Government Contributions

Although the Chinese government has so far held back from financially supporting contemporary art in China and some exhibitions are still closed down for censorship reasons (taboo subjects are still disparagement of Mao Zedong, the cultural revolution, Sexuality and nudes) China does increasingly invest in exhibitions of contemporary Chinese art abroad. Amongst others the exhibition 'Living in Time' in 2001 at the Hamburger Bahnhof station in Berlin, the 'Alors la Chine' show at the Centre Pompidou in Paris in 2003 and finally in 2005 the first participation at the Venice biannual with an official Chinese Pavillion were realised in cooperation with the Chinese ministry of culture. The Chinese government has not been interested in long-term support for culture and art in China itself until now, contemporary art is rather used as a prestigious political instrument to show a positive, as in modern and international image of China, to the world.

Media and art critics

Coverage of contemporary art in Chinese media has undoubtedly increased and even lifestyle magazines write about exhibitions and successful artists now. More comprehensive articles in however a descriptive rather than critical style appear in various Chinese art magazines as in 'Art World' (yishu shijie), 'Oriental Art' (dongfang yishu) or 'New Artist' (xin yishujia). International art magazines like 'Flash Art', 'Artforum' and 'Contemporary' by now report regularly on the Chinese art scene. The best magazine in English on contemporary Chinese art is 'Yishu' which is released quarterly in Taipei (Taiwan) with contributions by renowned connoisseurs of Chinese art.

Next to print media the Internet offers numerous platforms for debate on contemporary Chinese art. The leading one is the Chinese Internet page arts.tom.com which offers reliable information on grand openings, new publications and current issues of debate. Another important source of information are the numerous blogs by different Chinese artists and curators. In contrast to official media which is still subject to censorship discussions here can be quite controversial.

But China still lacks sound practices of constructive art reviews and art evaluations which could contribute greatly at this point. The art historian Zhu Qingsheng tries to improve this situation with his „year book project" at the University of Beijing which summarises the main events and points of discussion in the contemporary Chinese art scene for the preceding year. In Hongkong in turn the Asia Art Archive, a unique institution in this world, has undertaken to collect

Projekträume betreiben, als Museumskuratoren tätig sind oder in Zusammenarbeit mit Galerien oder finanzkräftigen Gebäudeentwicklern projektbezogen arbeiten. Dass sich häufig Bauträgerfirmen maßgeblich am Ausstellungswesen und an der Kunstproduktion beteiligen, ist ein spezifisch chinesisches Phänomen. Da eine staatliche Förderung zeitgenössischer Kunst noch kaum und ein Stiftungswesen wie wir es kennen gar nicht existiert, bietet eine Partnerschaft mit einer privaten Entwicklungsgesellschaft häufig einen guten, wenngleich nicht unproblematischen Weg, um auch größere Kunstprojekte kurz- oder längerfristig zu finanzieren. Dabei nutzen unabhängige Kuratoren gerade fertiggestellte Rohbauten befristet als Ausstellungsflächen und erhalten finanzielle Unterstützung für Equipment und Katalog. Aber auch Museen, so das Today Art Museum in Peking, oder Veranstaltungen wie die Triennale in Guangzhou, die in Zusammenarbeit mit dem Guangdong Art Museum durchgeführt wird, kooperieren mit Bauträgerfirmen – zeitgenössische Kunst ist im Land en vogue und suggeriert damit einen modernen Lebensstil, der sich gut verkaufen lässt; so profitieren beide Seiten von der Verbindung. Ein Beispiel: Die letzte Guangzhou-Triennale fand 2005 in einem Wohnviertel statt, wo ein von Rem Koolhaas konzipiertes Kunstmuseum entstand; der involvierte Bauträger veranstaltete zeitgleich nebenan Besichtigungen von neuen Wohnungen und warb mit dem Slogan „Hier treffen Sie beim Einkaufen im Supermarkt berühmte Künstler".

Das Engagement des Staates

Obwohl sich der chinesische Staat im eigenen Land bisher mit finanzieller Unterstützung von zeitgenössischer Kunst eher zurückhält und immer noch Ausstellungen aus Zensurgründen schließt (Tabuthemen sind nach wie vor die Verunglimpfung von Mao Zedong, die Kulturrevolution, Sexualität und nackte Körper), investiert er zunehmend in Ausstellungen zeitgenössischer chinesischer Kunst im Ausland. In Zusammenarbeit mit dem chinesischen Kulturministerium wurden unter anderem die Ausstellungen „Living in Time" 2001 im Hamburger Bahnhof in Berlin, die Schau „Alors, la Chine" im Centre Pompidou in Paris 2003 und zuletzt 2005 die erstmalige Teilnahme an der Biennale von Venedig mit einem offiziellen chinesischen Pavillon realisiert. Die chinesische Regierung ist bisher nicht an einer längerfristigen Förderung der Kunst und Kultur im eigenen Land interessiert, vielmehr dient ihr die zeitgenössische Kunst als prestigeträchtiges politisches Instrument, um ein positives, sprich modernes und internationales Image Chinas in der Welt zu propagieren.

Kunst und Kunstkritik in den Medien

Das Interesse der chinesischen Medien an der zeitgenössischen Kunst hat unzweifelhaft zugenommen, und inzwischen berichten selbst Lifestyle-Magazine über Ausstellungen und erfolgreiche Künstler. Gehaltvollere Beiträge, wenngleich meist eher beschreibender als kritischer Natur, finden sich in diversen chinesischen Kunstzeitschriften, so in „Art World" (Yishu shijie), „Oriental Art" (Dongfang yishu) oder „New Artist" (Xin yishujia). Internationale Kunst-

界的重要代表为更强调了独立思想的重要性，精心制作了另外的教学方案。文艺研讨会在延安举行，在这个标志性地方，毛泽东在1942发表了社会主义中国艺术的作用是服务社会。

虽然现今当代艺术家作为专业教师，艺术培训依然很保守，与校园外的生活很少有联系。

许多中国年轻人梦想成为艺术家，因为传统上来讲在中国艺术家拥有较高的社会地位，也因为他们渴望通过一点机遇和才华而让自己富有。

今天许多艺术家开着名车，住在豪华套间里，在提供美食的赞助饭店内与朋友一起聚餐，培养古老传统。最近几年在北京一些现代化餐馆里，一种新的美食文化逐渐发展起来，艺术家在那里消遣宴客。

具统计，北京是艺术家最多的聚集地，上海紧随其后。北京艺术界特有的特征是所谓的艺术家生活工作的艺术家村。圆明园画家村 紧邻北京西北的颐和园，在那里居住着在国际上享有盛名的许多艺术家象方力钧　和张大力，他们从上世纪80年代末期到90年代中期在那里创作。因此圆明园画家村被作为这类团体的原形。

如今最大艺术家聚居地在位于北京东北郊区通县　，大约有300多名艺术家居住于此。许多国际上著名和那些不太成功的艺术家被洼地，不动产　和便宜的物价以及远离城市乡村宁静所吸引而生活工作与此。通县拥有数座画廊和大型私人博物馆，　正不断开发当代艺术的基础设施。

在过去的几年中，许多长期漂泊海外的艺术家返回国内，希望在中国拥有自己的事业，在家乡成功。他们的经历更加快了中国艺术界的发展。

由于提供了参加展出和讨论的机会，对所有参与艺术的人来讲，上海和北京是国家利益和国际利益的重点。另一方面，这两个城市的本土和国际艺术市场的压力越来越大，许多艺术家很难摆脱这种压力而集中于他们的艺术创作。因为在中国艺术家几乎没任何私人和公有的资助，目前为止仅有两个艺术奖（一个是Ulli Sigg 设立的当代中国艺术奖，另一个是为毕业于高等院校毕业的青年设立的罗中立油画奖学金）。因此许多艺术家被迫快速的工作，创作出大量的作品以能够勉生计。

在其他地区的艺术家面临的压力相对较小，对他们来讲有可能产生优质艺术作品。这意味着在遥远的南方珠江三角洲和西部的四川可以看到艺术发展。

争论 与对话

中国艺术争论的集中点必然是对市场能力的分析以及对艺术的影响。另一个反映在相关艺术杂志和展出设计上的焦点是80年代的艺术及其对当今的显著冲击，如2006年秋天在深圳举行的当代艺术三年展上黄专先生回顾了艺术历史发展状况。上文提到的

all material on contemporary art in Asia and open this to the public. On the AAA website it is possible to research on catalogues, monographs, magazines and other material or to look up worldwide ongoing exhibitions or relevant events in connection with Asian art under the heading World Events.

Being an artist in China today

To achieve international standards in training of artists, critics and curators, academics have recently been discussing the out-of-date situation for universities and academies. Not long ago on the initiative of the 'Long March project group' important representatives of the contemporary art scene in China worked on an alternative Curricula with greater emphasis on indepentant thought; this workshop took place in Yanan, a deeply symbolic place where Mao Zedong in 1942 declared that in socialistic China the function of art is to serve society.

Although contemporary artists work as academy teachers today art training is still very conservative and has little relation to life outside the campus.
Many young Chinese dream of becoming artists because artists traditionally have a high social position in China but also because they hope, with a bit of luck and talent, to become very rich.
Many artists today drive expensive cars, live in glamourous lofts and cultivate the old tradition of patronising restaurants offering good food and of dining in company. In Beijing in particular a new gastronomic culture in stylishly decorated establishments has developed in recent years where the art crowd entertain for dinner.

Statistically Beijing has the greatest concentration of artists, directly followed by Shanghai. A special feature of Beijing's art scene are the so called artist villages in which artists live and work. Yuanmingyuan Artist Village close to the old Summer Palace in the north-west of Beijing, where many artists like Fang Lijun or Zhang Dali who have international fame today worked from the end of the 1980s to the mid-1990s, is considered the prototype for such communities.

Today the largest artists' colony with approximately 300 artists is in the Beijing suburb Tongxian in the north-east of the town. Many internationally famous as well as less successful artists live and work here attracted by low land, real estate and lease prices and by the almost rural tranquility far from the City. With several galleries and large private museums, Tongxian is busy developing an interesting infrastructure for contemporary art.
In the last couple of years many artists came back from long stays abroad wishing to have their share in the China boom at home. Their experiences further add to the fast developing art scene.

Thanks to the many opportunities offered for participation in exhibitions and discussions, Beijing and Shanghai are a main point of national and international interest for all people involved in art. On the other hand however, pressure

magazine wie „Flash Art", „Artforum" und „Contemporary" berichten inzwischen regelmäßig über die chinesische Kunstszene. Die beste englischsprachige Zeitschrift zur zeitgenössischen chinesischen Kunst ist wohl das vierteljährlich in Taipei (Taiwan) erscheinende Magazin „Yishu", in dem durchweg renommierte Kenner der chinesischen Kunst zu Wort kommen. Neben den Printmedien finden sich im Internet zahlreiche Plattformen, die der Debatte über die zeitgenössische chinesische Kunst dienen. Die chinesische Seite „arts.tom.com" ist hier führend und informiert verlässlich über Ausstellungseröffnungen, Neuerscheinungen und aktuelle Diskussionen. Eine weitere wichtige Informationsquelle sind die zahlreichen Blogs verschiedener chinesischer Künstler und Kuratoren. Anders als in den offiziellen Medien, die immer noch der Zensur unterliegen, wird hier des öfteren auch kontrovers diskutiert. Allerdings mangelt es in China noch immer an einer soliden Infrastruktur konstruktiver Kunstkritik und Kunstevaluierung, die gerade in der jetzt noch recht anarchischen Situation große Wichtigkeit besäße. Der Kunsthistoriker Zhu Qingsheng versucht hier mit einem Jahrbuch Abhilfe zu schaffen und stellt, angesiedelt an der Peking-Universität, jeweils die wichtigen Ereignisse und Diskussionen in der zeitgenössischen chinesischen Kunstszene für das vergangene Jahr zusammen. In Hongkong wiederum hat es sich die weltweit einzigartige Institution „Asia Art Archive" zur Aufgabe gemacht, sämtliche Materialien zur zeitgenössischen asiatischen Kunst zu sammeln und der Öffentlichkeit zugänglich zu machen. Auf der Webseite des AAA kann der Interessierte über Kataloge, Monografien, Zeitschriften und andere Materialien zur chinesischen Kunst recherchieren, sich aber unter „World Events" auch darüber informieren, wo auf der Welt aktuell Ausstellungen oder andere relevante Veranstaltungen zur asiatischen Kunst stattfinden.

Künstler werden und sein

Um auch in der Ausbildung von Künstlern, Kritikern und Kuratoren internationale Standards zu erreichen, wird in Akademikerkreisen in letzter Zeit verstärkt die antiquierte Situation an den Hochschulen und Akademien diskutiert. Erst kürzlich debattierten wichtige Vertreter der zeitgenössischen Kunstszene Chinas auf Initiative des Projektkollektivs „Long March" über alternative Curricula, die das selbstständige Denken in den Vordergrund stellen, und zwar an dem symbolträchtigen Ort Yanan, an dem Mao Zedong 1942 die Rolle der Kunst im sozialistischen China im Dienste der Gesellschaft zum Programm machte. Auch wenn an den Akademien inzwischen zeitgenössische Künstler als Lehrer arbeiten, ist die Ausbildung dort immer noch sehr konservativ und hat mit der Welt außerhalb des Campus wenig zu tun. Viele junge Chinesen träumen heute davon, Künstler zu werden, zum einen, weil der Künstler in China traditionell eine hohe gesellschaftliche Position besitzt, aber sicherlich auch, weil sie hoffen, mit ein bisschen Glück und Talent sehr reich werden zu können. Manche Künstler fahren heute teure Limousinen, bewohnen schicke Lofts und pflegen die althergebrachte Kultur des guten Essens in Gesellschaft in eigenen Restaurants. Besonders in Peking entwickelte sich eine neue Esskultur in stilvoll eingerichteten Etablissements, in denen sich die Artcrowd

尤伦斯当代艺术中心　计划2007年9月在北京举办以“回顾80年代”为主题的展出

至今，当代中国艺术反映了其自身状况以及其最近的历史，这种对话开始于海外如今引起中国公众的关注，这必定将为现代中国艺术的发展提供新的激励。

on local and international art markets in these towns is strong and many artists have difficulty escaping this pressure to concentrate on their art. Because there is hardly any public and private promotion of artists and so far only two art awards (the one created by Ulli Sigg called 'Chinese Contemporary Art Award' and the Luo Zhongli Scholarship for young graduates from academies) many artists are forced to work fast and produce lots of pieces to be able to even scrape a living.

Artists in other regions in China are under less pressure which makes it possible for them to produce better quality in art conception. This means that in remote places like the southern Pearl River Delta or in the west of the province Sichuan artistically very interesting developments can be observed.

Discussions and Discourse

A focal point of art discussion in China today is perforce analysis of market powers and their influence on art. Another focus both in relevant art magazines and for exhibition design is the 1980s art and its noticable impact today. For example in autumn 2006 Huang Zhuan reviewed historical developments at the OCT Contemporary Art Terminal in Shenzhen, and the Museum Ullens in Beijing mentioned earlier in the text is planning an opening exhibition in September 2007 on the subject 'review of the 1980's'.

By now contemporary art in China also reflects itself and its recent history, this discourse started abroad and is now gaining attention of the Chinese public which again will surely provide new incentive for contemporary Chinese art.

beim gemeinsamen Dinieren amüsiert. Statistisch ist in der Hauptstadt die Künstlerdichte am größten, direkt gefolgt von Shanghai. Charakteristisch für die Pekinger Kunstszene sind die sogenannten Künstlerdörfer, in denen Künstler leben und arbeiten – als Prototyp gilt das in der Nähe des Alten Sommerpalasts im Nordwesten der Stadt gelegene Yuanmingyuan Artist Village, in dem von Ende der 1980er bis Mitte der 1990er Jahre viele der heute international bekannten Künstler wirkten, wie Fang Lijun oder Zhang Dali. Heute befindet sich die größte Künstlerkolonie mit rund 300 Künstlern im Pekinger Vorort Tongxian im Nordosten der Stadt. Angezogen von den niedrigen Boden-, Immobilien- und Mietpreisen sowie der fast ländlichen Ruhe fernab der Innenstadt, leben und arbeiten dort sowohl international renommierte als auch weniger erfolgreiche Künstler. Mit mehreren Galerien und großen Privatmuseen entwickelt sich in Tongxian derzeit eine interessante Infrastruktur zeitgenössischer Kunst. In den letzten Jahren sind viele Künstler nach langen Auslandsaufenthalten in ihre Heimat zurückgekehrt, um vor Ort am Chinaboom teilzuhaben. Mit ihren Erfahrungen bereichern sie die ohnehin schon überaus bewegte Szene. Dank der vielfältigen Möglichkeiten der Ausstellungsbeteiligung und Diskussion gilt national und international Peking und Shanghai das Hauptinteresse aller Kunstinvolvierten. Auf der anderen Seite ist aber der Druck des lokalen und internationalen Kunstmarkts an diesen Standorten am stärksten, und manchem Künstler fällt es schwer, sich ihm zu entziehen, um sich ganz auf seine künstlerische Arbeit zu konzentrieren. Gerade weil es kaum öffentliche und private Förderungen für Künstler und bisher nur zwei Kunstpreise gibt (den von Ulli Sigg ins Leben gerufenen „Chinese Contemporary Art Award" und das „Luo Zhongli Stipendium" für junge Akademieabsolventen), sind viele Künstler schon aus ökonomischen Gründen gezwungen, schnell und viel zu produzieren. In anderen Regionen des Landes führen die Künstler dagegen ein weniger hektisches Leben, was nicht selten der konzeptionellen Qualität der künstlerischen Arbeiten zuträglich ist. Und so kann man etwa im südlichen Pearl River Delta oder in der westlichen Provinz Sichuan künstlerisch durchaus sehr interessante Positionen finden.

Debatten mit Perspektive

Einen Schwerpunkt der aktuellen Kunstdiskussion in China bildet zwangsläufig die kritische Auseinandersetzung mit der Macht des Marktes und ihren Folgen für die Kunst. Ein zweites Thema, sowohl in den einschlägigen Kunstmagazinen als auch für die Konzeption von Ausstellungen, ist die Kunst der 1980er Jahre und ihre bis heute spürbare Wirkung. So kuratierte im Herbst 2006 Huang Zhuan eine historische Rückschau im „OCT Contemporary Art Terminal" in Shenzhen, und im Herbst 2007 wird das bereits erwähnte Museum Ullens in Peking seine Eröffnungsausstellung einer Auseinandersetzung mit den 1980er Jahren widmen. Die zeitgenössische Kunst in China reflektiert also mittlerweile auch sich selbst und ihre junge Geschichte, ein Diskurs, der auf Umwegen über das Ausland nun wieder in der chinesischen Öffentlichkeit angekommen ist und der aktuellen chinesischen Kunst sicherlich neue interessante Impulse geben wird.

ALL THE ARTS ARE THE SAME – AND DIFFERENT
ALLE KUNST IST GLEICH – UND UNTERSCHIEDLICH
所以我的答案是所有艺术之间都是相同和不同的

AI WEIWEI – UTA GROSENICK

Ai Weiwei, born in 1957 in Beijing, is as artist, architect, and art promoter one of the most influential figures in the current cultural scene of the capital. He was the co-organizer of the avant-garde artist group The Stars, which drew for the first time, attention on Chinese contemporary art.

***Uta Grosenick:** What was it like to take part in the 1st Star exhibition back in 1979?*
***Ai Weiwei:** It was just after the Cultural Revolution, the whole society was like a dead society. It was under the communist ideology control. Anybody who's doing anything different can risk their life, be put in jail, or bear severe punishment. We were a bunch of young kids then, and we didn't believe in the old propaganda art. We started to practice our own type of expressions, which relates to artistic freedom, freedom of speech, freedom of exercise in individual feelings. It's a very important movement, because that movement was the core of any type of art.*

***G.:** When did you leave China? You were already exhibiting in the United States at the beginning of 1980s, is this before or after you move to New York?*
***Ai:** I did very little practice, my condition of being is really more observant, reading and also to have a real life in a complete different political social surrounding, rather than just being an artist. I very much enjoyed my very loose, no attachment condition in the United States.*

***G.:** Did you sense a shift in your artistic style after moving to the United States? How about after you moved back to China?*
***Ai:** Yes, before I went to United States, my style was very much a kind of post impressionist style. After I went to the United States, I was very much interested in the works of Marcel Duchamp, conceptual experimental art.*

***G.:** How did you become – in addition to your art activities – interested in architecture?*
***Ai:** I think architecture is a kind of activity which reflects the general condition of who we are and how we live in this*

Ai Weiwei, 1957 in Peking geboren, ist heute als Künstler, Architekt und Kunstpromoter die wohl einflussreichste Persönlichkeit der hauptstädtischen Kulturszene. Er war Mitorganisator des avantgardistischen Künstlerkollektivs „Die Sterne", mit dem die junge chinesische Kunst erstmals auf sich aufmerksam machte.

Uta Grosenick: Wie war es damals, an der ersten „Sterne"-Ausstellung 1979 mitzuwirken?
Ai Weiwei: Das war gleich nach der Kulturrevolution, und die ganze Gesellschaft war wie tot. Sie duckte sich unter der Dominanz der damaligen kommunistischen Ideologie. Jeder, der etwas „Abweichlerisches" tat, riskierte sein Leben oder zumindest das Gefängnis oder andere schwere Bestrafung. Wir waren damals eine Gruppe von Jugendlichen, die nichts von der alten Propagandakunst hielten. Wir begannen, unsere eigenen Ausdrucksformen zu praktizieren, und zwar im Hinblick auf künstlerische Freiheit, Redefreiheit, Freiheit des Auslebens persönlicher Gefühle. Es war eine sehr wichtige Bewegung, weil sie der Kern jeder Art von Kunst war.

G.: Wann haben Sie China verlassen? Sie stellten schon zu Beginn der 1980er Jahre in den Vereinigten Staaten aus, war das vor oder nach Ihrem Umzug nach New York?
Ai: Ich habe damals nur sehr wenige Arbeiten gemacht; mein Dasein bestand eigentlich mehr darin, zu beobachten, zu lesen und einmal wirklich zu leben, in einem ganz anderen politischen und gesellschaftlichen Umfeld, statt nur Künstler zu sein. Ich habe dieses sehr ungebundene Leben in den Vereinigten Staaten, ohne irgendwelche Verpflichtungen, sehr genossen.

G.: Hatten Sie das Gefühl, dass sich Ihr künstlerischer Stil nach Ihrem Umzug in die USA verändert hat? Und wie war es, nachdem Sie wieder nach China zurückgegangen sind?
Ai: Bevor ich in die Staaten ging, war mein Stil sozusagen postimpressionistisch. In den USA habe ich mich dann recht intensiv vor allem mit den Arbeiten von Marcel Duchamp befasst, mit der experimentellen Kunst und der Konzeptkunst.

艾未未，1957年出生于中国北京，集艺术家，建筑师，和艺术倡导者的多种身份，是当前北京文化界最有影响力的人物之一。他与别人一起创建了前卫艺术家团体星星画会，这个团体使中国当代艺术第一次引人关注。

问：您参加1979年第一届星星画展的原因是什么呢？

艾未未：文化大革命后，整个社会处于恐怖的共产主义意识的控制下，死气沉沉。任何人要做与之不同的事情要冒生命危险，或是被关进监狱，或是遭受严厉的惩罚，我们那时是一帮年轻人，当然不信仰旧的宣传艺术。我们开始去实践自己的表达方式，包括艺术自由，言论自由，个人情感表达的自由，那是非常重要的运动，它是所有艺术形式的精髓。

问：您是什么时候离开中国？在80年代初期您就在美国展出，是在来到美国前还是来到之后呢？

艾：那时没有多少实践，我当时的情况是多是观察和阅读，在一个完全不同的政治社会环境里真正的生活着，而不是仅仅作为艺术家。在美国，我非常放纵地生活着，没有其他因素左右。

问：移居美国之后，您意识到您的艺术风格的转变没有？ 返回中国之后的情况呢？

艾：是的，到美国之前我的风格是一种后印象派的，来到美国之后，我对观念实验艺术 Duchamp's 的作品很感兴趣。

问：除了您的艺术活动之外，您是怎么怎样又涉足建筑呢？

艾：我认为建筑是反映我们是谁以及我们是怎样生活在这个世界的总体情形的一种活动.从事建筑有一

world. It has a very philosophical reason behind the making of it. It shows the basic conditions of mental struggle and of our understanding of our own conditions.

***G.:** Which was the starting point of Chinese contemporary art?*
***Ai:** The starting point should be sometimes around 1979, the first Star exhibition. That time art reflects the current condition, the political social problems.*

***G.:** Is there a distinguishable Chineseness in Chinese contemporary art?*
***Ai:** I think today Chinese contemporary art reflects a very old and doctrine society. A society apart from international culture, fighting its way up to be part of globalism, the art today very much reflects that nature, and China's current conditions. Of course this very much reflects this Chineseness in there.*

***G.:** Is Chinese contemporary art a perpetuation or a lost of traditional Chinese art?*
***Ai:** In any social or political revolution, there is always on the surface a great change of the tradition, there's the overthrow of the old ideology and concepts, but at the same time I think tradition is something much deeper and much solid. Something like gravity it always comes back like a ghost. It's always there, no matter how dramatic the change can be. If we look back in history, any great change still shows the characters of traditions.*

***G.:** What do you think about the current worldwide increase of interest for Chinese art ?*
***Ai:** I think Chinese art has great passion and a variety of expressions, it offers a fresh aspect of today's world. Political, economical, and culturally tries to adjust its positions globally. It's a time for reshuffle, to find our own position on things. China today with a great political social change, the current art appears to be interesting.*

***G.:** What is the difference between Chinese and Western art?*
What do they have in common?
***Ai:** There's no difference between any art, all art are the same. But of course the art reflects the attitude, the understanding of the world, the weight, the traditional heritage, the expressions, the way to appreciate and to communicate. It always has some differences, not only between two cultures or different locations, even individual art are different. So the answer should be all the arts are the same and different.*

***G.:** Where will Chinese art be in 10, 25, 50 years?*
***Ai:** Nobody can predict the future, that's why we are still here. We always wonder, we always try to give a temporary answer to survive through this need and this eagerness of finding out so called temporary truth. But nobody can predict what the world will be like in 50 years.*

***G.:** Will the interest of the collectors last or move on to another subject?*
***Ai:** Same as the last question, nobody can predict the collectors, it all depends if there is others more interesting,*

G.: Wie kam es dazu, dass Sie sich – neben Ihren anderen künstlerischen Aktivitäten – für die Architektur interessieren?
Ai: Ich finde, Architektur spiegelt unsere allgemeinen Lebensumstände wider, wer wir sind und wie wir in dieser Welt leben. Dahinter steckt ein sehr philosophischer Ansatz. Architektur offenbart die Grundbedingungen unseres geistigen Strebens und unser Verstehen unserer eigenen Lage.

G.: Was war eigentlich der Ausgangspunkt der chinesischen Gegenwartskunst?
Ai: Der Ausgangspunkt dürfte tatsächlich die Zeit um 1979 und die erste „Sterne"-Ausstellung gewesen sein. Damals antwortete die Kunst auf die aktuelle Situation und die politischen und gesellschaftlichen Probleme.

G.: Gibt es etwas typisch Chinesisches an der chinesischen Gegenwartskunst?
Ai: Ich denke, die chinesische Gegenwartskunst reflektiert eine sehr alte und doktrinäre Gesellschaft. Eine von der internationalen Kultur abgeschottete Gesellschaft, die sich nach oben kämpft, um an der Globalisierung teilzuhaben. Die heutige Kunst spiegelt sehr deutlich diese Befindlichkeit und Chinas aktuelle Problematik. Natürlich zeigt sie damit etwas sehr typisch Chinesisches.

G.: Ist die chinesische Gegenwartskunst eine Fortsetzung oder ein Bruch mit der traditionellen chinesischen Kunst?
Ai: Bei jeder gesellschaftlichen oder politischen Revolution vollzieht sich an der Oberfläche immer eine große Veränderung der Tradition, ein Bruch mit alten Ideologien und Konzepten, aber gleichzeitig, ist die Tradition etwas viel Tiefgründigeres und Solideres. So etwas wie die Schwerkraft, sie ist immer da, ganz egal, wie dramatisch der Umbruch sein mag. Wenn wir auf die Geschichte zurückblicken, so scheint bei jeder großen Veränderung immer noch die Tradition durch.

G.: Was halten Sie von dem derzeit so starken Interesse an chinesischer Kunst?
Ai: Die chinesische Kunst bietet mit ihrer großen Leidenschaft und Ausdrucksvielfalt eine neue, frische Sichtweise der heutigen Welt. In politischer, wirtschaftlicher und kultureller Hinsicht versucht sie, ihre Positionen global anzupassen. Es ist Zeit für eine Neupositionierung, um unseren eigenen Standpunkt zu den Dingen zu finden. China macht zurzeit große politische und gesellschaftliche Veränderungen durch, und das macht die aktuelle Kunst so interessant.

G.: Was ist der Unterschied zwischen chinesischer und westlicher Kunst, und was sind ihre Gemeinsamkeiten?
Ai: Es gibt keine Unterschiede in der Kunst, alle Kunst ist gleich. Aber natürlich bildet jede Kunst eine Einstellung, ein Weltbild ab, das Gewicht und Vermächtnis der Tradition, die Ausdrucksweise, die Art, wie man etwas würdigt und wie man kommuniziert. Da gibt es immer gewisse Unterschiede, aber nicht nur zwischen zwei Kulturen oder verschiedenen Orten. Auch individuell unterscheidet sich die Kunst. Die Antwort müsste also lauten, dass alle Kunst gleich und unterschiedlich ist.

种很哲学的原因，它反映了精神奋斗和我们对自身认识的基本情况。

问：中国当代艺术的起点在那里呢？

艾：起点大约在1979年，第一届星星画展，那个时候的艺术折射了当时的环境，政治和社会问题。

问：中国当代艺术是不是有很明显的中国特性？

艾：我想中国今天的中国当代艺术反映了一个非常传统，教条的社会形态。这个社会在国际文化之外，并且在成为世界一体的一分子而努力着。今天的艺术多反映了这种特点以及中国现在的情形。当然当代艺术带有很明显的中国特性。

问：当代艺术是继承还是抛弃了传统艺术呢？

艾：所有的社会和政治变革，总是在表面上对传统有着很大的变化，颠覆了旧的意识形态和观念，但我认为在变革同时，传统的东西及其深入坚固，如重力一样，传统如幽灵一样回到变革中，无论怎样戏剧的变化。如果回顾历史，我们可以看到，任何巨大的变革依旧反映着传统的特征。

问：当前对中国现代艺术全球性的关注，您有什么看法？

艾：我想，中国艺术有着很大的热情和多种表达方式，为今天世界提供崭新的观点。它尝试在政治上，经济上和文化上调整自己的位置而使自己全球化。这也是我们寻找自己位置的依次变革。中国今天在政治和社会上有很大的变化，现实的艺术也似乎也在反映这种变化。

问：中西艺术有什么区别以及他们之间的共同点？

艾：任何艺术之间没有不同，所有的艺术都是相同的。艺术都反映了对世界，价值，传统遗产 以及表达方式的态度和认识，反映了欣赏和交流的方式。他们之间还是区别的，不仅是两种文化和不同地域，甚至个人艺术之间都是不同的，所以我的答案是所有艺术之间都是相同和不同的

问：在10年，25年，50年里，中国艺术的将会怎样呢？

艾：没有人可以预言未来的事情，这是因为我们仍然在这里。我们总在思考，总在尝试为满足这种需要和发现所谓的暂时的事实的热情给出一个临时的答案。但是没有人可以预测出50年后世界的样子

问：收藏家的兴趣还会持续吗？还是转到另一个领域？

艾：象上一个问题一样，没有人可以预测收藏家会怎么做，完全决定于在未来是否有存在更有潜力的，更有趣的活动。

things have more potential and more amusing activities.

***G.:** Is the interest of Chinese people in Western art as big as Western interest in Chinese art? Why?*

***Ai:** I think yes, Chinese has been much interested in Western art for the past 100 years, even in the communist region. China has a very limited source, but at that time still have strongest interest in what happened in the West. I think Western people's interest in Chinese art is very small and not even mentionable. It has only happened in the past few years and it's much exaggerated.*

***G.:** What can Western artists learn from Chinese artists? What can Chinese artists learn from Western artists?*

***Ai:** I think art is an individual act. In the west there is still a lot of artist behaving quite conservatively, even in the modernism context. In china artist are quite fresh and brave but lacking the background and more philosophical understanding of contemporary culture, so they have a lot to learn from each other.*

***G.:** Does the Chinese gallery system need to follow Western standards?*

***Ai:** I think gallery is a system of promoting and selling. Personally I don't know how it will be best for it to work, it doesn't have to follow any system until it creates a new system.*

***G.:** You are the founder of the non-profit China Art & Archives Warehouse. Did it turn out to be an alternative to the traditional commercial art market?*

***Ai:** Yes, China Art and Archives Warehouse functions as a platform for me to have a chance to choose the kind of artist and artwork, which I think has special qualities. I have the liberty not to look at things because that they are popular or have commercial quality. So I can really make decisions based on the works own character and own spiritual speciality. It really functions as one of the most important unique platforms for China's art.*

***G.:** Why are there so many new museums build in China?*

***Ai:** That's very governmental, it only shows governments stupidity there, as nation eager to speak the same language as the west. To be part of the so called modernity society, it's fake, it's wrongdoing. It only shows how stupid the governmental policy is.*

***G.:** What do you think of all the new established art fairs in China?*

***Ai:** It's good to bring consciousness and communication, and to try to work on the systems and necessary art, culture facilities. But of course it's a big financial interest behind it. So like anything happened today in the world, there's always a strong finical interest behind it, we just have to wait and see.*

***G.:** Why are there so few women artists in Chinese art?*

***Ai:** I think there's more women artist in Chinese art, maybe just less has been picked up. In school there's more female students. I know there's not lacking of women artist, but maybe the social economic condition, still not allows everybody to have equal opportunities, but there's no discrimination between sex agenda.*

G.: Wo wird die chinesische Kunst in zehn, 25, 50 Jahren stehen?

Ai: Niemand kann die Zukunft voraussagen, deshalb sind wir immer noch hier. Wir fragen immer und versuchen, eine vorläufige Antwort zu geben, aus dem Bedürfnis und der Begierde heraus, eine vorläufige Wahrheit ausfindig zu machen, zu überleben. Aber niemand weiß, wie die Welt in 50 Jahren aussehen wird.

G.: Wird das Interesse der Sammler von Dauer sein oder sich wieder auf etwas anderes verlagern?

Ai: Da gilt das Gleiche wie für die vorherige Frage, niemand kann das Verhalten der Sammler voraussagen. Es hängt alles davon ab, ob etwas anderes, Interessanteres kommt, andere Dinge mehr Potenzial oder mehr Spaß versprechen.

G.: Ist das Interesse der Chinesen an westlicher Kunst genauso groß wie das Interesse des Westens an der chinesischen Kunst?

Ai: Ich glaube ja. Die Chinesen interessieren sich schon seit 100 Jahren sehr für die westliche Kunst, sogar unter den Kommunisten. Damals waren die Informationsquellen in China sehr eingeschränkt, aber es herrschte trotzdem größtes Interesse daran, was im Westen vor sich ging. Umgekehrt glaube ich, dass im Westen das Interesse an der chinesischen Kunst sehr gering ist und gar nicht erwähnenswert. Es existiert überhaupt erst seit ein paar Jahren und wird stark überschätzt.

G.: Was können die westlichen Künstler von den chinesischen Künstlern lernen? Und umgekehrt?

Ai: Ich glaube, dass Kunst ein individueller Akt ist. Im Westen gebärden sich immer noch viele Künstler ziemlich konservativ, selbst im Kontext der Moderne. In China sind die Künstler ziemlich frisch und mutig, aber es fehlt ihnen an Hintergrundwissen und tieferem philosophischem Verständnis der modernen Kultur. So haben beide Seiten viel voneinander zu lernen.

G.: Sollte sich das chinesische Galeriesystem nach westlichen Standards richten?

Ai: Galerien sind ein Marketing- und Vertriebssystem. Ich persönlich weiß nicht, wie das am besten funktionieren wird.

G.: Sie sind Gründer des nicht-gewinnorientierten China Art & Archives Warehouse. Ist das eine Alternative zum traditionellen, kommerziellen Kunstmarkt?

Ai: Ja, das China Art & Archives Warehouse funktioniert für mich als Plattform, die mir die Chance bietet, Künstler und Kunstwerke auszuwählen, die in meinen Augen spezielle Qualitäten haben. Ich habe die Freiheit, mir Dinge nicht deshalb anzusehen, weil sie populär oder marktgerecht sind. So kann ich meine Entscheidungen wirklich auf den eigenen Charakter und die spirituelle Besonderheit der Werke gründen. Das CAAW ist tatsächlich eine der wichtigsten und ungewöhnlichsten Plattformen für Chinas Kunst.

G.: Wie kommt es, dass in China so viele neue Museen gebaut werden?

Ai: Das geht von staatlicher Seite aus und demonstriert nur den etwas sonderbaren Ehrgeiz der Regierung, als Nation

问：中国人的多西方艺术的兴趣和西方对中国艺术的兴趣一样大吗？为什么呢？

艾：我想是的。在过去100年里，即使是在共产党时期，中国人都对西方艺术饶有兴趣，虽然在那个时代，中国资源有限，但西方发生的事情仍有强烈的兴趣。我认为，西方人对中国艺术的兴趣很小甚至不值一提。西方人对中国艺术的兴趣仅仅从过去几年前开始，但是有点过于夸大。

问：西方艺术家可以从中国艺术家学习到什么？中国艺术家从西方艺术家那里呢？

艾：艺术是独立的艺术。在西方，仍然许多艺术家行为谨小慎微，即使在现代化的背景下。在中国艺术家经历充沛很大胆，但是缺少现代化的背景和对当代文化深刻的哲学认识，所以双方应该更多的彼此学习

问：中国的画廊体系需要模仿西方标准吗？

艾：我认为画廊是一个推销和销售体系。我个人是不知道它怎样去更好的去运转，我不会让它去模仿任何体系，直到我创立一种新的体系 。

问：您是非盈利性机构中国艺术文件仓库的创建人。它是传统商业艺术市场的另一种模式吗？

艾：是的，中国艺术文件仓库的功能是做为一个平台，让我去有机会去选择有艺术家和我认为有特殊品质的艺术作品，我有自由不去看那些大众的或者有商业性质的作品，所以基于作品的自身特点和精神特性，我能真正地作出决定。作为最重要独特的平台之一，它真正的为中国艺术发挥着作用。

问：为什么中国兴建如此多的新博物馆？

艾：那是政府的行为，仅仅表现政府的愚蠢，因为这个国家渴望和西方说一样的语言，成为所谓的现代社会的一部分。那是虚假 错误的做法，只是反映了政府政策的多么的愚蠢。

问：对你而言， 能自由独立的工作吗？

艾：是的，我一直是自由独立地工作着。我想有两种性质的自由和独立，对任何一个表达自己才华人来讲，那是最重要的。当然没有真正的自由。争取自由，争取独立，是最重要的艺术和政治方向。

问：你对中国所有新开的艺术博览会有什么看法？
艾：它有助于带来意念和交流，有助于建立体系和必要的艺术文化设施。然而其背后是巨大的经济。所以和今天发生在世界所有事情一样，其背后有着很强的经济，我们仅仅能去等待。

问：为什么中国艺术界的女艺术家很少呢？

艾：中国有很多的女艺术家，可能仅仅因为她们很少注意，学校里有许多女学生。我认为，并不是缺

G.: Is it possible for you to work free and independent today?
Ai: Yes, I have always been working free and independent. I think these are two qualities that are the most important qualities for anybody who deals with intellect. Of course there's no true condition of being free. But to fight for freedom, fight for liberty and fight for individuality that is the most artistic political position.

die gleiche Sprache zu sprechen wie der Westen, Teil der sogenannten modernen Gesellschaft zu sein.

G.: Was halten Sie von all den neu gegründeten Kunstmessen in China?
Ai: Es ist gut, für mehr Bewusstsein und Kommunikation zu sorgen und zu versuchen, an den Systemen und den notwendigen Kunst- und Kultureinrichtungen zu arbeiten. Aber natürlich steckt ein großes finanzielles Interesse dahinter. Wie bei allem, was heute auf der Welt passiert: Immer steckt ein starkes finanzielles Interesse dahinter – wir müssen einfach abwarten und sehen, was passiert.

G.: Warum gibt es so wenige Künstlerinnen in der chinesischen Kunst?
Ai: Ich glaube, es gibt gar nicht so wenige Künstlerinnen in der chinesischen Kunst, vielleicht finden sie bisher einfach nur weniger Beachtung. An den Hochschulen sind die Studentinnen in der Überzahl. Ich weiß, dass keineswegs ein Mangel an Künstlerinnen herrscht; womöglich bieten die sozio-ökonomischen Verhältnisse immer noch keine Chancengleichheit für alle, aber sexuelle Diskriminierung ist kein Thema mehr.

G.: Ist es Ihnen heute möglich, frei und unabhängig zu arbeiten?
Ai: Ja, ich habe immer frei und unabhängig gearbeitet. Ich denke, das sind die beiden wichtigsten Qualitäten für jeden, der sich intellektuell betätigt. Natürlich gibt es keinen Zustand echter Freiheit. Aber für die Freiheit und Individualität zu kämpfen, das ist die künstlerischste politische Position.

少女艺术家，而是在于政治经济环境，不允许人人都有平等的机会，但是也没有性别歧视.

ARTISTS
KÜNSTLER
艺术家

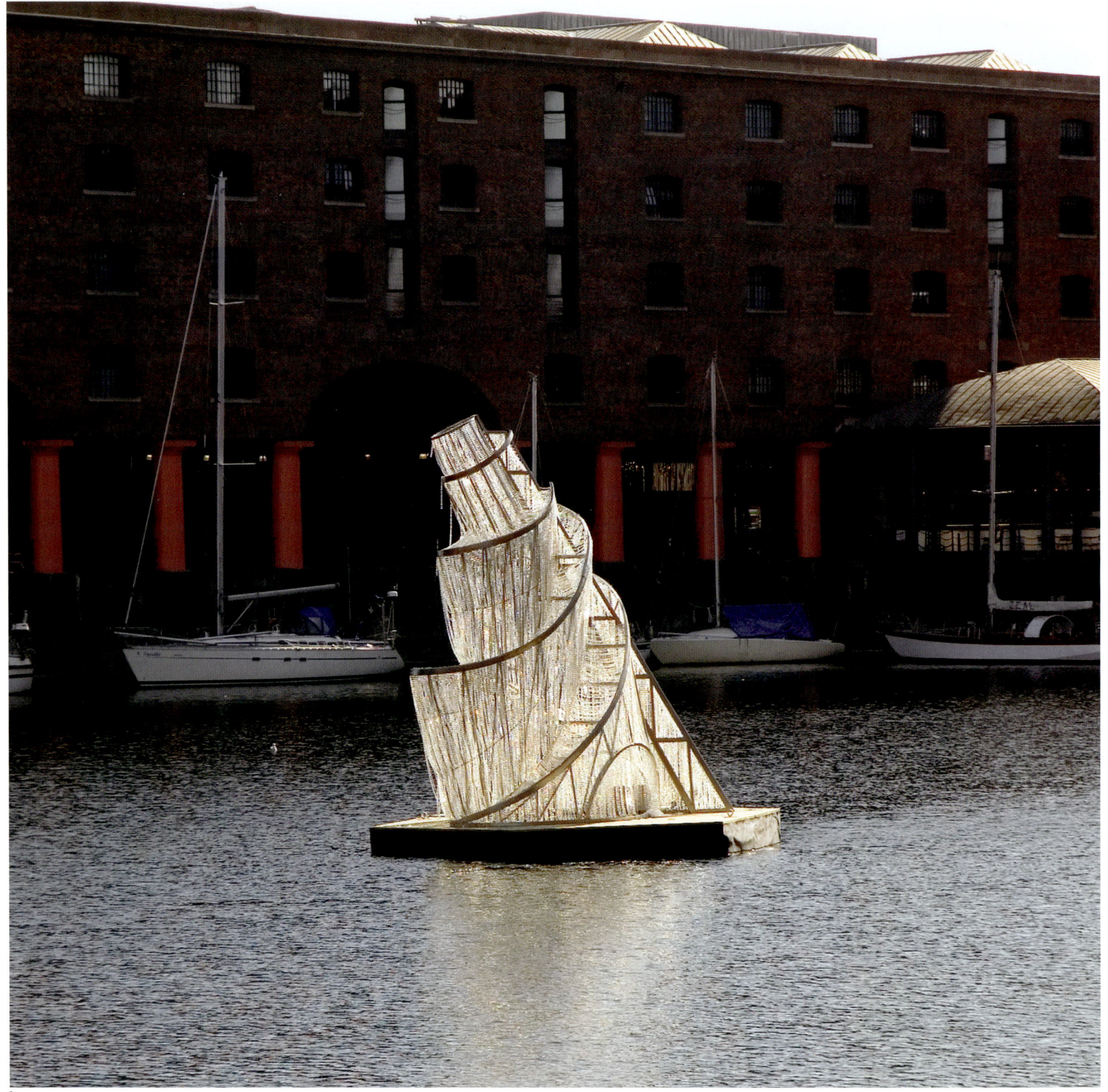

1

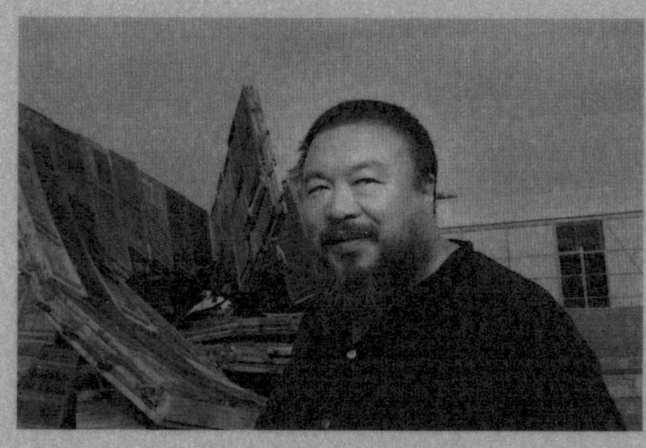

"I never place art apart from basic human rights – freedom of expression, for example. Also, it's the responsibility of individuals, and especially of artists, to speak out in what you believe in. This is as important as the strokes of paint, or other forms of art."

„Ich mache keinen Unterschied zwischen Kunst und grundlegenden Menschenrechten, wie der freien Meinungsäußerung zum Beispiel. Außerdem haben Individuen, und Künstler ganz besonders, die Verantwortung, sich für das einzusetzen, woran sie glauben. Das ist genauso wichtig wie Pinselstriche oder jede andere Form von Kunst."

"我从未在艺术中分离最基本的人权 —— 如表达的自由，同时，也是个体的责任，尤其对艺术家来说，说出其自己的信仰，这和画刷或其他艺术形式一样重要。"

Born in 1957 in Beijing, China. Lives and works in Beijing
Geboren 1957 in Peking, China. Lebt und arbeitet in Peking
1957年出生于北京中国，居住工作在北京

***Selected exhibitions* / Ausgewählte Ausstellungen** / 所选展览

1999 48. Biennale di Venezia, Venice, Italy
2004 "Ai Weiwei", Kunsthalle Bern, Berne, Switzerland
2006 "Fragments", Galerie Urs Meile, Beijing, China
15th Biennial of Sydney, Sydney, Australia
The 5th Asia-Pacific Triennial of Contemporary Art, Queensland Art Gallery, South Brisbane, Australia
2007 "ARCO'07", XXVI Feria Internacional de Arte Contemporáneo, Madrid, Spain
"We are the Future", 2nd Moscow Biennial of Contemporary Art, Former Lenin Museum, Moscow, Russia
"The Real Thing: Contemporary Art from China", Tate Liverpool, Liverpool, UK
documenta 12, Kassel, Germany

1999年 第48届威尼斯双年展，威尼斯
2004年 《艾未未》Kunsthalle Bern, 伯尔尼，瑞士
2006年 个展：《碎片》北京瑞士麦勒画廊北京
《第15届悉尼双年展》
《第5届三年亚洲和平的当代艺术昆士兰美术画廊三年展》南布里斯班, 澳洲
2007年 《第26届国际艺术博览会》马德里
《我们是未来, 第二届莫斯科当代艺术双年展》前列宁博物馆, 莫斯科, 俄罗斯
《真正的事:当代艺术从中国》泰特利物浦画廊, 利物浦，英国
第十二届德国文件展，卡塞尔，德国

***Selected publications* / Ausgewählte Publikationen** / 所选著作

Charles Merewether (ed.): "Ai Weiwei – Works: Beijing 1993–2003", Beijing 2003
"Ai Weiwei – Fragments", Galerie Urs Meile, Beijing/Lucerne 2006

Merewether, Charles（编者）:《艾未未--作品：北京1993-2003年》北京2003年
《艾未未 – 碎片》麦勒画廊，北京/卢塞恩2006年

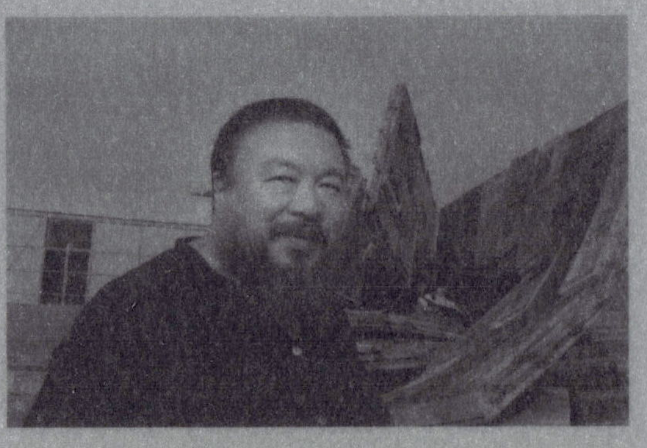

"I never place art apart from basic human rights - freedom of expression, for example. Also, it's the responsibility of individuals, and especially of artists, to speak out in what you believe in. This is as important as the strokes of paint, or other forms of art."

„Ich mache keinen Unterschied zwischen Kunst und grundlegenden Menschenrechten, wie der freien Meinungsäußerung zum Beispiel. Außerdem haben Individuen, und Künstler ganz besonders, die Verantwortung, sich für das einzusetzen, woran sie glauben. Das ist genauso wichtig wie Pinselstriche oder jede andere Form von Kunst."

"我从未在艺术中分离最基本的人权 — 如表达的自由，同时，也是个体的责任，尤其对艺术家来说，说出其自己的信仰，这和画刷或其他艺术形式一样重要。"

Born in 1957 in Beijing, China. Lives and works in Beijing
Geboren 1957 in Peking, China. Lebt und arbeitet in Peking
1957年出生于北京中国，居住工作在北京

Selected exhibitions / Ausgewählte Ausstellungen / 所选展览

1999 48. Biennale di Venezia, Venice, Italy
2004 "Ai Weiwei", Kunsthalle Bern, Berne, Switzerland
2006 "Fragments", Galerie Urs Meile, Beijing, China
15th Biennial of Sydney, Sydney, Australia
The 5th Asia-Pacific Triennial of Contemporary Art, Queensland Art Gallery, South Brisbane, Australia
2007 "ARCO'07", XXVI Feria Internacional de Arte Contemporáneo, Madrid, Spain
"We are the Future", 2nd Moscow Biennial of Contemporary Art, Former Lenin Museum, Moscow, Russia
"The Real Thing: Contemporary Art from China", Tate Liverpool, Liverpool, UK
documenta 12, Kassel, Germany

1999年 第48届威尼斯双年展，威尼斯
2004年 《艾未未》Kunsthalle Bern, 伯尔尼，瑞士
2006年 个展：《碎片》北京瑞士麦勒画廊北京
《第15届悉尼双年展》
《第5届三年亚洲和平的当代艺术昆士兰美术画廊三年展》南布里斯班，澳洲
2007年 《第26届国际艺术博览会》马德里
《我们是未来，第二届莫斯科当代艺术双年展》前列宁博物馆，莫斯科，俄罗斯
《真正的事：当代艺术从中国》泰特利物浦画廊，利物浦，英国
第十二届德国文件展，卡塞尔，德国

Selected publications / Ausgewählte Publikationen / 所选著作

Charles Merewether (ed.): "Ai Weiwei - Works: Beijing 1993-2003", Beijing 2003
"Ai Weiwei - Fragments", Galerie Urs Meile, Beijing/Lucerne 2006

Merewether, Charles（编著）：《艾未未—作品：北京1993-2003年》北京2003年
《艾未未 – 碎片》麦勒画廊，北京/卢塞恩2006年

AI WEIWEI 艾未未

[aɪ ueɪueɪ]

Since his emergence as an artist in the late 1970s, Ai Weiwei has been a prime mover in the Beijing art scene, combining his roles as artist, architect, and instigator to create new institutions as well as new art forms. Son of the renowned poet Ai Qing – who was celebrated during the early Communist period but then sent to Xinjiang in northwest China during the Cultural Revolution – Ai Weiwei grew up well aware of the irrationality of political movements and social upheavals. His family returned to Beijing in 1978, where he attended the Beijing Film Institute and helped organize "The Star" group, the first artist collective to present avant-garde art in China. In 1981, he moved to the United States where he immersed himself in experimental art movements, from Dadaism and Fluxus through Andy Warhol and the East Village scene, beginning to incorporate these ideas into his work.

Upon returning to China in 1993, Ai Weiwei soon became a central figure in Beijing's own East Village, embarking on publishing a series of texts, "Black Cover Book" (1994), "White Cover Book" (1995) and "Grey Cover Book" (1997) that featured interviews and texts by the artists of this mostly underground scene. Similarly, he founded China Art & Archives Warehouse, the first non-commercial venue in China to showcase conceptual art projects. On the occasion of the 2000 Shanghai Biennial, Ai Weiwei achieved his most notorious curatorial project, "Fuck Off!", a satellite show (co-curated with Feng Boyi) packed with critical and disturbing art works that achieved as much attention as the biennial itself.

By then, this artist was already gaining international attention for his own art works which meld a Dada sensibility with traditional Chinese antiquities and craftsmanship. Treating rare Han vases as ready-mades, Ai Weiwei dipped a series in white paint, a gesture that could either be interpreted as an act of destruction or a method of reinterpretation, resulting in such works as "Whitewash" (1993–2000), an installation of more than 100 of these urns. Likewise, he reconfigured authentic Ming furniture as

Seit er sich in den späten 1970er Jahren einen Namen machte, ist Ai Weiwei eine treibende Kraft der Pekinger Kunstszene: Er nutzt seine verschiedenen Rollen als Künstler, Architekt und Promoter, um nicht nur neue Kunstformen, sondern auch neue Institutionen zu schaffen. Als Sohn des berühmten Dichters Ai Qing – der zu Beginn der kommunistischen Ära noch gefeiert, während der Kulturrevolution aber nach Xianjiang in Nordwestchina verbannt worden war – wuchs Ai Weiwei mit der Erfahrung auf, wie irrational politische Bewegungen und gesellschaftliche Umwälzungen sein können. 1978 kehrte seine Familie nach Peking zurück, wo Ai das Beijing Film Institute besuchte und Mitorganisator der Gruppe „Die Sterne" wurde, des ersten Künstlerkollektivs, das in China mit Avantgardekunst an die Öffentlichkeit trat. 1981 ging er in die USA, wo er sich mit der modernen Kunst des Westens beschäftigte – von Dadaismus und Fluxus bis hin zu Andy Warhol und der East-Village-Szene – und begann, diese Ideen in seine eigene Arbeit zu integrieren.

1993 nach China zurückgekehrt, wurde Ai Weiwei rasch zu einer zentralen Figur in Pekings eigenem East Village. Er publizierte eine Reihe von Texten: „Black Cover Book" (1994), „White Cover Book" (1995) und „Grey Cover Book" (1997) präsentierten Interviews und Texte von Künstlern aus dieser Szene, die noch weitgehend im Untergrund wirkte. Außerdem gründete er als ersten nichtkommerziellen Ausstellungsort für Konzeptkunst-Projekte in China das schon bald berühmte China Art Archives & Warehouse. Und anlässlich der Shanghaier Biennale 2000 realisierte Ai Weiwei sein bis dahin skandalösestes kuratorisches Projekt: die Satelliten-show „Fuck Off!" (Ko-Kurator war übrigens Feng Boyi) – sie zeigte eine ganze Sammlung überaus kritischer und beunruhigender Kunst und erregte genau so viel Aufmerksamkeit wie die Biennale selbst.

Zu dieser Zeit erfuhr der Künstler bereits internationale Beachtung mit seinen eigenen Werken, in denen er Dada-Ansätze mit Kunsthandwerk aus der chinesischen Tradition verbindet. So nutzte Ai Weiwei kostbare Han-

自从作为70年代后艺术家的身份出现以后，艾未未容艺术家，建筑师，倡导者多种角色与一身，创建了新的文艺团体和新的艺术形式，是 北京艺术界的原动力。艾未未是著名诗人艾青之子，艾青在新中国初期很有名气，但在随后的文化大革命期间被遣送到中国西北的新疆地区—艾未未逐渐的完全明白了政治运动和社会动乱的荒唐。艾未未全家在1978年返回北京，就读于北京电影学院，并协助筹办星星画会，星星画会中国首个前卫艺术运动组织。1981年，艾移居美国，投身于试验艺术运动中，从达达派到激浪派，从Andy Warhol 到东村，那并开始将那些理念融合进作品。

艾未未于1993年返回国，立刻成为北京东村的领军人物，开始一系列的著作，《黑皮书》，《白皮书》，《灰皮书》，书中内容为采访录和一些地下艺术家的为文章。同时，艾未未成立了中国艺术文件仓库，中国首个非商业性质概念艺术作品陈列馆。在2000年的上海双年展上，与 冯博一策划的《不合作方式》饱受诟病，这个卫星展中有一件作品很有争论性，因此和展会同样受到关注。

那时，艾未未因其艺术作品如融合了达达主义的敏感性和传统中国古董和技术而引起国际上的关注。艾未未把一些珍贵的汉代花瓶当作很普通的处理了把它们仅在白色的涂料中，那种姿势既可以被解释成 破坏艺术，又可以被当作重新解释的方法，由此产生了如 由100等多个瓮组成的装置的系列作品，是。同样，他把明朝家具重新装配成及其畸形的艺术雕塑品。2006年的 是其众多技术实践的作品的顶峰，作品是由古代梁柱组成的大型雕塑，融合了中国传统的木工业技巧。

但艾未未对当代北京最有长远影响或许是在北京城中的众多的建筑设计。他的第一个作为建筑师的尝试是建造自己的房子，一座位于草场地 艺术区具有现代风格的传统庭院，整个建设工程在没有超过一百天。草场地艺术区现在是CAAW，麦勒画廊的展出

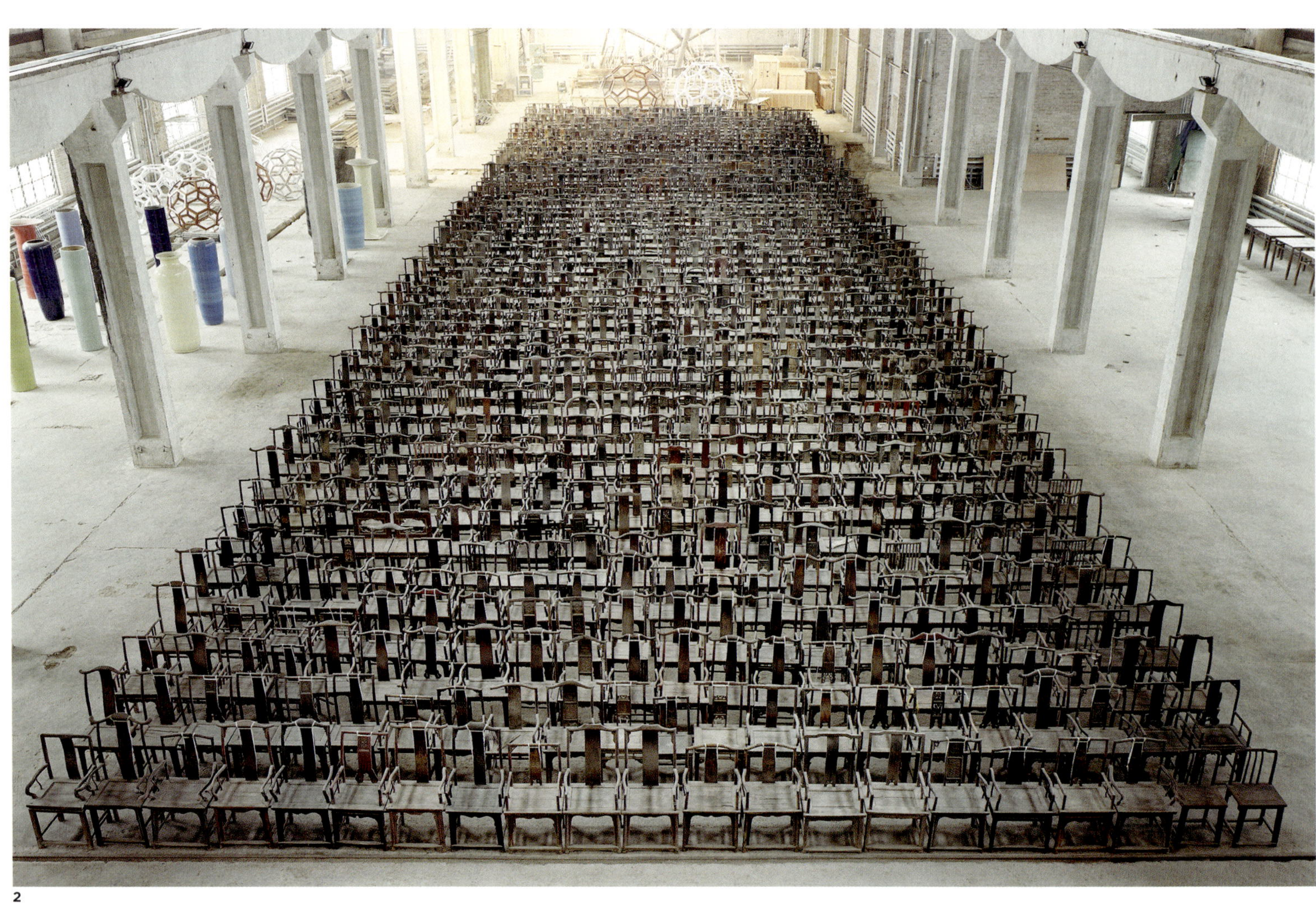

2

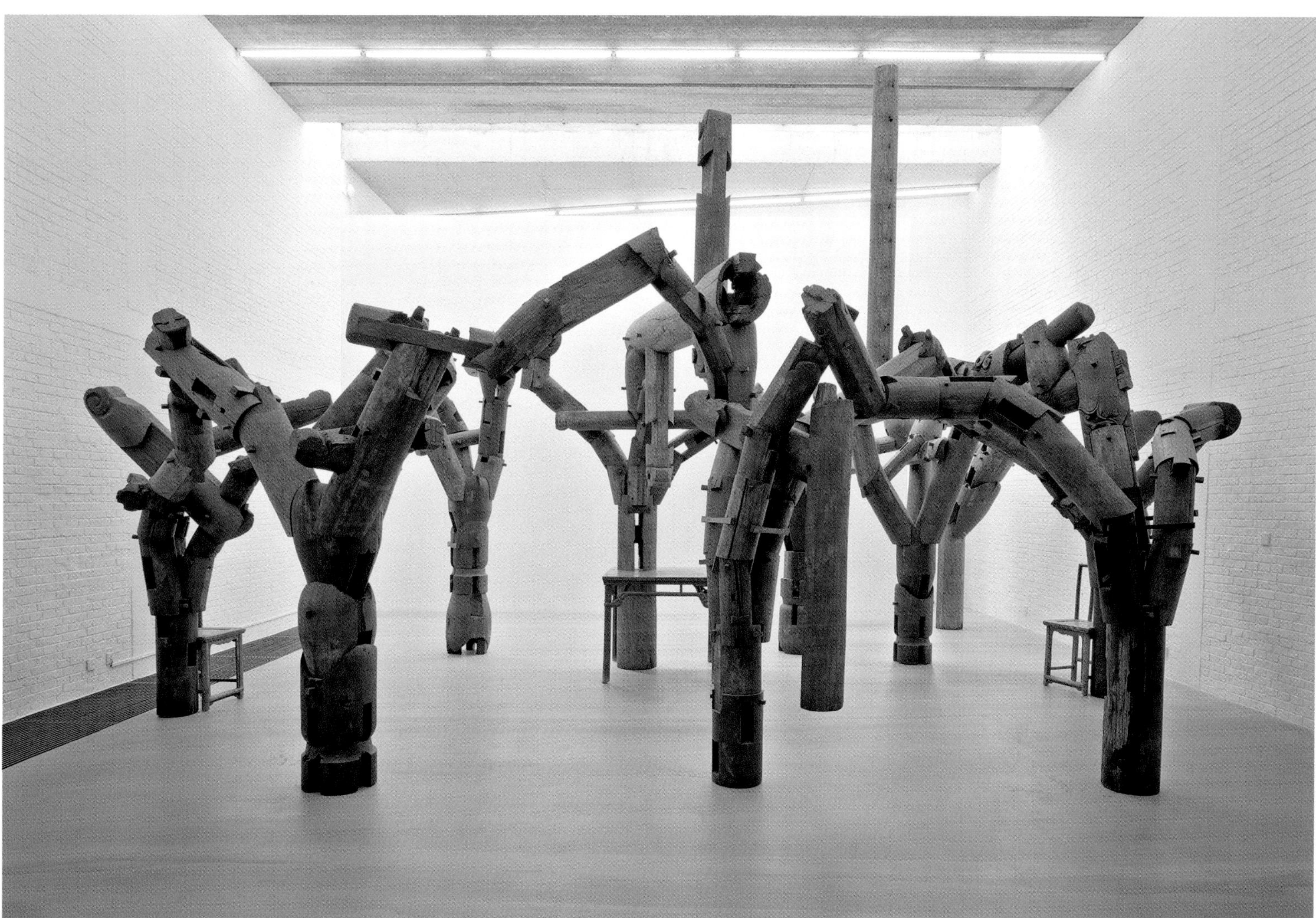

3

4

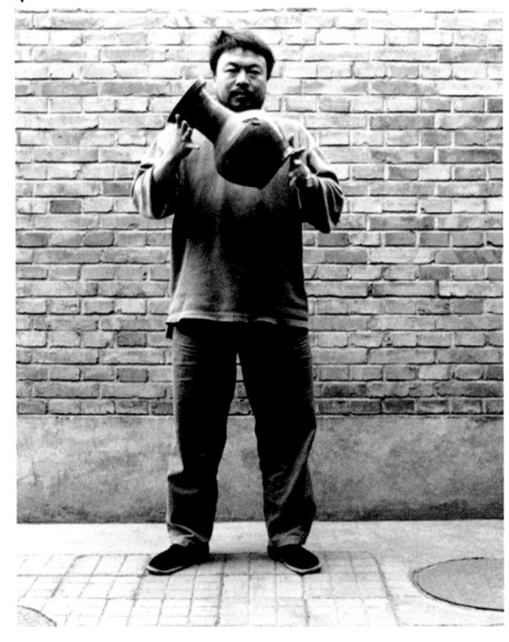

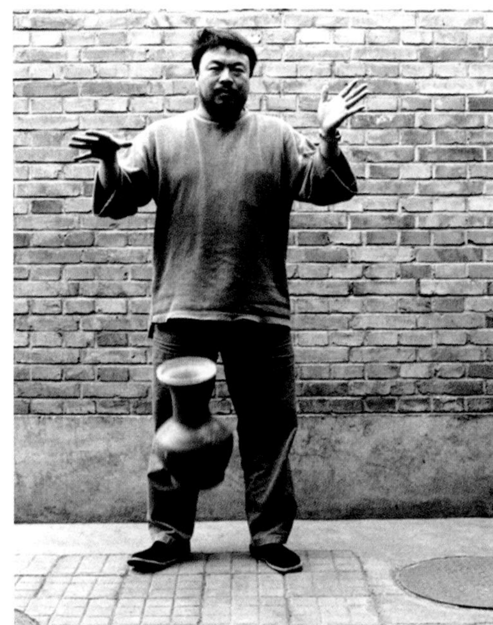

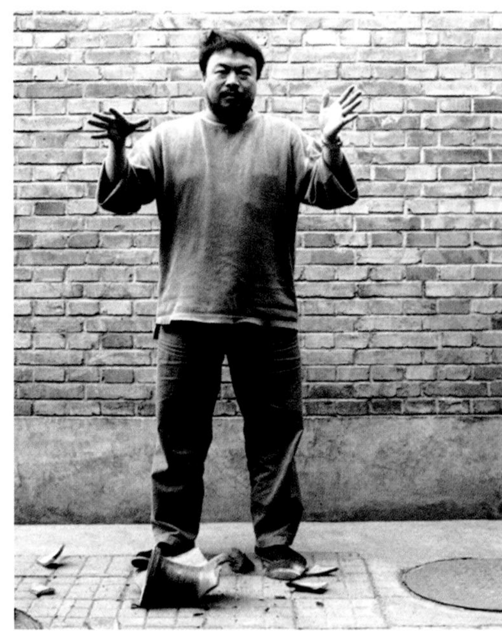

absurdly dysfunctional sculptures. "Fragments of a Temple" (2006), a massive sculptural form made from sections of antique beams and pillars melded together by traditional Chinese joinery, is the culmination of his numerous exercises in this technique.

But Ai Weiwei's most enduring impact on contemporary Beijing may be his numerous architectural projects around the city. His first venture as an architect was building his own home, a modern reinterpretation of a traditional courtyard house, in less than 100 days in the Caochangdi district, an area that now also features CAAW, Urs Meile Gallery and a new center for photography developed by the artist RongRong, all designed by Ai Weiwei. Now with an architectural practice of more than a dozen employees, the artist is working with the Swiss architectural firm Herzog & de Meuron on the design for the new Olympic Stadium, to be unveiled in 2008. By ever-challenging accepted ideas – in politics, art and design – Ai Weiwei has become the single most influential figure in Beijing's art scene today.

Vasen als Readymades, indem er eine Reihe davon in weiße Farbe tauchte – eine Geste, die man entweder als Akt der Zerstörung oder der Neuinterpretation deuten konnte. Dabei kamen Werke wie „Whitewash" (1993–2000) heraus, eine Installation aus über 100 solcher Gefäße. Oder er baute echtes Mobiliar aus der Ming-Periode zu absurden, funktionslosen Skulpturen um. In „Fragments of a Temple" (2006), einer wuchtigen skulpturalen Installation aus Bruchstücken alter Balken und Säulen, die in traditioneller chinesischer Schreinerkunst zusammengefügt wurden, kulminieren seine zahlreichen Experimente mit dieser Technik.

Am nachhaltigsten jedoch prägte Ai Weiwei das neue Peking durch seine zahlreichen Architekturvorhaben in der ganzen Stadt. Sein erstes Projekt als Architekt war der Bau seines eigenen Hauses: Die moderne Neuinterpretation eines traditionellen Hofhauses entstand in weniger als 100 Tagen im Bezirk Caochangdi. In dieser Gegend stehen heute auch das CAAW (China Art Archives & Warehouse), die Galerie Urs Meile und ein vom Künstlerkollegen RongRong konzipiertes neues Zentrum für Fotografie – alle nach Entwürfen von Ai Weiwei gebaut. Der Künstler betreibt inzwischen ein Architekturbüro mit über einem Dutzend Angestellter und arbeitet derzeit mit der schweizerischen Architekturfirma Herzog & de Meuron an der Gestaltung des neuen Olympiastadions, das 2008 eingeweiht werden soll. Indem er landläufige Vorstellungen immer wieder in Frage stellt – ob in Politik, Kunst oder Architektur –, ist Ai Weiwei zur einflussreichsten Persönlichkeit der aktuellen Pekinger Kunstszene geworden.

地，同时也是一个新的摄影中心，艺术区由荣荣创建，所有设计由艾完成，现在艾未未与瑞士建筑公司Herzog & de Meuron 一起设计新的奥林匹克体育馆，并和12个左右的建筑工人在进行实践，工程预计将于2008年交付使用。通过不断的挑战政治，艺术和设计上的传统观念，艾未未已经是北京艺术界唯一具有影响力的人物。

Barbara Pollack

5

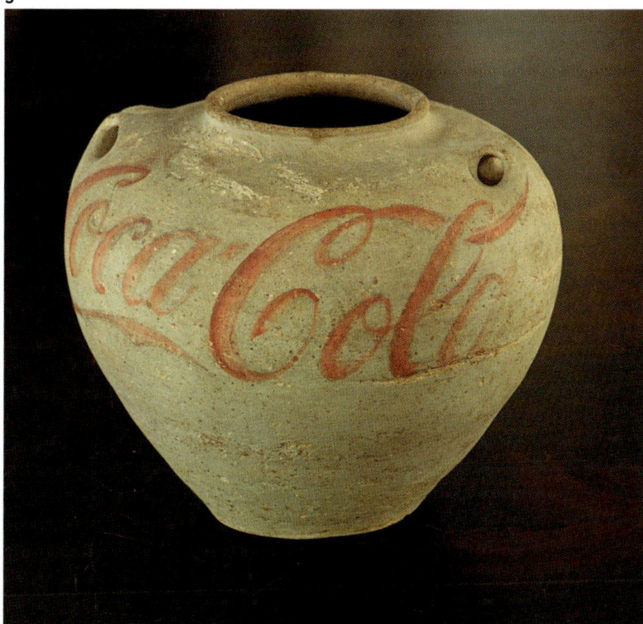

6

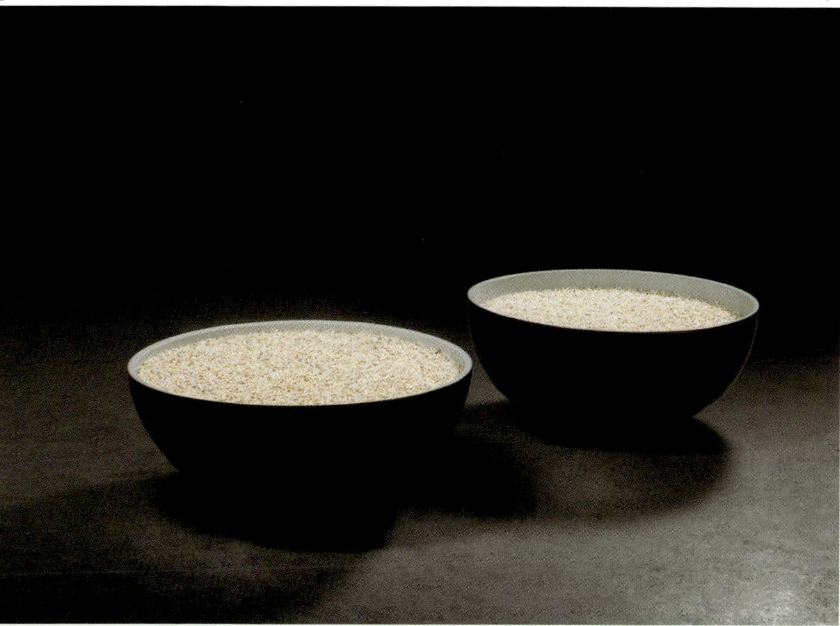

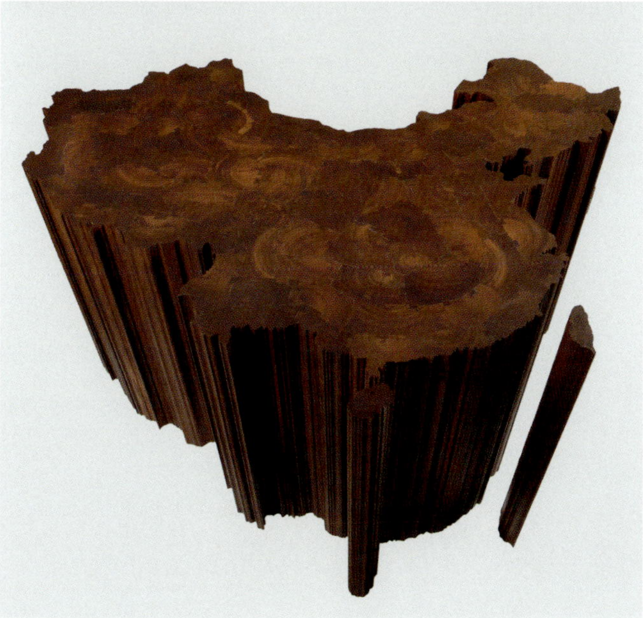

7

1 **Working Progress (Fountain of Light),** *2007*
In collaboration with Fake Studio, mixed media, installation view, "The Real Thing", Tate Liverpool
In Zusammenarbeit mit Fake Studio, Mixed media, Installationsansicht, „The Real Thing", *Tate Liverpool*
《灯光喷泉》2007年, 与Fake Studio合作, 混合媒介, 装置实景

2 **Fairytale,** *2007*
1001 chinese visitors, 1001 Qing Dynasty wooden chairs, Gottschalk-Halls and city area of Kassel
1001 chinesische Besucher, 1001 Holzstühle aus der Qing-Dynastie, Gottschalk-Hallen und Stadt Kassel
《童话》2007年, 1001个中国游客, 1001 张清朝椅子

3 **Fragments,** *2005*
Iron wood, Qing Dynasty tables, chairs, parts of beams and pillars, 850 x 700 x 500 cm, installation view
Holz, Stühle, Tische, Teile von Balken und Pfosten aus der Qing-Dynastie, 850 x 700 x 500 cm (Installationsansicht)
《碎片》2005年, 铁木, 清朝桌椅，梁、柱，850 x 700 x 500 cm, 装置实景

4 **Dropping a Han Dynasty Urn,** *1995/2004*
3 b/w prints, 212 x 143 cm each
3 Schwarzweißdrucke, je 212 x 143 cm
《掉汉瓶》1995/2004年, 3 b/w prints, 每幅212 x 143 cm

5 **Han Dynasty Urn with Coca-Cola Logo,** *1995*
Gouache on clay, 25 x 28 x 28 cm
Gouache auf Ton, 25 x 28 x 28 cm
《画着可口可乐商标的陶瓮》1995年, 陶上彩绘, 25 x 28 x 28 cm

6 **Bowl of Pearls,** *2006*
Coloured porcelain from Jingdezhen, half a ton of clear fresh water pearls, 100 cm diameter, 43 cm height
Farbiges Porzellan aus Jingdezhen, eine halbe Tonne helle Süßwasserperlen, Durchmesser 100 cm, Höhe 43 cm
《珍珠碗》2006年, 景德镇彩瓷、半吨淡水珍珠, 直径100 cm, 高43 cm

7 **Map of China,** *2006*
Iron wood (lignum vitae) from a destroyed Qing-Dynasty temple (1644–1911), 160 cm diameter, 80 cm height
Eisenholz (lignum vitae) von einem zerstörten Tempel aus der Qing-Dynastie (1644–1911), Durchmesser 160 cm, Höhe 80 cm
《中国地图》2006年，铁木取自一座毁坏的清朝寺庙中

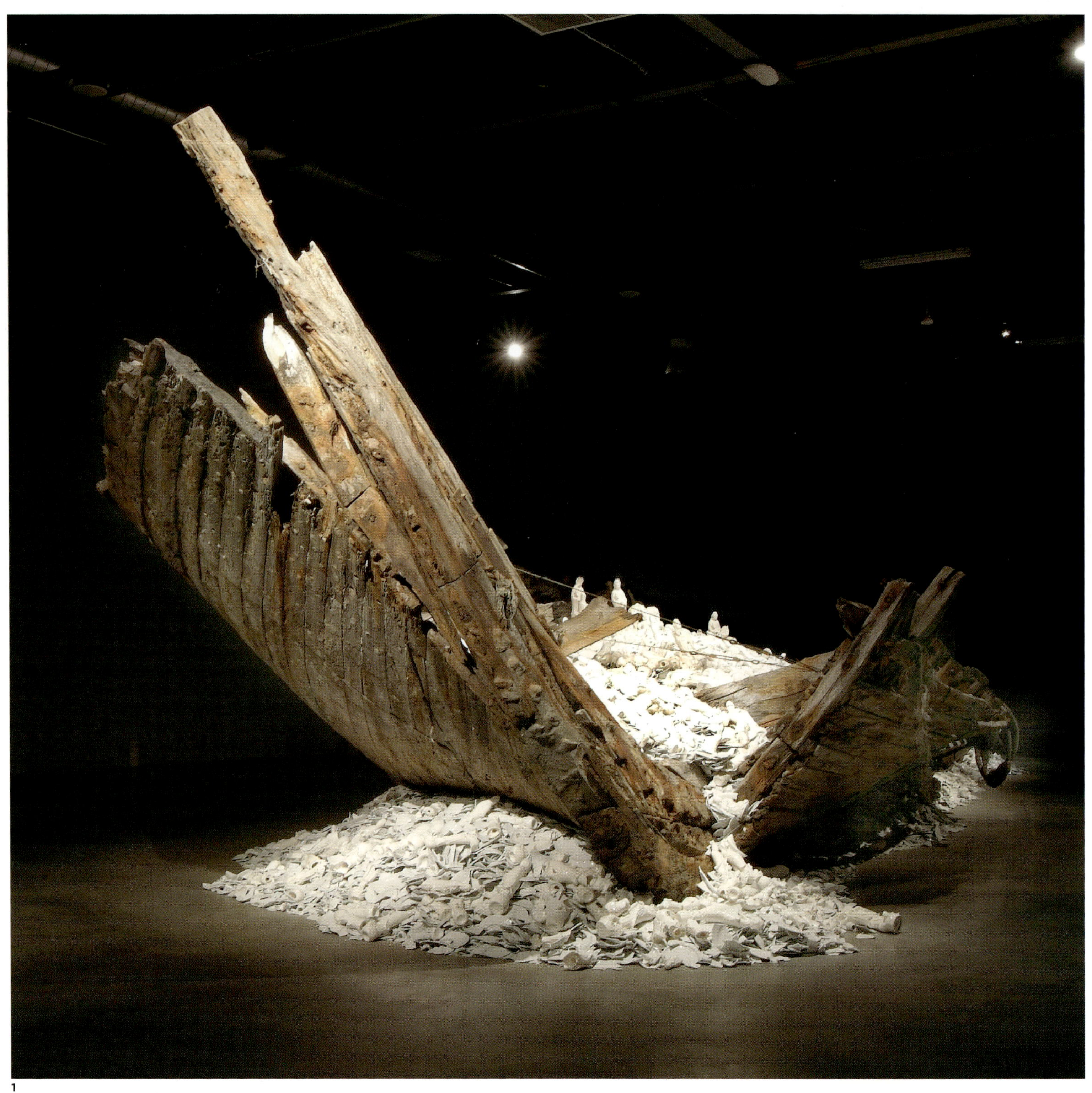

1

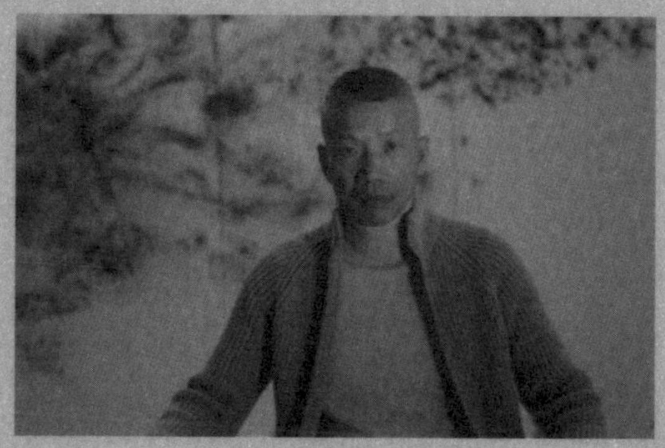

"As a Chinese you are always involved in history – an obligation I learned from my father who is art historian."

„Als Chinese ist man immer Teil der Geschichte – eine Verpflichtung, die ich von meinem Vater, der Kunsthistoriker ist, gelernt habe."

"中国人不能从历史中摆脱–这是我向我父亲学习的义务，他是艺术史学家。"

Born in 1957 in Quanzhou, China. Lives and works in New York, NY, USA
Geboren 1957 in Quanzhou, China. Lebt und arbeitet in New York, NY, USA
1957年出生于中国泉州。现居住工作于纽约, 美国

***Selected exhibitions* / Ausgewählte Ausstellungen / 所选展览**

2002 "Cai Guo-Qiang", Shanghai Art Museum, Shanghai, China
2003 "Ye Gong Hao Long: Explosion Project for Tate Modern", Tate Modern, London, UK
2006 "Cai Guo-Qiang: Head On", Sammlung Deutsche Bank, Deutsche Guggenheim Berlin, Berlin, Germany
"Cai Guo-Qiang on the Roof: Transparent Monument", Metropolitan Museum of Art, New York, NY, USA

2002年 《蔡国强》上海美术馆，上海
2003年 《叶公好龙：爆炸项目为Tate 现代》Tate 现代，伦敦
2006年 《蔡国强："Head On"》德意志银行收藏，德国古根海姆柏林，德国
《蔡国强在屋顶上：透明纪念碑》大城市艺术馆，纽约

***Selected publications* / Ausgewählte Publikationen / 所选著作**

Barry Schwabsky: "Tao and Physics: The Art of Cai Guo-Qiang", in: "Artforum", New York, Summer 1997
Eleanor Heartney: "Cai Guo-Qiang: Illuminating the New China", in: "Art in America", New York, May 2002
Holland Cotter: "Public Art Both Violent and Gorgeous", "New York Times", 14.9.2003
Jessica Dawson: "Cai Guo-Qiang's Ship Has Come in at Sackler", in: "The Washington Post", 14.11.2004
Bridget Goodbody: "The Peace Process", in: "ArtReview", London, November 2004

Schwabsky, Barry（著）:《道和物理：蔡国强的艺术》在《艺术论坛》纽约1997年
Heartney, Eleanor（著）:《蔡国强：照亮新中国》在《艺术与美国》纽约2002年5月
Cotter, Holland（著）:《公开艺术猛烈和华美》纽约时代周刊，2003年9月14日
Dawson, Jessica（著）:《蔡国强的船进来在Sackler》华盛顿邮报，2004年11月14日
Goodbody, Bridget（著）:《和平进程》艺术回顾，伦敦，2004年11月

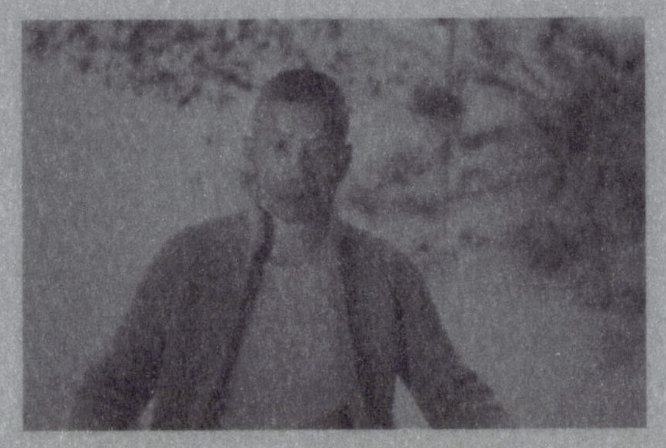

“As a Chinese you are always involved in history - an obligation I learned from my father who is art historian.”

„Als Chinese ist man immer Teil der Geschichte - eine Verpflichtung, die ich von meinem Vater, der Kunsthistoriker ist, gelernt habe.“

“中国人不能从历史中摆脱-这是我向我父亲学习的义务，他是艺术史学家。”

Born in 1957 in Quanzhou, China. Lives and works in New York, NY, USA
Geboren 1957 in Quanzhou, China. Lebt und arbeitet in New York, NY, USA
1957年出生于中国泉州。现居住工作于纽约，美国

Selected exhibitions / Ausgewählte Ausstellungen / 所选展览

2002 "Cai Guo-Qiang", Shanghai Art Museum, Shanghai, China
2003 "Ye Gong Hao Long: Explosion Project for Tate Modern", Tate Modern, London, UK
2006 "Cai Guo-Qiang: Head On", Sammlung Deutsche Bank, Deutsche Guggenheim Berlin, Berlin, Germany
"Cai Guo-Qiang on the Roof: Transparent Monument", Metropolitan Museum of Art, New York, NY, USA

2002年 《蔡国强》上海美术馆，上海
2003年 《叶公好龙：爆炸项目为Tate 现代》Tate 现代，伦敦
2006年 《蔡国强："Head On"》德意志银行收藏，德国古根海姆柏林，德国
《蔡国强在屋顶上：透明纪念碑》大城市艺术馆，纽约

Selected publications / Ausgewählte Publikationen / 所选著作

Barry Schwabsky: "Tao and Physics: The Art of Cai Guo-Qiang", in: "Artforum", New York, Summer 1997
Eleanor Heartney: "Cai Guo-Qiang: Illuminating the New China", in: "Art in America", New York, May 2002
Holland Cotter: "Public Art Both Violent and Gorgeous", "New York Times", 14.9.2003
Jessica Dawson: "Cai Guo-Qiang's Ship Has Come in at Sackler", in: "The Washington Post", 14.11.2004
Bridget Goodbody: "The Peace Process", in: "ArtReview", London, November 2004

Schwabsky, Barry（著）：《道和物理：蔡国强的艺术》在《艺术论坛》纽约1997年
Heartney, Eleanor（著）：《蔡国强：照亮新中国》在《艺术与美国》纽约2002年5月
Cotter, Holland（著）：《公开艺术猛烈和华美》纽约时代周刊，2003年9月14日
Dawson, Jessica（著）：《蔡国强的船进来在Sackler》华盛顿邮报，2004年11月14日
Goodbody, Bridget（著）：《和平进程》艺术回顾，伦敦，2004年11月

CAI GUOQIANG 蔡国强

[tsʰaɪ kuɔtɕʰiɑŋ]

The most famous works of Cai Guoqiang are like fireworks. The sound and light intensive effect of the respective staging as event will be documented by video footage too, but the pictures on exhibition are the smoke residue traces of pyrotechnical explosions. Spectacular installations between east and west, symbol and form enriched with dynamic and chaos are also part of the artist's repertoire who lives now in New York. Cai studied stage set design, spent some time in Japan and connects his Chinese roots and eastern tradition with the western world and the (existing or not existing) meaning related to a globally rapidly changing world. The individual seeks for the mystic of existence, the mental behind things and is looking for its place in universe. In every culture fire has something magic and holy, it is an original element, human beings learned to govern. And Cai is a perfect master in using fire as means of staging. The spectacular installations with title "Projects for Extra-terrestrials" comprise exclusively the individual and the extra-terrestrial, the unknown space of universe.

The traditional Chinese medicine used black powder as alchemical remedy – discovered accidentally when looking for immortality pills, but finally used to destroy lives. The hidden power of fire is full of beauty, but fugacious however, the explosions leave their traces on walls and become a remaining work of art in form of gunpowder drawings. On the other hand the social aspect of the firework is to be found: the shared experience of participants of a feast.

Cai Guoqiang's work is based on the old far eastern art of fortune telling, the traditional Chinese medicine and the philosophies of Dao and Chan. This tradition understands the whole universe as a chaotic entity – the Qi (energy) – which can be governed only by human beings' spirit. Cai uses the staged explosions to excite the power of Qi, liberates the human spirit and brings old ideas and values back to a new life. Chaos inspires him for extraordinary actions and works, making the spectators aware of disorientation and impersonal manner of the new global universal language – a vigorous impetus for reflection.

Die berühmtesten Arbeiten von Cai Guo-Qiang sind Feuerwerke. Die klang- und lichtintensive Wirkung der jeweiligen Inszenierung als Event wird zwar auch als Videoarbeit dokumentiert, die ausstellungsrelevanten Bilder sind aber die Schmauchspuren pyrotechnischer Explosionen. Ebenso gehören spektakuläre Rauminstallationen zwischen Ost und West, zwischen Symbol und Form, angereichert mit Dynamik und Chaos, zum Repertoire des heute in New York beheimateten Künstlers. Er hat Bühnendesign studiert, längere Zeit in Japan verbracht und verbindet seine chinesischen Wurzeln und die östliche Tradition mit der westlichen Welt und den (vorhandenen oder fehlenden) Sinnbezügen einer sich global rasant verändernden Situation. Das Individuum fragt nach dem Mythischen der Existenz, nach dem Spirituellen hinter den Dingen und befindet sich auf der Suche nach einem Platz im Universum.

Feuer ist wohl in jeder Kultur etwas Magisches und Heiliges, ein Ur-Element, das die Menschen zu beherrschen gelernt haben. Und Cai beherrscht es als inszenatorisches Mittel perfekt. In den mit „Projects for Extraterrestrials" betitelten Spektakeln geht es explizit um den Menschen und das Außerirdische, den unbekannten Raum des Universums.

In der chinesischen Medizin war Schwarzpulver ein alchimistisches Heilmittel – zufällig gefunden bei der Suche nach Unsterblichkeit, aber eingesetzt, um Leben zu zerstören. Die verborgene Macht des Feuers ist voller Schönheit und vergänglich, doch die Explosionen hinterlassen Spuren auf Wänden und werden in Schießpulver-Zeichnungen zu einem bleibenden Kunstwerk. Auf der anderen Seite steht der soziale Aspekt des Feuerwerks: das gemeinsame Erleben bei einem Fest aller Beteiligten.

Cai Guo-Qiangs Werk beruht auf der alten fernöstlichen Kunst der Wahrsagerei, der chinesischen Medizin und den Philosophien des Tao und Zen. In dieser Tradition wird das gesamte Universum als eine chaotische Gesamtheit, das Chi (Energie), verstanden, das nur vom Geist des Menschen kontrolliert werden kann. Mit seinen inszenierten Explo-

蔡国强的很著名的作品都象一堆焰火。虽然录像也记录了每个焰火的强烈声光效果，然而展出的照片上却是焰火爆炸好所留下的缕缕残烟。在东西方间的壮观的装置，虽然符号和形式富有动态感，而这个居住在纽约的艺术家的展示清单中，混乱仍是其中的一部分。他
在日本的大量时间学习舞台布景设计，并且将其中国根源和东方传统与西方世界连接在一起，这种存在或者不存在的内涵是与全球范围内迅速变化的世界有关。个体在探索事物背后的神秘存在和精神以及寻求事物在世间的位置。

在每个文化中，火具有一种魔力和神圣感，火是人类学习统治世界的原始元素之一。
作为舞台手法，蔡国强使用火来得心应手。大型装置《为外星人所作的计划》由个人和宇宙间未知外星空间所组成。

在中国传统医学中，黑火药被用作炼丹的材料-在寻求长生不老药时意外发明的，而黑火药却被用来摧毁生命。火的暗含的力量中充满着美感，但非常短暂，然而爆炸之后在墙上留下痕迹，成为火药绘画形式的遗留艺术作品。另一方面，也发现了焰火的社会意义：宴会参加者的共享经验。

蔡国强的作品创作基于古老远东的算命艺术、中国传统医学以及道禅哲学。传统认为，整个宇宙和人融为混乱的整体，气，只有人的意志才能驾驭。他使用分段爆炸来引发气的力量，解放人的心灵，把旧的观念和价值回归到新的生命形态中。混沌激发蔡国强做出非凡的举动和作品，使观众明白了新的全球共同语言的迷惑和非个人方式—这种语言强烈的促进了对过去的反思。

2006年，蔡国强在柏林展出了《Head On》，整个展览把其全部作品一分为三：焰火爆炸、火药绘画和空间装置，对于后者蔡选择凶野强壮的动物、在神化传说中英勇的象征：狼。这类动物通常被认

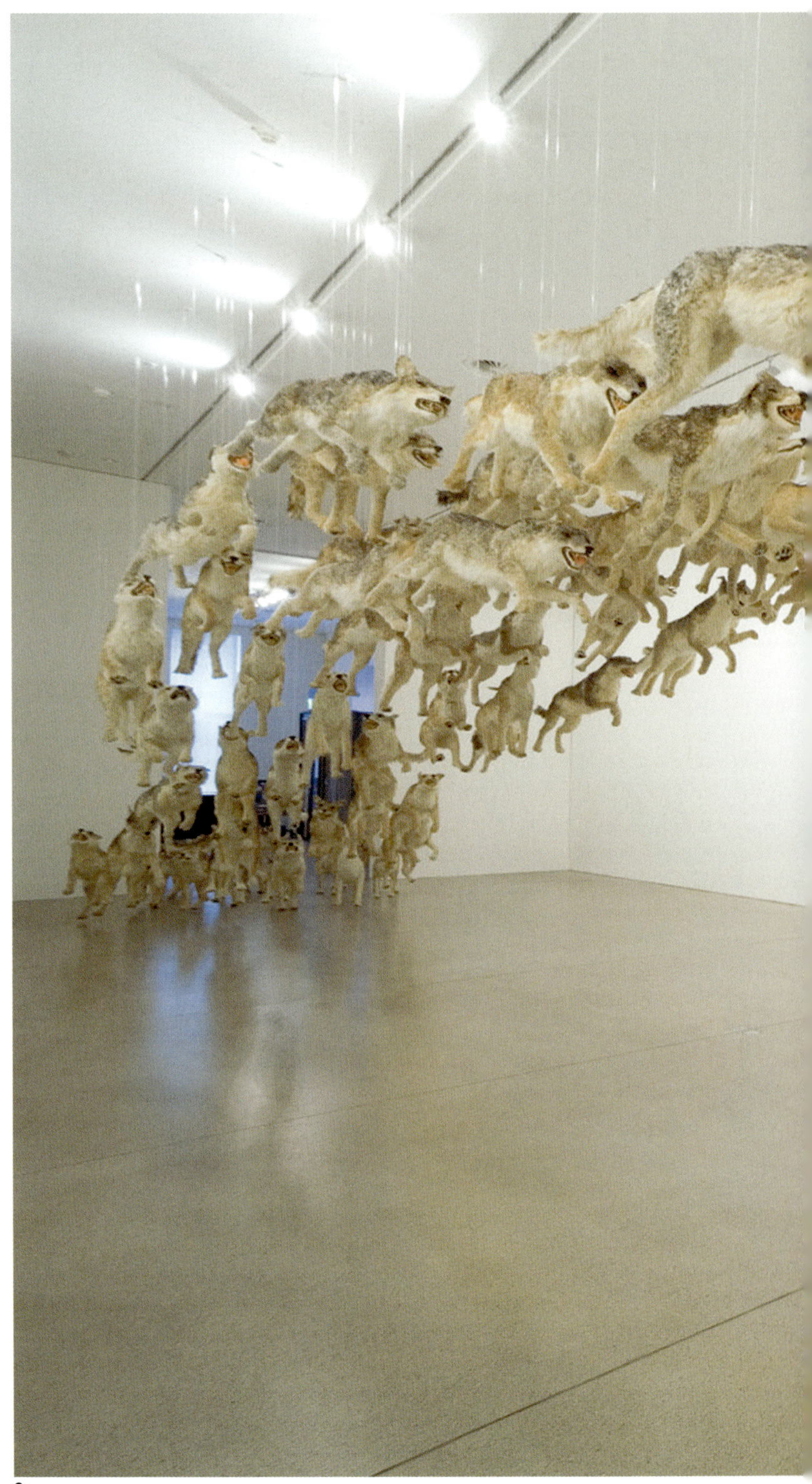

2

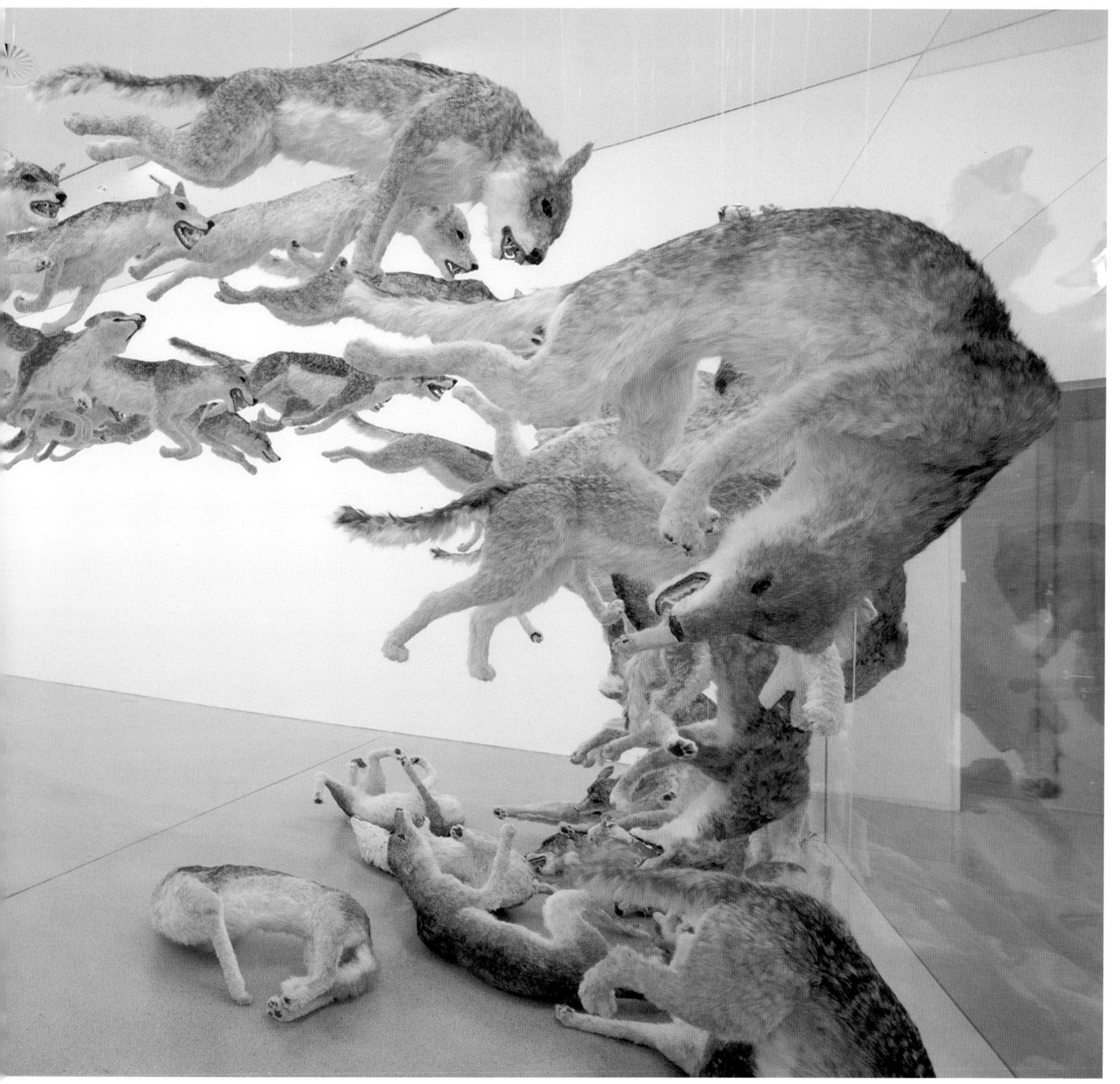

3

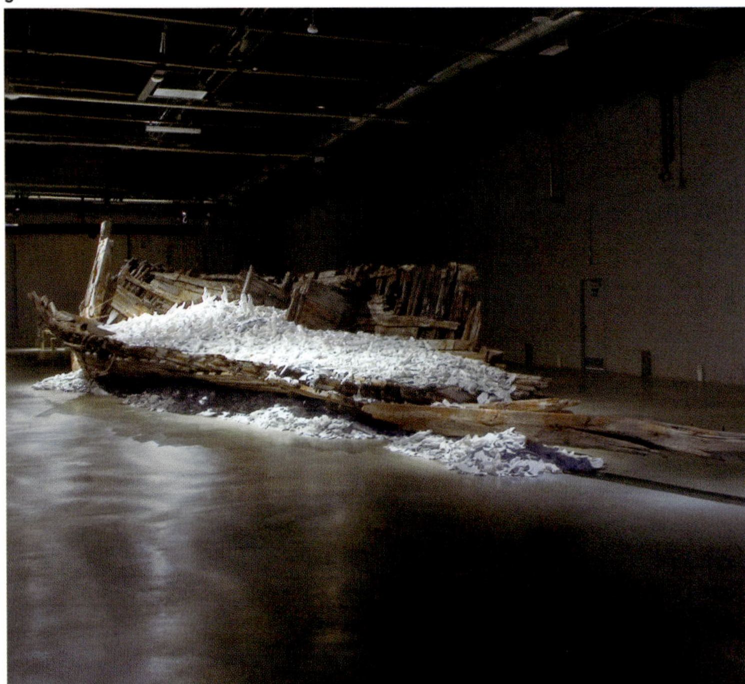

4

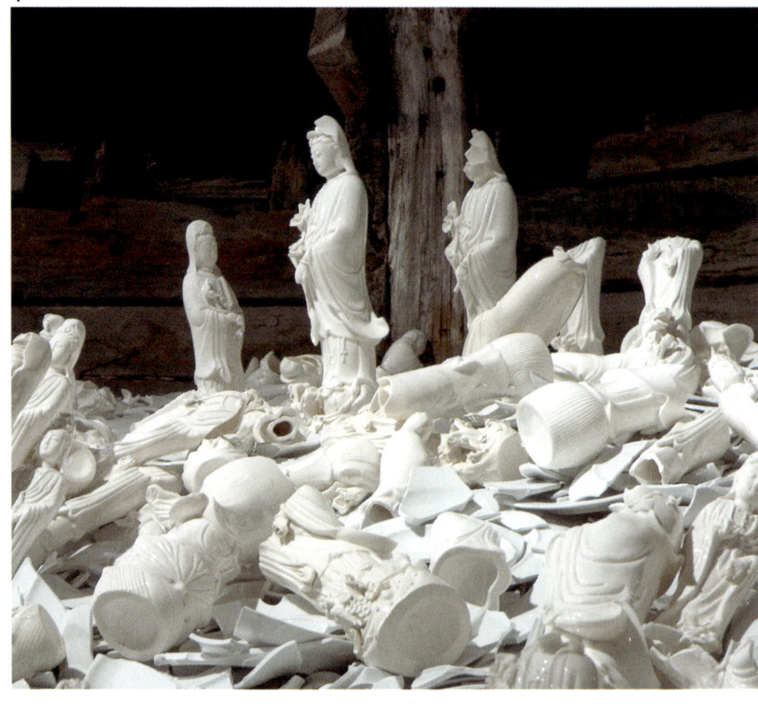

"Head On" (2006), Cai's exhibition in Berlin, was tripartite comprising the complete bandwidth of his œuvre: a firework explosion, a gunpowder drawing and a space installation. For the latter Cai chose a wild and strong animal, representing heroic features in myths: the wolf. This animal is regarded as being sociably living in prides – in Cai's installation such a pride forces its way wildly through the room, an organism full of energy, colliding with the wall again and again. The senseless and irrational is repeated as universal human tragedy being the thread through the history of mankind. Cai refers to the Zen concept of "tragic beauty" coming to life by most of our actions being completely senseless. Furthermore, his works have as subject subjective and universal reflections about the contradictory power of violence and beauty, of braveness and humour, destruction, fame and heroism among the eternal chaos. Cai was curator of the first-time presentation of the Chinese pavilion in Venice 2005, enhancing his current leading position as mediator of Chinese art.

sionen erweckt Cai die Kräfte des Chi, befreit den menschlichen Geist und belebt alte Ideen und Werte neu. Das Chaos inspiriert ihn zu ungewöhnlichen Aktionen und Arbeiten, durch die die Orientierungslosigkeit und Unverbindlichkeit der neuen globalen Weltsprache auch dem Publikum bewusst wird – ein kräftiger Anstoß zum Nachdenken.

Cais Berliner Ausstellung „Head On" (2006) war dreigeteilt und umspannte die ganze mediale Bandbreite seines Gesamtwerks: eine Feuerwerk-Explosion, eine Schießpulverzeichnung und eine Rauminstallation. Für letztere wählte Cai ein wildes, starkes Tier, das im Mythos auch heroische Charakterzüge trägt: den Wolf. Er gilt als gesellig und lebt im Rudel – in Cais Installation stürmt ein solches Wolfsrudel als ein einziger energiegeladener Organismus wie blind durch den Raum, um immer und immer wieder gegen die Wand zu prallen. Das Sinnlose und Unvernünftige wiederholt sich, als universelle menschliche Tragödie, quer durch die gesamte Menschheitsgeschichte. Cai beruft sich dabei auf das Zen-Konzept von der „tragischen Schönheit", die dadurch entsteht, dass die meisten unserer Handlungen völlig sinnlos sind. Darüber hinaus thematisieren seine weiteren Arbeiten zugleich subjektive wie allgemein gültige Reflektionen über die widersprüchlichen Kräfte von Gewalt und Schönheit, von Kühnheit und Humor, über Zerstörung, Ruhm und Heroismus inmitten des ewigen Chaos. Für die erstmalige Präsentation eines chinesischen Pavillons 2005 in Venedig trat Cai Guo-Qiang als Kurator auf, was seine aktuelle Führungsposition als Vermittler chinesischer Kunst unterstreicht.

为很骄傲的生物。蔡的装置中，此种骄傲随意的充斥着房间，精力旺盛的生物　　与冰冷死气的墙壁不断的冲突着。静态想象的图片代表着现实的场面。这种麻木和荒谬在世间人类的悲剧中重复着，也贯穿着人类的发展史。他通过我们无意义行为，把禅学中的“悲观美”融进生活中。此外他的作品以相对力量的客观和普遍的对应为主题，如永恒混沌中的暴力和美、勇敢和幽默、破坏和维护、名誉和英雄品质。蔡国强是首次在威尼斯双年展亮相的中国馆的策展人，突出他作为中国艺术调停人的主导作用。

Gregor Jansen

5

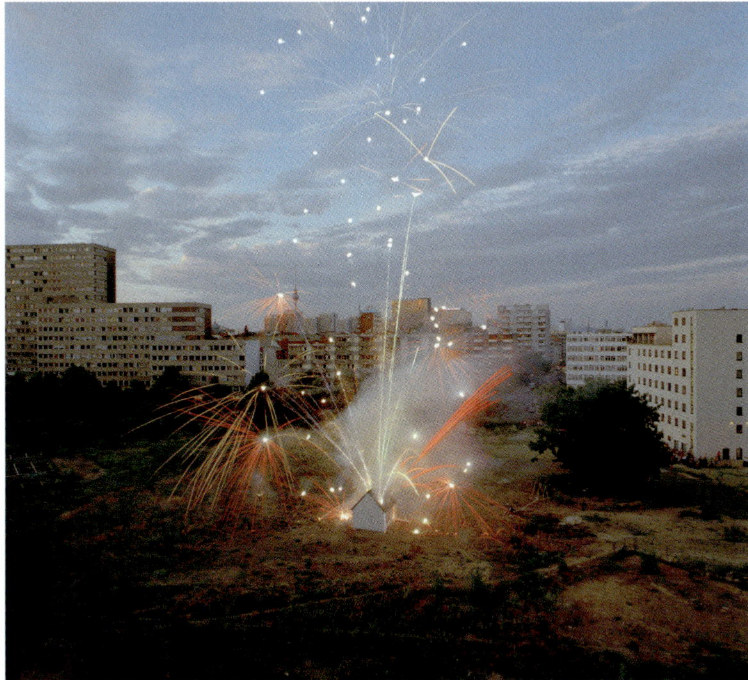

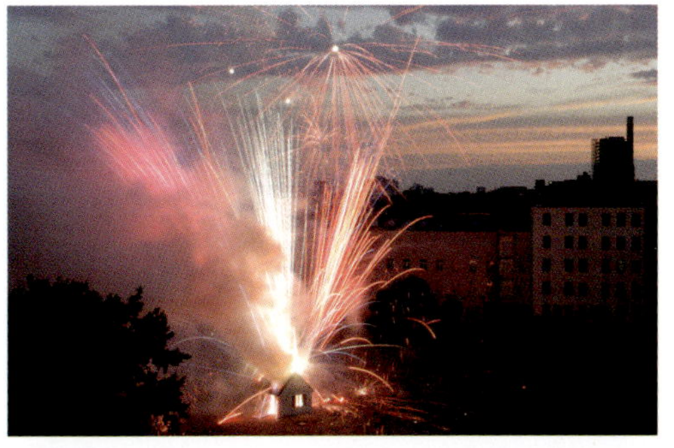

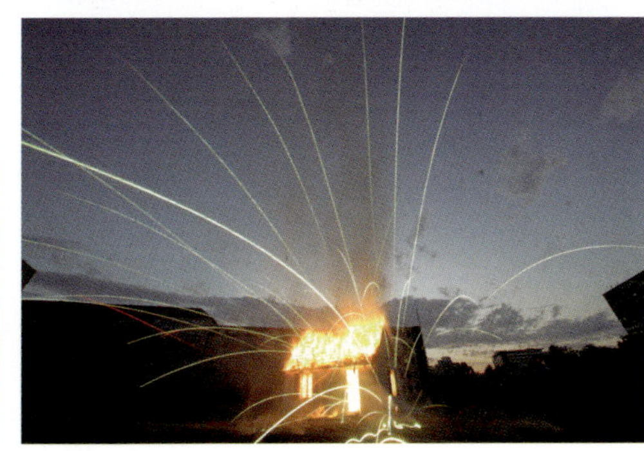

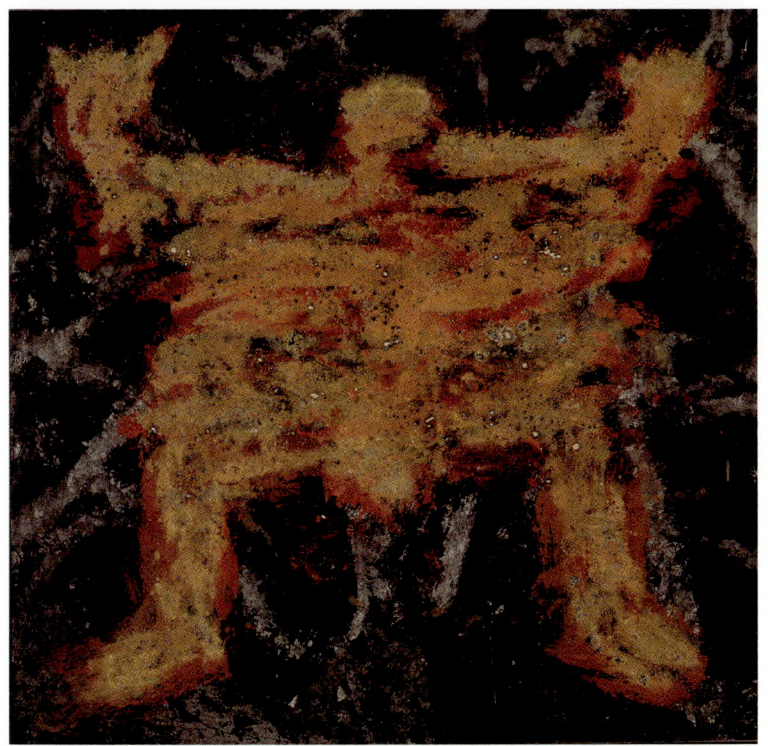

6

1 ***Reflection***, *2004*
Excavated boat, porcelains, 5.4 x 15 x 4.8 m
Geborgenes Boot, Porzellan, 5,4 x 15 x 4,8 m
《省》， 2004年, 挖掘的古舟, 瓷器, 5.4 x 15 x 4.8 m

2 ***Illusion II***, *2006*
Installation view "Head On", Deutsche Guggenheim Berlin
Commissioned by Deutsche Bank AG
Installationsansicht „Head On", Deutsche Guggenheim Berlin
Im Auftrag der Deutsche Bank AG
《幻想 II》2006年，装置实景 2006年，《迎面向前》，
德国古根海姆， 柏林，德意志银行委托

3 ***Reflection***, *2004*
Excavated boat, porcelains, 5.4 x 15 x 4.8 m
Geborgenes Boot, Porzellan, 5,4 x 15 x 4,8 m
《省》， 2004年, 挖掘的古舟, 瓷器， 5.4 x 15 x 4.8 m

4 ***Reflection***, *2004*
Excavated boat, porcelains (detail)
Geborgenes Boot, Porzellan (Detail)
《省》， 2004年, 挖掘的古舟, 瓷器，（详细）

5 ***Illusion II, Explosion Project***, 2006
Berlin 2006, commissioned by Deutsche Bank AG
Berlin 2006, im Auftrag der Deutsche Bank AG
《幻想 II》2006年 《爆炸 项目》2006年
柏林2006年， 德意志银行委托

6 ***Chu Wa Bang***, *1986*
Gunpowder, oil and ink on canvas, 155 x 150 cm
Schießpulver, Öl und Tusche auf Leinwand, 155 x 150 cm
《Chu Wa Bang》, 1986年, 火药, 布面油画和水墨,
155 x 150 cm

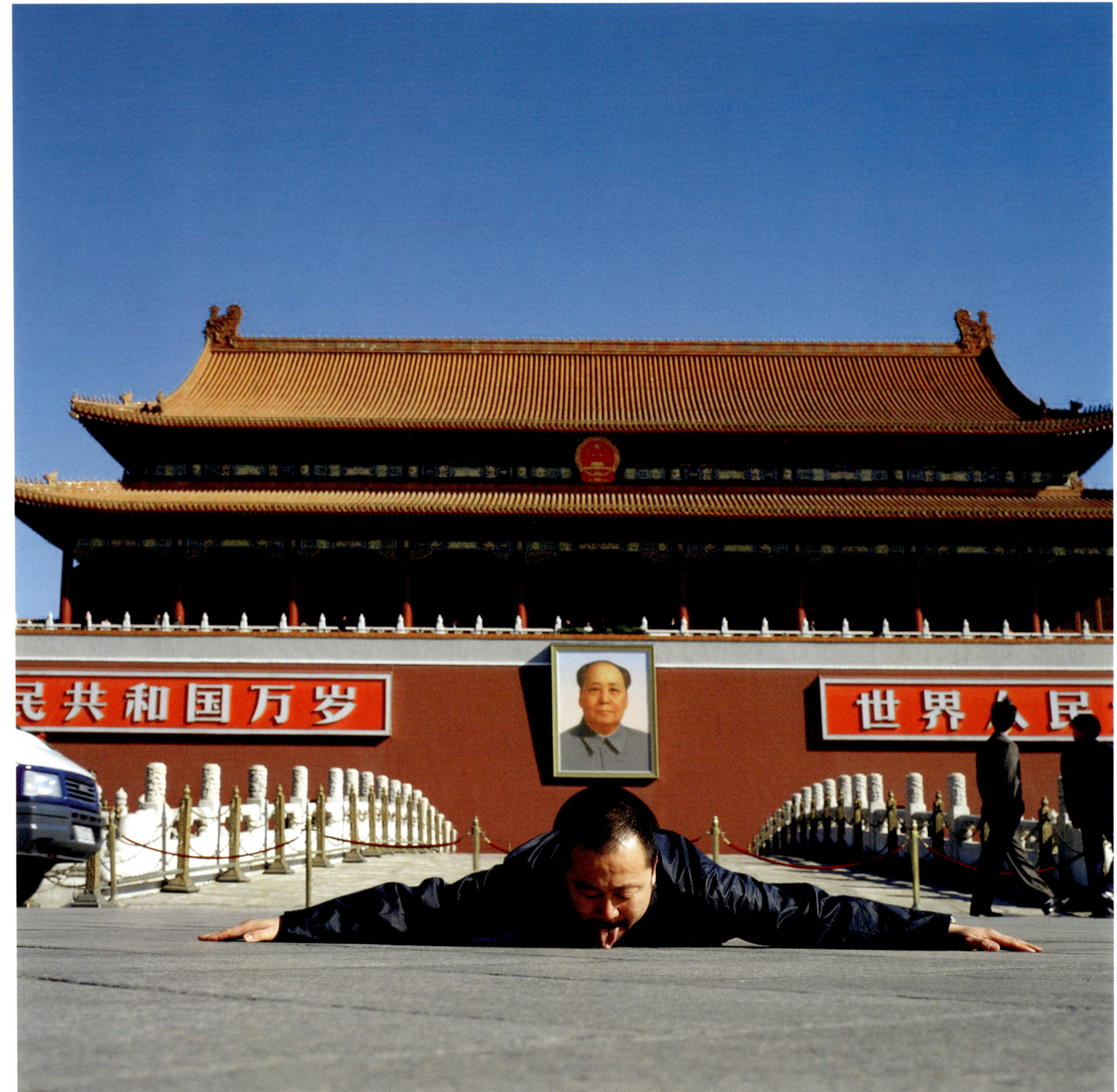

1

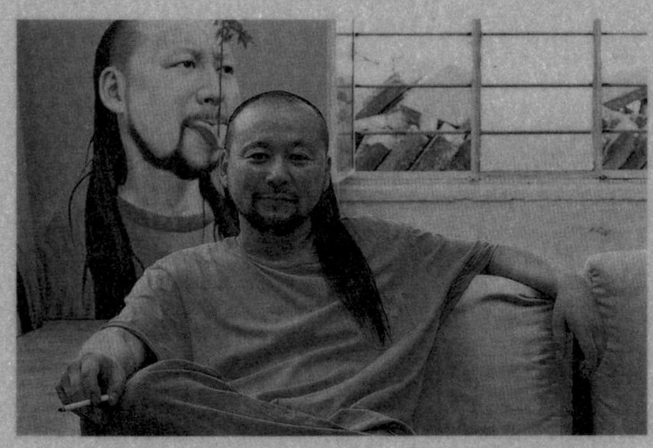

"Performance art is to find your offspring and the relation to the background of your roots."

„Performance-Kunst bedeutet, seinen eigenen Ursprung zu suchen und zu den eigenen Wurzeln zurückzukehren."

"做行为艺术一定要了解你的血缘、种族背景相关联，理清这条线索后再根据你目前的生存状态去发话。"

Born in 1967 in Suihua, Province Heilongjiang, China. Lives and works in Beijing
Geboren 1967 in Suihua, Provinz Heilongjiang, China. Lebt und arbeitet in Peking
1967年出生于中国绥化，黑龙江。现居住工作在北京

Selected exhibitions / **Ausgewählte Ausstellungen** / 所选展览

1994 "Virus Series: Trample the Face", solo performance, Beijing, China
2000 "Hot Pot, Kinesisk Samtidskunst, Chinese Contemporary Art", Kunstnernes Hus, Oslo, Norway
2002 Biennial of Sydney – The World May be Fantastic, Sydney, Australia
2003 "A Strange Heaven", Contemporary Chinese Photography, Vienna National Museum, Austria; National Gallery, Prague, Czech Republic
2006 "Cang Xin: Existence in Translation 1993–2006", 10 Chancery Lane Gallery, Beijing, China

1994年 《踩脸》北京东村， 中国
2000年 《火锅》中国当代艺术大展，挪威，奥斯陆
2002年 《悉尼双年展》澳大利亚，悉尼
2003年 《幻影天堂》中国当代摄影展，捷克，国家美术馆、法国，国家美术馆、奥地利，维也纳国家美术馆
2006年 《生存的转译 —— 苍鑫个展1993–2006》北京，程昕东当代艺术空间

Selected publications / **Ausgewählte Publikationen** / 所选著作

Cang Xin: "Existence in Translation", Beijing 2003
"Unusual scene report on necromancy", Shijiazhuang 2005

苍鑫（著）：《生命的转译》河北教育出版社，中国2003年
《异相景观一苍鑫巫术学报告》河北教育出版社，中国2005年

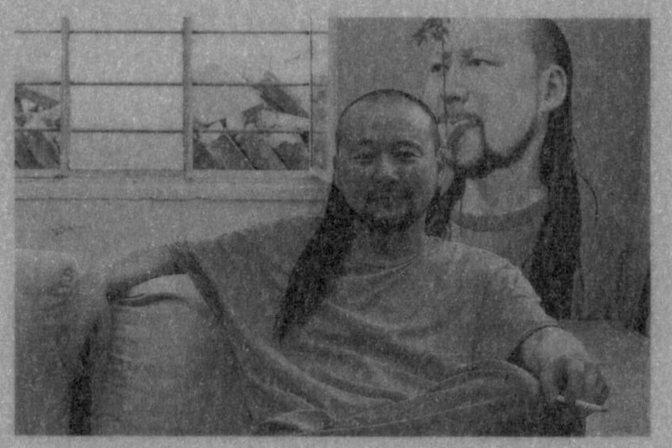

"Performance art is to find your offspring and the relation to the background of your roots."

„Performance-Kunst bedeutet, seinen eigenen Ursprung zu suchen und zu den eigenen Wurzeln zurückzukehren."

"做行为艺术一定要了解你的血缘，种族背景相关联，理清这条线索后再根据你目前的生存状态去发话。"

Born in 1967 in Suihua, Province Heilongjiang, China. Lives and works in Beijing
Geboren 1967 in Suihua, Provinz Heilongjiang, China. Lebt und arbeitet in Peking
1967年出生于中国绥化，黑龙江。现居住工作在北京

***Selected exhibitions* / Ausgewählte Ausstellungen / 所选展览**

1994	"Virus Series: Trample the Face", solo performance, Beijing, China
2000	"Hot Pot, Kinesisk Samtidskunst, Chinese Contemporary Art", Kunstnernes Hus, Oslo, Norway
2002	Biennial of Sydney - The World May be Fantastic, Sydney, Australia
2003	"A Strange Heaven", Contemporary Chinese Photography, Vienna National Museum, Austria; National Gallery, Prague, Czech Republic
2006	"Cang Xin: Existence in Translation 1993-2006", 10 Chancery Lane Gallery, Beijing, China

1994年	《踩脸》北京东村，中国
2000年	《火锅》中国当代艺术大展，挪威，奥斯陆
2002年	《悉尼双年展》澳大利亚，悉尼
2003年	《幻象天堂》中国当代摄影展，捷克，国家美术馆，法国，国家美术馆，奥地利，维也纳国家美术馆
2006年	《生存的转译 — 苍鑫个展1993-2006》北京，程昕东当代艺术空间

***Selected publications* / Ausgewählte Publikationen / 所选著作**

Cang Xin: "Existence in Translation", Beijing 2003
"Unusual scene report on necromancy", Shijiazhuang 2005

苍鑫（著）：《生命的转译》河北教育出版社，中国2003年
《异相景观一苍鑫巫术学报告》河北教育出版社，中国2005年

CANG XIN 苍鑫

[tshaŋ ɕin]

Cang Xin's experience of art creation has been based on performance art for more than a decade. As an important representative of Chinese performance art since the 1990s Cang Xin's performance art is doubtlessly a strong relationship between body and soul. He began his performances in Beijing's East Village in the 1990s with "Trample the Face" expressing his doubts of his own survival in his surroundings; the series "Communication" (since 1996) showed himself licking various items with his tongue, followed by the series "Identity Exchange" (since the late 1990s), in which the artist and different people exchange their clothing to borrow the symbolic status and identity related to their garments, to express the differences between soul and common nature in modern society.

In his series "The Unification of Heaven and Man" Cang Xin in fact redefines the meaning of performance art in his own way. His way is a kind of art shamanism, situated between the shaman, performance art and interaction of emotions, or in other words, art is for Cang Xin the modern expression of shamanism in the name of art. It can be said that Cang Xin has found his own individual way for his art, the core thereof lying in the search of performance art conception and the experience of identity of his individual roots in his native society. His latest work the "Shamanism" series – drawings and oil paintings – transgressing imagination, passes the soul concept of shamanism and supported by the role of the shaman and the modern psychologist the direct communication with other people's soul can be made.

Gradually Cang withdrew from the western conceptual art mode as for him the origins of action are to be sought more consciously in the innermost depth of one's soul. By constantly forcing his body past its perceived boundaries, he has repeatedly challenged, with his own experiences, existing concepts about art and the identity of the artist.

Cang Xin blickt heute auf mehr als zehn Jahre Performance-Kunst zurück. Als bedeutender Vertreter dieser Kunstrichtung in China betont er stark die Beziehung zwischen Körper und Seele. 1990 begann Cang in Pekings Künstlerviertel East Village mit „Trample the Face", das seine Zweifel am eigenen Überleben in dieser Umgebung ausdrückte. Die Serie „Communication" (seit 1996) zeigte ihn selbst in Situationen, in denen er verschiedene Gegenstände ableckt, und seit Ende der 1990er Jahre folgte „Identity Exchange": Cang Xin tauscht mit anderen Personen die Kleidung, um sich symbolisch den Status und die Identität des anderen auszuleihen und auf diese Weise die Unterschiede zwischen dem Individuum und dem Allgemeingültigkeitsanspruch der modernen Gesellschaft auszudrücken.

In „The Unification of Heaven and Man" definierte Cang die Bedeutung der Performance auf seine eigene Weise, denn für ihn ist sie angesiedelt zwischen Schamanismus, Kunst und emotionaler Interaktion, oder anders: Kunst ist für Cang der moderne Ausdruck für Schamanismus. Und er scheint für seine eigene Arbeit einen individuellen Weg gefunden zu haben, diese Konzeption sowie sein Kernthema, die schwierige Identitätserfahrung in seiner Heimatgesellschaft, umzusetzen. Sein jüngstes Werk, die „Schamanismus"-Serie – Zeichnungen und Ölgemälde –, geht allerdings schon darüber hinaus, lässt es doch das Konzept der eigenen Seele hinter sich, um stattdessen mithilfe des Schamanen und des modernen Psychologen eine direkte Kommunikation mit den Seelen anderer Menschen herbeizuführen.

Cang Xin zog sich nach und nach von den westlichen Formen der Konzeptkunst zurück, da er die Auffassung vertritt, dass der Ursprung der eigenen Handlungen bewusster im tiefsten Inneren der eigenen Seele zu erfahren ist. Indem er seinen eigenen Körper beständig dazu zwingt, über seine Grenzen hinauszugehen, fordert er immer wieder durch seine eigenen Erfahrungen die bestehenden Kunstauffassungen und die Identität des Künstlers heraus.

苍鑫十多年的艺术创作经历基本上都是以行为艺术的方式展开的。作为中国1990年代行为艺术的一个重要代表，苍鑫的行为艺术无疑具有一种很强烈的关于身体和灵异关系的实验性。从上世纪90年代初在北京“东村”的《踩脸》行为开始，表达了对自身生存境遇的质疑；1996年用舌头舔各种物品的《交流》系列，到90年代末与各种身份的人互换衣服的《身份互换》系列，假借象征外衣服饰的身份来验证灵魂之间在现代性社会可能的差异和共同的本质；以及他的《天人合一》系列等作品，苍鑫事实上用个人方式重新定义了行为艺术的含义。这种方式就是一种关于艺术的萨满想象，它介于巫、行为艺术和交感之间，换言之，苍鑫的艺术和身份也在巫师的受启、艺术家的表现和灵异学家的社会实验之间游动。艺术在苍鑫那里似乎不是一个纯粹的艺术，而是一个以艺术之名的萨满巫师的现代行为。可以说苍鑫走了一条自己独特的道路，这条道路的核心在于寻找行为艺术的观念基础和身体经验在本土社会的自我根源。

苍鑫最新创作的具有超验想象的《萨满》系列素描和油画等，是通过萨满的灵异观念，借助于巫师和现代科学家的角色，以及与他者直接的灵魂交流，逐渐摆脱了西方观念艺术的模式，更自觉地在内心灵魂深处寻找行为的思想原点，并且通过不断身体力行地超越身体边界，使自我经验不断挑战原有艺术观念和艺术家身份的边界。

Feng Boyi

2

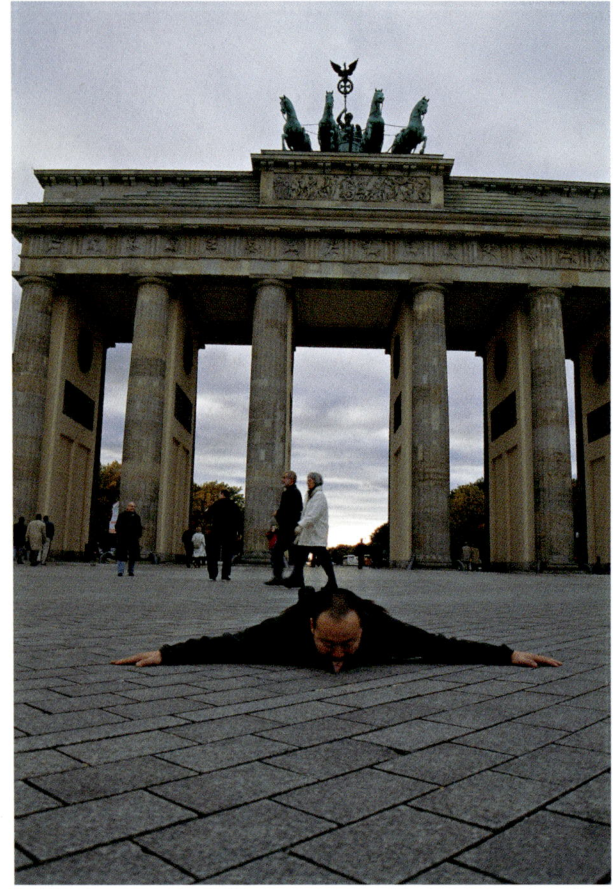

3

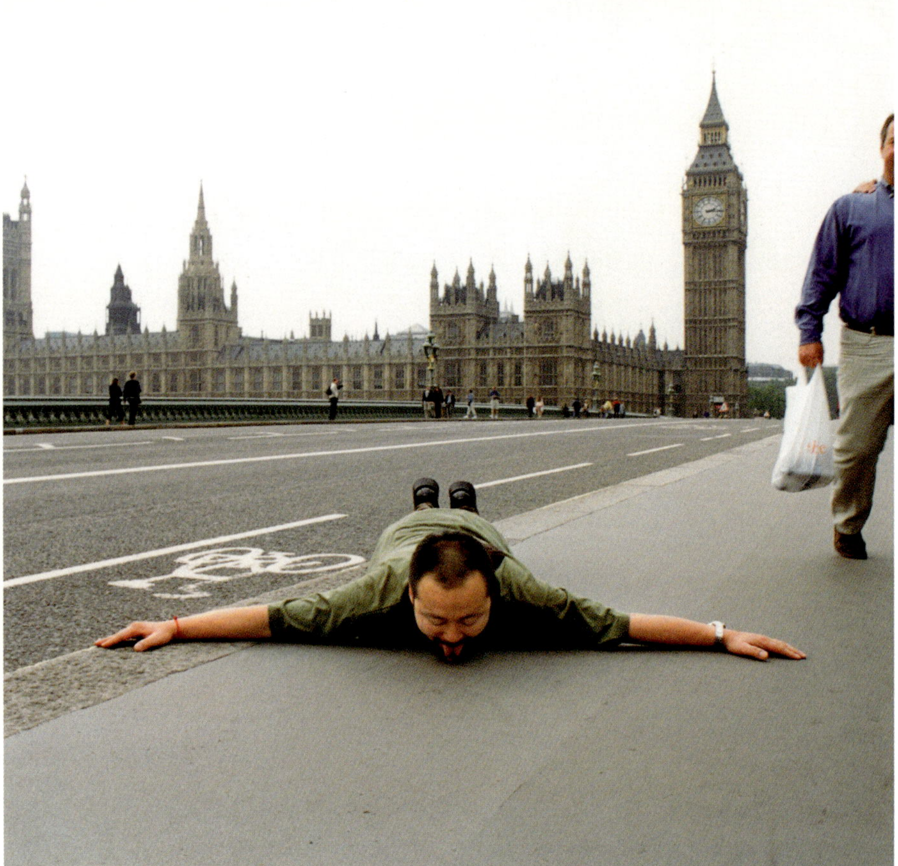

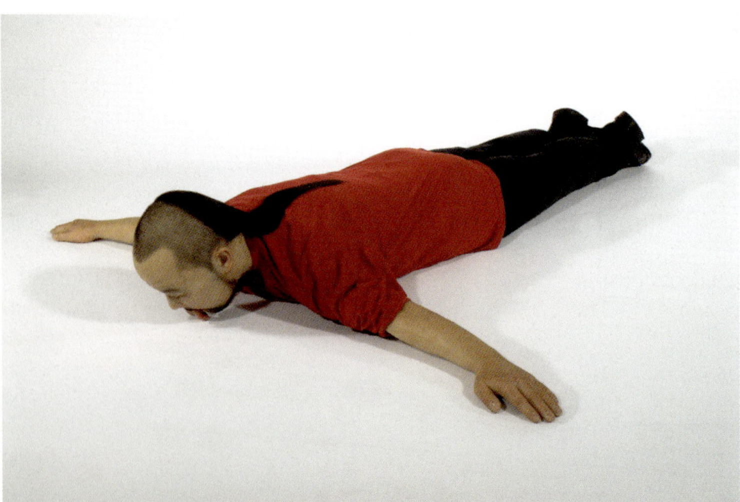

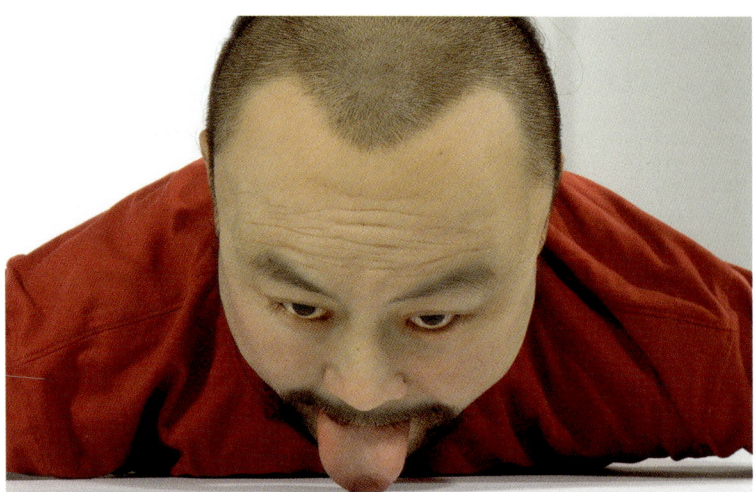

4

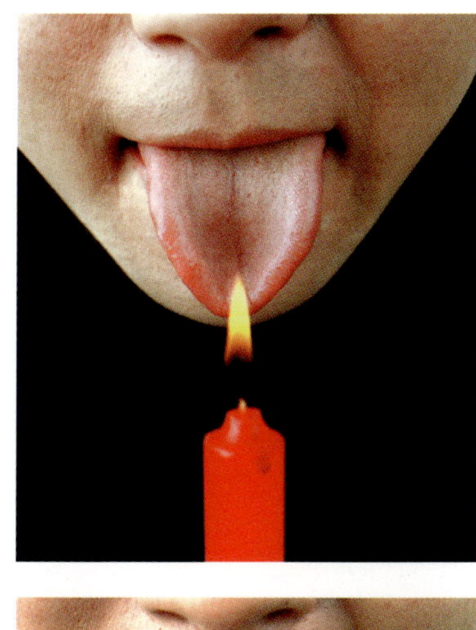
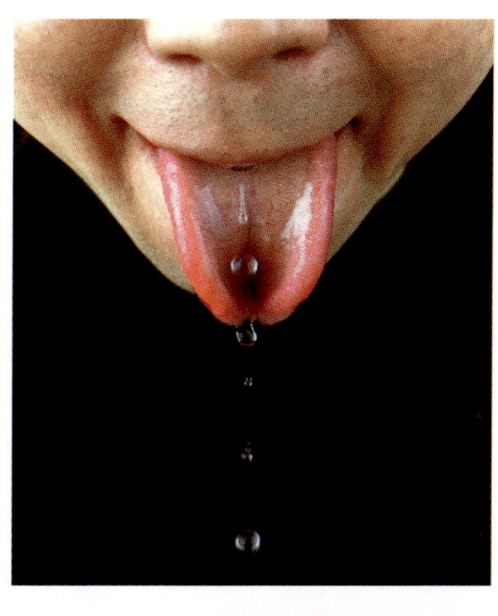
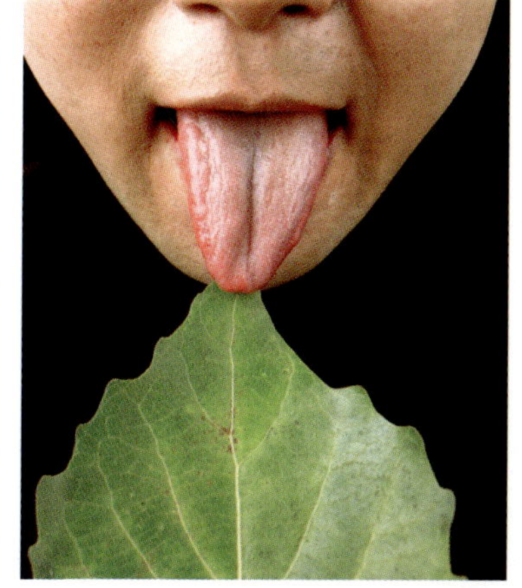
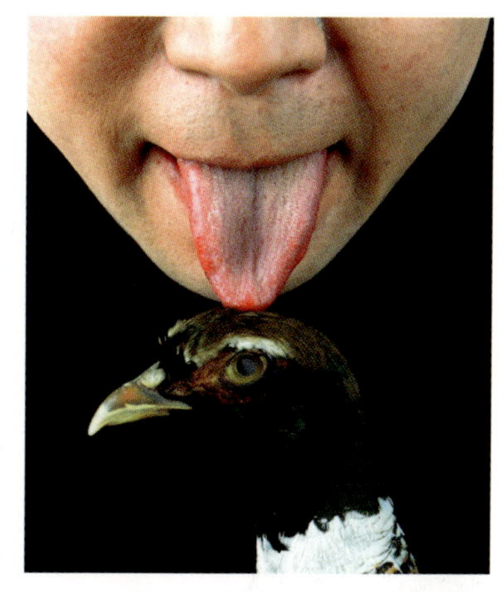
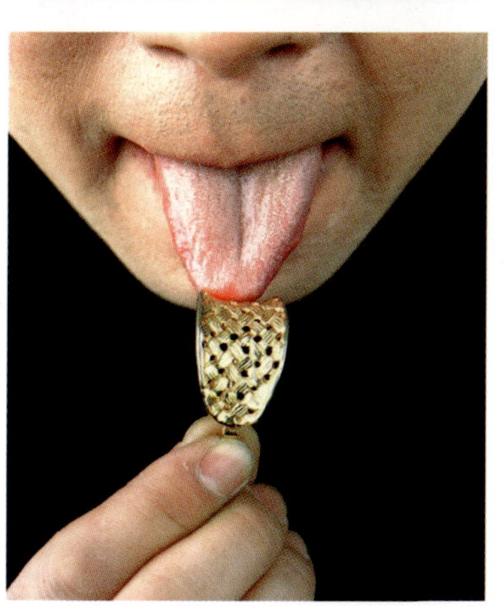
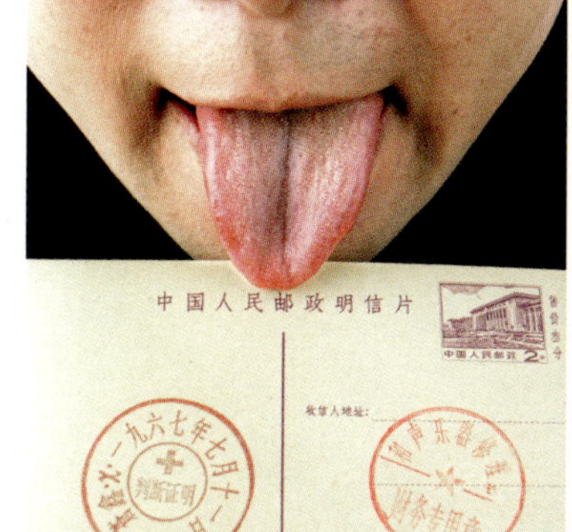

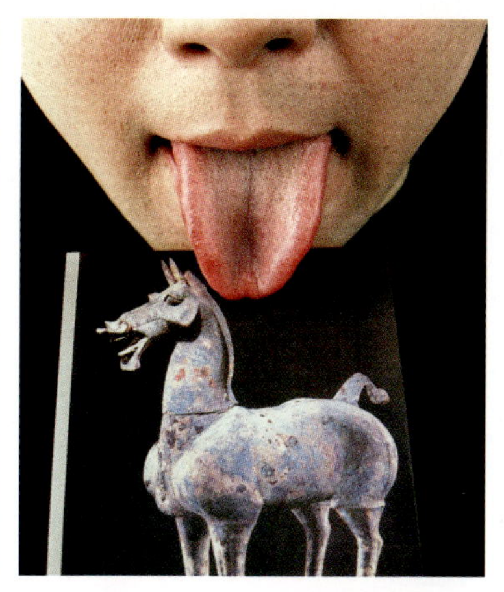
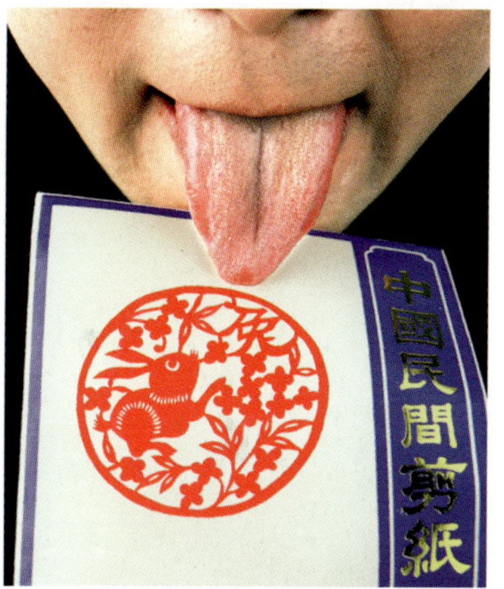

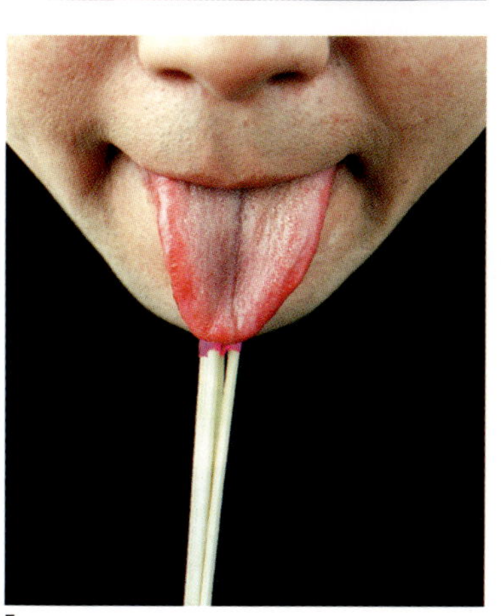
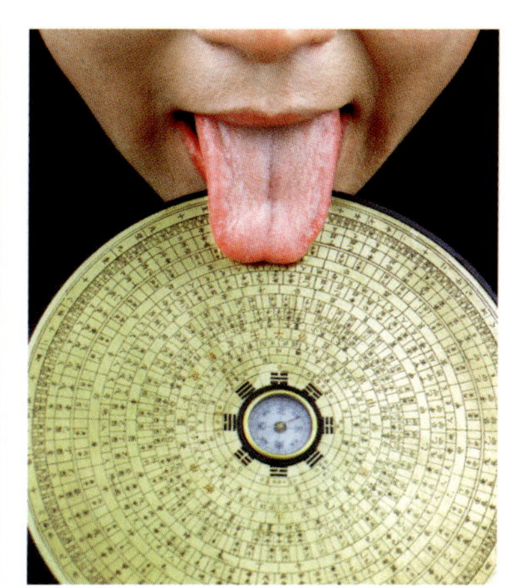
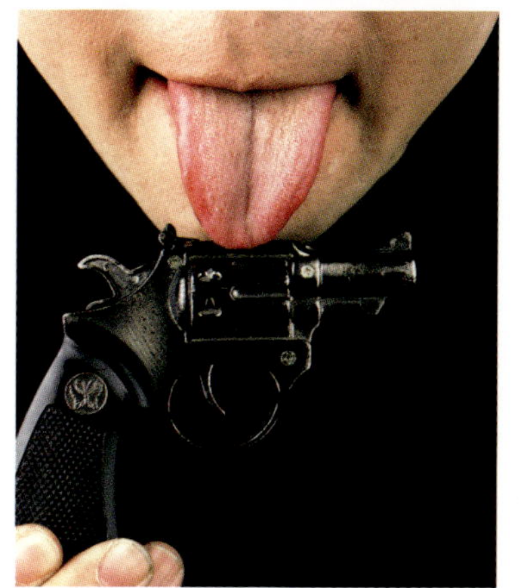
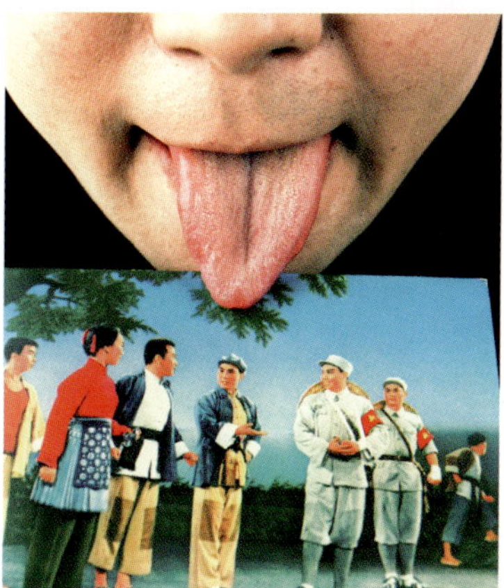

5

6

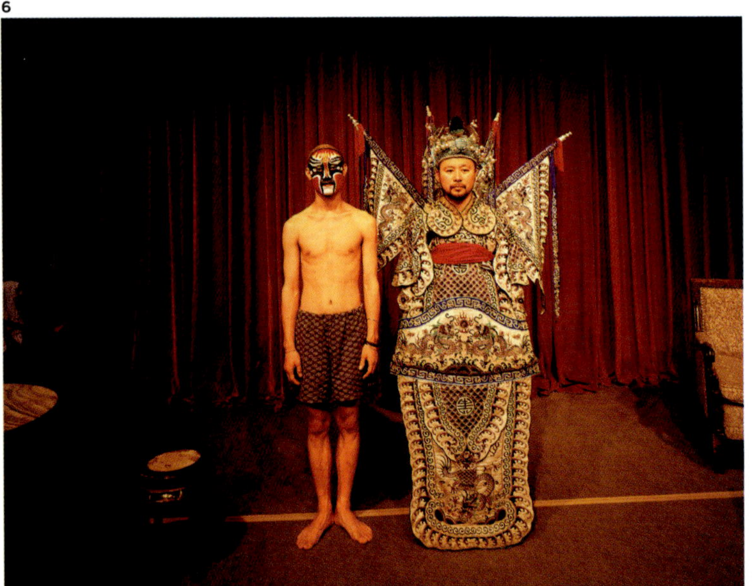

7

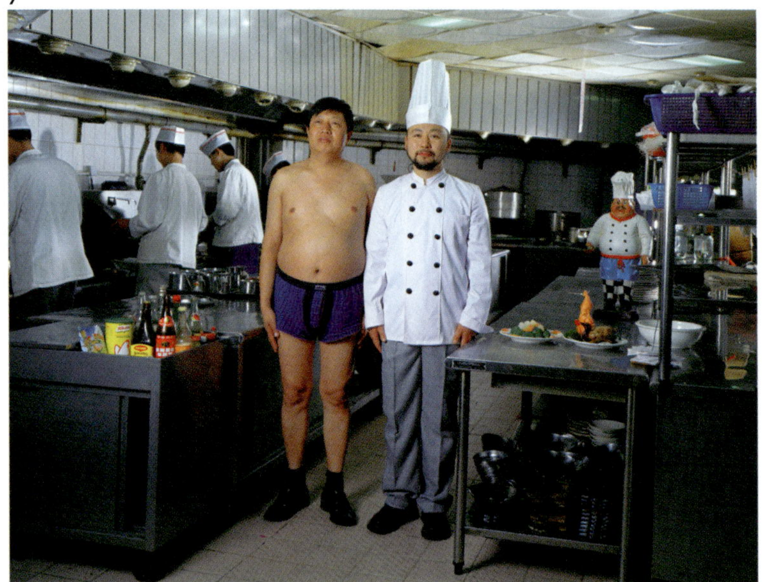

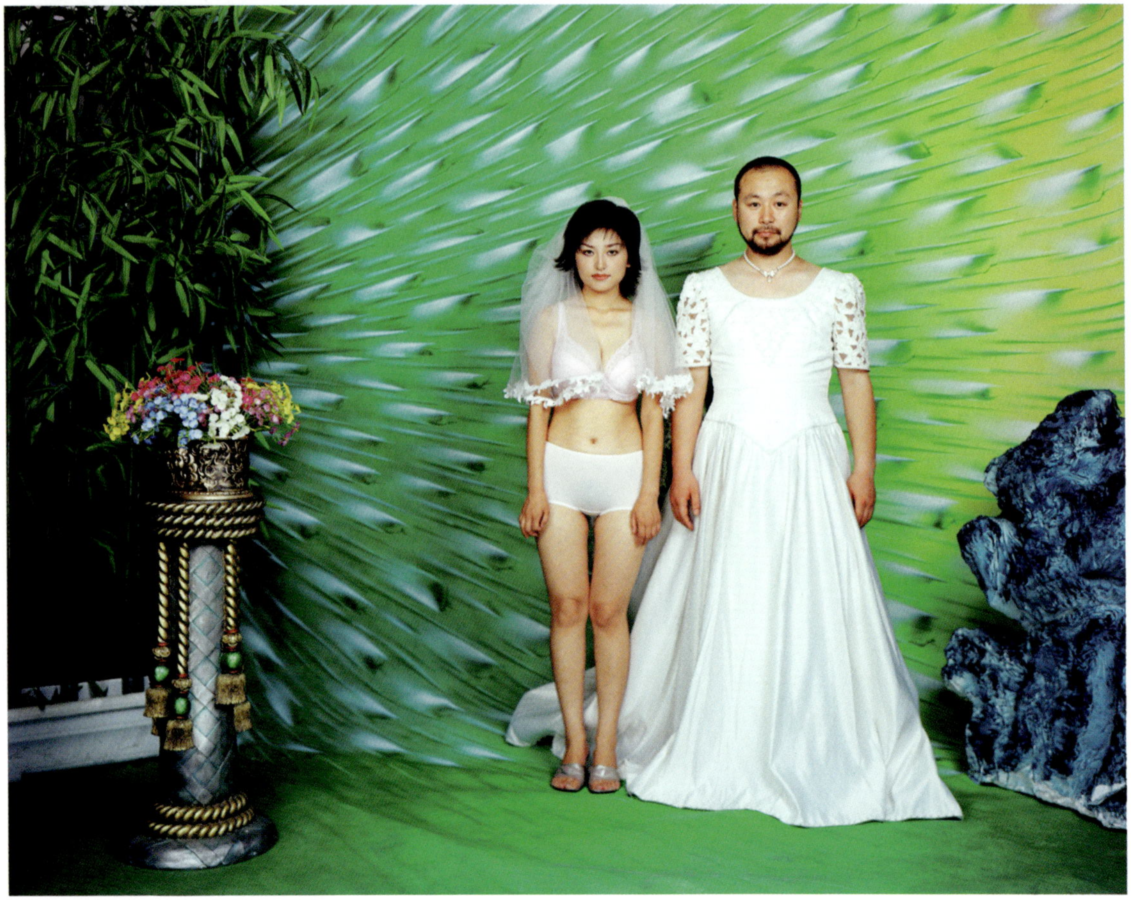

8

9

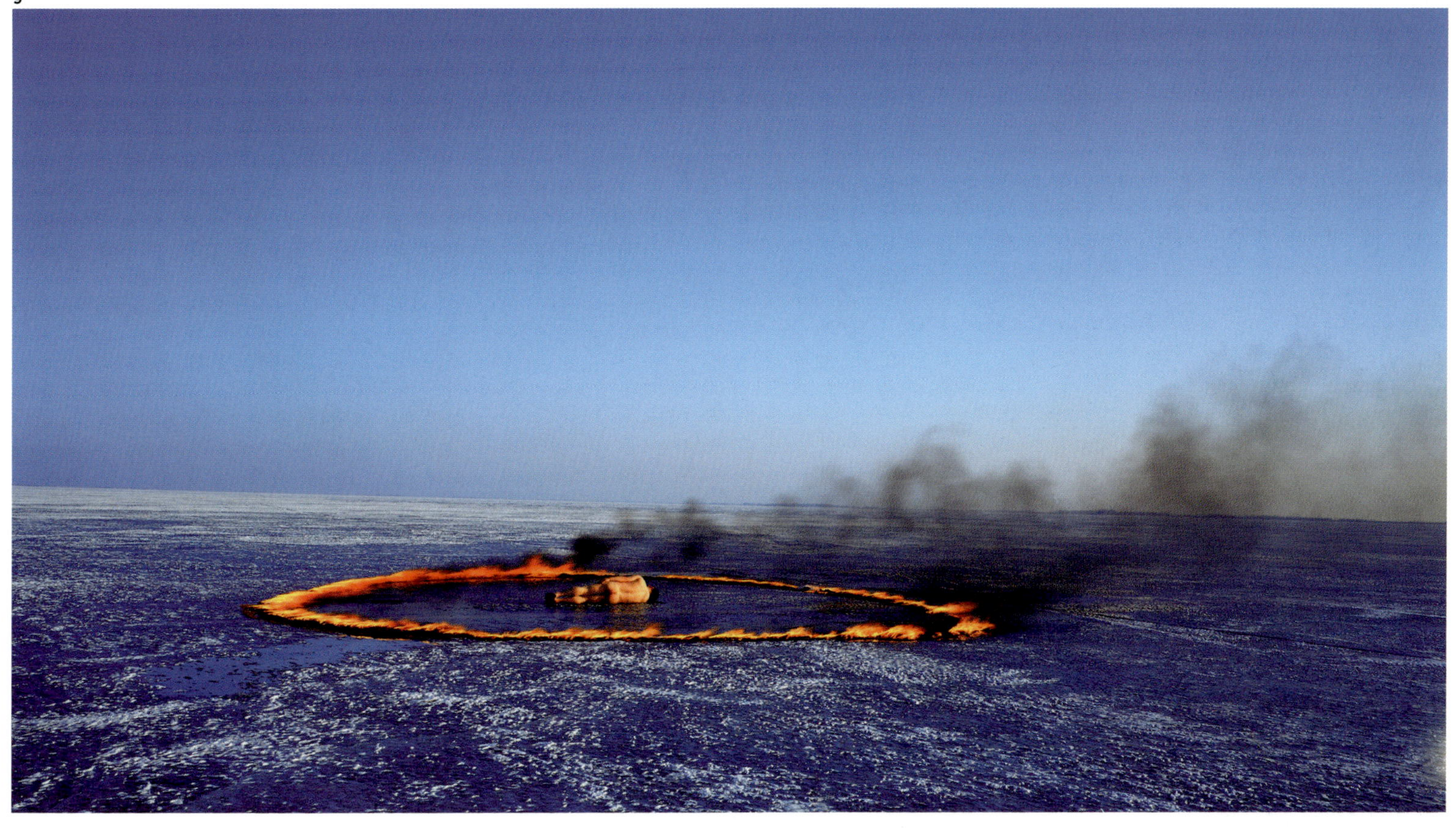

1 ***Communication Series – Tian'anmen***, *2002*
Performance
Performance
《交流系列 - 天安门》2002年, 表演

2 ***Communication Series – Brandenburger Tor***, *2003*
Performance
Performance
《交流系列 - 勃兰登堡门》2003年, 表演

3 ***Communication Series – London,*** *2001*
Performance
Performance
《交流系列 - 伦敦》, 2001年, 表演

4 ***Communication***, *2006*
Sculpture made of silica gel, 172 cm length
Skulptur aus Silica-Gel, Länge 172 cm
《交流》雕塑硅胶, 2006年, 长172 cm

5 ***Communication Series No. 2***, *1999*
Photographs, 60 x 50 cm each
Fotografien, je 60 x 50 cm
《交流系列No. 2》1999年, 摄影, 每幅60 x 50 cm

6 ***Identity Exchange Peking***, *2003*
Photograph, 105 x 85 cm
Fotografie, 105 x 85 cm
《身份互换-北京》2003年, 摄影, 105 x 85 cm

7 ***Identity Exchange Chef***, *2003*
Photograph, 105 x 85 cm
Fotografie, 105 x 85 cm
《身份互换-厨师》2003年, 摄影, 105 x 85 cm

8 ***Identity Exchange Wedding, Yellow***, *2003*
Photograph, 105 x 85 cm
Fotografie, 105 x 85 cm
《身份互换-婚礼》, 2003年, 摄影, 105 x 85 cm

9 ***Man and Sky as One Series – Fire Ring***, *2003*
Photograph, 127 x 250 cm
Fotografie, 127 x 250 cm
《天人合一》2003年, 摄影, 127 x 250 cm

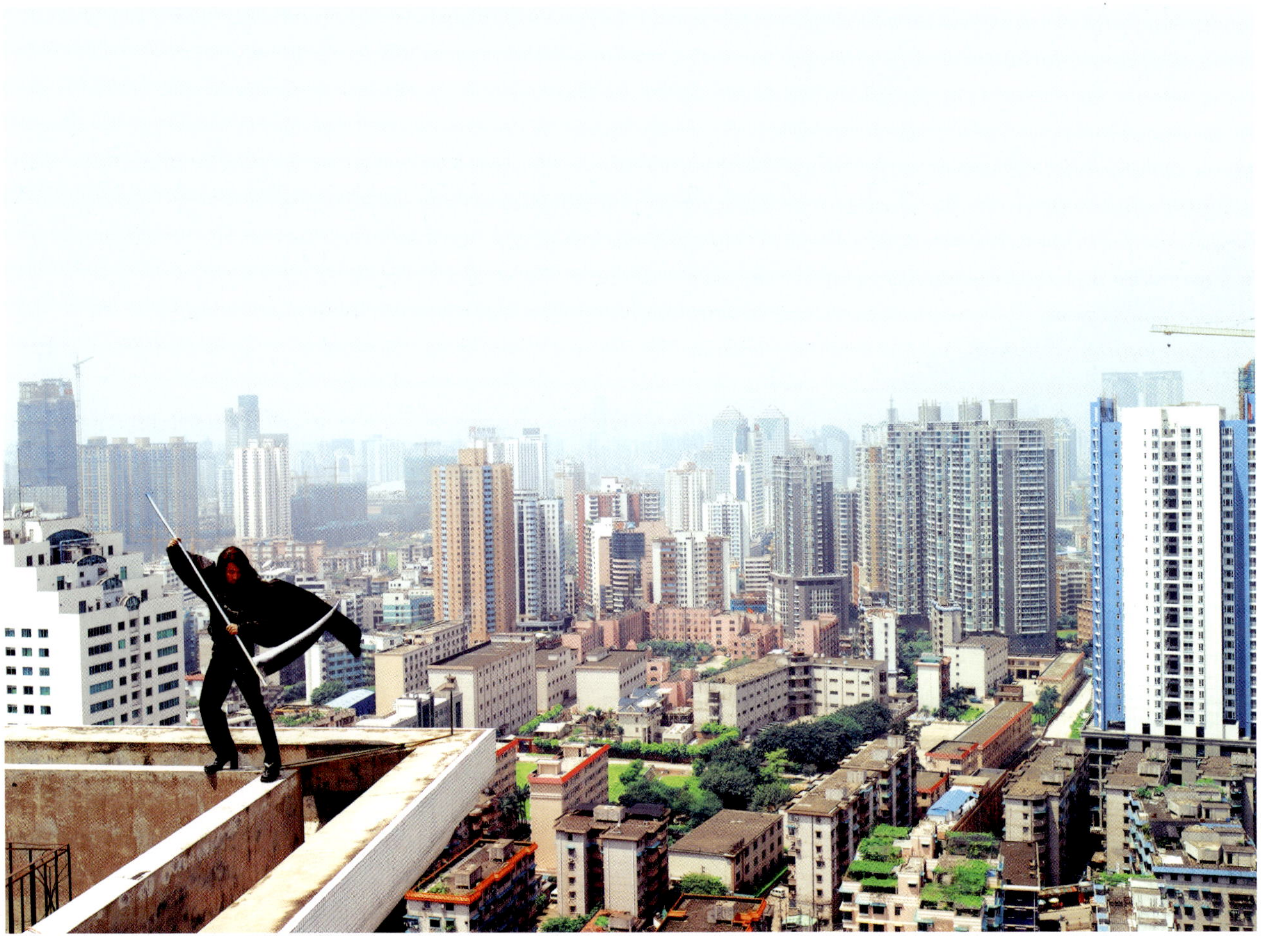

1

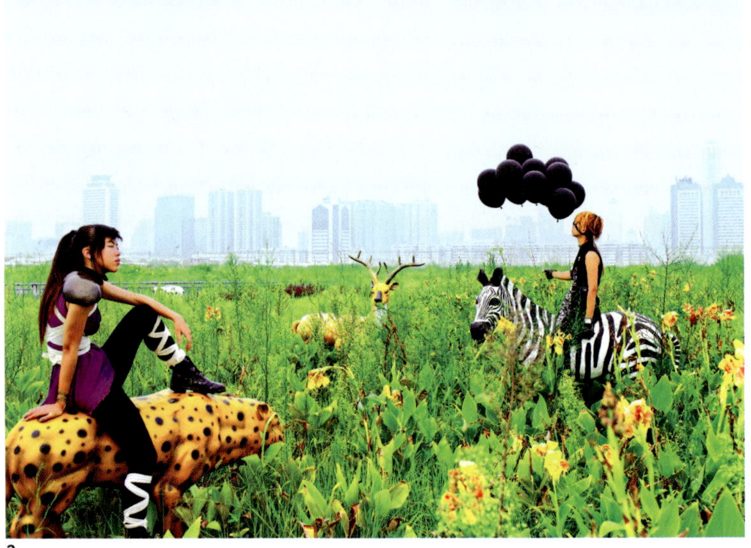

2

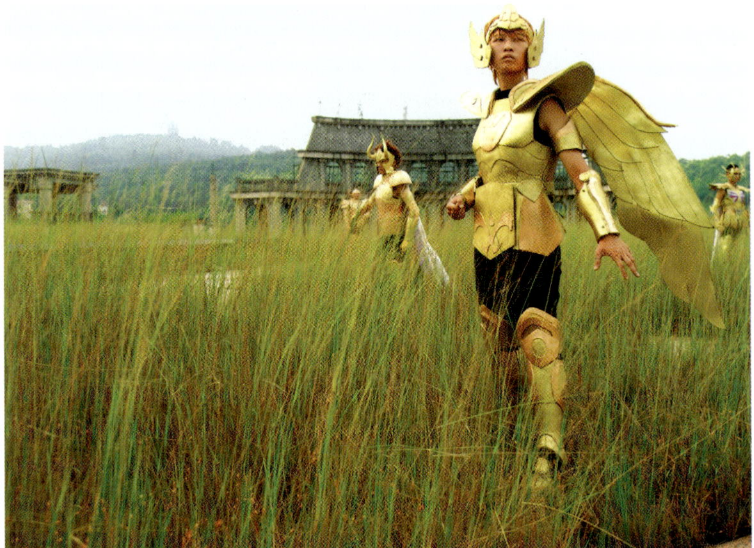

3

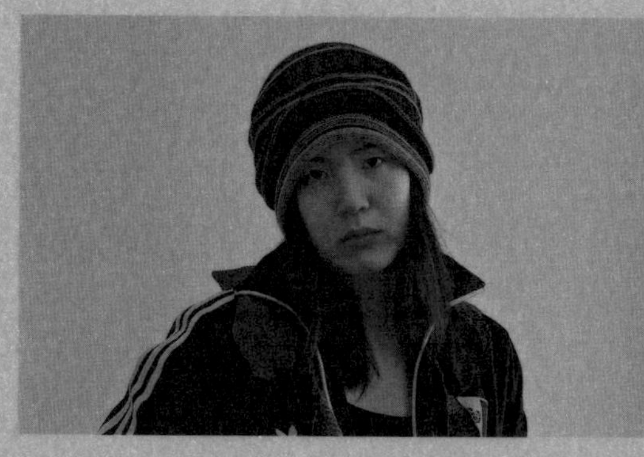

"Of course, these images of mine certainly don't present a very 'natural' face; they are all fabricated scenes, virtual emotions and experiences. They are to a greater or lesser degree made up, a collage of our realities, but I have to acknowledge that all of these hypotheses without exception come from my own real memories."

„Meine Arbeiten bieten ganz sicher keinen sehr ‚natürlichen' Anblick; es sind alles gestellte Szenen, virtuelle Emotionen und Erfahrungen, eine Collage aus Fragmenten unserer Realität, aber ich muss bekennen, dass all diese Fiktionen ausnahmslos meinen eigenen Erinnerungen entstammen."

"当然，我的图片的确不能表现一张自然的脸，他们都是乔装的，没有感情和经历但是他们或多或少的组合成我们现实中的 拼贴画，但我必须承认，所有这些臆想来自于我自己真实的 回忆。"

Born in 1978 in Guangzhou, China. Lives and works in Guangzhou and Beijing
Geboren 1978 in Guangzhou, China. Lebt und arbeitet in Guangzhou und Peking
1978年出生于广州，居住工作在广州和北京

***Selected exhibitions* / Ausgewählte Ausstellungen / 所选展览**

2005 "Cao Fei: CosPlayers", Lombard-Freid Projects, New York, NY, USA; Courtyard Gallery, Beijing, China
"Follow Me! Contemporary Chinese Art at the Threshold of the Millennium", Mori Art Museum, Tokyo, Japan
2006 "Cao Fei: HIP HOP", Lombard-Freid Projects, New York, NY, USA
"Da Zha Lan Project", The Museum of Modern Art, New York, NY, USA
15th Sydney Biennial, Sydney, Australia
2006/07 "China Power Station I", Battersea Power Station, Serpentine Gallery, UK, London; Astrup Fearnley Museum of Modern Art, Oslo, Norway
2007 52. Biennale di Venezia, Venice, Italy

2005年 曹 斐：《角色》Lombard-Freid Projects 纽约，四合苑画廊, 北京
《跟我来》东京森美术馆，东京
2006年 《嘻哈》纽约Lombard-Freid Projects和北京四合苑画廊合作展出展
《大栅栏计划》现代艺术馆，纽约
《第十五届悉尼双年展》悉尼，澳洲
2006/07年 中国电站I》蛇形画廊，巴特西电站伦敦英国 ; Astrup Fearnley现代美术馆 奥斯陆 挪威
2007年 第52届威尼斯双年展 威尼斯 意大利

***Selected publications* / Ausgewählte Publikationen / 所选著作**

Hou Hanru: "Cao Fei, a CosPlayer that recounts alternative histories", Sittard 2005
Hans Ulrich Obrist: "Cao Fei: First Take", in: "Artforum", New York, January 2006

侯瀚如（著）：《曹斐 是选择历史重述的角色》编目杂文, 领域博物馆，Sittard，荷兰
Obrist, Hans Ulrich（著）：《曹斐：第一作为》"Artforum" 艺术杂志，纽约2006年1月

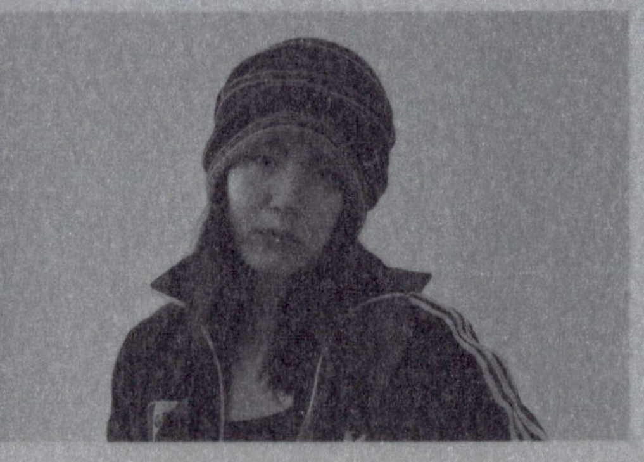

"Of course, these images of mine certainly don't present a very 'natural' face; they are all fabricated scenes, virtual emotions and experiences. They are to a greater or lesser degree made up, a collage of our realities, but I have to acknowledge that all of these hypotheses without exception come from my own real memories."

„Meine Arbeiten bieten ganz sicher keinen sehr ‚natürlichen' Anblick; es sind alles gestellte Szenen, virtuelle Emotionen und Erfahrungen, eine Collage aus Fragmenten unserer Realität, aber ich muss bekennen, dass all diese Fiktionen ausnahmslos meinen eigenen Erinnerungen entstammen."

"当然，我的图片的确不能表现一张自然的脸，他们都是乔装的，没有感情和经历但是他们或多或少的组合成我们现实中的 拼贴画，但我必须承认，所有这些臆想来自于我自己真实的 回忆。"

Born in 1978 in Guangzhou, China. Lives and works in Guangzhou and Beijing
Geboren 1978 in Guangzhou, China. Lebt und arbeitet in Guangzhou und Peking
1978年出生于广州，居住工作在广州和北京

Selected exhibitions / Ausgewählte Ausstellungen / 所选展览

2005	"Cao Fei: CosPlayers", Lombard-Freid Projects, New York, NY, USA; Courtyard Gallery, Beijing, China
	"Follow Me! Contemporary Chinese Art at the Threshold of the Millennium", Mori Art Museum, Tokyo, Japan
2006	"Cao Fei: HIP HOP", Lombard-Freid Projects, New York, NY, USA
	"Da Zha Lan Project", The Museum of Modern Art, New York, NY, USA
	15th Sydney Biennial, Sydney, Australia
2006/07	"China Power Station I", Battersea Power Station, Serpentine Gallery, UK, London; Astrup Fearnley Museum of Modern Art, Oslo, Norway
2007	52. Biennale di Venezia, Venice, Italy

2005年	曹 斐：《角色》Lombard-Freid Projects 纽约，四合苑画廊，北京
	《跟我来》东京森美术馆，东京
2006年	《嘻哈》纽约Lombard-Freid Projects和北京四合苑画廊合作展出展
	《大栅栏计划》现代艺术馆，纽约
	《第十五届悉尼双年展》悉尼，澳洲
2006/07年	中国电站I》蛇形画廊，巴特西电站伦敦英国 ；Astrup Fearnley现代美术馆 奥斯陆 挪威
2007年	第52届威尼斯双年展 威尼斯 意大利

Selected publications / Ausgewählte Publikationen / 所选著作

Hou Hanru: "Cao Fei, a CosPlayer that recounts alternative histories", Sittard 2005
Hans Ulrich Obrist: "Cao Fei: First Take", in: "Artforum", New York, January 2006

侯瀚如（著）：《曹斐 是选择历史重述的角色》编目杂文，锡城博物馆，Sittard，荷兰
Obrist, Hans Ulrich（著）：《曹斐：第一作为》"Artforum" 艺术杂志，纽约2006年1月

CAO FEI 曹 斐

[tshaʊ fei]

Cao Fei represents the best of the younger generation of Chinese artists, born in the advent of economic liberalization and with access to a wide range of cultural influences. She acutely observes and records the society around her – most often in the environs of her hometown of Guangzhou – though her methods are not strictly documentary. Instead this young woman artist highlights the fantasies, dreams and desires of this citizenry thrust into change over the past two decades, rather than merely describing the external details of their lives.

Since graduating from Guangzhou Academy of Fine Arts in 2001, Cao Fei has alternatively worked in performance, video and photography, often incorporating references to global popular culture in her content and aesthetic choices. In one of her early video and photograph projects, "Rabid Dogs" (2002), she unmasked the social climbing ambitions of her peers by staging an office situation filled with characters Burberry-clad humans made-up to resemble canines. For "CosPlayers" (2004), another project incorporating both, video and still images, the artist captures young people in Guangzhou at play, dressed as Japanese anime characters and enacting imaginary battles. Some of the wittiest images in this series follow the individuals home to their humble apartments where their parents are clearly confused by this cultish adoration of pop culture. Hip Hop, another cultural influence that has reached China, is the premise of a more recent project in which the artist invited ordinary people in various cities in the world, from Beijing to New York's Chinatown, to lip-synch and act out to rap music. The resulting videos, filled with awkward movements and embarrassing moments, embody the sometimes uncomfortable relationship of private individuals to popular culture, even when that culture promises easy and accessible modes of liberation.

At the same time, Cao Fei has also developed a series of works more closely related to documentary photography and cinéma vérité. Collaborating with her long-time partner Ou Ning, Cao Fei created in 2004 the "San Yuan Li" project, a

Cao Fei repräsentiert das Beste, was die jüngere chinesische Künstlergeneration zu bieten hat, die in den Beginn der wirtschaftlichen Liberalisierung hineingeboren wurde und Zugang zu einem breiten Spektrum kultureller Einflüsse hatte. Die junge Künstlerin beobachtet und dokumentiert ihr gesellschaftliches Umfeld ganz genau – meist in der Umgebung ihrer Heimatstadt Guangzhou –, auch wenn ihre Methoden nicht wirklich strikt dokumentarisch sind. Stattdessen beleuchtet Cao die Fantasien, Träume und Sehnsüchte einer Bevölkerung, die in den letzten beiden Jahrzehnten vom Wandel überrollt wurde, statt nur die äußeren Gegebenheiten ihres Lebens zu beschreiben.

Seit ihrem Abschluss an der Guangzhou Academy of Fine Arts 2001 hat Cao Fei abwechselnd mit Performances, Video und Fotografie gearbeitet und zahlreiche Verweise auf die globale Populärkultur in ihre inhaltliche und ästhetische Auswahl aufgenommen. In einem ihrer frühen Video- und Fotoprojekte, „Rabid Dogs" (2002), demaskierte sie die Aufstiegsambitionen ihrer Altersgenossen, indem sie Menschen in Burberry-Outfit mit geschminkten Hundegesichtern in inszenierten Bürosituationen auftreten ließ. In „CosPlayers" (2004), einem weiteren Projekt mit Videoaufnahmen und Stills, zeigt die Künstlerin, wie junge Leute aus Guangzhou in ihrer Freizeit als japanische Anime-Figuren verkleidet imaginäre Schlachten nachspielen. Einige der witzigsten Bilder aus dieser Serie entstehen, wenn sie die Mitspieler nach Hause in ihre bescheidenen Wohnungen begleitet, wo ihre Eltern deutlich verwirrt auf diesen Popkult reagieren.

Hiphop, ein weiterer popkultureller Einfluss, der längst auch China erreicht hat, gab den Anstoß zu einem neuen Projekt: Hier bringt die Künstlerin ganz normale Leute in verschiedenen Städten der Welt, von Peking bis zu New Yorks Chinatown, dazu, vor der Videokamera zu aggressivem Rap zu tanzen und mitzusingen. Die Videos voll unbeholfener Bewegungen und peinlicher Momente verkörpern die mitunter unbehagliche Beziehung des Einzelnen zur Populärkultur, selbst wenn diese Kultur überaus einfache und leicht zugängliche Wege der Befreiung verspricht.

曹 斐是中国最杰出的青年一代艺术家的代表, 他们生于经济自由, 并有机会更宽的受到文化的影响的年代。用不很专业的纪录片方式, 她敏锐地捕捉并记录下她周围的社会 -- 最多的地方是曹斐家乡广州的郊区。 反而这位年轻妇女艺术家有特别的去强调在过去二十年中公民渴望变化的愿望和幻想，而不仅仅记录着他们生活的外部环境。

曹斐2001年从广州美院毕业以后在创作交替地着行为，录像和摄影，常常把全球的流行文化融合进其作品内容和审美观中。在其早期的录像2002年摄影作品《饿狗》中，曹斐摘下积极向上的高贵面具, 走进一间办公室，里面充满着身穿防水雨衣打扮像狗的人。

在2004年另外一部融合录像和照片的作品《角色》中，曹斐捕捉了正在戏耍的广州年轻人，他们装扮得像日本卡通人物，在扮演着虚构的打斗情节。作品中的一些诙谐的形象也跟随这些年轻人进入他们简陋的住宅，他们的父母对儿女的流行文化的崇拜而烦恼着。另一个登陆中国的文化影响，《嘻哈》, 是更多作品的前奏，在作品中，曹斐邀请从北京到纽约的唐人街不同城市的普通人去假唱表演Rap。拍摄到的录像，充斥着笨拙的动作和尴尬的情节，具体表现了个体与流行文化的尴尬关系，即使那是是一种通往自由的简单可行的模式的文化。

同时，曹斐也创作了一组接近电影纪录片的作品。与欧宁长期合作，共同完成的是一部描述了城市快速变化的优美黑白影像诗篇《三元里计划》2004年，作品以切片的方式进行编辑。另一方面在2005年的《父亲》是对他父亲一部长期采访，一位著名的具有社会主义现实主义审美观的官方雕塑家，作品仅仅是逐渐地展示了两代艺术家之间的迥异。最近曹斐和欧宁又为一部追溯一个为2008年奥运会让路而强制现代化改造的北京破落胡同破坏过程的纪录片《大栅栏计划》揭幕。

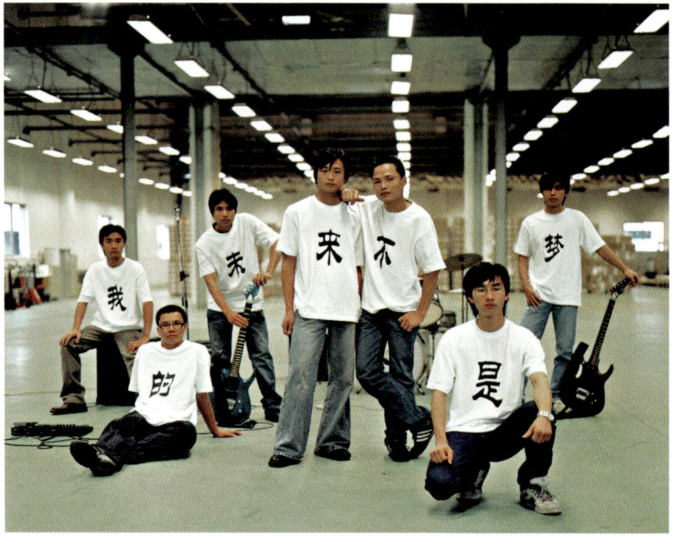

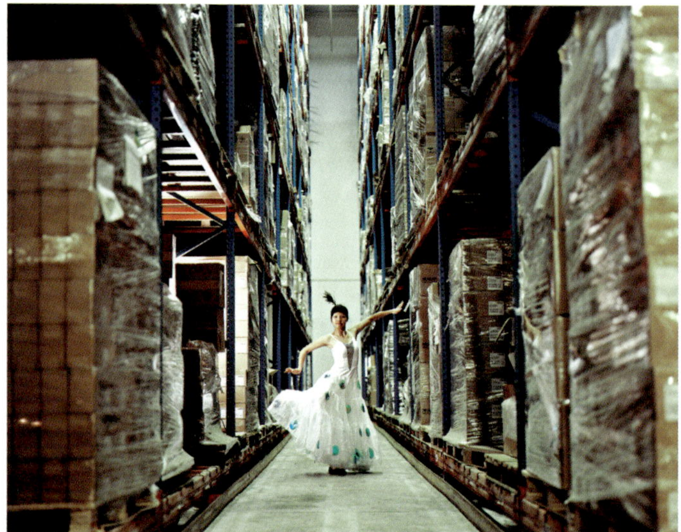

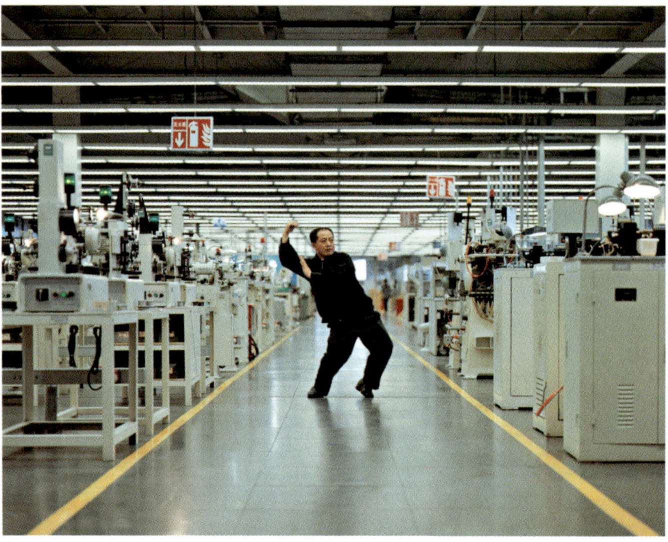

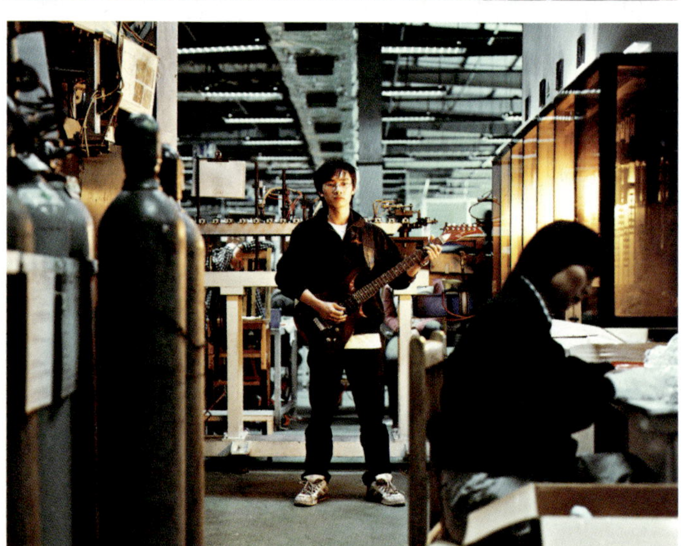

4

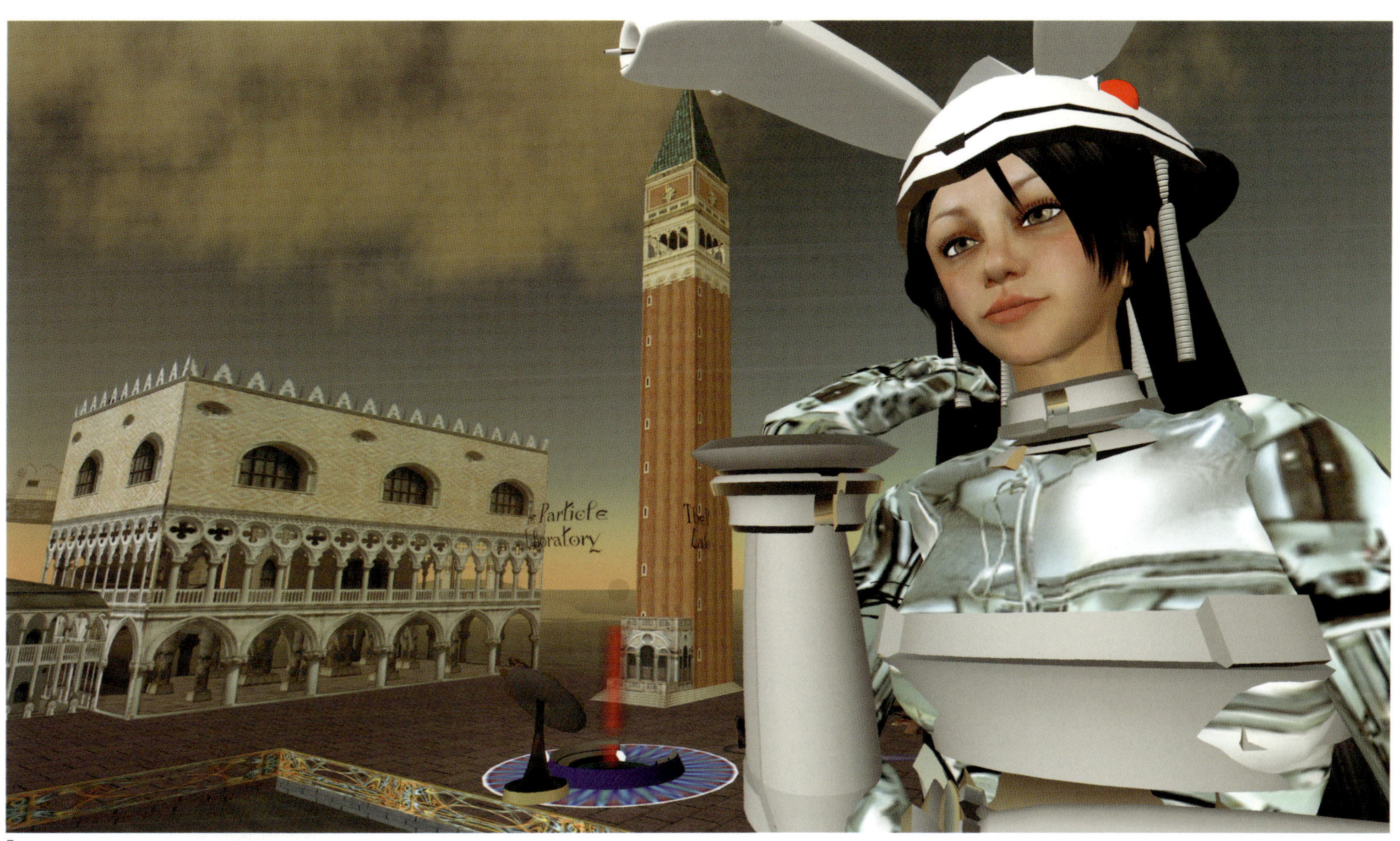

5

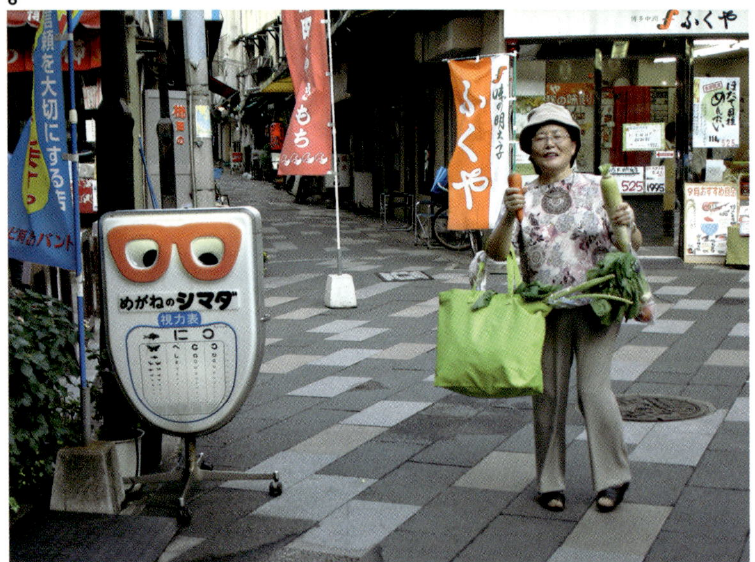

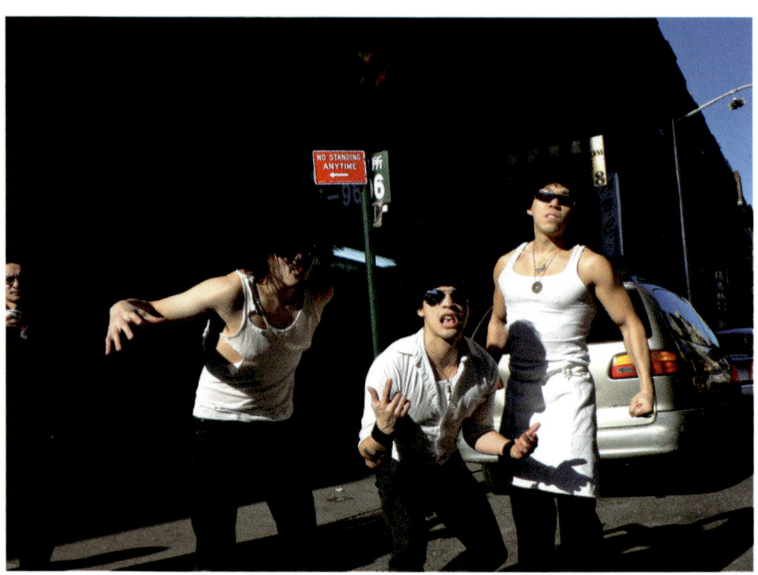

stunning black-and-white video portrait of a section of city undergoing rapid change, edited as a rapid fire compilation of images scored to a throbbing techno-beat. On the other hand, "Father" (2005), an extended interview with her own father, a successful official sculptor with a socialist realist aesthetic, only gradually reveals the tensions between these two generations of artists. Most recently, Cao Fei and Ou Ning unveiled the "Dazhalan project", a film that traces the destruction of a poor neighbourhood in Beijing, bulldozed to make way to modernize the city in time for the 2008 Olympics.

Cao Fei's two abiding concerns – fantasy and reality – come together in "SIEMENS Art Project 2006: What Are You Doing Here?", for which she won the young artist category of the annual China Contemporary Art Awards in 2006. In this installation, she traced the social conditions for workers in a Guangdong light bulb factory. In the midst of copious economic and social statistics, Cao Fei inserted a film in which she invites the workers to perform and dance to the music of their choice, a moment of spontaneity in stark contrast to the assembly line. It is a perfect example of the way this artist pushes the boundaries of documentary filmmaking to bring audiences closer to the humanity of a social situation.

Gleichzeitig hat Cao Fei eine Reihe von Arbeiten realisiert, die der Dokumentarfotografie und dem Cinéma Vérité näher stehen. In Zusammenarbeit mit ihrem langjährigen Partner Ou Ning schuf sie 2004 „San Yuan Li", ein eindringliches Schwarzweiß-Videoporträt eines Stadtteils im rapiden Wandel, in eine rasante Bildfolge geschnitten und mit hämmerndem Technobeat unterlegt. „Father" (2005) wiederum, ein ausführliches Interview mit ihrem eigenen Vater, einem erfolgreichen offiziellen Bildhauer des Sozialistischen Realismus, offenbart beiläufig die Spannungen zwischen den beiden Künstlergenerationen. Zuletzt präsentierten Cao Fei und Ou Ning das Projekt „Da Zha Lan": Der Film zeichnet den Abriss eines Armenviertels in Peking nach, das ein Opfer der Stadtmodernisierung für die Olympischen Spiele 2008 wurde.

Die Themen Fantasie und Realität, die Cao Fei durchgängig verfolgt, verschmelzen beispielhaft im „SIEMENS Art Project 2006: What Are You Doing Here?", für das sie 2006 den jährlich verliehenen China Contemporary Art Award in der Kategorie Nachwuchskünstler erhielt. In dieser Installation zeichnet sie die sozialen Bedingungen der Arbeiter in einer Glühbirnenfabrik in Guangdong nach. Zwischen umfängliche Wirtschafts- und Sozialstatistiken fügte Cao Fei einen Film ein, in dem sie die Arbeiterinnen und Arbeiter animiert, zu selbst gewählter Musik frei zu tanzen, ein Moment der Spontaneität, das im krassen Kontrast zu deren Fließbandarbeit steht – ein perfektes Beispiel dafür, wie die Künstlerin die Grenzen des Dokumentarfilms erweitert, um dem Publikum die menschliche Seite einer schwierigen gesellschaftlichen Situation näher zu bringen.

曹斐的两个长期关注：幻想与现实--在2006年的西门子艺术项目上实现了：《你在干什么》为曹赢得了2006年中国当代艺术奖中的最优秀年轻艺术家奖。在这个装置中，曹斐在广东一个灯泡厂中描绘了工人的社会地位，在大量的社会统计和经济统计数据中，曹插入了一部影片，影片中曹邀请工人们按他们自己的意愿选择音乐表演，跳舞，而另一瞬间则是装配线的静寂。这是一个非常好的例子，艺术家打破了传统纪录片的制片方式，使观众更能体会到社会的人性化。

Barbara Pollack

6

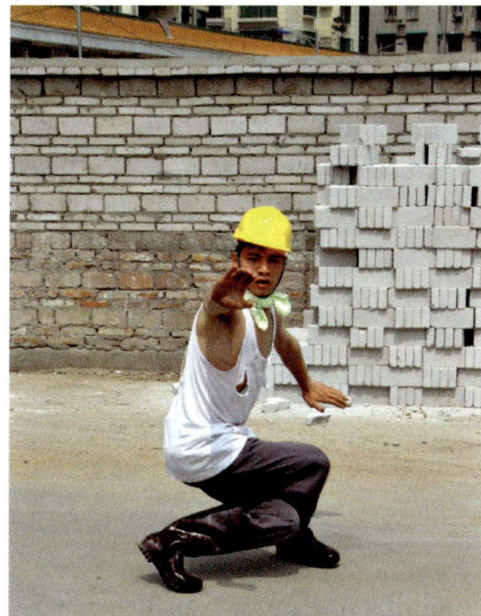

7

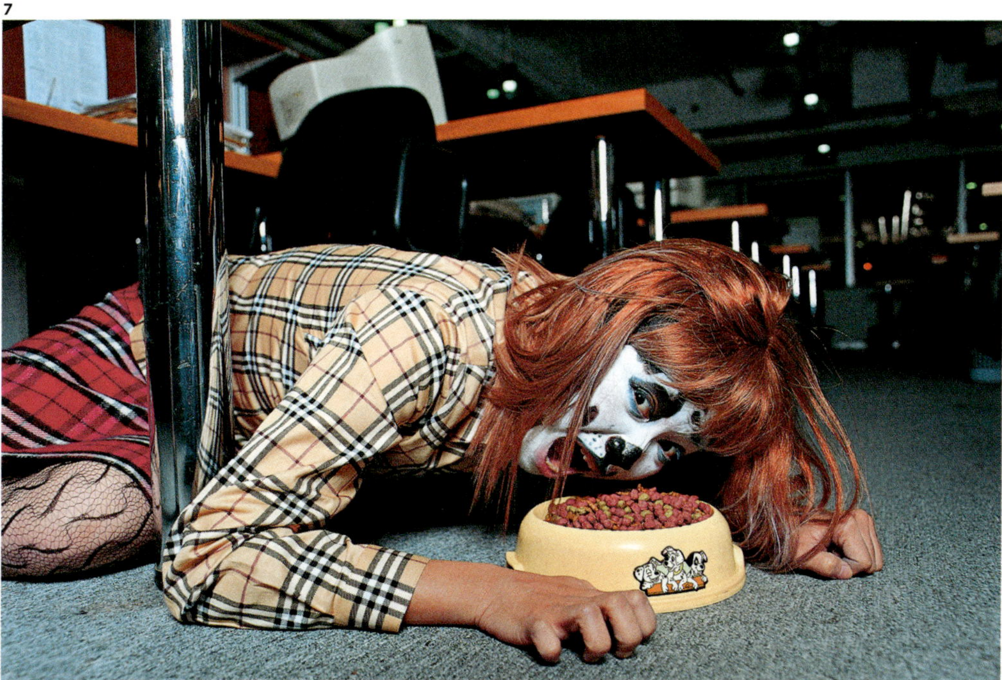

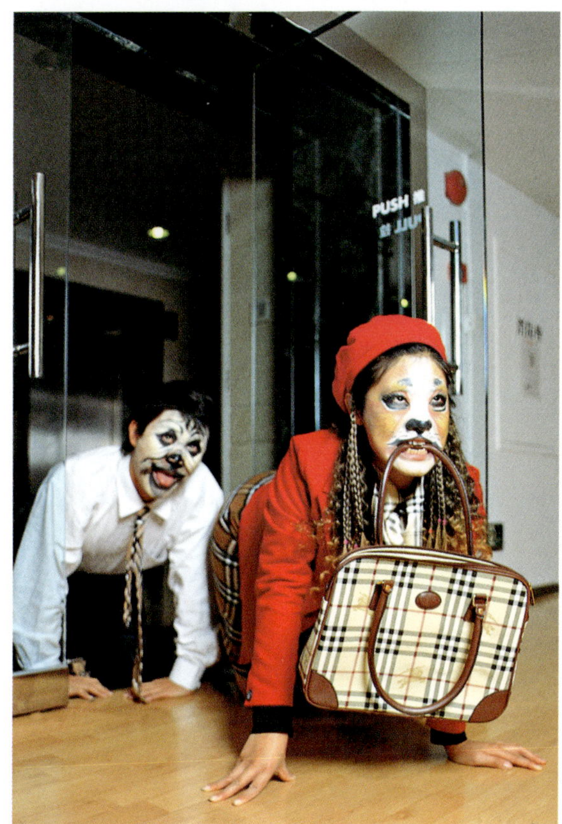

8

1 ***City Watcher***, *2004*
Photograph from the series "CosPlayers", 75 x 100 cm
Fotografie aus der Serie „CosPlayers", 75 x 100 cm
《城市看守人》2004年，《角色》系列的照片，75 x 100 cm

2 ***A Mirage***, *2004*
Photograph from the series "CosPlayers", 75 x 100 cm
Fotografie aus der Serie „CosPlayers", 75 x 100 cm
《海市蜃楼》2004年，《角色》系列的照片，75 x 100 cm

3 ***Golden Fighter's Despair***, *2004*
Photograph from the series "CosPlayers", 75 x 100 cm
Fotografie aus der Serie „CosPlayers", 75 x 100 cm
《金黄战士的绝望》2004年，《角色》系列的照片，75 x 100 cm

4 ***My Future is not a Dream***, *2006*
Video
Video
《我的未来不是梦》2006年，录像

5 ***China Tracy***, *2007*
Internet and installation project
Internet- und Installationsprojekt
《中国翠西》2007年，网和装置设计

6 ***Hip Hop Fukuoka***, *2005*
Video, 8 min
Video, 8 Min.
《嘻哈福冈》2005年，录像，8分

7 ***Rabid Dogs (Hungry Dog)***, *2002*
Video, 8 min 52 sec
Video, 8 Min. 52 Sek.
《狗》2002年，录像，8分52秒

8 ***Rabid Dogs (Dog Days)***, *2002*
Video, 8 min 52 sec
Video, 8 Min. 52 Sek.
《狗》2002年，录像，8分52秒

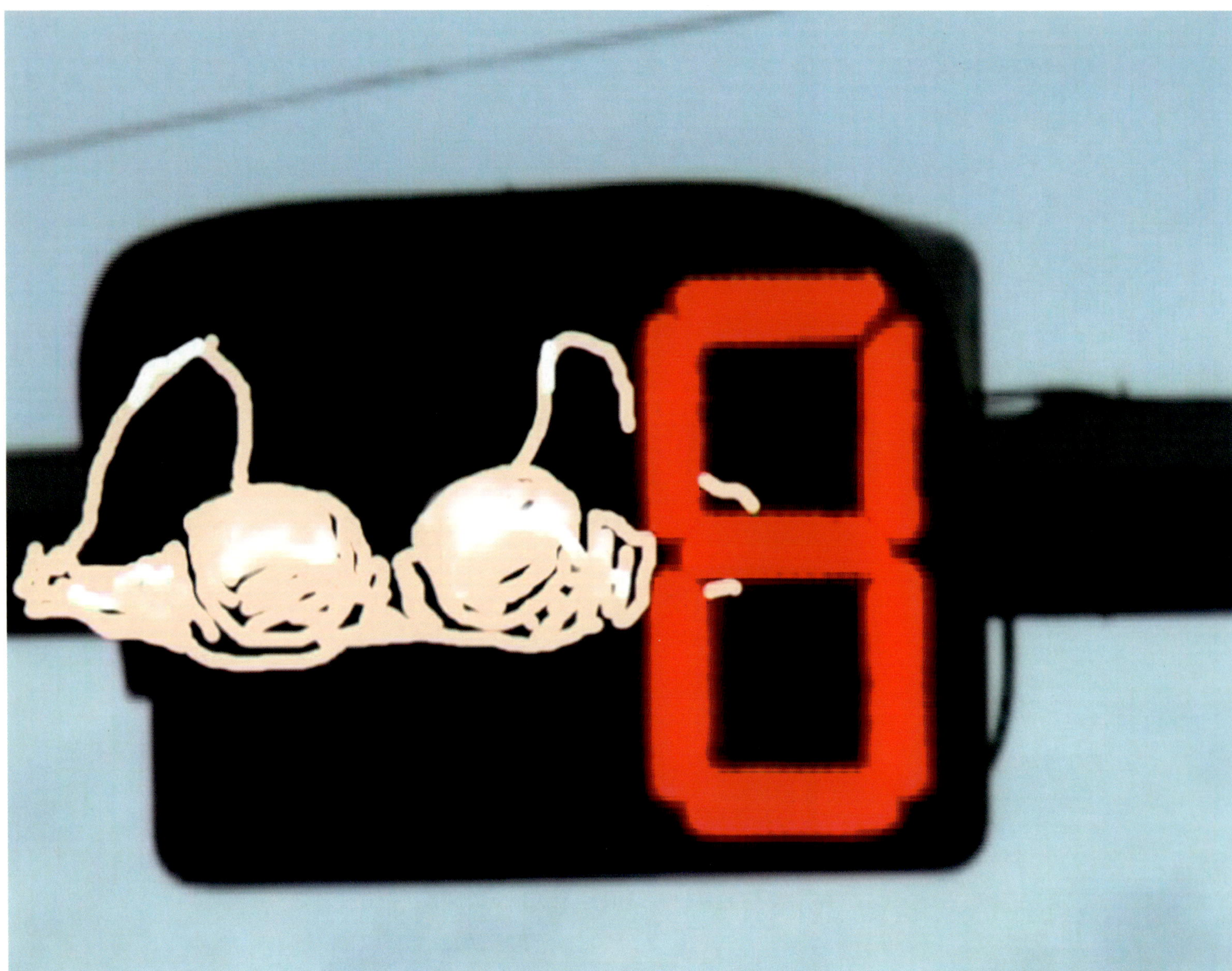

1

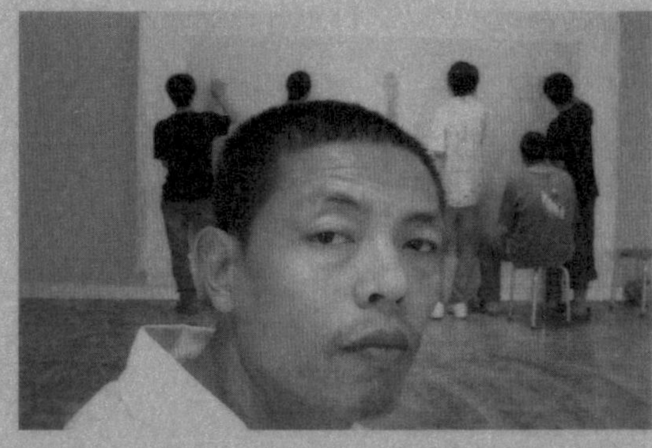

"I would like to say, that my knowledge of the world is just limited: there are many things I can see but still more I cannot see, there are many things I know but still more I don't know."

„Ich möchte ausdrücken, dass ich die Welt nur begrenzt kenne: Viele Dinge kann ich erkennen, aber noch mehr Dinge kann ich nicht erkennen, viele Dinge sehe ich, aber noch viel mehr Dinge sehe ich nicht."

"我想说，我对这个世界的了解是很有限的：我能看到许多事，但更多事我依然看不到，我了解许多事情，但更多的事情，我依然不了解。"

Born in 1962 in Shantou, China. Lives and works in Guangzhou
Geboren 1962 in Shantou, China. Lebt und arbeitet in Guangzhou
1962年出生于中国广东省汕头市，现在广州市住居工作

***Selected exhibitions* / Ausgewählte Ausstellungen / 所选展览**

2004 "Light As Fuck! Shanghai Assemblage 2000–2004", The National Museum of Art, Oslo, Norway
2005 "Follow Me! Chinese Art at the Threshold of the New Millennium", Mori Art Museum, Tokyo, Japan
2006 "Chen Shaoxiong, Art & Public", Cabinet PH, Geneva, Switzerland
2004–07 "Between Past and Future, New Photography and Video from China", International Center of Photography, New York, NY, USA (travelling exhibition)
2006/07 "China Power Station I", Battersea Power Station, Serpentine Gallery, UK, London; Astrup Fearnley Museum of Modern Art, Oslo, Norway
2007 "Visible and invisible, Known and Unknown", UniversalStudios, Beijing, China
"All About Laughter – Humour in Contemporary Art", Mori Art Museum, Tokyo, Japan

2004年 《轻而易举：上海拼图2000–2004》挪威国立美术馆，奥斯陆，挪威
2005年 《跟我学》森美术馆，东京，日本
2006年 《陈劭雄》《Art & Public – Cabinet PH》日内瓦，瑞士
2004–07年 《过去与未来之间—中国新影像展》 国际摄影中心 纽约 美国 （巡回展）
2006/07年 《中国电站I》蛇形画廊，巴特西电站 伦敦 英国； Astrup Fearnley 现代美术馆 奥斯陆 挪威
2007年 《看见的和看不见的，知道的和不知道的》U空间北京，北京
《笑之展 -- 当代艺术中的幽默》森美术馆，东京，日本

***Selected publications* / Ausgewählte Publikationen / 所选著作**

Hou Hanru: "Beyond the Cynical: China Avant-Garde in the 1990s", in: "AAP", vol. 3, no. 1, 1996
Chris Dreissen, Heidi van Mierlo (eds.): "Another Long March: Chinese Conceptual and Installation Art in the Nineties", Breda 1997
Rosalind Holmes: "Cityscapes, crazy consumption, and collective memory: Chen Shaoxiong's mimetic reality", in: "Yishu", Spring 2007

侯韩汝（著）:《在玩世不恭之外:中国先锋派在90 年代》AAP, 册 3, 第 1（1996年）
Dreissen, Chris/van Mierlo, Heidi（编者）:《另一次长征——20世纪90年代中国观念艺术》展览目册，布雷达，1997年
Holmes, Rosalind（著）:《都市风景、疯狂的消耗量和集体记忆：陈劭雄的模仿的现实》在《艺术》当代中国艺术杂志(春2007年)

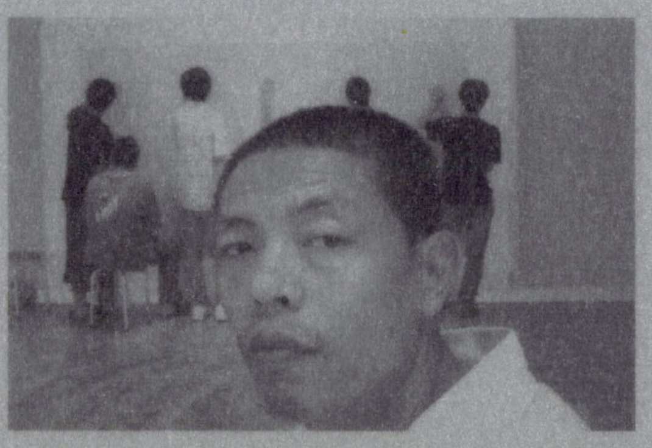

"I would like to say, that my knowledge of the world is just limited: there are many things I can see but still more I cannot see, there are many things I know but still more I don't know."

„Ich möchte ausdrücken, dass ich die Welt nur begrenzt kenne: Viele Dinge kann ich erkennen, aber noch mehr Dinge kann ich nicht erkennen, viele Dinge sehe ich, aber noch viel mehr Dinge sehe ich nicht."

"我想说，我对这个世界的了解是很有限的：我能看到许多事，但更多事我依然看不到，我了解许多事情，但更多的事情，我依然不了解。"

Born in 1962 in Shantou, China. Lives and works in Guangzhou
Geboren 1962 in Shantou, China. Lebt und arbeitet in Guangzhou
1962年出生于中国广东省汕头市，现在广州市住居工作

Selected exhibitions / Ausgewählte Ausstellungen / 所选展览

2004	"Light As Fuck! Shanghai Assemblage 2000-2004", The National Museum of Art, Oslo, Norway
2005	"Follow Me! Chinese Art at the Threshold of the New Millennium", Mori Art Museum, Tokyo, Japan
2006	"Chen Shaoxiong, Art & Public", Cabinet PH, Geneva, Switzerland
2004-07	"Between Past and Future, New Photography and Video from China", International Center of Photography, New York, NY, USA (travelling exhibition)
2006/07	"China Power Station I", Battersea Power Station, Serpentine Gallery, UK, London; Astrup Fearnley Museum of Modern Art, Oslo, Norway
2007	"Visible and invisible, Known and Unknown", UniversalStudios, Beijing, China
	"All About Laughter - Humour in Contemporary Art", Mori Art Museum, Tokyo, Japan

2004年	《轻而易举：上海拼图2000-2004》挪威国立美术馆，奥斯陆，挪威
2005年	《跟我学》森美术馆，东京，日本
2006年	《陈劭雄》《Art & Public - Cabinet PH》日内瓦，瑞士
2004-07年	《过去与未来之间—中国新影像展》国际摄影中心 纽约 美国（巡回展）
2006/07年	《中国电站I》蛇形画廊，巴特西电站 伦敦 英国；Astrup Fearnley 现代美术馆 奥斯陆 挪威
2007年	《看见的和看不见的，知道的和不知道的》U空间北京，北京
	《笑之展 — 当代艺术中的幽默》森美术馆，东京，日本

Selected publications / Ausgewählte Publikationen / 所选著作

Hou Hanru: "Beyond the Cynical: China Avant-Garde in the 1990s", in: "AAP", vol. 3, no. 1, 1996
Chris Dreissen, Heidi van Mierlo (eds.): "Another Long March: Chinese Conceptual and Installation Art in the Nineties", Breda 1997
Rosalind Holmes: "Cityscapes, crazy consumption, and collective memory: Chen Shaoxiong's mimetic reality", in: "Yishu", Spring 2007

侯瀚如（著）：《在玩世不恭之外：中国先锋派在90 年代》AAP，册 3，第 1（1996年）
Dreissen, Chris/van Mierlo, Heidi（编著）：《另一次长征——20世纪90年代中国观念艺术》展览目册，布雷达，1997年
Holmes, Rosalind（著）：《都市风景，疯狂的消耗量和集体记忆：陈劭雄的模仿的现实》在《艺术》当代中国艺术杂志（春2007年）

CHEN SHAOXIONG 陈劭雄

[tʂʰən ʂaʊɕiaʊ]

The main subject of the art works of Chen Shaoxiong is the Chinese accelerated urbanisation and the impact thereof on human perception. His preferred media is video and photography for his installation works, visualising the complex fabric of urban processes and revealing that the former linearity due to increasing marketisation of the country since the 1990s is not applicable to the view of present Chinese reality.

Chen's interest is especially attracted by things in his direct environment broaching the issue of China's dramatic change with his hometown Guangzhou in the south of China as an example. The centre of his work is the impact of the new and continuously changing reality on action and perception of each individual.

Chen uses artistic means for putting on top of each other several layers of space, time and meaning avoiding a uniform perspective. For him the potential of insight is held in the reality characterised by breaks, embracing interspaces and joints and not in the depiction of a unity. His target to challenge conventional views and horizons of experience; the spectator is agitated to find his own point of view of receptive experience.

"Streets" (since 1997), three dimensional photograph collages of urban scenes, are placed in real metropolis situations to transfer them in a third step by photographic means to two dimensional pictures. Real crossroads are melded with tableau like panoramas of cut out figures, advertisement spaces and vehicles to another fictive reality. Chen who consciously confuses the spectator and at the same time makes him sensitive, stages the urban space and broaches the issue of perception ambivalence, being unveiled as a construct of perception.

The installation "Ink City" (since 2005) a similar work, is a combination of ink paintings of urban scenes brought to life by means of slide projection and scenes of homely situation in a peep slide show manner. The spectator is in a simulated

Die künstlerischen Arbeiten Chen Shaoxiongs haben die chinesische Turbo-Urbanisierung und deren Auswirkungen auf die menschliche Wahrnehmung zum Thema. In seinen zumeist installativen Arbeiten, in denen er bevorzugt mit den Medien Video und Fotografie arbeitet, visualisiert er das komplexe Gefüge städtischer Prozesse und macht damit deutlich, dass die frühere Linearität in der Anschauung chinesischer Realitäten im Zuge der zunehmenden Ökonomisierung des Landes seit den 1990er Jahren keine Gültigkeit mehr besitzt.

Chen schenkt den Dingen in seiner unmittelbaren Umgebung besondere Aufmerksamkeit und thematisiert den dramatischen Wandel Chinas gern am Beispiel seiner Heimatstadt Guangzhou im Süden des Landes. Im Mittelpunkt seiner Arbeit stehen die Auswirkungen der neuen und sich kontinuierlich verändernden Wirklichkeit auf die Handlungen und Wahrnehmungen des Einzelnen.

Mit den künstlerischen Mitteln der Montage legt Chen stets mehrere Raum-, Zeit- und Bedeutungsschichten übereinander und vermeidet eine einheitliche Perspektive. Nicht die Darstellung einer Einheit, sondern die durch Brüche gekennzeichnete Realität und deren Zwischenräume und Nahtstellen bergen das Potenzial für Erkenntnis. Mit dem Ziel, herkömmliche Sehgewohnheiten und Erfahrungshorizonte herauszufordern, motiviert Chen den Betrachter dazu, seinen eigenen Zugang zu Wahrnehmungserlebnissen zu finden.

So stellt er mit „Streets" (seit 1997) dreidimensionale Fotocollagen städtischer Szenen in tatsächliche metropolitane Situationen, um sie in einem dritten Schritt fotografisch in eine zweidimensionale Darstellung zu überführen. Reale Straßenkreuzungen verschmelzen dabei mit tableauartigen Panoramen ausgeschnittener Figuren, Werbetafeln und Fahrzeugen zu einer gänzlich anderen fiktiven Realität. Den Betrachter bewusst verunsichernd und ihn zugleich sensibilisierend, inszeniert Chen den städtischen Raum und thematisiert die Ambivalenz der Wahrnehmung, die er als konzeptuelles Konstrukt entlarvt.

陈劭雄的艺术作品的主题是中国的激进的都市化进程，以及其对人感知的深刻影响。他偏好把视频和摄影两种媒介综合　　运用在其装置作品中，以呈现城市化进程中的复杂结构，揭示由于中国日益深化的市场化改革和城市化之间的关系，因为上世纪90年代并不能反映当今中国的现实。

陈劭雄的主要关注中国高速变化的直接环境，以在位于中国南部的他的家乡广州为例。日新月异、不断持续的变化的现实对个体行为和思想上影响是其作品的中心。

为避免观众单调的观点，陈劭雄运用艺术手法处理了空间、时间和意义。对他而言，顿悟的可能性约束在由突变而形成的特征化现实中，潜藏在现实和过去的空隙中和交接处，而非在整体的描述中。挑战传统经验的观点和视野局限是其目标，观众也可以在其直观经验中欣喜地发现自己的观点。

《街景》把立体城市风景摄影拼贴画放置在现实的都市环境中，然后再拍摄成平面照片。现实中的十字路口与由剪贴的人物、广告空间、车流组成场面融为一体，形成另一幅虚构的现实。陈劭雄在有意地干扰观众，而同时使其敏感、展现城市空间，并　引出因意识结构的凸现而导致意识矛盾心理的话题。

装置《墨水城市》也是类似的作品，描写城市风景的水墨画的幻灯片和家庭环境的西洋景的组合，给观众一种处于对应的公共和私人仿真空间中的感觉。动画片和装置策略的逼真的直接性，无论是浏览视觉表面还是自己亲身体验，都可以感觉到一种真实感，多维因素的存在而使内部结构相互对立。

在其视频装置《视力矫正器》中，陈阐明现实的感觉(我们难以　完成这种处理信息的方式)需要一种个人策略--需要在调节和短暂的坐标之间颤动--但这种策略却不会揭示现实的本来面目。

2

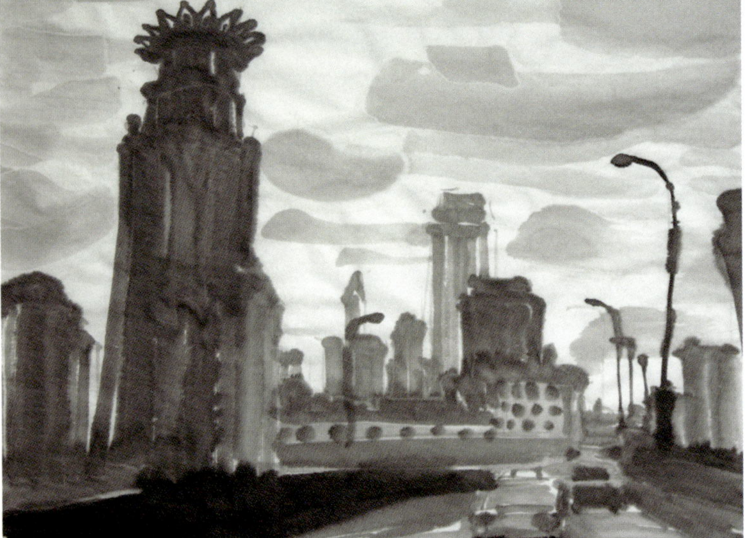

3

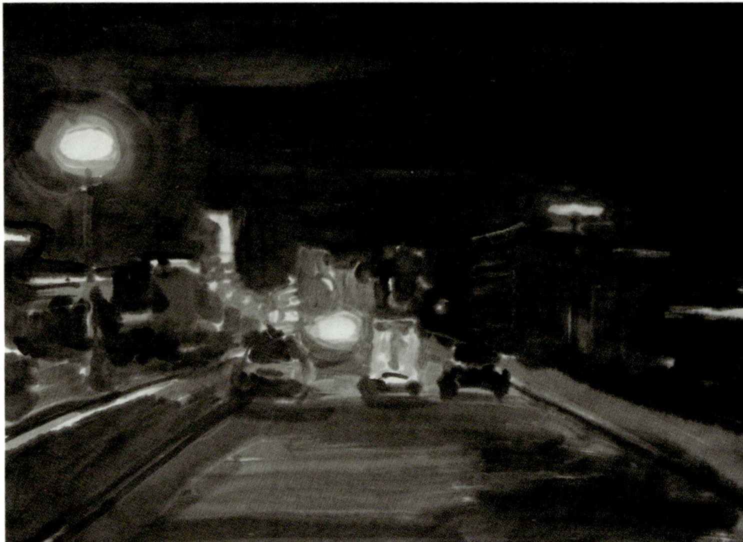

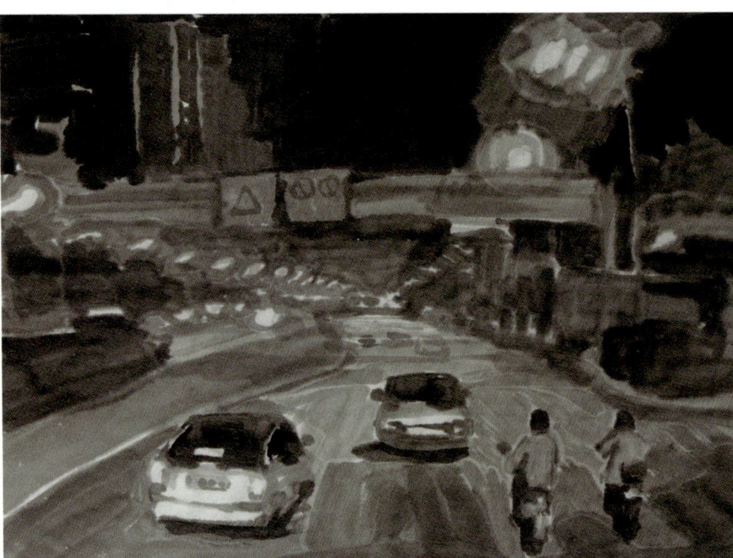

4

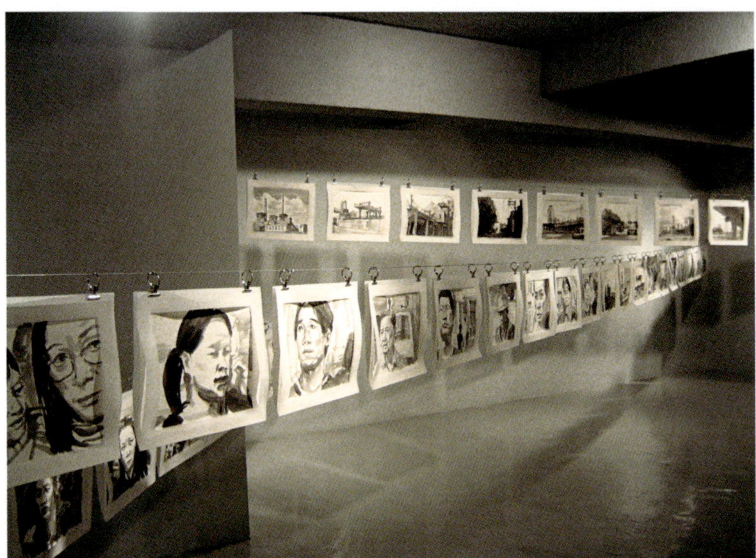

5

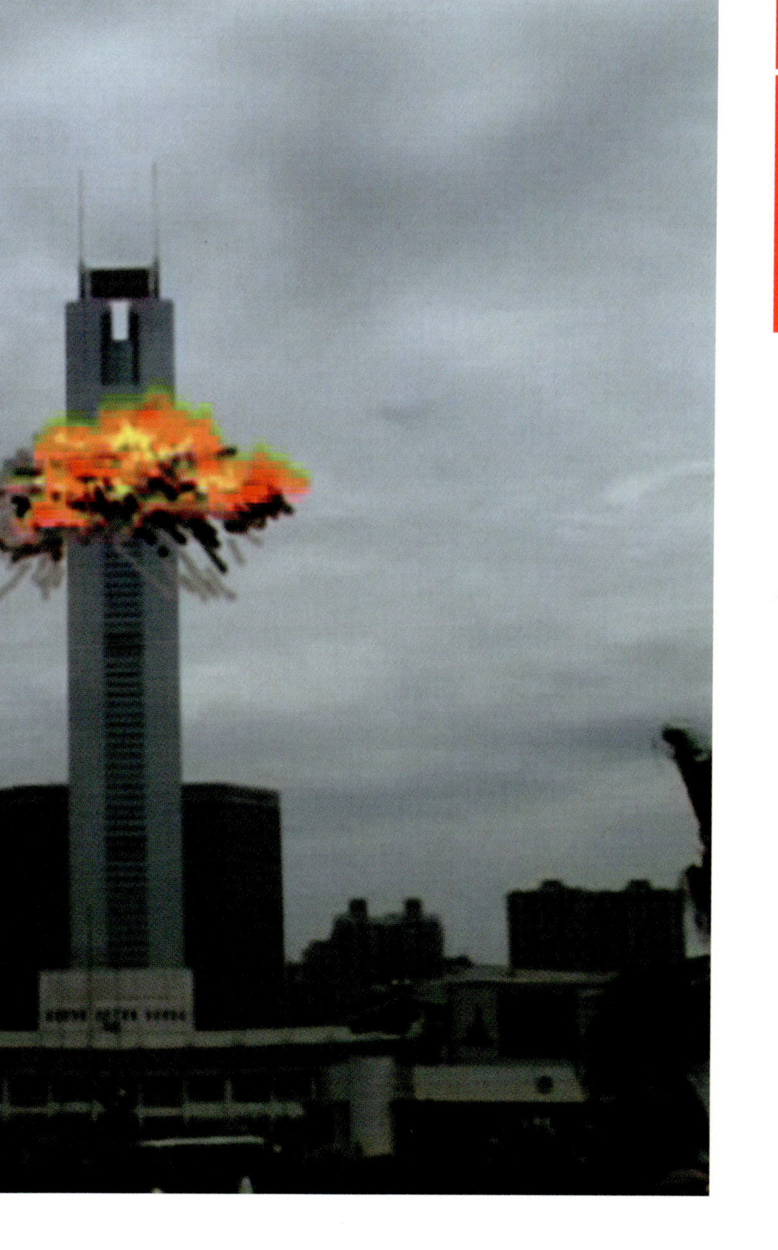

6

7

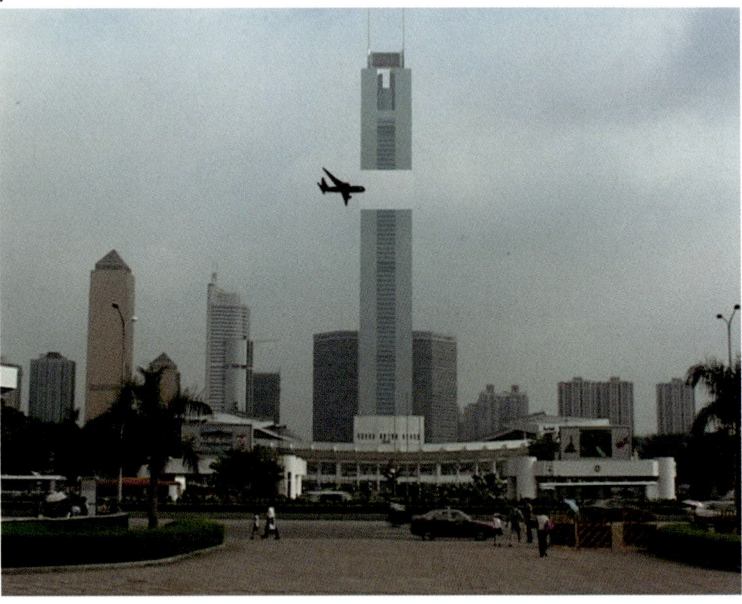

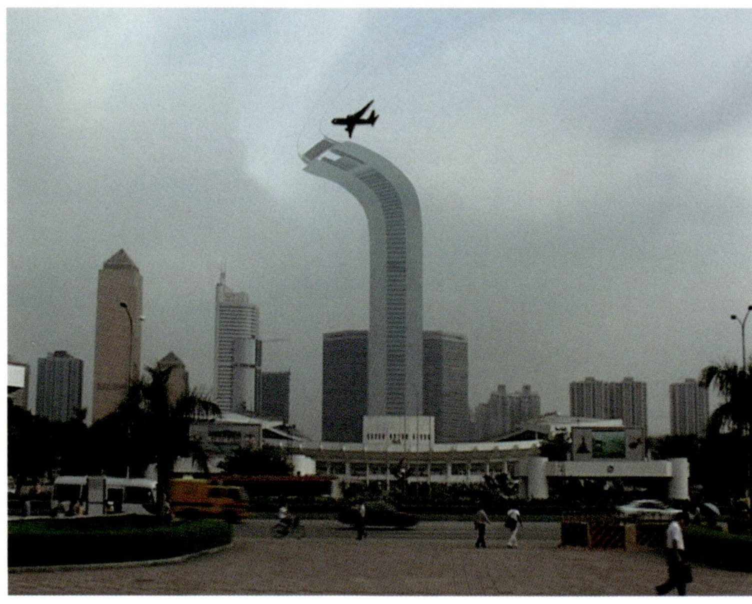

room which looms between the corresponding public and privacy. Due to the animated pictures and the imminent directness of such installation strategies the perception of reality does not only result from viewing visual surfaces but as well as from bodily experience, making inner structures virulent as further dimensions. In his video installation "Sight Adjusters" (1996) Chen Shaoxiong demonstrates that the perception of reality – the dealing with information falling down on us, – requires personal strategies vibrating between adjustment and temporary position fixing but never unveiling the ultimate truth.

For Chen, art is a means of communication, being accessible for many and not just limited to an adept circle of arty people. As member at the beginning of the 1990s in Guangzhou founded south China work group "Big Tail Elephant", the common denominator thereof being the critical discussion of the rapid urbanisation aspects, Chen is interested in the interaction with the city. In the 1990s he surprised visitors of a public toilet with a voyeur-like video installation. The use of a provocative and humouristic language also characterises him as member of the "Big Tail Elephant" group. In his video "Anti-terror Variety" (2002) he invents intelligent high buildings being able to draw aside to avoid attacking aircrafts and the catastrophe of a collision.

In ähnlicher Weise funktioniert die Installation „Ink City" (seit 2005), in der der Künstler Tuschebilder städtischer Szenen mittels Diaprojektion zum Leben erweckt und mit Guckkasten-Dioramen häuslicher Situationen kombiniert. Der Betrachter befindet sich in einem simulierten Raum, der sich zwischen den korrespondierenden Sphären Öffentlichkeit und Privatheit auftut. Aufgrund der animierten Bilder und der immanenten Direktheit resultiert die Wahrnehmung der Realität nicht mehr nur aus der Betrachtung visueller Oberflächen, sondern auch aus körperlicher Erfahrung, in der innere Strukturen als weitere Dimension virulent werden. Wie Chen in seiner Videoinstallation „Sight Adjusters" (1996) zeigte, verlangt die Wahrnehmung der Realität, sprich der Umgang mit den auf uns einstürzenden Informationen, nach persönlichen Strategien, die zwischen Anpassung und temporärer Standortbestimmung oszillieren und niemals endgültige Wahrheiten enthüllen.

Kunst ist für Chen Mittel der Kommunikation und soll nicht nur einem eingeweihten Zirkel Kunstkundiger, sondern möglichst vielen zugänglich sein. Als Mitglied der Arbeitsgruppe „Big Tail Elephant", die sich Anfang der 1990er Jahre im südchinesischen Guangzhou formierte und deren gemeinsamer Nenner die kritische Auseinandersetzung mit Aspekten der Turbo-Urbanisierung ist, interessiert ihn die direkte Interaktion mit der Stadt – so überraschte er in den 1990er Jahren die Besucher einer öffentlichen Toilette mit einer voyeuristischen Videoinstallation. Auch der Einsatz einer provokativen und humoristischen Sprache weist ihn als Mitglied der „Großschwanzelefanten" aus. So erfindet er in dem Video „Anti-terror Variety" (2002) intelligente Hochhäuser, denen es durch geschicktes Ausweichen gelingt, den attackierenden Flugzeugen und damit der Katastrophe zu entgehen.

在陈劭雄的心中，艺术是一种交流方式，因为艺术被大众接受，而非仅仅局限在在艺术圈里。20世纪90年代，广州出现了一个叫做大尾象工作组艺术团体，该团体以批评激进的城市化进程为主要特征，陈劭雄是成员之一，他关注城市化进程与城市的相互作用。在90年代，他的一部偷窥公厕视频装置而让观众瞠目结舌。

因为煽他也运用煽动性和幽默语言，所以把陈劭雄归入大尾象工作组的成员。在视频装置《反恐象棋》(2002年)中，他发明了一栋智能楼宇，这种建筑能防止飞机的袭击和碰撞而带来的灾难。

Birgit Hopfener

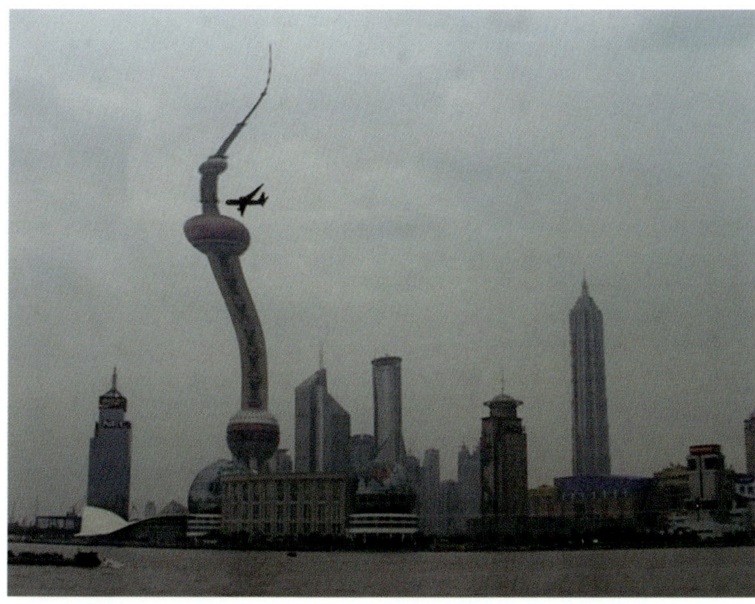

8

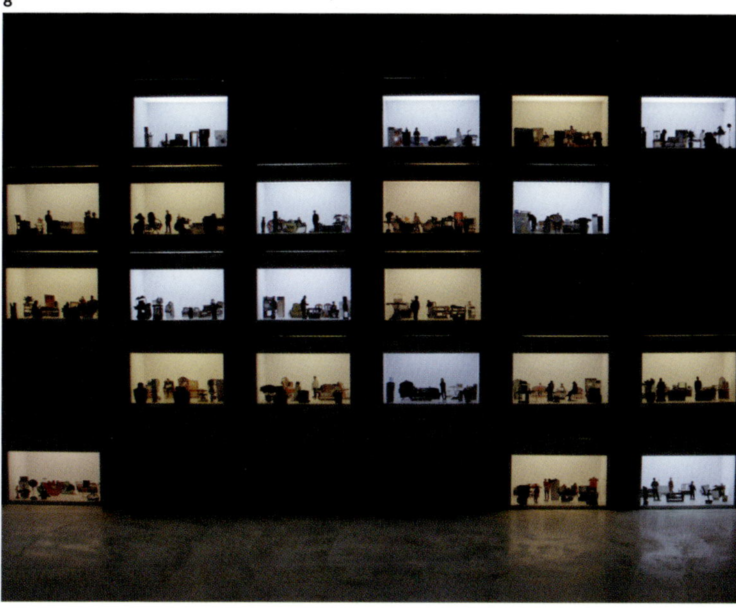

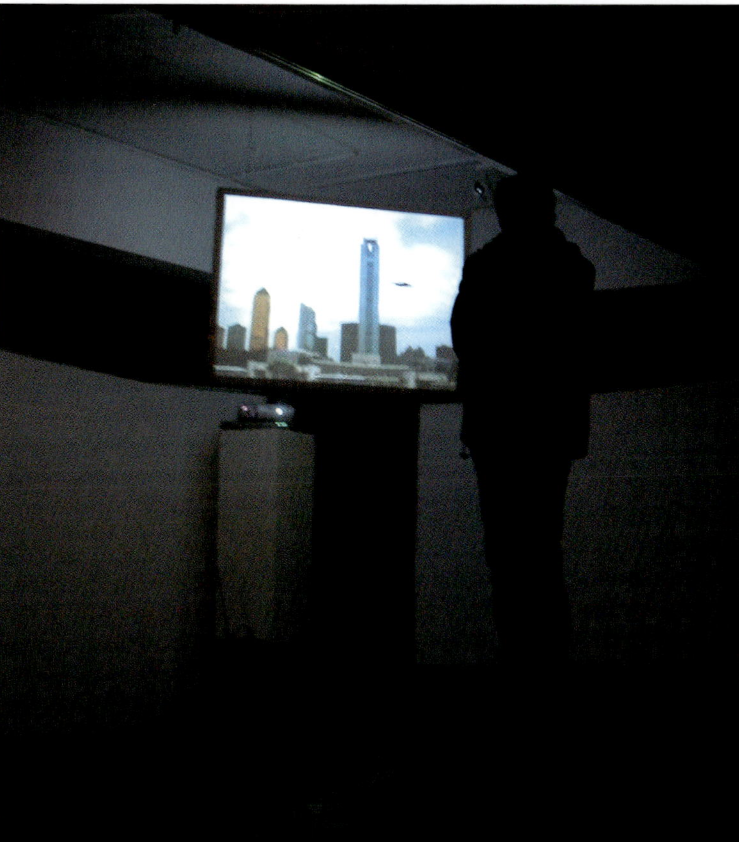

9

1 ***Windows XP***, *2002*
Colour video, 2 min
Windows XP, 2002, Video, Farbe, 2 Min.
《Windows XP》2002年, 彩色录像, 2分钟

2–4 ***Ink City***, *2005*
B/w video, 3 min
Video, schwarzweiß, 3 Min.
《墨水城市》2005年, 黑白录像, 3分钟

5 ***Ink City***
Ink on paper, 30 x 40 cm each, installation view "Ink City"
Tusche auf Papier, je 30 x 40 cm, Installationsansicht „Ink City“
水墨画, 每幅30 x 40 cm, 《墨水城市》装置实景, "墨水城市"

6 ***Windows XP***, *2002*
Colour video, 2 min
Video, Farbe, 2 Min.
《Windows XP》2002年, 彩色录像, 2分钟

7 ***Anti-terror Variety***, *2002*
Colour video, 5 min 14 sec
Video, Farbe, 5 Min. 14 Sek.
《花样反恐》, 2002年, 彩色录像, 5分14秒

8 ***Homescape***, *2005*
Photo collage, 100 boxes, 30 x 30 x 55 cm each
Fotocollage, 100 Kisten, je 30 x 30 x 55 cm
《家景》, 2005年, 照片拼贴画, 100 箱, 每幅30 x 30 x 55 cm

9 ***Windows XP***, *2002*
Colour video, 2 min (installation view)
Video, Farbe, 2 Min. (Installationsansicht)
《Windows XP》, 2002年, 彩色录像, 2分钟, 装置实景

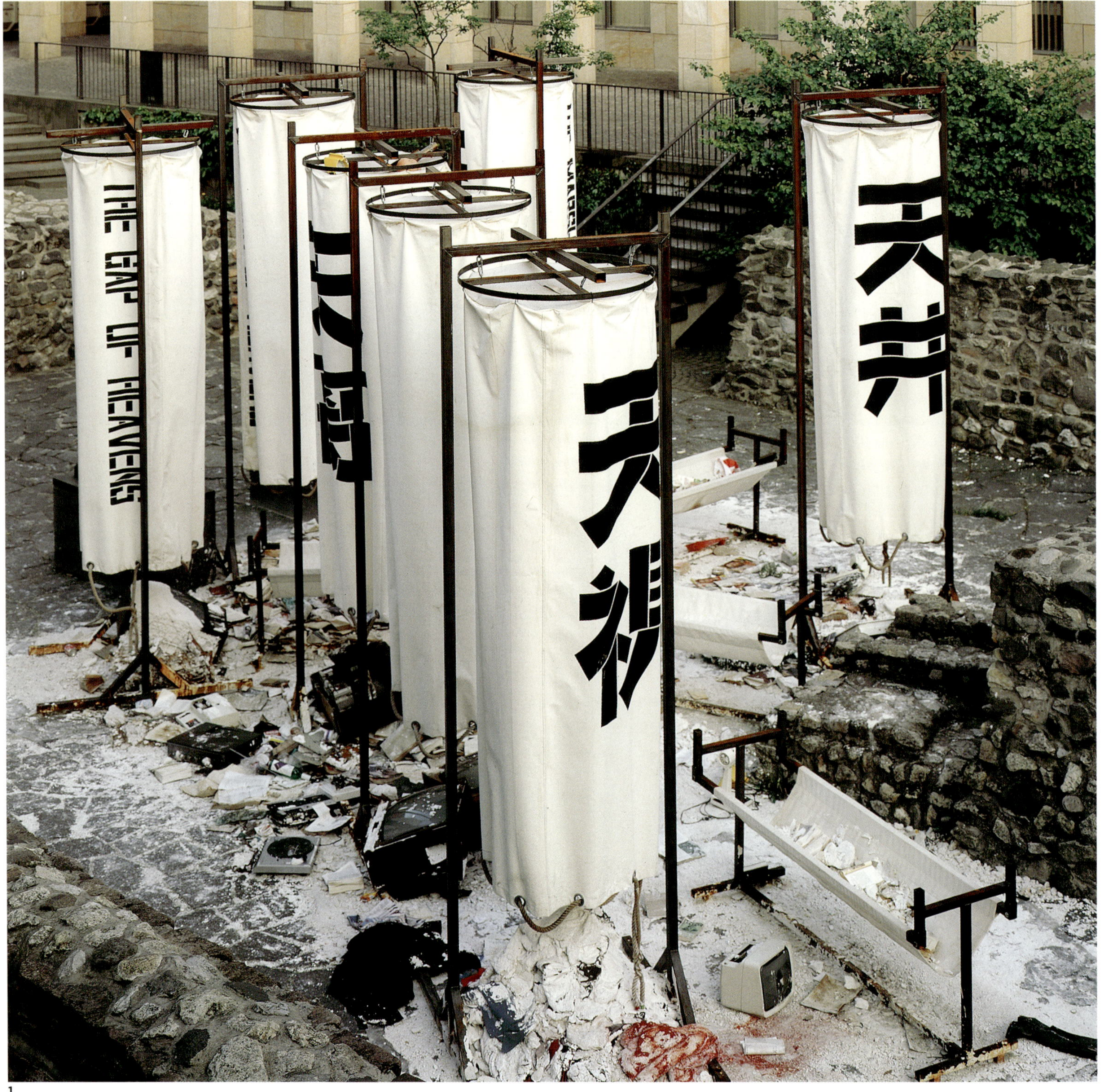

1

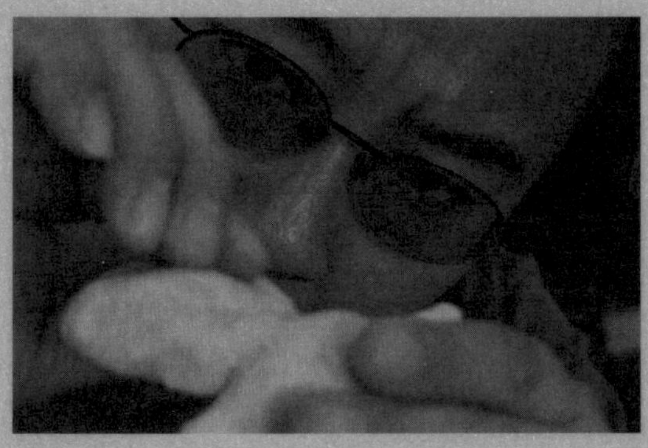

"You can only arrive at your objective opinion by understanding the East and being involved in the West. Observe the world by examining yourself."

„Man kann nur eine objektive Position erreichen, wenn man zugleich den Osten versteht und in den Westen verstrickt ist. Beobachte die Welt, indem du dich selbst untersuchst."

"只有当你认识了东方，并也了解了西方之后，才能真正确立你自己的观点。在审视世界的同时，也检验自我。"

Born in 1955 in Shanghai, China. Died 2000 in Paris, France
Geboren 1955 in Shanghai, China. Gestorben 2000 in Paris, Frankreich
1955年出生于中国上海，2000年在巴黎逝世

Selected exhibitions **/ Ausgewählte Ausstellungen /** 所选展览

1996 "Chen Zhen", Centre international d'Art contemporain de Montréal, 11e édition des 100 Jours d'art contemporain de Montréal, Canada
1998 "Jue Chang/Fifty Strokes to Each", Tel Aviv Museum of Art, Helena Rubinstein Pavilion for Contemporary Art, Tel Aviv, Israel
2001 "Chen Zhen", Serpentine Gallery, London, UK
2002 "Chen Zhen. Metaphors of the Body", National Museum of Contemporary Art, Athens, Greece
2006 "Chen Zhen", Shanghai Art Museum, Shanghai, China
2007 "Chen Zhen. Der Körper als Landschaft", Kunsthalle Wien, Vienna, Austria

1996年 《陈箴》蒙特利尔国际当代艺术中心蒙特利尔当代艺术100天第11版 加拿大
1998年 《绝唱 -- 各打五十大板》特拉维夫艺术博物馆，以色列
2001年 《陈箴》蛇形画廊，伦敦，英国
2002年 《陈箴-身体隐喻》希腊国家博物馆，雅典，希腊
2006年 《陈箴》上海美术馆，上海
2007年 《陈箴。身体作为风景》维也纳艺术馆，维也纳，奥地利

Selected publications **/ Ausgewählte Publikationen /** 所选著作

Chen Zhen, Carolyn Christov-Bakargiev, Daniel Buren: "Chen Zhen – Hopeful Monster", Turine 2000
"Chen Zhen. In Praise of Black Magic", Turine 2000
Guy & Myriam Ullens Foundation (ed.): "Alles onder de hemel/All under heaven. China Now!", Antwerp 2003
Jean-Hubert Martin: "Zhen Chen", Prato 2003

陈箴/Christov-Bakargiev, Carolyn/Buren, Daniel（著）:《陈箴 -- 有希望的怪物》都灵 2000年
《陈箴。在黑魔术称赞》展览目册，都灵2000年
Guy & Myriam Ullens Foundation（编者）:《天堂之下》安特卫普2003年
Martin, Jean-Hubert（著）:《陈箴》Prato 2003年

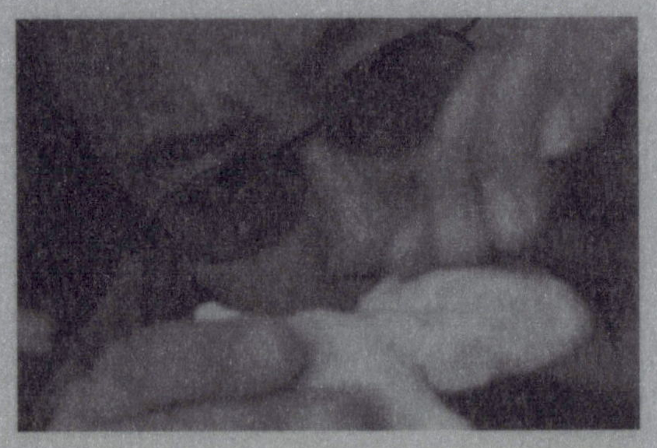

"You can only arrive at your objective opinion by understanding the East and being involved in the West. Observe the world by examining yourself."

„Man kann nur eine objektive Position erreichen, wenn man zugleich den Osten versteht und in den Westen verstrickt ist. Beobachte die Welt, indem du dich selbst untersuchst."

"只有当你认识了东方，并也了解了西方之后，才能真正确立你自己的观点。在审视世界的同时，也检验自我。"

Born in 1955 in Shanghai, China. Died 2000 in Paris, France
Geboren 1955 in Shanghai, China. Gestorben 2000 in Paris, Frankreich
1955年出生于中国上海，2000年在巴黎逝世

Selected exhibitions / Ausgewählte Ausstellungen / 所选展览

1996 "Chen Zhen", Centre international d'Art contemporain de Montréal, 11e édition des 100 Jours d'art contemporain de Montréal, Canada
1998 "Jue Chang/Fifty Strokes to Each", Tel Aviv Museum of Art, Helena Rubinstein Pavilion for Contemporary Art, Tel Aviv, Israel
2001 "Chen Zhen", Serpentine Gallery, London, UK
2002 "Chen Zhen. Metaphors of the Body", National Museum of Contemporary Art, Athens, Greece
2006 "Chen Zhen", Shanghai Art Museum, Shanghai, China
2007 "Chen Zhen. Der Körper als Landschaft", Kunsthalle Wien, Vienna, Austria

1996年 《陈箴》蒙特利尔国际当代艺术中心蒙特利尔当代艺术100天第11版 加拿大
1998年 《绝唱 — 各打五十大板》特拉维夫艺术博物馆，以色列
2001年 《陈箴》蛇形画廊，伦敦，英国
2002年 《陈箴-身体隐喻》希腊国家博物馆，雅典，希腊
2006年 《陈箴》上海美术馆，上海
2007年 《陈箴。身体作为风景》维也纳艺术馆，维也纳，奥地利

Selected publications / Ausgewählte Publikationen / 所选著作

Chen Zhen, Carolyn Christov-Bakargiev, Daniel Buren: "Chen Zhen - Hopeful Monster", Turine 2000
"Chen Zhen. In Praise of Black Magic", Turine 2000
Guy & Myriam Ullens Foundation (ed.): "Alles onder de hemel/All under heaven. China Now!", Antwerp 2003
Jean-Hubert Martin: "Zhen Chen", Prato 2003

陈箴/Christov-Bakargiev, Carolyn/Buren, Daniel（著）：《陈箴 — 有希望的怪物》都灵 2000年
《陈箴。在黑魔术称赞》展览目册，都灵2000年
Guy & Myriam Ullens Foundation（编者）：《天堂之下》安特卫普2003年
Martin, Jean-Hubert（著）：《陈箴》Prato 2003年

CHEN ZHEN 陈箴

[tʂʰən tʂən˨]

Everybody is drumming as loud as possible. In 1999 at the Biannial of Venice Chen Zhen also made noise: as a simple means of protest against the conflicts on earth he offered the traditional Zen practice: two conflicting parties are to be beaten with fifty strokes to each, in the hope to bring them to terms. The understanding of the other's position should help to find the self-awareness – a kind of empathic self therapy. "Jue Chang – Fifty Strokes to Each" the title of an enormous installation, provides the spectators with beds and chairs, covered with hides to beat on with wooden plugs like on drums.

Interaction and reaction in the spell of violence and power are the guiding theme of Chen Zhen, sculptor and installation artist. For him art is a liberating and depurification process picking out the subjective examination of the socialising world as central theme. Chen used the word "trans-experience" – for the exchange between cultures and societies. Being a child of the cultural revolution he experienced himself the slanders of Chinese tradition, initiated by Mao turning again more intensely than before to tradition after the end of Mao's rule.

His unpretentious works criticising society deem to be understood as spiritual remedies towards the dominant materialism in the western world and the obsessive consumption accompanying it.

Chen was one of the avant-garde generation leaving China in the mid 1980s. He went to Paris, where his interest was attracted by common things of daily life like beds, chairs, pots, vases, abacus, mattresses and so on, already used items changing due to the encounter with the west. He arranged these simple objects in space dimension like accumulative installations, where those daily objects won a new purely spiritual identity being in contrast to their original function. The spectator is often interactively involved –by starting these things to move or to make noise – becomes a partner in this search for identity within or towards a foreign culture.

Jeder trommelt so laut er kann. Auch Chen Zhen machte richtig Krach: Als simples Mittel gegen die Konflikte der Welt bot er 1999 auf der Biennale in Venedig eine alte Zen-Praxis an, nach der an zwei streitende Parteien jeweils 50 Schläge auszuteilen sind, in der Hoffnung, dass sie dadurch zur Vernunft kommen. Die Einsicht in die Position des Anderen soll die Selbsterkenntnis fördern – eine Art empathischer Eigentherapie. „Jue Chang – Fifty Strokes to Each", so der Titel der gewaltigen Installation, stellt dem Publikum mit Tierhäuten bespannte Betten und Stühle zur Verfügung, auf die es mit Holzpflöcken wie auf Trommeln Hiebe austeilen kann.

Interaktion und Reaktion im Zirkel von Gewalt und Macht waren die Leitmotive des Bildhauers und Installationskünstlers Chen Zhen. Er verstand Kunst als einen befreienden und reinigenden Prozess, der die subjektive Auseinandersetzung mit der sozialisierenden Welt thematisiert. Chen sprach von „Trans-Erfahrung" zwischen den Kulturen und Gesellschaften. Als Kind der Kulturrevolution erlebte er am eigenen Leib die von Mao angestoßenen Schmähungen der chinesischen Tradition, um sich dieser nach dem Ende von Maos Herrschaft dann umso stärker zuzuwenden.

Seine unprätentiösen gesellschaftskritischen Arbeiten lassen sich mitunter als spirituelle Heilsangebote gegen den im Westen dominanten Materialismus und den zwanghaften Konsum verstehen, der mit ihm einhergeht.

Chen gehörte zu jenem Teil der chinesischen Avantgarde, der das Land Mitte der 1980er Jahre verließ. Er emigrierte nach Paris. Dort interessierte ihn, wie sich aus dem Osten stammende, schon benutzte Alltagsgegenstände wie Bett, Stuhl, Töpfe, Vasen, Abakus, Matratzen usw. in der Begegnung mit dem Westen verändern. Er arrangierte diese schlichten Objekte in raumgreifenden, akkumulativen Installationen, wobei sie eine im Gegensatz zur ursprünglichen Objekt-Funktion vollkommen neue, rein spirituelle Identität gewannen. Der Besucher wird häufig interaktiv miteinbezogen und – etwa indem er Dinge in Bewegung

人人都在自吹自擂，在1999年的威尼斯双年展上陈箴也高声谈论：以一种抗议世间冲突的纯朴方式，他提出传统禅学理念；一有冲突，给冲突双方各打五十大板，最终归于统一. 换位思考可以有助于发现自我意识-通过移情达到的自我治疗的目的。大型装置作品《绝唱 -- 各打五十大板》，中无数只悬吊在空间里的“床鼓”与“椅鼓”而组成的一个大型装置作品，邀请观众们参与到其中，并用“手”击鼓的形式。

魔咒的暴力和能量里的交感和感应是雕塑家、装置艺术家陈箴的主题。对他而言，艺术是解放和净化的过程，以提炼出社会化世界的主观检验作为中心思想。陈用“融超经验”来表达文化和社会思想的交流。在文化大革命中，儿童时代的他亲身体验了对中国传统的批判文化，这由毛泽东首先发起，在毛统治结束以后，而发展的更加激烈。

他批评社会的低调作品，通常被当作是西方世界主导的物质主义和强迫消费的精神良药。在上世纪80年代中期，陈箴是离开中国的先锋艺术家之一。他来到了巴黎，对日常生活中的普通用品产生了兴趣，如床、椅子、水壶、花瓶、算盘、床垫等一些由于西方文化的碰撞早已改变的东西。这些普通的物品被排列在装置里，与其原有的功能相比，它们获得了全新的精神性。观众也常常也相应参与其中，或是动手搬移，或是评头论足，和艺术家一起共同对外来文化进行自我探索。

陈箴的作品根源于道学，道家理论认为，宇宙由阴阳两部分组成，两者势力均衡。甚至东西医学的不同以及佛教的灵性和理性的西方文化都是陈的创作对象。相当重要的人体是陈关注的核心，由于他身患恶疾，痛苦是他作品中的另一个关键元素。

陈箴把人体作为一个神秘的内部景观来考虑，无数的元素长期和谐协作而使人体平静运转。鉴于古老的传统仪式（或仅仅是旧家具）陈用特定的方式比

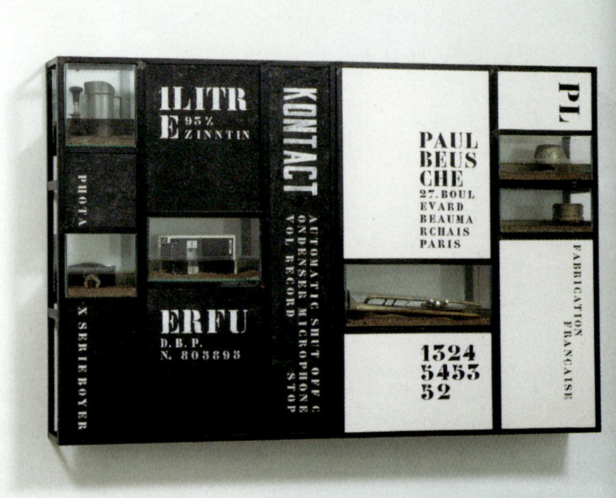
1LITR
E 95%
ZINNTIN
PHOTA
ERFU
D. B. P.
N. 803893
X SERIE BOYER
KONTACT
AUTOMATIC SHUT OFF C
ONDENSER MICROPHONE
VOL RECORD STOP
PAUL
BEUS
CHE
27.BOUL
EVARD
BEAUMA
RCHAIS
PARIS
1324
5453
52
PL
FABRICATION
FRANCAISE

2

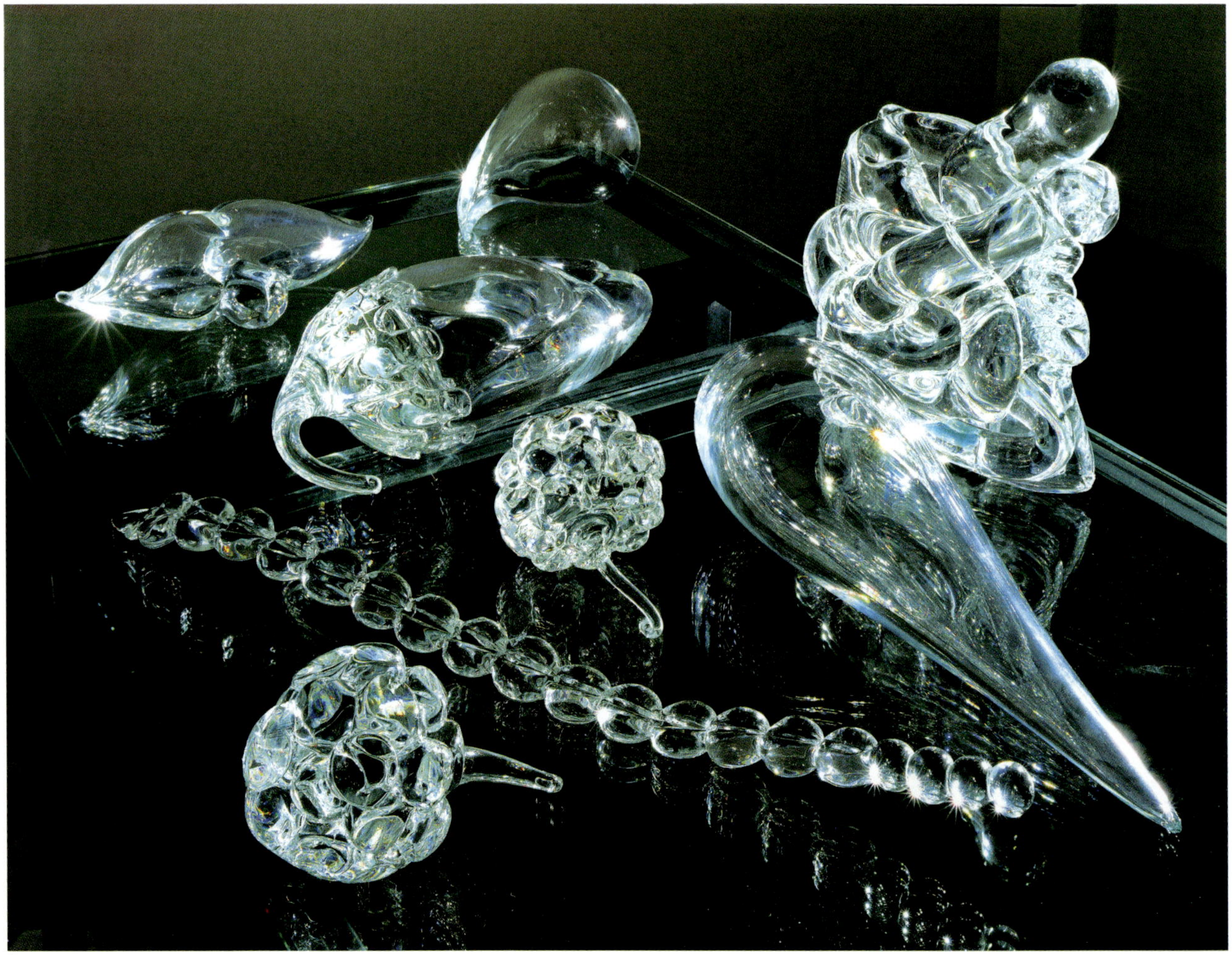

3

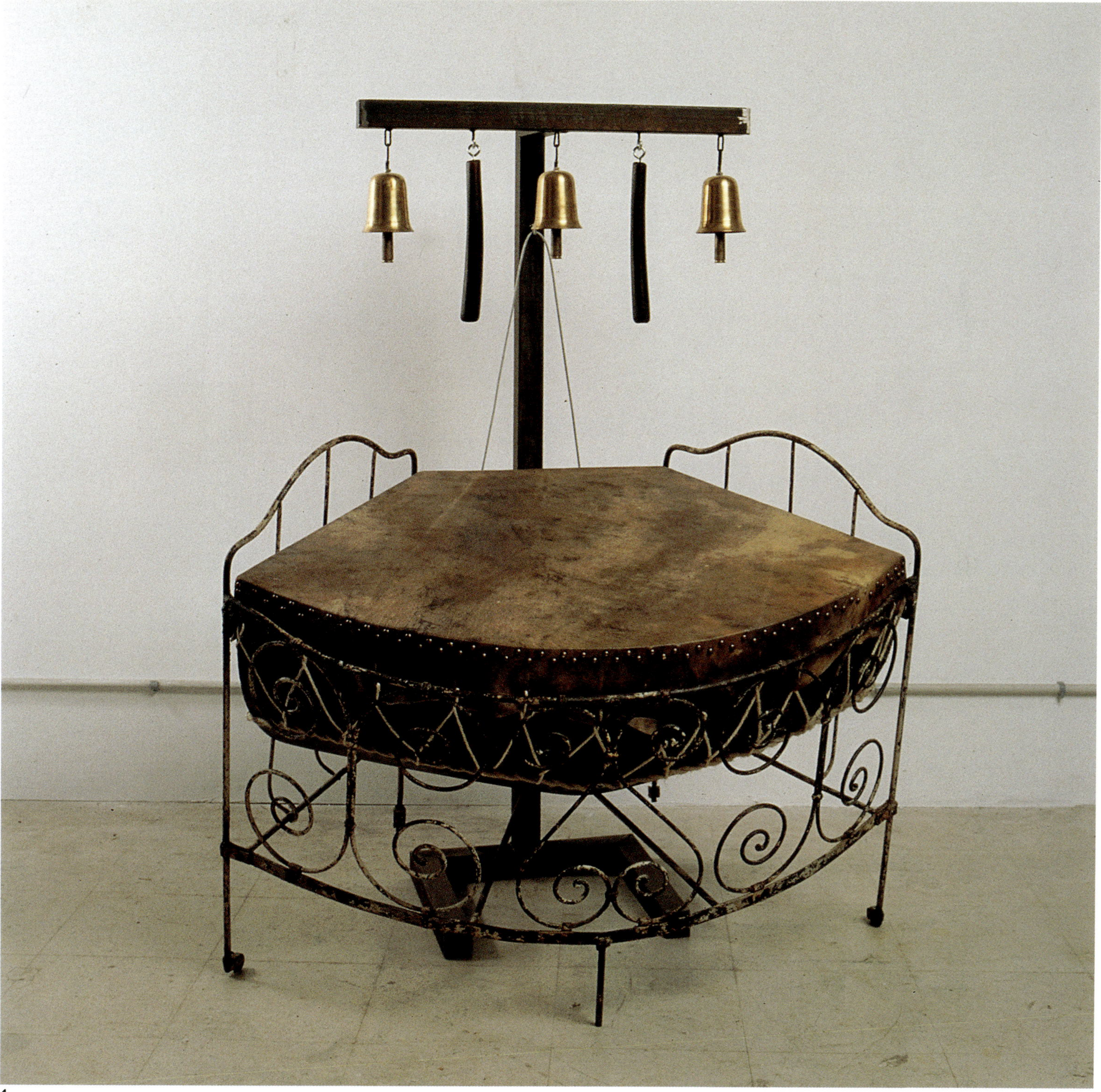

4

5

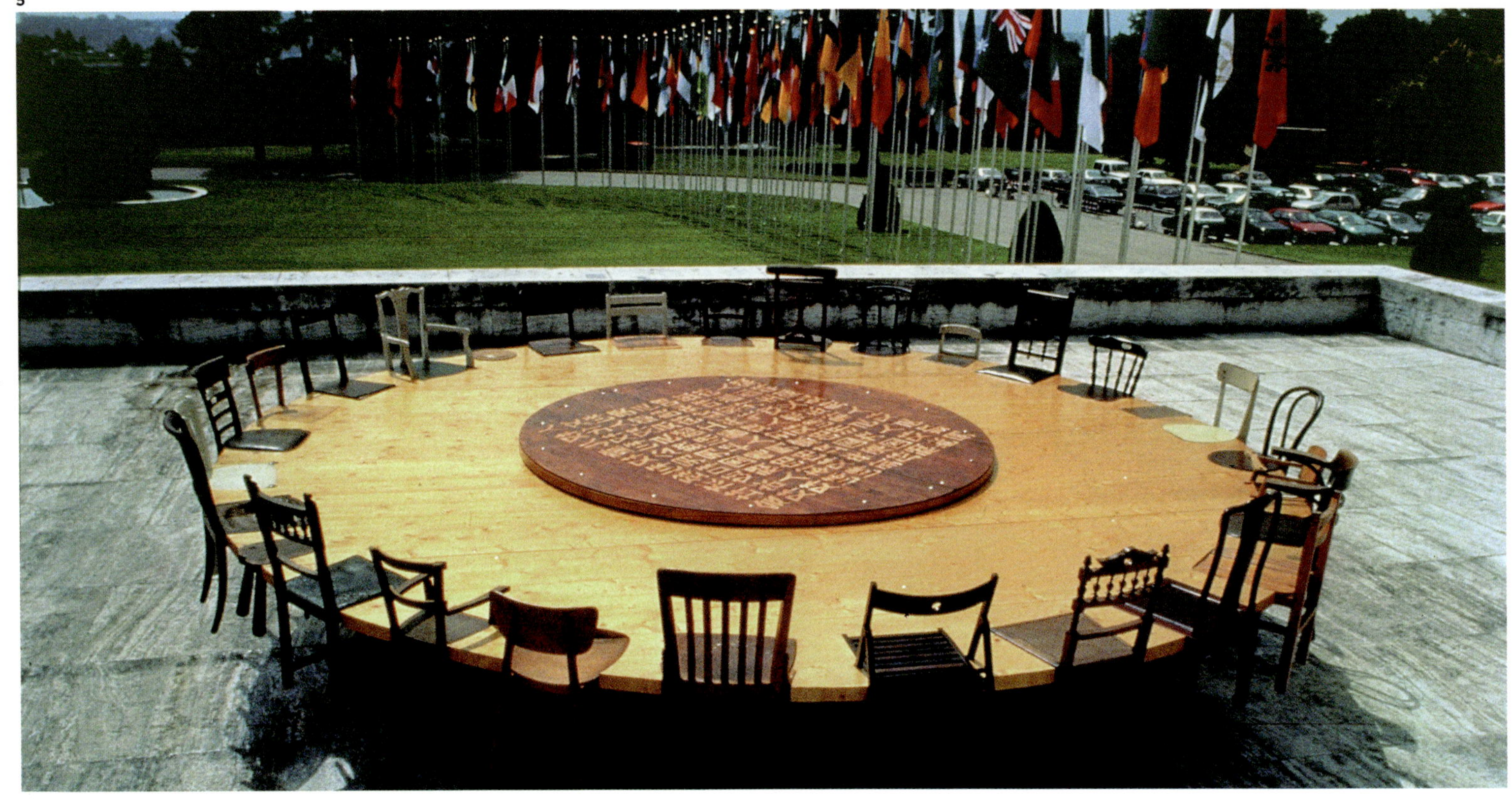

Chen's works may have their roots in Daoism having Yin and Yang as two equal parts of the cosmic oneness. Even the differences between western and eastern medicine as well as Buddhist spirituality and the rationally dominated western culture are objects of the artist. Not least the human body was the centre of Chen's interest, due to his own serious illness, pain being another key element of his work.

Chen regarded the human body as a mysterious inner landscape, working in peace as long as the numerous elements cooperate in harmony. Considering old traditional rites (or just old furniture) Chen confronts the obsolete old with the coveted new, characterising globalisation in common, but the situation of Asian cities and the Chinese high speed urbanization as well. "Transexperience" was an artistic process, Chen Zhen based on transfer and experiments but also on use and melding. The "trans-experience" as necessary act of resistance is a hybrid and parasitic attitude of art towards the world.

setzt und Geräusche auslöst – zum Partner auf der ernsten Suche nach Identität innerhalb oder gegenüber einer fremden Kultur.

Womöglich sind Chens Arbeiten im Taoismus verwurzelt, für den Yin und Yang zwei gleichberechtigte Seiten der kosmischen Einheit darstellen. Auch die Unterschiede zwischen westlicher und östlicher Medizin sowie zwischen buddhistischer Spiritualität und der rational dominierten westlichen Kultur beschäftigten den Künstler. Doch nicht zuletzt stand der menschliche Körper im Zentrum von Chens Interesse, sicher auch wegen der eigenen schweren Erkrankung, sodass ein weiteres Schlüsselelement seines Werks der Schmerz ist. Für Chen war der Leib eine rätselhafte Innenlandschaft, ein Organismus, der friedlich arbeitet, solange seine zahlreichen Elemente harmonisch zusammenwirken.

Mit dem Aufgreifen traditioneller Rituale (oder auch nur von Möbeln) konfrontierte Chen das obsolete Alte mit dem begehrten Neuen und charakterisierte damit die Globalisierung allgemein, aber auch die Situation der asiatischen Städte und die chinesische Hochgeschwindigkeitsurbanisierung im besonderen. „Trans-expérience" war für Chen Zhen ein künstlerisches Verfahren, das vorrangig auf Transfer und Experiment setzte, aber ebenso auf Anwendung und Verschmelzung. Die „Trans-Erfahrung" als ein notwendiger Akt des Widerstands, aber auch als eine hybride und parasitäre Haltung der Kunst gegenüber der Welt.

较了已经湮灭、新的以及和全球化中的之间的区别和联系。“融超经验”是一项艺术过程，陈依据转换和经验当然还有运用了融合。“融超经验”作为必要的艺术抗争，是以混杂和寄生的态度看待世界。

Gregor Jansen

6

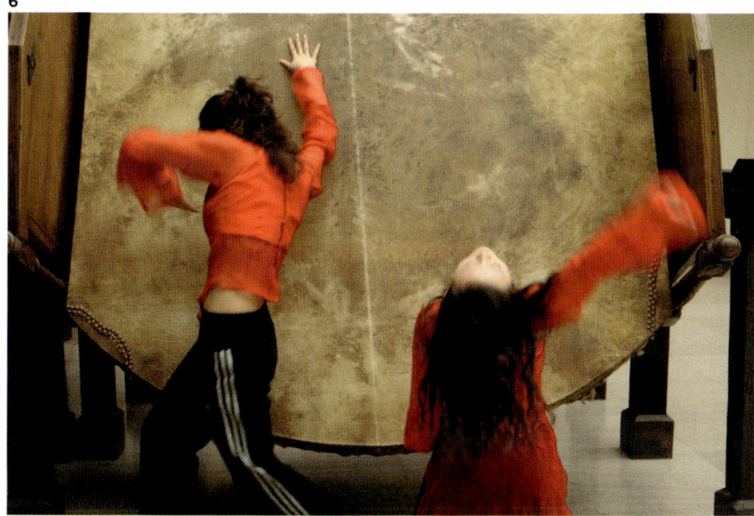

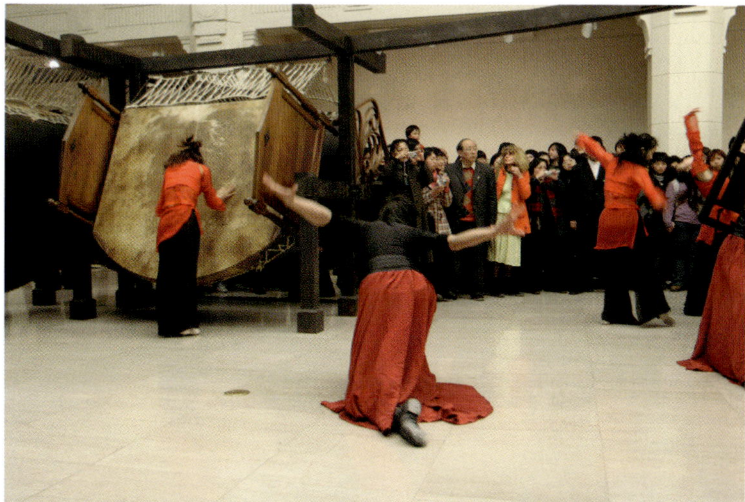

1 ***Sacrifice in the Heaven's Well***, *1993*
Metal, plaster, canvas, objects, 450 x 800 x 1200 cm, exhibition view, "Prospect 93", Frankfurter Kunstverein and Schirn Kunsthalle, Frankfurt, Germany
Metall, Gips, Leinwand, Objekte, 450 x 800 x 1200 cm, Ausstellungsansicht, „Prospect 93", Frankfurter Kunstverein und Schirn Kunsthalle, Frankfurt, Germany
《天井祭》1993年, 金属, 石膏, 帆布等, 450 x 800 x 1200 cm, 展览实景

2 ***L'autel – Le dépôt/Le repos***, *1992*
Metal, water, sand, glass, wood, acrylic paint, objects, 119 x 181 x 31 cm
Metall, Wasser, Sand, Glas, Holz, Acrylfarbe, Objekte, 119 x 181 x 31 cm
《借尸还魂》1992年, 金属, 水, 沙子, 玻璃, 木头, 丙烯颜料, 实物, 119 x 181 x 31 cm

3 ***Crystal Landscape of Inner Body***, *2000*
Crystal, metal, glass, 95 x 70 x 190 cm; Kristall, Metall, Glas, 95 x 70 x 190 cm
《水晶体内风景》2000年, 水晶，金属, 玻璃，95 x 70 x 190 cm

4 ***Un-interrupted Voice***, *1998*
Children's bed, bells, wood, metal, skin and drawings, 170 x 160 x 80 cm
Kinderbett, Glocken, Holz, Metall, Haut und Zeichnungen, 170 x 160 x 80 cm
《不间断的声音》1998年, 儿童床，铃铛，金属，木头等, 170 x 160 x 80 cm

5 ***Round Table***, *1995*
Wood, chairs from five continents, metal, 180 x 550 x 550 cm, installation view, "Dialogue of Peace", UN Building, Geneva, Switzerland
Holz, Stühle von fünf Kontinenten, Metall, 180 x 550 x 550 cm, Installationsansicht, „Dialogue of Peace", UN-Gebäude, Genf, Schweiz
《双圆桌》1995年，木头, 五大洲的椅子, 金属, 180 x 550 x 550 cm, 装置实景

6 ***Jue Chang – Dancing Body-Drumming Mind***, *2000*
Wood, iron, chairs, beds, leather, ropes, nails, 2.44 x 18 x 14 m, installation view, Shanghai Art Museum
Holz, Eisen, Stühle, Betten, Leder, Seile, Nägel, 2,44 x 18 x 14 m, Installationsansicht, Shanghai Art Museum
《绝唱-身体隐喻》2000年, 木头, 铁, 椅子, 床, 皮革, 绳, 钉子, 石头, 2.44 x 18 x 14 m, 装置实景

7 ***Un monde accroché/détaché***, *1990*
99 objects hanged in a burnt forest, exhibition view, "Chine demain pour hier", Pourrières, France
99 Objekte in einem abgebrannten Wald aufgehängt, Ausstellungsansicht, „Chine demain pour hier", Pourrières, Frankreich
《世界连接了/解开了》1990年, 99 物体悬挂在燃烧的树林里，展览实景

8 ***Jue Chang – Fifty Strokes to Each***, *1999*
Wood, iron, chairs, beds, leather, ropes, nails, stone, 2.44 x 9,80 x 10 m, installation view, Tel Aviv Museum of Art, Tel Aviv, Israel
Holz, Eisen, Stühle, Betten, Leder, Seile, Nägel, Stein, 2,44 x 9,80 x 10 m, Installationsansicht, Tel Aviv Museum of Art, Tel Aviv, Israel
《绝唱 — 各打五十大板》1999年, 木头, 铁, 椅子, 床, 皮革, 绳, 钉子, 石头, 2.44 x 9.80 x 10 m, 装置实景

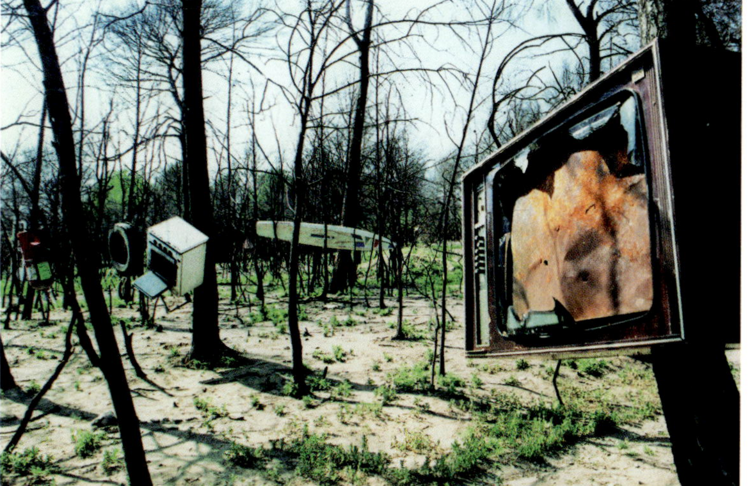

7

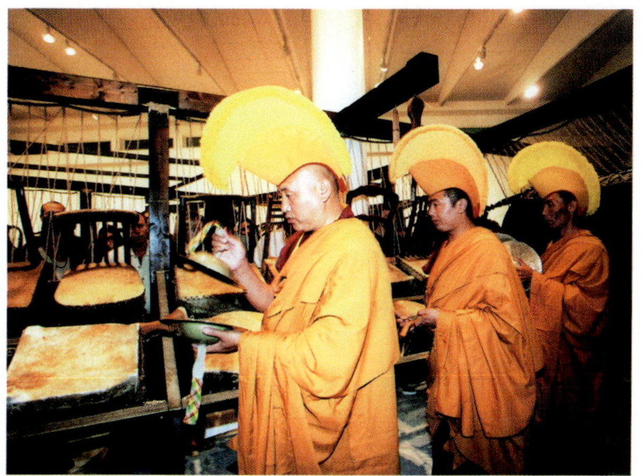

8

1

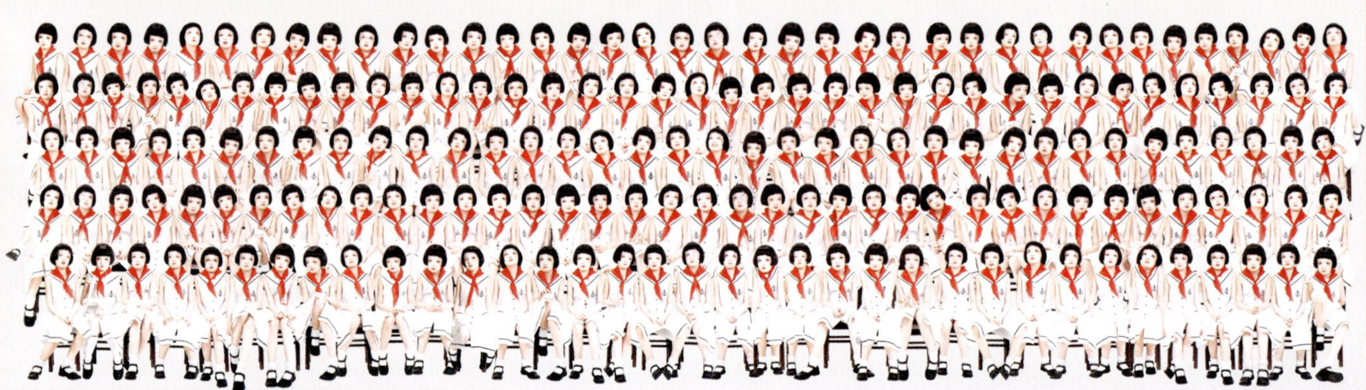

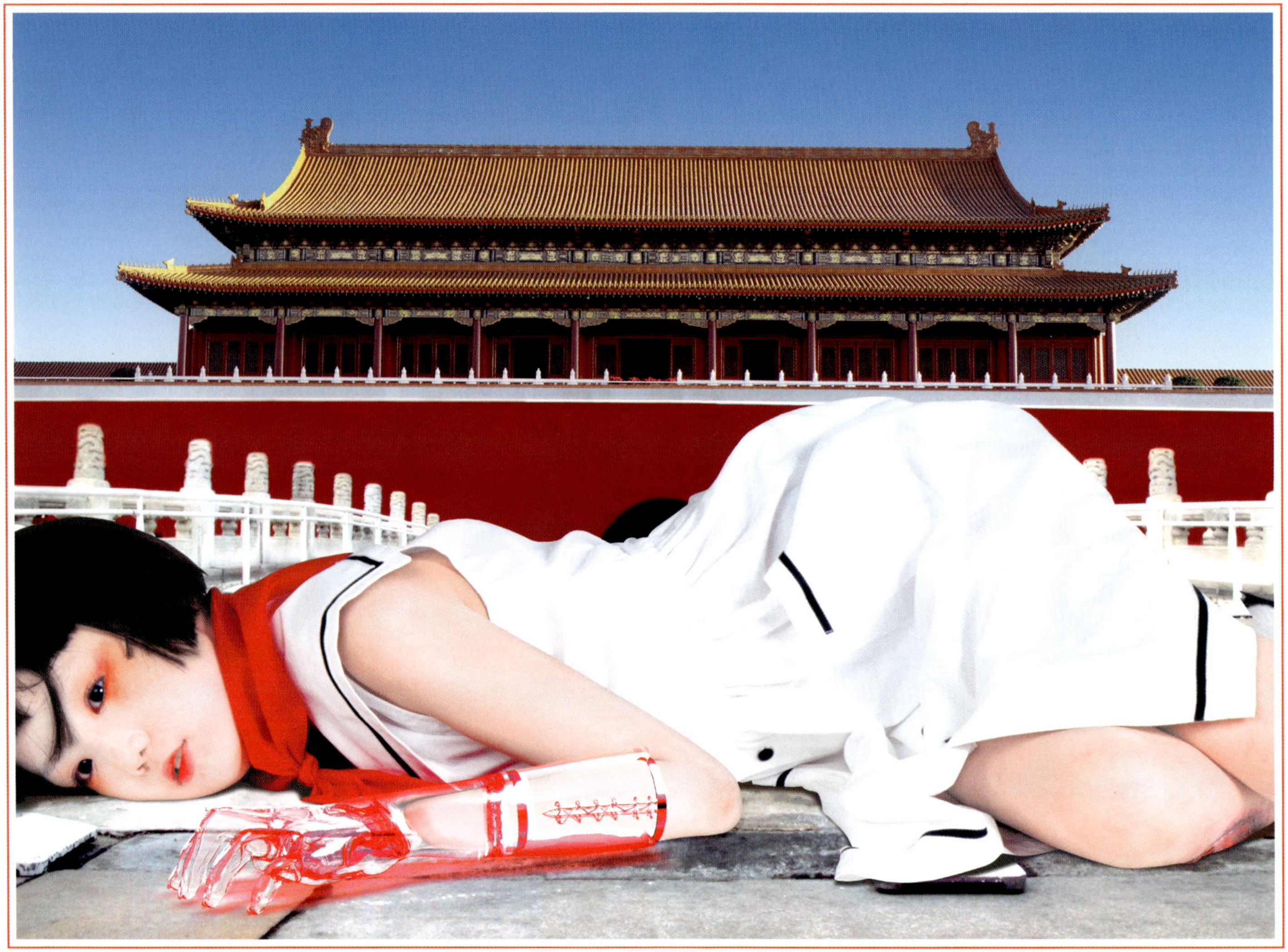

2

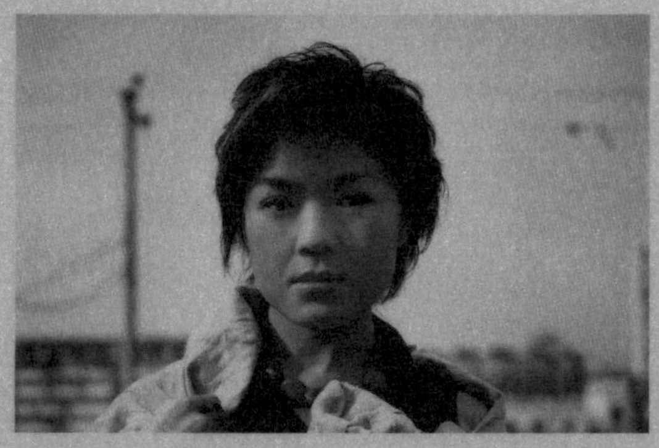

"Every minute, every second, people are in different spaces doing the same thing, or different things. Some of the things they do excite my interest, because within a certain relative period of time they can alter the function of the space."

„In jeder Minute und jeder Sekunde befinden sich Leute in unterschiedlichen Räumen, während sie das Gleiche tun oder auch etwas anderes. Einige ihrer Handlungen erregen mein Interesse, denn innerhalb einer gewissen Zeitspanne können sie die Funktion des Raums verändern."

"每分，每秒，不同空间的人们做着相同或者不同的事情。他们做得有些事情能激发我的兴趣，因为在一定相对的时期内，他们能改变空间的作用。"

Born in 1970 in Heilongjiang, China. Lives and works in Beijing
Geboren 1970 in Heilongjiang, China. Lebt und arbeitet in Peking
1970年出生于黑龙江。她居住工作在北京

Selected exhibitions **/ Ausgewählte Ausstellungen /** 所选展览

2001	"Constructed Reality: Beijing Conceptual Photography", Hong Kong Arts Center, Hong Kong, China
	"Cross-Pressure: Contemporary Photography and Video from Beijing", Finnish Museum of Photography, Helsinki, Finland
2002	"Chinart: Contemporary Art from China", Museum Küppersmühle, Duisburg, Germany
	"Under Construction/New Dimensions of Asian Art", Tokyo Opera City Art Gallery, Tokyo, Japan
2003	"Alors, la Chine?", Centre Georges Pompidou, Paris, France
2004	"Cui Xiuwen/Kan Xuan", Musée d'Art Contemporain, Bordeaux, France
2004–07	"Between Past and Future, New Photography and Video from China", International Center of Photography, New York, NY, USA (travelling exhibition)
2005–07	"Mahjong – Chinesische Gegenwartskunst aus der Sammlung Sigg", Kunstmuseum Bern, Berne, Switzerland; Hamburger Kunsthalle, Hamburg, Germany; Museum der Moderne, Salzburg, Austria

2001年	《建构的真实：北京观念摄影展 》，香港艺术中心，香港
	《多重压力：当代北京摄影和录影》，摄影芬兰博物馆，赫尔辛基
2002年	《中国艺术：中国当代艺术》杜伊斯堡
	《建设中：亚洲艺术新维度》东京歌剧城市美术画廊, 东京
2003年	《那么中国呢？》蓬皮杜文化艺术中心现代艺术馆法国巴黎
2004年	《崔岫闻/阚萱 影像作品展》波尔多博物馆，波尔多，法国
2004–07年	《过去与未来之间—中国新影像展》 国际摄影中心 纽约 美国（巡回展）
2005–07年	《麻将》西克中国当代艺术收藏展 伯尔尼美术馆 瑞士；汉堡美术馆 汉堡 德国；萨尔茨保现代美术馆 奥地利

Selected publications **/ Ausgewählte Publikationen /** 所选著作

Wenil Rhee, Peter Weibl, Gregor Jansen (eds.): "ThermoCline of Art: New Asian Waves", Ostfildern-Ruit 2007

Rhee, Wenil/Weibl, Peter/Jansen, Gregor（编者）:《艺术温跃层：亚洲新浪潮，艺术和媒介技术中心ZKM Zentrum für Kunst und Medientechnologie》， Ostfildern-Ruit 2007年

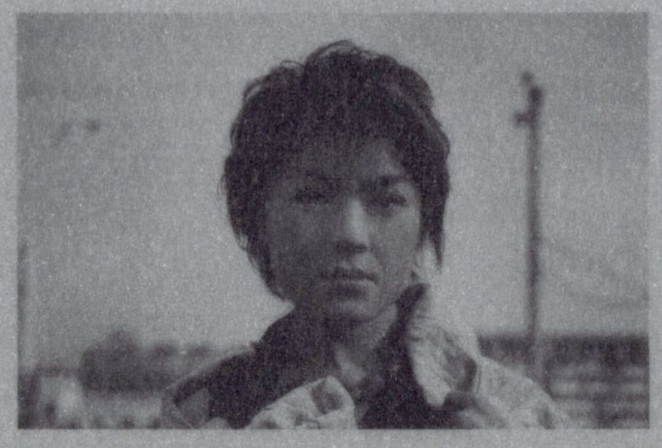

"Every minute, every second, people are in different spaces doing the same thing, or different things. Some of the things they do excite my interest, because within a certain relative period of time they can alter the function of the space."

„In jeder Minute und jeder Sekunde befinden sich Leute in unterschiedlichen Räumen, während sie das Gleiche tun oder auch etwas anderes. Einige ihrer Handlungen erregen mein Interesse, denn innerhalb einer gewissen Zeitspanne können sie die Funktion des Raums verändern.“

"每分，每秒，不同空间的人们做着相同或者不同的事情。他们做得有些事情能激发我的兴趣，因为在一定相对的时期内，他们能改变空间的作用。"

Born in 1970 in Heilongjiang, China. Lives and works in Beijing
Geboren 1970 in Heilongjiang, China. Lebt und arbeitet in Peking
1970年出生于黑龙江。她居住工作在北京

Selected exhibitions / Ausgewählte Ausstellungen / 所选展览

2001	"Constructed Reality: Beijing Conceptual Photography", Hong Kong Arts Center, Hong Kong, China
	"Cross-Pressure: Contemporary Photography and Video from Beijing", Finnish Museum of Photography, Helsinki, Finland
2002	"Chinart: Contemporary Art from China", Museum Küppersmühle, Duisburg, Germany
	"Under Construction/New Dimensions of Asian Art", Tokyo Opera City Art Gallery, Tokyo, Japan
2003	"Alors, la Chine?", Centre Georges Pompidou, Paris, France
2004	"Cui Xiuwen/Kan Xuan", Musée d'Art Contemporain, Bordeaux, France
2004-07	"Between Past and Future. New Photography and Video from China", International Center of Photography, New York, NY, USA (travelling exhibition)
2005-07	"Mahjong - Chinesische Gegenwartskunst aus der Sammlung Sigg", Kunstmuseum Bern, Berne, Switzerland; Hamburger Kunsthalle, Hamburg, Germany; Museum der Moderne, Salzburg, Austria

2001年	《建构的真实：北京观念摄影展 》，香港艺术中心，香港
	《多重压力：当代北京摄影和录影》，摄影芬兰博物馆，赫尔辛基
2002年	《中国艺术：中国当代艺术》杜伊斯堡
	《建设中：亚洲艺术新维度》东京歌剧城市美术画廊，东京
2003年	《那么中国呢？》蓬皮杜文化艺术中心现代艺术馆法国巴黎
2004年	《崔岫闻/阚萱 影像作品展》波尔多博物馆，波尔多，法国
2004-07年	《过去与未来之间—中国新影像展》国际摄影中心 纽约 美国（巡回展）
2005-07年	《麻将》西克中国当代艺术收藏展 伯尔尼美术馆 瑞士；汉堡美术馆 汉堡 德国；萨尔茨堡现代美术馆 奥地利

Selected publications / Ausgewählte Publikationen / 所选著作

Wenli Rhee, Peter Weibl, Gregor Jansen (eds.): "ThermoCline of Art: New Asian Waves", Ostfildern-Ruit 2007

Rhee, Wenli/Weibl, Peter/Jansen, Gregor（编者）：《艺术温跃层：亚洲新浪潮，艺术和媒介技术中心ZKM Zentrum für Kunst und Medientechnologie》，Ostfildern-Ruit 2007年

CUI XIUWEN 崔岫闻

[tsʰueɪ ɕiouuən]

Cui Xiuwen first studied design in Northeast Normal University in Harbin and then oil painting in the Central Academy of Fine Arts in Beijing. A group of paintings that she made in the late 1990s took sexuality – often female homosexuality – as their subject; her explicit (though never graphic) depictions of embracing couples and the sexual awakening of pubescent girls created a stir in Beijing's art world. But it was a short documentary video called "Ladies' Room" (2000) that established Cui Xiuwen's reputation as a daring experimental artist (a daring feminist artist to some critics). With a hidden camcorder she secretly filmed activities in a ladies' bathroom in one of Beijing's most fashionable hotels. The camcorder focuses on a limited area in front of a row of mirrors, where young prostitutes stopped frequently over a long night. So there they were, quickly examining their faces and fixing their make-up, and adjusting their bras under their blouses. Their movements were brisk and impersonal. There is little verbal exchange between them and no emotional expression on their faces. These young women are at work, and that is all. The only dramatic tension in the video is generated by a uniformed cleaning lady who silently watches these glamorous young girls from the dark background. Although some art critics have praised "Ladies' Room" as a social critique of commercial sex in today's China, Cui Xiuwen's interest lies in representing a social space which is both public and secret, and which belongs to women alone.

Since 2000 Cui Xiuwen has created a considerable body of videos and photographs around three themes related to women's interiority. Each has its roots in Cui's earlier works, but it has developed into the core of a group of interrelated works. The first theme is private female behaviour in public space. A representative work in this group is the 2002 video "Underground", which focuses on a female passenger in a Beijing subway who keeps touching and tearing off chapped skin from her lips for more than 20 minutes. In Cui's words, the woman's unconscious act transforms the underground "into a public space of private necessity."

Cui Xiuwen studierte zunächst Design an der Northeast Normal University in Harbin und dann Ölmalerei an der Central Academy of Fine Arts in Peking. Eine Gruppe von Gemälden, die sie in den späten 1990er Jahren schuf, beschäftigte sich mit dem Thema Sexualität – und zwar häufig mit weiblicher Homosexualität. Ihre offenherzigen (wenn auch nie drastischen) Bilder von Paaren, die sich umarmen, oder vom sexuellen Erwachen pubertierender Mädchen erregten in der Pekinger Kunstszene einiges Aufsehen. Aber es war eine kurze Videodokumentation mit dem Titel „Ladies' Room" (2000), die Cui Xiuwens Ruf als kühne Experimentalkünstlerin (oder, wie einige Kritiker fanden, kühne feministische Künstlerin) begründete. Mit einem versteckten Camcorder hatte sie das Geschehen auf einer Damentoilette in einem der schicksten Hotels von Peking gefilmt. Das Objektiv hielt einen festen Raumausschnitt vor einer Spiegelreihe im Fokus, wo junge Prostituierte im Laufe einer langen Nacht häufig Zwischenaufenthalte einlegen: Sie studieren ihr Gesicht, reparieren ihr Make-up und rücken ihren BH unter der Bluse zurecht. Ihre Bewegungen sind energisch und unpersönlich, auf den Gesichtern ist kein Gefühlsausdruck zu sehen, und verbalen Austausch zwischen ihnen gibt es kaum. Diese jungen Frauen sind einfach bei der Arbeit, das ist alles. Die einzige dramatische Spannung in dem Video bewirkt eine uniformierte Toilettenfrau, die die glamourösen Damen aus dem dunklen Hintergrund beobachtet. Auch wenn einige Kunstkritiker „Ladies' Room" als beißende Sozialkritik am käuflichen Sex im heutigen China interpretieren, war Cui Xiuwen eher daran interessiert, einen gesellschaftlichen Raum darzustellen, der zugleich öffentlich und verborgen ist und allein den Frauen gehört.

Seit dem Jahr 2000 hat Cui Xiuwen eine stattliche Anzahl von Videos und Fotos rund um drei Themen geschaffen, die alle mit dem weiblichen Seelenleben zu tun haben. Jedes dieser Themen wurzelt in Cuis früheren Werken, hat sich aber jeweils zum Kern einer Gruppe zusammenhängender Werke weiterentwickelt. Der erste Themenkreis, der sich schon in „Ladies' Room" so eindringlich artikulierte, nimmt sich des persönlichen Verhalten von Frauen an öffentlichen

崔岫闻先在哈尔滨的东北师大学习设计，后又在北京的中央美术学院学习油画。她在上世纪九十年代后期的一组油画作品将性，尤其是女同性恋作为主题。她对拥抱中的情侣和思春期少女的性觉醒的直白描述，尽管没有直接描写，仍然在当时的北京艺术界引起了轰动。然而使她作为一名大胆的试验艺术家而声名鹊起的则是她的一部名为《洗手间》（2000年）的记录短片，而对于一些批评家来说，她则是一名大胆的女性主义艺术家。她使用一部藏起来的摄像机偷拍了北京一家最时尚的夜总会的女洗手间中发生的事。摄像机对准一排镜子前方的有限区域。在一个漫长夜晚中，年轻的坐台小姐们频繁的停留在镜子前，迅速地检查自己的容颜并补妆，以及调整在上衣里面的胸罩。她们的动作轻快而冷淡，彼此之间几乎没有言语交流而且全都面无表情。这些年轻的小姐们只是在工作而已。片中唯一的戏剧张力来自一名穿制服的清洁女工，她在昏暗的背景中默默地注视着这些年轻迷人的小姐们。尽管部分艺术批评家称赞《洗手间》是对当今中国性交易的一种社会批判，但至少对崔岫闻而言，她的兴趣不过是想描绘一个既是公共的、又是私人的，而且仅仅属于女人的社会场所，仅此而已。

从2000年开始，围绕着三个与女性内在世界相关的主题，崔岫闻创作了大量录像及摄影作品。每个主题都源自其早期作品，但同时又发展成为一组相关作品的核心。第一个主题为女性在公共空间的行为，这已经在《洗手间》中有力地表现过，其代表作品为2002年的录像作品《地下铁》。作品将镜头对准了一位北京地铁上的女性乘客，长达 20 多分钟的时间里，这名妇女不停地触摸并撕下嘴唇上裂开的皮。用崔岫闻的话来说，这位妇女的下意识动作将地铁转化成为一个“私人需求的公共空间”。

第二个主题则为女性的身体及性解放《TOOT》，（2001 年）、青春期（《程程和贝贝》，2001年）以及性关系的社会性《两次》，（2001年）。第三类作品则将第二个主题与崔岫闻自身的童年记

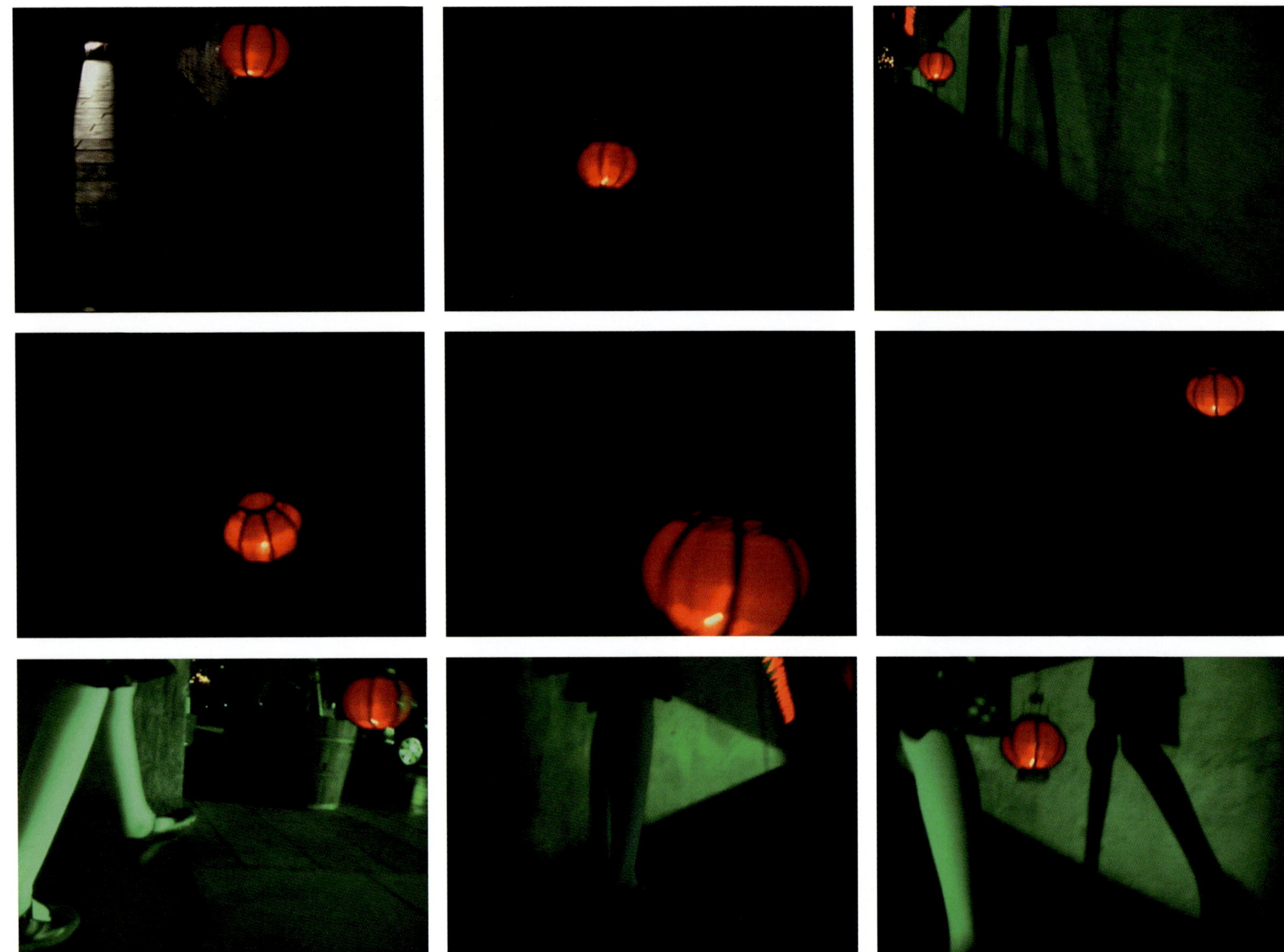

3

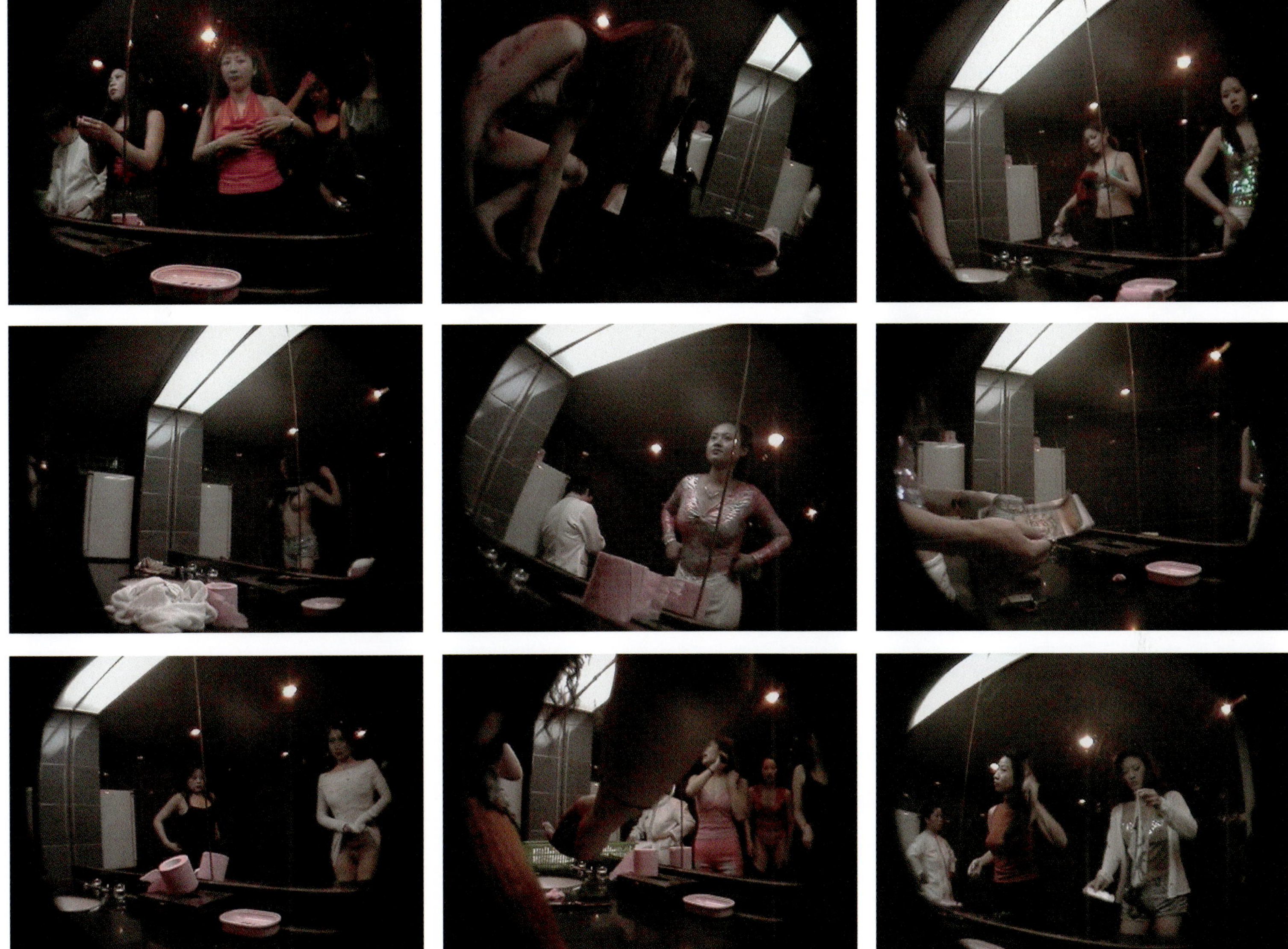

4

5
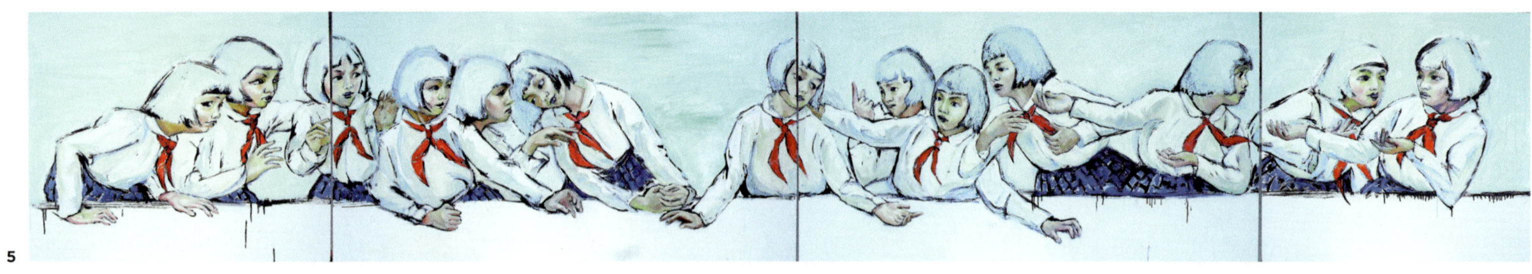

6
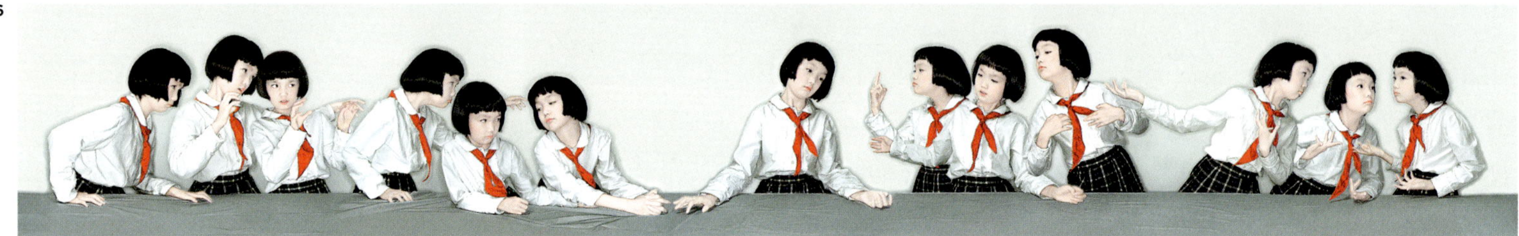

The second theme is the female body and sexual liberation ("TOOT"), puberty ("Chengcheng & Beibei"), and the sociality of sexual relationships ("Twice", all 2001).

A third group of works combines this second theme with Cui's own memory of her childhood. In a series of ambitious works since 2003, including "Sanjie" (2003), "One Day in 2004" (2004), and "Drifting Lantern" (2005), Cui employs a teenage actress with a face like her own. Wearing a white dress and a Young Pioneer's red scarf, she is fresh and innocent; the future seems to belong to her. Yet in the images this girl is either dwarfed by the towering red walls of the Forbidden City or multiplied and transformed into a maze-like virtual landscape. She is helplessly alone, confused and scared. As a result, these works, as well as Cui's most recent photographic series "Angel" (2006), have a strong autobiographical voice, resurrecting the artist's memory of her mixed beliefs, hopes, dreams, and fears.

Orten an. Repräsentativ dafür ist das Video „Underground" von 2002: Es konzentriert sich auf eine Passagierin in der Pekinger U-Bahn, die über 20 Minuten lang ihre aufgesprungenen Lippen befingert und dabei kleine Hautfetzen abzupft. In Cuis Worten: Das unbewusste Tun der Frau verwandelt die U-Bahn „in einen öffentlichen Raum privater Notwendigkeit".

Das zweite Thema handelt vom weiblichen Körper und der sexuellen Befreiung („TOOT"), der Pubertät („Chengcheng & Beibei") und dem sozialen Charakter sexueller Beziehungen („Twice", alle 2001). Eine dritte Werkgruppe verknüpft dann schließlich diesen zweiten Themenschwerpunkt mit Cuis Erinnerungen an die eigene Kindheit. Zu diesem Zweck setzte die Künstlerin seit 2003 in einer Serie ambitionierter Arbeiten, zu denen „Sanjie" (2003), „One Day in 2004" (2004) und „Drifting Lantern" (2005) gehören, eine Schauspielerin im Teenageralter ein, die ihr ähnlich sieht. Mit einem weißen Kleid und dem roten Halstuch der Jungen Pioniere wirkt sie, für sich genommen, frisch und unschuldig; die Zukunft scheint ihr zu gehören. Doch in den Bildzusammenhängen erscheint das Mädchen dann entweder zwergenhaft vor den alles überragenden roten Mauern der Verbotenen Stadt, oder sie wirkt, vervielfacht, wie in eine eigene verwirrende virtuelle Landschaft verwandelt, die sie hilflos, verlassen, verwirrt und verängstigt macht. Dieser stark autobiographische Impetus kommt auch in Cuis jüngster Fotoserie „Angle" (2006) zum Ausdruck – diese Arbeiten erwecken die Erinnerungen der Künstlerin an ihre früheren Überzeugungen, Hoffnungen, Träume und Ängste zu neuem Leben.

忆结合起来。在 2003 年以来的一系列挑战性作品中，包括《三界》（2003 年），《2004 的某一天》（2004 年）以及《飘灯》（2005 年），崔岫闻雇用了一位面孔像她自己的十来岁的女演员。穿着白色衣服，戴着少先队员的红领巾的女孩青涩而天真，似乎未来就属于她一样。图像中的女孩在紫禁城高耸的红墙下缩小，抑或嬗变、复制成一幅迷宫似的虚幻风景。她无助而孤独，迷惑而害怕。结果，这些作品和崔岫闻最新的摄影系列《天使》（2006年）一样，都具有强烈的自传色彩，作者混淆的信仰、希望、梦想以及恐惧都在作品中被唤醒。

Wu Hung

7

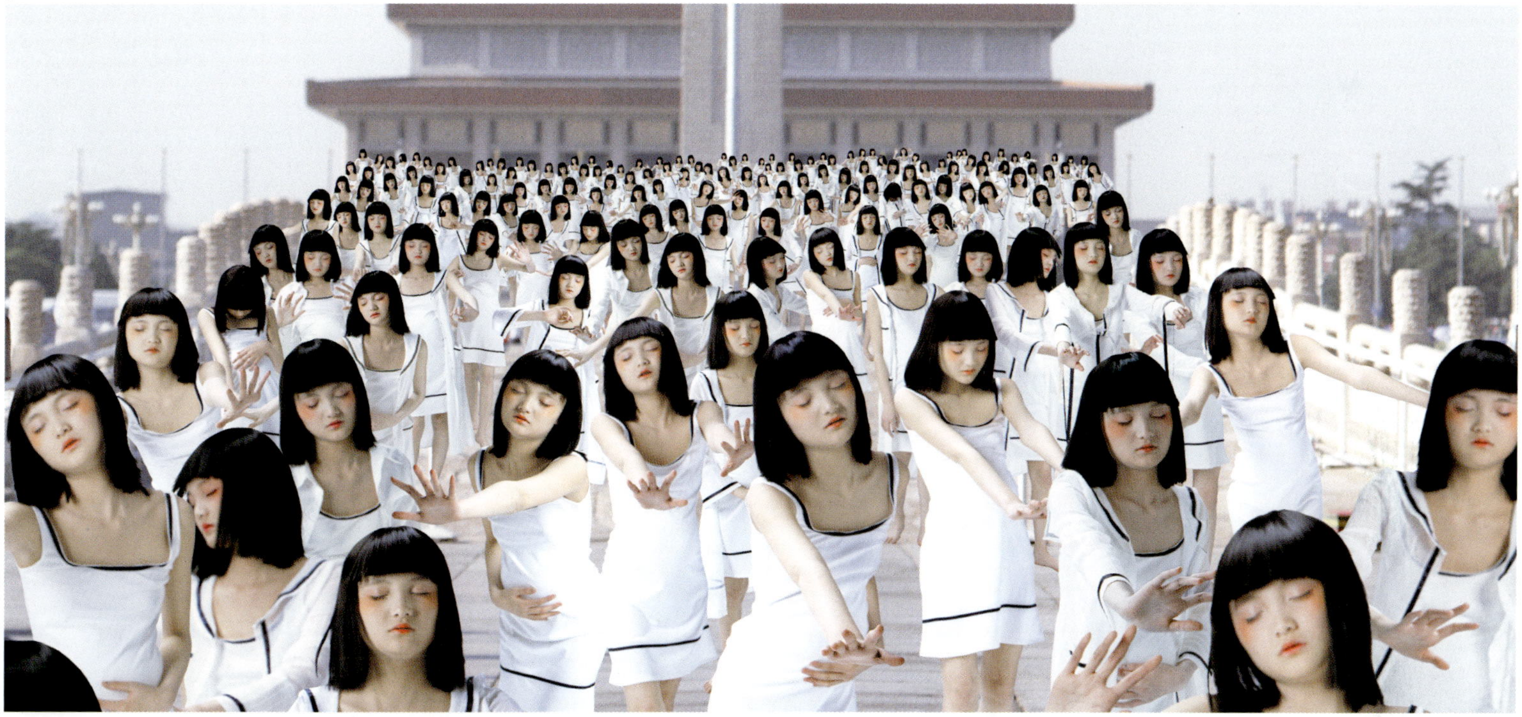

8

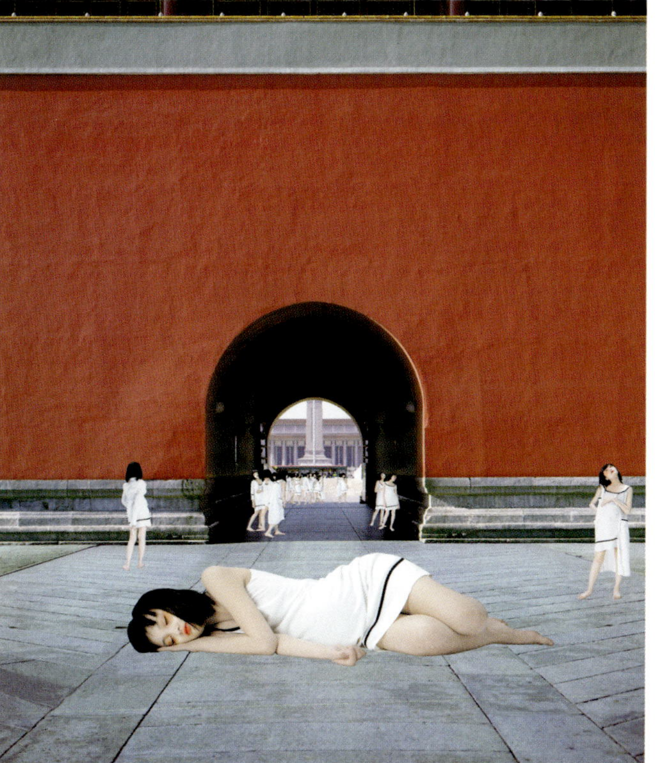

1 ***One day in 2004 No. 2***, *2004*
C-print, 93 x 304 cm
C-print, 93 x 304 cm
《2004年的某一天No. 2》2004年， C-印刷，
93 x 304 cm

2 ***One day in 2004 No. 6***, *2004*
C-print, 132 x 176 cm
C-print, 132 x 176 cm
《2004年的某一天No. 6》2004年, C-印刷,
132 x 176 cm

3 ***Drifting Lantern***, *2005*
Video, 27 min
Video, 27 Min.
《飘灯》2005年, 录像, 27分

4 ***Ladies' Room***, *2000*
Video, 6 min 12 sec
Video, 6 Min. 12 Sek.
《洗手间》2000年, 录像, 6分 12秒

5 ***Sanjie***, *2003*
Painting, 100 x 600 cm
Gemälde, 100 x 600 cm
《三界》2003年, 油画, 100 x 600 cm

6 ***Sanjie***, *2003*
C-print, 97 x 560 cm
C-print, 97 x 560 cm
《三界》2003年, C-印刷, 97 x 560 cm

7 ***Angel No. 3***, *2006*
C-print, 138 x 290 cm
C-print, 138 x 290 cm
《 天使No. 3》2006年, C-印刷, 138 x 290 cm

8 ***Angel No. 11***, *2006*
C-print, 170 x 120 cm
C-print, 170 x 120 cm
《天使No. 11》2006年, C-印刷, 170 x 120 cm

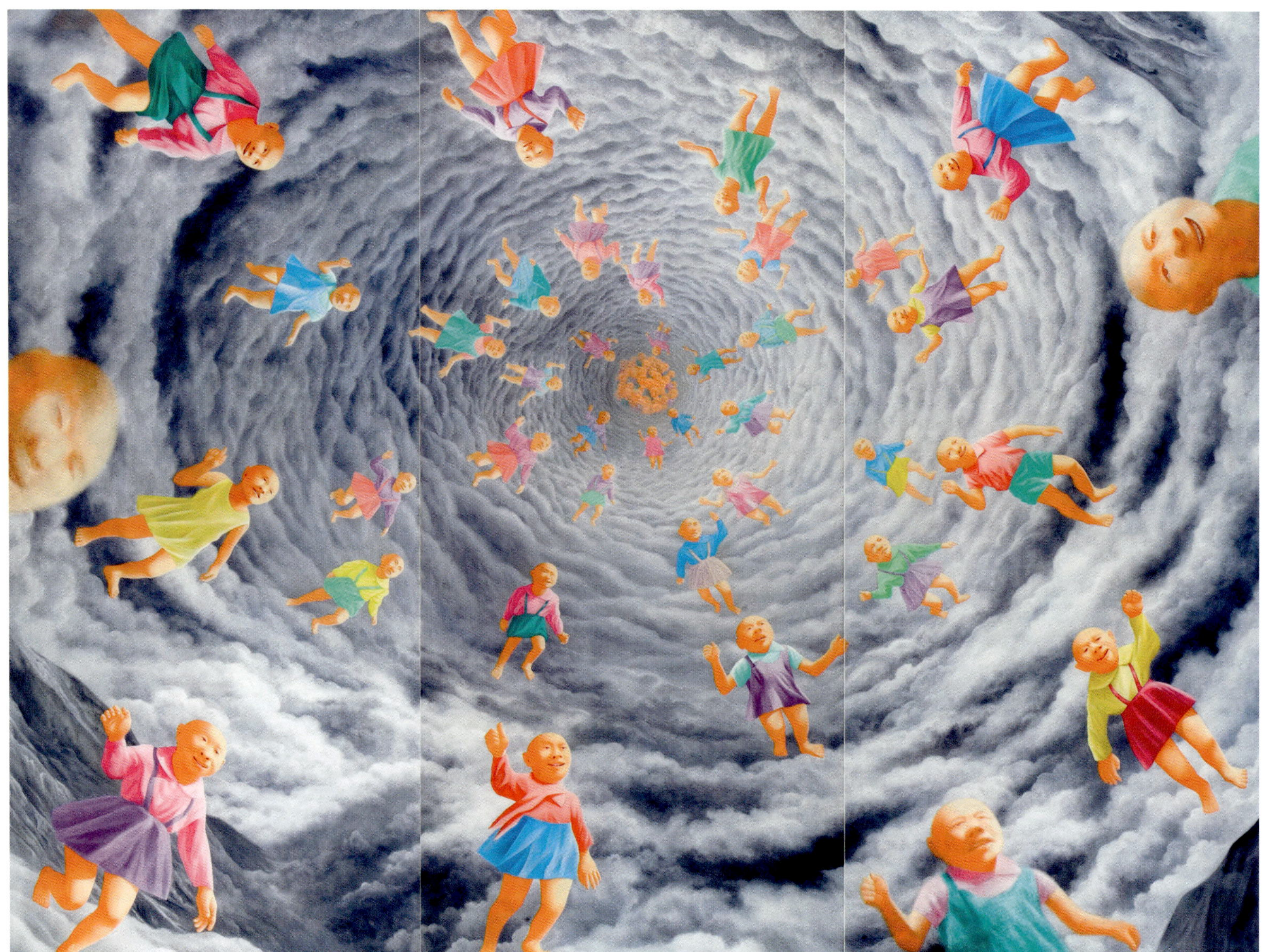

1

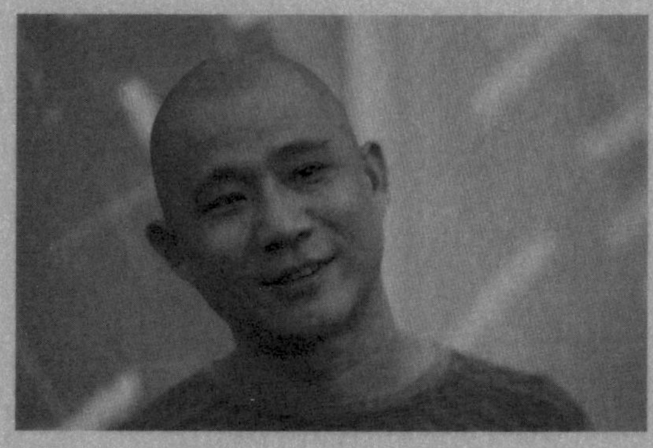

"To me, the significance of a shaven head is the annihilation of individuality allowing for a rendering of the essence of humanity."

„Das Bedeutsame an einem kahlen Kopf ist für mich die Auslöschung der Individualität, die es möglich macht, die eigentliche Essenz des Menschlichen wiederzugeben."

"对我，光头的意义是个性的泯灭，就表现人类本而言。"

Born in 1963 in Handan, Hebei Province, China. Lives and works in Beijing
Geboren 1963 in Handan, Provinz Hebei, China. Lebt und arbeitet in Peking
1963年出生于中国河北省邯郸，现于北京居住工作

***Selected exhibitions* / Ausgewählte Ausstellungen /** 所选展览

1999 48. Biennale di Venezia, Venice, Italy
2002 "Fang Lijun – Between Beijing & Dalí, Woodcuts & Paintings 1989–2002", Ludwig Forum für Internationale Kunst, Aachen, Germany
2003 "Alors, la Chine!", Centre Georges Pompidou, Paris, France
2005–07 "Mahjong – Chinesische Gegenwartskunst aus der Sammlung Sigg", Kunstmuseum Bern, Berne, Switzerland; Hamburger Kunsthalle, Hamburg, Germany; Museum der Moderne, Salzburg, Austria
2006 "Fang Lijun, TODAY!", Today Art Museum, Beijing, China
"Fang Lijun", Kupferstichkabinett, Staatliche Museen zu Berlin, Berlin, Germany

1999年 第48届威尼斯双年展，威尼斯，意大利
2002年 《方力钧 – 北京和搭理之间，木刻和绘画1989–2002年》路德维希论坛为国际艺术，亚琛，德国
2003年 《中国怎么样！》乔治 蓬皮杜现代艺术中心，巴黎，法国
2005–07年 《麻将》西克中国当代艺术收藏展，伯尔尼美术馆，瑞士；汉堡美术馆，汉堡，德国；萨尔茨保现代美术馆 奥地利
2006年 《今日方力钧，！》今日美术馆，北京，中国
《方力钧》铜板画陈列室柏林国家博物馆，德国

***Selected publications* / Ausgewählte Publikationen /** 所选著作

Michael Sullivan: "Art and Artists of Twentieth Century China", Berkeley/Los Angeles 1996
"Fang Lijun", Hunan 2001
"Fang Lijun", Shijiazhuang 2006

Sullivan, Michael（著）：《二十世纪之中国艺术和艺术家》伯克利 / 洛杉矶 1996年
《方力钧》湖南 2001年
《方力钧》石家庄 2006年

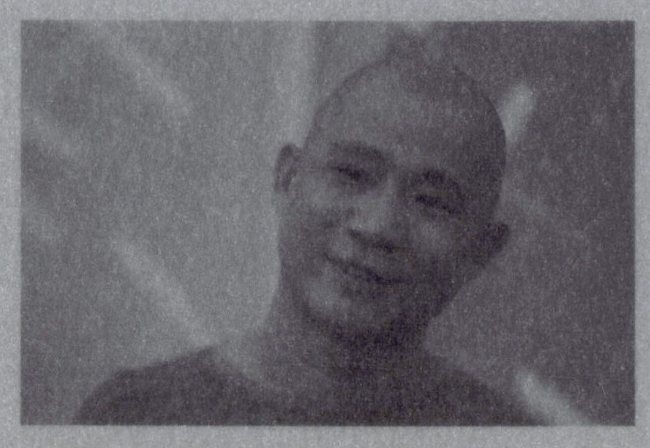

"To me, the significance of a shaven head is the annihilation of individuality allowing for a rendering of the essence of humanity."

„Das Bedeutsame an einem kahlen Kopf ist für mich die Auslöschung der Individualität, die es möglich macht, die eigentliche Essenz des Menschlichen wiederzugeben."

"对我，光头的意义是个性的泯灭，就表现人类本而言。"

Born in 1963 in Handan, Hebei Province, China. Lives and works in Beijing
Geboren 1963 in Handan, Provinz Hebei, China. Lebt und arbeitet in Peking
1963年出生于中国河北省邯郸，现于北京居住工作

Selected exhibitions / Ausgewählte Ausstellungen / 所选展览

1999 48. Biennale di Venezia, Venice, Italy
2002 "Fang Lijun - Between Beijing & Dali, Woodcuts & Paintings 1989-2002", Ludwig Forum für Internationale Kunst, Aachen, Germany
2003 "Alors, la Chine!", Centre Georges Pompidou, Paris, France
2005-07 "Mahjong - Chinesische Gegenwartskunst aus der Sammlung Sigg", Kunstmuseum Bern, Berne, Switzerland; Hamburger Kunsthalle, Hamburg, Germany; Museum der Moderne, Salzburg, Austria
2006 "Fang Lijun, TODAY!", Today Art Museum, Beijing, China
"Fang Lijun", Kupferstichkabinett, Staatliche Museen zu Berlin, Berlin, Germany

1999年 第48届威尼斯双年展，威尼斯，意大利
2002年 《方力钧－北京和搭理之间，木刻和绘画1989-2002年》路德维希论坛为国际艺术，亚琛，德国
2003年 《中国怎么样!》乔治 蓬皮杜现代艺术中心，巴黎，法国
2005-07年 《麻将》西克中国当代艺术收藏展，伯尔尼美术馆，瑞士；汉堡美术馆，汉堡，德国；萨尔茨堡现代美术馆 奥地利
2006年 《今日方力钧，!》今日美术馆，北京，中国
《方力钧》铜版画陈列室柏林国家博物馆，德国

Selected publications / Ausgewählte Publikationen / 所选著作

Michael Sullivan: "Art and Artists of Twentieth Century China", Berkeley/Los Angeles 1996
"Fang Lijun", Hunan 2001
"Fang Lijun", Shijiazhuang 2006

Sullivan, Michael（著）：《二十世纪之中国艺术和艺术家》伯克利 / 洛杉矶 1996年
《方力钧》湖南 2001年
《方力钧》石家庄 2006年

FANG LIJUN 方力钧

[faŋ litɕuən]

Fang Lijun's highly original (and widely imitated) painterly language is synonymous with one perceived power of contemporary art in China – its ability to capture and distill socio-political dispositions into iconic images. Fang grew up in Handan, an industrial city 450 kilometers south of Beijing where his father worked for the railroad. Fang entered a vocational school and studied ceramics, emerging a few years later as a petty entrepreneur on the newly open provincial markets. His early training in painting, through which he met the critic Li Xianting, then also in Handan, led him to apply to the Central Academy of Fine Arts, gaining a rare seat in the printmaking department in 1985. Early paintings from his mid-1980s "Country Muse" series play on the trend toward Rustic Realism then popular and foreshadow through their expansive pictorial planes and yellowed palettes a number of themes that would later emerge as his distinguishing features.

Fang settled into an orthodox realist training with classmates including Hong Hao and Liu Wei (the elder). Partially owing to his close relationship with Li Xianting, his work was selected for inclusion in the 1989 "China/Avant-Garde exhibition" at the National Gallery despite his status as a student and his contribution of monochrome charcoal drawings. Yet in these late student works, which also included canvases "Oil Painting I" and "Oil Painting II" (1988/89), the signature motif of the bald-headed man begins to emerge. The figures in these works are nominally farmers from Fang's native province Hebei, heads turned and shoulders slouched, evoking a quiet desperation. The farmers come easily to stand for an entire generation rendered bored simpletons by the excesses of the Cultural Revolution. Needless to say, bald-headed Fang Lijun has always perceived himself to be part of this generation.

After the upheavals of 1989 had run their course, Fang moved unemployed to a shoddy village home near the Old Summer Palace (Yuanmingyuan), a far-flung nature-filled park where he had spent student days learning to "paint from life". The area soon emerged as China's first

Fang Lijuns eigenständige malerische Sprache steht für eine offenkundige Stärke der chinesischen Gegenwartskunst – ihre Fähigkeit, soziopolitische Tendenzen einzufangen und zu visionären Ikonen zu destillieren. Aufgewachsen in Handan, einer Industriestadt 450 km südlich von Peking, wo sein Vater bei der Eisenbahn arbeitete, erlernte Fang an einer Berufsschule die Porzellanmalerei und tauchte einige Jahre später als Kleinunternehmer auf den neu eröffneten Provinzmärkten auf. Die Begegnung mit dem damals ebenfalls in Handan ansässigen Kritiker Li Xianting brachte ihn auf die Idee, sich bei der Central Academy of Fine Arts zu bewerben, wo er 1985 einen der begehrten Studienplätze im Fachbereich Druckgrafik erhielt. Seine frühen Gemälde aus der Mitte der 1980er Jahre entstandenen Serie „Country Muse" spielen mit dem damals populären Trend zum Rustikalen Realismus und deuten in ihrer großzügigen Flächigkeit und gelbdominierten Farbpalette bereits eine Reihe von Eigenschaften an, die sich später als seine Erkennungsmerkmale herausbilden sollten.

Fang durchlief eine orthodoxe Ausbildung zusammen mit Kommilitonen wie Hong Hao und Liu Wei (dem Älteren). Nicht zuletzt dank Li Xianting fand sein Frühwerk in der Ausstellung „China/Avant-Garde" 1989 in der National Gallery Berücksichtigung, obwohl er noch Student war und sein Beitrag lediglich aus monochromen Kohlezeichnungen bestand. In diesen Studentenarbeiten, zu denen auch die Gemälde „Oil Painting I" und „Oil Painting II" (1988/89) gehörten, begann der Glatzkopf als charakteristisches Motiv in Erscheinung zu treten. Die Figuren in diesen Werken sind Bauern aus Fangs Heimatprovinz Hebei, die mit abgewandten Köpfen und hängenden Schultern eine stille Verzweiflung vermitteln und durchaus für eine ganze Generation stehen, die durch die Exzesse der Kulturrevolution zu gelangweilten Einfallspinseln degradiert wurde. Der selbst kahlköpfige Fang Lijun hat sich stets als Teil dieser Generation verstanden.

Nach den Unruhen von 1989 zog er, arbeitslos, in ein schäbiges Dorfhaus in der Nähe des Alten Pekinger Som-

方力钧的高度原始的（也是普遍模仿）绘画语言是中国当代艺术感知力的同义词--其将社会政治意义捕捉并升华入肖像画中。方力钧二十年一如既往的光头形象是他的梦想者身份的象征。

少年时代的方力钧从未想过走进艺术世界这个高雅领域。他在邯郸长大，一个距离北京南450公里的工业城市，他的父亲在铁路上工作。文革结束后方力钧进入一所技校学习陶瓷技术，而几年之后，他却成为一个精明的企业家。他早年学习油画，也因此结识了评论家栗宪庭，随后也是在邯郸，栗宪庭指引他去报考中央美院，1985年成为该校版画系少数学生之一。他80年代中期的《乡恋》利用乡村现实主义的趋势而受到欢迎，从作品中大气的画面和黄颜色中可以预示了许多主题，这些主题在后来都是他杰出特征。

方力钧与同学洪浩和刘炜一起接受正统的现实主义训练。部分因为与栗宪庭的亲密关系，尽管他还是学生，作品也是单色木炭素描，但还是选入在中国美术馆举行的中国现代艺术大展(1989年）。然而在这些晚期的学生作品中，光头男人主题开始出现，当然也包括作品《油画1》和《油画2》。创作于1988年作品里人物形象取自其家乡河北的农民，他们转着头，肩膀下垂着，一副绝望的样子。这些农民代表着由文化大革命而产生一代无聊的傻子。毫无疑问，光头方力钧也早已意识到自己是这代人中的一个受骗者。

1989年天安门事件结束以后，方没有工作，搬到圆明园村，在学生时期就在那个广阔的公园里体验“油画来源于生活”。当方力钧走出困境时，这个地方不久就形成了中国第一个后89　艺术家村。同时，他的作品也有了新的转变，画面他的脑袋变大了，（也许受1989年展览上耿建翌笑着头的影响）并且打着哈欠。栗宪庭将这风格总结为“玩世现实主义”，指这些油画所表现的倦怠和错误方向。错误方向，讽刺地讲，证明是不断攀升的事业的基

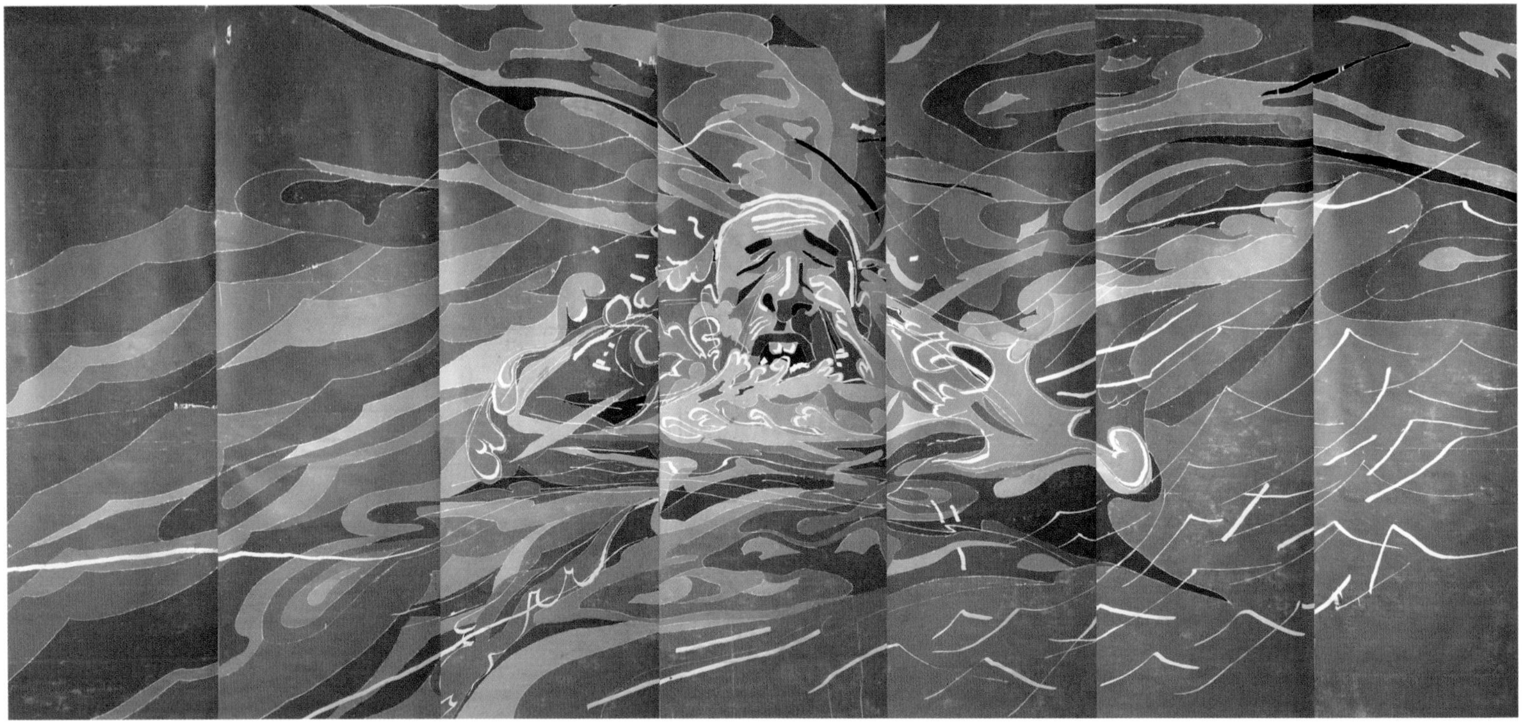

2

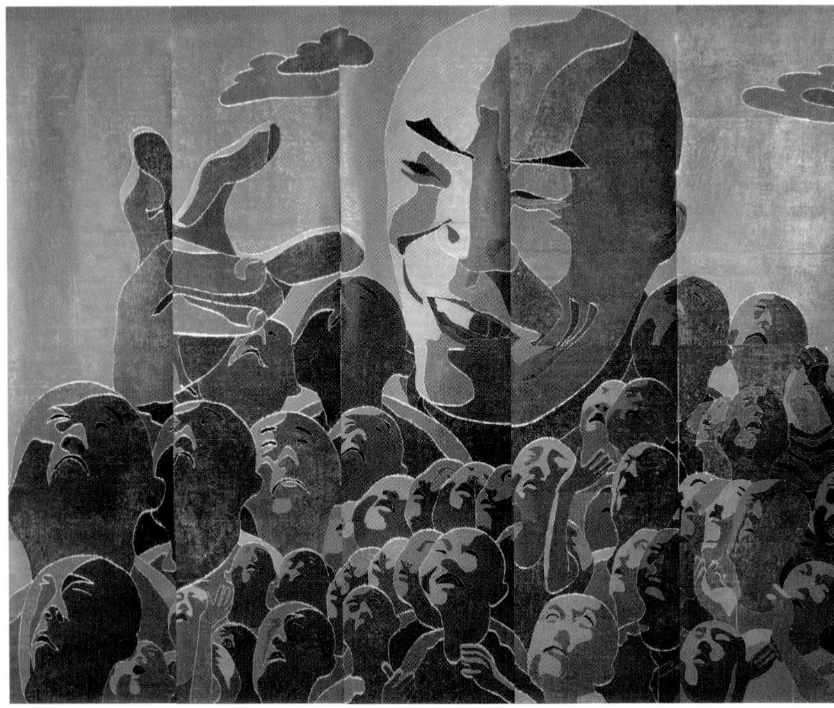

3

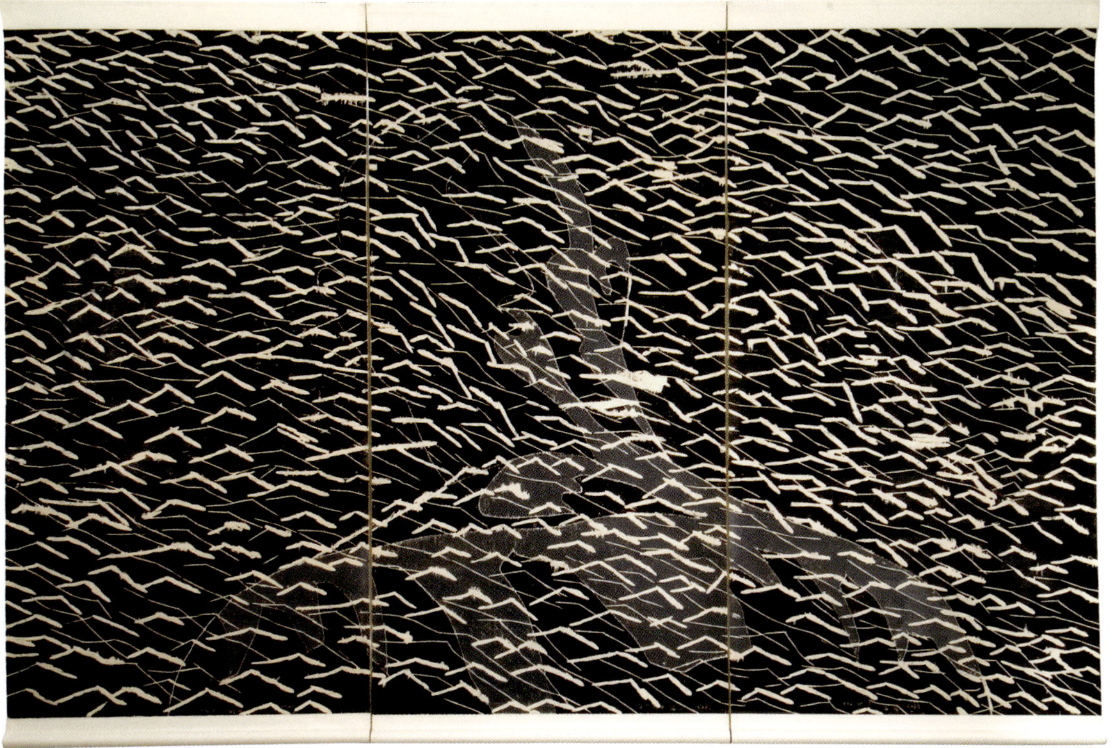

4

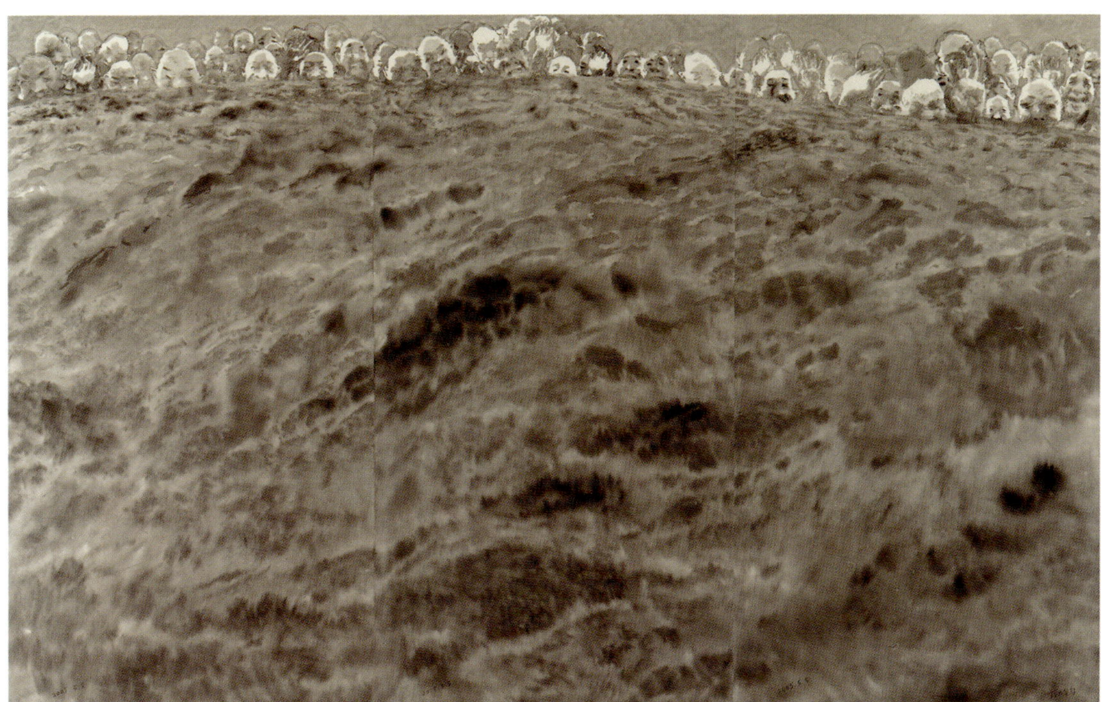

5

6

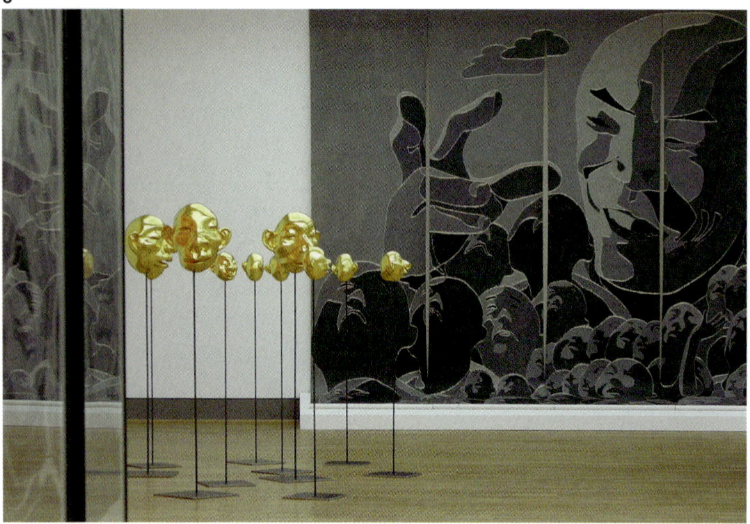

7

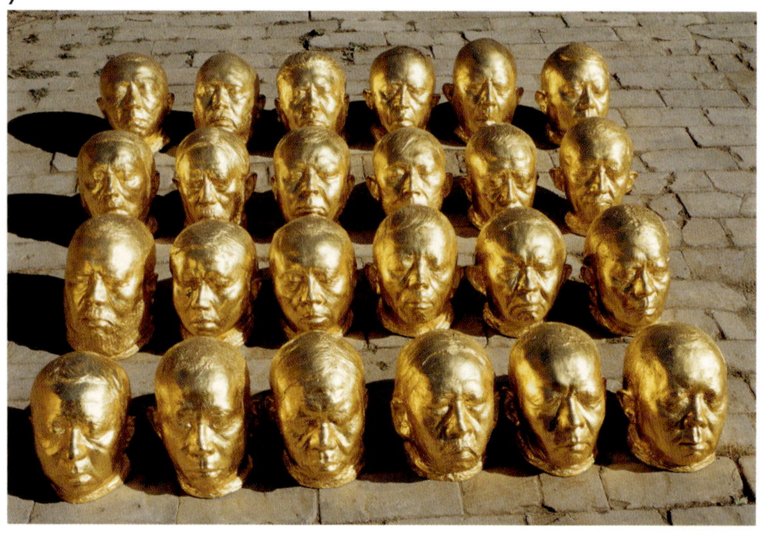

post-1989 artists' village, as would-be Fang Lijuns came out of the woodwork. Meanwhile, Fang's heads grew in size and assumed their signature yawns. Li Xianting labeled the style Cynical Realism, speaking to the listlessness and misdirection these canvases seem to embody. A misdirection, ironically, that would prove the basis for an upwardly mobile career; by 1993 his yawning heads had been featured in the Venice Biennale and on the cover of the "New York Times Magazine".

Fang Lijun soon moved his studio to Songzhuang, far on the eastern fringes of Beijing. He was joined there by Li Xianting and a number of his Yuanmingyuan artistic peers including Liu Wei and Yue Minjun. Water emerged as a major element in his work, and the solitary, bald swimmer as a major motif, floating in the boundless space of the ocean. Fang spent the period between summer 1997 and February 1998 in Amsterdam, producing a series of canvases for a solo exhibition at the Stedelijk Museum in which he returns to the greens and yellows of his earliest paintings. Upon his return to Beijing, he began to experiment with the woodcut printing techniques in which he had trained at the Academy, producing a major series of works named simply by their dates of completion. His oil palette also began to grow brighter, sunset red figures and cobalt blue backgrounds dotted by shining flowers, as Fang's attention turned from post-Tian'anmen despair to pre-Olympic frenzy.

In this decade Fang Lijun has emerged domestically as a paragon of urban style in a way possible only in the last few years. His shaven head and leather pants have featured in movies like the 2002 romantic comedy "Green Tea". And his work is instantly recognizable by the urban elites who despite ever-increasing prosperity can still identify with the existential anomie it summons.

merpalasts mit seinem abgelegenen Park, in dem er während seiner Studentenzeit gelernt hatte, „nach dem Leben zu malen". Die Gegend entwickelte sich nach 1989 rasch zu Chinas erstem Künstlerdorf. Derweil nahm Fangs Werk eine neue Wendung: Seine Köpfe wurden immer größer und entwickelten ihr typisches Gähnen. Li Xianting etikettierte Fangs Stil als Zynischen Realismus, womit er auf die Unlust und Desorientierung anspielte, die aus diesen Gemälden sprach. Doch eben diese Desorientierung erwies sich als Ausgangspunkt einer steilen Karriere. 1993 erschienen Fangs gähnende Köpfe bereits auf der Biennale von Venedig und auf dem Cover des „New York Times Magazine".

Fang Lijun verlegte sein Atelier bald nach Songzhuang, am östlichen Stadtrand von Peking. Dort stießen Künstlerkollegen aus Yuanmingyuan zu ihm, darunter Liu Wei und Yue Minjun, aber auch Li Xianting. Wasser wurde nun zu einem Hauptelement in Fangs Arbeiten und der einsame, kahlköpfige Schwimmer in der Weite des Ozeans zu einem wiederkehrenden Motiv. Vom Sommer 1997 bis Februar 1998 produzierte Fang in Amsterdam eine Gemäldeserie für eine Einzelausstellung im Stedelijk Museum, bei der er auf die Grün- und Gelbtöne seiner frühesten Bilder zurückgriff. Nach seiner Rückkehr nach Peking begann er mit Holzschnitttechniken zu experimentieren, zugleich wurde seine Ölpalette zunehmend bunter – etwa mit Figuren in Sonnenuntergangsrot und leuchtenden Blumen vor kobaltblauem Hintergrund –, als seine Verzweiflung über die Ereignisse auf dem Platz des Himmlischen Friedens allmählich doch durch die allgemeine Hektik im Vorfeld der Olympiade abgelöst wurde.

In diesem Jahrzehnt ist Fang Lijun in China zur Leitfigur eines urbanen Stils geworden. Sein Glatzkopf und seine Lederhosen waren sogar in Filmen wie der romantischen Komödie „Green Tea" von 2002 zu bewundern. Und sein Werk hat einen hohen Wiedererkennungswert bei den städtischen Eliten, die sich trotz ihres wachsenden Wohlstands immer noch mit dem existenziellen Gefühl der Sinnlosigkeit identifizieren können, das Fang heraufbeschwört.

础；1993年他的那些打着哈欠的脑袋在威尼斯双年展展出，也刊登在《纽约时报》封面上，并有配以 Andrew Solomon 撰写的文章《他们的讽刺，幽默可以挽救中国》。

不久方力钧将工作室搬到北京东边的宋庄。栗宪庭和许多圆明园艺术家朋友们也搬到那里，如岳敏君和刘炜等。水是作品中的主要元素，而浮动在无边海洋中孤独的光头泳者则是主题。1997年夏天到1998年二月期间，方力钧在阿姆斯特丹度过，期间创作了一系列油画，这些作品展示在国家美术馆举行的个展上。作品也回归到早期油画中的绿黄颜色。回到北京以后，方力钧开始用试验木刻印刷创作，这些技巧他曾在学校学习过，主要作品仅简单地以完作日期命名。作品色彩也开始变得更加鲜艳，闪耀的花朵装点着晚霞色的人物和钴蓝的背景，方力钧已将天安门事件后的悲怆转移到奥林匹克奥运会前的喜悦中。

在当前十年里，方力钧在国内是城市风格的典范，而仅在最近几年里这种方法才可实现。他的餐馆可以看作是看作他对温和的云南兴趣转到盘子上，他在云南拥有一间画室。他的光头和皮裤已经在电影上展示，如2002年的浪漫喜剧《绿茶》。方力钧作品马上受到城市精英的认可，他们尽管不断发展，但仍然认同影片所宣扬的存在社会失范。

Philip Tinari

8

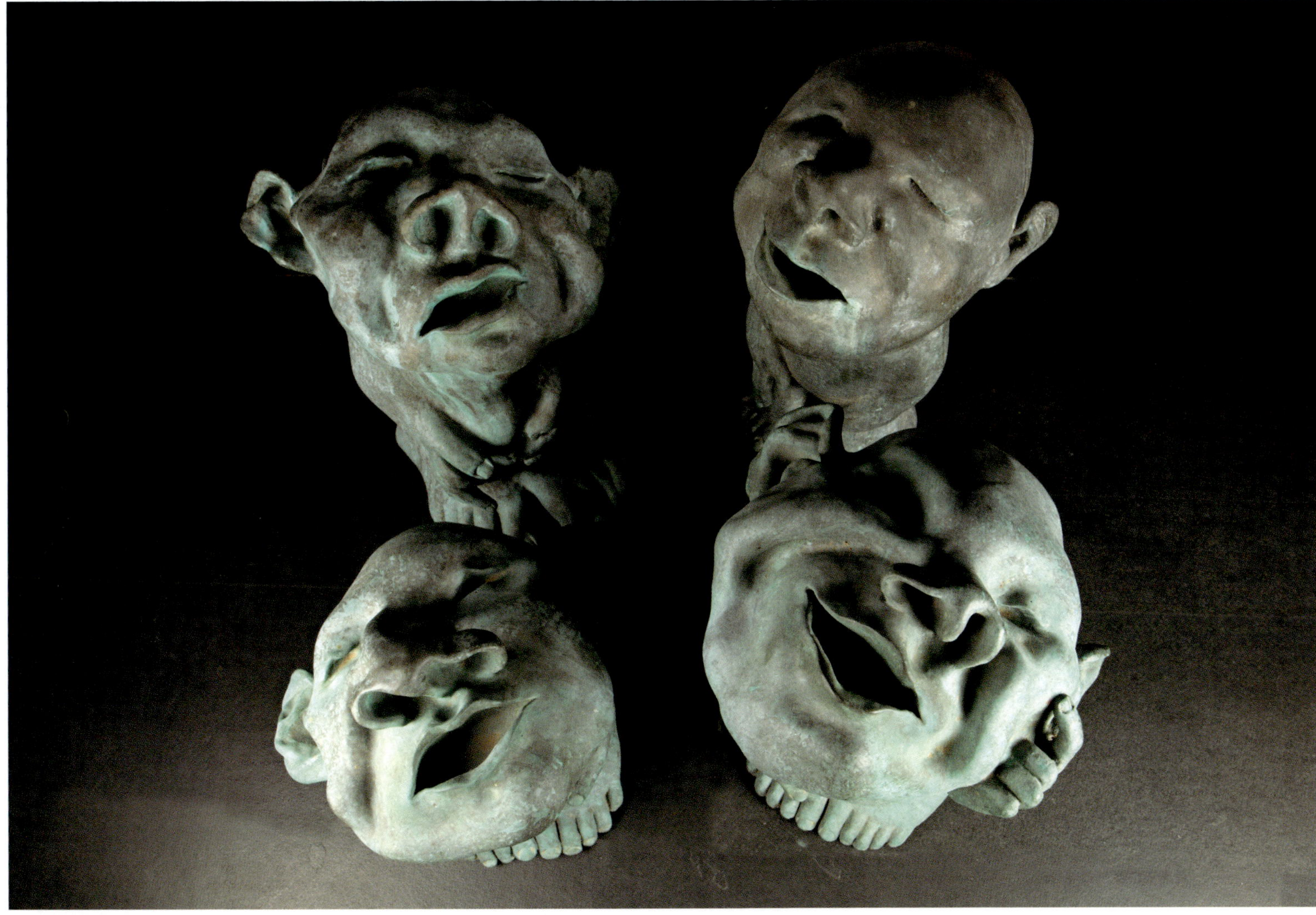

1 ***30th Mary**, 2006*
Oil on canvas, 400 x 525 cm
Öl auf Leinwand, 400 x 525 cm
2006年五月30日, 布面油画, 400 x 525 cm

2 ***2003.3.1**, 2003*
Woodblock prints, ink on 8 paper, fabric scrolls with wooden dowels, 400 x 852 cm
Holzschnitt, Tusche auf 8 Rollen aus Papier und Stoff mit Holzstäben, 400 x 852 cm
《2003.3.1》 2003年 水墨木刻印刷, 8页，纺织布卷轴，带有木销 布面油画, 400 x 852 cm

3 ***1999.6.1**, 1999*
Woodblock prints, ink on 5 paper, fabric scrolls with wooden dowels, 491 x 606 cm
Holzschnitt, Tusche auf 5 Rollen aus Papier und Stoff mit Holzstäben, 491 x 606 cm
《1999.6.1》 1999年 水墨木刻印刷, 5页，纺织布卷轴，带有木销 布面油画, 491 x 606 cm

4 ***1996. No. 17**, 1996*
Woodblock prints, ink on 3 paper, fabric scrolls with wooden dowels, 262 x 366 cm
Holzschnitt, Tusche auf 3 Rollen aus Papier und Stoff mit Holzstäben, 262 x 366 cm
《1996年 No. 17》1996年 水墨木刻印刷, 3页，纺织布卷轴，
带有木销 布面油画, 262 x 366 cm

5 ***Untitled (Swimmers)**, 2006*
Inkwash on paper mounted on canvas, 132 x 213 cm
Tusche auf Papier auf Leinwand aufgezogen, 132 x 213 cm
无题 （游泳）2006年 纸上稀释，装裱在布面上。布面油画, 132 x 213 cm

6 *Exhibition view, "Fang Lijun – Woodcuts and Drawings",*
SMBK, Kupferstichkabinett Staatliche Museen zu Berlin, Berlin, 2006
Ausstellungsansicht, „Fang Lijun – Holzschnitte und Zeichnungen",
SMBK, Kupferstichkabinett Staatliche Museen zu Berlin, Berlin, 2006
展览现场图《方力钧 – 木刻和绘画展》

7 ***24 Portraits**, 2006*
Goldfoil, copper, iron plate, life-size
Goldfolie, Kupfer, Eisenplatte, lebensgroß
《24 肖像》2006年, 真人等大，金箔、铜、铁板

8 ***Nature Group**, 2006*
Bronze, approx. 35 x 25 x 25 cm each
Bronze, je ca. 35 x 25 x 25 cm
《自然团体》2006年, 青铜, 每幅估计 35 x 25 x 25 cm, 青铜

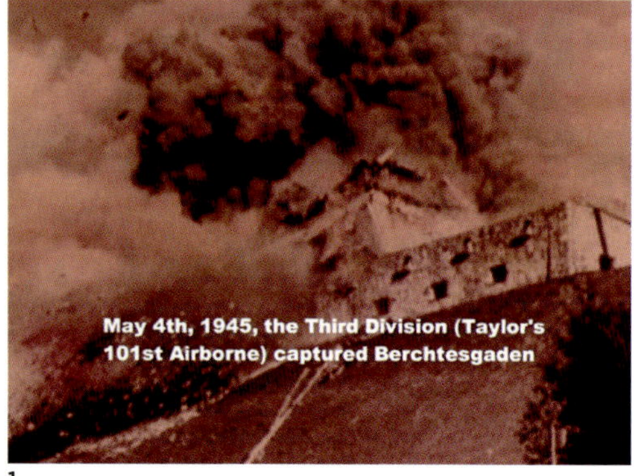
May 4th, 1945, the Third Division (Taylor's
101st Airborne) captured Berchtesgaden

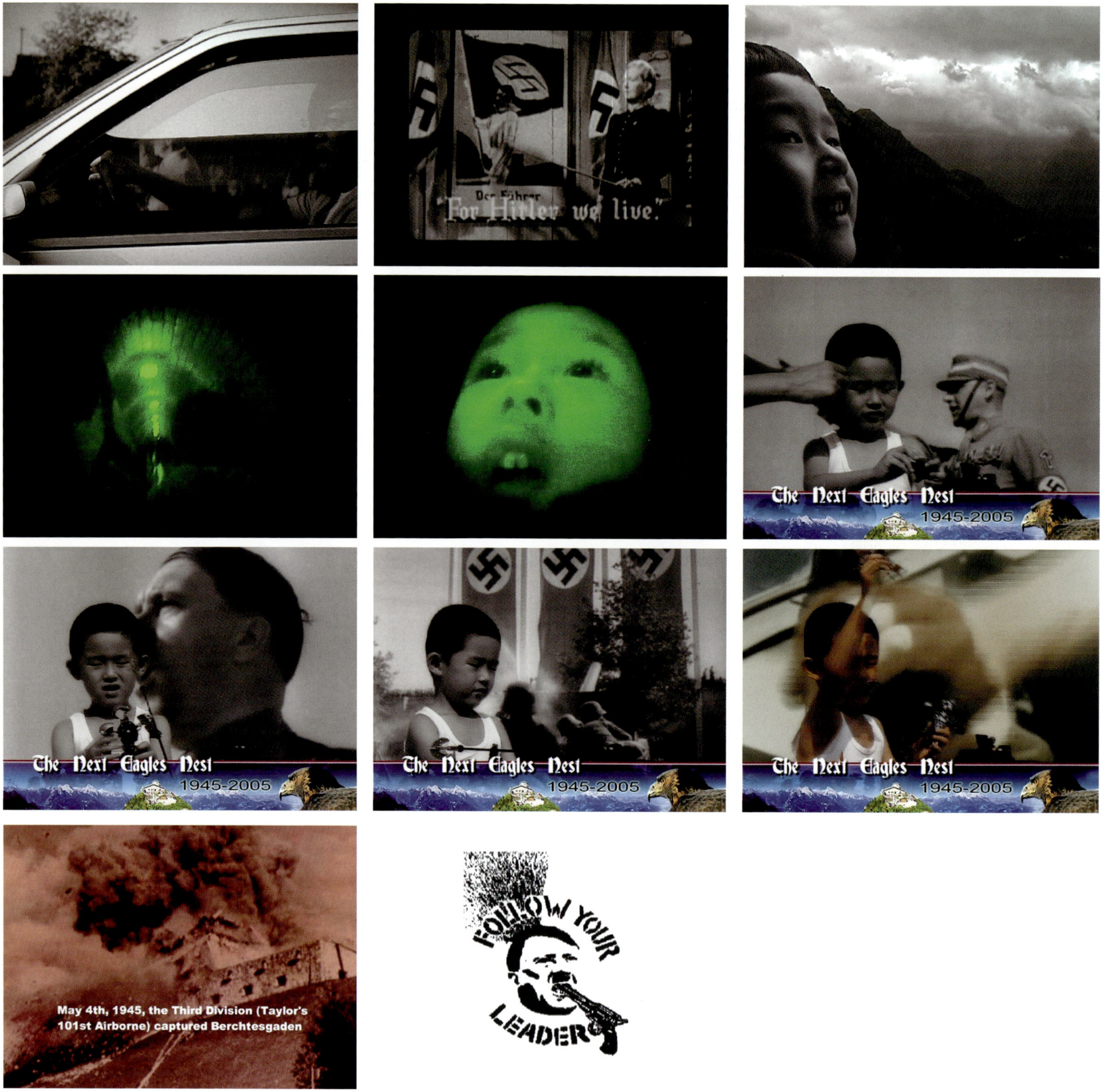

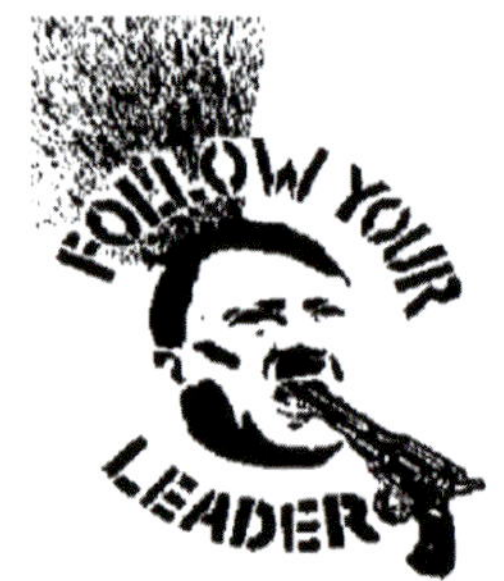
FOLLOW YOUR
LEADER

1

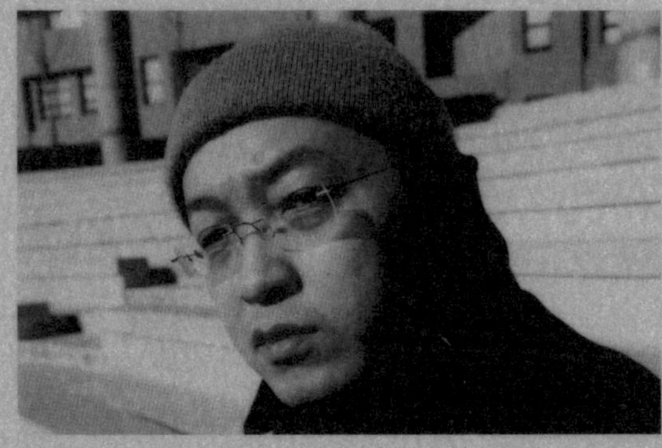

"Since I had always believed art originated from games, why don't I just bring games back into art?"

„Da ich schon immer geglaubt habe, dass sich Kunst aus dem Spiel entwickelt hat, warum sollte ich dann nicht das Spiel zurück in die Kunst bringen?"

"既然我总是认为艺术来源游戏，为什么我不能把游戏融入艺术呢?"

Born in 1966 in Beijing, China. Lives and works in Beijing
Geboren 1966 in Peking, China. Lebt und arbeitet in Peking
1966年出生于中国北京，现在北京居住工作

***Selected exhibitions* / Ausgewählte Ausstellungen / 所选展览**

1997 documenta 10, Kassel, Germany
2001 "Living in Time", Hamburger Bahnhof, Berlin, Germany
2002 First Guangzhou Triennale, Guangzhou, China
2003 "Past Virtualized – Future Cloned: Feng Mengbo 1994–2003", MOCA Museum, Taipei, Taiwan
2004–07 "Between Past and Future, New Photography and Video from China", International Center of Photography, New York, NY, USA (travelling exhibition)
2005–07 "Mahjong – Chinesische Gegenwartskunst aus der Sammlung Sigg", Kunstmuseum Bern, Berne, Switzerland; Hamburger Kunsthalle, Hamburg, Germany; Museum der Moderne, Salzburg, Austria

1997年 《第十届文献展》卡塞尔，德国
2001年 《生活在此时：中国当代艺术展》柏林、汉堡火车站柏林，德国
2002年 《广州三年展》广州，中国
2003年 《虚拟过去-复制未来：冯梦波1994-2003》当代美术馆，台北，台湾
2004-07年 《过去与未来之间—中国新影像展》国际摄影中心 纽约 美国（巡回展）
2005-07年 《麻将》西克中国当代艺术收藏展，伯尔尼美术馆 瑞士；汉堡美术馆 汉堡，德国；萨尔茨保现代美术馆，奥地利

***Selected publications* / Ausgewählte Publikationen / 所选著作**

Wu Hung, Feng Boyi (eds.): "The First Guangzhou Triennial – Reinterpretation: A Decade of Experimental Chinese Art (1990–2000)", Guangzhou 2002
"Past Virtualized – Future Cloned: Feng Mengbo 1994–2003", Taipei 2003
"Feng Mengbo: built to order", Hong Kong 2006

巫鸿和冯博一（编者）:《首届广州三年展-重新解读: 中国实验艺术十年（1990-2000）》展册，广州 2002年
《虚拟过去-复制未来: 冯梦波1994-2003》展册, 台北 2003年
《冯梦波: 订制》展册, 香港 2006年

"Since I had always believed art originated from games, why don't I just bring games back into art?"

„Da ich schon immer geglaubt habe, dass sich Kunst aus dem Spiel entwickelt hat, warum sollte ich dann nicht das Spiel zurück in die Kunst bringen?"

"既然我总是认为艺术来源游戏，为什么我不能把游戏融入艺术呢?"

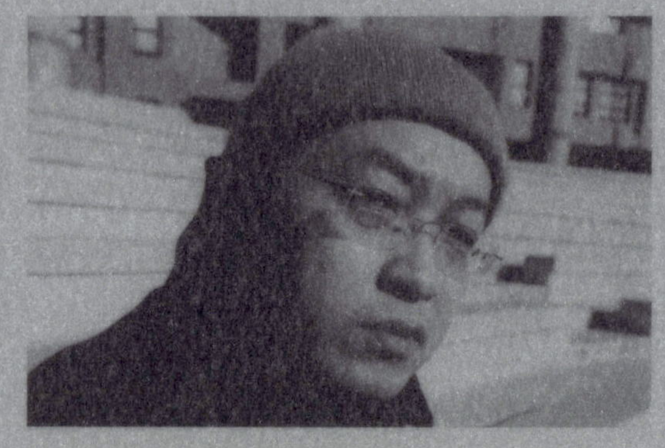

Born in 1966 in Beijing, China. Lives and works in Beijing
Geboren 1966 in Peking, China. Lebt und arbeitet in Peking
1966年出生于中国北京，现在北京居住工作

Selected exhibitions / Ausgewählte Ausstellungen / 所选展览

1997 documenta 10, Kassel, Germany
2001 "Living in Time", Hamburger Bahnhof, Berlin, Germany
2002 First Guangzhou Triennale, Guangzhou, China
2003 "Past Virtualized - Future Cloned: Feng Mengbo 1994-2003", MOCA Museum, Taipei, Taiwan
2004-07 "Between Past and Future, New Photography and Video from China", International Center of Photography, New York, NY, USA (travelling exhibition)
2005-07 "Mahjong - Chinesische Gegenwartskunst aus der Sammlung Sigg", Kunstmuseum Bern, Berne, Switzerland; Hamburger Kunsthalle, Hamburg, Germany; Museum der Moderne, Salzburg, Austria

1997年 《第十届文献展》卡塞尔，德国
2001年 《生活在此时：中国当代艺术展》柏林，汉堡火车站柏林，德国
2002年 《广州三年展》广州，中国
2003年 《虚拟过去-复制未来：冯梦波1994-2003》当代美术馆，台北，台湾
2004-07年 《过去与未来之间—中国新影像展》国际摄影中心 纽约 美国 （巡回展）
2005-07年 《麻将》西克中国当代艺术收藏展，伯尔尼美术馆 瑞士；汉堡美术馆 汉堡，德国；萨尔茨堡现代美术馆，奥地利

Selected publications / Ausgewählte Publikationen / 所选著作

Wu Hung, Feng Boyi (eds.): "The First Guangzhou Triennial - Reinterpretation: A Decade of Experimental Chinese Art (1990-2000)", Guangzhou 2002
"Past Virtualized - Future Cloned: Feng Mengbo 1994-2003", Taipei 2003
"Feng Mengbo: built to order", Hong Kong 2006

巫鸿和冯博一（编者）：《首届广州三年展-重新解读：中国实验艺术十年（1990-2000）》展册，广州 2002年
《虚拟过去-复制未来：冯梦波1994-2003》展册，台北 2003年
《冯梦波：订制》展册，香港 2006年

FENG MENGBO 冯梦波

[fɤŋ mɤŋpuɔ]

Feng Mengbo, multi media artist whose work comprises painting, photography as well as digital video and computer art, is fond of games associating it with art. The starting point of his artistic discussion of virtual worlds and global interconnectedness is his passion for video games. Feng Mengbo uses computer technology and popular killer games similarly as tools, material and projection surface, humorously delivering works of subtly ironic comments of phenomenona of global mass culture and of recent Chinese history.

In the early 1990s Feng Mengbo started oil painting of screenshots of video games on canvas. The portraits of Mao Zedong and other heroes of the revolution are to be found side by side with Ninjas and pawn dinosaurs. In his series "Taxi! Taxi! – Mao Zedong I–III" (1994) the artist alienates a well-known portrait of Chairman Mao who, instead of waving the Red Guards calls a Yellow Cab. With this kind of profanatory depiction of an icon the artist catapults Mao playfully into presence and raises him on the same level as citizens of Chinese metropolises.

Feng Mengbo's first interactive work "My Private Album" (1996) originated in his intention to digitalise old photographs of his family to store them safely. In the end this work resulted in a comprehensive documentation on CD-ROM, containing apart from Feng's family photographs scans of postcards, deeds, books as well as film clips the cut surface reflecting the individual and cultural memory of China's 20th century.

The second CD-ROM installation "Taking Mt. Doom By Strategy" (1997) with its video game "Doom" as playground is used by Feng to revoke the phantoms of the Cultural Revolution, by connecting the popular game with clips of the picturised revolutionary opera "Taking Tiger Mountain by Strategy" into an interactive synthesis. The game being a mass media entertainment for the global youth as well as the movie being a means of propaganda for the young Red Guards are characterised by heroism, violence and

Der Multimediakünstler Feng Mengbo, dessen Werk Malerei, Fotografie sowie digitale Video- und Computerkunst umfasst, liebt das Spiel und setzt es in Beziehung zur Kunst. Ausgangspunkt seiner künstlerischen Auseinandersetzung mit virtuellen Welten und globaler Vernetzung ist seine Leidenschaft für das Videospiel. Mit viel Humor nutzt Feng Computertechnologie und populäre Killerspiele gleichermaßen als Werkzeug, Material und Projektionsfläche und liefert mit seinen Arbeiten subtil ironische Kommentare zu Phänomenen globaler Massenkultur und der jüngeren chinesischen Geschichte.

In den frühen 1990er Jahren begann Feng Mengbo Screenshots von Videospielen mit Öl auf Leinwand zu malen. Die Konterfeis von Mao Zedong und anderen Revolutionshelden tauchen neben Ninjas und Dinosauriern als Spielfiguren auf. In der Serie „Taxi! Taxi! – Mao Zedong I–III" (1994) verfremdet der Künstler eine bekannte Aufnahme des Großen Vorsitzenden, indem er Mao nicht mehr den Roten Garden zuwinken, sondern ein Yellow Cab herbeirufen lässt. Mit diesem Akt der Profanierung einer Ikone katapultiert er Mao auf spielerische Weise in die Gegenwart und stellt ihn auf eine Augenhöhe mit den Bewohnern der chinesischen Metropolen.

Feng Mengbos erste interaktive Arbeit „My Private Album" (1996) geht ursprünglich darauf zurück, dass er alte Fotos seiner Familie digitalisieren wollte, um sie zu sichern. Am Ende entstand daraus eine umfangreiche Dokumentation auf CD-ROM, die neben Fengs Familienbildern auch Scans von Postkarten, Urkunden, Büchern sowie Filmausschnitte enthält und an der Schnittstelle von individuellem und kulturellem Gedächtnis das 20. Jahrhundert in China widerspiegelt.

In der zweiten CD-Rom Installation „Taking Mt. Doom By Strategy" (1997) dient Feng das brutale Videospiel „Doom" als Spielfläche, auf der er die Gespenster der Kulturrevolution wachruft. Er verbindet dabei das überaus populäre Spiel mit Clips aus der verfilmten Revolutionsoper „Taking

冯梦波，多栖艺术家，作品种类涉及油画、摄影以及数字录像和电脑艺术，喜爱电子游戏，并将此和艺术联系起来。他对虚拟世界和全球互联的艺术讨论的出发点是其对电子游戏的热情。冯梦波以电脑技术和流行的类似于杀手游戏为工具、素材和放映面，所产生的幽默作品，微妙地讽刺了全球大众文化现象和中国当代发展。

90年代早期，冯梦波开始在画布上绘制电子游戏截屏的油画。毛泽东和其他革命英雄的肖像画上，可以看到他们的两边分别站着日本武士和和典当恐龙。在他的作品系列《出租车！ 出租车！ – 毛泽东 I-III“》中(1994年)，毛主席不是在向红卫兵挥手致意，而是在招手去叫一辆出租车。通过这样一种有点亵渎伟人的手法，艺术家将毛泽东推向前台，放在一个都是普通市民的角度。

冯梦波的首部互动作品《我的照相簿》（1996年），是艺术家为了安全储存其家庭老照片而将之数字化，后来就形成了这部作品。在最后，这部作品形成了一个综合的CD驱动的文件包含冯的家庭照片，明信片、票据和书籍的扫描件以及放映个20世纪个人和文化记忆的短片剪辑。

冯梦波在第二部CD-驱动装置《智取毁灭战士》(1997年)中以电子游戏《毁灭战士》为舞台，并将之与京剧《智取威虎山》的电影片段连伟互动的整体，把人带入了文化大革命的记忆之中。这部以全球青少年为对象的大众娱乐游戏和那部红卫兵的教训宣传影片都带有英雄主义、暴力和流血冲突的标记。冯梦波将这部作品比作创作方法以及力量和暴力的形式，而与历史现象没有任何平行，也没有带有历史的标记。

冯梦波将这种互动视作游戏与参与的交互作用。装置是一部《Q4U》 （2000-2002年）基于网络戏《雷神之槌III》的作品，观众要接受艺术家是这部游戏中唯一的形象，而同时在场外与其对战。其中

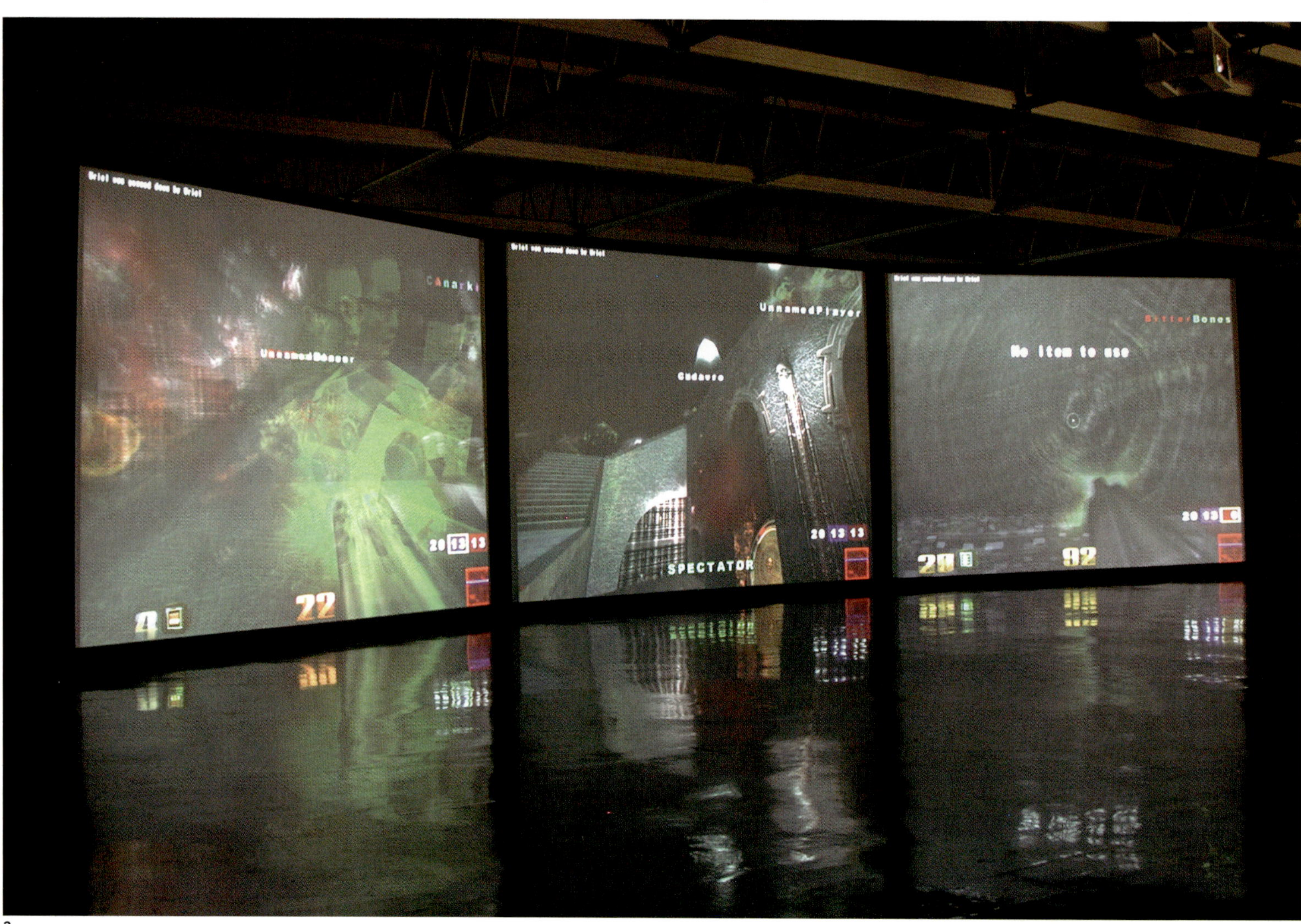

2

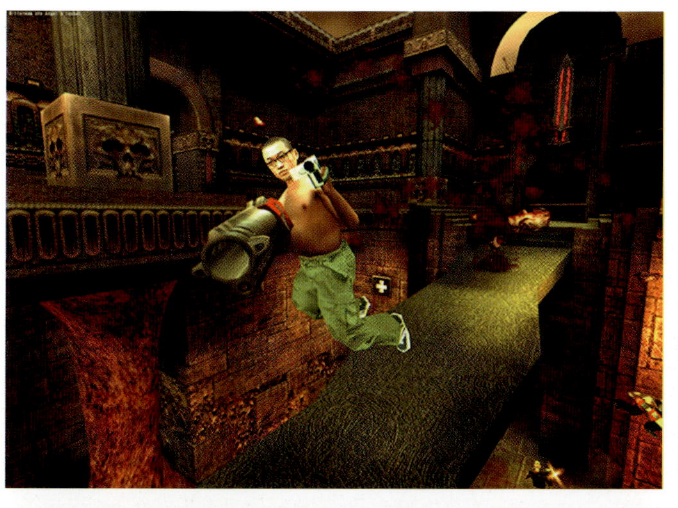
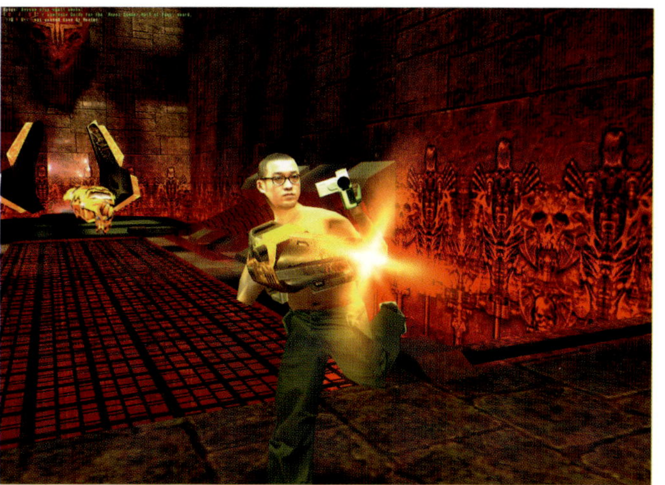
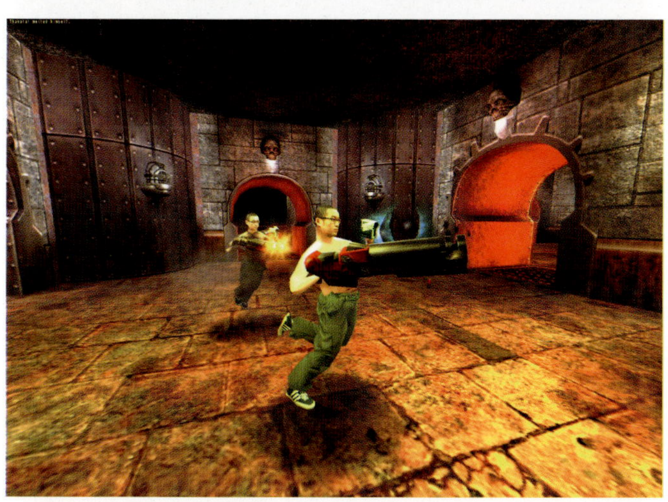
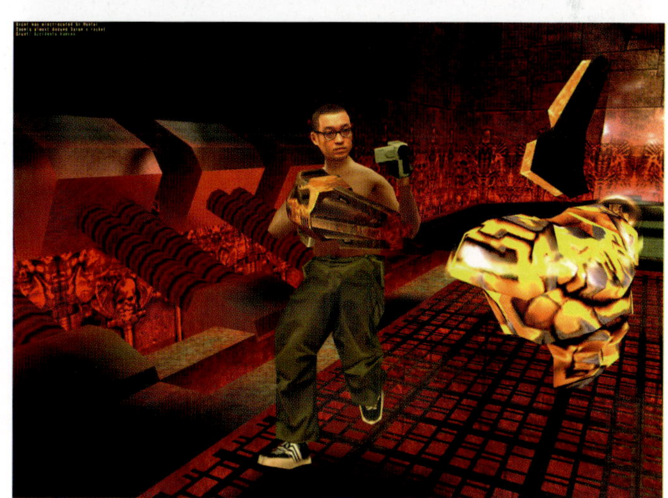
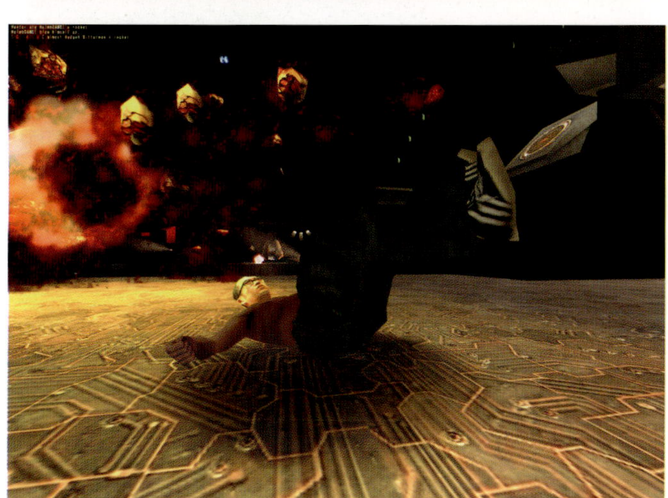
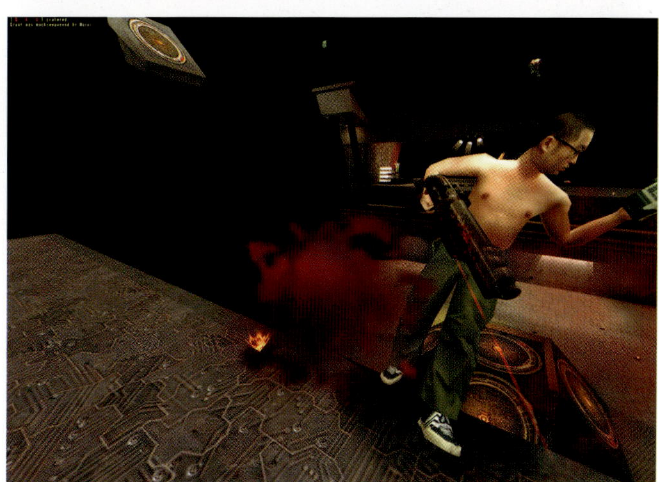

3

4

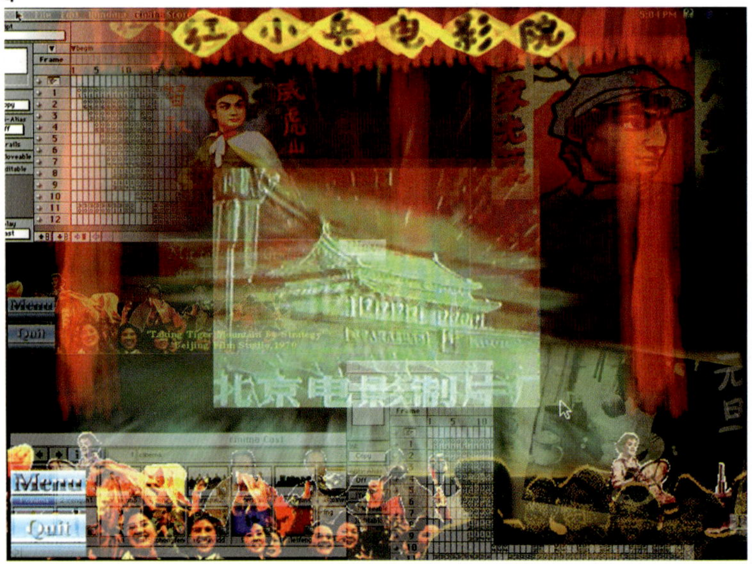

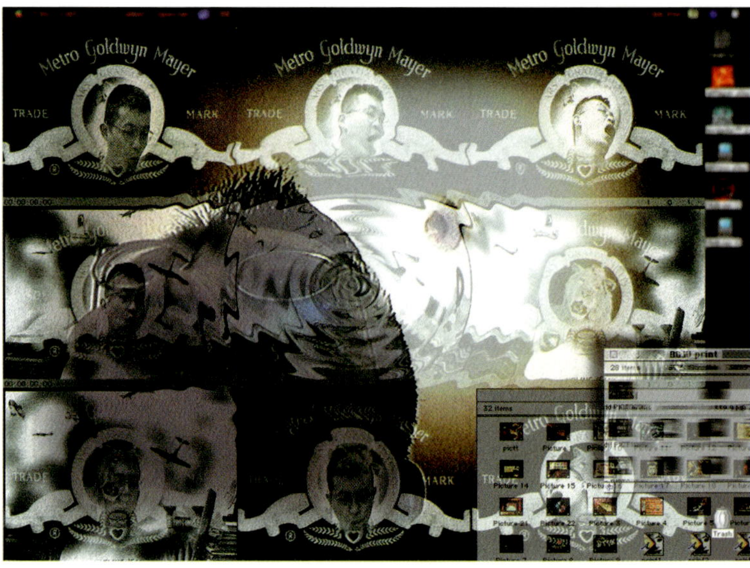

bloody conflicts. Feng refers with this work to a machinery of manipulation as well as to forms of power and violence without any direct parallels to historical phenomenona or to qualify them.

Feng Mengbo regards interaction as interchangeable for participation and game. His installation "Q4U" (2000–2002) based on the brutal internet game "Quake III Arena" the spectator is demanded to adopt the identity of the artist whose character being the only avatar of the game and to act simultaneously against him. The animated self-portrait depicts Feng stripped to the waist and in army trousers, holding a digital camera in one hand and a weapon in the other one. On three linked computers a multiple player version is installed, projected large-sized enabling the spectators of the exhibition to compete with the global internet community on the virtual level of the game. Feng Mengbo's virtual self-portrait incorporates friend and enemy simultaneously according to a single rule: to kill or to be killed.

Another traditional type of play is represented by Piying, the Chinese galanty show. This play becoming extinct, Feng Mengbo dedicates comprehensive research. One of the artist's latest works, the documentary multi-channel film installation "Donkey_ment" (2007) shows a galanty show performance form three different points of view being understood as a plea against the cultural oblivion.

Tiger Mountain by Strategy" zu einer interaktiven Synthese. Sowohl das Spiel, ein Massenunterhaltungsmedium der globalen Jugend, als auch der Film, ein Erziehungs- und Propagandamittel für die jungen Roten Garden, sind von Heroismus, Gewalt und blutigen Konflikten geprägt. Ohne direkte Parallelen zu ziehen oder gar zwischen historischen Phänomenen zu relativieren, verweist Feng mit dieser Arbeit auf Mechanismen der Manipulation sowie Formen von Macht und Gewalt.

Interaktion ist für Feng Mengbo Synonym für Partizipation und Spiel. In der installativen Arbeit „Q4U" (2000–2002), die auf dem brutalen Internetspiel „Quake III Arena" basiert, wird der Betrachter aufgefordert, die Identität des Künstlers, dessen Avatar im Spiel der einzige Charakter ist, anzunehmen und gleichzeitig gegen diesen zu spielen. Das animierte Selbstbildnis zeigt Feng mit nacktem Oberkörper und Armeehose, in der einen Hand eine DigiCam, in der anderen die Waffe haltend. Auf drei vernetzten Computern ist eine Mehrspielerversion installiert, die zudem großformatig projiziert wird und es Ausstellungsbesuchern vor Ort ermöglicht, mit der globalen Internet-Community auf der virtuellen Ebene des Spiels in Wettbewerb zu treten. Feng Mengbos virtuelles Selbstbildnis verkörpert Freund und Feind zugleich, denn es gilt nur eine Regel: töten oder getötet werden.

Eine sehr alte Form des Spiels repräsentiert das Piying, das chinesische Schattentheater. Dieser aussterbenden Spielkultur widmet Feng Mengbo umfangreiche Recherchen, und eine seiner neuesten Arbeiten: Die dokumentarische Mehrkanal-Filminstallation „Donkey_ment" (2007) zeigt eine Schattenspielaufführung aus drei Perspektiven und ist als Appell gegen das kulturelle Vergessen zu verstehen.

的动画形象是：冯裸着上身，下身穿着军裤，左手持数码相机，右手拿着一件武器。

在三台互联的电脑上都安装了多媒体播放器，用来放映大幅图像，以便让展览上的观众与世界各地的玩家们一起进行这个游戏。冯梦波的虚拟形象根据唯一的规则：不是你死就是我亡，来同时区别朋友和敌人。

另一个传统型的戏剧以中国的皮影戏《拼音》展示。这种艺术现在基本上已经几乎不存在了，冯梦波对他进行了全面的研究。冯梦波最新的作品《Donkey_ment》(2007)是一个多道电影装置，从三个不同角度表演皮影戏，这些被看作文化消逝的祈求。

Birgit Hopfener

4

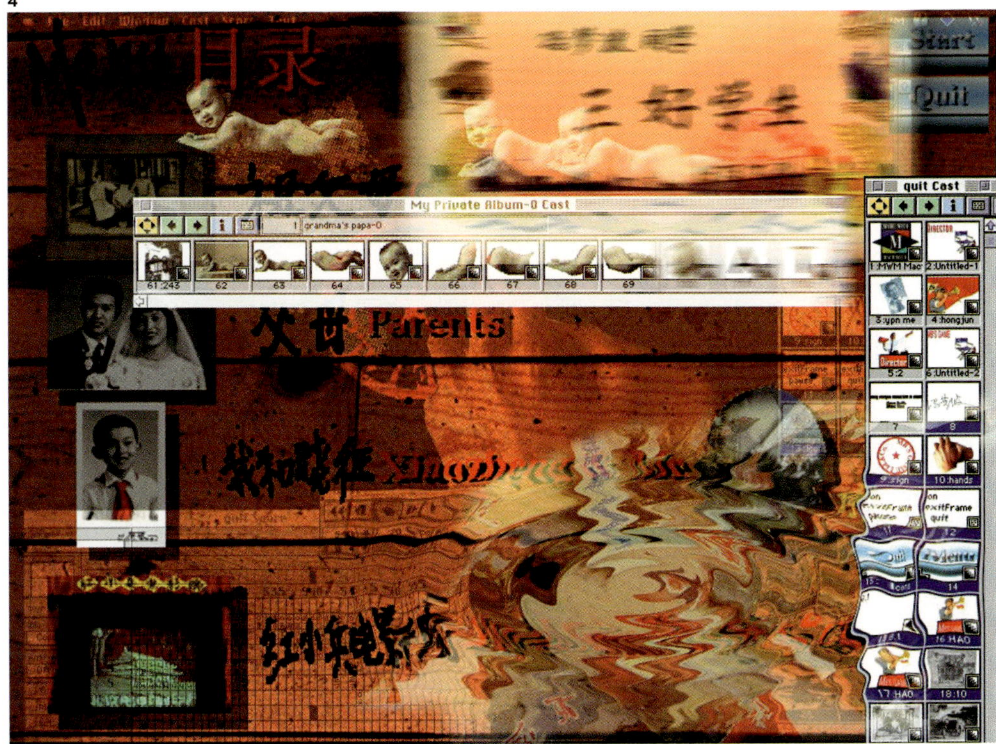

1 ***The Next Eagle's Nest***, *2005*
Movie installation, MIDI sequence software, MIDI interface, MIDI to contact by Doepfer, electronic controlled stage with curtains and lighting, seats, 30 min
Film-Installation, MIDI Sequence-Software, MIDI Interface, MIDI von Doepfer, elektronisch steuerbare Bühne mit Vorhängen und Beleuchtung, Sitze, 30 Min.
《下一个鹰巢》2005年，电影装置，MIDI 软件，MIDI 界面，30分钟

2 ***Q4U***, *2000–2002*
Video game, interactive installation, performance, internet project, 3 projections, sound system, SpeedPad game keyboard
Videospiel, interaktive Installation, Performance, Internetprojekt, 3 Projektionen, Ton, SpeedPad Spielkonsole
《Q4U》2000–2002年，电子游戏，互动装置/表演/网络项目，3 付投影设备，声音系统，SpeedPad 游戏键盘

3 ***Shot***, *2003*
Photographs from "Q4U", 74 x 100 cm each
Fotografien von „Q4U", je 74 x 100 cm
《射击》2003年，拍自《Q4U》，每幅74 x 100

4 ***My Private Album***, *1996*
Video game, interactive installation, 1 Macintosh, stage with curtains
Videospiel, interaktive Installation, 1 Macintosh Computer, Bühne mit Vorhängen
《我的照相簿》1996年，电子游戏，互动装置，1台 麦克金森机，配有幕布

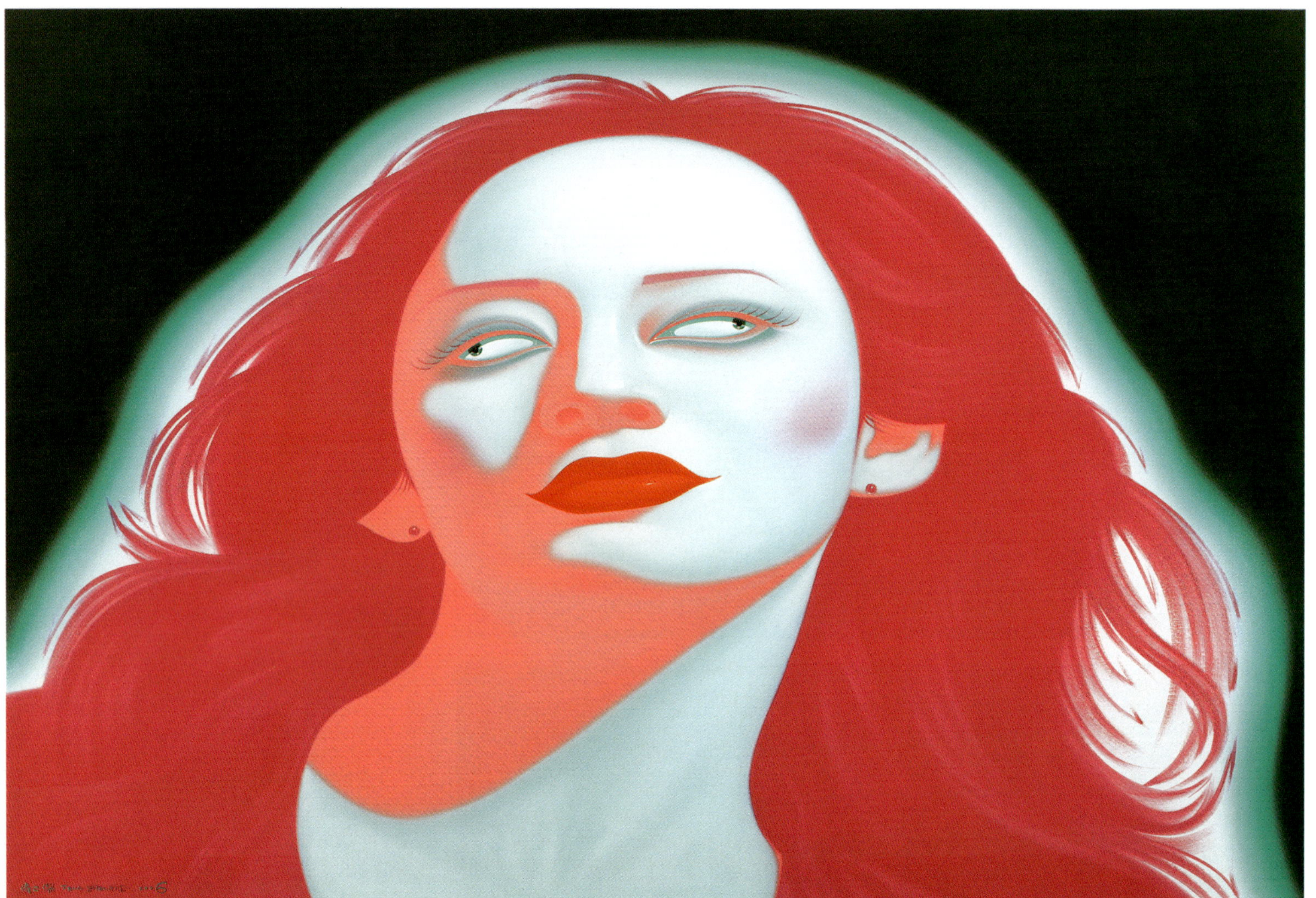

1

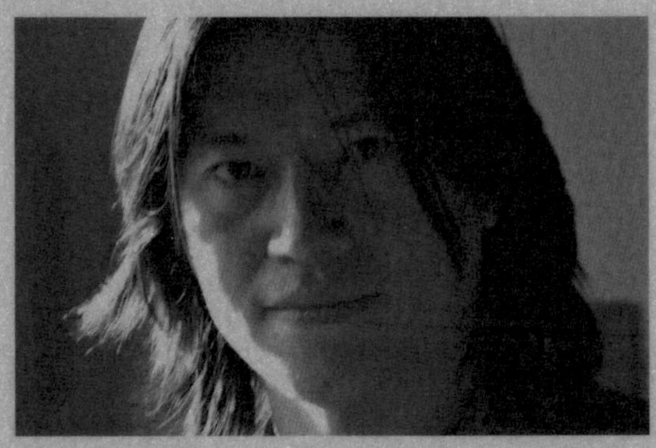

"On the one hand, I also felt that popular culture had an unusually great vitality. Perhaps I found all this perplexing myself and was therefore anxious to find out what actually lay beneath the surface and why it had such great influence."

„Ich spürte, dass die Popkultur eine außergewöhnlich starke Vitalität besaß. Vielleicht fand ich das alles selbst verwirrend und wollte darum unbedingt herausfinden, was wirklich unter der Oberfläche lag und weshalb es einen so großen Einfluss ausübte."

"一方面而言，我也认为流行文化有着非同一般的巨大生命力。也许因为发现了这种复杂性，所以我渴望探寻这种文化表面下的本质以及其巨大影响力原因。"

Born in 1968 in Sichuan Province, China. Lives and works in Beijing
Geboren 1968 in der Provinz Sichuan, China. Lebt und arbeitet in Peking
1968年出生于四川省，现于北京居住工作

Selected exhibitions **/ Ausgewählte Ausstellungen /** 所选展览

1996 "Recounting of Skin", Art Museum of Capital Normal University, Beijing, China
2001 "Coolness", Common Ground Art Gallery, Windsor, Canada
2002 "Paintings 1996–2001", 314 International Art Centre, Bergen, Norway
"Paintings of Feng Zhengjie", M. K. Ciurlionis National Museum of Art, Kaunas, Lithuania
2003 "Regards vers l'Est, Regards vers l'Ouest", Albert Benamou Gallery, Paris, France
2005 "Paintings of Feng Zhengjie", Marella Art Contemporary, Milan, Italy
Prague Biennale 2, Prague, Czech Republic
2007 "Thermocline of Art: New Asian Waves", ZKM (Center for Art and Media), Karlsruhe, Germany

1996年 《皮肤的叙述》首都师范大学美术馆，北京 北京
2001年 《酷》Common Ground 画廊，温莎，加拿大
2002年 《油画1996–2001》314基金会卑尔根 挪威
《俸正杰油画展》M.K Ciurlionis 国立美术馆，考那斯，立陶宛
2003年 《东张西望》阿尔贝•贝纳木，巴黎，法国
2005年 《俸正杰油画展》Marella当代艺术画廊，米兰，意大利
布拉格双年展 布拉格 捷克共和国
2007 《艺术温跃层：亚洲新浪潮》艺术与媒体中心，卡尔斯鲁厄，德国

Selected publications **/ Ausgewählte Publikationen /** 所选著作

Li Xianting: "Seven Chinese Artists and Contemporary Chinese Art after Political Pop", in: "Contemporary Art from China", Vancouver 1998
"Feng Zhengjie", Bologna 2006

栗宪庭（著）:《七个中国艺术家和政治波普后的当代中国艺术》于Force, Yvonne 和 Carmen Zita（策展人）:《当代艺术从中国》（展册），温哥华1998年
千葉 成夫（著）:《这些女孩看到什么?》于《俸正杰》Grafiche Damiani, 意大利2006年

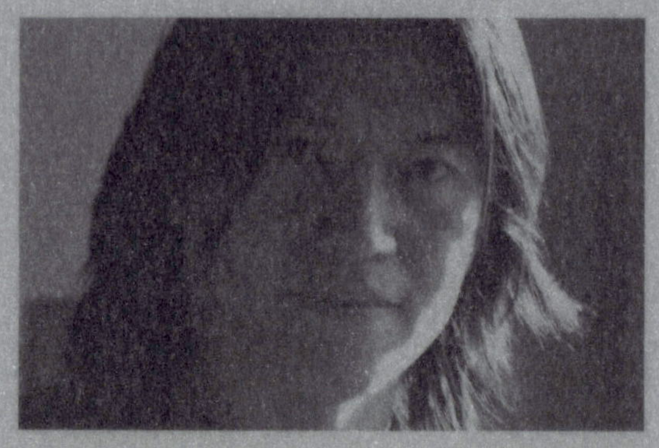

"On the one hand, I also felt that popular culture had an unusually great vitality. Perhaps I found all this perplexing myself and was therefore anxious to find out what actually lay beneath the surface and why it had such great influence."

„Ich spürte, dass die Popkultur eine außergewöhnlich starke Vitalität besaß. Vielleicht fand ich das alles selbst verwirrend und wollte darum unbedingt herausfinden, was wirklich unter der Oberfläche lag und weshalb es einen so großen Einfluss ausübte."

"一方面而言，我也认为流行文化有着非同一般的巨大生命力。也许因为发现了这种复杂性，所以我渴望探寻这种文化表面下的本质以及其巨大影响力原因。"

Born in 1968 in Sichuan Province, China. Lives and works in Beijing
Geboren 1968 in der Provinz Sichuan, China. Lebt und arbeitet in Peking
1968年出生于四川省，现于北京居住工作

Selected exhibitions / Ausgewählte Ausstellungen / 所选展览

1996 "Recounting of Skin", Art Museum of Capital Normal University, Beijing, China
2001 "Coolness", Common Ground Art Gallery, Windsor, Canada
2002 "Paintings 1996–2001", 314 International Art Centre, Bergen, Norway
"Paintings of Feng Zhengjie", M. K. Ciurlionis National Museum of Art, Kaunas, Lithuania
2003 "Regards vers l'Est, Regards vers l'Ouest", Albert Benamou Gallery, Paris, France
2005 "Paintings of Feng Zhengjie", Marella Art Contemporary, Milan, Italy
Prague Biennale 2, Prague, Czech Republic
2007 "Thermocline of Art: New Asian Waves", ZKM (Center for Art and Media), Karlsruhe, Germany

1996年 《皮肤的叙述》首都师范大学美术馆，北京 北京
2001年 《酷》Common Ground 画廊，温莎，加拿大
2002年 《油画1996-2001》314基金会卑尔根 挪威
《俸正杰油画展》M.K Ciurlionis 国立美术馆，考那斯，立陶宛
2003年 《东张西望》阿尔贝•贝纳木，巴黎，法国
2005年 《俸正杰油画展》Marella当代艺术画廊，米兰，意大利
布拉格双年展 布拉格 捷克共和国
2007 《艺术温跃层：亚洲新浪潮》艺术与媒体中心，卡尔斯鲁厄，德国

Selected publications / Ausgewählte Publikationen / 所选著作

Li Xianting: "Seven Chinese Artists and Contemporary Chinese Art after Political Pop", in: "Contemporary Art from China", Vancouver 1998
"Feng Zhengjie", Bologna 2006

栗宪庭（著）：《七个中国艺术家和政治波普后的当代中国艺术》于Force, Yvonne 和 Carmen Zita（策展人）：《当代艺术从中国》（展册），温哥华1998年
千叶 成夫（著）：《这些女孩看到什么？》于《俸正杰》Grafiche Damiani，意大利2006年

FENG ZHENGJIE 俸正杰

[fɤŋ ʈʂɤŋtɕiɛ]

Feng Zhengjie belongs to a generation of artists that came of age in reaction to the Political Pop style that had developed through the late 1980s and emerged triumphant in the wake of 1989. Trained at the Sichuan Academy just as the "Southwest Painting Group" was beginning to disperse, he was deeply influenced by the early experimental styles of his mentors Zhang Xiaogang and Zhou Chunya. The lasting import of his work however has been to create an autonomous painterly language based on, yet distinctly refractive of, contemporary commercial visual culture in China.

Feng Zhengjie's late student paintings begin to demonstrate an interest in anatomical deconstruction and psychological analysis. His "Life" series (1991) broke common forms from his training in oil painting down into basic manifestations as amoeba-like blobs. His "Dissection" series, begun upon his graduation to the Academy's MFA program in 1992, superimposes diagrammed, planar surfaces onto otherwise "finished" neoclassical compositions, labeling the anatomical parts that he renders in black line drawings. The feeling created harkens back to Cubism, but is also vaguely reminiscent of some of the best of the '85 New Wave conceptual paintings, by artists like Zhang Peili and Wang Guangyi. The directness and planarity of this series can also be seen as subversive of realism, a trend still worthy of debunking in the minds of many artists. This series fades into psychology in paintings like his early attention-getters "Marriage Advertisement" and "Graduated in This Year" (both 1992), group portraits of the artist with friends and classmates.

Towards the end of his graduate studies, Feng Zhengjie began a series now dubbed "Recounting of Skin" (1996) in which the nude female form appears ulcerated in gory reds and greens against backgrounds of patterned dots and squares. Critic Li Xianting saw in these works an implicit reference to Lu Xun's line about the effete late Qing scholars whose erudition led them to describe "an ulcer as gaudy as peach blossoms," an indictment of Chinese

Feng Zhengjie gehört einer Künstlergeneration an, die gerade den Kinderschuhen entwuchs, als in den späten 1980er Jahren der Polit-Pop im Gefolge des Geschehens von 1989 seinen Durchbruch erlebte. Er besuchte die Sichuan Academy, als sich die „Southwest Painting Group" aufzulösen begann, und wurde stark von den frühen, experimentellen Stilen seiner Mentoren Zhang Xiaogang und Zhou Chunya beeinflusst. Die bleibende Bedeutung seines Werks besteht jedoch in der Entwicklung einer autonomen Malsprache, die sich auf die kommerzielle visuelle Kultur der chinesischen Gegenwart stützt, sie aber in deutlich gebrochener Form wiedergibt.

Die späten Gemälde aus Feng Zhengjies Studentenzeit lassen bereits ein Interesse an anatomischer Dekonstruktion und psychologischer Analyse erkennen. Seine „Life"-Serie (1991) löste konventionelle Formen in Öl in amöbenartige Kleckse auf. In seiner „Dissection"-Serie, die er nach seiner Aufnahme in den Meister-Studiengang der Akademie 1992 begann, überlagert er klassizistische Kompositionen mit diagrammatischen Flächen, wobei er die anatomischen Partien als schwarze Linienzeichnungen ausführt und beschriftet. Die Wirkung erinnert an den Kubismus, aber auch ein wenig an einige der besten konzeptuellen Gemälde des '85er New Wave von Künstlern wie Zhang Peili und Wang Guangyi. Die Unmittelbarkeit und Flächigkeit dieser Serie kann auch als Subversion des Realismus gedeutet werden, eines Trends, der nach Meinung vieler Künstler immer noch der Demontage bedarf. Mit seinen Frühwerken „Marriage Advertisement" und „Graduated in This Year" (beide 1992) – Gruppenporträts des Künstlers mit Freunden und Kommilitonen –, die große Aufmerksamkeit erregten, verflüchtigt sich diese Serie ins Psychologische.

Gegen Ende seines Meister-Studiums nahm Feng Zhengjie eine Serie in Angriff, die unter dem Titel „Recounting of Skin" (1996) bekannt wurde. In ihr erscheint der weibliche Akt in blutrünstig-geschwürähnlichen Rot- und Grüntönen vor einem Hintergrund aus Punkten und Quadraten. Der Kritiker Li Xianting sah in diesen Arbeiten eine Anspielung auf Lu

政治波普运动在80年代末期发展起来，在1989年取得巨大的成功，俸正杰属于这一时期成长起来的艺术家。当西南艺术研究群体开始解散时，方力均还在四川美院学习，深深受到其导师张晓刚，周春芽等艺术家的早期试验风格的影响。作品的长期模仿而形成了自己独特的画风，这种风格建立在中国当代商业和视觉文化上，虽然很难折射出。

俸正杰的学生时代晚期作品开始显现出他对结构剖析和心理分析的兴趣。在《生命》系列中，可以看出他与学院时期所掌握的一般艺术形式的决裂，而用象阿米巴似的斑点的方法来表达主题。《解剖》系列创作于1992年，是其考入四川美院美术硕士的一幅作品。作品将二维图解表层叠加在其他"成品"新古典主义作品上，解剖部分已用黑线粉刷，并贴上标签。所产生的效果似乎让人回归了立体派的世界中，但是也有些85新具象画家作品的模糊的回忆，如艺术家张培力和王广义。该系列作品的直接性和平面性基本上颠覆现实主义，虽然在许多艺术家的观念中现实主义依然可用来揭露事实真相。这部作品将心理学渐渐融入油画中，与早期的亮点作品《征婚广告》和与同窗好友的集体画像《今年毕业》有些相似。

在硕士学习末期，俸正杰开始创作《皮肤的叙述》系列作品。画面中在点状和正方形背景下，裸体女人身体溃烂成血淋淋的红色和绿色。评论家栗宪庭在观看作品时，指出了其图鲁迅一部作品的微妙联系：行将就木的晚清学者博学广识，却将溃疡描述为"溃烂之处，艳如桃李"，控诉着中国传统无力对抗现代化现实。在栗宪庭将皮肤系列描述为"艳俗"后不久，他就创制了"艳俗艺术"定义以俸正杰为首的有意低俗油画派别，但这个画派存在时间不长。

在俸全部作品中，当属《浪漫旅程》最为艳丽俗气。经过多年的体验和升华，他的绘画语言符合当代生活的视觉标准。在这部作品中，他特别地讽刺

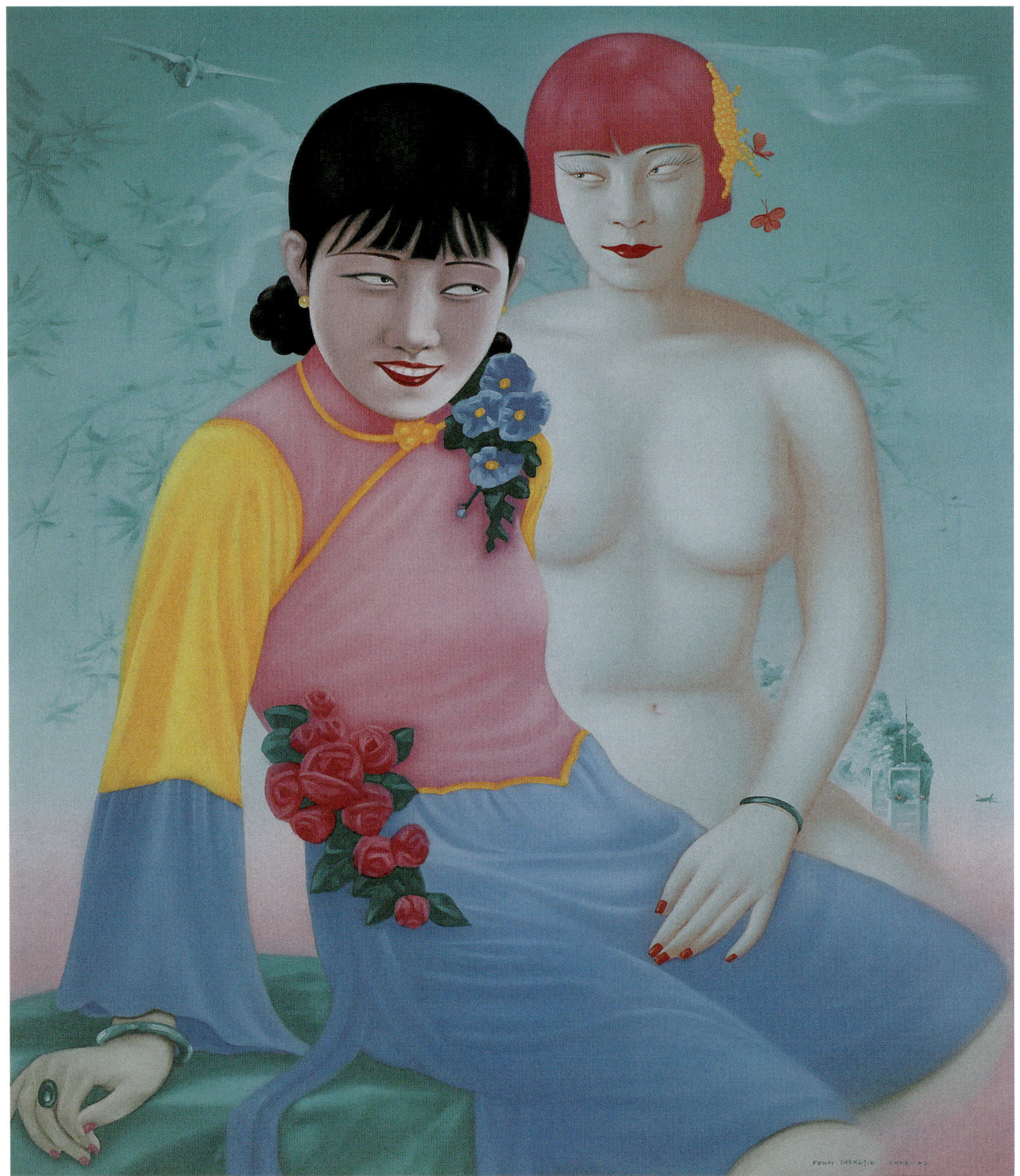

3

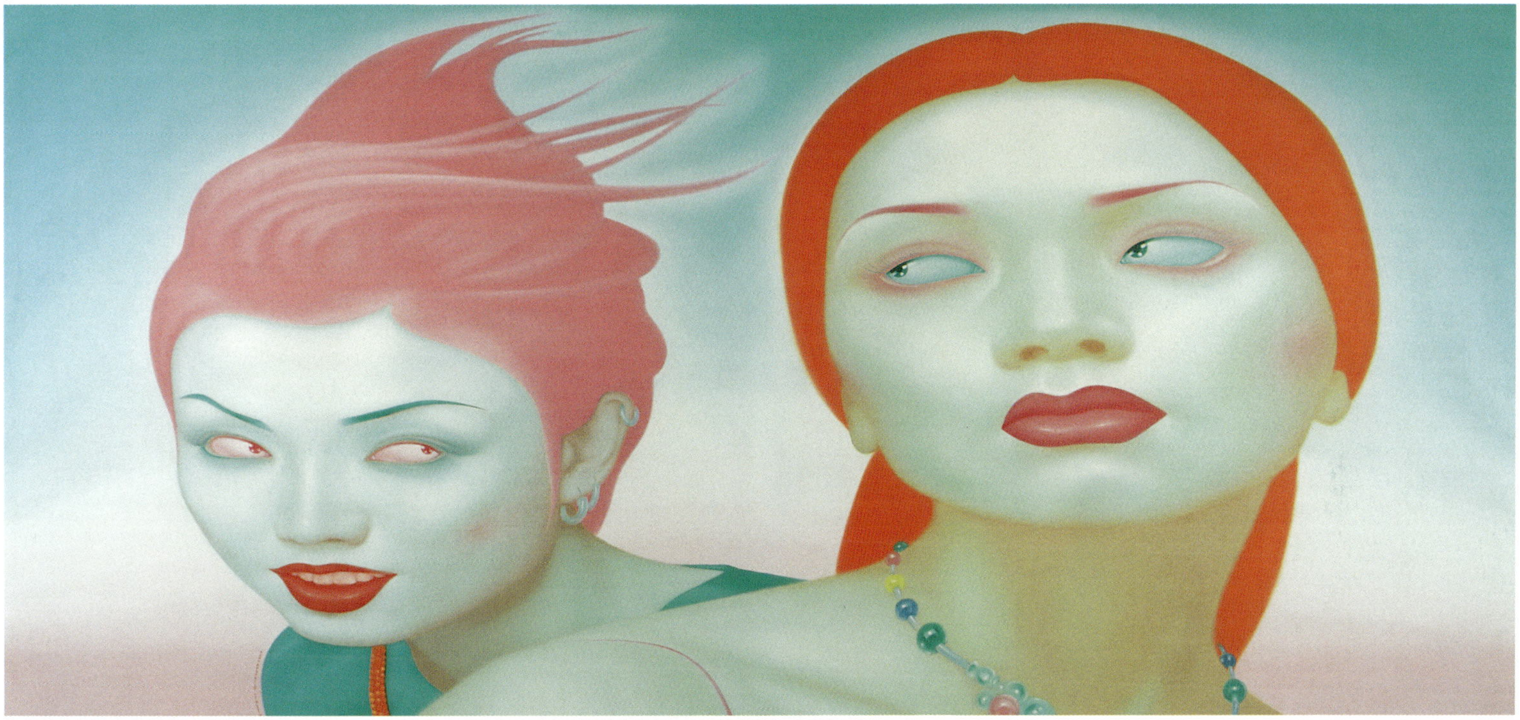

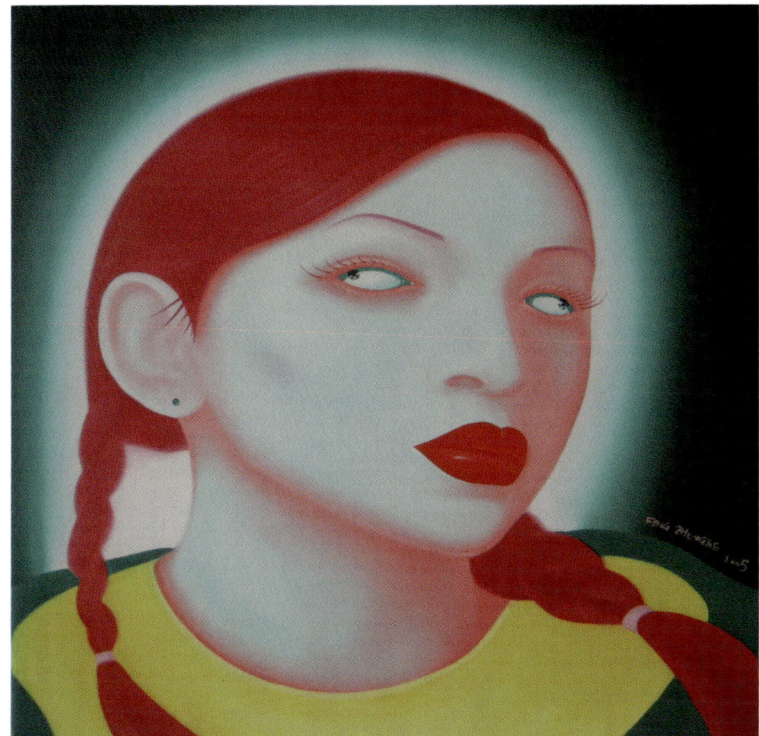

4

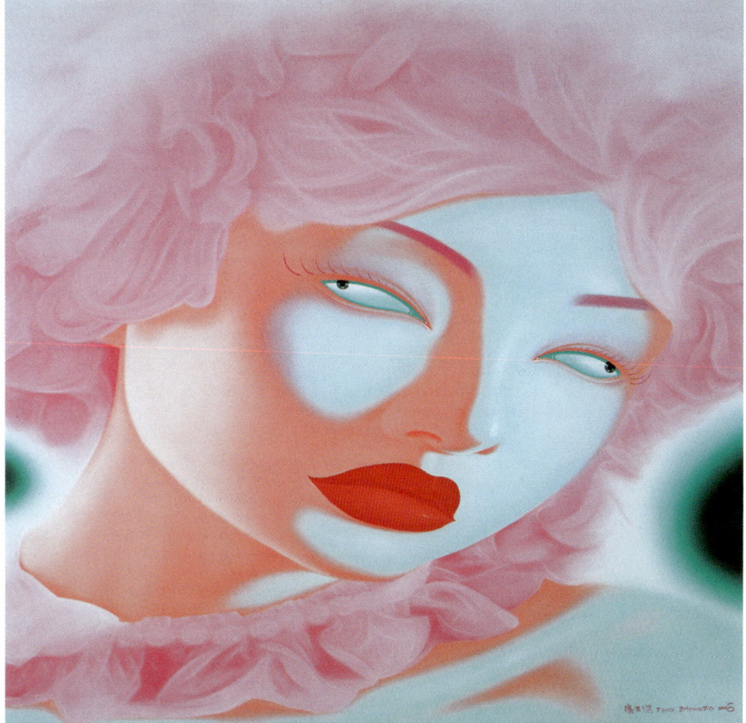

5

6

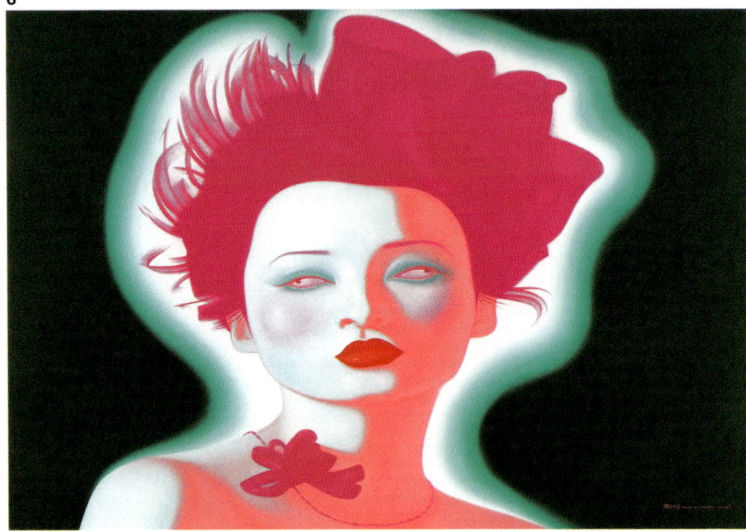

7

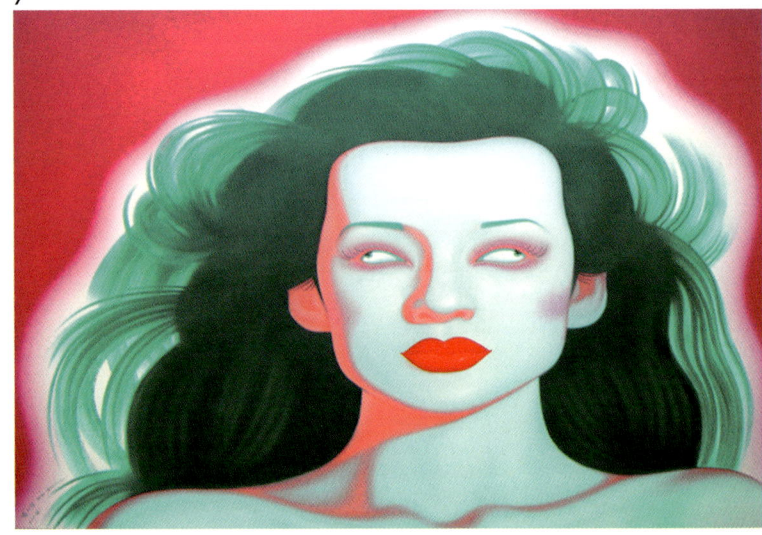

tradition's inability to confront modern realities. For Li Xianting, describing this skin series as "gaudy", led soon to his coinage of the phrase Gaudy Art to describe a short-lived school of intentionally tacky paintings with Feng Zhengjie as its head.

The most recognizably gaudy in Feng Zhengjie's œuvre belong to his "Romantic Trip" series (1996–1999), where his painterly language, developed over years of experimentation and refinement, meets up with the visual meat of contemporary life. Specifically, he satirizes in this series the 1990's wedding portrait, a genre at once emblematic and symptomatic of the dreams of bourgeois materiality that emerged in a China then beginning to boom. (New couples in that decade would often spend large amounts of money on photo shoots depicting them in high Western wedding garb.) All traces of the deconstructive skepticism that marked his early work disappear, as his attention turns to representing jubilant couples wearing silly smirks in the brightest colors he could allow himself. Gaudy art thus continues the work of Political Pop in its basic stance – an elite critique of mass (commercial) culture.

Feng Zhengjie's recent work – a sprawling series of portraiture entitled simply "China" (since 2003) serves as a gloss on his entire career. Its reds and greens derive from the colors he pioneered in the "Recounting of Skin" series, and its subject matter – pretty young things striking poses – counterfeit, glorify, and ultimately sublimate the visual conventions of advertising into the realm of abstract form.

Xuns Bemerkung über die verweichlichten Gelehrten der späten Qing-Periode, die sich in ihrer Gelehrsamkeit dazu verstiegen, „ein Geschwür so kitschig wie Pfirsichblüten" zu beschreiben – eine Kritik an der Unfähigkeit der chinesischen Traditionalisten, sich mit der Realität auseinanderzusetzen. Li Xianting prägte dafür den treffenden Begriff Gaudy Art (grelle Kitschkunst) und begründete damit eine kurzlebige Schule vorsätzlich kitschiger Malerei mit ihm selbst an der Spitze.

In Feng Zhengjies Schaffen zeigt sich der Kitschfaktor am deutlichsten in der Serie „Romantic Trip" (1996–1999), in der seine über Jahre entwickelte Malsprache auf die visuelle Substanz des modernen Lebens trifft. Er persifliert darin die Hochzeitsbilder der 1990er, ein Genre, das sinnbildlich und zugleich symptomatisch für die Träume des spießbürgerlichen Materialismus steht, die zu Beginn des Wirtschaftsbooms in China florierten (damals gaben frisch verliebte Paare oft viel Geld für Fotoaufnahmen aus, die sie in aufwändiger westlicher Hochzeitstracht zeigten). Alle Spuren des dekonstruktivistischen Skeptizismus, der Fengs Frühwerk prägte, verschwanden, als er seine Aufmerksamkeit der Darstellung freudestrahlender, debil grinsender Pärchen zuwandte – und das in den grellsten Farben, die ihm zur Verfügung standen. Fengs Gaudy Art setzt das Werk des Polit-Pop von der Intention her fort – als elitäre Kritik an der Massen- und Kommerzkultur.

Feng Zhengjies neuere Arbeiten – eine ausufernde Porträtserie mit dem schlichten Titel „China" (seit 2003) – bilden gleichsam den krönenden Hochglanzanstrich seiner gesamten Laufbahn. Ihre Rot- und Grüntöne zitieren die Farben, die er in der Serie „Recounting of Skin" erstmals verwendete, und ihre Motive – hübsche junge Frauen, die sich in Pose werfen – imitieren und glorifizieren die visuellen Konventionen der Werbung und heben sie ins Reich der abstrakten Form.

了90年代婚纱照，婚纱照一出现在中国，就被认为是资产阶级梦想的象征，随后就流行起来。(那时的新婚夫妇常常乐于花费大笔钱在这上面，照片上的他们常常身着高档西方婚纱)。而他早期作品中解析性怀疑论的痕迹都无影无踪，而以最鲜艳的色彩表现面带假笑的喜气洋洋的夫妇。因而就基本态度 -- 对大众（商业）文化的无情批评 -- 来讲，艳俗艺术是政治波普的继续。

俸正杰近作《中国》为一部无计划延伸的肖像画系列，也被看作他整个事业生涯的一个亮点。红绿色彩来源于《皮肤的叙述》，而其主题搔 首弄姿的年轻美女则模仿、美化了广告视觉手法并最终将之升华入抽象形式的世界中。

Philip Tinari

8

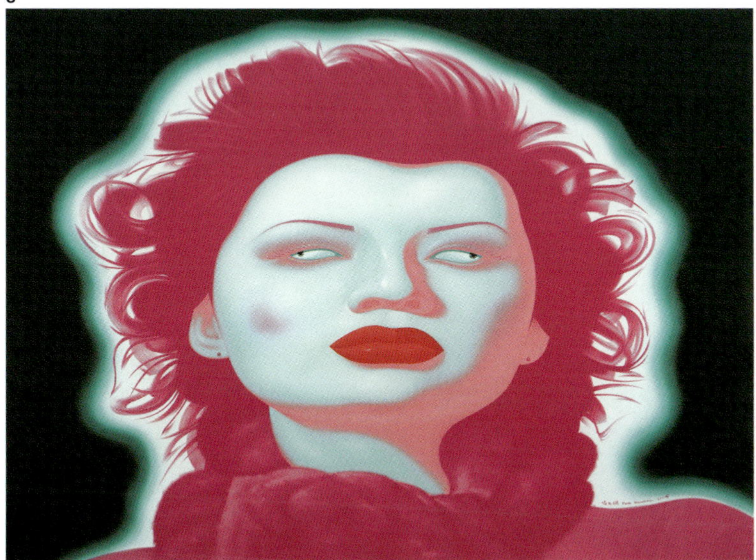

9

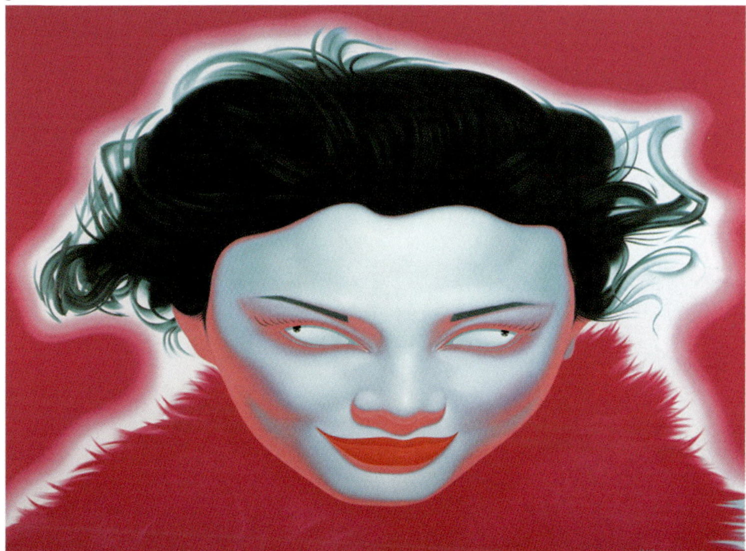

1 ***Chinese Portrait L Series 2006 No. 10***, *2006*
Oil on canvas, 210 x 300 cm; Öl auf Leinwand, 210 x 300 cm
《中国肖像L系列 2006 No. 10》2006年, 布面油画，210 x 300 cm

2 ***Butterfly in Love***, *2003*
Oil on canvas, 130 x 110 cm; Öl auf Leinwand, 130 x 110 cm
《爱上的蝴蝶》2003年 布面油画, 130 x 110 cm

3 ***China 2000–2002 No. 20***, *2001*
Oil on canvas, 210 x 450 cm; Öl auf Leinwand, 210 x 450 cm
《中国 2000–2002 No. 20》2001年, 布面油画，210 x 450 cm

4 ***Chinese Portrait 2005 No. 22***, *2005*
Oil on canvas, 91 x 91 cm; Öl auf Leinwand, 91 x 91 cm
《中国肖像 2005 No. 22》2005年, 布面油画，91 x 91 cm

5 ***Chinese Portrait K Series No. 08***, *2006*
Oil on canvas, 210 x 210 cm; Öl auf Leinwand, 210 x 210 cm
《中国肖像K系列 2006 No. 08》2006年, 布面油画，210 x 210 cm

6 ***Chinese Portrait L Series 2006 No. 02***, *2006*
Oil on canvas, 210 x 300 cm; Öl auf Leinwand, 210 x 300 cm
《中国肖像L系列 2006 No. 02》2006年, 布面油画，210 x 300 cm

7 ***Chinese Portrait L Series 2006 No. 11***, *2006*
Oil on canvas, 210 x 300 cm; Öl auf Leinwand, 210 x 300 cm
《中国肖像L系列 2006 No. 11》2006年, 布面油画，210 x 300 cm

8 ***Chinese Portrait P Series 2006 No. 01***, *2006*
Oil on canvas, 300 x 400 cm; Öl auf Leinwand, 300 x 400 cm
《中国肖像P系列 2006 No. 01》2006年, 布面油画，300 x 400 cm

9 ***Chinese Portrait P Series 2006 No. 02***, *2006*
Oil on canvas, 300 x 400 cm; Öl auf Leinwand, 300 x 400 cm
《中国肖像P系列 2006 No. 02》2006年, 布面油画，300 x 400 cm

10 ***China 2005 No. 13***, *2005*
Oil on canvas, 150 x 150 cm; Öl auf Leinwand, 150 x 150 cm
《中国2005 No. 13》2005年, 布面油画，150 x 150 cm

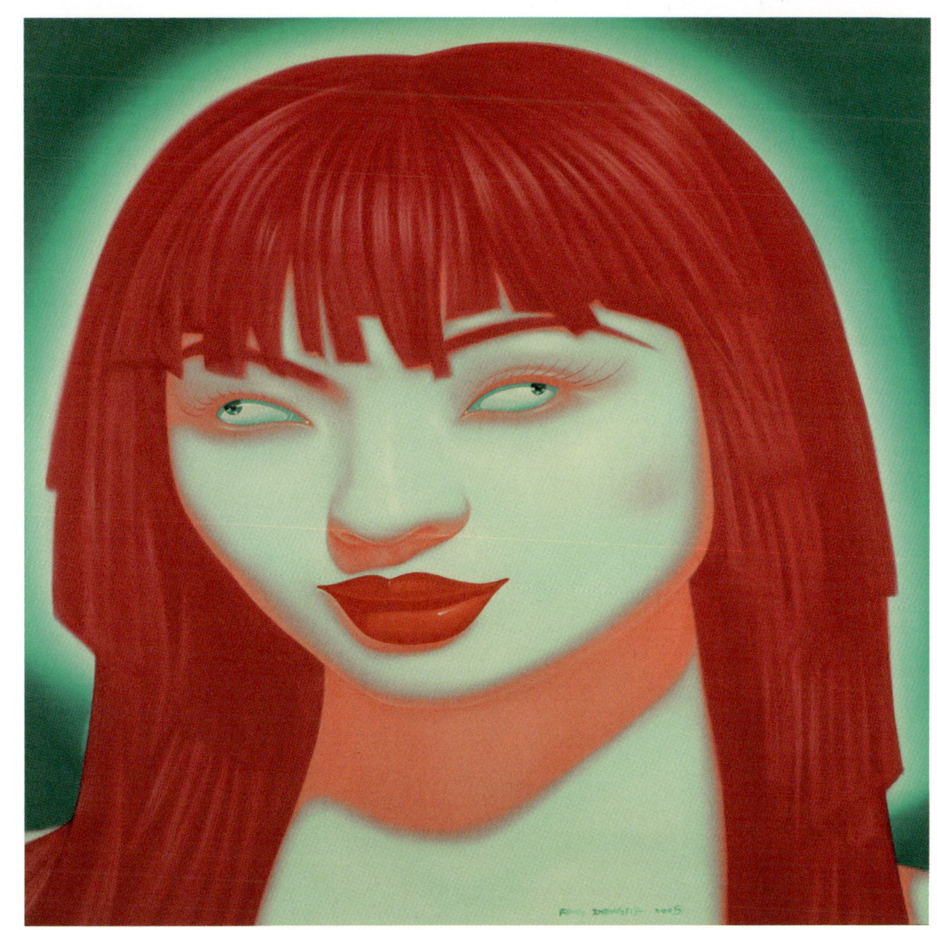

10

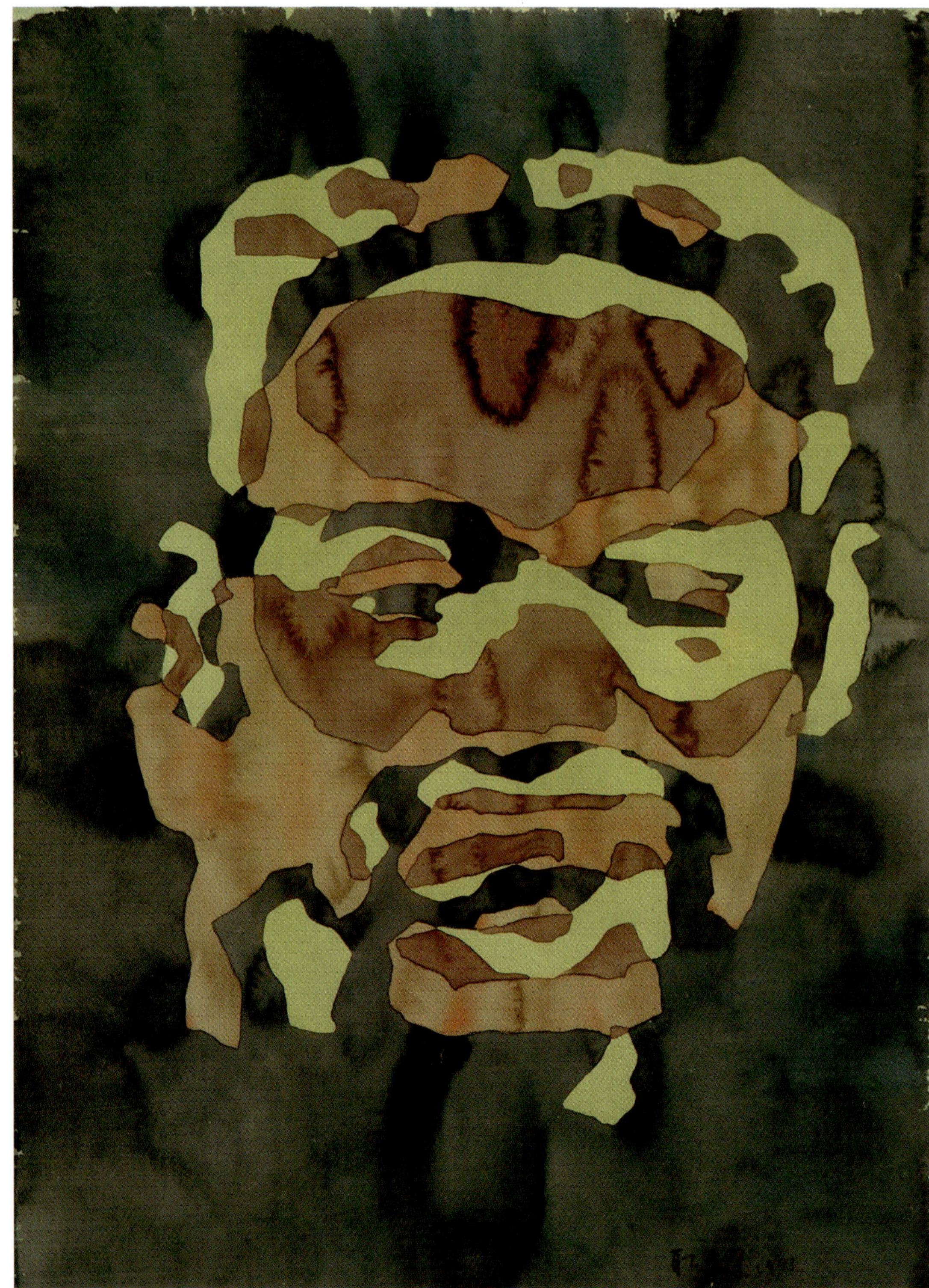

1

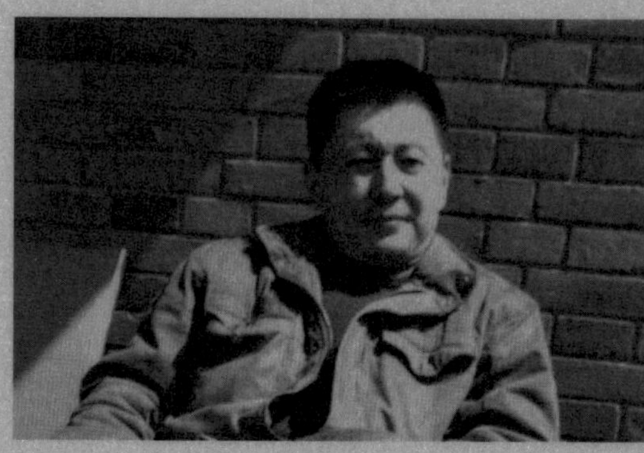

"What to say?"

„Was soll ich sagen?“

“什么说?”

Born in 1962 in Zhengzhou, Henan Province, China. Lives and works in Hangzhou
Geboren 1962 in Zhengzhou, Provinz Henan, China. Lebt und arbeitet in Hangzhou
1962年出生于河南郑州，中国。住居工作在杭州

***Selected exhibitions* / Ausgewählte Ausstellungen / 所选展览**

2002	“Pause”, Gwangju Biennial 2002, Gwangju, Korea
	First Guangzhou Triennial, Guandong Museum of Art, Guangzhou, China
2003	“Chinese Maximalism”, Millennium Art Museum, Beijing, China
2005	“Zooming into Focus: Chinese Contemporary Photography & Video from the Haudenschild Collection”, National Art Museum of China, Beijing, China
2005–07	“Mahjong – Chinesische Gegenwartskunst aus der Sammlung Sigg”, Kunstmuseum Bern, Berne, Switzerland; Hamburger Kunsthalle, Hamburg, Germany; Museum der Moderne, Salzburg, Austria
2006	“Shu: Reinventing Books in Contemporary Chinese Art”, China Institute Gallery, New York, NY, USA

2002年	《第四届光州双年展》韩国，光州
	《观看》首届广州三年展，广东美术馆，广州
2003年	《合成现实》远洋艺术中心，北京
2005年	《聚焦》北京，中国美术馆；
2005–07年	《麻将》西克中国当代艺术收藏展 伯尔尼美术馆 瑞士；汉堡美术馆 汉堡 德国；萨尔茨保现代美术馆 奥地利
2006年	《书:重创书在当代中国艺术》中国院画廊，纽约

***Selected publications* / Ausgewählte Publikationen / 所选著作**

“Contemporary Chinese Art Criticism Series: A Study on ‘New Figurative Art’”, Changchun 1999
Bernhard Fibicher, Matthias Frehner: “Mahjong: Contemporary Chinese Art from the Sigg Collection”, Ostfildern-Ruit 2005
Karen Smith: “Nine Lives: The Birth of Avant-Garde Art in New China”, Zurich 2005
“Shu: Reinventing books in contemporary Chinese art”, New York 2006

《当代中国艺术批评系列：关于‘新形象的艺术的’一项研究》长春1999年
Fibicher, Bernhard/Frehner, Matthias（编者）:《麻将一西克的当代艺术收藏展》Ostfildern-Ruit 2005年
Smith, Karen（著）:《当代艺术的九个文化英雄》苏黎世 2005年
《书：重创书在当代中国艺术》中国院画廊，纽约2006年

"What to say?"

„Was soll ich sagen?"

"什么说?"

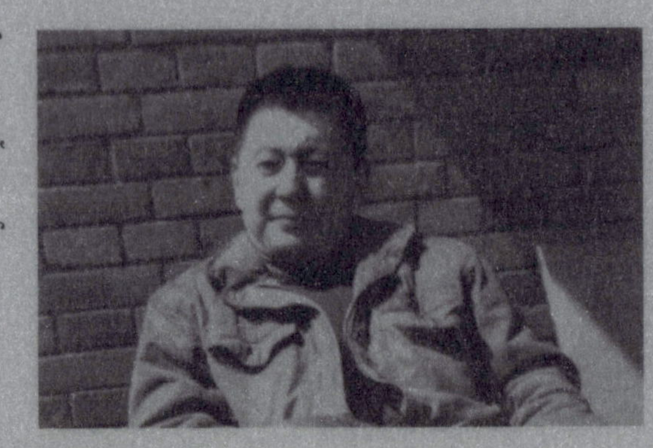

Born in 1962 in Zhengzhou, Henan Province, China. Lives and works in Hangzhou
Geboren 1962 in Zhengzhou, Provinz Henan, China. Lebt und arbeitet in Hangzhou
1962年出生于河南郑州，中国。住居工作在杭州

Selected exhibitions / Ausgewählte Ausstellungen / 所选展览

2002	"Pause", Gwangju Biennial 2002, Gwangju, Korea
	First Guangzhou Triennial, Guandong Museum of Art, Guangzhou, China
2003	"Chinese Maximalism", Millennium Art Museum, Beijing, China
2005	"Zooming into Focus: Chinese Contemporary Photography & Video from the Haudenschild Collection", National Art Museum of China, Beijing, China
2005–07	"Mahjong – Chinesische Gegenwartskunst aus der Sammlung Sigg", Kunstmuseum Bern, Berne, Switzerland; Hamburger Kunsthalle, Hamburg, Germany; Museum der Moderne, Salzburg, Austria
2006	"Shu: Reinventing Books in Contemporary Chinese Art", China Institute Gallery, New York, NY, USA

2002年	《第四届光州双年展》韩国，光州
	《观看》首届广州三年展，广东美术馆，广州
2003年	《合成现实》远洋艺术中心，北京
2005年	《聚焦》北京，中国美术馆；
2005–07年	《麻将》西克中国当代艺术收藏展 伯尔尼美术馆 瑞士；汉堡美术馆 汉堡 德国；萨尔茨堡现代美术馆 奥地利
2006年	《书：重创书在当代中国艺术》中国院画廊，纽约

Selected publications / Ausgewählte Publikationen / 所选著作

"Contemporary Chinese Art Criticism Series: A Study on 'New Figurative Art'", Changchun 1999
Bernhard Fibicher, Matthias Frehner: "Mahjong: Contemporary Chinese Art from the Sigg Collection", Ostfildern-Ruit 2005
Karen Smith: "Nine Lives: The Birth of Avant-Garde Art in New China", Zurich 2005
"Shu: Reinventing books in contemporary Chinese art", New York 2006

《当代中国艺术批评系列：关于'新形象的艺术的'一项研究》长春1999年
Fibicher, Bernhard/Frehner, Matthias（编者）：《麻将—西克的当代艺术收藏展》Ostfildern-Ruit 2005年
Smith, Karen（著）：《当代艺术的九个文化英雄》苏黎世 2005年
《书：重创书在当代中国艺术》中国院画廊，纽约2006年

GENG JIANYI 耿建翌

[kɤŋ tɕiɛni]

Geng Jianyi was painting big and bold laughing heads as early as 1985, pioneering the Cynical Realism movement in Chinese contemporary art. Instead of conforming to this very movement that would later take over the Chinese contemporary art scene in the 1990s, he embarked on a versatile and complex conceptual art practice. Today he is celebrated as a leading conceptual artist of the country and his involvement in the experimental art group "Chi She" in Hangzhou from 1986 to 1987 was an indispensable contribution to the 85's movement, an explosion of contemporary art experiments inspired by the influx of Western philosophical theories into China.

In many of Geng's signature works from the early 90s to the mid 90s, the art-making process was the concept itself and often involved self-imposed, fabricated or mathematical rules and a stretched, repetitive and almost mind-numbing course of action in order to preclude meaning, emotion and interpretation. In "How Powerful is the Word" (1997/98), he toiled for hours blotting out all characters apart from "of" in a book, and afterwards replicated a book of the same size with all blank papers, filled the new book with squares written in places corresponding to those of "ofs" in the former book.

Such deliberately tedious, ritualistic and almost seemingly idiotic approaches to art gave rise to a term "grey humor", which defined art practices popular from the late 80s to the mid 90s. To a certain extent, they resembled scientific experiments, except that these were experiments carried out by artists in order to investigate issues related to the society and the paradoxical relationship between individuals and the society as a system. That explained the sociological dimension in Geng's practice.

In 1993, in a project called "Marriage Law", the Hangzhou-based artist invited a group of 20 people, which included his friends and friends of friends, to participate in a written test that he drafted based on the marital laws in China since the founding of the country and the verdicts

Geng Jianyi malte schon 1985 große und ausdrucksvolle lachende Gesichter und wurde damit zum Pionier des Zynischen Realismus in der zeitgenössischen chinesischen Kunst. Doch statt sich in dieser erfolgreichen Bewegung bequem einzurichten, die Chinas Kunstszene in den 1990er Jahren dominieren sollte, wählte er einen abwechslungsreicheren Weg: Er wurde der führende Konzeptkünstler des Landes. Sein Engagement in der experimentellen Künstlergruppe „Chi She" in Hangzhou von 1986 bis 1987 war ein unentbehrlicher Beitrag zur 85er-Bewegung, die als erste in China stürmisch die Anregungen moderner Kunst und Philosophie aus dem Westen aufgriff und mit ihnen experimentierte.

Bei vielen der charakteristischen Werke Gengs aus der Zeit von Anfang bis Mitte der 1990er Jahre lieferte der Schaffensprozess selbst den konzeptionellen Ansatz. Oft mit eigens dafür erfundenen oder mathematischen Regeln und mit einem ausgesprochen pedantischen Vorgehen bemühte sich Geng, aus seiner Arbeit jeden tieferen Sinn, jedes höhere Gefühl und vor allem jedwede Interpretationsmöglichkeit zu eliminieren. Für „How Powerful is the Word" (1997/98) plagte sich der Künstler, um aus einem Buch alle Schriftzeichen bis auf ein ganz bestimmtes, besonders häufig vorkommendes zu tilgen. Anschließend nahm er ein Buch der gleichen Größe und Ausstattung, aber mit leeren Seiten, und setzte darin Quadrate an jene Stellen, die im ersten die verbliebenen Schriftzeichen einnahmen.

Für diese mühevolle, vorsätzlich ritualisierte und scheinbar widersinnige Herangehensweise, die von den späten 1980er Jahren bis Mitte der 1990er Jahre eine gewisse Popularität genoss, wurde später der Begriff „grauer Humor" geprägt. Der Ansatz dieses Humors hatte eine gewisse Ähnlichkeit mit wissenschaftlichen Experimenten. Allerdings handelte es sich dabei eben nicht um Experimente von Wissenschaftlern, sondern von Künstlern, die die oft paradoxe Beziehung zwischen Individuen und Gesellschaft auf ihre Weise erforschten. Immerhin erklärt sich so die soziologische Dimension in Gengs Arbeit.

早在 1985 年，耿建翌就开始绘制巨幅面带狂笑的作品，引领中国当代艺术的玩世现实主义运动。他并未将这一之后在上世纪九十年代盛行于中国当代艺术界的运动继续下去，而是开始着手于多样而复杂的概念艺术实践。如今他被称作中国的概念艺术家领袖，而他于 1986 年至 1987 年在杭州参加的试验艺术团体“池社”，则为 85 美术运动做出了不可或缺的贡献 -- 西方哲学理论流入中国后所激发的当代艺术试验的爆发。

从上世纪九十年代初期到中期，在许多耿建翌的署名作品中，为了排除意图、情感以及解释，艺术创作过程本身便是概念，并且常常涉及自加的、虚构的或精确的规则，以及延伸的、反复的乃至意识麻木的行为过程。在作品《怎一个“OF”字了得》（1997-1998 年）中，他不辞辛劳地花费数小时将一本书内除“的”外的所有字符用墨水涂掉，然后复制了一本相同尺寸而且全部为空白页的书，并在新书内与原书中“的”相应的地方填上方块。

这种刻意冗长、仪式化而且近乎白痴般艺术表现方法引出了一个术语 --“灰色幽默”，该术语为上世纪八十年代后期到九十年代中期所盛行的艺术实践作出了定义。在某种程度上，这些实践类似于科学试验，只不过做试验的是艺术家，而试验目的是研究社会相关的，以及个人和作为整体的社会之间的荒谬关系相关的问题。这就解释了耿建翌作品中的社会学维度。

1993 年，在一个名为《婚姻法》的项目中，这位杭州艺术家邀请了 20 位观众，包括他的朋友及朋友的朋友，参加他根据建国以来的中国婚姻法以及最高人民法院关于婚姻的决议起草的书面测验。这次活动在一间中学教室中举行，而试卷被设计成类似小传单的形状。这次活动引发了一场激烈争论，争论内容涉及法律、婚姻、家庭以及一个结构正在经历巨大变化的社会体系中的保守与开放。在一个根据实事创作的作品《他是谁？》（1994 年）中，

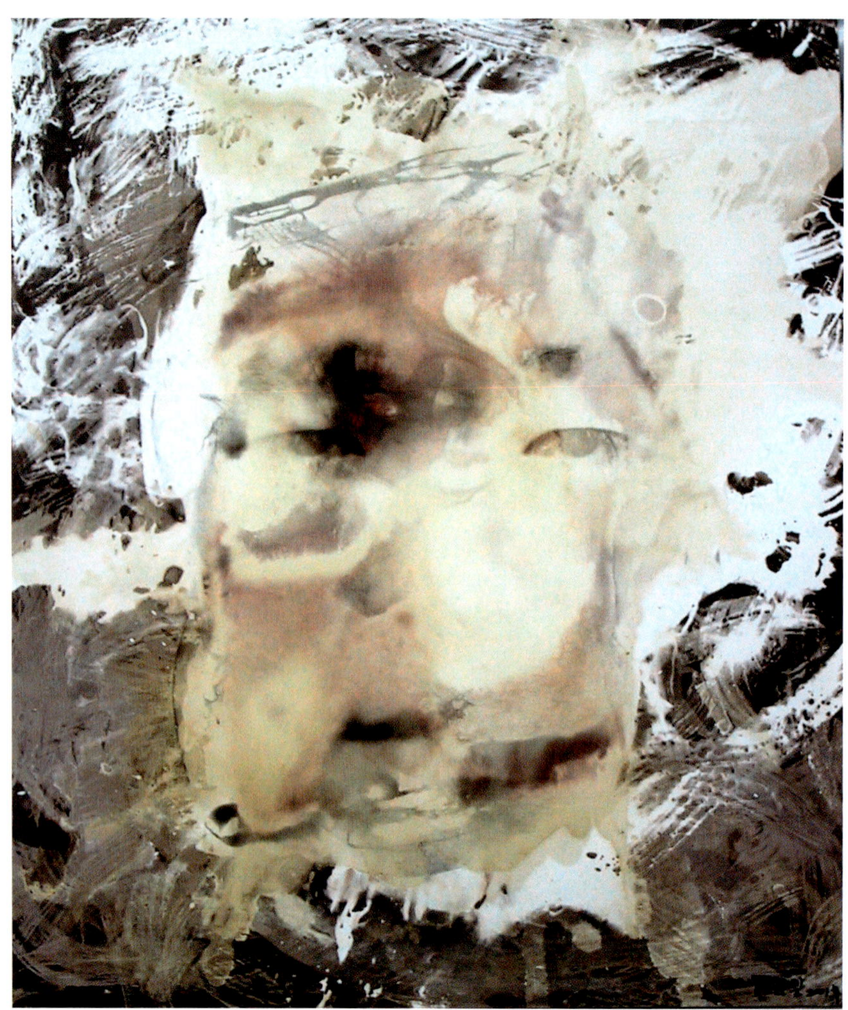

2

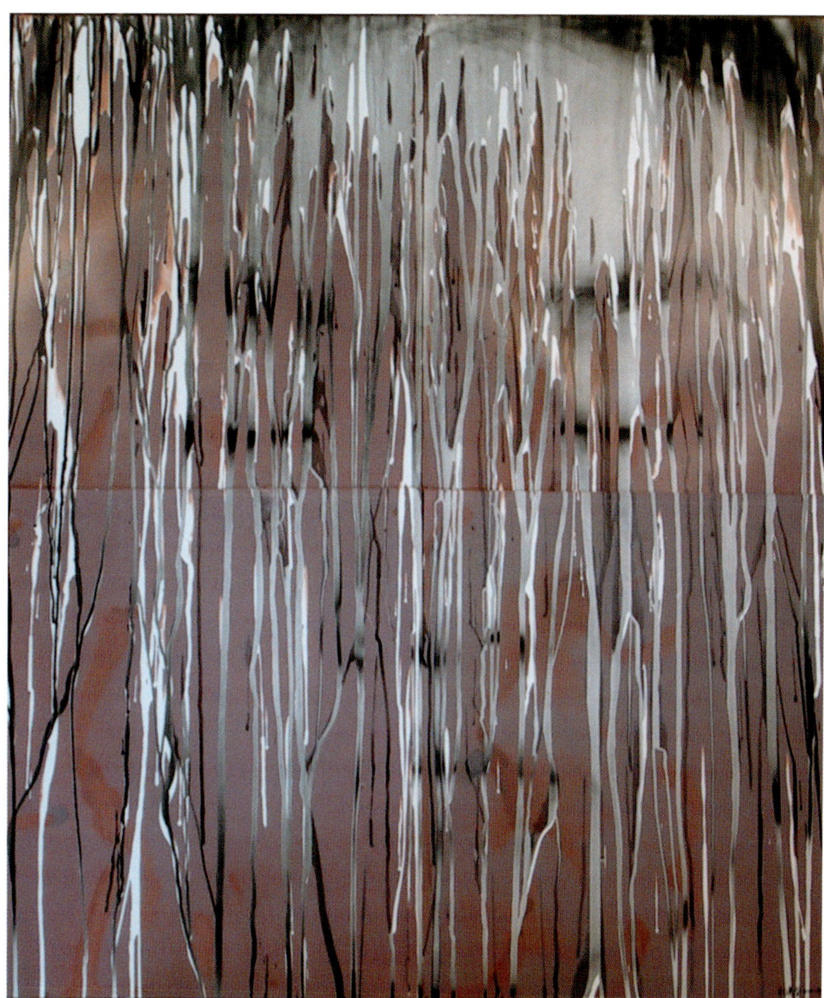

3

4

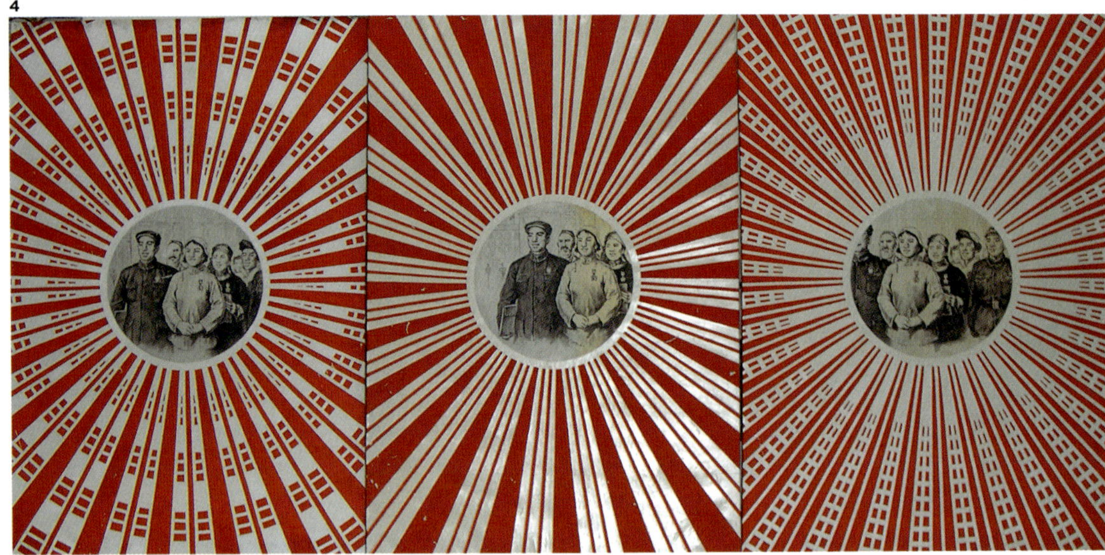

of the Supreme People's Court concerning marriage. The event took place in a middle school classroom and the examination paper was designed to look like a small leaflet. The happening provoked a heated discussion about laws, marriage, family as well as the rigidity and openness of the system in a society whose structure was undergoing drastic transformation. In "Who Is He?"(1994), based on a true event, Geng invited his neighbours to fill out a form and make a sketch each describing the same person. The very person in question is a friend of Geng who visited him when he was not around but was spotted by his neighbours. As his neighbours tried to tell Geng who had visited him without knowing this person's name, Geng was amazed by how different the descriptions of the same person could be and how it reflected deeper social imprints. Geng then proceeded to develop this art project from it.

Geng continues to examine mechanisms that shape our own system of knowing and thinking. In a recent series of installations called "Book Without Words" in 2006, Geng devised a group of books of nothing but blank pages and no words. Powered by motors, the books are opened up and flipped through automatically in different ways. The books have taken on a life of their own, even though they are completely deprived of content. Geng belonged to a generation who grew up through the Cultural Revolution, in which books were considered nothing but toxic, Geng's humour in this body of works is more grave than grey.

Für sein Projekt mit dem Titel „Marriage Law" lud der in Hangzhou lebende Künstler 1993 eine Gruppe von 20 Leuten, darunter Freunde sowie Freunde von Freunden, zu einem schriftlichen Test ein. Er hatte ihn auf Grundlage der Ehegesetze in China seit der Gründung des Landes und der Urteile des Obersten Gerichtshofs zum Thema Ehe konzipiert. Die Prüfung fand im Klassenzimmer einer Mittelschule statt, und die Prüfungsarbeit war wie eine kleine Broschüre gestaltet. Dieses Happening löste eine hitzige Diskussion aus: nicht nur über Gesetze, Ehe und Familie, sondern auch über die Starrheit oder Offenheit des Systems in einer Gesellschaft, deren Strukturen sich im dramatischen Umbruch befanden. „Who Is He?" (1994) wiederum lag folgendes Geschehen zugrunde: Ein Freund von Geng war zu Besuch gekommen, als Geng selbst nicht zu Hause war. Aber die Nachbarn hatten ihn gesehen. Geng bat sie nun, den Besucher, dessen Namen sie nicht kannten, mittels eines Formulars und einer Skizze zu beschreiben. Geng war verblüfft, wie unterschiedlich die verschiedenen Beschreibungen ein und derselben Person ausfielen und in welchem Maß sie ganz offensichtlich tiefe soziale Prägungen spiegelten. Grund genug für ihn, den Vorfall in ein Kunstprojekt zu überführen.

Jenen Mechanismen, die unser Wissens- und Denksystem prägen, gilt nach wie vor das konzeptionelle Interesse Gengs. 2006 zeigte er in einer Serie von Installationen mit dem Titel „Book Without Words" eine Anzahl von Büchern mit vollständig leeren Seiten. Von Motoren angetrieben, öffnen sich die Bücher selbsttätig und werden automatisch in unterschiedlicher Weise durchblättert. Obwohl jedes Inhalts beraubt, bekommen die Bücher dabei eine Art Eigenleben. Mit dieser Serie beweist Geng nun eher schwarzen als grauen Humor, gehört er doch einer Generation an, die während der Kulturrevolution aufwuchs – zu einer Zeit also, in der Bücher als pures Gift galten.

耿建翌邀请他的邻居填写一份表格并画一份草图以描写同一个人。这个人是耿建翌的朋友，这位朋友曾经拜访耿建翌，没有遇到主人却遇到了邻居。而当不知客人姓名的邻居们试图告诉耿建翌是谁来拜访他时，耿建翌惊异于对同一个人的描述的差异之大，及其所反应出的更深的社会印记。于是，他根据此事创作了这个作品。

耿建翌继续测试塑造我们自己的知识与思考体系的机制。最近在一个名为《无字书》（2006年）的装置作品中，他设计了一组只有空白页面、空无一字的书。这些书由电动机提供动力，以不同的方式打开并翻页。尽管这些书完全没有内容，但却具有了自己的生命。耿建翌是历经了文革的一代，而那时书籍完全被当作毒素。耿建翌在这种作品载体中的幽默比灰色更深重。

Carol Lu

5

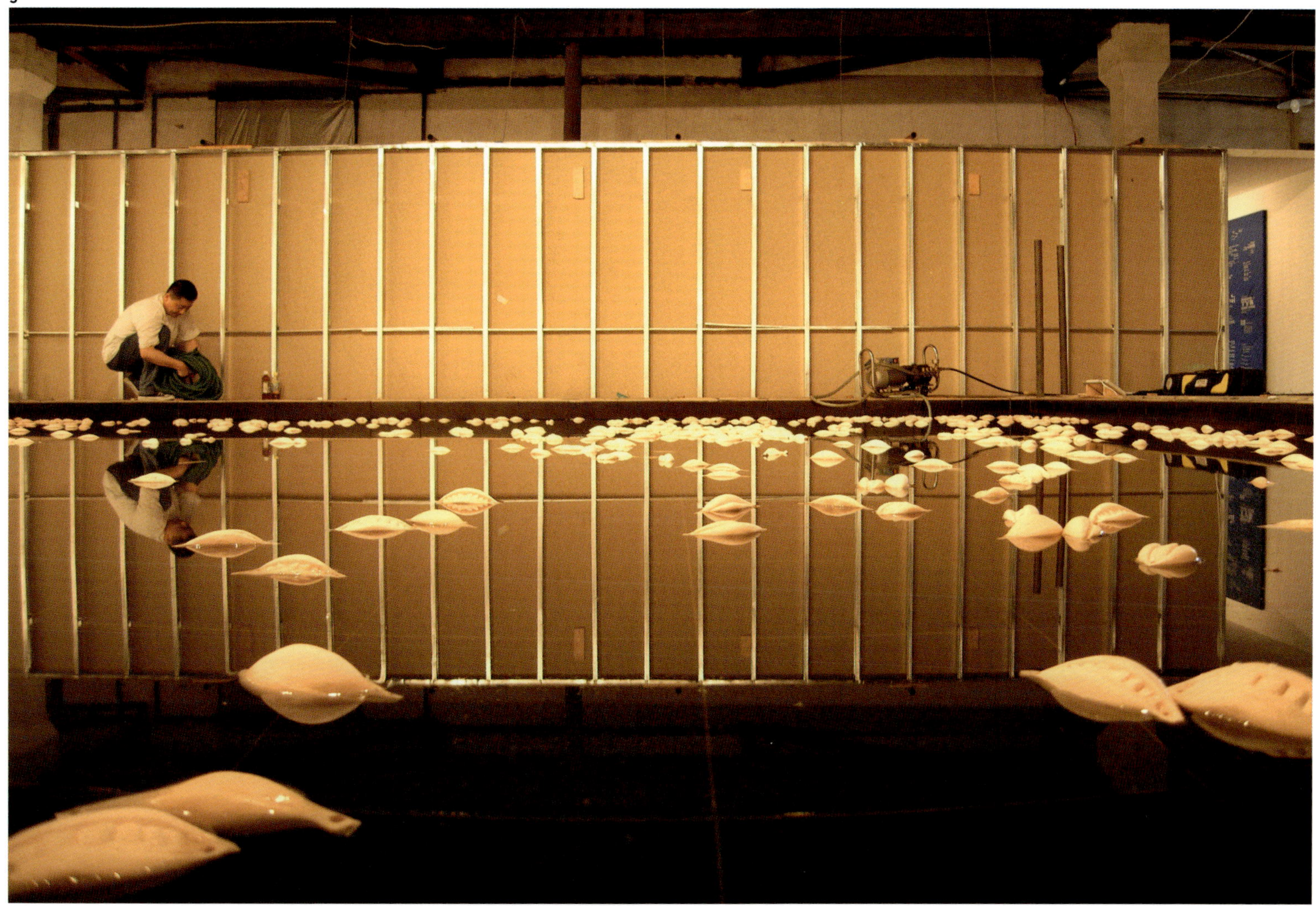

1 ***Face***, *1993*
Watercolour on paper, 74 x 52 cm
Aquarell auf Papier, 74 x 52 cm
《面孔》1993年，纸面水彩，74 x 52 cm

2 ***Visible Face***, *2001*
Photograph, 61 x 51 cm
Fotografie, 61 x 51 cm
《可看见的面孔》2001年，摄影，61 x 51 cm

3 ***Face is washed away***, *2001*
Photograph, 61 x 51 cm
Fotografie, 61 x 51 cm
《洗去的面孔》2001年，摄影，61 x 51 cm，四部

4 ***Eternal Rays of the Sun***, *1992*
Oil on canvas, 195 x 393 cm, 3 panels
Öl auf Leinwand, 195 x 393 cm, 3-teilig
《永放光芒》1992年，布面油画，195 x 293 cm，三部

5 ***Happy Pond***, *2005*
Installation, silica gel
Installation, Silicagel
《开心池》2005年，装置，硅胶等

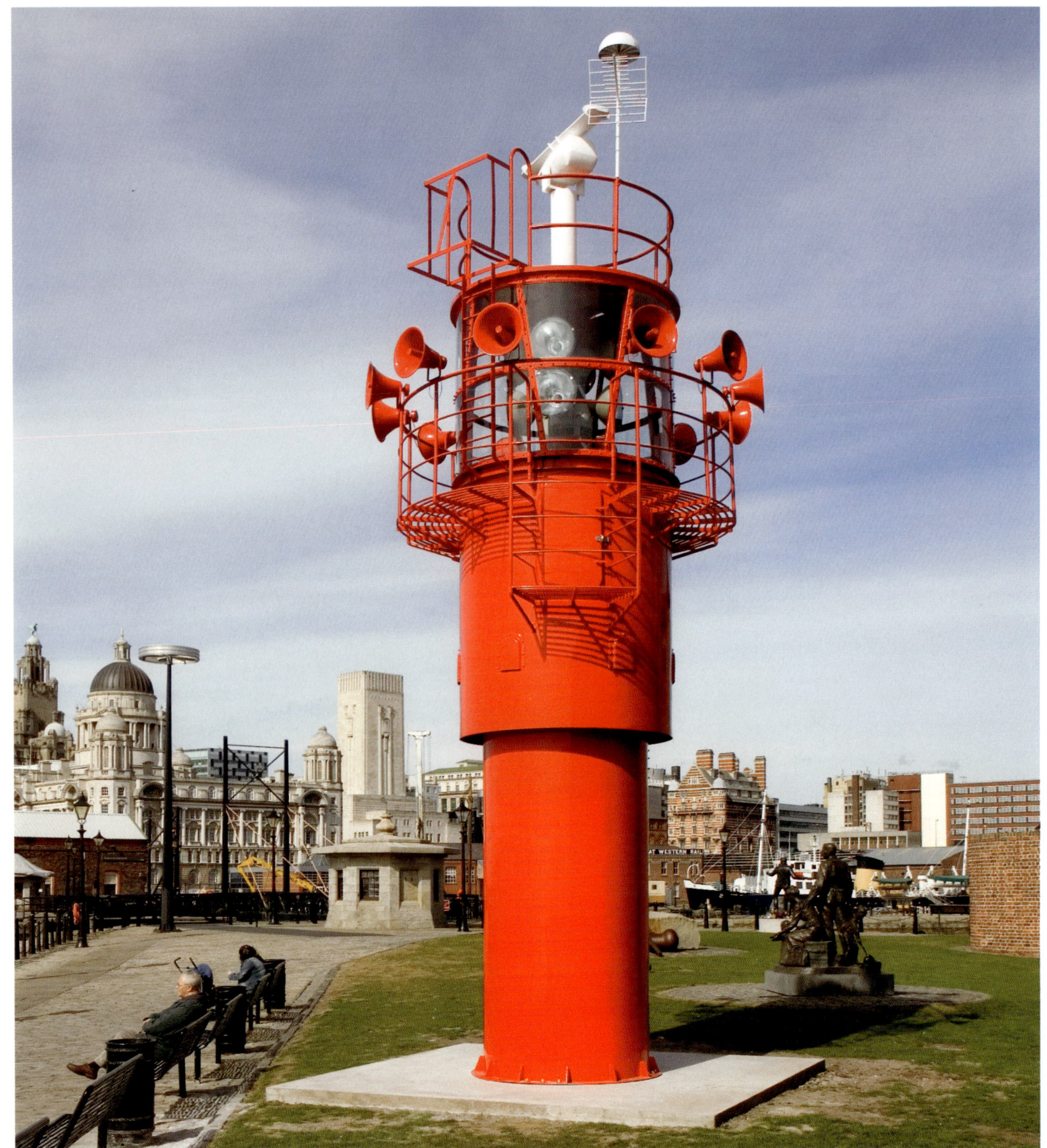

1

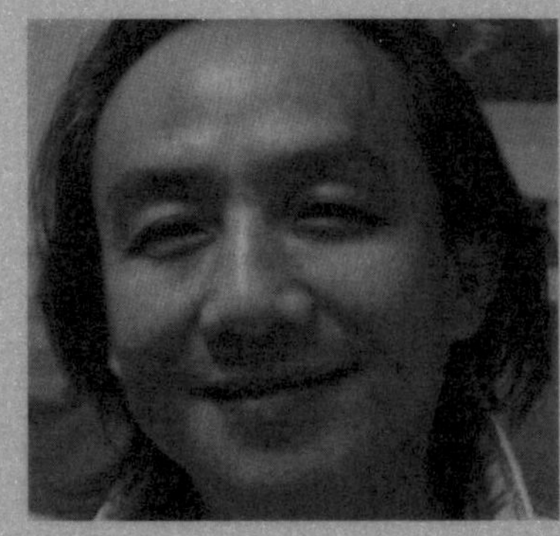

"To me, in an artwork, there is neither a beginning nor a conclusion."

„Für mich gibt es in einem Kunstwerk weder einen Anfang noch ein Ende."

"对我而言，艺术 没有起点也没有终点。"

Born in 1962 in Beijing, China. Lives and works in Beijing
Geboren 1962 in Peking, China. Lebt und arbeitet in Peking
1962年出生于北京，中国。居住工作在北京

Selected exhibitions **/ Ausgewählte Ausstellungen /** 所选展览

2002 "Pause", Gwangju Biennial 2002, Gwangju, Korea
First Guangzhou Triennial, Guandong Museum of Art, Guangzhou, China
2004–07 "Between Past and Future, New Photography and Video from China", International Center of Photography, New York, NY, USA (travelling exhibition)
2005–07 "Mahjong – Chinesische Gegenwartskunst aus der Sammlung Sigg", Kunstmuseum Bern, Berne, Switzerland; Hamburger Kunsthalle, Hamburg, Germany; Museum der Moderne, Salzburg, Austria

2002年 《暂停》，第四届光州双年展，光州，韩国
首届广州三年展，广东美术馆，广州
2004–07年 《过去与未来之间—中国的新影像展》国际摄影中心 纽约 美国（巡回展）
2005–07年 《麻将》西克中国当代艺术收藏展 伯尔尼美术馆 瑞士；汉堡美术馆 汉堡 德国；萨尔茨保现代美术馆 奥地利

Selected publications **/ Ausgewählte Publikationen /** 所选著作

Thierry Raspail: "The Monk and the Demon: Chinese Contemporary Art", Musée d'Art Contemporain, Lyon 2004
Bernhard Fibicher, Matthias Frehner (eds.): "Mahjong: Contemporary Chinese Art from the Sigg Collection", Ostfildern-Ruit 2005
Karen Smith: "Nine Lives: The Birth of Avant-Garde Art in New China", Zurich 2005
"Create History – Commemoration Exhibition of Chinese Modern Art in 1980s", Guangdong 2006

Raspail, Thierry（著）:《修道士和邪魔：中国当代艺术》当代艺术博物馆，里昂，法国2004年
Fibicher, Bernhard/Frehner, Matthias（编者）：《麻将－西克的当代艺术收藏展》Ostfildern-Ruit 2005年
Smith, Karen（著）:《当代艺术的九个文化英雄》苏黎世 2005年
《创造历史: 中国20世纪80年代的现代艺术》广东 2006年

"To me, in an artwork, there is neither a beginning nor a conclusion."

„Für mich gibt es in einem Kunstwerk weder einen Anfang noch ein Ende."

"对我而言，艺术 没有起点也没有终点。"

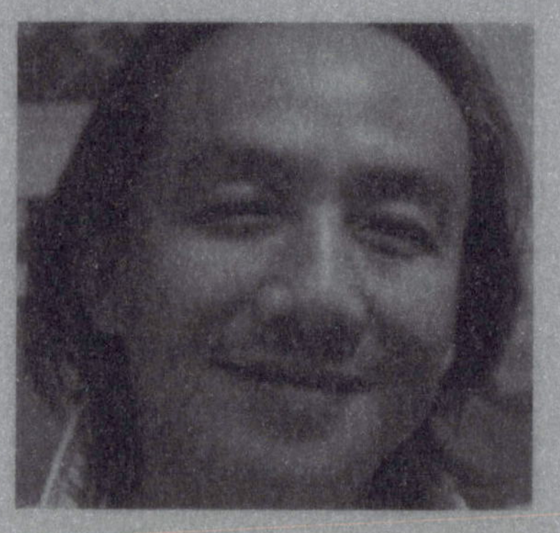

Born in 1962 in Beijing, China. Lives and works in Beijing
Geboren 1962 in Peking, China. Lebt und arbeitet in Peking
1962年出生于北京，中国。居住工作在北京

Selected exhibitions / Ausgewählte Ausstellungen / 所选展览

2002 "Pause", Gwangju Biennial 2002, Gwangju, Korea
First Guangzhou Triennial, Guandong Museum of Art, Guangzhou, China
2004-07 "Between Past and Future, New Photography and Video from China", International Center of Photography, New York, NY, USA (travelling exhibition)
2005-07 "Mahjong - Chinesische Gegenwartskunst aus der Sammlung Sigg", Kunstmuseum Bern, Berne, Switzerland; Hamburger Kunsthalle, Hamburg, Germany; Museum der Moderne, Salzburg, Austria

2002年 《暂停》，第四届光州双年展，光州，韩国
首届广州三年展，广东美术馆，广州
2004-07年《过去与未来之间—中国的新影像展》国际摄影中心 纽约 美国（巡回展）
2005-07年《麻将》西克中国当代艺术收藏展 伯尔尼美术馆 瑞士；汉堡美术馆 汉堡 德国；萨尔茨堡现代美术馆 奥地利

Selected publications / Ausgewählte Publikationen / 所选著作

Thierry Raspail: "The Monk and the Demon: Chinese Contemporary Art", Musée d'Art Contemporain, Lyon 2004
Bernhard Fibicher, Matthias Frehner (eds.): "Mahjong: Contemporary Chinese Art from the Sigg Collection", Ostfildern-Ruit 2005
Karen Smith: "Nine Lives: The Birth of Avant-Garde Art in New China", Zurich 2005
"Create History - Commemoration Exhibition of Chinese Modern Art in 1980s", Guangdong 2006

Raspail, Thierry（著）：《修道士和邪魔：中国当代艺术》当代艺术博物馆，里昂，法国2004年
Fibicher, Bernhard/Frehner, Matthias（编著）：《麻将—西克的当代艺术收藏展》Ostfildern-Ruit 2005年
Smith, Karen（著）：《当代艺术的九个文化英雄》苏黎世 2005年
《创造历史：中国20世纪80年代的现代艺术》广东 2006年

GU DEXIN 顾德新

[ku tɤɕin]

Gu Dexin's work is no easy feast. Grotesque images, loud colors, especially that of red and foul smell often characterizes Gu Dexin's site-specific installations, which typically involves blood-dripping animal hearts or brains, big or small chunks of meat, fresh or dried, rotting fruits such as strawberries, bananas, and most often apples of different colors. His infatuation with the darker sides of materials, particularly those of flesh, and anything that tantalizes human senses, started as early as the mid 80s, a few years prior to the emergence of Young British Artists, whose first group exhibition was inaugurated in 1988. He toiled in a plastic factory for about a year purely for first-hand investigation into the nature and sculptural possibilities of plastic. Subsequently he produced an intense body of spine-chilling and highly dramatic sculptural objects made of plastic after different degrees of burning and molding. They were first-rate props for horror movies, gaudy, full of vivid details, gruesome textures and sinister shapes, easily mistaken for tangled up human intestines or a cluster of ghostly jungle.

It was around the same time that he was involved in another experiment of equally extreme nature. Together with two other artists, they formed the "Xinkedu" (New Measurement Group) Group, which still stands firmly as a beacon in the Chinese contemporary art world today. Xinkedu Group was a collective platform for non-object based art experiments that investigated the world in a self-invented analytical, methodical and quantitative format. The group existed from 1988 to 1995 and was an indispensable contribution to the rational discourse prevalent in contemporary art practice at that time, which introduced logic, analysis too and eliminated human and emotional traces in art. It was a significant counterpoint to the overblown idealism and revolutionary realism in art of the former decades.

Since the early 1990s, Gu Dexin has been constantly invited to work ad hoc for a great number of international exhibitions in a complexity of sites from churches, casinos all the way to former military bases. In all of his projects,

Gu Dexins Werk ist keine leichte Kost. Schreiende Farben – besonders Rot – und eklige Gerüche sind charakteristisch für seine Installationen, zu denen typischerweise bluttriefende Tierherzen oder -hirne, größere oder kleinere frische oder getrocknete Fleischklumpen sowie faulendes Obst (wie Erdbeeren, Bananen und am häufigsten Äpfel) gehören. Seine Begeisterung für die dunklen Seiten der Materialien, ganz besonders von Fleisch und für alles, was die menschlichen Sinne irritiert, entwickelte sich schon Mitte der 1980er Jahre, noch vor der Formierung der Young British Artists, deren erste Gruppenausstellung 1988 stattfand. Gu schuftete fast ein Jahr lang in einer Kunststofffabrik, um die Beschaffenheit und die bildhauerischen Möglichkeiten des Werkstoffs professionell kennen zu lernen. Anschließend schuf er eine packende Sammlung gruseliger und hochdramatischer Objekte aus bizarr verschmortem und verformtem Plastik. Sie hätten ideale Requisiten für Horrorfilme abgegeben: grellbunt, mit ausdrucksvollen Details, schaurigen Texturen und unheimlichen Formen – Knäueln menschlicher Eingeweide oder einem Stück Urwald nicht unähnlich.

Zur gleichen Zeit engagierte Gu sich bei einem nicht minder extremen Experiment. Zusammen mit zwei anderen Künstlern gründete er die Gruppe „Xinkedu" (New Measurement Group), die bis heute wie ein Leuchtturm aus der zeitgenössischen Kunstszene Chinas herausragt. Sie war eine kollektive Plattform für nicht objektbezogene Kunstvorhaben, die die Welt auf eine selbsterdachte, analytisch-methodisch-quantitative Weise vermaß. Die Gruppe bestand von 1988 bis 1995 und leistete einen wesentlichen Beitrag zu jenem wichtigen rationalen Diskurs, der damals Logik und Analyse in die Kunst einbrachte, während er zugleich alle allzu menschlichen und emotionalen Spuren aus ihr tilgte. Die Gruppe setzte einen bedeutsamen Kontrapunkt zum schwülstigen Idealismus und sozialistischen Realismus der vorausgegangenen Jahrzehnte.

Seit Anfang der 1990er Jahre wurde Gu Dexin immer wieder zu einer Vielzahl internationaler Ausstellungen an den verschiedensten Orten eingeladen: ob nun in Kirchen,

顾德新的作品决不是轻松的筵席。怪诞的形象、艳丽的色彩（尤其是红色）以及难闻的气味常常是他特定场所装置作品的特色。其装置作品常常涉及滴血的动物心脏或脑髓、大块小块鲜肉或干肉、腐烂的水果（如草莓、香蕉，但最常见的还是各种颜色的苹果）。他醉心于素材较为阴暗的一面，尤其是肉以及其他任何刺激人类感官事物的阴暗面。他的这种偏执开始于上世纪八十年代中期，比（余震）YBA 的出现早了数年，而后者的第一组展览于 1988 年举行。他在一家塑料工厂内耗费了整整一年的时间，纯粹为了进行关于塑料的特质以及雕塑可能性的第一手调查。随后他通过将塑料进行不同程度的融化和成型，创作了大量令人毛骨悚然而又极其生动的塑料雕塑作品。这些作品是一流的恐怖电影道具，花哨、充满生动的细节、可憎的材质和凶恶的形状，很容易让人错认为缠结的人肠或一片可怕的丛林。

大约同一时间，顾德新还从事另一关于同等极端性质的尝试。他与另外两位艺术家一道组建了"新刻度"小组，而该小组如今依然作为中国当代艺术界的灯塔稳固地矗立着。"新刻度"小组是一个为基于无对象的艺术试验提供的集体平台，这些试验以自创的分析、方法及量化形式对世界展开调查。小组存在于 1988 至 1995 年，为当时当代艺术实践中盛行的理性论述做出了不可磨灭的贡献。这些论述将逻辑和分析引入到艺术当中，并消除了在艺术中人为的和感情的因素。主要针对过去数十年间艺术界的浮夸风及革命现实主义，意义深远。

从上世纪九十年代早期开始，顾德新不断地接到大量来自国际展览的创作邀请，而他的创作地点则极其复杂，从教堂、赌场直到前军事基地一应俱全。在他所有的项目中，当地的历史和自然一直是他概念中的主要考虑之一，而在顾德新对于易腐烂素材的表现中，生命的毁灭、无法忍受的场景和腐烂毁坏的气味仍然占据首要位置。在他的作品《2005 年 11 月 26 日》（2005 年）中，他将三大块猪

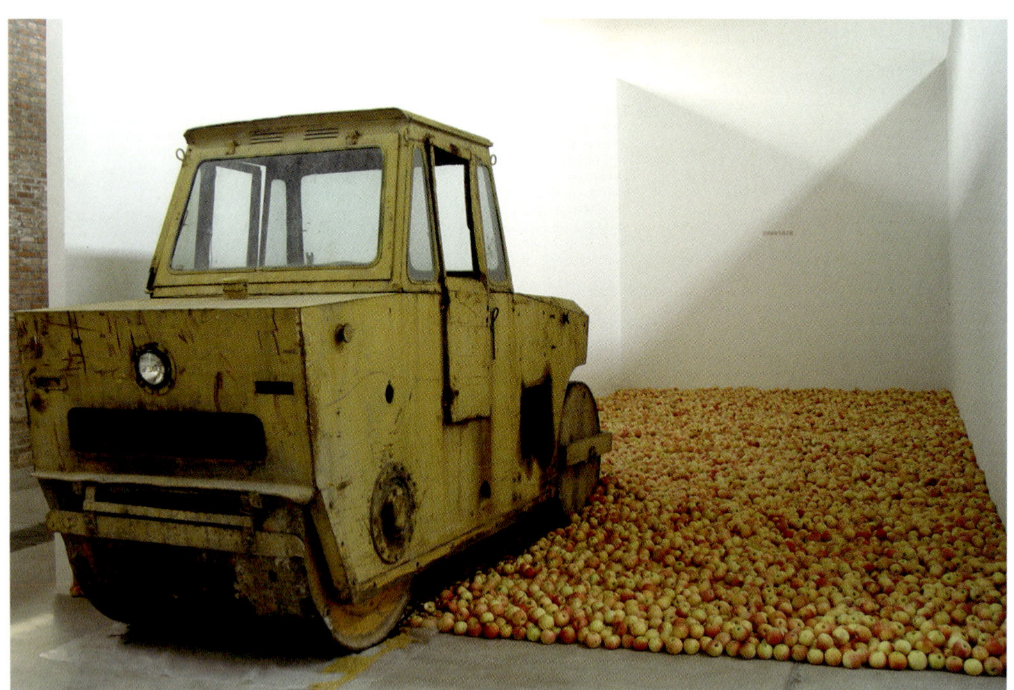

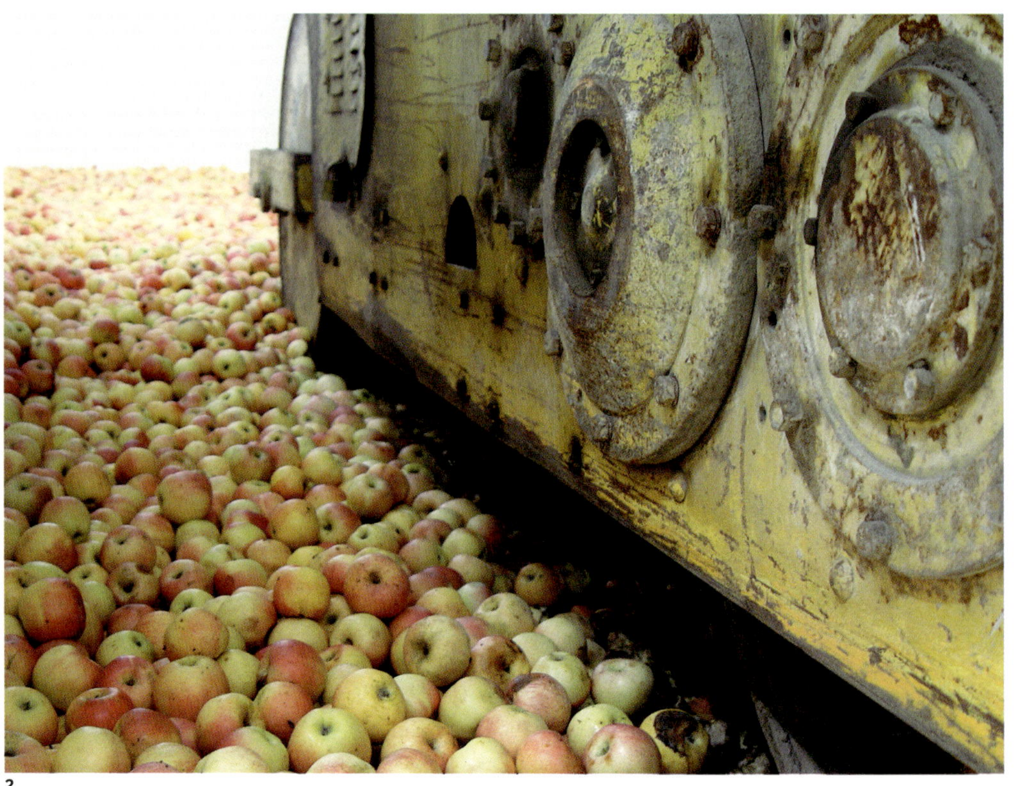

2

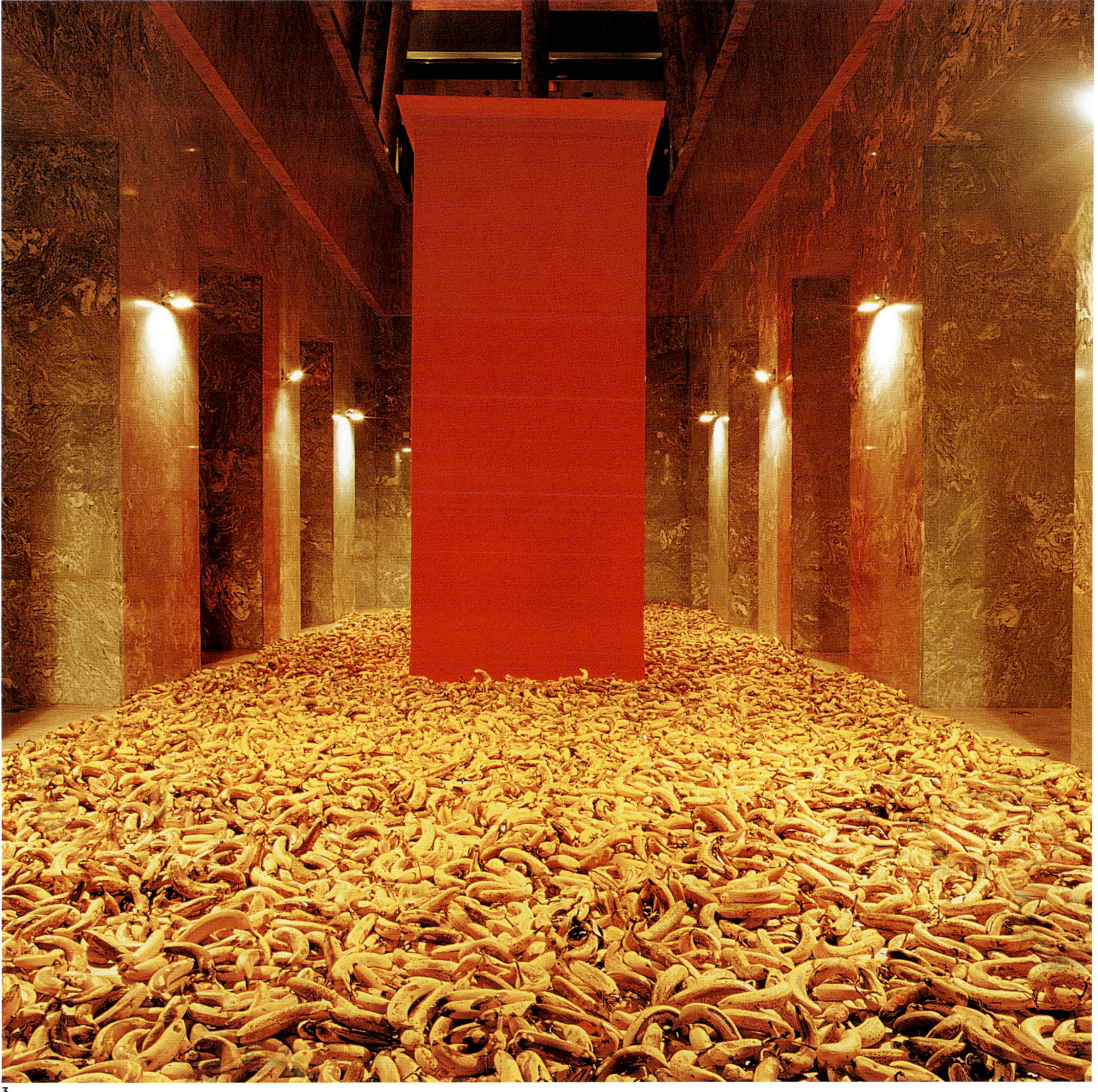

3

4

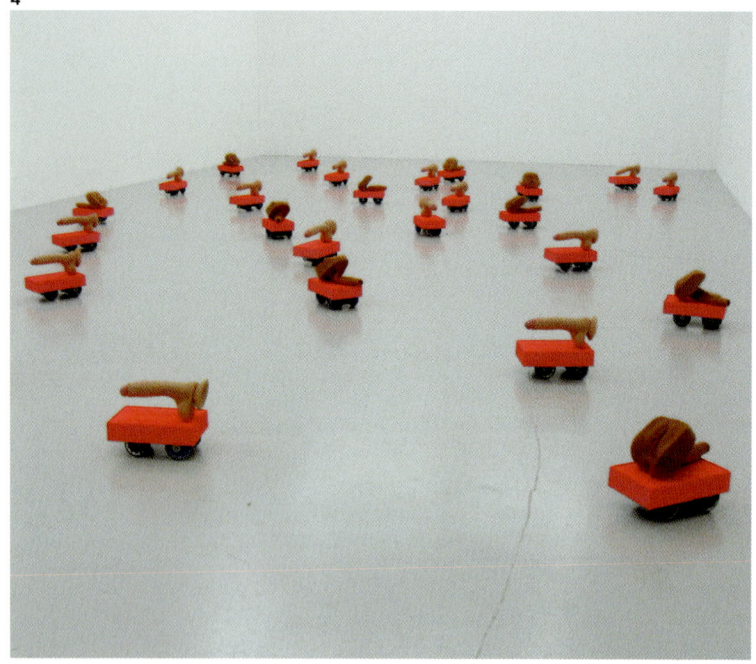

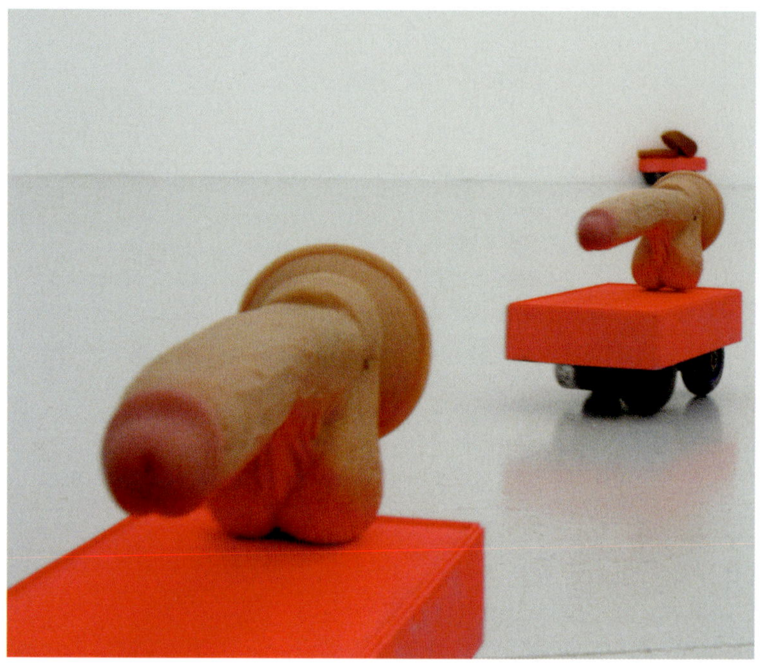

the history and nature of the location has always been one of the primary concerns for his conception, while the perish of life and the unbearable sights and smells of decay and destruction continue to take the central stage in Gu's plays on perishable materials. In his work "November 26, 2005" (2005), he soaked three big trucks of meat in a pool of perfume and let them grow moldy with time. This mixing of two incompatible smells was revolting and embodied the paradox of life that the artist reveals with foresight and a right dose of sarcasm.

In works where there were no flesh or fresh fruits, Gu substitutes with singing toy figures or sex toys on motors, which are all powered by battery that runs out eventually. The passage of time is a crucial element in his works, which are all named after the date of making, a sensible format without revealing too much interpretation of the work from the artist himself. In fact, as a rule, the artist refuses to give any interview or interpretation for any of his work.

Casinos oder ehemaligen Militärstützpunkten. Und bei all seinen Projekten bezog Gu stets die Geschichte und das Wesen der jeweiligen Lokalität als wesentlichen Gesichtspunkt in seine Konzeption mit ein. Parallel dazu stehen das Versiegen des Lebens und die oft unerträglichen Ansichten und Gerüche von Verwesung und Zerstörung weiterhin im Mittelpunkt seiner spielerischen Arbeiten mit verderblichen Materialien. Für „November 26, 2005" (2005) lud er drei Lkw-Ladungen Fleisch in ein Becken voller Parfüm und ließ sie darin vor sich hinmodern. Das abstoßende Gemisch aus zwei unvereinbaren Gerüchen verkörpert für ihn das Paradox des Lebens, das er immer wieder mit gehörigem Sarkasmus aufzeigt.

Bei Arbeiten, die ohne Fleisch und Obst auskommen, verwendet Gu singende Spielzeugfiguren oder motorisierte Sexspielzeuge – alle von Batterien angetrieben, die irgendwann ihren Geist aufgeben. Das Verstreichen der Zeit ist ein entscheidendes Element in Gus Werken, die als Titel nur ihr Entstehungsdatum tragen – ein sinnvoller Kunstgriff, der kaum etwas über die Deutung des Werks durch den Künstler selbst preisgibt. Und konsequent weigert sich Gu Dexin, Interviews zu geben oder Interpretationen zu seinen Arbeiten zu liefern.

肉浸入香水池中并让其随时间腐烂发臭。两种相反的味道混合在一起令人作呕，传达出艺术家通过远见和恰到好处的讽刺所揭示的生命悖论。在那些没有肉和新鲜水果的作品里，顾德新用歌能唱歌的玩具人物或电动性玩具取而代之，均由电池供电并且电力最终将用完。时间的流逝是其作品中的一个关键元素。他总是在作品完成后为作品命名，而且自己并不对作品进行太多的解释，这无疑是种明智的方式。事实上，他通常拒绝对自己的任何作品做出评价或解释。

Carol Lu

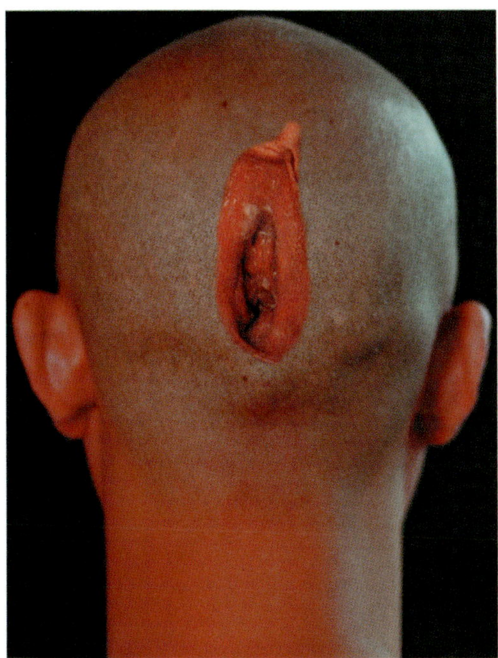

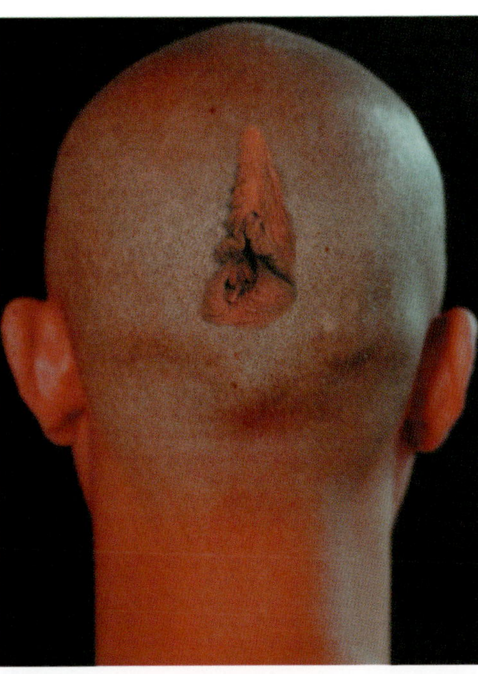

1 ***30th March 2007**, 2007*
Steel, sound device, beacon device, engine, oil paint (installation view)
Stahl, Geräuschvorrichtung, Leuchtturmanlage, Motor, Ölanstrich (Installationsansicht)
《2007年3月30日》，钢材，音响设备，灯塔照明设备，电动机，油漆

2 ***2nd September 2006**, 2006*
Bulldozer, apples, wood (installation view)
Bulldozer, Äpfel, Holz (Installationsansicht)
《2006年9月2日》2006年，压路机，苹果.，木材，（装置图）

3 ***5th March 2005**, 2005*
Bananas, wood, oil paint, stainless steel, notebook computer, glass, golden frame, picture (installation view)
Bananen, Holz, Ölfarbe, Edelstahl, Notebook, Glas, Goldrahmen, Bild (Installationsansicht)
《2005年3月5日》2005年，香蕉，木材，油漆，不锈钢，苹果，钢材。笔记本电脑。玻璃，金色画框，手捏肉照片（装置图/细节）

4 ***4th March 2006**, 2006*
Genitalia, electric toy car, wood (installation view)
Genitalien, elektrisches Spielzeugauto, Holz (Installationsansicht)
《2006年3月4日》2006年，性工具. 电动玩具车. 木材（装置图）

5 ***30th October 1999**, 1999*
Computer synthesis picture, mixed media
Computerbild, mixed media
《1999年10月30日》1999年 电脑合成图片，金色床，木材，地毯，塑料，性工具，电动机，金色画框，照明设备

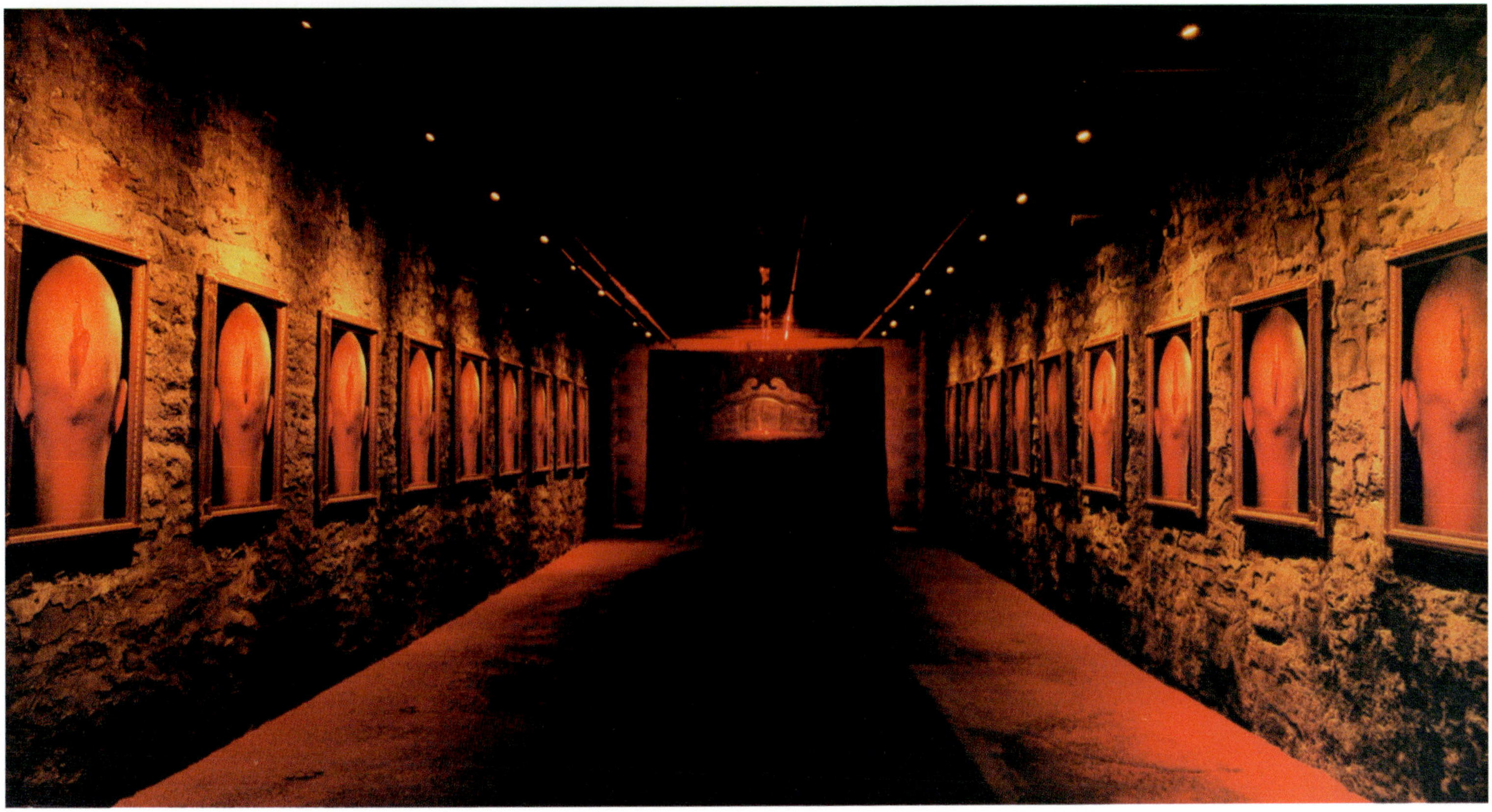

5

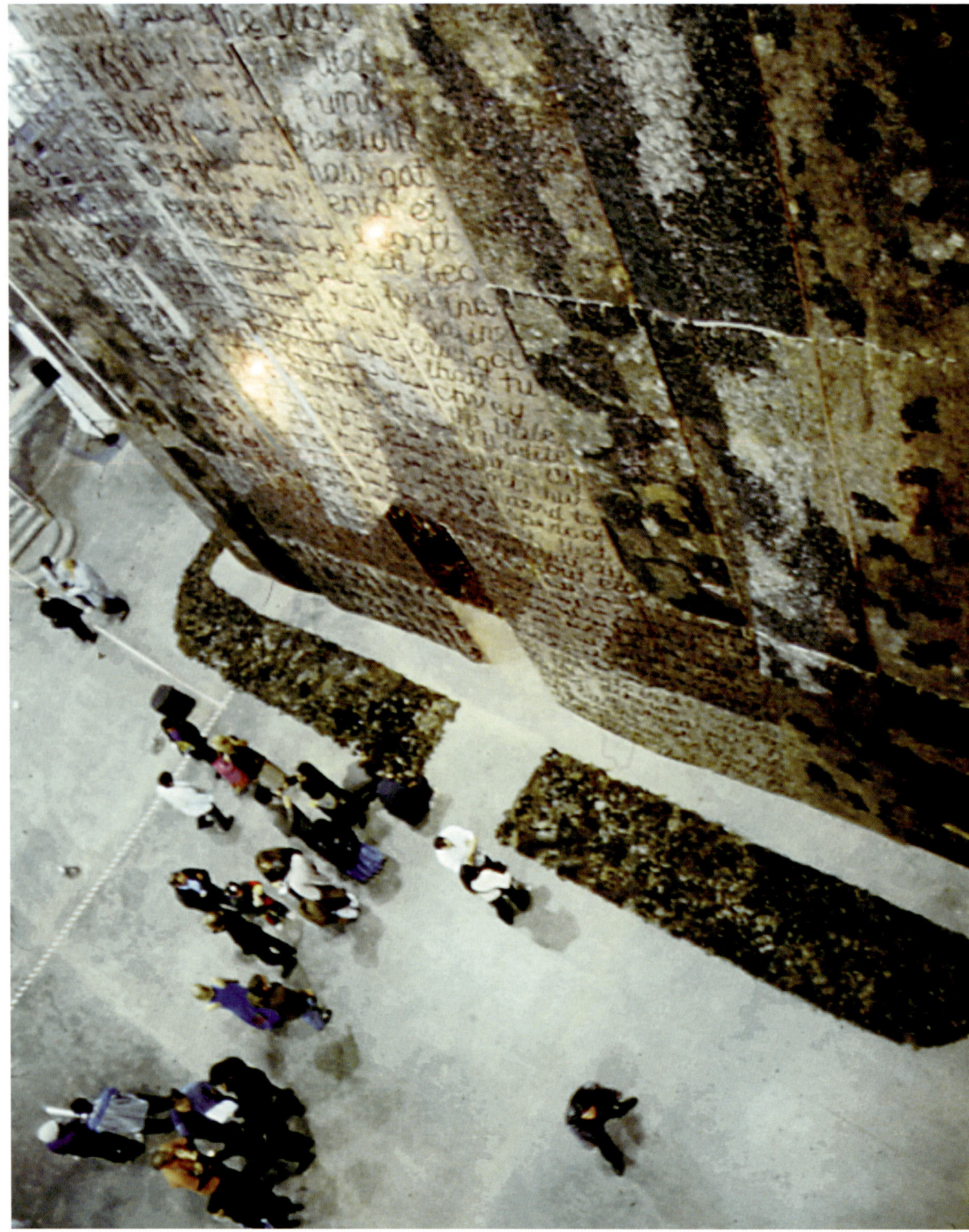

1

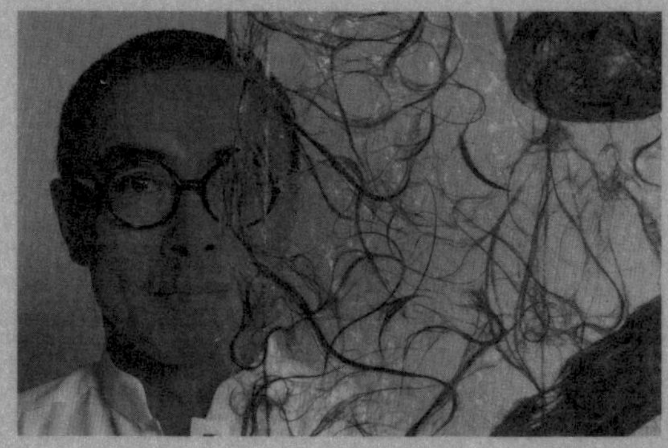

"I'm not interested in direct political issues at all. I absorb most current political issues, fashions and trends, but only use those elements in my art that are of eternal significance to the human spirit, and are, therefore, timeless."

„Ich interessiere mich überhaupt nicht für tagespolitische Fragen. Ich nehme die meisten aktuellen politischen Themen, Moden und Trends auf, verarbeite in meiner Kunst aber nur die Elemente, die von ewiger Bedeutung für den menschlichen Geist und damit zeitlos sind."

"我对直接的政治问题丝毫没有兴趣。我从最新的政治问题、风尚及潮流中吸取元素，但仅仅是将这些对于人类精神领域而言具有永恒的意义的元素运用到我的艺术中；因此这些元素是永恒的。"

Born in 1955 in Shanghai, China. Lives and works between New York, NY, USA, and Shanghai
Geboren 1955 in Shanghai, China. Lebt und arbeitet in New York, NY, USA, und Shanghai
1955 年出生于上海，居住工作往返于纽约和上海之间

Selected exhibitions / **Ausgewählte Ausstellungen** / 所选展览

2000 "United Nations – Great Wall of the Millennium", Art Center, New York State University, Buffalo, NY, USA
2001 "Wenda Gu's Wedding Life", Haus der Kulturen der Welt, Berlin, Germany
"Translation & Intersection: Wenda Gu's New Installations", National Gallery of Australia, Canberra, Australia
2003/04 "Wenda Gu: Middle Kingdom to Biological Millennium", University of North Texas, Denton; Kansas Art Institute, Kansas City; Institute of Contemporary Art, Maine College of Art, Portland, USA
2005–07 "Mahjong – Chinesische Gegenwartskunst aus der Sammlung Sigg", Kunstmuseum Bern, Berne, Switzerland; Hamburger Kunsthalle, Hamburg, Germany; Museum der Moderne, Salzburg, Austria

2000年 《联合国—世纪长城》美国布法罗，纽约州立大学艺术中心
2001年 《古文达的婚姻生活：德国》德国柏林，世界文化宫
《翻译和再翻译：谷文达的新装置》澳大利亚堪培拉，澳大利亚国家美术馆
2003/04年 《谷文达—从中央帝国到生物时代》美国，北德克萨斯大学，2003年，美国堪萨斯市，堪萨斯艺术学院，2003年，缅因艺术学院当代艺术系2004年
2005–07年 《麻将》西克中国当代艺术收藏展 伯尔尼美术馆 瑞士；汉堡美术馆 汉堡 德国；
萨尔茨保现代美术馆 奥地利

Selected publications / **Ausgewählte Publikationen** / 所选著作

Michael Kampen O'Riley: "Art Beyond the West", London 2001
Peter Osborne: "Conceptual Art", London 2002
Mark H. C. Bessire: "Wenda Gu – Art from Middle Kingdom to Biological Millennium", Cambridge 2003
Janet Marquardt, Stephen Eskilson: "Frames of Reference – Art, History, and the World", London 2004

Kampen O'Riley, Michael（著）：《西方以外的艺术》伦敦2001年
Osborne, Peter（著）：《概念艺术》伦敦2002年
Bessire, Mark H. C.（著）：《谷文达—从中央帝国到生物时代的艺术》剑桥2003 年
Marquardt, Janet/Eskilson, Stephen（著）：《参考框架—艺术、历史及世界》伦敦2004年

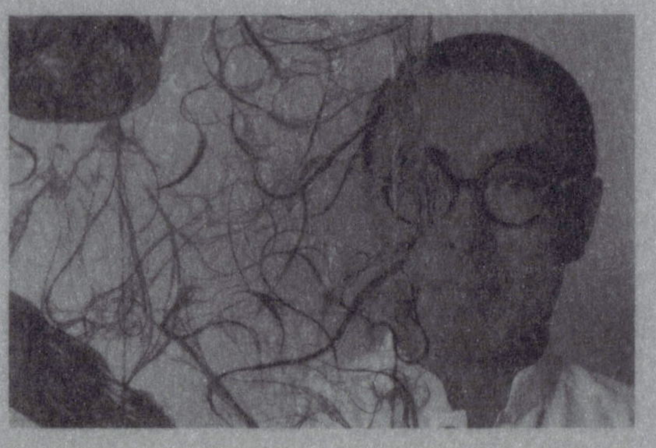

"I'm not interested in direct political issues at all. I absorb most current political issues, fashions and trends, but only use those elements in my art that are of eternal significance to the human spirit, and are, therefore, timeless."

„Ich interessiere mich überhaupt nicht für tagespolitische Fragen. Ich nehme die meisten aktuellen politischen Themen, Moden und Trends auf, verarbeite in meiner Kunst aber nur die Elemente, die von ewiger Bedeutung für den menschlichen Geist und damit zeitlos sind."

"我对直接的政治问题丝毫没有兴趣。我从最新的政治问题，风尚及潮流中吸取元素，但仅仅是将这些对于人类精神领域而言具有永恒的意义的元素运用到我的艺术中：因此这些元素是永恒的。"

Born in 1955 in Shanghai, China. Lives and works between New York, NY, USA, and Shanghai
Geboren 1955 in Shanghai, China. Lebt und arbeitet in New York, NY, USA, und Shanghai
1955 年出生于上海，居住工作往返于纽约和上海之间

Selected exhibitions / Ausgewählte Ausstellungen / 所选展览

2000 "United Nations - Great Wall of the Millennium", Art Center, New York State University, Buffalo, NY, USA
2001 "Wenda Gu's Wedding Life", Haus der Kulturen der Welt, Berlin, Germany
"Translation & Intersection: Wenda Gu's New Installations", National Gallery of Australia, Canberra, Australia
2003/04 "Wenda Gu: Middle Kingdom to Biological Millennium", University of North Texas, Denton; Kansas Art Institute, Kansas City; Institute of Contemporary Art, Maine College of Art, Portland, USA
2005-07 "Mahjong - Chinesische Gegenwartskunst aus der Sammlung Sigg", Kunstmuseum Bern, Berne, Switzerland; Hamburger Kunsthalle, Hamburg, Germany; Museum der Moderne, Salzburg, Austria

2000年 《联合国—世纪长城》美国布法罗，纽约州立大学艺术中心
2001年 《古文达的婚姻生活：德国》德国柏林，世界文化宫
《翻译和再翻译：谷文达的新装置》澳大利亚堪培拉，澳大利亚国家美术馆
2003/04年 《谷文达—从中央帝国到生物时代》美国，北德克萨斯大学，2003年，美国堪萨斯市，堪萨斯艺术学院，2003年，缅因艺术学院当代艺术系2004年
2005-07年 《麻将》西克中国当代艺术收藏展 伯尔尼美术馆 瑞士；汉堡美术馆 汉堡 德国；萨尔茨堡现代美术馆 奥地利

Selected publications / Ausgewählte Publikationen / 所选著作

Michael Kampen O'Riley: "Art Beyond the West", London 2001
Peter Osborne: "Conceptual Art", London 2002
Mark H. C. Bessire: "Wenda Gu - Art from Middle Kingdom to Biological Millennium", Cambridge 2003
Janet Marquardt, Stephen Eskilson: "Frames of Reference - Art, History, and the World", London 2004

Kampen O'Riley, Michael（著）：《西方以外的艺术》伦敦2001年
Osborne, Peter（著）：《概念艺术》伦敦2002年
Bessire, Mark H. C.（著）：《谷文达—从中央帝国到生物时代的艺术》剑桥2003 年
Marquardt, Janet/Eskilson, Stephen（著）：《参考框架—艺术，历史及世界》伦敦2004年

GU WENDA 谷文达

[ku uənda]

Gu Wenda was a pioneer of New Art in China. He was awarded his master's degree in 1981 from the ink painting department of Zhejiang Academy, where he continued to teach until 1987. At Zhejiang Academy, he discovered western philosophy, which had a surprising impact upon his aesthetic strategy. The result was an on-going series of astonishing experiments using ink on paper, but on a scale never seen before seen in China. This coalition of calligraphy and brush painting remains an icon of the age in which it was created, radically avant-garde in spirit. Gu Wenda built his international career on the special foundation of his approach of western and Chinese philosophy.

Gu Wenda was never satisfied with obvious answers to the questions he posed, and after following the closure of his first solo show in Xi'an in 1986, he immediately accepted a visiting fellowship at the University of Minnesota (1989–1990). He devoted the first two years in the US to mastering English, and absorbing a wider range of theoretical debates. He returned to the studio with enthusiasm in 1991 to begin the project "Oedipus Refound", which took him almost three years to complete. This work revolved around the collection of women's sanitary towels and related stories from the women who supplied them.

Where calligraphy was a major element of his formative training, it was natural that language would present itself as a choice for the material content of a major work. This was "United Nations" (1993–2004), a series of large-scale installations formed of floor-to-ceiling sheets of human hair delicately sculpted into the form of myriad linguistic texts. It comprises ten separate site-specific works for Poland (1993), Italy and The Netherlands (1994), Israel and the US (1995), Sweden and Britain (1996), Taiwan, Hong Kong and Africa (1997), China and Canada (1998), Korea and France (2000), Australia (2001), with new projects in other parts of these countries in between and on to 2004. The use of hair proved extremely controversial, highlighting deep divisions at large in the world today that have little to do with nationality and everything to do with ethnic traits,

Gu Wenda war ein Pionier der Neuen Kunst in China. 1981 machte er seinen Abschluss am Fachbereich Tuschmalerei der Zhejiang Academy, wo er anschließend bis 1987 als Dozent tätig war. Dort entdeckte er auch die westliche Philosophie für sich – mit verblüffenden Auswirkungen auf seine weitere ästhetische Strategie. Das Ergebnis war eine fortlaufende Serie erstaunlicher Experimente mit Tusche auf Papier, allerdings in einem Maßstab, wie man ihn in China bis dahin nicht kannte. Diese Verbindung von Kalligraphie und Tafelmalerei bleibt mit ihrem radikal avantgardistischen Ansatz einzigartig in ihrer Entstehungszeit. Gu Wendas Annäherung an westliche und chinesische Philosophie bildet das besondere Fundament seiner internationalen Karriere.

Gu Wenda gab sich nie mit nahe liegenden Antworten auf die Fragen, die sich ihm stellten, zufrieden. Gleich nach seiner ersten Einzelausstellung in Xi'an 1986 nahm er das Angebot einer Gastprofessur an der University of Minnesota (1989/90) an. Seine ersten beiden Jahre in den USA verbrachte er damit, Englisch zu lernen und ein breites Spektrum theoretischer Debatten auf sich wirken zu lassen. 1991 kehrte er dann voll Tatkraft ins Atelier zurück, um das Projekt „Oedipus Refound" in Angriff zu nehmen. Bis zu dessen Vollendung vergingen fast drei Jahre. Es handelt sich dabei u. a. um eine Sammlung von Damenbinden, verknüpft mit den Geschichten jener Frauen, die sie ihm zur Verfügung stellten.

Die Kalligraphie hat in Gu Wendas Ausbildung eine wichtige Rolle gespielt. Und da lag es nahe, die Sprache selbst zum substanziellen Thema eines größeren Werks zu machen. So entstand unter dem Titel „United Nations" (1993–2004) eine Serie großformatiger Installationen aus raumhohen Vorhängen; kunstvoll aus Menschenhaar jedweder ethnischen Herkunft hergestellt, sind sie zugleich mit kryptischen Texten und Zeichen verknüpft. Das Projekt umfasst separate ortsspezifische Werke für Polen (1993), Italien und die Niederlande (1994), Israel und die USA (1995), Schweden und Großbritannien (1996), Taiwan, Hongkong und Afrika (1997), China und Kanada (1998), Korea und Frank-

谷文达是中国前卫艺术运动的领军人之一。他于1981年获得浙江美术学院（现中国美术学院）山水画专业硕士学位，并在该学院任教至 1987年。在浙江美院期间，他对西方哲学进行了探索，这段时期对其审美取向产生了巨大的影响。由此成就了仍在持续令人称奇的“试验水墨”作品系列，这些作品在中国以前所未有的规模出现。这种书法与国画的拼接如今仍然是其创作年代的一个时代标志，是一种彻头彻尾的前卫意识。这种拼接再加上其独特的中西方哲学性符号，奠定了谷文达国际性声誉事业的基石。

对于自己引发的问题，谷文达从不满足于表面答案。1986年，他在西安的第一个个人作品展闭幕后，立即接受了明尼苏达大学的访问学者的邀请（1989-1990年）。他将在美国的前两年投入到掌握英语学习中，同时吸收了广泛的理论。1991 年他带着满腔热情返回自己的工作室，并开始了一个耗时约三年的创作--《重新发现俄底浦斯》系列。该主题围绕着对妇女的卫生巾征集及发生在提供这些卫生巾的妇女身上的故事。

书法是谷文达所接受传统培训中的主要元素，因此语言便自然而然的成为了其一份主要作品的素材，这件作品便是《联合国》（1993-2004年）。该作品是一系列的大型装置，由从天花板到地板的床单上精细地盘成无数的语言文字的人类头发所构成。《联合国》包含十件独立针对当地而作的作品，分别是波兰（1993年）、意大利及荷兰（1994年）、以色列及美国（两件）（1995年）、瑞典及英国（1996年）、台湾、香港及非洲（1997年）、中国及加拿大（1998年）、韩国及法国（2000年），以及澳大利亚（2001年），同时也包括其间直至 2004年在这些国家的其他部分所创作的新作品。作品中人发的使用引发了激烈的争论，彰示了当今世界上普遍存在的文化深深鸿沟，这些鸿沟与国家无关，而与种族特性、宗教信仰、文化礼仪及传统信奉息息相关。《联合国》试图彰

2

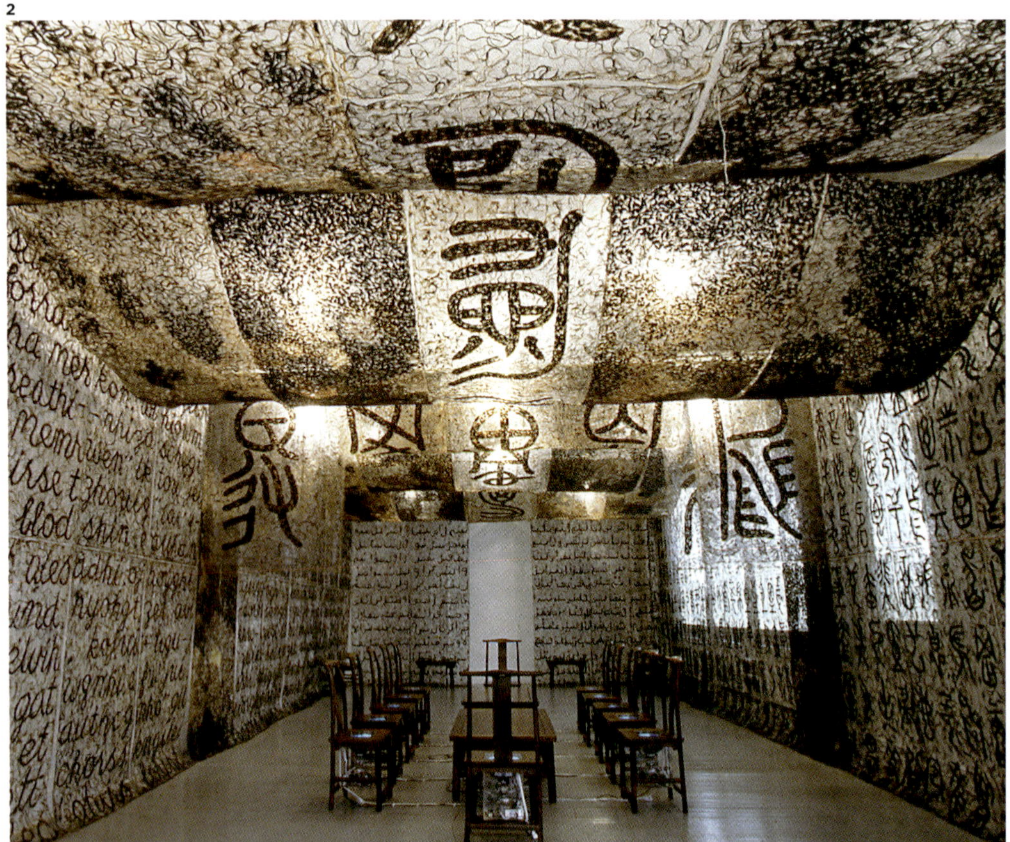

3

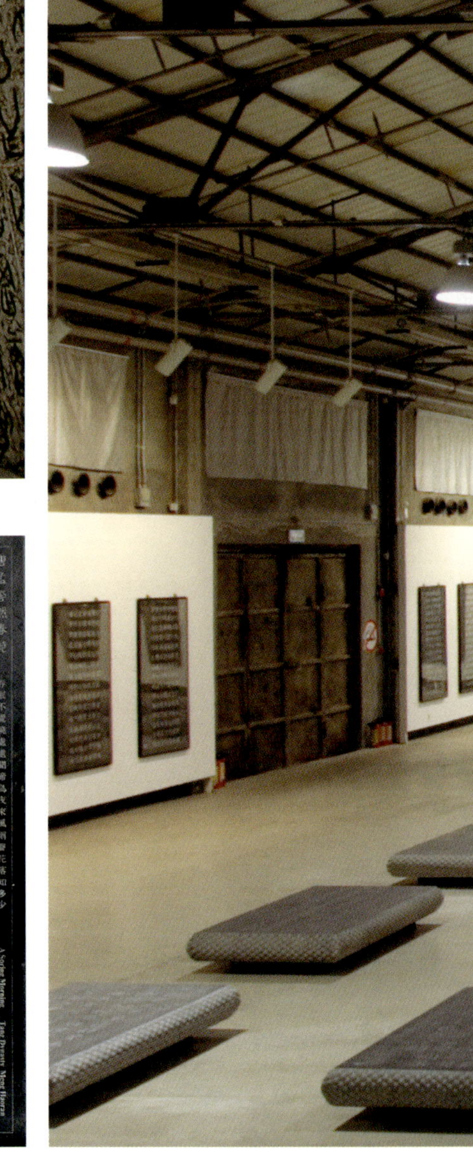

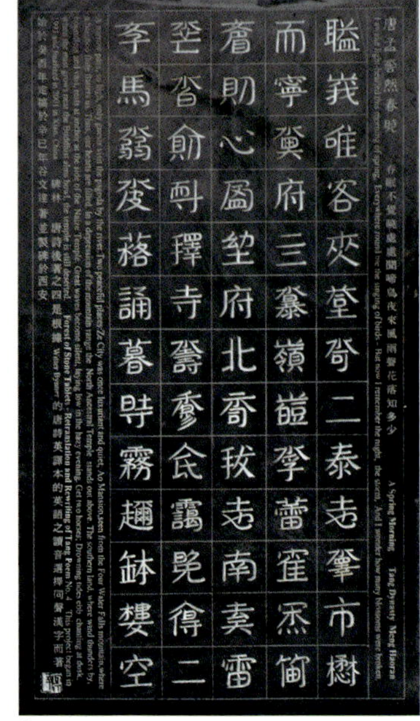

4

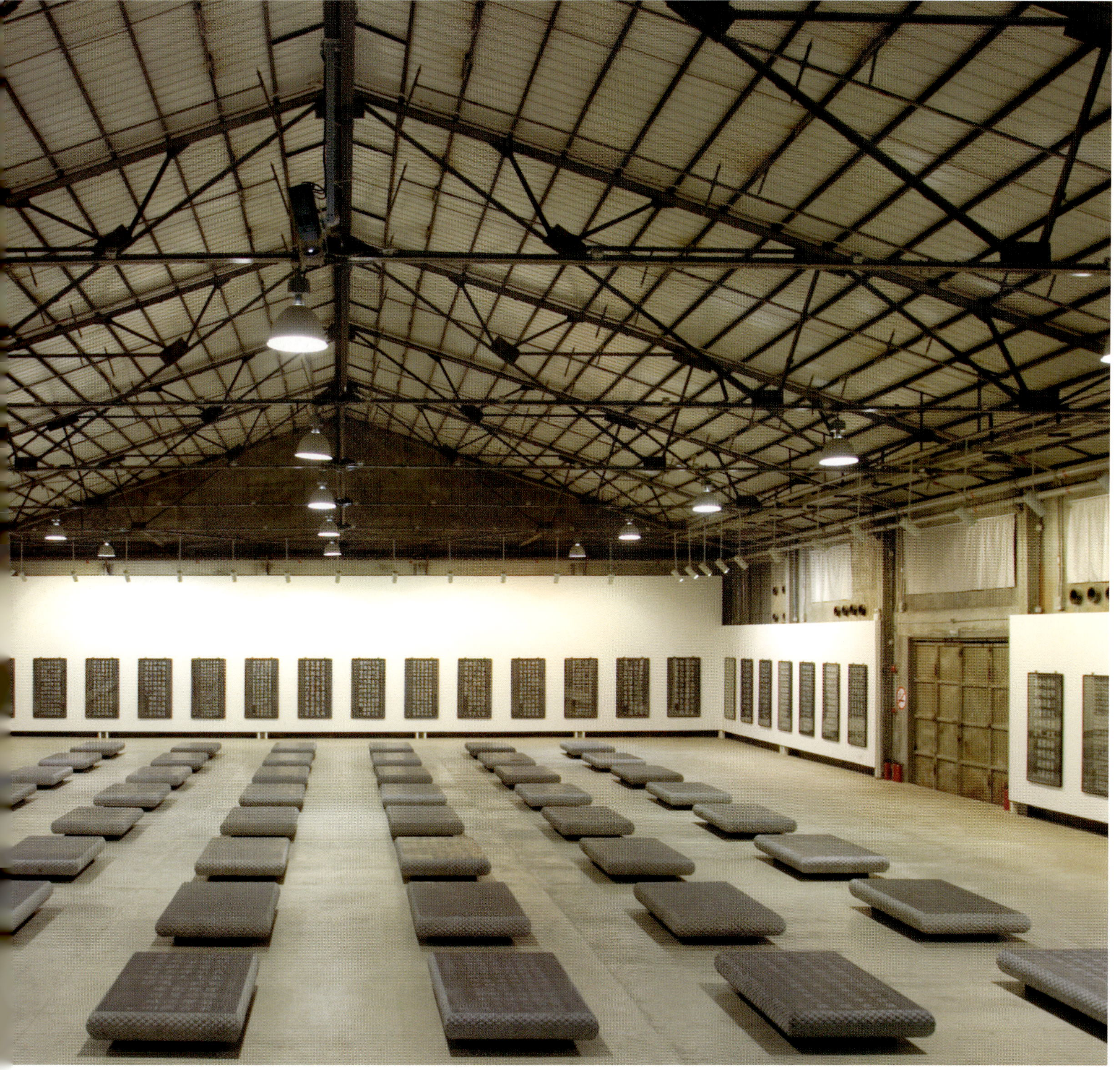

5

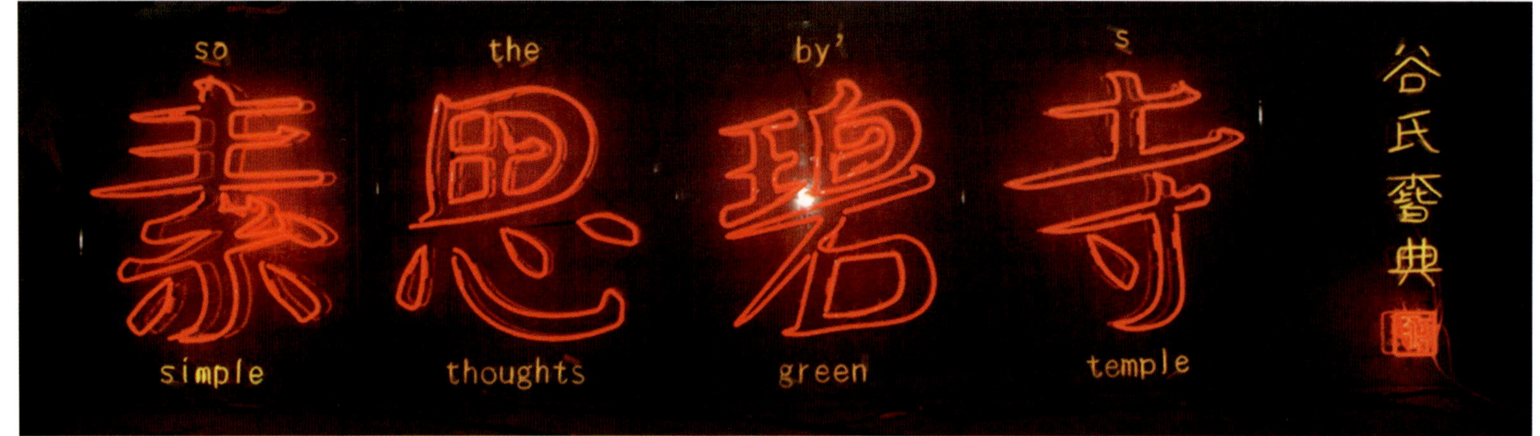

religious faiths, cultural rituals and traditional beliefs. "United Nations" attempted to highlight universal issues of identity in the context of globalisation, and to look at the nature of that globalisation, its motivating forces and effects.

Simultaneously, from 1993, Gu Wenda implemented work on a second monumental project. This major endeavour is the twelve-year process of creating "Forest of Stone Steles – Retranslation and Rewriting of Tang Dynasty Poems", where a complex round of aural and aliteral translations were carved on each of fifty magnificent "jade king" steles. This word game is a complex conundrum for a non-Chinese audience, which has little or no knowledge of the way in which the translation of Chinese characters is open to manipulation and compromise. Gu Wenda substitutes a conventional visual read of meaning with an unconventional focus on the multiplicity of possible characters – and the meaning of these – suggested by the pronunciation alone. Here he demonstrates how cultural relativism has been applied to readings of Chinese culture, and how in every single culture, language, written as spoken, embodies the specific cultural characteristics so entirely as to define us.

These were not the only projects to occupy Gu Wenda in recent years. The process of producing these monumental projects prompted offshoots from the ideas described above. "Ink Alchemy" (2000–2003) perfected a technique for producing a rich permanent ink from powdered Chinese hair, whilst "Tea Alchemy" (1999–2001) transformed green tea leaves into sheets of paper for ink painting.

reich (2000) sowie Australien (2001), wobei bis 2004 noch weitere Arbeiten entstanden, die sich auf jeweils andere Regionen dieser Länder beziehen. Mit seiner Verwendung von „internationalem" Menschenhaar löste Gu Wenda heftige Kontroversen aus – was ein Schlaglicht auf die tiefen Gräben innerhalb der modernen Welt wirft, die wenig mit Nationalitäten, dafür aber sehr viel mit ethnischen Besonderheiten, Glauben, kulturellen Ritualen und traditionellen Haltungen zu tun haben. „United Nations" war ein Versuch, allgemeingültige Identitätsfragen im Kontext der Globalisierung zu beleuchten und das Wesen dieser Globalisierung, ihre Triebkräfte und Wirkungen, genauer zu betrachten.

Gleichzeitig arbeitete Gu Wenda ab 1993 an einem zweiten monumentalen Projekt, dem „Forest of Stone Steles – Retranslation and Rewriting of Tang Dynasty Poems". In einem zwölfjährigen Arbeitsprozess meißelte Gu einen komplexen Zyklus akustischer und schriftloser Rückübersetzungen von ins Englische übertragenen Tang-Poemen in 50 prachtvolle „Jadekönig"-Stelen. Die gemeißelten Wortspiele sind eine harte Nuss für ein nichtchinesisches Publikum, das wenig oder nichts darüber weiß, wie stark die Übersetzung chinesischer Schriftzeichen Manipulationen und Kompromissen unterworfen sein kann. An die Stelle der konventionellen Lesung nach der eindimensionalen Bedeutung der Zeichen setzt Gu Wenda die Vielzahl möglicher Bedeutungen, die sich allein aus der Aussprache ergeben. Er demonstriert damit, wie ein gewisser kultureller Relativismus bei der Interpretation der chinesischen Kultur zum Tragen gekommen ist – und in jeder Kultur verkörpert die Sprache, ob geschrieben oder gesprochen, die spezifischen kulturellen Besonderheiten so vollständig, dass sie uns geradezu definiert.

Gu Wenda war in all diesen Jahren ungemein produktiv. Die Arbeit an den genannten Großprojekten brachte verschiedene Ableger hervor. Für „Ink Alchemy" (2000–2003) stellte er farbsatte dauerhafte Tusche aus pulverisiertem chinesischem Haar her, und für „Tea Alchemy" (1999–2001) verwandelte er grüne Teeblätter in Papierbögen für die Tuschemalerei.

示全球化有关身份普遍的问题，并试图看到全球化的本质、驱动力以及影响。

与此同时，自 1993年起，谷文达还着手于另一代表作的创作 -- 他将十二年的努力投入到《碑林・唐诗后著》的创作中。五十首唐诗复杂的音译及意译的中英对译文本被分别雕刻到五十块“墨玉王”青石碑上。这个文字游戏对于中国人以外的观众而言是个难解之谜，鉴于他们对中文字符在翻译过程中的处理及折衷方式知之甚少或根本一无所知。谷文达摒弃了传统读文知意的阅读方式，而代之以另一种非传统的强调字符可能多样性的阅读方式以及字符的含义，仅由发音所联想到的含义。他借此作品论证了如何将文化相对论运用到中国文化的读物中，以及在每种单一文化中书面语言及口头语言是如何将特定的文化特性完全地传达出来的，正如语言定位我们本身那样。

谷文达近年来的作品不仅于此。创作这些代表作的过程同时也激发了源于上述观念的一些分支作品的创意。《墨炼金术》（2000-2003年）完善了一种技术，以中国人的头发粉末为原料制成一种饱满的墨汁；而《茶炼金术》（1999-2001年）则是将绿茶茶叶制成水墨画使用的宣纸。

Karen Smith

6

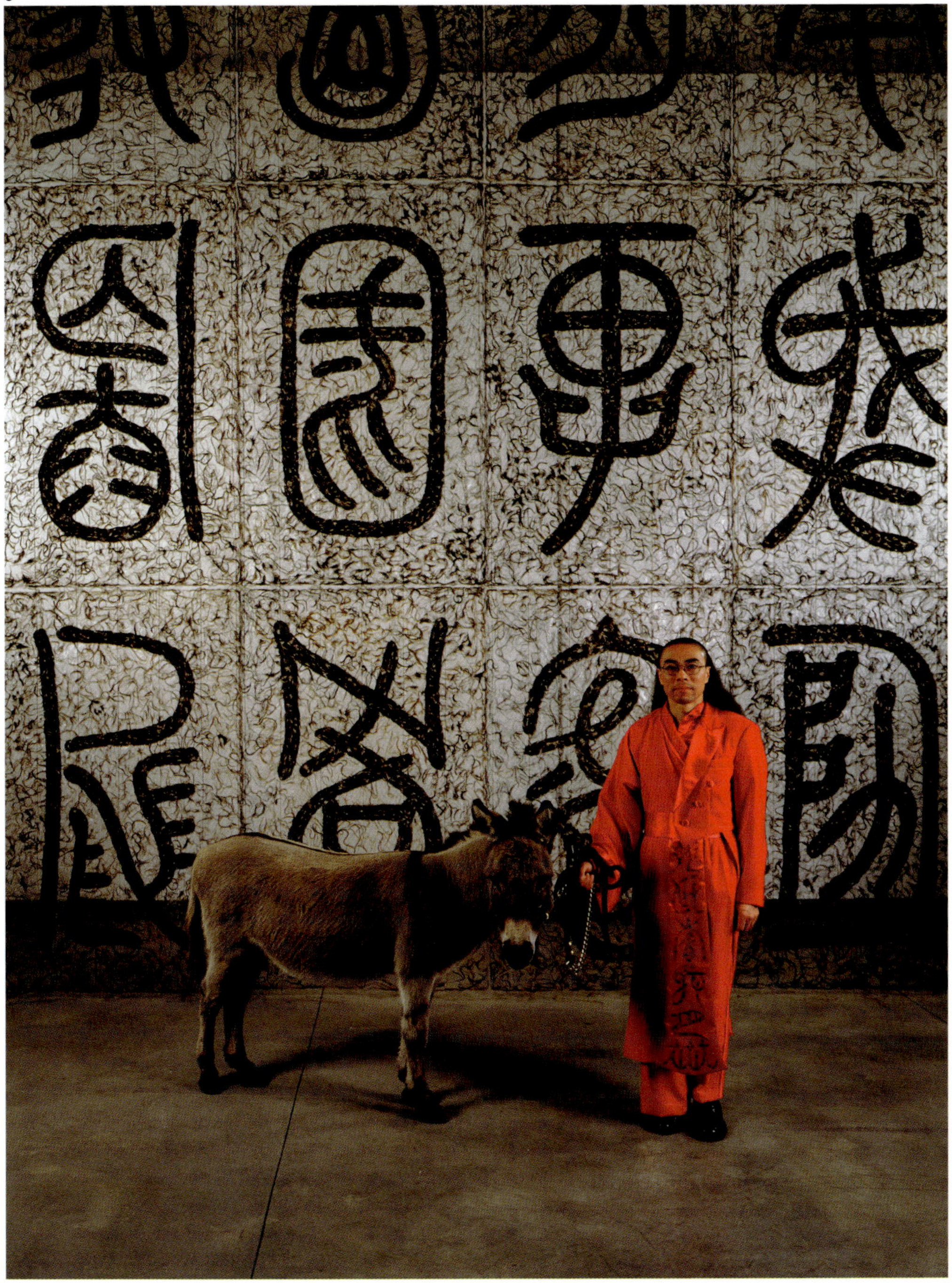

7

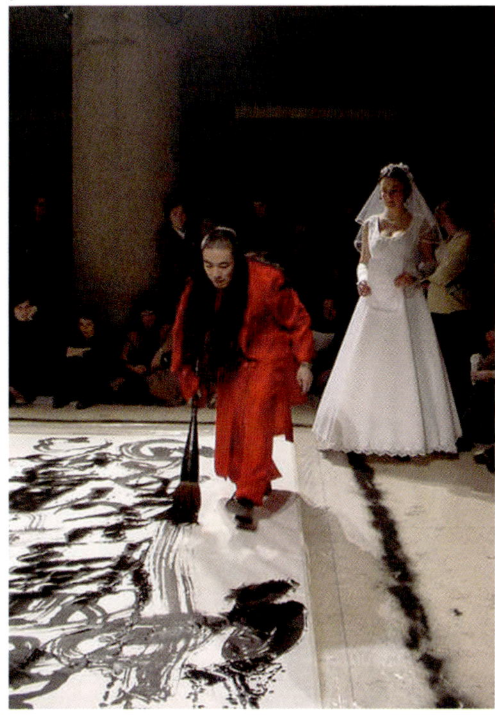

1 ***United Nations – Africa Monument: The Praying Wall of the World**, 1997*
Installation view, 2nd Johannesburg Biennial
Installationsansicht, 2. Johannesburg Biennale
《联合国---非洲纪念碑：祈祷之墙》1997年，装置实景

2 ***Forest of Stone Steles No. 4**, 1999*
Stone, 190 x 120 x 20 cm; Stein, 190 x 120 x 20 cm
《碑林--No. 4》1999年，石质，190 x 120 x 20 cm

3 ***Forest of Stone Steles – Retranslation and Rewriting of Tang Dynasty Poems**, 1993–2005*
Installation view; Installationsansicht
《碑林-唐诗后著》1993-2005年，装置实景

4 ***United Nations – China Monument: Temple of Heaven**, 1997/98*
Installation with screens of human hair, 1587 x 396 x 609 cm
Installation aus Menschenhaar, 1587 x 396 x 609 cm
《联合国--中国纪念碑：天坛》1997/98年，发幕装置，1587 x 396 x 609 cm

5 ***Cultural Transference – Sotheby's**, 2006*
Installation, 150 x 500 cm
Installation, 150 x 500 cm
《文化迁移 - 苏富比》2006年，装置，150 x 500 cm

6 ***Confucius' Diary**, 2006*
Performance, Vancouver
Performance, Vancouver
《孔子日记》2006年，表演，温哥华

7 ***Wenda Gu's Marriage Life #4**, 2001*
Performance, Haus der Kulturen der Welt, Berlin
Performance, Haus der Kulturen der Welt, Berlin
《谷文达的婚姻生活#4》2001年，表演，世界文化宫，柏林

柔和的主调容易让 Mr. Hong 进入宁静的沉思中

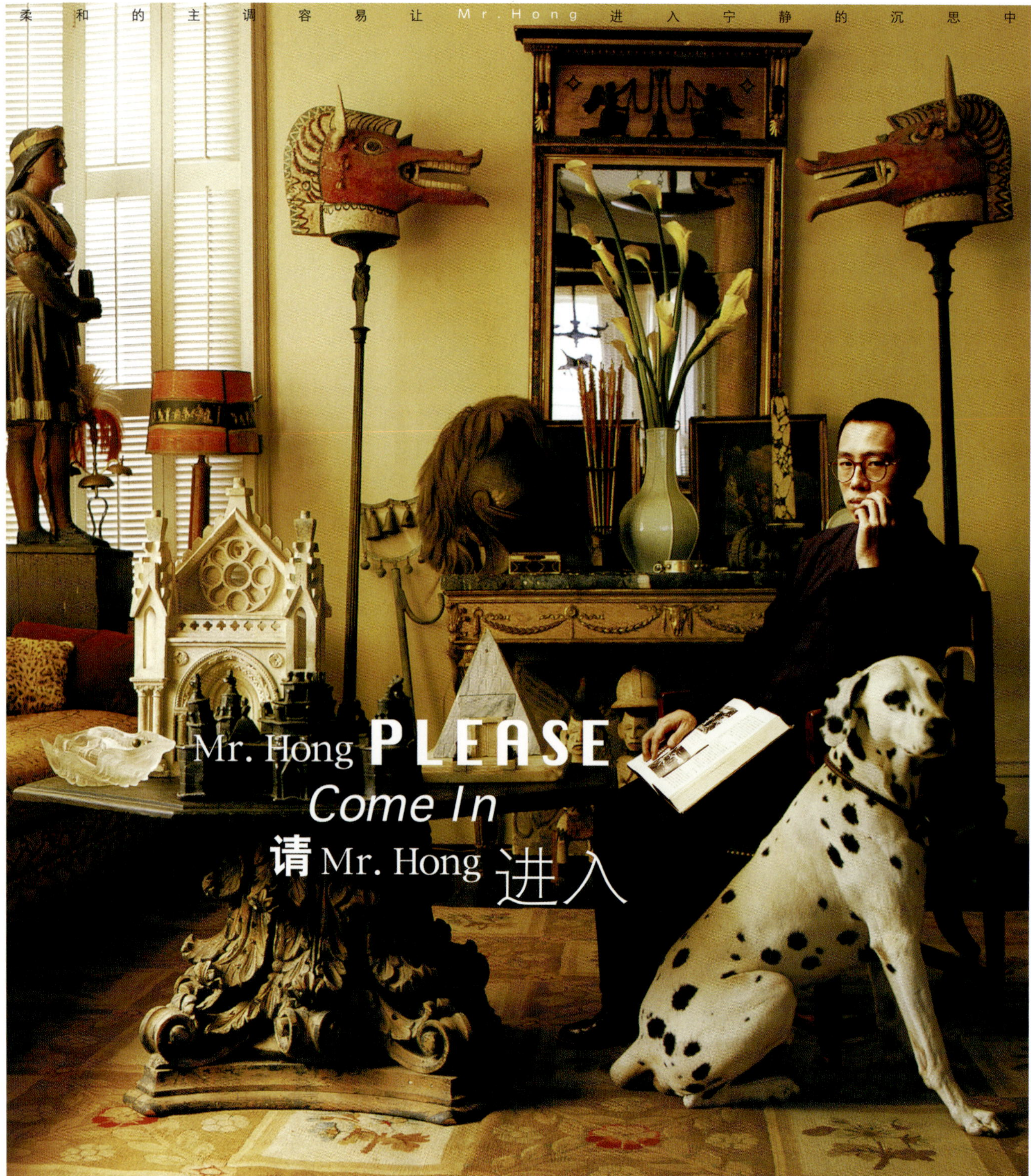

Mr. Hong PLEASE Come In

请 Mr. Hong 进入

1

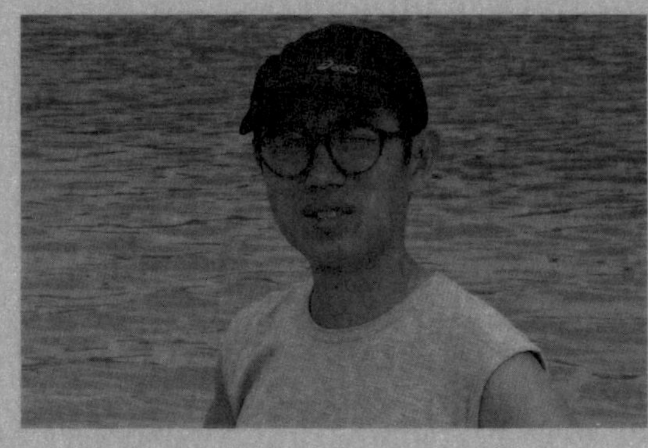

"I question the relationship between individual and collective identity, which conjures the expression 'We are what we consume, and what we consume makes us unique.'"

„Ich stelle die Frage nach dem Zusammenhang zwischen individueller und kollektiver Identität und komme zu dem Schluss: ‚Wir sind, was wir konsumieren, und was wir konsumieren, macht uns einzigartig.' "

"我质疑个人与集体身份之间的关系，这种关系总是让我想起这样一句话：'我们就是我们所消费的东西，我们所消费的东西使我们区别于他人。'"

Born in 1964 in Beijing, China. Lives and works in Beijing
Geboren 1964 in Peking, China. Lebt und arbeitet in Peking
1964 年出生于北京，中国。居住工作在北京

Selected exhibitions **/ Ausgewählte Ausstellungen /** 所选展览

2000 "Inside Out: New Chinese Art", Asia Society/P.S.1 Contemporary Art Center, New York, NY, USA
Shanghai Biennial, Shanghai Art Museum, Shanghai, China
2002 First Guangzhou Triennial, Guangdong Museum of Art, Guangzhou, China
2003 "Rencontres d'Arles", Arles, France
2004–07 "Between Past and Future: New Photography and Video from China", International Center of Photography, New York, NY, USA (travelling exhibition)
2006 "Since 2000: Printmaking Now", The Museum of Modern Art, New York, NY, USA
2007 "Passion for Art", Sammlung Essl, Klosterneuburg, Austria

2000年 《蜕变与突破：中国新艺术展》，美国纽约，亚洲协会美术馆 P.S.1 当代艺术中心，旧金山现代艺术博物馆
《海上，上海—上海双年展》中国，上海美术馆
2002年 《第一届广州三年展》，中国广州，广东美术馆
2003年 《洪浩作品在阿尔勒国际摄影节》，法国阿尔勒
2004–07年 《过去与未来之间—中国新影像展》国际摄影中心 纽约 美国（巡回展）
2006年 《自 2000 年起：当代版画》美国纽约，现代艺术博物馆
2007年 《艺术激情》Sammlung Essl美术博物馆，克罗斯特纽堡，奥地利

Selected publications **/ Ausgewählte Publikationen /** 所选著作

Ai Weiwei (ed.): "Chinese Artists: Texts and Interviews – Chinese Contemporary Art Awards", Hong Kong 2002
Zhu Qi (ed.): "Chinese Avant-Garde Photography Since 1990", Changsha 2004
Christina Yu: "Knowledge and Illusion: On Hong Hao's Recent Work", in: "Yishu", 5, No. 2, Taipei 2006
Zhang Zhaohui: "Our Stuff – On Hong Hao's New Work in Derailing Becomes Trendy", Changsha 2006

艾未未(编者):《中国艺术家：文本和采访 – 中国当代艺术褒奖》香港2002 出版
朱其（编者):《1990 年以来的中国先锋摄影》长沙2004 年出版
Yu, Christina（著）:《知识与幻想：洪浩的近期作品》在《艺术》第 5 卷，2006 年 6 月第 2 号，台北
张朝晖（著）:《我们的东西—从洪浩的新作说起》在《当叛逆沦为时尚》2006 年，湖南美术出版社

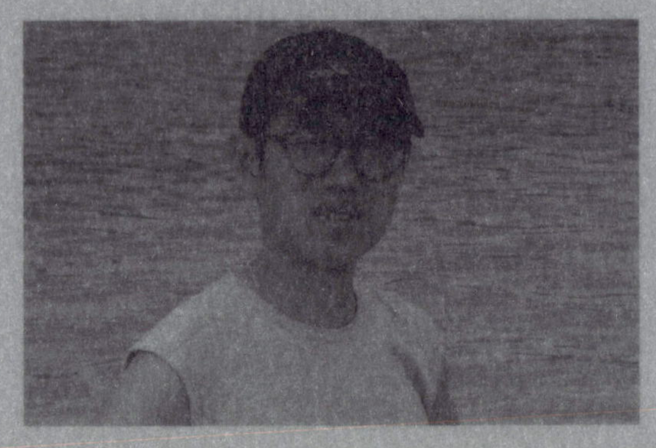

"I question the relationship between individual and collective identity, which conjures the expression 'We are what we consume, and what we consume makes us unique.'"

„Ich stelle die Frage nach dem Zusammenhang zwischen individueller und kollektiver Identität und komme zu dem Schluss: ‚Wir sind, was wir konsumieren, und was wir konsumieren, macht uns einzigartig.'"

"我质疑个人与集体身份之间的关系，这种关系总是让我想起这样一句话：'我们就是我们所消费的东西，我们所消费的东西使我们区别于他人。'"

Born in 1964 in Beijing, China. Lives and works in Beijing
Geboren 1964 in Peking, China. Lebt und arbeitet in Peking
1964 年出生于北京，中国。居住工作在北京

Selected exhibitions / Ausgewählte Ausstellungen / 所选展览

2000	"Inside Out: New Chinese Art", Asia Society/P.S.1 Contemporary Art Center, New York, NY, USA
	Shanghai Biennial, Shanghai Art Museum, Shanghai, China
2002	First Guangzhou Triennial, Guangdong Museum of Art, Guangzhou, China
2003	"Rencontres d'Arles", Arles, France
2004-07	"Between Past and Future: New Photography and Video from China", International Center of Photography, New York, NY, USA (travelling exhibition)
2006	"Since 2000: Printmaking Now", The Museum of Modern Art, New York, NY, USA
2007	"Passion for Art", Sammlung Essl, Klosterneuburg, Austria

2000年	《蜕变与突破：中国新艺术展》，美国纽约，亚洲协会美术馆 P.S.1 当代艺术中心，旧金山现代艺术博物馆
	《海上，上海—上海双年展》中国，上海美术馆
2002年	《第一届广州三年展》，中国广州，广东美术馆
2003年	《洪浩作品在阿尔勒国际摄影节》，法国阿尔勒
2004-07年	《过去与未来之间—中国新影像展》国际摄影中心 纽约 美国（巡回展）
2006年	《自 2000 年起：当代版画》美国纽约，现代艺术博物馆
2007年	《艺术激情》Sammlung Essl美术博物馆，克罗斯特纽堡，奥地利

Selected publications / Ausgewählte Publikationen / 所选著作

Ai Weiwei (ed.): "Chinese Artists: Texts and Interviews - Chinese Contemporary Art Awards", Hong Kong 2002
Zhu Qi (ed.): "Chinese Avant-Garde Photography Since 1990", Changsha 2004
Christina Yu: "Knowledge and Illusion: On Hong Hao's Recent Work", in: "Yishu", 5, No. 2, Taipei 2006
Zhang Zhaohui: "Our Stuff - On Hong Hao's New Work in Derailing Becomes Trendy", Changsha 2006

艾未未（编著）：《中国艺术家：文本和采访 — 中国当代艺术奖》香港2002 出版
朱其（编著）：《1990 年以来的中国先锋摄影》长沙2004 年出版
Yu, Christina（著）：《知识与幻想：洪浩的近期作品》在《艺术》第 5 卷，2006 年 6 月第 2 号，台北
张朝晖（著）：《我们的东西—从洪浩的新作说起》在《当叛逆沦为时尚》2006 年，湖南美术出版社

HONG HAO 洪浩

[xʊŋ xaʊ]

When Hong Hao graduated from the printmaking department of Beijing's Central Academy of Fine Arts in 1989, he recreated a silk-screen studio in his tiny apartment in the city centre. Hong Hao had a vision of printmaking that would occupy him for the next eight years: 31 individual leaves for a private encyclopaedia of Chinese cultural and socio-political history, including humorous takes on philosophy, ideology, medicine, and consumerism, as well as several revolutionary adaptations of cartographic world order. All was executed with meticulous attention to detail that today is a primary characteristic of his work.

In 1997, having put the final chapter of the encyclopaedia to bed, Hong Hao turned his attention to the tide of consumerism sweeping China. This was encouraging new individual aspirations pivoted on a range of exciting new social identities made possible by economic reform, in addition to a wealth of consumer items that were read as badges of success. Hong conducted this phase of expression using photography. First, he turned the lens upon himself in a series of kitsch quips at the vulgar excess of modern-day aspirations. Captions like "Mr. Hong, please come in" play implicitly to a nouveau elite eager to join the club.

From the late 1990s, Hong Hao supplemented satire with a degree of sobriety, now tackling the cultural misunderstanding between "China" and the "West". "The Tour Guide Series" (1999–2000) places Hong Hao in the principle role again; one familiar to all visitors who have taken package tours to China. The postcard picturesque compositions of happy foreigners at historic sites spotlight cultural attitudes of how China perceives itself; the image it seeks to project, and how it is perceived by the outside world. Hong Hao next applied this same philosophy to a series of photographic works that recreate famous classical paintings as contemporary records of similar journeys through the life of the times: yesteryear replaced by today.

Latterly, Hong Hao undertook a mapping of his own world in "My Things": a dazzling array of personal possessions

Nach seinem Abschluss am Fachbereich Grafik der Pekinger Central Academy of Fine Arts 1989 baute sich Hong Hao in seiner winzigen Wohnung im Stadtzentrum eine Seidensiebdruckerei nach. Er hatte eine druckgrafische Vision, die ihn die nächsten acht Jahre beschäftigen sollte: 31 Einzelblätter für seine persönliche Enzyklopädie der kulturellen und soziopolitischen Geschichte Chinas, mit humoristischen Interpretationen von Philosophie, Ideologie, Medizin und Konsumismus sowie einigen revolutionären Umstellungen der kartographischen Weltordnung. Das alles führte er mit einer pedantischen Detailgenauigkeit aus, die bis heute ein grundlegendes Charakteristikum seines Werks ist.

1997, nachdem das letzte Kapitel der Enzyklopädie unter Dach und Fach war, wandte Hong Hao seine Aufmerksamkeit der Konsumwelle zu, die China überschwemmte. Sie fördert individuelle Ambitionen, die sich um aufregend neue gesellschaftliche Identitäten drehen. Möglich wurde das alles durch wirtschaftliche Reformen und eine bis dahin unbekannte Flut von Konsumgütern, deren Besitz als Erfolgssymbol gilt. In dieser Phase wählte Hong Hao die Fotografie als Ausdrucksmittel. Zuerst richtete er die Linse auf sich selbst – in einer Reihe verkitschter Karikaturen der vulgären Exzesse zeitgenössischer Aufstiegsträume. Bildunterschriften wie „Mr. Hong please come in" wenden sich an eine neureiche Elite, die darauf brennt, dazuzugehören.

Ab den späten 1990er Jahren wurden Hong Haos Satiren deutlich ernsthafter – er wandte sich nun den kulturellen Missverständnissen zwischen China und dem Westen zu. In „The Tour Guide Series" (1999–2000) spielt er selbst wieder die Hauptrolle und zwar eine, die jedem, der je als Pauschaltourist in China unterwegs war, vertraut sein dürfte. Die pittoresk-postkartentauglichen Kompositionen mit fröhlichen Ausländern an historischen Schauplätzen beleuchten kulturelle Haltungen: Wie China sich selbst sieht, welches Bild es zu vermitteln sucht und wie es von der Außenwelt gesehen wird. Anschließend setzte Hong Hao diesen Impetus auch in eine Serie fotografischer Werke um, die berühmte klassische Gemälde als moderne Dokumente

毕业于北京的中央美术学院版画系院（1989年）后，洪浩在其位于市中心的小阁楼里布置了一间丝网版画工作室，拥有了一幅占据其人生随后八年的版画幻想：一部关于中国文化及社会政治史的三十一页的个人“藏经”，包括关于哲学、意识形态、医药及保护消费者利益运动的幽默的意见，以及将世界地图的顺序进行革命性的一些调整。所有的创作过程中都极为注重细节，而如今这也成为其作品的主要特点之一。

1997年，在结束“藏经”的最后一章以后，洪浩开始其注意力转移到了当时席卷中国的保护消费者利益运动上。经济改革使一类令人兴奋的崭新社会身份成为可能，同时大量的消费品被解读为成功的标识，这些都激发了一种新的个人欲望。洪浩使用摄影作为这一阶段的表达形式。首先，在一个戏谑讽刺作品系列中他将镜头对准了自己，对世俗中过度的欲望进行了讽刺。类似《洪先生请进》的标题含蓄地对渴望加入社交阶层的新近社会精英进行了调侃。

从九十年代后期开始，洪浩在其讽刺作品中加入了一定程度的清醒元素，如今则着眼于“中国”与“西方”之间的文化误解。《游行指南系列》再次将洪浩作为主演，所有曾经随团到中国旅游的人都不会对此感到陌生。开心的外国游客在历史景点上所构成的明信片式的独特风景集中显示了各种文化态度：中国对自身的认识，试图设计的形象，以及外部世界又是如何看到中国的。接着，洪浩又将相同的哲学运用到一个摄影作品系列中，作品通过不同时期的生活 -- 今天取代从前，将著名的传统绘画作品用当代相似旅程的记录进行再创作。

近来，洪浩在《我的东西》中采用了他自身世界的形态：眼花缭乱的排列着他不厌其烦的分类并罗列的个人用品--纸张、日常家用品、艺术书籍、《长征在潘家园》中所搜集的纪念品（潘家园是北京传说中的跳蚤市场）以及大量的货币合集，全部以 1:1

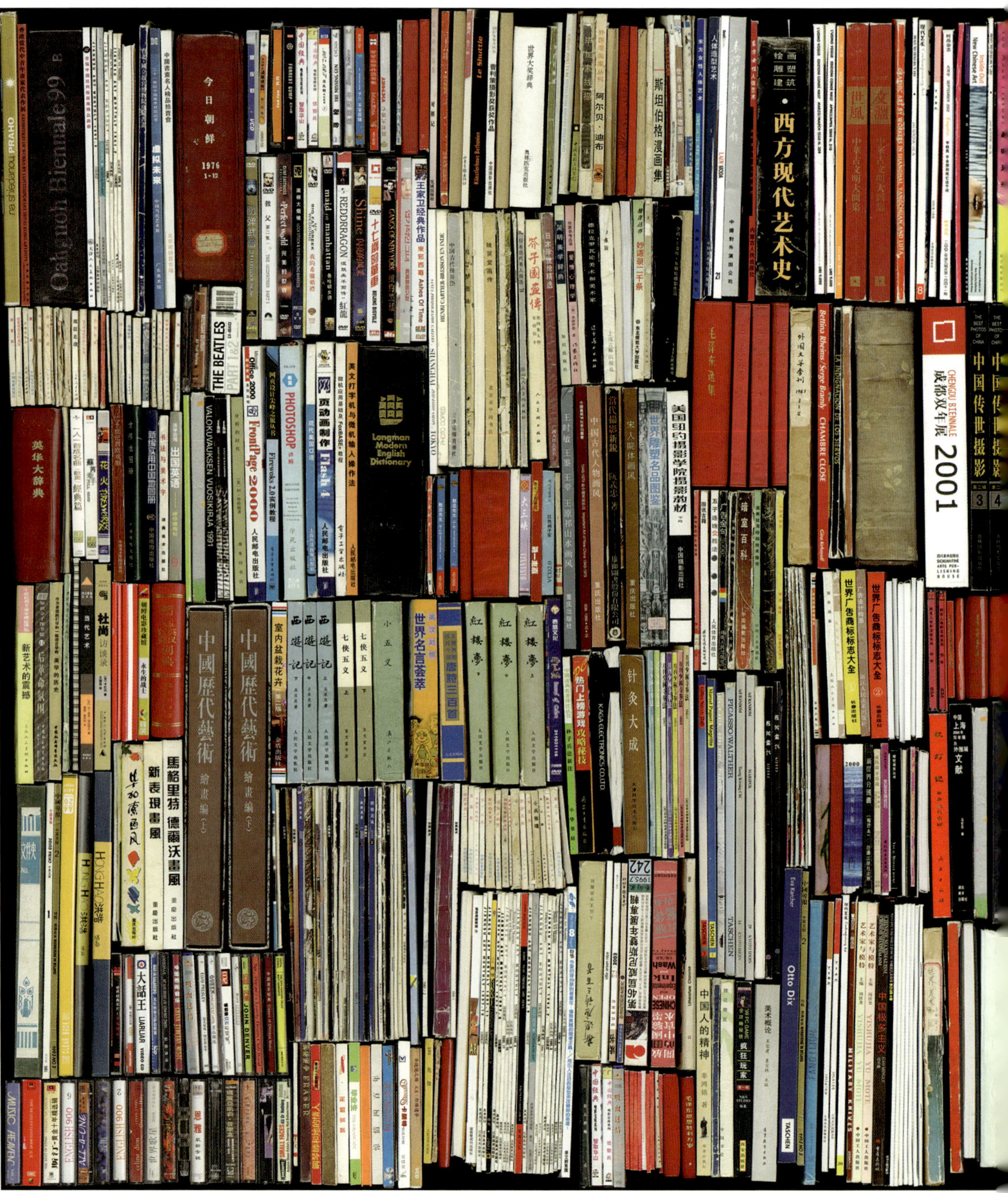

Oangnoh Biennale99
今日朝鲜 1976 1-12
西方现代艺术史
斯坦伯格漫画集
世界大笑辞典
芥子园画传
英华大辞典
THE BEATLES
PHOTOSHOP
FrontPage 2000
Longman Modern English Dictionary
VALOKUVAUKSEN VUOSIKIRJA 1991
世界雕塑名品图鉴
毛泽东选集
成都双年展 2001
CHENGDU BIENNALE
中国传世摄影
中國歷代藝術 繪畫編
西遊記
七俠五义
世界名言荟萃
紅樓夢
针灸大成
新表現畫風
馬格里特 德爾沃書風
大話王
JOHN DENVER
PICASSO/WALTHER
TASCHEN
Otto Dix
中国人的精神
美术概论
世界广告商标标志大全
MUSIC HEAVEN

2

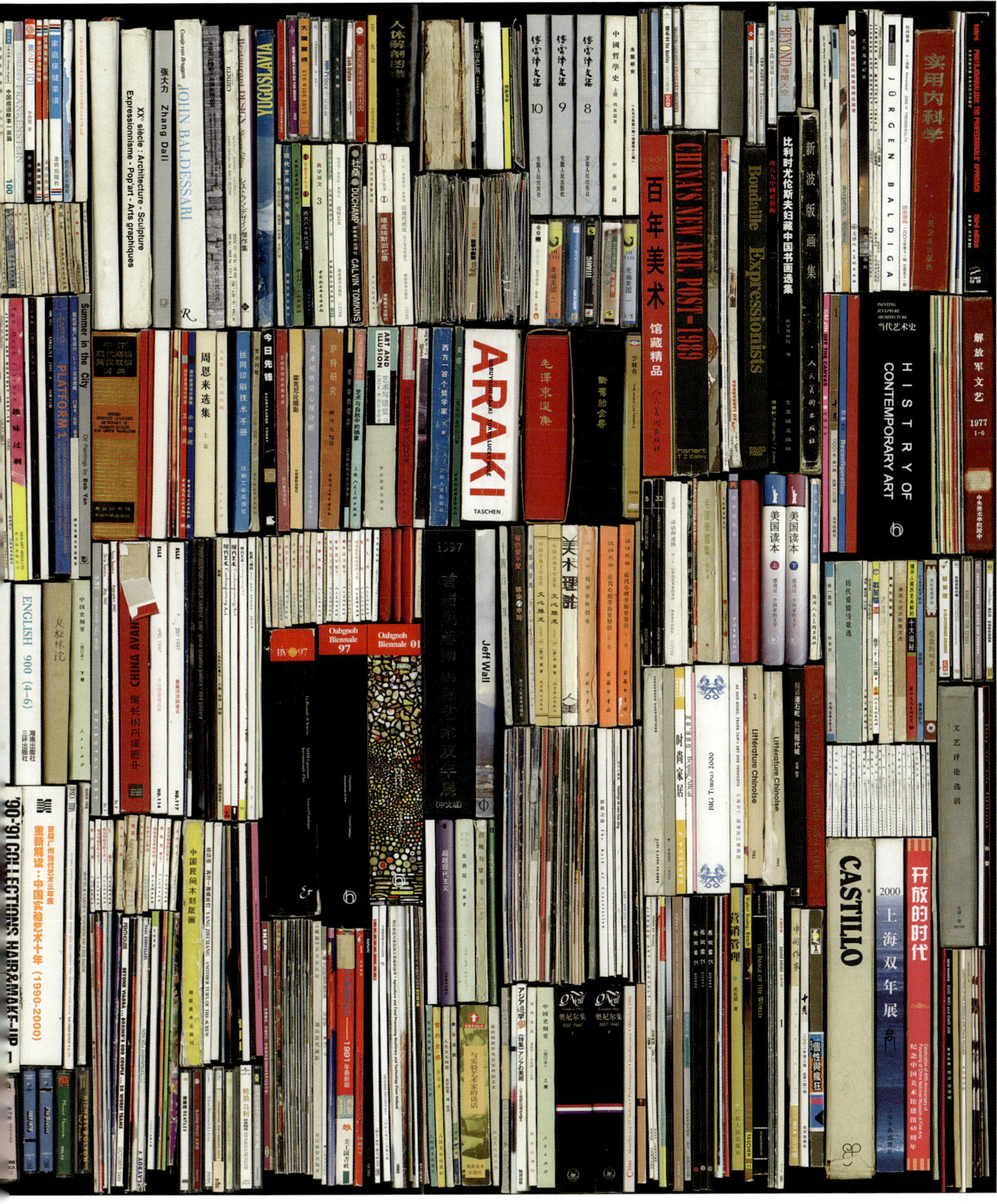
YUGOSLAVIA
JOHN BALDESSARI
张大力 Zhang Dali
XXe siècle : Architecture · Sculpture
Expressionnisme · Pop'art · Arts graphiques
人体解剖图谱
傅雷译文集 10
傅雷译文集 9
傅雷译文集 8
中国哲学史
DUCHAMP
CALVIN TOMKINS
百年美术 馆藏精品
CHINA'S NEW ART, POST-1989
Boudaille Expressionists
比利时尤伦斯夫妇藏中国书画选集
新波版画集
JÜRGEN BALDIGA
实用内科学
PHOTOJOURNALISM: THE PROFESSIONAL'S APPROACH
Summer in the City
PLATFORM 1
周恩来选集
今日先锋
萨特研究
ARAKI
TASCHEN
毛泽东选集
HISTORY OF CONTEMPORARY ART
当代艺术史
解放军文艺 1977
ENGLISH 900 (4-6)
CHINA AVANT
Oahgnoh Biennale 97
Oahgnoh Biennale 01
Jeff Wall
美术理论
美国读本
历代爱情诗歌选
时尚家居
Littérature Chinoise
文艺评论选辑
CASTILLO
2000 上海双年展
开放的时代
'90-'91 COLLECTIONS HAIR&MAKE-UP
重新解读：中国实验艺术十年（1990-2000）
中国民间木刻版画
超越现代主义
营销管理
中国史纲要
奥尼尔集

3

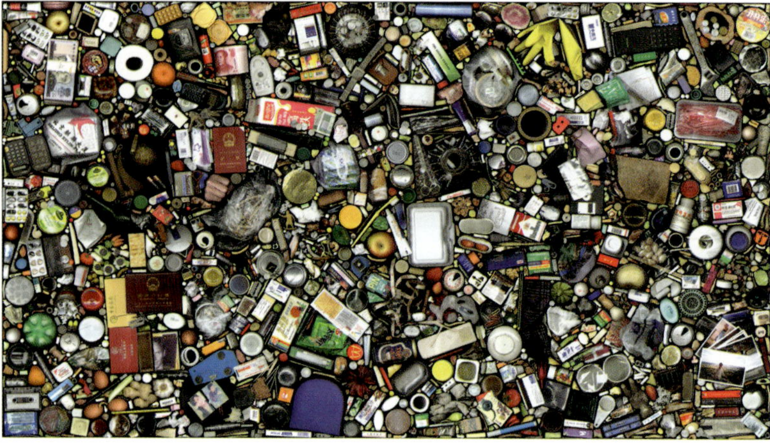

4

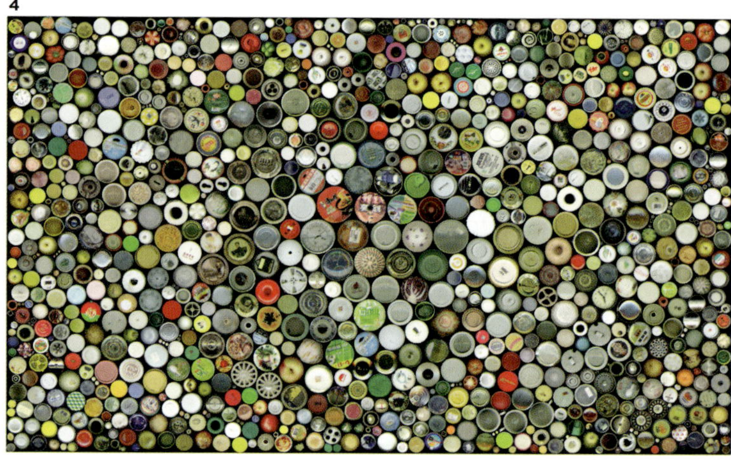

painstakingly categorised into batches – private papers; daily household items; art books; relics collected on expeditions in Panjiayuan (Beijing's legendary flea market), and a mass composite of currencies – all scanned on a 1:1 scale. "My Things" (2001–2006) takes on consumer culture from a delightfully non-partisan angle.

Hong Hao has collaborated on projects with conceptual artist Yan Lei. In 1997, using the alias Ielnay and Oahgnoh – their names spelt backwards – the pair applied Hong Hao's finely-tuned printing skills, to fabricating a letter from Kassel's Documenta office. They then sent a letter to hundreds of artists nationwide, outlining a forthcoming visit by Documenta curators. Documenta was then perceived as the apogee of international art events. The art world's excitement was as unrestrained as the rage that ensued when the prank was exposed. Ever alert to new phenomenon affecting the contemporary art world in China, in 2006, for a project commissioned by Taikang Life (Beijing), the artists negotiated a life insurance policy against the possibility of "crazed artistic self-harming" in the manner of van Gogh: a provocative send-up of all that the State once censured as the spiritually polluting traits of modern art.

von Reisen durch das Leben der Zeit nachstellen: Die Gegenwart nimmt den Platz der Vergangenheit ein.

Neuerdings hat sich Hong Hao an eine gründliche Inventarisierung seiner eigenen Welt gemacht: Mit „My Things" (2001–2006) präsentiert er eine überwältigende Sammlung persönlicher Besitztümer, die er säuberlich sortiert hat: in private Unterlagen, alltägliche Haushaltsgegenstände, Kunstbücher, Mitbringsel von Ausflügen nach Panjiayuan (Pekings legendärem Flohmarkt) und eine Sammlung verschiedener Währungen – alles im Maßstab 1:1 gescannt. Trotz der privaten Perspektive nähert sich „My Things" der Konsumkultur aus einem erfrischend unvoreingenommenen Blickwinkel.

Hong Hao realisierte auch gemeinsame Projekte mit dem Konzeptkünstler Yan Lei. 1997 machten die beiden sich unter den Künstlernamen Ielnay und Oahgnoh – ihre Namen rückwärts buchstabiert – Hong Haos hochentwickelte drucktechnische Fertigkeiten zunutze: Sie fälschten einen Brief des Kasseler Documenta-Büros und verschickten ihn landesweit an Hunderte von Künstlern, um ihnen einen bevorstehenden Besuch von Documenta-Kuratoren anzukündigen – wobei die Documenta als das Spitzenereignis des internationalen Kunstzirkus gilt. Die Aufregung in der Kunstwelt war ebenso groß wie der Zorn, der sich entlud, als der Streich aufflog. 2006 handelten die Künstler – stets offen für neue Phänomene, die Chinas zeitgenössische Kunstszene betreffen – für ein Projekt im Auftrag von Taikang Life (Peking) eine Lebensversicherungspolice für den Fall einer „Selbstverstümmelung in künstlerischer Umnachtung" à la van Gogh aus: eine provokative Parodie auf all das, was der Staat seinerzeit als moralisch verderblichen Einfluss der modernen Kunst zensierte.

的比例进行扫描。《我的东西》从一个令人愉悦的无党派视角表现了消费文化。

洪浩曾经与概念艺术家颜磊进行数次合作。1997年，他们以 Ielnay 和Oahgnoh（他们二人姓名拼音的逆序书写）名义，运用洪浩娴熟的版画技巧伪造了卡塞尔文献展的邀请信。他们接着向全国成百上千的艺术界人士发出信函，概述了文献展策划人即将进行的访问。文献展当时被当作遥远的国际艺术始建的代名词。当恶作剧被揭穿时，来自艺术界的愤怒和之前的兴奋一样不可遏制。藉着对影响当代中国艺术界的新现象永远的警惕，2006年，为了由泰康人寿（北京）所举办《一件作品》，二人协商了一种保险策略，为梵高式“疯狂艺术家的自残”的可能性进行保险：一种对过去被国家斥之为现代艺术的精神污点的挑悻讽刺。

Karen Smith

5

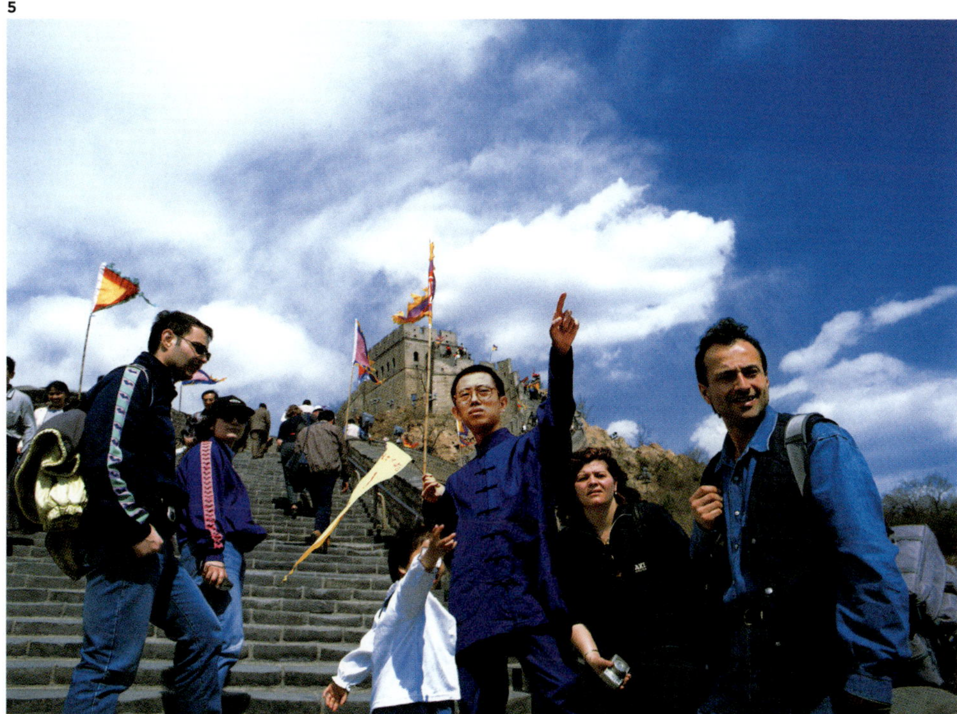

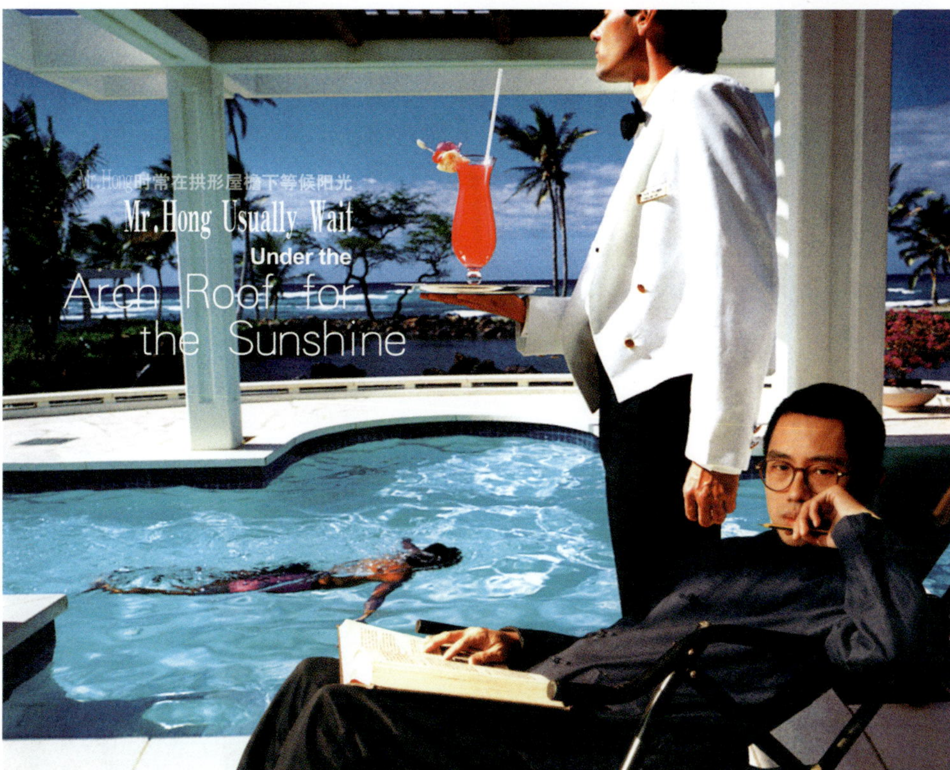

6

1 ***Mr. Hong please come in***, *1998*
Photograph, 138 x 120 cm
Fotografie, 138 x 120 cm
《洪先生请进》1998年, 摄影, 138 x 120 cm

2 ***My Things No. 7***, *2004*
Photograph, 120 x 210 cm
Fotografie, 120 x 210 cm
《我的东西 No. 7》2004年，摄影，120 x 210 cm

3 ***My Things No. 1***, *2001/02*
Photograph, 120 x 210 cm
Fotografie, 120 x 210 cm
《我的东西 No. 1》2001/02年, 摄影, 120 x 210 cm

4 ***My Things About Circle No. 3***, *2006*
Photograph, 165 x 270 cm
Fotografie, 165 x 270 cm
《我的东西 No. 3》2006, 摄影, 165 x 270 cm

5 ***The Great Wall***, *1999*
Photograph, 120 x 160 cm
Fotografie, 120 x 160 cm
《长城》1999年，摄影，120 x 160 cm

6 ***Mr. Hong usually waits under the arch roof for the sunshine***, *1998*
Photograph, 120 x 150 cm
Fotografie, 120 x 150 cm
《洪先生时常在拱形屋檐下等候光照》1998, 摄影, 120 x 150 cm

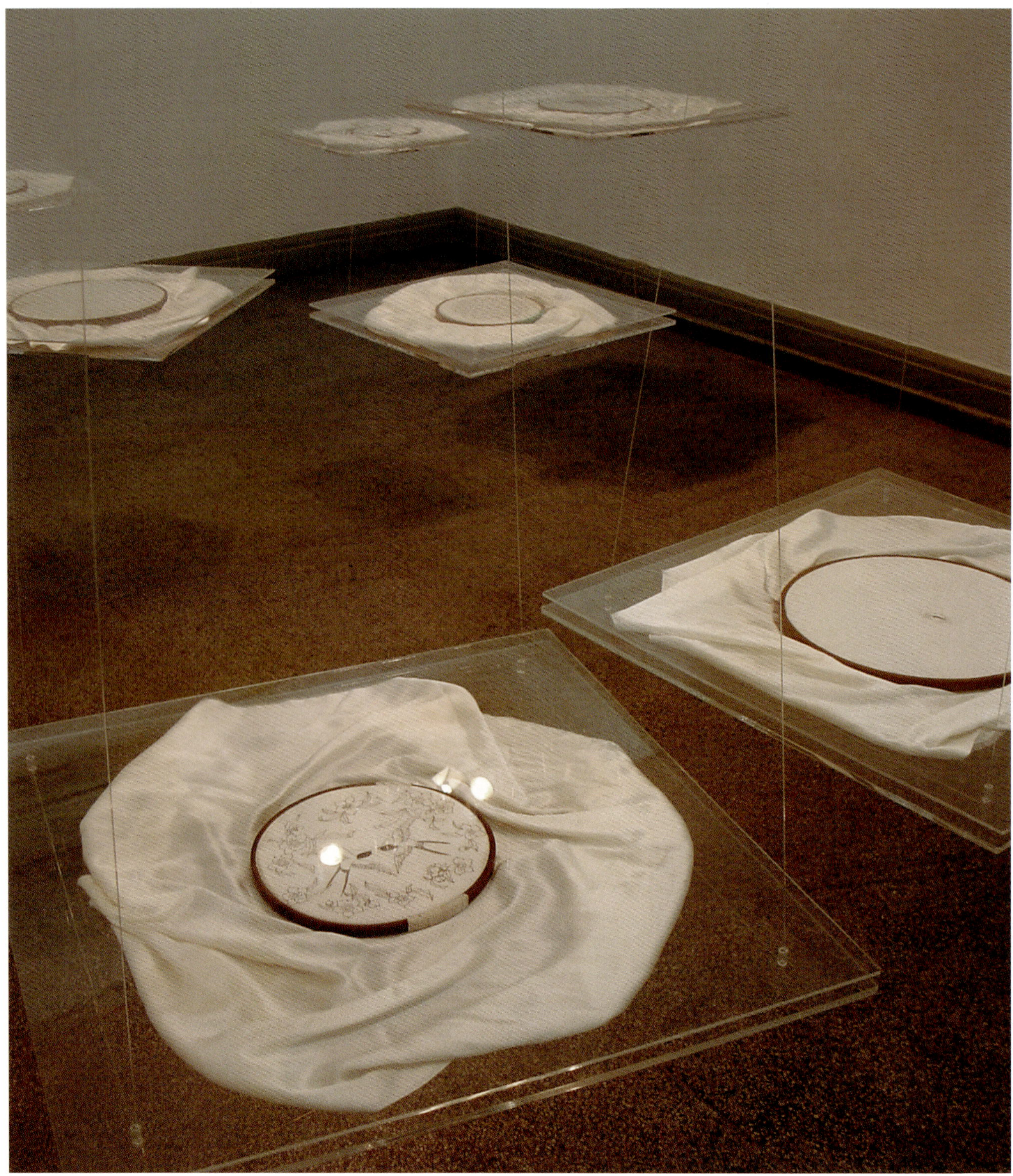

1

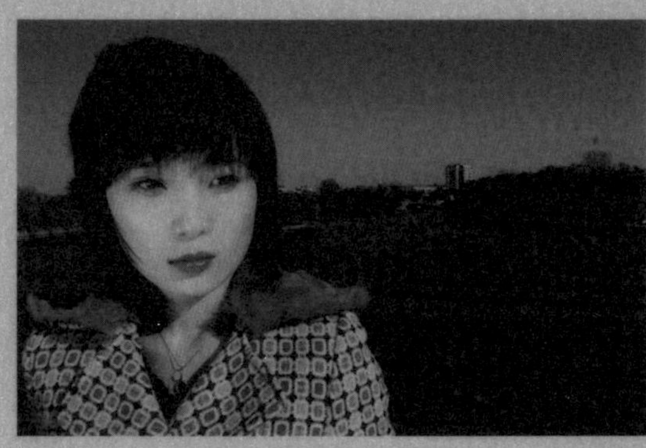

"I choose the materials and forms of my art: they don't choose me."

„Ich wähle die Materialien und Formen meiner Kunst aus, und nicht umgekehrt."

"我选择我的艺术的题材及形式，而不是它们选择我。"

Born in 1977 in Harbin, China. Lives and works in Beijing
Geboren 1977 in Harbin, China. Lebt und arbeitet in Peking
1977年出生于哈尔滨，中国。居住工作在北京

***Selected exhibitions* / Ausgewählte Ausstellungen / 所选展览**

2004 "N12 New Painting-No. 2", Central Academy of Fine Arts Gallery, Beijing, China
2005–07 "Mahjong – Chinesische Gegenwartskunst aus der Sammlung Sigg", Kunstmuseum Bern, Berne, Switzerland; Hamburger Kunsthalle, Hamburg, Germany; Museum der Moderne, Salzburg (Austria)
2006 "Body", Heng Contemporary Art Space, Nanjing, China
"Replacement", Chinese Contemporary, Beijing, China
"The Self-made Generation", Zendai Museum of Modern Art, Shanghai, China
2007 "China Welcomes You", Kunsthaus Graz, Graz, Austria
documenta 12, Kassel, Germany

2004年 《N12 新绘画-第二回展》中国北京，中央美术学院美术馆
2005–07年 《麻将一西克的当代艺术收藏展》瑞士伯尔尼，伯尔尼美术博物馆
2006年 《身体》中国南京，恒当代艺术空间
《代替》中国北京，中国当代画廊
《自我造局》中国上海，上海证大现代艺术馆
2007年 《中国欢迎你》格拉茨美术馆 格拉茨 奥地利
第十二届德国文件展 卡塞尔 德国

***Selected publications* / Ausgewählte Publikationen / 所选著作**

Wu Penghui: "Manner and Image", in: "Art World", Beijing, November 2003
Karen Smith: "Cultural Revolution", in: "Spoon", Paris/London, November/December 2005
Stacey Duff: "Broken Flowers", in: "Time Out", Beijing, March 2006
Luo Ke: "Love Faith Which Can't Be Sent", in: "Bookzine", Beijing, May 2006

兀鹏辉（著）:《风格与图像》《艺术世界》2003 年 11 月
Smith, Karen（著）:《文化大革命》在："Spoon"，巴黎-伦敦2005 年 11 月 / 12 月
Duff, Stacey（著）:《破碎的花朵》在："Time Out Beijing"（英文版）北京2006 年 3 月
洛恪（著）:《送不出去的爱之信仰》在《杂志书》北京2006 年5 月，第 140-3 页

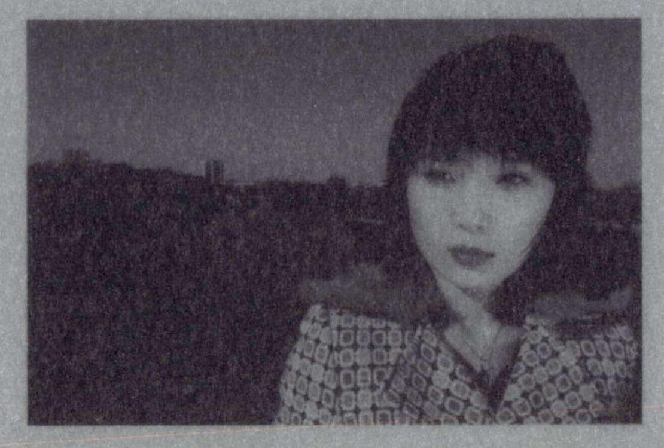

"I choose the materials and forms of my art: they don't choose me."

„Ich wähle die Materialien und Formen meiner Kunst aus,
und nicht umgekehrt."

"我选择我的艺术的题材及形式，而不是它们选择我。"

Born in 1977 in Harbin, China. Lives and works in Beijing
Geboren 1977 in Harbin, China. Lebt und arbeitet in Peking
1977年出生于哈尔滨，中国。居住工作在北京

Selected exhibitions / Ausgewählte Ausstellungen / 所选展览

2004	"N12 New Painting-No. 2", Central Academy of Fine Arts Gallery, Beijing, China
2005–07	"Mahjong - Chinesische Gegenwartskunst aus der Sammlung Sigg", Kunstmuseum Bern, Berne, Switzerland; Hamburger Kunsthalle, Hamburg, Germany; Museum der Moderne, Salzburg (Austria)
2006	"Body", Heng Contemporary Art Space, Nanjing, China
	"Replacement", Chinese Contemporary, Beijing, China
	"The Self-made Generation", Zendai Museum of Modern Art, Shanghai, China
2007	"China Welcomes You", Kunsthaus Graz, Graz, Austria
	documenta 12, Kassel, Germany

2004年	《N12 新绘画-第二回展》中国北京，中央美术学院美术馆
2005-07年	《麻将一西克的当代艺术收藏展》瑞士伯尔尼，伯尔尼美术博物馆
2006年	《身体》中国南京，恒当代艺术空间
	《代替》中国北京，中国当代画廊
	《自我造局》中国上海，上海证大现代艺术馆
2007年	《中国欢迎你》格拉茨美术馆　格拉茨　奥地利
	第十二届德国文件展　卡塞尔　德国

Selected publications / Ausgewählte Publikationen / 所选著作

Wu Penghui: "Manner and Image", in: "Art World", Beijing, November 2003
Karen Smith: "Cultural Revolution", in: "Spoon", Paris/London, November/December 2005
Stacey Duff: "Broken Flowers", in: "Time Out", Beijing, March 2006
Luo Ke: "Love Faith Which Can't Be Sent", in: "Bookzine", Beijing, May 2006

吴鹏辉（著）：《风格与图像》《艺术世界》2003 年 11 月
Smith, Karen（著）：《文化大革命》在："Spoon"，巴黎-伦敦2005 年 11 月 / 12 月
Duff, Stacey（著）：《破碎的花朵》在："Time Out Beijing"（英文版）北京2006 年 3 月
洛格（著）：《送不出去的爱之信仰》在《杂志书》北京2006 年5 月，第 140-3 页

HU XIAOYUAN 胡晓媛

[xu ɕiaʊyɛn]

Hu Xiaoyuan is as kooky as Björk, as mignon as Audrey Hepburn. The defining traits of these personalities – an intense individualism and a beguiling honesty – partner equally in shaping Hu Xiaoyuan's art. Not trained as a painter – she graduated from the design department of the Central Academy of Fine Arts (2002) – Hu Xiaoyuan's first endeavours as an independent artist were with oil paint, but the flat expanse of a canvas, brush marks and pigment, didn't get to the core of what she wanted to express. The small series of paintings she produced prior to liberating herself from the conventions attached to the medium, touch upon subject matter that would resurface in subsequent conceptual works – "A Keepsake I Cannot Give Away" (2005/06) and "Mine" (2004). Compared against the listless tone in which the content of these paintings is articulated, the conceptual realm clearly allows ways and means of expression far more stimulating in nature.

The transition to this new realm began at the end of 2004, when, having decided upon her first project, Hu Xiaoyuan began to let her hair down – literally. By January 2005, this modern-day Rapunzel's locks were long enough for her purposes: she shaved them off, preserving the waist-long strands for use as silken embroidery threads to create "A Keepsake I Cannot Give Away".

China has a long tradition of embroidery, evidenced by a rich legacy of imperial gowns. It is also an important folk tradition. Specific combinations of stitch and pattern represent the defining characteristics of a minority people; as much decoration as emblem of ethic identity. Even today, young minority girls embroider to demonstrate a nimbleness of fingers desired of a prospective wife.

Adopting the stance of a modern young woman – modern by Chinese standards, despite the entrenched attitudes towards women that remain – Hu Xiaoyuan invokes this maidenly tradition only to adulterate the modesty and virtue it was designed to embody by introducing images certain to make a chaste maiden blush. Familiar metaphors

Hu Xiaoyuan erscheint so überspannt wie Björk und so niedlich wie die junge Audrey Hepburn. Die kennzeichnenden Wesenszüge dieser beiden Persönlichkeiten – ein ausgeprägter Individualismus und unwiderstehliche Ehrlichkeit – prägen Hu Xiaoyuans Kunst zu gleichen Teilen. Sie, die keine formale Ausbildung zur Malerin hat, sondern lediglich einen Abschluss im Fachbereich Design der Central Academy of Fine Arts (2002), unternahm ihre ersten Versuche als selbstständige Künstlerin mit Ölfarbe.

Aber die plane Fläche einer Leinwand, die Pinselstriche und Pigmente drangen nicht zum Kern dessen vor, was sie ausdrücken wollte. Die kleine Serie von Gemälden, die sie schuf, bevor sie sich von den Konventionen des Mediums befreite, berührte Themen, die in späteren Konzeptarbeiten wieder auftauchen sollten – etwa in „A Keepsake I Cannot Give Away" (2005/06) und „Mine" (2004). Doch während sich diese Themen im Rahmen der Gemälde noch mit einer gewissen Lustlosigkeit artikulieren, eröffnet die Welt der Konzeptkunst Hu Xiaoyuan ganz offensichtlich weit anregendere Ausdruckswege und -möglichkeiten.

Der Eintritt in diese neue künstlerische Welt begann Ende 2004, als sich Hu entschloss, für ihr erstes neues Projekt Haare zu lassen – im Januar 2005 war die Haarpracht dieses modernen Rapunzels endlich lang genug für ihre Zwecke: Sie rasierte sie ab und verwendete die taillenlangen Strähnen als seidiges Stickgarn für „A Keepsake I Cannot Give Away".

China hat eine lange Stickereitradition, was schon das reiche Erbe kaiserlicher Gewänder deutlich macht. Zugleich ist die Stickerei eine wichtige traditionelle Volkskunst. Bestimmte Kombinationen von Stichen und Mustern verkörpern die grundlegenden Wesenszüge ethnischer Minderheiten und dienen damit nicht nur der Dekoration, sondern auch als Symbol der Identität. Noch heute pflegen die Mädchen mancher Volksgruppen die Stickerei, um jene Fingerfertigkeit zu erlernen, die bei einer zukünftigen Ehefrau als wünschenswert gilt.

如Björk一样乖僻，如Audrey Hepburn一样可爱，这就是胡晓媛。强烈的个人主义及伪善的诚实--这些个性的标志性特点在胡晓媛的艺术中平分秋色。胡晓媛并非学画出身，她于 2002 年毕业于中央美术学院设计系，油画是其作为一个独立艺术家的首次尝试，然而平整宽阔的画布、画刷痕迹及颜料无法达到她想要表达的核心。在将自己从传统的材质解放出来以前，她所创作的一小部分画作所涉及到的题材能够在其之后的概念作品《送不出去的信物》和《我的》中再次看到。这些作品的内容掺杂着怠慢的风格，与之相比，作品的概念领域上的表达方法及方式在本质上更具冲击性。

向这一新领域的过渡开始于 2004 年末。决定了自己的首个项目以后，胡晓媛开始留长头发。到 2005 年 1 月为止，这位当代的拉普耶鲁的“梯子”已经留到她需要的长度：她剪下头发，将齐腰的头发当作刺绣的丝线使用，创作了《送不出去的信物》。

大量遗留下来的龙袍见证了中国悠久的刺绣历史。刺绣同时也是一项重要的民族传统。针线和图案的特定组合代表着一个少数民族的鲜明特色，装饰越多则德望越高。甚至到了今天，年轻的少数民族少女依旧进行着刺绣，以展现其贤妻应当具备的巧手。

胡晓媛以一名摩登（中式标准，抛开那些遗留下来且难以改变的对待妇女的态度）女郎的姿态出现，利用这些女红传统对其本来应该蕴含着的谦虚和美德进行篡改。她的刺绣图案绝对能让一位贞洁的少女脸红。求爱的鸳鸯、羞涩圣洁的花蕾含苞欲放，这些熟悉的爱情意喻与另一幅刺绣成双结对，而后者则迫不及待地描述了对她自己身体的一瞥 -- 一个乳头，臀部的曲线，以及在卷在她私处周围的薄薄毛发。

胡晓媛继续作画，主要是在纸上 -- 精致的水彩，素描及拼贴的组合，这些均采取了个人图画日记的

2

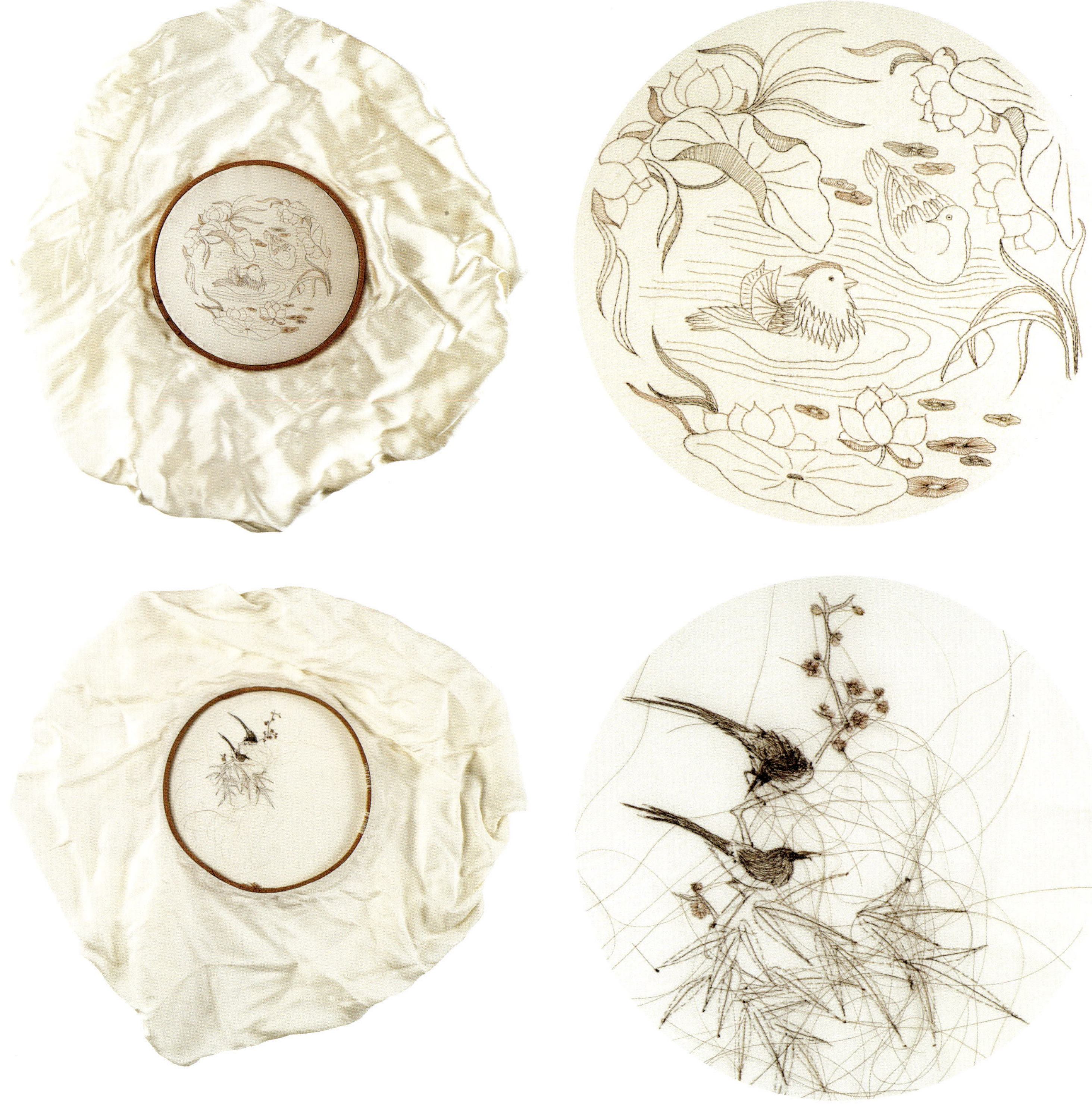

3

4

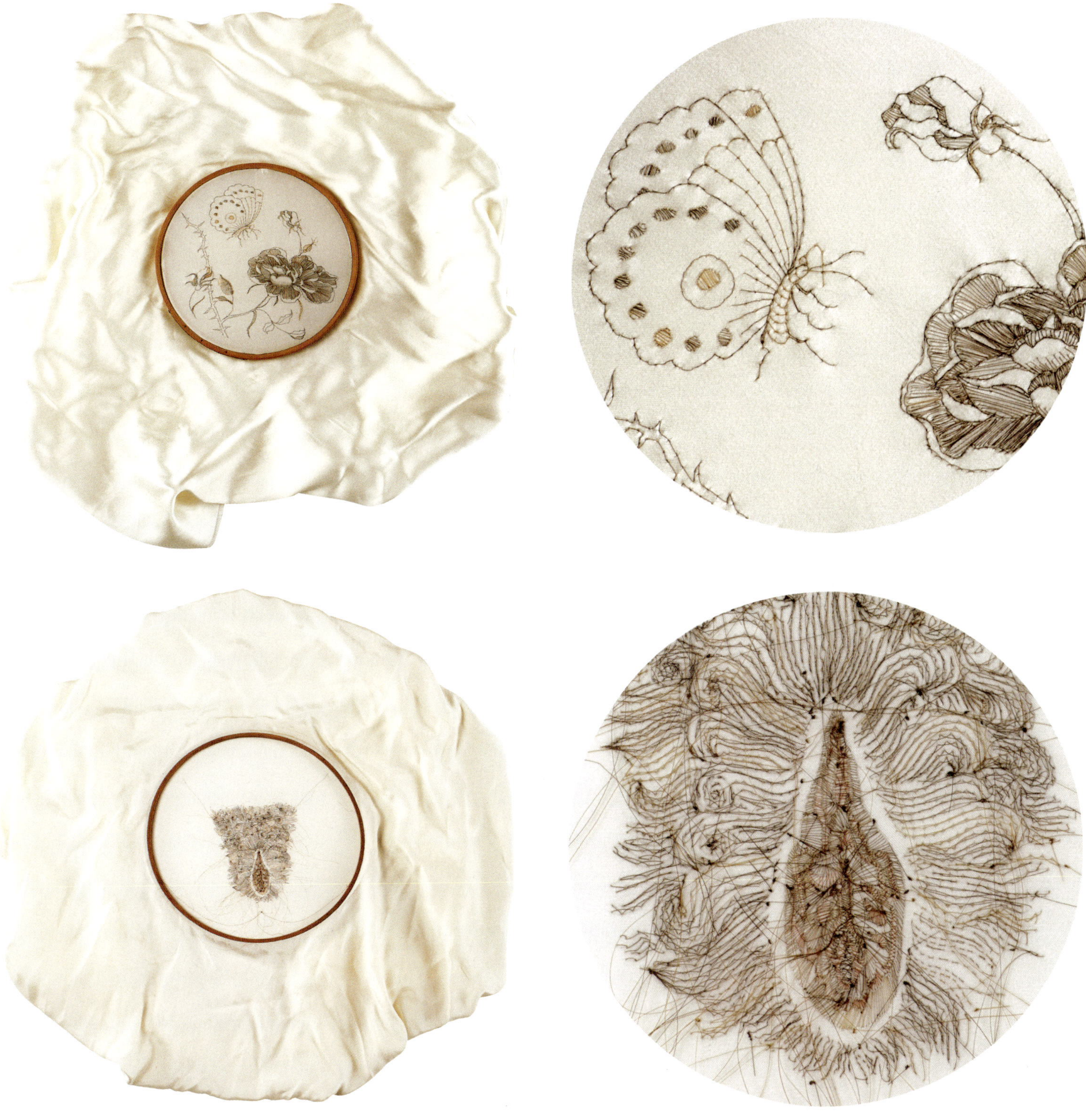

5

6

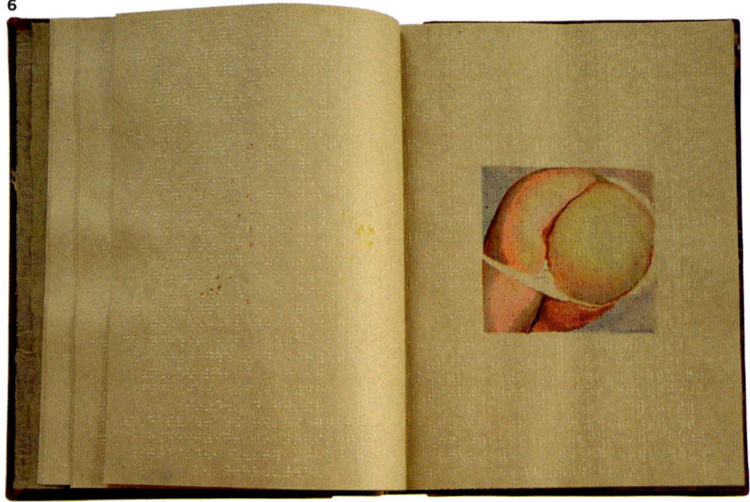

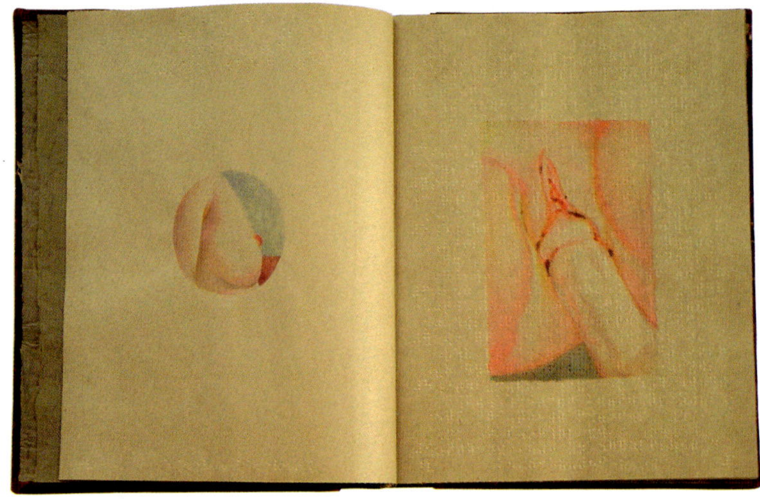

for love – courting Mandarin ducks, shy virgin buds about to burst into bloom – are paired with a second embroidery that depicts a tantalizing glimpse of her own body – a nipple, the curve of her hip, a mist of pubic hair curling around her genitalia.

Hu Xiaoyuan continues to paint, primarily on paper – delicate watercolours, combined with drawing and collage, techniques also used to create "Mine" (2004), which take the form of personal pictorial diaries. Her most recent work is a second experiment in mapping "woman". "The Times" (2006) comprise three vertical hangings, representing three specific women: Hu Xiaoyuan, her mother, and her grandmother. For these works, two layers of semi-transparent gauze are sandwiched together to contain a selection of personal objects all carefully sewn within. The range of items – a gauze kerchief, socks, sunglasses from Hu Xiaoyuan, house keys that hung round her neck as a school-child, and a love letter from her first boyfriend; for her mother a dowry pillow, coloured lights bought to decorate the home, herbal medicines, an abacus, and her wallet; for her grandmother a handful of objects left behind when she passed away (1996) – suggests the changing nature of the eras to which each of the women belongs. Hu Xiaoyuan is a young artist, in a tiny minority of women artists in China, but who has made a remarkable start to her career.

Dem bis in unsere Tage starr verwurzelten Frauenbild zum Trotz nimmt Hu Xiaoyuan aus der Haltung einer modernen jungen Frau heraus (modern nach chinesischen Maßstäben) auf diese mädchenhafte Tradition nur Bezug, um die Bescheidenheit und Tugend, die diese verkörpern soll, zu entwürdigen, indem sie sie mit Bildern kombiniert, die jede keusche Maid erröten lassen würden. Vertraute Symbole für die Liebe – balzende Mandarin-Enten, jungfräuliche Knospen kurz vor der Blüte – werden mit einer zweiten Stickerei kombiniert, die verführerische Blicke auf den Körper der Künstlerin gewährt: hier eine Brustwarze, dort die Rundung ihrer Hüfte, da eine Wolke von Schamhaaren, die sich um ihre Geschlechtsteile locken.

Hu Xiaoyuan malt auch weiterhin, vorwiegend auf Papier – zarte Aquarelle, kombiniert mit Zeichnungen und Collagen. In solcher Mischtechnik gestaltete sie auch ihre Arbeit „Mine" (2004), und zwar in Form sehr persönlicher Bildtagebücher. Ihr jüngstes Werk ist ein weiteres Experiment in ihrem Projekt der Kartographierung der Frau – „The Times" (2006) umfasst drei „Vorhänge", die drei Frauen und drei Generationen verkörpern: Hu Xiaoyuan, ihre Mutter und ihre Großmutter. Die Werke bestehen jeweils aus zwei Lagen transparenter Gaze, zwischen denen eine Auswahl persönlicher Gegenstände angeordnet und sorgfältig eingenäht ist. Die Bandbreite der Gegenstände verweist auf die Wechselhaftigkeit der Zeiten, denen diese Frauen angehörten und angehören – ein hauchzarter Gazeschal, Socken, eine Sonnenbrille von Hu Xiaoyuan, Hausschlüssel, die sie als Schulkind um den Hals trug, und ein Liebesbrief von ihrem ersten Freund; für ihre Mutter ein Aussteuer-Kissen, farbige Lämpchen, die sie kaufte, um ihr Heim zu dekorieren, Kräuterheilmittel, ein Abakus und ihre Brieftasche; für ihre Großmutter eine Handvoll Gegenstände, die diese bei ihrem Tod (1996) hinterließ. Hu Xiaoyuan gehört zur winzigen Minderheit chinesischer Künstlerinnen, hat aber, so jung sie ist, einen bemerkenswerten Karrierestart geschafft.

形式同样被用于创作《我的》（2004 年）的技巧。她最新的作品又一次尝试描绘"女人"。《那时光》（2006 年）由三条垂直落下的布纱构成，分别代表三个不同年龄的女人：胡晓媛、她的母亲、以及她的外婆。作品中，两层半透明的薄纱叠在一起，将一些个人物品细致地缝在里面。物品的包括：一方纱巾、袜子、胡晓媛的墨镜、上学时挂在脖子上的家门钥匙以及初恋男友的情书；她母亲的物品包括作为嫁妆的枕头、买来装饰家里的彩色灯泡、草药、一把算盘以及钱包；她外婆的物品则是一些外婆（1996 年）的遗物——代表着每个女人所生长的不同时代。胡晓媛是一位年轻的艺术家，在中国女性艺术家只是一小部分，然而她已经在自己的事业上迈出了非凡的第一步。

Karen Smith

7

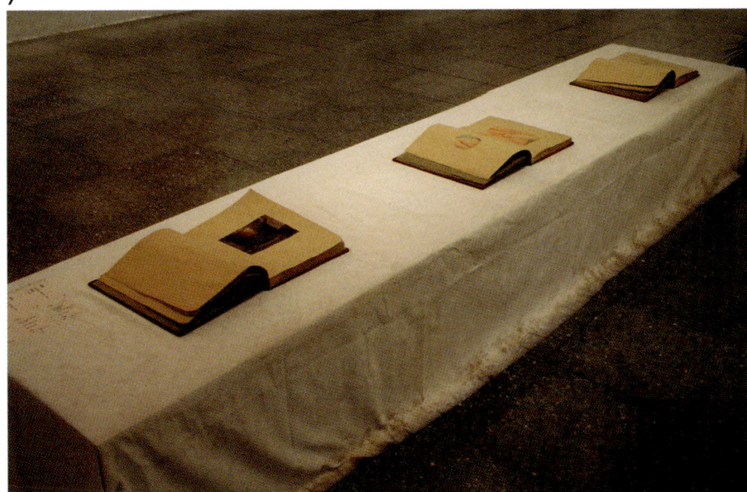

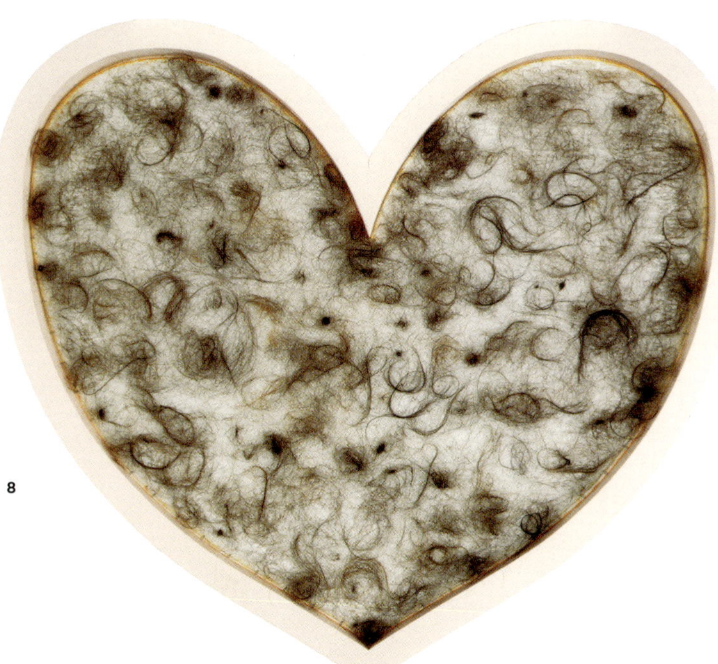

8

1 ***A Keepsake I Cannot Give Away****, 1/1/2005–17/3/2006*
The artist's own hair, white twill-weave silk, old embroidery frame (installation view)
Haar der Künstlerin, weiße Seide, alter Stickrahmen (Installationsansicht)
《送不出去的信物》05-1-1-17/3/2006，头发，白色真丝布料，老绣花绷子，装置实景

2 ***A Keepsake I Cannot Give Away – Yun Yang Xi Lian****, 1/1/2005–17/3/2006*
The artist's own hair, white twill-weave silk, old embroidery frame, 23.5 cm diameter (detail)
Haar der Künstlerin, weiße Seide, alter Stickrahmen, Durchmesser 23,5 cm (Detail)
《送不出去的信物》05-1-1-17/3/2006，头发，白色真丝布料，老绣花绷子，直径23.5 cm（详细）

3 ***A Keepsake I Cannot Give Away – Zhu Mei Shuang Xi****, 1/1/2005–17/3/2006*
The artist's own hair, white twill-weave silk, old embroidery frame, 30 cm diameter (detail)
Haar der Künstlerin, weiße Seide, alter Stickrahmen, Durchmesser 30 cm (Detail)
《送不出去的信物》05-1-1-17/3/2006，头发，白色真丝布料，老绣花绷子，直径30 cm（详细）

4 ***A Keepsake I Cannot Give Away – Die Lian Hua****, 1/1/2005–17/3/2006*
The artist's own hair, white twill-weave silk, old embroidery frame, 17 cm diameter (detail)
Haar der Künstlerin, weiße Seide, alter Stickrahmen, Durchmesser 17 cm (Detail)
《送不出去的信物》05-1-1-17/3/2006，头发，白色真丝布料，老绣花绷子，直径17 cm（详细）

5 ***A Keepsake I Cannot Give Away – Xuan Hua Jia Die****, 1/1/2005–17/3/2006*
The artist's own hair, white twill-weave silk, old embroidery frame, 31 cm diameter (detail)
Haar der Künstlerin, weiße Seide, alter Stickrahmen, Durchmesser 31 cm (Detail)
《送不出去的信物》05-1-1-17/3/2006，艺术家自己的发丝，白色真丝布料，老绣花绷子，直径31 cm（详细）

6 ***Mine****, 2004*
Braille bibles – St. Mark, watercolour, 31.5 x 24.5 cm each book
Bibel in Braille-Schrift – Markus, Aquarell, jedes Buch 31,5 x 24,5 cm
《我的》2004年，盲文圣经（马可福音），水色，每本尺寸31.5 x 24.5 cm

7 ***Mine****, 2004*
Braille bibles – St. Mark, watercolour, 31.5 x 24.5 cm each book (installation view)
Bibel in Braille-Schrift – Markus, Aquarell, jedes Buch 31,5 x 24,5 cm (Installationsansicht)
《我的》2004年，盲文圣经（马可福音），水色，每本尺寸31.5 x 24.5 cm，装置实景

8 ***My family****, 6/10/2005–13/11/2006*
Lost hair by metabolism in the whole year belong to my papa, my mum, my younger brother, my younger brother's girlfriend, my sweetheart and me, wood, gloss household paint, resin, 110 x 113 cm
Durch Stoffwechsel während eines Jahres ausgefallenes Haar von meinem Papa, meiner Mama, meinem jüngeren Bruder, der Freundin meines jüngeren Bruders, meines Liebsten und mir. Holz, Lack, Haushaltsfarbe, Kunstharz, 110 x 113 cm
《我的家族》2005年10月6日-2006年11月13 日 ，本作由所用材料为头发，家用颜料和树脂等，为了那些发丝，我花了一年多时间收集了我父母，弟弟及他的女友，我的宝贝以及我自己所掉下的头发，木材， 漆，油漆，人造树脂， 尺寸110 x 113 cm

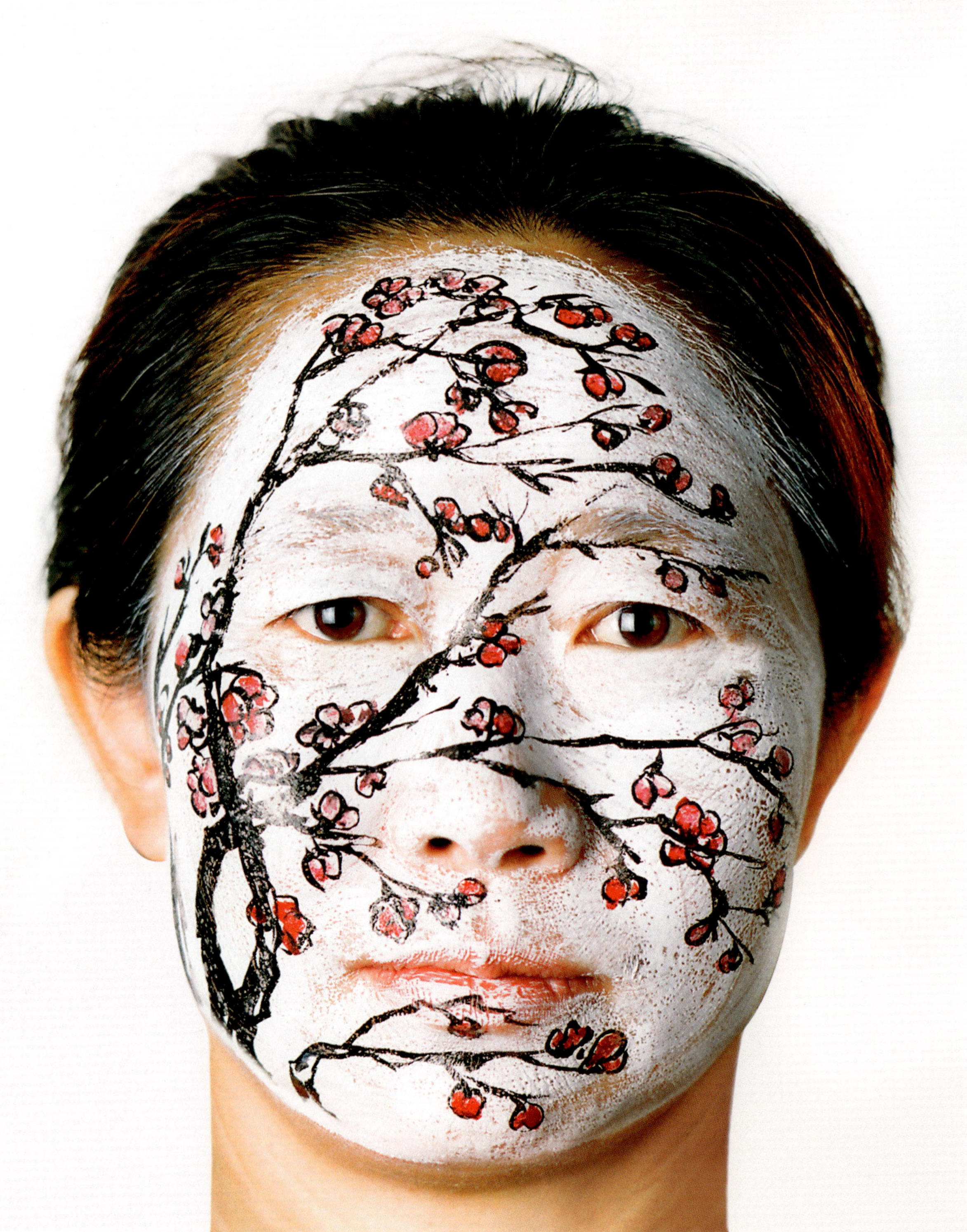

1

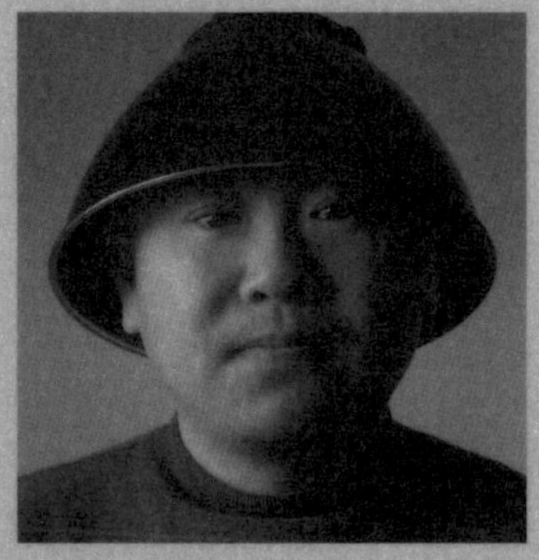

"I have always had the impression that I am on a long and arduous voyage in search of my own 'little garden': a modern incarnation of ancient Daoist thought."

„Ich hatte von jeher den Eindruck, dass ich mich auf einer langen, beschwerlichen Reise oder auf der Suche nach meinem eigenen ‚kleinen Garten' befinde: einer modernen Inkarnation des alten daoistischen Denkens."

"我总是感觉自己正在一条漫长而艰辛的路上，追寻着我自己的'小花园'：一个古代道家思想的现代化身。"

Born in 1966 in Jilin, China. Lives and works in Beijing and Changchun
Geboren 1966 in Jilin, China. Lebt und arbeitet in Peking und Changchun
1966年出生于中国吉林，中国。居住工作在北京和长春

***Selected exhibitions* / Ausgewählte Ausstellungen / 所选展览**

2003 Prague Biennial, Prague, Czech Republic
Brazil São Paulo Image Biennial Exhibition, São Paulo, Brazil
2004 "China, the body everywhere", Musée d'Art Contemporain, Marseille, France
"China – New Filming World", Filming Center, New York, Museum of Contemporary Art, Chicago, IL, USA
2004–07 "Between Past and Future, New Photography and Video from China", International Center of Photography, New York, NY, USA (travelling exhibition)
2005 "Out of the Red 2 – The Photographic Session", Marella Arte Contemporanea, Milan, Italy
2007 "Made in China", Louisiana Museum of Modern Art, Humlebæk, Denmark

2003年 《布拉格双年展》捷克布拉格
《巴西圣保罗影像双年展》巴西圣保罗
2004年 《身体中国》法国马赛，现代艺术博物馆
《中国新摄影》美国纽约，国际摄影中心；芝加哥，当代艺术博物馆
2004–07年 《过去未来之间一中国新摄影和录影》美国，西雅图艺术博物馆；英国伦敦，维多利亚与爱伯特博物馆
2005年 《红色之外一2 摄影展》意大利米兰，玛蕊拉画廊
2007年 《中国制造》路易斯安那现代艺术馆 Humlebæk，丹麦

***Selected publications* / Ausgewählte Publikationen / 所选著作**

"Body Tattoo, Landscape 2001", in: Edward Lucie-Smith: "Art Tomorrow", Paris 2002
Wu Hung (ed.): "The First Guangzhou Triennial – Reinterpretation: A Decade of Experimental Chinese Art 1990–2000", Chicago 2002
Huang Yan: "The History of Landscape, About Zen Art, Report on Sociological Impressions Taken From Demolitions Between 1993 to 2002, Note on Ink Painting in Huang Yan 1990–2006", Beijing 2006

《纹身- 风景2001年》, 在: Lucie-Smith, Edward:《明天艺术》巴黎 2002年
巫鸿（编者):《首届广州三年展一重新解读：中国实验艺术十年 1990-2000年》芝加哥2002年
黄岩:《风景的历史》《关于禅艺术》《报告关于社会学印象被采取从爆破在1993 年到2002 年之间》《笔记关于墨水绘画》在：
《黄岩个展 1990年到2006年》北京2006年

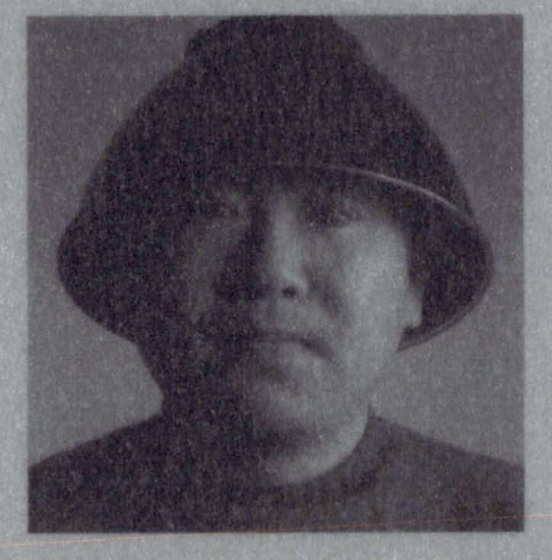

"I have always had the impression that I am on a long and arduous voyage in search of my own 'little garden': a modern incarnation of ancient Daoist thought."

„Ich hatte von jeher den Eindruck, dass ich mich auf einer langen, beschwerlichen Reise oder auf der Suche nach meinem eigenen ‚kleinen Garten' befinde: einer modernen Inkarnation des alten daoistischen Denkens."

"我总是感觉自己正在一条漫长而艰辛的路上，追寻着我自己的'小花园'：一个古代道家思想的现代化身。"

Born in 1966 in Jilin, China. Lives and works in Beijing and Changchun
Geboren 1966 in Jilin, China. Lebt und arbeitet in Peking und Changchun
1966年出生于中国吉林，中国。居住工作在北京和长春

Selected exhibitions / Ausgewählte Ausstellungen / 所选展览

2003	Prague Biennial, Prague, Czech Republic
	Brazil São Paulo Image Biennial Exhibition, São Paulo, Brazil
2004	"China, the body everywhere", Musée d'Art Contemporain, Marseille, France
	"China – New Filming World", Filming Center, New York, Museum of Contemporary Art, Chicago, IL, USA
2004-07	"Between Past and Future, New Photography and Video from China", International Center of Photography, New York, NY, USA (travelling exhibition)
2005	"Out of the Red 2 – The Photographic Session", Marella Arte Contemporanea, Milan, Italy
2007	"Made in China", Louisiana Museum of Modern Art, Humlebaek, Denmark

2003年	《布拉格双年展》捷克布拉格
	《巴西圣保罗影像双年展》巴西圣保罗
2004年	《身体中国》法国马赛，现代艺术博物馆
	《中国新摄影》美国纽约，国际摄影中心；芝加哥，当代艺术博物馆
2004-07年	《过去未来之间—中国新摄影和录影》美国，西雅图艺术博物馆；英国伦敦，维多利亚与爱伯特博物馆
2005年	《红色之外—2 摄影展》意大利米兰，玛蕾拉画廊
2007年	《中国制造》路易斯安那现代艺术馆 Humlebaek，丹麦

Selected publications / Ausgewählte Publikationen / 所选著作

"Body Tattoo, Landscape 2001", in: Edward Lucie-Smith: "Art Tomorrow", Paris 2002
Wu Hung (ed.): "The First Guangzhou Triennial – Reinterpretation: A Decade of Experimental Chinese Art 1990-2000", Chicago 2002
Huang Yan: "The History of Landscape, About Zen Art, Report on Sociological Impressions Taken From Demolitions Between 1993 to 2002, Note on Ink Painting in Huang Yan 1990-2006", Beijing 2006

《纹身一 风景2001年》，在：Lucie-Smith, Edward：《明天艺术》巴黎 2002年
巫鸿（编者）：《首届广州三年展—重新解读：中国实验艺术十年 1990-2000年》芝加哥2002年
黄岩：《风景的历史》《关于禅艺术》《报告关于社会学印象被采取从爆破在1993 年到2002 年之间》《笔记关于墨水绘画》在：《黄岩个展 1990年到2006年》北京2006年

HUANG YAN 黄岩

[xuaŋ iɛn]

Throughout a twenty-year career, Huang Yan has demonstrated a diverse use of media and approach, although in recent years diversity is primarily represented by the grounds to which he applies his on-going series of Chinese paintings. He is also a published poet.

Like most Chinese artists, Huang Yan's first experiments with contemporary art took the form of oil paintings, of a style and content that gently mocked Revolutionary Realism, the official style of art that directed all artistic expression in the Mao era (1949–1976) and which immediately preceded the dawn of the avantgarde. But equally, similar to many other artists desirous of achieving their own language of expression, Huang Yan soon broke with the picture plain to create object-based pieces, photographic works, installations, and text-based projects. Huang Yan has always been prolific. His experiments have been far-ranging, yet are all part of this search for a distinctive contemporary language that further has its roots in the techniques and aesthetics that belong to ancient Chinese cultural traditions and philosophies. In this way, Huang Yan draws on the past to comment upon the present moment.

Since embarking on the "Chinese Painting" series he has been aided by his wife Zhang Tiemei. It is a creative coupling that sees Huang Yan conceive, and his wife execute, the works. The collaboration has achieved a large body of work using familiar subject matter from Chinese (ink) painting. The delicately painted images bare hallmarks of traditional techniques: an array of brush strokes, a flow, drag and deliberate stutter of lines, soft pools of distinctly Chinese mineral pigment, and seemingly casual dots that caress the surface of a landscape, leading the eye through the composition. Yet, whilst Huang Yan's theme pivots on the ink tradition, these are clearly modern works with a distinctly contemporary twist. Huang Yan is primarily a conceptual artist.

Zhang Tiemei's brush skills were essential when, in 1999, Huang Yan used his own torso and limbs as the "ground", in

Im Laufe seiner 20-jährigen Karriere hat Huang Yan eine große Vielseitigkeit in der Wahl seiner Medien und Techniken bewiesen. In den letzten Jahren zeigt sich dies hauptsächlich in der Vielfalt der Malgründe, auf die er seine fortlaufende Serie von Gemälden aufträgt. Er hat übrigens auch Gedichte veröffentlicht.

Wie die meisten chinesischen Künstler experimentierte Huang Yan mit der modernen Kunst zuerst in Form von Ölgemälden, die in Stil und Inhalt den Sozialistischen Realismus mild bespöttelten. Dieser offizielle Kunststil bestimmte den gesamten künstlerischen Impetus der Mao-Ära (1949–1976) – bis eben zum Aufbruch der Avantgarde. Und wie viele andere Künstler, die sich nun um eine persönliche Sprache bemühten, verabschiedete sich Huang Yan bald von der konventionellen Malerei, um stattdessen Objektkunst, fotografische Werke, Installationen und textbasierte Projekte zu schaffen. Er war immer sehr produktiv, und seine Experimente sind breit gefächert, aber stets Teil seiner Suche nach einer unverwechselbaren zeitgenössischen Ausdrucksform, die dennoch in den Techniken und der Ästhetik der uralten chinesischen Kulturtraditionen und Philosophien wurzelt. So schöpft Huang Yan aus der Vergangenheit, um die Gegenwart zu kommentieren.

Seit Beginn der Serie „Chinese Painting" unterstützt ihn seine Frau Zhang Tiemei bei der Arbeit. Diese kreative Paarung sieht so aus, dass Huang Yan seine Werke konzipiert und seine Frau sie ausführt. Aus diesem Zusammenwirken ist bereits eine große Zahl von Arbeiten hervorgegangen, die vertraute Themen aus der chinesischen (Tusche-)Malerei aufgreifen. Die zart gepinselten Bilder tragen Kennzeichen traditioneller Techniken: eine Ansammlung von Pinselstrichen, ein Fließen, Ziehen und gewolltes Flattern der Linien, weiche Lachen chinesischer Pigmente und scheinbar zufällige Punkte, die die Oberfläche einer Landschaft zärtlich abtasten und das Auge durch die Komposition leiten. Doch obwohl Huang Yans Ästhetik in der Tuschetradition gründet, sind dies klar zeitgenössische Arbeiten mit spürbar modernem Flair. Denn in erster Linie ist er Konzeptkünstler.

黄岩在自己二十年的职业生涯中，论证了多种媒介和方法的使用，而近年来则主要以正在从事的国画系列作品为代表。他同时还是一位出版过作品的诗人。

如同大多数中国艺术家一样，黄岩的首次当代艺术尝试采用了油画的形式。他的油画的风格和内容柔和地嘲笑革命的现实主义，则是在毛泽东时代（1949-1976年）指引所有艺术表达并随即揭开了前卫艺术序章的官方艺术风格。然而和其他许多希望找到自己表达语言的　艺术家们一样，黄岩很快与仅仅是基于物体的绘画作品决裂、为了创作摄影作品、装置及文字作品。黄岩一直是位多产的艺术家。他所尝试的范围广泛，全面探求一种技巧与美学都源自古代中国的文化传统及哲学思想的独特当代语言。黄岩以这种方式借古讽今。从着手于《国画》系列起，他的妻子张铁梅开始对他进行协助。这是一次创造性的联手 -- 黄岩对作品进行构思，而他的妻子则负责执行。他们使用常见的国画（水墨）作品主题，共同合作创作了大量的作品。这些精细绘制的图像带有传统技巧的特点：放眼其作品，攒簇、拖笔、提按、渲染及点擢等技巧运用自如。尽管黄岩的作品主题以传统水墨为轴心，而这些明显带有现代手法的作品却无疑属于当代作品。黄岩在根本上是一位概念艺术家。

1999 年，在一个组摄影作品系列中，黄岩将自己的躯体和四肢当作“画布”，此时张铁梅的笔法技巧就成为基础。在十二幅图像中，黄岩从脖子到手腕上都画上了中国山水画，就好像后来的日本黑社会分子一样。尽管是静态的照片，但一具鲜活的躯体却依然给其上所画的图像注入了生命力，人体的凸凹则给山水画增添了层次感。

与此同时，《国画》系列同时也被带到了帆布上。第一眼看上去，整个画面仿佛是一整块固体颜料 -- 红色、橙色、绿色、蓝色以及白色 -- 仅由一条缝在帆布表面的拉链分割开来，以及仅能辨认的极其

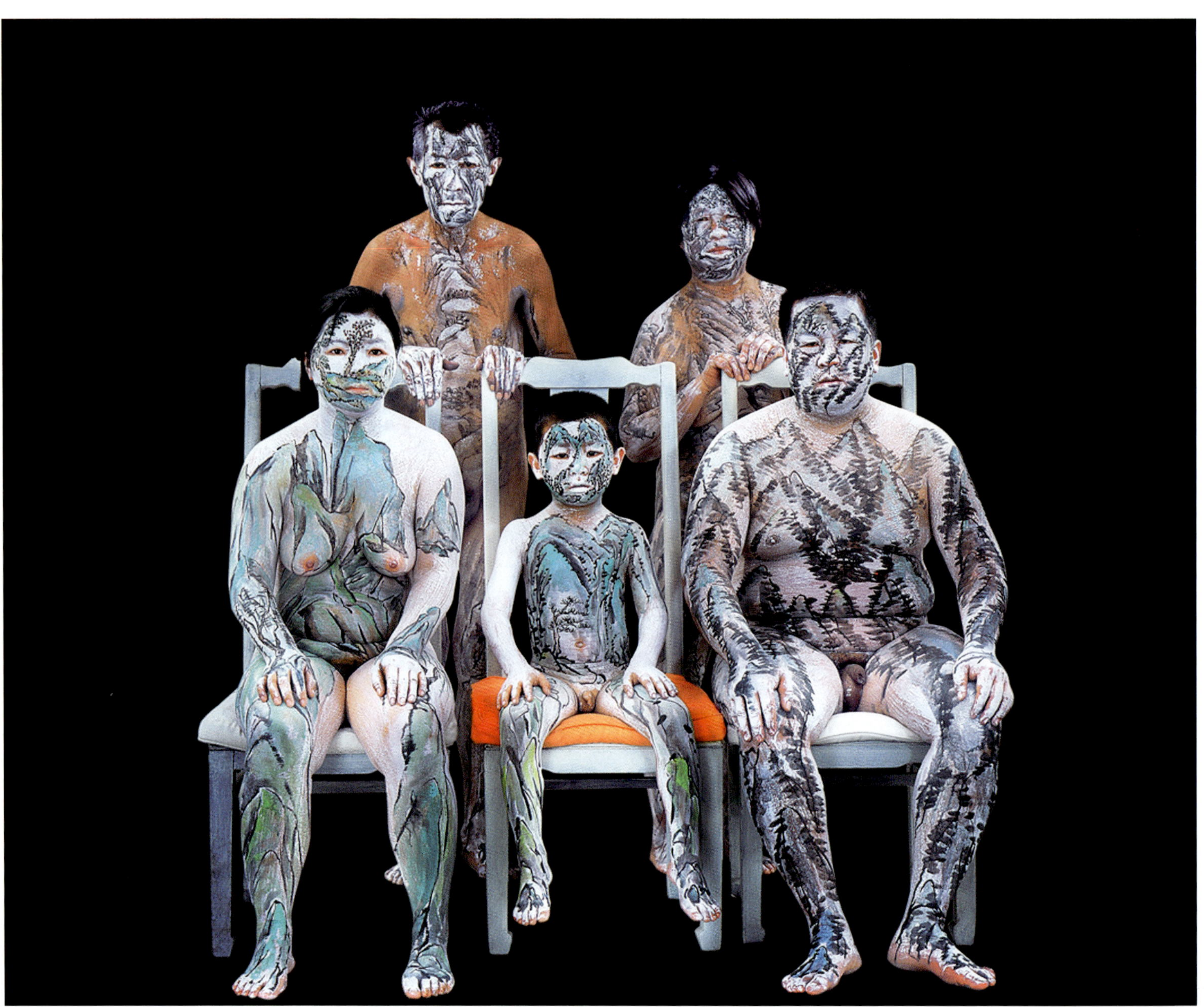

2

3

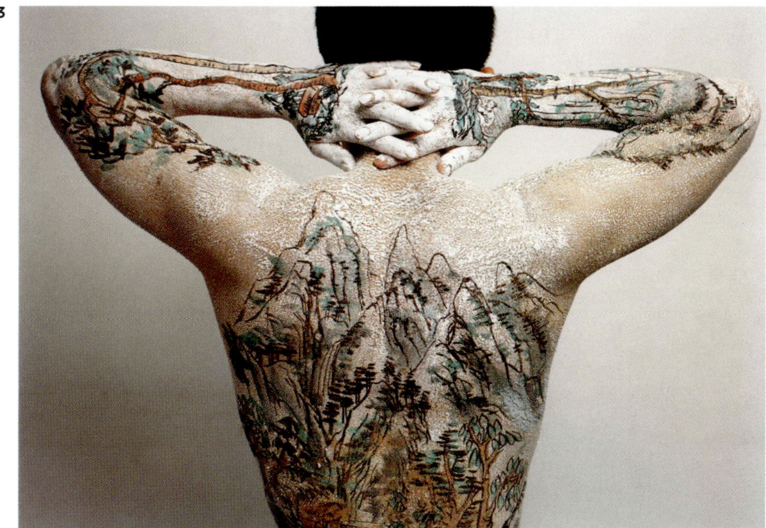

4

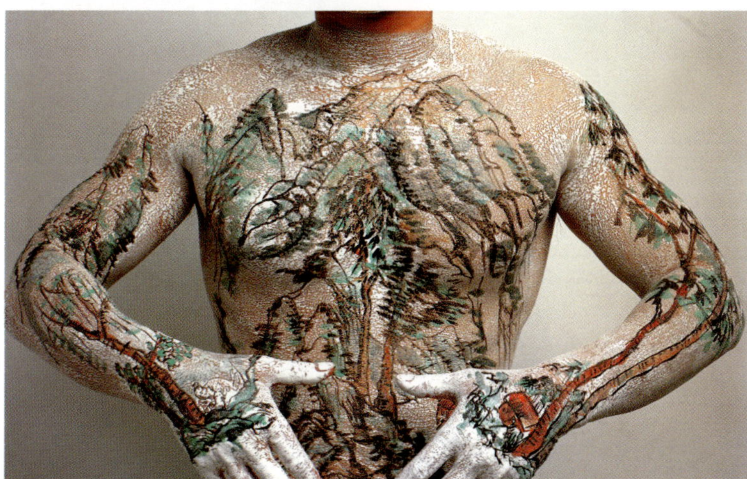

5

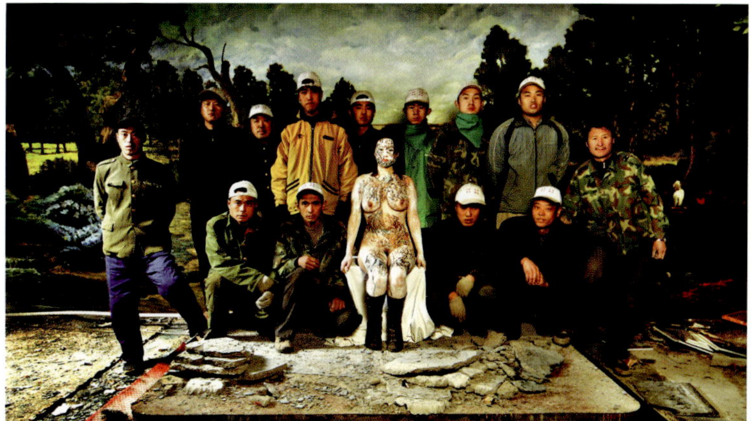

6

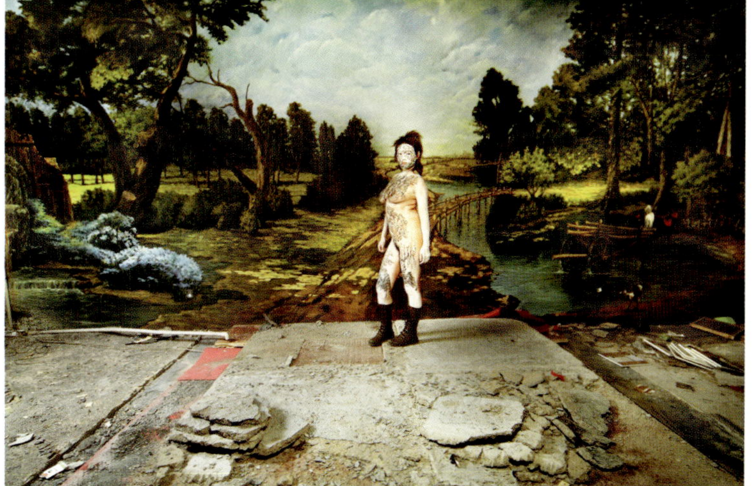

7

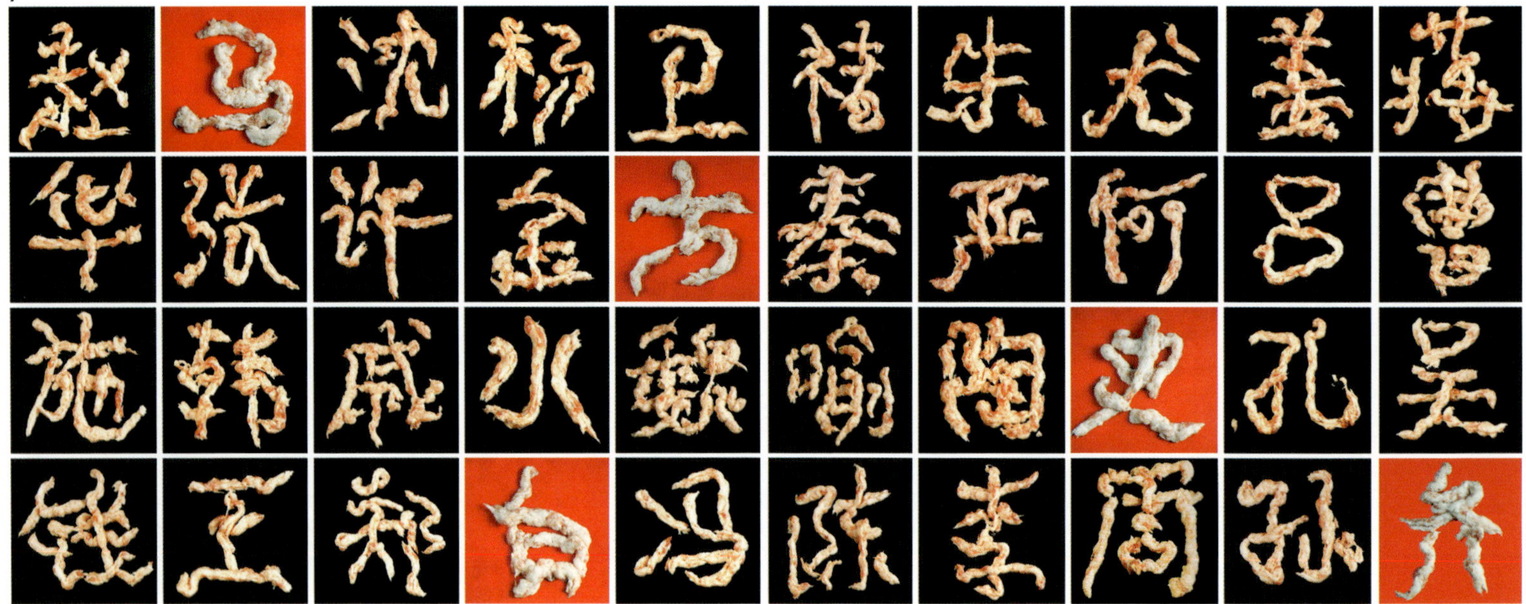

a series of photographic works. Across twelve images, he is tattooed from neck to waist with a Chinese landscape, like a latter-day Japanese "yakusa". Even with a still photograph, a living body breathes life into the painted image, whilst the curved surface of the human armature adds depth to the landscape.

Simultaneously, the "Chinese Painting" series was also brought to canvas. Here, at first glance, the entire picture plane appears to be one solid block of colour – red, orange, green, blue, white – broken only by a zip fastener sewn to the surface of the canvas, and of a closely matched hue as to be barely obvious. Viewers are intended to pull back the zip fastening to uncover the scroll painting hidden inside: a secret world in miniature that evokes the aura of secrecy, the "hidden" treasures of a classical painting, which are the rewards of careful contemplation. The meditation complete, the zip can be closed, the secret kept safe until one wishes to journey again. These works, and the Chinese painting on ox bones and porcelain busts, have been overshadowed by the popularity of the photographic versions of "Chinese Landscape: Tattoo" (1999), and more recently the "Four Seasons" (2004). Recent works continue in this vein using a similar variety of mediums as vehicles for this expansive exploration.

Zhang Tiemeis Kunstfertigkeit mit dem Pinsel spielte eine wesentliche Rolle, als Huang Yan 1999 seinen eigenen Torso und seine Gliedmaßen als „Malgrund" für eine Serie von Fotoarbeiten hergab. Die zwölf Bilder zeigen ihn vom Hals bis zur Taille mit einer chinesischen Landschaft tätowiert, beinahe wie ein japanischer Yakusa. Selbst auf dem unbewegten Foto haucht der Körper dem Gemälde noch Leben ein, während die Unebenheiten der menschlichen Gestalt der Landschaft Tiefe verleihen.

Parallel dazu wurde die Serie „Chinese Painting" auch auf die Leinwand gebannt. Hier wirkt die ganze Bildebene auf den ersten Blick wie ein geschlossener Farbblock – Rot, Orange, Grün, Blau, Weiß –, unterbrochen nur durch einen auf die Leinwand aufgenähten Reißverschluss in einem so exakt angepassten Farbton, dass man ihn kaum wahrnimmt. Der Betrachter muss den Reißverschluss aufziehen, um das dahinter verborgene Rollbild zu enthüllen: eine versteckte Miniaturwelt, die eine Aura des Geheimnisvollen heraufbeschwört, die „verborgenen" Schätze eines klassischen Gemäldes, die dem aufmerksamen Betrachter als Belohnung winken. Nach dieser meditativen Versenkung kann der Reißverschluss wieder geschlossen werden, um das Geheimnis sicher zu bewahren, bis man die Reise erneut antreten möchte. Diese Werke und Huangs/Zhangs Malerei auf Ochsenknochen und Porzellanbüsten wurden durch die Popularität der fotografischen Versionen von „Chinese Landscape: Tattoo" (1999) und „Four Seasons" (2004) etwas in den Schatten gedrängt. Neuere Werke führen diesen Ansatz fort, indem sie ähnlich vielfältige Untergründe als Vehikel für ausgedehnte Entdeckungsreisen nutzen.

相近的色调所构成。观众需要拉开拉链才能揭开藏在里面的卷轴画：充满神秘气息的微缩秘密世界，一幅传统绘画的“秘密”宝藏，这些都是仔细观察的回报。结束了冥想之后，可以再将拉链拉上，“密宝”则将保持安全直至有人希望再次启程。与摄影作品版《中国山水：纹身》（1999年）以及更近期的《四季》（2004年）的声望相比，这些作品以及在牛骨上的国画和半身瓷器等则显得黯然失色。他近期的作品继续了这种脉络，使用相似的介质作为他在广袤艺术中探险的工具。

Karen Smith

8

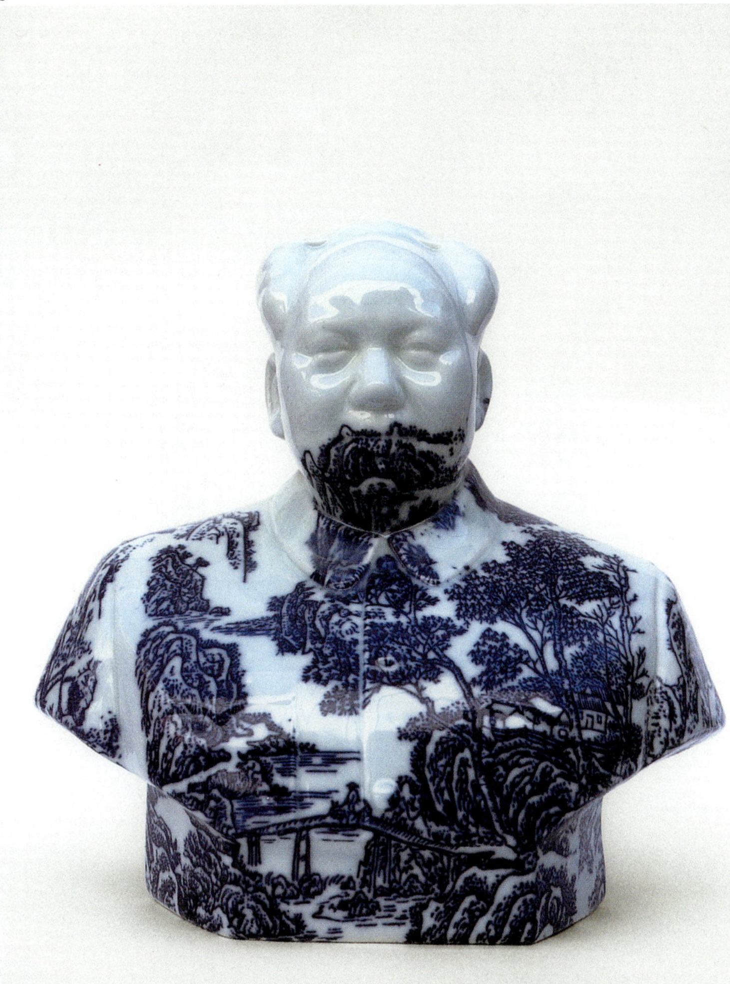

9

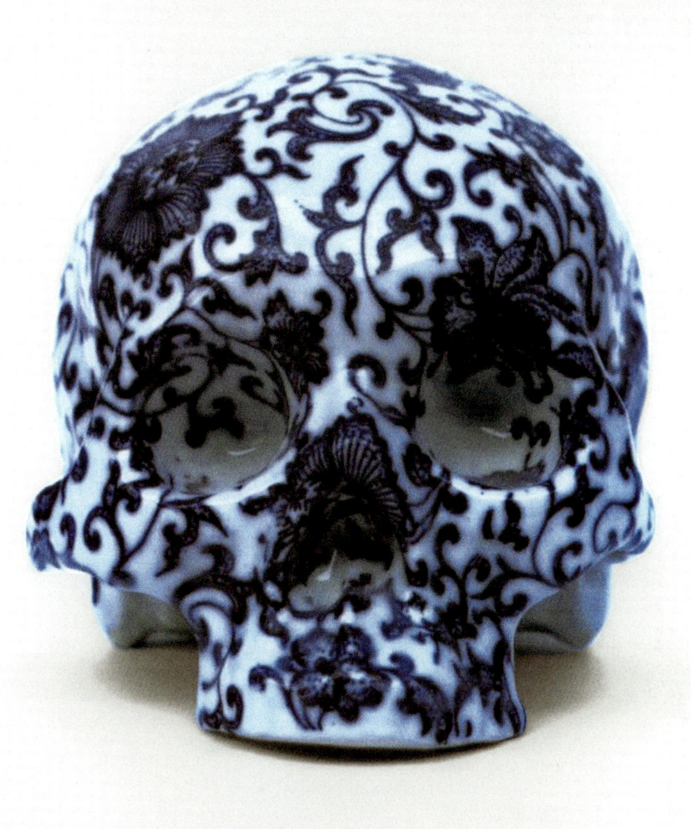

1 ***Face – Plum***, *2004*
Photograph, 150 x 120 cm
Fotografie, 150 x 120 cm
《竹纹脸》2004年, 摄影, 150 x 120 cm

2 ***Model's family Landscape No. 8***, *2006*
Photograph, 120 x 150 cm
Fotografie, 120 x 150 cm
《模特家庭 No. 8》2006年, 摄影, 120 x 150 cm

3 ***Chinese Shanshui Tattoo 13***, *1999*
Photograph, 150 x 120 cm
Fotografie, 150 x 120 cm
《中国山水纹身十三》1999年, 摄影, 150 x 120 cm

4 ***Chinese Shanshui Tattoo 6***, *1999*
Photograph, 150 x 120 cm
Fotografie, 150 x 120 cm
《中国山水纹身六》1999年, 摄影, 150 x 120 cm

5 ***Farmer Landscape***, *2005*
Photograph, 127 x 190 cm
Fotografie, 127 x 190 cm
《农夫风景》2005年, 摄影, 127 x 190 cm

6 ***Dismantle Landscape 5***, *2005*
Photograph, 127 x 190 cm
Fotografie, 127 x 190 cm
《取消风景之5》2005年, 摄影, 127 x 190 cm

7 ***Calligraphy on Meat, The Hundred Chinese Family Names***, *2000*
Photograph, 100 x 300 cm
Fotografie, 100 x 300 cm
《百家姓》2000年, 摄影, 100 x 300 cm

8 ***Landscape Mao Zedong Image No. 1***, *2003*
Ceramic, 30 x 25 x 12 cm
Keramik, 30 x 25 x 12 cm
《毛主席系列No. 1》2003年, 陶质, 30 x 25 x 12 cm

9 ***Rough Veins Skull No. 1***, *2003*
Ceramic, 25 x 20 x 20 cm
Keramik, 25 x 20 x 20 cm
《粗砺的静脉头骨No. 1》2003年，陶质，25 x 20 x 20 cm

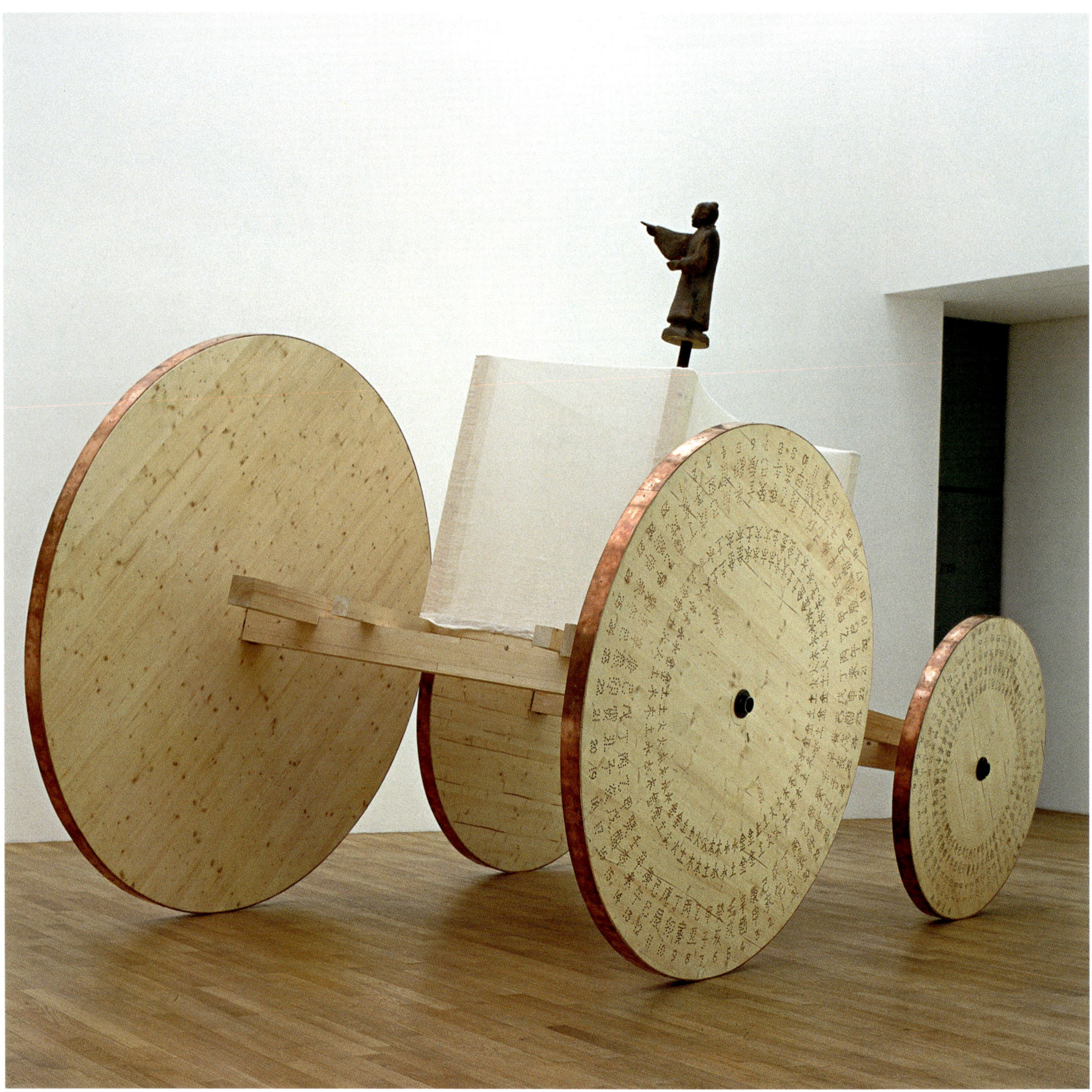

1

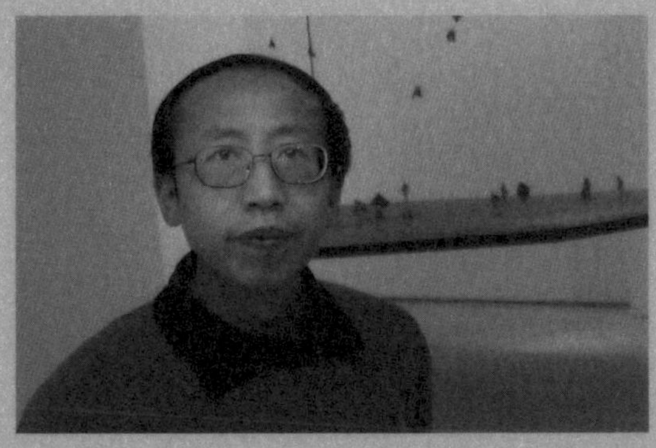

"In reality freedom of art has become impossible today. How can the artist withdraw from market control and influences of artistic fashions?"

„In Wirklichkeit ist heute die Freiheit der Kunst unmöglich geworden. Wie kann sich der Künstler der Kontrolle des Marktes und dem Einfluss künstlerischer Moden entziehen?"

"在如今的现实生活中，艺术的自由已经不可能。艺术家怎么能逃避市场的控制和艺术风尚的影响呢?"

Born in 1954 in Xiamen, China. Lives and works in Paris, France
Geboren 1954 in Xiamen, China. Lebt und arbeitet in Paris, Frankreich
1954年出生于中国厦门，现居住工作于巴黎，法国

***Selected exhibitions* / Ausgewählte Ausstellungen / 所选展览**

1997	"Huang Yong Ping", De Appel, Amsterdam, The Netherlands
	"Péril de mouton", Fondation Cartier pour l'Art Contemporain, Paris, France
1999	"Taigong Fishing: Willing to Bite the Bait", Jack Tilton Gallery, New York, NY, USA
	"Crane's legs, Deer's Tracks", Project Gallery at CCA, Kitakyushu, Japan
2003	"Un cane italiano", Galerie Beaumontpublic, Luxembourg, Luxembourg
2005-07	"House of Oracles: A Huang Yong Ping Retrospective", Walker Art Center, Minneapolis, MI; MASS MoCA, North Adams, MA, USA; Vancouver Art Gallery, Vancouver, Canada

1997年	《黄永砯》De Appel 阿姆斯特丹，荷兰
	《羊祸》Cartier当代艺术基金会，巴黎，法国
1999年	《太公钓鱼，愿者上钩》纽约 Jack Tilton画廊 美国
	《鹤腿，鹿迹》北九州当代艺术中心 横滨 日本
2003年	《意大利狗》Beaumontpublic 画廊，卢森堡
2005-07年	《神殿之屋》黄永砯回顾展，Walker艺术中心，马萨诸塞博物馆，美国；温哥华美术馆 温哥华 加拿大

***Selected publications* / Ausgewählte Publikationen / 所选著作**

"Huang Yong Ping: Cinq questions à des artistes non occidentaux", in: "Art Press", Nr. 136, Paris, May 1989
Dominique Aube: "Huang Yong Ping", in: "Art Press", Nr. 149, Paris, July/August 1990
Fei Da Wei, Huang Yong Ping: "Promenade in Asia", Tokyo 1997

Huang Yong Ping（著）:《Cinq questions a des artistes non occidentaux》Art Press 136页，巴黎 五月刊 1989年
Aube, Dominique（著）:《黄永砯》, Art Press 149页 巴黎 七、八月刊 1990年
费大为，黄永砯（编者）:《散步在欧洲》东京 1997年

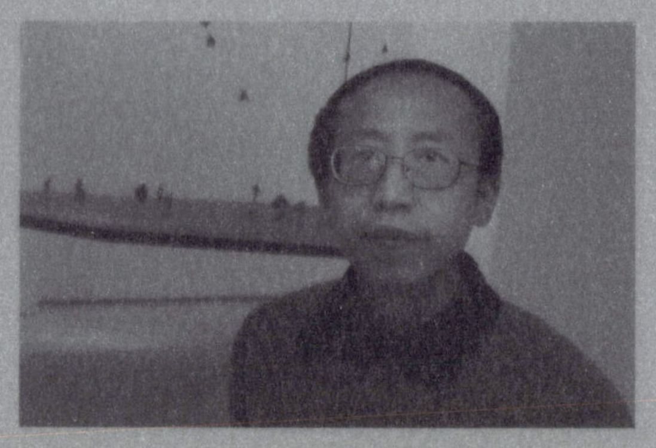

"In reality freedom of art has become impossible today. How can the artist withdraw from market control and influences of artistic fashions?"

„In Wirklichkeit ist heute die Freiheit der Kunst unmöglich geworden. Wie kann sich der Künstler der Kontrolle des Marktes und dem Einfluss künstlerischer Moden entziehen?"

"在如今的现实生活中，艺术的自由已经不可能。艺术家怎么能逃避市场的控制和艺术风尚的影响呢?"

Born in 1954 in Xiamen, China. Lives and works in Paris, France
Geboren 1954 in Xiamen, China. Lebt und arbeitet in Paris, Frankreich
1954年出生于中国厦门，现居住工作于巴黎，法国

Selected exhibitions / Ausgewählte Ausstellungen / 所选展览

1997	"Huang Yong Ping", De Appel, Amsterdam, The Netherlands
	"Péril de mouton", Fondation Cartier pour l'Art Contemporain, Paris, France
1999	"Taigong Fishing: Willing to Bite the Bait", Jack Tilton Gallery, New York, NY, USA
	"Crane's legs, Deer's Tracks", Project Gallery at CCA, Kitakyushu, Japan
2003	"Un cane italiano", Galerie Beaumontpublic, Luxembourg, Luxembourg
2005-07	"House of Oracles: A Huang Yong Ping Retrospective", Walker Art Center, Minneapolis, MI; MASS MoCA, North Adams, MA, USA; Vancouver Art Gallery, Vancouver, Canada

1997年	《黄永砯》De Appel 阿姆斯特丹，荷兰
	《羊祸》Cartier当代艺术基金会，巴黎，法国
1999年	《太公钓鱼，愿者上钩》纽约 Jack Tilton画廊 美国
	《鹤腿，鹿迹》北九州当代艺术中心 横滨 日本
2003年	《意大利狗》Beaumontpublic 画廊，卢森堡
2005-07年	《神殿之屋》黄永砯回顾展，Walker艺术中心，马萨诸塞博物馆，美国；温哥华美术馆 温哥华 加拿大

Selected publications / Ausgewählte Publikationen / 所选著作

"Huang Yong Ping: Cinq questions à des artistes non occidentaux", in: "Art Press", Nr. 136, Paris, May 1989
Dominique Aube: "Huang Yong Ping", in: "Art Press", Nr. 149, Paris, July/August 1990
Fei Da Wei, Huang Yong Ping: "Promenade in Asia", Tokyo 1997

Huang Yong Ping（著）：《Cinq questions a des artistes non occidentaux》Art Press 136页，巴黎 五月刊 1989年
Aube, Dominique（著）：《黄永砯》，Art Press 149页 巴黎 七，八月刊 1990年
费大为，黄永砯（编著）：《散步在欧洲》东京 1997年

HUANG YONG PING 黄永砯

[xuaŋ jʊŋpʰiŋ]

Huang Yong Ping is French, but his Chinese offspring characterises his works like the Great Wall the northern empire. His tendency towards comprehensive works of art as well as to towards monumental strengthen his works like a bulwark, reaching often the frontiers of the feasible – resulting from time to time in censuring measures. Huang's sculptures made of natural material are in fact ironically fanciful installations, enriched by historical references, whimsical artefacts, cheerful animal associations and symbols of intercultural conflicts. With "Le théâtre du monde", an installation of 1993/94, living turtles, snakes, grasshoppers and beetles are to be found together in big cages. Unavoidingly the main subject in these terrariums is to eat and to be eaten, a metaphor for the living space of different ethnic groups.

In 1986 Huang was one of the founding members of the "Xiamen Dada Group", whose radical actions aimed at radically questioning and destroying art as well as artistic value added creations – expressing the deep scepticism about the system and the values of social political coinage in general. The group manifested in heartless exhibitions and public incinerations of artworks its biting criticism. But due to the democratic movement the context of system imminent parameters declined. Today this period is regarded as one of the most innovative phases of recent art history in Asia. Huang like others was forced in 1989 to leave China and settled down in Paris. His 1987 paper clusters made of Chinese and western art books, which were thrown and tumbled in a washing machine made him abruptly famous. He intended to produce pure art being clear and chaotic at the same time – thus being unseizable for art history which sets up values especially in the west.

Huang's subject is the post colonialism. How can the individual stand its ground within the cultural evolution without abandoning the cultural heritage of an artist? – the central question in the work of Huang Yong Ping. In the exile being a new homeland as well, he found his very own impetus and awareness that the political has to

Huang Yong Ping ist Franzose, wiewohl seine chinesische Herkunft sein Werk kennzeichnet wie die Große Mauer das Nordreich. Der Hang zum Gesamtkunstwerk wie zum Monumentalen festigen wie ein Bollwerk seine Arbeiten, die häufig an die Grenzen des Machbaren stoßen – wozu bisweilen auch Zensurmaßnahmen gehören. Huangs aus natürlichen Materialien hergestellte Skulpturen sind in Wahrheit meist ironisch verspielte Installationen, angereichert mit historischen Verweisen, skurrilen Artefakten, heiteren Tierassoziationen und interkulturellen Konfliktsymbolen. Bei „Le théâtre du monde", einer Installation von 1993/94, befinden sich lebende Schildkröten, Schlangen, Heuschrecken und Käfer gemeinsam in großen Käfigen. Unvermeidlich geht es in diesen Terrarien ums Fressen und Gefressenwerden, metaphorisch um den Lebensraum verschiedener ethnischer Gruppen.

Im Jahr 1986 war Huang Gründungsmitglied der „Xiamen Dada Group", deren radikale Aktionen zum Ziel hatten, die Kunst ebenso wie jede künstliche Mehrwertschöpfung rigoros in Frage zu stellen und zu zerstören – Ausdruck tiefen Zweifels am System und den Werten gesellschaftspolitischer Prägung überhaupt. In lieblos arrangierten Ausstellungen und öffentlichen Kunstwerkverbrennungen manifestierte die Gruppe ihre scharfe Kritik. Mehr und mehr zerfiel im Zuge der damaligen Demokratiebewegung der Kontext systemimmanenter Parameter. Heute sprechen viele von der innovativsten Phase der jüngeren Kunstgeschichte Asiens. Wie andere sah Huang sich 1989 gezwungen, das Land zu verlassen. Er ließ sich in Paris nieder. Seine 1987 in einer Waschmaschine gewaschenen, vom Wasser zusammengepappten Papierklumpen aus chinesischen und westlichen Kunstbüchern machten ihn schlagartig berühmt. Reine Kunst wollte er produzieren, klar und chaotisch zugleich – ungreifbar für die Werte setzende Kunsthistorie, die vor allem eine des Westens ist.

Huangs Thema ist der Postkolonialismus. Wie lässt sich die eigene Identität innerhalb der kulturellen Entwicklung behaupten, ohne dass man als Künstler sein kulturelles Erbe

黄永砯是法籍华人，所以他的作品中有北部帝国长城的特色。他艺术作品中趋向综合以及不朽的风格，强化了其壁垒的作用，直到达到一种可行的境界, 有时这是责难的结果。黄永砯的由天然材料制作而成的雕塑，实际上是具有讽刺意义的想象性装置，而历史的概述，奇怪的人工艺术品，欢乐的动物联想和不同文化间矛盾的符号而丰富了其艺术作品。在1993/94年的装置《世界剧场》中，活生生的龟、蛇、蝗虫和甲虫集于一个大笼子里。这些动物培植箱的小动物，不可避免地，处于吃食和被吃食的角色，隐喻着不同种族的生存空间。笼子里分布着残留的杂物，象征着侵略性的文化霸权主义。创造一个充满符号的新真实或者 创造一个隐喻意识的事实瞬间，对黄而言总是很重要的。

1986年黄和他人一起创建了厦门达达组织，他们激进的行为，旨在质疑和摧毁艺术和艺术价值创造 以表达了对社会政治制度体系和价值总体上深深的怀疑。这个团体在户外展出和公开焚烧艺术作品，尖锐地讽刺社会。但是由于民主运动和其因素的即刻衰落，今天那个时期被认为亚洲当代艺术史上最具创新的阶段。黄和其他艺术家被迫离开中国定居在巴黎。他把中外艺术书籍扔入洗衣机中。立刻使其名声远扬。他同时在创作清晰而混乱的纯艺术--因此与艺术史的价值观不合拍的，尤其是在西方世界。

黄的主题是后殖民主义。个体在没有抛弃艺术家的文化传统的条件下，怎样立足于文化发展过程里呢？-关键问题是黄永砯的作品。在其流亡中，他有了自己新的国家，因此 发现了他自己真正动力，意识到政治对国际艺术文化关系中的主导作用。

Jimmy Durham 早已知道 国际文化艺术不过是西方文化和艺术的创新而已，这对以黄永砯为代表的优秀中国青年艺术家而言是却是碰撞。他经常以及到中国传统圣贤体系的《易经》，中国古典哲学中的一个重要元素。在与Joseph Beuys、Jannis

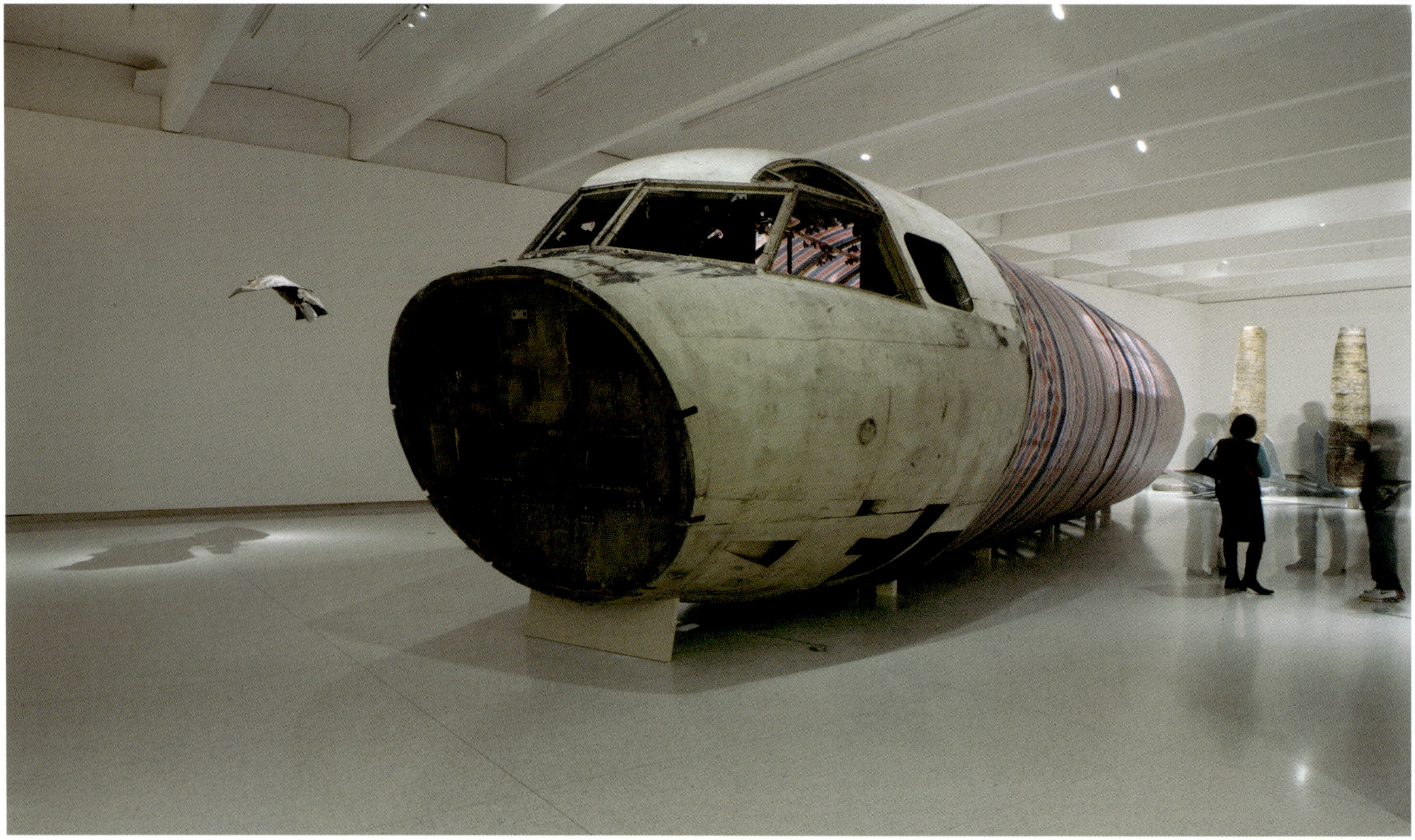

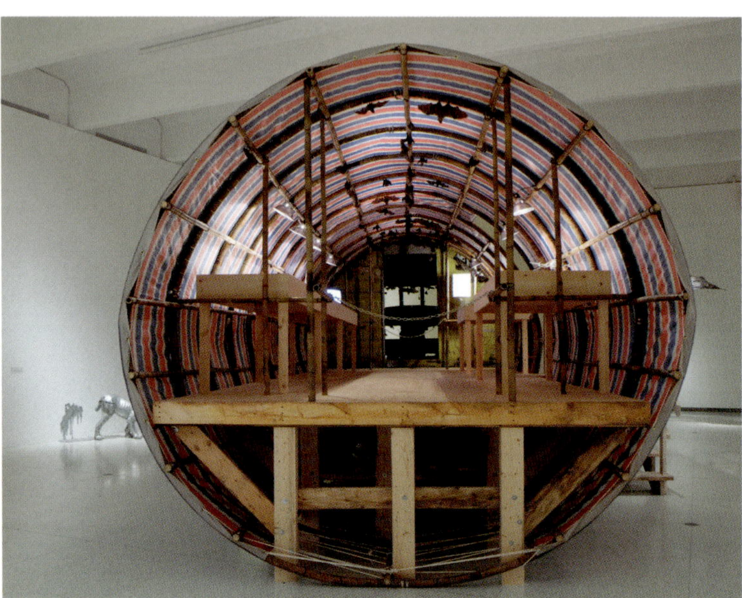

2

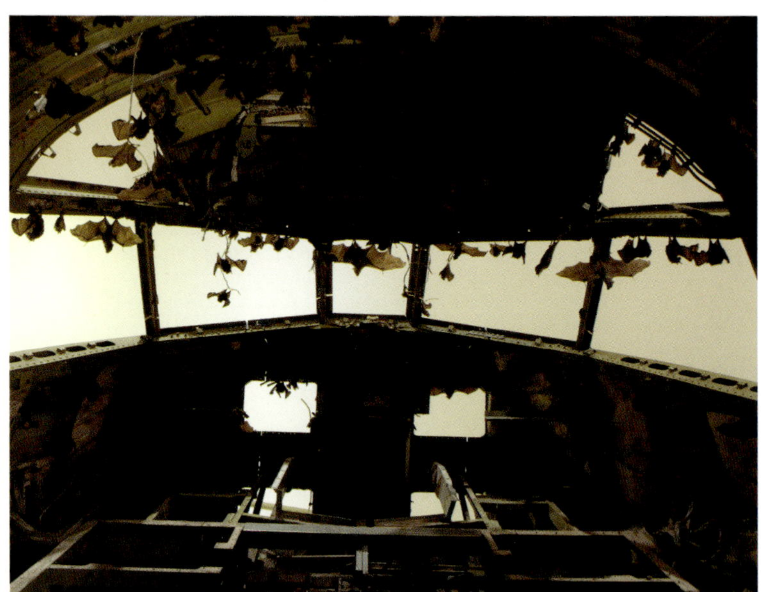

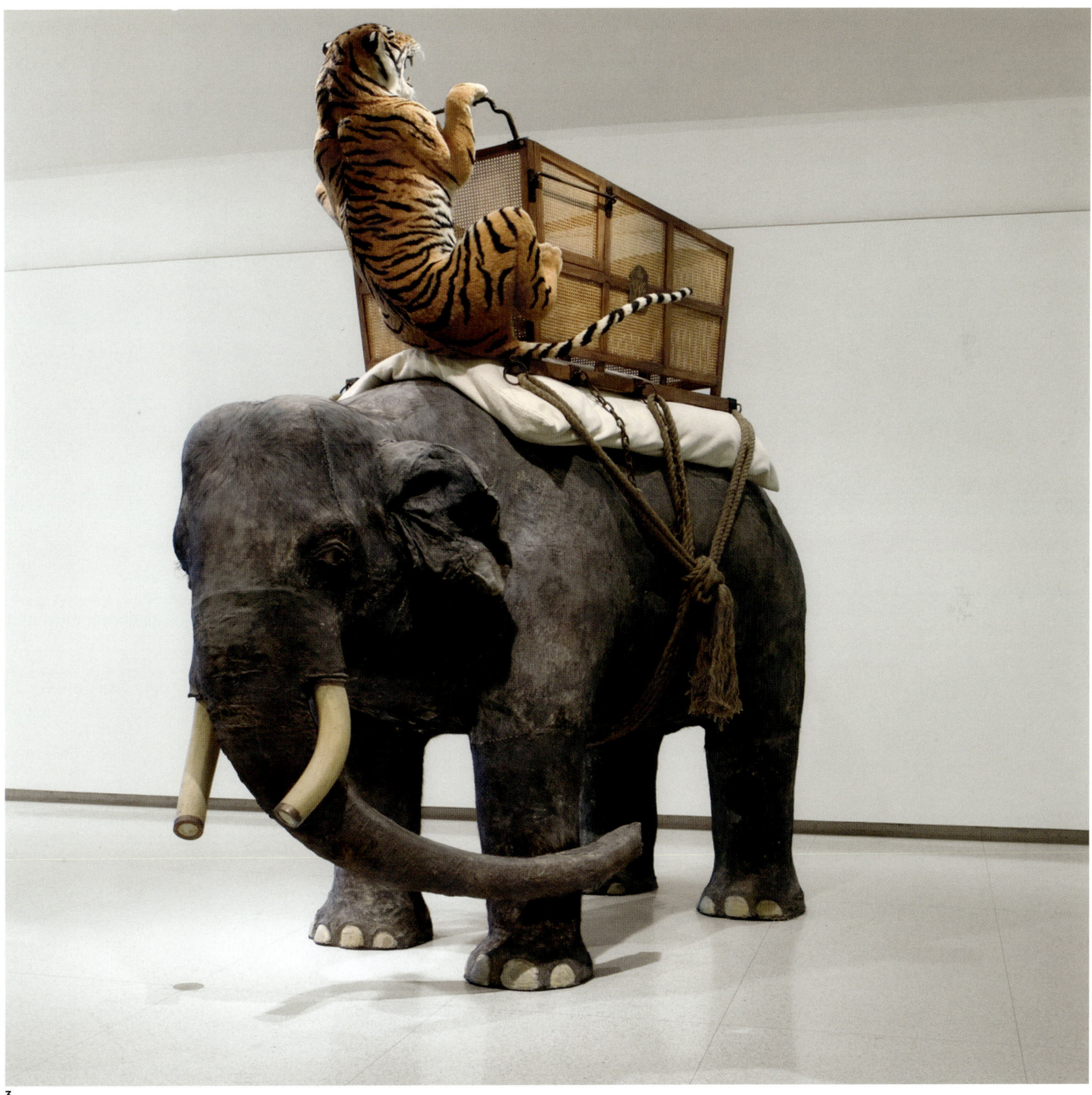

3

4

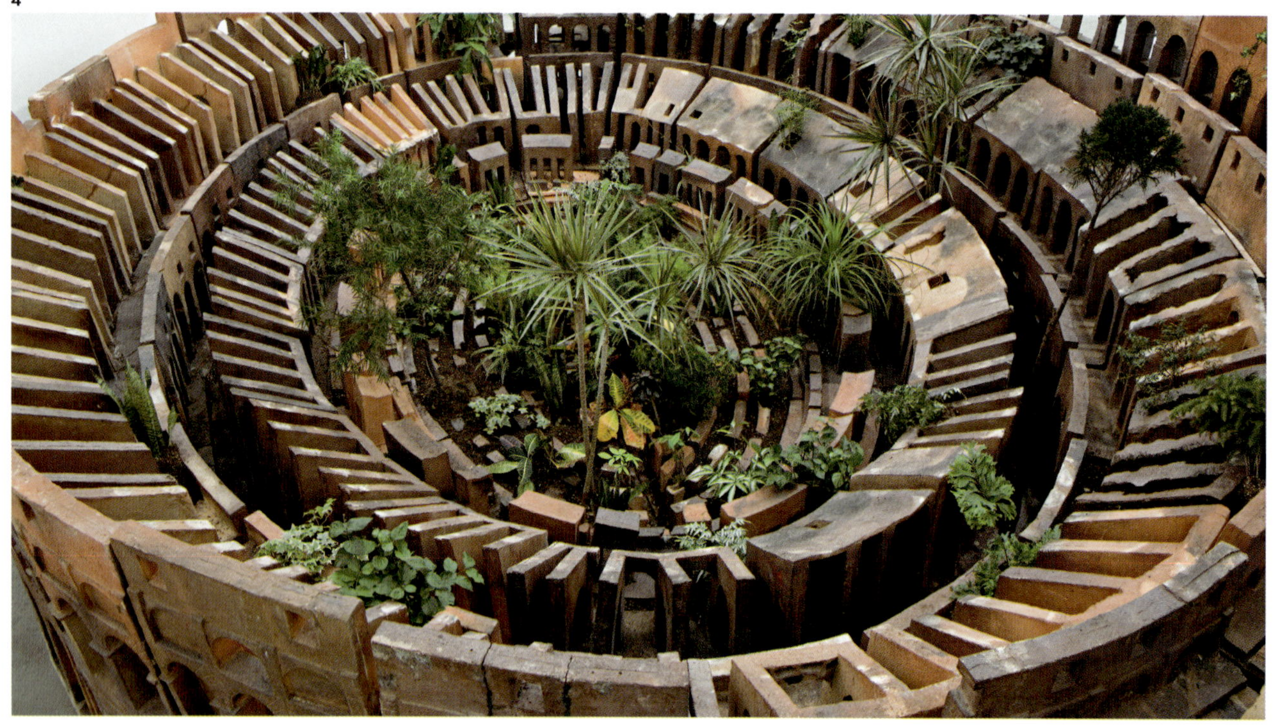

be predominant in internationally artistic-cultural relationships.

Jimmy Durham already knew the international culture and art are an invention of the west, being a confrontation for young Chinese artists with Huang as being one of their most prestigious. He refers often to the old Chinese oracle system of Yijing (Book of Changes), an important element of classic Chinese philosophy. His comment from 1991 is typical: "In fact, the freedom of art of today has become impossible. One has to identify with certain criteria. But how to continue, how to go on with one's work?"

Huang's multiple project "Bat Project" (since 2001) related radically to political reality, is the reconstruction of an American reconnaissance aircraft, which was forced to land after a collision with a Chinese jet over the Chinese airspace, resulting in a severe diplomatic crisis. Finally, the solution was the deconstruction of the American EP3, which could be transported in pieces back to the USA – with the side effect of being inspected thoroughly by the Chinese prior to transport. Huang reconstructed this paradox procedure and exhibited the result in several pieces in China – each time accompanied by protest of the officials. Huang is fascinated by the reverse of technological power: the powerlessness of the existential obedience thereof.

aufgibt? Das ist eine zentrale Frage im Werk Huang Yong Pings. Im Exil, das zugleich eine neue Heimat darstellt, fand er seinen ureigenen Antrieb und die Erkenntnis, dass das Politische in den internationalen künstlerisch-kulturellen Beziehungen vorrangig bleiben muss.

Mit der westlichen Erfindung einer internationalen Kultur und Kunst sahen sich auch die jungen chinesischen Künstler konfrontiert, und Huang in besonderem Maße. Er beruft sich oft auf das alte chinesische Weissagungssystem Yi Ching (das Buch der Wandlungen), ein wichtiges Element der klassischen chinesischen Philosophie. Bezeichnend ist sein Kommentar von 1991: „In Wirklichkeit ist heute die Freiheit der Kunst unmöglich geworden. Man muss sich mit bestimmten Kriterien identifizieren. Aber wie fährt man fort, wie arbeitet man weiter?"

Ganz radikal auf die politische Realität bezogen ist sein mehrteiliges „Bat Project" (seit 2001), in dem er ein amerikanisches Aufklärungsflugzeug rekonstruierte, das nach dem Zusammenstoß mit einem chinesischen Jet im chinesischen Luftraum 2001 zur Notlandung gezwungen wurde, was eine schwere diplomatische Krise zur Folge hatte. Die Lösung war schließlich die Demontage der amerikanischen EP3, sodass sie zerlegt zurück in die USA geschafft werden konnte – mit dem Nebeneffekt, dass die Chinesen das Fluggerät zuvor ausgiebig inspizieren konnten. Diesen paradoxen Vorgang rekonstruierte Huang und stellte das Ergebnis in mehreren Teilen in China aus – jedesmal unter Protest von offizieller Seite. Den Künstler fasziniert die Kehrseite technologischer Macht: die Ohnmacht durch die existentielle Abhängigkeit von ihr.

Kounellis, Enzo Cucchi、Anselm Kiefer 讨论中，他对项目《我们还应当建一座大教堂?》有如下评论：“实际上，如今的艺术自由已经不可能实现。人必须认同某种价值标准。但是如何继续自己的创作呢？由于《易经》，我寻找思想上的慰藉的过程，表达了自己的选择。在如今的时代中，《易经》提供给我们另一种信息形式，它超越了现实世界，超越了当带大众媒体所刻画的现实。那是另一种真实。”

他的多组件项目《蝙蝠计划》(自2001年)，激进地讲述了政治现实，这个项目重现了一架美国侦察飞机在中国领空上与一架中国飞机相撞之后，被迫登陆，因而导致了一场严重的外交危机。最后，双方的解决方案是肢解这架 EP3飞机, 然后分件运回美国，在运输之前由中方完全监控相关情况。黄重现了这一复杂的程序，并在中国分几部分展示这个结果-每次都有官方的反对。黄痴迷于这种科技力量的逆转：对此只能服从，而毫无他法。

Gregor Jansen

5

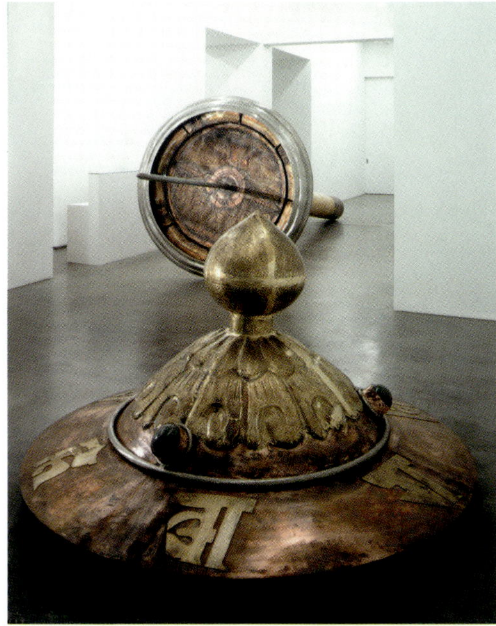

6

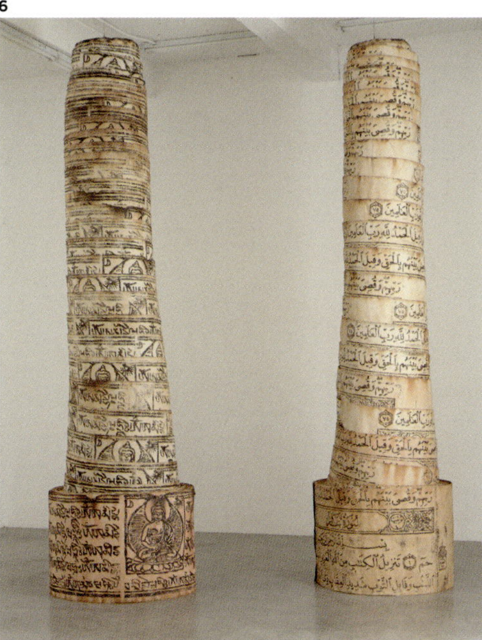

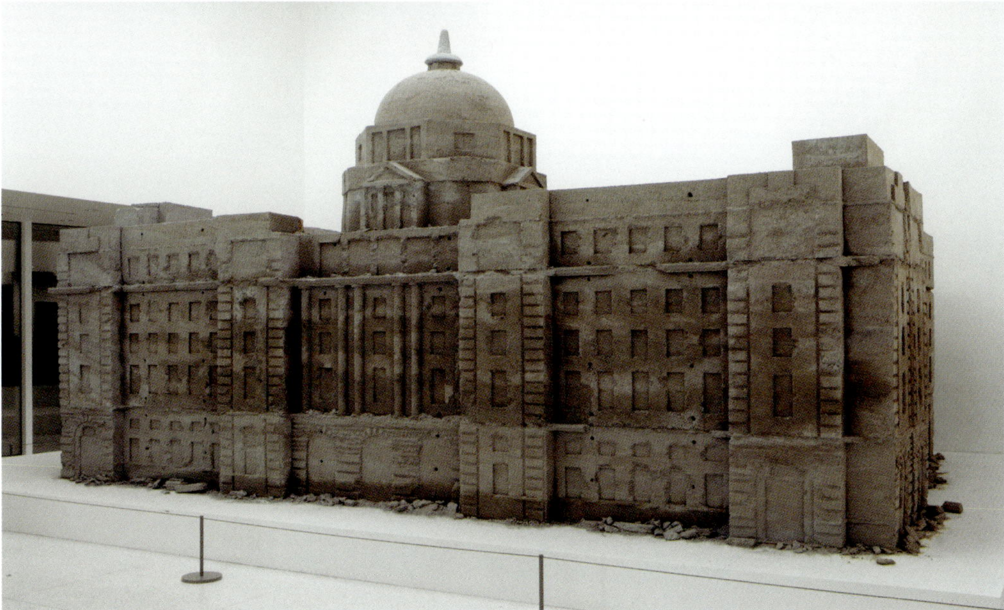

7

1 ***Sixty Year Cycle Chariot***, *1999–2000*
Copper, iron, wood, cloth, 315 x 411 x 236 cm
Kupfer, Eisen, Holz, Stoff, 315 x 411 x 236 cm
《六十甲子车》1999-2000年，黄铜，铁，木料，布，
315 x 411 x 236 cm

2 ***Bat Project IV***, *2004/05*
Mixed media, 2.5 m diameter, 10 m length
Mixed media, Durchmesser 2,5 m, Länge 10 m
《蝙蝠计划IV》2004/05年，混合媒介，直径2.5 m，长10 m

3 ***11 June 2002 – The Nightmare of George V***, *2002*
Concrete, reinforced steel, animal skins, paint, fabric cushion, plastic, wood, cane seat, 244 x 356 x 168 cm
Beton, Panzerstahl, Tierhäute, Farbe, Stoffpolster, Kunststoff, Holz, Korbstuhl, 244 x 356 x 168 cm
《2002年6月11日乔治五世的噩梦》2002年，水泥，钢筋，动物皮，颜料，垫子 塑料，木料，藤椅，244 x 356 x 168 cm

4 ***Colosseum***, *2007*
Ceramic, soil, and plants, 226 x 556 x 758 cm
Keramik, Erde, Pflanzen, 226 x 556 x 758 cm
《角斗场》2007年，陶土，泥土，和颜料，226 x 556 x 758 cm

5 ***"Om Mani Padme Hum"***, 2002
Installation view, Gladstone Gallery, New York
Installationsansicht, Gladstone Gallery, New York
"六字真言"，2002年，装置实景

6 ***Two Typhoons***, *2001*
Burnt paper, 406 x 114 x 114 cm each
Mit Feuer bearbeitetes Papier, je 406 x 114 x 114 cm
《两个大风》2001年，过干纸，每幅，406 x 114 x 114 cm

7 ***Bank of Sand / Sand of Bank***, *2000–2005*
Sand, concrete, 350 x 608 x 438 cm, installation view, Walker Art Center, Minneapolis
Sand, Zement, 350 x 608 x 438 cm, Installationsansicht, Walker Art Center, Minneapolis
《沙的金行/金行的沙》，2005年，沙，水泥，
350 x 608 x 438 cm 装置实景

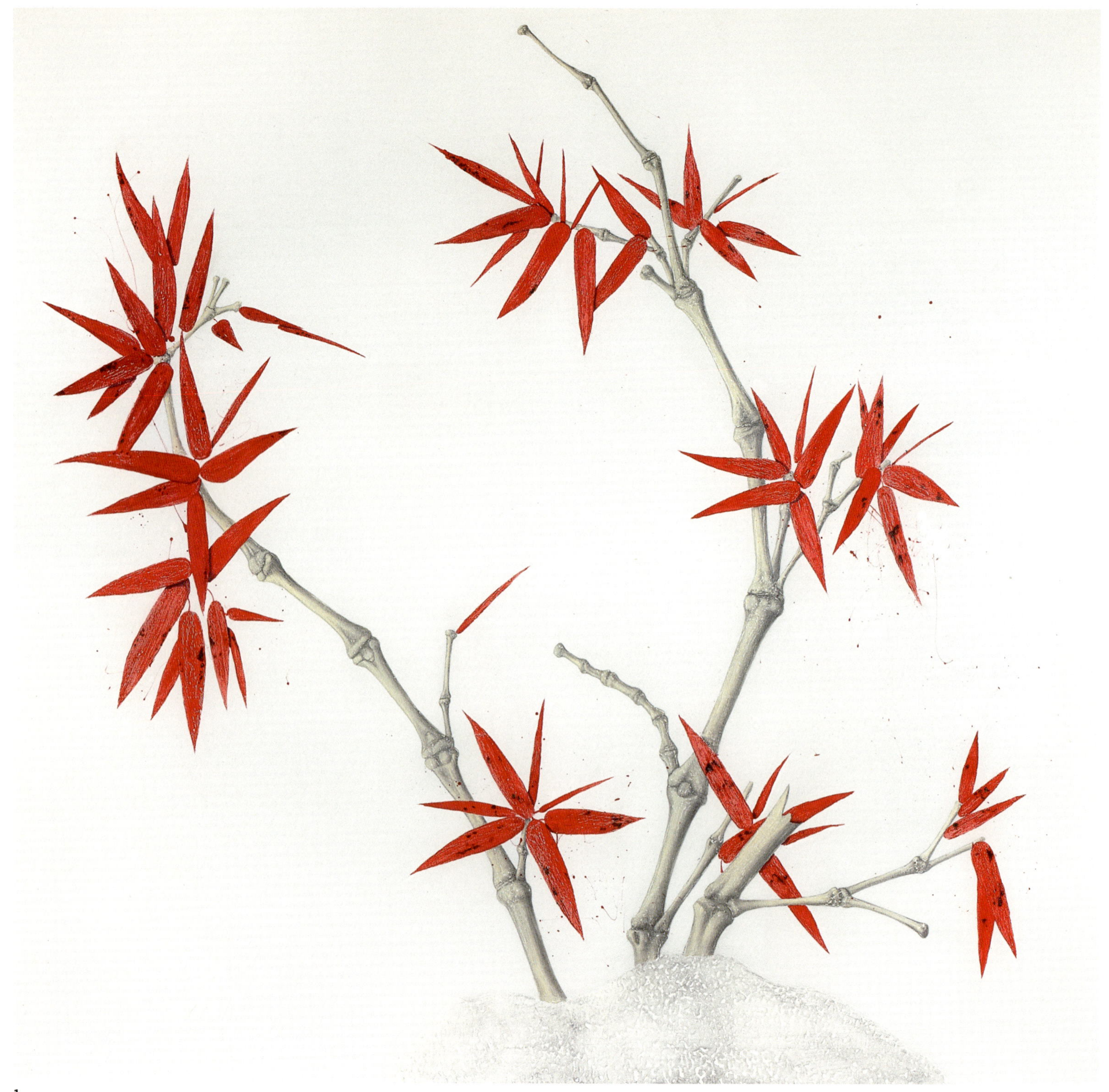

1

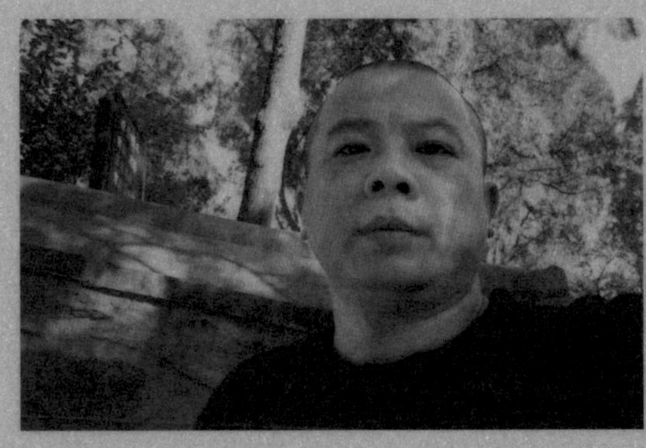

"Each person has the infinite space of freedom to be happy or to suffer. In this rule we can see our own originality, and slowly promote the process of our own mind boundary."

„Jeder Mensch hat einen unbegrenzten Freiraum, um entweder glücklich zu sein oder zu leiden. Daran können wir unsere Originalität erkennen und langsam die Grenzen unseres Geistes erweitern."

"我们每个人都有无限的自由空间，快乐或痛苦. 在这个游戏规则中见到自己的本性，体会心灵境界慢慢提升的过程。"

Born in 1968 in Nantong, Jiangsu Province, China. Lives and works in Beijing
Geboren 1968 in Nantong, Provinz Jiangsu, China. Lebt und arbeitet in Peking
1968 年出生于中国南通，江苏省，现生活工作于北京

Selected exhibitions / Ausgewählte Ausstellungen / 所选展览

1997 "This other realism", Haus der Kulturen der Welt, Berlin, Germany
2000 Shanghai Biennial, Shanghai Art Museum, Shanghai, China
2001 Chengdu Biennial, Chengdu Museum of Contemporary Art, Chengdu, China
2005 "Ji Dachun", Posco Art Museum, Seoul, Korea
2007 "Ji Dachun", Kunstmuseum Bern, Berne, Switzerland

1997年 《其他的现代主义》，德国，柏林，世界文化宫
2000年 《上海双年展》，中国，上海美术馆
2001年 《成都双年展》中国，成都现代艺术馆
2005年 《季大纯》，韩国首尔、Posco Art Museum
2007年 《季大纯》，瑞士伯尔尼美术馆

Selected publications / Ausgewählte Publikationen / 所选著作

"Ji Dachun", Hong Kong 2005
"Ji Dachun", Beijing 2006

《季大纯》Hong Kong 2005年
《季大纯》北京，今日美术馆出版, 2006年

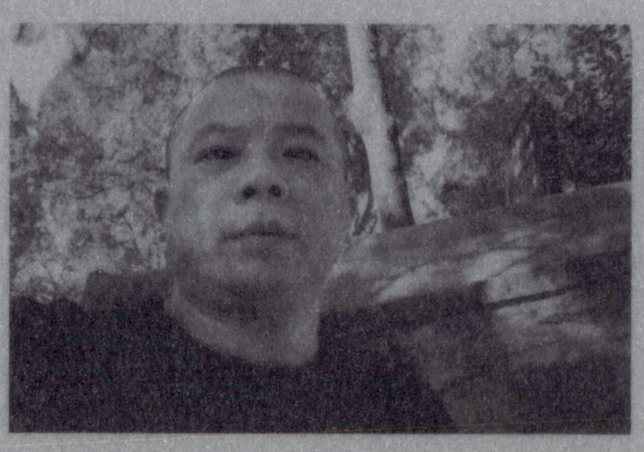

"Each person has the infinite space of freedom to be happy or to suffer. In this rule we can see our own originality, and slowly promote the process of our own mind boundary."

„Jeder Mensch hat einen unbegrenzten Freiraum, um entweder glücklich zu sein oder zu leiden. Daran können wir unsere Originalität erkennen und langsam die Grenzen unseres Geistes erweitern."

"我们每个人都有无限的自由空间，快乐或痛苦。在这个游戏规则中见到自己的本性，体会心灵境界慢慢提升的过程。"

Born in 1968 in Nantong, Jiangsu Province, China. Lives and works in Beijing
Geboren 1968 in Nantong, Provinz Jiangsu, China. Lebt und arbeitet in Peking
1968 年出生于中国南通，江苏省，现生活工作于北京

Selected exhibitions / Ausgewählte Ausstellungen / 所选展览

1997 "This other realism", Haus der Kulturen der Welt, Berlin, Germany
2000 Shanghai Biennial, Shanghai Art Museum, Shanghai, China
2001 Chengdu Biennial, Chengdu Museum of Contemporary Art, Chengdu, China
2005 "Ji Dachun", Posco Art Museum, Seoul, Korea
2007 "Ji Dachun", Kunstmuseum Bern, Berne, Switzerland

1997年 《其他的现代主义》，德国，柏林，世界文化宫
2000年 《上海双年展》，中国，上海美术馆
2001年 《成都双年展》中国，成都现代艺术馆
2005年 《季大纯》，韩国首尔，Posco Art Museum
2007年 《季大纯》，瑞士伯尔尼美术馆

Selected publications / Ausgewählte Publikationen / 所选著作

"Ji Dachun", Hong Kong 2005
"Ji Dachun", Beijing 2006

《季大纯》Hong Kong 2005年
《季大纯》北京，今日美术馆出版，2006年

JI DACHUN 季大纯

[tɕi tatʂʰuən]

Ji Dachun, a profilic artist, melds in his works the Chinese haphazardly simple and humorous view of human life. His characters in his still life paintings manifest a traditional Chinese Literati painting the Chinese in thought and an ideal condition of the Eastern mood, but with a fresh new feeling. His representative works are the "Bencao gangmu" (Book of Chinese herbs, 2003), "Omega", "Just to the Point" (both 2006) and others.

In his works past and present are to be found, the past being easily seen in the past of the individual as private experiences which are easy to define, however the present is filled with game-like humour, the destiny of each individual being indefinite, nearly stochastically transforming their own status, going through with being airborne by different times.

Ji Dachun's work structure possesses a kind of intrinsic life vein, which causes a link between these scattered individuals and items, quite the same as China's living style of the masses. People, landscapes and timeless outer appearance of signs demonstrate his search for "reality likeness" which passes and joins together in a new linguistic environment outstanding freedom under the contemporary Chinese kind of "indefiniteness", one kind of infinite change, unable to grasp. "The indefiniteness" is according to Ji Dachun not a kind of form but the very concrete and subtle experience of life. In fact it manifests towards the trivially mediocre somehow impossible satire and banter, this kind of joke and banter is addressed to the average "masses" sometimes to the "Old Master" or "Leader" the Chinese were following in the past, sometimes addressed to the annoying and negative circumstances of life, creating the "masses". His magic imaginativeness achieves a mixture of time and space, of historical people and people of the presence in subtle and ambiguous relations. This realistic culturally pointed view does not seek the relation to the corresponding reality, but seeks the reality as a kind of projection of former images.

Der überaus produktive Ji Dachun verarbeitet in seinem Werk die für China typische einfache und humoristische Sicht des menschlichen Lebens. In seinen Figuren manifestiert sich auf neue, frische Weise die traditionelle Literatenmalerei, die das im Fernen Osten geläufige Ideal eines vergeistigten Menschenbildes zu erreichen sucht. Wichtige Werke Jis sind u. a. „Bencao gangmu" (2003), „Omega" und „Just to the Point" (beide 2006).

In Jis Schaffen spielen Vergangenheit und Gegenwart eine Rolle, wobei die Vergangenheit, die ihn interessiert, mit den Erfahrungen des Einzelnen identisch und damit leicht definierbar ist. Die Gegenwart dagegen ist für Ji von spielerischem Humor erfüllt, der das Schicksal jedes Einzelnen gänzlich undefiniert in einer gleichsam luftigen Schwebe hält, in der vieles möglich und offen scheint.

Ji Dachuns Werk wird durch eine Lebensader gespeist, die eine Art Verbindung zwischen den disparaten Elementen seiner Wahrnehmung bewirkt und damit einem in China verbreiteten Lebensgefühl entspricht. Seine Menschen, Landschaften und Zeichen demonstrieren seine Suche nach einer Wirklichkeit, die nur vergeht, um sich in einem neuen linguistischen Kontext von immenser Freiheit, nach Maßgabe der gegenwärtig typisch chinesischen Undefiniertheit zu konstituieren – eine Art stetiger Wandel, der nicht greifbar ist. „Undefiniertheit" ist Ji Dachun zufolge keine Frage der Form, sondern eine sehr konkrete und subtile Lebenserfahrung, die sich gegenüber trivialen Mittelmäßigkeiten dadurch auszeichnet, dass sie sich nahezu grenzenlos in ihrer Ironie einmal an die gewöhnlichen „Massen", ein andermal an jene „Alten Meister" oder „Führer" richten kann, denen die Chinesen in der Vergangenheit gern folgten. Bisweilen nimmt Ji mit ihr auch die nervenden Lebensumstände aufs Korn, die das „Volk" kreiert. Seine Vorstellungsgabe führt Gestalten aus Vergangenheit und Gegenwart quer durch Zeit und Raum in mehrdeutigen Beziehungen zusammen. Gleichwohl ist Ji ein Realist, der die Wirklichkeit nicht im historisch Konkreten wirksam sieht, sondern in dessen Projektion in Form überlieferter Bilder.

季大纯是个多产的艺术家，在创作中融和了中国人随意、淡泊而幽默的人生观。他的人物与静物作品除了利用了中国传统文人绘画的资源之外，重在意念与意境中体现中国的东方情怀，从而别有一番新鲜的语感。其代表作有《本草纲目》、《欧米伽》、《点到为止》、《年轻的心》等等。

他的作品中具有“过去”和“现在”二个部分，“过去”往往有迹可寻，每个人在“过去”中的经历往往是具有确定的形象；但“现在”的部分则充满了游戏性的幽默，每个人在“现在”的命运都是不确定的，几乎随机地变换自己的身份，穿行于不同时空中。他在作品结构上有一种内在的生活脉络，使得这些分散的人物和器物之间气息贯通，构成浑然一体的中国式的生存众生相。人物和景物形象和没有明确时代标示的服饰装束，都显示了他的绘画跨出了中国以往写实主义对于“似真性”追求之后，在一个新的语境中的自由穿越与拼合，从而凸现了中国当下的一种“不确定性”的状态，一种无法把握的无限变动。

“不确定性”对于季大纯来说，决不是一种形式，而是一种具体而微的生活经验。实际上是体现出对琐碎平庸的不可奈何的现状的讽刺与戏谑，这种戏仿与戏谑，有些是指向平庸的“众数”，有些是指向中国人以往所侍奉的“大师”、“领袖”，也有些是指向造成“众数”的无聊和消极的生活环境。他瑰奇的想象力使得时间与空间、历史人物与现时人物之间出现了一种混杂、微妙和暧昧的关系。其现实文化针对性不是在对应的现实关系中去寻找，而是在一种既往的形象中寻找现实对它的投影。

Feng Boyi

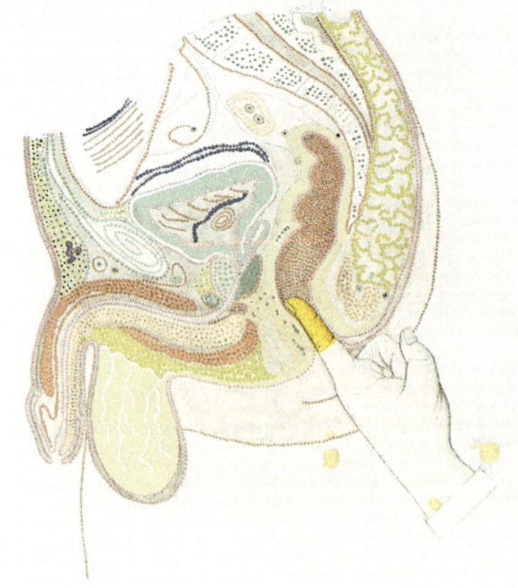

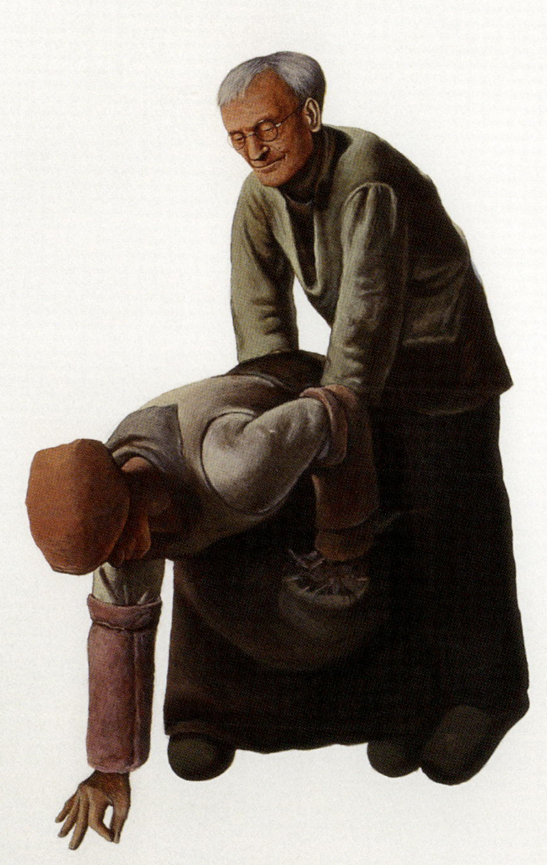

3

4

5

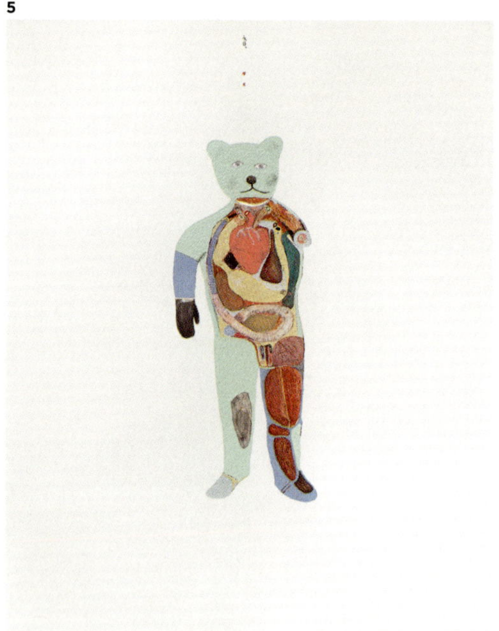

6

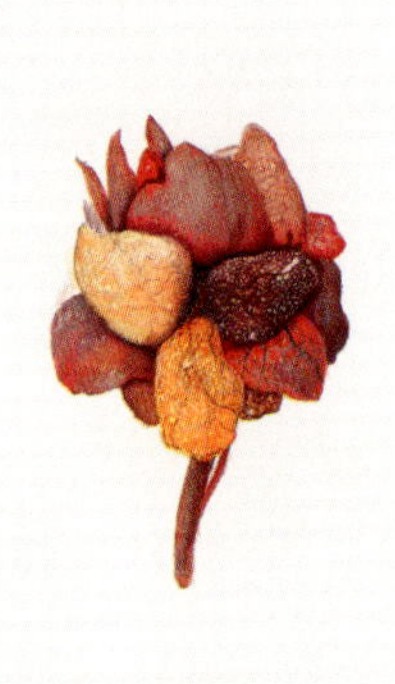

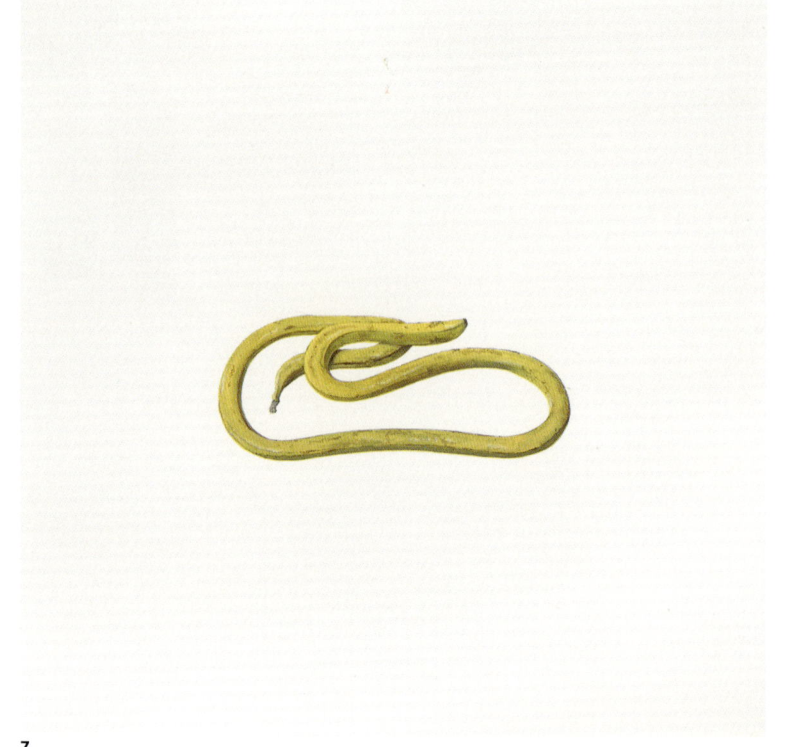

7

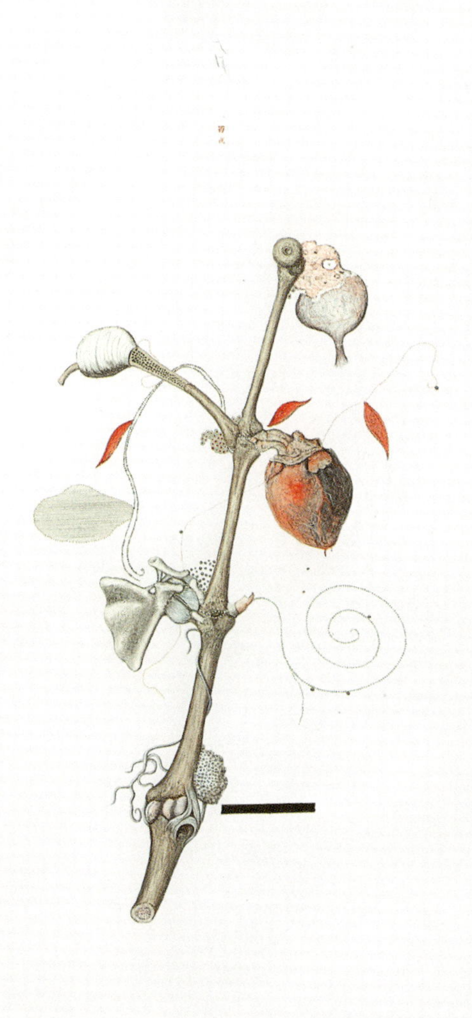

1 ***Mona Lisa Kill Kill***, *2004*
Acrylic on canvas, 140 x 140 cm
Acryl auf Leinwand, 140 x 140 cm
《蒙那里杀杀》2004年, 布面丙稀, 140 x 140 cm

2 ***Go Through the Motions***, *2006*
Acrylic on canvas, 140 x 110 cm
Acryl auf Leinwand, 140 x 110 cm
《通过行動》2006年, 布面丙稀, 140 x 110 cm

3 ***Sigh Picking Wheat***, *2006*
Acrylic on canvas, 150 x 150 cm
Acryl auf Leinwand, 150 x 150 cm
《拾穗者在叹息》2006年, 布面丙稀, 150 x 150 cm

4 ***Red Man, Red Fox, Yellow Demon***, *2004*
Mixed media on canvas, 150 x 110 cm
Mixed media auf Leinwand, 150 x 110 cm
《红人红狐黄夜叉》2004年, 布面混合材料, 150 x 110 cm

5 ***Animal Dissection***, *2006*
Acrylic on canvas, 150 x 110 cm
Acryl auf Leinwand, 150 x 110 cm
《动物解剖》2006年, 布面丙烯, 150 x 110 cm

6 ***Dirty Red Flower***, *2003*
Acrylic on canvas, 150 x 110 cm
Acryl auf Leinwand, 150 x 110 cm
《臟红花》2003年, 布面丙烯, 150 x 110 cm

7 ***Omega***, *2006*
Acrylic on canvas, 150 x 150 cm
Acryl auf Leinwand, 150 x 150 cm
《欧米伽》2006年, 布面丙烯, 150 x 150 cm

8 ***Hearts of Youth***, *2006*
Acrylic on canvas, 150 x 110 cm
Acryl auf Leinwand, 150 x 110 cm
《年轻的心》2006年, 布面丙烯, 150 x 110 cm

9 *Exhibition view*
Ausstellungsansicht
展览实景

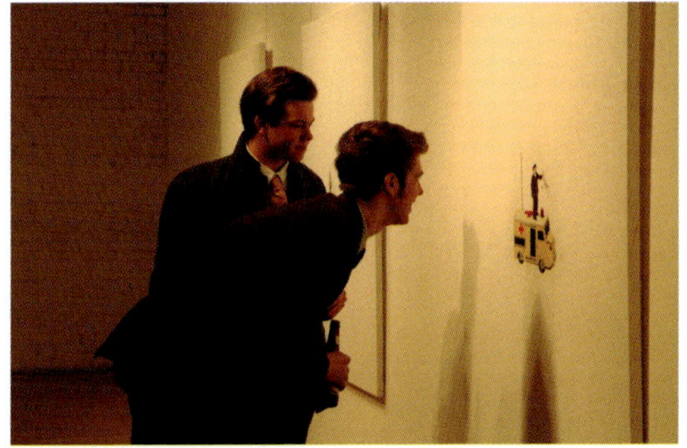

9

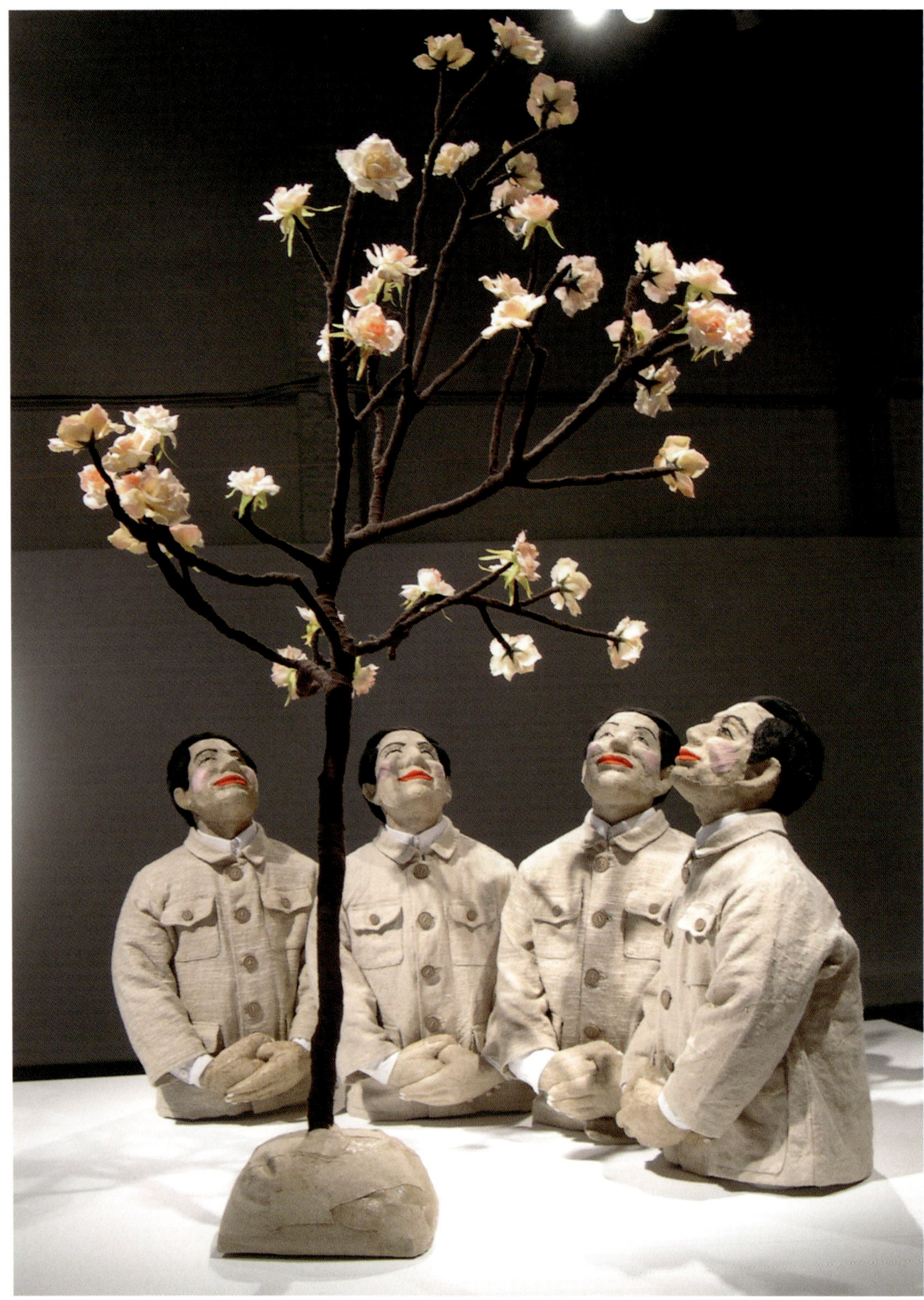

1

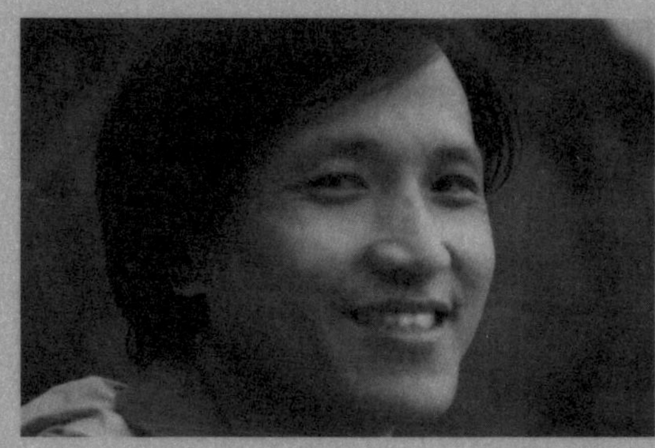

"As an artist, I pay attention to the changes in our life, and I care more on the changing process of our attitude in this changing circumstance and the conjunction between China and the world. This is why I painted these paintings."

„Als Künstler achte ich auf die Veränderungen in unserem Leben und interessiere mich für den Prozess des Wandels unserer Einstellungen dabei und für die Verbindung zwischen China und der Welt. Das ist der Grund, warum ich diese Bilder male."

"作为艺术家，我注意生活的变化，而我更关注在不断变化的环境中，我们对变化过程的态度以及中国和世界的衔接。这就是我画这些油画的原因。"

Born in 1959 in Shanghai, China. Lives and works in Shanghai
Geboren 1959 in Shanghai, China. Lebt und arbeitet in Shanghai
1959年出生于中国上海，现于上海生活工作

***Selected exhibitions* / Ausgewählte Ausstellungen /** 所选展览

1996 "Begegnung mit China, Neuerwerbungen der Sammlung Ludwig", Ludwig Forum für internationale Kunst, Aachen, Germany
1998 "Ji Wenyu", Vermont Studio Center, Johnson, VT, USA
2002 "Money and Value – the Last Taboo", Swiss Expo '02, Arteplage Biel, Biel, Switzerland
2003 "Sweeter than Honey", Esplanade, Singapore, Singapore
2006 "Dressing Up Before Going Out", Museum 52, London, UK
6th Shanghai Biennale, Shanghai

1996年 《中国当代艺术展会•回眸中国》，路德维希博物馆科隆，德国
1998年 《计文于》佛蒙特艺术工作室中心画廊佛蒙特，美国
2002年 《金钱和价值－最后的禁忌》瑞士
2003年 《比蜜甜》Esplanade, 新加坡
2006年 《打扮好了再出门》52美术馆，伦敦，英国
第六届上海双年展，上海

***Selected publications* / Ausgewählte Publikationen /** 所选著作

"Ji Wenyu", Shanghai 2004
Uta Grosenick, Sine Bepler (eds.): "ShanghART Gallery 10 Years", Cologne 2006

《计文于》展册，上海2004年
Grosenick, Uta/Bepler, Sine （编者）:《10年的香格纳画郎》科隆2006

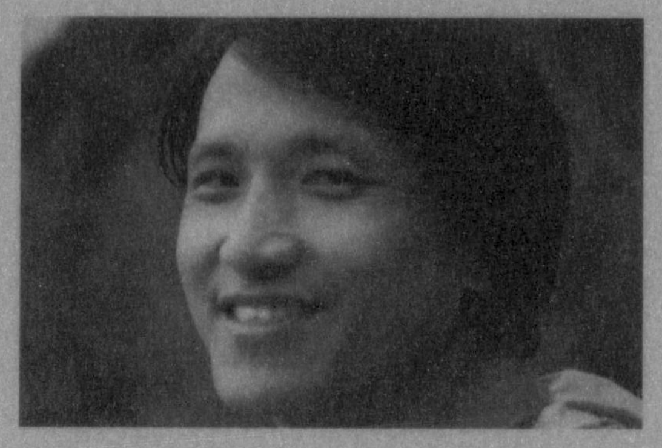

"As an artist, I pay attention to the changes in our life, and I care more on the changing process of our attitude in this changing circumstance and the conjunction between China and the world. This is why I painted these paintings."

„Als Künstler achte ich auf die Veränderungen in unserem Leben und interessiere mich für den Prozess des Wandels unserer Einstellungen dabei und für die Verbindung zwischen China und der Welt. Das ist der Grund, warum ich diese Bilder male."

"作为艺术家，我注意生活的变化，而我更关注在不断变化的环境中，我们对变化过程的态度以及中国和世界的衔接。这就是我画这些油画的原因。"

Born in 1959 in Shanghai, China. Lives and works in Shanghai
Geboren 1959 in Shanghai, China. Lebt und arbeitet in Shanghai
1959年出生于中国上海，现于上海生活工作

Selected exhibitions / Ausgewählte Ausstellungen / 所选展览

1996 "Begegnung mit China, Neuerwerbungen der Sammlung Ludwig", Ludwig Forum für internationale Kunst, Aachen, Germany
1998 "Ji Wenyu", Vermont Studio Center, Johnson, VT, USA
2002 "Money and Value – the Last Taboo", Swiss Expo '02, Arteplage Biel, Biel, Switzerland
2003 "Sweeter than Honey", Esplanade, Singapore, Singapore
2006 "Dressing Up Before Going Out", Museum 52, London, UK
6th Shanghai Biennale, Shanghai

1996年 《中国当代艺术展会•回眸中国》，路德维希博物馆科隆，德国
1998年 《计文于》佛蒙特艺术工作室中心画廊佛蒙特，美国
2002年 《金钱和价值—最后的禁忌》瑞士
2003年 《比蜜甜》Esplanade，新加坡
2006年 《打扮好了再出门》52美术馆，伦敦，英国
第六届上海双年展，上海

Selected publications / Ausgewählte Publikationen / 所选著作

"Ji Wenyu", Shanghai 2004
Uta Grosenick, Sine Bepler (eds.): "ShanghART Gallery 10 Years", Cologne 2006

《计文于》展册，上海2004年
Grosenick, Uta/Bepler, Sine （编者）：《10年的香格纳画廊》科隆2006

JI WENYU 计文于

[tɕi wənjy]

Ji Wenyu's paintings over the last fifteen years maintain a consistent sensibility and set of interests which might be described as interrogating the cultural rhythms of the new China. He does this through a seemingly knowing appropriation of kitsch images deriving from traditional visual forms, contemporary commercial culture, and current government propaganda. While these materials appear in the work of many contemporary Chinese painters, Ji Wenyu manages to montage them and put them into relief in a manner distinct, creating celebratory yet eerie odes that register just one shade off from their real-life inspirations.

Ji Wenyu's paintings from the early and mid-1990s take up the Chinese encounter with Western art history and pop culture. They ape images ranging from Botticelli's "Venus" and Rubens' "Rape of the Daughters of Leucippus" to Disney's Mickey Mouse. The paintings satirizing commercial brands do so by incorporating logos into traditional visual genres like New Year's cards, wishing the viewer quick and easy fortune. The paintings that play on Western art do so, for example, by putting three Mona Lisas clad in a qipao, a military jacket, and a nightgown in front of a mountainous landscape that includes the Great Wall, or juxtaposing a Chinese ceramic garbage can with Jeff Koons' sealed vacuum cleaners.

More recent works appear as collages of everyday objects less than collections of overt political or art-historical symbols. In his relentlessly gaudy palette, Ji runs through a lexicon of the newly ordinary: Windows 2000 compatible laptop computers, Guangming brand milk cartons, high-rise condominium buildings, bottles of red wine and peanut oil. The ordinary is infused with the political, a tactic most obvious in paintings like "Shanghai Food" (2002), in which a smiling George W. Bush and Jiang Zemin (in a famous photo taken at the APEC Summit in Shanghai shortly after September 11, 2001) smile out over a table of dumplings and bread. The characters "Shanghai Snacks" appear across the top of the canvas, in a quaint Socialist-era font. Around this time, a frame motif began to appear in Ji Wenyu's

Im Anliegen seiner Gemälde ist sich Ji Wenyu über die letzten 15 Jahre hinweg treu geblieben; es lässt sich vielleicht mit Hinterfragung der kulturellen Rhythmen des neuen China beschreiben. Ji setzt dies um, indem er sich ganz offenkundig all den visuellen Kitsch aneignet, der sich von traditionellen künstlerischen Formen, aus der zeitgenössischen Kommerzkultur und der aktuellen Regierungspropaganda ableitet. Zwar tauchen solche Elemente im Werk vieler zeitgenössischer Maler auf, doch Ji Wenyu gelingt es, sie auf ganz eigene Weise herauszuarbeiten und damit zugleich feierliche wie unheimliche Oden zu schaffen, deren Wirkung nur eine (allerdings entlarvende) Nuance neben der ihrer Vorbilder aus der realen Welt liegt.

Ji Wenyus Gemälde von Anfang und Mitte der 1990er Jahre greifen die chinesische Begegnung mit der westlichen Kunstgeschichte und Popkultur auf und verwenden dabei Ikonen, die von Botticellis „Die Geburt der Venus" und Rubens' „Der Raub der Töchter des Leukippos" bis zu Walt Disneys Micky Maus reichen. Diejenigen seiner Bilder, die kommerzielle Marken persiflieren, integrieren deren Logos in traditionelle Bildgattungen wie Neujahrskarten, die schlicht und einfach Glück wünschen. Und bei den Gemälden mit westlichen Ikonen platziert Ji etwa drei Mona Lisas im Qipao, dem traditionellen chinesischen Gewand, einer Militärjacke und im Nachthemd vor eine Gebirgslandschaft mit Chinesischer Mauer oder eine chinesische Keramikmülltonne neben Jeff Koons' Vitrinen-Staubsauger.

Ji Wenyus neuere Arbeiten präsentieren sich dagegen eher als gemalte Collagen aus Alltagsgegenständen. Mit seiner schonungslos knallbunten Farbpalette arbeitet er sich durch ein ganzes Lexikon des mittlerweile auch in China Alltäglichen: Windows-2000-kompatible Laptops, Guangming-Milchkartons, Hochhaus-Wohnblocks, Rotwein- und Erdnussölflaschen. Das Alltägliche ist dabei vom Politischen infiltriert, was am offensichtlichsten in Gemälden wie „Shanghai Food" (2002) wird, das George W. Bush und Jiang Zemin (nach einem berühmten Foto vom APEC-Gipfel in Shanghai kurz nach dem 11. September 2001) zeigt, die

在过去十五年中，计文于的油画中保持着一贯的敏感性，质疑新中国文化节奏的变化。通过对传统视觉形式、当代商业文化或当前政府宣传品上的庸俗图片重新创作，他做到了。若其他众多画家也使用相同的素材，计文于则将之剪辑组合并以独特的方式让平常的事物变得引人注目，呈现出喜庆但怪异的歌功颂德场面。

计文于早中期的油画开始让其与西方艺术史和波普文化发生碰撞。摹写的油画包括从波堤切利的《维纳斯》、鲁本斯的《劫夺留西帕斯的女儿》到迪斯尼的《米老鼠》。计文于将商业标志和带有中国传统视觉风俗画融合起来，以此达到讽刺商业品牌的目的，如祝愿好运的新年贺卡。那些戏谑西方艺术的油画也是如此，如在以崇山峻岭中的长城为背景的画面中，三个蒙娜丽莎分别身穿旗袍、军装和晚礼服。

他的近期作品是以日常生活为主题的抽象拼贴画，而非对政治或艺术史标记简单的收集。在他的花花绿绿的调色盘里，计文于以新日常品为创作素材：Windows 2000兼容手提电脑，光明牛 奶箱，高高耸立的公寓楼，红酒瓶和花生油瓶。在油画《上海食品》中，日用品与政治融合一起，这种策略非常明显。画面上满脸笑容的布什和江泽民（该照片拍摄于2001年9月11日后的上海APEC峰会）对着桌面上的饺子和面包开心的笑着；“上海快餐”四个字，以闪亮的社会主义时期的字体显示在画布顶端。大约就在这时，计的作品中开始呈现出一种结构主题：怪异的笑脸。

从2000年起，他的作品风格有所转变，但依然掩藏在本质视觉形式里，如宣传海报或对联。计文于的艺术语言是以墨守成规、半诗歌的中国人节奏为基础，因此相当尖锐。如果宣传标语上的五言和七言对联是对经典诗歌的幽默模仿，那计文于的讽刺对联（有时是重写，有些就是简单地修改）则反过来是模仿的模仿。如对联“端起酒杯喝喝喝，抓起东

2

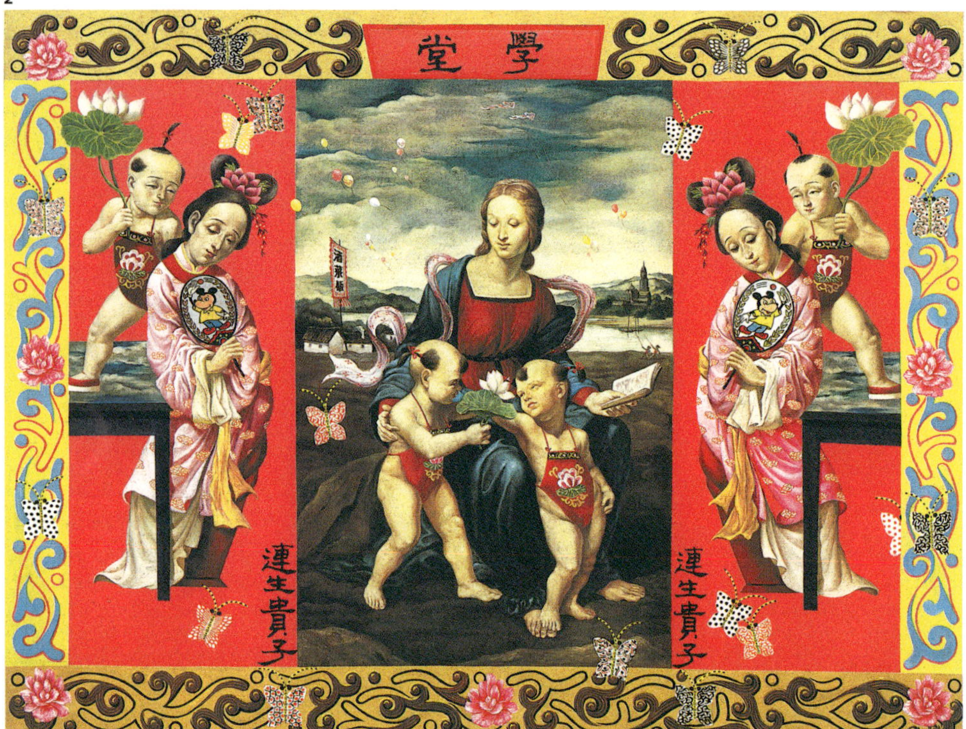

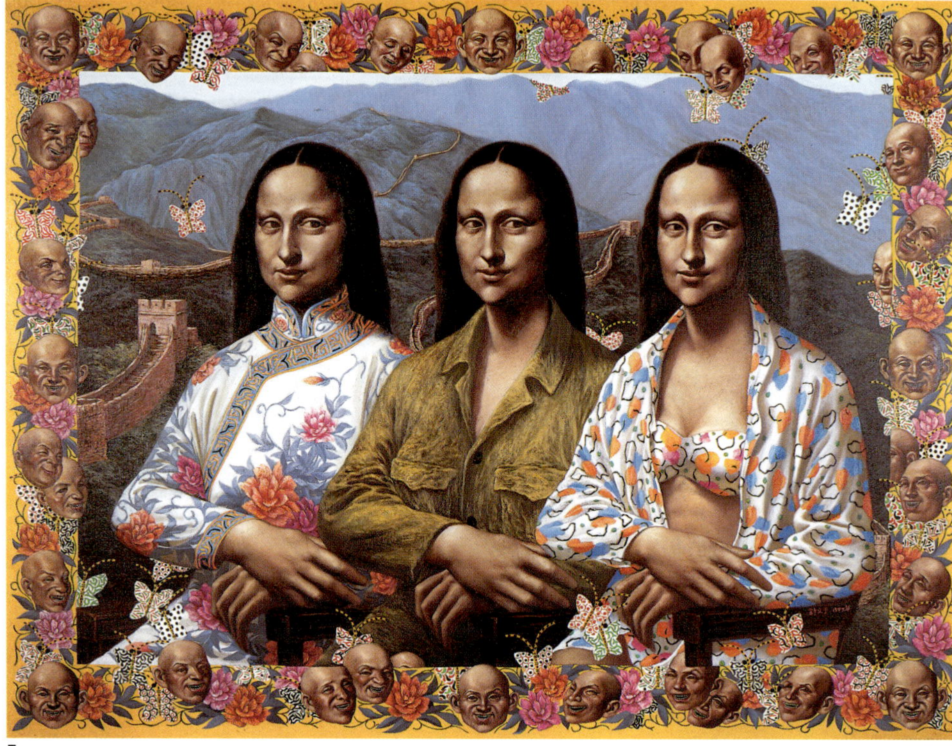

3

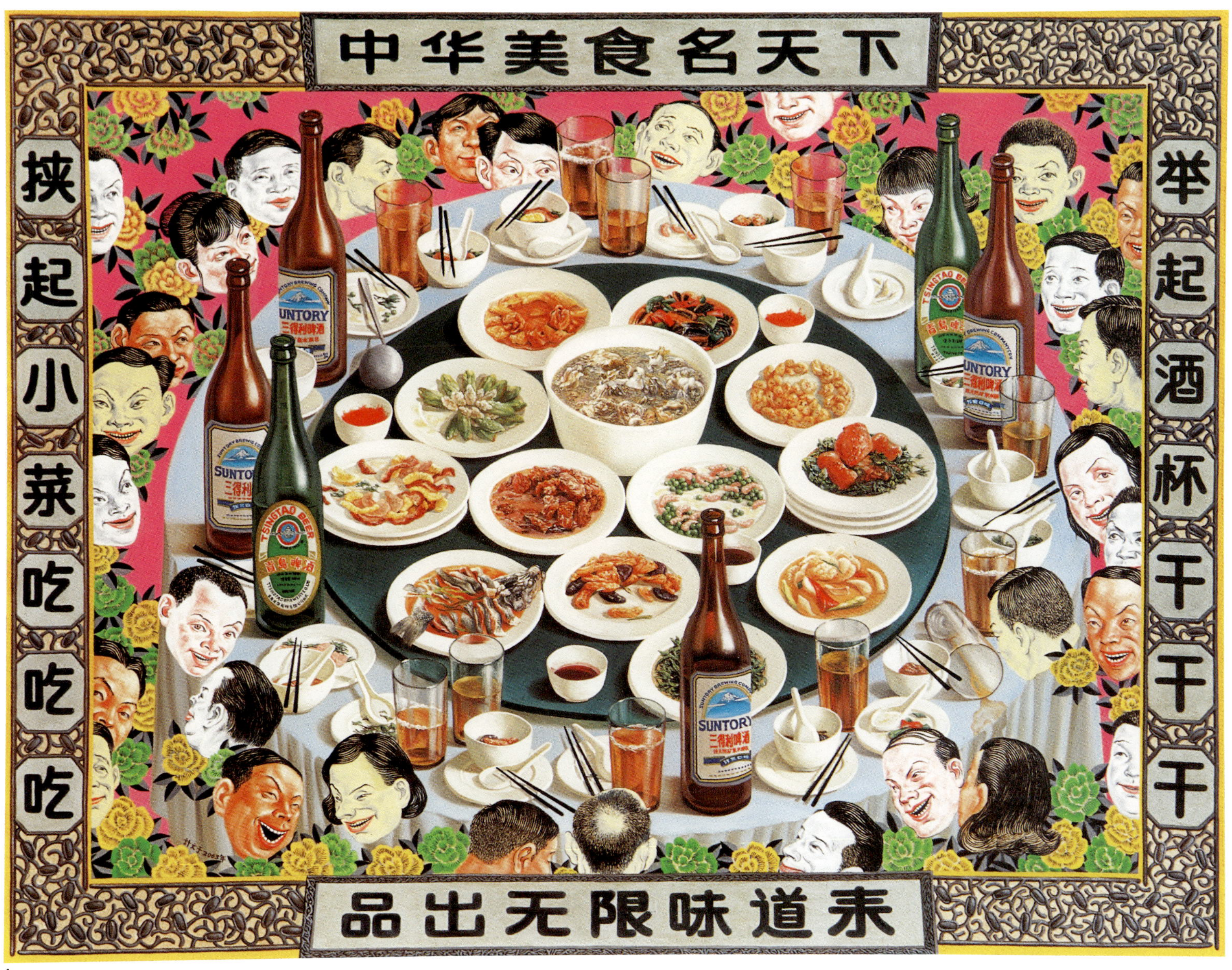

4

5

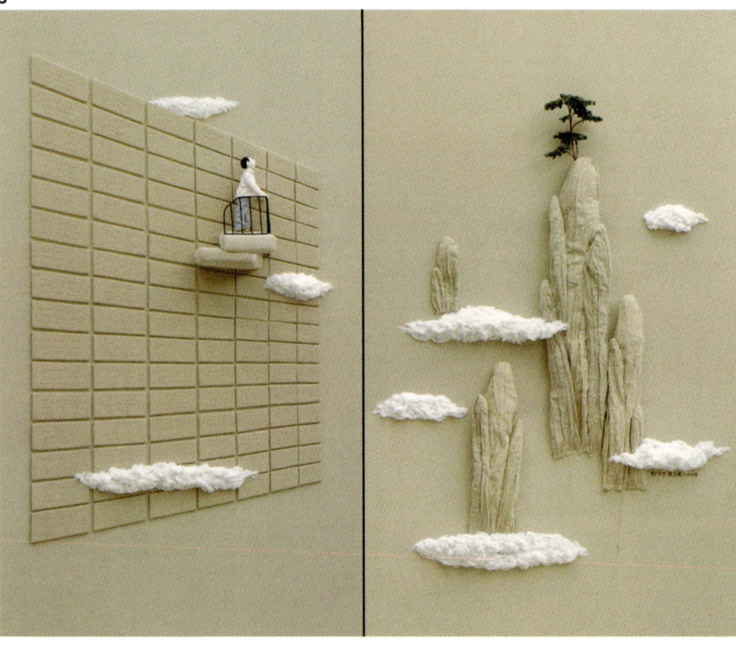

6

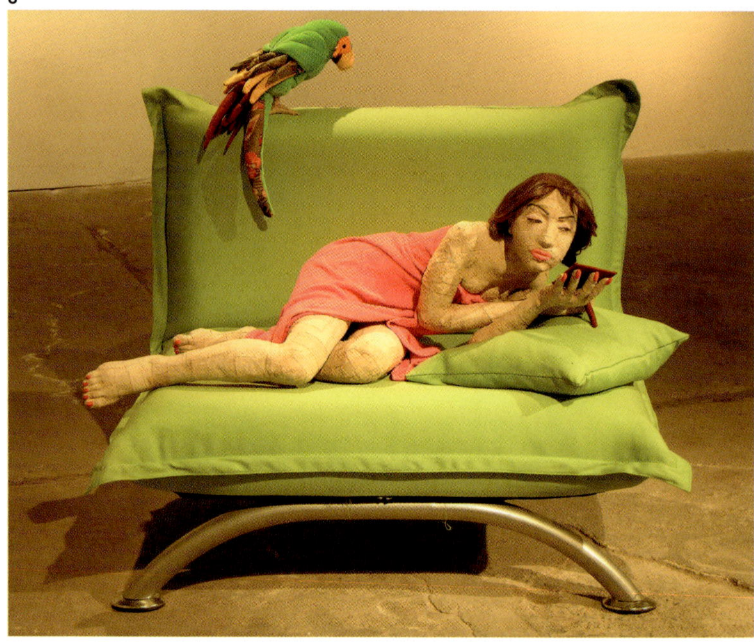

work, whereby a border of eerie, smiling faces surround some of his compositions.

Since 2000, his works have taken a linguistic turn, although one still masked in essentially visual forms such as propaganda posters or the poetic couplets (duilian) hung on either side of doors at the Spring Festival. Ji Wenyu's painted words are stinging, based on the rhythms of bureaucratic, semi-poetic Chinese. If the five and seven character couplets in which propaganda slogans are often expressed are a travesty of classical poetry, Ji's ironic couplets – sometimes rewritten, others simply appropriated – are in turn travesties of these travesties, overly simple to the point of axiomatic idiocy. In sentences like "Pick Up the Wineglass and Drink Drink Drink; Grab the Food and Eat Eat Eat" as in labels such as "Leaders Cut the Ribbon," he exposes the logics and tautologies that drive Chinese state and society.

Trained not in the academy system but at a municipal arts-and-crafts school in Shanghai, his compositions – includremain inflected by a folk sensibility associated with things like the New Year's calendars common throughout China in the twentieth century. Perhaps owing to his cosmopolitan Shanghai identity, these images are able to resonate at once with a knowing native audience and a curious international one. As Ji Wenyu has said of his country, "We are in the process of linking up with the western world. What the west has, we must have. What the west lacks we must also have. Our lives are sweeter than honey."

sich über einen Tisch voller Teigtaschen und Brot hinweg anlächeln; über den oberen Rand des Gemäldes verlaufen die Bildzeichen für „Shanghai Snacks" in einer altmodischen Schrifttype aus der sozialistischen Ära. Etwa zur gleichen Zeit umschließt Ji auch erstmals einige seiner Kompositionen mit einem Rahmen aus unheimlich lächelnden Gesichtern.

Seit 2000 hat Jis Werk eine Wende zur Sprachlichkeit genommen, die visuelle Formen maskiert, wie bei Propagandaplakaten oder den poetischen Reimpaaren (duilian), die man zum Frühlingsfest beiderseits der Türen anbringt. Ji Wenyus bissige gemalte Worte basieren auf den Rhythmen des halbdichterischen Bürokratenchinesisch. Propagandaslogans werden in China für gewöhnlich in Form von Fünf- und Sieben-Zeichen-Reimen ausgedrückt: Sieht man sie als Travestie der klassischen Poesie, so sind jene ironischen Reime, die Ji sich darauf macht, ihrerseits Travestien von Travestien, extrem vereinfacht bis hin zum offensichtlichen Schwachsinn. Mit Sentenzen wie „Heb das Weinglas und trink trink trink; greif das Essen und iss iss iss" oder „Führer durchschneiden das Band" stellt er die Phraseologie bloß, die den chinesischen Staat und seine Gesellschaft trägt.

Ji Wenyu wurde nicht im Akademiesystem, sondern an einer städtischen Kunsthandwerksschule in Shanghai ausgebildet, weshalb seine Arbeiten von einer bodenständigen volkstümlichen Sensibilität geprägt sind. Vielleicht hat es mit seiner kosmopolitischen Shanghaier Identität zu tun, dass er beim heimischen Publikum ebenso Anklang findet wie beim internationalen – oder wie er selbst sagt: „Wir sind dabei, uns an die westliche Welt anzukoppeln. Was der Westen hat, müssen wir auch haben. Was dem Westen fehlt, müssen wir erst recht haben. Unser Leben ist süßer als Honig."

西吃吃吃”以及横幅“领导剪彩”，揭露了中国政权和社会的逻辑方式和繁文缛节。

虽然他毕业于上海市工艺美术学校而非艺术院校，但他的作品也受到与民间感性相关事物的影响，如90年代中国流行新年挂历。也许因为其国际化上海人的身份，这些图像因此立即引起本国观众和海外观众的共鸣。计文于谈到祖国时说：我们正处在与西方国家连为一体的进程中。西方有的东西，我们也必须有。西方所没有的，我们也仍然有。我们的生活比蜜还要甜美。

Philip Tinari

7

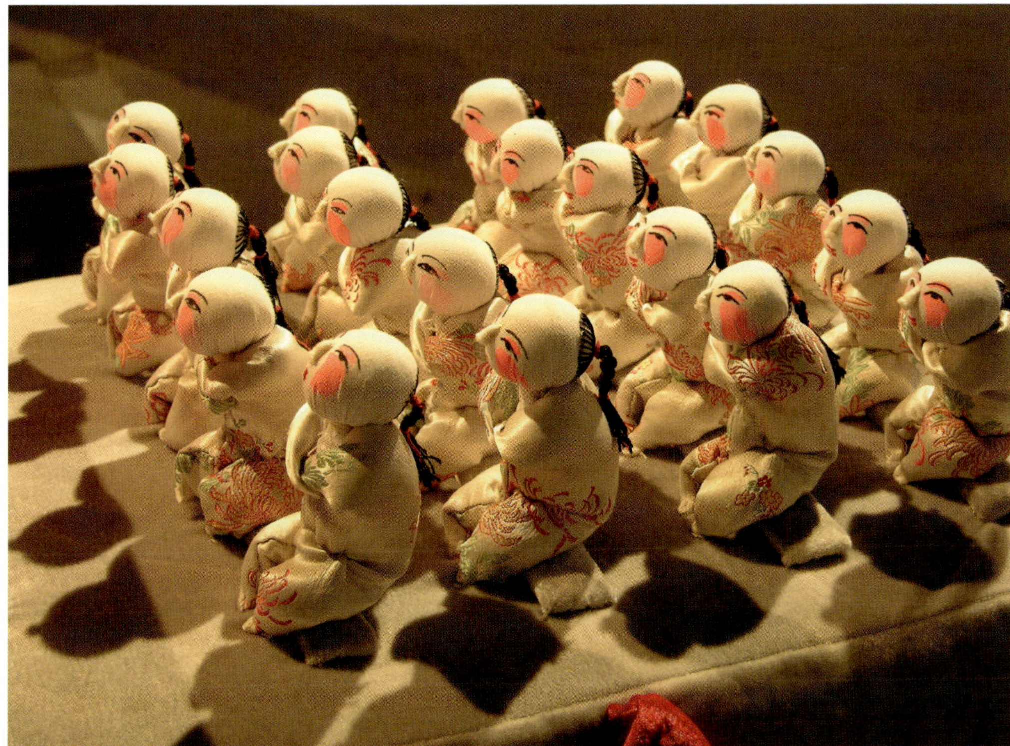

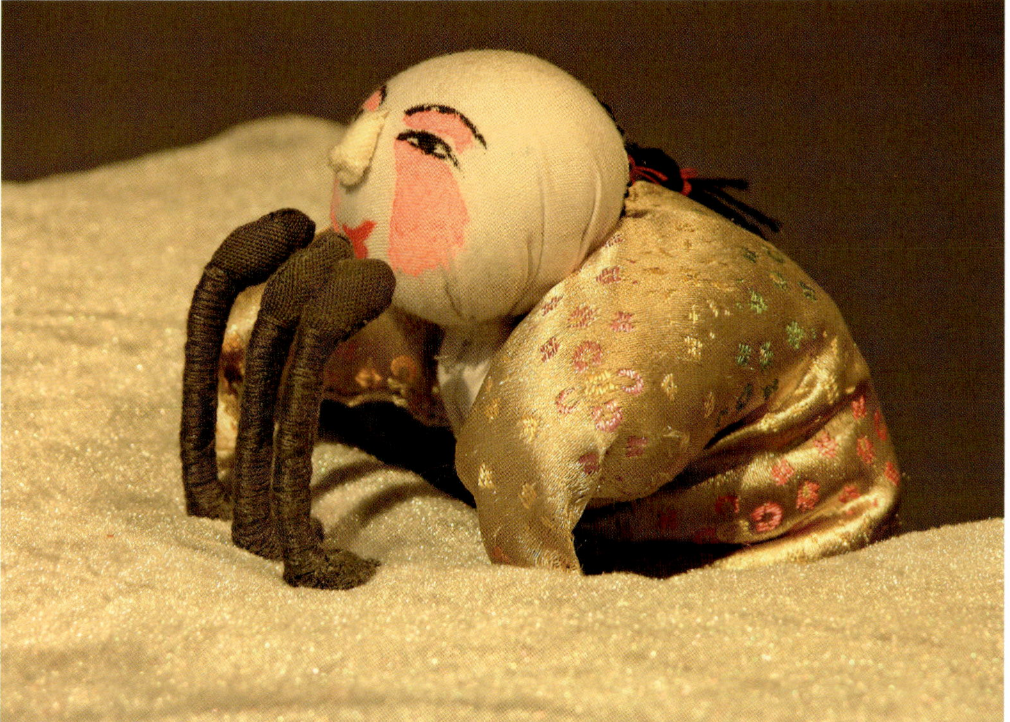

8

1 ***Enjoy flowers***, *2005*
In collaboration with Zhu Weibing, linen, stone, insulative packing materials, fake flowers, latex, iron, wood, 140 x 140 x 142 cm
In Zusammenarbeit mit Zhu Weibing, Leinen, Stein, Isoliermaterial, künstliche Blumen, Latex, Eisen, Holz, 140 x 140 x 142 cm
《赏花》（与朱卫兵和合作）2005年，亚麻，石头，绝缘包装材料，假花，乳胶，铁，木料 140 x 140 x 142 cm

2 ***Teaching next generation***, *1996*
Oil on canvas, 89 x 116 cm
Öl auf Leinwand, 89 x 116 cm
《教育下一代》1996年，布面油画，89 x 116 cm

3 ***Mona Lisa in China***, *1995*
Oil on canvas, 89 x 116 cm
Öl auf Leinwand, 89 x 116 cm
《中国的蒙娜丽莎》1995年，布面油画，89 x 116 cm

4 ***Chinese food is well known in the world***, *2003*
Oil on canvas, 114 x 146 cm
Öl auf Leinwand, 114 x 146 cm
《中国食物世界闻名》2003年，布面油画，114 x 146 cm

5 ***Watch the view***, *2005*
In collaboration with Zhu Weibing, corrugated paper, gauze, linen, sponge, 300 x 250 x 30 cm
In Zusammenarbeit mit Zhu Weibing, gewelltes Papier, Gaze, Leinen, Schwamm, 300 x 250 x 30 cm
《观景》（与朱卫兵和合作）2005，瓦楞纸，沙布，亚麻布，海绵，300 x 250 x 30 cm

6 ***Make beautiful***, *2005*
In collaboration with Zhu Weibing, linen, fabric, latex, insulative packing materials, chair, 108 x 88 x 106 cm
In Zusammenarbeit mit Zhu Weibing, Leinen, Stoff, Latex, Isoliermaterial, Stuhl, 108 x 88 x 106 cm
《打扮好了再出门》（与朱卫兵和合作）2005年，亚麻，纺织物，乳胶，绝缘包装物，椅子，108 x 88 x 106 cm

7 ***Meeting***, *2006*
In collaboration with Zhu Weibing, newspaper, corrugated paper, plush, sponge, 90 x 63 x 52 cm
In Zusammenarbeit mit Zhu Weibing, Zeitungspapier, gewelltes Papier, Plüsch, Schwamm, 90 x 63 x 52 cm
《小巴拉子开会了》（与朱红兵合作）2006年，报纸，瓦楞纸，填充棉，丝绒，布料，海棉，90 x 63 x 52 cm

8 ***Meeting***, *2006*
In collaboration with Zhu Weibing, newspaper, corrugated paper, plush, sponge, 90 x 63 x 52 cm (detail)
In Zusammenarbeit mit Zhu Weibing, Zeitungspapier, gewelltes Papier, Plüsch, Schwamm, 90 x 63 x 52 cm (Detail)
《小巴拉子开会了》（与朱红兵合作），2006年，报纸，瓦楞纸，填充棉，丝绒，布料，海棉，90 x 63 x 52 cm（详细）

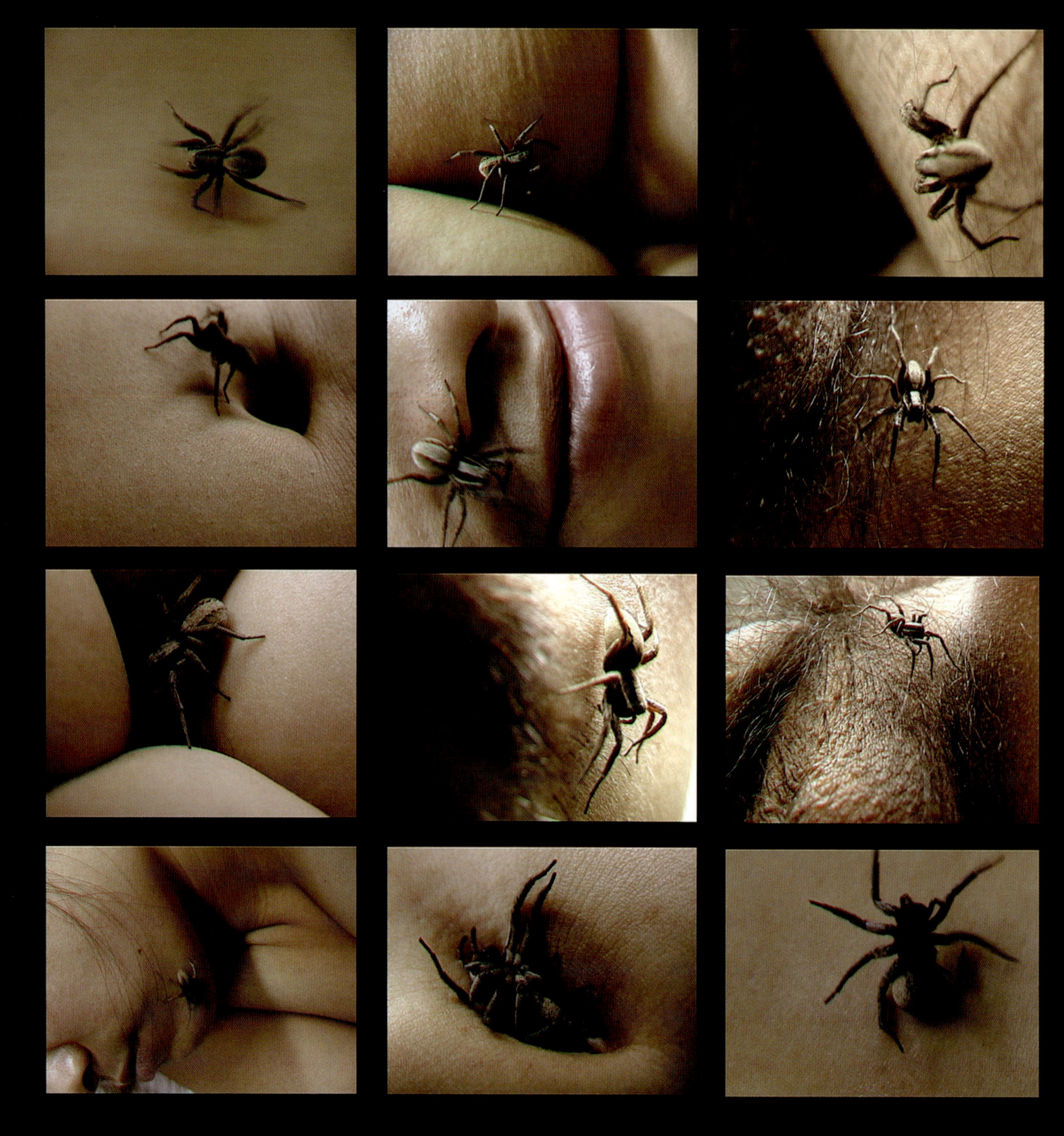

1

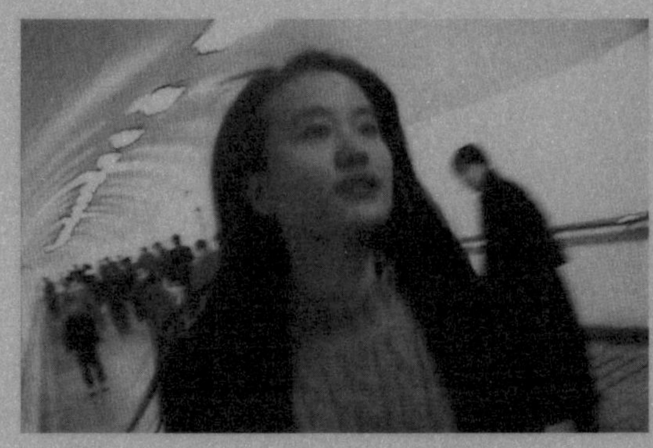

“Emotions are small intervals of time that have a beginning and an end. All my videos can free us from pre-established ideas that we have gained through education.”

„Emotionen sind kleine Zeitintervalle mit einem Anfang und einem Ende. Alle meine Videos können uns von überkommenen Ideen befreien, die wir durch unsere Erziehung erworben haben.“

“情感是一小段时光间隔，有起点也有终点。我的录像能将把我们从先前观念中解放出来，那些从教育中获得的观念。”

Born in 1972 in Xuancheng, China. Lives and works in Beijing and Amsterdam, The Netherlands
Geboren 1972 in Xuancheng, China. Lebt und arbeitet in Peking und Amsterdam, Niederlande
1972年出生于中国安徽宣城，现于北京和阿姆斯特丹居住工作

***Selected exhibitions* / Ausgewählte Ausstellungen /** 所选展览

2001 “Fantasia-1”, space im A, Seoul, Korea
2002 “C'est pas du cinema”, Studio national des arts contemporains, Fresnoy, France
2003 “Alors, la Chine?”, Centre Georges Pompidou, Paris, France
2004 “Kan Xuan and Cui Xiuwen”, Museum d'Art contemporain, Bordeaux, France
2005 “A Molecular History of Everything”, Australian Centre for Contemporary Art, Melbourne, Australia
2006 “A happy girl”, Ikon Gallery, Birmingham, UK
2007 52. Biennale di Venezia, Venice, Italy

2001年 《幻想曲1》首尔，韩国
2002年 《这不是电影》国立弗莱诺瓦制作室 法国
2003年 《中国怎么样?》蓬皮杜艺术中心，巴黎，法国
2004年 《阚萱和崔岫闻影像作品展》波尔多博物馆，波尔多，法国
2005年 《事物的历史》澳大利亚当代艺术中心悉尼，澳大利亚
2006年 《开心女孩》伊肯美术馆，伯明翰，英国
2007年 第52届威尼斯双年展，威尼斯，意大利

***Selected publications* / Ausgewählte Publikationen /** 所选著作

Bernhard Fibicher, Matthias Frehner (eds.): “Mahjong. Chinesische Gegenwartskunst aus der Sammlung Sigg”, Ostfildern-Ruit 2005

Fibicher, Bernhard/Frehner, Matthias （编著）：《麻将—希客收藏的中国当代艺术展》斯图加特2005年

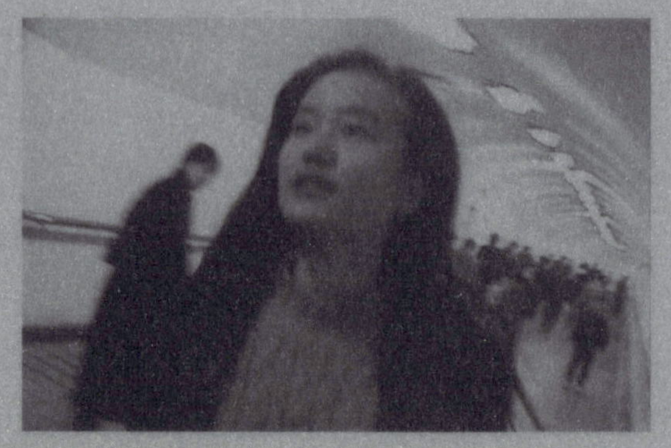

"Emotions are small intervals of time that have a beginning and an end. All my videos can free us from pre-established ideas that we have gained through education."

„Emotionen sind kleine Zeitintervalle mit einem Anfang und einem Ende. Alle meine Videos können uns von überkommenen Ideen befreien, die wir durch unsere Erziehung erworben haben."

"情感是一小段时光间隔，有起点也有终点。我的录像能将把我们从先前观念中解放出来，那些从教育中获得的观念。"

Born in 1972 in Xuancheng, China. Lives and works in Beijing and Amsterdam, The Netherlands
Geboren 1972 in Xuancheng, China. Lebt und arbeitet in Peking und Amsterdam, Niederlande
1972年出生于中国安徽宣城，现于北京和阿姆斯特丹居住工作

Selected exhibitions / Ausgewählte Ausstellungen / 所选展览

2001 "Fantasia-1", space im A, Seoul, Korea
2002 "C'est pas du cinema", Studio national des arts contemporains, Fresnoy, France
2003 "Alors, la Chine?", Centre Georges Pompidou, Paris, France
2004 "Kan Xuan and Cui Xiuwen", Museum d'Art contemporain, Bordeaux, France
2005 "A Molecular History of Everything", Australian Centre for Contemporary Art, Melbourne, Australia
2006 "A happy girl", Ikon Gallery, Birmingham, UK
2007 52. Biennale di Venezia, Venice, Italy

2001年 《幻想曲1》首尔，韩国
2002年 《这不是电影》国立弗莱诺瓦制作室 法国
2003年 《中国怎么样?》蓬皮杜艺术中心，巴黎，法国
2004年 《阚萱和崔岫闻影像作品展》波尔多博物馆，波尔多，法国
2005年 《事物的历史》澳大利亚当代艺术中心悉尼，澳大利亚
2006年 《开心女孩》伊肯美术馆，伯明翰，英国
2007年 第52届威尼斯双年展，威尼斯，意大利

Selected publications / Ausgewählte Publikationen / 所选著作

Bernhard Fibicher, Matthias Frehner (eds.): "Mahjong. Chinesische Gegenwartskunst aus der Sammlung Sigg", Ostfildern-Ruit 2005

Fibicher, Bernhard/Frehner, Matthias （编著）：《麻将—希客收藏的中国当代艺术展》斯图加特2005年

KAN XUAN 阚萱

[kʰan ɕyɛn]

Kan Xuan is one of the most important female video artists in China, working with installation and performance elements, and additionally known for her photographs. The appeal of her art lies between experienced and imagined reality, the frontiers thereof being floating. In a world of unlimited possibilities being understood not as a total of given facts but of a continuously recreating cosmos in our consciousness, Kan Xuan's works represent the mirror of her personal experiences. To broaden and sharpen her own conception as well as the one of the spectator, the artist focuses on the intimate and often neglected details. She is neither interested in things as they are, but in the mutual relationship and the comprehensive relationship network, nor the representation of reality but in the presence of a potential world which shall become absorbable through her works.

The emotional and cognitive potential for activation being imminent in her films are optimised by Kan Xuan, using performance and installation elements as artistic articulation whereby the artist is the protagonist in most cases. Kan Xuan is fond of the game with all senses, challenging the perception of her self and of the spectator by repeating obsessive-like actions and manipulating sense of sight by certain techniques as slowing down, colour manipulation and striking sounds.

Kan Xuan surpasses frontiers and appeals to the sensitivity and imagination of the spectator. Her often extreme and confusing but brave representations being a discussion, by all means of her own physicality examine social and psychological conventions and questioning them at the same time. For Kan Xuan the subject is, like the relationship of things among each other are to be understood only in relation to a world, oscillating between meaningfulness and emptying of meaning. Kan's works touch the spectator by their confrontational directness moving between states of tension and relaxation, the confirmation and resolution of the self. In the black and white video "Or everything" (2005) being almost meditative in its effect, the artist

Kan Xuan, eine der wichtigsten Video-Künstlerinnen in China, arbeitet mit installativen und performativen Elementen, ist aber auch für ihre Fotografien bekannt. Die Wirkung ihrer Kunst entfaltet sich im Raum zwischen erlebter und imaginierter Wirklichkeit, wobei die Grenzen zwischen beiden Sphären fließend sind. In einer Welt des unendlich Möglichen, die man nicht als die Summe gegebener Tatsachen, sondern als einen sich kontinuierlich im Bewusstsein neu generierenden Kosmos verstehen kann, funktionieren Kan Xuans Arbeiten als Spiegel ihrer persönlichen Erfahrungen. Denn um ihre eigene Wahrnehmung ebenso wie die des Betrachters zu weiten und zu schärfen, richtet die Künstlerin ihren Fokus vor allem auf das Intime und oftmals Übersehene. Nicht die Dinge an sich interessieren sie, sondern deren Beziehungen zueinander und zum umfassenden Beziehungsgeflecht, nicht die Repräsentation des Realen, sondern die Präsenz der möglichen Welt, die in ihren Arbeiten erfahrbar werden soll.

Das bewegten Bildern immanente emotionale und kognitive Aktivierungspotenzial optimiert Kan Xuan in ihrer künstlerischen Artikulation mit performativen und installativen Elementen, wobei Performances mit ihr selbst als Protagonistin häufig den Ausgangspunkt bilden. Die Künstlerin liebt das Spiel mit allen Sinnen, fordert die Wahrnehmung ihrer selbst und des Betrachters durch sich wiederholende, obsessiv anmutende Handlungen heraus und manipuliert Seh- und Hörsinn durch den Einsatz technischer Mittel, etwa der Verlangsamung und Farbmanipulation sowie mittels eindringlicher Sounds.

Kan Xuan überschreitet dabei Grenzen und appelliert an das Einfühlungsvermögen und die Vorstellungskraft des Betrachters. Ihre häufig extremen, verstörenden und mutigen Darbietungen, in denen sie sich mit ihrer eigenen Körperlichkeit auseinandersetzt, untersuchen soziale und psychologische Konventionen und stellen sie zugleich in Frage. Wie die Dinge untereinander, so ist auch das Subjekt bei Kan Xuan stets nur in Relation zu einer Welt zu verstehen, die zwischen Bedeutungsgebung und Bedeu-

阚萱是中国最重要的女录像艺术家之一，创作装置作品和表演艺术，尤以摄影为人所知。
介于经验和想象之间的现实，以及两者之间正摇摆的界限是阚萱艺术作品魅力所在。在一个无限可能的世界中，阚萱的作品将艺术家的个人经验呈现于世人，那个世界不是已有的现实事物而是在我们意识中不断创造的的世界。

为使自己以及观众的观念变得更开阔、更敏锐，阚萱将视角关注于常常被人遗忘的微妙细节。她对事情的本身不感兴趣，但是关心其中相互关系和错综复杂的关系网；她对现实的表象不感兴趣，但关心融于其作品中的潜在世界的表象。
阚萱运用表演和装置作为艺术衔接方法，为她的影片精心选择了瞬间即可激发的情感和感知潜能，而在那些艺术方法中，她在多数情况下是其中的主角。阚萱对游戏非常喜爱，通过连续重复同一个动作来挑战自己和观众的视觉；运用特定的技巧如放慢速度、颜色处理以及制造声音，而达到操纵视觉感的目的。

阚萱超越了艺术的边界，而且吸引着观众的意识和想象力。她以全部的感官观察社会和心理习惯，同时也在不断地质疑它们，而那种极端令人费解但大胆的表现方式却引人争论。

对阚萱而言，作品的主题介于有意义和无意义之间，类似于事物之间的相互关系只有在某个世界中才可理解。

在阚萱的作品中，矛盾的直接性在紧张和松弛、确定和分解的状态间移动，而令观众感动。在黑白录像《亦或所有》，艺术家将佛殿上的雕塑处理的象在水上一样，而使其栩栩如生，好像几乎象真的一般。这可理解为佛学教义（阚萱曾全面修习过）和“空”及“逝”的暗示，而“空”则是佛徒得以“悟”的途径。

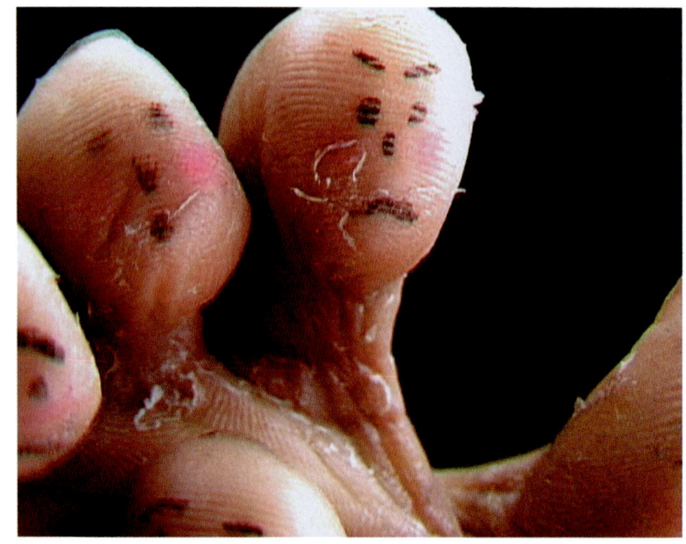

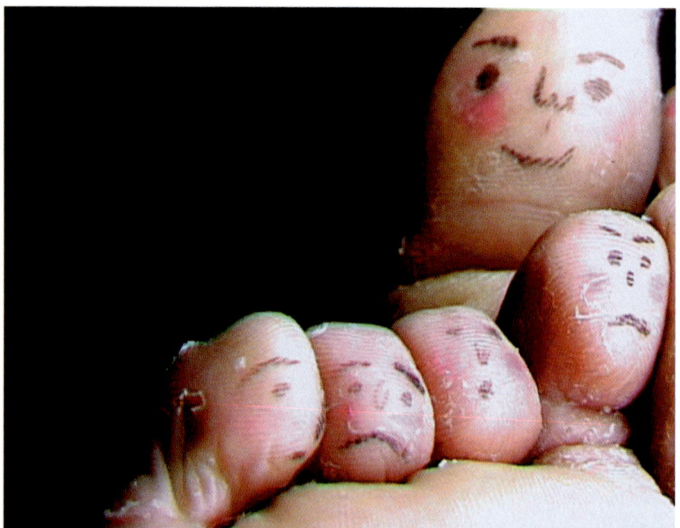

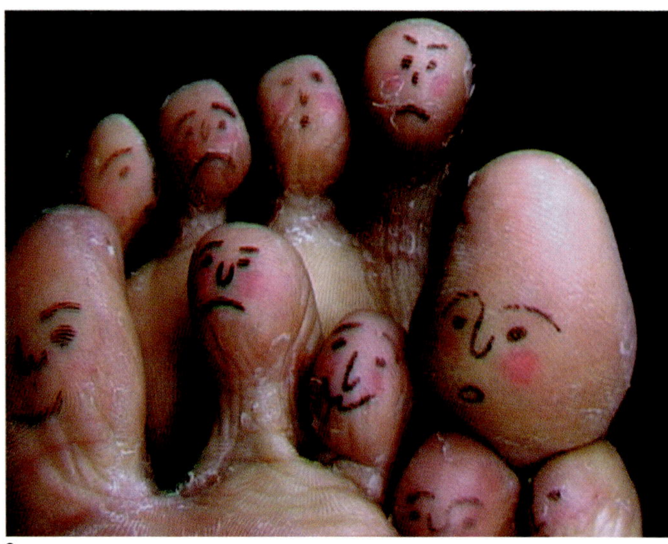

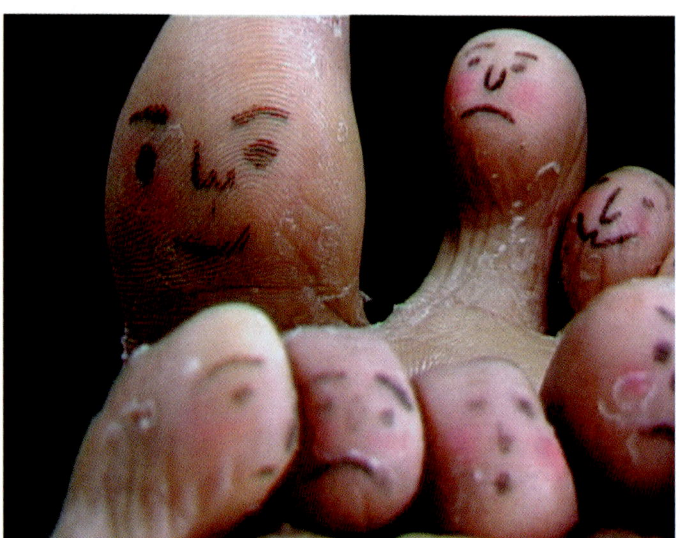

2

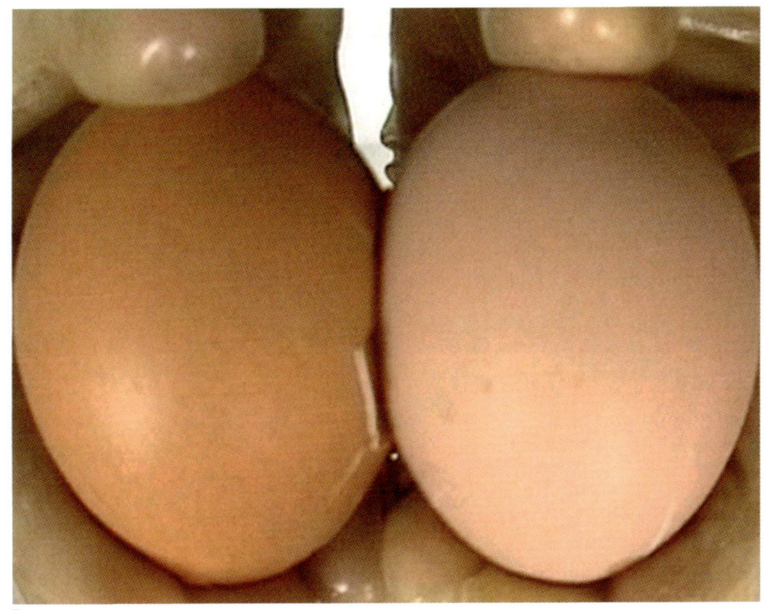

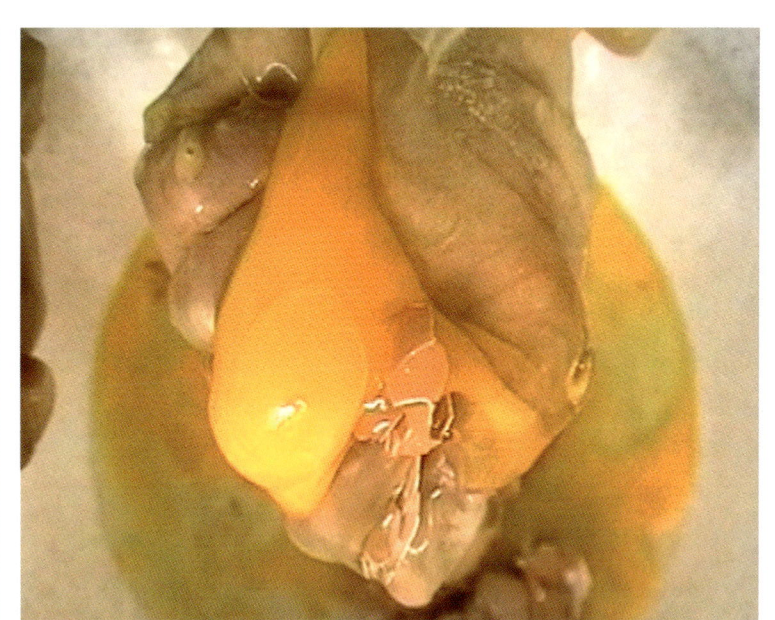

3

4

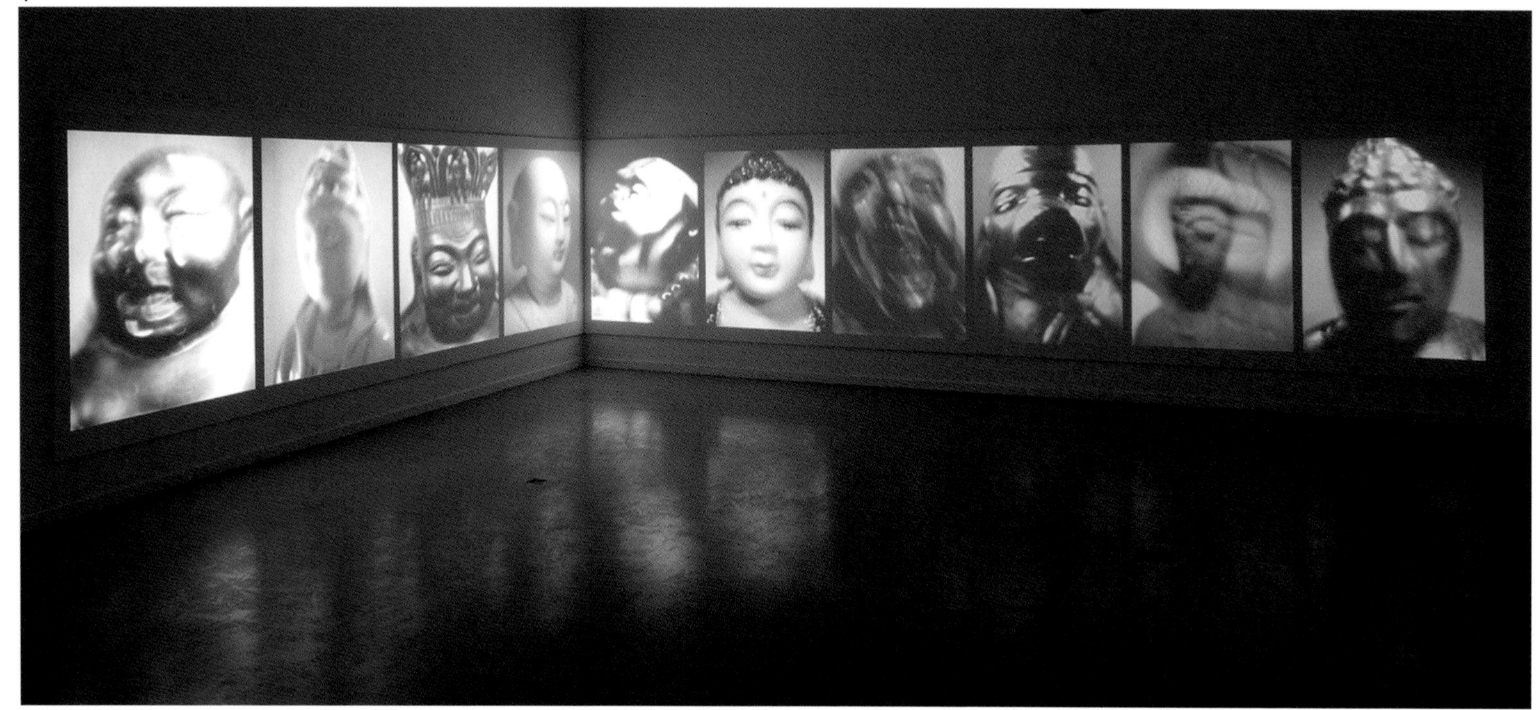

animates statues of the Buddhist pantheon in a way that they seem to be like a reflection on water. This can be understood as reference to the Buddhist teaching – Kan Xuan was comprehensively studying – and its paradigm of the emptiness, the fugaciousness, that emptiness the Buddhist is seeking for to achieve enlightenment.

The video work "Kan Xuan! – Yes!" (1999) being irritating and confusing shows the artist bustling through a subway of an underground station as being followed by herself shouting her name and answering herself. Did she try to express that the own existence is perceptible only in the ambivalence of self assurance and distance?

The black and white video work "Objects" (2003) shows different items of daily life like coins, stones, pills, apples and milk slowly falling down, and immersing in water kept in a transparent recipient. A soft female voice names the items and describes their medial by techniques created colourfully in white, grey and black. By constituting a temporary unity of real and fictitious world conventional structures of experience are questioned and the spectators get sensitised to the items no matter how they are received by their senses.

tungsentleerung oszilliert. Kans Arbeiten berühren den Betrachter durch ihre konfrontative Direktheit und bewegen sich zwischen Zuständen der An- und Entspannung, der Bestätigung und Auflösung des Selbst. Beinahe meditativ in seiner Wirkung ist das Schwarzweißvideo „Or everything" (2005), in dem die Künstlerin Figuren des buddhistischen Pantheons so animiert, dass sie wie Spiegelungen auf einer Wasseroberfläche wirken. Man kann dies als Referenz an die buddhistische Lehre – mit der Kan sich umfassend beschäftigt hat – und deren Paradigma der Leere verstehen, jene Leere, die der Buddhist zu begreifen sucht, um Erleuchtung zu erlangen.

Irritierend und verstörend war die Videoarbeit „Kan Xuan! – Yes!" (1999), die die Künstlerin durch eine Unterführung eines U-Bahnhofs hetzend zeigt, wie von sich selbst verfolgt, dabei ihren eigenen Namen laut ausrufend und sich selbst antwortend. Versucht sie damit auszudrücken, dass die eigene Existenz nur in der ständigen Ambivalenz zwischen Vergewisserung und Abstand begreifbar ist?

Die schwarzweiße Videoarbeit „Objects" (2003) präsentiert verschiedene alltägliche Dinge wie Münzen, Steine, Pillen, Äpfel und Milch beim langsamen Fallen und Eintauchen in einen durchsichtigen Behälter mit Wasser. Eine sanfte Frauenstimme nennt die Dinge beim Namen und beschreibt ihre mediale, also ihre durch technische Mittel erzeugte Farbigkeit in den Tönen weiß, grau und schwarz. Indem reale und fiktive Welt eine temporäre Einheit bilden, werden herkömmliche Erfahrungsstrukturen in Frage gestellt und die Betrachter für die Gegenstände, wie immer sie auch den Sinnen erscheinen mögen, sensibilisiert.

录像《阚萱！哎！》（1999年）却是一部令费解的作品。阚萱自己在人潮涌动的地铁里穿行，一边跑一边喊着自己的名字“阚萱”，接着又自己“哎”一声应答自己的喊声。难道她要表达：只有在自我肯定和疏远的矛盾情感之中，才可觉察自我存在吗？

黑白录像作品《物体》（2003年）则展示了生活日常生活中的小物品，如硬币、石头、药丸、苹果和牛奶等，这些物品被分别缓慢地扔下透明容器中，随后便浸没在水中。同时，一个柔和的女声根据声音描述每个物体的颜色，由于录像是黑白的，颜色只呈现于黑、白和灰色之间。通过让现实与虚幻世界的临时共存，传统的经验结构受到质疑，而无论观众怎样感知物体，对它们变得敏感。

Birgit Hopfener

1 ***Looking looking looking for****, 2001*
Video, 2 min 42 sec
Video, 2 Min. 42 Sek.
《找啊找》2001年, 录像, 2 分 42秒

2 ***Chorus****, 2001*
Video, 1 min 48 sec
Video, 1 Min. 48 Sek.
《合唱队》2001年, 录像, 1分钟 48秒

3 ***Egg****, 1999*
Video, 5 min
Video, 5 Min.
《鸡蛋》1999年，录像，5分钟

4 ***Or everything****, 2005*
Video, 24 min 12 sec
Video, 24 Min. 12 Sek.
《亦或所有》2005年, 录像, 24分12秒

5 ***A happy girl****, 2001*
Video, 1 min
Video, 1 Min.
《快乐女孩》2001年，录像, 1分钟

5

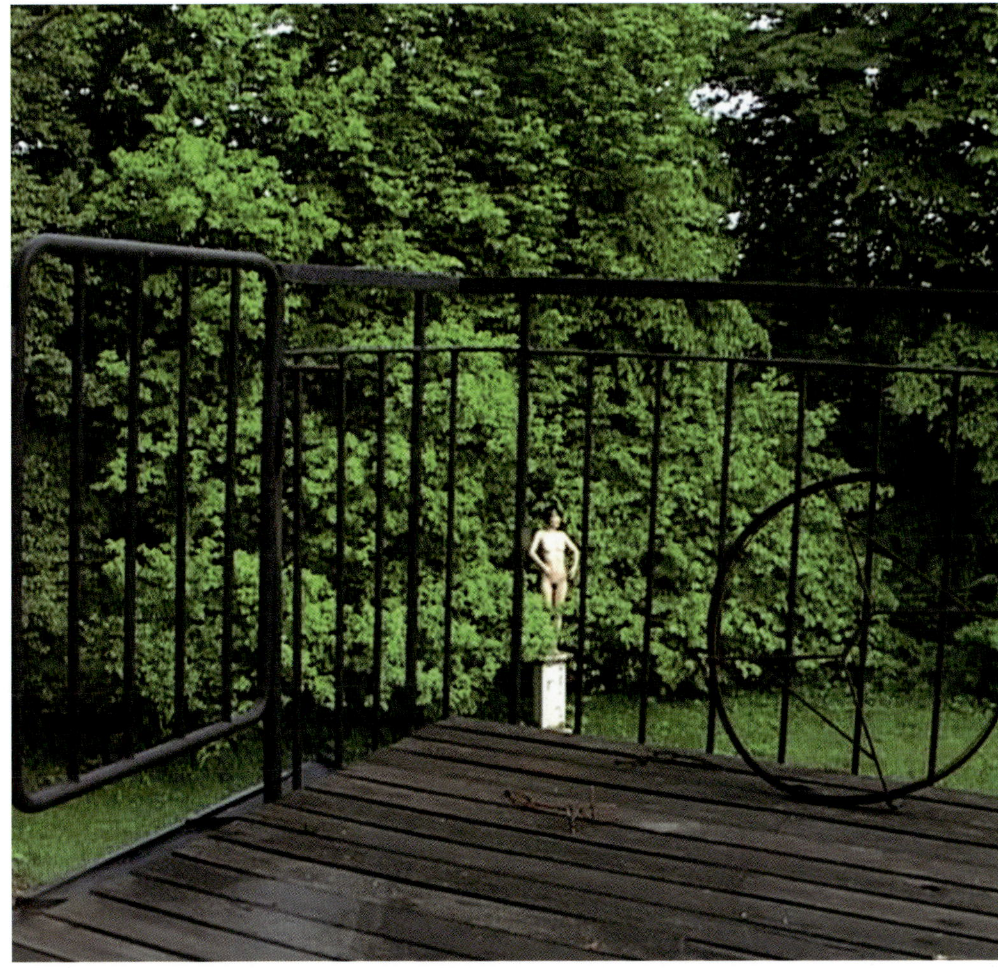

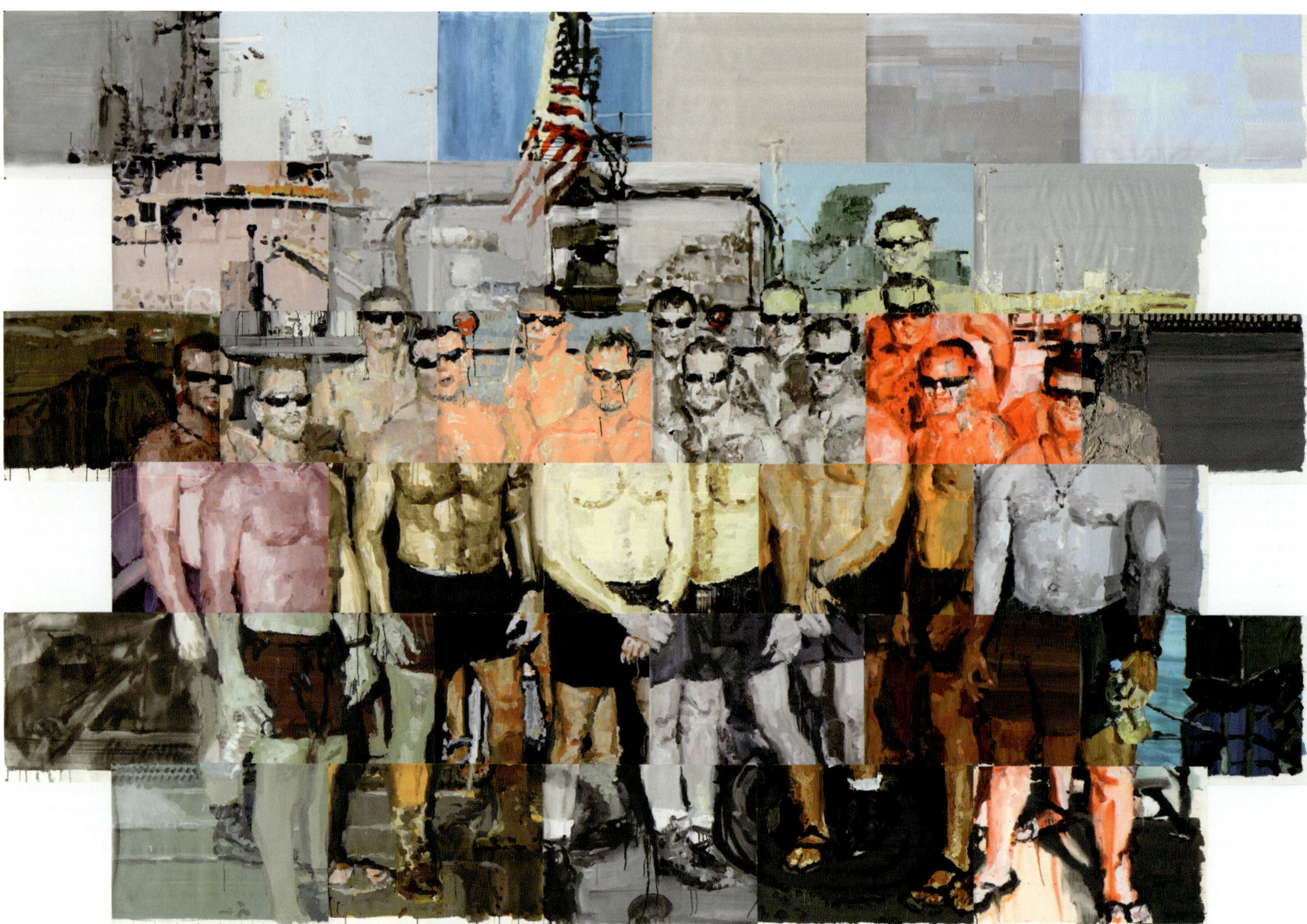

1

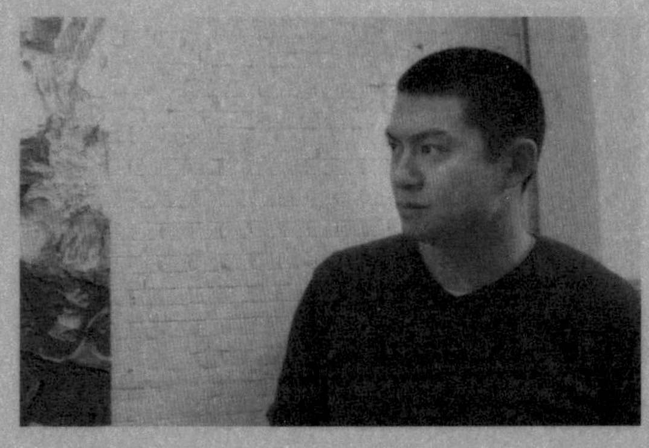

"When a judgement already results in a conclusion, I offer new contradictions and insert a new problem."

„Wenn ein Urteil bereits in eine Schlussfolgerung mündet, kann ich daran neue Widersprüche und eine neue Problemstellung aufzeigen."

"当一个判断已经有了结论的时候，我可能会提出新的矛盾，
在里面放置新的问题。"

Born in 1973 in Beijing, China. Lives and works in Beijing
Geboren 1973 in Peking, China. Lebt und arbeitet in Peking
1973年出生，居住工作于北京

***Selected exhibitions* / Ausgewählte Ausstellungen / 所选展览**

2003 "Left Hand – Right Hand", 798 Space, Beijing, China
2004 "Li Songsong 2001–2004", China Art & Archives Warehouse (CAAW), Beijing, China
2005–07 "Mahjong – Chinesische Gegenwartskunst aus der Sammlung Sigg", Kunstmuseum Bern, Berne, Switzerland; Hamburger Kunsthalle, Hamburg, Germany; Museum der Moderne, Salzburg, Austria
2006 "Li Songsong – Hypnogenesis", Galerie Urs Meile, Lucerne/Beijing, Switzerland/China
"Altered, Stitched and Gathered", P.S.1 Contemporary Art Center, New York, NY, USA
2007 "China Now", Sammlung Essl, Klosterneuburg, Austria
2nd Moscow Biennial, Moscow, Russia

2003年 《左手与右手 一中德当代艺术联展》北京，大山子艺术区
2004年 《李松松 2001一2004》北京，中国艺术文件仓库
2005-07年《麻将一希客收藏的中国当代艺术展》伯尔尼美术馆/瑞士、汉堡美术馆/德国
2006年 《李松松一催眠》北京/瑞士卢塞恩，麦勒画廊，主要的群展包括
《改变，缝合与聚集》美国，P.S.1
2007年 《今日中国》Sammlung Essl美术博物馆，克罗斯特纽堡, 奥地利
第二届 莫斯科双年展 莫斯科 俄罗斯

***Selected publications* / Ausgewählte Publikationen / 所选著作**

"Li Songsong's works 2001–2004", Beijing 2004
"Li Songsong – Hypnogenesis", Lucerne 2006

《李松松作品2001-2004》，2004年
《李松松一催眠》，2006 年

"When a judgement already results in a conclusion, I offer new contradictions and insert a new problem."

„Wenn ein Urteil bereits in eine Schlussfolgerung mündet, kann ich daran neue Widersprüche und eine neue Problemstellung aufzeigen."

"当一个判断已经有了结论的时候，我可能会提出新的矛盾，在里面放置新的问题。"

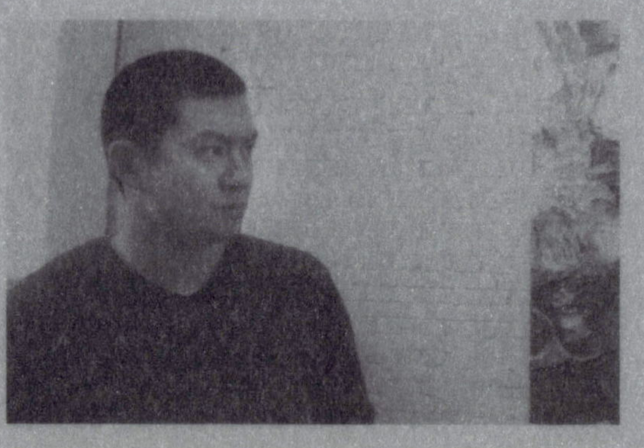

Born in 1973 in Beijing, China. Lives and works in Beijing
Geboren 1973 in Peking, China. Lebt und arbeitet in Peking
1973年出生，居住工作于北京

Selected exhibitions / Ausgewählte Ausstellungen / 所选展览

2003	"Left Hand - Right Hand", 798 Space, Beijing, China
2004	"Li Songsong 2001-2004", China Art & Archives Warehouse (CAAW), Beijing, China
2005-07	"Mahjong - Chinesische Gegenwartskunst aus der Sammlung Sigg", Kunstmuseum Bern, Berne, Switzerland; Hamburger Kunsthalle, Hamburg, Germany; Museum der Moderne, Salzburg, Austria
2006	"Li Songsong - Hypnogenesis", Galerie Urs Meile, Lucerne/Beijing, Switzerland/China "Altered, Stitched and Gathered", P.S.1 Contemporary Art Center, New York, NY, USA
2007	"China Now", Sammlung Essl, Klosterneuburg, Austria 2nd Moscow Biennial, Moscow, Russia

2003年	《左手与右手 一中德当代艺术联展》北京，大山子艺术区
2004年	《李松松 2001—2004》北京，中国艺术文件仓库
2005-07年	《麻将一希客收藏的中国当代艺术展》伯尔尼美术馆/瑞士，汉堡美术馆/德国
2006年	《李松松一催眠》北京/瑞士卢塞恩，麦勒画廊，主要的群展包括 《改变，缝合与聚集》美国，P.S.1
2007年	《今日中国》Sammlung Essl美术博物馆，克罗斯特纽堡，奥地利 第二届 莫斯科双年展 莫斯科 俄罗斯

Selected publications / Ausgewählte Publikationen / 所选著作

"Li Songsong's works 2001-2004", Beijing 2004
"Li Songsong - Hypnogenesis", Lucerne 2006

《李松松作品2001-2004》，2004年
《李松松一催眠》，2006 年

LI SONGSONG 李松松

[li sʊŋsʊŋ]

As a young artist born in the early seventies, Li Songsong's creations continuously discuss the problem of relationships between public images and the transformation of them into paintings. These pictures and images are mainly based on aspects of Chinese and world history, events and human beings. His process of transforming them into oil paintings has nothing to do with the official Chinese efforts to use art as an instrument for teaching and propagating to inspire people's heart with eulogies. Li's works have nothing in common with criticism or disclosing certain epochs of history as it was common among certain artists until the 90s nor does he expose himself by satirical questions. His attitude towards pictures is an objective one, in other words he uses interesting historical pictures as inspiration and not as judgment of historic events according to existing opinions. His work is simply the transforming of the visual factors into an objective, simple work expressing the vigour of history. His representative works are "In God We Trust", "Cuban Sugar", "The Happiness" (all 2006), "My Homeland" (2004) and "Black Car" (2005).

This transformation of history does not only offer us a new point of view of historical memory but simultaneously offers a new method of pondering the historical linguistic of our memory. This attitude of the young artist is a reflection on the collective memory and the individual one, distinguishing him from the former generation of artists. This manner decides, to a great extent, the degree of reality and depth of a narration, and the viewer is captured by the space of historical reality of public images and the feeling of the non-concrete boundary between. The large brushstrokes and the joyful language of oil painting as means of distance seeks a new kind of implication and annotation of history, and opens the spectator new space for conclusions and reflection on history.

Der junge, in den 1970er Jahren geborene Künstler Li Songsong setzt sich in seinen Arbeiten mit den wechselseitigen Beziehungen zwischen öffentlichen, vor allem fotografischen Darstellungen und deren Übertragung in die Malerei auseinander. Die Fotografien, auf die Li dabei zurückgreift, beziehen sich hauptsächlich auf Aspekte der Geschichte Chinas und der Welt, auf Ereignisse und Menschen. Sein Prozess der Umformung dieser offiziellen Bilder in Ölgemälde hat jedoch nichts gemein mit dem offiziellen Pathos chinesischer Propaganda, derzufolge Kunst dazu dienen soll, die Menschen zu unterweisen und Lobeshymnen auf den Staat zu singen. Ebensowenig aber stimmt Li in den Tenor der Kritik oder die Bloßlegung bestimmter historischer Epochen ein, wie es bis in die 1990er Jahre hinein viele Künstler taten. Lis Haltung gegenüber den Bildern, mit denen er arbeitet, ist vielmehr objektiv – er lässt sich durch interessante historische Aufnahmen inspirieren, ohne durch sie geschichtliche Ereignisse be- oder verurteilen zu wollen. Er ist bemüht, sichtbare Faktoren in objektive, einfache Bildwerke umzuwandeln, die die Kraft und Wirkung der Geschichte ausdrücken sollen. Zu Lis bekannten Arbeiten gehören „In God We trust", „Cuban Sugar", „The Happiness" (alle 2006), „My Homeland" (2004) und „Black Car" (2005).

Eine solche Umformung und Umwandlung der Geschichte bietet uns nicht nur einen neuen Blickwinkel auf das geschichtliche Gedächtnis, sondern auch eine neue Methode, um die historische Sprache unserer eigenen Erinnerung zu überdenken. Indem er über das kollektive Gedächtnis und die Erinnerung des Einzelnen reflektiert, unterscheidet sich dieser junge Künstler von seinen Vorgängern. Seine besondere Sichtweise macht den Grad der historischen Realität in öffentlichen Darstellungen deutlich und das Gefühl des nicht konkreten Grenzbereichs, der in ihnen liegt. Lis kräftige Pinselstriche und die frohe Sprache seiner Ölgemälde suchen als Mittel der Distanz eine neue Form, Geschichte zu implizieren und zu annotieren. Zugleich eröffnen sie dem Betrachter einen neuen Raum für eigene Schlussfolgerungen und regen ihn an, selbst über die Geschichte nachzudenken.

作为70年代出生的年轻艺术家，李松松的创作一直在探讨公共图像与绘画之间的转换关系问题。这些图像基本上是有关中国或世界历史、事件、人物等方面的摄影照片。他在转换到油画的过程中，既没有按照中国官方对艺术作品要求歌颂式的鼓舞人心的宣传教化的功能，也没有延续上世纪90年代以来的有些艺术家对某一历史片段或批判揭露，或质疑反讽等惯常的表现方式，而是采用一种意象的相对客观的态度。换句话说，他在对他感兴趣的历史图像资源的利用上，没有做过多的似乎已成定论的历史价值判断，只是在视觉的因素上将感受到历史的客观、朴素、直接的力量转换或移植到画面上。其代表作有《我们相信上帝》、《古巴糖》、《长眠就是幸福》、《我的祖国》、《黑车》等。

这种转换不仅为我们提供了一个重新思考历史记忆的视角，也提供了一个重新思考历史语境中记忆认同的方式。呈现了中国年轻一代艺术家在对待历史的集体记忆和个人记忆上与前几代艺术家的差异与不同的态度和立场。这个态度在很大程度上决定了叙述本身的真实程度与深度，使观者获得了一种介于公共的历史图像的真实与非具体之间界限关系的感受。大笔触、写意性的油画语言，也使在这种间隔当中相对充分地寻求到历史的某种新的寓意和诠释，抑或也是将对历史的判断余地和思考空间更多地留给了观众。

Feng Boyi

2

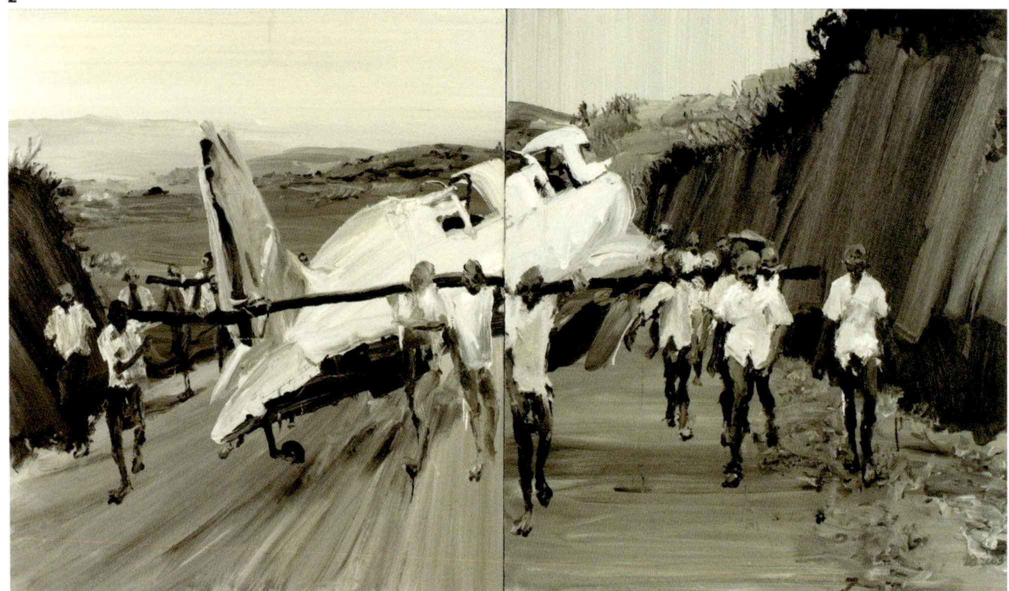

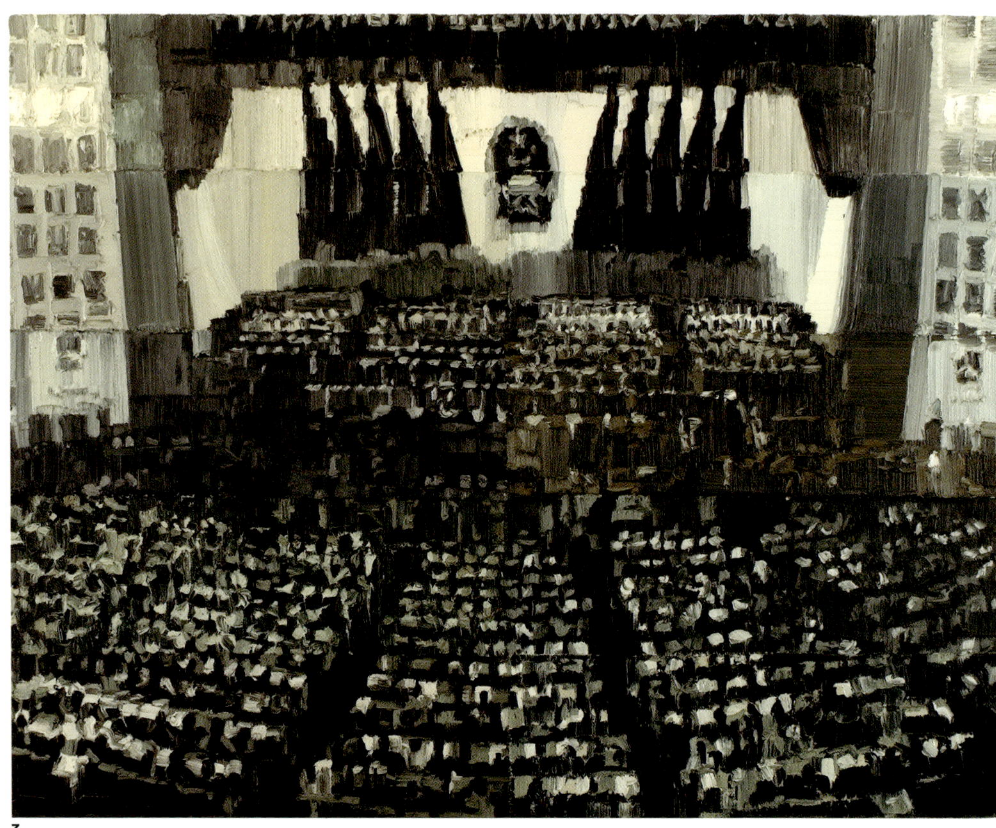

3

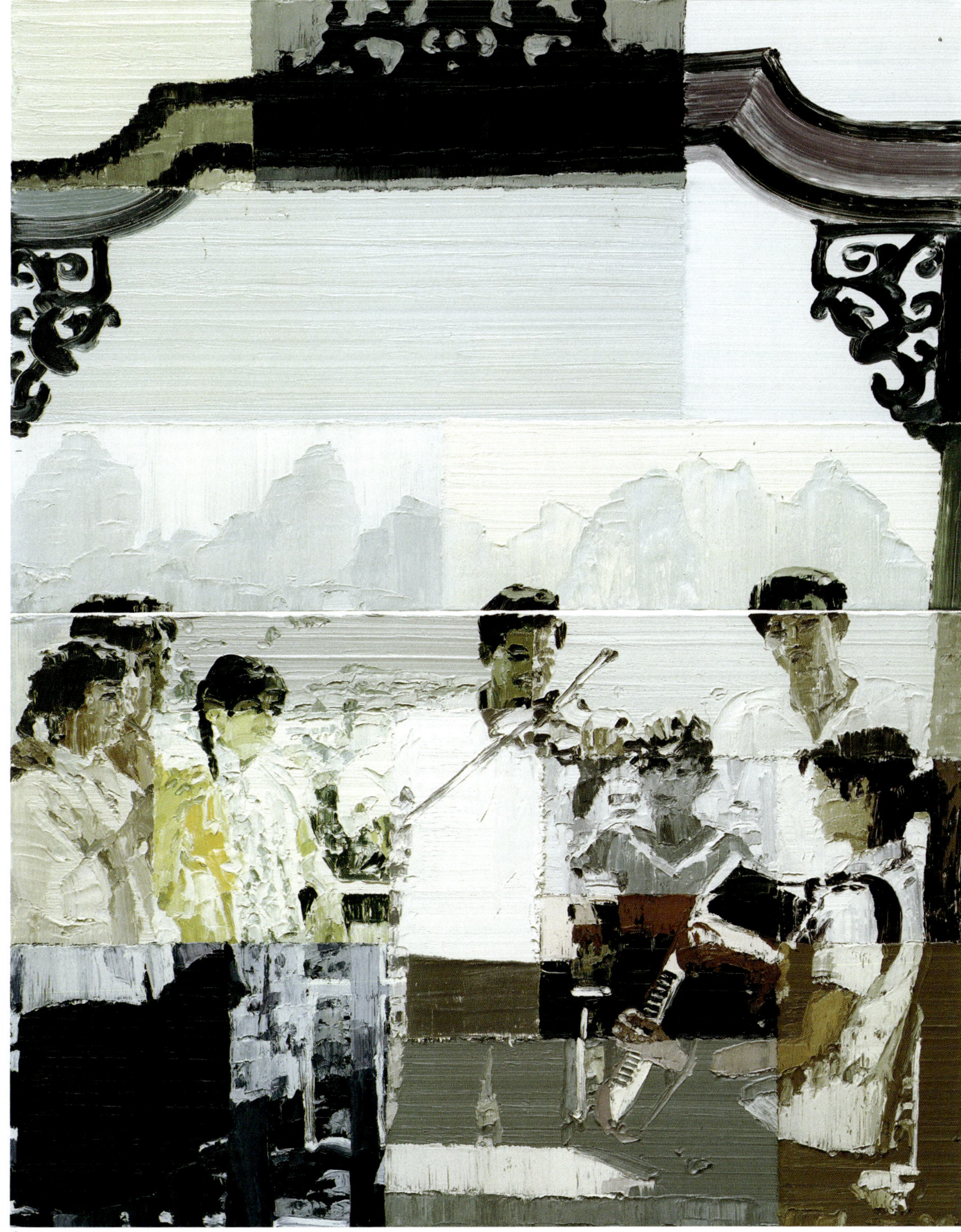

4

5

环球比基尼小姐大赛今日开幕

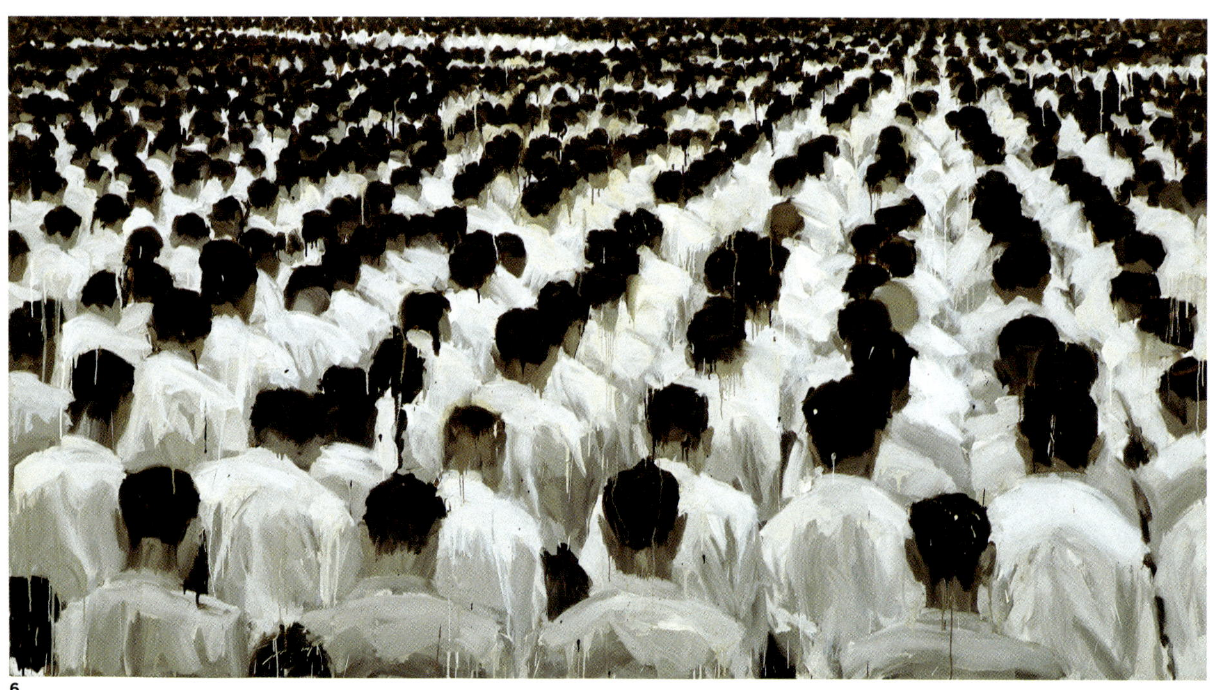

6

8

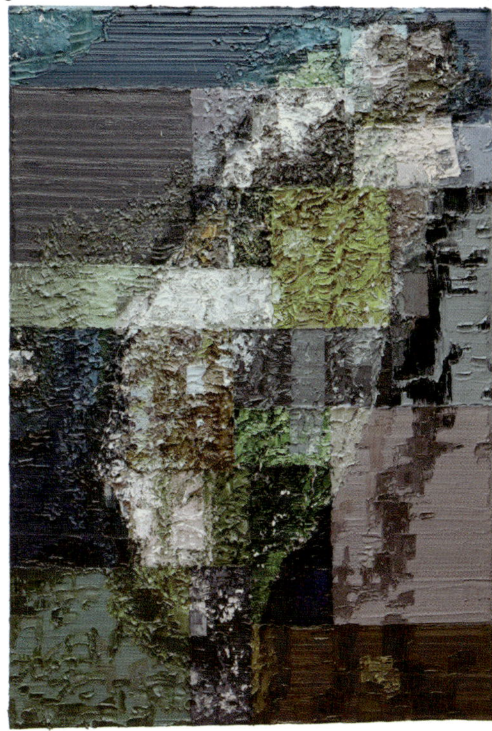

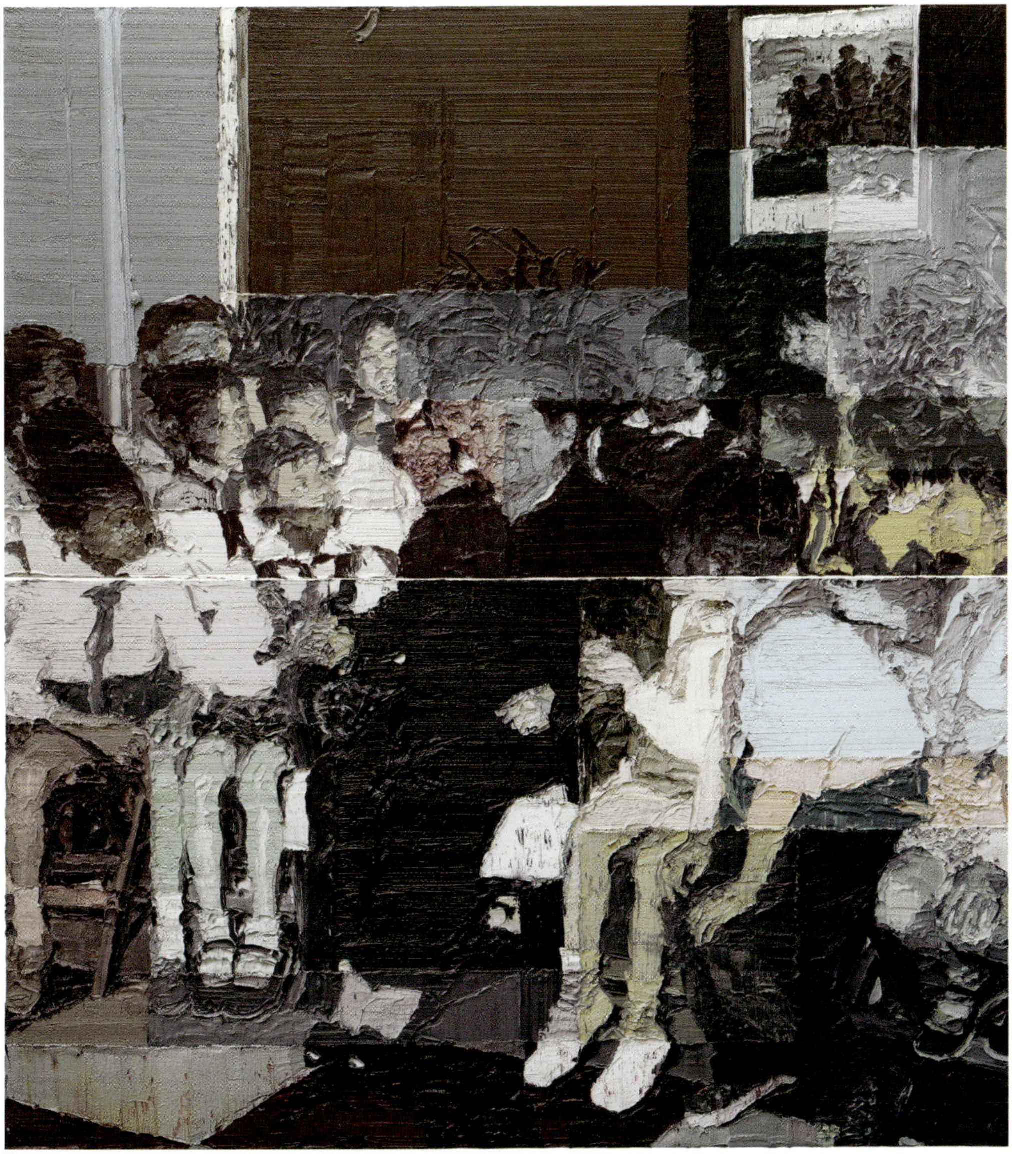

7

1 ***In God We Trust**, 2006*
Acrylic and ink on paper, mounted on canvas, 429 x 609 cm
Acryl und Tusche auf Papier, auf Leinwand aufgezogen, 429 x 609 cm
《我们信昂的神》2006年，纸上丙烯和水墨，429 x 609 cm

2 ***Gift**, 2003*
Oil on canvas, 180 x 300 cm; Öl auf Leinwand, 180 x 300 cm
《礼物》2003年，布上油画，180 x 300 cm

3 ***The Decameron**, 2004*
Oil on canvas, 170 x 210 cm; Öl auf Leinwand, 170 x 210 cm
《十日谈》2004年，布上油画，170 x 210 cm

4 ***Wonderful Life**, 2004*
Oil on canvas, 260 x 200 cm; Öl auf Leinwand, 260 x 200 cm
《美好生活》2004年，布上油画，260 x 200 cm

5 ***Gift**, 2007*
Oil on canvas, 230 x 350 cm; Öl auf Leinwand, 230 x 350 cm
《礼物》2007年，布上油画，230 x 350 cm

6 ***The Square**, 2001*
Oil on canvas, 180 x 320 cm; Öl auf Leinwand, 180 x 320 cm
《广场》2001年，布上油画，180 x 320 cm

7 ***Qingling's Young Pioneers**, 2005*
Oil on canvas, 203 x 203 cm; Öl auf Leinwand, 203 x 203 cm
《庆龄与少先队员》2005年，布上油画，203 x 203 cm

8 ***National Geographic**, 2006*
Oil on canvas, 313 x 192 cm; Öl auf Leinwand, 313 x 192 cm
《国家地理》2006年，布上油画，313 x 192 cm

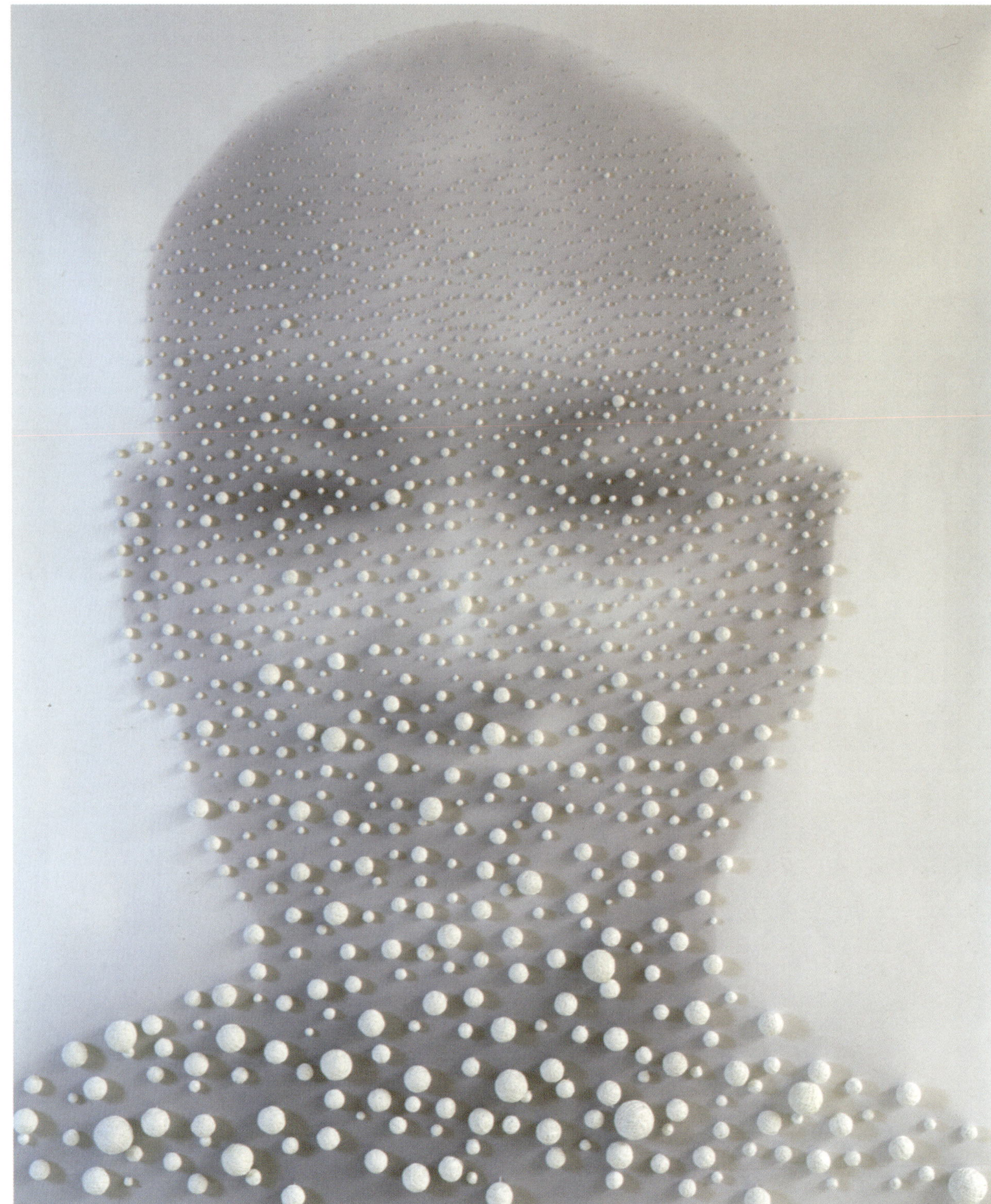

1

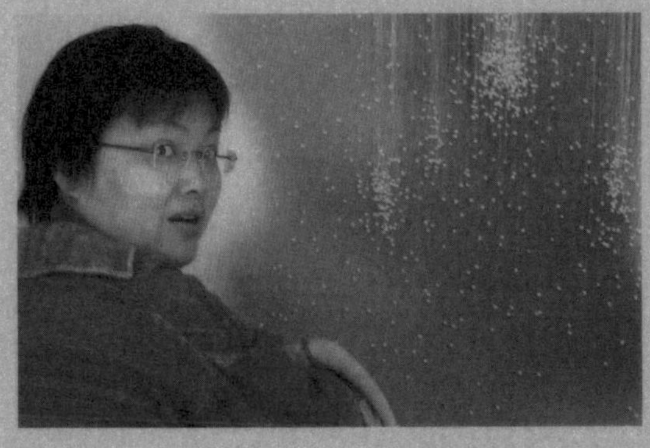

"Only in the process of working slowly can I eventually express myself. My situation is like drinking tea: you understand how and what it is only after drinking it."

„Ich kann mich bestenfalls in einem langsamen Arbeitsprozess ausdrücken. Es ähnelt dem Teetrinken: Man versteht erst nach dem Trinken, was Tee ist."

"只有在工作时，我才能慢慢的最终的表达自己。我就好像喝茶：只有在品茶后，才能茶的味道和品质。"

Born 1961 in Taiyuan, China. Lives and works in Beijing
Geboren 1961 in Taiyuan, China. Lebt und arbeitet in Peking
1961年出生于中国山西太原，现在北京定居工作

***Selected exhibitions* / Ausgewählte Ausstellungen / 所选展览**

2002 2. Fukuoka Asian Art Triennale, Fukuoka Asian Art Museum, Fukuoka, Japan
2004 "Non Zero", Beijing Tokyo Art Projects, Beijing, China
2004–07 "Between Past and Future, New Photography and Video from China", International Center of Photography, New York, NY, USA (travelling exhibition)
2005 "Lin Tianmiao", Courtyard Gallery, Beijing, China
2005–07 "Mahjong – Chinesische Gegenwartskunst aus der Sammlung Sigg", Kunstmuseum Bern, Berne, Switzerland; Hamburger Kunsthalle, Hamburg, Germany; Museum der Moderne, Salzburg, Austria

2002年 第二届福冈三年展，福冈亚洲艺术博物馆，日本
2004年 《非零》东京艺术工程，北京
2004–07年《过去将来－中国当代摄影》始于美国纽约及亚洲学会的国际摄影中心的巡回展
2005年 《王功新/林天苗新作展》四合院艺术中心 北京
2005–07年《麻将》西克中国当代艺术收藏展 伯尔尼美术馆 瑞士 ；汉堡美术馆 汉堡 德国；萨尔茨保现代美术馆 奥地利

***Selected publications* / Ausgewählte Publikationen / 所选著作**

Chris Werner, Qiu Ping, Marianne Pitzen (eds.): "Die Hälfte des Himmels: Chinesische Künstlerinnen", Bonn 1998
Liao Wen: "Tumultuous History of China's Feminist Values and Art", in: "Chinese Type Contemporary Art Online Magazine", vol. 1.2 , 1998
Karen Smith: "Lin Tianmiao: Non Zero", Hong Kong 2004
Britta Erickson: "Here? Or there?: Wang Gongxin & Lin Tianmiao", Hong Kong 2005

Werner, Chris/Qiu Ping/Pitzen, Marianne（编者）:《半边天-当代中国女艺术》波恩1998年
Liao Wen（著）:《中国的女权价值和艺术的喧哗的历史》在：《中国型当代艺术网上杂志》，第卷1 号2 1998年1月.
Smith, Karen（著）:《林天苗：非零》香港 2004年
Erickson, Britta（著）:《这里?或那里?：王功新 和 林天苗》香港 2005年

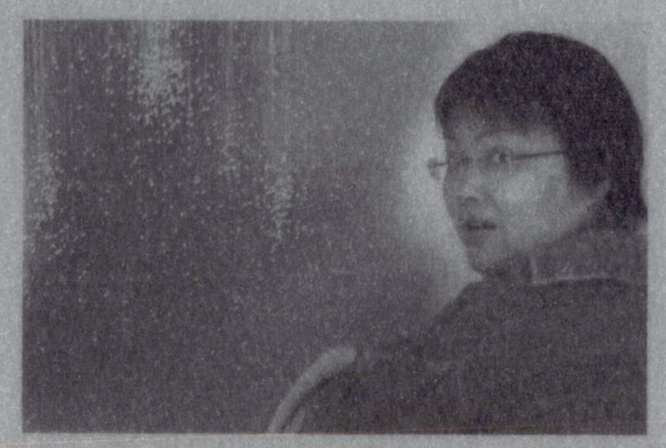

"Only in the process of working slowly can I eventually express myself. My situation is like drinking tea: you understand how and what it is only after drinking it."

„Ich kann mich bestenfalls in einem langsamen Arbeitsprozess ausdrücken. Es ähnelt dem Teetrinken: Man versteht erst nach dem Trinken, was Tee ist."

"只有在工作时，我才能慢慢的最终的表达自己。我就好像喝茶：只有在品茶后，才能茶的味道和品质。"

Born 1961 in Taiyuan, China. Lives and works in Beijing
Geboren 1961 in Taiyuan, China. Lebt und arbeitet in Peking
1961年出生于中国山西太原，现在北京定居工作

Selected exhibitions / Ausgewählte Ausstellungen / 所选展览

2002 2. Fukuoka Asian Art Triennale, Fukuoka Asian Art Museum, Fukuoka, Japan
2004 "Non Zero", Beijing Tokyo Art Projects, Beijing, China
2004–07 "Between Past and Future, New Photography and Video from China", International Center of Photography, New York, NY, USA (travelling exhibition)
2005 "Lin Tianmiao", Courtyard Gallery, Beijing, China
2005–07 "Mahjong – Chinesische Gegenwartskunst aus der Sammlung Sigg", Kunstmuseum Bern, Berne, Switzerland; Hamburger Kunsthalle, Hamburg, Germany; Museum der Moderne, Salzburg, Austria

2002年 第二届福冈三年展，福冈亚洲艺术博物馆，日本
2004年 《非零》东京艺术工程，北京
2004-07年 《过去将来一中国当代摄影》始于美国纽约及亚洲学会的国际摄影中心的巡回展
2005年 《王功新/林天苗新作展》四合院艺术中心 北京
2005-07年 《麻将》西克中国当代艺术收藏展 伯尔尼美术馆 瑞士；汉堡美术馆 汉堡 德国；萨尔茨堡现代美术馆 奥地利

Selected publications / Ausgewählte Publikationen / 所选著作

Chris Werner, Qiu Ping, Marianne Pitzen (eds.): "Die Hälfte des Himmels: Chinesische Künstlerinnen", Bonn 1998
Liao Wen: "Tumultuous History of China's Feminist Values and Art", in: "Chinese Type Contemporary Art Online Magazine", vol. 1.2., 1998
Karen Smith: "Lin Tianmiao: Non Zero", Hong Kong 2004
Britta Erickson: "Here? Or there?: Wang Gongxin & Lin Tianmiao", Hong Kong 2005

Werner, Chris/Qiu Ping/Pitzen, Marianne（编著）:《半边天-当代中国女艺术》波恩1998年
Liao Wen（著）:《中国的女权价值和艺术的喧哗的历史》在:《中国型当代艺术网上杂志》, 第卷1 号2 1998年1月.
Smith, Karen（著）:《林天苗：非零》香港 2004年
Erickson, Britta（著）:《这里?或那里?：王功新 和 林天苗》香港 2005年

LIN TIANMIAO 林天苗

[lin tʰiɛnmaʊ]

The aesthetic of winding, coiling and wrapping is the unmistakable label of Lin Tianmiao. Her installation works are a combination of things wound or wrapped in white yarn with the media photography and video. "Bound-Unbound", the title of her first solo exhibition in 1997, exhibiting her installation of the same title, discloses the core of her art. Beyond the process of winding her works are always on the narrow dislocating ridge between the complementary poles of adoption and disentanglement – the individual experience arising in between.

The main subjects in Lin Tianmiao's work are processes of individualisation within the given social structures. Apart from material experiences, the socially coded relationships and ties of the Chinese society are picked out as a central theme. Her first installation "Proliferation of Thread Winding" (1995), one of her earliest artistic works, consists of white wound balls of yarn being spread on the floor around a brass bed and connected with the mattress by needles holding the loose ends of these threads. The needles side by side evoke the deceiving image of a soft bed, reminiscent of a fluffy fur. The documentation of the winding process being displayed on a monitor at the end of the bed enhances the fourth dimension of time when disclosing the process of winding to the spectator.

An oversized pair of paper trousers is hanging from the ceiling, perforated with numerous needles in the pubic area. Lin Tianmiao picking up the traditional Chinese concept of the two complementary poles – yin for the female principle and yang for the male one – as central theme in her installation "Proliferation of Thread Winding", and though her selection of daily life items from the homely surrounding as well as the actions like winding, weaving and binding are often interpreted as female, Lin refuses the gender specific interpretation as to short sighted. The core of her artistic inventions are the given circumstances and structure, embossing the individual and determining the human existence itself.

Die Ästhetik des Wickelns, Aufwickelns und Einwickelns ist Lin Tianmiaos unverwechselbares Markenzeichen. In ihren installativen Arbeiten kombiniert sie mit weißem Garn Geoder Umwickeltes mit den Medien Fotografie und Video. „Bound-Unbound", so der Titel ihrer ersten Soloschau im Jahr 1997, in der sie ihre gleichnamige Installation zeigte, trifft den Kern ihrer Kunst. Über den Produktionsprozess des Wickelns hinaus bewegen sich ihre Arbeiten stets auf dem schmalen, sich ständig verschiebenden Grat zwischen den komplementären Polen Anpassung und Loslösung – dazwischen entsteht individuelle Erfahrung.

Hauptthema in Lin Tianmiaos Werk sind Individualisierungsprozesse innerhalb der gegebenen gesellschaftlichen Strukturen. Neben materiellen Erfahrungen thematisiert sie die sozial kodierten Bindungen in der chinesischen Gesellschaft. Ihre erste Installation „Proliferation of Thread Winding" (1995), die zugleich zu ihren frühesten künstlerischen Arbeiten zählt, besteht aus weißen gewickelten Garnknäueln, die auf dem Boden um ein Messingbett verteilt und mit diesem verbunden sind, indem die losen Fadenenden durch Nadelöhre gefädelt und die Nadeln in die Matratze gestochen wurden. Durch das enge Nebeneinander der Nadeln wirkt das Bett trügerisch weich und erinnert an ein flaumiges Fell. Mit der Dokumentation des Wickelprozesses, die auf einem Bildschirm am Kopfende des Betts zu sehen ist, akzentuiert Lin die vierte Dimension der Zeit, die sich dem Betrachter über den Nachvollzug des Wickelvorgangs erschließt.

Von der Zimmerdecke hängt eine papierene überdimensionale Hose herab, die im Schambereich mit zahllosen Nadeln perforiert ist. Obwohl die Künstlerin das traditionelle chinesische Konzept der beiden komplementären Pole, des weiblichen Prinzips Yin und des männlichen Yang, in „Proliferation of Thread Winding" thematisiert und ihre Wahl von Alltagsgegenständen aus dem häuslichen Umfeld sowie die Tätigkeiten des Wickelns, Webens und Flechtens häufig als weiblich interpretiert werden, lehnt Lin eine rein genderspezifische Interpretation als zu kurzgreifend ab.

林天苗作品的缠绕、盘绕和包装的美感是其明显的特征。她的装置作品都是 通过 白纱线把视频和照片缠绕或者包扎在一起而组合而成。1997年，她的首个个展《缠了,再剪开》（展览名与其中一件作品同名），揭示其艺术的核心。而作品远非简单的捆绑那么简单，而是组成部分相互补充融为一体 --创作中个人的经验再其中得以升华。

在原有的社群结构中的个性化进程是林天苗作品的主题。除物质经验外，社会礼俗关系和中国社会关系也是其主题之一。她的一个最早的艺术作品，也是其首座装置作品《缠的扩散》(1995年)，白色的缠绕的线球，分布在一张铜床旁边的地板上，那些错乱的线头穿在一根根针上，针连着床垫。并排着的根根银针，不禁让人想起一张柔软舒适的床、想起毛茸茸的毛皮。安装在床尾的监视器记录着整个缠绕过程，在观众观看这个过程时候，而增强了时间的第四维度感。

一条特大纸裤悬挂在天花板上，阴部处有着数不清的针孔。林天苗在其装置PTW中选择中国传统概念中相互对立的两极作为其作品的两极：阴代表雌性原理，而阳代表着雄性。虽然她的日常生活的选自家居环境和那些通常都是女性所作的缝补编织活，而林天苗否认性别解释的目光短浅。她的艺术创作的核心是浮现个体和决定个体存在的特定环境和结构。

装置《缠了-再剪开》中，白色纱线把100多件家庭物品缠绕一起，分布在一张帆布前，帆布由并排悬挂着的纱线构成，上面映现着象征性模仿切线的动作。事物的本来形式依然可以透过蚕丝依稀可辨，而同时却脱离了本来环境和用途。这样事物就看可以 达到一种新的审美维度和审美特性。物体的背后，储存记忆、时间和能量惹人注意，而非在阅读一个修饰万分的物体。她的兴趣不在于已有的概念，而是在可能拓宽视野新的记忆概念。

2

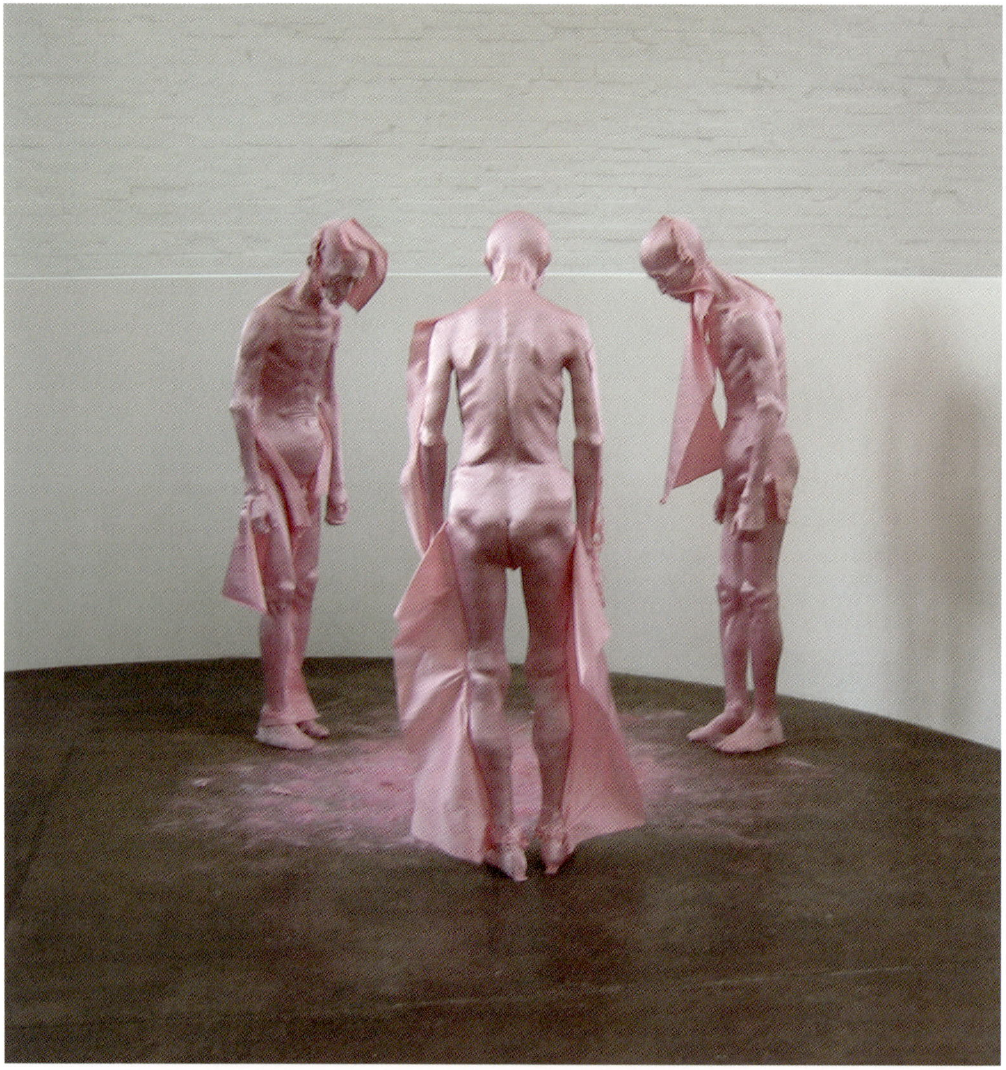

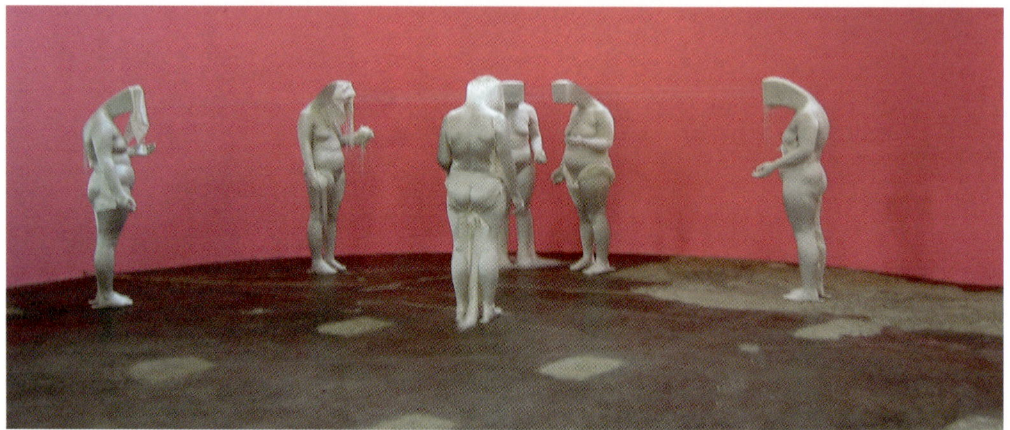

3

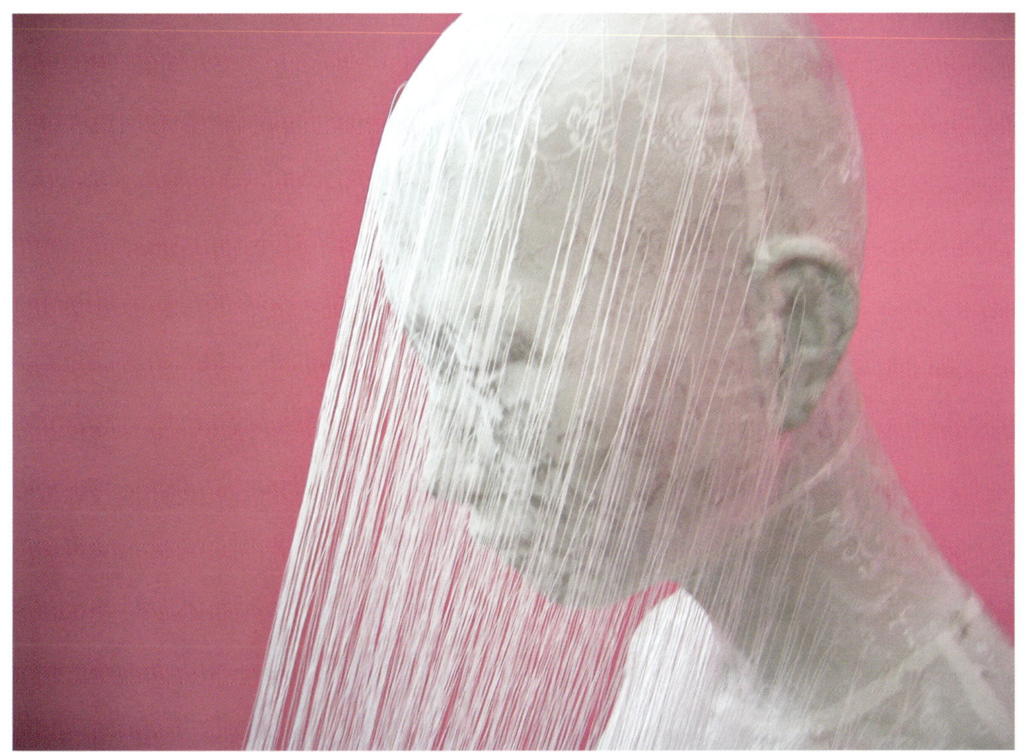

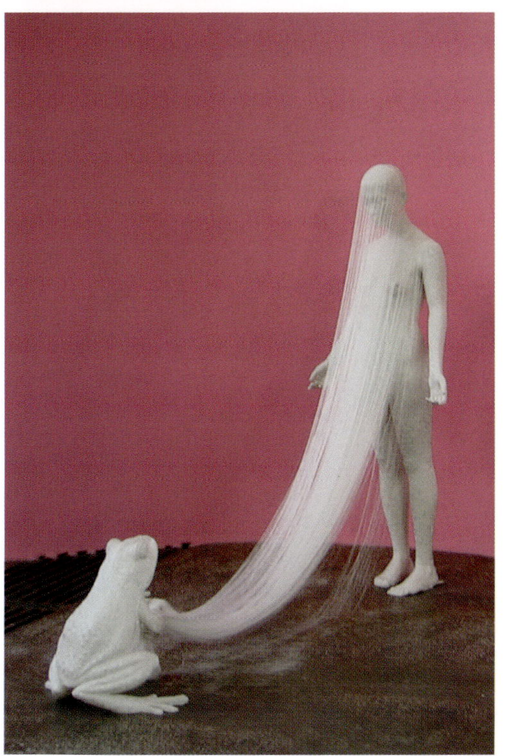

4

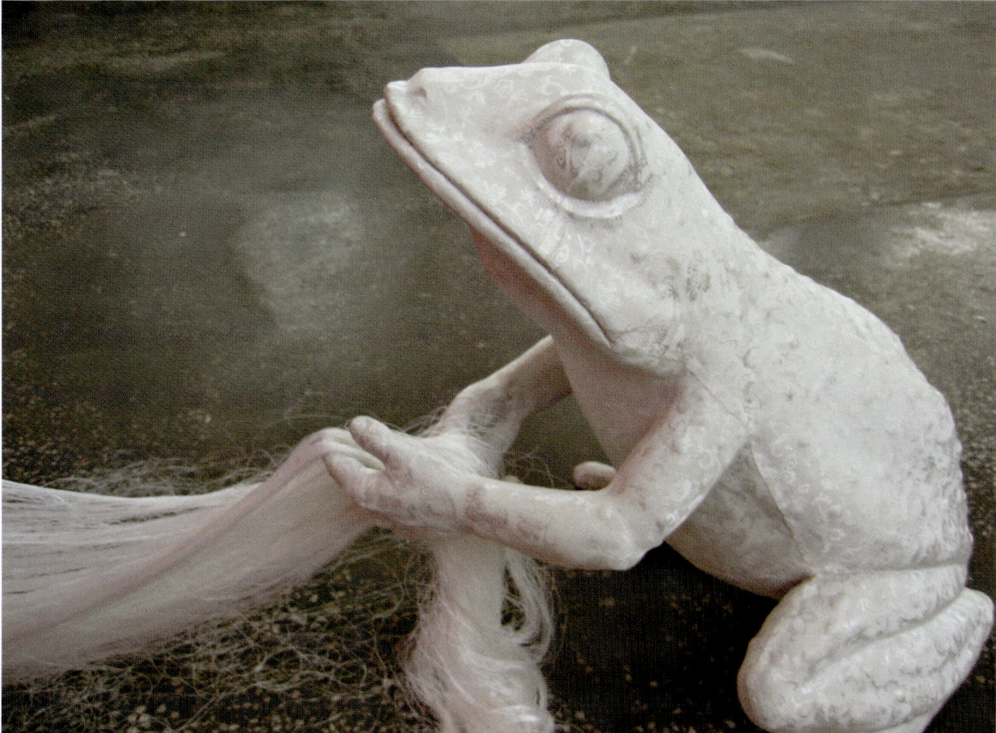

5

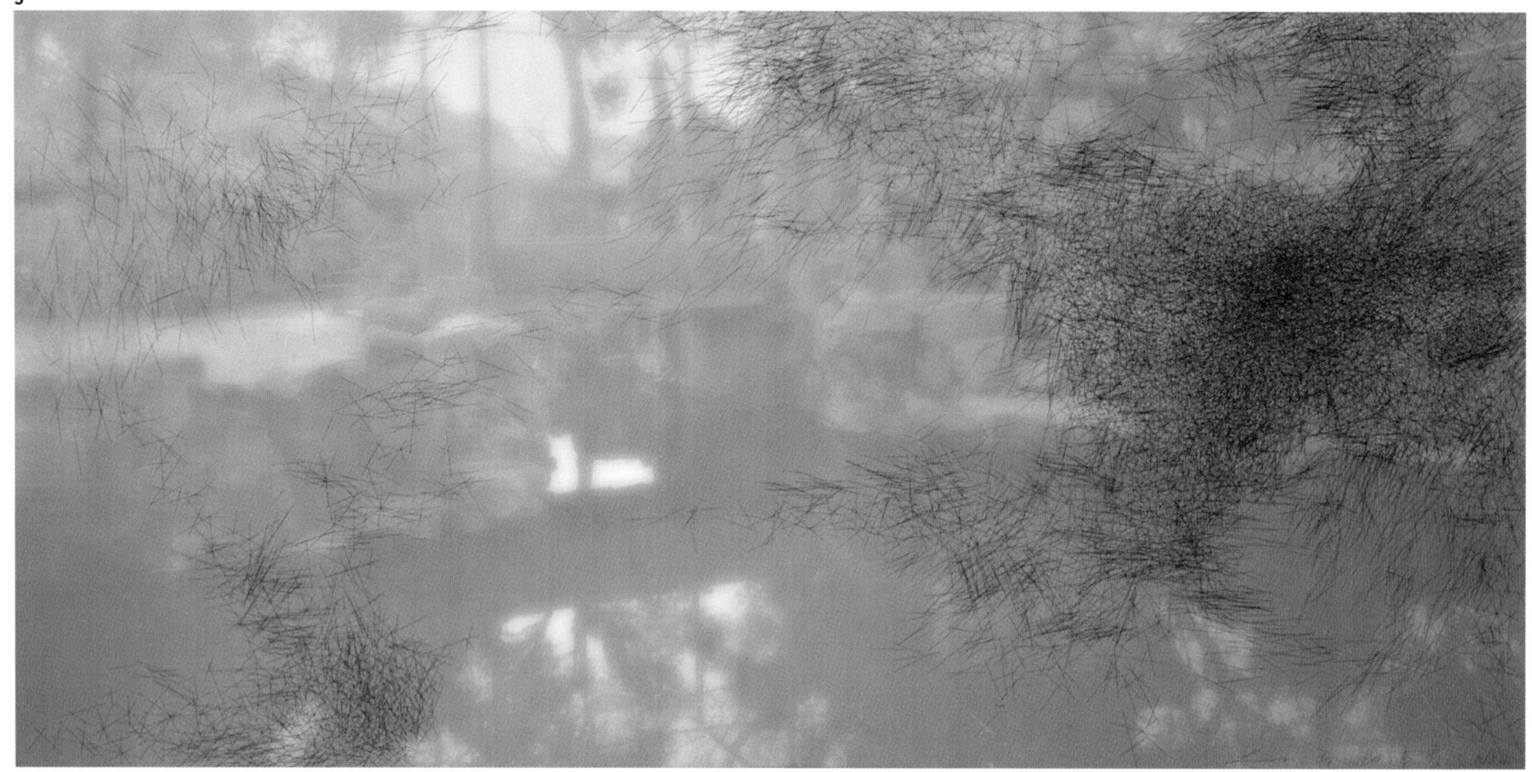

The installation "Bound-Unbound" (1995–1997) consists of over 100 household items wound with white yarn, being spread in front of a canvas, built of threads hanging down side by side the projection of the action of cutting yarns being symbolically simulated. The original form of things is still recognizable through the cocoon of yarn but at the same time deprived of context and former use. In this way things get a new aesthetic dimension and identity. The things behind, stored experiences, time and energy come to the fore instead of reading a figurative object. The artist's interest lies not on the given, but on the conception as a chance for new experiences broadening the horizon.

The process of work is constitutive in Lin Tianmiao's art the traceable visualisation of the idea behind the work being the utmost target. Winding is like a relaxing meditation for Lin Tianmiao, an opportunity to allow her thoughts to ramble. The action and the examination of the material offer experiences on the area of conflict between distance and integration, they can be understood as care of the self in context with social, familial, and natural relations.

Im Mittelpunkt ihrer künstlerischen Interventionen stehen vielmehr die gegebenen Umstände und Strukturen, die das Individuum prägen und die menschliche Existenz an sich bestimmen.

Die Installation „Bound-Unbound" (1995–1997) besteht aus über hundert mit weißem Garn umwickelten Haushaltsgegenständen, die Lin im Raum vor einer Leinwand auslegt, die sich aus dicht nebeneinander herabhängenden Fäden bildet und auf der die Projektion der Tätigkeit des Zerschneidens von Garn symbolisch simuliert wird. Durch den Garnkokon sind die Dinge zwar formal noch in ihrer ursprünglichen Form erkennbar, gleichzeitig aber ihrem Kontext enthoben und ihres ehemaligen Nutzwerts beraubt. Sie erhalten eine neue ästhetische Dimension und Identität. Nicht mehr das Lesen eines figurativen Objekts, sondern das Dahinter, die gespeicherte Erfahrung, Zeit und Energie stehen im Vordergrund. Nicht das Gegebene, sondern die Vorstellung als Möglichkeit neuer, horizonterweiternder Erfahrung interessiert die Künstlerin.

Bei Lin Tianmiao ist der Arbeitsprozess werkkonstituierend und die nachvollziehende Visualisierung der dahinter stehenden Idee oberstes Ziel. Das Wickeln ist für Lin entspannende Meditation, eine Möglichkeit, die Gedanken schweifen zu lassen. Die Tätigkeit und die Auseinandersetzung mit dem Material bieten Erfahrungen im Spannungsfeld zwischen Abstand und Integration und können als Pflege des eigenen Ichs im Kontext der gesellschaftlichen, familiären und natürlichen Bezüge verstanden werden.

创作的过程是林天苗艺术不可或缺的一部分，而作品蕴含的观点的可追寻性是其至上目标。对她而言，缠线是一种悠闲的沉思，而有机会去放飞自己的心灵。距离与整体的矛盾，是自我与社会、家庭和自然的关系。

Birgit Hopfener

6

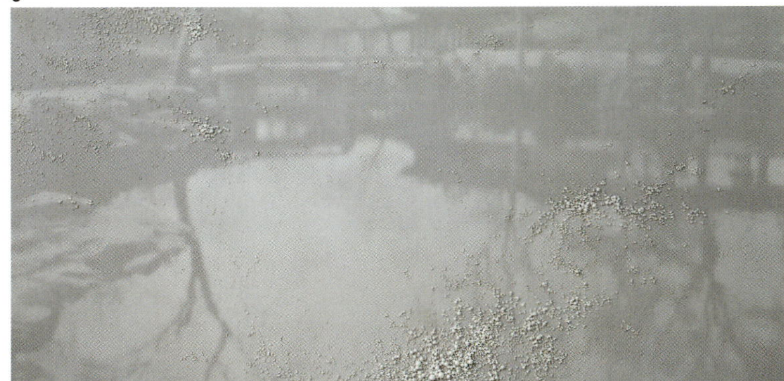

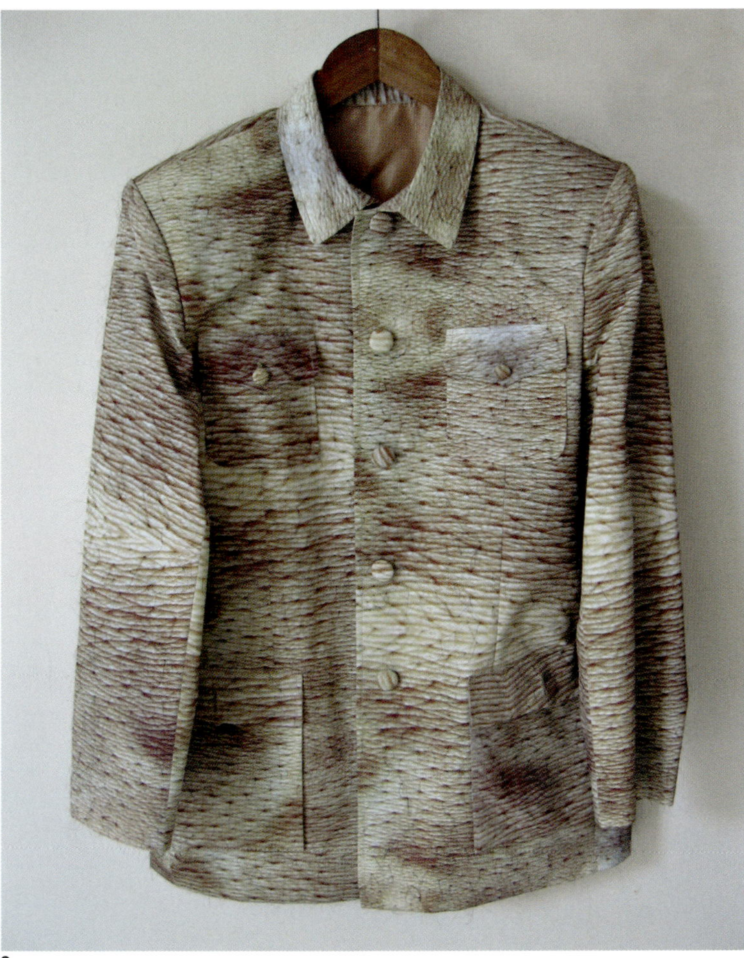

8

7

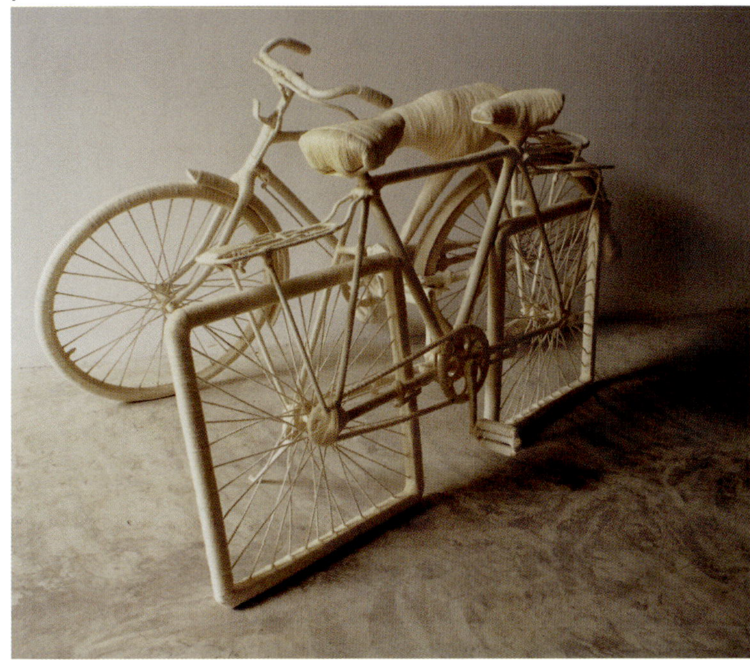

1 ***Focus***, *2001*
Digital photograph, thread, hair, 160 x 130 cm
Digitale Fotografie, Faden, Haar, 160 x 130 cm
《聚焦》2001年, 数字摄影，线，头发，160 x 130 cm

2 ***Endless***, *2004*
Installation
Installation
《不零》2004年, 装置

3 ***Chatting***, *2004*
Installation
Installation
《闲谈》2004年, 装置

4 ***Initiator***, *2004*
Installation
Installation
《创始人》2004年, 装置

5 ***Seeing Shadow***, *2005*
Digital photograph and embroidery on canvas, 144 x 284 x 8 cm
Digitale Fotografie und Stickerei auf Leinwand, 144 x 284 x 8 cm
《看影》2005年，数字照片和布面刺绣，144 x 284 x 8 cm

6 ***Seeing Shadow***, *2005*
Digital photograph and embroidery on canvas, 89.5 x 178 cm
Digitale Fotografie und Stickerei auf Leinwand, 89,5 x 178 cm
《看影》2005年，数字照片和布面刺绣，89.5 x 178 cm

7 ***Bicycle***, *2001*
Installation
Installation
《自行车》2001年，装置

8 ***Skin***, *2005*
Mixed media, life-size
Mixed media, lebensgroß
《皮肤》2005年，混合材料，真人大小

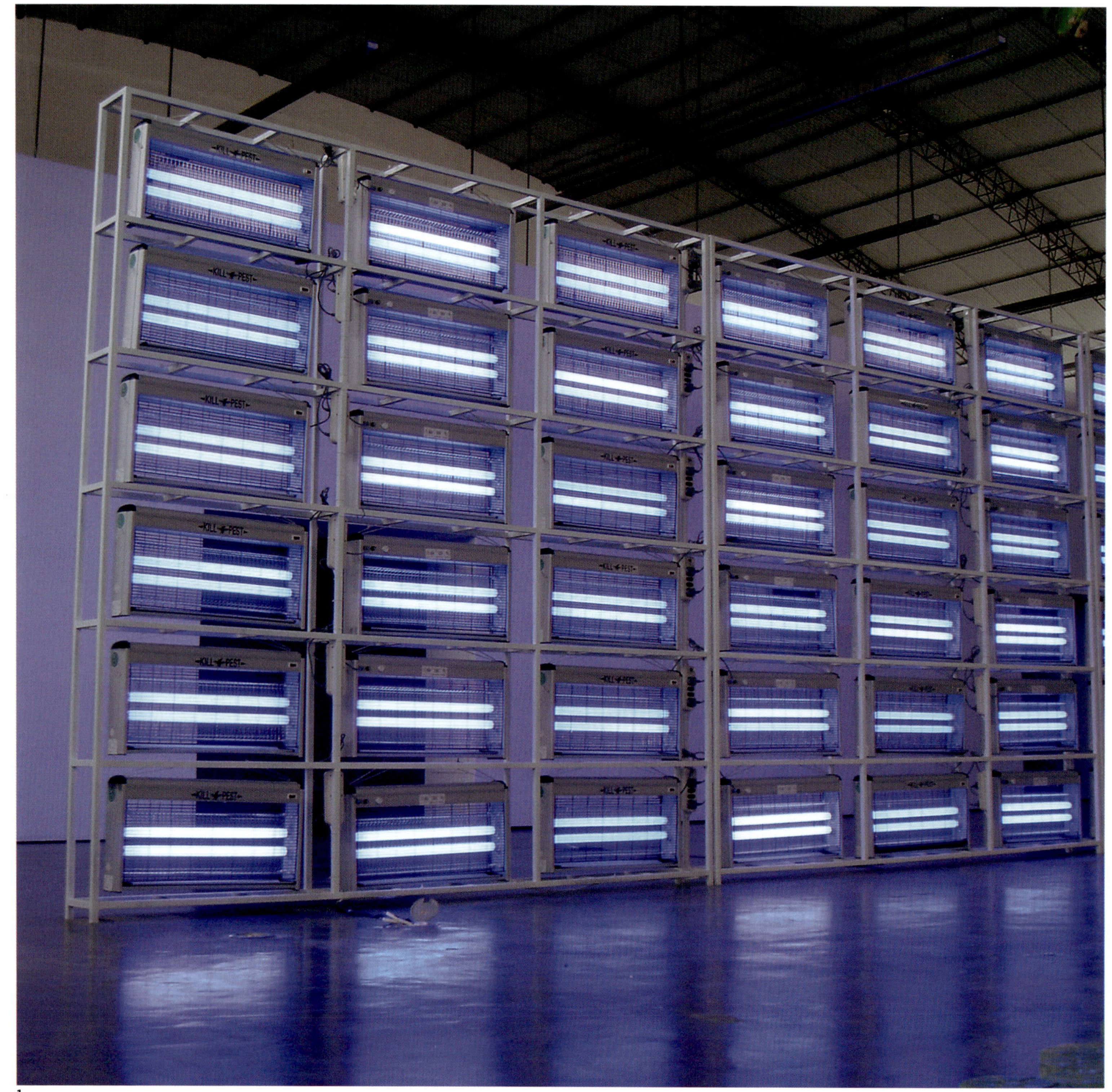

1

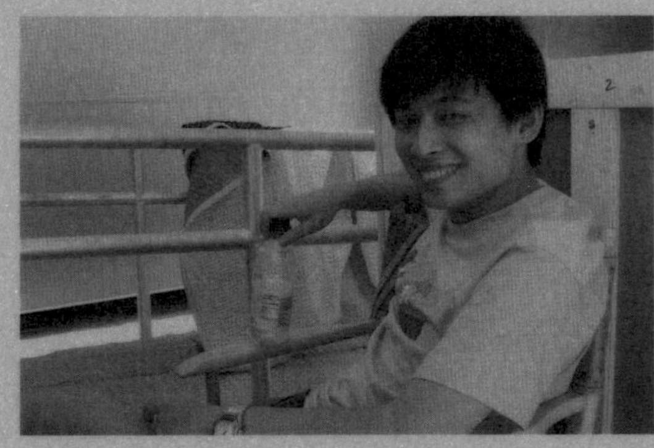

"Your role model is yourself."

„Dein Vorbild, das bist du selbst."

"你的偶像是你自己。"

Born in 1976 in Changzhou, Jiangsu Province, China. Lives and works in Beijing
Geboren 1976 in Changzhou, Provinz Jiangsu, China. Lebt und arbeitet in Peking
1976年出生于中国江苏省常州市，现住居在北京

***Selected exhibitions* / Ausgewählte Ausstellungen / 所选展览**

2004 "Image Beyond Image – Liu Ding's Photography Exhibition", Rooseum, Malmö, Sweden
2005 "Complete Art Experience Project No. 6 – Playground of Authorship", University of Rochester, New York, NY, USA
Archaeology of the Future – the 2nd Triennial of Chinese Art, Nanjing Museum, Nanjing, China
2006 "Samples from the Transition – Products", L. A. Gallery, Frankfurt, Germany
"Alllooksame?", Fondazione Sandretto Re Rebaudengo, Turine, Italy
"China Power Station Part 1", Battersea Power Station, Serpentine Gallery, London, UK
The 4th Seoul International Media Art Biennial, Seoul Museum of Art, Seoul, Korea
2007 "Thermocline of Art", ZKM (Center for Art and Media), Karlsruhe, Germany

2004年 《象外之象》刘鼎摄影展，Rooseum美术馆，马尔默，瑞典
2005年 《联合现场项目No. 6 -- 锦囊妙计》罗切斯特大学画廊, 纽约
《未来考古学 -- 第二届中国艺术三年展》南京美术馆 南京
2006年 《转型期的标本 -- 产品》L.A.画廊，法兰克福，德国
《看上去都一样》中日韩当代艺术展，都灵, 意大利
《中国电站第一站》巴特西发电站，蛇形画廊，伦敦，英国
《第四届韩国首尔媒体艺术双年展》首尔市立美术馆，首尔
2007年 《艺术温跃层》德国艺术与媒体中心，卡斯鲁尔厄，德国

***Selected publications* / Ausgewählte Publikationen / 所选著作**

"The Second Guangzhou Triennial", Guangzhou 2005
"Alllooksame?", Fondazione Sandretto Re Rebaudengo, Turine 2006
"Fancy Dream", Milan 2006
"Touching The Stone", Cologne 2006

《第二届广州三年展》岭南美术出版社 广东美术馆 广州，2005年
《看上去都一样》中日韩当代艺术展，都灵, 意大利，2006年
《幻想》Damiani, 米兰2006年
《摸着石头》科隆2006年

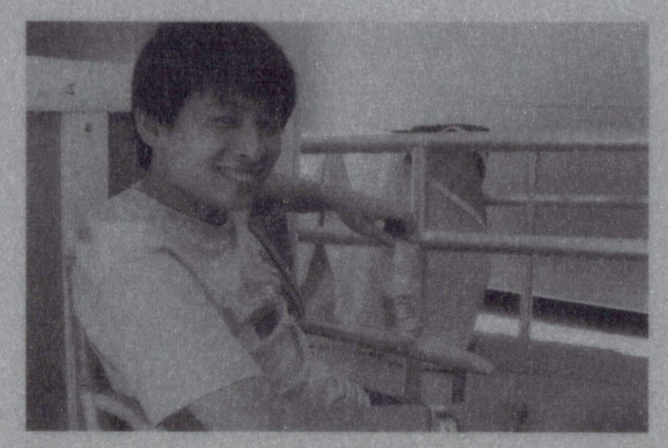

"Your role model is yourself."

„Dein Vorbild, das bist du selbst."

"你的偶像是你自己。"

Born in 1976 in Changzhou, Jiangsu Province, China. Lives and works in Beijing
Geboren 1976 in Changzhou, Provinz Jiangsu, China. Lebt und arbeitet in Peking
1976年出生于中国江苏省常州市，现住居在北京

Selected exhibitions / Ausgewählte Ausstellungen / 所选展览

2004 "Image Beyond Image - Liu Ding's Photography Exhibition", Roosseum, Malmö, Sweden
2005 "Complete Art Experience Project No. 6 - Playground of Authorship", University of Rochester, New York, NY, USA
Archaeology of the Future - the 2nd Triennial of Chinese Art, Nanjing Museum, Nanjing, China
2006 "Samples from the Transition - Products", L. A. Gallery, Frankfurt, Germany
"Alllooksame?", Fondazione Sandretto Re Rebaudengo, Turine, Italy
"China Power Station Part 1", Battersea Power Station, Serpentine Gallery, London, UK
The 4th Seoul International Media Art Biennial, Seoul Museum of Art, Seoul, Korea
2007 "Thermocline of Art", ZKM (Center for Art and Media), Karlsruhe, Germany

2004年 《象外之象》刘鼎摄影展，Roosseum美术馆，马尔默，瑞典
2005年 《联合现场项目No. 6 一 锦囊妙计》罗切斯特大学画廊，纽约
《未来考古学 一 第二届中国艺术三年展》南京美术馆 南京
2006年 《转型期的标本 一 产品》L.A.画廊，法兰克福，德国
《看上去都一样》中日韩当代艺术展，都灵，意大利
《中国电站第一站》巴特西发电站，蛇形画廊，伦敦，英国
《第四届韩国首尔媒体艺术双年展》首尔市立美术馆，首尔
2007年 《艺术温跃层》德国艺术与媒体中心，卡斯鲁尔厄，德国

Selected publications / Ausgewählte Publikationen / 所选著作

"The Second Guangzhou Triennial", Guangzhou 2005
"Alllooksame?", Fondazione Sandretto Re Rebaudengo, Turine 2006
"Fancy Dream", Milan 2006
"Touching The Stone", Cologne 2006

《第二届广州三年展》岭南美术出版社 广东美术馆 广州，2005年
《看上去都一样》中日韩当代艺术展，都灵，意大利，2006年
《幻想》Damiani，米兰2006年
《摸着石头》科隆2006年

LIU DING 刘鼎

[liou tiŋ]

Liu Ding has a talent in translating an idea into a visual spectacle and creating objects, installations and scenes that transport viewers to different aesthetic and sensual realms and surreal worlds. From 2000 to 2003, he glued empty capsules of different sizes and colours to make small, minimalist sculptural objects and forms such as white and yellow mushrooms and a short brown column that he jokingly named "Brown Sugar". When exhibited, the mushrooms had been randomly scattered on the ground or displayed as a piece of precious antique in a glass case lit from within. They are glistening, attractive, fragile, and almost seem like they could be creatures straight from a lab of a science fiction film or from a fairy tale.

He believes in the power of omens and is always on the look out for even the smallest indications of social changes and transformations and their potential impact. In "Grey Goo" (2003), a title he took from a technique of genetic modification and engineering, he constructed two mounds, one big, one small, of green capsules. Like a prophet he placed a stuffed crow, a symbol of death and bad fortune in Chinese culture, on the top of the taller hill. The installation occupied a single room that was lit with icy white spotlight and echoed a sense of menace.

In his works, Liu never gives out his position easily or unambiguously yet he conscientiously articulates his sociological, philosophical and humanistic concerns in art that draws empathy from viewers. He always succeeds in building up enough glamour and charisma around his installations that they become temporary illusions and outlets for escapism. In "Treasure" (2005), he dug a two-meter deep hole on the floor of a small gallery project room and placed at the bottom of the gap a big pile of fake jewelry. As they were lit from underneath, a strong beam of light shot straight out of the crack to the ceiling in the dim room that was painted in a dark shade of pink. Viewers were involuntarily lured to the side of the crack, to peek inside and discover the glistening jewellery as if suddenly encountering a wonder. This is the magical power of the

Liu Ding schafft mit seinen Objekten, Installationen und Szenen visuelle Schauspiele, die ihre Betrachter in sehr unterschiedliche ästhetische und sinnliche Sphären und Welten entführen. So klebte er zwischen 2000 und 2003 leere Kapseln unterschiedlicher Größe und Farbe zu kleinen minimalistischen Objekten und Formen zusammen, etwa zu weißen und gelben Pilzen und einer kurzen braunen Säule, die er scherzhaft „Brown Sugar" nannte. Bei Ausstellungen wurden die Pilze willkürlich auf dem Boden verstreut oder aber wie kostbare Preziosen in einer von innen beleuchteten Vitrine präsentiert. Die glänzenden, reizvollen und fragilen Objekte wirken beinahe wie Kreationen aus einem Science-Fiction-Labor – oder einem Märchen.

Liu Ding glaubt tatsächlich an die Macht von Omina und hält beständig Ausschau nach den kleinsten Hinweisen auf gesellschaftliche Veränderungen und Umbrüche und ihre potenziellen Auswirkungen. Für „Grey Goo" (2003 – der Titel ist von einem Begriff aus der Nano- und Gentechnologie abgeleitet) konstruierte er zwei kegelförmige Anhäufungen aus grünen Kapseln, die eine größer als die andere. Wie ein Schamane oder Prophet setzte er eine ausgestopfte Krähe auf die Spitze des höheren Kegels; sie gilt in der chinesischen Kultur als Symbol für Tod und Unglück. In einem Raum mit frostig weißem Scheinwerferlicht untergebracht, strahlte die Installation etwas äußerst Bedrohliches aus.

Liu gibt seine Position in seinen Werken nie einfach oder unzweideutig zu erkennen, artikuliert aber seine gesellschaftlichen, philosophischen und humanistischen Anliegen durchaus zuverlässig, und zwar in einer Weise, die beim Betrachter Anteilnahme weckt. Und es gelingt ihm immer, seine Installationen mit so viel Glamour und Charisma zu umgeben, dass sie zu kurzlebigen Illusionen und Ventilen für Eskapismus werden. Für „Treasure" (2005) grub er ein zwei Meter tiefes Loch in den Boden eines kleinen Galerie-Projektraums und deponierte darin einen großen Haufen unechten Schmucks. Diesen beleuchtete er von unten, sodass ein starker Lichtstrahl aus dem Loch bis zur Decke des schummerigen Raums hinaufschoss, der in einem dunklen

将创意转化为看得见的展品，创作物品、装置及布景，将观众带入不同的美学和感官领域及超现实世界 —— 在这些方面，刘鼎拥有独特的天赋。从2000年到 2003 年，他将各种尺寸、不同颜色的空胶囊粘合起来，制成小型的极简抽象主义雕塑物品和形体，例如白色和黄色的蘑菇，一个美其名曰为“红糖”的褐色矮柱等。在展出时，他将这些蘑菇任意散布在地面上，或者将其作为一块珍贵的古董碎片放在一个里面发光的玻璃瓶内。这些胶囊作品闪闪发光、充满魅力而又脆弱，就仿佛是直接从科幻里的实验室中取出的物种，抑或是来自童话世界。

他相信预兆的力量，并且随时留意哪怕是最细微的社会改变及变化迹象，以及这些改变和变化的潜在影响。在《灰色粘质》（标题取自一项基因改良及基因工程技术）中，他用绿色胶囊堆建了一大一小两个小丘。他好像一位先知那样，将一只乌鸦标本放置在较高的小丘上，而在中国文化中，乌鸦是死亡和厄运征兆。该装置作品占据了一整间房间，房间由冰冷的白色聚光灯所照亮，散发着危险的气息。

在自己的作品中，刘鼎从不轻易或明确地表现自己的立场，而是他引人入胜的艺术中谨慎地在阐明自己对社会学、哲学以及人文学的关注。他总能在其装置作品周围成功地营造足够的魅力及感召力，并使其成为暂时逃离现实的幻想和出口。在《转型期的标本 —— 宝藏》（2005 年）中，他在一间小的画廊项目房间里挖了一个两米深的洞，在洞的底部放置了一大堆假珠宝。当从下面照亮这些珠宝时，一道强光径直穿出洞口并照到昏暗房间内漆着粉红色阴影的天花板上。观众不知不觉中就被吸引到洞边，偷看里面，然后发现那些闪闪发光的珠宝，就仿佛突然遇到了一个奇迹。这就是艺术家的魔力，他已经完美地掌握了材料的表现形式、形状、材质、空间以及制造奇迹的公式。

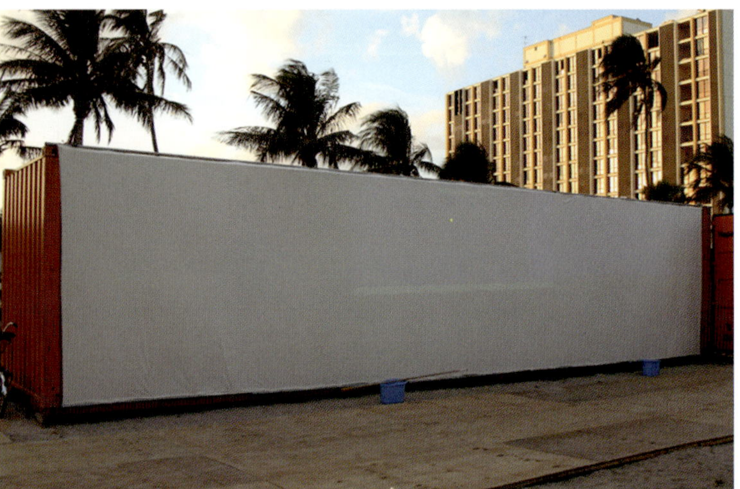

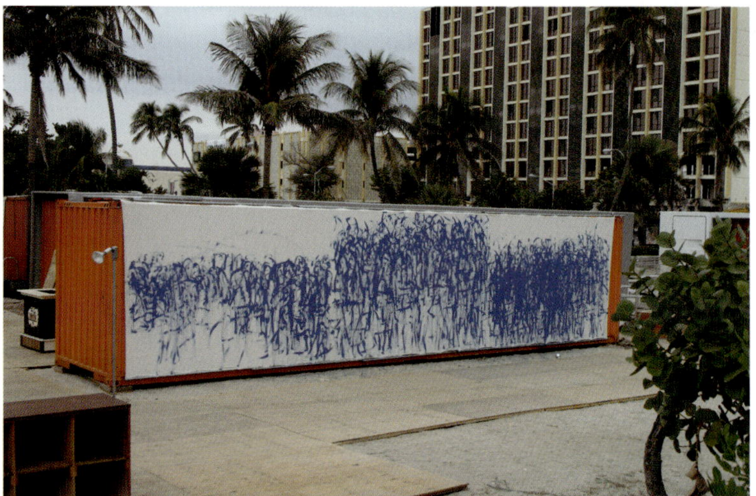

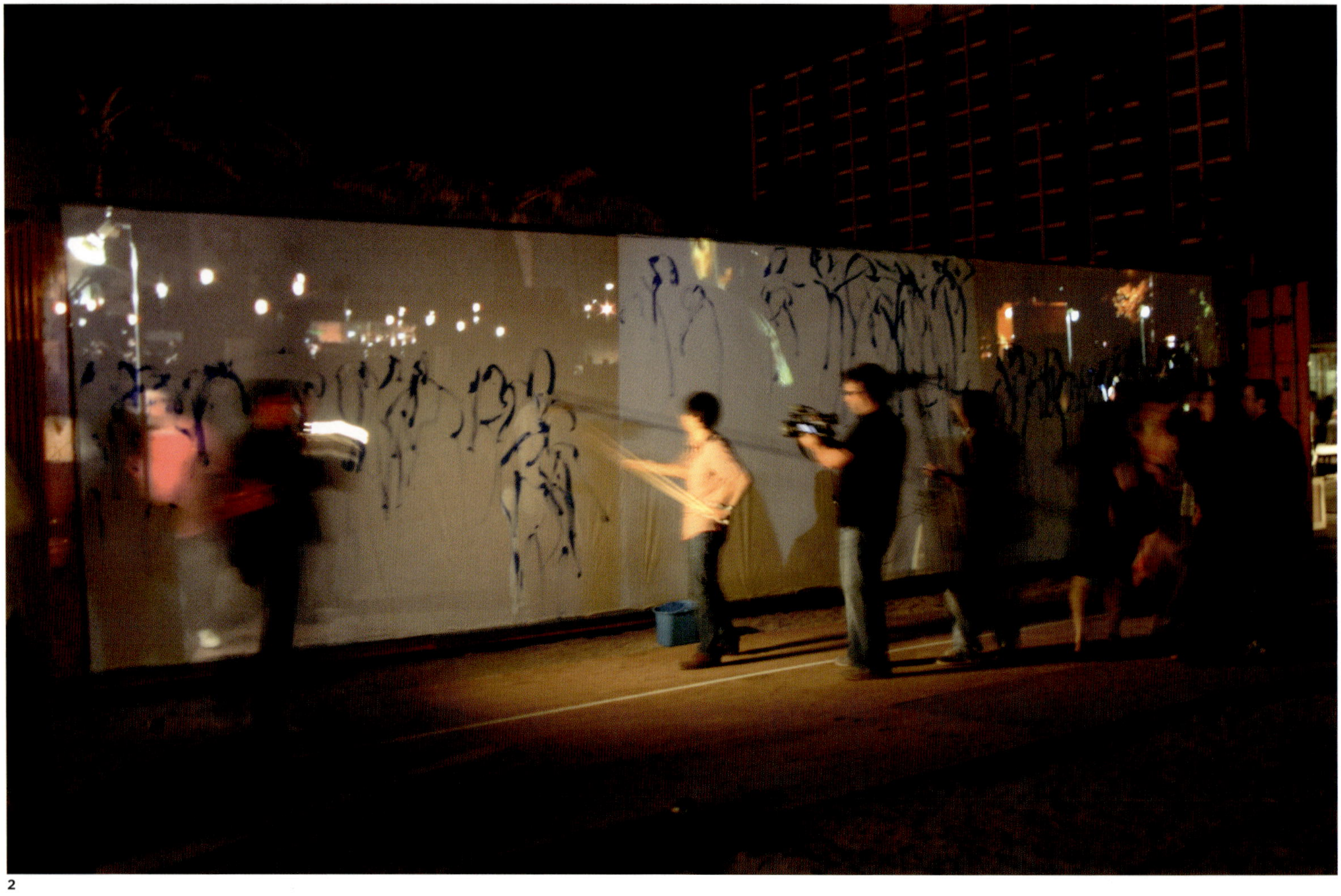

2

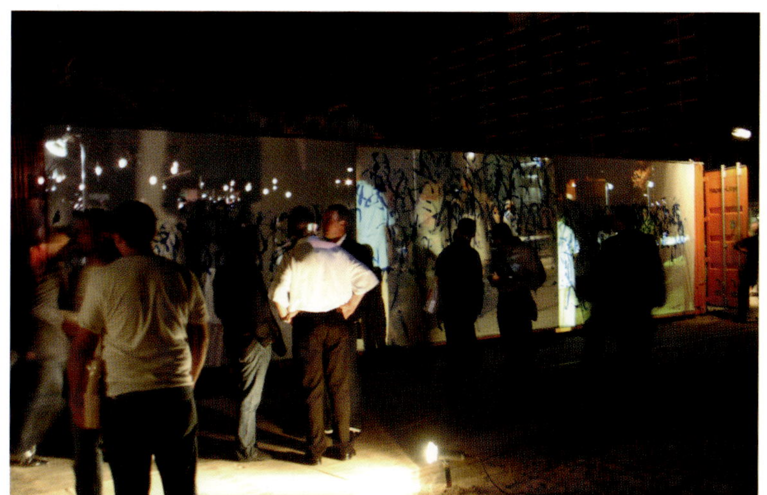

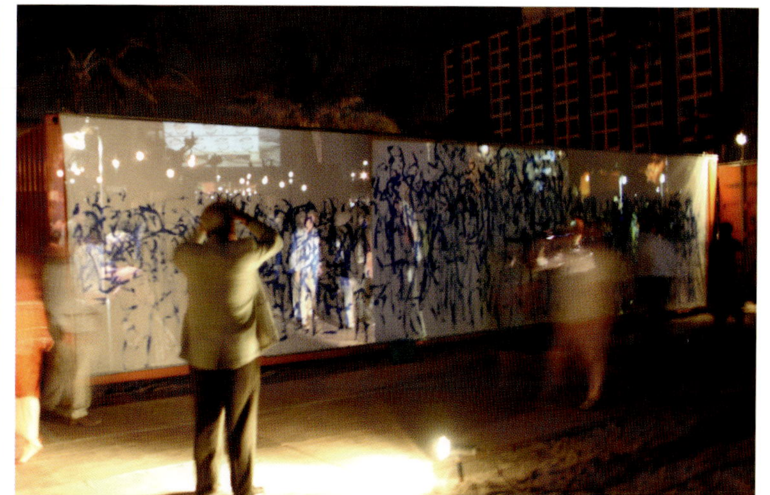

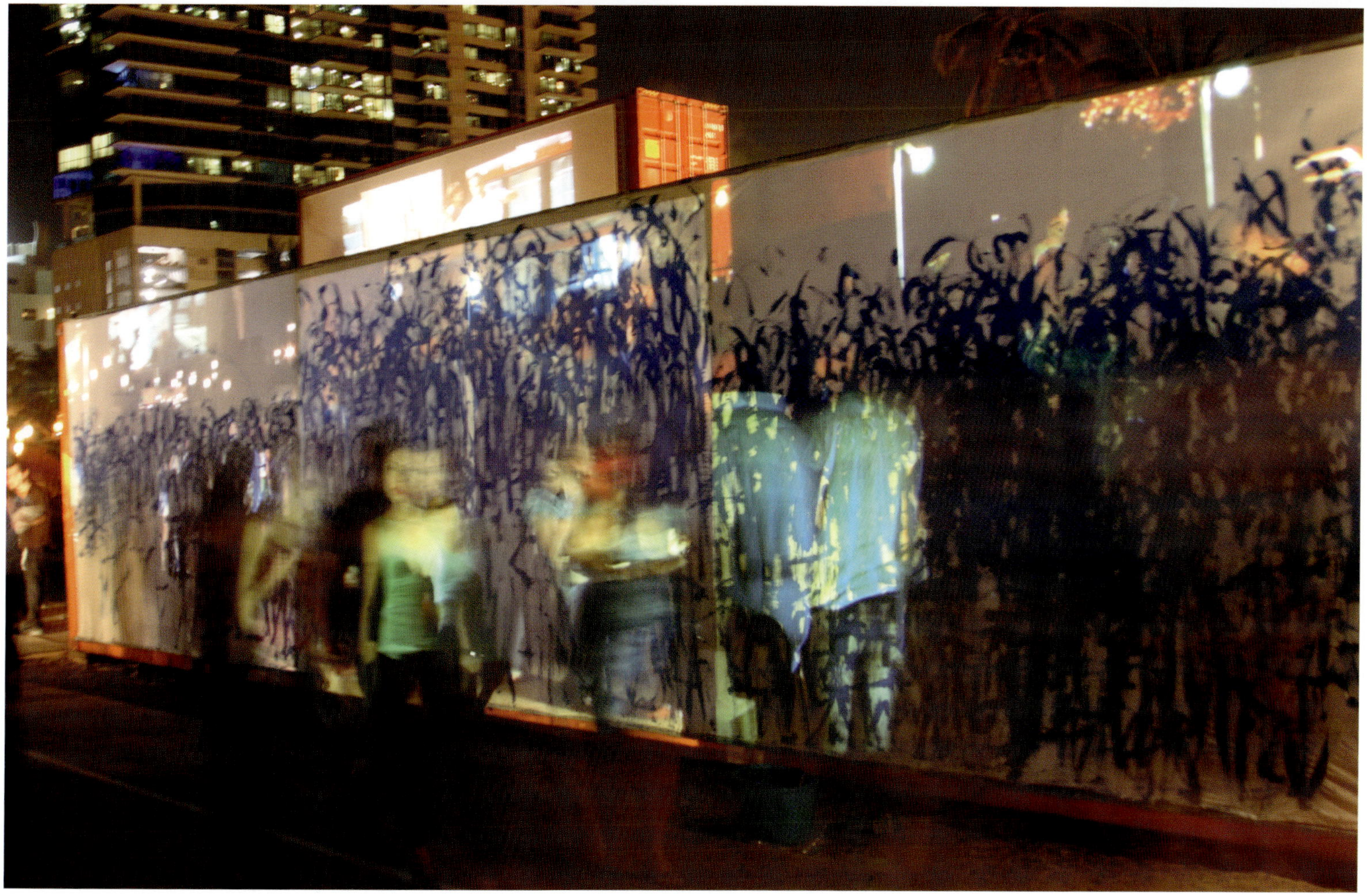

3

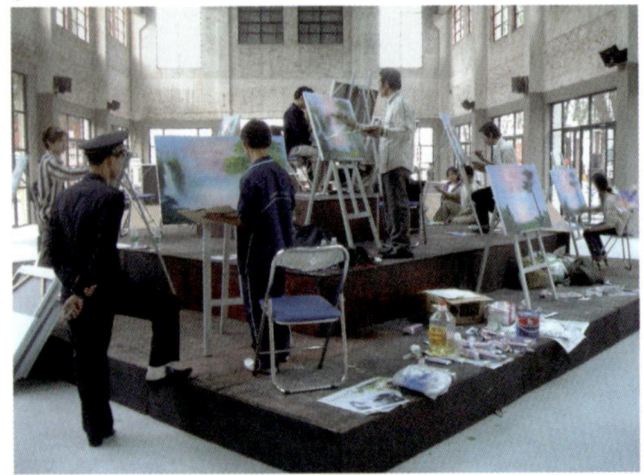

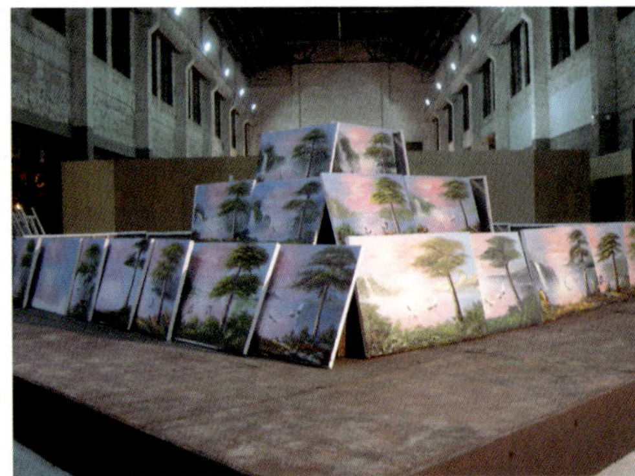

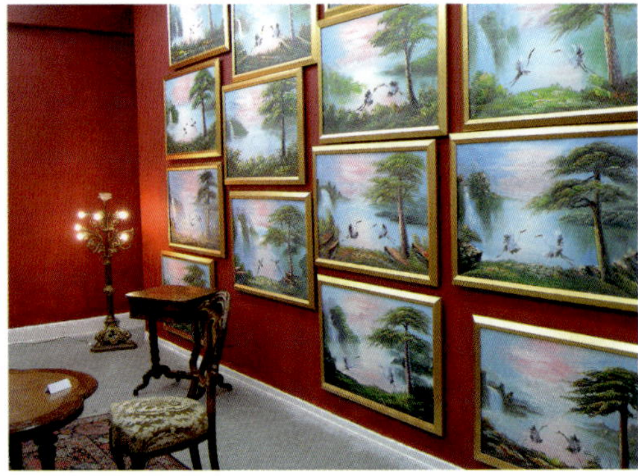

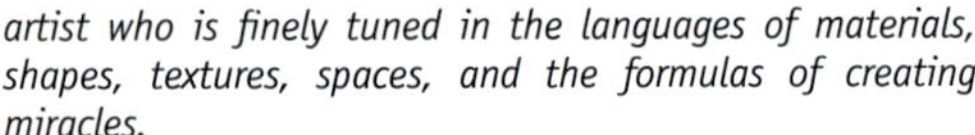

artist who is finely tuned in the languages of materials, shapes, textures, spaces, and the formulas of creating miracles.

He pulls out a rich range of sources and references for his magic making. In "Products" (2005/06), he collaborated with 13 painters from Dafencun, a famed village in south China thriving on exporting mass produced reproductions of oil paintings, especially those of Western masters to the Western market. He invited them into the museum and had them perform their assembly line production routine. He built a three-layer pyramid-shaped podium as an elevated working station for the painters, who were positioned on different levels depending on their range of importance in the hierarchy of production. Sticking to their strict regime of labour division in terms of who paints what on each painting, the 13 painters produced 40 elaborate paintings based on a highly decorative folk-looking landscape painting within a few hours of performance. The paintings were put up with gold frames, shipped to Frankfurt for his solo exhibition, since paintings of this kind usually end up in a Western home. These paintings were then displayed in salon style, filling up the walls of a gallery room furnished with 18th century German bourgeois fixtures. This fantasy-like splendour of this room installation is interwoven with, and enriched by, complex discussions not only of the nature of international trading, the status of third world countries as international factories, the isolation and vulnerability of such manufacturing economy, labour relationships and the division of low art and high art, but also of the world-wide circulation of visual culture.

Rosaton gestrichen war. Die Besucher fühlten sich unweigerlich an den Rand der Grube gelockt, um hineinzuspähen – und entdeckten den glitzernden Schmuck ganz so, als seien sie auf ein Wunder gestoßen. Die magische Kraft dieses Künstlers besteht darin, sich in den Sprachen der Materialien, Formen, Texturen und Räume und in Rezepten zur Schaffung kleinerer und größerer Wunder bestens auszukennen.

Liu Ding schöpft aus einem reichen Fundus von Quellen und Verweisen, um derlei Magie zu schaffen. Bei „Products" (2005/06) arbeitete er mit 13 Malern aus Dafencun zusammen. Dieses bekannte Dorf in Südchina lebt vom Export serienmäßig produzierter Kopien von Ölgemälden, vorwiegend Reproduktionen westlicher Meister für den westlichen Markt. Liu Ding lud die Maler ins Museum ein und ließ sie ihre routinierte Fließbandproduktion dort als Performance vorführen. Er baute dazu ein dreistufiges, pyramidenförmiges Podium als Arbeitsbühne für die Maler, die je nach ihrer Bedeutung in der Produktionshierarchie auf den verschiedenen Stufen platziert wurden. Die 13 Maler hielten sich an die ihnen gewohnte strikte Arbeitsteilung, wonach jeder nur bestimmte Teile eines Gemäldes ausführt, und produzierten in wenigen Stunden 40 aufwändig ausgeführte Versionen eines äußerst dekorativen, volkstümlich anmutenden Landschaftsgemäldes. Die Gemälde wurden dann (goldgerahmt) zu Liu Dings Einzelausstellung nach Frankfurt verschifft, da Produkte dieser Art normalerweise in westlichen Wohnzimmern landen. In Frankfurt stellte man die Werke in einem Salon-Ambiente aus: dicht an dicht an den Wänden eines Galerieraums, der mit gutbürgerlichem deutschem Mobiliar aus dem 18. Jahrhundert eingerichtet war. Die überspannte Pracht dieser Rauminstallation ging einher mit komplexen Diskussionen, die sich nicht nur um das Wesen des internationalen Handels, den Status von Drittweltländern als internationale Fabriken, die Anfälligkeit einer solchen Fertigungswirtschaft, die Beziehungen zwischen Arbeitgebern und -nehmern sowie die Unterscheidung zwischen höherer und niederer Kunst drehten, sondern auch um die weltweite Verbreitung visueller Kultur überhaupt.

其魔幻创作取材于各种丰富的资源和资料。在《转型期的标本 -- 产品》（2005-2006 年）中，他与 13 位来自大芬村的画家进行合作。大芬村是位于中国南部的一个村庄，以向西方市场出口大量生产的油画，尤其是西方大师们的油画的复制品而闻名。他将画家们请到博物馆内，并请他们演示他们的流水作业生产程序。他建造了一个三层的金字塔状的梯台作为画家们的高架工作台，而画家们则根据各自在作品层次中的重要性被安排在不同的高度上。在数小时的表演过程中，13 位画家们严格遵守各自画作品对应部分的分工制度，并根据一幅极富装饰性且具有民族特色的风景画，生产出 40 幅精致的画作。由于这些画作的去处常常是某一户西方家庭，因此采用了金框镶边，并被运往法兰克福的刘鼎个展。随后，这些画作以沙龙风格在一间摆放着十八世纪德国中产阶级家具的画廊房间展出，并布满了房间的墙壁。该室内装置作品魔幻般的光彩与各种复杂的讨论相交织并为这些讨论所丰富。讨论的内容不仅包括国际商贸的本质、第三世界国家作为世界工厂的状况、这种制造业经济的孤立性和脆弱性、劳动关系以及低级艺术与高级艺术的区分，还包括视觉文化全球性流通。

Carol Lu

4

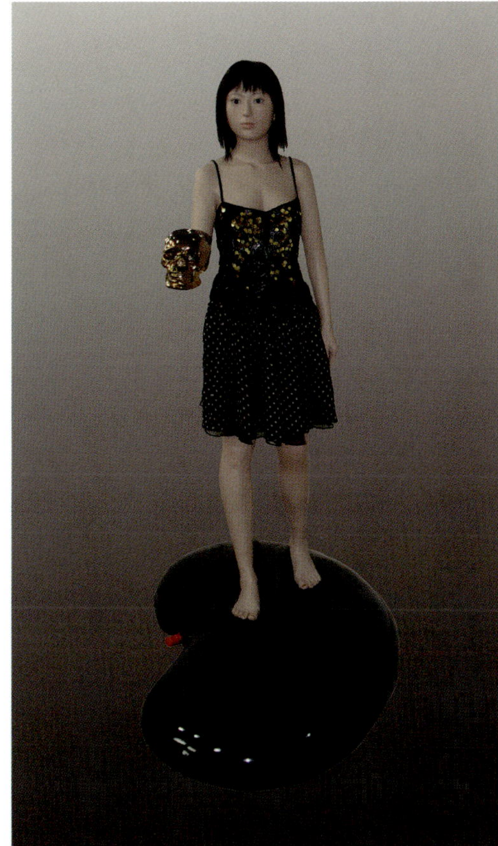

5

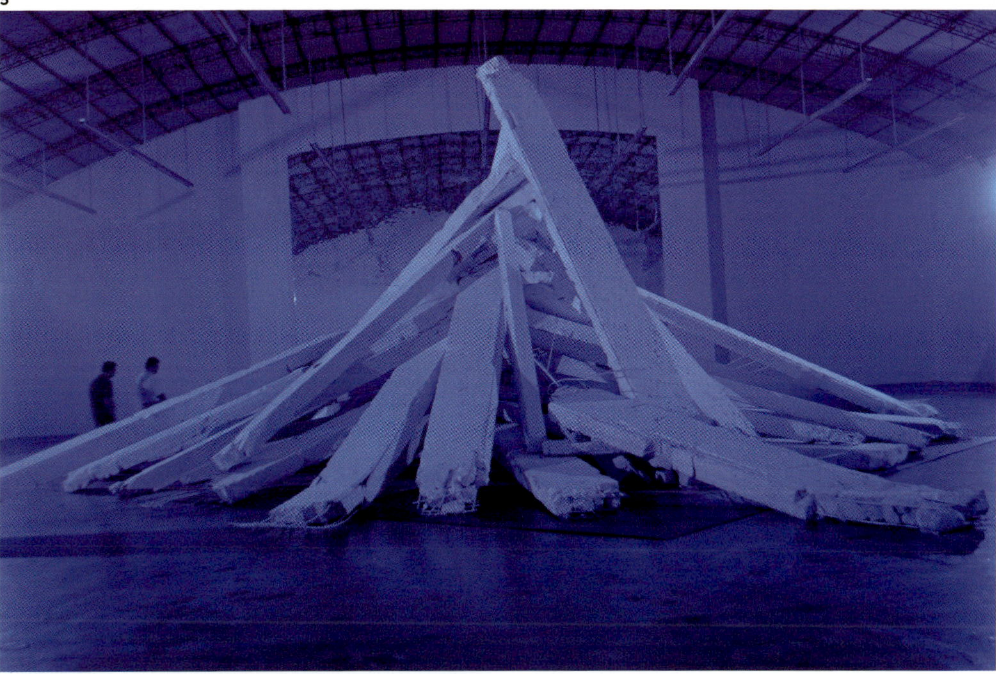

6

1 ***It's a War***, *2006*
60 insect killers, 30 mosquito bats, 260 x 830 x 40 cm
Insektenvernichter, 30 Fliegenklatschen, 260 x 830 x 40 cm
《战争》2006年, 60 只灭蚊器, 30 只电蚊拍,
260 x 830 x 40 cm

2 ***Tracing the Wind and the Shadows***, *2006*
Painting and video performance, Art Basel Miami Beach, Miami, FL, 2006
Malerei- und Video-Performance, Art Basel Miami Beach, Miami, FL, 2006
《追踪风和阴影》2006年, 油画和录像表演

3 ***Samples from the Transition, Products***, *2005*
Performance and installation, 2nd Guangzhou Triennial 2005
Performance und Installation, 2. Guangzhou Triennale 2005
《转型期的标本--产品》2005年, 表演和装置

4 ***A Girl Holding a Skull on a Kidney***, *2007*
Resin, porcelain, fabric, 180 x 120 x 75 cm
Kunstharz, Porzellan, Stoff, 180 x 120 x 75 cm
《站在肾上持骷髅的女孩》2007年，树脂，瓷器, 纺织物,
180 x 120 x 75 cm

5 ***Tiger***, *2007*
Concrete beams, mirror, steel plates, tiger skin, blue fluorescent lights (installation view)
Betonpfeiler, Spiegel, Stahlplatten, Tigerfell, blaues fluoreszierendes Licht (Installationsansicht)
《老虎》2007年，水泥棒，镜子，钢盘, 虎皮，蓝色荧光灯，装置实景

6 ***Tiger***, *2007*
Concrete beams, mirror, steel plates, tiger skin, blue fluorescent lights (installation view, detail)
Betonpfeiler, Spiegel, Stahlplatten, Tigerfell, blaues fluoreszierendes Licht (Installationsansicht, Detail)
《老虎》2007年，水泥棒，镜子，钢盘, 虎皮，蓝色荧光灯，装置实景, 详细

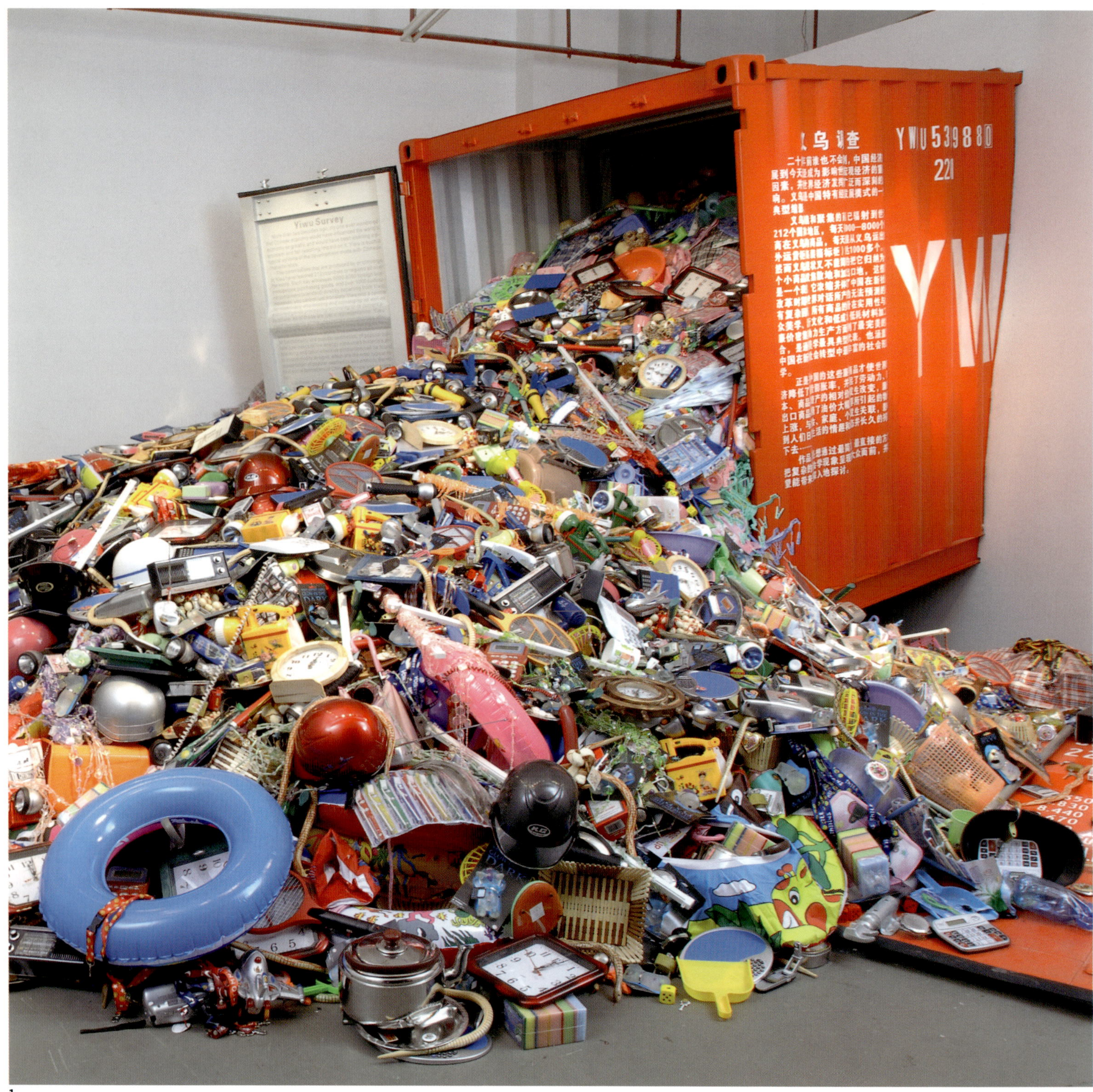

1

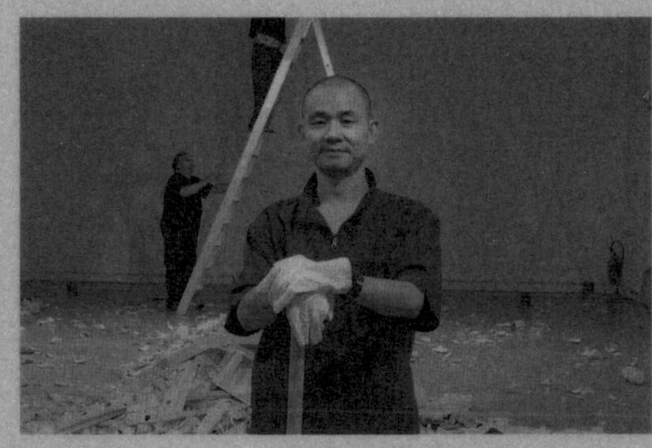

"Art is as rich and colourful as life..."

„Die Kunst ist so reich und bunt wie das Leben ..."

"艺术象生活一样丰富多彩…"

Born in 1962 in Ji'an, Jiangxi Province, China. Lives and works in Shanghai
Geboren 1962 in Ji'an, Provinz Jiangxi, China. Lebt und arbeitet in Shanghai
1962年出生于中国江西吉安，居住工作在上海

***Selected exhibitions* / Ausgewählte Ausstellungen /** 所选展览

2003 "What Do You Really Know About Yourself: Porcelain Works by Liu Jianhua", ShanghART Gallery, Shanghai, China
2004 "A Secret History of Clay: From Gauguin to Gormley", Tate Liverpool, Liverpool, UK
2005 "Only One Wall", Beijing Commune, Beijing, China
"The Elegance of Silence: Contemporary Art From East Asia", Mori Art Museum, Tokyo, Japan
2006 "Anomalous Thoughts – Liu Jianhua's Solo Exhibition", Galleria Continua, Beijing, China
Singapore Biennial 2006: Belief, Singapore, Singapore
Shanghai Biennial 2006: HyperDesign, Shanghai Art Museum, China
2007 2nd Moscow Biennial, Moscow, Russia

2003年 《你真的认识吗》-- 刘建华作品展》上海·香格纳画廊
2004年 《泥土的秘密：从高更到葛姆雷英国》利物浦泰特美术馆
2005年 《只有一面墙》北京公社艺术空间
《寂静的典雅》东亚当代艺术展 森美术馆 东京
2006年 《异想：刘建华个展》北京常青画廊 北京
《梦想》新加坡双年展，新加坡
《超设计》上海双年展，上海美术馆
2007年 第二届莫斯科双年展 俄罗斯

***Selected publications* / Ausgewählte Publikationen /** 所选著作

"Chinese Art (1979–1999)", Hong Kong 2000
"Dreams and Conflicts – The Dictatorship of the Viewer", Milan 2003
"Sex Pots – Eroticism in Ceramics", Piscataway 2003
"Shanghai Biennale 2006: HyperDesign", Shanghai 2006

《中国艺术：1979–1999》香港2000年
《梦想与冲突 -- 观者的独立视角》米兰2003年
《性罐》Piscataway 2003年
《超设计》上海双年展，上海美术馆，上海2003年

"Art is as rich and colourful as life..."

„Die Kunst ist so reich und bunt wie das Leben ..."

"艺术象生活一样丰富多彩…"

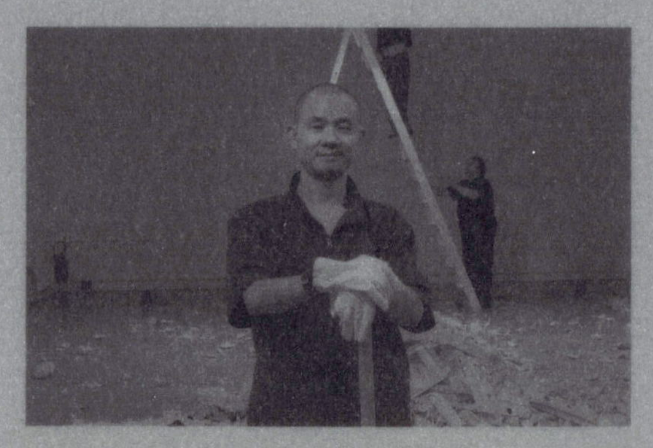

Born in 1962 in Ji'an, Jiangxi Province, China. Lives and works in Shanghai
Geboren 1962 in Ji'an, Provinz Jiangxi, China. Lebt und arbeitet in Shanghai
1962年出生于中国江西吉安，居住工作在上海

Selected exhibitions / Ausgewählte Ausstellungen / 所选展览

2003 "What Do You Really Know About Yourself: Porcelain Works by Liu Jianhua", ShanghART Gallery, Shanghai, China
2004 "A Secret History of Clay: From Gauguin to Gormley", Tate Liverpool, Liverpool, UK
2005 "Only One Wall", Beijing Commune, Beijing, China
"The Elegance of Silence: Contemporary Art From East Asia", Mori Art Museum, Tokyo, Japan
2006 "Anomalous Thoughts - Liu Jianhua's Solo Exhibition", Galleria Continua, Beijing, China
Singapore Biennial 2006: Belief, Singapore, Singapore
Shanghai Biennial 2006: HyperDesign, Shanghai Art Museum, China
2007 2nd Moscow Biennial, Moscow, Russia

2003年 《你真的认识吗》-- 刘建华作品展》上海・香格纳画廊
2004年 《泥土的秘密：从高更到葛姆雷英国》利物浦泰特美术馆
2005年 《只有一面墙》北京公社艺术空间
《寂静的典雅》东亚当代艺术展 森美术馆 东京
2006年 《异想：刘建华个展》北京常青画廊 北京
《梦想》新加坡双年展，新加坡
《超设计》上海双年展，上海美术馆
2007年 第二届莫斯科双年展 俄罗斯

Selected publications / Ausgewählte Publikationen / 所选著作

"Chinese Art (1979-1999)", Hong Kong 2000
"Dreams and Conflicts - The Dictatorship of the Viewer", Milan 2003
"Sex Pots - Eroticism in Ceramics", Piscataway 2003
"Shanghai Biennale 2006: HyperDesign", Shanghai 2006

《中国艺术：1979-1999》香港2000年
《梦想与冲突 — 观者的独立视角》米兰2003年
《性罐》Piscataway 2003年
《超设计》上海双年展，上海美术馆，上海2003年

LIU JIANHUA 刘建华

[liou tɕiɛnxua]

Liu Jianhua is one of the few porcelain-based artists in China who has the combined edges of being proficient in the language of porcelain through his years of labor in a porcelain studio in Jingdezhen, the famed porcelain town in China and later being trained in an art school as a sculptor. He first became known in the early 1990s for his bright-color, headless and armless porcelain female torsos tightly wrapped in Qipao dresses, appearing in sexually charged postures and placed on big traditionally patterned plates. These works had a wide appeal to a largely Western audience who found analogy between his works and their exotic view of what the Oriental has to offer.

His profound understanding of porcelain proved to be liberating in his following practice, in which he reversed the idea of porcelain making as a craft that requires a high degree of precision and refinement. Instead, he cast a large quantity of everyday objects, anything he can find, from pillows, bottles, computer keyboards, hammers, to hamlets and so on in downright white porcelain. They were stripped of any color, any detail, any text, any logo, any pattern, any personality, and any indication of hierarchy in their former forms, and were all returned to their most basic and democratic forms. He deliberately preserved the rough edges of these duplicates and any imperfections from the production procedure. He made room-size installations by displaying these objects and the results generated a barren, humble yet powerful feeling. Their grassroots visual quality almost has a pride that shines through the coarseness and their unfinished and unfurnished surfaces.

In his recent site-specific installations, he took an even more radical approach towards these innocent objects by dumping a considerable amount of them onto the floor of the exhibition space and smashing them hard and thoroughly with a shovel. He then laid out these broken bits and pieces in the shape of a space shuttle of an enormous size. ("Dream", 2005) It's interesting to see the conceptual dimension gradually taking over the material dimension in the years of Liu Jianhua's practice, to such a point that

Liu Jianhua verfügt als einer von wenigen Porzellankünstlern in China über eine Doppelqualifikation: Durch jahrelange Tätigkeit in einer Porzellanwerkstatt der berühmten chinesischen Porzellanstadt Jingdezhen ist er in der Technik der Porzellanbearbeitung bewandert und erlernte später noch an einer Kunstschule die Bildhauerei. Zu Beginn der 1990er Jahre wurde er bekannt durch Darstellungen bunter, kopf- und armloser Frauenkörper, die sich in engen Qipao-Kleidern und sexuell aufreizenden Posen auf großen, traditionell gemusterten Tellern räkelten. Diese Arbeiten fanden vor allem beim westlichen Publikum großen Anklang, das in Lius Werk sicher eigene Erwartungen an das exotisch Fernöstliche bestätigt sah.

Lius profunder „Porzellanverstand" erwies sich in seinem weiteren Schaffen als befreiend: Er räumte nun mit der Vorstellung auf, dass die Porzellanherstellung ein Kunsthandwerk sei, das ein hohes Maß an Genauigkeit und Verfeinerung erfordere. Stattdessen goss er eine Vielzahl von Alltagsgegenständen – von Kopfkissen und Flaschen über Computertastaturen und Hämmer bis zu Helmen – in schlichtem weißem Porzellan nach. Dadurch beraubte er die Vorlagen aller Farbe, aller Details, aller charakteristischen Muster und jedes Hinweises auf die vormalige Hierarchie der Dinge, der sie zugeordnet waren, und führte sie so auf ihre grundlegenden demokratischen Formen zurück. Die rauen Kanten der Abgüsse und etwaige, im Produktionsverfahren entstandene Unvollkommenheiten ließ er absichtlich bestehen. Aus all diesen Objekten gestaltete er raumgroße Installationen, die Kargheit, Bescheidenheit und zugleich eine gewisse Kraft ausstrahlen. Die schlichte optische Anmutung vermittelt einen eigenen Stolz, der durch die Grobheit der unbearbeiteten und schmucklosen Oberflächen hindurchscheint. Bei seinen neueren ortsbezogenen Installationen ging Liu noch radikaler mit seinen Fundstücken um, indem er sie in großer Zahl auf den Boden des Ausstellungsraums kippte und sie brutal und gründlich mit einer Schaufel zertrümmerte. Dann fügte er die Bruchstücke zur Gestalt eines riesigen Spaceshuttles zusammen („Dream", 2005).

在中国，刘建华是少数基于瓷器创作的艺术家之一。在景德镇（中国著名的瓷器之都）一家瓷器创作室里数年的工作使他得以精通瓷器的表现形式，而后在一所艺术学校接受的雕刻培训使他具备双重优势。在上世纪九十年代凭借一组色泽明亮、没有头部和手臂的残缺女性瓷器作品，他首次为人所知是。作品中的模型紧紧裹着旗袍，做出性感的姿势，放在绘有传统图案的大型托盘上。这些作品能够广泛吸引大多西方观众的注意，他们能够在刘建华的作品和他们对东方异国风情想象之间找到相同的地方。

在刘建华接下来的实践中，他对瓷器的深刻理解得到了证实和释放。他颠覆了瓷器制造作为艺术品必须需要高度精确和完美的传统观念。相反地，他以大量的日用品为素材制作纯白瓷器，这些物品可能是他能够找到的任何事物，从枕头、瓶子、电脑键盘、锤子到村庄等等一应俱全。这些事物被抽离了原先的任何色彩、细节、文字、标识、图案、个性及层次特征，并被还原成它们最基本、最平等的形态。他特意保留了这些复制品的粗糙边缘及所有在制作过程中留下的瑕疵。通过展示这些物品，他制作了房间大小的装置作品，营造出单调、粗陋却强有力的感觉。透过作品的粗糙及其未经琢磨和修饰的表面，作品的草根视觉品质甚至闪耀着一种荣耀。

在近年的特定场所装置作品中，刘建华甚至对这些单纯的物品用更为激进的方式处理。他将大量物品倾倒在展览场所的地板上，然后使用一柄铁铲猛烈、彻底地粉碎它们。接着，他将这些碎块和碎片摆成一艘巨型宇宙飞船的形状。《梦想》，2005年）刘建华的数年实践由概念维度取代了物质维度，直至瓷器本身在他的作品中微不足道，而目睹这一过程非常有趣。通过解构瓷器表现形式并减弱自己所接受的瓷器制作培训的影响，他为自己的概念赋予了潜能和力量。

2

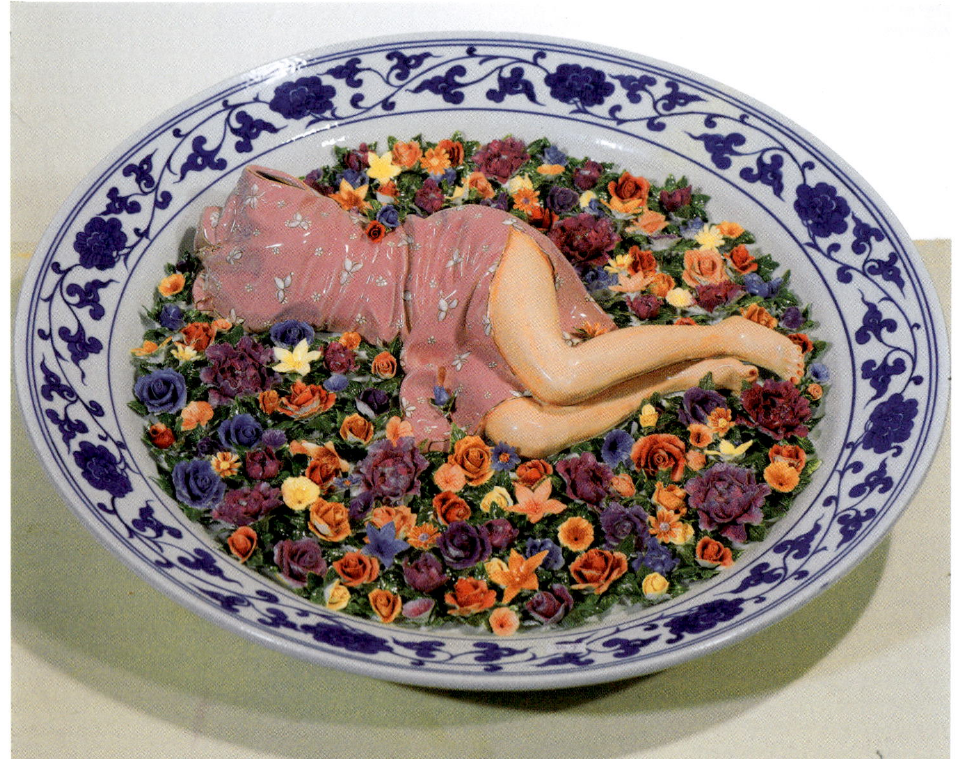

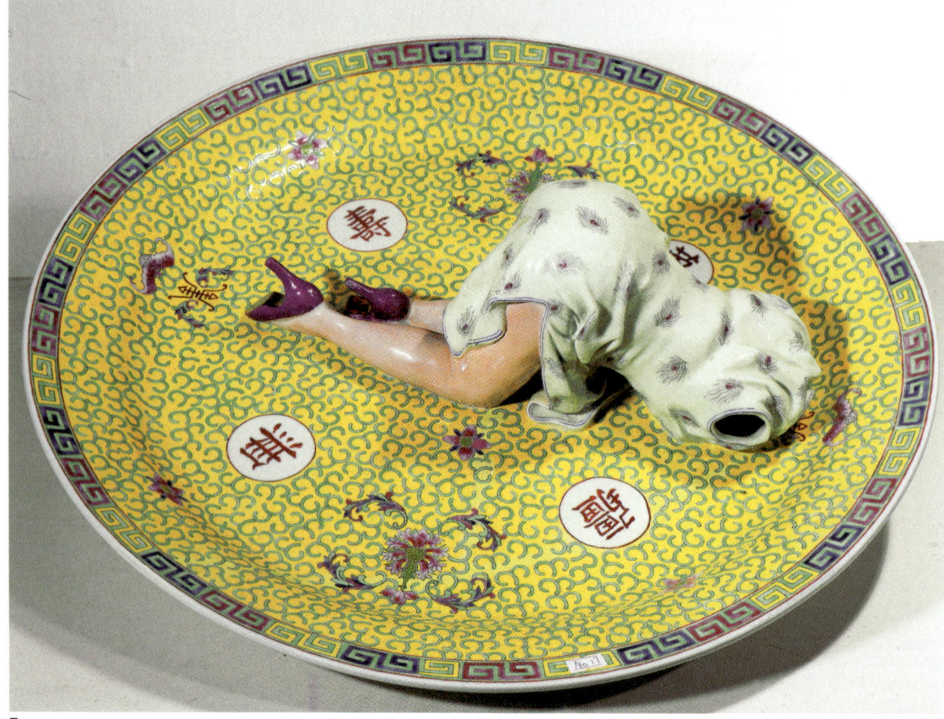

3

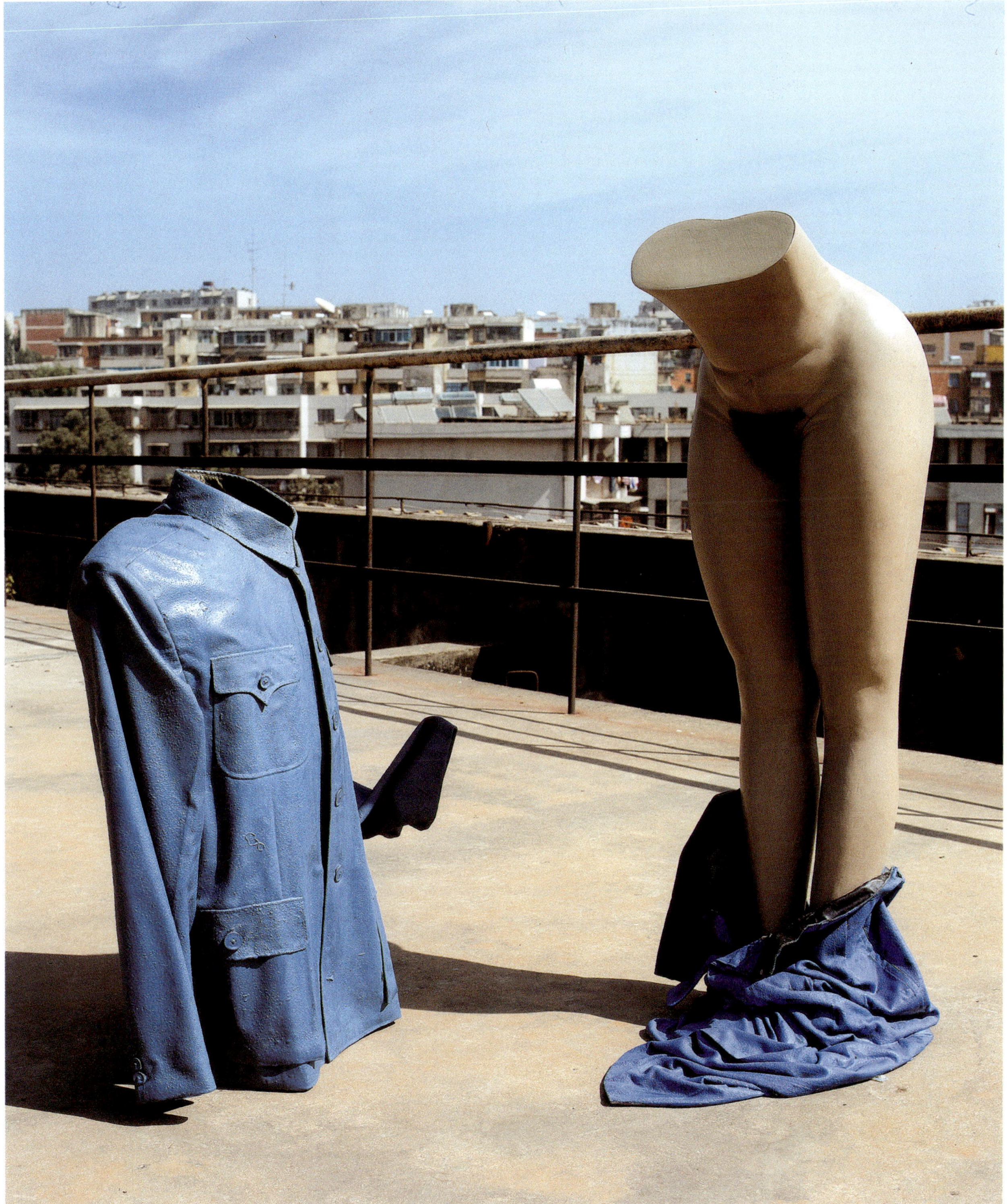

4

5

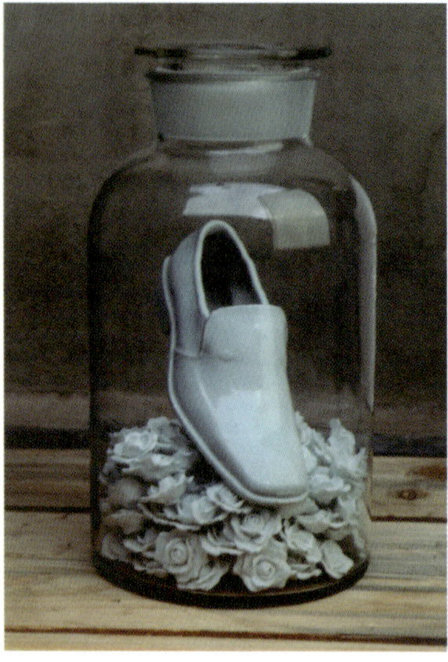

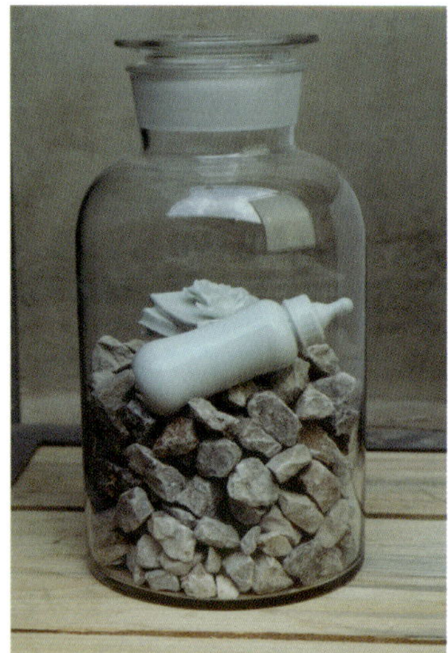

6

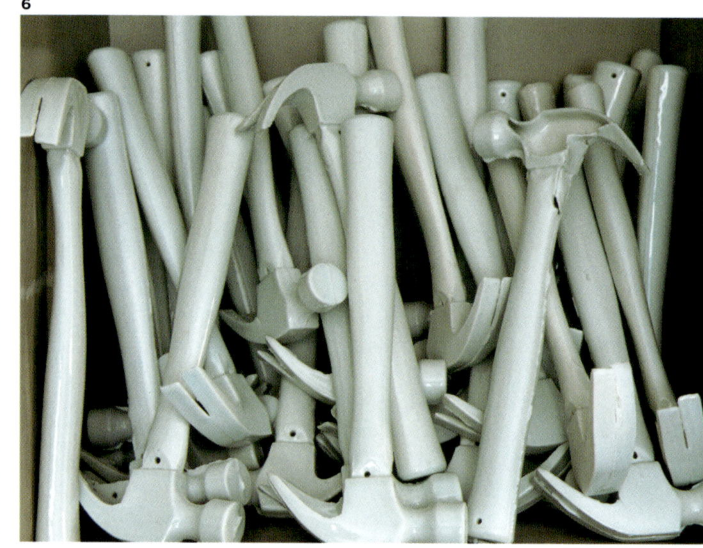

porcelain in itself is no longer of much importance in his work. By his deconstructing the language of porcelain and relenting any of the training he had received as a porcelain maker, he has invested his concepts with potency and strength.

His relocation to Shanghai from Yunnan has also exerted a strong impact on his way of thinking, which was evident in his work "Can You Tell Me?"(2006) He raised 50 questions engraved into 50 opened books made of stainless steel. The questions touch upon issues, consequences and predictions of modernization and relentless urban construction and development in the metropolitan of Shanghai. In this work, he retrieved his sensitivity to the beauty of object making and still life and empowered these books with a timeless quality and a sense of authority.

The changing skyline of Shanghai was also a source of inspiration for another work "Reflection-Mirror Illusion" (2006), which imitated and portrayed skylines of Shanghai, Beijing and Shenzhen in a strip of flat and zigzag porcelain installation that is usually suspended and attached to the middle of the gallery wall. It resembled a reflection of the cities' dramatic skyline in the water, as if the whole vision of China's urbanization were nothing more than an illusion.

Es ist bemerkenswert, wie in Liu Jianhuas Schaffen die materielle Dimension mit den Jahren allmählich der konzeptionellen weicht, bis zu einem Punkt, an dem das Porzellan selbst kaum mehr eine Bedeutung für sein Werk hat. Indem er die Sprache des Werkstoffs dekonstruiert und die eigene Herkunft als Porzellanmacher von sich abschüttelt, entwickelt Liu eine neue Kraft und Intensität für seine radikalen Konzepte.

Auch sein Umzug von Yunan nach Shanghai hat seine Denkweise stark beeinflusst, was in der Arbeit „Can You Tell Me?" (2006) deutlich zum Ausdruck kommt. Darin stellt er 50 Fragen, die in 50 offene Bücher aus Edelstahl eingraviert sind. Diese Fragen betreffen Probleme, Konsequenzen und Prognosen der Modernisierung und der unaufhaltsamen Bau- und Erschließungswut in der Metropole Shanghai. Mit diesem Werk gewann er sein Empfinden für die Schönheit der Objektgestaltung und des Stilllebens zurück, wodurch den Büchern etwas Zeitloses und Gewichtiges anhaftet.

Die Veränderungen der Skyline von Shanghai inspirierten Liu zu dem Werk „Reflection-Mirror Illusion" (2006): Diese Installation bildet die Skylines von Shanghai, Peking und Shenzhen als flachen Streifen aus gezacktem Porzellan nach, der mittig auf einer Galeriewand installiert wird – es entsteht der Eindruck einer Wasserspiegelung der dramatischen Stadtlandschaften, als sei die ganze Vision der chinesischen High-Speed-Urbanisierung nichts weiter als ein Trugbild.

从云南搬迁到上海同样对他思考方式的产生了强烈影响。在他的作品《你能告诉我吗？》（2006年）中尤为明显。他将 50个问题分别刻在 50本打开的，用不锈钢做成的书上。50个问题分别涉及上海都市的现代化、冷漠的城市建筑及发展的问题、结果及预言。在此作品中，他重新找回了对于物品制作和静止生命的美的敏感，并将永恒的品质和权威感赋予这些书。上海变化的轮廓同时也是他另一个作品《水中倒影》（2006年）的灵感来源。作品中他使用通常是悬附在画廊墙壁中央的一条平直而又高低不齐的瓷器装置，模仿和描绘上海、北京和深圳的轮廓，看上去似乎是这些城市的生动轮廓在水中的倒影，彷佛中国都市化的全景不过是一场幻影而已。

Carol Lu

7

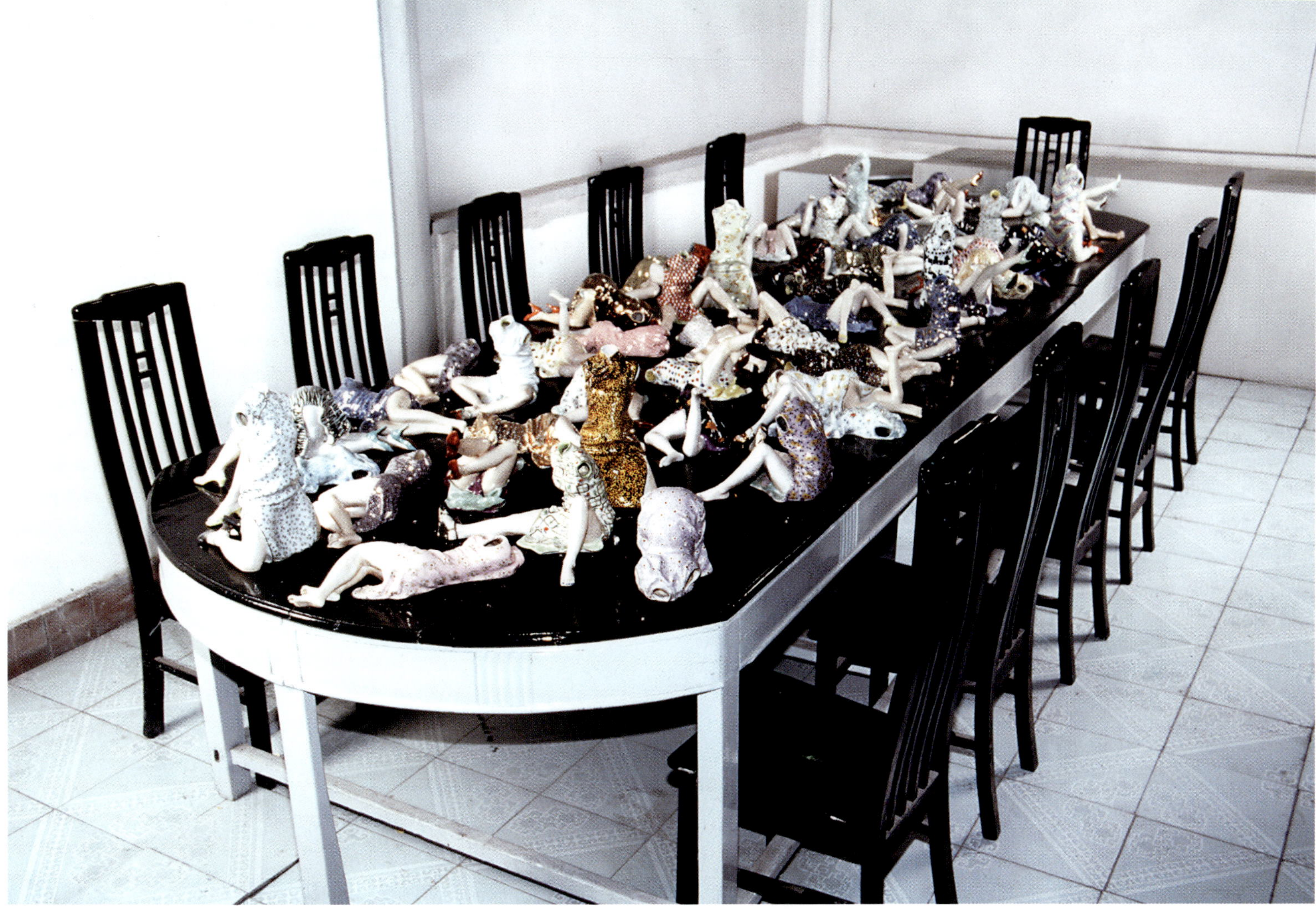

1 ***Yiwu Survey**, 2006*
Small merchandise, container, dimensions variable
Kleinwaren, Container, Maße variabel
《义乌调查方案》2006年, 小商品，钢托, 尺寸可变

2 ***Merriment**, 1999–2001*
Porcelain, 57 x 57 x 23 cm
Porzellan, 57 x 57 x 23 cm
《嬉戏》1999-2001年, 瓷器, 57 x 57 x 23 cm

3 ***Merriment**, 1999–2001*
Porcelain, 57 x 57 x 23 cm
Porzellan, 57 x 57 x 23 cm
《嬉戏》1999-2001年, 瓷器, 57 x 57 x 23 cm

4 ***Disharmony**, 1994–1997*
Mixed media, 130 x 150 x 120 cm
Mixed media, 130 x 150 x 120 cm
《不协调系列》1994-1997年, 混合材料, 130 x 150 x 120 cm

5 ***Sustainable Trapezoid Scenery**, 2003*
Mixed media, 480 x 500 x 350 cm (details)
Mixed media, 480 x 500 x 350 cm (Details)
《可以延续的梯形风景》2003年，混合材料,
480 x 500 x 350 cm, 详细

6 ***Regular – Fragile**, 2003*
Porcelain, dimensions variable
Porzellan, Maße variabel
《日常·易碎》2003年, 瓷，尺寸不一

7 ***Merriment**, 1999–2001*
Porcelain, dimensions variable
Porzellan, Maße variabel
《嬉戏》1999-2001年, 瓷，尺寸不一

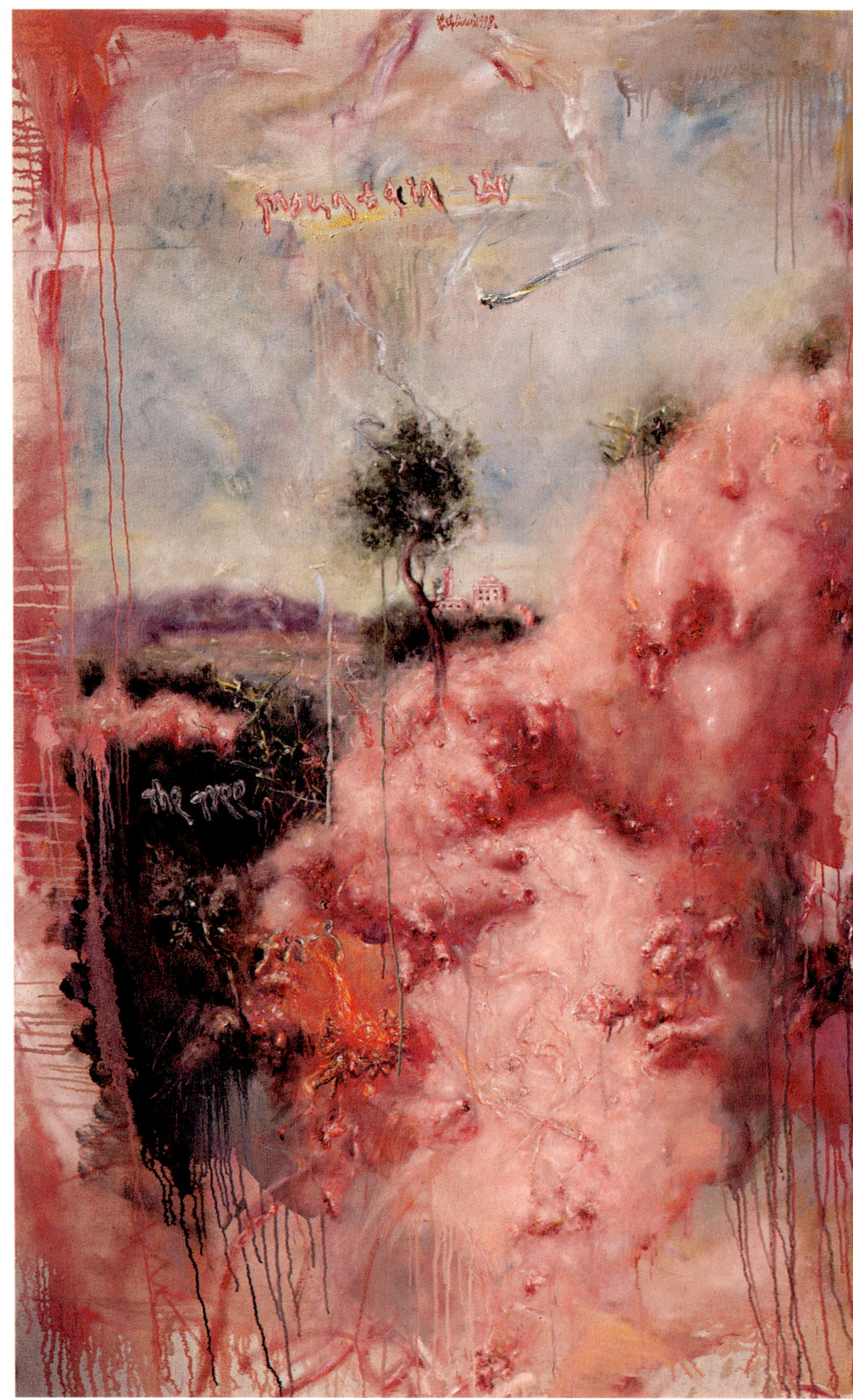

1

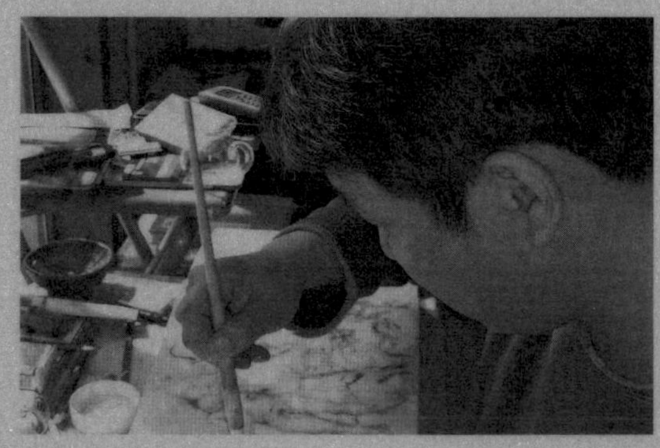

"I never like to theorise about my art. I just like to work, at home, at my own pace, doing my own thing."

„Ich theoretisiere nicht gern über meine Kunst. Mir gefällt es einfach, zu Hause in meinem eigenen Tempo meinen eigenen Vorstellungen zu folgen."

"我从来不喜欢将我的艺术理论化。我只是喜欢工作，呆在在家里，以我自己的步调，做自己的事情。"

Born in 1965 in Beijing, China. Lives and works in Beijing
Geboren 1965 in Peking, China. Lebt und arbeitet in Peking
1965年出生于中国北京，居住工作在北京

Selected exhibitions **/ Ausgewählte Ausstellungen /** 所选展览

2000 "Inside Out: New Chinese Art", P.S.1 Contemporary Art Center, New York, NY, USA
2001 "Towards a New Image: Twenty Years of Contemporary Chinese Painting", Beijing, Shanghai, Chengdu (travelling exhibition)
2002 First Guangzhou Triennial, Guangdong Art Museum, Guangzhou, China
2005 "Always to the Front – China Contemporary Art", Kuandu Museum of Fine Arts, Taipei, Taiwan
"Works on Paper", Shanghai Gallery of Art, Shanghai, China
2006 "Flowers Fall, Streams Flow", Red Bridge Gallery, Shanghai, China

2000年 《蜕变突破：华人新艺术》纽约亚洲协会美术馆、P.S.1 开展，旧金山
2001年 《新形象：中国当代绘画二十年》中国北京.上海.成都.广州巡展
2002年 《首届广州当代艺术三年展》中国广州，广东美术馆
2005年 《明日，不回眸 -- 中国当代艺术》台北，关渡美术馆
《纸上作品展》中国上海，外滩三号沪申画廊
2006年 《落花•流水》中国上海，红桥画廊（个展)

Selected publications **/ Ausgewählte Publikationen /** 所选著作

Francesca Dal Lago: "Personal Mao: Reshaping an Icon in Contemporary Chinese Art – Chinese Political and Cultural Leader Mao Zedong", in: "Art Journal", Summer 1999

Dal Lago, Francesca（著）：《毛泽东的画像在现代艺术中再应用》Art 杂志 1999年夏季版所选展览

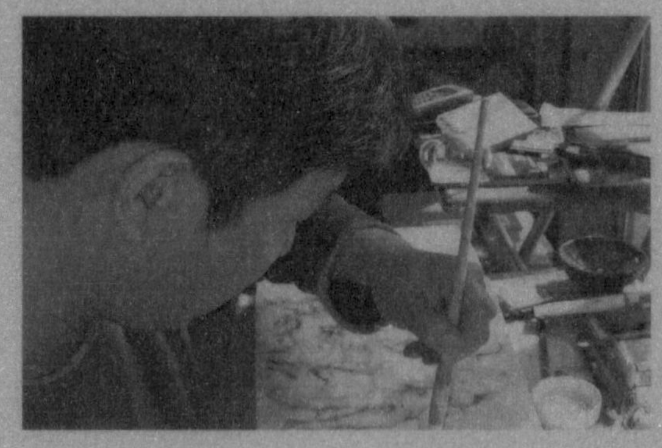

"I never like to theorise about my art. I just like to work, at home, at my own pace, doing my own thing."

„Ich theoretisiere nicht gern über meine Kunst. Mir gefällt es einfach, zu Hause in meinem eigenen Tempo meinen eigenen Vorstellungen zu folgen."

"我从来不喜欢将我的艺术理论化。我只是喜欢工作，呆在家里，以我自己的步调，做自己的事情。"

Born in 1965 in Beijing, China. Lives and works in Beijing
Geboren 1965 in Peking, China. Lebt und arbeitet in Peking
1965年出生于中国北京，居住工作在北京

Selected exhibitions / Ausgewählte Ausstellungen / 所选展览

2000 "Inside Out: New Chinese Art", P.S.1 Contemporary Art Center, New York, NY, USA
2001 "Towards a New Image: Twenty Years of Contemporary Chinese Painting", Beijing, Shanghai, Chengdu (travelling exhibition)
2002 First Guangzhou Triennial, Guangdong Art Museum, Guangzhou, China
2005 "Always to the Front – China Contemporary Art", Kuandu Museum of Fine Arts, Taipei, Taiwan
"Works on Paper", Shanghai Gallery of Art, Shanghai, China
2006 "Flowers Fall, Streams Flow", Red Bridge Gallery, Shanghai, China

2000年 《蜕变突破：华人新艺术》纽约亚洲协会美术馆，P.S.1 开展，旧金山
2001年 《新形象：中国当代绘画二十年》中国北京.上海.成都.广州巡展
2002年 《首届广州当代艺术三年展》中国广州，广东美术馆
2005年 《明日，不回眸 -- 中国当代艺术》台北，关渡美术馆
《纸上作品展》中国上海，外滩三号沪申画廊
2006年 《落花•流水》中国上海，红桥画廊（个展）

Selected publications / Ausgewählte Publikationen / 所选著作

Francesca Dal Lago: "Personal Mao: Reshaping an Icon in Contemporary Chinese Art – Chinese Political and Cultural Leader Mao Zedong", in: "Art Journal", Summer 1999

Dal Lago, Francesca（著）：《毛泽东的画像在现代艺术中再应用》Art 杂志 1999年夏季版所选展览

LIU WEI 刘炜

[liou ueɪ]

Liu Wei is demonstrably one of the most innovative painters at work in China today. Every painting he produces is painstakingly thrashed out, often requiring months of intense work to attain the desired complexity and directness. Liu Wei is distinct amongst contemporary Chinese artists in the pleasure he derives from working on paper; primarily as drawings, but beginning in 2003, as a series of unique mixed-media woodblock prints.

In a typical drawing, Liu Wei allows his vision to unfold in a tangled scrawl of figures and forms not dissimilar to those that characterise his canvas paintings. These deft doodlings blend ink and watercolour with impasto clusters of coloured chalk to give life, grotesque though it may be, to his favourite things. Pigs, people, cucumbers, more pigs, scribbled phrases and strange fruit meet in the fantastic chaos of Liu Wei's world. For all their apparent schoolboy spontaneity, the paper works, like the paintings, take months to refine. At times, the picture frame, even the glass mount serves as an extension of the paper. Here, the thick, coarse surrounds Liu Wei prefers are carved in spurts of nervous chiselling which always enhances the main work. These paperworks are like a working manual to the artist's thought processes: essential reading for a broader appreciation of Liu Wei's canvas painting.

Liu Wei graduated from the mural painting department of Beijing's Central Academy of Fine Arts in 1989. He started working on canvas immediately after, and by the early 1990s was hailed as a leader of the Cynical Realism movement. Whilst Cynical Realism was characterized by symbols of social malaise and political posturing, Liu Wei's subjects rested closer to home. Best known early works include "Two Drunken Painters" (1990) and "Father Watching Peking Opera" (1992), in which satire is tartly aligned with the artist's personal experience. By 1994, Liu Wei was clearly over superficial "China politics", determinedly hacking out his own direction. A fascination with the blacker side of human nature emerged now in a series of large risqué compositions created for the São Paulo Biennial

Liu Wei ist zweifellos einer der innovativsten Künstler, die heute in China tätig sind. Jedes seiner Gemälde ist mit äußerster Sorgfalt ausgeführt, oft braucht er Monate intensivster Arbeit, um die angestrebte Komplexität und Deutlichkeit zu erreichen. Von anderen chinesischen Gegenwartskünstlern unterscheidet sich Liu Wei schon dadurch, dass er besonders gern auf Papier arbeitet – zuerst in Form von Zeichnungen, seit 2003 aber auch mit Holzschnitten, die er in einer einzigartigen Mischtechnik gestaltet.

In einer für ihn typischen Zeichnung entfaltet Liu Wei seine Vision in einem verschlungenen Gewirr von Figuren und Formen, wie sie ähnlich auch auf seinen Gemälden auftauchen. Tusche und Aquarellfarben kombiniert er dabei mit dick aufgetragener farbiger Kreide, um seinen Lieblingsdingen (mitunter groteskes) Leben einzuhauchen. Schweine, Menschen, Gurken, hingekritzelte Phrasen und seltsame Früchte begegnen einander im fantastischen Chaos von Liu Weis Kosmos. Trotz ihrer vermeintlich schuljungenhaften Spontaneität nimmt die Perfektionierung dieser Papierarbeiten wie der Gemälde viel Zeit in Anspruch. Manchmal nutzt Liu Wei auch das Passepartout und den Bildrahmen als Fortsetzung des Papiers. Die groben Fassungen, die er bevorzugt, bearbeitet er gleichsam mit energischen Hieben, um seine Vision noch besser zur Geltung zu bringen. Die Papierarbeiten sind gewissermaßen ein Arbeitshandbuch zum kreativen Prozess und damit fast schon eine Pflichtlektüre, um auch Liu Weis Malerei auf Leinwand umfassend begreifen zu können.

1989 machte Liu Wei seinen Abschluss am Fachbereich Wandmalerei der Central Academy of Fine Arts von Peking. Er begann sogleich, auf Leinwand zu arbeiten und wurde schon in den frühen 1990er Jahren als führende Kraft des Zynischen Realismus gefeiert. Doch während der Zynische Realismus von Symbolen der gesellschaftlichen Misere und des Politiktheaters geprägt war, suchte sich Liu Wei persönlichere Motive. Zu seinen bekanntesten Frühwerken gehören „Two Drunken Painters" (1990) und „Father Watching Peking Opera" (1992), die persönliche Erfahrungen des

刘炜绝对是当今中国最具创新性的画家之一。他的每件作品都历经苦心推敲，通常潜心工作数月，以期达到想要的复杂丰富及率直达意。刘炜在当代中国艺术家中独树一帜，他沉浸在纸上工作的乐趣中，作品以绘画为主。但从 2003 年起，其作品以一系列具有独特风格的综合材料的木版画为主。在一幅代表作中，刘炜让自己的视野在缠结的纷乱图形中展开，这与他的油画作品不无相同。这些随意而有些怪异的涂鸦混和了水墨、水彩及彩色粉笔笔画，赋予其喜爱的事物以生命。猪肉、人、黄瓜、更多猪肉、潦草的短语及怪异的水果，混和在刘炜稀奇古怪乱七八糟的世界里。而为了这些看起来像是小学男生所作的一派天真的作品，他常常要像在画布上那样在纸上花费数月的时间进行修饰。到后来常常是连画框，甚至装画的玻璃都成了纸张的延伸。这时，刘炜所喜爱的厚重、粗糙的边缘装饰上刻满了情绪爆发的凿痕，并且通常能够使其作品得到升华。这些纸上作品恰似一份艺术家思索过程的说明书：更加广泛地欣赏刘炜油画的必须读物。

刘炜于 1989 年毕业于北京的中央美术学院版画系。随后他开始在帆布上作画，并且在上世纪九十年代初期被称作"玩世现实主义"运动的发起人之一。"玩世现实主义"以社会疾病及政治姿态的符号为特征，与此同时刘炜的题材更加贴近家庭。他最为著名的早期作品包括《两个酒醉的画家》（1990 年）以及《看京剧的父亲》（1992 年），作品中包含着辛辣的讽刺以及作者的亲身经历。到了 1994 年，刘炜明显跳出了肤浅的"中国"政治波普，决心探求自己的方向。在他为《圣保罗双年展》所作的一系列大型带色情元素的作品中，已经显现出一种伴随着人类本质的黑暗面的独特魅力。在一段短时期内，衣着暴露的女人（像被剥光了的职业妓女那样妖艳）成为其作品的必然题材。

到了上世纪九十年代中期，刘炜释放自己的本能，尝试各种材质及形式。细腻的勾勒如今变成了爆炸性的颜料涂抹，创作、再创作，且不论是否惹人厌

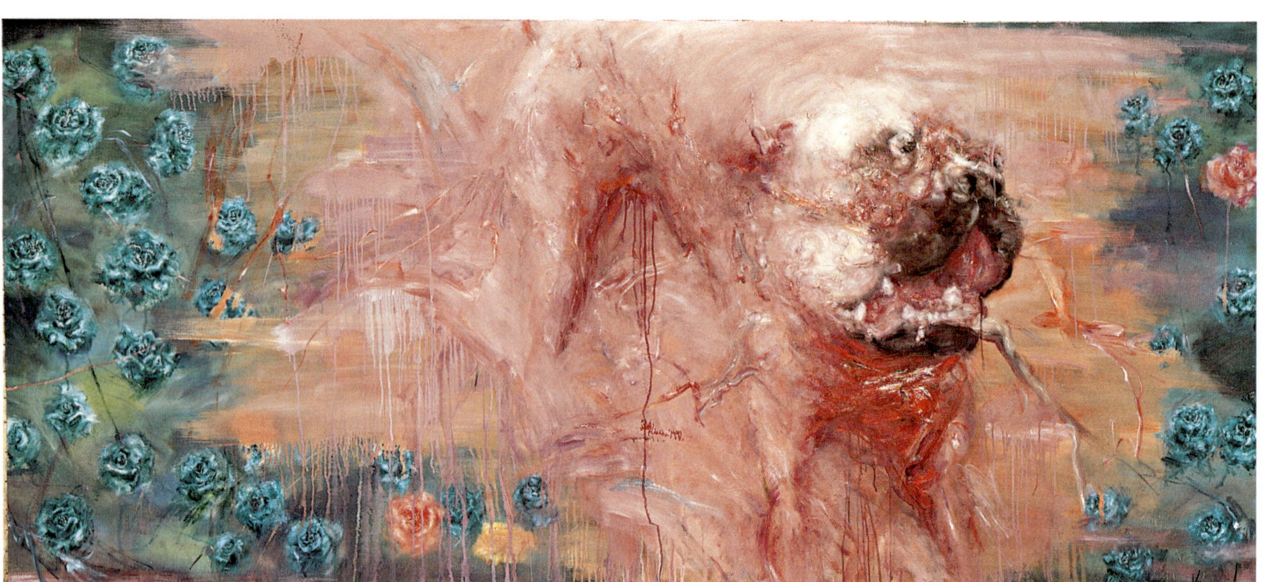

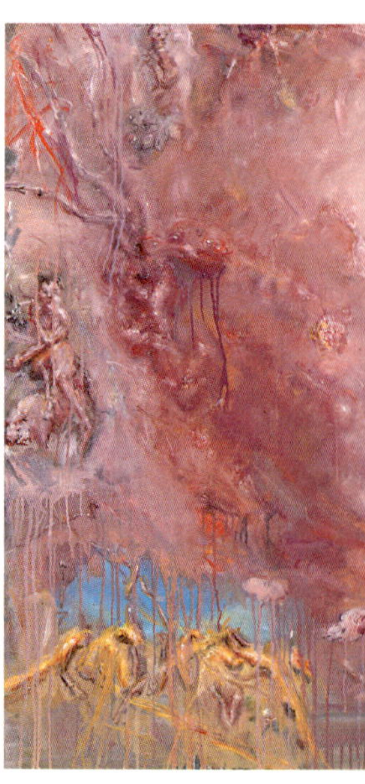

2

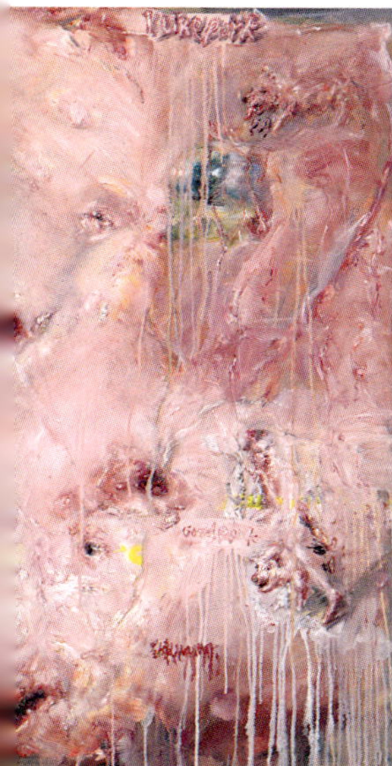

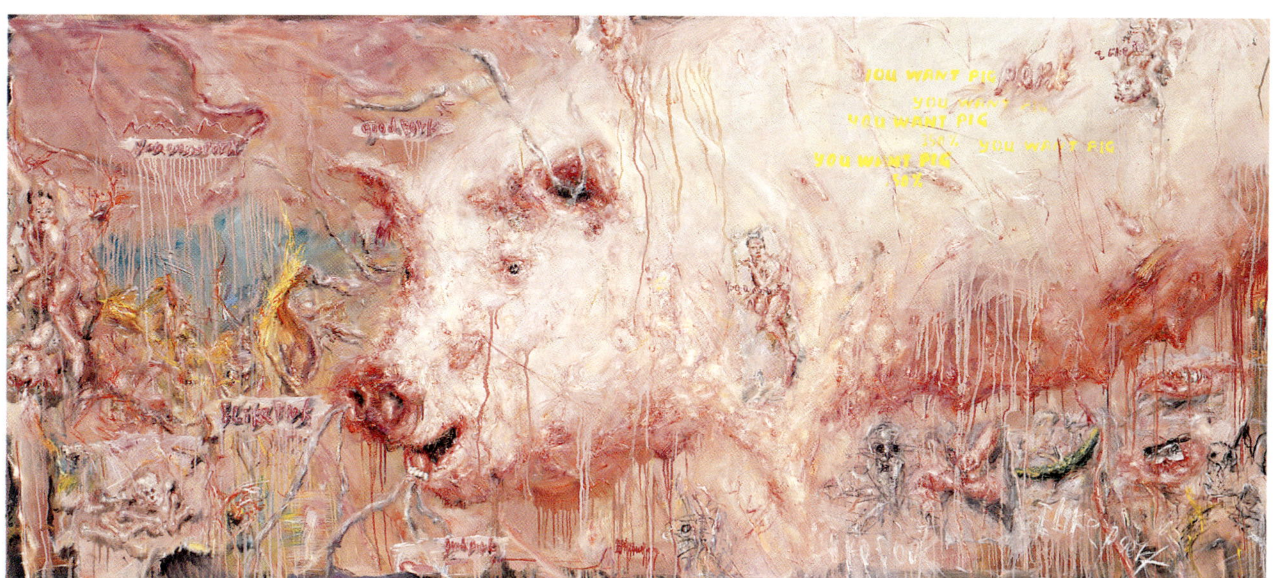
YOU WANT PIG
PORK
YOU WANT PIG
YOU WANT PIG
YOU WANT PIG
YOU WANT PIG

3

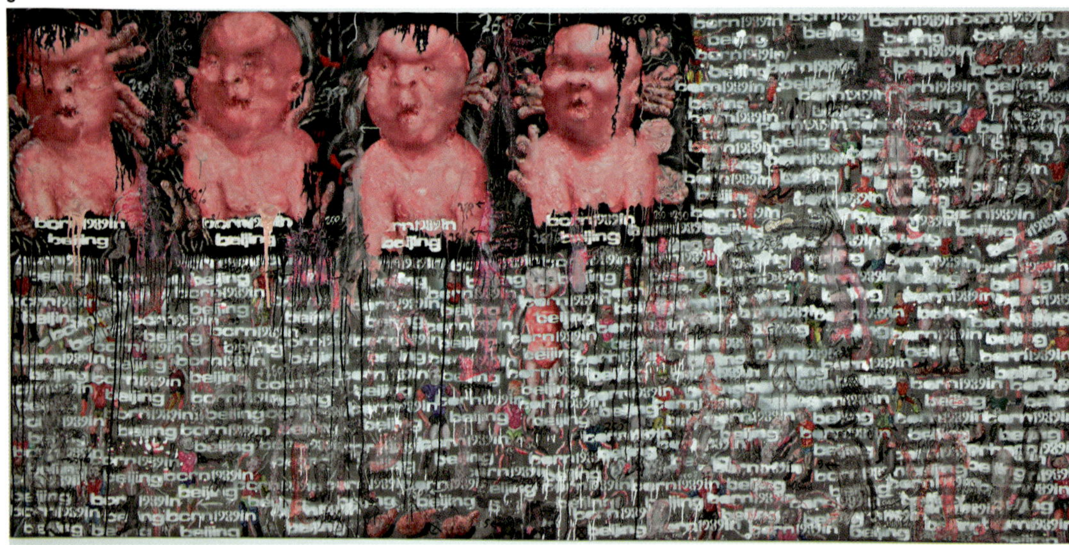

("Swimmers", "Bathing Beauty"). For a brief period, scantily dressed women – voluptuous like wily courtesans stripped bare – became a dominant fixture of his work.

By the mid-1990s, Liu Wei was giving free rein to his instinct to experiment with texture and form. Smooth brushwork now bowed out to explosive mounds of pigment, worked and reworked to achieve a tactile, if repulsive, sense of flesh. First applied to his metaphoric approach to human form, the technique is at its best in abrasive depictions of grossly bloated pigs – a fetishist fascination that continued through to the new millennium accompanied by the much-vaunted phrase "You like pork!". Liu Wei extrapolated this further to banana-munching females, vulgarly bespoked businessmen, and even the sullied pastoral landscapes and dying blooms of neglected flora that were the subject of his first solo show in China (2005). Liu Wei's subject matter offers no apologies for the sentiments it sows. Eschewing obvious China motifs, the works are uncannily evocative of the age: an uncompromising, peremptory comment on the social climate. Acutely sensitive to life in general, Liu Wei remains impervious to the mounting pressure that commercial forces are exerting upon the contemporary art world in China. In a culture that is perforce so polite in public, his art is a breath of fresh, if at times caustic, air.

Malers in beißende Satire verwandeln. Schon 1994 hatte Liu Wei die oberflächliche „China-Politisiererei" ganz klar überwunden und bahnte sich entschlossen seinen eigenen Weg. Wie sehr ihn die dunklere Seite der menschlichen Natur fasziniert, zeigte sich damals in einer Serie großer gewagter Kompositionen, die er für die Biennale von São Paulo (u. a. „Swimmers" und „Bathing Beauty") schuf. Für kurze Zeit bildeten spärlich bekleidete Frauen ein beherrschendes Element seines Werks – sinnlich und raffiniert entblätterte Kurtisanen.

Mitte der 1990er Jahre begann Liu Wei dann, ungehemmt mit Texturen und Formen zu experimentieren. Die glatten Pinselstriche machten explosiven Pigmenthäufungen Platz, die immer und immer wieder bearbeitet wurden, um eine greifbare, wenn auch vielleicht abstoßende „Fleischlichkeit" zu vermitteln. Zuerst setzte er diese Technik zur metaphorischen Annäherung an die menschliche Gestalt ein, doch am besten kommt sie in seinen provokanten Abbildungen abartig aufgeblähter Schweine zur Geltung – eine geradezu fetischistische Faszination, die sich bis ins neue Jahrtausend fortsetzte, stets begleitet von der Direktive: „You like pork"! In gleicher Weise führte Liu Wei bananenmampfende Frauen, vulgär gewandete Manager und auch die besudelten ländlichen Idyllen einer verwahrlosten Flora vor, die Gegenstand seiner ersten Einzelausstellung in China waren (2005). Lius Kunst rechtfertigt sich nicht für die Gefühle, die sie weckt. Obwohl er in seinen Arbeiten augenscheinlich auf typisch chinesische Motive verzichtet, sind sie mit schlafwandlerischer Sicherheit auf ihre Zeit bezogen: ein kompromissloser, kategorischer Kommentar zum herrschenden gesellschaftlichen Klima. So sensibel Liu Wei das Leben im Allgemeinen wahrnimmt, so unempfänglich ist er für den wachsenden Druck, den kommerzielle Interessen auf Chinas aktuelle Kunstszene ausüben. In einer Kultur, die sich offiziell (gezwungenermaßen) nach wie vor artig gibt, wirkt seine Kunst wie eine frische und mitunter beißende Brise.

恶，直至达到一种质感 -- 肉的质感。这种技巧在他首次运用时达到极致，他将严重发胀的猪肉隐喻性地刻画成接近人体形状 -- 一种贯穿到新千年的恋物情结的魔力，伴随着一句极尽吹嘘之能事的短语：“你喜欢肉！”在他自己的首个中国个展的题材（2005年）中，刘炜依旧延续着这种创作方法：咀嚼香蕉的女人，外表庸俗的商人，甚至是被玷污的田园式风景或不被注意的植物上的枯萎花朵等。刘炜的题材内容对其所播种的情绪不做任何辩解。离开了明显的中国题材，这些作品神秘地让人想起其所处的时代：一种对社会风气毫不妥协的强硬态度。刘炜敏锐地关注大众的生活，丝毫不为商业化施加在当代中国艺术领域上的压力所动。在一种与人为善的文化中，他的艺术作品尽管不时夹杂着腐蚀的气息，但仿佛又是一股清新的空气。

Karen Smith

4

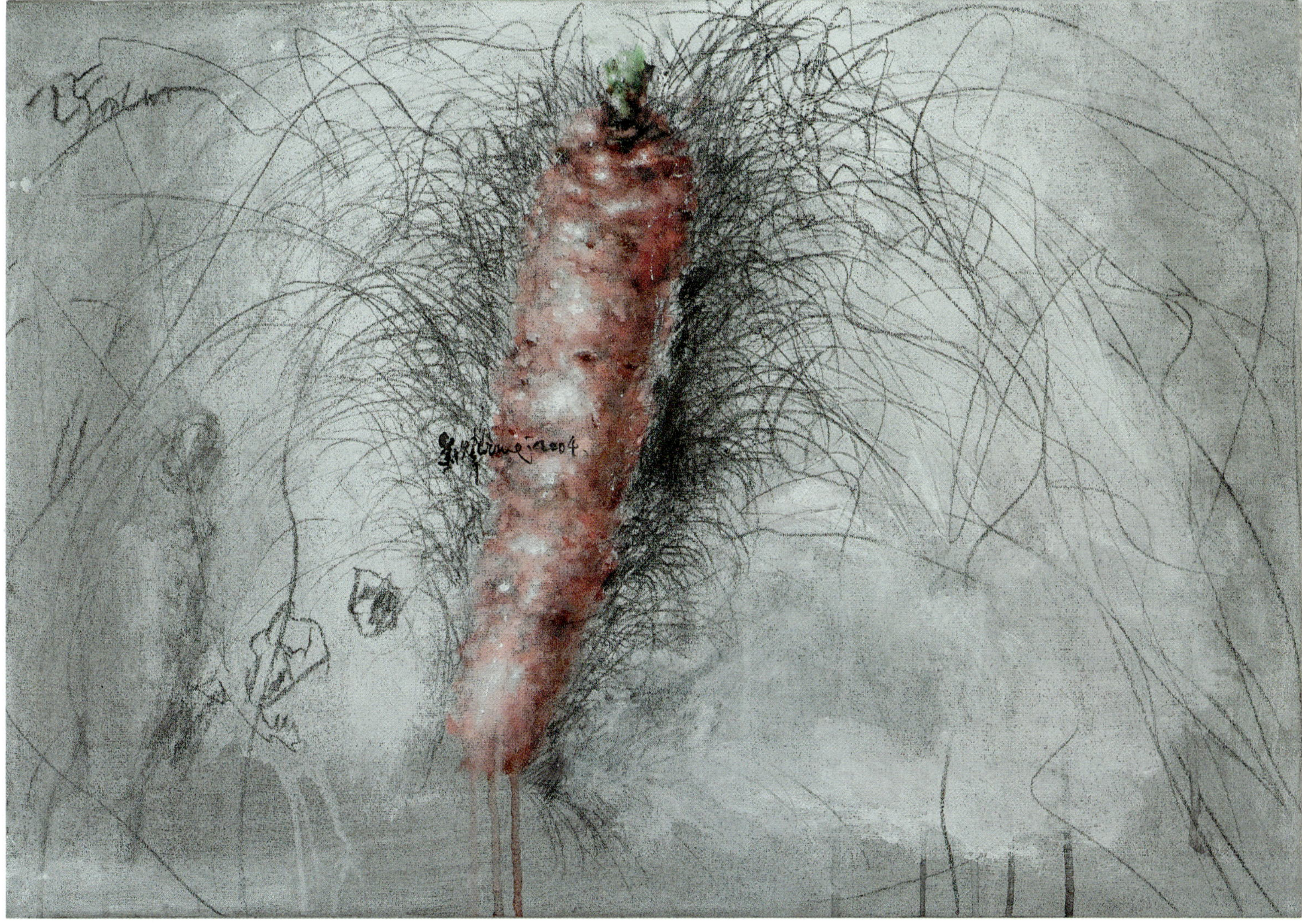

1 ***Untitled***, *1998*
Oil on canvas, 200 x 100 cm
Öl auf Leinwand, 200 x 100 cm
《无题》1998年, 布面油画, 200 x 100 cm

2 ***Untitled (Triptych)***, *1997*
Oil on canvas, 120 x 260 cm, 120 x 140 cm, 120 x 260 cm
Öl auf Leinwand, 120 x 260 cm, 120 x 140 cm, 120 x 260 cm
《无题》(三联) 1997年, 布面油画, 120 x 260 cm, 120 x 140 cm, 120 x 260 cm

3 ***Born 1989 in Beijing***, *1995/96*
Oil on canvas, 150 x 300 cm
Öl auf Leinwand, 150 x 300 cm
《1989年生于北京》1995/96年, 布面油画, 150 x 300 cm

4 ***Untitled***, *2004*
Acrylic on canvas, 50 x 70 cm
Acryl auf Leinwand, 50 x 70 cm
《无题》2004年, 布面丙烯, 50 x 70 cm

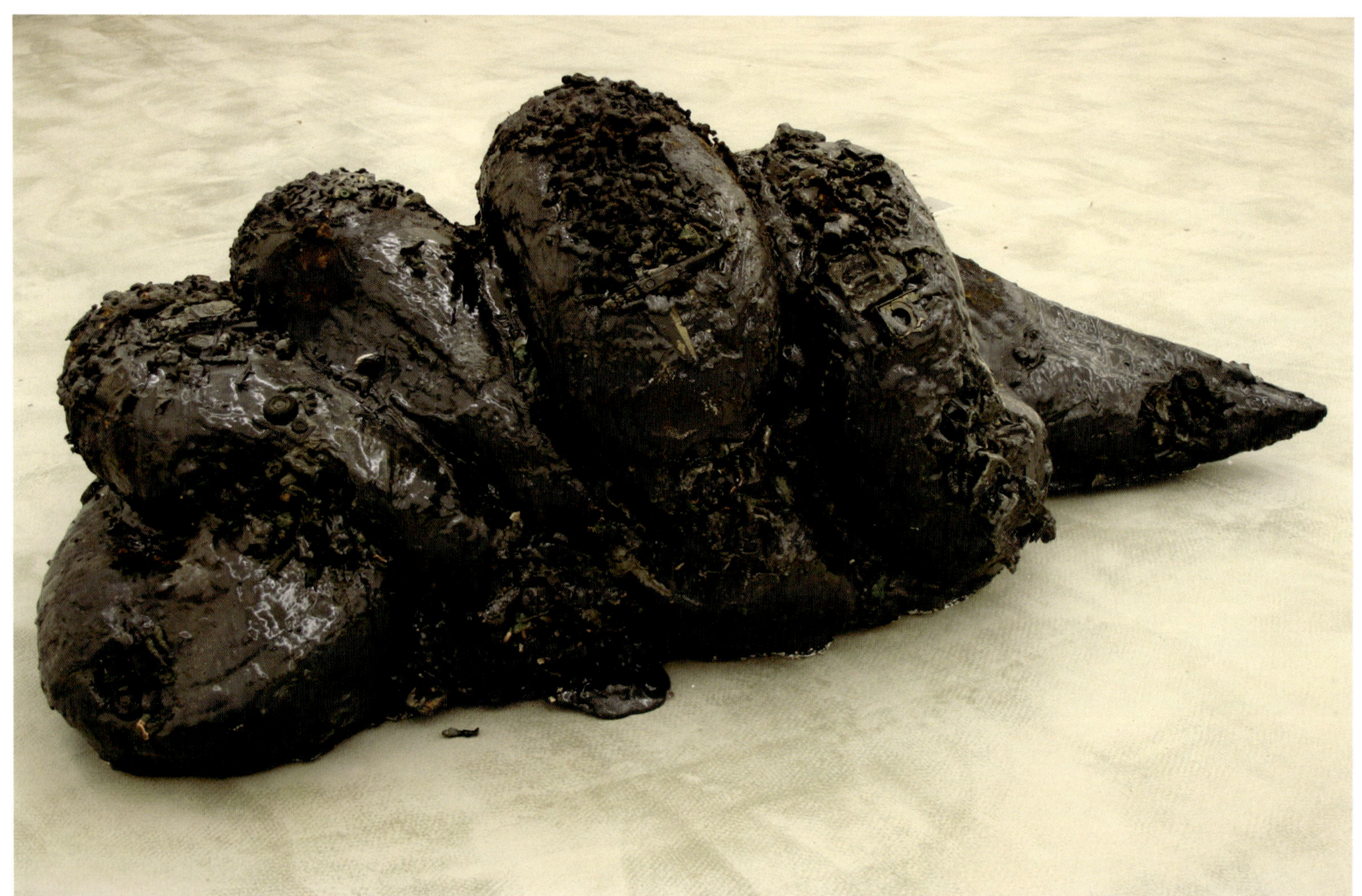

1

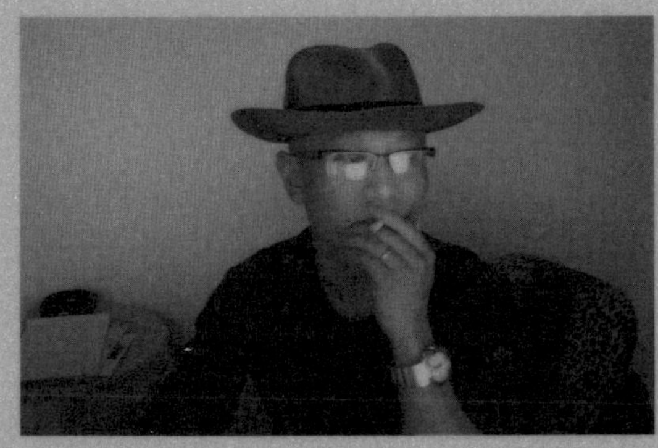

"I don't know what I'm supposed to be interested in. Can an artist really go deeper into things? What will be the result? People often don't know if you do something well, only that you have done it. So what?"

„Ich weiß nicht, woran ich interessiert sein soll. Kann ein Künstler wirklich tiefer in die Dinge eindringen? Was kommt dabei heraus? Die Leute wissen oft nicht, ob du etwas gut machst, nur dass du es gemacht hast. Na und?"

"我不知道我应该对什么感兴趣。艺术家真的看什么都很深入吗？结果又将会怎么样？人们常常不知道你是否能做好一件事，除非你做给他们看。那又如何？"

Born in 1972 in Beijing, China. Lives and works in Beijing
Geboren 1972 in Peking, China. Lebt und arbeitet in Peking
1972 年出生于中国北京，居住工作在北京

Selected exhibitions **/ Ausgewählte Ausstellungen /** 所选展览

1999 "Revolutionary Capitals: Beijing in London", Institute of Contemporary Art, London, UK
2000 "House, Home, Family", 4/F Yuexing Furniture Corporation, Shanghai, China
2001 "Manic Ecstasy", Impression Gallery, Hangzhou, China
2002 First Guangzhou Triennial, Guangdong Art Museum, Guangzhou, China
2003 "Second-hand Reality", Today Museum of Art, Beijing, China
2004 Techniques of the Visible: Fifth International Shanghai Biennial, Shanghai Art Museum, Shanghai, China
2004–07 "Between Past and Future, New Photography and Video from China", International Center of Photography, New York, NY, USA (travelling exhibition)

1999年 《北京在伦敦：革命之都》英国伦敦，当代艺术中心
2000年 《家？》中国上海，月星家具广场 4 楼
2001年 《附体》中国杭州，印象画廊
2002年 《首届广州三年展》中国广州，广东美术馆
2003年 《二手现实》中国北京，今日美术馆
2004年 《影像生存：第五届上海双年展》中国上海，上海美术馆
2004–07年 《过去将来一中国当代摄影》始于美国纽约及亚洲学会的国际摄影中心的巡回展

Selected publications **/ Ausgewählte Publikationen /** 所选著作

Bernhard Fibicher, Matthias Frehner (eds.): "Mahjong. Chinesische Gegenwartskunst aus der Sammlung Sigg", Ostfildern-Ruit 2005

Fibicher, Bernhard/Frehner, Matthias（编者）:《麻将一西克的当代艺术收藏展》Ostfildern-Ruit 2005年

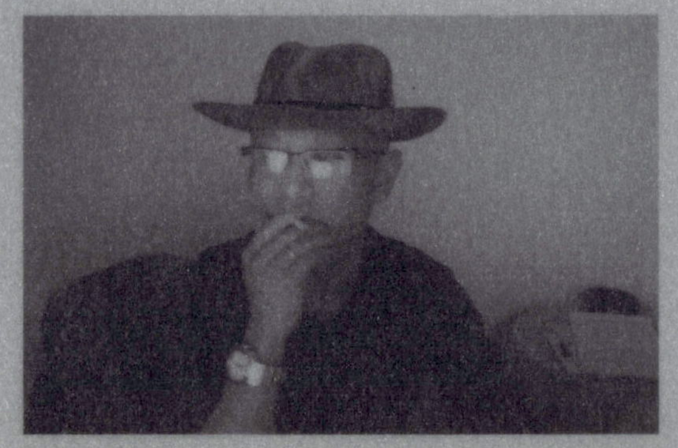

"I don't know what I'm supposed to be interested in. Can an artist really go deeper into things? What will be the result? People often don't know if you do something well, only that you have done it. So what?"

„Ich weiß nicht, woran ich interessiert sein soll. Kann ein Künstler wirklich tiefer in die Dinge eindringen? Was kommt dabei heraus? Die Leute wissen oft nicht, ob du etwas gut machst, nur dass du es gemacht hast. Na und?"

"我不知道我应该对什么感兴趣。艺术家真的看什么都很深入吗？结果又将会怎么样？人们常常不知道你是否能做好一件事，除非你做给他们看。那又如何？"

Born in 1972 in Beijing, China. Lives and works in Beijing
Geboren 1972 in Peking, China. Lebt und arbeitet in Peking
1972 年出生于中国北京，居住工作在北京

Selected exhibitions / Ausgewählte Ausstellungen / 所选展览

1999 "Revolutionary Capitals: Beijing in London", Institute of Contemporary Art, London, UK
2000 "House, Home, Family", 4/F Yuexing Furniture Corporation, Shanghai, China
2001 "Manic Ecstasy", Impression Gallery, Hangzhou, China
2002 First Guangzhou Triennial, Guangdong Art Museum, Guangzhou, China
2003 "Second-hand Reality", Today Museum of Art, Beijing, China
2004 Techniques of the Visible: Fifth International Shanghai Biennial, Shanghai Art Museum, Shanghai, China
2004-07 "Between Past and Future, New Photography and Video from China", International Center of Photography, New York, NY, USA (travelling exhibition)

1999年 《北京在伦敦：革命之都》英国伦敦，当代艺术中心
2000年 《家？》中国上海，月星家具广场 4 楼
2001年 《附体》中国杭州，印象画廊
2002年 《首届广州三年展》中国广州，广东美术馆
2003年 《二手现实》中国北京，今日美术馆
2004年 《影像生存：第五届上海双年展》中国上海，上海美术馆
2004-07年 《过去将来－中国当代摄影》始于美国纽约及亚洲学会的国际摄影中心的巡回展

Selected publications / Ausgewählte Publikationen / 所选著作

Bernhard Fibicher, Matthias Frehner (eds.): "Mahjong. Chinesische Gegenwartskunst aus der Sammlung Sigg", Ostfildern-Ruit 2005

Fibicher, Bernhard/Frehner, Matthias（编者）：《麻将－西克的当代艺术收藏展》Ostfildern-Ruit 2005年

LIU WEI 刘韡

[liou ueɪ]

Liu Wei cut his artistic teeth in late 1999 in the groundbreaking, artist-initiated exhibition titled "Post-Sense Sensibility: Alien Bodies and Delusion". This was held in the basement of a residential apartment block in Beijing: Liu Wei's contribution, a video installation titled "Hard To Restrain", worked perfectly against the low-ceiling labyrinth of underground rooms. "Hard To Restrain" was unquestionably innovative for the times: in defiance of the trend to produce ever-bigger artworks, this multi-screen work was presented via a jumbled cluster of miniature CCTV monitors. The content comprised looped sequences of scuttling naked figures, filmed from afar so their form was abstracted. The sequences were played back at high speed so the motion equated with that of angry flies. Where the theme of the exhibition focused on the contemporary social experience of individual existence, Liu Wei's image of man made animal was succinct.

Liu Wei has since proved himself diverse in output. In general, he favours site-specific installations but since 2004 has also turned his hand to painting – or perhaps "anti-painting" is more apt a description. His approach begins with computer-generated drawings that are enlarged on canvas as dramatic, minimal land- and city-scapes. The steel-grey monochrome of these compositions suggests clinical visions of modern living, which of itself implies alienation. In terms of style and practice, Liu Wei exhibits a casual, almost off-hand approach to the observations of trends in contemporary culture and art – urban chaos, architectural concepts, the objects of desire, and the obsession with possession – that he expresses. This is to be expected of the younger generation of Chinese artists, largely free of the socio-political regimentation of the mind imposed upon their elders.

Since the early 2000s, Liu Wei has made installation his primary focus but has also produced several photographic works. His adaptation of the human form in the black and white photographic series titled "Contemporary Landscape" was a focal point of the 2002 Shanghai Biennial.

Seine ersten künstlerischen Sporen verdiente sich Liu Wei Ende 1999 mit seiner Teilnahme an der wegweisenden künstlerinitiierten Ausstellung „Post-Sense Sensibility: Alien Bodies and Delusion". Sie fand im Keller eines Wohnblocks in Peking statt: Liu Weis Beitrag, eine Videoinstallation mit dem Titel „Hard To Restrain", passte perfekt in dieses Labyrinth unterirdischer Räume mit ihren niedrigen Decken. „Hard To Restrain" war für seine Zeit fraglos innovativ: Dem allgemeinen Trend zur Produktion immer größerer Kunstwerke zum Trotz präsentierte sich dieses Multiscreen-Werk als eine Ansammlung von Videoüberwachungsmonitoren im Miniaturformat. Darauf zu sehen: Endlossequenzen mit herumhastenden nackten Gestalten, aus so großer Entfernung aufgenommen, dass ihre Formen abstrahiert erschienen. Die Sequenzen wurden im Zeitraffertempo abgespielt, sodass die Bewegung an aufgescheuchte Fliegen erinnerte. Während das Thema der Ausstellung auf die zeitgenössische gesellschaftliche Erfahrung der individuellen Existenz abhob, steuerte Liu Wei ein prägnantes Bild des zum Tier herabgewürdigten Menschen bei.

Seither hat sich Liu Weis Produktion als ausgesprochen abwechslungsreich erwiesen. Generell bevorzugt er ortsspezifische Installationen. Seit 2004 hat er sich aber auch der Malerei zugewandt – obwohl hier vielleicht „Anti-Malerei" eine treffendere Bezeichnung wäre. Er geht von computergenerierten Zeichnungen aus, die er auf der Leinwand zu dramatisch-minimalistischen Landschaften und Skylines vergrößert. Die stahlgraue Monochromie dieser Kompositionen beschwört klinische Visionen vom modernen Leben herauf, wobei die Entfremdung gleich mitgedacht ist.

In puncto Stil und Technik bringt Liu Wei seine Beobachtungen der Trends in der zeitgenössischen Kultur und Kunst – urbanes Chaos, Architekturkonzepte, Objekte der Begierde, zwanghafte Besitzgier – auf ungezwungene, ja fast beiläufige Weise zum Ausdruck; recht typisch für die jüngere Generation chinesischer Künstler, die weitgehend von der soziopolitischen Reglementierung des Geistes befreit sind, wie sie ihren Vorläufern noch aufoktroyiert wurde.

刘韡的艺术生涯始于 1999 年年末一个极富创造力的艺术展览，展览名为《后感性—异形与妄想》，是在一个北京居民住宅楼的地下室举行的。刘韡的作品，一个名为《难以抑制》的影像装置，在地下室迷宫般的低天花板下取得了很好的效果。毋需质疑，《难以抑制》具有时代性的创新：当时的趋势是作品越做越大，而这件多屏幕作品却与之背道而驰，通过杂乱地放置大量微型闭路电视监视器而进行展示。作品内容由奔窜的裸体人影的循环片段组成，由于是从远处拍摄，所以人影显得抽象化。片段用高速进行播放，因此片中愤怒的奔窜与装置的动作产生了语义联系。在这个关注当代个体存在的社会体验的展览中，刘韡的人与动物类比的影像简明扼要。

自此刘韡证明了自己创作的多样化。一般来说，他喜欢在特定场所的装置，但自从 2004年起，他也涉猎绘画——也许“反绘画”是个更恰当的说法。他的绘画手法始于计算机制出的图画，这些图画被放大到帆布上成为富于表现力的陆地景色或城市景色的微缩。这些作品中单一的青灰色暗示了现代生活的病态景象，而颜色本身也意味着孤独。就风格和实践而言，刘韡展示了对他所表达的当代文化和艺术——城市的混乱、建筑思想、欲望的目标以及伴随着占有的困惑——的趋势观察的一种随意乃至无礼的探讨。这只能在中国年轻一代的艺术家身上看到，因为他们大多都没有受到强加于其先一辈的社会政治统治对意识的影响。

自 2000 年年初起，刘韡就将装置展作为他的首要兴趣，但同时他也完成了数个摄影作品。他在黑白摄影系列《当代风景》中对人类形体的改写成为了 2002年 上海双年展的焦点。摄影也表现为装置展的一个特征，但在例如《爱它，咬它！》和《发现》（都为2006年）的作品中，它们只作为物体集合的补充。这里的物体主要来自非艺术资源：《爱它，咬它！》使用了牛皮条，这种除了成为狗咬胶的主要原料之外没多少商业价值的东西被当作

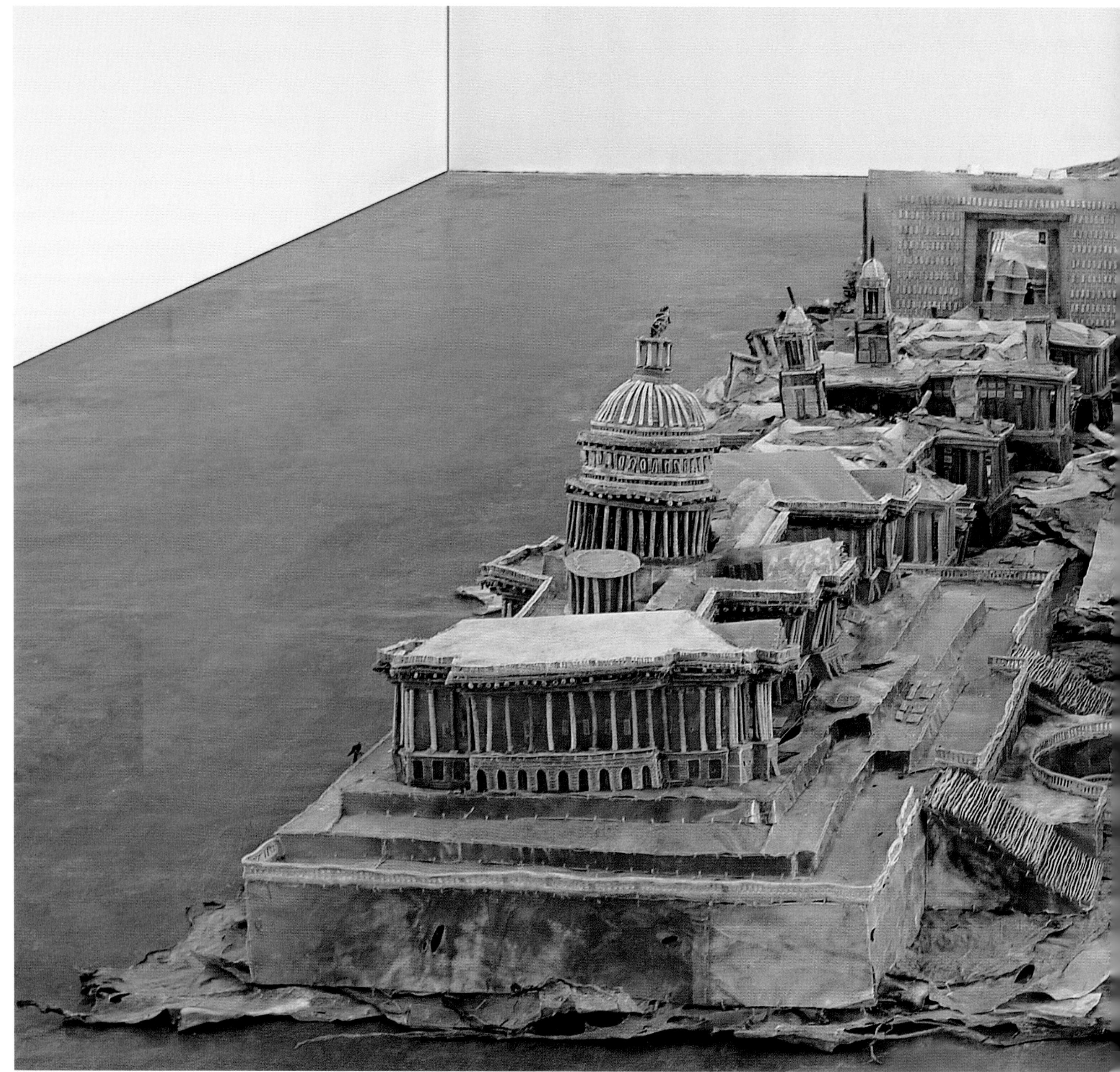

2

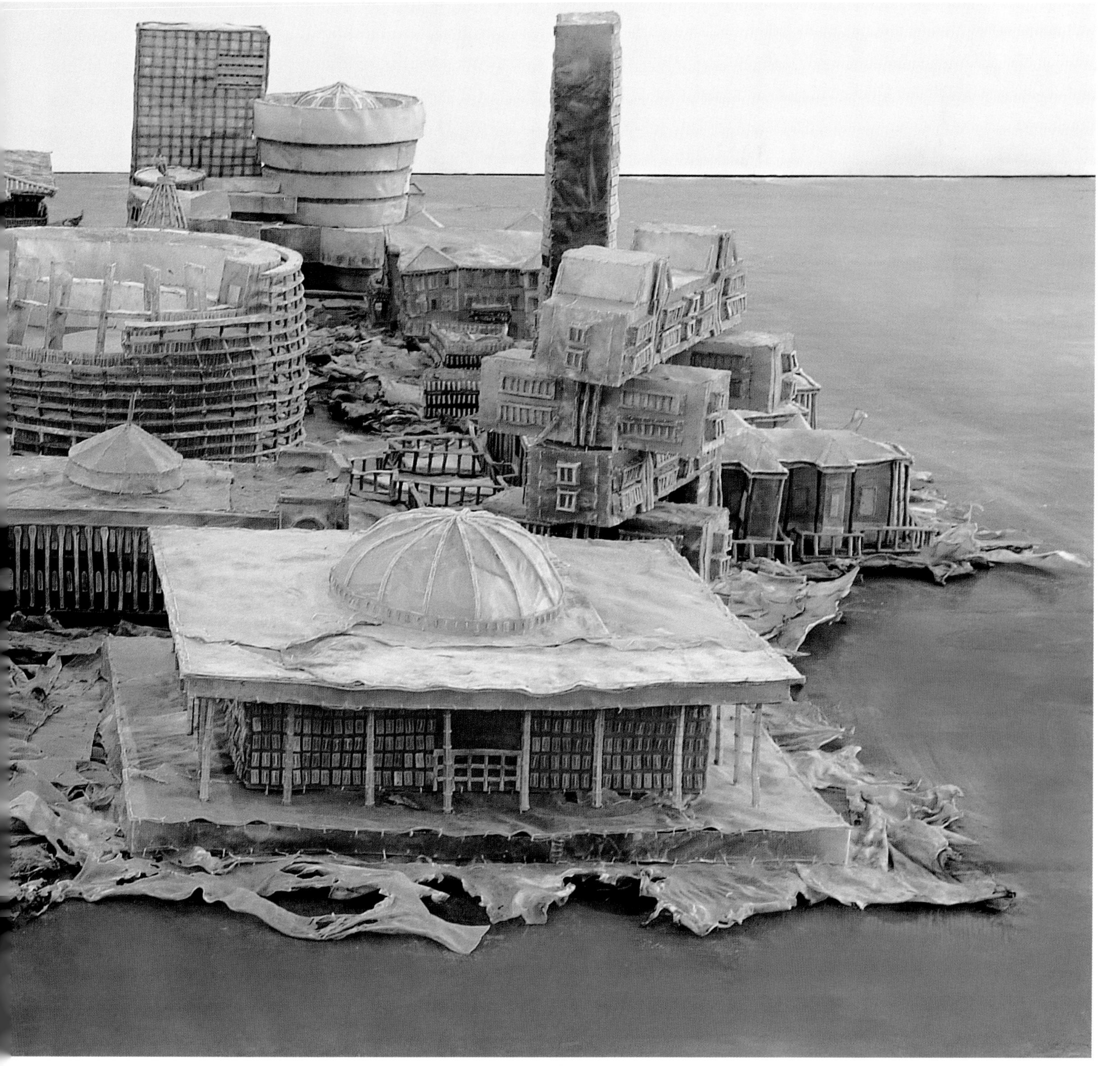

3

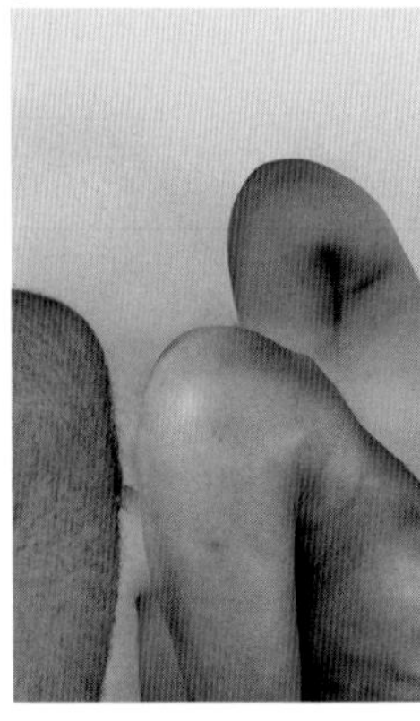
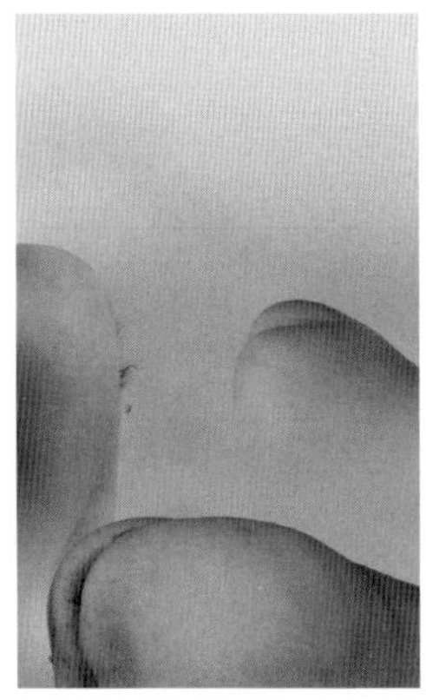
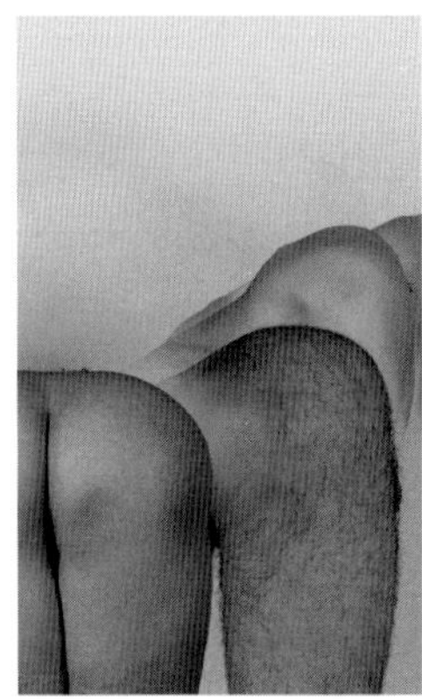
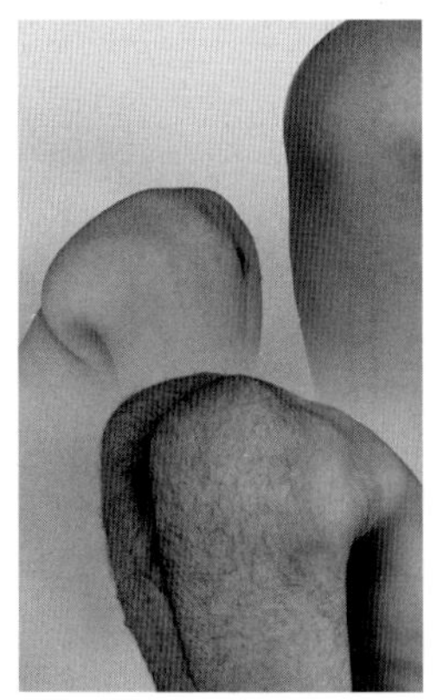
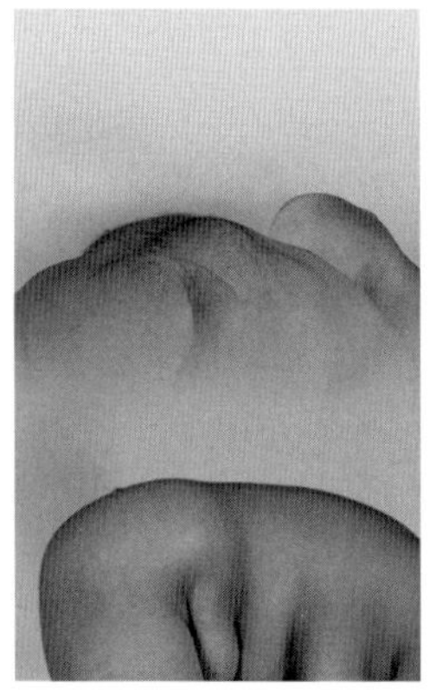
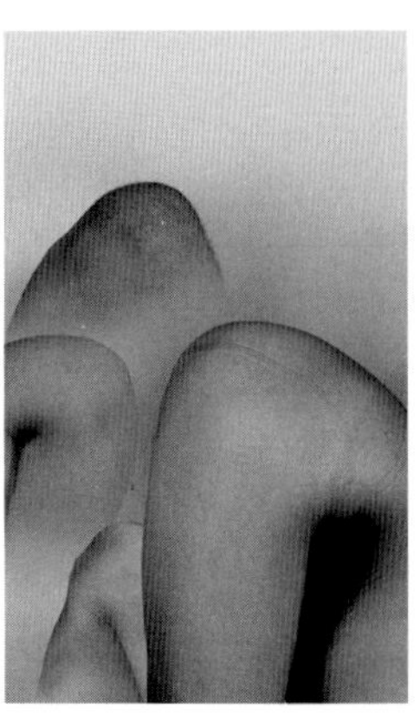

Photographs also appear as a feature of installation works, but in works like "Love It! Bite It!" and "Discovery" (both 2006), they play second fiddle to the assembly of objects. The objects here are primarily appropriated from non-art sources: "Love It! Bite It!" employs strips of rawhide, a substance of little commercial value beyond being the primary ingredient of canine treats, as the material form of scale models of global architectural icons. Despite being fortified by strenuous seams, the material softens in the air reducing these cultural powerhouses to fatuous, impotent symbols of a national prowess that belongs to a bygone era little relevant to the global age.

"Missiles" (2005/06) employs household chinaware as the individual segments for military missiles, presented in crates designed to suggest the same military function. In keeping with the military feel, Liu Wei stencilled these forms with the phrase "Property of L. W". This first appeared on a small series of paintings that created a clever repeat pattern using the image of Mickey Mouse in the guise of army camouflage (2004/05). It was used again in "Discovery" claim ownership of a group of found objects, random examples of debris whose status as art form is sealed by the artist's stamp. The thread that connects this diverse body of work is Liu Wei's questioning of what constitutes aesthetic value and worthy subject matter. This explains the unsavoury array of decayed teeth in "Perfect World" (2001), his use of ready-mades in "Discovery", the unvarnished bodies that form the "Landscape" series, and the animal skins that are the subject of the "Fur" paintings (2003/04). There is a raw, unpolished aspect to all these works. For some artists this might indicate uncertainty or weakness, for Liu Wei it is a strategy that knows neither prejudice nor inhibition about what constitutes art in the modern world.

Seit Beginn des neuen Jahrtausends hat Liu Wei den Schwerpunkt seiner Arbeit auf Installationen gelegt, aber auch fotografische Werke geschaffen. Seine Adaption der menschlichen Gestalt in der Schwarzweißfotoserie „Contemporary Landscape" erregte auf der Shanghai Biennale 2002 großes Interesse. Fotos erscheinen auch als Elemente in seinen Installationen; in Werken wie „Love It! Bite It!" und „Discovery" (beide von 2006) treten sie gegenüber der Objektsammlung in den Hintergrund. Diese Objekte stammen in erster Linie aus nicht-künstlerischen Quellen: Bei „Love It! Bite It!" dienen Streifen aus Rohleder, einem minderwertigen Material (abgesehen von seiner Verwendung für Hundebeißspielzeug), als Baustoff für maßstäbliche Modelle globaler Architektur-Ikonen. Obwohl durch massive Nähte verstärkt, weicht das Material an der Luft allmählich auf und degradiert so diese kulturellen „Großwerke" zu albernen, kraftlosen Symbolen der nationalen Tüchtigkeit einer vergangenen Ära, die für das globale Zeitalter belanglos ist.

„Missiles" (2005/06) verwendet Haushaltsporzellan als Segmente militärischer Geschosse und präsentiert diese in Kisten, die auf ebendiese militärische Funktion verweisen. Passend versah Liu Wei die Missiles mit der schablonierten Aufschrift „Property of L. W.". Diese Besitzdeklaration erschien übrigens zuerst auf einer kleinen Serie von Gemälden, die in einem raffinierten Wiederholungsmuster Mickymäuse in militärischen Tarnanzügen präsentierten (2004/05). Dann tauchte sie bei „Discovery" erneut auf, um das Eigentum an einer Gruppe von Fundobjekten zu beanspruchen, bei denen es sich um Trümmerteile handelt, deren Kunststatus durch den Stempel des Künstlers besiegelt wird. Der rote Faden, der sich durch all diese vielfältigen Arbeiten zieht, ist Liu Weis Frage, worin eigentlich der ästhetische Wert und die „Kunstwürdigkeit" eines Gegenstands begründet liegen. Das erklärt auch die unappetitliche Aufreihung verrotteter Zähne in „Perfect World" (2001), oder seine Verwendung von Readymades in „Discovery" sowie die „ungeschminkten" Körper der „Landscape"-Serie und die Tierfelle, die Gegenstand der „Fur"-Gemälde (2003/04) sind. All diesen Werken ist etwas Rohes, Ungeschliffenes eigen. Bei anderen Künstlern könnte man dies als Hinweis auf Unsicherheit oder Schwäche deuten. Bei Liu Wei jedoch kommt damit eine Strategie zum Ausdruck, die weder Vorurteile noch Hemmungen kennt, wenn es um die Frage geht, worin Kunst in der modernen Welt besteht.

全球标志性建筑比例模型的材料形式。尽管经过努力拼接加强，这些材料在空气中依然逐渐软化，将这些文化源泉减弱为国家力量愚笨、无力的符号，而国家力量是属于以前的年代，和全球时代已没多大关系。

《导弹》（2005-2006年）采用了家用的瓷器作为军队导弹的各个单独部分，并将其装在设计于表示军事用途的容纳导弹的板条箱内。为了和军事打击题材一致，刘韡在这些形体上印制了“刘韡财产”字样。这种方式第一次出现在一个小的绘画系列中，画上借军事迷彩创作了一个灵巧的米老鼠图案（2004-2005年）。在《发现》这个作品上这种方法又一次得到使用，以用来表示一组拿来物品的所属随便拣来的碎片以艺术的形式被戳上艺术家的印鉴。刘韡对是什么构成美学价值并值得作为题材的质问成为连接这些丰富的作品形式的线索。这就解释了《完美世界》（2001年）中令人不适的腐朽牙齿组合，《发现》中使用的现成品，《风景》系列中不加掩饰的人体，以及作为《毛皮》绘画（2003-2004年）的主题的动物皮。所有这些作品都具有原始、未打磨的外表。对有些艺术家来说，这可能表示不坚定或软弱，但对刘韡来说只是一种策略，对于现代社会中的艺术组成既没有偏见，也没有禁忌。

Karen Smith

4

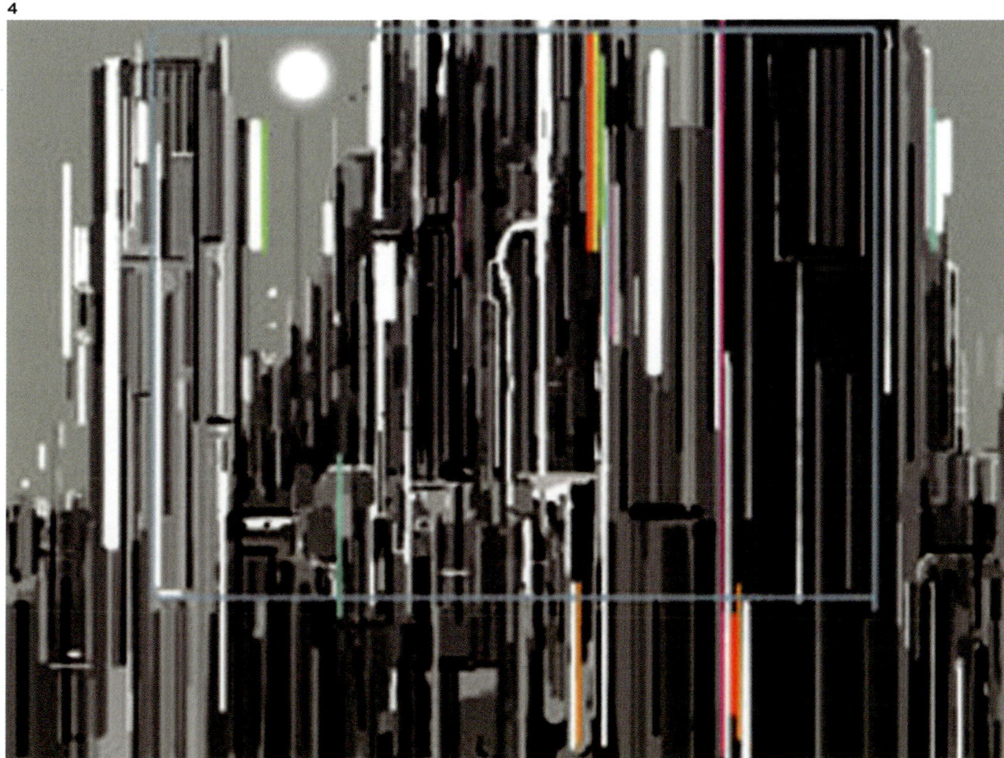

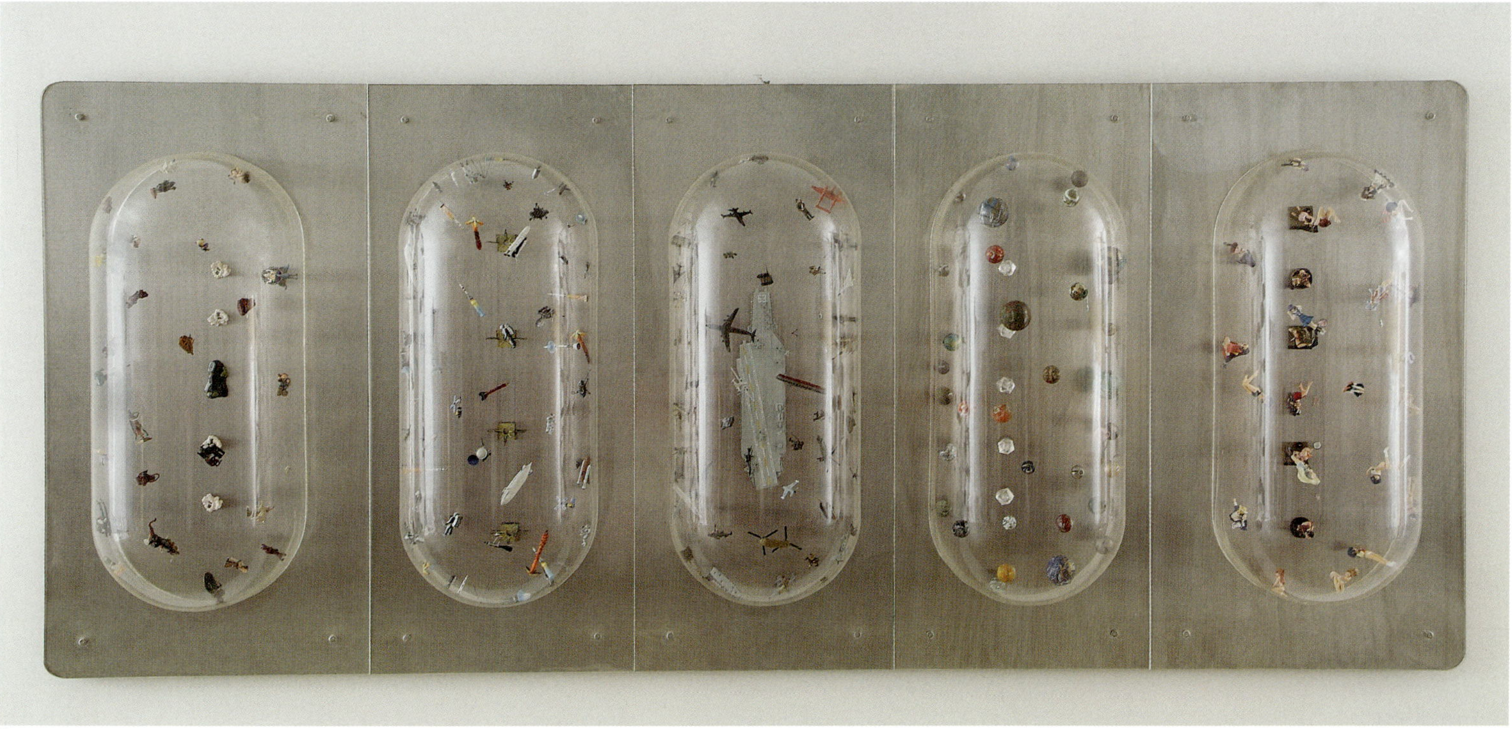

1 ***Indigestion II***, *2005*
Installation, 200 x 120 x 100 cm
Installation, 200 x 120 x 100 cm
《消化不良II》2005年, 装置, 200 x 120 x 100 cm

2 ***Super Structure***, *2005–2007*
Installation from Edible Dog Chews
Installation aus Hundekauknochen
《超级建筑》2005–2007年, 装置

3 ***It Looks Like a Landscape***, *2004*
Digital b/w photographs, 300 x 180 cm each
Digitale Schwarzweißfotografien, je 300 x 180 cm
《风景》2004年, 数码黑白照片, 每幅300 x 180 cm

4 ***Purple III No. 5***, *2006*
Oil on canvas, 310 x 380 cm
Öl auf Leinwand, 310 x 380 cm
《紫色III No. 5》2006年, 布面油画, 310 x 380 cm

5 ***Capacity II***, *2004*
Stainless steel, toys, glass containers, 310 x 160 cm
Edelstahl, Spielzeug, Glasbehälter, 310 x 160 cm
《生产能力II》2004年，不锈钢，玩具，琉璃箱，310 x 160 cm

5

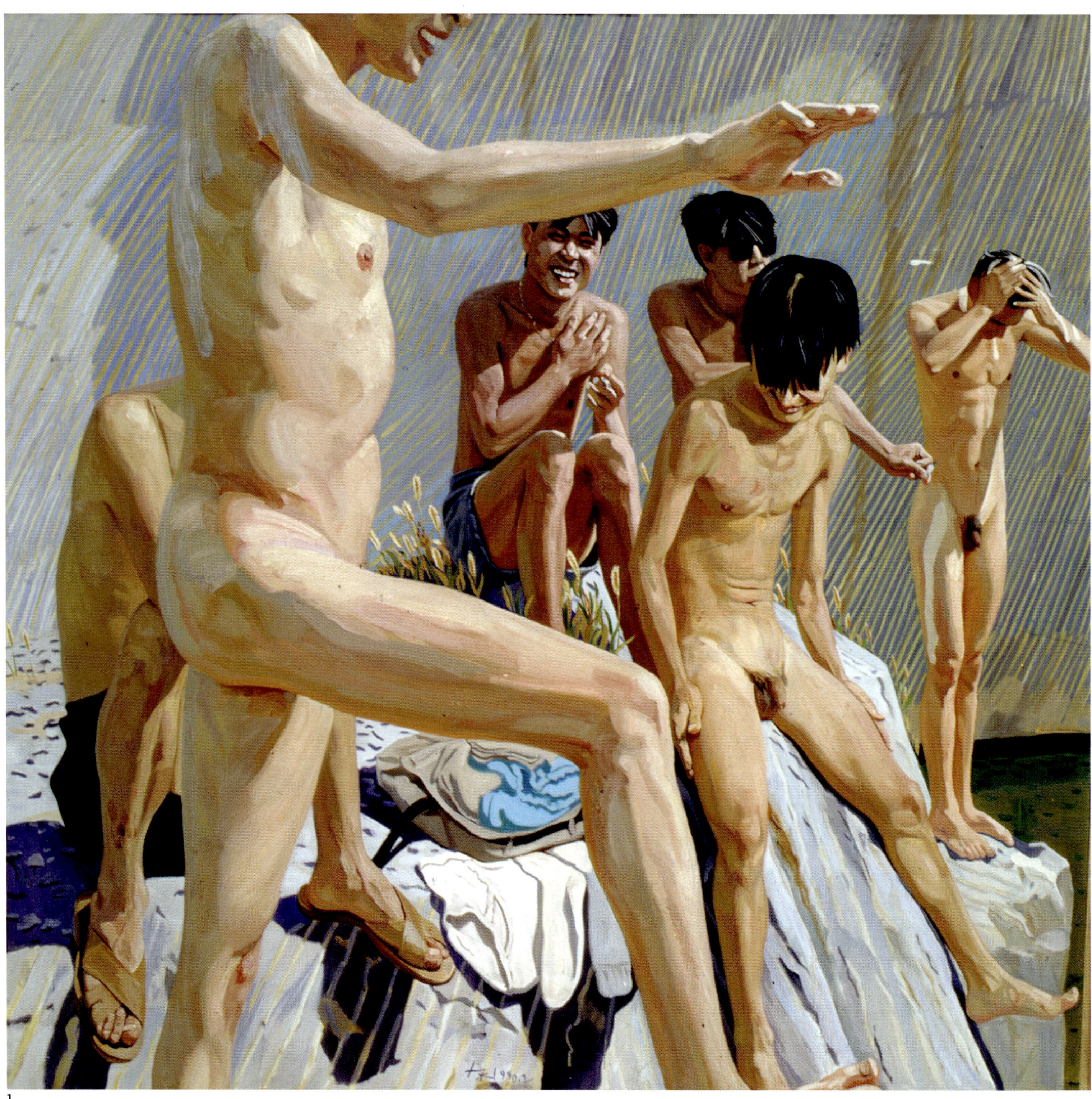

1

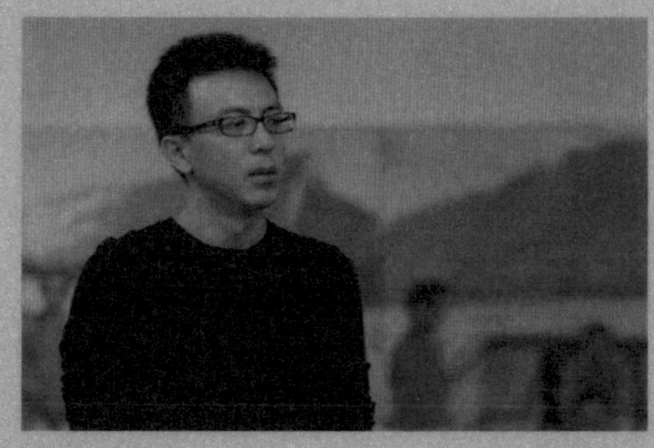

"'The Three Gorges New Immigration' was created in 2004 when I went there. The picture expresses the real works site of the Three Gorges, the demolition of the rocks, the migrating people each different in manner, naïve and mischievous children."

„'The Three Gorges New Immigration' geht auf das Jahr 2004 zurück, als ich am Drei-Schluchten-Damm war … Das Bild drückt die Zerstörung des Felsens aus, die Vertreibung der Menschen, naive und freche Kinder."

"《三峡新移民》创作于2004年，那时我正来到那里。图片描写了三峡 的真实工作场地，千疮百孔的岩石，神情迴异的移民，天真淘气的孩童。"

Born in 1963 in Jincheng, Liaoning Province, China. Lives and works in Beijing
Geboren 1963 in Jincheng, Provinz Liaoning, China. Lebt und arbeitet in Peking
1963 年出生于中国辽宁金城镇，居住工作于北京

***Selected exhibitions* / Ausgewählte Ausstellungen / 所选展览**

1992 "China's New Art, Post 1989", Hong Kong Arts Centre, Hong Kong, China
1997 47. Biennale di Venezia, Venice, Italy
2000 Shanghai Biennial Art Exhibition, Shanghai, China
2003 "Alors, la Chine?", Centre Georges Pompidou, Paris, France
2005 "The Wall: Reshaping Contemporary Chinese Art", Millennium Art Museum, Beijing, China
2006 "The Three Gorges Project – Paintings by Liu Xiaodong", Asian Art Museum, San Francisco, CA, USA

1992年 《后'89中国前卫艺术展》汉雅轩香港
1997年 第47届威尼斯双年展，威尼斯
2000年 上海双年展
2003年 《中国怎么样?》蓬皮杜艺术中心，巴黎
2005年 《墙：重解中国当代艺术》奥尔布赖特-诺克斯艺术画廊，水牛城，美国
2006年 《三峡项目》亚洲美术馆，旧金山，美国

***Selected publications* / Ausgewählte Publikationen / 所选著作**

Jean-Marc Decrop (ed.): "Liu Xiaodong", with contributions by Charles Merewether and Wu Hung, Hong Kong 2005

《刘小东》刘小东（作者），Charles Merewether（撰稿），Jean-Marc Decrop（编辑），Wu Hung（编辑），2005年

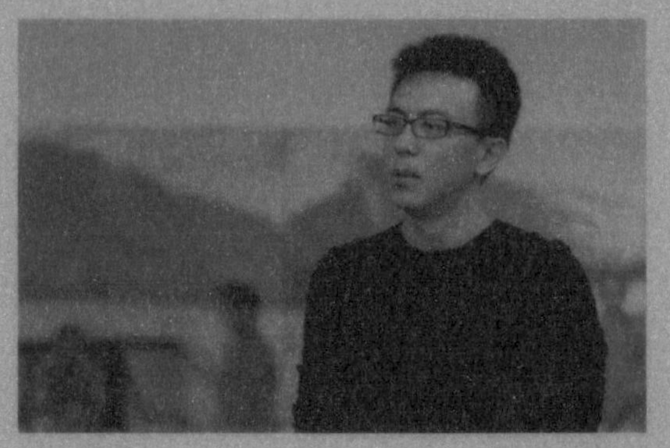

"'The Three Gorges New Immigration' was created in 2004 when I went there. The picture expresses the real works site of the Three Gorges, the demolition of the rocks, the migrating people each different in manner, naïve and mischievous children."

„'The Three Gorges New Immigration' geht auf das Jahr 2004 zurück, als ich am Drei-Schluchten-Damm war ... Das Bild drückt die Zerstörung des Felsens aus, die Vertreibung der Menschen, naive und freche Kinder."

"《三峡新移民》创作于2004年，那时我正来到那里。图片描写了三峡 的真实工作场地，千疮百孔的岩石，神情迥异的移民，天真淘气的孩童。"

Born in 1963 in Jincheng, Liaoning Province, China. Lives and works in Beijing
Geboren 1963 in Jincheng, Provinz Liaoning, China. Lebt und arbeitet in Peking
1963 年出生于中国辽宁金城镇，居住工作于北京

Selected exhibitions / Ausgewählte Ausstellungen / 所选展览

1992 "China's New Art, Post 1989", Hong Kong Arts Centre, Hong Kong, China
1997 47. Biennale di Venezia, Venice, Italy
2000 Shanghai Biennial Art Exhibition, Shanghai, China
2003 "Alors, la Chine?", Centre Georges Pompidou, Paris, France
2005 "The Wall: Reshaping Contemporary Chinese Art", Millennium Art Museum, Beijing, China
2006 "The Three Gorges Project - Paintings by Liu Xiaodong", Asian Art Museum, San Francisco, CA, USA

1992年 《后'89中国前卫艺术展》汉雅轩香港
1997年 第47届威尼斯双年展，威尼斯
2000年 上海双年展
2003年 《中国怎么样?》蓬皮杜艺术中心，巴黎
2005年 《墙：重解中国当代艺术》奥尔布赖特-诺克斯艺术画廊，水牛城，美国
2006年 《三峡项目》亚洲美术馆，旧金山，美国

Selected publications / Ausgewählte Publikationen / 所选著作

Jean-Marc Decrop (ed.): "Liu Xiaodong", with contributions by Charles Merewether and Wu Hung, Hong Kong 2005

《刘小东》刘小东（作者），Charles Merewether（撰稿），Jean-Marc Decrop（编辑），Wu Hung（编辑），2005年

LIU XIAODONG 刘小东

[liou ɕiaʊtʊŋ]

Liu Xiaodong is the preeminent realist painter working in China today though he came to prominence with the Cynical Realist movement of the early 1990s. An art trend associated with the malaise and despair experienced in the aftermath of the Tian'anmen Square incident, Cynical Realism included such widely disparate painters as Fang Lijun, Liu Wei and Zhang Xiaogang. But of this group, only Liu Xiaodong resolutely remained faithful to the realist tradition, focusing on the everyday experiences affecting ordinary people in China.

Trained at the Central Academy of Fine Arts in Beijing, where he is currently a professor, Liu Xiaodong found his own approach to realism in 1988. As opposed to the socialist realism of the Cultural Revolution or the idealized classicism enforced by the academy, he developed a more aggressive brushstroke that perfectly suited his direct approach to his subjects. Liu Xiaodong was also equally trained in both Chinese and western traditions, earning a masters' degree from the Central Academy in 1995 and another from the Complutense University in Madrid in 1999. His style has often been compared to that of Lucian Freud and Eric Fischl.

Instead of dealing with idealistic dreams and national pride, Cynical Realism depicted the banal details, even negative qualities, arising in everyday life. In his early paintings, working from photographs, Liu Xiaodong first depicted the lives of his circle of friends, then expanded to include urban denizens and migrant workers. Even when he picks ordinary people as his focus, he portrays them in a harsh light, using garish colours and emphasizing unflattering characteristics.

In more recent years, Liu Xiaodong has addressed broader social issues with his work. In "Battlefield Sketches: The New Eighteen Arhats" (2004), the artist painted nine life-size portraits of Chinese soldiers and nine of Taiwanese soldiers to form of suite of 18 paintings addressing the gulf between the two countries. Spending time on military

Liu Xiaodong ist heute der herausragende realistische Maler in China, nachdem er sich ursprünglich im Zynischen Realismus der frühen 1990er Jahre einen Namen gemacht hatte – einer Kunstbewegung, in der sich die allgemeine Beklommenheit und Verzweiflung nach dem Massaker auf dem Platz des Himmlischen Friedens spiegelte und der so unterschiedliche Maler wie Fang Lijun, Liu Wei und Zhang Xiaogang angehörten. Von ihnen blieb jedoch allein Liu Xiaodong seiner realistischen Herkunft unbeirrbar treu: Er konzentriert sich bis heute auf die alltäglichen Erfahrungen gewöhnlicher Menschen in China.

Liu Xiaodong, der die Central Academy of Fine Arts in Peking besuchte, an der er zurzeit auch als Dozent tätig ist, fand 1988 zu seiner eigenen Form des Realismus. Im Gegensatz zum Sozialistischen Realismus der Kulturrevolution oder dem idealisierten Klassizismus, der an der Akademie vorherrschte, entwickelte er einen aggressiveren Pinselstrich, der perfekt zu seiner direkten Herangehensweise an seine Motive passt. Liu Xiaodong ist sowohl in der chinesischen als auch in der westlichen Tradition versiert: Neben dem Master der Central Academy in Peking aus dem Jahr 1995 verfügt er über einen zweiten Abschluss an der Universidad Complutense in Madrid aus dem Jahr 1999. Sein Stil wurde schon oft mit dem von Lucian Freud und Eric Fischl verglichen.

Statt sich mit idealistischen Träumen und Nationalstolz aufzuhalten, bildete der Zynische Realismus die banalen Details und auch die negativen Seiten des Alltagslebens ab. In seinen frühen Gemälden, die auf Fotografien basierten, stellte Liu Xiaodong zunächst das Leben seines Freundeskreises dar, um dann seinen Aktionsradius auf Stadtbewohner und Wanderarbeiter zu erweitern. Selbst wenn er ganz alltägliche Menschen in den Brennpunkt stellt, porträtiert er sie in grellem Licht und schrillen Farben und unter Hervorhebung ihrer unvorteilhaften Züge.

In den letzten Jahren greift Liu Xiaodong in seinen Arbeiten auch weiter reichende gesellschaftliche Fragen auf.

刘小东是北京艺术界中杰出的现实主义画家，上世纪90年代初期的泼皮艺术运动让其引人注目。泼皮艺术是一种艺术趋向，与天安门事件所形成的悲伤经历紧密相连，方力钧、刘炜张晓刚等都属于泼皮艺术家。但是他们这个群体中，仅有刘小东依旧皈依于现实主义传统，着眼于影响普通人日常经历。

刘小东曾在中央美院学习，而如今却是那里的教授，1988年他在寻找到通向现实主义的自己的策略。不用于文化大革命中社会现实主义和学院派的理想现实主义，他的粗犷不羁的笔调，极好的与主题协调。刘小东既受过中国传统和西方传统教育，1995年取得中央美院的硕士学位，1999年取得马德里的康普鲁登塞大学硕士学位。其格调常常与Lucian Freud 和Eric Fischl相提并论。

泼皮艺术没有去涉及理想主义梦想和民族骄傲，而是描述日常生活中平凡的细节甚至相反的品质。其早期的绘画中，以摄影为蓝本，刘小东先是描写了他朋友圈中的生活方式，然后扩展到城市居民和农民工。甚至把普通人作为其焦点时，他以一种刺眼的亮光，运用鲜艳的色彩去强调坦率的特性。

最近几年中，刘小东在其作品中讲述了广泛的社会主题。在《战地写生—新十八罗汉像》中，艺术家绘画i了9个真人大小的大陆士兵和9个台湾士兵的肖像，以说明两岸间的差异。刘小东在两岸的军事主题上花费了大量精力，通过对军对的人性化处理，而使这个装置成为一座象征意义的桥梁　　同时，刘小东开始与其伟大的创作，一组五幅的绘画，作品讲述了三峡大坝对当地居民的影响。最大的一幅，《三峡新移民》2005年，长33英尺，高9英尺。作品中，一群当地居民站在即将冲毁他们家园的江水边，这些人面部表情复杂。在其作品中，有一种由主题所引起的紧迫性，而陈小东的直接从大自然或者现场创作的事实又加速了这种迫切性。

Barbara Pollack

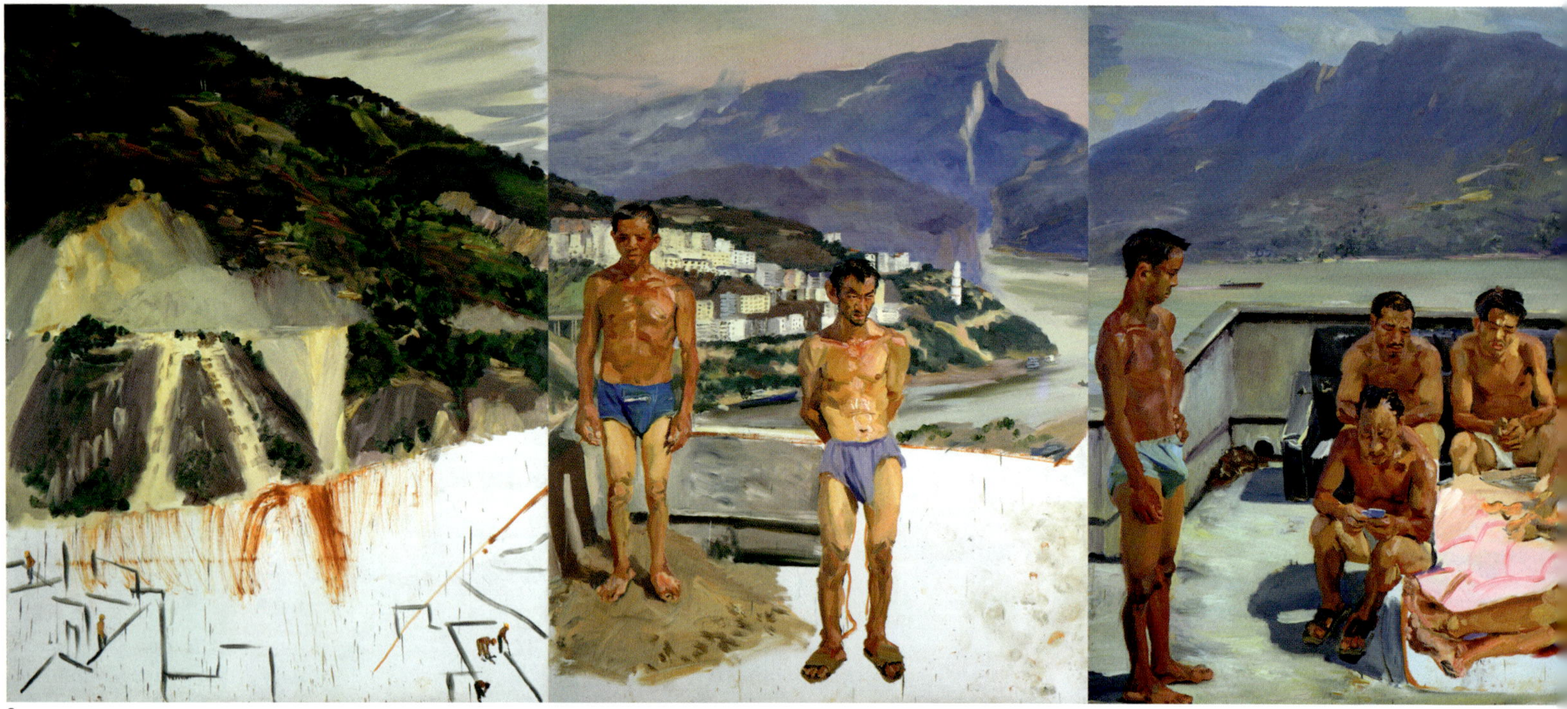

2

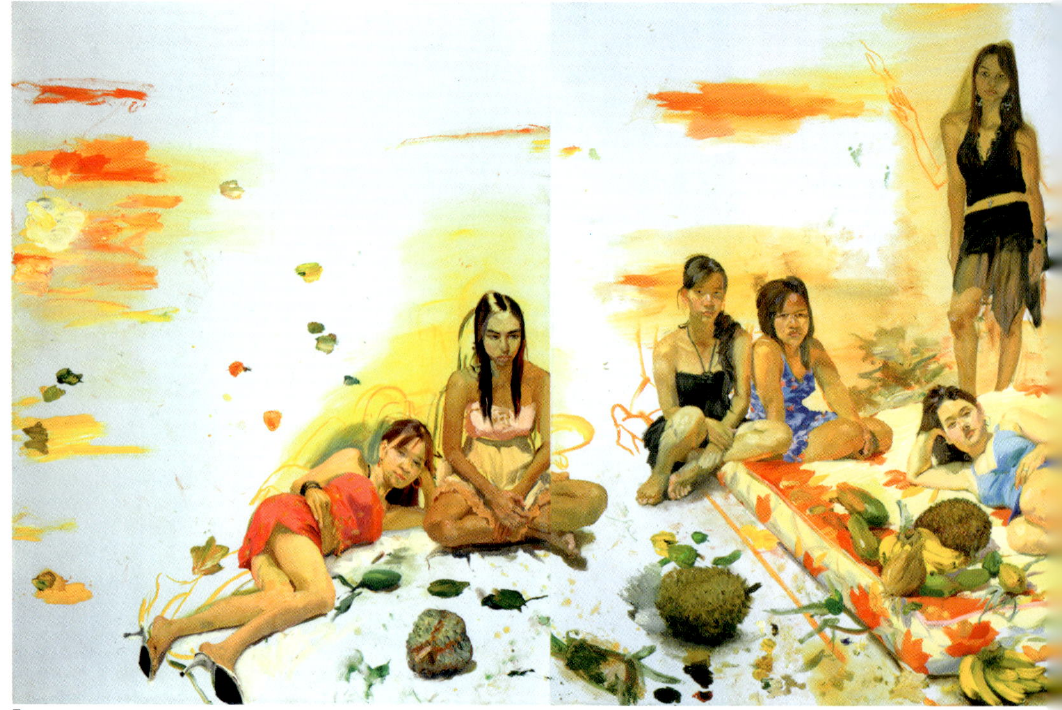

3

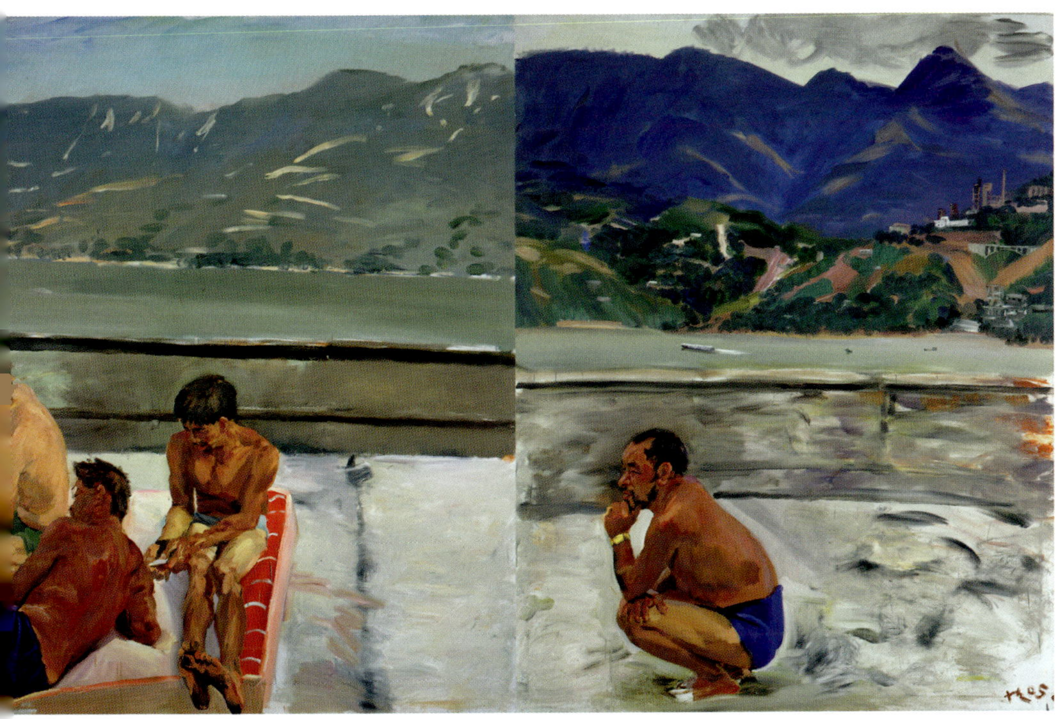

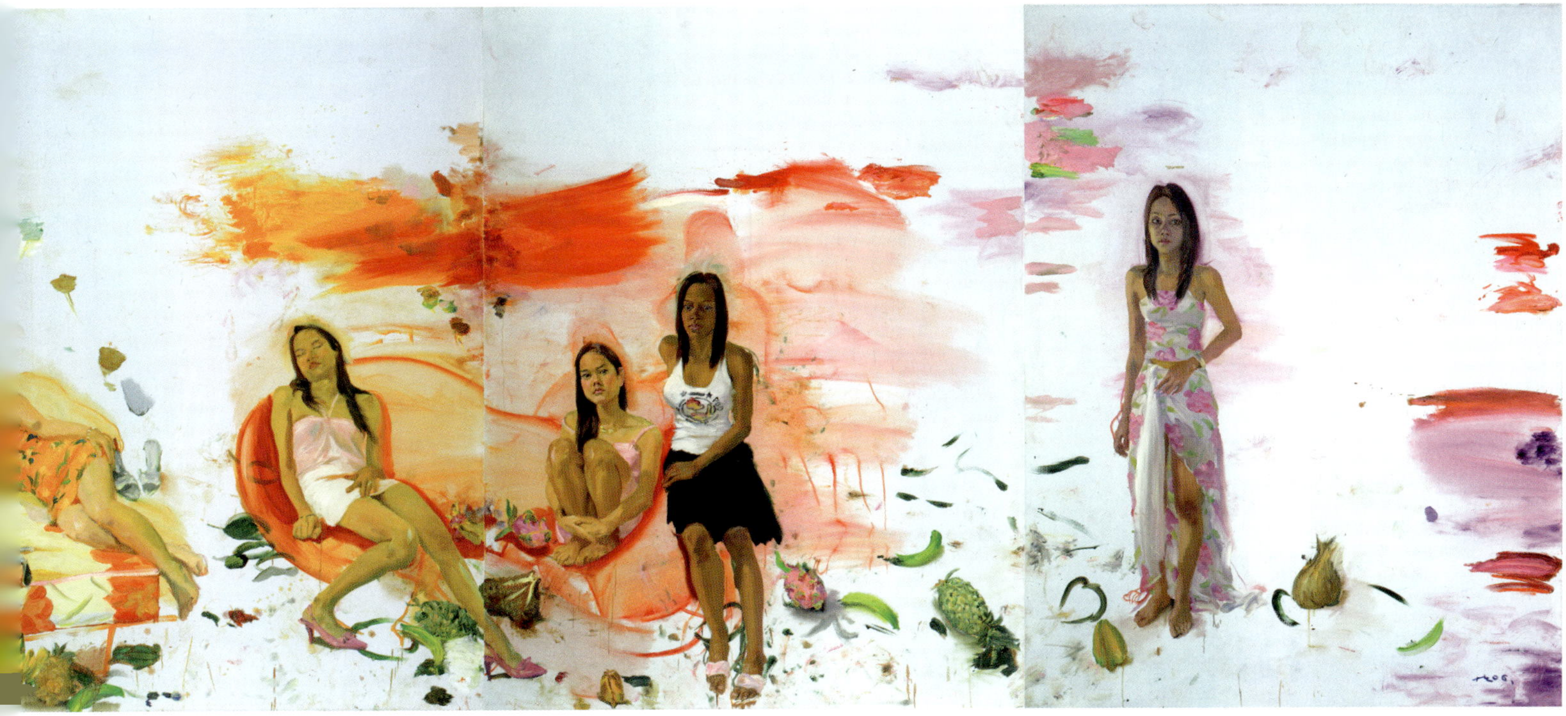

4

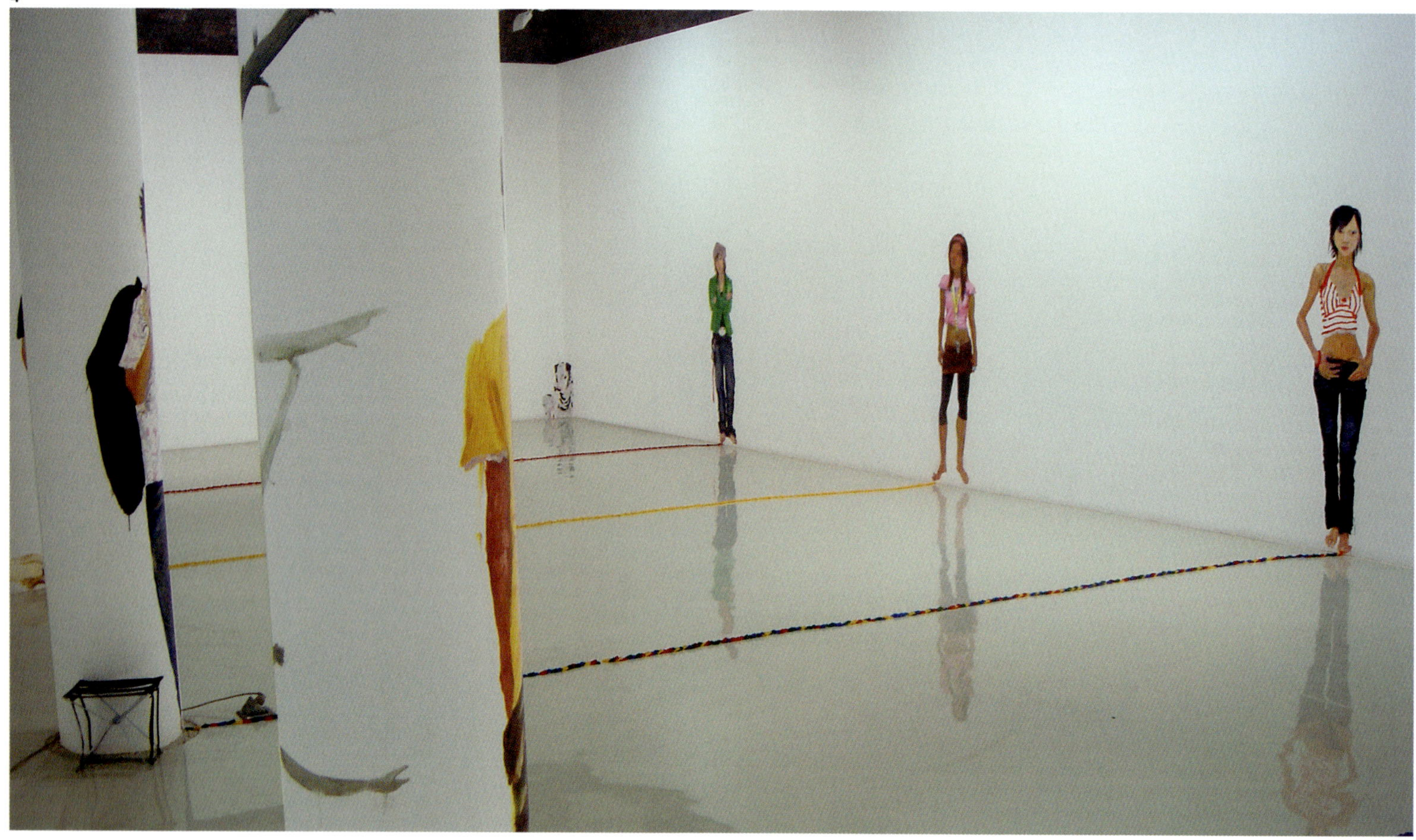

bases on both sides of the Strait, the artist came up with this installation which symbolically forms a bridge by humanizing the military. At the same time, Liu Xiaodong began work on his grandest undertaking, a series of five monumental paintings, addressing the impact on the local population caused by the building of the Three Gorges Dam. The largest painting in the suite, "Three Gorges: Newly Displaced Population" (2005), measures 33 feet long and 9 feet high. It depicts the reactions on the faces of a group of people standing at the edge of the water which will soon wash away their homes. There is urgency in this work, fuelled by the subject matter, but accelerated by the fact that the artist now works on-site and directly from nature.

Für seine „Battlefield Sketches: The New Eighteen Arhats" (2004) malte der Künstler eine Serie mit neun lebensgroßen Porträts von chinesischen und neun von taiwanesischen Soldaten als Kommentar zu der Kluft zwischen den beiden Ländern. Liu Xiaodong fand nach einiger Zeit auf Militärbasen beiderseits der Taiwan-Straße zu dieser Bildlösung, die eine symbolische Brücke zwischen den verfeindeten Brüdern schlägt, indem sie dem Militär ein menschliches Antlitz verleiht.

Gleichzeitig begann Liu mit der Arbeit an seinem bislang umfangreichsten Projekt, einer Serie von fünf Monumentalgemälden über die Auswirkungen des Drei-Schluchten-Damms auf die betroffene Bevölkerung. Das größte Gemälde der Serie, „Three Gorges: Newly Displaced Population" (2005), 10 m lang und 2,75 m hoch, zeigt die Reaktionen in den Gesichtern der Menschen, die am Rand des Wassers stehen, das bald ihre Häuser wegspülen wird. Die Eindringlichkeit des Werkes verdankt sich nicht nur der Thematik, sondern auch der Tatsache, dass der Künstler jetzt vor Ort und direkt nach der Natur arbeitet.

5

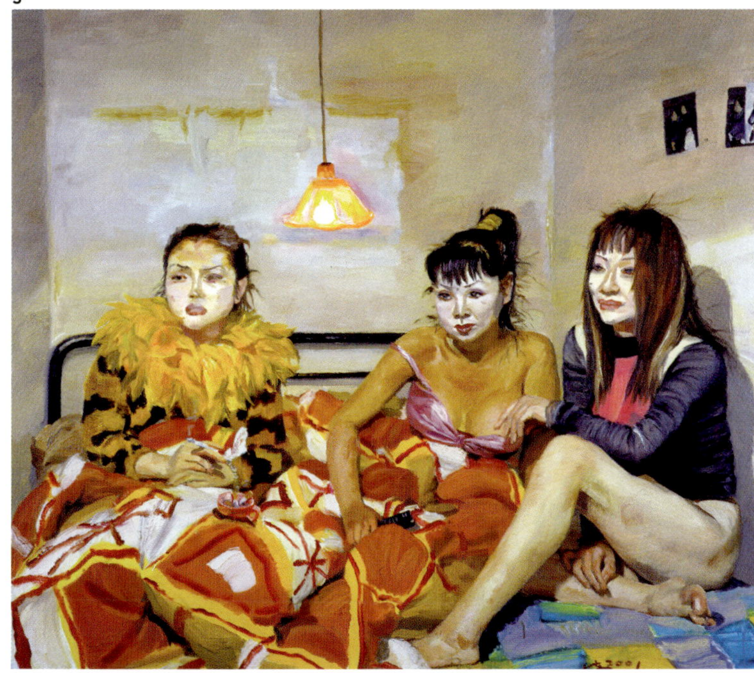

6

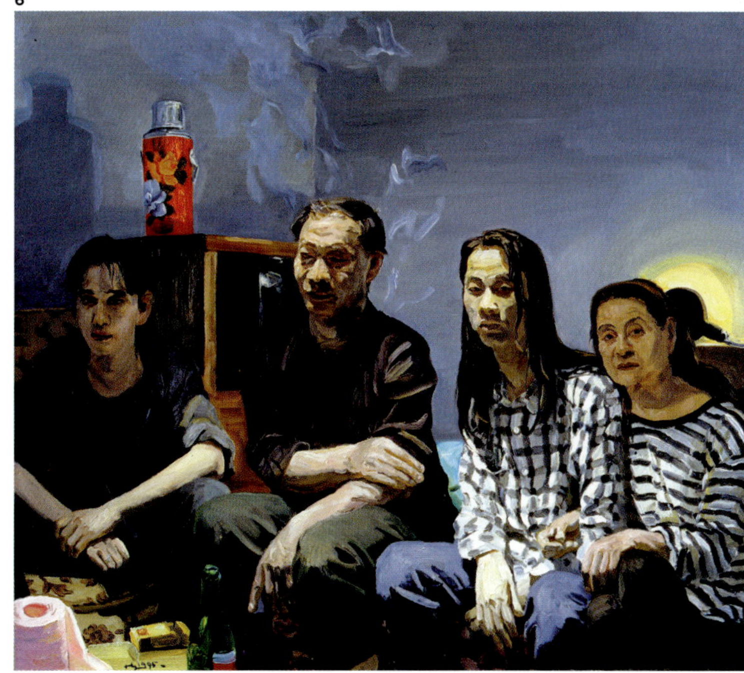

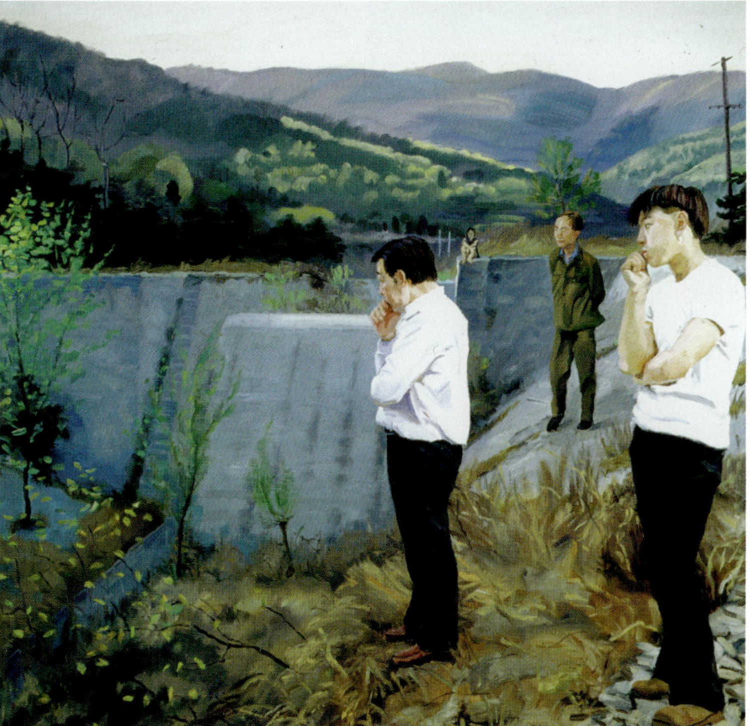

7

1 ***Showered in Sunlight**, 1990*
Oil on canvas, 180 x 195 cm
Öl auf Leinwand, 180 x 195 cm
《阳光普照》1990年, 布面油画, 180 x 195 cm

2 ***Hot Bed No. 1**, 2005*
Oil on canvas, 2.6 x 10 m
Öl auf Leinwand, 2,6 x 10 m
《温床 No. 1》2005年, 布面油画, 2.6 x 10 m

3 ***Hot Bed No. 2**, 2005*
Oil on canvas, 2.6 x 10 m
Öl auf Leinwand, 2,6 x 10 m
《温床 No. 2》2005年, 布面油画，2.6 x 10 m

4 ***Domino**, 2006*
Acrylic on wall (installation view)
Acrylic auf Wand (Installationsansicht)
《多米诺》2006年, 墙上丙烯，装置实景

5 ***Three girls watching TV**, 2001*
Oil on canvas, 137 x 152 cm
Öl auf Leinwand, 137 x 152 cm
《三个女孩看电视》2001年, 墙上油画, 137 x 152 cm

6 ***Sons**, 1995*
Oil on canvas, 150 x 170 cm
Öl auf Leinwand, 150 x 170 cm
《儿子》1995年, 布面油画, 150 x 170 cm

7 ***Watching**, 2000*
Oil on canvas, 200 x 200 cm
Öl auf Leinwand, 200 x 200 cm
《观看》2000年, 布面油画, 200 x 200 cm

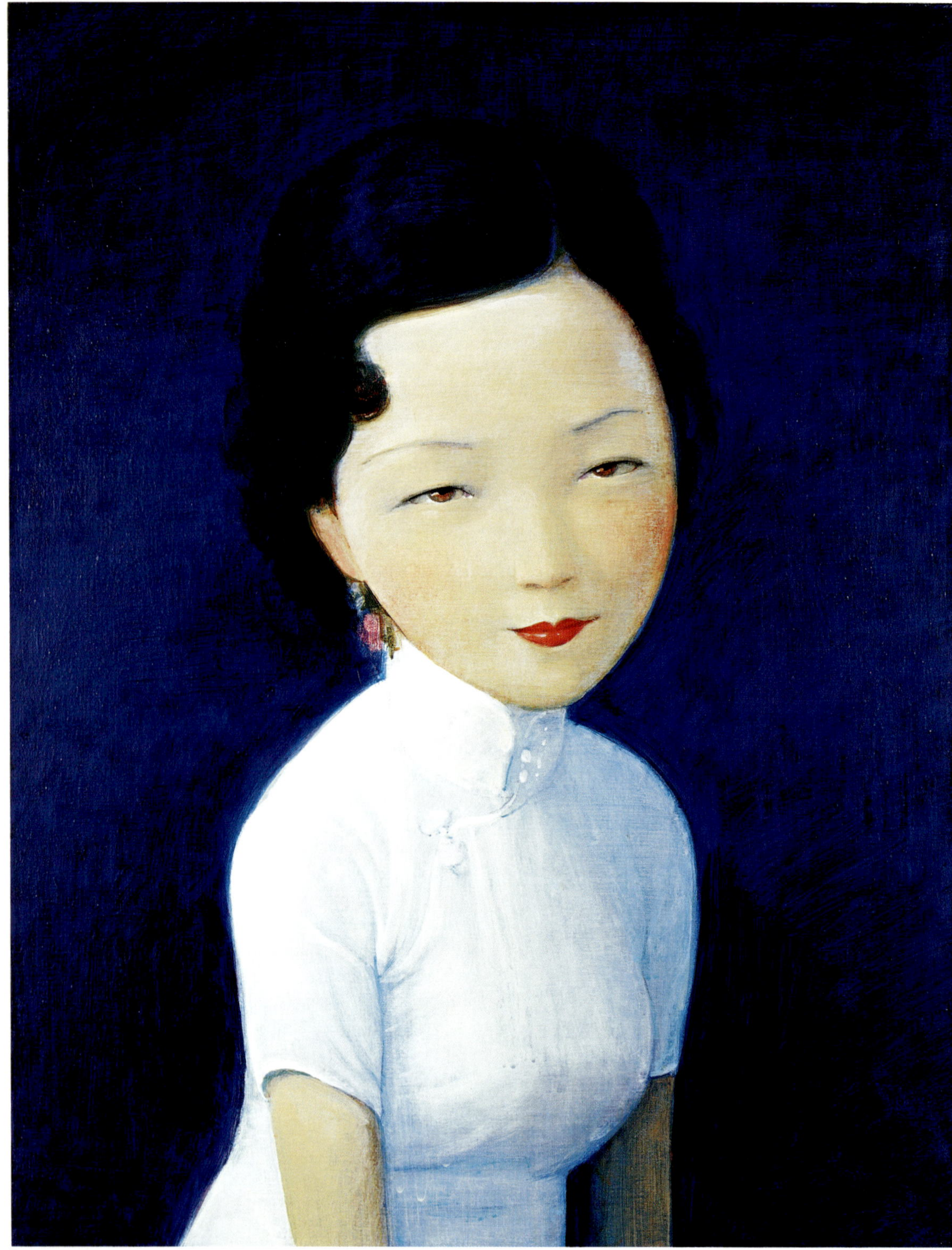

1

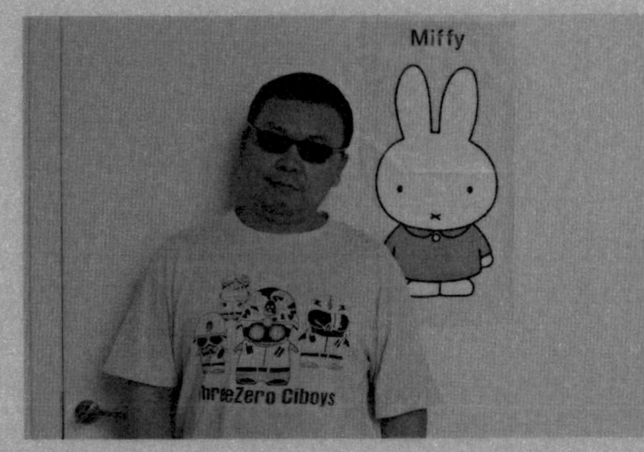

"They say I am not mature yet and I still keep the feelings of my childhood."

„Man sagt, dass ich noch nicht reif sei, dabei habe ich mir lediglich etwas Kindliches bewahrt."

"你说我不成熟，我还觉得是童心未泯呢。"

Born in 1964 in Beijing, China. Lives and works in Beijing
Geboren 1964 in Peking, China. Lebt und arbeitet in Peking
1964 年出生于中国北京。住居工作于北京

***Selected exhibitions* / Ausgewählte Ausstellungen /** 所选展览

1993 "Interieur", Galerie Taube, Berlin, Germany
1995 "New Anecdotes of Social Talk", Art Gallery of the International Palace, Beijing, China
1998 "It's Me! Forbidden City Taimiao, Beijing – Mondrian in China", Art Gallery of the International Palace, Beijing, China
2003 "Left Hand, Right Hand", 798 Space, Beijing, China
2005 "Liu Ye", Tomio Koyama Gallery, Tokyo, Japan
2006 "Temptations", Sperone Westwater, New York, NY, USA
2007 "Liu Ye", Johnen + Schöttle, Cologne, Germany
"Liu Ye", Kunstmuseum Bern, Berne, Switzerland

1993年 《刘野个展》德国柏林Taube画廊
1995年 《世说新语》中国北京
1998年 《是我》中国北京
2003年 《左手，右手》北京
2005年 《刘野》小山登美夫画廊，东京，日本
2006年 《诱惑》Sperone Westwater画廊，纽约，美国
2007年 《刘野》Johnen + Schöttle美术馆 科隆 德国
《刘野》伯尔尼艺术博物馆 伯尔尼 瑞士

***Selected publications* / Ausgewählte Publikationen /** 所选著作

"Red Yellow Blue", Hong Kong 2003

《红，黄，兰》展册，艺术画廊，香港2003年

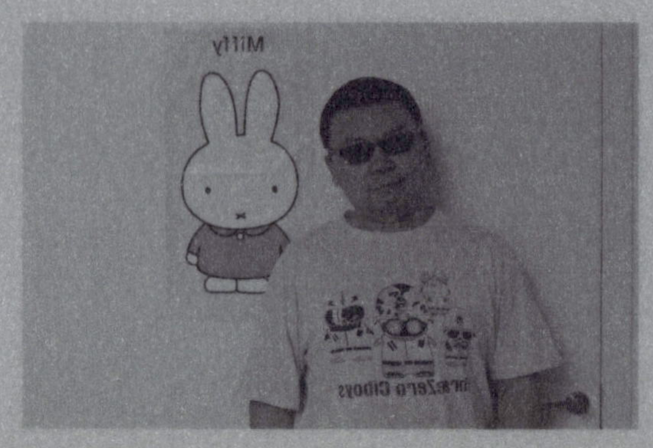

"They say I am not mature yet and I still keep the feelings of my childhood."

„Man sagt, dass ich noch nicht reif sei, dabei habe ich mir lediglich etwas Kindliches bewahrt."

"你说我不成熟，我还觉得是童心未泯呢。"

Born in 1964 in Beijing, China. Lives and works in Beijing
Geboren 1964 in Peking, China. Lebt und arbeitet in Peking
1964 年出生于中国北京。住居工作于北京

Selected exhibitions / Ausgewählte Ausstellungen / 所选展览

1993	"Interieur", Galerie Taube, Berlin, Germany
1995	"New Anecdotes of Social Talk", Art Gallery of the International Palace, Beijing, China
1998	"It's Me! Forbidden City Taimiao, Beijing – Mondrian in China", Art Gallery of the International Palace, Beijing, China
2003	"Left Hand, Right Hand", 798 Space, Beijing, China
2005	"Liu Ye", Tomio Koyama Gallery, Tokyo, Japan
2006	"Temptations", Sperone Westwater, New York, NY, USA
2007	"Liu Ye", Johnen + Schöttle, Cologne, Germany
	"Liu Ye", Kunstmuseum Bern, Berne, Switzerland

1993年	《刘野个展》德国柏林Taube画廊
1995年	《世说新语》中国北京
1998年	《是我》中国北京
2003年	《左手，右手》北京
2005年	《刘野》小山登美夫画廊，东京，日本
2006年	《诱惑》Sperone Westwater画廊，纽约，美国
2007年	《刘野》Johnen + Schöttle美术馆 科隆 德国
	《刘野》伯尔尼艺术博物馆 伯尔尼 瑞士

Selected publications / Ausgewählte Publikationen / 所选著作

"Red Yellow Blue", Hong Kong 2003

《红，黄，兰》展册，艺术画廊，香港2003年

LIU YE 刘野

[liou jɤ]

Liu Ye spent a happy childhood. His father was a writer of children's books, his mother a language teacher at high school. During his playschool time he was skilled in painting and his teacher, being convinced of Liu's talent, excited his interest in art. At that time Liu thought of airplanes in a dark blue sky, big canons on the yellow soil, warships on a blue ocean, fervent sun and sunflowers in bright yellow and his paintings were a composition thereof mainly in red, yellow and blue.

His father owned a collection of famous children's books and his grandmother told him fairytales at night when he was still a little boy, feeding him with stories of fantasia and miracles. Therefore, Liu Ye lived in a world of fantasia and miracles and refused to grow up, even as an adult. But simultaneously there is an adult Liu Ye dedicated to philosophy as philosophy gives him rational rigorous thought. Liu Ye's passion of fairytales and philosophy is in equal measure and his paintings are settled between the two poles of the feelings of his childhood and philosophy, seeking for a balance between them lifelong.

At the age of 15 Liu enrolled at the department of industrial design at Beijing School of Arts & Crafts and during his studies got acquainted with the style of Piet Mondrian (1872–1944) which impressed him deeply. Until present his works still reflect the influence of this painter. In 1986 Liu Ye passed the entrance examination at the Mural Department of the Central Academy of Fine Arts and not having graduated from his studies yet he applied for the entrance examination at Kunsthochschule Berlin in Germany. After spending four years abroad studying at Plastic Arts department, and painting in the new style of expressionism he was awarded the master degree in 1994 returning to China thereafter.

Regarding Liu Ye's works superficially they evoke the impression of being manga-like or just illustration, however, his style is influenced by traditional painting applying stroke by stroke, layer by layer diligently. For Liu Ye, Jan van Eyck,

Liu Yes Kindheit verlief offenbar sehr glücklich. Sein Vater war Autor von Kinderbüchern, seine Mutter Sprachlehrerin an einer höheren Schule. Schon während der Grundschulzeit tat sich Liu als geschickter Zeichner hervor, weshalb sein Lehrer, von seinem Talent überzeugt, versuchte, in ihm das Interesse für Kunst zu wecken. Damals dachte Liu allerdings, wie er erzählte, vor allem an silberne Flugzeuge am tiefblauen Himmel, an Kanonen auf gelber Erde, an Kriegsschiffe auf dem Ozean, an glühende Sonne und leuchtend gelbe Sonnenblumen, sodass er für seine frühen Bilder hauptsächlich die Farben Rot, Blau und Gelb verwendete.

Liu Yes Vater besaß eine große Sammlung berühmter Kinderbücher, und seine Großmutter erzählte ihm abends fantasievolle Geschichten über wundersame Begebenheiten – vielleicht erklärt dieser Hintergrund, weshalb Liu sich in gewisser Weise weigerte, erwachsen zu werden, während sich der faktisch irgendwann erwachsene Liu Ye der Philosophie zuwandte, um sich in einem rigorosen rationalen Denken zu üben. Zwischen diesen beiden Extremen – der kindlichen Leidenschaft für Märchen und dem Wunsch nach einer strengen Philosophie – ist Liu Yes gesamtes bisheriges Werk angesiedelt, und der Künstler ist fortwährend bemüht, zwischen beiden Polen eine Balance herzustellen.

Schon mit 15 Jahren schrieb sich Liu an der Beijing School of Arts and Crafts ein. Während seiner Studienzeit machte er sich insbesondere mit Piet Mondrian (1872–1944) vertraut, der ihn tief beeindruckt hat, und bis heute reflektieren seine Arbeiten den Einfluss dieses Malers. 1986 legte Liu Ye die Aufnahmeprüfung für die Abteilung Wandmalerei der Central Academy of Fine Arts ab, bewarb sich aber noch vor seinem Abschluss um die Aufnahme an der Hochschule der Künste in Berlin. Seinen vierjährigen Aufenthalt, bei dem er vor allem Bildhauerei und Malerei im neuen expressionistischen Stil studierte, schloss Liu als Magister Artium ab und kehrte 1994 nach China zurück.

Auf den ersten, oberflächlichen Blick wirken Liu Yes Arbeiten beinahe wie Comics oder konventionelle Illustrationen,

刘野有一个幸福的童年。他的父亲是一位儿童文学作家，母亲则是高中的语文教师。刘野在幼儿园的时候，就是班里画得最好的小孩，老师认为他很有天分，引起了他对艺术的兴趣。那时候，他想到的都是蔚蓝天里的飞机、黄土地上的大炮、蓝蓝大海上的军舰、火红的太阳、嫩黄色的向日葵等等，一一成了他画画的题材，而红、黄、蓝三原色，也就自然成为他用的最多的颜色。

小时候，父亲拥有许多儿童名著的藏书，祖母又常在晚上给刘野说童话故事，他的小脑袋因而塞满了许多奇观异想。从此，有一个爱幻想的小男孩儿，顽强地蛰伏在刘野日益长大的身躯里，而且一直拒绝长大。那个小男孩儿的刘野，迷恋童话，因为童话赋予他感性的想像空间。同时，另一个成人的刘野，则沉醉于哲学，因为哲学带给他理性的严谨思维。刘野对于童话和哲学具有一种相同的热情，而他的绘画创作，忽悠摆荡在这感性与理智的两极之间，这一辈子都必需非常努力地去寻求自己的平衡点。

刘野15岁进入北京工艺美术学校工业设计系，在这段求学生涯中，他认识了风格派的蒙德里安(Piet Mondrian, 1872-1944)作品，对他一生产生很大影响，甚至，蒙德里安式的绘画，日后还一再出现在他的绘画里。1986年刘野考上了中央美术学院壁画系，1989年美院尚未毕业，他就申请到德国柏林艺术学院去参加考试，之后在造型艺术系留学了四年，画过新表现主义的风格，1994年获得硕士学位后他就立刻回国。
刘野的作品表面上看起来像漫卡通或插画，他却是以古典主义的精神，一笔笔、一层层，很严肃地去画画。法兰德斯北方文艺复兴的Jan van Eyck (1395-1441)或者17世纪荷兰的风俗画家Johannes Vermeer van Delft (1632-1675)才是他真正的启蒙大师。Jean-Baptiste-Siméon Chardin, (1699-1779)处理静物的疏离而冷静态度，也是刘野心仪的对象。

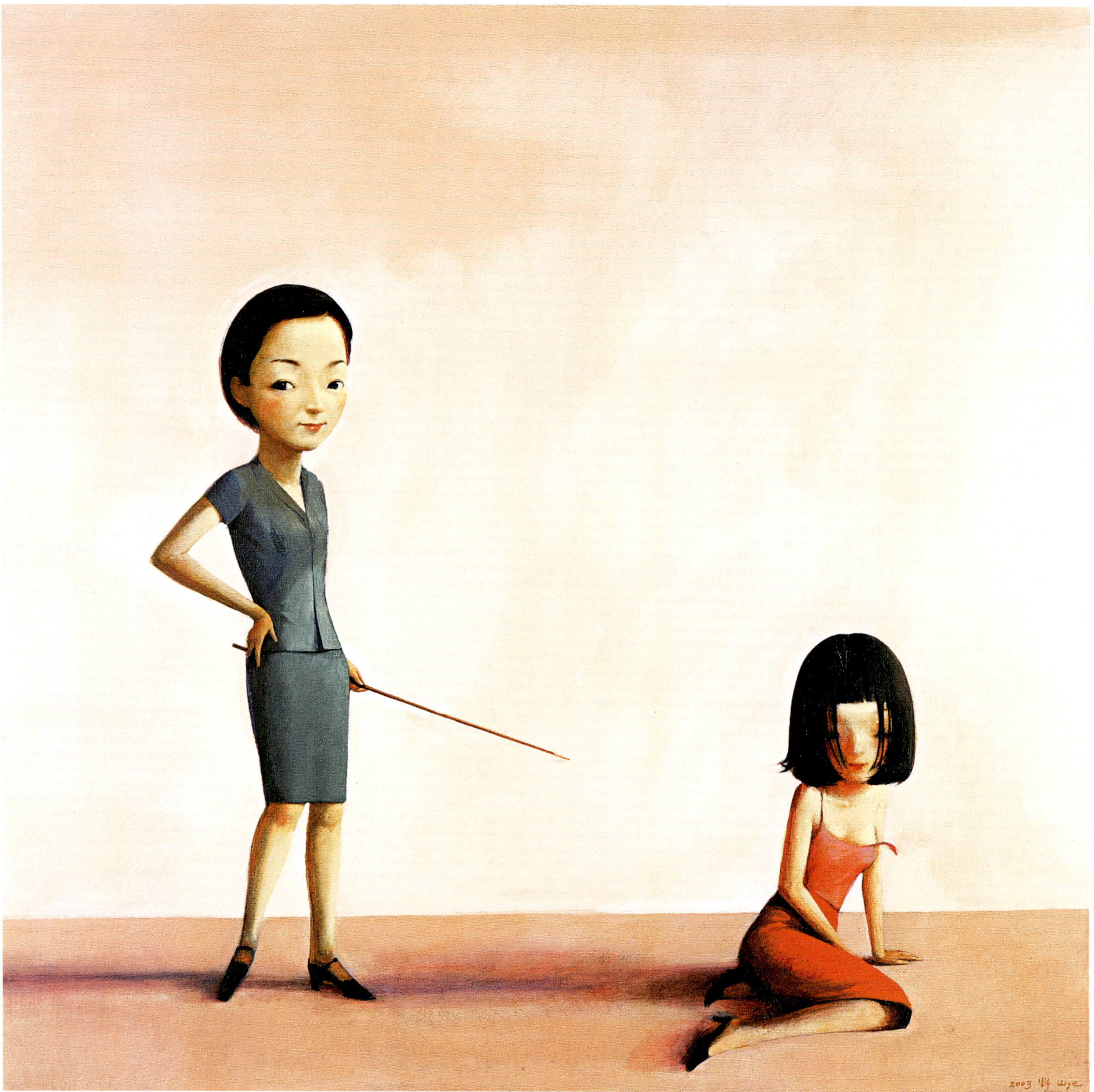

2

3

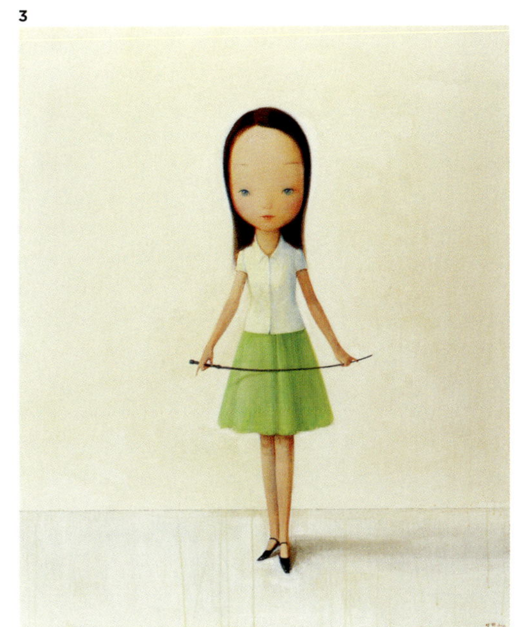

4

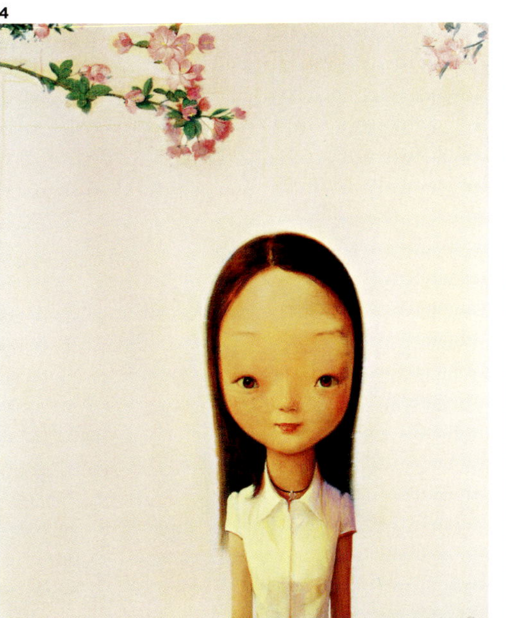

5

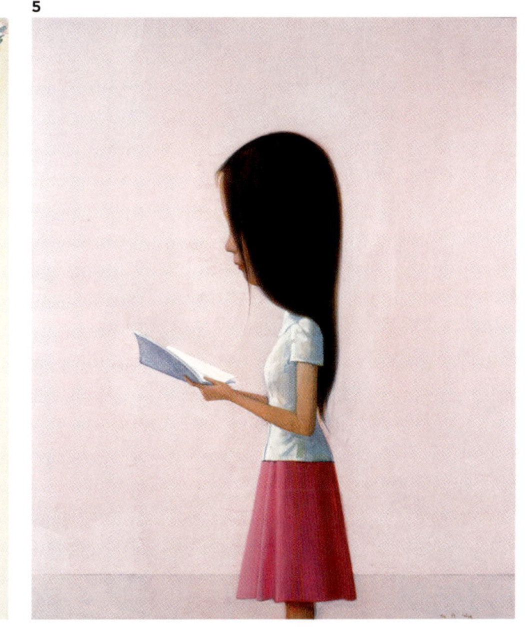

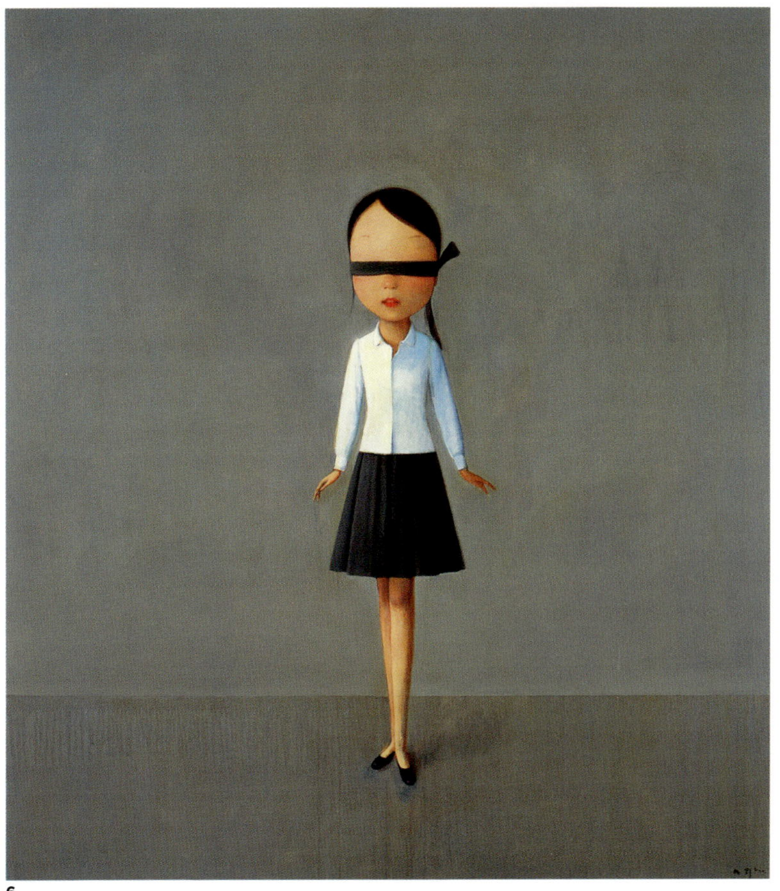

6

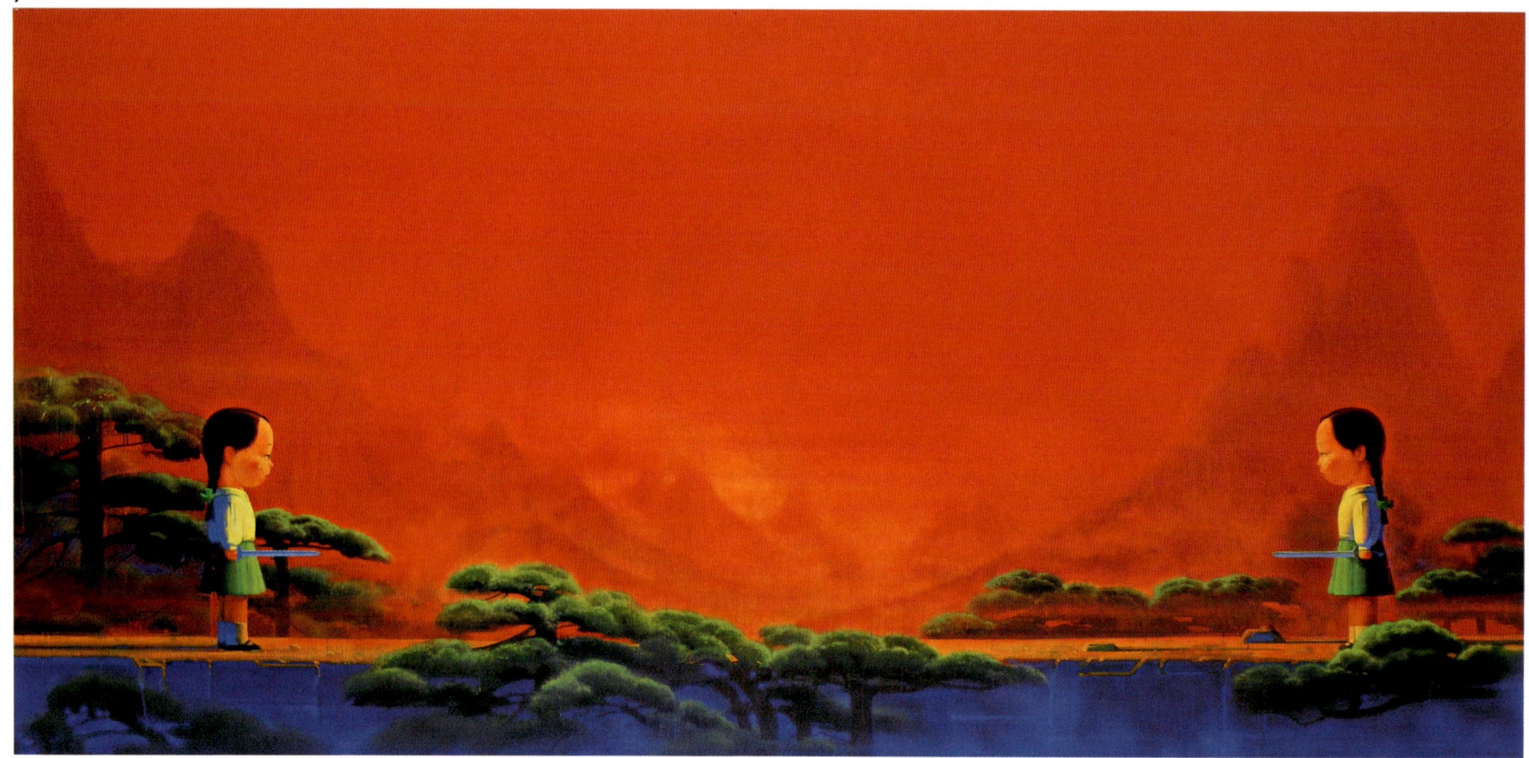

Dutch painter of the Northern Renaissance (1385–1441) or the Dutch painter of the 17th century Jan Vermeer van Delft (1632–1675), depicting scenes of Dutch life are the two real outstanding masters of the Age of Enlightenment. The distinct and prosaic style of Jean-Baptiste Siméon Chardin's (1699–1779) still life paintings influenced Liu Ye in his works, also.

Young boy Liu Ye, who started to realise his dream, was searching for the pure beauty of form in his "Composition with Square" (1998). He continued to paint his childhood dreams in "Killing me softly" (2002) depicting a girl with a knife in her hand and in "Sleepwalker" (2006) showing the little rabbit of Dick Bruna from its backside.

Further works reflecting the influence of childhood memories are the shivering "Snow White" (2006) or "Smoking Ruan Linyu" (2002). Liu Ye paints approximately only ten pictures per year. He lives among his pictures of love, peace and beauty and similar to Gong Qijun's movies doesn't care about mainstreams of art.

doch beim genauen Hinsehen bemerkt man, dass er, ganz im Stil der traditionellen Malerei, sorgfältig Linie um Linie und Schicht für Schicht auf die Leinwand bringt. Liu Ye interpretiert seine Vorbilder, die beiden Niederländer Jan van Eyck (1385–1441) und Jan Vermeer van Delft (1632–1675), die in strenger und klarer Manier Szenen aus dem Alltag wiedergaben, als zwei herausragende Meister der Aufklärung, doch auch die Nüchternheit der Stillleben eines Jean-Baptiste Siméon Chardin (1699–1779) beeinflusste Liu Ye bei den eigenen Arbeiten.

Das ewige Kind Liu Ye, als es seinen Kunsttraum zu realisieren begann, begab sich auf die Suche nach reiner Schönheit etwa in „Composition with Square" (1998) und malte seine Kindheitsträume in Bildern wie „Killing me softly" (2002), auf dem ein Mädchen mit einem Messer in der Hand zu sehen ist, in „Sleepwalker" (2006), das den kleinen Hasen Miffy von Dick Bruna von hinten zeigt, in „Snow White" (2006) oder „Smoking Ruan Linyu" (2002). Liu Ye malt im Jahr an die zehn Bilder über Liebe, Frieden und Schönheit, lebt ganz mit und in ihnen und schert sich so wenig wie Gong Qijun in seinen Filmen um Modeströmungen in der Kunst.

梦想起飞的小男孩儿刘野，复制在1998年《方格子的构图》里，他追求纯粹的形式美，不论是《温柔的杀我》中拿刀的小女孩，还是《梦游者》背对观众的Dick Bruna的小兔子，就连站在雪地中发抖的《白雪公主》，或者喷云吐雾的《吸烟的阮玲玉》，都是那个住在他身体里的小男孩儿的投影。每年平均只画十张画的刘野，他生活在自己创造的大爱、和平与唯美的画境之中，就像宫崎骏创作动画时一样，他们从来不在乎什么是主流的艺术。

Victoria Lu

8

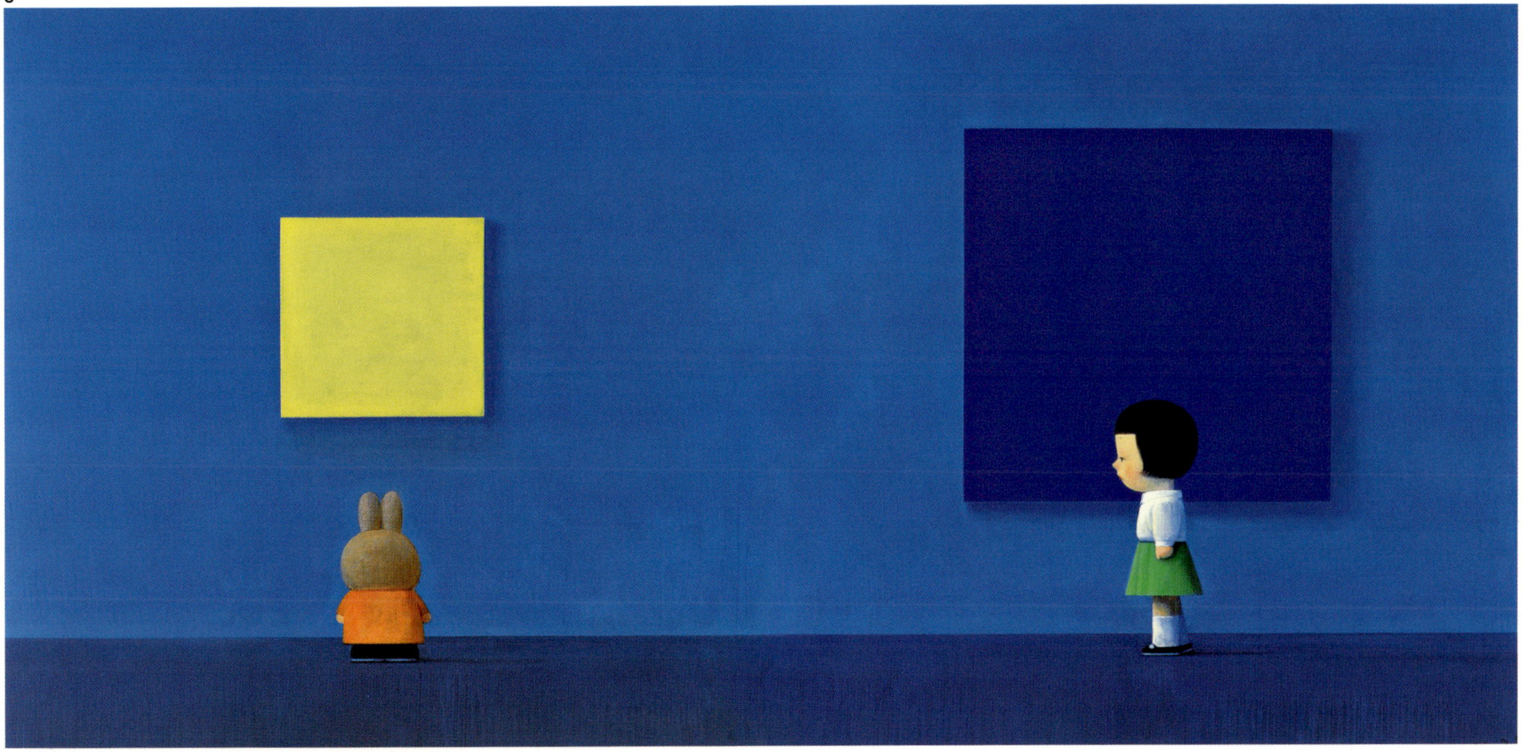

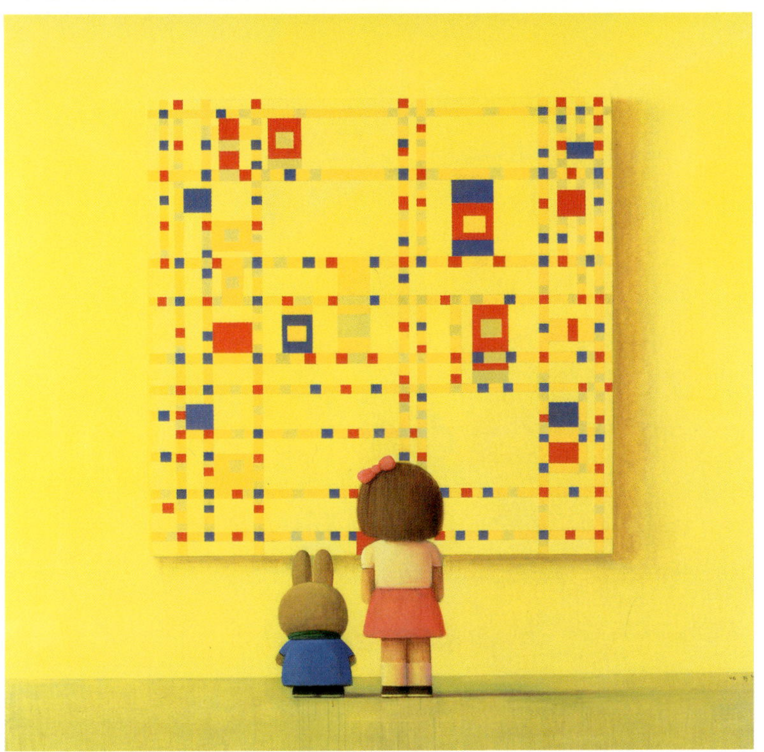

9

1 ***Ruan Ling-Yu***, *2002*
Acrylic and oil on canvas, 60 x 45 cm; Acryl und Öl auf Leinwand, 60 x 45 cm
《阮玲玉》2002年, 布面油画和丙烯，60 x 45 cm

2 ***Pink***, *2003*
Acrylic and oil on canvas, 90 x 90 cm; Acryl und Öl auf Leinwand, 90 x 90 cm
《粉》2003年, 布面油画和丙烯，90 x 90 cm

3 ***Who is afraid of Madame L***, *2005*
Acrylic and oil on canvas, 100 x 80 cm; Acryl und Öl auf Leinwand, 100 x 80 cm
《谁害怕L 女士?》2005年, 布面油画和丙烯, 100 x 80 cm

4 ***Portrait of L***, *2004*
Acrylic and oil on canvas, 100 x 80 cm; Acryl und Öl auf Leinwand, 100 x 80 cm
《L的肖像》2004年, 布面油画和丙烯, 100 x 80 cm

5 ***Banned Book***, *2006*
Acrylic and oil on canvas, 100 x 80 cm; Acryl und Öl auf Leinwand, 100 x 80 cm
《禁书》2006年, 布面油画和丙烯, 100 x 80 cm

6 ***Composition with Black, White and Grey***, *2006*
Acrylic and oil on canvas, 160 x 140 cm; Acryl und Öl auf Leinwand, 160 x 140 cm
《黑白灰》2006年, 布面油画和丙烯, 160 x 140 cm

7 ***Sword***, *2001/02*
Acrylic and oil on canvas, 180 x 360 cm; Acryl und Öl auf Leinwand, 180 x 360 cm
《剑》，2001/02年, 布面油画和丙烯, 180 x 360 cm

8 ***International Blue***, *2006*
Acrylic and oil on canvas, 210 x 420 cm; Acryl und Öl auf Leinwand, 210 x 420 cm
《国际蓝》, 2006年, 布面油画和丙烯, 210 x 420 cm

9 ***Once Upon a Time on Broadway***, *2005/06*
Acrylic and oil on canvas, 210 x 210 cm; Acryl und Öl auf Leinwand, 210 x 210 cm
《百老汇往事》2005/06年, 布面油画和丙烯, 210 x 210 cm

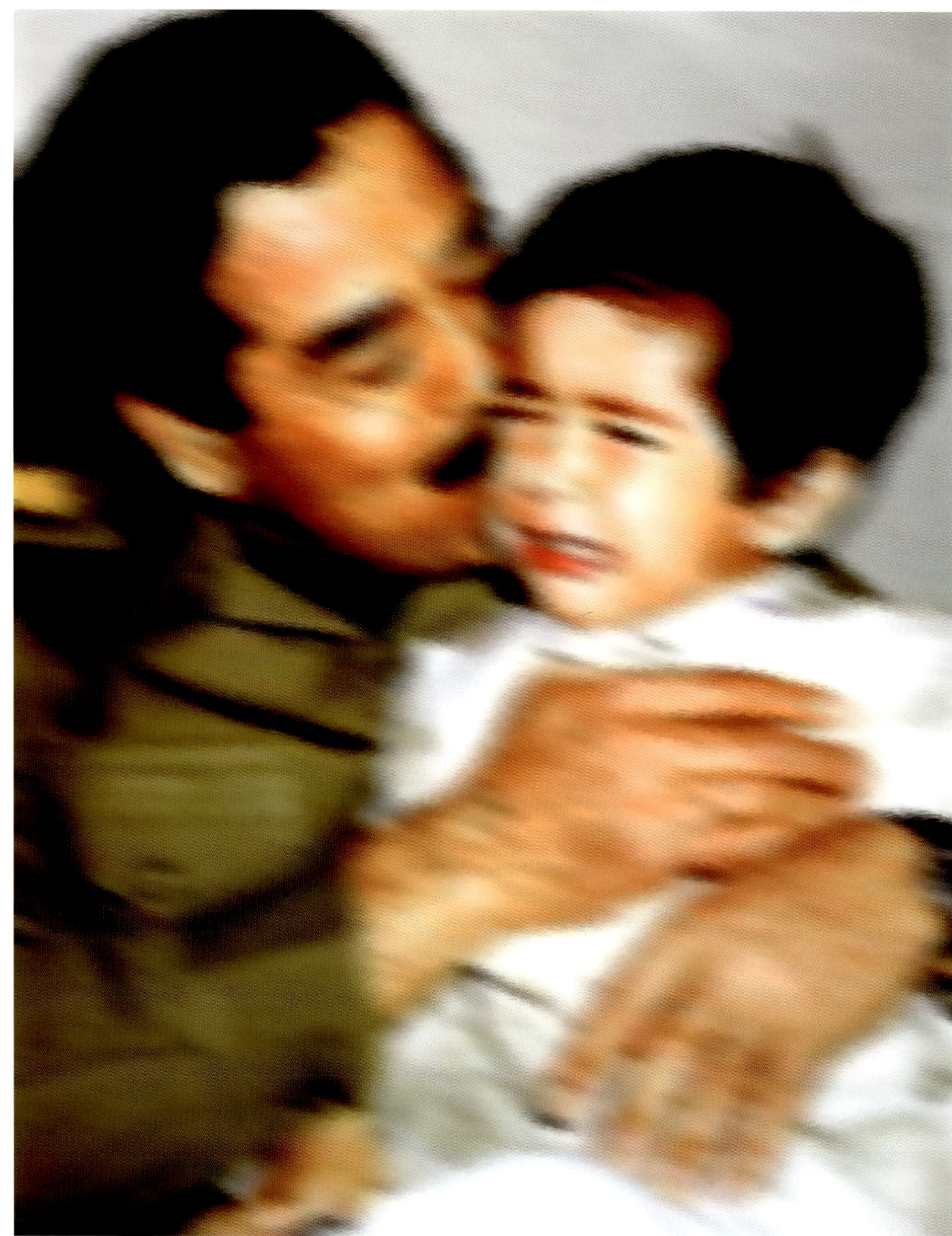

1

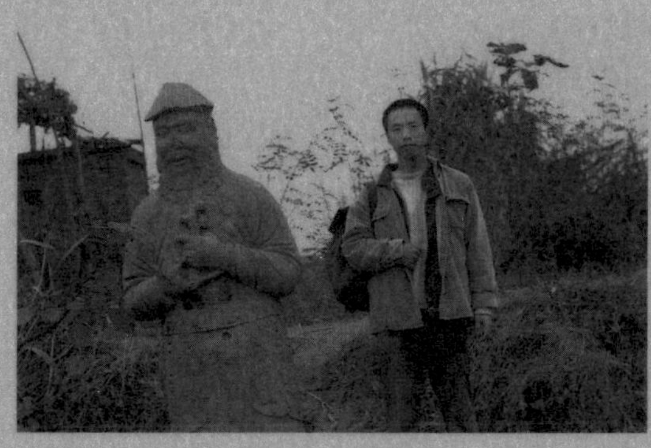

"I am not a humanist. I photograph these people to show the helpless absurdities of human existence."

„Ich bin kein Humanist. Ich fotografiere diese Menschen, um die hilflose Absurdität der menschlichen Existenz aufzuzeigen."

"我非人道主义者。我拍摄这些人目的在于展示人类存在的无助的荒谬。"

Born in 1969 in Hebei Province, China. Lives and works in Beijing
Geboren 1969 in der Provinz Hebei, China. Lebt und arbeitet in Peking
1969年出生于中国河北省,现在北京居住工作

***Selected exhibitions* / Ausgewählte Ausstellungen /** 所选展览

2001 "The Chinese", Central Academy of Fine Arts, Beijing, China
2002 "Sagamihara City – 2nd Annual Asian Photo Festival", Sagamihara, Japan
2003 "Liu Zheng – Rencontres d'Arles", Photography Festival Arles, France
2004 "Die Chinesen – Fotografie und Video aus China", Kunstmuseum Wolfsburg, Wolfsburg, Germany
2005 The 6th Gwangju Biennale 2006, Gwangju, Korea
2006 "Under The Sun", Art Beijing 2006, Beijing, China

2001年 《国人》中央美院 北京，中国
2002年 《相模原市综合摄影展》相模原市，日本
2003年 《阿尔勒摄影节》法国阿尔勒。
2004年 《国人》沃尔斯堡美术馆 德国
2005年 《热风变奏曲》第六届光洲双年展，韩国
2006年 《太阳底下》艺术北京，北京，中国

***Selected publications* / Ausgewählte Publikationen /** 所选著作

"China New Photo", in: "Photographers International", no. 41, 1998
Jonathan Goodman: "Human, Demonic and Divine in the Photographs of Liu Zheng", in: "Art on Paper", vol. 4, no. 3, 2000
Wu Hung: "Photographing Deformity: Liu Zheng and his Photo Series 'My Countrymen'", in: "Public Culture", vol. 13, no. 3, 2001
Meg Maggio: "A contrary vision", interview with Liu Zheng, in: "Asian Art News", vol. 12, no. 4, July/August 2002

《中国新摄影》摄影师国际版 第41期（1998）
Goodman, Jonathan （著）:《刘铮摄影中的人、鬼、神》Art on Paper 第四卷第三期，2000年一月和二月合刊
巫鸿（著）:《拍影残疾:刘铮和他的摄影系列‘国人’》, 公开文化, 第13卷, 刊3, 2001年
Maggio, Meg 著:《刘铮访谈》, 亚洲艺术新闻 2002年七、八月

"I am not a humanist. I photograph these people to show the helpless absurdities of human existence."

„Ich bin kein Humanist. Ich fotografiere diese Menschen, um die hilflose Absurdität der menschlichen Existenz aufzuzeigen."

"我非人道主义者。我拍摄这些人目的在于展示人类存在的无助的荒谬。"

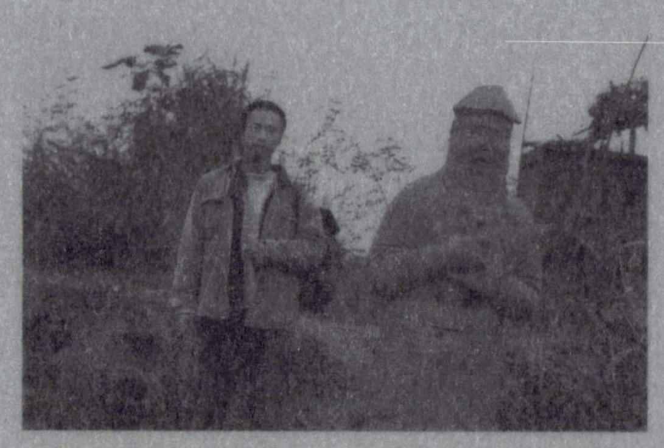

Born in 1969 in Hebei Province, China. Lives and works in Beijing
Geboren 1969 in der Provinz Hebei, China. Lebt und arbeitet in Peking
1969年出生于中国河北省，现在北京居住工作

Selected exhibitions / Ausgewählte Ausstellungen / 所选展览

2001 "The Chinese", Central Academy of Fine Arts, Beijing, China
2002 "Sagamihara City - 2nd Annual Asian Photo Festival", Sagamihara, Japan
2003 "Liu Zheng - Rencontres d'Arles", Photography Festival Arles, France
2004 "Die Chinesen - Fotografie und Video aus China", Kunstmuseum Wolfsburg, Wolfsburg, Germany
2005 The 6th Gwangju Biennale 2006, Gwangju, Korea
2006 "Under The Sun", Art Beijing 2006, Beijing, China

2001年 《国人》中央美院 北京，中国
2002年 《相模原市综合摄影展》相模原市，日本
2003年 《阿尔勒摄影节》法国阿尔勒。
2004年 《国人》沃尔斯堡美术馆 德国
2005年 《热风变奏曲》第六届光州双年展，韩国
2006年 《太阳底下》艺术北京，北京，中国

Selected publications / Ausgewählte Publikationen / 所选著作

"China New Photo", in: "Photographers International", no. 41, 1998
Jonathan Goodman: "Human, Demonic and Divine in the Photographs of Liu Zheng", in: "Art on Paper", vol. 4, no. 3, 2000
Wu Hung: "Photographing Deformity: Liu Zheng and his Photo Series 'My Countrymen'", in: "Public Culture", vol. 13, no. 3, 2001
Meg Maggio: "A contrary vision", interview with Liu Zheng, in: "Asian Art News", vol. 12, no. 4, July/August 2002

《中国新摄影》摄影师国际版 第41期（1998）
Goodman, Jonathan（著）：《刘铮摄影中的人、鬼、神》Art on Paper 第四卷第三期，2000年一月和二月合刊
巫鸿（著）：《拍摄残疾：刘铮和他的摄影系列'国人'》，公开文化，第13卷，刊3，2001年
Maggio, Meg 著：《刘铮访谈》，亚洲艺术新闻 2002年七，八月

LIU ZHENG 刘铮

[liou ʈʂɤŋ]

The scope, ambition and seriousness of Liu Zheng's photographic projects set him apart from nearly every other photographer working in China today. Liu came to art through technology, particularly optics, his specialization at the army-run Beijing Institute of Technology where he studied in the late 1980s. He established an early record as abnormal, in one case following a PLA instructor whom he knew as a proficient photographer everywhere the man went. His first job after college, with the Beijing municipal mining bureau, sent him photographing miners in the city's own tiny mines. Refusing to account for the vast quantities of extra film he had commandeered from the bureau for his own project, Liu Zheng quit this job as he would a number of successive gigs. This chosen alienation from normal society was perhaps the basis for his epic series "Guoren" (a May Fourth-era nationalist term for Chinese compatriots), alternately translated "My Countrymen" and, after Robert Frank, "The Chinese".

Realized over the course of a long series of travels, "The Chinese" (1994–2001) comprises one hundred black-and-white photographs which together offer a stirring portrait of the underbelly of Chinese society at the turn of the millennium. Comparisons to Diane Arbus and August Sander have been drawn. Shot partially during Liu's time as a photojournalist for the "Workers' Daily", these images portray temple clowns, transvestites, fire breathers, prisoners, ethnic minorities, and corpses, framed in a tone of no-nonsense seriousness rarely and with a subtle technical virtuosity rarely evident in photographic work from the mid-1990s. His relationship to his subjects also bears mentioning – unlike the scads of quasi-documentary, digitally manipulated, staged, and performance-based photography that characterize the era, Liu Zheng's portraits derive often from a lived relationship to his consenting sitters. Others images are staged, but the boundary between artifice and documentation is never made clear.

The experience of photographing these often wretched scenes also deeply altered the artist's own subjectivity,

Liu Zheng hebt sich durch Umfang, Ehrgeiz und Ernsthaftigkeit seiner fotografischen Projekte von fast allen anderen Fotografen ab, die derzeit in China tätig sind. Liu kam durch die Technik zur Kunst, genauer gesagt durch die Optik, sein Hauptfach am militärischen Beijing Institute of Technology, wo er in den späten 1980er Jahren studierte. Er erwarb sich schon dort den Ruf, ein wenig besessen zu sein – so folgte er einem Ausbilder, der ihm als fähiger Fotograf bekannt war, für eine Weile auf Schritt und Tritt. Seine erste Anstellung nach dem College, beim Pekinger Bergbauamt, führte ihn in die winzigen Minen der Stadt, wo er die Bergleute fotografierte. Nach Querelen um gewaltige Mengen zusätzlichen Filmmaterials, das er vom Bergbauamt für seine eigenen Zwecke abgezweigt hatte, gab Liu Zheng diesen Job auf, wie auch eine Reihe weiterer kurzfristiger Arbeitsverhältnisse. Diese selbst gewählte Entfremdung von der normalen Gesellschaft legte vielleicht den Grundstein für seine monumentale Serie „Guoren" (ein nationalistischer Begriff für chinesische Landleute der Ära des 4. Mai), die mal als „My Countrymen", mal, nach Robert Frank, als „The Chinese" übersetzt wird.

„The Chinese" (1994–2001) entstand im Laufe mehrerer Reisen und umfasst 100 Schwarzweißfotografien, die ein erschütterndes Bild von den Niederungen der chinesischen Gesellschaft um die Jahrtausendwende zeichnen. Sie brachte Liu Vergleiche mit Diane Arbus und August Sander ein. Die Bilder, die er teils während seiner Zeit als Fotojournalist für „Workers' Daily" schoss, porträtieren Tempelclowns, Transvestiten, Feuerschlucker, Häftlinge, ethnische Minderheiten und Leichen, in nüchterner Seriosität und subtiler technischer Virtuosität, wie sie bei fotografischen Arbeiten ab Mitte der 1990er Jahre selten zu finden ist. Erwähnenswert ist auch Lius Beziehung zu seinen Modellen – anders als bei vielen quasi-dokumentarischen, digital bearbeiteten, inszenierten und performance-basierten Fotografien, die prägend für die Zeit sind, sind Liu Zhengs Porträts häufig das Resultat einer gelebten Beziehung zu seinen Modellen. Und auch, wo die Bilder gestellt sind, wird die Grenze zwischen Kunstgriff und Dokumentation nie deutlich.

刘铮摄影作品的角度、志向和严肃性而使其与其他当代摄影师与众不同。刘铮技术出身，后转行艺术领域。80年代末他在北京理工大学学习，对光学尤为精通。他的摄影事业纯属偶然，他曾经追随一位解放军讲师，那位老师是摄影专家，去过很多地方。大学毕业后的第一个单位是北京市矿务局，单位分派他去当地的一个小煤矿区拍摄矿工的生活。为拍摄其自己的项目作品，他向局里申请了许多胶片，而他却拒绝解释这些大量胶片的用途，于是刘铮辞去这份工作。他选择的远离正常社会的生活，也许是他史诗般系列作品《国人》（五四运动时期民族主义者对同胞的称呼）的创作基础，也有人将之翻译为《我的同胞》。

1994年到2001年在长期的旅行历程之后，他组织了一百多幅黑白照片，这些照片生动的描绘了千禧年之交中国底层社会的芸芸众生。这些创作类似于Diane Arbus 和August Sander 的作品。这些照片部分是其供职于工人日报期间拍摄，以一种正经的严肃腔调和90年代摄影作品中所体现的微妙技术鉴赏力，描绘了僧侣 农民、僧侣、流浪者、囚犯、富人、乞丐、戏子、舞女、诗人、未亡人、残疾人、变性人、死尸、干尸等。他所涉及的主题也尤值得一提，与那个时期标记性的准记录性、数字处理和编排的和表演性的摄影作品不同，刘铮的绘画常常来源于模特的现场表演。其他图片拍摄完成，但是艺术作品和文件记录之间的边界永远不可能泾渭分明。这些常常是污秽场面的摄影实践也深刻地改变着艺术家自己的主观性，也让他更近地面对着死亡、残疾和不满。

创作这些作品时，刘铮认识了荣荣，随后年轻的艺术家记录了东村艺术家的表演活动。他们两人一起创办了《新摄影》杂志，虽然发行时间不长，但是影响很大，1996年到1997年共发行了四期，上面登载了青年概念艺术家的影印作品。
其他两个史诗般的系列作品《革命》和《三界》仍未完成。前者采用剧本编排的摄影形式，呈现

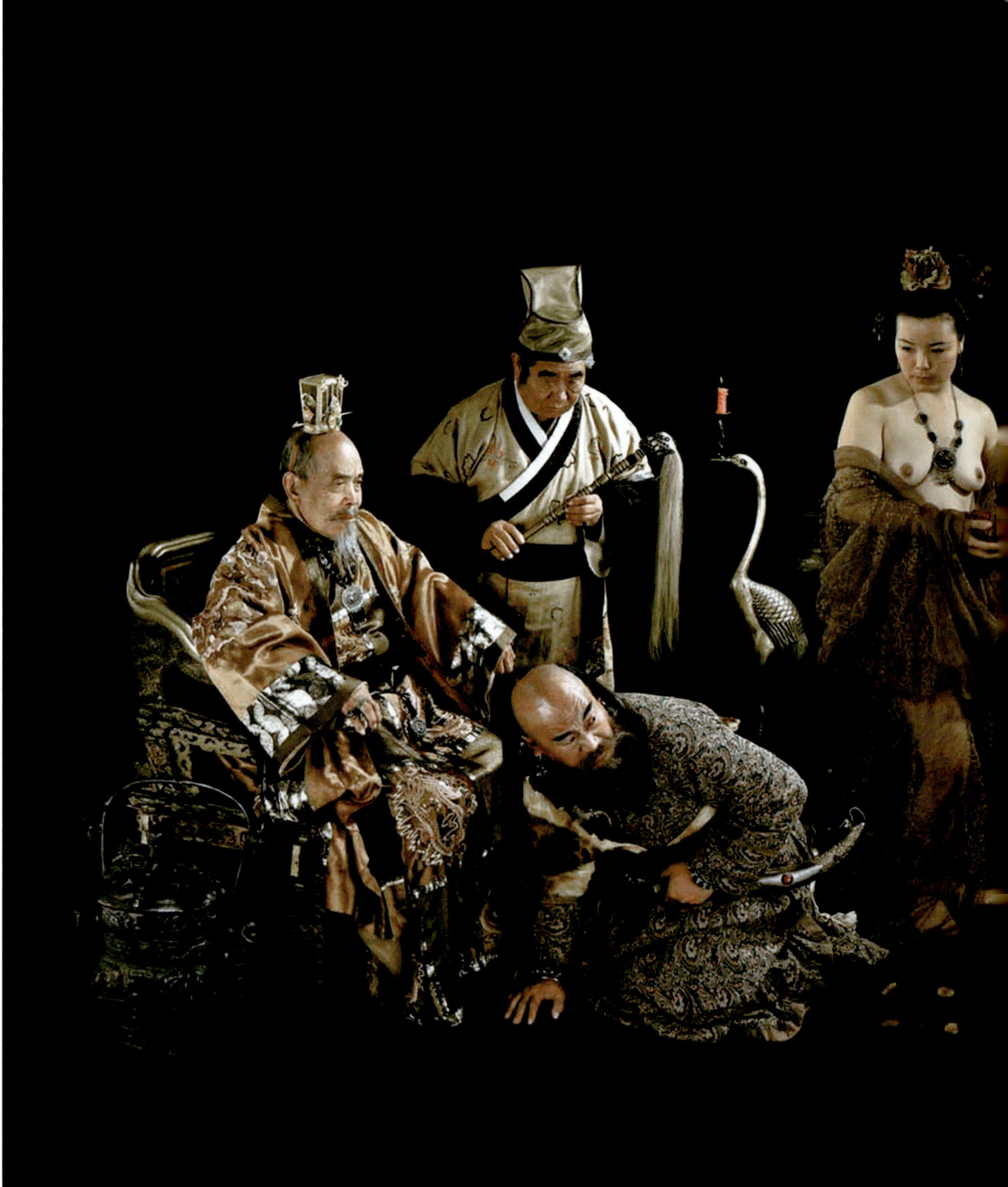

2

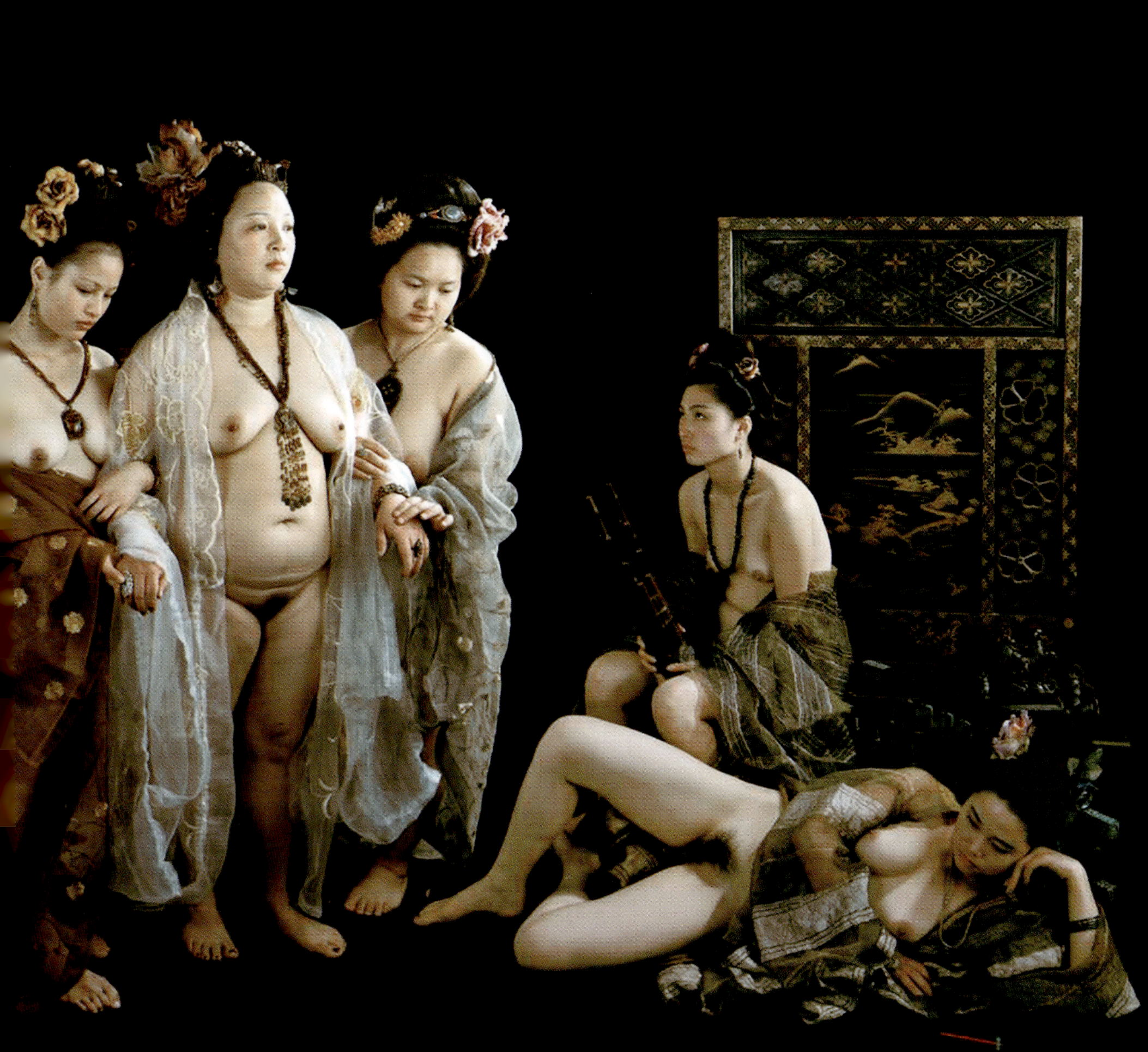

3

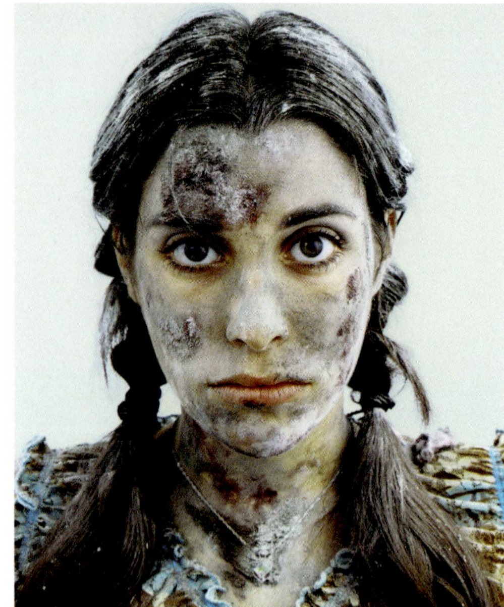

4

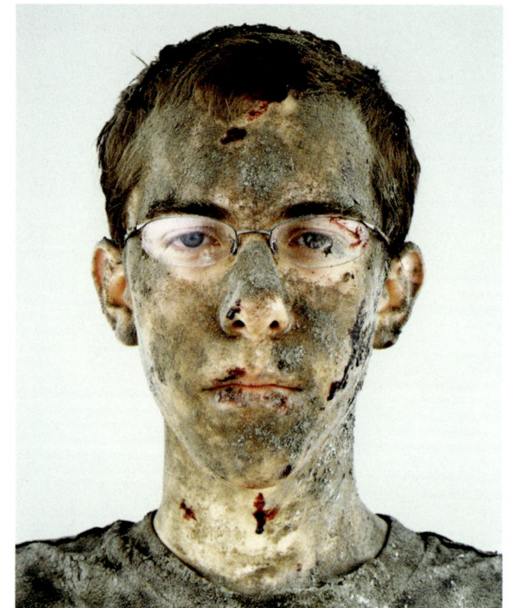

5

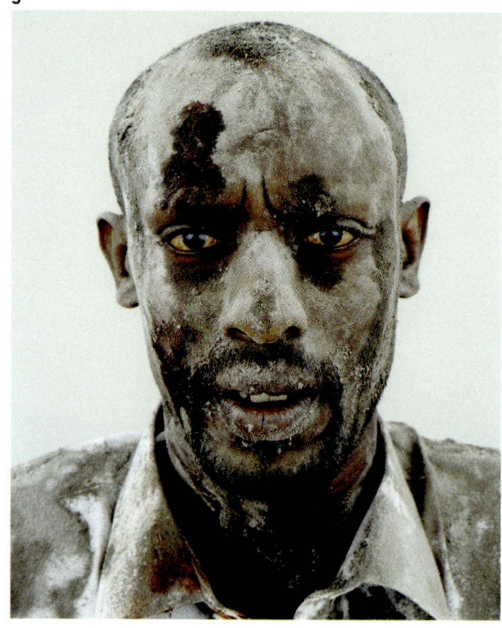

bringing him into close confrontation with death, disability, and disaffection. While working on "The Chinese", Liu Zheng made the acquaintance of RongRong, then a young photographer chronicling the performances of the East Village artists. Together they launched a short-lived but highly influential magazine called "Newphoto", its four issues produced in 1996 and 1997 and consisting of photocopied versions of works by young conceptual photographers crudely stapled together.

Two other epic series remain incomplete, "Revolution" and "Three Realms". The former resorts to highly scripted photographic forms to present overly fabricated tableaux of revolutionary scenes, sometimes modified in the direction of soft pornography. "Three Realms" (named for the Buddhist concept of separate spheres of existence for humans, deities, and suffering souls) includes a number of sub-series such as "Peking Opera" (1997) and "Four Beauties" (2004). In the "Peking Opera"-photographs, canonical scenes from classical dramas are modified as the female players are stripped of their clothes. These photographs have recently provoked criticism from cultural conservatives, a full decade after their completion. "Survivor" (2005) portrays bedraggled foreigners with ashen faces, in apparent reference to 9/11 news photographs. His most recent series "Under the Sun" (2006) entails a Richteresque compilation of images ranging from topless women on a speedboat to the injured Che Guevara. Some of the images are staged, others are rephotographed and digitally altered.

Der Blickwinkel des Fotografen änderte sich durch die Erfahrung, diese häufig elenden Szenen zu fotografieren, die ihn eng mit Tod, Behinderung und Unvermögen konfrontierten. Während seiner Arbeit an „The Chinese" machte Liu Zheng die Bekanntschaft von RongRong, der damals als junger Fotograf die Performances der East-Village-Künstler dokumentierte. Zusammen gründeten sie ein kurzlebiges, aber sehr einflussreiches Magazin namens „Newphoto", dessen vier Ausgaben 1996 und 1997 erschienen und aus fotokopierten und behelfsmäßig zusammengehefteten Reproduktionen der Arbeiten junger Konzeptfotografen bestanden.

Zwei weitere monumentale Serien sind bis heute unvollendet: „Revolution" und „Three Realms". Erstere präsentiert, minuziös ausgearbeitet, konstruierte Tableaus revolutionärer Szenen, die sich bisweilen der Softpornografie nähern. „Three Realms" (nach der buddhistischen Vorstellung unterschiedlicher Lebenssphären für Menschen, Gottheiten und leidende Seelen) umfasst eine Reihe von „Unterserien" wie „Peking Opera" (1997) und „Four Beauties" (2004). „Peking Opera" wandelt bekannte Szenen aus klassischen Dramen ab, indem Liu die weiblichen Mitwirkenden ihrer Kleidung beraubt; gerade diese Fotografien wurden noch unlängst von Kulturkonservativen kritisiert – ein volles Jahrzehnt nach ihrer Entstehung. „Survivor" (2005) porträtiert derangierte Ausländer mit aschgrauen Gesichtern, offensichtlich auf Nachrichtenfotos vom 11. September 2001 anspielend. Liu Zhengs jüngste Serie „Under the Sun" (2006) kompiliert in Richterscher Manier Bilder von barbusigen Frauen auf einem Speedboat bis hin zum verwundeten Che Guevara; einige sind gestellt, andere abfotografiert und digital überarbeitet.

了虚构的由真人表演的革命场景，有时带有软色情场面。作品《三界》（佛学概念中三个独立的存在方　式：人、神、鬼）包含许多子系列　作　品，如《京剧》（1997年）和《四美图》（2004年）。在《京剧》摄影作品中，艺术家改编了经典戏剧场景，女演员大部分身体裸露着。这些作品在完成整整十年之后，最近却招致了传统文化的批评。在最近9/11新闻摄影参考中，幸存者肖像画中的外国人满是灰尘，脸色苍白。最近的系列作品《太阳底下》继承了Richteresque　的编辑方式，从游艇上坦胸露背的女人到受伤的切.格瓦拉。其中的一些照片被拿去展出，而其他的或是重新拍摄或是被数字处理。

Philip Tinari

6

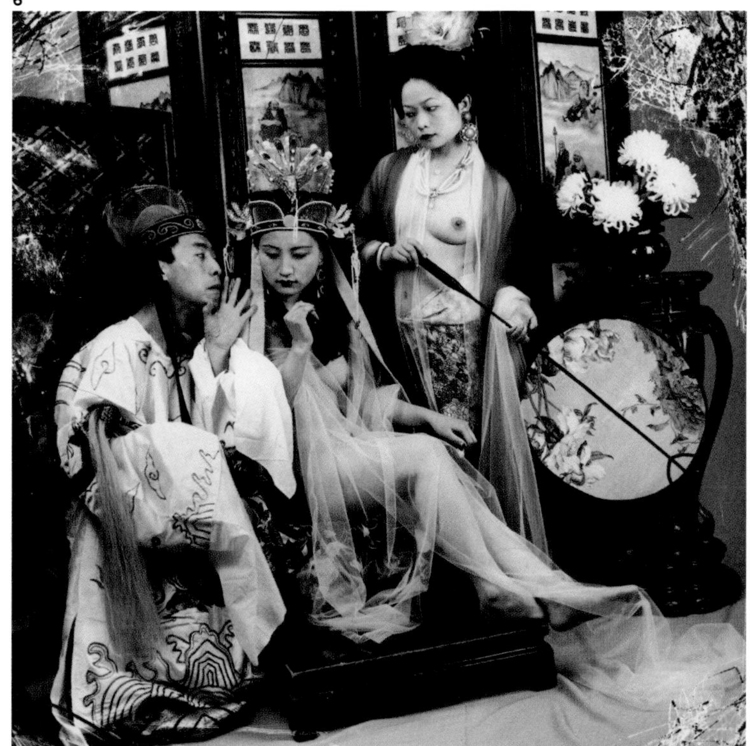

7

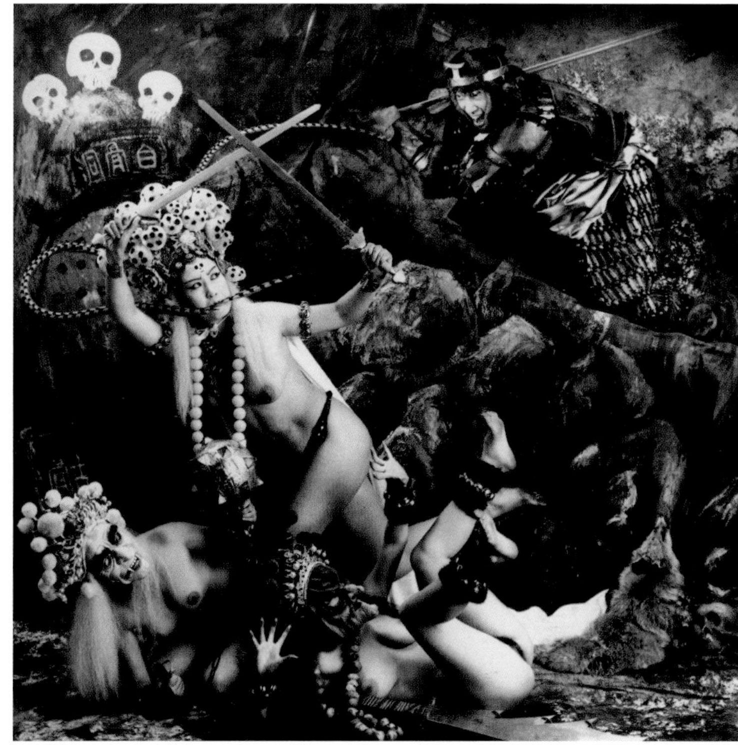

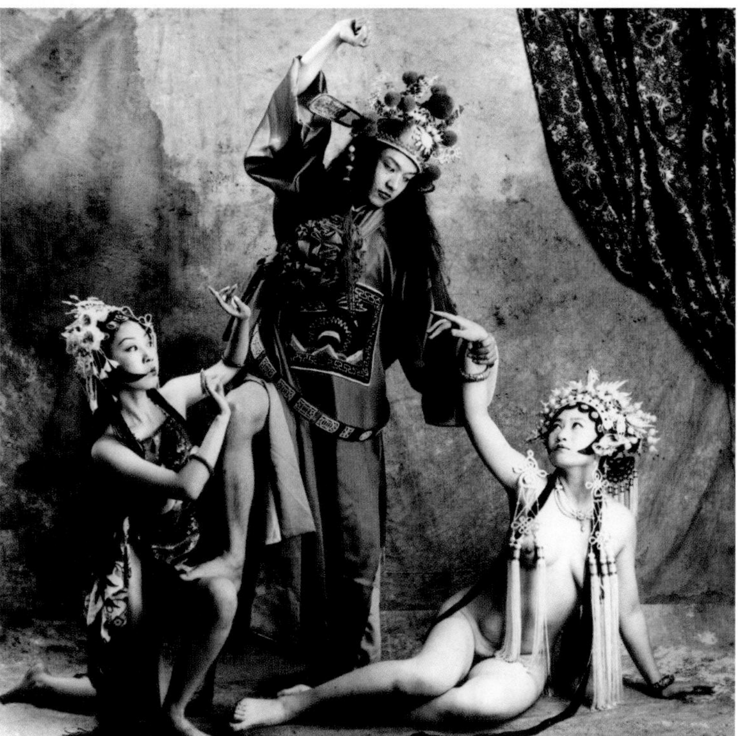

8

1 ***Saddam***, *2004*
C-print, 140 x 100 cm; C-print, 140 x 100 cm
《撒旦》2004年, C-印刷, 140 x 100 cm

2 ***Four Beauties***, *2003*
C-print, 100 x 200 cm; C-print, 100 x 200 cm
《四美图》2003年, C-印刷, 100 x 200 cm

3 ***Survivor No. 4***, *2005*
C-print, 220 x 160 cm; C-print, 220 x 160 cm
《受害者No. 4》2005年, C-印刷, 220 x 160 cm

4 ***Survivor No. 8***, *2005*
C-print, 220 x 160 cm; C-print, 220 x 160 cm
《受害者No. 8》2005年, C-印刷, 220 x 160 cm

5 ***Survivor No. 3***, *2005*
C-print, 220 x 160 cm; C-print, 220 x 160 cm
《受害者No. 3》2005年, C-印刷, 220 x 160 cm

6 ***Peking Opera – Self Portrait***, *1997*
Gelatin silver print, 46 x 46 cm; Silbergelatineabzug, 46 x 46 cm
《京剧-自画像》1997年, 明胶银版印刷, 46 x 46 cm

7 ***Peking Opera – Quelling the White Bonded Demon***, *1997*
Gelatin silver print, 46 x 46 cm; Silbergelatineabzug, 46 x 46 cm
《京剧 - 三打白骨精》1997年, 明胶银版印刷, 46 x 46 cm

8 ***Peking Opera – Beating the Princess***, *1997*
Gelatin silver print, 46 x 46 cm; Silbergelatineabzug, 46 x 46 cm
《京剧—醉打金枝》1997年, 明胶银版印刷, 46 x 46 cm

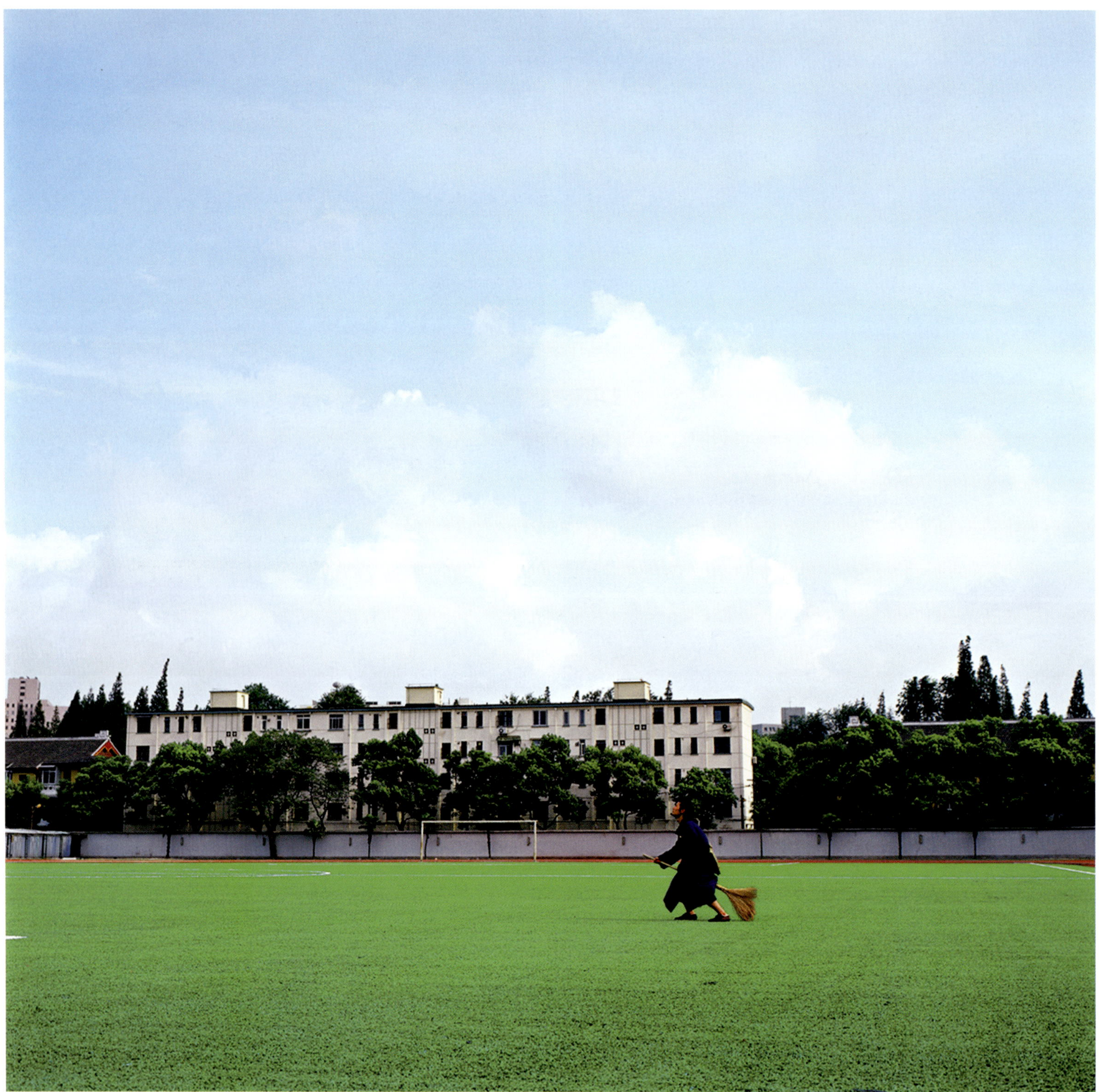

1

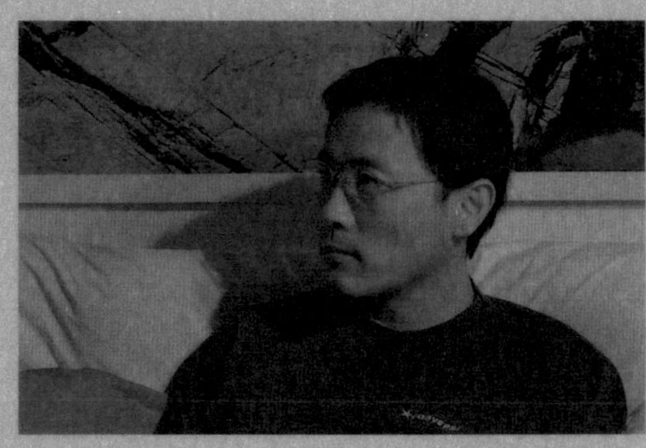

"If I was going to write a novel, I wish my writing would be a 'science fiction' which was bound to become a science novel."

„Wenn ich einen Roman schreiben würde, wünschte ich, es wäre ‚Science-Fiction', die zu einem Wissenschaftsroman werden müsste."

"如果写小说的话，我希望写一种即将成为科幻小说的"科幻小说。"

Born in 1968 in Changchun, China. Lives and works in Shanghai
Geboren 1968 in Changchun, China. Lebt und arbeitet in Shanghai
1968年出生于中国吉林长春，现生活和工作于上海

***Selected exhibitions* / Ausgewählte Ausstellungen / 所选展览**

2000 "Uncooperative Approach (Fuck Off!)", Eastlink Gallery, Shanghai, China
2001 "Living in Time – Contemporary Artists from China", Nationalgalerie im Hamburger Bahnhof , Museum für Gegenwartskunst, Berlin, Germany
2002 First Guangzhou Triennial, Guangdong Museum of Art, Guangzhou, China
2003 "Echigo – Tsumari Art Triennial, 2003", Niigata, Japan
"Fabricated Paradises", Le Parvis centre d'art contemporain, Pau, France
2005 "Out of Sight", De Appel, Amsterdam, The Netherlands
2007 "Thermocline of Art: New Asian Waves", ZKM (Center for Art and Media), Karlsruhe, Germany

2000年 《不和作方式》上海东廊，上海
2001年 《生活在此时：中国当代艺术展》柏林汉堡火车站，当代美术馆，柏林，德国
2002年 《首届广州三年展 -- 重新解读：中国实验艺术十年（1990-2000年）》广东美术馆，广州
2003年 越后妻有三年展，新潟，日本
《自制天堂》Le Parvis当代艺术中心，波城，法国
2005年 《视线之外》De Appel 基金会，阿姆斯特丹，荷兰
2007年 《艺术温跃层：亚洲新浪潮》德国艺术与媒体中心，卡斯鲁尔厄，德国

***Selected publications* / Ausgewählte Publikationen / 所选著作**

"Beyond Boundaries: Shanghai Gallery of Art '04 – '05", Shanghai 2005

《超越界限 -- 沪申画廊2004-2005》，沪申画廊，上海 2005年

"If I was going to write a novel, I wish my writing would be a 'science fiction' which was bound to become a science novel."

„Wenn ich einen Roman schreiben würde, wünschte ich, es wäre ‚Science-Fiction', die zu einem Wissenschaftsroman werden müsste."

"如果写小说的话，我希望写一种即将成为科幻小说的"科幻小说。"

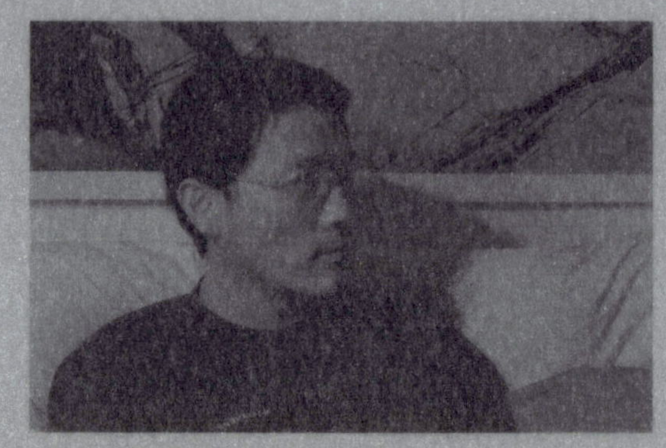

Born in 1968 in Changchun, China. Lives and works in Shanghai
Geboren 1968 in Changchun, China. Lebt und arbeitet in Shanghai
1968年出生于中国吉林长春，现生活和工作于上海

Selected exhibitions / Ausgewählte Ausstellungen / 所选展览

2000 "Uncooperative Approach (Fuck Off!)", Eastlink Gallery, Shanghai, China
2001 "Living in Time – Contemporary Artists from China", Nationalgalerie im Hamburger Bahnhof , Museum für Gegenwartskunst, Berlin, Germany
2002 First Guangzhou Triennial, Guangdong Museum of Art, Guangzhou, China
2003 "Echigo – Tsumari Art Triennial, 2003", Niigata, Japan
"Fabricated Paradises", Le Parvis centre d'art contemporain, Pau, France
2005 "Out of Sight", De Appel, Amsterdam, The Netherlands
2007 "Thermocline of Art: New Asian Waves", ZKM (Center for Art and Media), Karlsruhe, Germany

2000年 《不合作方式》上海东廊，上海
2001年 《生活在此时：中国当代艺术展》柏林汉堡火车站，当代美术馆，柏林，德国
2002年 《首届广州三年展 — 重新解读：中国实验艺术十年（1990-2000年）》广东美术馆，广州
2003年 越后妻有三年展，新潟，日本
《自制天堂》Le Parvis当代艺术中心，波城，法国
2005年 《视线之外》De Appel 基金会，阿姆斯特丹，荷兰
2007年 《艺术温跃层：亚洲新浪潮》德国艺术与媒体中心，卡斯鲁尔厄，德国

Selected publications / Ausgewählte Publikationen / 所选著作

"Beyond Boundaries: Shanghai Gallery of Art '04 - '05", Shanghai 2005

《超越界限 — 沪申画廊2004-2005》，沪申画廊，上海 2005年

LU CHUNSHENG 陆春生

[lu ʈʂʰuənʂɤŋ]

Although originally studying sculpture at China National Academy of Fine Arts in Hangzhou, Lu Chunsheng since 1999 started experimenting with a camera. Nowadays, he is one of the most important photographers and filmmakers in China.

His first video work, "The Curve Can Cough" (2000), captures pedestrians as they walk between buildings from a bird's eye view. The series of photographs entitled "I Want to be a Gentleman" from 2000 represents men standing on tall pillars almost like on a museum display in an industrial area, while the photograph "Water" from the same year shot the man in a night gown standing still and relaxed while water accumulates around him.

"Trotsky Murdered in Summer, Gentlemen in Financial Circles Got More Depressed" (2003) is a video that takes Trotsky as a symbol not necessarily sticking to the historical relevance of the story. He uses the symbol of the top hat and Trotsky to tell the story dealing with ideas of destiny and collective memory.

The artist's interests in the Industrial Era and the urban texture of everyday life can be seen in his use of image narration and his setting of scenes. Furthermore, at times his work becomes a labyrinth-like story of emotion, actions without particular aim or direction.

In 2005 his series of photographs "Xiao" made in narrative sequences show odd scenes in an urban environment. "Carlin" series shows a person riding on a broom and includes other images of the broom in different urban settings. Another photography piece called "One of the Most Foolish Attacks Against Science Fiction" is about the idea that one cannot forecast the future. "The First White Person to be Pushed Down #1" shows a white man encircled with group of people on an edge of the cliff.

Lu Chunsheng's own unique film language can be seen in the video titled "The History of Chemistry 1" (2004), a work

Nachdem er ursprünglich Bildhauerei an der China National Academy of Fine Arts in Hangzhou studiert hatte, begann Lu Chunsheng ab 1999 mit der Kamera zu experimentieren. Inzwischen ist er einer der bedeutendsten Fotografen und Filmemacher Chinas.

In seiner ersten Videoarbeit „The Curve Can Cough" (2000) fing er Fußgänger, die zwischen Gebäuden umhergingen, aus der Vogelperspektive ein. Die Fotoserie „I Want to Be a Gentleman" aus dem Jahr 2000 zeigt Männer auf hohen Pfeilern in einem Industriegebiet stehend – fast wie in einer Museumsausstellung. Die Fotoserie „Water" aus dem selben Jahr stellt einen Mann im Nachthemd dar, der ruhig und entspannt dasteht, während sich Wasser um ihn ausbreitet.

Das Video „Trotzky Murdered in Summer, Gentlemen in Financial Circles Got More Depressed" (2003) hält sich nicht notwendigerweise an die historische Relevanz des Themas, vielmehr nutzt der Künstler die Symbole Zylinder und Trotzki, um eine Geschichte zu erzählen, in der es vor allem um Schicksal und kollektive Erinnerung geht.

Lus Interesse am Industriezeitalter und der urbanen Textur des Alltagslebens wird daran deutlich, wie er bildhaftes Erzählen und die Schauplätze seiner Szenarien einsetzt. Sein Werk gerät dabei mitunter zu einer labyrinthisch verschlungenen, emotionalen Erzählung voller Handlung, doch ohne spezielle Zielsetzung oder Richtung.

2005 zeigte Lus Fotoserie „Xiao", in erzählerischer Abfolge geschossen, seltsame Szenen in städtischer Umgebung. Die Serie „Carlin" zeigt jemanden, der auf einem Besen reitet, der auch in anderen städtischen Szenarien wieder auftaucht. Eine Fotoarbeit mit dem Titel „One of the Most Foolish Attacks Against Science Fiction" thematisiert die Einsicht, dass sich die Zukunft nicht voraussagen lässt, während „The First White Person to be Pushed Down #1" einen weißen Mann am Rand einer Steilküste zeigt, der von einer Menschenmenge eingekesselt ist.

虽然最初在杭州的中国美院学习雕塑，但是陆春生从1999年开始用摄像机创作。如今，陆春生是中国最重要的摄影师和电影制片人之一。

他的首部录像作品《会咳嗽的曲线》(2001年)以鸟瞰的镜头捕捉院子里人们循着路径穿行时的情景。自2000年开始拍摄的组照《我想做一个绅士》，衰败的工业建筑物前，9个男人站在很高的方形柱上，就像是博物馆里被展出的雕像一般。而同年的摄影系列《水》也是选择一种类似的场景：水泥广场上面站立着一位穿着白大褂睡衣的人，从他的脚底下正慢慢地渗出一滩水，照片记录着水正在渐渐地扩大的过程。录像《托洛茨基在夏天被谋杀，金融界的先生们变得更沮丧了》把托洛茨基描述为与历史没有多少联系的标志。他以礼帽和托洛茨基为符号讲述命运和集体记忆的故事。

从图像叙述和场景中。我们可以看出他对工业合金钢和日常生活中的纺织品的兴趣。另外，他的作品象在讲述一个充满感情而无方向的费解的故事。2005年的组照《Xiao》由叙述　性的片断组成，揭示城市环境中的奇怪现象。《女巫》系列上一张照片上一个人跨在扫帚上，而其他照片拍摄了不同城市场景中的扫帚。而另一个摄影作品《对科幻小说最愚蠢的抨击之一是认为它不能预测未来》讲述了未　来不可预　测的观　点。而《第一个被推下的白人》则展示了峭壁边上的被一群人围着的白人。

从全球展映的录像作品《化学史之一》(2004年)中，陆春生独特的电影语言可见一斑。在《化学史》中，艺术家缓缓地移动着摄像机，以获得纯朴稳定的全景镜头，捕捉无名人群的经历。当这群年轻人离开神秘的大陆开始航行时，录像达到了高潮，在船长的带领下来到航程的终点工业大中心。录像虽然无语，但是精心的场景和音乐选择，录像的每一幕都能勾起观众心中复杂的感情。最后一幕中，年轻的小伙子，手持锤子，象征着文明的开端。

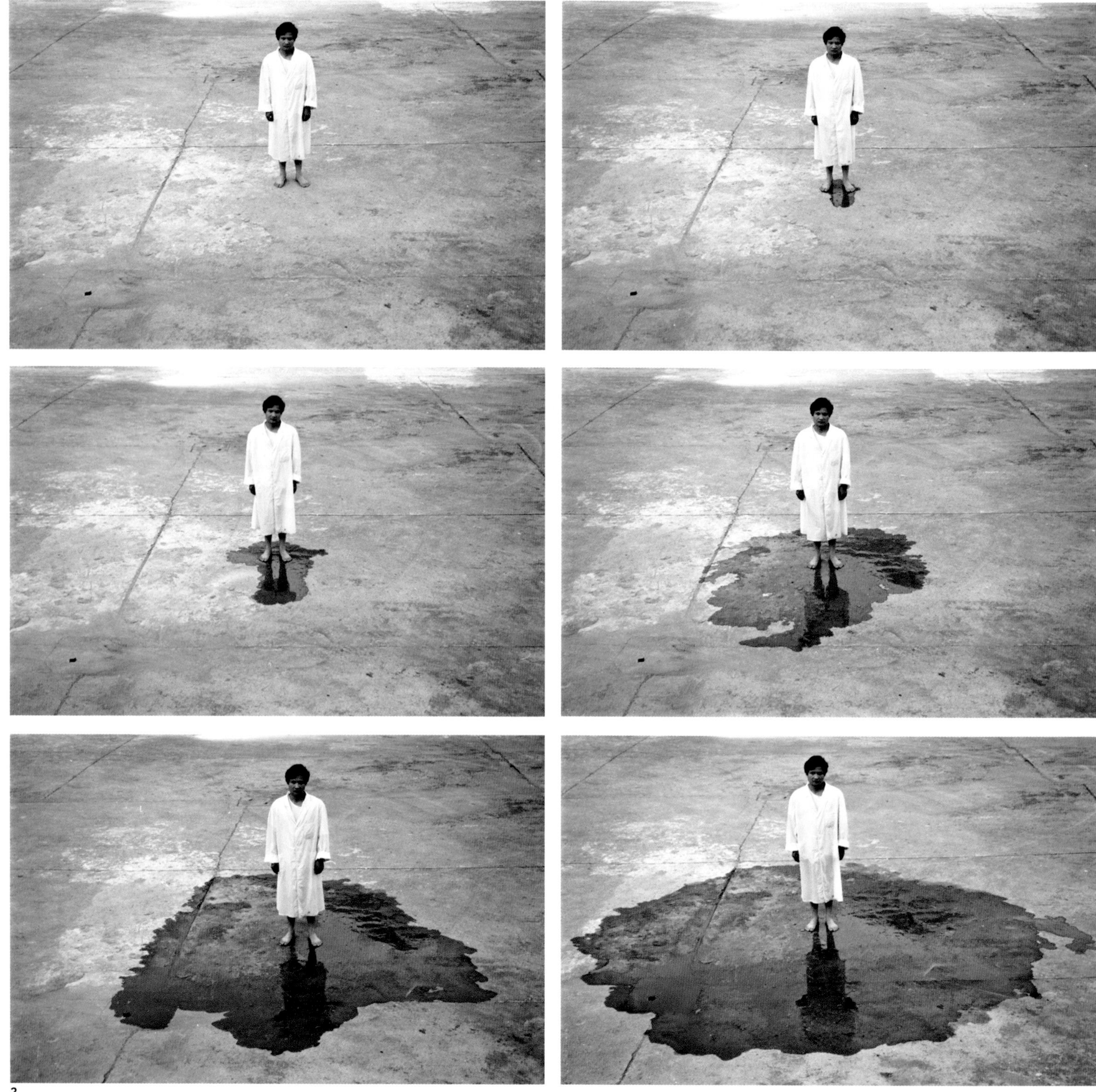

2

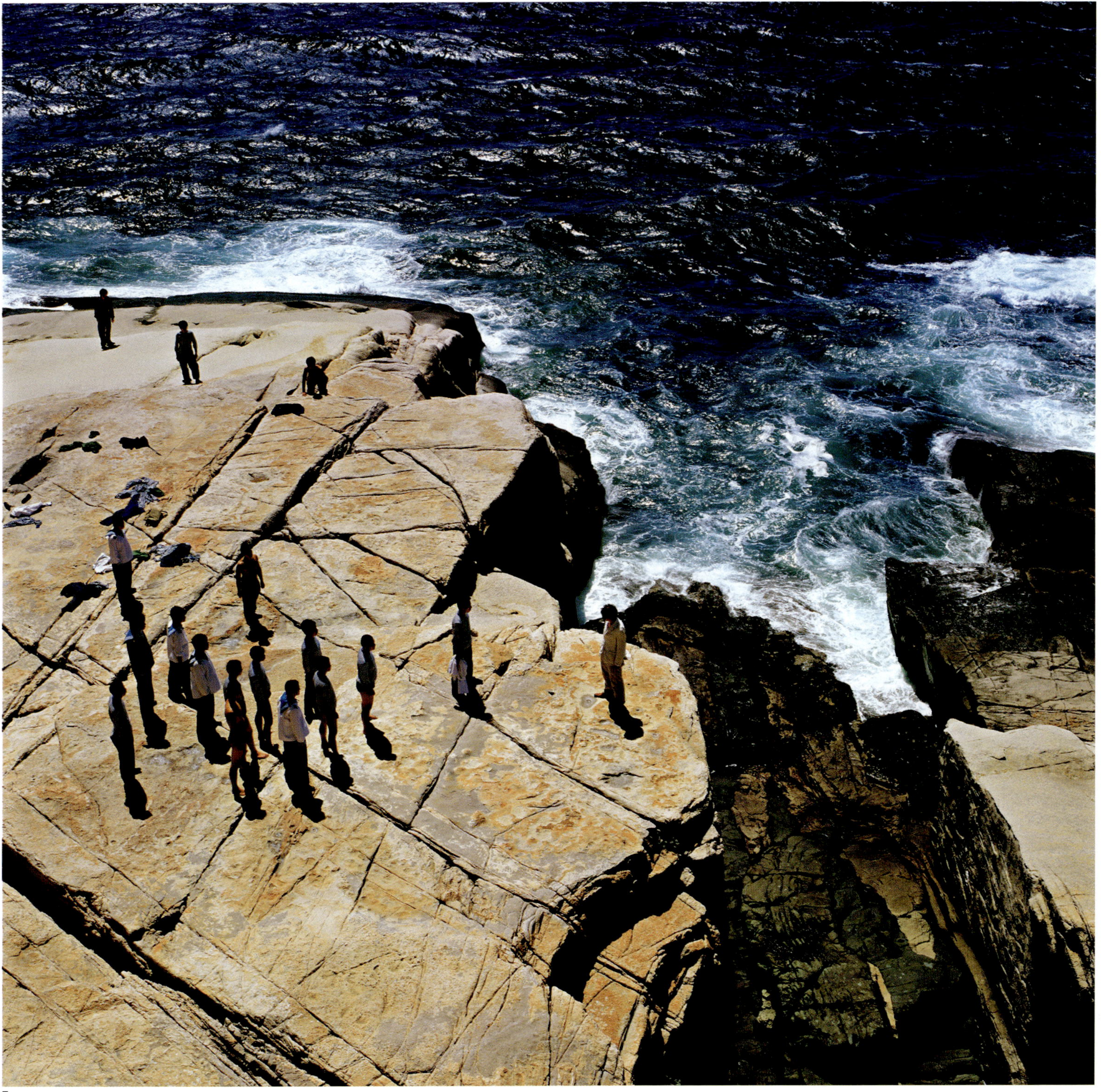

3

4

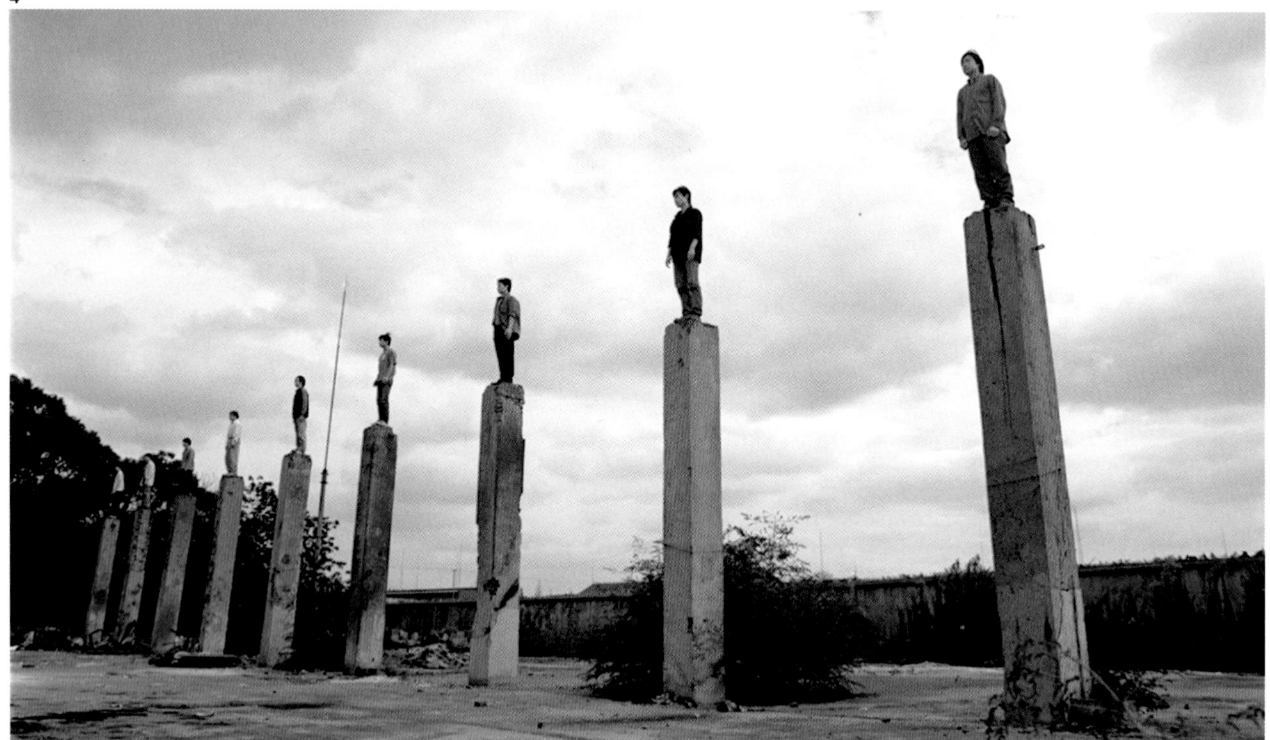

that has been shown worldwide. In "History of Chemistry" the artist moves the camera very slowly, making simple and stable uncut pan shots, capturing the experiences of a group of unknown people. The video develops as this group of young men start on a voyage from an ambiguous land, under the lead of a captain taking them ultimately to an industrial complex. Without words but with a delicate selection of scenes and music, each scene in the video incites complex emotions in the viewer. The last scene shows a young man with hammer in hand symbolizing the start of civilization.

In "The History of Chemistry 2: Excessively Restrained Mountaineering Enthusiasts" (2006) he shows a stronger use of narrative. Lu Chunsheng's video uses both its title and the narrative structures to tell a science fiction themed, urban story full of bizarre situations. The story seems to end without a specific or clear result when a group of people get imprisoned, however the actual story is about the world and how unfamiliar and distanced it can be sometimes.

Lu Chunshengs ureigene filmische Sprache wird vor allem in dem Videofilm „The History of Chemistry 1" (2004) deutlich, einem Werk, das weltweit Aufmerksamkeit fand. Der Künstler bewegt darin die Kamera sehr langsam, in einfachen, ruhigen, ungeschnittenen Schwenks, um die Erlebnisse einer Gruppe junger Männer einzufangen, die unter Führung eines Kapitäns aus einem unbestimmten Land zu einer Reise aufbrechen, die sie am Ende zu einem Industriekomplex führt. Ohne Sprache, aber mit sorgfältig ausgewählter Szenenabfolge und Musik, löst jede Szene des Videos beim Betrachter komplexe Emotionen aus. Die Schlussszene zeigt einen jungen Mann mit einem Hammer in der Hand, der für den Beginn der Zivilisation steht.

In „The History of Chemistry 2: Excessively Restrained Mountaineering Enthusiasts" (2006) tritt das erzählerische Element noch deutlicher hervor. Lu Chunshengs Video vermittelt sowohl durch seinen Titel als auch durch seine Erzählstrukturen eine urbane Science-Fiction-Geschichte voll bizarrer Situationen. Die Geschichte scheint ohne eindeutiges oder klares Ergebnis zu enden – zwar werden die anonymen Protagonisten zum Schluss eingekerkert, doch die eigentliche Fabel handelt von unserer Welt und davon, wie unvertraut und unzugänglich sie uns bisweilen ist.

《化学史第二过于拘谨的登山爱好者》(2006年)显示他对叙事手法的娴熟运用。陆春生的录像运用标题加叙述结构双重手法讲述了一个以科幻为主题，光怪陆离的城市故事最后这群人被投入监狱，结局含糊留有悬念，而故事却反应了我 们的这个世界，有的时候让人感到陌生而遥远。

Biljana Ciric

5

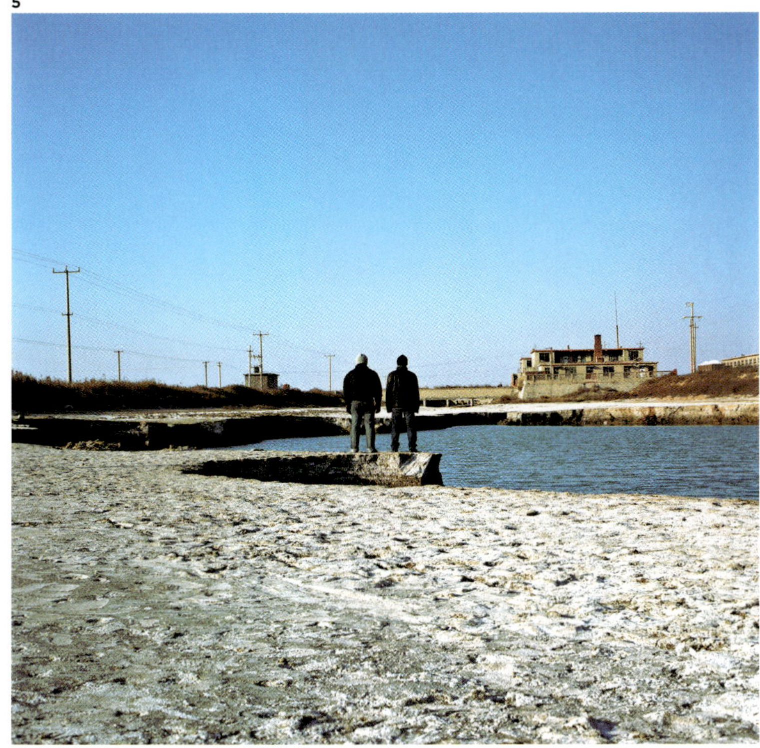

6

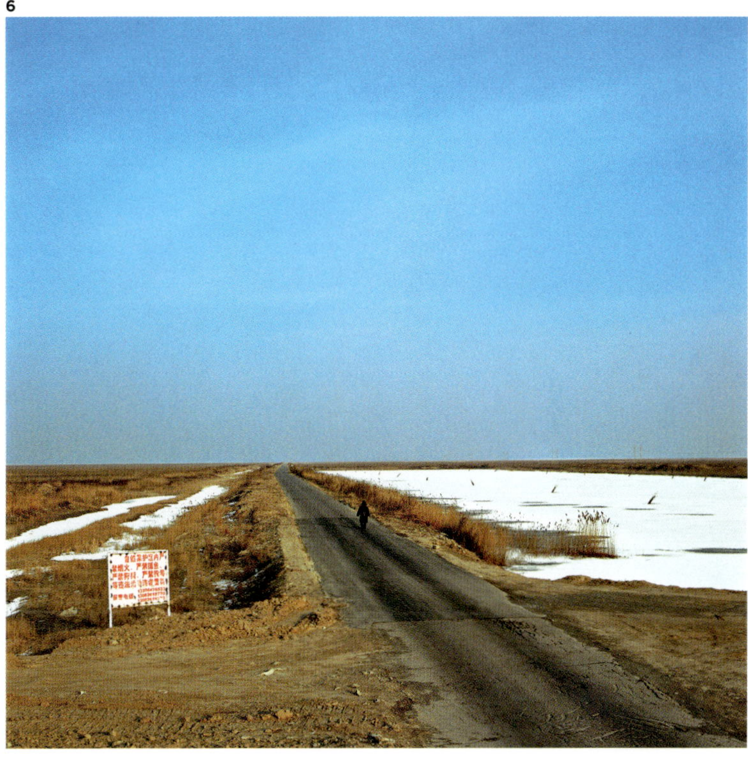

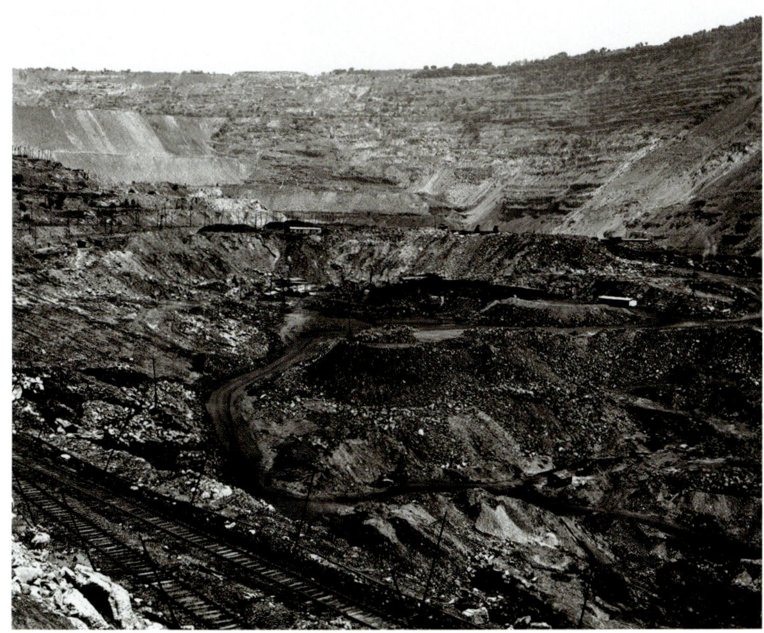

7

1 ***One of the most stupid attacks against science fiction is that it is unable to forecast the future – the witch 2***, *2005*
Photograph, 124 x 124 cm; Fotografie, 124 x 124 cm
《对科幻小说最愚蠢的抨击之一是认为它不能预测未来 --巫婆 2》2005年, 摄影, 124 x 124 cm

2 ***Water***, *2000*
Photographs, 70 x 100 each; Fotografien, je 70 x 100
《水》2000年, 摄影, 每幅, 70 x 100 cm

3 ***One of the most stupid attacks against science fiction is that it is unable to forecast the future – the first white man who is pushed down***, *2005*
Photograph, 124 x 124 cm; Fotografie, 124 x 124 cm
《对科幻小说最愚蠢的抨击之一是认为它不能预测未来 -- 被推挤下来的第一白人》2005年, 摄影, 124 x 124 cm

4 ***I want to be a gentleman***, *2000*
Photograph, 70 x 100 cm; Fotografie, 70 x 100 cm
《我要做绅士》2000年，摄影，70 x 100 cm

5 ***One of the most stupid attacks against science fiction is that it is unable to forecast the future – Gothic***, *2005*
Photograph, 124 x 124 cm; Fotografie, 124 x 124 cm
《对科幻小说最愚蠢的抨击之一是认为它不能预测未来》2005年，摄影, 124 x 124 cm

6 ***One of the most stupid attacks against science fiction is that it is unable to forecast the future – the postman delivering letters to the nature reserve***, *2005*
Photograph, 124 x 124 cm; Fotografie, 124 x 124 cm
《对科幻小说最愚蠢的抨击之一是认为它不能预测未来》2005年, 摄影, 124 x 124 cm

7 ***One of the most stupid attacks against science fiction is that it is unable to forecast the future – the witch 1***, *2005*
Photograph, 124 x 124 cm; Fotografie, 124 x 124 cm
《对科幻小说最愚蠢的抨击之一是认为它不能预测未来 ----巫婆 1》2005年, 摄影, 124 x 124 cm

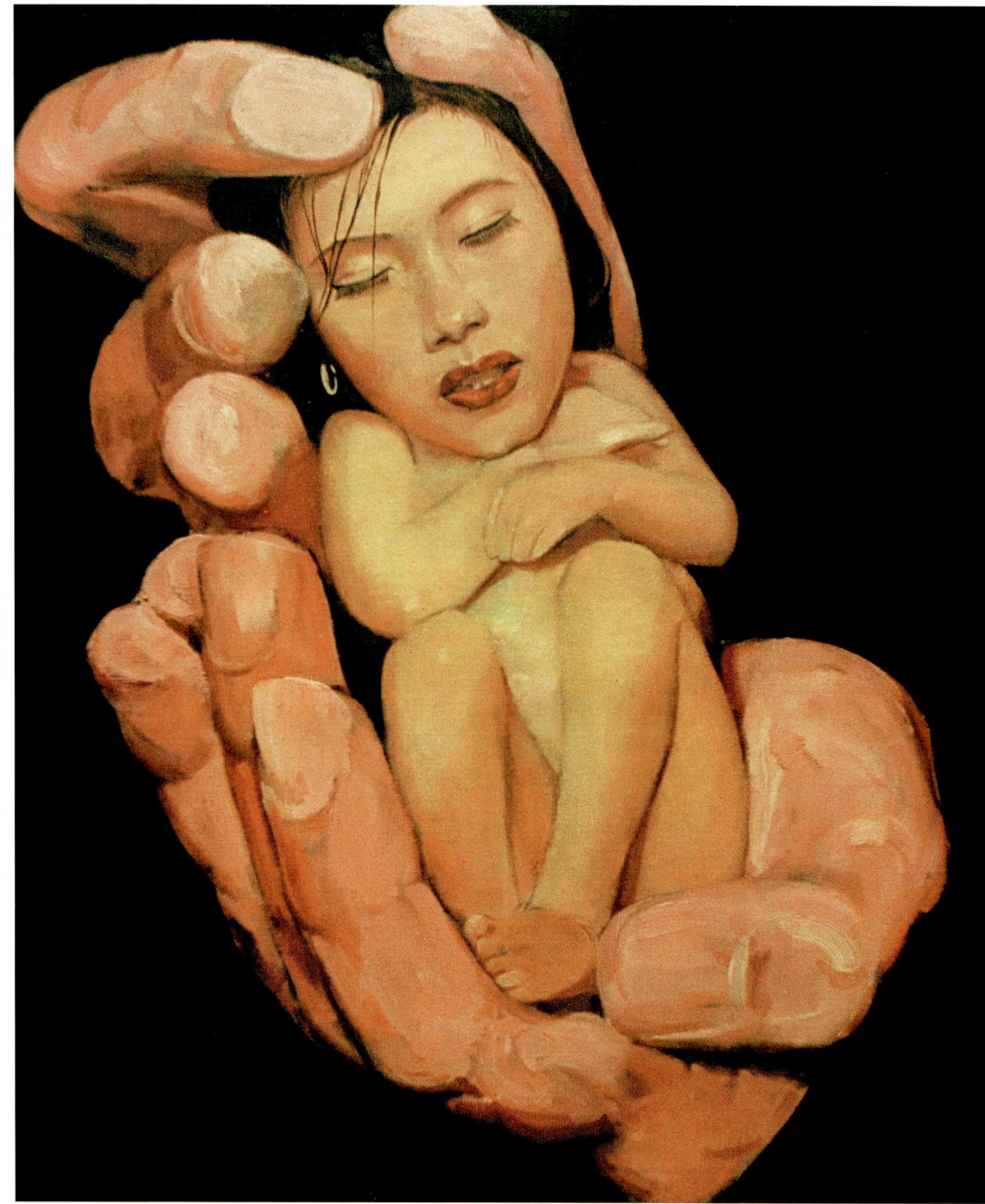

1

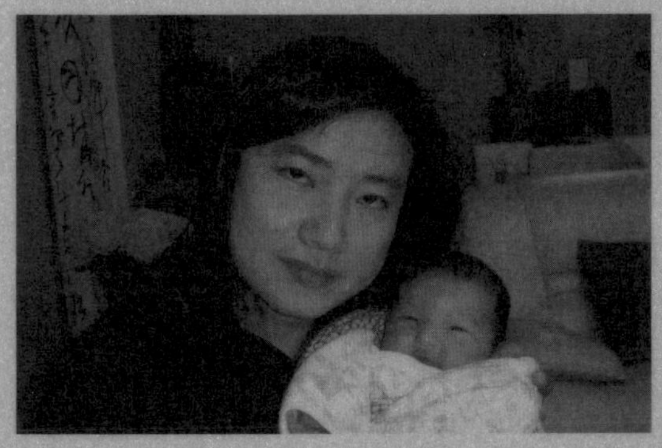

"I want to explore a series of questions in various forms. And these questions are raised through the fundamental question of sexual ambiguity. Such an ambiguity is not just visual or physical but more psychological and spiritual. It transcends such issues as social, cultural, and racial differences, just as space and time."

„Ich möchte eine Reihe von Fragen sondieren, die sich aus der Grundfrage der sexuellen Mehrdeutigkeit ergeben, die nicht nur eine optische oder körperliche, sondern eher eine seelische und geistige ist. Sie transzendiert gesellschaftliche, kulturelle und ethnische Unterschiede ebenso wie Raum und Zeit."

"我想要探索一系列多种形式的问题。而这些问题起源于性模糊性的基本问题。此类的模糊性不在于视觉和物质上，而更多的在于心理和精神上。其超越了社会， 文化和种族差别等主题，因为它超越了时空。"

Born in 1969 in Huangshi, Hubei Province, China. Lives and works in Beijing
Geboren 1969 in Huangshi, Provinz Hubei, China. Lebt und arbeitet in Peking
1969年出生于中国湖北黄石，现居住工作于北京

***Selected exhibitions* / Ausgewählte Ausstellungen / 所选展览**

1998	"Inside Out: New Chinese Art", Asia Society, P.S.1 Center for Contemporary Art, New York, NY, USA
2000	Gwangju Biennial, Gwangju, Korea
2001	7th Istanbul Biennial, Istanbul, Turkey
2002	First Guangzhou Triennial, Guangdong, China
2003	"Ma Liuming", Fukuoka Asian Art Museum, Fukuoka, Japan
2004–07	"Between Past and Future, New Photography and Video from China", International Center of Photography, New York, NY, USA (travelling exhibition)

1998年	《蜕变与突破：中国新艺术展》亚洲协会美术馆, P.S.1当代艺术中心, 纽约, 美国
2000年	《光洲双年展》光洲, 韩国
2001年	《第七届伊斯坦布尔双年展》伊斯坦, 土耳其
2002年	《首届广州三年展》广东, 中国
2003年	《马六明》个展　福冈亚洲艺术博物馆，日本
2004–07年	《过去与未来之间—中国新影像展》国际摄影中心, 纽约, 美国（巡回展）

***Selected publications* / Ausgewählte Publikationen / 所选著作**

Qian Zhijian: "Performing bodies: Zhang Huan, Ma Liuming, and performance art in China", interview, in: "Art Journal", 1999
Julia Laetitia Colman: "Ma Liuming: Experiencing the Unexpected", ed. by Yuko Hasegawa, New York/Beijing/London 2005

Qian Zhijian（著）:《行为的身体：张洹，马六明和行为艺术在中国》采访，艺术杂志，1999年夏
Colman, Julia Laetitia（著）:《马六明：体验 突如其来的》長谷川祐子（编者）纽约/北京/伦敦年

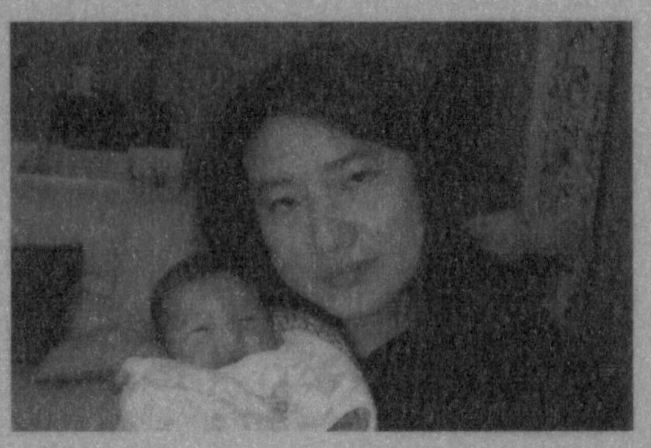

"I want to explore a series of questions in various forms. And these questions are raised through the fundamental question of sexual ambiguity. Such an ambiguity is not just visual or physical but more psychological and spiritual. It transcends such issues as social, cultural, and racial differences, just as space and time."

„Ich möchte eine Reihe von Fragen sondieren, die sich aus der Grundfrage der sexuellen Mehrdeutigkeit ergeben, die nicht nur eine optische oder körperliche, sondern eher eine seelische und geistige ist. Sie transzendiert gesellschaftliche, kulturelle und ethnische Unterschiede ebenso wie Raum und Zeit."

"我想要探索一系列多种形式的问题。而这些问题起源于性模糊性的基本问题。此类的模糊性不在于视觉和物质上，而更多的在于心理和精神上。其超越了社会、文化和种族差别等主题，因为它超越了时空。"

Born in 1969 in Huangshi, Hubei Province, China. Lives and works in Beijing
Geboren 1969 in Huangshi, Provinz Hubei, China. Lebt und arbeitet in Peking
1969年出生于中国湖北黄石，现居住工作于北京

Selected exhibitions / Ausgewählte Ausstellungen / 所选展览

1998	"Inside Out: New Chinese Art", Asia Society, P.S.1 Center for Contemporary Art, New York, NY, USA
2000	Gwangju Biennial, Gwangju, Korea
2001	7th Istanbul Biennial, Istanbul, Turkey
2002	First Guangzhou Triennial, Guangdong, China
2003	"Ma Liuming", Fukuoka Asian Art Museum, Fukuoka, Japan
2004–07	"Between Past and Future, New Photography and Video from China", International Center of Photography, New York, NY, USA (travelling exhibition)

1998年	《蜕变与突破：中国新艺术展》亚洲协会美术馆，P.S.1当代艺术中心，纽约，美国
2000年	《光州双年展》光州，韩国
2001年	《第七届伊斯坦布尔双年展》伊斯坦，土耳其
2002年	《首届广州三年展》广东，中国
2003年	《马六明》个展 福冈亚洲艺术博物馆，日本
2004–07年	《过去与未来之间—中国新影像展》国际摄影中心，纽约，美国（巡回展）

Selected publications / Ausgewählte Publikationen / 所选著作

Qian Zhijian: "Performing bodies: Zhang Huan, Ma Liuming, and performance art in China", interview, in: "Art Journal", 1999
Julia Laetitia Colman: "Ma Liuming: Experiencing the Unexpected", ed. by Yuko Hasegawa, New York/Beijing/London 2005

Qian Zhijian（著）：《行为的身体：张洹，马六明和行为艺术在中国》采访，艺术杂志，1999年夏
Colman, Julia Laetitia（著）：《马六明：体验 突如其来的》長谷川祐子（编著）纽约/北京/伦敦年

MA LIUMING 马六明

[ma lioumiŋ]

A pioneer of performance art, Ma Liuming was one of the first artists to explore the power and poetry of public nudity in China, a country where such behavior was strictly forbidden. As such, he has also been the target of government censorship, unable to perform in his own country for most of his career.

Trained as an oil painter, Ma Liuming graduated from Hubei Academy of Fine Arts in 1991. Two years later, he was one of the founders of Beijing East Village, an artists colony on the outskirts of Beijing that was a mecca for experimental art forms in the early 1990s. Here, Ma Liuming collaborated with Zhang Huan and Zhu Ming and staged his earliest performances such as "Fen-Ma Liuming's Lunch I" (1994), in which he sat, completely nude, sucking a plastic tube that was attached to his penis. For works like this, the artist was arrested in 1994 and held for two months in jail. Many of the other artists fled the village in response to this police action.

But Ma Liuming only proceeded further with his work, developing his own performance persona – Fen-Ma Liuming, a hybrid figure of male and female components – to match his own uniquely androgynous appearance. In his performances as Fen-Ma Liuming, this artist interrogates the ways that gender is normally identified and sexually is rigidly controlled, particularly in a country that historically has been as repressive as China. Always appearing in long hair and make-up, he conveys the convincing appearance of a female, until he cuts away his apparel, revealing his male genitalia. In many works, he challenges audiences to interact with his ambiguous figure. In one performance as Fen-Ma Liuming that was staged in museums internationally throughout the late-1990s, Ma sat motionless and naked on a platform holding a camera release-switch in his hand. As he continuously snapped the shutter, viewers were per mitted to pose with the artist, often touching his body or taking off their own clothes, in response to his complete passivity.

Ma Liuming ist ein Pionier der Performance-Kunst und gehörte zu den ersten Künstlern, die die Kraft und Poesie der Nacktheit in China ausloteten, als dergleichen dort strikt verboten war. Er wurde zur Zielscheibe der staatlichen Zensur und konnte sich in seiner Heimat lange nicht künstlerisch betätigen.

Ma Liuming studierte Ölmalerei an der Hubei Academy of Fine Arts und machte 1991 seinen Abschluss. Zwei Jahre später war er Mitbegründer des East Village, einer Künstlerkolonie am Stadtrand von Peking, die zu Beginn der 1990er Jahre zum Mekka für experimentelle Kunstformen wurde. Hier arbeitete Ma Liuming mit Zhang Huan und Zhu Ming zusammen und inszenierte seine frühesten Performances, wie z. B. „Fen-Ma Liuming's Lunch I" (1994): Bei diesem „Mittagessen" saß er völlig nackt da und lutschte an einem Plastikschlauch, dessen anderes Ende auf seinem Penis steckte. Für Arbeiten wie diese wurde der Künstler 1994 verhaftet und zwei Monate ins Gefängnis gesperrt, eine Polizeiaktion, die viele andere Künstler veranlasste, das East Village fluchtartig zu verlassen.

Ma Liuming aber setzte seine Arbeit fort und entwickelte eine eigene Performance-Persönlichkeit – Fen-Ma Liuming, ein Mischwesen aus männlichen und weiblichen Komponenten –, die zu seiner androgynen Erscheinung passt. Durch seine Performances in dieser Kunstgestalt stellt der Künstler die Art und Weise in Frage, wie normalerweise die Geschlechtsidentität bestimmt und die Sexualität strikt gemaßregelt wird, insbesondere in einem Land, das in der Vergangenheit so repressiv war wie China. Fen-Ma tritt stets mit langem Haar und Make-up auf und vermittelt überzeugend das Bild einer Frau, bis er seine Kleidung aufschneidet und seine männlichen Genitalien entblößt. Bei vielen seiner Aktionen fordert er das Publikum dazu auf, mit dieser uneindeutigen Gestalt zu interagieren – so saß Fen-Ma einmal bei einer Performance, die er in den späten 1990er Jahren in verschiedenen internationalen Museen durchführte, bewegungslos und nackt auf einem Podest und hielt einen Kamera-Fernauslöser in der Hand. Während

行为艺术先锋马六明是中国首位探索公共裸体的力量和诗意的艺术家，而此类行为在中国严令禁止。因此，他也是政府当局审查当局的监控对象，而不能在自己的国家中表演自己主要作品。

1991年，马六明毕业于湖北美术学院，所学专业为油画。两年以后，和别人一起创立了艺术家沙龙组织"北京东村"，该组织位于北京市郊，在上世 纪90年代初期是实 验艺 术形式的圣地。那里马六明与张洹和朱冥合作开始了其早期的艺术表演如《芬—马六明午餐》，作品中他全裸而坐，阴茎上连接着一根塑料管，而他吮舔着另一头。因为进行类似的行为表演，1994年，芬•马被当局逮捕，在监狱中度过了两个月。这一事件，也让许多其他艺术家纷纷离开东村。

而马却继续着其作品创作，形成了自己的女妆男身表演形象 —— 芬-马六明—与其自己独特 的雌雄通体的 形象相符。在其芬-马六明的表演中，艺术家询问了正常鉴别性别差异的方法以及性被严格控制，尤其在象中国一样历史上对性非常保守的国家。马总是留着长长的头发，浓妆淡抹，让人看起来是一副女性的样子，而直到扔掉外衣，露出男性生殖器，才让人知道他的本性。在他的众多作品中，其模糊的形象挑战着观众的反映。在90年代末期的，芬—马六明的一个表演在国际性的博物馆里展出，马手里拿着一部摄像机，面无表情，裸体着坐在展台上。他不断按动着，观众可向其摆着姿势，常常触摸着他的肌体，或为响应这种完全放纵，观众也脱下他们的衣服。

在其作品中，摄影起着重要作用，而文件也常常成为艺术品。在《芬•马六明 走长城》中，马六明赤着脚在 长城漫步，他雇请的专业摄影师则捕捉着这一过程。油画也是马六明作品的重要部分。自2000年起，他创作了《婴儿》系列，其中是一个烦恼可笑的形象，婴儿身体上长着一张芬•马六明的脸庞。 最近，他研究了产道，在一系列油画中，他似

2

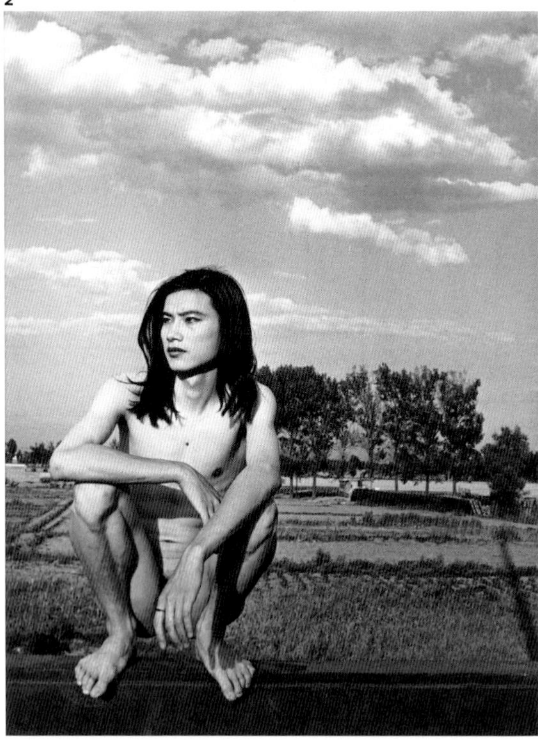

3

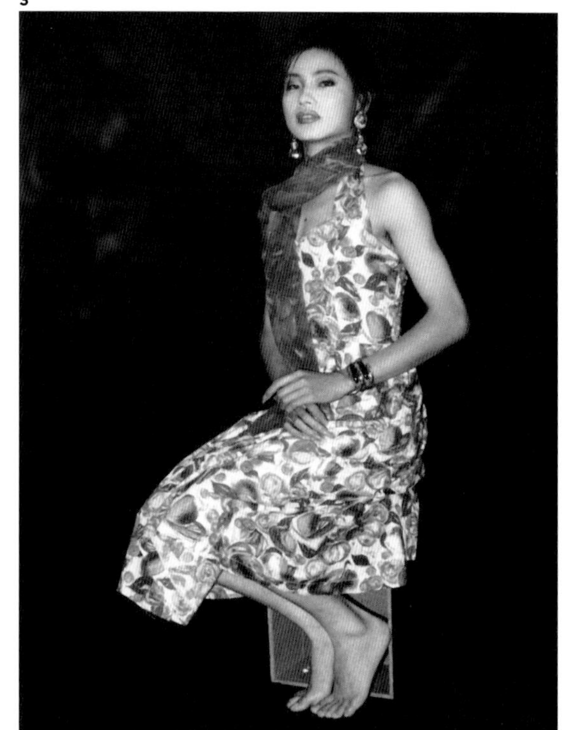

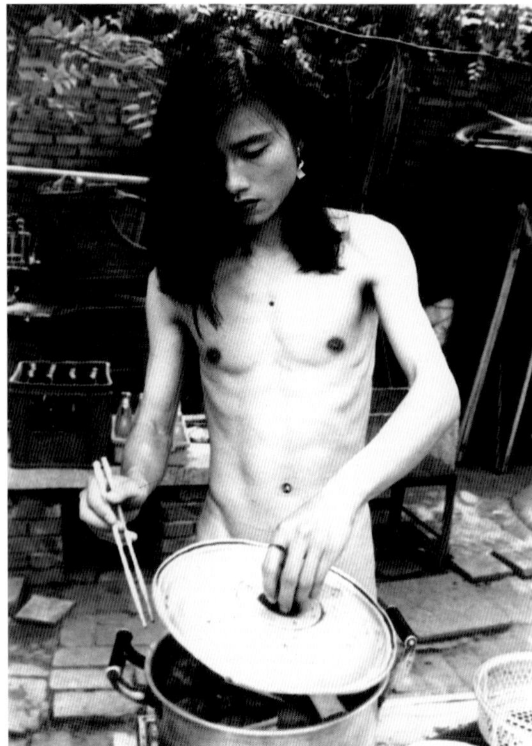

4

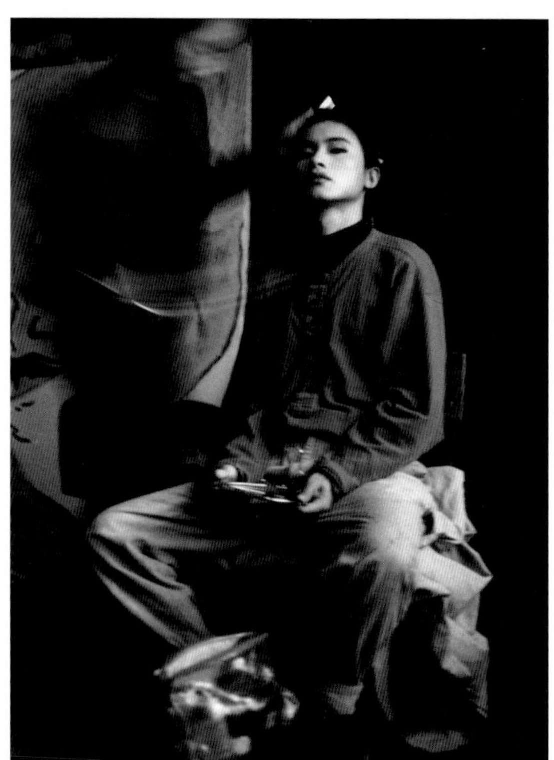

5

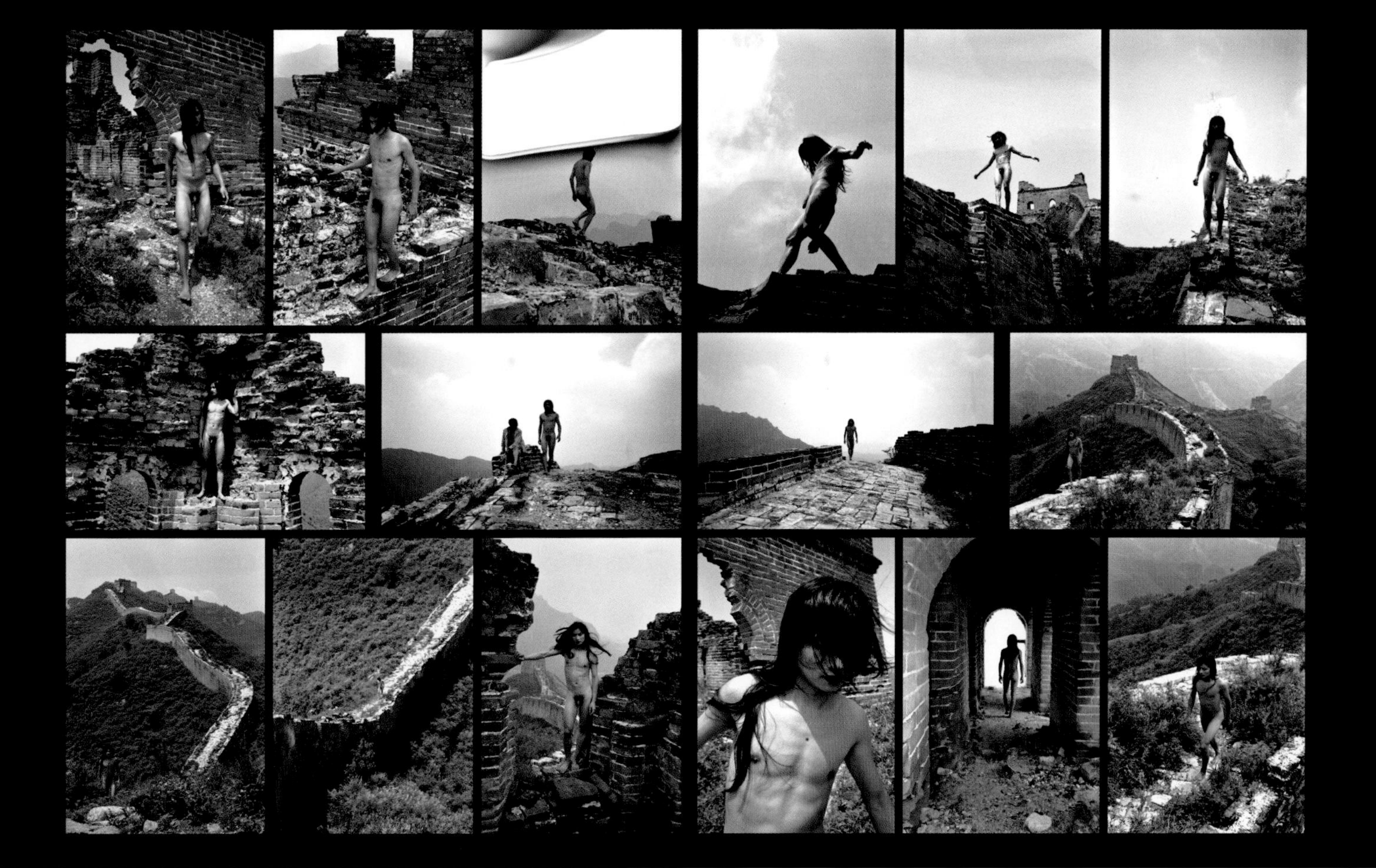

6

7

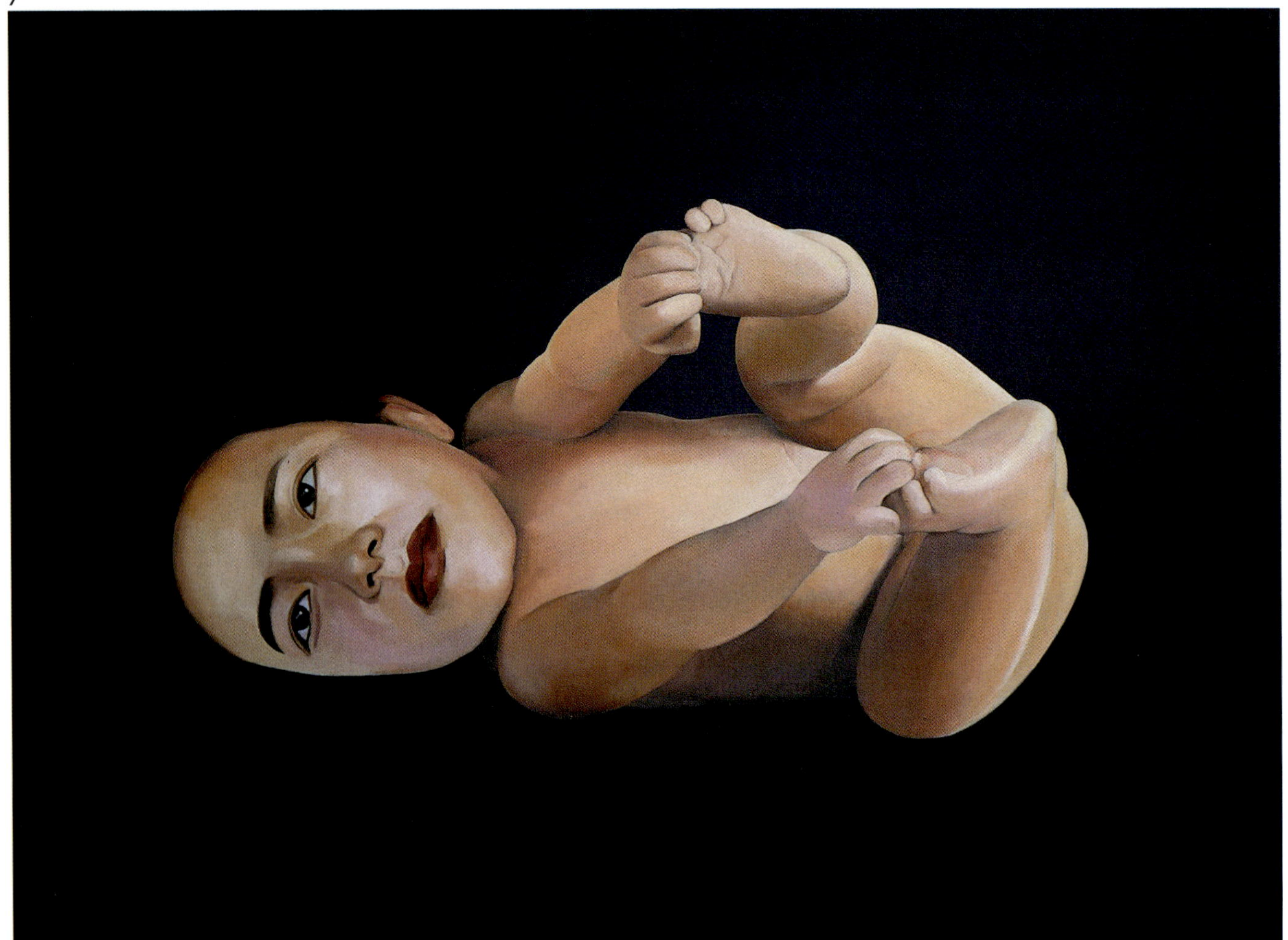

Photography plays an important role in Ma Liuming's work with documentation often serving as artworks in their own right. In Fen-Ma Liuming "Walks on the Great Wall" (1998), the artist hired a professional photographer to capture his barefoot trek along this ancient artifice. Painting is also a key component in Ma's output. Since 2000, he has developed his "Baby series", in which the face of Fen-Ma appears on an infant's body, a surrealistic image that is both disturbing and laughable. More recently, he has investigated the birth canal, in a series of paintings that seem to view the world through slits. Throughout these various mediums, Ma Liuming continues to investigate the limits of provocation, seducing his audience into an inquiry of more intriguing matters.

er diesen immer wieder betätigte, durften die Zuschauer mit dem Künstler posieren, wobei viele ihn berührten oder sogar selbst ihre Kleidung ablegten – in Reaktion auf seine vollständige Passivität.

Die Fotografie spielt eine wichtige Rolle in Ma Liumings Werk, denn die Dokumentationen seiner Darbietungen werden oft zu eigenständigen Kunstwerken. Für Fen-Ma Liuming „Walks on the Great Wall" (1998) ließ sich der Künstler von einem Profifotografen ablichten, während er unbekleidet und barfuß über das uralte Bauwerk spazierte. Auch die Malerei ist eine Schlüsselkomponente in Mas Schaffen. Seit 2000 entwickelt er seine „Baby-Serie", bei der das Gesicht von Fen-Ma auf einen Babykörper montiert erscheint, ein surrealistisches Bild, das beunruhigend und lächerlich zugleich wirkt. Neuerdings befasst sich Ma Liuming in einer Reihe von Gemälden, die die Welt durch Schlitze zu betrachten scheinen, mit dem Geburtskanal. In all diesen Medien testet er immer wieder die Grenzen der Provokation aus und verführt sein Publikum dazu, sich immer faszinierenderen Themen zuzuwenden.

通过切口来观察世界。通过这些媒介，马六明继续研究这些刺激物的局限性，诱导观众对更多有兴趣的事物产生疑问。

Barbara Pollack

8

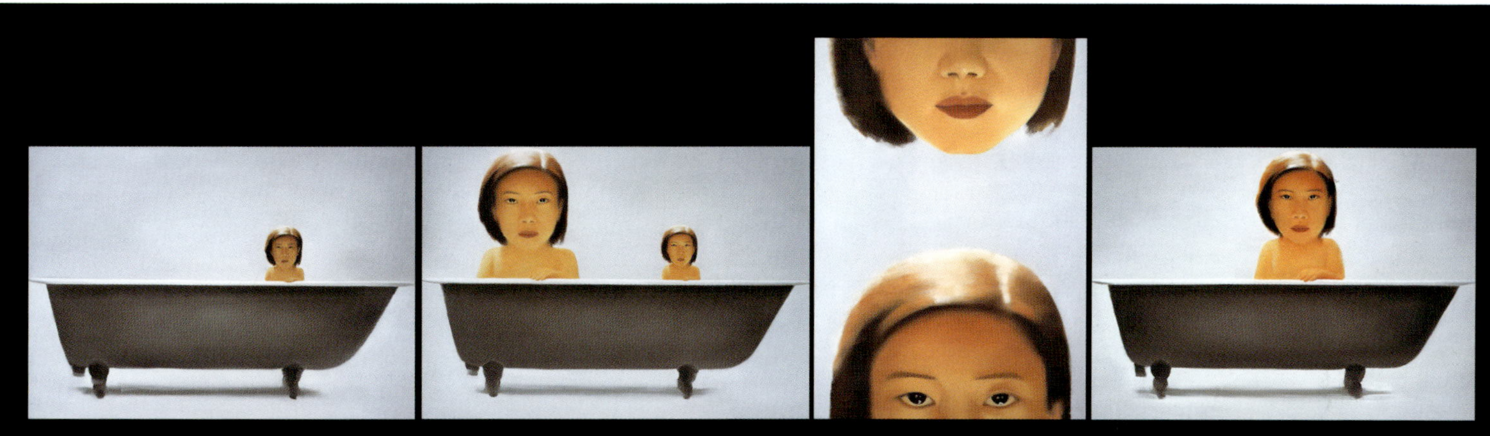

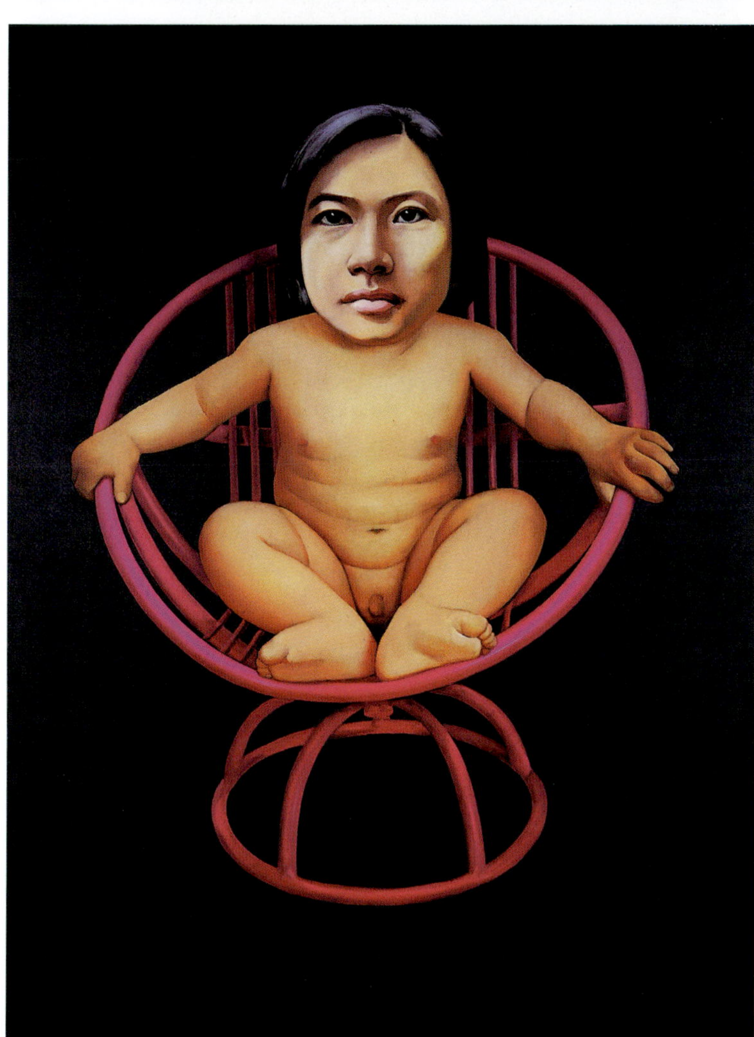

9

1 ***Baby No. 1***, *1993*
Oil on canvas, 90.5 x 75.5 cm
Öl auf Leinwand, 90,5 x 75,5 cm
《婴儿》系列 No. 1, 1993年，布面油画，90.5 x 75.5 cm

2 ***Fen-Ma Liuming II***, *1994*
Performance, Beijing
Performance, Peking
《芬•马 六明II》，1994年，表演，北京

3 ***Fen-Ma Liuming I***, *1993*
Performance, Beijing
Performance, Peking
《芬•马 六明I》，1993年，表演，北京

4 ***Fen-Ma Liuming's Lunch II***, *1994*
Performance, Beijing
Performance, Peking
《芬•马 六明的午餐II》，1994年，表演，北京

5 ***Fen-Ma Liuming I***, *1993*
Performance, Beijing
Performance, Peking
《芬•马 六明I》，1993年，表演，北京

6 ***Fen-Ma Liuming walks on the Great Wall***, *1998*
Performance, Beijing
Performance, Peking
《芬•马 六明在长城上行走》，1998年，表演，北京

7 ***Baby No. 4***, *1999*
Oil on canvas, 150 x 200 cm
Öl auf Leinwand, 150 x 200 cm
《婴儿》系列 No. 4, 1999年，布面油画，150 x 200 cm

8 ***No. 33 A – B – C – D***, *2005/06*
Oil on canvas, 100 x 140 cm each
Öl auf Leinwand, je 100 x 140 cm
《婴儿》系列 No. 33 A - B - C - D, 2005/06年，布面油画，
每幅100 x 140 cm

9 ***Baby No. 7***, *1998*
Oil on canvas, 180 x 139 cm
Öl auf Leinwand, 180 x 139 cm
《婴儿》系列 No. 7, 1998年，布面油画，180 x 139 cm

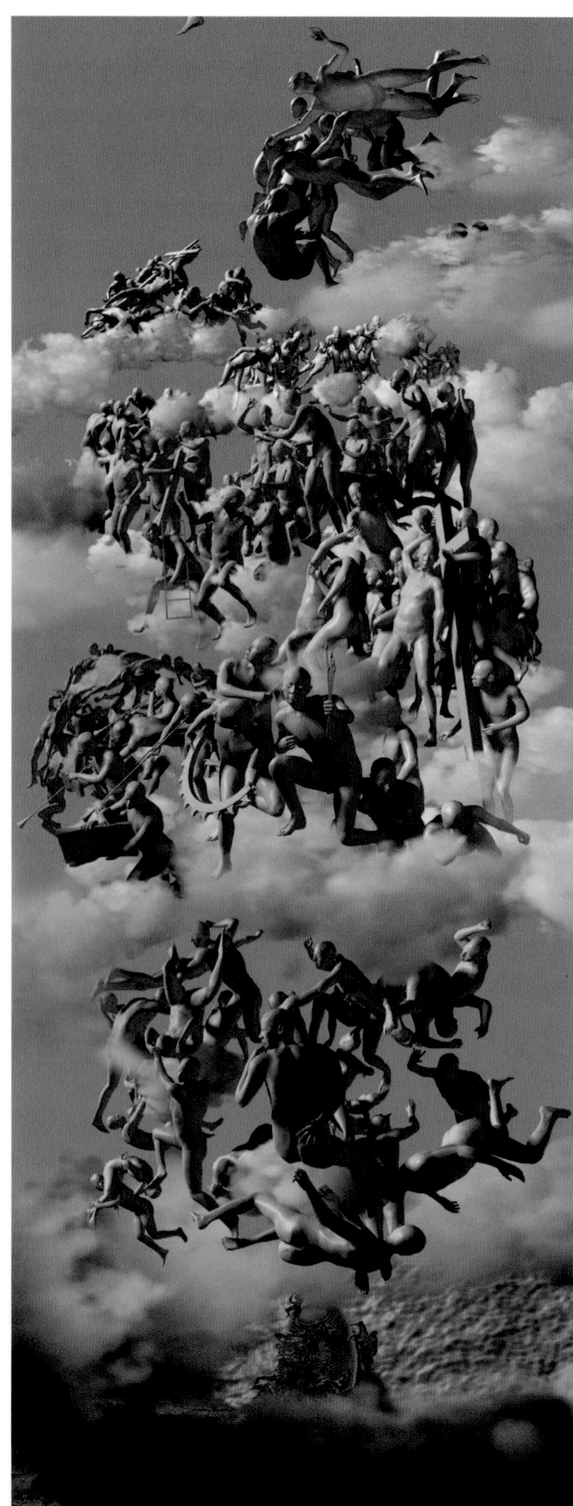

1

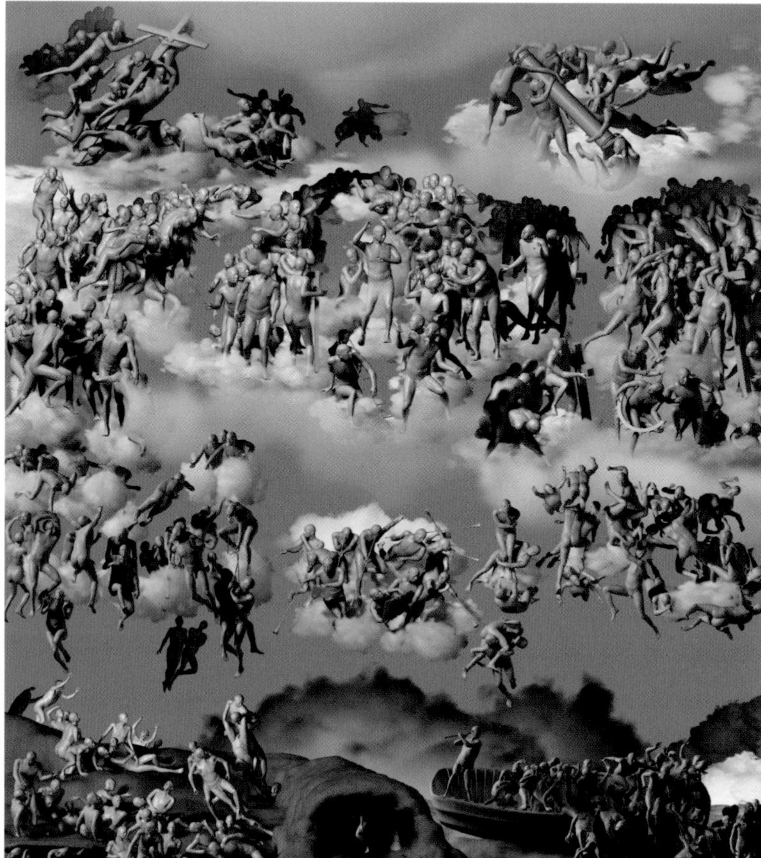

2

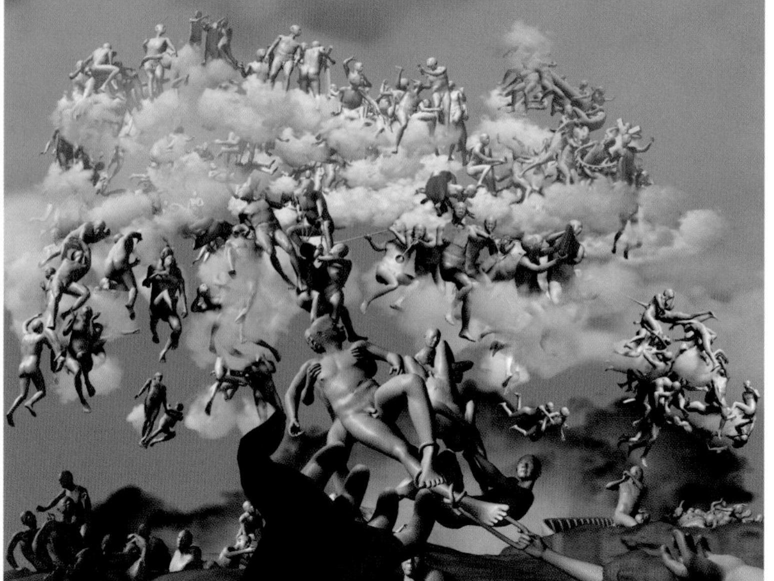

3

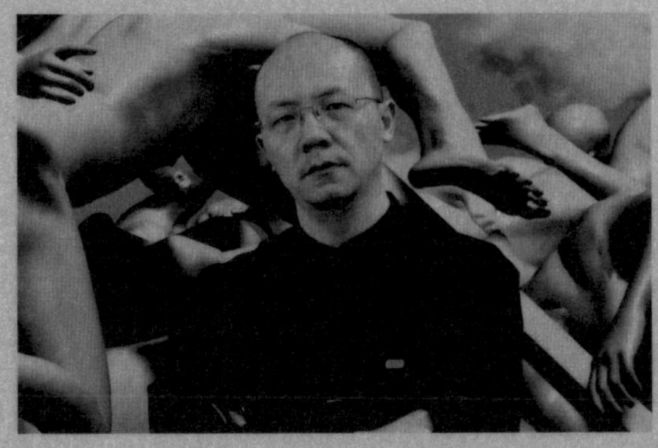

"By combining up to 70 digital pictures, I reconstruct the way the eye works, but simultaneously I destroy the illusion of an authentic representation of reality."

„Indem ich bis zu 70 Digitalfotos kombiniere, bilde ich die Funktionsweise des Auges nach, zerstöre aber gleichzeitig die Illusion einer authentischen Wiedergabe der Realität."

"由结合70 张数字式图片，我重建眼睛运作的方式，但同时我毁坏现实的真实的表现方法的幻觉。"

Born in 1964 in Wuxi Jiangsu, China. Lives and works in Beijing
Geboren 1964 in Wuxi Jiangsu, China. Lebt und arbeitet in Peking
1964年出生于无锡，江苏，中国。居住工作在北京

***Selected exhibitions* / Ausgewählte Ausstellungen / 所选展览**

2004 "The Last Judgment in Cyberspace", Walsh Gallery, Chicago, IL, USA
"Sightseeing", SCA Gallery, Sydney College of the Arts, Sydney, Australia
"Le Printemps de Chine", Musée CRAC Alsace, Altkirch, France
"Rivka Rinn and Miao Xiaochun", White Space, Beijing, China
"Pinyao in Paris", National Library, MK2, Paris, France
"Phantasmagoria", Walsh Gallery, Chicago, IL, USA
2006 "China Contemporary", Museum Boijmans Van Beuningen, Rotterdam, The Netherlands

2004年 《虚拟最后的审判》芝加哥，Walsh画廊
《观光》SCA画廊，悉尼的艺术学，悉尼
《中国的春天》博物馆 CRAC 阿尔萨斯，Altkirch
《Rivka Rinn 和缪晓春》白色空间，北京
《品要在巴黎》国际图书馆，MK2，巴黎
《幻影》芝加哥，Walsh画廊
2006年 《当代中国》荷兰鹿特丹，波宁根美术馆

***Selected publications* / Ausgewählte Publikationen / 所选著作**

Bernhard Fibicher, Matthias Frehner (eds.): "Mahjong. Chinesische Gegenwartskunst aus der Sammlung Sigg", Ostfildern-Ruit 2005
"European Photography", Nr. 76, Göttingen 2005

Fibicher, Bernhard/Frehner, Matthias（编者）：《麻将一西克的当代艺术收藏展》，Ostfildern-Ruit 2005年
《欧洲摄影》，第76号，格廷根 2005年

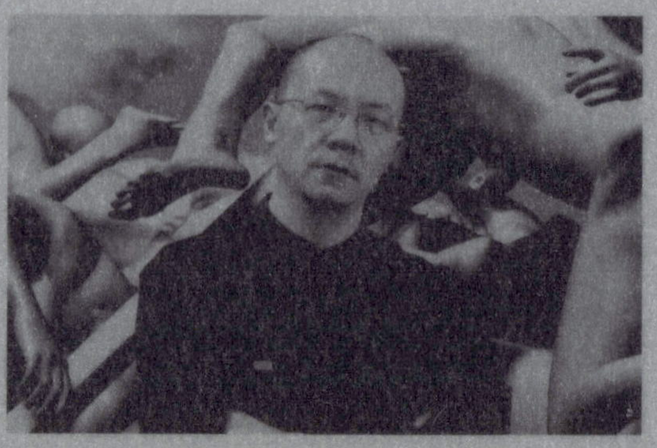

"By combining up to 70 digital pictures, I reconstruct the way the eye works, but simultaneously I destroy the illusion of an authentic representation of reality."

„Indem ich bis zu 70 Digitalfotos kombiniere, bilde ich die Funktionsweise des Auges nach, zerstöre aber gleichzeitig die Illusion einer authentischen Wiedergabe der Realität."

"由结合70 张数字式图片，我重建眼睛运作的方式，但同时我毁坏现实的真实的表现方法的幻觉。"

Born in 1964 in Wuxi Jiangsu, China. Lives and works in Beijing
Geboren 1964 in Wuxi Jiangsu, China. Lebt und arbeitet in Peking
1964年出生于无锡，江苏，中国。居住工作在北京

Selected exhibitions / Ausgewählte Ausstellungen / 所选展览

2004 "The Last Judgment in Cyberspace", Walsh Gallery, Chicago, IL, USA
"Sightseeing", SCA Gallery, Sydney College of the Arts, Sydney, Australia
"Le Printemps de Chine", Musée CRAC Alsace, Altkirch, France
"Rivka Rinn and Miao Xiaochun", White Space, Beijing, China
"Pinyao in Paris", National Library, MK2, Paris, France
"Phantasmagoria", Walsh Gallery, Chicago, IL, USA
2006 "China Contemporary", Museum Boijmans Van Beuningen, Rotterdam, The Netherlands

2004年 《虚拟最后的审判》芝加哥，Walsh画廊
《观光》SCA画廊，悉尼的艺术学，悉尼
《中国的春天》博物馆 CRAC 阿尔萨斯，Altkirch
《Rivka Rinn 和缪晓春》白色空间，北京
《品要在巴黎》国际图书馆，MK2，巴黎
《幻影》芝加哥，Walsh画廊
2006年 《当代中国》荷兰鹿特丹，波宁根美术馆

Selected publications / Ausgewählte Publikationen / 所选著作

Bernhard Fibicher, Matthias Frehner (eds.): "Mahjong. Chinesische Gegenwartskunst aus der Sammlung Sigg", Ostfildern-Ruit 2005
"European Photography", Nr. 76, Göttingen 2005

Fibicher, Bernhard/Frehner, Matthias（编者）：《麻将－西克的当代艺术收藏展》，Ostfildern-Ruit 2005年
《欧洲摄影》，第76号，格廷根 2005年

MIAO XIAOCHUN 缪晓春

[miaʊ ɕiaʊʈʂhun]

Born in 1964, Miao Xiaochun received his art education at Kunsthochschule Kassel, Germany, after studying art history in Beijing's Central Academy of Arts and working as a freelance painter for five years. He returned to China in 1999 to teach at the newly established Department of Photography and New Media at his alma mater. As a result of this background, his photographs betray a painter's observation of the world, but also attest to a strong desire to expand the field of photography through digital technology.

Since the late 1990s, Miao Xiaochun has created a large body of works related to his experience in foreign or Chinese cities, which can be roughly divided into four groups or periods. The initial group consists of his graduation works in Kunsthochschule Kassel. This is a series of black-and-white photographs, each with a life-size mannequin as its central character. Dressed as an ancient Chinese gentleman, the figure has Miao Xiaochun's face and is created as the artist's alter-ego. Autobiographical in nature, these photographs embody Miao Xiaochun's personal experience while he was a foreign student in Germany.

Miao Xiaochun created a second group of photographs after he returned to China in 1999 and exhibited them in a one-man show in the Gallery of the Central Academy of Fine Arts in 2001. The exhibition's title, "From East to West and Back Again", defines it as a sequel to the previous exhibition. This significance is again established by the statue, which appears in each photograph as well as in a sculptural form in an installation. Situated in the Chinese environment, however, the meaning of the ancient gentleman is complicated: it now often signifies Miao's "culture shock" upon returning to his country after five years, during which time China underwent rapid globalization and commercialization.

The third period started in 2002, when Miao began to create large, colourful photographs with the help of digital technology. Whereas these works constantly evoke earlier

Der 1964 geborene Miao Xiaochun studierte zunächst Kunstgeschichte an der Central Academy of Arts in Peking und arbeitete dann fünf Jahre als freier Maler, bevor er zur Kunstausbildung an die Kunsthochschule Kassel in Deutschland ging. 1999 kehrte er nach China zurück, um am neu gegründeten Fachbereich für Fotografie und Neue Medien seiner Alma Mater zu unterrichten. Dank dieser Vorgeschichte verraten seine Fotografien die Betrachtungsweise des Malers, zeugen aber zugleich vom starken Interesse, das Gebiet der Fotografie durch die Digitaltechnik zu erweitern.

Seit Ende der 1990er Jahre hat Miao Xiaochun zahlreiche Arbeiten vorgelegt, die mit seinen Erfahrungen in ausländischen und chinesischen Städten zu tun haben. Sie lassen sich grob in vier Gruppen oder Perioden unterteilen: Die erste Gruppe entstand als Abschlussarbeit an der Kunsthochschule Kassel. Es handelt sich um eine Serie von Schwarzweißfotografien, deren zentrale Figur eine lebensgroße Gliederpuppe ist. Wie ein chinesischer Gelehrter aus alter Zeit gekleidet, trägt sie Miao Xiaochuns Gesichtszüge – gleichsam das Alter Ego des Künstlers. Diese autobiografischen Fotografien verarbeiten Miao Xiaochuns persönliche Erfahrungen als ausländischer Student in Deutschland. 1999 nach China zurückgekehrt, schuf Miao Xiaochun eine zweite Serie von Fotografien, die er 2001 bei einer Einzelausstellung in der Galerie der Central Academy of Fine Arts zeigte. Der Ausstellungstitel „From East to West and Back Again" definiert sie als Fortsetzung der früheren Arbeiten, zumal wiederum in jeder Fotografie und auch in einer skulpturalen Installation das schon bekannte Double des Künstlers auftaucht. Im Kontext des chinesischen Umfelds kompliziert sich die Bedeutung des Gelehrten jedoch: Jetzt verweist er eher auf Miaos „Kulturschock" bei seiner Rückkehr in die Heimat nach fünf Jahren, in denen China eine rasante Globalisierung und Kommerzialisierung durchgemacht hat.

Miaos dritte Werkperiode begann 2002, als er mit Hilfe der Digitaltechnik großformatige Farbfotografien produzierte. Wenngleich diese Arbeiten auf frühere Themen und Bilder

缪晓春出生于1964年，在北京的中央美术学院学习艺术史，并作为自由画家工作五年，随后在卡塞尔艺术学院接受了他的艺术教育。他于 1999 年回国，在其母校新设的摄影与数码媒体系任教。由于具有这样的背景，他的摄影不但透露出来自画家的看待世界的视角，同时也突显其通过数码技术扩展摄影领域的强烈愿望。

从上世纪九十年代后期开始，缪晓春创作了与其国外或国内城市经历相关的大量作品，这些作品大致可以分为四个阶段。最初的作品包括他在卡塞尔艺术学院的毕业作品。这是一系列黑白摄影作品，每幅都以一个真人大小的服装模特作为中心角色。角色穿着古代中国先生的服装，具有缪晓春的脸孔，并作为这位艺术家的另一面被创造出来。这些摄影作品具有自传的特质，表达出缪晓春作为一名留学生在德国的个人经历。

在1999年回国以后，缪晓春创作了第二组摄影作品，并于2001年在中央美院画廊的个展上展出了这些作品。这次展览主题为《从东到西，从西到东》，并被定义为前一次展览的续篇。出现于每幅摄影作品，并且在一件装置作品中以雕塑形式出现的一个雕像再次确立了这层含义。然而，处于中国环境下，古代先生的意义变得复杂：它如今常常表现出缪晓春在时隔五年回国以后的“文化震惊”，而在此期间中国经历了快速的全球化和商业化。

第三阶段开始于2002年，缪晓春开始借助数码技术创作大型的彩色摄影作品。尽管这些作品不断地令人想起他早期的题材和影像，例如中国社会不断深入的商业化，古代先生的孤独以及传统和现代文化之间的对比，作品越来越复杂的构成反映出艺术家对于体裁和技术革新日益浓厚的兴趣。他将画面置于极长作品中的趋势已经在之前的一个阶段中显现出来，而如今他则是特意地将这种构成风格同中国古代卷轴画相结合。

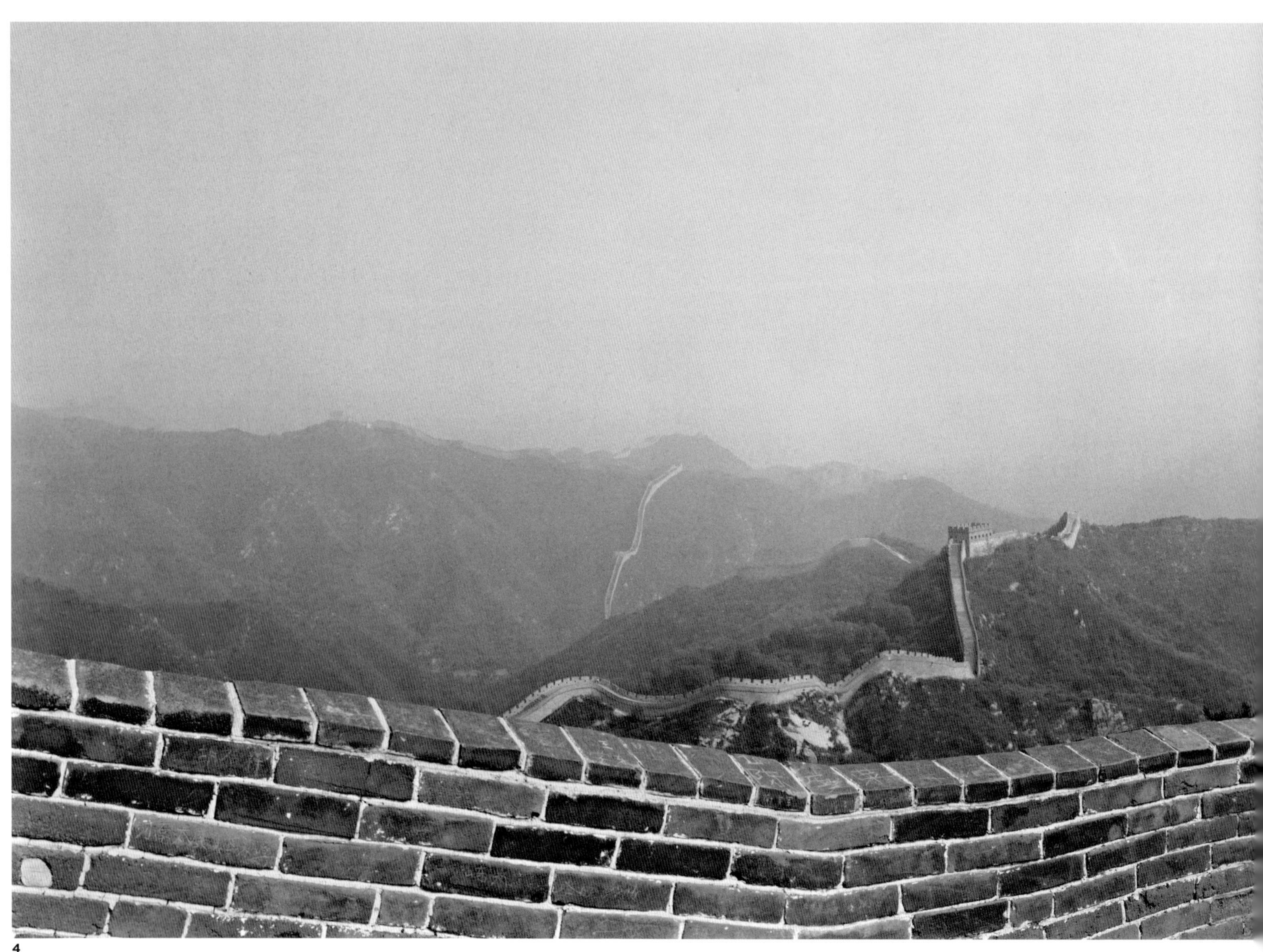

4

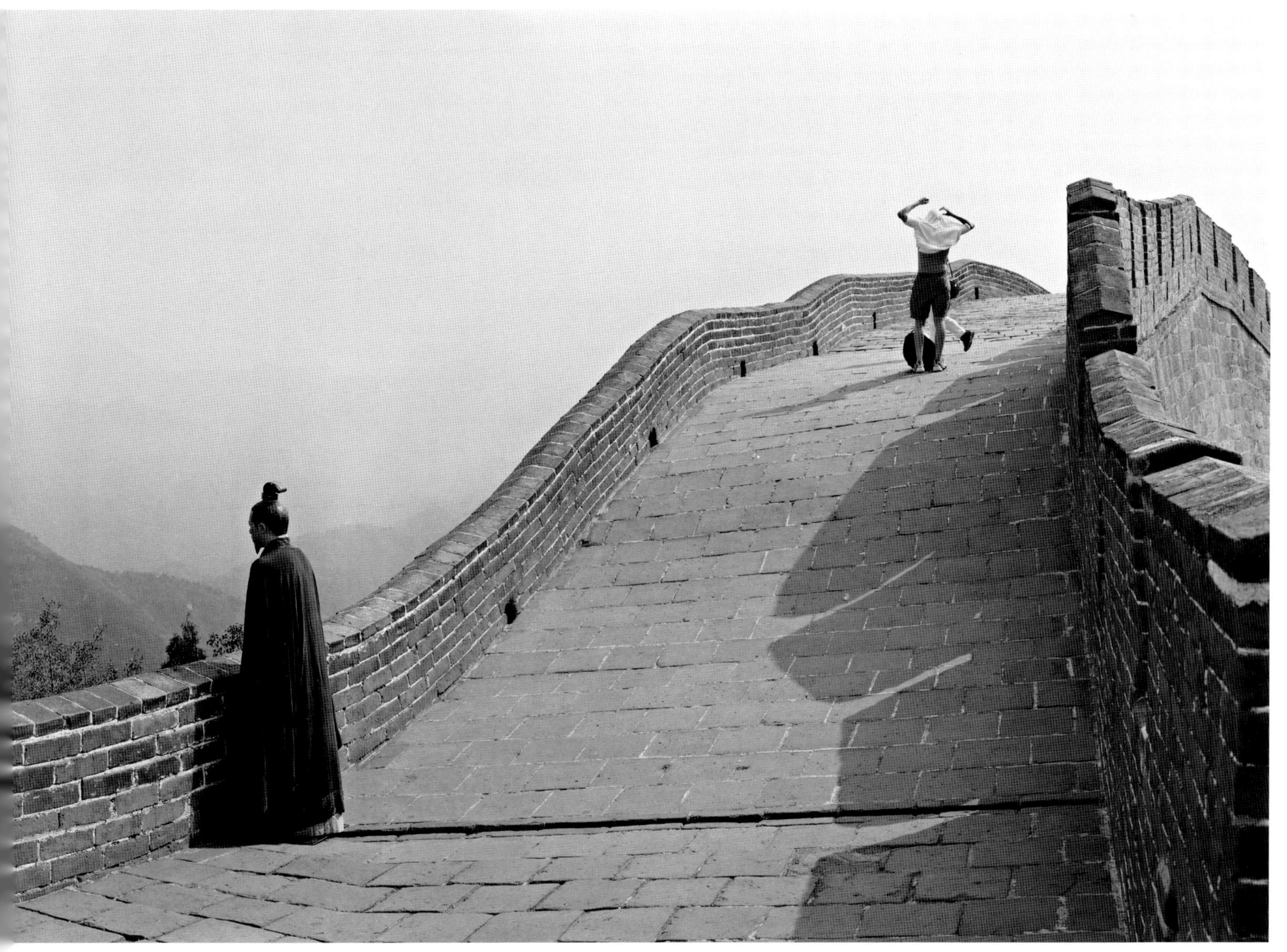

5

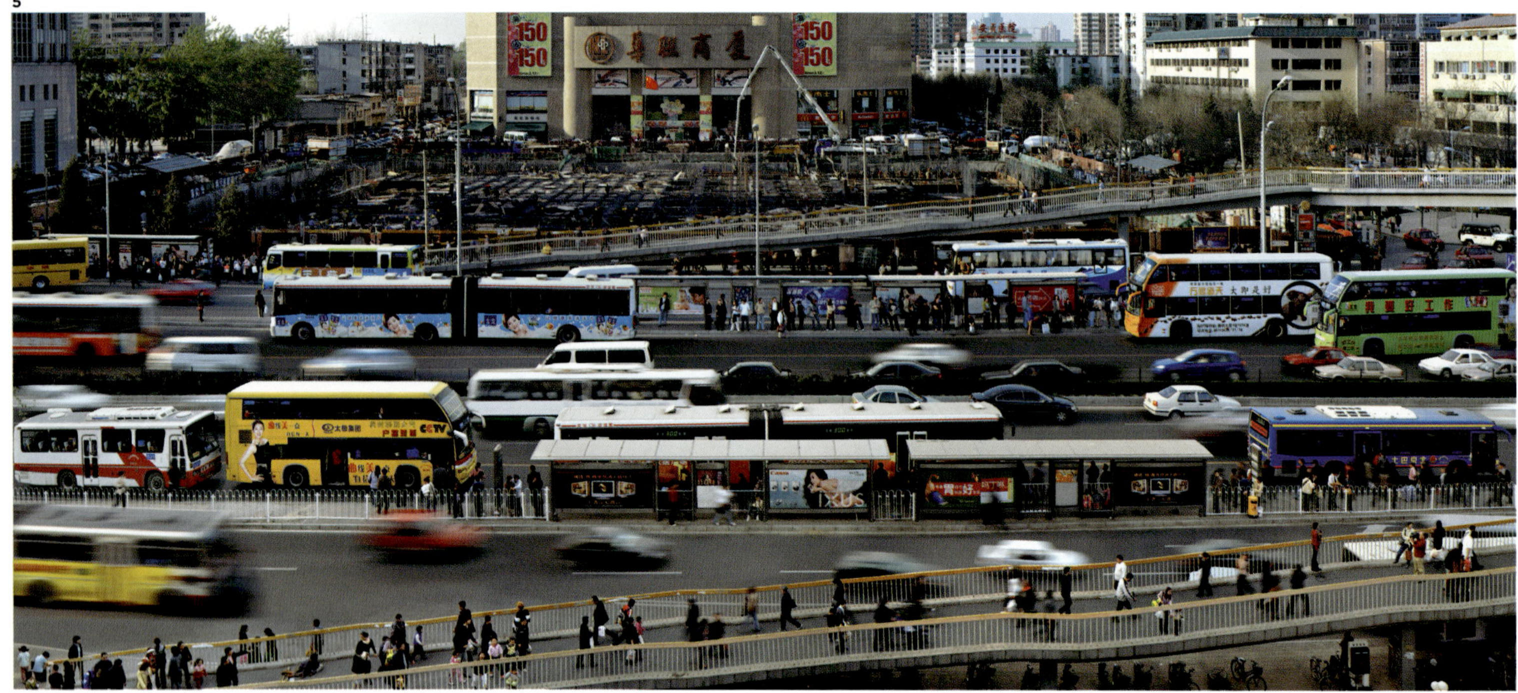

themes and images – the deepening commercialization of Chinese society, the solitude of the ancient gentleman, and the contrast between traditional and contemporary culture – their increasingly complex compositions reflect the artist's heightened attraction to stylistic and technical innovations. His tendency to frame a picture in an overly long composition was already evident in the previous period, but now Miao Xiaochun self-consciously connected this compositional style with ancient Chinese scroll painting.

This third period reached its end with the disappearance of the mannequin from his large-format, computer-manipulated photographs, which take the life of a city as the main subject of representation. At the same time, he also began an ambitious project which translates Michelangelo's "Last Judgement" into multiple compositions and a video. The project was motivated by Miao's desire to explore the internal space of the masterpiece and represent the individual perspectives of the painted figures. Through a complex process of image translation and manipulation, he created a 3D digital model of a figure based on his own image, bestowing it with different gestures and movements, and integrated these 3D figures into a virtual space according to the composition of "The Last Judgement". Once he had achieved this 3D spatial construct, he, or a built-in camera lens he controlled, could not only view the composition from numerous internal positions, but could also assume vantage points outside the constructed pictorial space.

zurückgreifen – die zunehmende Kommerzialisierung der chinesischen Gesellschaft, die Einsamkeit des altmodischen Gelehrten und den Kontrast zwischen traditioneller und zeitgenössischer Kultur –, so spiegeln ihre immer komplexeren Kompositionen zugleich die verstärkte Beschäftigung des Künstlers mit stilistischen und technischen Innovationen. Die Tendenz, seine Bilder extrem querformatig anzulegen, war schon vorher erkennbar, aber nun setzt Miao Xiaochun dieses kompositorische Stilmittel ausdrücklich in Bezug zu alten chinesischen Rollbildern. Und in dieser dritten Schaffensperiode verschwindet auch schließlich sein Alter Ego aus den riesigen computerbearbeiteten Fotografien, deren zentrales Motiv das Leben einer Stadt ist.

Parallel dazu nahm Miao ein äußerst ehrgeiziges Unternehmen in Angriff, nämlich Michelangelos „Jüngstes Gericht" in eine komplexe Bild- und Video-Komposition zu transponieren. Dahinter steckte der Wunsch, den inneren Raum des Meisterwerks zu ergründen und die individuellen Blickwinkel der gemalten Figuren darzustellen. Durch einen komplexen Prozess der Bildtransformation und -bearbeitung schuf er ein digitales 3D-Modell einer Figur, die auf seiner eigenen Erscheinung basierte. Er stattete sie mit verschiedenen Gesten und Bewegungen aus und integrierte sie in einen virtuellen Raum nach dem Vorbild des „Jüngsten Gerichts". Innerhalb dieses Raums kann eine mobile steuerbare Kameralinse die Komposition aus zahlreichen inneren Positionen heraus betrachten, aber auch Standpunkte außerhalb des konstruierten Bildraums einnehmen.

第三阶段伴随着服装模特在他作品中的消失而结束，他如今创作大型计算机处理的摄影作品，而这些作品将城市的生命作为表达的主题。与此同时，他还开始了一项雄心勃勃的项目，将米开朗基罗的《最后的审判》转换成为多个组成成分，然后再将这些成分转换成为一部动画作品。该项目的创意来源于缪晓春希望发掘这一杰作的"内在"空间，以及表达作品人物的"个别"视角的愿望。通过一个图像转换和处理的复杂过程，他根据自己的形象创作了一个三维数字模型人物，并赋予其各种姿势和动作，并将这些三维人物根据《最后的审判》的组成整合成为一个虚拟空间。当他完成了这个三维空间构造以后，他，或者说他所控制的一个内置相机镜头不仅能够从无数的"内部位置"观看这一作品，同样也能够在所构造的图形空间外部的有利位置进行观看。

Wu Hung

6

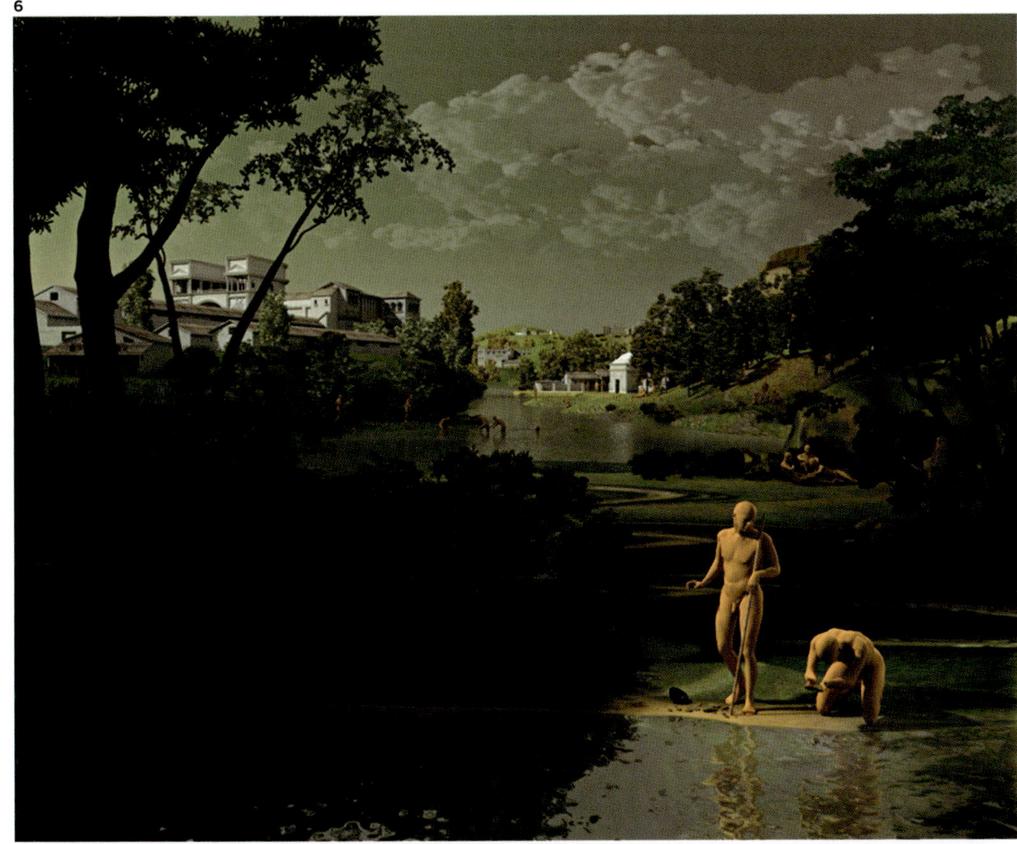

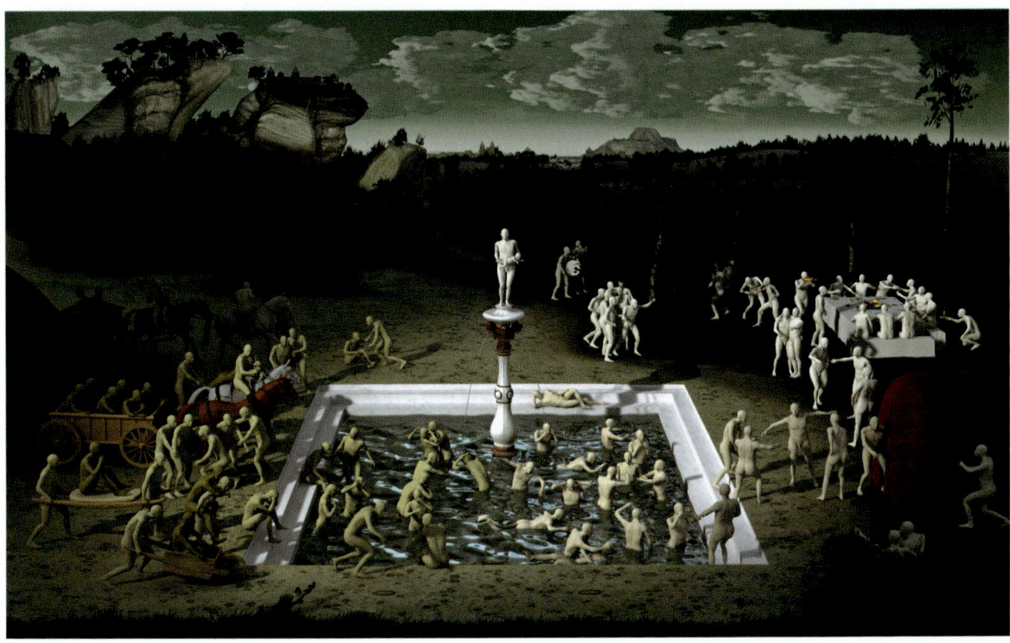

7

1 ***The Last Judgement in Cyberspace – The Side View***, *2006*
C-print, 160 x 428 cm
C-print, 160 x 428 cm
《虚拟最后审判–侧视图》C–印刷品, 160 x 428 cm

2 ***The Last Judgement in Cyberspace – The Front View***, *2006*
C-print, 418 x 360 cm
C-print, 418 x 360 cm
《虚拟最后审判–正视图》C–印刷品, 418 x 360 cm

3 ***The Last Judgement in Cyberspace – The Below View***, *2006*
C-print, 385 x 480 cm
C-print, 385 x 480 cm
《虚拟最后审判–仰视图》C–印刷品, 385 x 480 cm

4 ***The Great Wall two thousand years ago***, *2001*
B/w photograph, 127 x 360 cm
Schwarzweißfotografie, 127 x 360 cm
《两千多年前的长城》2001年, 摄影, 127 x 360 cm

5 ***Orbit***, *2005*
C-print, 217 x 480 cm
C-print, 217 x 480 cm
《轨道运动》2005年, C–印刷品, 217 x 480 cm

6 ***Landscape with Diogenes***, *2007*
C-print, 170 x 204 cm
C-print, 170 x 204 cm
《有戴奥真尼斯的风景》2007年, C–印刷品, 170 x 204 cm

7 ***The Fountain of Youth***, *2007*
C-print, 228 x 360 cm
C-print, 228 x 360 cm
《青春泉》2007年, C–印刷品, 228 x 360 cm

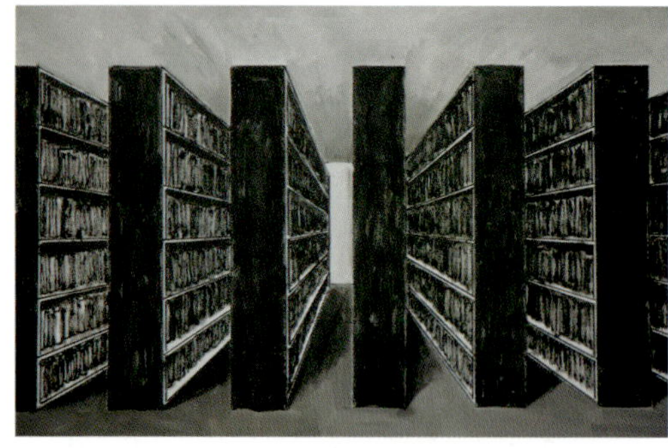
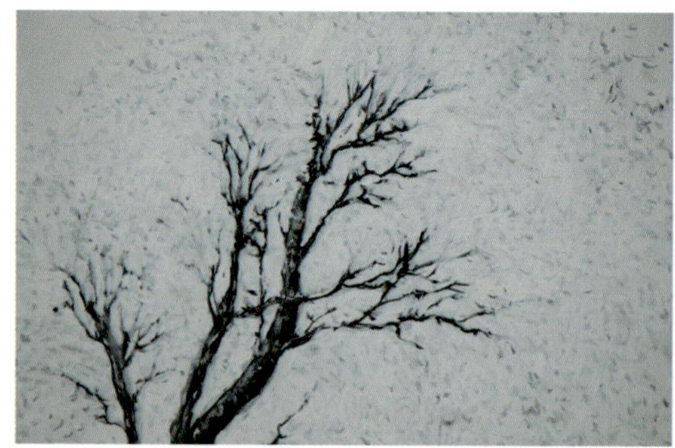
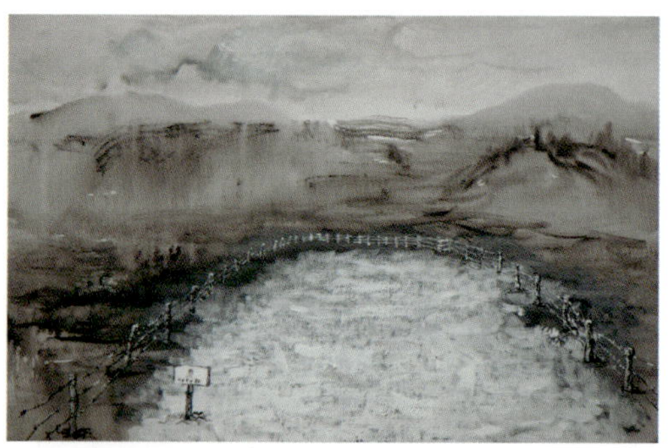
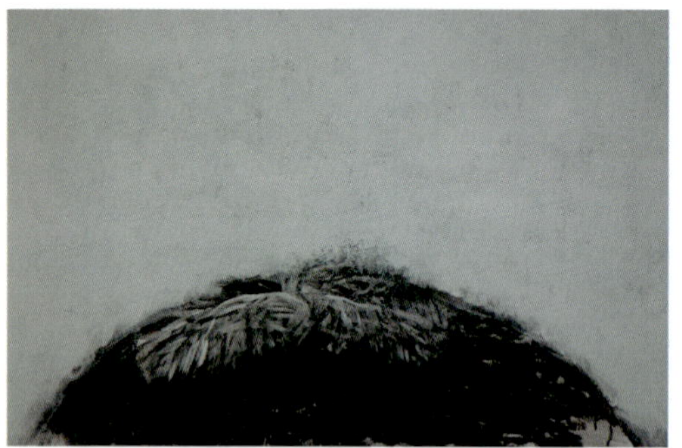
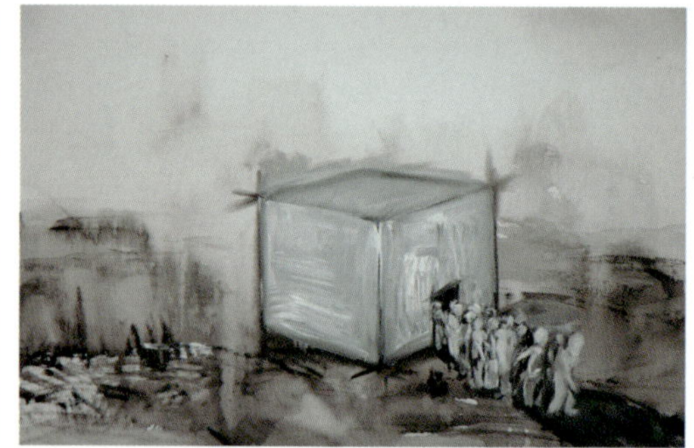
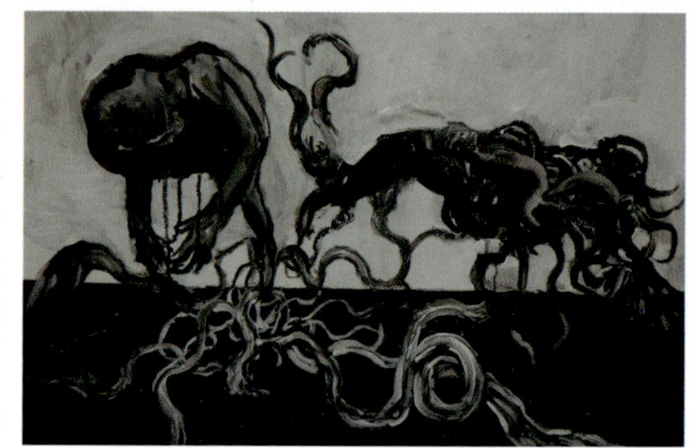
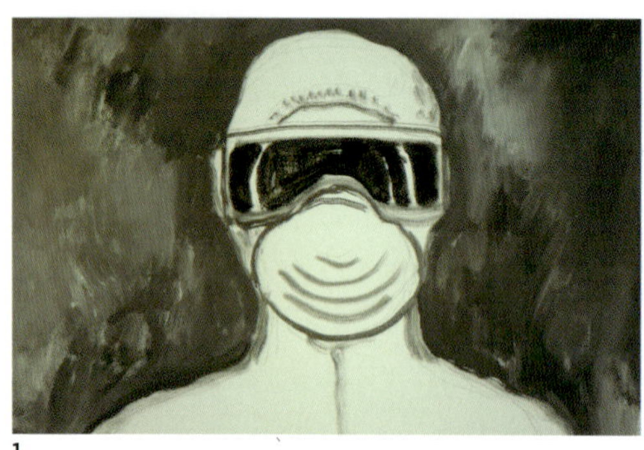
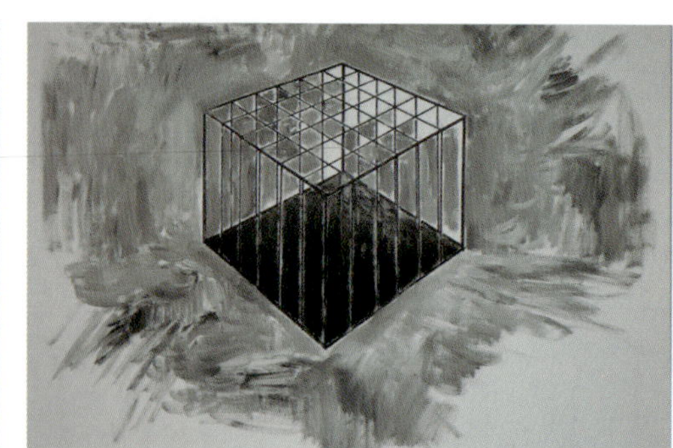
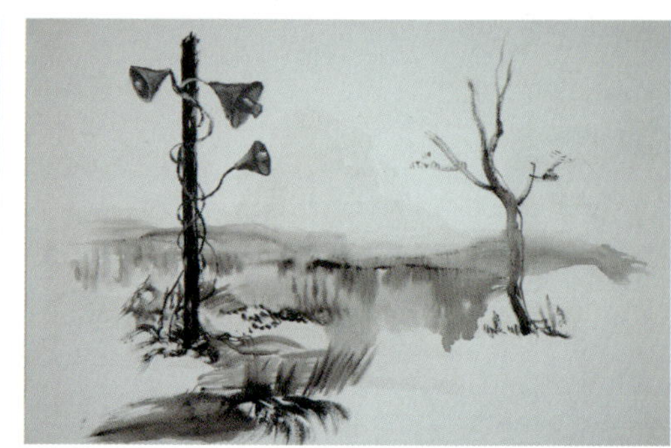

1

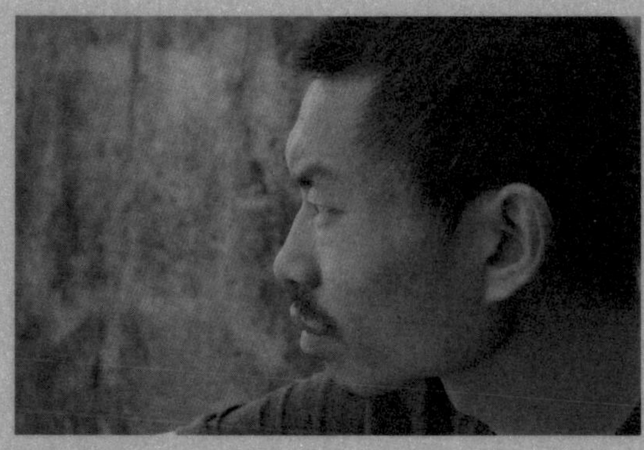

"Life itself is a narrative, it is a contradictory thing. Memory and forgetting are struggling eternally to each other in time. My artworks seem to be like a piece of shredded paper from my memories."

"Das Leben selbst ist eine widersprüchliche Geschichte. Erinnerung und Vergessen kämpfen für immer miteinander. Meine Werke erscheinen mir wie ein Stück zerfetztes Papier meiner Erinnerungen."

"生活是记叙文，它是一件矛盾的事。记忆和忘记及时奋斗永恒地互相。我的艺术品似乎是象切细的纸张从我的记忆，从涌现忘记的那些想像力。"

Born in 1972 in Chengdu, Sichuan Province, China. Lives and works in Shanghai
Geboren 1972 in Chengdu, Provinz Sichuan, China. Lebt und arbeitet in Shanghai
1972年出生于中国四川成都。 住居工作在上海

Selected exhibitions **/ Ausgewählte Ausstellungen /** 所选展览

2000 "Tale of two Cities", Asia Contemporary Art, London, UK
2003 "New landscapes, new portraits – Shen Xiaotong, Qiu Anxiong", Hanart TZ Gallery, Hong Kong, China
2004 "24 Artists from Germany and China", Alexander Ochs Gallery, Beijing, China
2006 "MoCA Envisage 2006", Museum of Contemporary Art, Shanghai, China
2006/07 "China Power Station I", Battersea Power Station, Serpentine Gallery, London, UK; Astrup Fearnley Museum of Modern Art, Oslo, Norway

2000年 《两城故事》，亚洲当代艺术画廊，伦敦
2003年 《邱黯雄　沈晓彤：新造像　新山水》，汉雅轩画廊，香港
2004年 《中德当代艺术展》，北京空白空间画廊，北京，中国
2006年 《上海当代艺术馆文献展2006》上海当代艺术馆 中国
2006/07年《中国电站I》蛇形画廊，巴特西电站 伦敦 英国；Astrup Fearnley 现代美术馆 奥斯陆 挪威

Selected publications **/ Ausgewählte Publikationen /** 所选著作

Joris Escher, Martijn Kielstra (eds.): "The Chengdu Movement", Amsterdam 2000

Escher, Joris/Kielstra, Martijn（编者）：《成都運動》阿姆斯特丹2000年

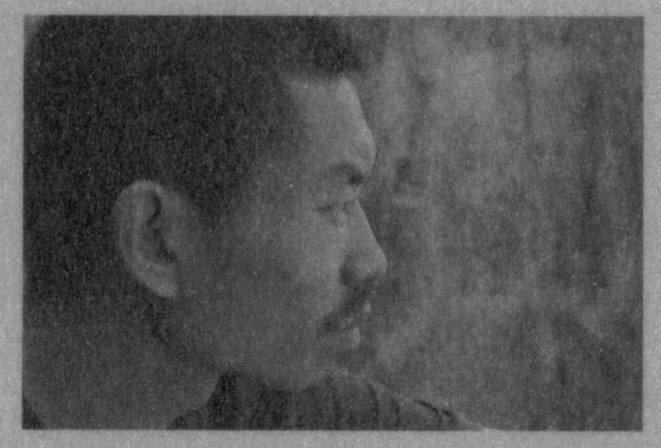

"Life itself is a narrative, it is a contradictory thing. Memory and forgetting are struggling eternally to each other in time. My artworks seem to be like a piece of shredded paper from my memories."

"Das Leben selbst ist eine widersprüchliche Geschichte. Erinnerung und Vergessen kämpfen für immer miteinander. Meine Werke erscheinen mir wie ein Stück zerfetztes Papier meiner Erinnerungen."

"生活是记叙文，它是一件矛盾的事。记忆和忘记及时奋斗永恒地互相。我的艺术品似乎是象切细的纸张从我的记忆，从涌现忘记的那些想像力。"

Born in 1972 in Chengdu, Sichuan Province, China. Lives and works in Shanghai
Geboren 1972 in Chengdu, Provinz Sichuan, China. Lebt und arbeitet in Shanghai
1972年出生于中国四川成都。 住居工作在上海

Selected exhibitions / Ausgewählte Ausstellungen / 所选展览

2000	"Tale of two Cities", Asia Contemporary Art, London, UK
2003	"New landscapes, new portraits – Shen Xiaotong, Qiu Anxiong", Hanart TZ Gallery, Hong Kong, China
2004	"24 Artists from Germany and China", Alexander Ochs Gallery, Beijing, China
2006	"MoCA Envisage 2006", Museum of Contemporary Art, Shanghai, China
2006/07	"China Power Station I", Battersea Power Station, Serpentine Gallery, London, UK; Astrup Fearnley Museum of Modern Art, Oslo, Norway

2000年	《两城故事》，亚洲当代艺术画廊，伦敦
2003年	《邱黯雄 沈晓彤：新造像 新山水》，汉雅轩画廊，香港
2004年	《中德当代艺术展》，北京空白空间画廊，北京，中国
2006年	《上海当代艺术馆文献展2006》上海当代艺术馆 中国
2006/07年	《中国电站I》蛇形画廊，巴特西电站 伦敦 英国；Astrup Fearnley 现代美术馆 奥斯陆 挪威

Selected publications / Ausgewählte Publikationen / 所选著作

Joris Escher, Martijn Kielstra (eds.): "The Chengdu Movement", Amsterdam 2000

Escher, Joris/Kielstra, Martijn（編者）：《成都運動》阿姆斯特丹2000年

QIU ANXIONG 邱黯雄

[tɕ^{h}iou anɕiʊŋ]

Qiu Anxiong, graduating in 1994 from the Sichuan Art Academy, worked for some time at a planning company, but the restrictions there made him return soon to his hometown Chengdu, where he regularly met artists like He Duoling, Zhou Chunya, Zhang Xiaogang, and Shen Xiaotong. The meeting point was a small tavern he had opened for the artists to have a place for discussing art, and playing Rock music together. From 1998 to 2003 Qiu Anxiong went to Germany to attend Kunsthochschule Kassel, Germany, where he graduated in 2003. In 2004 he returned to China where he worked as teacher at Shanghai Normal University and established his own studio. For his first video footage "Jiangnan Poem", he borrowed the camera from Yang Fudong, a video artist from Shanghai.

Due to his deep interest in traditional Chinese literature, philosophy, and religions, Qiu Anxiong started to study earnestly the Chinese Classics and techniques of traditional ink painting. In the beginning of his studies he already transmitted the ink painting techniques to abstract oil painting. During his stay in Germany he came in contact with the new art media like electronics, which opened the door to a new line of creation possibilities. Back to China in his hometown which is full of legends and myths he started to use these new media for a remake of his edition of art, finding a new interface for east and west culture, and giving the traditional Chinese painting a new appearance by electronic media.

In fact, Qiu Anxiong started in 2004 to draw a modern fairytale, called "New Shan Hai Jing" (New Classic of Mountains and Seas), added writings in style of classical Chinese annotations, and had this painting handmade and gave it friends and relatives. He then experimented with the two ink paintings "In the Sky" and "Butterfly Effect" (both 2005) as animated cartoon and created with this film of 30 minutes the "New Shan Hai Jing". This was the start of his career. The cartoon made him known in 2006 as China's first famous media artist among the new generation on the contemporary Chinese art scene.

Qiu Anxiong beendete 1994 sein Studium an der Sichuan Art Academy. Danach arbeitete er einige Zeit für eine Planungsfirma, kehrte aber schon bald wegen der strengen Vorschriften in seine Heimatstadt Chengdu zurück, wo er regelmäßig mit Künstlern wie He Duoling, Zhou Chunya, Zhang Xiaogang und Shen Xiaotong zusammenkam. Als Treffpunkt diente eine kleine Schenke, die er für die Künstler eröffnet hatte, um einen Ort für Diskussionen zu schaffen und gemeinsam Rockmusik spielen zu können. Von 1998 bis 2003 war Qiu Anxiong in Deutschland an der Kunsthochschule Kassel, an der er 2003 seinen Abschluss machte. 2004 kehrte er nach China zurück, wo er als Lehrer an der Shanghai Normal University arbeitete und gleichzeitig sein eigenes Studio einrichtete. Für seine erste Videoaufnahme „Jiangnan Poem" lieh er sich von Yang Fudong, einem Videokünstler aus Shanghai, die Kamera.

Angestoßen durch sein Interesse an traditioneller chinesischer Literatur, Philosophie und Religion begann Qiu Anxiong ernsthaft die chinesischen Klassiker und die Technik der traditionellen Tuschemalerei zu studieren. Zu Beginn seiner Studien übertrug er letztere noch einfach auf abstrakte Ölgemälde. Doch während seines Deutschlandaufenthalts war Qiu mit den neuen technischen Errungenschaften zur Produktion von Kunst in Berührung gekommen, was ihm völlig neue Möglichkeiten eröffnete. Nach China zurückgekehrt, begann er darum in seiner Heimatstadt, die erfüllt von Legenden und Mythen ist, diese Techniken für eine Neuorientierung seiner Kunst zu nutzen. Er hatte einen Schnittpunkt zwischen östlicher und westlicher Kultur gefunden und wollte der traditionellen chinesischen Malerei mithilfe der elektronischen Medien ein neues Erscheinungsbild geben.

2004 begann Qiu ein modernes Märchen zu entwickeln, das er „New Shan Hai Jing" (New Classic of Mountains and Seas) nannte. Er fügte diesem Kommentare im Stil klassischer chinesischer Bücher hinzu und ließ die Zeichnungen von Hand anfertigen, um sie anschließend an Freunde und Verwandte zu verteilen. Danach experimentierte er mit zwei Tuschezeichnungen – „In the Sky" und „Butterfly Effect"

1994年邱黯雄毕业于四川美术学院，之后一度在深圳的设计公司工作，但受不了拘束，不久就回到老家成都。那段期间，他和何多苓、周春芽、张晓刚、沈晓彤等艺术家常常聚在一起，甚至开了一家“小酒馆”作为大家聚会的场所，大夥儿一起谈艺术，一起玩摇滚音乐。1998年至2003年邱黯雄远赴德国卡塞尔大学艺术学院留学，2004年回国任教于上海师范大学，并且在上海成立自己的工作室。他拍第一部录像影片《江南错》的器材，还是向也定居在上海的影像艺术家杨福东去商借的。

原本对中国古典文学、哲学和宗教文化深感兴趣的邱黯雄，熟读经书也深谙水墨画的技巧。早期他曾经以中国水墨技法画抽象的油画，然而他在德国求学期间接触到电子媒体的新媒体艺术，却为他打开了一条崭新的创作路线，将他的中国神话原乡，用电子媒介的素材重新诠释出他的版本，将原本平行的东西文化找到了交错点，将传统的中国绘画赋予了电子版的新媒体形貌。

其实，邱黯雄从2004年便开始绘制现代怪兽《新山海经》，加上文言文的注解，手工订制成册，分送给众亲好友。经历《空中的》和《蝴蝶效应》两部水墨动画片的实验，一部集大成的30分钟长度的《新山海经》使得他横空出世，成为中国当代艺坛2006年最受瞩目的新媒体艺术家。

古籍《山海经》包括南山经卷、西山经卷、北山经卷等，是一部描写奇人异兽的中国神话，共记录了历史、地理、宗教等方面的320种事物。邱黯雄在古典版本的基础上，创造了他想象的新奇人异兽，例如他把现代文明的新生事物融合了长鼻喷火的大象，形成的新怪兽“唐坦”，就是大象和坦克车的混合体。邱黯雄以半年的时间亲自制作，他一共手绘了六千张原稿，增补了不少反映新时代的内容，他打算一集一集出片，每一集收纳30至40个描写对象。

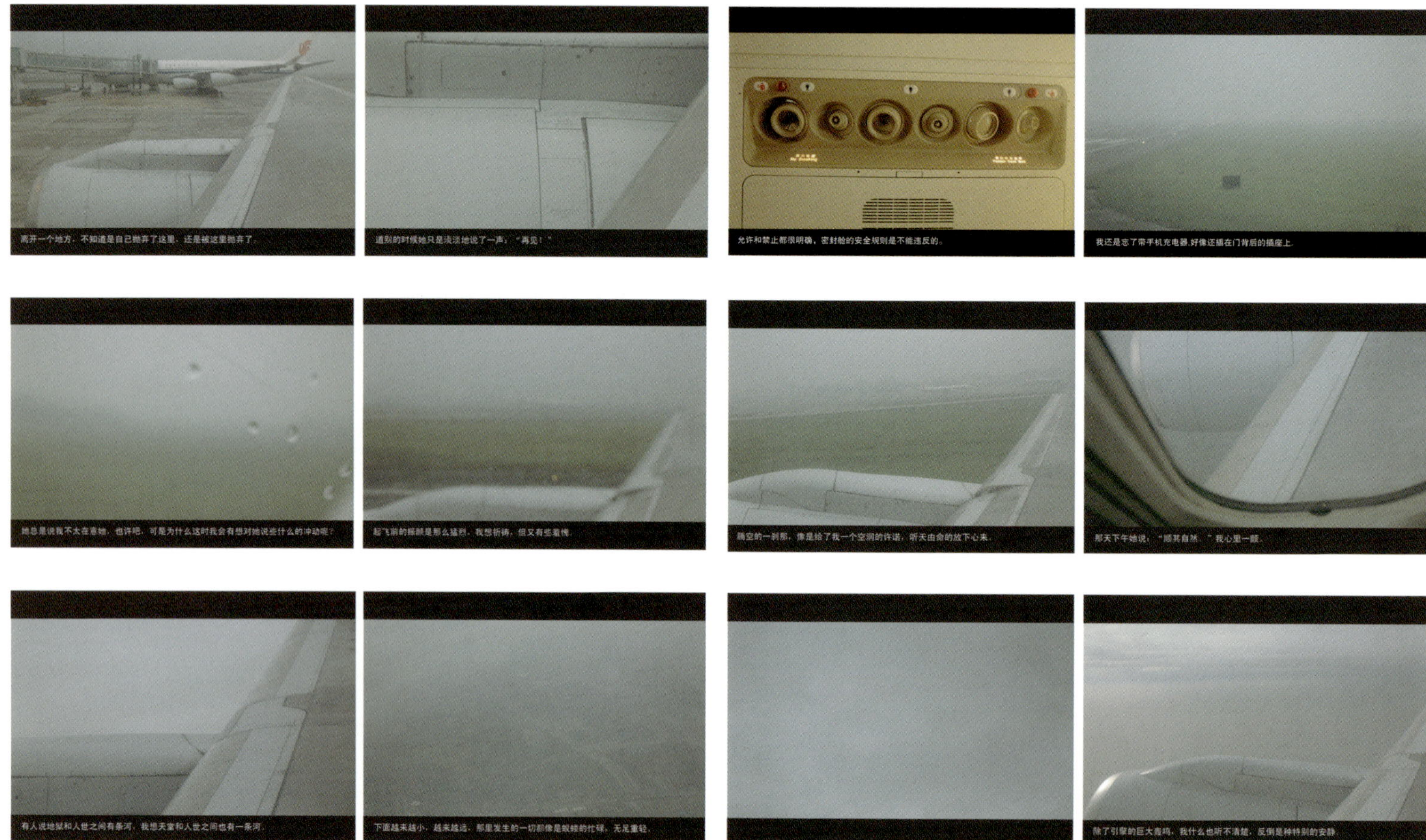
离开一个地方，不知道是自己抛弃了这里，还是被这里抛弃了。
道别的时候她只是淡淡地说了一声："再见！"
允许和禁止都很明确，密封舱的安全规则是不能违反的。
我还是忘了带手机充电器,好像还插在门背后的插座上。
她总是说我不太在意她，也许吧，可是为什么这时我会有想对她说些什么的冲动呢？
起飞前的振颤是那么猛烈，我想祈祷，但又有些羞愧。
腾空的一刹那，像是给了我一个空洞的许诺，听天由命的放下心来。
那天下午她说："顺其自然。"我心里一颤。
有人说地狱和人世之间有条河，我想天堂和人世之间也有一条河。
下面越来越小，越来越远，那里发生的一切都像是蚊蝇的忙碌，无足重轻。
除了引擎的巨大轰鸣，我什么也听不清楚，反倒是种特别的安静。

2

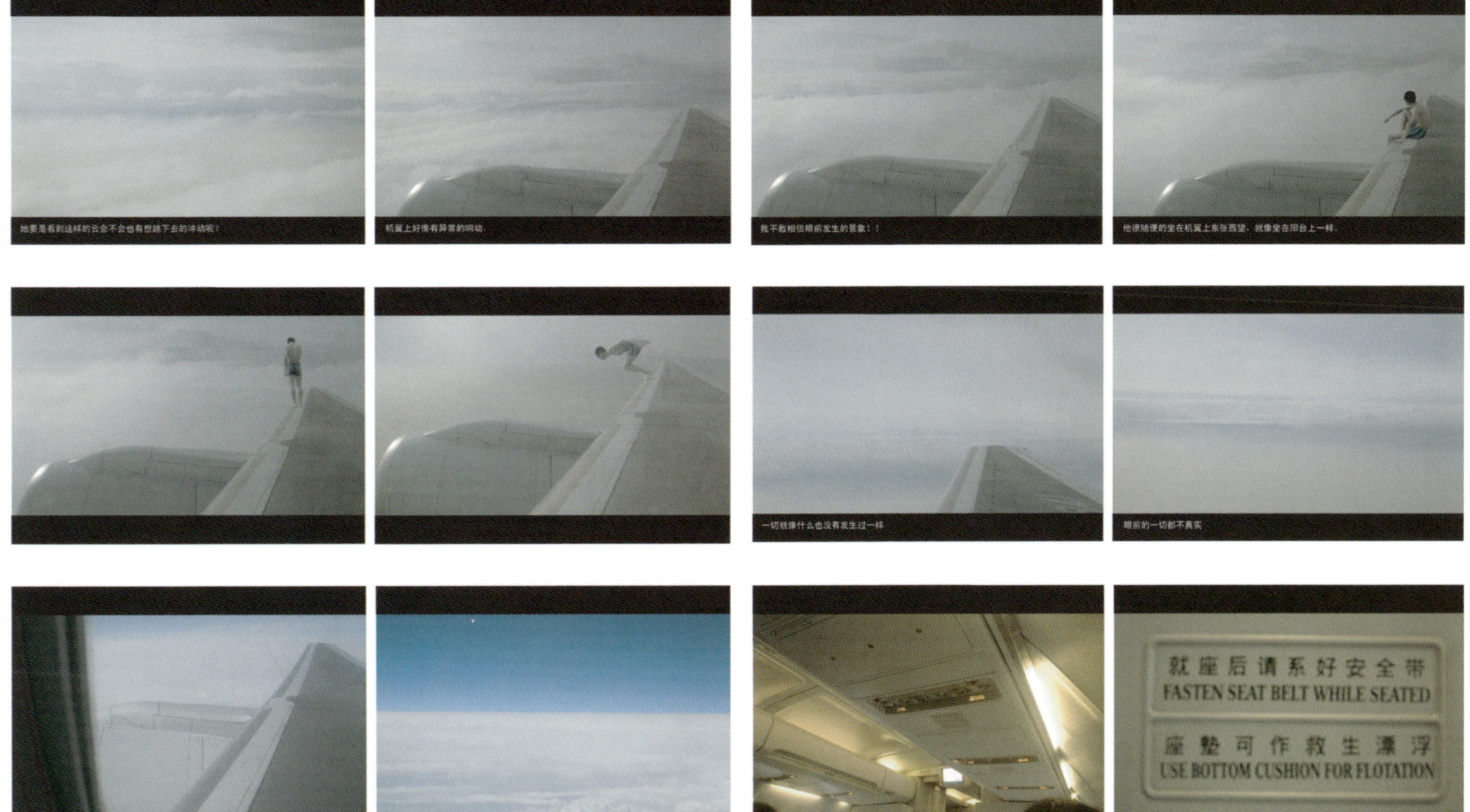
她要是看到这样的云会不会也有想跳下去的冲动呢？
机翼上好像有异常的响动。
我不敢相信眼前发生的景象！！
他很随便的坐在机翼上东张西望，就像坐在阳台上一样。
一切就像什么也没有发生过一样
眼前的一切都不真实
阳光是那样强烈，刚才的情景历历在目，那么清晰，又像是一个刚做完的梦。
天堂就在窗外，仿佛伸手可及，其实那是个距离的幻像，舱外是另一个世界，咫尺天涯
机舱里一切如常，电视里的港产片还在播放着。
就座后请系好安全带
FASTEN SEAT BELT WHILE SEATED
座垫可作救生漂浮
USE BOTTOM CUSHION FOR FLOTATION
待会儿下飞机是不是要给她打个电话，说我平安到达了。

3

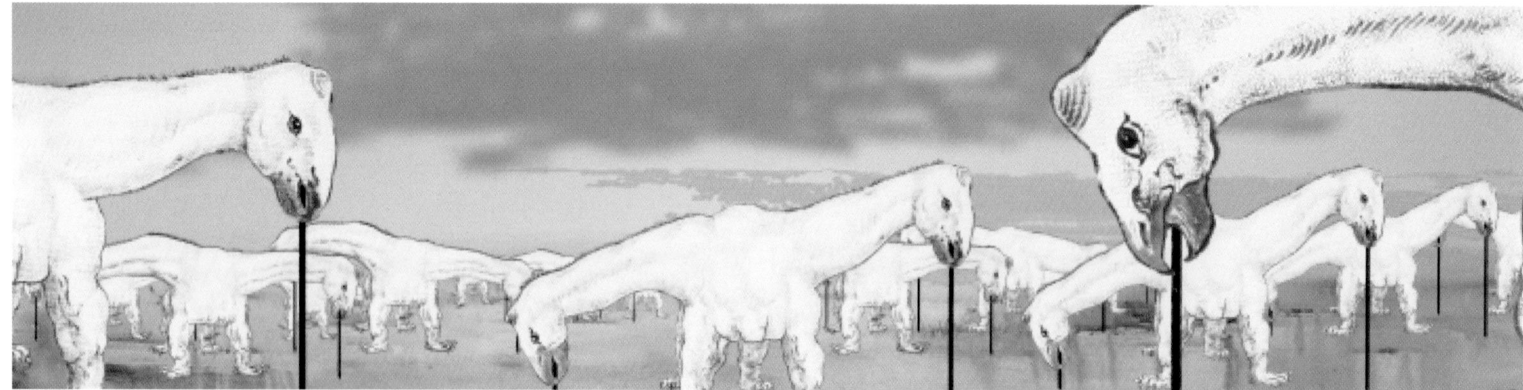

The classic "Shan Hai Jing" comprised chapters of the southern mountains, the western and northern ones, one part of the book described strange and alien human beings and monsters, providing history, geography and religions of more than 320 kinds. Qiu Anxiong created his own strange beings and monsters based on this classical writing, born from his own fantasy. One of this new kind of monsters is "Tang Tan", an elephantlike being with a long proboscis in form of flames, representing a mixture of the old legend and modern civilisation. In fact it is a mixture of elephant and tank. Qiu Anxiong worked on this project of "New Shan Hai Jing" about half a year, drawing himself more than 6000 sketches based on the original book, inserted issues of modern civilisation as reflection of the old tales. He intends to issue one series of cartoons after another each composed of 30 to 40 subjects.

Qiu Anxiong plans to establish his own creation of art, a new system of world view which is neither western style nor based on systems of psychology, but offers a new system of pure sensual cognition, transcending the continuous learning and knowledge and finally returning to the all embracing conditions of life. Qiu Anxiong's ink painting cartoons meld eastern philosophy and western humour based on the Chinese Classics of monsters opening a world of imagination and miracles without frontiers.

(beide 2005) – und entwickelte daraus einen Zeichentrickfilm von 30 Minuten Länge, ebenfalls mit dem Titel „New Shan Hai Jing". Damit schaffte er den Karrieredurchbruch und war 2006 der berühmteste Medienkünstler der neuen chinesischen Künstlergeneration.

Das ursprüngliche „Shan Hai Jing" handelt von den südlichen, westlichen und nördlichen Bergen, von seltsamen Geschöpfen und Ungeheuern, von Geschichte, Geografie und religiösen Bräuchen. Über 320 verschiedene Einträge finden sich in diesem alten Buch, nach dessen Vorlage Qiu Anxiong seine eigenen fremdartigen Wesen und Ungeheuer gestaltete, die seiner Fantasie entsprangen. Eines dieser neuen Ungeheuer ist „Tang Tan", mit seinem langen Rüssel in Form von Flammen ein elefantenähnliches Wesen, das eine Mischung aus den alten Legenden und der modernen Zivilisation verkörpert. Tatsächlich wirkt dieses Wesen wie eine Mischung aus Elefant und Panzer. Qiu Anxiong arbeitete am Projekt des „New Shan Hai Jing" mehr als ein halbes Jahr, zeichnete selbst über 6000 Entwürfe auf der Grundlage des Originalbuchs und fügte, gleichsam als Reflexion der alten Erzählungen, Hinweise auf die Probleme der modernen Zivilisation ein. Qiu plant, dieses Projekt kontinuierlich fortzusetzen, als eine Abfolge von Serien, von denen jede 30 bis 40 Themen abdecken soll.

Qiu Anxiong hat den Ehrgeiz, eine ganz eigene Kunstgattung zu erschaffen, ein neues System der Weltsicht, das weder auf westlichen Anschauungen noch auf Psychologie basieren soll, sondern eine Methodik der reinen Sinneswahrnehmung anstrebt, die das beständige Lernen und Wissen transzendiert und schließlich zu den allumfassenden Bedingungen des Lebens zurückkehrt. Qiu Anxiongs Tuschemalerei verschmilzt östliche Philosophie und westlichen Humor. Auf der Grundlage der chinesischen Klassiker über Ungeheuer eröffnet er eine neue Welt der Imagination und Wunder ohne Grenzen.

邱黯雄企图透过他的艺术创作建立起一个观察世界的系统，一个非西方式的、非理性科学的系统，而是一个纯感性认知的符号系统，透过知识的不断累积和学习，而最终回归到生命本来的完整状态。邱黯雄的水墨动画片，交融了东方式的哲理和西方式的幽默，在中国古典神怪传奇的基础上，揭开喻示了人们无限想象的神奇世界。

Victoria Lu

3

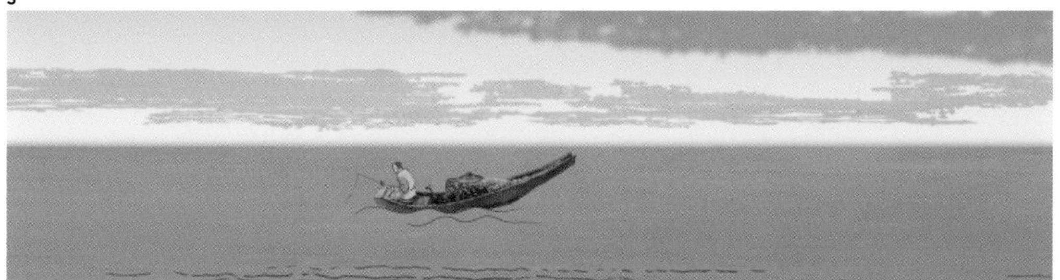

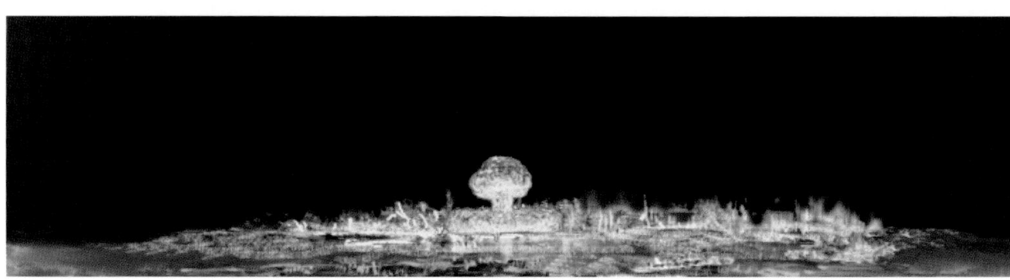

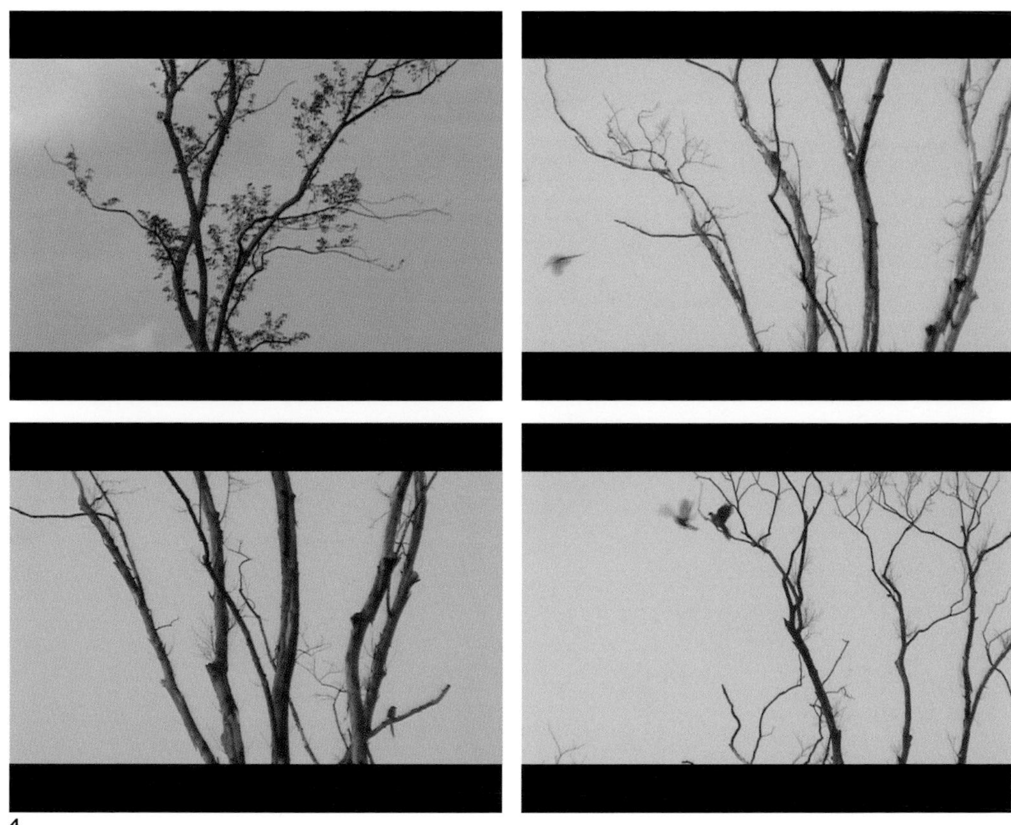

4

1 ***Flight to South***, *2006*
Animation, 9 min 18 sec
Animation, 9 Min. 18 Sek.
《雁南》2006年, 动画, 9分 18秒

2 ***Air-tight Cabinet***, *2005*
Photo installation
Foto-Installation
《密封舱》2005年, 照片装置

3 ***New Book of Mountains and Seas***, *2006*
Animation, 30 min 5 sec
Animation, 30 Min. 5 Sek.
《新山海经》2006年, 动画, 30分 5秒

4 ***Jiang Nan Poem***, *2005*
Video, 12 min 45 sec
Video, 12 Min. 45 Sek.
《江南错》2005年, 录像, 12分 45秒

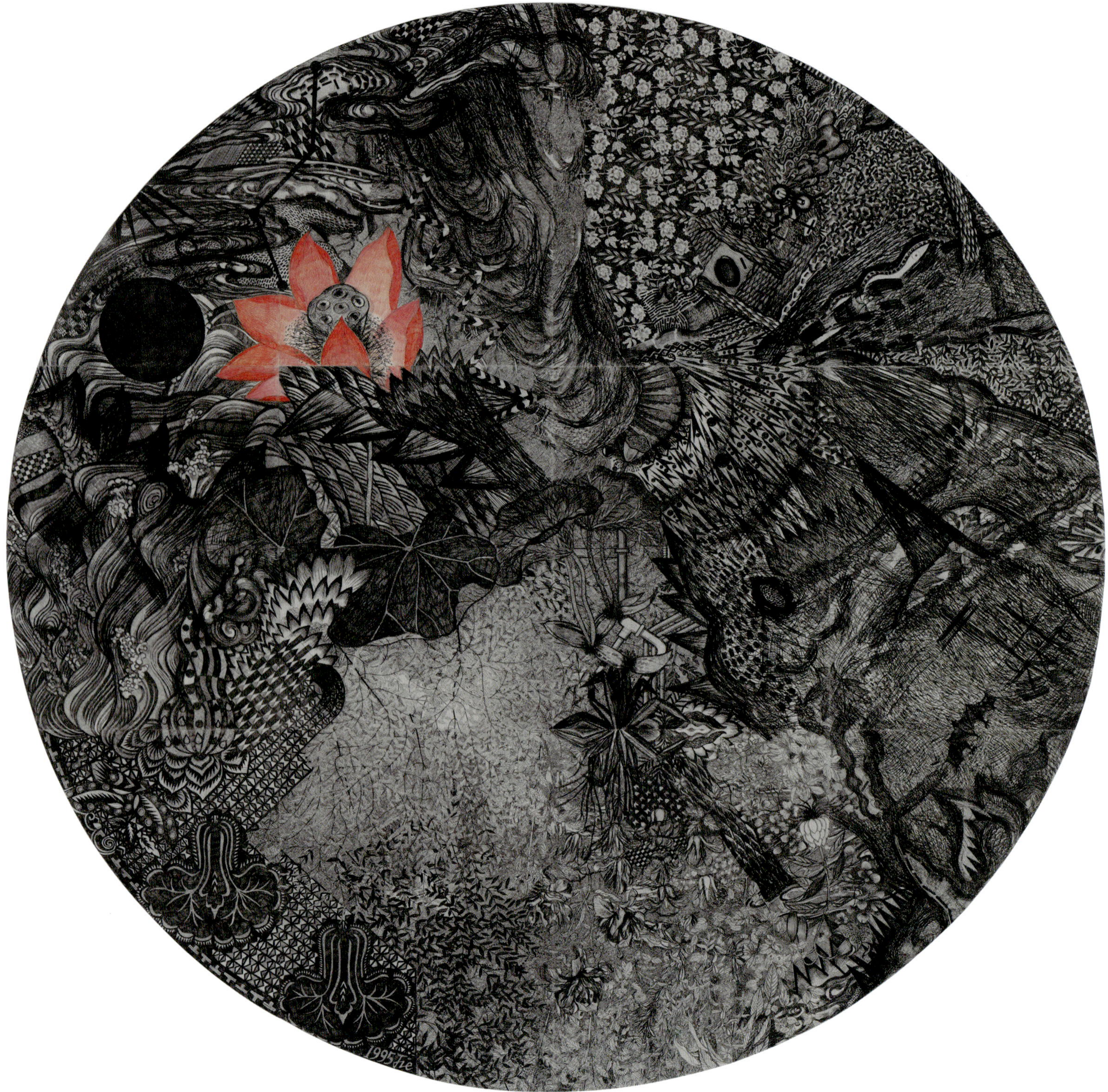

1

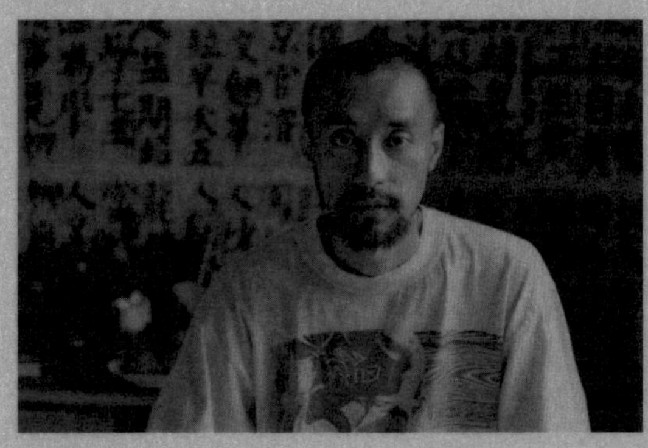

"Success is cherishing the positive point of view, the ability of moving from one defeat towards another defeat."

„Der Erfolg schätzt die positive Anschauung, die Fähigkeit, von einer Niederlage zur nächsten zu schreiten."

"成功就是怀着积极的心态，从一个失败走向另一个失败的能力。"

Born in 1961 in Shanghai, China. Lives and works in China, France and Switzerland
Geboren 1961 in Shanghai, China. Lebt und arbeitet in China, Frankreich und der Schweiz
1961年出生于中国上海。住居工作在中国、法国、瑞士

***Selected exhibitions* / Ausgewählte Ausstellungen /** 所选展览

1999 "Somewhere one", attitudes - espace d'arts contemporains, Geneva, Switzerland
2003 "Colours make the wall", Factory Secheron, Geneva, Switzerland
2005 "Discover - Rediscover", Musée Rath, Geneva, Switzerland
2006 "MoCA Envisage 2006", Museum of Contemporary Art, Shanghai, China

1999年 《他乡》Attitudes 画廊 日内瓦
2003年 《用颜色组成的墙》Sécheron 旧工厂 日内瓦
2005年 《重新再发现》Rath 艺术馆 日内瓦
2006年 《上海当代艺术馆文献展2006》上海当代艺术馆，中国

***Selected publications* / Ausgewählte Publikationen /** 所选著作

Thomas Schunke: "Qiu Jie", Geneva 1998

Schunke, Thomas（著）：《邱节》，日内瓦1998年

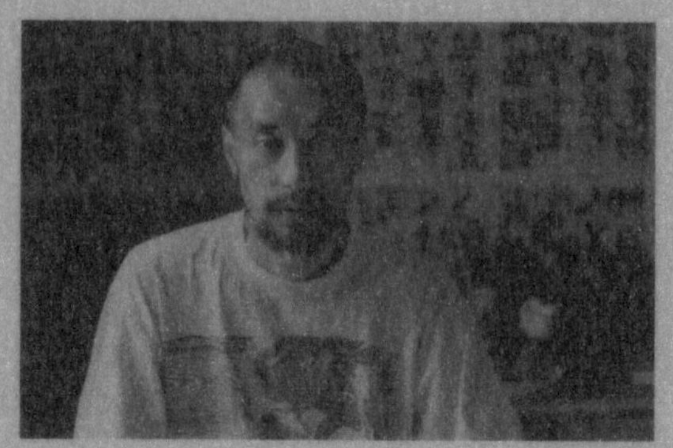

"Success is cherishing the positive point of view, the ability of moving from one defeat towards another defeat."

„Der Erfolg schätzt die positive Anschauung, die Fähigkeit, von einer Niederlage zur nächsten zu schreiten."

"成功就是怀着积极的心态，从一个失败走向另一个失败的能力。"

Born in 1961 in Shanghai, China. Lives and works in China, France and Switzerland
Geboren 1961 in Shanghai, China. Lebt und arbeitet in China, Frankreich und der Schweiz
1961年出生于中国上海。住居工作在中国，法国，瑞士

Selected exhibitions / Ausgewählte Ausstellungen / 所选展览

1999 "Somewhere one", attitudes - espace d'arts contemporains, Geneva, Switzerland
2003 "Colours make the wall", Factory Secheron, Geneva, Switzerland
2005 "Discover - Rediscover", Musée Rath, Geneva, Switzerland
2006 "MoCA Envisage 2006", Museum of Contemporary Art, Shanghai, China

1999年 《他乡》Attitudes 画廊 日内瓦
2003年 《用颜色组成的墙》Sécheron 旧工厂 日内瓦
2005年 《重新再发现》Rath 艺术馆 日内瓦
2006年 《上海当代艺术馆文献展2006》上海当代艺术馆，中国

Selected publications / Ausgewählte Publikationen / 所选著作

Thomas Schunke: "Qiu Jie", Geneva 1998

Schunke, Thomas（著）：《邱节》，日内瓦1998年

QIU JIE 邱节

[tɕʰiou tɕiɛ]

Qiu Jie grew up with his grandparents, then went to Switzerland where the language barrier made him feel the loneliness of human life. His paintings, regardless of his childhood or foreign environment, display frequently an unconscious kind of hope, an intense expression of desire being the driving force in his precisely realistic style, linked to the endurance and unequalled patience of people in the world. Qiu Jie's pseudonym "Hermit in a foreign country" reflects his feelings while staying in a foreign country for many years; his homeland has been near and far in inexhaustible memories.

People of Qiu Jie's generation have the same experience of the environment of a great epoch, but Qiu Jie's experience is different from artists of the same generation. For him reality is a detailed and pointedly weaving and depicting without the personal feelings of joy, anger, dolefulness and cheerfulness as if he is holding a mirror which reflects only the traces of time cycles.

Analysing Qiu Jie's art cannot be done without going to and fro in the mighty stream of history sometimes startled by inundating wild waves, sometimes going downstream or smooth and uneventful, in other words, he unceasingly grafts the realistic surface which he experiences being on the ordinate axis of history which forms the boundary of the picture revolved by his axis feeling and causes the individual to see through space and time without localisation.

In the early 1990s he created his first giant drawing, melding the institutional solid sketch skill with political propaganda posters of the Great Cultural Revolution and wall newspaper, the content being the new reality of the metropolis after starting the reform.

Before Qiu Jie composes giant drawings of combined types he doesn't make sketches but starts from one corner, and with a winding technique drills into time, slowly lays out like continuously without any stops until the scope of the broad area can then truly pull open the spatial curtain.

Qiu Jie wuchs bei seinen Großeltern auf und zog später in die Schweiz, wo er durch die Sprachbarriere die Grunderfahrung menschlicher Einsamkeit machte. Aber unabhängig von seiner Kindheit oder dem Erlebnis des Fremdseins, wohnt seinen Arbeiten häufig eine unterschwellige Form der Hoffnung inne, ein starker Ausdruck des Verlangens, das wohl die treibende Kraft hinter seinem präzisen realistischen Stil ist. Qiu Jies Pseudonym „Hermit in a foreign country" (Einsiedler im fremden Land) spiegelt sein Selbstverständnis während seines Aufenthalts im Ausland wider, als seine Heimat in seinen unerschöpflichen Erinnerungen über mehrere Jahre hinweg nah und fern zugleich war.

Chinesen aus Qiu Jies Generation teilen die Erfahrung, Zeitzeuge einer großen Epoche zu sein, aber Qius Umgang damit unterscheidet ihn von den Künstlern seines Alters. Für ihn ist die Realität stets detailliert und exakt, darum stellt er sie emotionslos, unter Verzicht auf Freude, Wut, Kummer oder Heiterkeit dar, so als ob er ihr einen Spiegel vorhalten würde, der lediglich ihre Spuren reflektiert. Man kann seine Kunst nicht verstehen, ohne den mächtigen Strom der Geschichte zu berücksichtigen, den manchmal wilde Wellen peitschen, während er zu anderen Zeiten ruhig und ereignislos dahinfließt. Qiu Jie bildet unaufhörlich und realistisch von seinem Standort aus die Oberflächen ab, die er wahrnimmt, und bringt den Betrachter dazu, gleichsam durch Zeit und Raum hindurch zu blicken.

In den frühen 1990er Jahren schuf er seine erste große Zeichnung, worin er die soliden tradierten Zeichentechniken mit der Ästhetik der politischen Propaganda-Poster der Kulturrevolution und der Ära der Wandzeitung verband – thematisch ging es ihm um die veränderte Realität der Metropole nach dem Beginn der gesellschaftlichen Neuordnung. Bevor Qiu Jie sich an seine riesigen Gemälde macht, fertigt er keine Skizzen an, vielmehr beginnt er an einer Ecke des Malgrunds gleichsam mit einer kontinuierlichen Erforschung der Zeit, die dazu führt, dass die breite Panoramaleinwand räumliche Dimensionen eröffnet. Diese Form der traditionellen Landschaftsmalerei, etwa von Jing Hao,

1961年出生于上海的邱节，从小在祖父母身边成长，之后移居瑞士，开始时语言的隔阂，那种独自面对人生的孤寂感，不论在童年，还是到异乡，在他的画面里，经常不自觉地流露出一种渴望，强烈的表达欲望，这种为了和世人沟通所展现出的无比耐心和持久力，是他精密写实风格的原动力。邱节的号“他乡山人”也反映了他的心情，长年在他乡索居，故国于他，是既近又远的无尽回忆。

邱节的同代人，他们经历的大时代环境是一样的，但是邱节和他同辈的艺术家所不同者，是他很少以批判的立场回顾他的过往。现实于他，只是点点滴滴细节的编织与描述，不带他个人喜怒哀乐的感怀，好比他持著一面镜子，单纯地反映出时间流转过去的痕迹。

分析邱节的艺术，无法避免穿梭在历史的洪流之中，有时惊滔骇浪，有时顺流而下，或者风平浪静，总之，他在历史的纵轴上，不断嫁接他所经历的现实平面，形成轴心式旋转的画境，使人难以一眼看穿其时空的定位。例如他在1990年代初创作的首幅巨型素描，融合了学院派扎实的素描功力，和文革时期的政治宣传画和大字报的型式，内容却是改革开放以后的都会新现实，交错成复杂而多元的叙事文本，每一小方块里都隐藏著大家共有的某些过去。这种跨越时空的编辑手法，既记实也抽象，乍看很明确的叙述情节，细究起来语式本身却又相当暧昧浑沌，随时隐匿著荒谬或突兀的意外。

邱节在创作这类组合式的巨型素描之前，从不打草稿，由一个角落开始，以钻入时间邃道的蜿蜒前进手法，慢慢铺陈开来，似乎是一种无尽止的继续，直到有了广阔的面积范围，才能够真正拉开空间的帏幕。这种承继五代「荆关董巨」山水画的传统，才是“他乡山人”作为今之古人的核心精神。所以，邱节的记实，和西方传统的写实主义并无直接的渊源，反而是荆浩在他的《笔法记》中所强调的“图真”理念，先要描绘形似之真，进而表现神

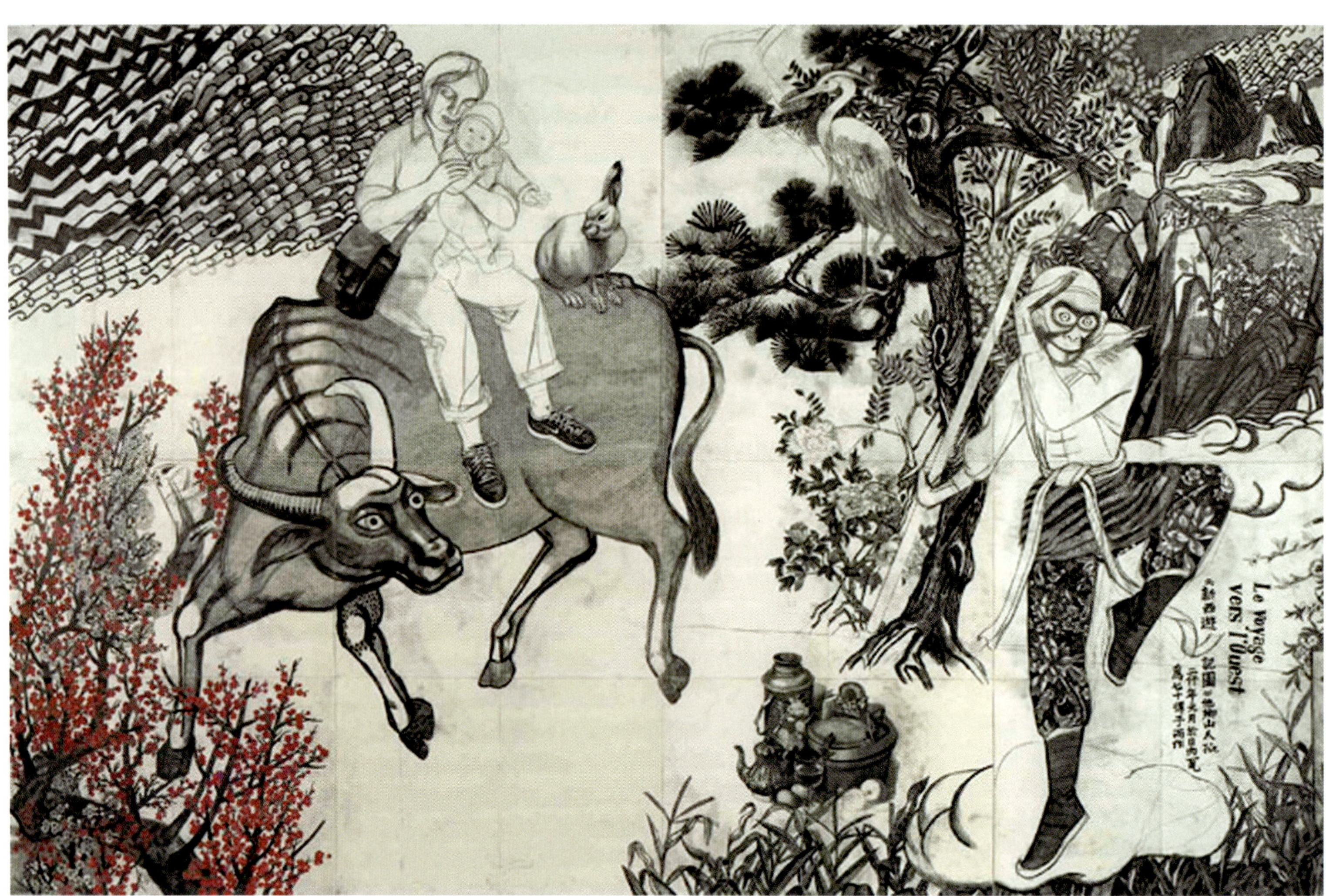

2

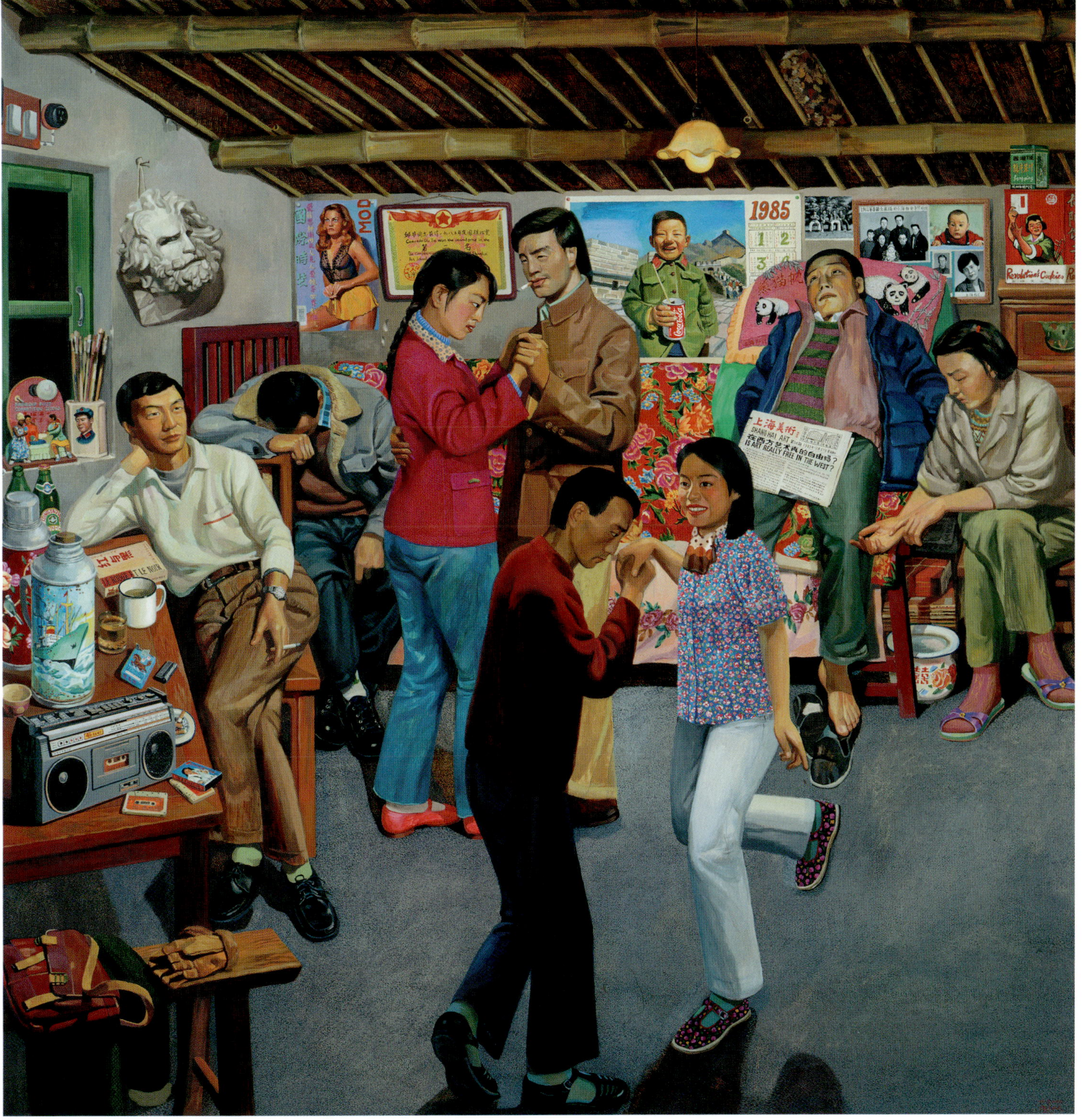
1985
上海美術
SHANGHAI ART
在西方艺术真的自由吗？
IS ART REALLY FREE IN THE WEST?
Revolution Cookies

3

4

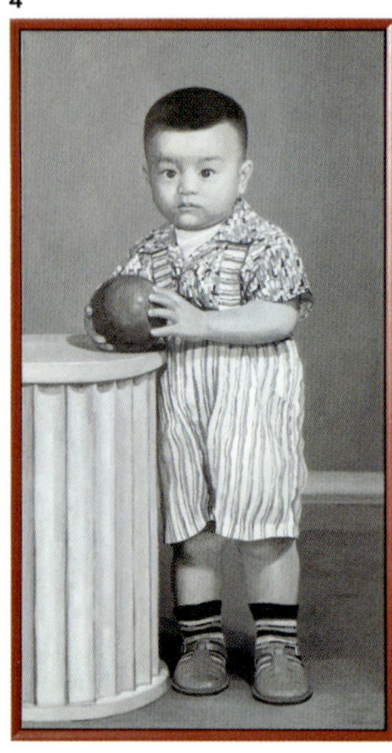
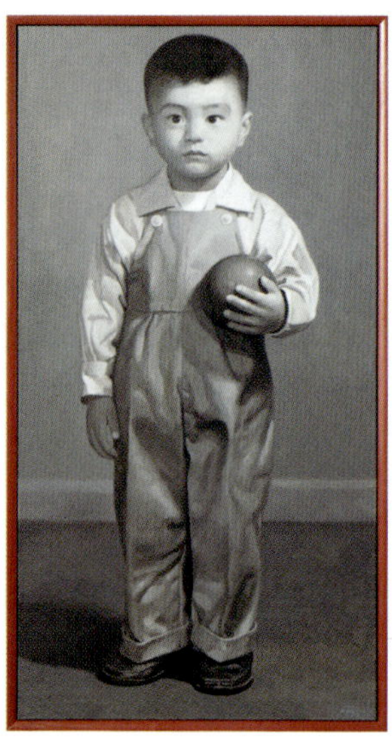
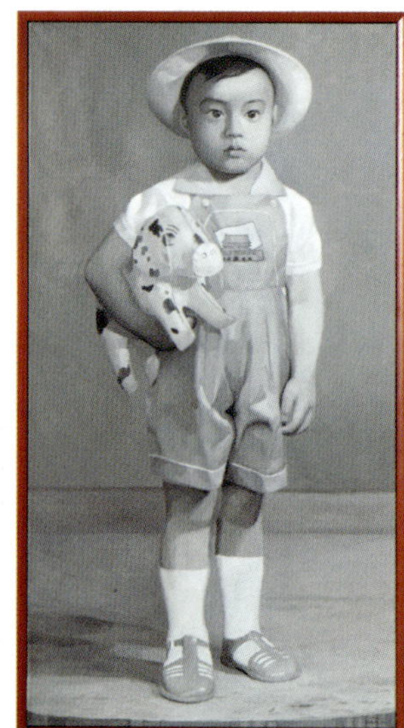
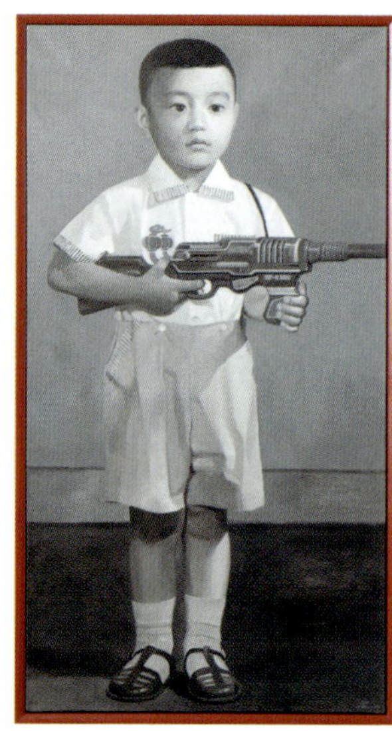
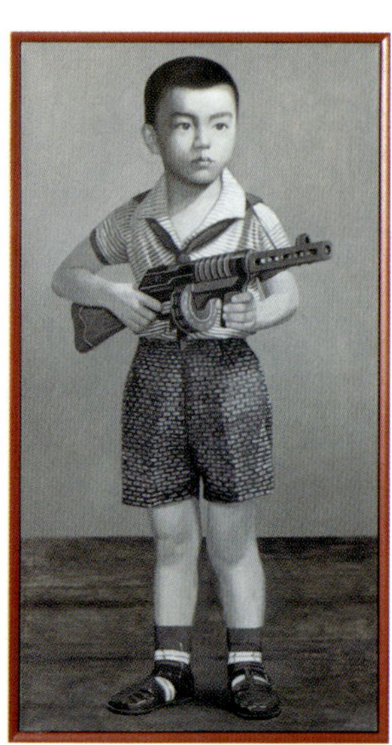

This kind of inherited traditional landscape painting of Jing Hao, Guan Tong, Dong Yuan, Ju Ran of the Five Dynasties (906–960) and the spirit thereof is incorporated in Qiu Jie's paintings of present being the "Hermit in a foreign country". Therefore, Qiu Jie's recorded reality and western traditional realism are without direct origin, but instead Jing Hao's idea of enhancing the truth as described in his "Record of Brush Technique" is to be found, which means to draw first according to reality and then to express the spiritual beauty according to Jing Hao's "Four categories" being "spirit, excellence miraculous, and skill" which are the essential standards for jugding the aesthetic of a painting.

Apart from giant drawings Qiu Jie is infatuated with ultra big oil paintings of mural criterion, his oil paintings and drawings are picture crystallisations of human life, history and memory, and therefore he doesn't adhere to the technique of "reflecting reality" like Italian painters of the 15th century Renaissance style but uses the Chinese landscape painting style of the multi-spots migration perspective idea. If the western origin is to be sought in Qiu Jie's oil paintings the Northern Renaissance of Flanders can be traced, being a far distant relative to Qiu Jie's precisely realistic style full of mystery and symbols.

Guan Tong, Dong Yuan, Ju Ran aus den Fünf Dynastien (906–960) wird in Qiu Jies aktuellen Werken des „Hermit in a foreign country" besonders deutlich. Qiu Jies Realismus hat also wenig mit dem westlichen gemein, sondern leitet sich eher von Jing Haos Idee ab, die Wahrheit zu erweitern, wie er es in seiner „Studie der Pinseltechnik" beschrieben hat. Danach zeichnet der Künstler zunächst nach der Realität, ehe er dann nach der spirituellen Schönheit der Dinge arbeit, wobei er Jings „Vier Kategorien" folgt, die die essentiellen Standards zur Beurteilung der Ästhetik eines Gemäldes darstellen.

Qiu Jie besticht daneben auch mit Ölgemälden von wandbildhaften Ausmaßen, überdimensionalen Formfindungen für das menschliche Leben, die Geschichte und die Erinnerung des Menschen. Auch hier folgt er nicht etwa der idealisierten, zentralperspektivischen Wiedergabe der Realität, wie sie die italienischen Renaissance-Künstler des 15. Jahrhunderts pflegten, sondern bedient sich wieder der klassischen chinesischen Perspektivenauffassung der „mehrfach fließenden Punkte". Sucht man nach westlichen Einflüssen in Qiu Jies Gemälden, trifft man allenfalls auf Spuren der nördlichen Renaissance Flanderns, die wie ein entfernter Verwandter des präzise realistischen Stils von Qiu Jie voller Geheimnis und Symbole ist.

似之美，即荆浩所谓的“四品”，是一种以「神、妙、奇、巧」作为评断标准的审美观。

除了巨幅素描画，邱节对壁画尺度的超大油画也十分醉心，他的油画和素描都是他对个人生命经历记忆的图像结晶，因而不像15世纪意大利文艺复以降所采取定点线性透视的“再现真实”的表现手法，邱节使用的是中国山水画中的多点移动透视的观念，由于是记忆的图像，所以光线也是散乱的不规律组合。如果一定要为邱节的油画寻找他的西方渊源，那么法兰德斯的北方文艺复兴，应该可以算是邱节那充满了符号和隐喻性的精密写实风格的远亲了。

Victoria Lu

5

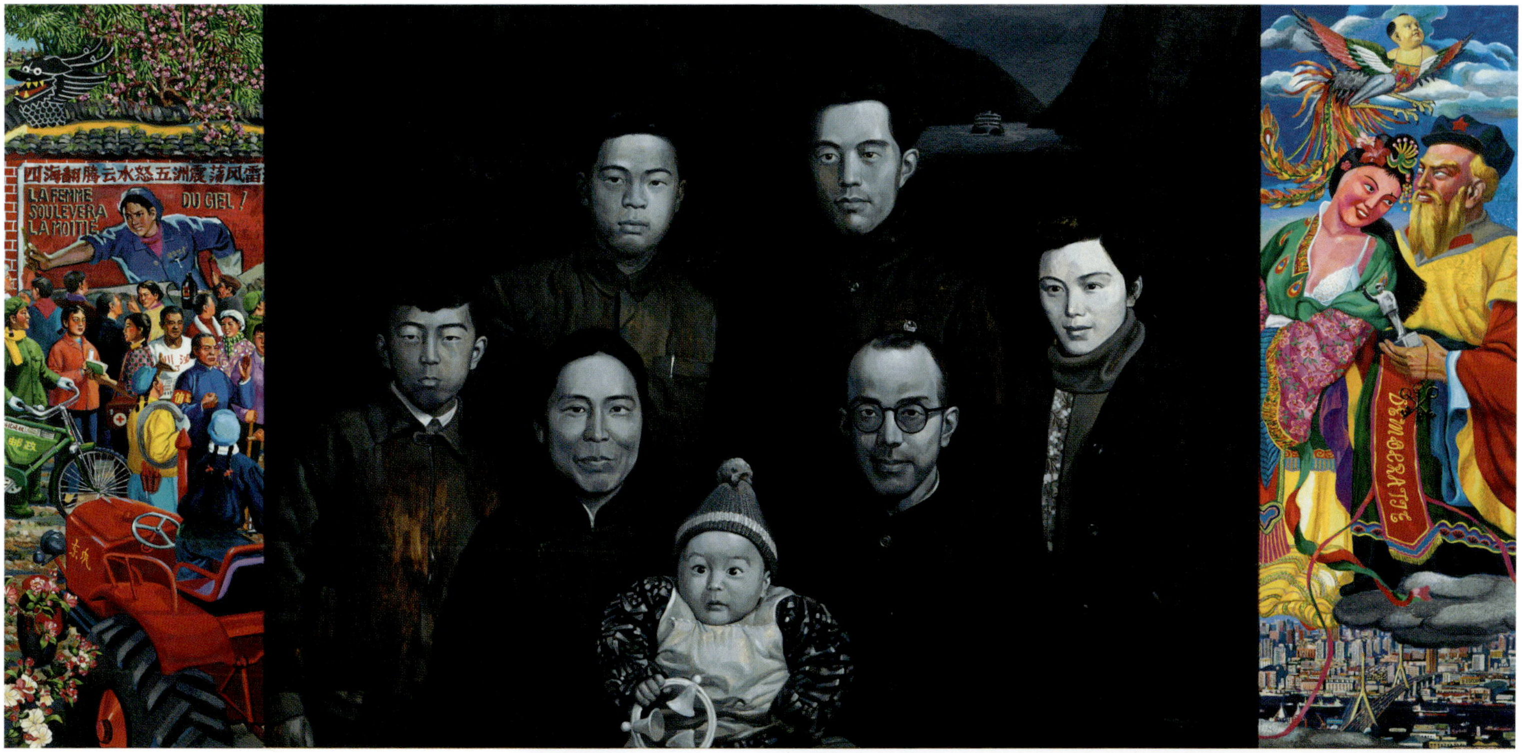

1 ***Round drawing***, *1995*
Lead on paper, 356 cm diameter
Bleistift auf Papier, 356 cm Durchmesser
《圆的图画》1995年, 铅笔画, 直径356 cm

2 ***Pèlerinage vers l'ouest***, *2000*
Lead on paper, 224 x 336 cm
Bleistift auf Papier, 224 x 336 cm
《新西游记》2000年, 铅笔画, 224 x 336 cm

3 ***The Dance***, *2000*
Oil on canvas, 220 x 200 cm
Öl auf Leinwand, 220 x 200 cm
《舞》2000年, 布面油画, 220 x 200 cm

4 ***Childhood series***, *1997*
Oil on canvas, 101 x 52 cm each
Öl auf Leinwand, je 101 x 52 cm
《儿童时代》1997年, 布面油画, 每幅101 x 52 cm

5 ***The Return***, *2000*
Oil on canvas, 110 x 221 cm
Öl auf Leinwand, 110 x 221 cm
《回归》2000年, 布面油画, 110 x 221 cm

6 ***Caca Boudin***, *2004*
Oil on canvas, 240 x 360 cm
Öl auf Leinwand, 240 x 360 cm
《Caca Boudin》2004年, 布面油画, 240 x 360 cm

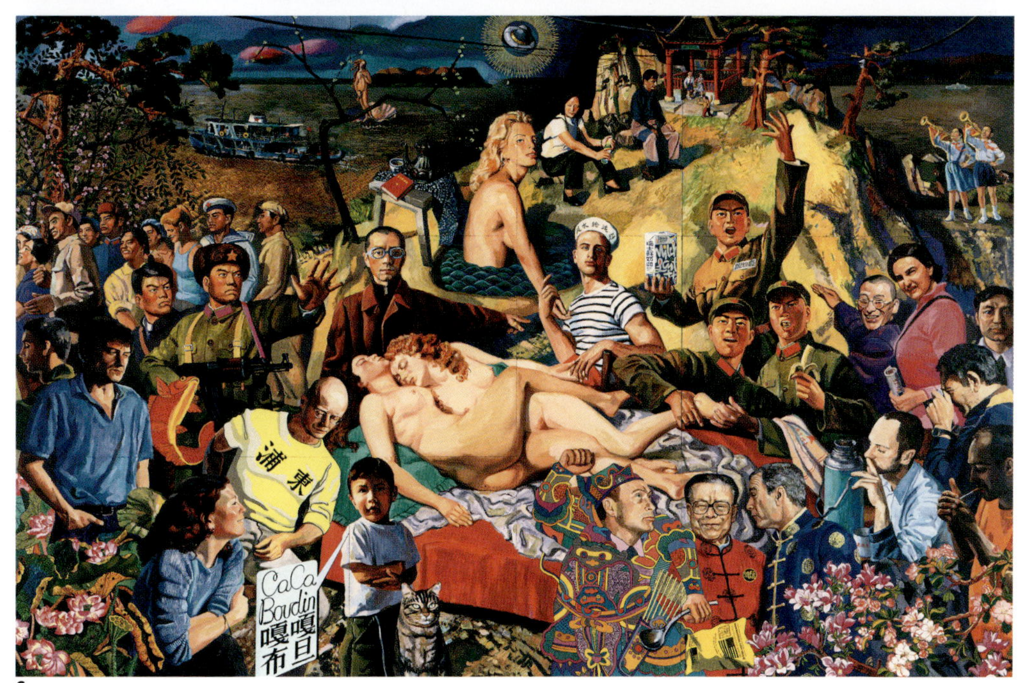

6

1

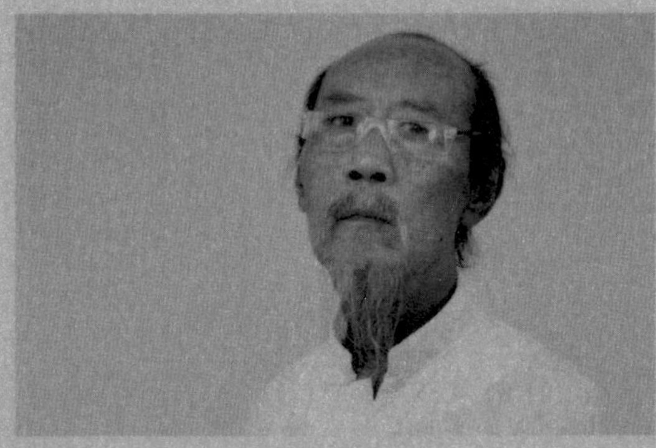

"My pursuit goes beyond the visible. I also strive for completeness and vividness in the objects that are painted. Among them there is space, as long as spectators can enter this space they will feel the painting is well done."

„Meine Ziele liegen jenseits des Sichtbaren. Ich strebe auch nach Vollständigkeit und Lebendigkeit der gemalten Objekte. Zwischen ihnen ist Raum; solange die Betrachter in diesen Raum eintreten können, haben sie das Gefühl, dass das Gemälde gut gemacht ist."

"我的追求超越视觉范围。我也力求所画物体的完整性和生动感。当观众进入物体间的空间时，他们就会立刻感受这些油画的完美。"

Born in 1940 in Sichuan Province, China. Lives and works in Shenzhen
Geboren 1940 in der Provinz Sichuan, China. Lebt und arbeitet in Shenzhen
1940年出生于中国四川省，现在深圳居住工作

***Selected exhibitions* / Ausgewählte Ausstellungen /** 所选展览

2001 "The Inward Eye: Transcendence in Contemporary Art", Contemporary Art Museum Houston, Houston, TX, USA
2003 "New Zone – Chinese Art", Zacheta National Gallery of Art, Warszaw, Poland
"Einbildung – Das Wahrnehmen in der Kunst", Kunsthaus Graz, Graz, Austria
2006 "The Sublime is Now", Museum Franz Gertsch, Burgdorf, Switzerland
2007 "The Year of the Golden Pig – Contemporary Chinese Art from the Sigg Collection", Lewis Gluckman Gallery, University College, Cork, Ireland
"White Out", Künstlerhaus Palais Thurn und Taxis, Bregenz, Austria; Stadtgalerie Saarbrücken, Saarbrücken, Germany

2001年 《内向的眼睛：当代艺术中的超越》当代美术馆，休斯顿，美国
2003年 《新地带中国艺术》Zacheta 国家美术馆，华沙，波兰
《想象 – 艺术中的发觉》格拉茨艺术院，奥地利
2006年 《升华是现在》Franz Gertsch 博物馆，布格多夫，瑞士
2007年 《金猪的年 – Sigg收藏的当代中国艺术》Lewis Gluckman 画廊，大学学院，黄柏，爱尔兰
《白色出》Palais Thurn und Taxis 艺术院，布雷根茨，奥地利 / 市画廊萨尔布吕肯，萨尔布吕肯，德国

***Selected publications* / Ausgewählte Publikationen /** 所选著作

Dieter Ronte, Walter Smerling, Evelyn Weiss (eds.): "China! Zeitgenössische Malerei", Cologne 1996
Chang Tsong-zung: "Beyond the Middle Kingdom: An Insider's View", in: Gao Minglu (ed.): "Inside Out: New Chinese Art", Berkeley 1998
"Qiu Shihua", Kunsthalle Basel, 1999

Ronte, Dieter/Smerling, Walter/Weiss, Evelyn（著）:《中国！当代绘画》Cologne 1996年
Chang Tsong-zung（著）:《中王国以上：知情人的景色》于高明潞(编者):《蜕变突破：华人新艺术》（展册目)，伯克利 1998年
《邱世华》展册 Kunsthalle巴塞尔1999年

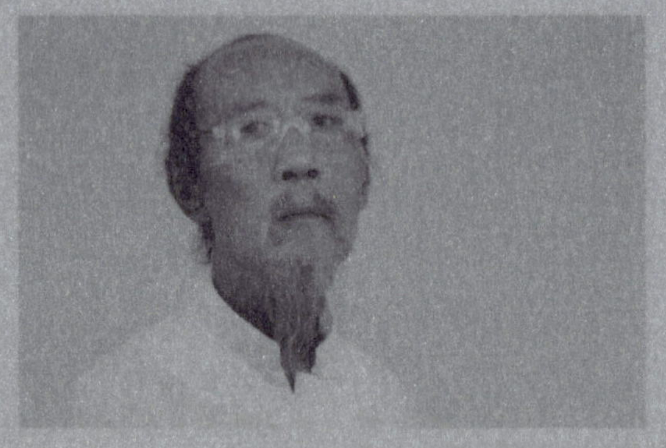

"My pursuit goes beyond the visible. I also strive for completeness and vividness in the objects that are painted. Among them there is space, as long as spectators can enter this space they will feel the painting is well done."

„Meine Ziele liegen jenseits des Sichtbaren. Ich strebe auch nach Vollständigkeit und Lebendigkeit der gemalten Objekte. Zwischen ihnen ist Raum; solange die Betrachter in diesen Raum eintreten können, haben sie das Gefühl, dass das Gemälde gut gemacht ist."

"我的追求超越视觉范围。我也力求所画物体的完整性和生动感。当观众进入物体间的空间时，他们就会立刻感受这些油画的完美。"

Born in 1940 in Sichuan Province, China. Lives and works in Shenzhen
Geboren 1940 in der Provinz Sichuan, China. Lebt und arbeitet in Shenzhen
1940年出生于中国四川省，现在深圳居住工作

Selected exhibitions / Ausgewählte Ausstellungen / 所选展览

2001 "The Inward Eye: Transcendence in Contemporary Art", Contemporary Art Museum Houston, Houston, TX, USA
2003 "New Zone – Chinese Art", Zacheta National Gallery of Art, Warszaw, Poland
"Einbildung – Das Wahrnehmen in der Kunst", Kunsthaus Graz, Graz, Austria
2006 "The Sublime is Now", Museum Franz Gertsch, Burgdorf, Switzerland
2007 "The Year of the Golden Pig – Contemporary Chinese Art from the Sigg Collection", Lewis Gluckman Gallery, University College, Cork, Ireland
"White Out", Künstlerhaus Palais Thurn und Taxis, Bregenz, Austria; Stadtgalerie Saarbrücken, Saarbrücken, Germany

2001年《内向的眼睛：当代艺术中的超越》当代美术馆，休斯顿，美国
2003年《新地带中国艺术》Zacheta 国家美术馆，华沙，波兰
《想象 – 艺术中的发觉》格拉茨艺术院，奥地利
2006年《升华是现在》Franz Gertsch 博物馆，布格多夫，瑞士
2007年《金猪的年 – Sigg收藏的当代中国艺术》Lewis Gluckman 画廊，大学学院，肯柏，爱尔兰
《白色出》Palais Thurn und Taxis 艺术院，布雷根茨，奥地利 / 市画廊萨尔布吕肯，萨尔布吕肯，德国

Selected publications / Ausgewählte Publikationen / 所选著作

Dieter Ronte, Walter Smerling, Evelyn Weiss (eds.): "China! Zeitgenössische Malerei", Cologne 1996
Chang Tsong-zung: "Beyond the Middle Kingdom: An Insider's View", in: Gao Minglu (ed.): "Inside Out: New Chinese Art", Berkeley 1998
"Qiu Shihua", Kunsthalle Basel, 1999

Ronte, Dieter/Smerling, Walter/Weiss, Evelyn（著）：《中国！当代绘画》Cologne 1996年
Chang Tsong-zung（著）：《中王国以上：知情人的景色》于高明潞（编著）：《蜕变突破：华人新艺术》（展册目），伯克利 1998年
《邱世华》展册 Kunsthalle巴塞尔1999年

QIU SHIHUA 邱世华

[tɕʰiou ʂixua]

The oil paintings of Qiu Shihua exist as empty palimpsests onto which the viewer can, with time, project his or her own vision. These inscrutable compositions, in a seemingly infinite range of whites and off-whites, reveal their figurative essences only to the most patient of onlookers. To these few, however, the paintings resonate with a power with a depth that draws on both Chinese representational conventions and Impressionist understandings of the relationship between object and image. To be sure, his images never depict anything extraordinary, returning time and again to the motifs of skies and sunsets, fields and forests, and yet suspending these in a tense, existential indeterminacy.

Qiu Shihua was trained in orthodox Socialist Realism at the Xi'an Academy of Fine Arts in the early years of the People's Republic, graduating in 1962. He spent the ensuing 22 years in Tongchuan, a coal-mining town in Shaanxi province, painting signs for a movie theater and watching one political movement fade into another. At times he would paint billboards ten meters long, humbly honing his representational technique on this frightening scale. In 1984 – already 44 years old – Qiu moved to Shenzhen, then a newly opened "special economic zone" filtering Hong Kong-style capitalism into the Mainland, taking a job with a trading company. In 1987 he visited France, beginning a long string of short residences in Europe and the United States. Throughout the 1980s, he concerned himself mainly with landscape painting, refined, dimly toned, and yet still somehow resonating with the grandiosity of Socialist Realism.

The monochrome landscapes for which Qiu Shihua is best known grow out of a series in 1990 and 1991 which cast natural scenes and objects in a dim, dusky light. Perhaps owing to his encounter with a Daoist sage in 1991 (Qiu has been a lifelong practitioner of Daoist meditation), his works grew brighter and yet less clear, taking on a luminescence that Qiu's longtime dealer Johnson Chang has compared to a pre-dawn sky. Although he rarely comments on his own

Die Ölgemälde von Qiu Shihua existieren als leere Palimpseste, auf die Betrachter ihre eigenen Visionen projizieren können. Diese unergründlichen Kompositionen in einer scheinbar unendlichen Palette von gebrochenen Weißtönen offenbaren ihr figuratives Wesen nur den geduldigsten Betrachtern. Für diese wenigen jedoch pulsieren die Gemälde mit einer Kraft und Tiefe, die sowohl aus Traditionen der chinesischen gegenständlichen Kunst als auch aus der impressionistischen Auffassung der Beziehung zwischen Objekt und Bild herrühren. Dabei stellen seine Bilder nie Außergewöhnliches dar, sondern kehren immer wieder zu den Motiven Himmel und Sonnenuntergang oder Feld und Wald zurück, lassen diese aber in spannungsgeladener, existenzieller Unbestimmtheit gleichsam schweben.

Qiu Shihua wurde in den frühen Jahren der Volksrepublik an der Xi'an Academy of Fine Arts im orthodoxen Sozialistischen Realismus ausgebildet und machte 1962 seinen Abschluss. Die nächsten 22 Jahre verbrachte er in Tongchuan, einer Kohlebergbaustadt in der Provinz Shaanxi, wo er Kinoschilder malte und miterlebte, wie eine politische Bewegung von der nächsten abgelöst wurde. Damals malte er Plakatwände von zehn Metern Länge und perfektionierte an diesem einschüchternden Maßstab nebenher seine Darstellungstechnik. 1984 – im Alter von immerhin schon 44 Jahren – zog Qiu nach Shenzen, damals eine neu eröffnete „Sonderwirtschaftszone", die den Hongkong-Kapitalismus in gefilterter Form nach Festland-China einsickern ließ, und nahm dort eine Stelle bei einer Handelsgesellschaft an. 1987 besuchte er Frankreich, als Auftakt einer langen Reihe von Kurzaufenthalten in Europa und den USA. In den 1980er Jahren beschäftigte sich Qiu hauptsächlich mit Landschaftsmalerei: verfeinert und in gedämpften Tönen zwar, doch noch immer von der Grandiosität des Sozialistischen Realismus beeinflusst.

Die monochromen Landschaften, für die Qiu Shihua am bekanntesten ist, sind aus einer Serie der Jahre 1990 und 1991 entstanden, die Naturszenen und -motive in gedämpftes Dämmerlicht tauchte. Vielleicht infolge seiner

邱世华的油画是一幅幅空缈的重写本，观众可在上投射自己想象的东西。这些耐人寻味的、表面上是无限的白色和灰白色的作品，只有耐心的观众才可读懂其深刻内涵。但是这些油画中，很少能共鸣起一种力量和深度，对中国写意传统深度和对印象主义中物体和图像的关系的理解的深度。但有一点是可以肯定的，他的画中从未描写超凡的物质，而是反复地回归到天空，夕阳，田野和森林主旨中，并将之处于紧张、存在的不确定性的状态。

邱世华出生于1940年，建国后在西安美术学院接受正统的社会主义现实主义教育，1962年大学毕业。随后，在陕西省的煤城铜川生活了22年，他在一家剧院从事美术工作，见证了一个又一个政治运动的潮起潮落。那时他能绘制十米长的标语牌，因此也逐渐地练就了其惊人的写意技巧。在1984年，时年已44岁的邱世华移居深圳，在一家贸易公司谋到一份工作，那时的深圳刚刚成为经济特区，资本主义渗入大陆的产物。1987年出访法国，开始了在欧洲的美国的短暂逗留。整个80年代期间，他主要绘制精致而沉闷风景画，但是仍可反映社会现实主义的宏伟风格。

1990年到1991年期间，邱世华绘制了最著名的单色风景画，并形成了一个系列，作品中阴晦朦胧的光线笼罩着自然景色和物体。1991年也许因为他遇上了一位道家圣人（他长期修习道教），其作品风格而变化的更加明朗但是仍有一点模糊，似乎照耀在冷光之下。邱世华的长期经纪人Johnson Chang将之比作黎明前的天空。虽然他极少对自己的作品发表评论，而在1997年邱世华解释自己的以前作品"大部分关注于情感"，之后的作品着眼于"原始，经历的根源。"因此，他的油画是与历史和历史联系的一次睿智的对话，它在临时的制作和展示框架外仍保留着本质的力量。

在一段时间内，中国当代艺术家常常机械地将具有象征和寓意内容植入艺术作品中，有时很贴切但常

2

3

work Qiu Shihua did issue a statement in 1997 explaining that while his previous paintings "were mostly concerned with emotions," his works thereafter would tackle "origin, the genesis of experience." As a result, his paintings come to seem at once savvy dialogues with history and context that retain their power outside the temporal frameworks of production and display.

In a moment where Chinese contemporary art often implies the rote marshalling of symbols and icons into compositions sometimes poignant but rarely subtle, Qiu Shihua's work has proven a welcome exception to such norms. In their formal, tonal, and figurative nuance, Qiu Shihua's paintings offer a thoughtful respite from the daily parade of images, calling the viewer to join the artist on a higher plane.

Begegnung mit einem taoistischen Weisen im Jahr 1991 (Qiu hat sein Leben lang taoistische Meditation praktiziert) wurden seine Werke danach heller, doch weniger klar, und nahmen eine Leuchtkraft an, die Qius langjähriger Händler Johnson Chang mit dem Leuchten des Himmels vor Tagesanbruch verglichen hat. Qiu Shihua, der sein Werk nur selten kommentiert, erklärte 1997, seine früheren Gemälde hätten „vorwiegend mit Gefühlen" zu tun gehabt, während sich seine Arbeiten danach mit „dem Ursprung, der Entstehung von Erfahrungen" befassten. So wirken seine Gemälde zugleich wie clevere Dialoge mit der Geschichte, die ihre Ausdruckskraft auch jenseits des zeitlichen Rahmens ihrer Entstehung und Präsentation bewahren.

Zu einer Zeit, in der sich die chinesische Gegenwartskunst oft darin erschöpft, Symbole und Ikonen routiniert zu Kompositionen zusammenzubauen, die mitunter packend, aber selten subtil sind, hat sich Qiu Shihuas Werk als bereichernde Ausnahme von dieser Regel bewährt. In ihrer formalen, tonalen und figurativen Nuanciertheit bieten Qiu Shihuas Gemälde eine besinnliche Ruhepause von der täglichen Bilderflut und laden den Betrachter ein, dem Künstler auf eine höhere Ebene zu folgen.

常是很不得要领，而邱世华的作品却是例外。也许因为这个原因，他能在欧洲重要的机构里举行个人展览，如巴塞尔艺术节（1999年）和艺术之家（杜塞尔多夫2004年）。在形式、音调和寓意的细微差别上，邱世华的油画短暂的截取了日常照片场景，而使观众在更高水平上与艺术家保持一致。

Philip Tinari

5

6

1 ***Untitled**, 2001*
Oil on canvas, 108 x 82 cm
Öl auf Leinwand, 108 x 82 cm
《无题》2001年, 布面油画, 108 x 82 cm

2 ***Untitled**, 2003*
Oil on canvas, 86.5 x 108 cm
Öl auf Leinwand, 86,5 x 108 cm
《无题》2003年, 布面油画，86.5 x 108 cm

3 ***Wooded pasture**, 1996*
Oil on canvas, 153 x 307 cm
Öl auf Leinwand, 153 x 307 cm
《生长树木的牧场地》1996年, 布面油画，153 x 307 cm

4 ***Untitled**, 2001*
Oil on canvas, 50 x 95 cm
Öl auf Leinwand, 50 x 95 cm
《无题》2001年, 布面油画，50 x 95 cm

5 ***Untitled**, 1992*
Oil on paper, 110 x 167 cm
Öl auf Papier, 110 x 167 cm
《无题》1992年, 纸面油画，110 x 167 cm

6 ***Untitled**, 1992*
Oil on paper, 110 x 169 cm
Öl auf Papier, 110 x 169 cm
《无题》1992年, 纸面油画，110 x 169 cm

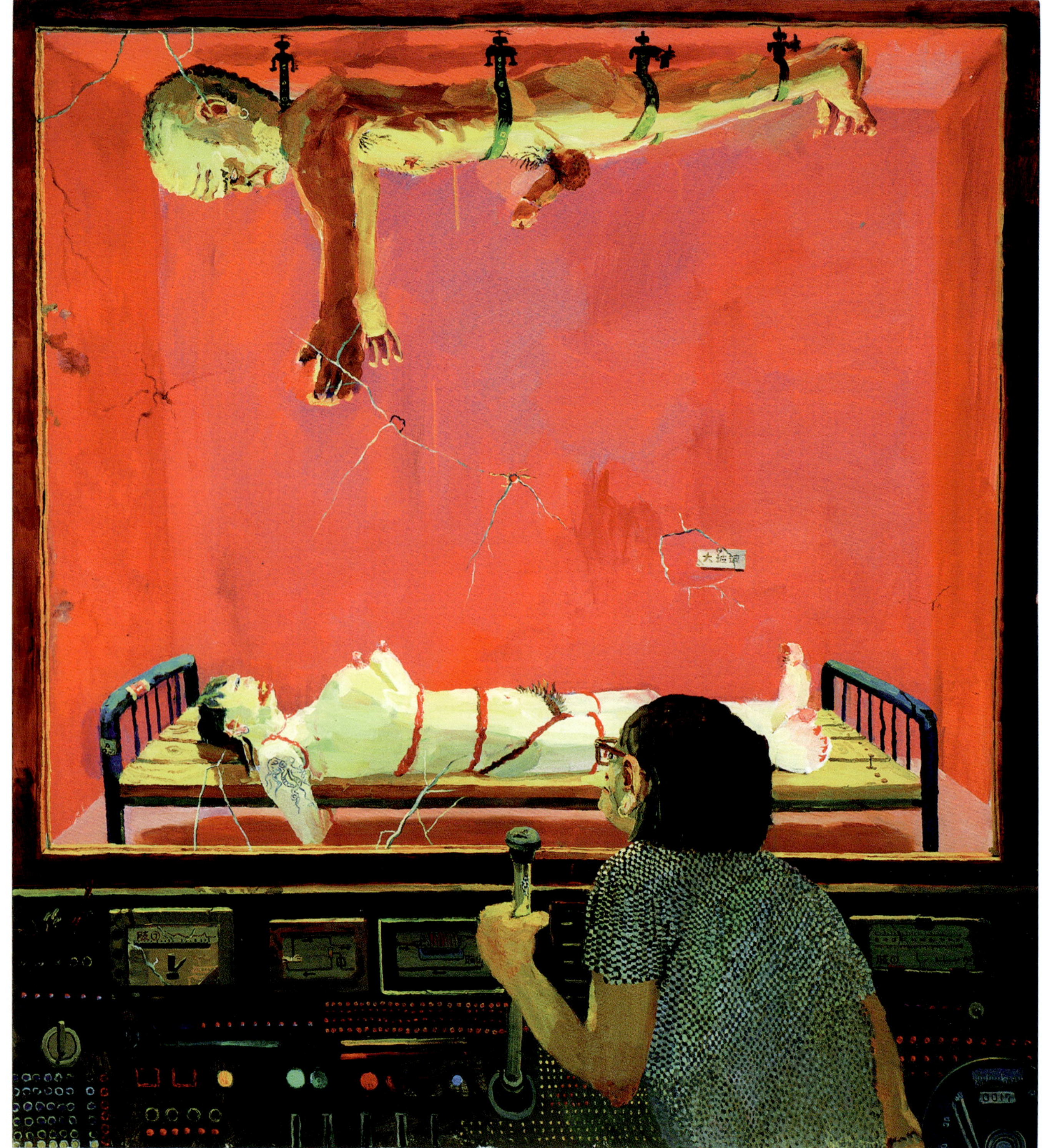

1

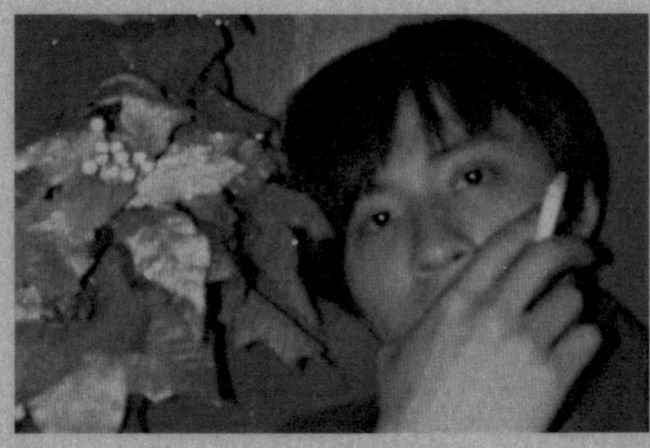

"I always hope that my paintings don't look like paintings, but more like objects on the wall collecting dust and acquiring the weathered look of time."

„Ich hoffe immer, dass meine Gemälde nicht wie Gemälde aussehen, sondern eher wie Objekte an der Wand, die Staub ansammeln und mit der Zeit Patina ansetzen."

"我常常希望我的油画看起来不像油画，而总希望它们是墙壁上的布满灰尘饱经沧桑的物体。"

Born in 1977 in Harbin, China. Lives and works in Beijing
Geboren 1977 in Harbin, China. Lebt und arbeitet in Peking
1977年出生于中国哈尔滨，现居住工作于北京

Selected exhibitions **/ Ausgewählte Ausstellungen /** 所选展览

2003 "The Third Chinese Oil Painting Exhibition", National Museum of Fine Arts, Beijing, China
2004 "Together", Chinablue Gallery, Beijing, China
2005 "Welcome, Welcome", Base Gallery, Tokyo, Japan
"Naughty Kids", Star Gallery, Beijing, China
"SCAPES: the 'CENTURY' and the 'PARADISE'" – 2005 Chengdu Biennial, Chengdu, China
2005–07 "Mahjong – Chinesische Gegenwartskunst aus der Sammlung Sigg", Kunstmuseum Bern, Berne, Switzerland; Hamburger Kunsthalle, Hamburg, Germany; Museum der Moderne, Salzburg, Austria
2007 "The Real Thing: Contemporary Art from China", Tate Liverpool, Liverpool, UK

2003 年 《第三届中国油画精品展》中国美术馆，北京，中国
2004年 《在一起》环碧堂画廊，北京，中国
2005年 《欢迎欢迎》Base 画廊，东京，日本
《坏孩子的天空》星空间，北京，中国
《景观：世纪与天堂》第二届成都双年，成都，中国
2005–07年 《麻将》西克中国当代艺术收藏展，伯尔尼美术馆 瑞士；汉堡美术馆，汉堡，德国；萨尔茨保现代美术馆 奥地利
2007年 《真货：中国当代艺术》泰特美术馆，利物浦，英国

Selected publications **/ Ausgewählte Publikationen /** 所选著作

"Qiu Xiaofei: Heilongjiang Box", with essays by Karen Smith and Pi Li, Shijiazhuang 2006
"The Real Thing", Liverpool 2007

《仇晓飞一黑龙江盒子》专论，Karen Smith 和 Pi Li撰文，石家庄2006年
《真货》展册 泰特美术馆，利物浦2007年

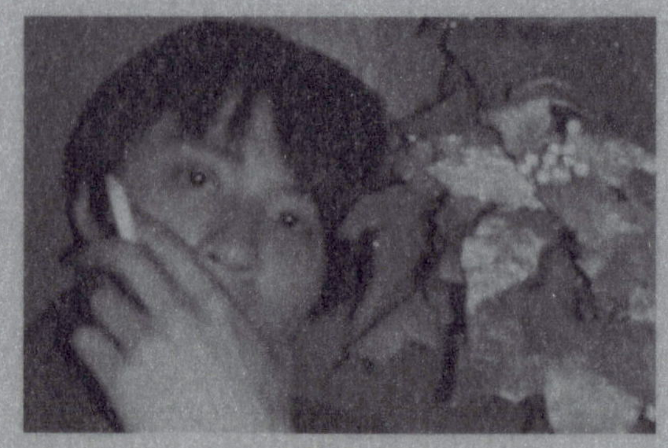

"I always hope that my paintings don't look like paintings, but more like objects on the wall collecting dust and acquiring the weathered look of time."

„Ich hoffe immer, dass meine Gemälde nicht wie Gemälde aussehen, sondern eher wie Objekte an der Wand, die Staub ansammeln und mit der Zeit Patina ansetzen."

"我常常希望我的油画看起来不像油画，而总希望它们是墙壁上的布满灰尘饱经沧桑的物体。"

Born in 1977 in Harbin, China. Lives and works in Beijing
Geboren 1977 in Harbin, China. Lebt und arbeitet in Peking
1977年出生于中国哈尔滨，现居住工作于北京

Selected exhibitions / Ausgewählte Ausstellungen / 所选展览

2003	"The Third Chinese Oil Painting Exhibition", National Museum of Fine Arts, Beijing, China
2004	"Together", Chinablue Gallery, Beijing, China
2005	"Welcome, Welcome", Base Gallery, Tokyo, Japan
	"Naughty Kids", Star Gallery, Beijing, China
	"SCAPES: the 'CENTURY' and the 'PARADISE'" - 2005 Chengdu Biennial, Chengdu, China
2005–07	"Mahjong – Chinesische Gegenwartskunst aus der Sammlung Sigg", Kunstmuseum Bern, Berne, Switzerland; Hamburger Kunsthalle, Hamburg, Germany; Museum der Moderne, Salzburg, Austria
2007	"The Real Thing: Contemporary Art from China", Tate Liverpool, Liverpool, UK
2003 年	《第三届中国油画精品展》中国美术馆，北京，中国
2004年	《在一起》环碧堂画廊，北京，中国
2005年	《欢迎欢迎》Base 画廊，东京，日本
	《坏孩子的天空》星空间，北京，中国
	《景观：世纪与天堂》第二届成都双年，成都，中国
2005–07年	《麻将》西克中国当代艺术收藏展，伯尔尼美术馆 瑞士；汉堡美术馆，汉堡，德国；萨尔茨堡现代美术馆 奥地利
2007年	《真货：中国当代艺术》泰特美术馆，利物浦，英国

Selected publications / Ausgewählte Publikationen / 所选著作

"Qiu Xiaofei: Heilongjiang Box", with essays by Karen Smith and Pi Li, Shijiazhuang 2006
"The Real Thing", Liverpool 2007

《仇晓飞—黑龙江盒子》专论，Karen Smith 和 Pi Li撰文，石家庄2006年
《真货》展册 泰特美术馆，利物浦2007年

QIU XIAOFEI 仇晓飞

[tɕʰiou ɕiaʊfei]

Qiu Xiaofei's painterly practice is based on a refined kind of mimesis, creating facsimiles of everyday objects that bear nostalgic traces of the hand. One of his first publicly circulated series, "Photo Album" (2002), recreates the pages from a book of pictures of his childhood in Harbin, tiny black-and-white photographic compositions painted onto the black background of an album leaf. The first and last paintings in the series depict the front and back covers of the album. Other early paintings re-capture images from old postcards, or stock images of the famous Beijing buildings of an earlier era, like the Xidan Telegraphic Building on Chang'an Avenue. Before he had even graduated from the Central Academy, Qiu Xiaofei had set upon a style based on memory and disappearance, aiming to recapture moments and objects from his 1980s childhood.

More recently Qiu Xiaofei has applied this compositional strategy to three-dimensional objects, turning wooden boxes into old radios and televisions, plain desks into aged pieces of furniture strewn with papers and photographs. For "Art Class", displayed in a 2007 exhibition at Tate Liverpool, he fabricated an entire painting studio, like those of his alma mater, the Central Academy of Fine Arts, from wood and cardboard. Ten easels hung with canvases faced a plaster bust, the floor littered with used tubes of paint, sketchbooks, discarded beverages. Upon close inspection these objects reveal themselves to have been created in paint, and from the reverse, the trompe d'œil effect becomes entirely obvious, as Qiu Xiaofei left the back side of these objects blank. Smaller scale works have duped the forms of doors or electrical outlets, represented in this same crafty vocabulary.

Qiu is in many ways a logical heir to his professor, mentor, and fellow north-easterner Liu Xiaodong, whose innovation of turning the lens of Socialist Realism onto scenes of the everyday was the basis for a vibrant school of painting in the 1990s. His path to art was indirect, as he entered the affiliated high school of the Central Academy mainly for lack of the Beijing residence papers that would allow him

Qiu Xiaofeis malerisches Werk basiert auf einer verfeinerten Form einer Mimesis, die Nachahmungen alltäglicher Gegenstände mit nostalgischen Gebrauchsspuren schafft. Eine seiner ersten öffentlich gezeigten Serien, „Photo Album“ (2002), reproduziert die Seiten eines Fotoalbums aus seiner Kindheit in Harbin: winzige, schwarzweiße fotografische Kompositionen, auf den schwarzen Untergrund einer Albumseite gemalt. Das erste und das letzte Gemälde der Serie stellen die vorderen und hinteren Einbanddeckel des Albums dar. Andere frühe Gemälde lassen Bilder von alten Postkarten wiedererstehen oder klassische Darstellungen berühmter Pekinger Gebäude, wie etwa des Xidan-Telegrafenamts in der Chang'an-Avenue. Schon vor seinem Abschluss an der Central Academy hatte sich Qiu Xiaofei auf einen Stil festgelegt, der Erinnerung und Verschwinden thematisiert und darauf abzielt, Augenblicke und Gegenstände aus seiner Kindheit in den 1980er Jahren wiederzubeleben.

In jüngerer Zeit wendet Qiu Xiaofei diese kompositorische Methode auch auf dreidimensionale Objekte an, indem er Holzkisten in alte Radios und Fernseher verwandelt und schlichte Tische in alte Möbelstücke, die mit Papieren und Fotos übersät sind. Für „Art Class“, 2007 auf einer Ausstellung in der Tate Liverpool vorgestellt, baute er ein komplettes Maleratelier – wie die Ateliers in seiner Alma Mater, der Central Academy of Fine Arts – aus Holz und Pappe nach: zehn Staffeleien mit Leinwänden vor einer Gipsbüste, inmitten von benutzten Farbtuben, Skizzenblöcken und Getränkebehältern, die auf dem Boden liegen. Bei genauerer Betrachtung entpuppen sich diese Objekte selbst als nur aus Farbe geschaffen, und von hinten wird der Trompe-l'œil-Effekt ganz offensichtlich, da Qiu Xiaofei die Rückseite der Gegenstände unbemalt ließ. Kleinformatigere Werke imitieren auf ähnliche Weise Türen oder Steckdosen, stets in derselben gewitzten Bildsprache ausgeführt.

Qiu ist in mancher Hinsicht der logische Erbe seines ebenfalls aus dem Nordosten stammenden Professors und Mentors Liu Xiaodong, dessen Anregung, die Linse des

仇晓飞的美术实践基于精致的模仿，摹写那些能勾起怀旧感觉的日常物品。他的首部公开发行的作品系列《相册》(2002年)，重新创作了他哈尔滨童年时的一本相册。他把微型的黑白照片画在黑色底色的相页上。这组油画系列的第一幅和最后一幅分别为相册的首尾封面。类似的，另一幅早期的油画也截取了老明信片和票具上早期北京的著名建筑，如长安街上的西单电影大楼。早在毕业于中央美院之前，仇晓飞就开始基于记忆和泯灭事物的风格的创作，以重新体验他80年代童年时期的瞬间和物体。

最近，他又将这种创作方法应用于三维物体，木质盒子雕刻成老式的收音机和电视机，普通桌子上布满了报纸和照片而俨然一副陈旧的家具。在2007年泰特美术馆展示的作品《艺术课堂》中，他模仿其母校中央美院的样子制作了一间画室，从木材到纸板。十个画架上悬挂着帆布，对面是一尊塑料半身雕像，地板上乱七八糟的散落着用过的颜料管、写生本、丢弃的饮料盒。仔细观察这些东西，将会发现这些东西是画出来的，从反面看来，错觉图像效果就非常明显，因为仇晓飞在物体的背面留白。在小幅的作品中也采用相同的手法处理门和电源插座。

仇晓飞在许多方面继承了他的j教授、导师和同乡的刘小东的思维方式，刘创新地将社会主义现实主义视角转移到日常生活中，这一创新也是90年代院校派油画风格发转变的基础。仇晓飞进入艺术之路并非一帆风顺的，因为没有北京户口，所以报考了面向全国招生的中央美院附中，随后顺利进入美院；他的真正热情来源其朋克音乐。刘小东是观察现实的画家，而仇却是以流逝的记忆为主题的画家，如作品《艺术课堂》的创作　基本上以　其早年学生生活记忆为蓝本。与当今青年一代常常关注城市变化的现象相比，仇晓飞的这一策略非常特别。他的作品的采用一种“抗议忘记”数年前的现实的方式，在一种激烈的变化的联系中回归到过往的历史中。在2004年到2005年戏剧市场高涨之后，随着这种

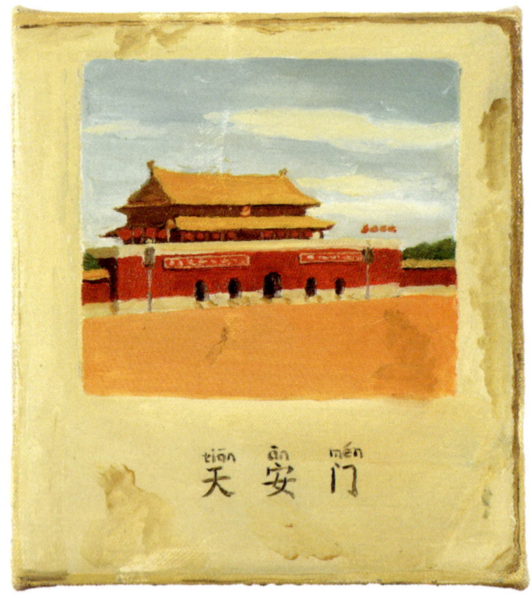

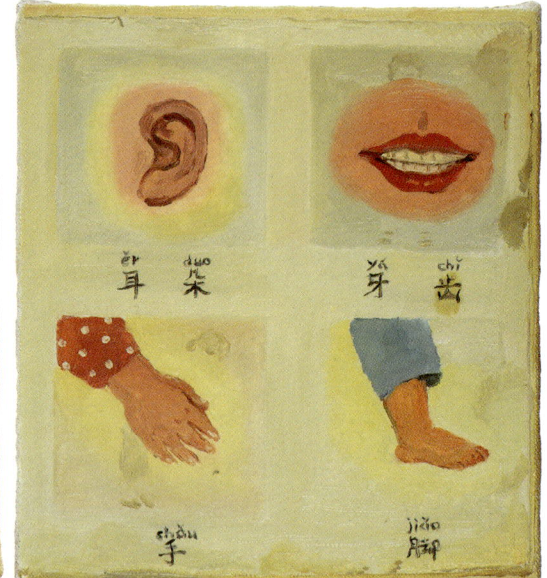

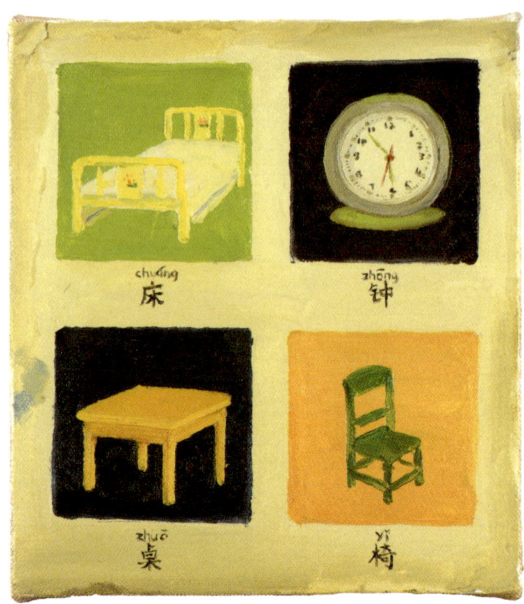

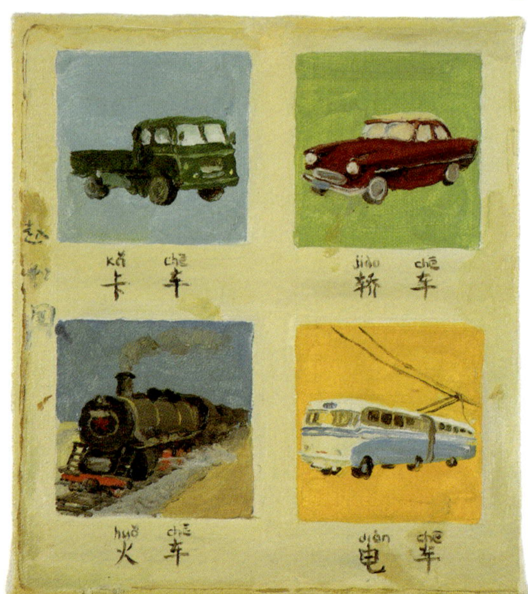

2

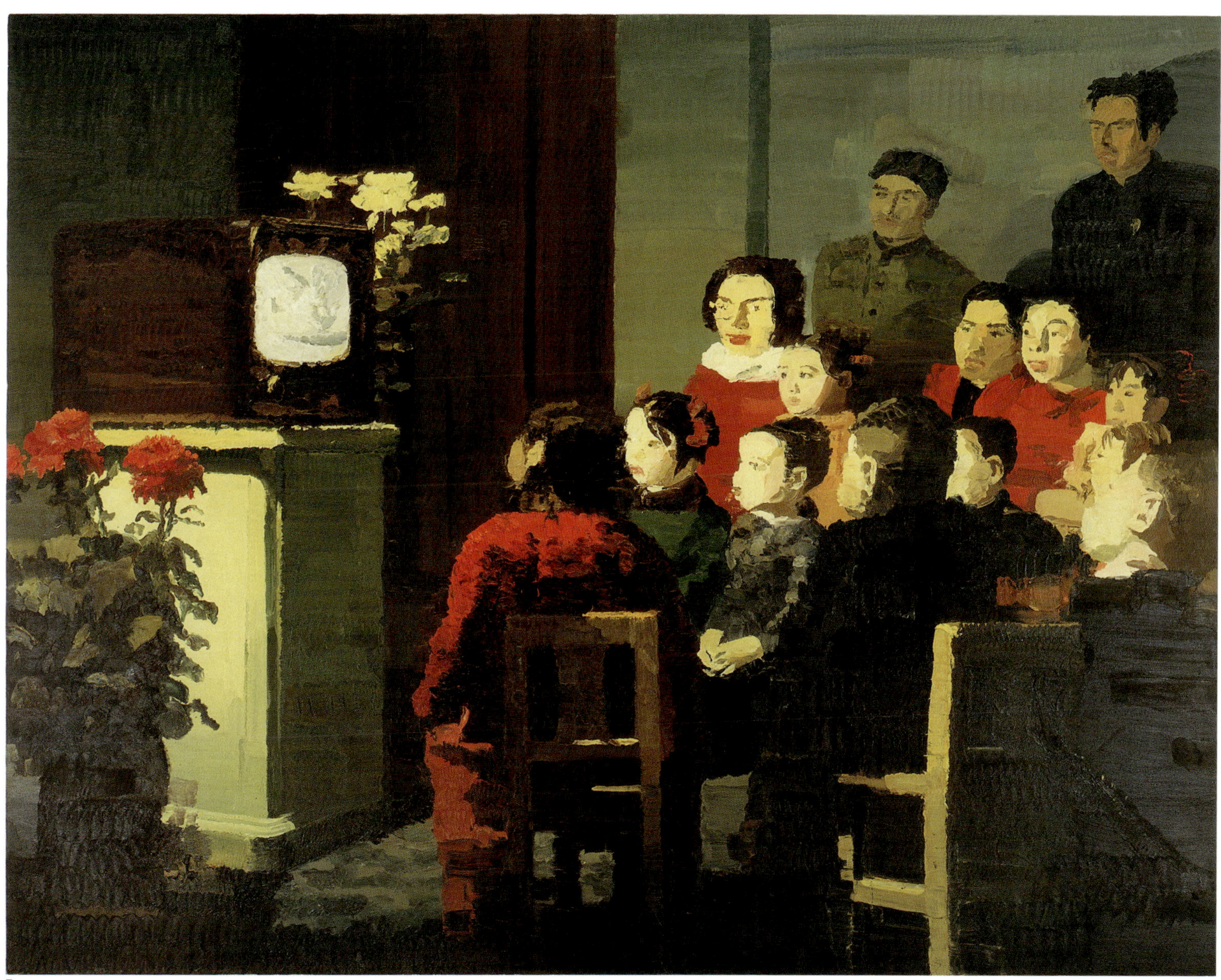

3

4

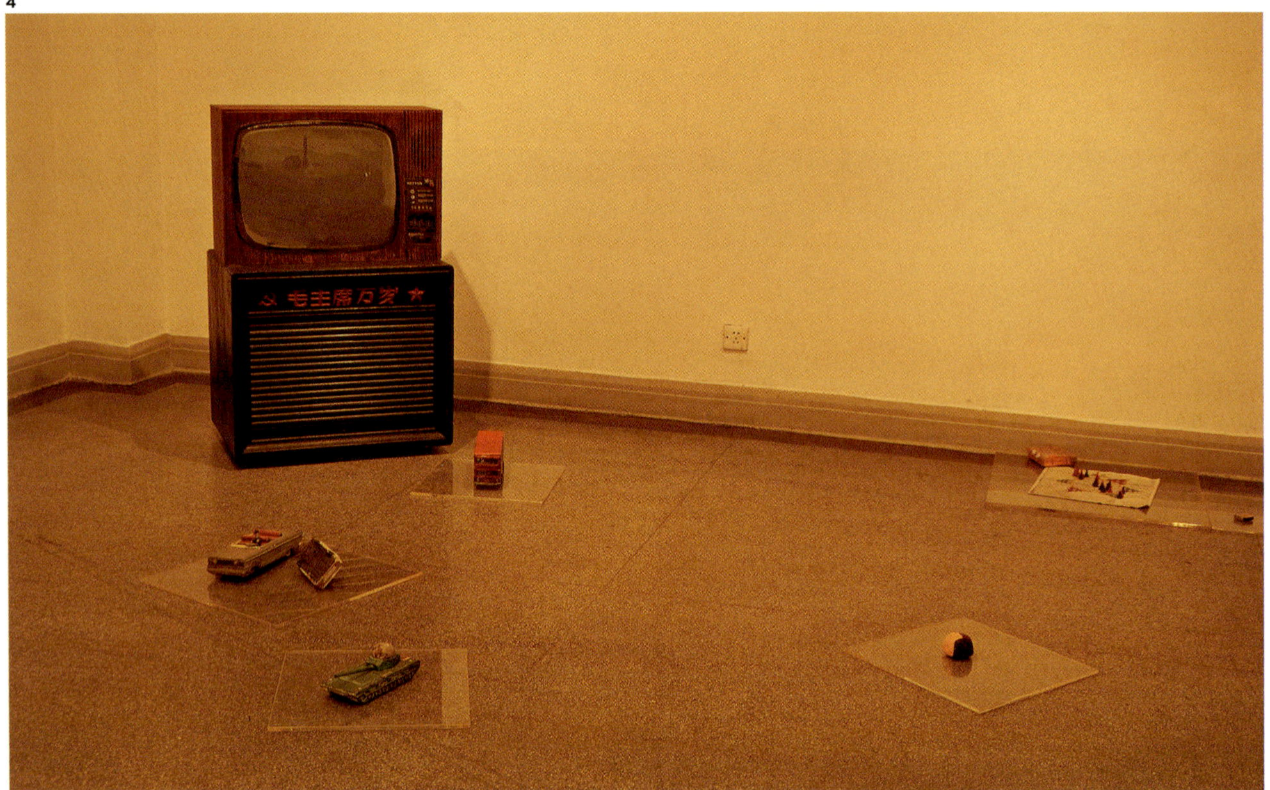

to attend a local school; his real passion through much of his schooling lay with punk music. Where Liu Xiaodong is a painter of observed realities, Qiu Xiaofei has become a painter of fading memories, basing compositions such as "Art Class" purely on his recollections of his earlier life. It is an uncommon strategy, particularly among a younger generation often more concerned with the unending parade of new urban phenomena. His work is in some ways a "protest against forgetting" the realities of just a few years ago, which in a context of such heated change come to seem like ancient history.

Qiu Xiaofei is in a sense the first painter to have emerged after the dramatic market upswing of 2004/05, axiomatically at home with the implications of this new environment on young artists. A 2002 graduate of the Central Academy, he formed a group called "N12" with eleven of his fellow-traveling classmates including Song Kun and his partner Hu Xiaoyuan (the latter of whom was featured in documenta 12) all working in varieties of this contemporary yet nostalgic realism.

Sozialistischen Realismus einmal auf Szenen des Alltags zu richten, in den 1990er Jahren zum Ausgangspunkt einer sehr dynamischen malerischen Schule wurde. Qiu kam auf Umwegen zur Kunst: An die Oberschule der Central Academy ging er hauptsächlich deshalb, weil ihm die Pekinger Meldebescheinigung fehlte, mit der er eine örtliche Schule hätte besuchen dürfen. Während seiner Schulzeit galt seine wahre Liebe lange der Punkmusik. Während Liu Xiaodong ein Maler der vorgefundenen Realität ist, ist Qiu Xiaofei zum Maler der verblassenden Erinnerungen geworden: Kompositionen wie „Art Class" gehen ganz und gar auf seine Erinnerungen an frühere Abschnitte seines Lebens zurück – eine ungewöhnliche Strategie, vor allem innerhalb der jüngeren Generation, die sich oft mehr für die endlose Parade neuer urbaner Phänomene interessiert. Qius Werk ist eine Art „Protest gegen das Vergessen" von Realitäten, die erst wenige Jahre zurückliegen, im Kontext des hektischen aktuellen Wandels aber bereits aus grauer Vorzeit zu stammen scheinen.

In gewissem Sinne war Qiu Xiaofei der erste Maler, der nach dem dramatischen Marktaufschwung von 2004/05 die immense Bedeutung dieses neuen Umfelds für junge Künstler erkannte. Nach seinem Abschluss an der Central Academy 2002 gründete er mit elf Mitstudenten eine Gruppe namens „N12". Alle pflegen eigene Versionen dieses zeitgenössischen und doch nostalgischen Realismus – dazu gehören u. a. Song Kun und seine Partnerin Hu Xiaoyuan, die auf der Documenta 12 vertreten ist.

新环境对年轻艺术家们暗示，仇晓飞在某种意义上是第一位在国内崭露头角的艺术家。2002年毕业于中央美院后，他和其他11位旅行伙伴一起创建了N12组织，其中就包括宋琨和胡晓远（后者作品入选第七届德国文件展）所有成员都以这种现代却怀旧的现实主义风格创作着。

Philip Tinari

5

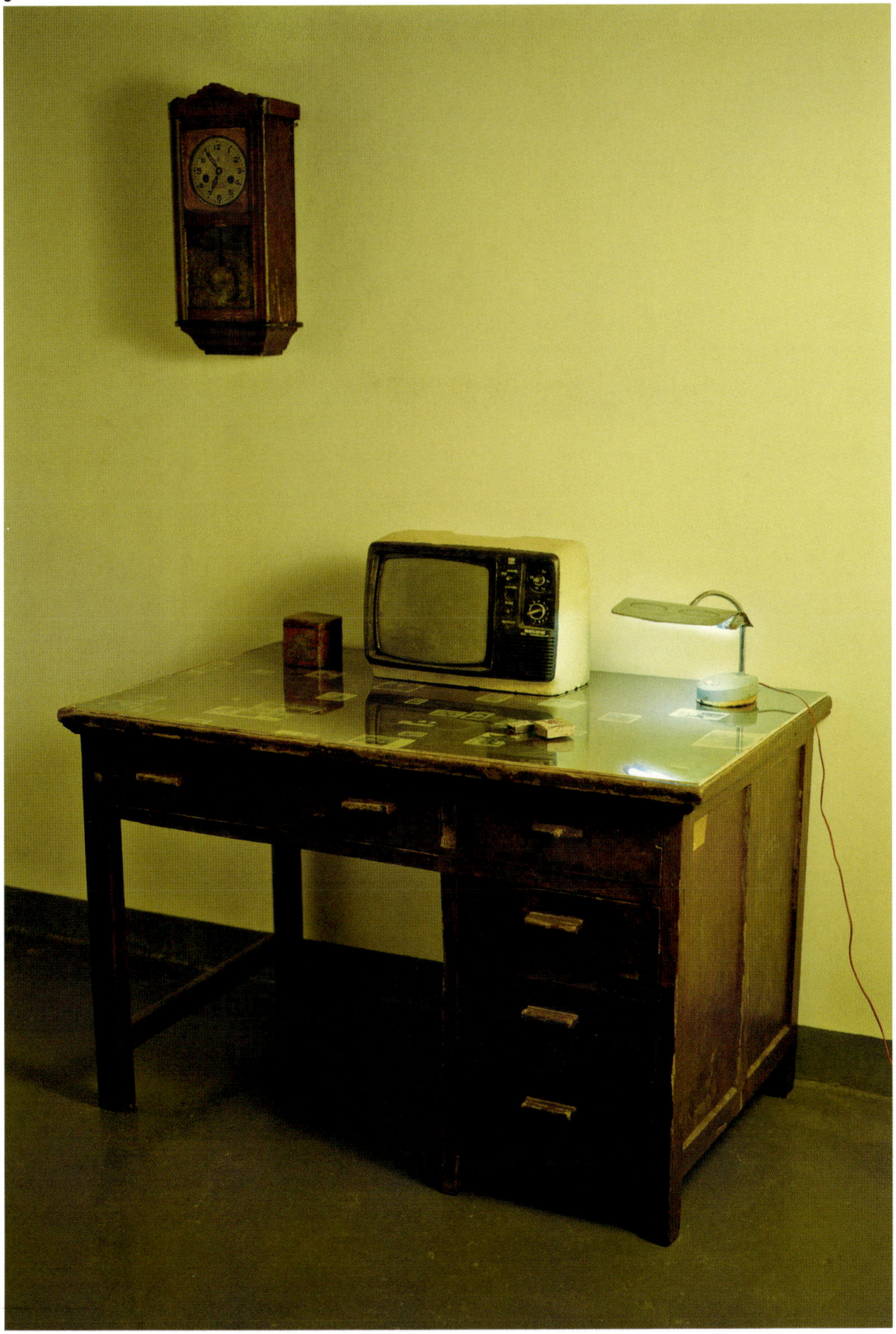

6

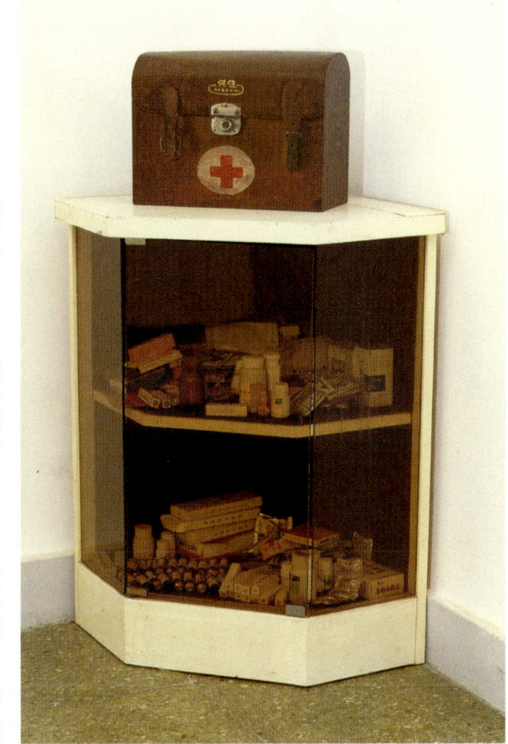

1 ***Madness***, *2003*
Oil on canvas, 180 x 160 cm
Öl auf Leinwand, 180 x 160 cm
《疯狂》2003年, 布面油画, 180 x 160 cm

2 ***Learning To Read Through Pictures***, *2003*
Oil on canvas, 23 x 23 cm each
Öl auf Leinwand, je 23 x 23 cm
《学会读通过图片》2003年, 布面油画， 每幅 23 x 23 cm

3 ***Watching***, *2004*
Oil on canvas, 200 x 250 cm
Öl auf Leinwand, 200 x 250 cm
《看电视》2004年, 布面油画, 200 x 250 cm

4 ***Hei Long Jiang Box***, *2006*
Installation view
Installationsansicht
《黑龙江盒子》2006年, 装置实景

5 ***Almost 7 o'clock***, *2005*
Acrylic on glass fibre reinforced plastic (installation view)
Acryl mit Fiberglas verstärktem Kunststoff (Installationsansicht)
《快七点了》2005年, 玻璃纤维丙烯, 装置实景

6 ***At the clinic***, *2005*
Mixed media, oil colour (installation view)
Mixed media, Ölfarbe (Installationsansicht)
《在诊所》2005年, 混合媒介, 油彩， 装置实景

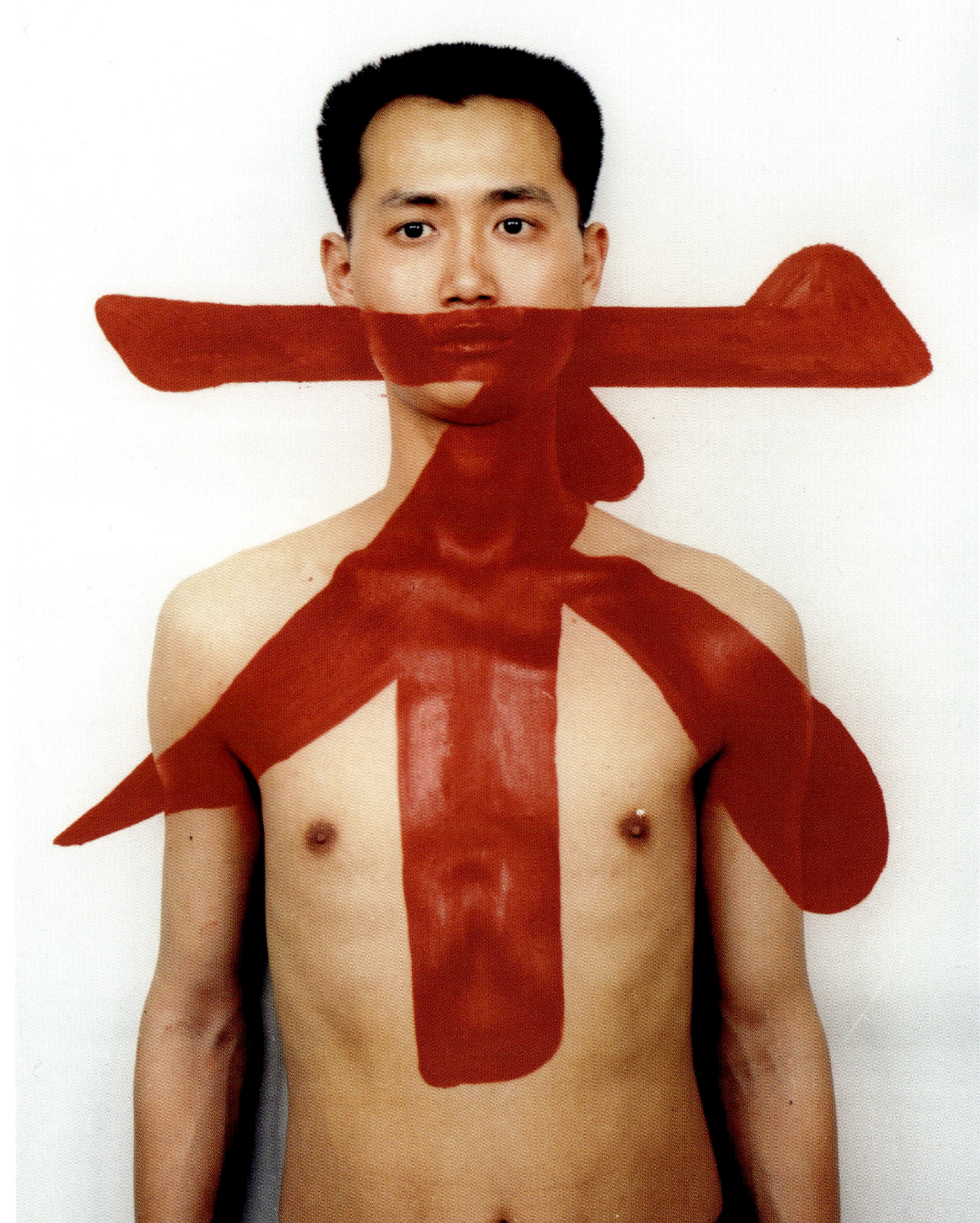

1

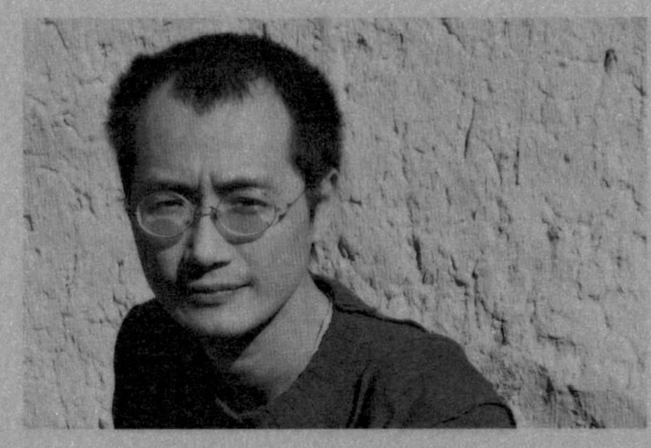

"So the new Long March for us is actually an active search on our own initiative to seek a modernity, which belongs to us, to seek a modernity that we want."

„Der neue Lange Marsch bedeutet für uns tatsächlich eine eigene Initiative, eine Moderne zu finden, die zu uns gehört. Wir suchen die Moderne, die wir wollen."

"新长征对我们而言，实际上是积极探索自身追求现代性的主动性，它属于我们，去寻找我们所需要的现代性。我们主要关注哪种新试验方式可以呈现于其他人，而非从别人那里获取新的方式。"

Born in 1969 in Zhangzhou, China. Lives and works in Beijing and Hangzhou
Geboren 1969 in Zhangzhou, China. Lebt und arbeitet in Peking und Hangzhou
1969年出生于中国福建省漳州，现于北京和杭州工作居住

Selected exhibitions / **Ausgewählte Ausstellungen** / 所选展览

1999 "Innate Forces, mixed media works by Qiu Zhijie", Art Beatus Gallery, Vancouver, Canada
2001 "Qiu Zhijie: Invisibility," Ethan Cohen Fine Arts, New York, NY, USA
2004 "Qiu Zhijie: Social Portraits", Court Yard Gallery, Beijing, China
2004–07 "Between Past and Future, New Photography and Video from China", International Center of Photography, New York, NY, USA (travelling exhibition)
2007 "Made in China", Louisiana Museum of Modern Art, Humlebæk, Denmark

1999年 《内在元素》精艺轩，温哥华
2001年 《消失：邱志杰作品展》伊森恩艺廊，纽约
2004年 《社会肖像》四合院画廊，北京
2004-07年 《过去与未来之间—中国新影像展》国际摄影中心 纽约 美国（巡回展）
2007年 《中国制造》路易斯安那现代艺术馆 Humlebæk, 丹麦

Selected publications / **Ausgewählte Publikationen** / 所选著作

"Young Chinese Contemporary Art/Junge chinesische zeitgenössische Kunst", Vienna 2005
"The shape of time", New York 2007
Christina Yu: "Light Writing, Qiu Zhijie's New Works", at: www.bjartlab.com, 2007

HangART-7 出版 2。年轻中国当代艺术, Basis 维也纳 2005年
《时间的形态》前波画廊，展册，纽约 2007年
Yu, Christina（著）：《轻的文字;邱志杰的新作品》网上出版 www.bjartlab.com, 2007年

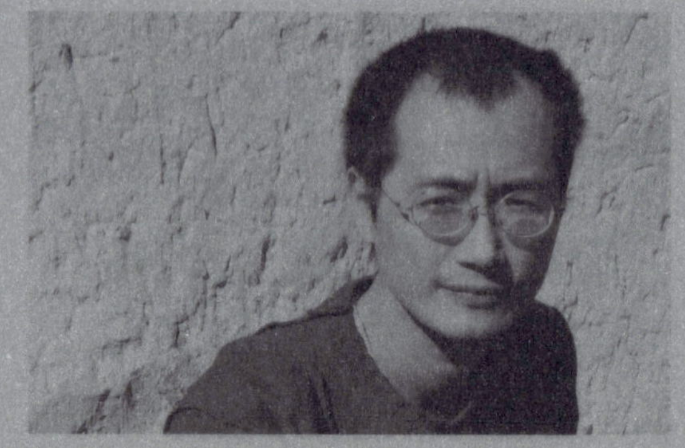

"So the new Long March for us is actually an active search on our own initiative to seek a modernity, which belongs to us, to seek a modernity that we want."

„Der neue Lange Marsch bedeutet für uns tatsächlich eine eigene Initiative, eine Moderne zu finden, die zu uns gehört. Wir suchen die Moderne, die wir wollen."

"新长征对我们而言，实际上是积极探索自身追求现代性的主动性，它属于我们，去寻找我们所需要的现代性。我们主要关注哪种新试验方式可以呈现于其他人，而非从别人那里获取新的方式。"

Born in 1969 in Zhangzhou, China. Lives and works in Beijing and Hangzhou
Geboren 1969 in Zhangzhou, China. Lebt und arbeitet in Peking und Hangzhou
1969年出生于中国福建省漳州，现于北京和杭州工作居住

Selected exhibitions / Ausgewählte Ausstellungen / 所选展览

1999	"Innate Forces, mixed media works by Qiu Zhijie", Art Beatus Gallery, Vancouver, Canada
2001	"Qiu Zhijie: Invisibility," Ethan Cohen Fine Arts, New York, NY, USA
2004	"Qiu Zhijie: Social Portraits", Court Yard Gallery, Beijing, China
2004-07	"Between Past and Future, New Photography and Video from China", International Center of Photography, New York, NY, USA (travelling exhibition)
2007	"Made in China", Louisiana Museum of Modern Art, Humlebaek, Denmark

1999年	《内在元素》精艺轩，温哥华
2001年	《消失：邱志杰作品展》伊森恩艺廊，纽约
2004年	《社会肖像》四合院画廊，北京
2004-07年	《过去与未来之间—中国新影像展》国际摄影中心 纽约 美国（巡回展）
2007年	《中国制造》路易斯安那现代艺术馆 Humlebaek, 丹麦

Selected publications / Ausgewählte Publikationen / 所选著作

"Young Chinese Contemporary Art/Junge chinesische zeitgenössische Kunst", Vienna 2005
"The shape of time", New York 2007
Christina Yu: "Light Writing, Qiu Zhijie's New Works", at: www.bjartlab.com, 2007

HangART-7 出版 2。年轻中国当代艺术, Basis 维也纳 2005年
《时间的形态》前波画廊，展册，纽约 2007年
Yu, Christina（著）：《轻的文字：邱志杰的新作品》网上出版 www.bjartlab.com, 2007年

QIU ZHIJIE 邱志杰

[tɕ^{h}iou ʈʂztɕiɛ]

Qiu Zhijie, born into a scholar's family, is an artist difficult to categorise. Learning calligraphy as a boy under the guidance of his grandfather, his teenage years coincided with China's opening to the West. Qiu, interested in philosophy not only studied the writings of Karl Marx, Friedrich Nietzsche, Jean-Paul Sartre but also of Lu Xun, the Chinese activist and famous writer who also provided him with the intellectual background for his later works.

In 1988 he enrolled in the Printmaking Department of the Zhejiang Academy of Fine Arts in Hangzhou, where he graduated in 1992. In 1989 he was given support to travel abroad, but the travel restriction after the June Fourth Movement shuttered his ambitions and he stayed in China. At this time he started to collaborate with Wu Shanzhuan and Zhang Peili executing a series of anti-establishment activities designed to eradicate "the personal" from their artwork.

Since his graduation Qiu Zhijie experimented with an impressive range of media and styles, making him difficult to be categorised in the Chinese art scene. He is calligrapher, painter, stone carver, computer and video artist as well as curator and teacher. By putting traditional Chinese art in a conceptual context, and raising questions about the essence of the traditions he has inherited and studied, Qiu Zhijie has made himself into one of the most thought provoking artists active in China today. He has presented his works within China and abroad like 1998 at the "Inside – Out" exhibition at New York and San Francisco, followed by exhibitions in Asia and the West. His calligraphy work "A one thousand time copy of Lantingxu" (1990–1997), a writing of the same text on one single sheet of rice paper after the famous work of Wang Xizhi, composed in 353 and being a masterpiece of calligraphy and prose, resulted in a blackened paper finally, the different 50 stages of Qiu's writing being documentated by photography. This kind of rewriting the same characters can be compared to Zen-Buddhist meditation.

Qiu Zhijie, in eine Gelehrtenfamilie hineingeboren, lässt sich als Künstler nur schwer einordnen. Als Kind erlernte er die Kalligraphie unter der Anleitung seines Großvaters, und seine Jugendjahre fielen mit der Öffnung Chinas gegenüber dem Westen zusammen. Qiu, der sich für Philosophie interessiert, studierte nicht nur die Schriften von Karl Marx, Friedrich Nietzsche und Jean-Paul Sartre, sondern auch von Lu Xun, dem chinesischen Querdenker und berühmten Schriftsteller – so erklärt sich der intellektuelle Hintergrund seiner späteren Arbeiten.

1988 schrieb sich Qiu an der Zhejiang Academy of Fine Arts, Abteilung für Druckkunst ein, wo er 1992 seine Studien abschloss. 1989 hatte er bereits die Zusage für ein Stipendium für eine Auslandsreise erhalten, doch die Reisebeschränkungen nach den Ereignissen auf dem Platz des Himmlischen Friedens machten seine Pläne zunichte und er musste in China bleiben. Damals begann seine Zusammenarbeit mit Wu Shanzhuan und Zhang Peili. Gemeinsam wurden sie gegen das Establishment in einer Weise aktiv, die zum Ziel hatte, „das Persönliche" aus ihrer Kunstproduktion auszulöschen.

Seit seinem Hochschulabschluss experimentiert Qiu Zhijie mit einer großen Vielfalt an Medien und Stilen, was es schwer macht, ihn in der chinesischen Kunstszene einzuordnen. Er ist Kalligraph, Maler, Steinschnitzer, Computer- und Video-Künstler, aber auch Kurator und Professor für Kunst. Indem er die traditionelle chinesische Kunst in einen konzeptuellen Kontext stellt und überkommene Traditionen hinterfragt, wurde Qiu zu einem der provokantesten Künstler, der alles konventionelle Denken anzweifelt. Seine Werke waren und sind in China ebenso wie im Ausland zu sehen – „Inside – Out" (1998) in New York und San Francisco –, und er ist durch zahlreiche Ausstellungen in Asien und westlichen Ländern präsent. Sein Kalligraphiewerk „A One Thousand Time Copy of Lantingxu" (1990–1997), bei dem er ein und denselben Text des berühmten Wang Xizhi aus dem Jahre 353, ein Meisterwerk der Kalligraphie und Dichtkunst, auf ein einziges Blatt Reispapier tausendfach

邱志杰，出生于一个学者家庭，是一个难以归类的艺术家。孩提时代，他在祖父的指导下学习书法，他的青少年时代与改革开放同步进行。在哲学方面，邱不仅学习马克思、尼采和萨特的思想，而且还有著名活动家和作家鲁迅的思想，这些其近作理论基础。

1988年，他考入浙江美院版画系，1992年毕业。1989年别人资助他去国外，但是六四运动之后的旅行管制打击了他的抱负，仍呆在中国。也就是在那时他开始与吴山专和张培力合作开展了一系列反个人主义活动，以消除他们艺术作品中的"个性"。

自毕业以后，邱志杰用多种介质和风格试验艺术，因此在中国艺术界中，很难将他归类哪个艺术流派。他是一个书法家、画家、石雕匠、电脑和视频艺术家以及策展人和教师。通过将中国传统艺术置于观念联系中，并且质疑他继承和学习的传统艺术的本质，邱志杰成为活跃在中国中最有思想创造力的艺术家之一。他的作品在国内外展出，如1998年的《蜕变与突破：中国新艺术》，该展在纽约和旧金山以及亚洲和欧洲巡回展出。书法作品《重复书写一千遍兰亭序》(1990–1997年)是作者用单张宣纸摹写了王羲之的《兰亭序》(创作于公元353年，是书法和诗歌的杰作)，同时用录像记录该过程的前五十遍，最终作品呈现方式是被写黑的纸本原件和记录变化过程的照片和录像。这种重写相同的字可比作禅宗的冥想。

除书法以外，他的录像装置如《西方》(1999年)，根据前南斯拉夫中国大使馆轰炸事件创作，是一部互动式CD-ROM项目，展示了这个多才多艺的艺术家另一面。但是，书法仍然是其作品的核心。摄影作品如《纹身I》和《纹身II》(1994)　和《四季》系列作品(2007年在前波画廊展览)，将美学和书法艺术组合起来，邱志杰用闪光灯书写了24节气的传统标志，照片描绘了从北京到澳门和英国的场景和景色。

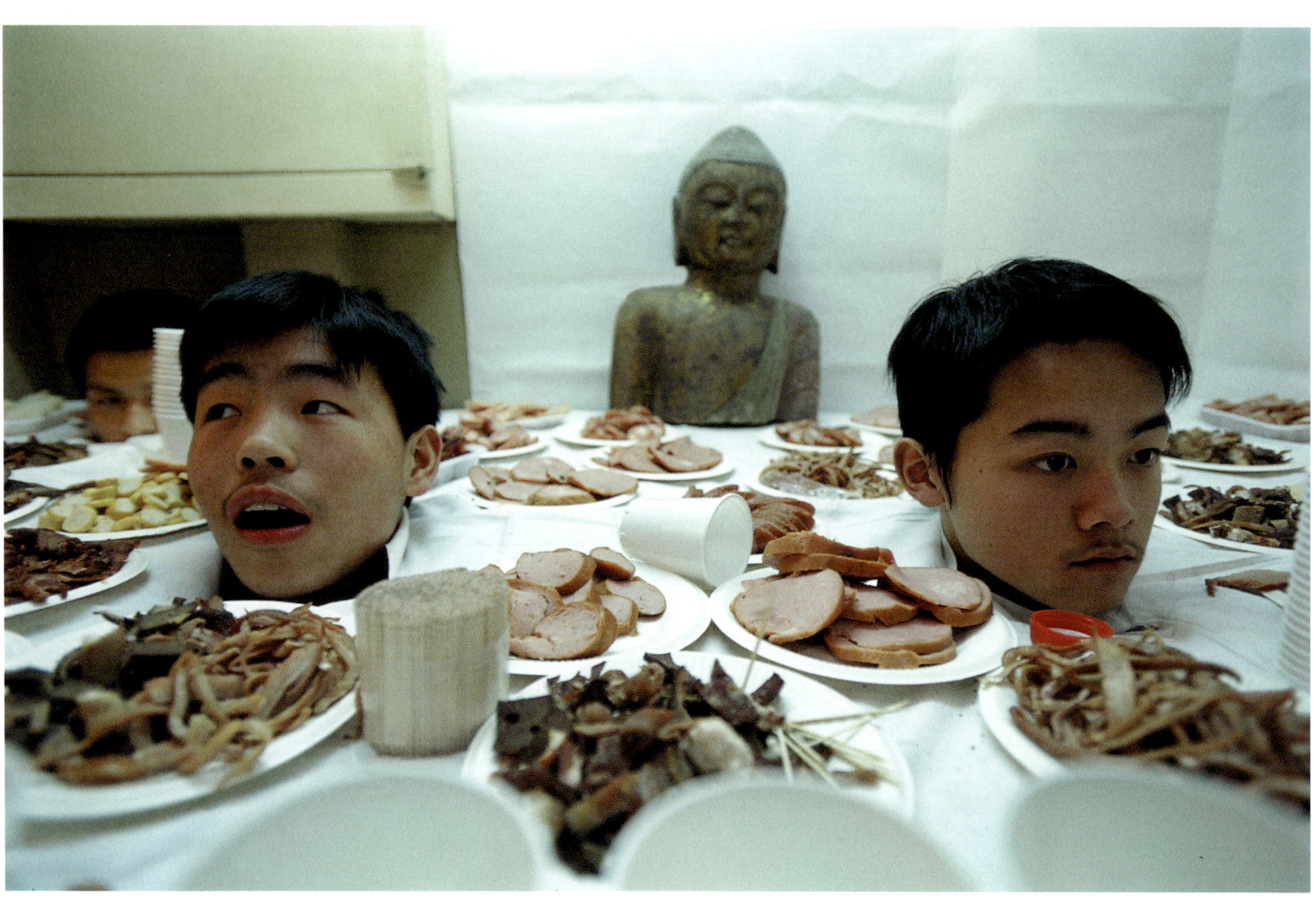

2

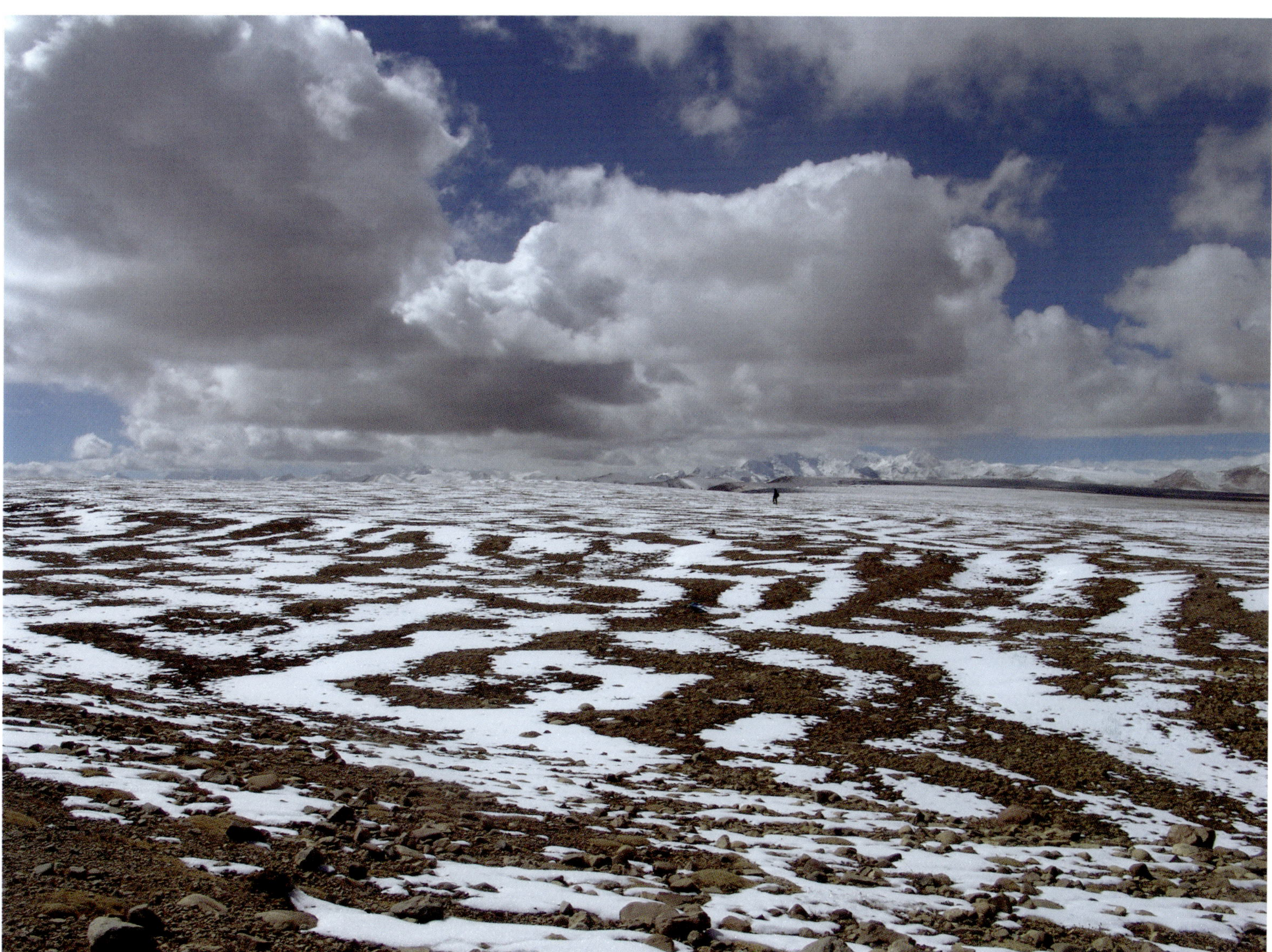

3

4

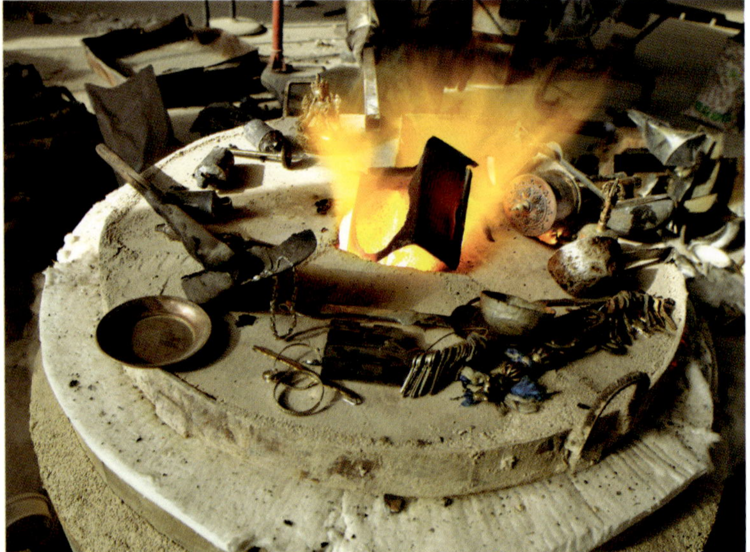

5

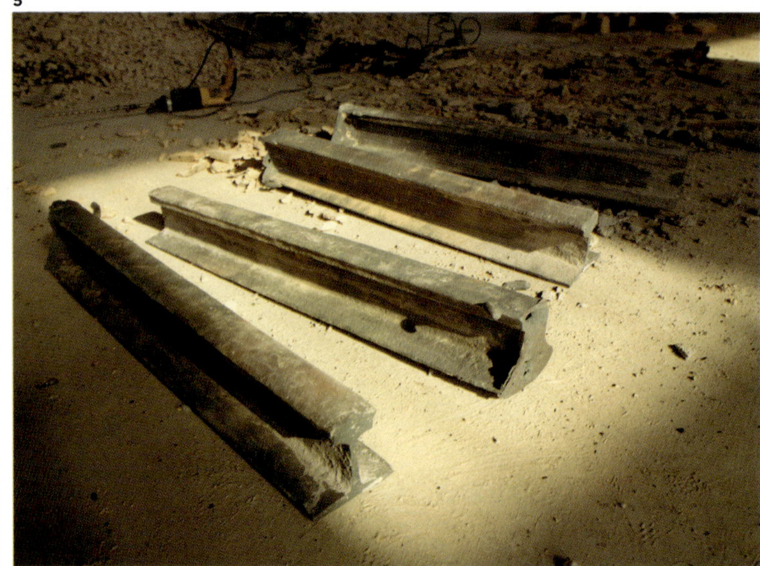

Apart from his calligraphy his video installations like "The West" (1999) caused by the bombing of the Chinese Embassy in former Yugoslavia, an interactive CD-ROM-project, shows another facet of this multitalented artist. But calligraphy still is the core of his works. Photographs are like the series "Tattoo I" and "Tattoo II" (1994) and the series "The Four Seasons" (2007) combines aesthetics and calligraphy, as traditional signs of the seasons (altogether 24 season "markers") are written by flashlight on the photos, depicting scenes and landscapes from Beijing to Macau and England. Qiu Zhijie's work is interdisciplinary like his interests, and as he is not focussed on just one media – he keeps the role of an unpredictable and challenging artist of today's China contemporary art scene.

niederschrieb, bis am Ende nur noch ein tiefschwarzes Papier zu sehen war, dokumentierte er durch Fotografien der 50 einzelnen Phasen. Diese Form der ständigen Wiederholung einer einzigen Tätigkeit erinnert stark an eine Zen-Meditation.

Neben der Kalligraphie widmet sich Qiu in seinen Video-Arbeiten aktuellen Themen wie der Bombardierung der chinesischen Botschaft im ehemaligen Jugoslawien, die er zu einem interaktiven CD-ROM-Projekt mit dem Titel „The West" (1999) zusammenfasste – eine weitere Facette dieses Multitalents. Die Kalligraphie bleibt jedoch das Kernstück seiner Arbeiten. In Fotoserien wie „Tattoo I" und „Tattoo II" (1994) sowie „The Four Seasons" (2007) kombiniert Qiu Fotoästhetik und Kalligraphie in neuer Form, indem er auf Fotos, die Szenen und Landschaften von Peking bis Macao und England zeigen, traditionelle Schiftzeichen, die für die Jahreszeiten stehen (insgesamt 24), mit Blitzlicht schrieb. Qiu Zhijies Werke sind ebenso interdisziplinär angelegt wie seine Interessen, und da er sich nicht auf ein einziges Medium konzentriert, wird er im heutigen China auch weiterhin die Rolle des unberechenbaren und herausfordernden Künstlers spielen.

邱志杰的作品和其兴趣一样多种多样，他没有专注于某一介质。在中国艺术界中，他依然是难以捉摸，具有挑战性的艺术家。

Victoria Lu

6

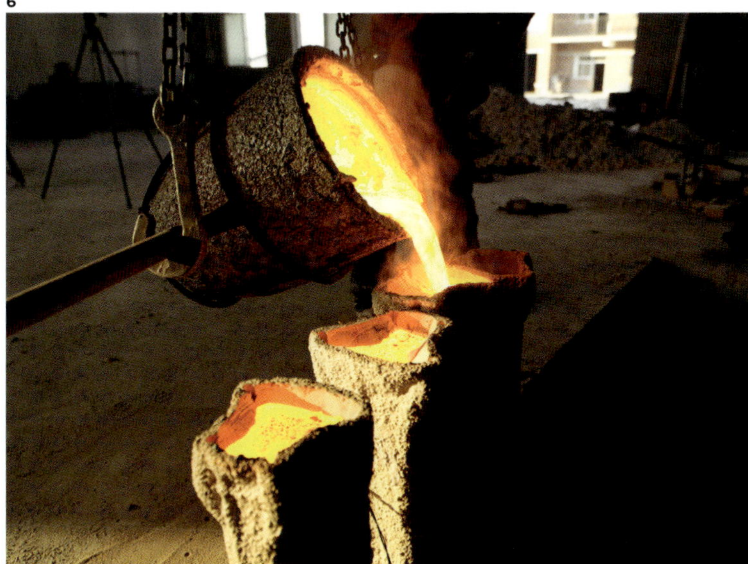

7

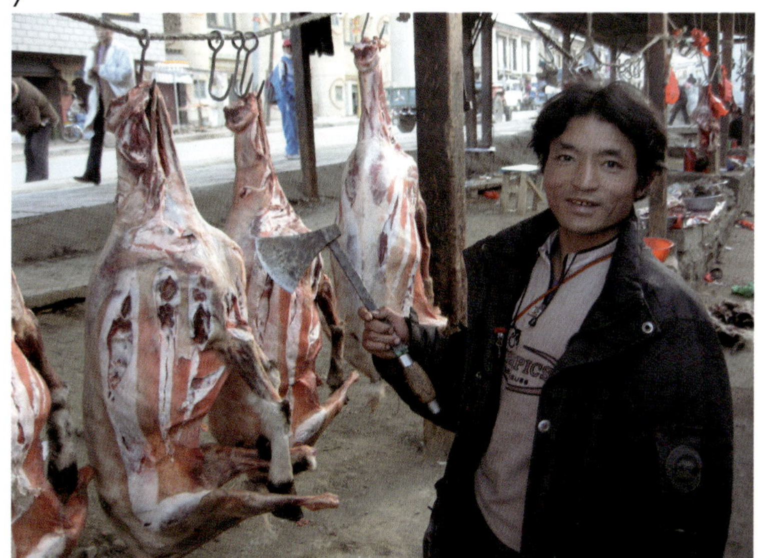

1 ***Tattoo II**, 1994*
Photograph, 180 x 140 cm
Fotografie, 180 x 140 cm
《纹身2》1994年，摄影, 180 x 140 cm

2 ***All the Meat here is clean**, 2001*
Performance
Performance
《狂欢・这里的肉是干净的》2001年, 表演

3–8 ***The Railway from Lhasa to Kathmandu**, 2006/07*
Performance, video
Performance, Video
《拉萨到加德满都的铁路》2006/07年, 表演，录像

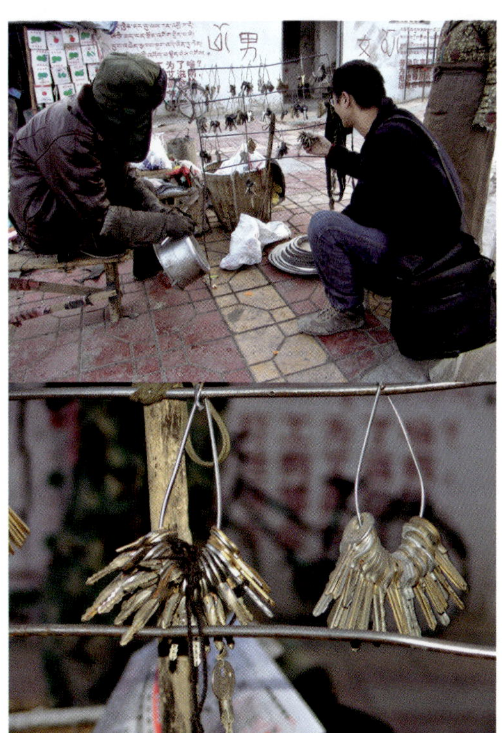

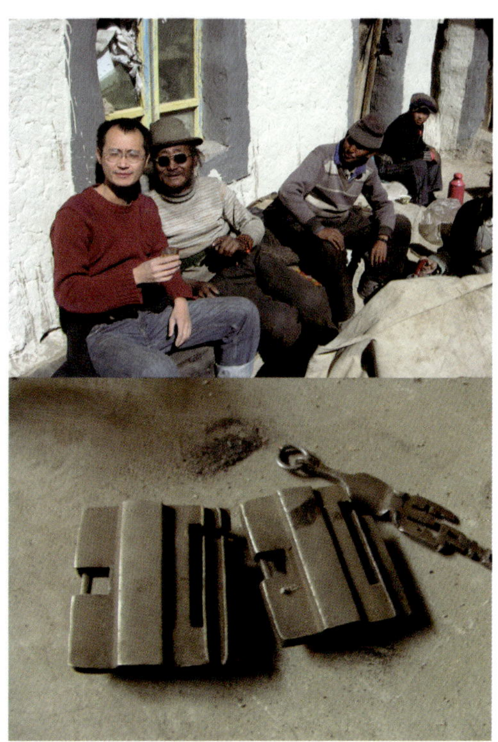

8

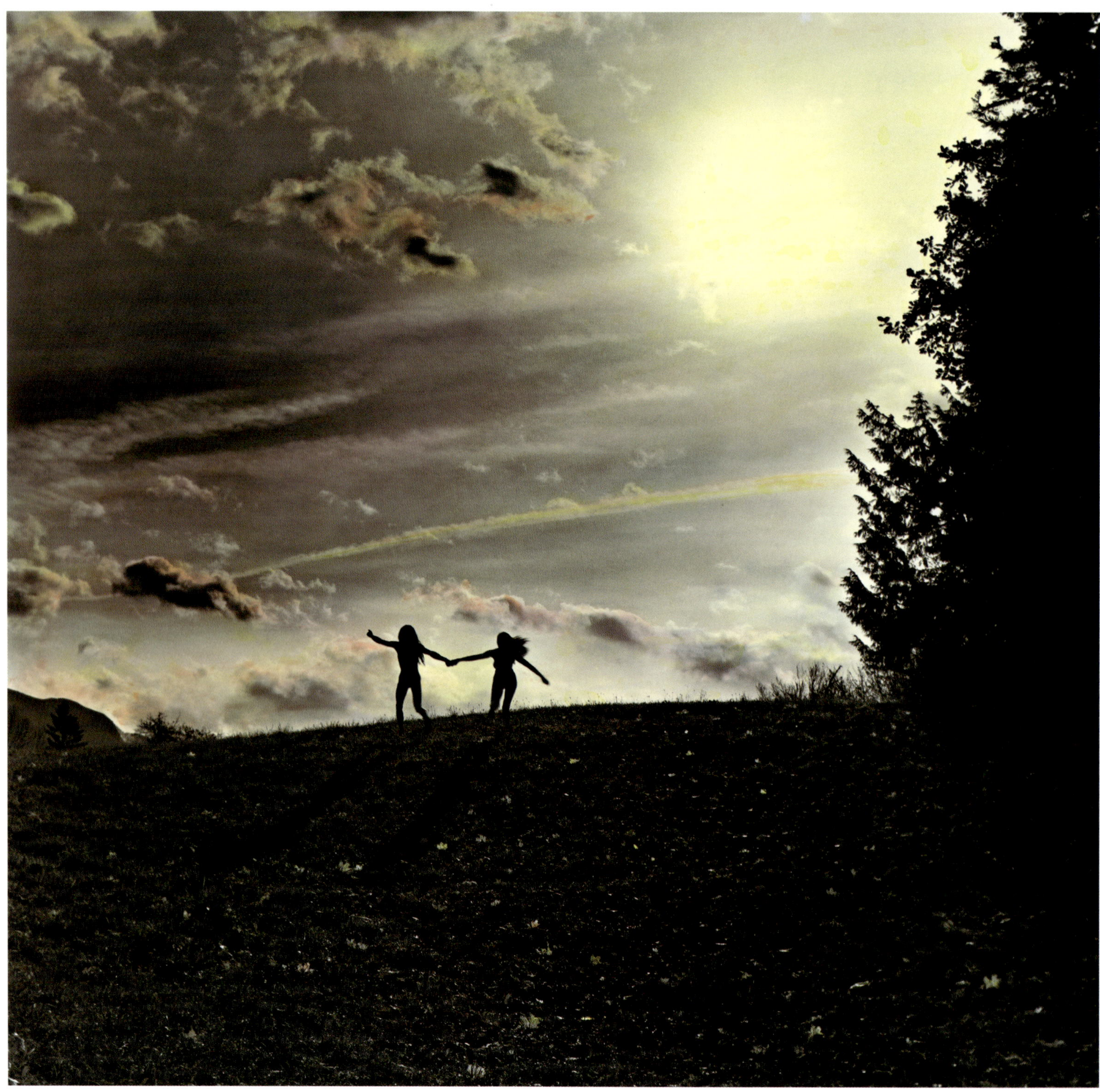

1

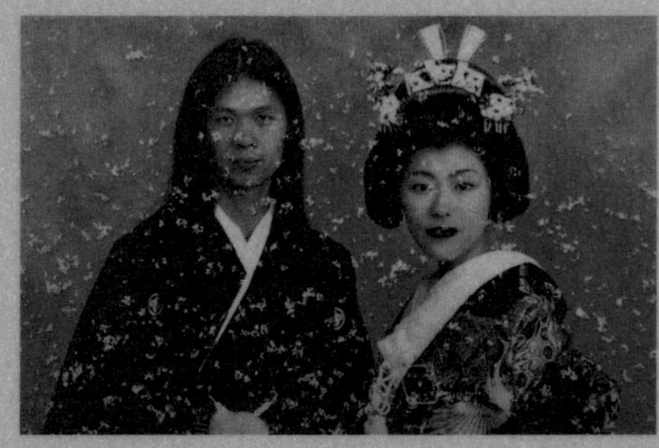

"People, who go to visit those places, cannot perceive the world of our experience. That world does not exist anywhere in the real world. You can only possess that world with us in our photos."

„Menschen, die diese Orte besuchen, können die Welt unserer Erfahrungen nicht wahrnehmen. Sie existiert nirgends. Diese Welt kann man sich nur mit uns in unseren Fotos aneignen."

"去过那些地方人们并不能感悟到我们经历中的世界，那个世界存在于现实世界之外，人们只能通过我们的照片去了解，认知。"

RongRong, born in 1968 in Zhangzhou, China; Inri, born in 1973 in Kanagawa, Japan
The artists live and work in Beijing
RongRong, geboren 1968 in Zhangzhou, China; Inri, geboren 1973 in Kanagawa, Japan
Die Künstler leben und arbeiten in Peking
1968年荣荣出生于中国漳州。1973年映里生于日本神奈川。二人共同定居工作在北京

Selected exhibitions / **Ausgewählte Ausstellungen** / 所选展览

2004–07 "Between Past and Future, New Photography and Video from China", International Center of Photography, New York, NY, USA (travelling exhibition)
2005 "Über Schönheit", Haus der Kulturen der Welt, Berlin, Germany
"De Zomer van Middelburg", Museum van Hedendaagse Kunst, Antwerp, Belgium
"A Strange Heaven", Helsinki City Art Museum, Helsinki, Finland
2005–07 "Mahjong – Chinesische Gegenwartskunst aus der Sammlung Sigg", Kunstmuseum Bern, Berne, Switzerland; Hamburger Kunsthalle, Hamburg, Germany; Museum der Moderne, Salzburg, Austria

2004–07年《过去与未来之间—中国新影像展》国际摄影中心 纽约 美国（巡回展）
2005年 《关于秀丽》，文化房子，柏林
《中堡的夏》，当代艺术博物馆, 安特卫普
《奇怪的天堂》，赫尔辛基市美术馆, 赫尔辛基
2005–07年 《麻将》西克中国当代艺术收藏展 伯尔尼美术馆 瑞士；汉堡美术馆，汉堡，德国；萨尔茨保现代美术馆 奥地利

Selected publications / **Ausgewählte Publikationen** / 所选著作

Guy & Myriam Ullens Foundation (ed.): "Alles onder de hemel/All under heaven. China now!", Antwerp 2003
Bernhard Fibicher, Matthias Frehner (eds.): "Mahjong. Chinesische Gegenwartskunst aus der Sammlung Sigg", Ostfildern-Ruit 2005
Wu Hung (ed.): "RongRong and Inri: Tui-Transformation", Hong Kong 2005

Guy & Myriam Ullens Foundation（编者）：《天堂之下》China now!, 安特卫普 2003年
Fibicher, Bernhard/Frehner, Matthias（编者）：《麻将一西克的当代艺术收藏展》Ostfildern-Ruit 2005年
巫鸿（编者）：《荣荣和映里:蜕变革》香港 2005年

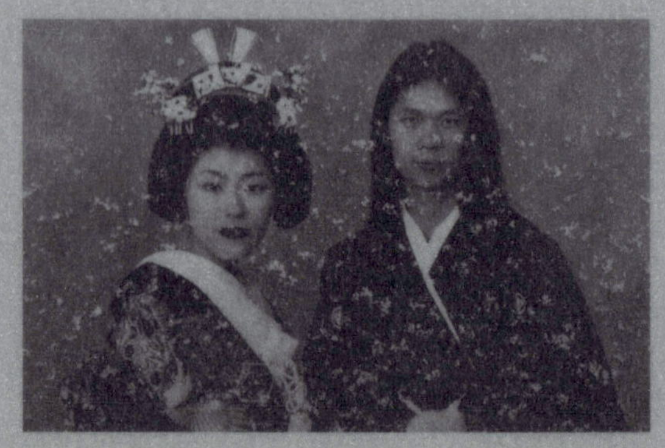

"People, who go to visit those places, cannot perceive the world of our experience. That world does not exist anywhere in the real world. You can only possess that world with us in our photos."

„Menschen, die diese Orte besuchen, können die Welt unserer Erfahrungen nicht wahrnehmen. Sie existiert nirgends. Diese Welt kann man sich nur mit uns in unseren Fotos aneignen."

"去过那些地方人们并不能感悟到我们经历中的世界，那个世界存在于现实世界之外，人们只能通过我们的照片去了解，认知。"

RongRong, born in 1968 in Zhangzhou, China; Inri, born in 1973 in Kanagawa, Japan
The artists live and work in Beijing
RongRong, geboren 1968 in Zhangzhou, China; Inri, geboren 1973 in Kanagawa, Japan
Die Künstler leben und arbeiten in Peking
1968年荣荣出生于中国漳州。1973年映里生于日本神奈川。二人共同定居工作在北京

Selected exhibitions / Ausgewählte Ausstellungen / 所选展览

2004–07	"Between Past and Future, New Photography and Video from China", International Center of Photography, New York, NY, USA (travelling exhibition)
2005	"Über Schönheit", Haus der Kulturen der Welt, Berlin, Germany
	"De Zomer van Middelburg", Museum van Hedendaagse Kunst, Antwerp, Belgium
	"A Strange Heaven", Helsinki City Art Museum, Helsinki, Finland
2005–07	"Mahjong - Chinesische Gegenwartskunst aus der Sammlung Sigg", Kunstmuseum Bern, Berne, Switzerland; Hamburger Kunsthalle, Hamburg, Germany; Museum der Moderne, Salzburg, Austria

2004–07年	《过去与未来之间—中国新影像展》国际摄影中心 纽约 美国（巡回展）
2005年	《关于秀丽》，文化房子，柏林
	《中堡的夏》，当代艺术博物馆，安特卫普
	《奇怪的天堂》，赫尔辛基市美术馆，赫尔辛基
2005–07年	《麻将》西克中国当代艺术收藏展 伯尔尼美术馆 瑞士；汉堡美术馆，汉堡，德国；萨尔茨堡现代美术馆 奥地利

Selected publications / Ausgewählte Publikationen / 所选著作

Guy & Myriam Ullens Foundation (ed.): "Alles onder de hemel/All under heaven. China now!", Antwerp 2003
Bernhard Fibicher, Matthias Frehner (eds.): "Mahjong. Chinesische Gegenwartskunst aus der Sammlung Sigg", Ostfildern-Ruit 2005
Wu Hung (ed.): "RongRong and Inri: Tui-Transformation", Hong Kong 2005

Guy & Myriam Ullens Foundation（编者）：《天堂之下》China now!，安特卫普 2003年
Fibicher, Bernhard/Frehner, Matthias（编者）：《麻将—西克的当代艺术收藏展》Ostfildern-Ruit 2005年
巫鸿（编者）：《荣荣和映里:蜕变革》香港 2005年

RONGRONG & INRI 荣荣和映里

[ʐʊŋ ʐʊŋ]

RongRong arrived in Beijing in 1992 with wide-open eyes and a newly purchased camera. A farm boy from the southeastern province of Fujian, who had never left home before. In Beijing he attended photography classes and became quite good at making the kind of arty, sentimental pictures favoured by popular photo magazines. A drastic change took place in his life and career in 1993, when he moved into a tumble-down village on the city's east fringe. Later known as Beijing's East Village, it would become home to an artistic community that produced some of the most daring works in contemporary Chinese art, before it was closed down by the local police in June 1994.

In the East Village RongRong photographed avant-garde performances – Ma Liuming's "Fen-Ma Liuming's Lunch", Zhang Huang's "12 Square Meters and 65 Kilograms", and others. The importance of these images lies not only in documenting these performances, which have become "classics" of contemporary Chinese art, but also in signifying the emergence of a new kind of photography through forging an intimate relationship between photography and performance. This relationship continued to underlie several series of photographs that RongRong created after the East Village community dispersed, including "Wedding Gown" (1997–2000) and "Ghost Village" (1999–2000). He increasingly appeared before his camera, acting while recording his acts; the strong performance quality of these photos resonated with his personal life.

A new theme entered RongRong's art shortly after the mid-90s: he was fascinated by the numerous half-demolished houses in Beijing, which provided this rapidly developing city with a major visual spectacle. The torn images of glamorous pin-ups left on the broken walls especially attracted him. The incompleteness of these images declares loss and propels the viewer to imagine the life and psyche of the previous occupants of the demolished houses.

Inri graduated from the Nippon Photography Institute in 1994 and worked for the famous newspaper "Asahi

RongRong kam 1992 mit offenem Blick und einer frisch erworbenen Kamera nach Peking. Es war das erste Mal, dass der Bauernjunge aus der südöstlichen Provinz Fujian von Zuhause fort war. In Peking besuchte er Kurse für Fotografie und reüssierte bald mit pseudokünstlerischen, sentimentalen Fotos, die populäre Fotomagazine schätzten. Die Wende in seinem Leben und seiner Karriere kam 1993, als er in ein verfallenes Dorf am Ostrand der Stadt zog. Das Dorf, das später als Pekings East Village zu Ruhm gelangte, wurde Heimat einer Künstlergemeinde, die einige der gewagtesten Werke der zeitgenössischen chinesischen Kunst hervorbrachte, bevor sie im Juni 1994 von der örtlichen Polizei aufgelöst wurde.

Im East Village fotografierte RongRong Avantgarde-Performances – Ma Liumings „Fen-Ma Liuming's Lunch", Zhang Huangs „12 Square Meters and 65 Kilograms" und andere. Die Bedeutung dieser Bilder lag nicht nur darin, dass sie diese Performances dokumentierten, die zu Klassikern der chinesischen Gegenwartskunst geworden sind, sondern vor allem darin, dass sie eine intime Beziehung zwischen Fotografie und Performance herstellten. Dieser neue Ansatz schlug sich auch in den folgenden Fotoserien nieder, die RongRong nach der Auflösung der East-Village-Künstlerkolonie schuf, darunter „Wedding Gown" (1997–2000) und „Ghost Village" (1999–2000). Zunehmend trat er nun auch selbst als Performer vor die eigene Kamera.

Ab Mitte der 1990er Jahre tauchte dann ein neues Thema in RongRongs Arbeiten auf: die vielen teilabgerissenen Häuser in Peking, die vor dem Hintergrund der rasanten Stadtentwicklung ein bemerkenswertes visuelles Schauspiel boten. Ganz besonders reizten ihn die zerfetzten, ehedem glamourösen Pin-ups an halb zertrümmerten Wänden. Das Fragmentarische dieser Bilder kündet vom Verlust und lädt den Betrachter ein, sich Leben, Denken und Fühlen der einstigen Bewohner der abgerissenen Häuser vorzustellen.

Inri machte 1994 ihren Abschluss am Nippon Photography Institute und arbeitete die folgenden drei Jahre für die

带着新买的相机和一双好奇的眼睛，荣荣于 1992 年抵达北京。他是一名来自东南省份福建的农家男孩，并且在此之前从未离开过家园。在北京，他参加了摄影班，并且逐渐变得非常擅长于拍摄那种流行摄影杂志所钟意的艺术性感伤图片。1993 年，在搬到北京东部郊区一个破破烂烂的小村庄以后，他的生活和事业发生了剧烈的变化。后来被称作北京"东村"的这个小村庄在 1994 年 6 月被当地警方关闭，而在此之前这里则是一个艺术团体的家园，该团体创作了部分最大胆的当代中国艺术作品。

在东村期间，荣荣用相机拍摄了艺术家们的前卫表演——马六明《芬·马六明的午餐》，张洹的《12 平米》和《65 公斤》以及其他作品。这些图片的重要性不仅在于记录了这些已成为当代中国艺术"经典"的行为，同时也在于意味着一种新式摄影的出现，而这种新式摄影则致力于达成摄影和表演之间的紧密联系。这种联系继续成为荣荣在东村团体消失后所创作的若干摄影系列的基础，作品包括《婚纱》（1997-2000 年）以及《废墟》（1999-2000 年）。他越来越频繁地出现在自己的镜头前，表演并记录这些表演；这些摄影作品中强烈的表演性质与他的个人生活产生共鸣。
20世纪九十年代中期后不久，荣荣的艺术中多了一个新的主题：他被北京大量处于半毁坏状态的房屋所吸引，这些废屋给这个快速发展的城市提供了主要的视觉风景。尤其是在破墙上残留漂亮挂件的破损图像尤其另他着迷。这些不完整的图像宣示着了过往的逝去，并促使观众去想象这些废屋旧主人的生活和心灵。

映里 1994 年毕业于日本写真艺术专门学校，随后的三年内为著名的报纸《朝日新闻》工作。在厌倦了给名人拍摄肖像以后，她于 1997 年辞职并成为一名自由摄影家。她在 1999 年和 2000 年所创作的三组作品，包括《灰色地带》，《1999, 东京》和《MAXIMAX》，奠定了她作为一名年轻的天才

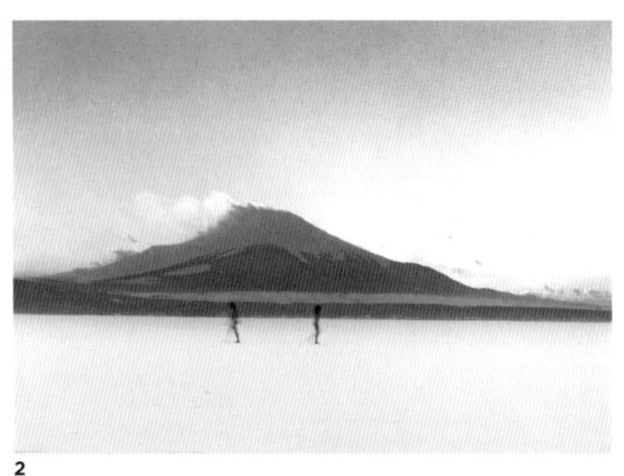
2

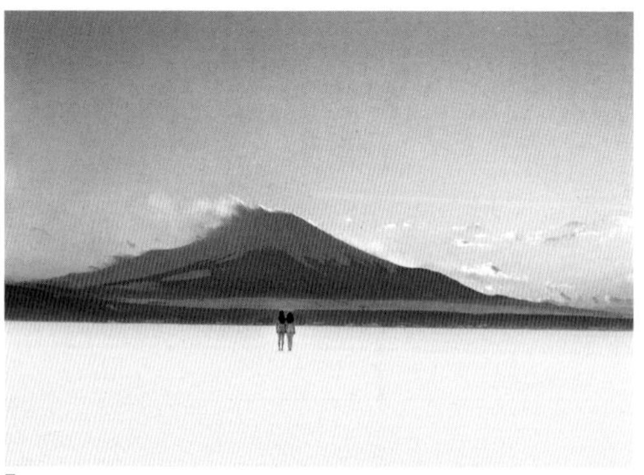
3

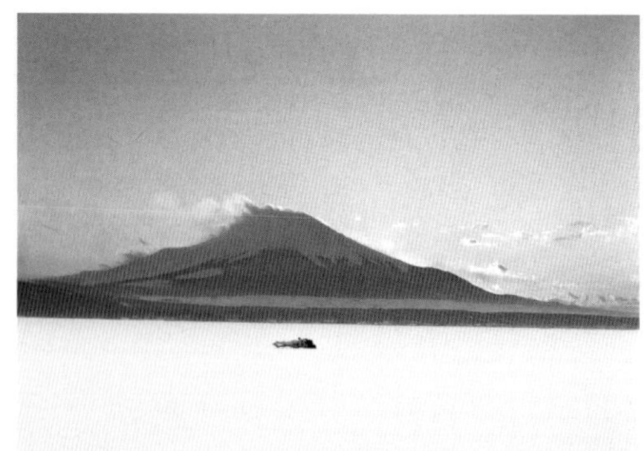
4

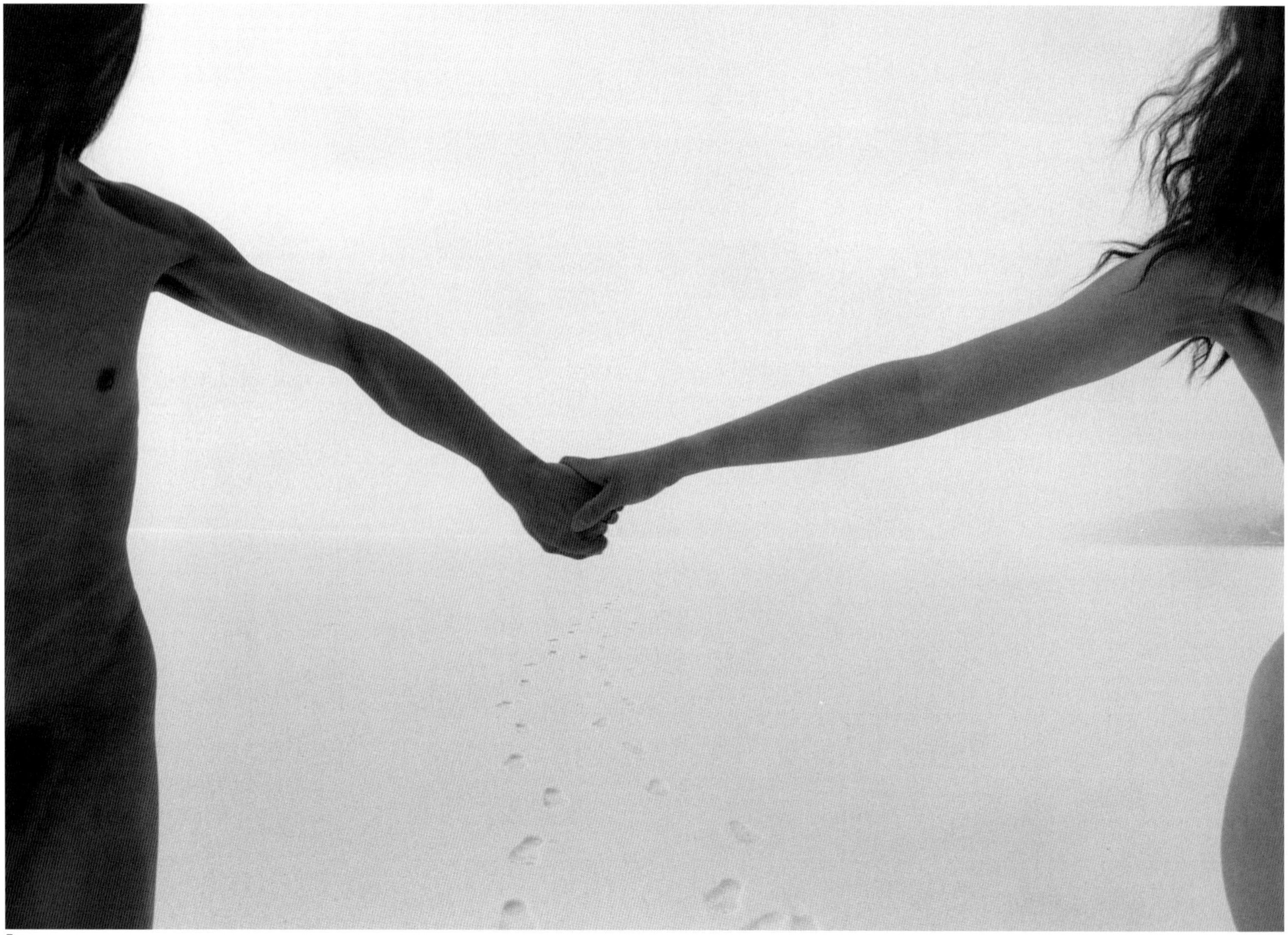

5

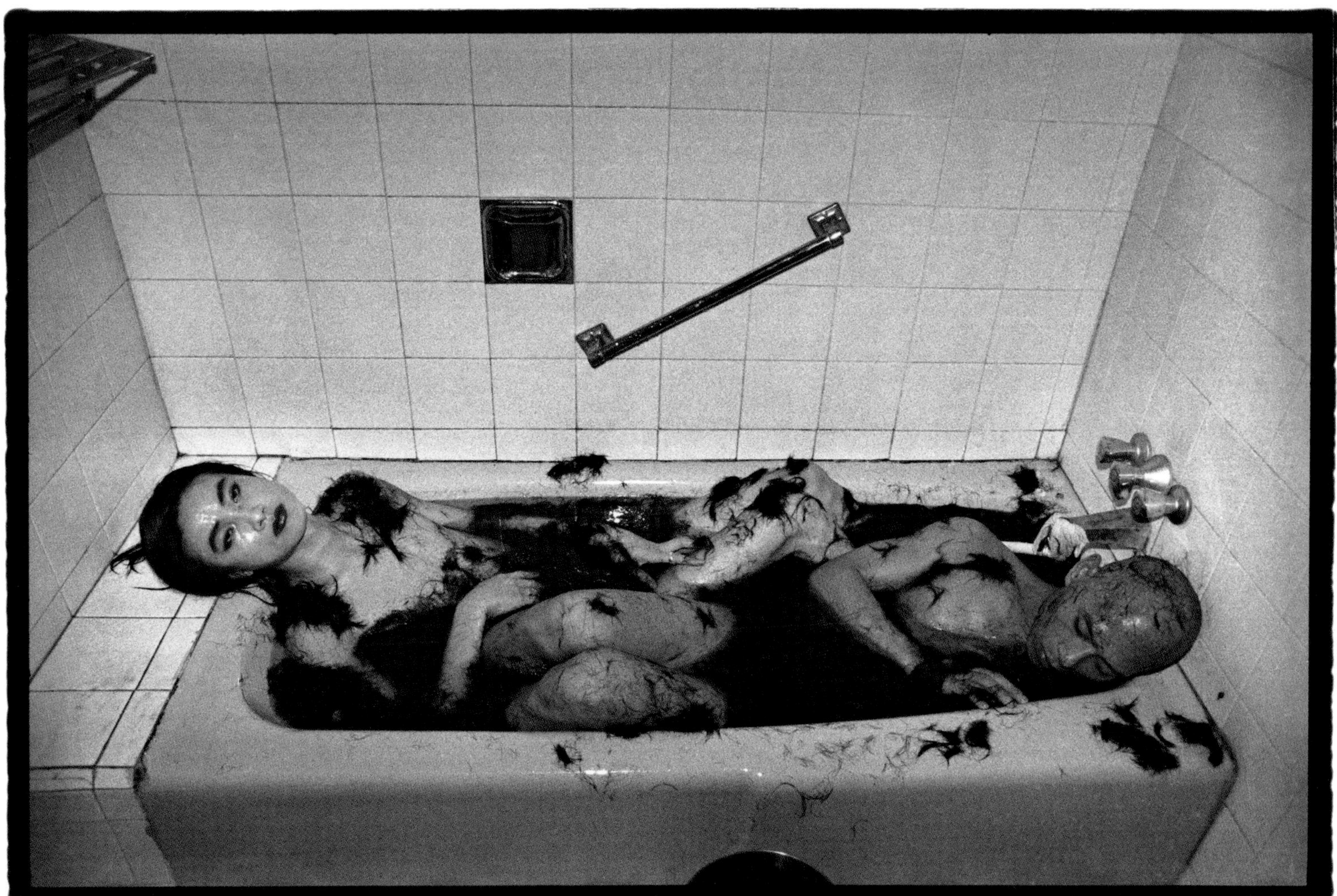

6

7

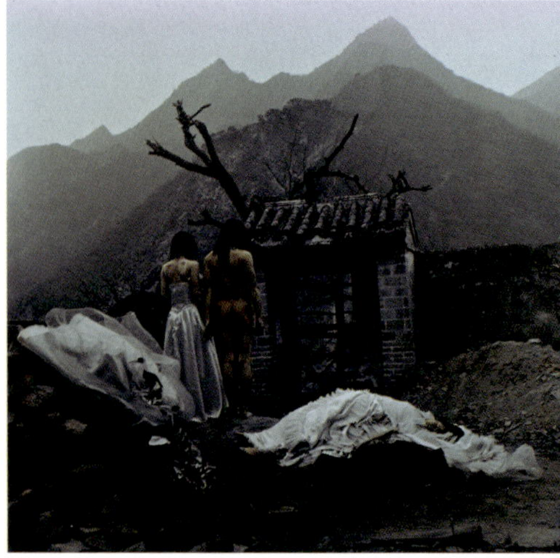

8

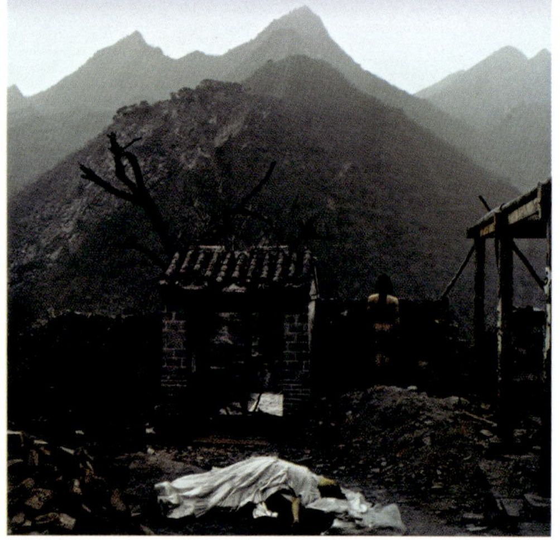

9

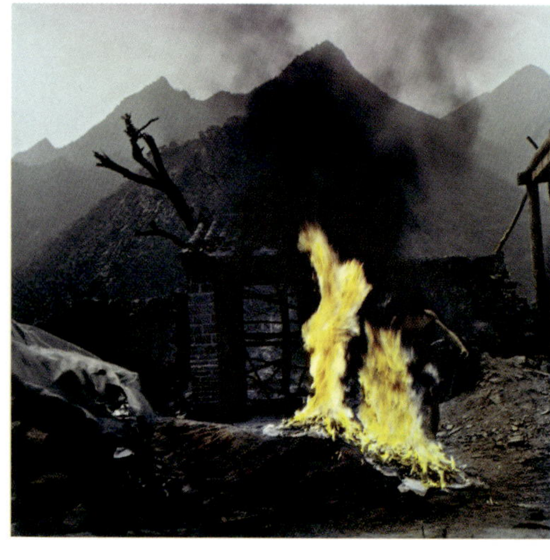

Shimbun" for the next three years. Tired of taking portraits of celebrities, she quit her job in 1997 to become a freelance photographer. Three series of works she created in 1999 and 2000, including "Gray Zone", "Tokyo" and "MAXIMAX", established her position as a gifted young photographer capable of discovering her subject's psychological depth. But if these three series are characterized by a strong feeling of fin-de-siècle, the photographs she created together with RongRong since 2000 have taken love and beauty as their central theme. In the winter of 2001 they made a memorable trip to Mount Fuji. Dancing and running naked on a frozen lake at the foot of the sacred mountain, they used an automatic camera to record their movements. The result is an extraordinary series of photographs, astonishingly beautiful in representing both romantic love and landscape.

The most recent exhibition of RongRong and Inri included the photographs they took in Liulitun, a small village near Beijing where they lived for about two years from 2000 to 2002 (RongRong moved in there in 1995). Most of these works are fragments of daily life. Inri presented her photographs in the exhibition as galley proofs. There is no spatial coherence or sequential narrative; the only constant is the eye behind the camera. The last series of works in the show documents a private "funeral" she and RongRong held for the place in 2003, when their courtyard house at Liulitun was finally razed.

berühmte Zeitung „Asahi Shimbun". 1997 war sie es leid, immer nur Porträts von Prominenten zu knipsen, und kündigte ihren Job, um als freiberufliche Fotografin tätig zu werden. 1999 und 2000 schuf sie drei größere Serien, darunter „Grey Zone" (1999), und etablierte sich damit als talentierte junge Fotografin mit einer besonderen Begabung, die psychischen Tiefen ihrer Modelle auszuloten. Diese Serien waren von einer starken Fin-de-siècle-Stimmung durchdrungen. Dagegen widmen sich die Fotografien, die sie seit 2000 zusammen mit RongRong schuf, zunächst den Themen Liebe und Schönheit. So unternahmen die beiden im Winter 2001 einen Ausflug zum Berg Fuji; eine automatische Kamera zeichnete auf, wie sie nackt auf dem gefrorenen See am Fuß des heiligen Bergs umhertanzten und -rannten. Die Fotoserie stellt sowohl die romantische Liebe als auch die Landschaft in verblüffender Schönheit dar.

In ihrer jüngsten Ausstellung zeigten RongRong und Inri u.a. ihre Fotografien aus Liulitun, einem kleinen Dorf in der Nähe von Peking, wo sie von 2000 bis 2002 zusammen lebten (RongRong war 1995 hierher gezogen). Die meisten dieser Arbeiten sind Schnappschüsse aus dem alltäglichen Leben dort. Inri präsentierte ihre Fotos in der Ausstellung als Druckfahnen. Es gibt keine räumliche Kohärenz oder erzählerische Abfolge; die einzige Konstante ist das Auge hinter der Kamera. Die Ausstellung endete mit einer Werkserie, die eine private „Bestattungsfeier" dokumentiert, mit der RongRong und Inri ihres Hinterhofhauses in Liulitun gedachten, das 2003 abgerissen wurde.

摄影师的地位，她以发掘主题的心理深度见长。然而，如果说这三个系列以强烈的“世纪末”感为特色，那么她和荣荣从 2000 年开始创作的摄影作品则将爱和美作为他们的中心题材。2001 年冬季，他们进行了难忘的富士山之旅。在圣洁的山峰下，山脚下的冰湖上，他们赤裸着奔跑、跳跃，而一部自动相机则拍下了他们的活动。这是一组非同凡响的摄影系列，浪漫的爱情和美丽的风景同样令人惊艳。

荣荣和映里最近的展览中收纳了他们在“六里屯”所拍摄的作品。“六里屯”是在北京附近的一个小村庄，从 2000 年到 2002 年（荣荣于 1995 年搬到这里）他们在这里生活了大约两年。这些作品的绝大部分是日常生活的片断。在展览中，映里将她的摄影作品以毛样展出。作品中并没有空间的一致或连续的叙述，唯一不变的只有相机后的眼睛。他们在六里屯所住的四合院最终被夷为平地，而展览中最后一个作品系列，则记录了她和荣荣在 2003 年为这个地方所举行的私人“葬礼”。

Wu Hung

10

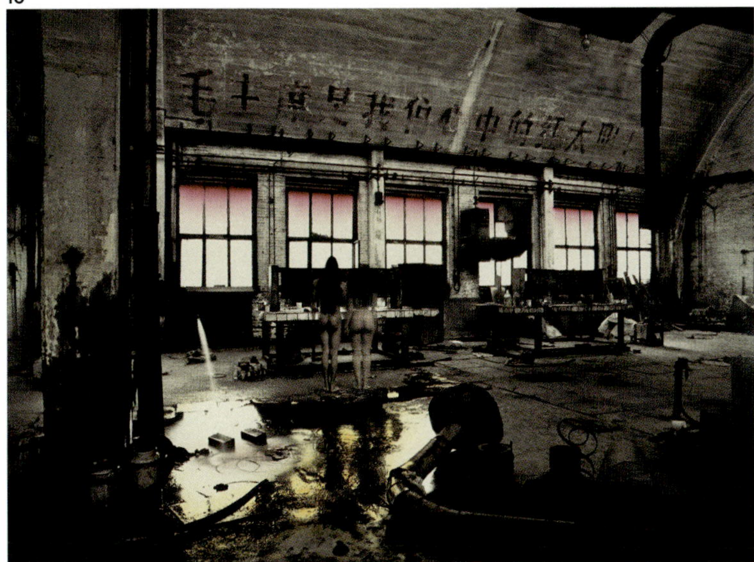

11

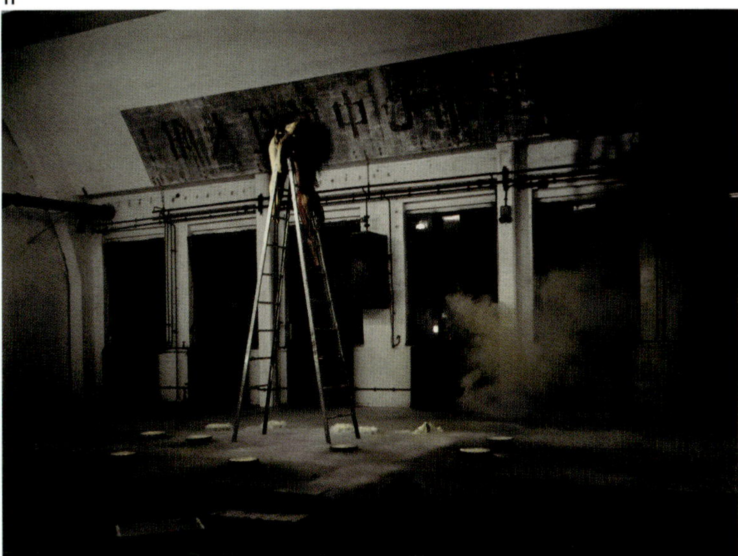

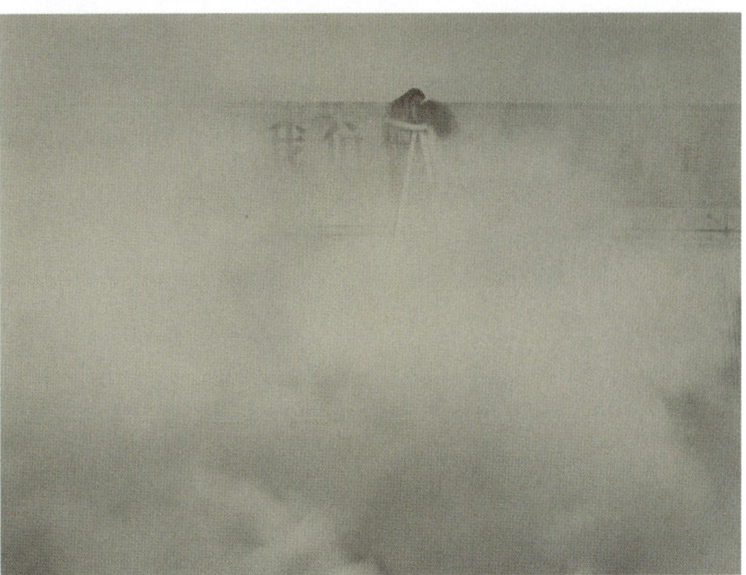

12

1 ***In Bad Goisern, Austria, No. 6****, 2001*
Hand-dyed silver gelatin print, 100 x 100 cm; handkolorierter Silbergelatineabzug, 100 x 100 cm
《在奥地利 Bad Goisern No. 6》2001年, 手染明胶银版印刷, 100 x 100 cm

2 ***In Fujisan, Japan, No. 12****, 2001*
Gelatin silver print, 42.5 x 46.5 cm; Silbergelatineabzug, 42,5 x 46,5 cm
《在日本富士山No. 12》2001年, 明胶银版印刷, 42.5 x 46.5 cm

3 ***In Fujisan, Japan, No. 13****, 2001*
Gelatin silver print, 42.5 x 46.5 cm; Silbergelatineabzug, 42,5 x 46,5 cm
《在日本富士山No..13》2001年, 明胶银版印刷, 42.5 x 46.5 cm

4 ***In Fujisan, Japan, No. 14****, 2001*
Gelatin silver print, 42.5 x 46.5 cm; Silbergelatineabzug, 42,5 x 46,5 cm
《在日本富士山No. 14》2001年, 明胶银版印刷, 42.5 x 46.5 cm

5 ***In Fujisan, Japan, No. 10****, 2001*
Gelatin silver print, 42.5 x 46.5 cm; Silbergelatineabzug, 42,5 x 46,5 cm
《在日本富士山No. 10》2001年, 明胶银版印刷, 42.5 x 46.5 cm

6 ***1995, No. 43****, 1995*
Gelatin silver print, 100 x 150 cm; Silbergelatineabzug, 100 x 150 cm
《1995, No. 43》1995年, 明胶银版印刷, 100 x 150 cm

7 ***2000, No. 1 Beijing****, 2000*
Hand-dyed on gelatin silver print, 100 x 100 cm; handkolorierter Silbergelatineabzug, 100 x 100 cm
《2000, No. 1 北京》2000年, 手染明胶银版印刷, 100 x 100 cm

8 ***2000, No. 3 Beijing****, 2000*
Hand-dyed on gelatin silver print, 100 x 100 cm; handkolorierter Silbergelatineabzug, 100 x 100 cm
《2000, No. 3 北京》2000年, 手染明胶银版印刷, 100 x 100 cm

9 ***2000, No. 4 Beijing****, 2000*
Hand-dyed on gelatin silver print, 100 x 100 cm; handkolorierter Silbergelatineabzug, 100 x 100 cm
《2000, No. 4 北京》2000年, 手染明胶银版印刷, 100 x 100 cm

10 ***We are here, No. 1****, 2002*
Hand-dyed on gelatin silver print, 100 x 136 cm; handkolorierter Silbergelatineabzug, 100 x 136 cm
《我们在这里No. 1》2002年, 手染明胶银版印刷, 100 x 136 cm

11 ***We are here, No. 4****, 2002*
Hand-dyed on gelatin silver print, 100 x 136 cm; handkolorierter Silbergelatineabzug, 100 x 136 cm
《我们在这里No. 4》2002年, 手染明胶银版印刷, 100 x 136 cm

12 ***We are here, No. 5****, 2002*
Hand-dyed on gelatin silver print, 100 x 136 cm; handkolorierter Silbergelatineabzug, 100 x 136 cm
《我们在这里No. 5》 2002年, 手染明胶银版印刷, 100 x 136 cm

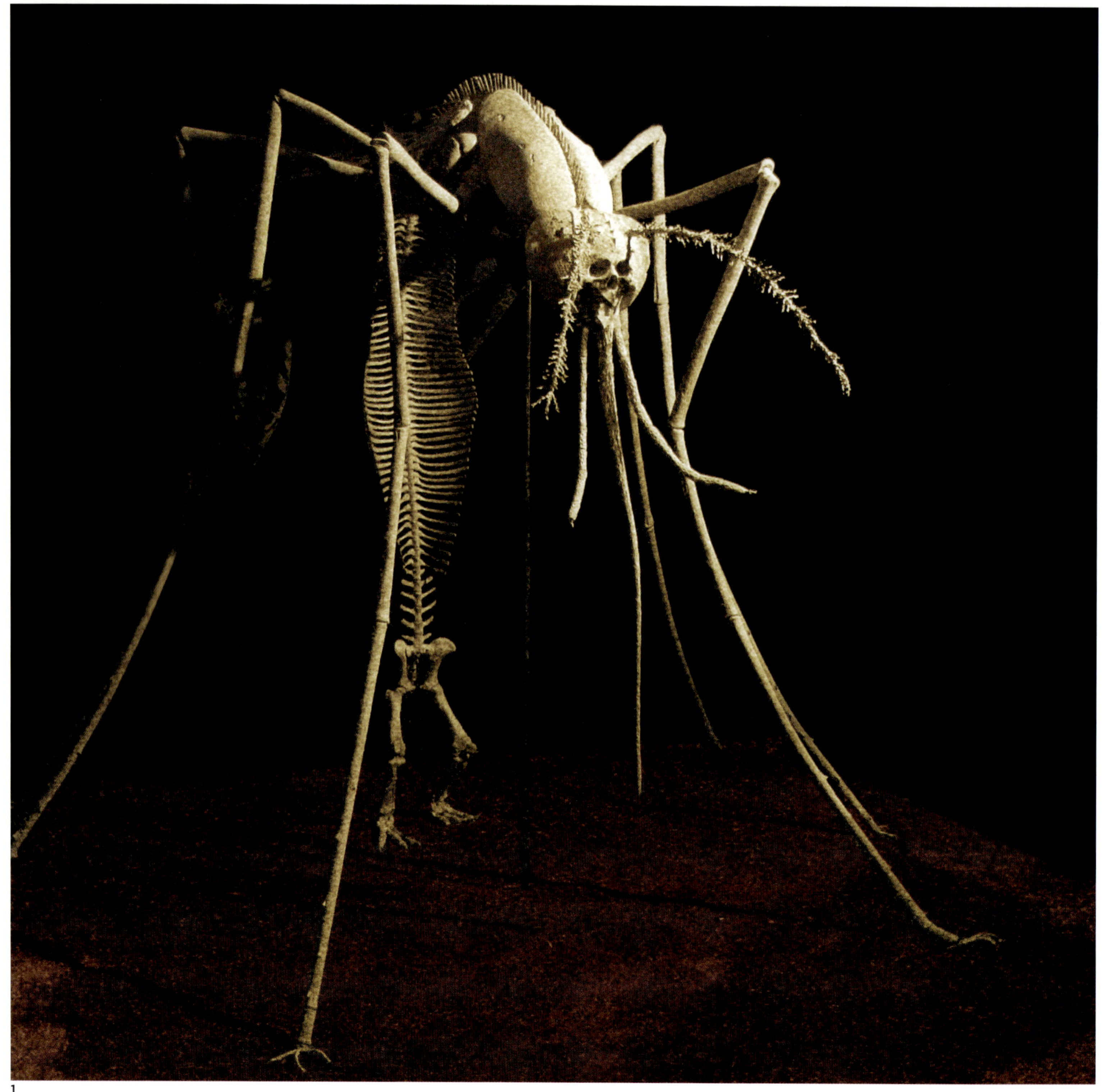

1

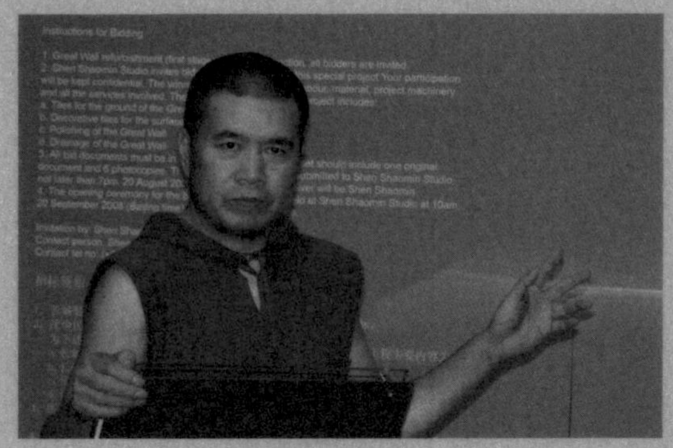

"I want to use the fundamental relationship between beasts and people as a way to think about human survival from the very essence of life. Did rats give the bubonic plague to human beings, or did humans develop it themselves?"

„Ich möchte die Beziehung zwischen Tieren und Menschen als Weg nutzen, über das menschliche Überleben an sich nachzusinnen. Haben die Ratten den Menschen die Pest gebracht, oder haben wir sie selbst produziert? All das ist bedenkenswert."

"我想运用动物与人的基本关系去思考人类生存中的生活本质。是老鼠将黑死病传染给人类，还是人类自己创造了黑死病了呢?"

Born in 1956 in Heilongjiang Province, China. Lives and works in Beijing and Sydney, Australia
Geboren 1956 in der Provinz Heilongjiang, China. Lebt und arbeitet in Peking und Sydney, Australien
1956年出生于黑龙江省,现居在北京和悉尼居住工作

***Selected exhibitions* / Ausgewählte Ausstellungen / 所选展览**

1995 "Dialogue", East West Gallery, Melbourne, Australia
2001 "Transplantation", Asia-Australia Arts Center, Sydney, Australia
2003 "Science Fictions", Singapore Art Museum, Singapore
2004 The 1st Architectural Biennial Beijing, Beijing, China
2006 "Scary Monsters", Osage Contemporary Art Space, Hong Kong, China
"From Polar Region to Tiexi District: Contemporary Art in Northeastern China", Guangdong Museum, Guanzhou, China
2007 "Thermocline of Art: New Asian Waves", ZKM (Center for Art and Media), Karlsruhe, Germany

1995年 《对话》东西画廊，墨尔本，澳大利亚
2001年 《移植》亚澳艺术中心，悉尼，澳大利亚
2003年 《科学的虚构》新加坡美术馆，新加坡
2004年 《首届中国国际建筑双年展》，北京 中国
2006年 《惊骇异物》奥沙艺术空间，香港，中国
《从"极地"到"铁西区"》东北当代艺术展，广东美术馆，广州
2007年 《艺术温跃层：亚洲新浪潮》艺术与媒体中心,卡尔斯鲁厄,德国

***Selected publications* / Ausgewählte Publikationen / 所选著作**

Bernhard Fibicher, Matthias Frehner (eds.): "Mahjong. Chinesische Gegenwartskunst aus der Sammlung Sigg", Ostfildern-Ruit 2005

Fibicher, Bernhard/Frehner, Matthias（编者）：《麻将-西克当代艺术收藏展》，Ostfildern-Ruit 2005

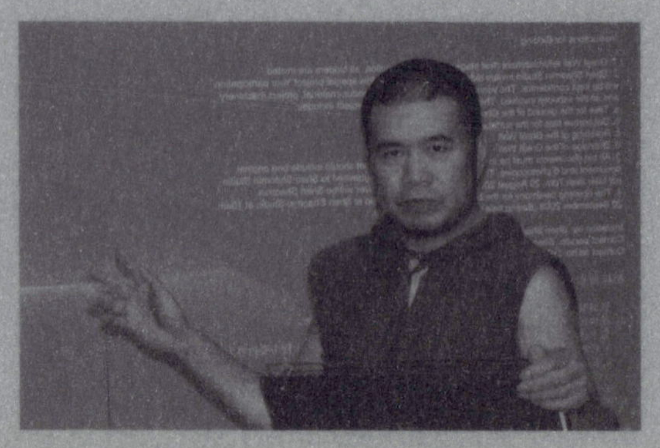

"I want to use the fundamental relationship between beasts and people as a way to think about human survival from the very essence of life. Did rats give the bubonic plague to human beings, or did humans develop it themselves?"

„Ich möchte die Beziehung zwischen Tieren und Menschen als Weg nutzen, über das menschliche Überleben an sich nachzusinnen. Haben die Ratten den Menschen die Pest gebracht, oder haben wir sie selbst produziert? All das ist bedenkenswert."

"我想运用动物与人的基本关系去思考人类生存中的生活本质。是老鼠将黑死病传染给人类，还是人类自己创造了黑死病了呢?"

Born in 1956 in Heilongjiang Province, China. Lives and works in Beijing and Sydney, Australia
Geboren 1956 in der Provinz Heilongjiang, China. Lebt und arbeitet in Peking und Sydney, Australien
1956年出生于黑龙江省，现居住在北京和悉尼居住工作

Selected exhibitions / Ausgewählte Ausstellungen / 所选展览

1995	"Dialogue", East West Gallery, Melbourne, Australia
2001	"Transplantation", Asia-Australia Arts Center, Sydney, Australia
2003	"Science Fictions", Singapore Art Museum, Singapore
2004	The 1st Architectural Biennial Beijing, Beijing, China
2006	"Scary Monsters", Osage Contemporary Art Space, Hong Kong, China
	"From Polar Region to Tiexi District: Contemporary Art in Northeastern China", Guangdong Museum, Guanzhou, China
2007	"Thermocline of Art: New Asian Waves", ZKM (Center for Art and Media), Karlsruhe, Germany

1995年	《对话》东西画廊，墨尔本，澳大利亚
2001年	《移植》亚澳艺术中心，悉尼，澳大利亚
2003年	《科学的虚构》新加坡美术馆，新加坡
2004年	《首届中国国际建筑双年展》，北京 中国
2006年	《惊骇异物》奥沙艺术空间，香港，中国
	《从"极地"到"铁西区"》东北当代艺术展，广东美术馆，广州
2007年	《艺术温跃层：亚洲新浪潮》艺术与媒体中心，卡尔斯鲁厄，德国

Selected publications / Ausgewählte Publikationen / 所选著作

Bernhard Fibicher, Matthias Frehner (eds.): "Mahjong. Chinesische Gegenwartskunst aus der Sammlung Sigg", Ostfildern-Ruit 2005

Fibicher, Bernhard/Frehner, Matthias（编者）：《麻将-西克当代艺术收藏展》，Ostfildern-Ruit 2005

SHEN SHAOMIN 沈少民

[ʂən ʂaʊmin]

Since 2002, Shen Shaomin has been a sculptor in bone, piecing together exotic creatures that resonate with the ancient Chinese bestiary even as they arouse profoundly contemporary fears about genetic modification and even terrorism. His sculptures, under the series name "Unknown Creatures" (since 1993), fabricate nonexistent beings, preserving them as if they are extinct animals in a natural history museum. They arouse a curiosity almost spiritual in nature, as the viewer is left to wonder what became of an animal that in fact never was.

In works like "Unknown Creature – Three-Headed Monster" (2003) and "Unknown Creature No. 12 – Mosquito" (2004), Shen Shaomin cobbles together from bone and glue skeletons of compelling proportions. At nearly seven meters long, three-headed monster stands upon eight legs, its ribs cresting into a pointy spine that runs the length of its back. Upon closer inspection, each and every bone appears to be engraved in Chinese and English with sayings culled from sacred texts. Shen Shaomin's "Mosquito" is scarier still – a shrunken torso flows down into a stream of emaciated legs, with giant fangs sprouting from its tiny face. Unlike the work of Korean artist Hyungkoo Lee (featured in that country's Venice pavilion in 2007) whereby skeletons of recognizable beasts deriving from cartoons are fabricated from synthetic materials, Shen Shaomin's frightening creatures are fictional in origin and yet "real" in materiality.

Born in China's far northeast, Heilongjiang province, Shen Shaomin emigrated to Australia in 1989, shortly after a solo show at the National Art Museum of China. His distance from the mainland scene of the 1990s – maintained in Sydney along with other Chinese artists like Guan Wei and A Xian – allowed for some perspective when he again became active in China in the early part of this decade. His Australian career did not progress very far, confined to a string of shows with "Mary Reibey Interiors & Gallery" through the mid-1990s, and culminating with a presentation at the Asia-Australia Arts Center in 2001. Like many Chinese artists who scattered abroad in the wake of

Seit 2002 baut Shen Shaomin als Bildhauer Knochen zu Kreaturen zusammen, in denen das alte chinesische Bestiarium durchschimmert, während sie zugleich moderne Ängste vor genetischen Manipulationen und sogar Terrorismus wecken. Seine Skulpturen der Serie „Unknown Creatures" (seit 1993) sind artifizielle Wesen, die wie ausgestorbene Arten in einem naturgeschichtlichen Museum konserviert sind. Sie wecken beim Betrachter eine fast schon spirituelle Neugier, indem sie ihn dazu bringen, sich zu fragen, was aus einem Tier geworden ist, das in Wirklichkeit nie gelebt hat.

Für Werke wie „Unknown Creature – Three-Headed Monster" (2003) und „Unknown Creature No. 12 – Mosquito" (2004) bastelte Shen Shaomin aus Knochen und Klebstoff Skelette von überwältigenden Dimensionen zusammen. Das fast sieben Meter lange dreiköpfige Monster steht auf acht Beinen und seine Rippen laufen nach oben hin in ein spitzstacheliges Rückgrat aus. Aus der Nähe ist zu erkennen, dass in jeden einzelnen Knochen chinesische und englische Zitate aus heiligen Schriften graviert sind. Noch unheimlicher wirkt Shens Moskito – sein Schrumpftorso geht nach unten in eine Vielzahl spindeldürrer Beine über, während aus dem winzigen Kopf gigantische Fänge sprießen. Anders als die Arbeiten des koreanischen Künstlers Hyungkoo Lee, der im koreanischen Pavillon der Biennale von Venedig 2007 zu sehen war und aus synthetischen Materialien Skelette zu wiedererkennbaren Comicfiguren zusammensetzt, sind Shen Shaomins verstörende Kreaturen in ihrem Ursprung fiktional, doch von ihrer Materialität her äußerst „real".

Shen Shaomin, in Chinas entlegenem Nordosten in der Provinz Heilongjiang geboren, wanderte 1989, kurz nach einer Einzelausstellung im National Art Museum of China, nach Australien aus. Seine Distanz zur chinesischen Szene der 1990er Jahre – die er in Sydney mit anderen chinesischen Künstlern wie Guan Wei und A Xian teilte – verschaffte ihm einen besonderen Blickwinkel, als er zu Beginn des neuen Jahrtausends wieder in seiner Heimat tätig wurde. Seine australische Karriere ist nicht sonderlich weit gediehen und beschränkte sich auf eine Reihe von Ausstellungen bei

从2002年起，沈少民开始骨刻雕塑。拼接外来动物让人回想中国古老的寓言故事，产生对修改基因的彻骨害怕，甚至令人联想到恐怖主义。他在雕塑作品《未知生物》（2002年）中虚构了无名物种，并将之保存起来，似乎它们是自然博物馆中灭绝的动物一般。他们唤起了人类精神上的好奇性，让观众来去思考动物将变成实际上并不存在的东西。

在类似系列作品《未知生物》：《三头怪物》和《未知生物》：蚊子，是沈少民按比例将骨头和胶质骨架组合而成。接近七米长的《三头怪物》，八只脚立在地上，肋骨伸展入尖尖的脊骨，这样才支撑着尾部的长度。靠近观察，每一根骨头上都用中英文刻上了神话传 说寓言典故。沈少民的《蚊子》更令人恐惧—缩小的躯体垂 下 一 串 瘦弱的腿中，同时小小的脸上眦出巨大的牙齿。

与韩国艺术家 Hyungkoo Lee的作品（2007年在威尼斯的韩国展馆上展出）不同，Lee的作品中那些动物来源卡通，动物的骨骼由合成材料构成，而沈少民的那些可怕的动物虽然在现实中并不存在，但材料却是真实的。

1956年，沈少民出生于中国遥远的东北黑龙江省的一个城市，1989年在参加完在全国美术馆的个展短短一段时间后，他就移居澳洲。他与90时期大陆艺术界的距离给他提供了形成某些观点的空间---他与其他中国艺术家仍然继续着那个时 期的创作，如关伟等，在这个十 年早期，他又开始在中国艺术界活跃起来。他的澳洲事业并未更深的发展，在90 年代中期仅仅局限于在玛利亚画廊的一连串的展览，并于2001年参加 亚澳艺术中心展出，达到了其事业 的顶峰。象许多在1989年觉醒而流离海外的中国艺术家一样，他决定在新千禧年开始回到祖国发展自己的事业。他开始以更大的比例创作其《未知生物》系列作品，与卢塞恩-北京麦勒画廊建立的稳定的合作，让 其可以 继续进行其艺术试验创作。

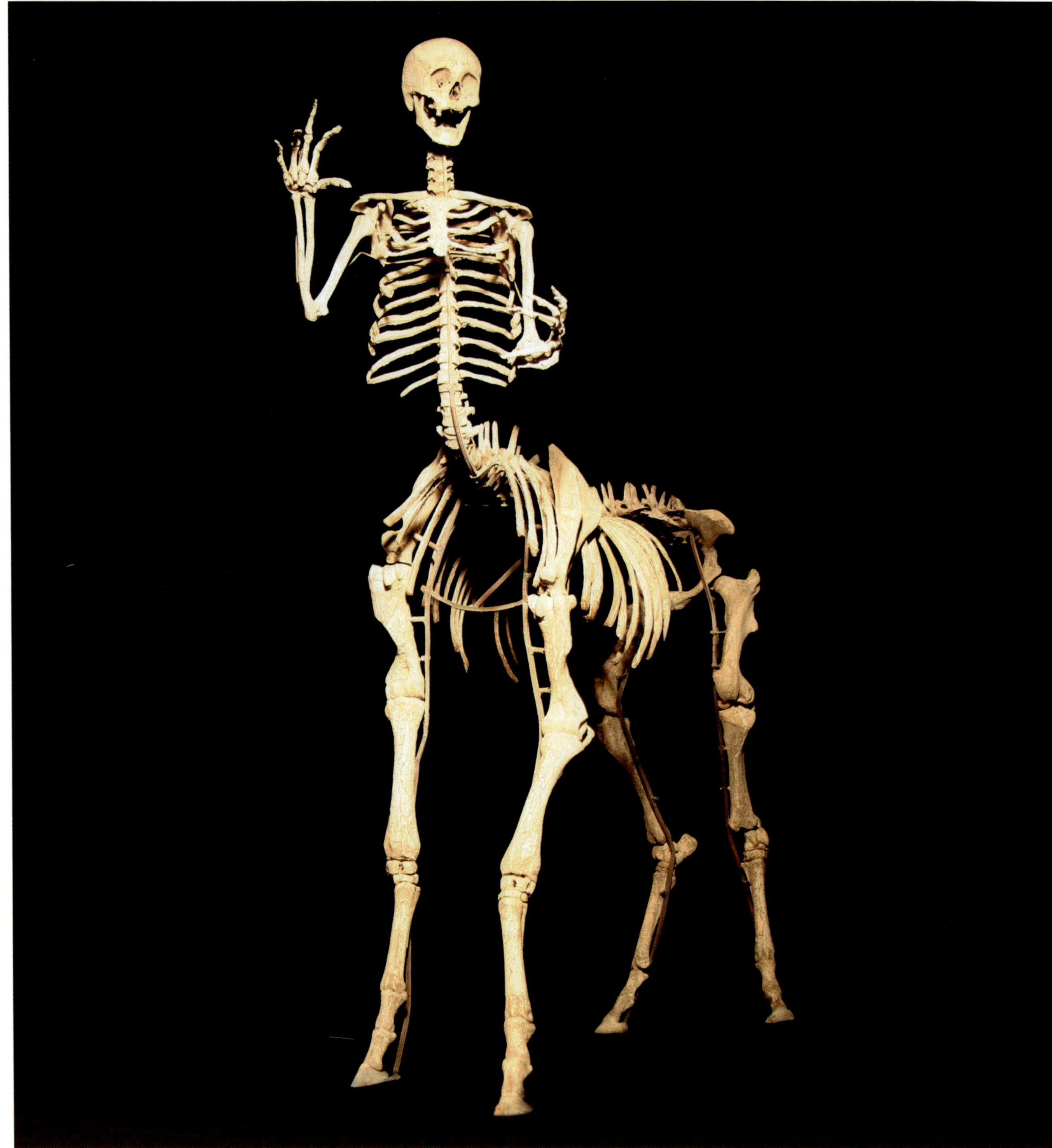

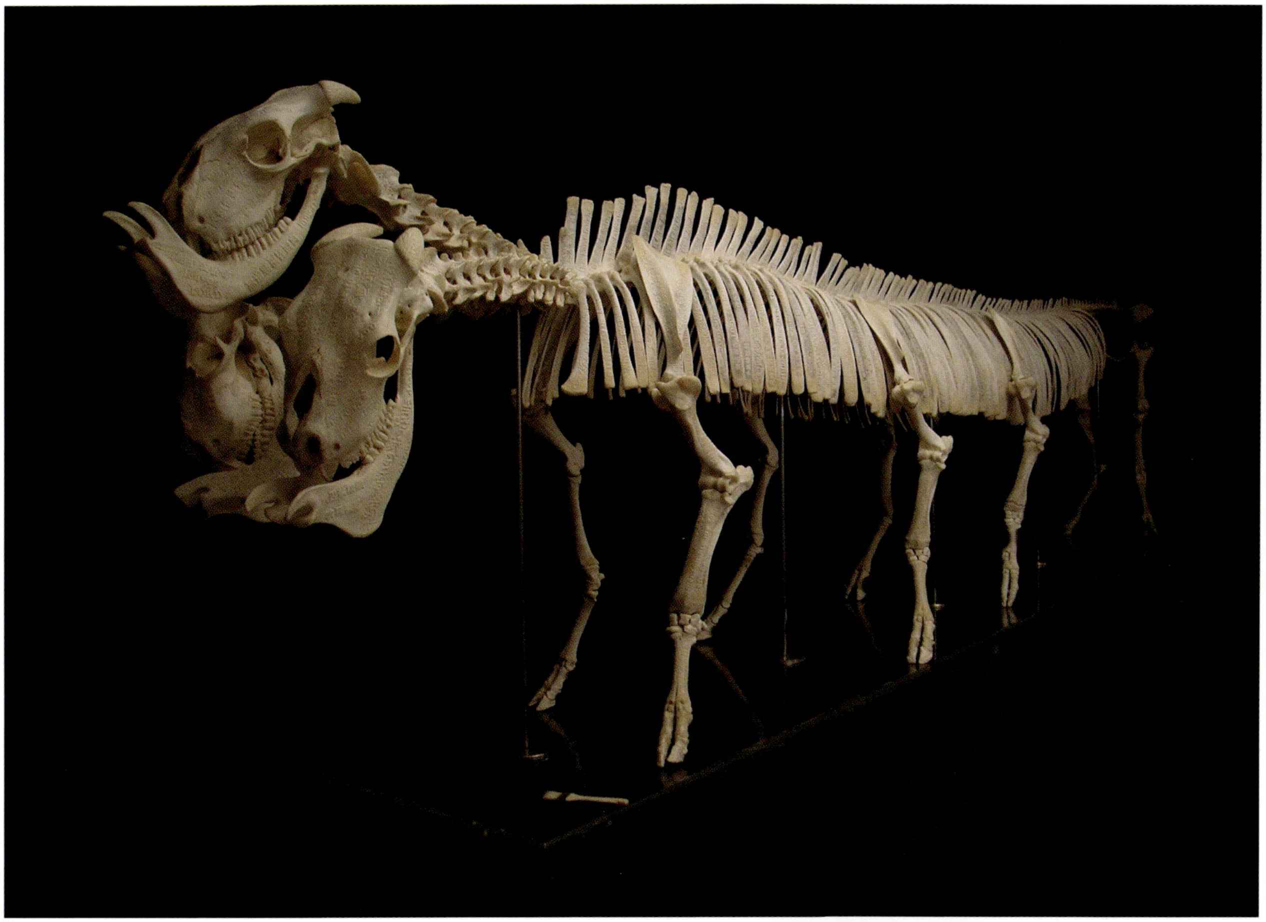

3

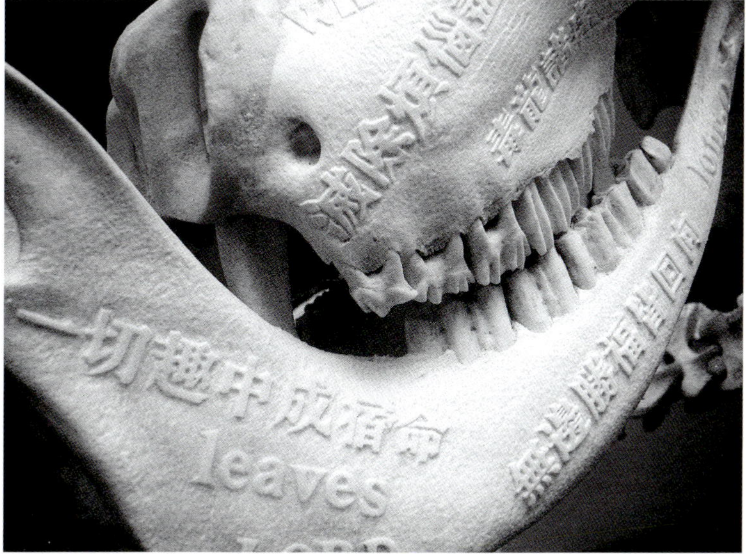

4

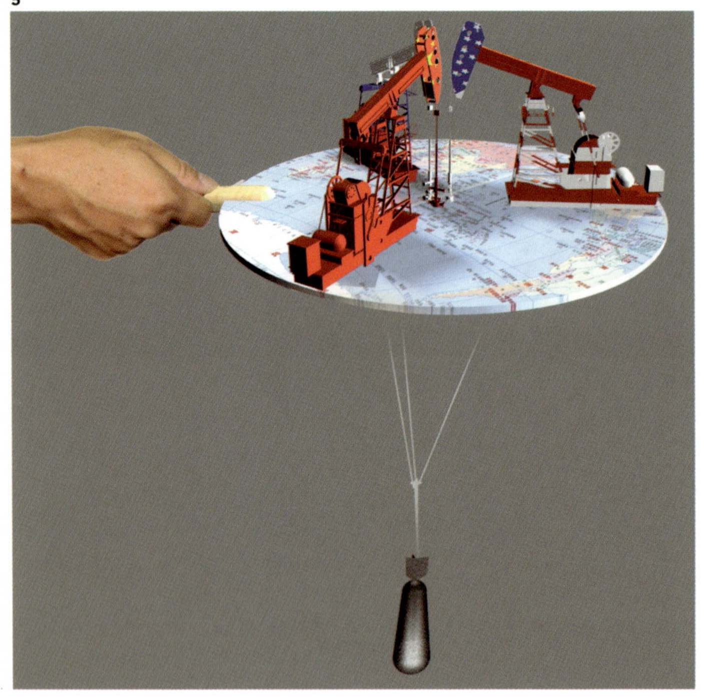

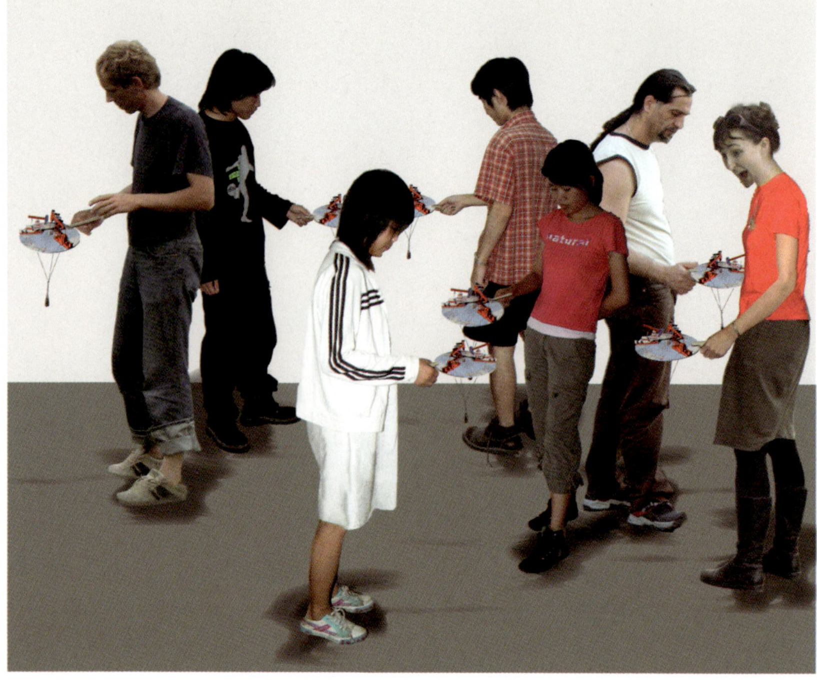

1989, he decided at the opening of the new millennium to return home to work.

Shen Shaomin is interesting for not being part of any recognizable school or trend in contemporary Chinese art. He did not train at one of the nation's elite academies, nor did he spend his formative years engaged in some close-knit group of painters in a far-off province-stock biographical elements for many of his generational peers. And although his beasts evoke some of the experiments with human and animal bodies that characterized the "Post-Sense Sensibility" movement of the late 1990s, they grow out of a sensibility, and a trajectory, all Shen's own.

„Mary Reibey Interiors & Gallery" Mitte der 1990er Jahre und gipfelte in einer Präsentation im Asia-Australia Arts Center 2001. Wie viele chinesische Künstler, die nach den Geschehnissen von 1989 ins Ausland gingen, entschloss er sich schließlich, wieder in seine Heimat zurückzukehren.

Shen Shaomin gehört, so weit zu erkennen ist, keiner Schule oder Richtung der chinesischen Gegenwartskunst an, er hat an keiner der Eliteakademien des Landes studiert und seine prägenden Jahre nicht in irgendeiner verschworenen Künstlergemeinde in einer abgelegenen Provinz verbracht – Stationen, die die Biografien vieler Künstler seiner Generation prägten. Und obwohl seine Bestien an manche Experimente mit Menschen- und Tierkörpern aus der „Post-Sense Sensibility"-Bewegung der späten 1990er Jahre erinnern, sind sie doch aus Shens ureigener Sensibilität und Lebensgeschichte erwachsen.

有意思的是，沈少民并不属于当代中国艺术界中任何一个院校派别或风格。与许多同龄人的经历一样，他未在专业艺术院校学习过，也未在某个偏远的省份的画家团体中度过其蜕变期。虽然他创造的动物唤起了人与 动物体的试验，这是 90年代末期后感性 运动的标记，但是这些作品已经超越了沈民自 己所有的敏感性和 轨迹。

Philip Tinari

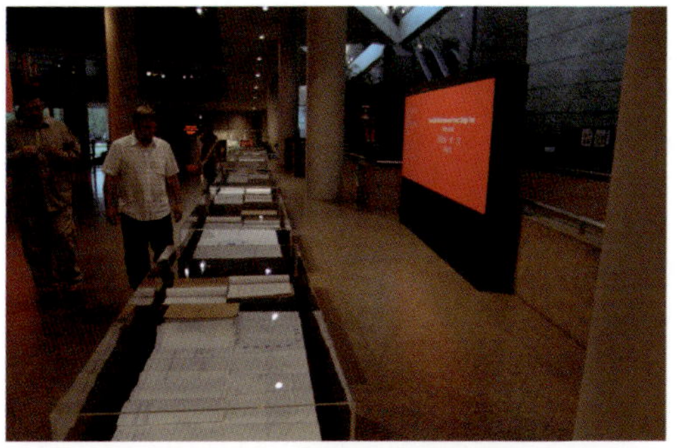

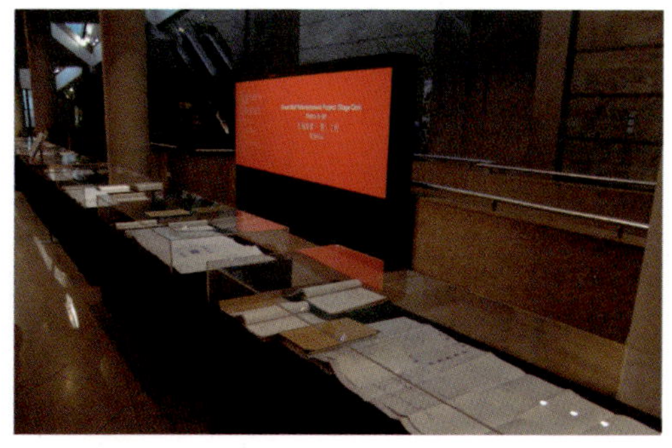

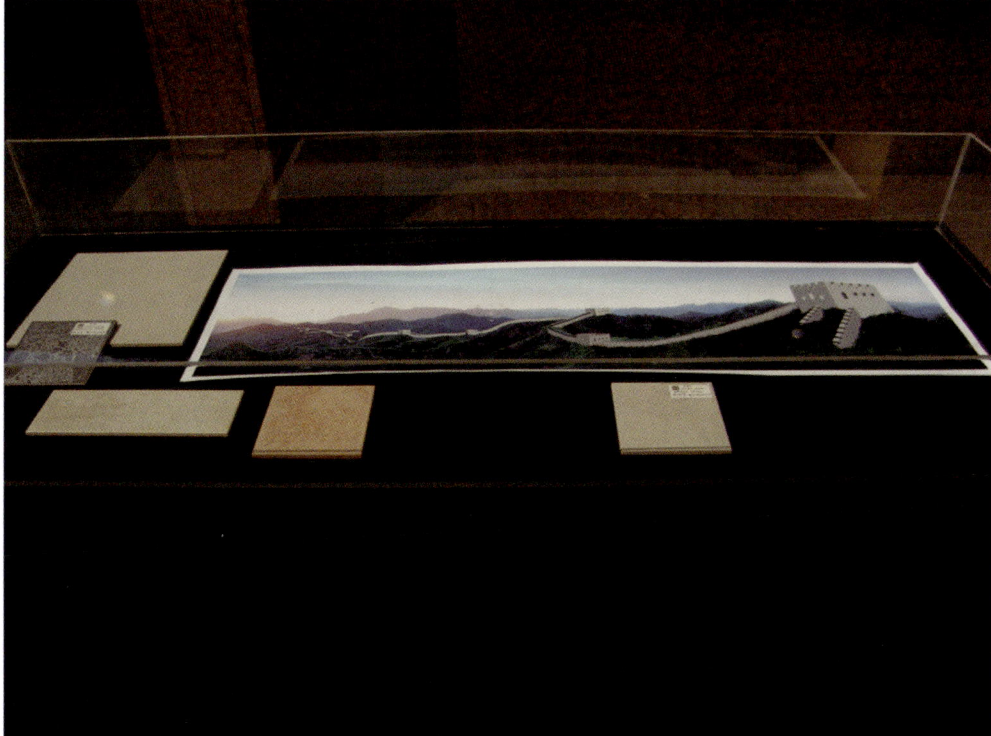

6

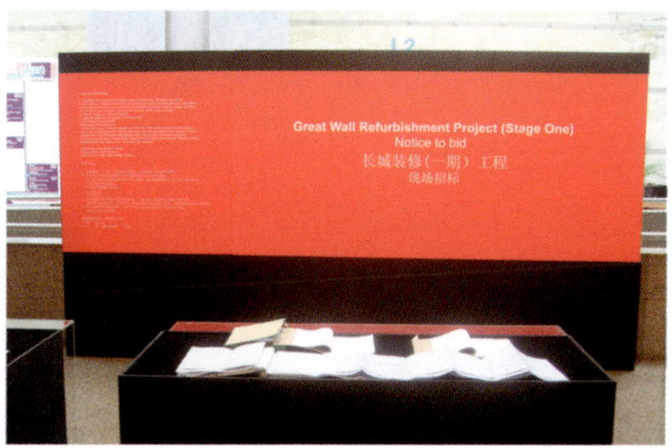

1 ***Unknown Creature No. 12 – Mosquito***, *2004*
Bone, bonemeal, glue, 240 x 240 x 230 cm
Knochen, Knochenmehl, Leim, 240 x 240 x 230 cm
《未知生物第12 - 蚊子》2004年，骨骼，骨粉，胶，
240 x 240 x 230 cm

2 ***Centaur***, *2005*
Bone, bonemeal, glue, 165 x 60 x 300 cm
Knochen, Knochenmehl, Leim, 165 x 60 x 300 cm
《半人半马怪》2005年，骨骼，骨粉，胶，165 x 60 x 300 cm

3 ***Unknown Creature – Three-Headed Monster***, *2003*
Bone, bonemeal, glue, 670 x 70 x 130 cm
Knochen, Knochenmehl, Leim, 670 x 70 x 130 cm
《未知生物--三头怪物》2003年，骨骼，骨粉，胶，
670 x 70 x 130 cm

4 ***Unknown Creature – Three-Headed Monster***, *2003*
Bone, bonemeal, glue (detail)
Knochen, Knochenmehl, Leim (Detail)
《未知生物--三头怪物》2003年，骨骼，骨粉，胶，
670 x 70 x 130 cm（详细）

5 ***Oil Gaming Machine***, *2006*
Plastic, 30 cm diameter
Kunststoff, 30 cm Durchmesser
《游戏机》2006年，塑料，直径30 cm

6 ***Great Wall Refurbishment Project***, *2005*
Blueprint (installation view)
Lichtpause (Installationsansicht)
《长城复原计划》2005年，设计图，装置实景

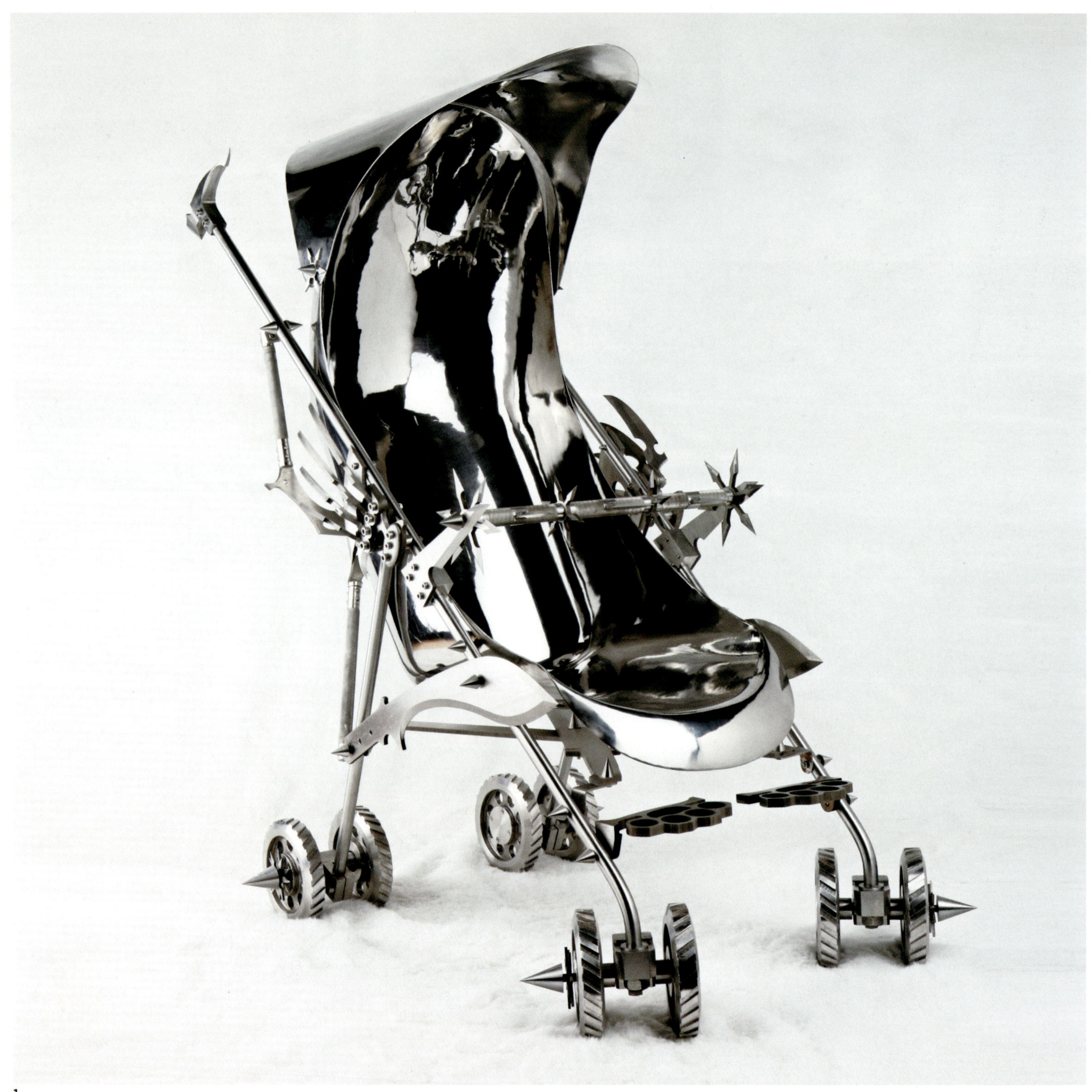

1

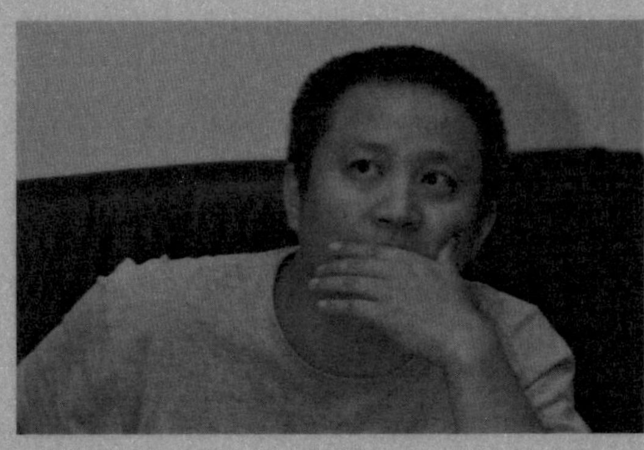

"I create works to anatomise the reality of society, but my interest is an analysis of human pathology."

„Ich schaffe Werke, um die gesellschaftliche Realität zu sezieren, mein Interesse gilt dabei aber einer Analyse der menschlichen Pathologie."

"我通过作品的创作来解剖现实社会中的是是非非，
而我更愿意分析人的病状根源。"

Born in 1969 in Dangyang, Hubei Province, China. Lives and works in Wuhan
Geboren 1969 in Dangyang, Provinz Hubei, China. Lebt und arbeitet in Wuhan
1969年5月出生于中国湖北当阳。居住工作在武汉

***Selected exhibitions* / Ausgewählte Ausstellungen / 所选展览**

2003	"Alors, la Chine?", Centre Georges Pompidou, Paris, France
2005-07	"Mahjong – Chinesische Gegenwartskunst aus der Sammlung Sigg", Kunstmuseum Bern, Berne, Switzerland; Hamburger Kunsthalle, Hamburg, Germany; Museum der Moderne, Salzburg, Austria
	"Shanghai Cool: Creative Production", Duolun Museum of Modern Art, Shanghai, China
2006	Shanghai Biennial, Shanghai, China
	"Halong Kellong Product Launch", Platform Gallery, Beijing, China
	"Na Zha Baby Boutique", Saatchi Collection, London, UK; Chambers Fine Art, New York, NY, USA

2003年	《中国怎么样?》蓬皮杜文化艺术中心，巴黎
	《人工 呼吸》三合艺术中心，北京
2005-07年	《麻将》一中国当代艺术希客伯尔尼美术博物馆，伯尔尼
	《上海酷：创意再生产》国际艺术展。上海多伦现代美术馆
2006年	上海双年展
	《哈克龙产品品投放市场》四合院画廊 北京
	《哪吒儿童用品》Saatchi 展览馆伦敦以及前波画廊，纽约

***Selected publications* / Ausgewählte Publikationen / 所选著作**

"Na Zha Baby Care Guide", New York 2006
Amy Michael: "Shi Jinsong at Chambers", in: "Art in America", November 2006

《哪吒儿童用品》前波画廊, 纽约2006年
Michael, Amy（著）：《史金淞在前波画廊》艺术在美国, 2006年11月

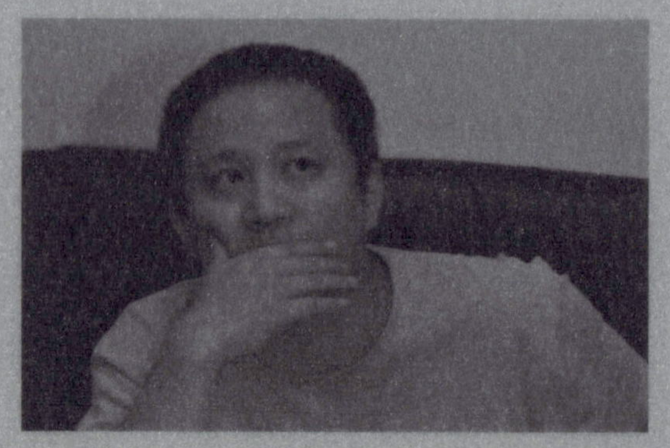

"I create works to anatomise the reality of society, but my interest is an analysis of human pathology."

„Ich schaffe Werke, um die gesellschaftliche Realität zu sezieren, mein Interesse gilt dabei aber einer Analyse der menschlichen Pathologie."

"我通过作品的创作来解剖现实社会中的是是非非，而我更愿意分析人的病状根源。"

Born in 1969 in Dangyang, Hubei Province, China. Lives and works in Wuhan
Geboren 1969 in Dangyang, Provinz Hubei, China. Lebt und arbeitet in Wuhan
1969年5月出生于中国湖北当阳。居住工作在武汉

Selected exhibitions / Ausgewählte Ausstellungen / 所选展览

2003	"Alors, la Chine?", Centre Georges Pompidou, Paris, France
2005-07	"Mahjong - Chinesische Gegenwartskunst aus der Sammlung Sigg", Kunstmuseum Bern, Berne, Switzerland; Hamburger Kunsthalle, Hamburg, Germany; Museum der Moderne, Salzburg, Austria
	"Shanghai Cool: Creative Production", Duolun Museum of Modern Art, Shanghai, China
2006	Shanghai Biennial, Shanghai, China
	"Halong Kellong Product Launch", Platform Gallery, Beijing, China
	"Na Zha Baby Boutique", Saatchi Collection, London, UK; Chambers Fine Art, New York, NY, USA

2003年	《中国怎么样?》蓬皮杜文化艺术中心，巴黎
	《人工 呼吸》三合艺术中心，北京
2005-07年	《麻将》一 中国当代艺术希客伯尔尼美术博物馆，伯尔尼
	《上海酷：创意再生产》国际艺术展。上海多伦现代美术馆
2006年	上海双年展
	《哈克龙产品品牌投放市场》四合院画廊 北京
	《哪吒儿童用品》Saatchi 展览馆伦敦以及前波画廊，纽约

Selected publications / Ausgewählte Publikationen / 所选著作

"Na Zha Baby Care Guide", New York 2006
Amy Michael: "Shi Jinsong at Chambers", in: "Art in America", November 2006

《哪吒儿童用品》前波画廊，纽约2006年
Michael, Amy（著）：《史金淞在前波画廊》艺术在美国，2006年11月

SHI JINSONG 史金淞

[ʂz tɕinsʊŋ]

Futuristic sculptures too dangerous to touch are a specialty of Shi Jinsong. With their razor-like edges and gleaming stainless steel surfaces, these sculptures look like props from a science fiction movie, but they are also inspired by ancient Chinese symbols and rituals.

Shi Jinsong is obsessed with issues of control and extreme manipulation, reformulated as everyday design objects. In fact, he originally called his sculptures "prototypes", as in "Office Equipment-Prototype No. 1" (2004), a kidney-shaped stainless steel computer station and chair in which the computer controls were also torture devices. These prototypes were a continuation of the investigation that this artist had initiated with his "Secret Book of Cool Weapons" (2002), where he transformed recognizable corporate logos into a selection of ancient weaponry. For the groundbreaking exhibition "Alors, la Chine?", at the Centre Pompidou in 2003, he departed from his usual use of stainless steel and presented "A Life of Sugar", an installation made of caramel designed to melt over the course of the show.

More recently Shi Jinsong has created full-scale installations, emulating store displays and entertainment arcades. In 2005, he created "Na Zha Baby Boutique" with sculptures, blueprints, and photographs, for an outrageously unsafe line of baby products. These include a deadly baby carriage; an extremely dangerous cradle; and a needle-decorated pacifier. The chosen brand name, Na Zha, refers to the Chinese folklore character, a trickster with supernatural powers and flair for fashion, who has become the symbol for the God of Lotteries and Gambling in the new Chinese global economy.

In 2006, Shi Jinsong launched his "Halong Kellong" product line at the Shanghai Biennale, a pseudo-realistic entertainment in a form reminiscent of a Chinese dragon Melding together the design of a Harley Davidson, a tractor and shipping containers, the installation housed a Karaoke room, a dining buffet and a movie screening facility, a

Futuristische Skulpturen, zu gefährlich zum Anfassen, sind eine Spezialität von Shi Jinsong. Mit ihren rasiermesserscharfen Kanten und glänzenden Edelstahlflächen wirken sie wie Requisiten aus einem brutalen Science-Fiction-Film, sind aber zugleich von uralten chinesischen Symbolen und Ritualen inspiriert.

Shi Jinsong ist besessen von Fragen der Kontrolle und extremen Manipulation, die er in alltägliche Designobjekte umformuliert. Anfangs bezeichnete er seine Skulpturen als „Prototypen", so bei „Office Equipment-Prototype No. 1" (2004), einer Computerstation samt Nierentisch und Stuhl aus Edelstahl, bei der die Bedienungselemente zugleich als Folterinstrumente fungierten. Mit diesen Prototypen setzte er jene Gedankengänge fort, die er mit seinem „Secret Book of Cool Weapons" (2002) erstmals formuliert hatte, für das er bekannte Unternehmenslogos in ein Sammelsurium antik anmutender Waffen verwandelte. Bei der wegweisenden Ausstellung „Alors, la Chine?" im Centre Pompidou 2003 verzichtete Shi sogar auf den Einsatz von Edelstahl und präsentierte stattdessen mit „A Life of Sugar" eine Installation aus Karamell, die im Verlauf der Ausstellung allmählich dahinschmelzen sollte.

In letzter Zeit hat Shi Jinsong lebensgroße Installationen geschaffen, die Ladenausstellungen und Spielhallen nachempfunden sind. So kreierte er 2005 die berühmt gewordene „Na Zha Baby Boutique" mit Skulpturen, Blaupausen und Fotografien rund um eine haarsträubend gefährliche Kollektion von Babyartikeln. Dazu gehörten ein mörderischer Kinderwagen, eine lebensgefährliche Wiege und ein nadelspitzer Schnuller. Der Markenname „Na Zha" verdankt sich einer Gestalt der chinesischen Volkssage, einem Spitzbuben mit übernatürlichen Kräften und modischem Flair, der in Chinas neuer globaler Wirtschaft als Gott des Lotterie- und Glücksspiels gilt.

2006 stellte Shi Jinsong auf der Shanghai-Biennale seine Produktlinie „Halong Kellong" vor, einen pseudorealistischen Event-Room, der ein wenig wie ein überdimensionierter

未来派雕塑因风险较高而无人涉及，但史金淞长于此。这些雕塑的剃刀般的边刃以及闪闪发亮的不锈钢表面，使人看起来就像科幻剧中的小道具，而这些作品是受古代中国的象征和而启发而产生。

史金淞被控制和极端的操纵等问题而困扰着，再用日常设计物的形式来表示。事实上，当初他就称作他的雕塑为刑具，如《2004设计1号-刑具》，电脑掌控的肾形不锈钢电脑桌和椅子也是刑讯设备。史开始对这些刑具进行了展开了更一步的调查，反映在其作品《冷兵器》。这是一座把著名公司的标志改造成部分古代冷兵器的雕塑。2003参加的在法国蓬皮杜文化艺术中心举办的《中国怎么样？》上，史金淞放弃平常使用的不锈钢材料，用麦芽糖制做了常见的生活用品的模型，创作了《甜蜜生活》。

最近史金淞仿效商店展览和娱乐厅的拱廊，创作了与原物一样大小的装置。2005年，因为儿童用品的恶劣的不安全，他创作了《哪吒儿童用品》，作品中有雕塑，蓝图和照片，包含致命的婴儿车，极其危险的摇篮，针状的奶嘴等。其所选品牌，哪吒，来自于具有非凡本领和力量的神话人物，现在已经中国全球经济化转变的象徵。

2006年，史金淞在上海双年展上展出了其《哈克龙》，一场在形似传说中国龙的装　置里举行的冒充现实的娱乐表演，装置的设计融合哈雷摩托车和农用拖拉机，集装箱于一体，里面设有卡拉-OK 厅，西式自助餐具以及电影放映室等。这是一个青年文化的幻想空间，甚至连上海的商业中心都没有其时尚流行，哈克龙的名字，大概翻译自你好--克隆，讽刺地夸耀了批评中国设计是快速复制品的权威批评。史金淞计划按照哈雷德路线开发其“哈克龙”系列生产品，如夹克，腰带和其他除摩托车以外产品。

Barbara Pollack

2

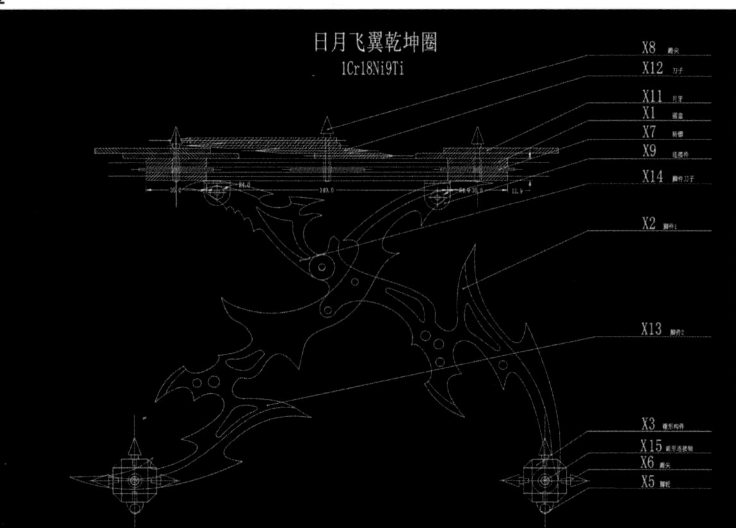

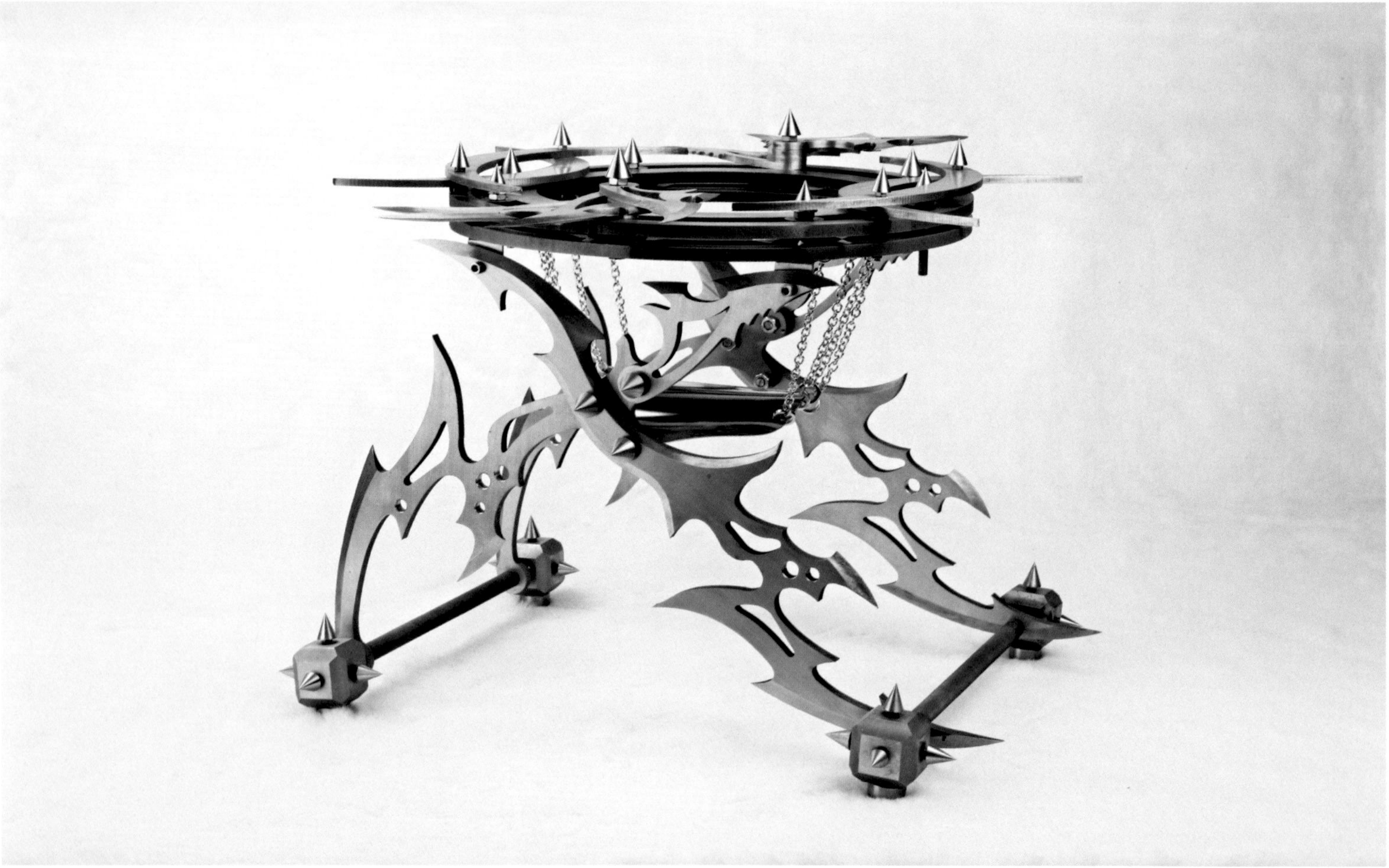

3

4

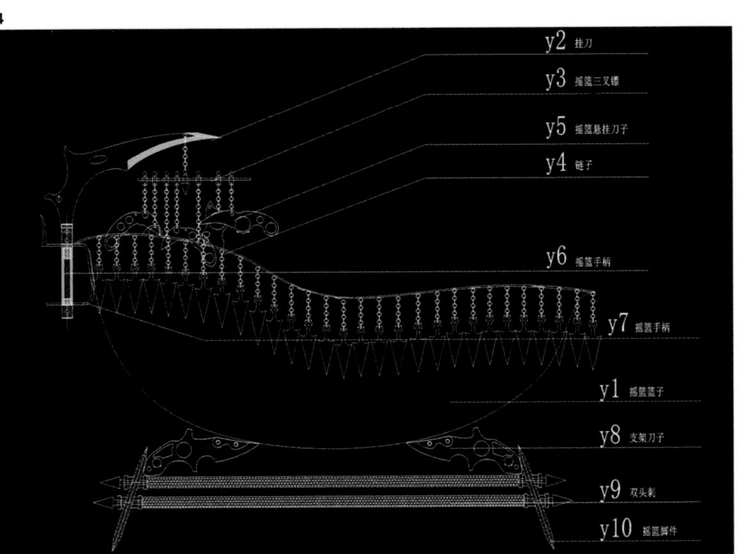
y2 挂刀
y3 摇篮三叉镖
y5 摇篮悬挂刀子
y4 链子
y6 摇篮手柄
y7 摇篮手柄
y1 摇篮篮子
y8 支架刀子
y9 双头刺
y10 摇篮脚件

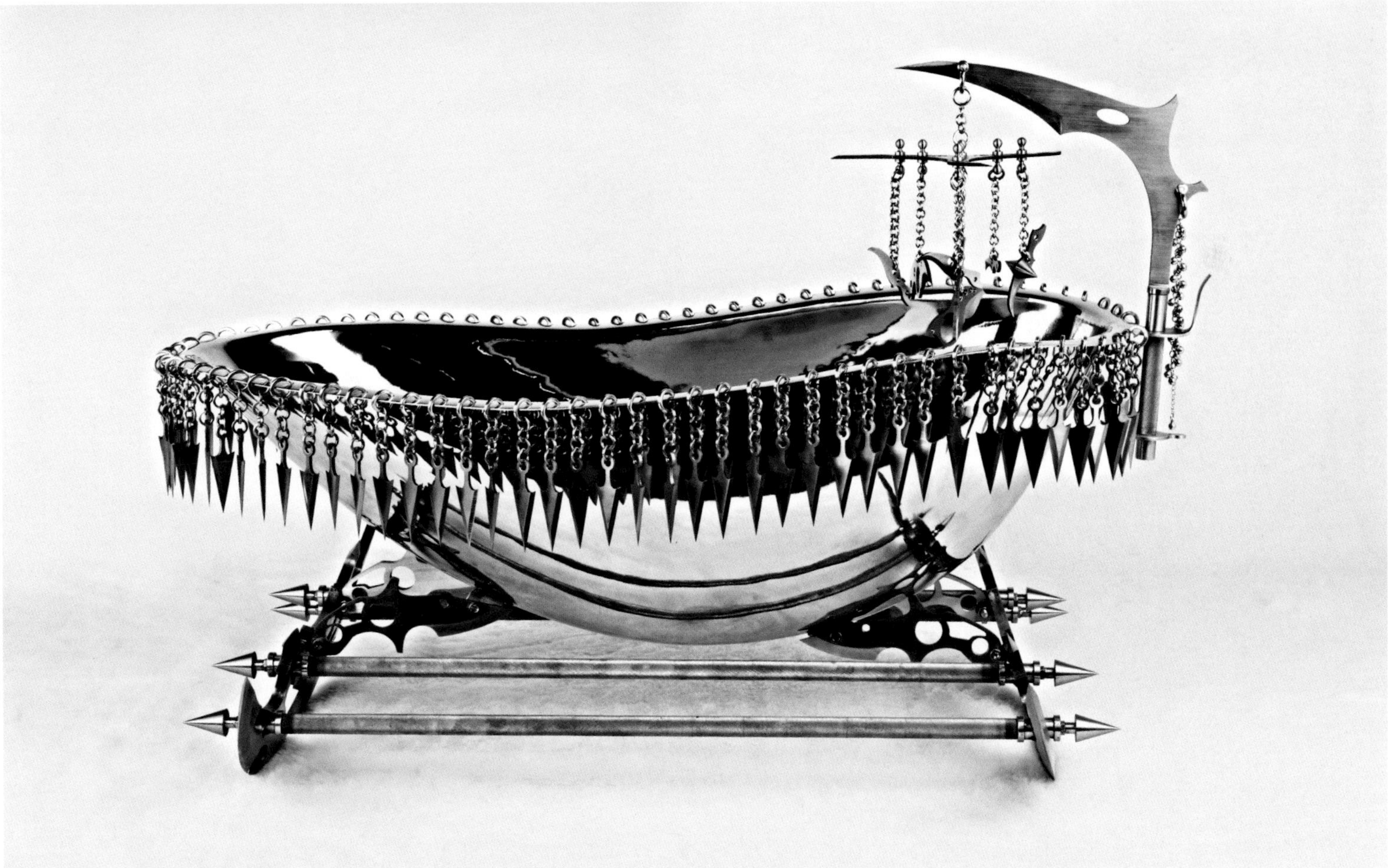

5

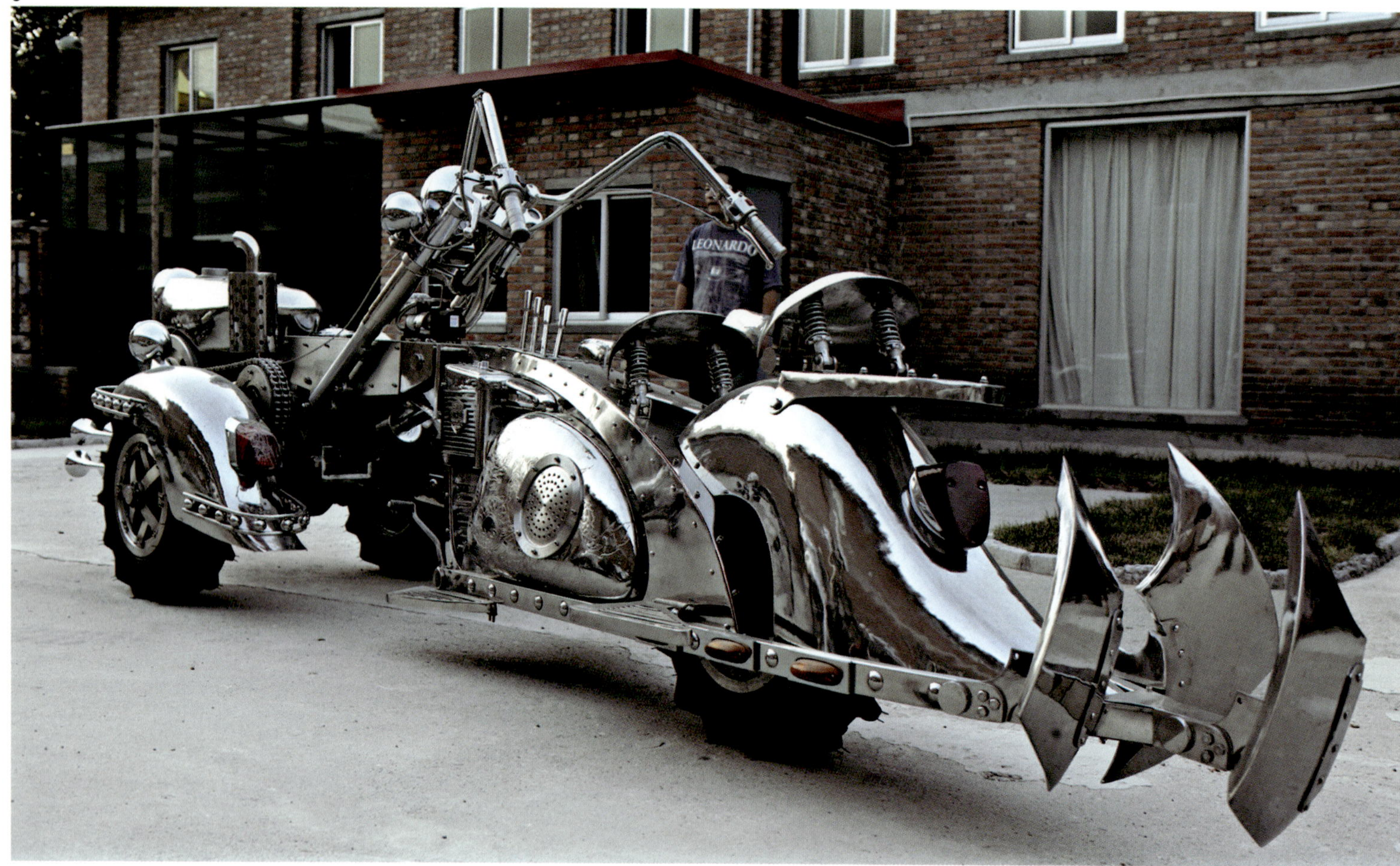

fantasy space of youth culture even more fashionable and cool than those emporiums already existing in cities like Shanghai. The name "Halong Kellong", roughly translates as "Hello-Clone", ironically flaunting the standard criticism of Chinese design as merely production of "knock-offs."

Shi Jinsong plans to develop his own "Halong Kellong" product series along the lines of Harley Davidson's output of jackets, belt buckles, and ephemera in addition to their motorcycles.

chinesischer Drachen gestaltet ist. Die Installation kombiniert einen Zwitter aus Harley Davidson und Traktor mit mehreren Containern und beherbergt einen Karaoke-Raum, eine Erfrischungsbar und einen Filmvorführbereich. Dieser Fantasieraum für die Jugendkultur wirkt noch modischer und cooler als die Vergnügungscenter, die in Städten wie Shanghai bereits existieren. Der Name „Halong Kellong" lässt sich in etwa als „Hallo Klon" übersetzen, eine ironische Anspielung auf das verbreitete Urteil, das chinesische Design erschöpfe sich in Raubkopien.

Shi Jinsong plant die Fortentwicklung seiner Halong-Kellong-Produktserie im Sinn jenes Sortiments an Jacken, Gürtelschnallen und anderen kurzlebigen Modeartikeln, mit denen z. B. die Firma Harley Davidson die Produktion ihrer Motorräder begleitet.

7

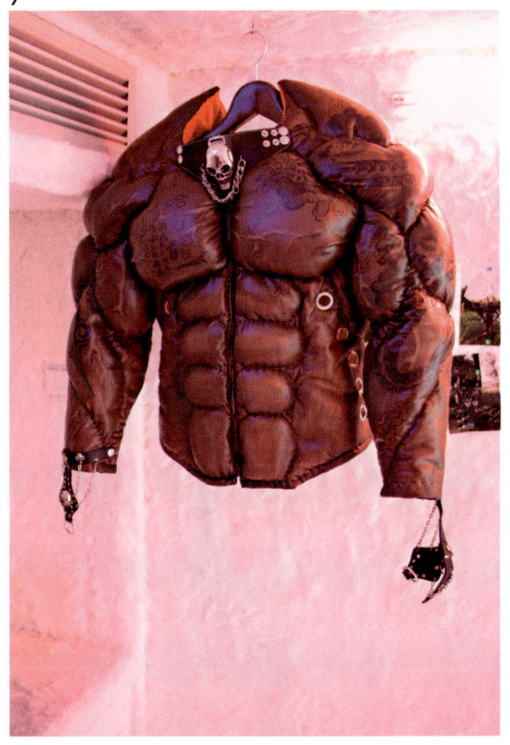

8

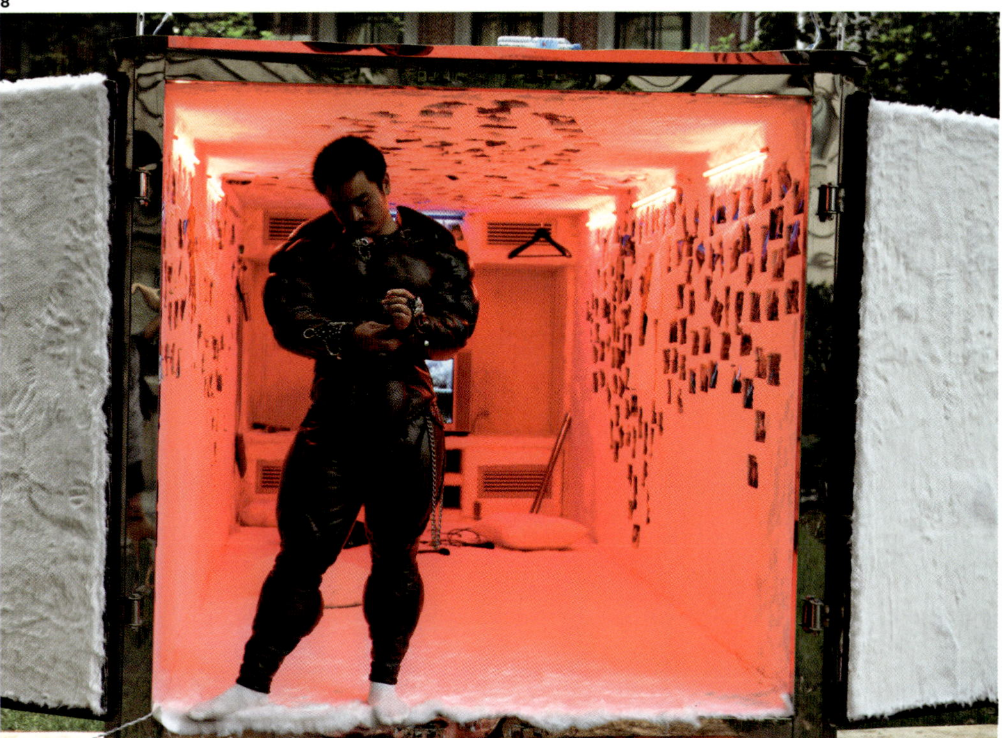

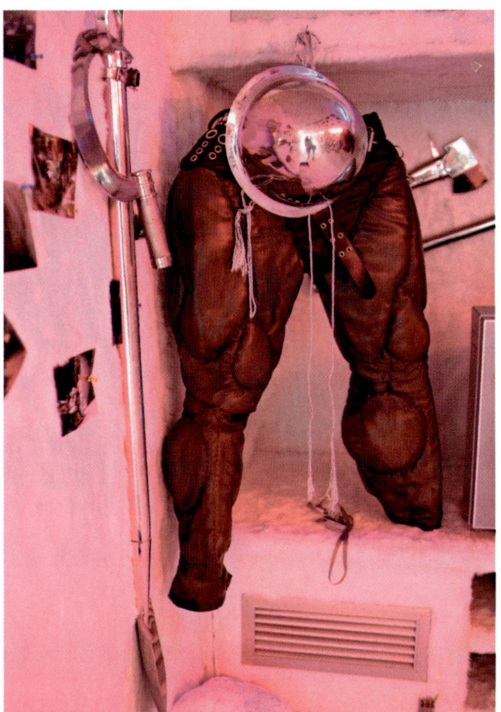

9

1 ***Na Zha's Baby Stroller***, *2005*
Stainless steel, 110 x 81 x 110 cm
Edelstahl, 110 x 81 x 110 cm
《那吒婴孩车》2005年, 不锈钢, 110 x 81 x 110 cm

2 ***Na Zha's Walker***, *2005*
Drawing in form of a blueprint, 198 x 90 cm
Zeichnung in Form eines Lichtdrucks, 198 x 90 cm
《那吒学步车》2005年, 蓝图, 198 x 90 cm

3 ***Na Zha's Walker***, *2005*
Stainless steel, 61 x 48 x 72 cm
Edelstahl, 61 x 48 x 72 cm
《那吒学步车》2005年, 不锈钢, 61 x 48 x 72 cm

4 ***Na Zha's Cradle***, *2005*
Drawing in form of a blueprint, 198 x 90 cm
Zeichnung in Form eines Lichtdrucks, 198 x 90 cm
《那吒摇篮》2005年, 蓝图, 198 x 90 cm

5 ***Na Zha's Cradle***, *2005*
Stainless steel, 81 x 62 x 61 cm
Edelstahl, 81 x 62 x 61 cm
《那吒摇篮》2005年, 不锈钢, 81 x 62 x 61 cm

6 ***Halong Kellong No. 1***, *2003–2005*
Stainless steel, 135 x 130 x 450 cm
Edelstahl, 135 x 130 x 450 cm
《哈克龙 No. 1》, 2003-2005年, 不锈钢等综合材料, 135 x 130 x 450 cm

7 ***Halong Kellong***, *2003–2006*
Muscle clothing, artificial leather, rayon, colour painting, brands
Muskelkleidung, Kunstleder, Synthetik, farbige Bemalung, Marken
《哈克龙-肌肉服》2003-2006年，人造皮革、人造棉、彩绘、及各种商标

8 ***Halong Kellong – KTV container with room***, *2003–2006*
Stainless steel, synthetic fibre, performance
Edelstahl, synthetische Fasern, Performance
《哈克龙-KTV集装箱包房》2003-2006年，不锈钢、人造毛，表演

9 ***Halong Kellong***, *2003–2006*
Muscle clothing, trousers, artificial leather, rayon, colour painting, brands
Muskelkleidung, Hose, Kunstleder, Synthetik, farbige Bemalung, Marken
《哈克龙-肌肉服》2003-2006年，裤，人造皮革、人造棉、彩绘、及各种商标

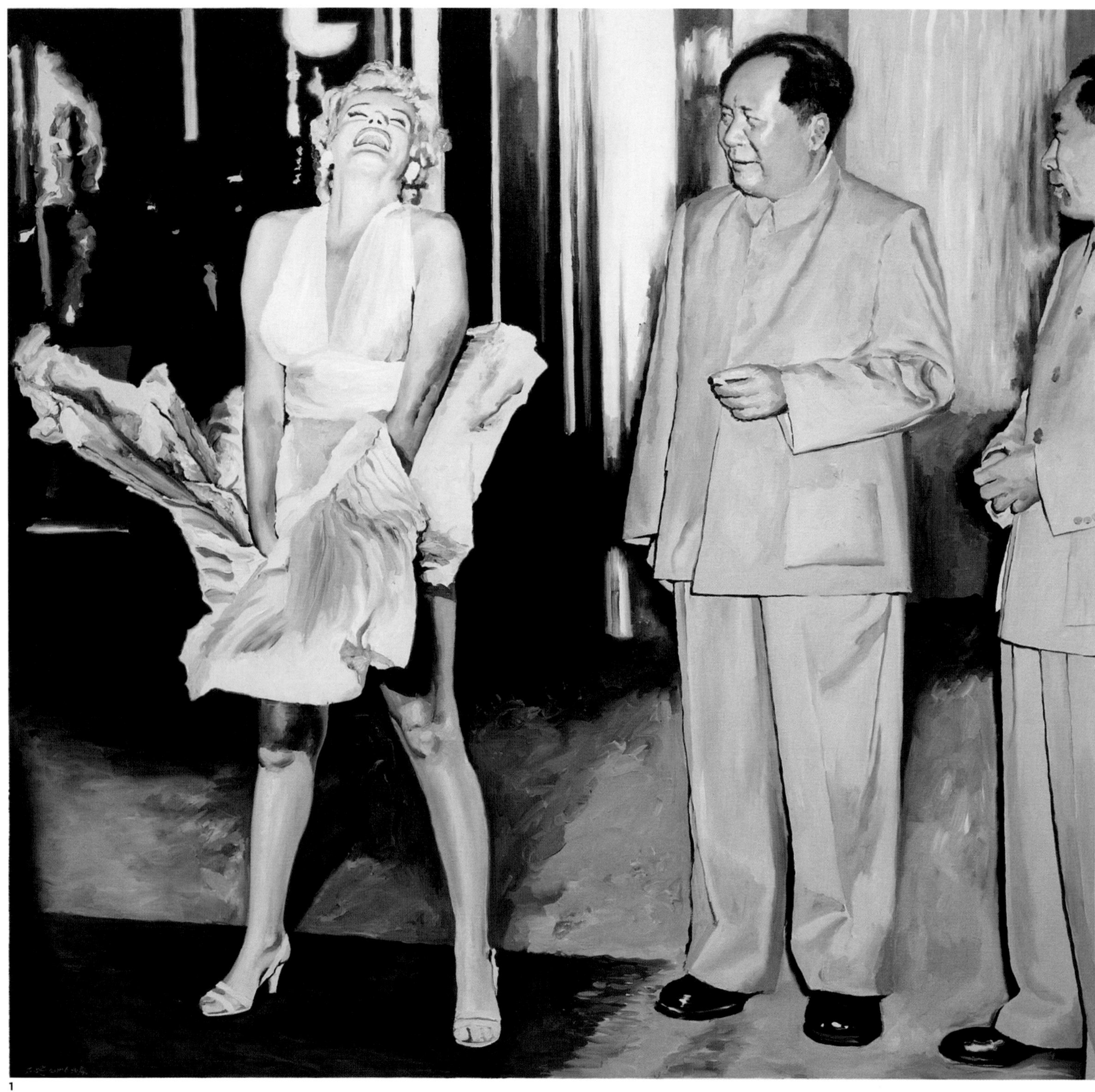

1

"This kind of different and absurd image concoction which can deeply penetrate promulgates a kind of absurdity or a thing resembling the true one as in the eyes of each individual there is a different explanation."

„Diese Art des absurden Bildgebräus, das tief in einen eindringen kann, verkündet, dass es für jedes Ding in den Augen jedes Individuums eine gänzlich andere Erklärung gibt."

"这种差异的、荒谬影像的臆造能更深入地揭示一种荒谬，或者一种类似于真理的东西，这在每个人的眼中都会有不同的解释。"

Born in 1969 in Yingkou, Liaoning Province, China. Lives and works in Beijing
Geboren 1969 in Yingkou, Provinz Liaoning, China. Lebt und arbeitet in Peking
1969出生于中国辽宁省营口市。现生活工作于北京

***Selected exhibitions* / Ausgewählte Ausstellungen / 所选展览**

2001 "Fake – Reality, Shi Xinning's works", Fun Gallery, Beijing, China
2003 "China's Art Today", Marella Arte Contemporanea, Milan, Italy
2004 "Chinese photographic paintings", China Art Seasons Gallery, Beijing, China
2005–07 "Mahjong – Chinesische Gegenwartskunst aus der Sammlung Sigg", Kunstmuseum Bern, Berne, Switzerland, Hamburger Kunsthalle, Hamburg, Germany, Museum der Moderne, Salzburg, Austria

2001年 《捏造・真实》石心宁作品展，北京
2003年 《中国艺术现在》意大利米兰
2004年 《中国影像绘画》北京
2005–07年 《麻将》西克中国当代艺术收藏展 伯尔尼美术馆 瑞士；汉堡美术馆 汉堡 德国；萨尔茨保现代美术馆 奥地利

***Selected publications* / Ausgewählte Publikationen / 所选著作**

Lorenzo Sassoli de Bianchi: "China Contemporary Painting", Bologna 2005
"Road map of drawing", Hong Kong 2006

Sassoli de Bianchi, Lorenzo:《中国当代绘画》，出版 2005年
《绘画路线图》，出版 2006年

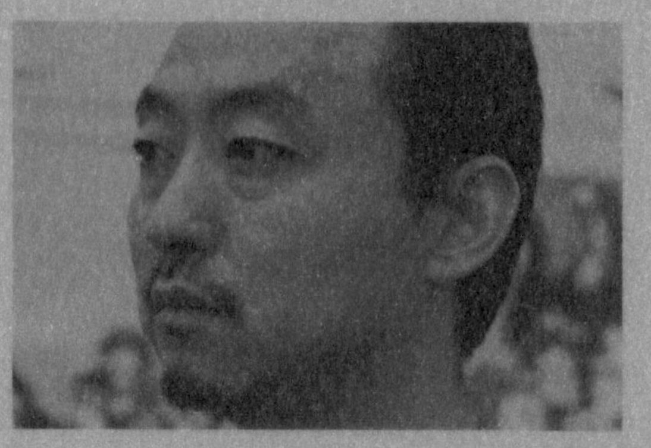

"This kind of different and absurd image concoction which can deeply penetrate promulgates a kind of absurdity or a thing resembling the true one as in the eyes of each individual there is a different explanation."

„Diese Art des absurden Bildgebräus, das tief in einen eindringen kann, verkündet, dass es für jedes Ding in den Augen jedes Individuums eine gänzlich andere Erklärung gibt."

"这种差异的，荒谬影像的臆造能更深入地揭示一种荒谬，或者一种类似于真理的东西，这在每个人的眼中都会有不同的解释。"

Born in 1969 in Yingkou, Liaoning Province, China. Lives and works in Beijing
Geboren 1969 in Yingkou, Provinz Liaoning, China. Lebt und arbeitet in Peking
1969出生于中国辽宁省营口市。现生活工作于北京

Selected exhibitions / Ausgewählte Ausstellungen / 所选展览

2001 "Fake - Reality, Shi Xinning's works", Fun Gallery, Beijing, China
2003 "China's Art Today", Marella Arte Contemporanea, Milan, Italy
2004 "Chinese photographic paintings", China Art Seasons Gallery, Beijing, China
2005-07 "Mahjong - Chinesische Gegenwartskunst aus der Sammlung Sigg", Kunstmuseum Bern, Berne, Switzerland, Hamburger Kunsthalle, Hamburg, Germany, Museum der Moderne, Salzburg, Austria

2001年 《捏造・真实》石心宁作品展，北京
2003年 《中国艺术现在》意大利米兰
2004年 《中国影像绘画》北京
2005-07年 《麻将》西克中国当代艺术收藏展 伯尔尼美术馆 瑞士；汉堡美术馆 汉堡 德国；萨尔茨堡现代美术馆 奥地利

Selected publications / Ausgewählte Publikationen / 所选著作

Lorenzo Sassoli de Bianchi: "China Contemporary Painting", Bologna 2005
"Road map of drawing", Hong Kong 2006

Sassoli de Bianchi, Lorenzo:《中国当代绘画》，出版 2005年
《绘画路线图》，出版 2006年

SHI XINNING 石心宁

[ʂi ɕinnŋ]

The works of Shi Xinning are mainly based on the collection and research of domestic photographs, posters and documents of historical value resulting in "fabrication, distortion", but he also uses the master pieces of western Avant-garde; photographs from current magazine editions and also older mannered photos since the foundation of "the China after 1949" as resources.

His representative works are "Duchamp Retrospective Exhibition in China" (2000/01), "Mourning Che Guevara" (2001), "Miracle of the 20th Century" (2002), "Yalta No. 2" (2006) and so on. This kind of imagination and method is derived from his knowledge of composition and making of traditional paintings, his challenge and rebellion against narrative rules and evaluating judgment. As the picture being mutual in the relationship it is the solution and subversion of the meaning and value of the original picture. In other words he uses in his works the methodology of Postmodernism, an attempt to eliminate the relational explanation pattern between the original and the facsimile, the surface layer and the deeper layer, the reality and the non-reality, which can be seen from the diversion and fictionalisation of photos and representative works of old masters, resulting in a combination of historically poetic sense and the Chinese real difficulties – a kind of collating playful effect surpassing the copy.

This kind tampers the classic manner in the interior of the classics, promulgating regularly the cognition pattern limitation, but delivering a challenge for the authority of the uniform narration. This causes the familiar sounding detailed works to offer a short moment of distorted history which is unreliable, thus the viewer cannot help smiling as even the core of his work is thought provoking. These picture resources were the companions of Shi Xinning's memory as he grew up. Therefore if it is said that he is concocting pictures, or in other words he is cleaning up his passing visualized memory and experience, this kind of memory and experience is not only the one of an individual in China simultaneously, it is a commonly collective one.

Die Arbeiten von Shi Xinning basieren meist auf der Rezeption von einheimischen Fotos, Postern und Dokumenten mit historischer Bedeutung, die aber nach ihrer „Reproduktion" durch den Künstler gewisse Verzerrungen aufweisen. Außerdem greift er auf Abbildungen von Schlüsselwerken der westlichen Avantgarde, Bildmaterial aus aktuellen Zeitschriften und alte Fotografien, die kurz nach der Gründung der Volksrepublik China 1949 entstanden sind, zurück.

Zu Shis bedeutenden Werken zählen neben „Duchamp Retrospective Exhibition in China" (2000/01) vor allem „Mourning Che Guevara" (2001), „Miracle of the 20th Century" (2002) und „Yalta No. 2" (2006). Sein Ideenreichtum und seine Methodik entspringen zwei Wurzeln: einem stupenden Wissen über die Komposition und Herstellung traditioneller chinesischer Bilder sowie seiner Auflehnung gegen narrative Regeln und bewertende Urteile. Shis Version eines vorgefundenen Bildes stellt den Umsturz von Bedeutung und Wert des Originals dar. Er benutzt Mittel der Postmoderne, um das relationale Erklärungsmuster zwischen dem Original und der Reproduktion zu eliminieren, zwischen Oberfläche und Tiefe, zwischen Sein und Schein – er fiktionalisiert also spielerisch seine Vorlagen und kombiniert dabei eine poetische historische Sinnhaftigkeit mit den realen Schwierigkeiten des aktuellen China.

Shi stellt den klassischen Wunsch, Eindeutiges und Verbindliches zu schaffen, in Frage, indem er die Begrenztheit solcher Wahrnehmungsmuster offenlegt und an der Autorität einer einheitlichen Erzählung zweifelt. Auf den ersten Blick wirken seine detailreichen Gemälde vertraut – um sogleich den Anschein der offensichtlichen Geschichte zu verzerren, die immer unzuverlässig ist. Bei dieser Provokation spart Shi die eigene Arbeit keineswegs aus, sondern stellt auch sie mit einem Schmunzeln zur Diskussion. Shi schöpft aus Bildquellen, die ihn seit Jugendzeiten begleiten. Und indem er all diese vergänglichen visualisierten Erinnerungen und Erfahrungen auf seine Weise bereinigt, mündet diese „Vergangenheitsbewältigung" eines einzelnen Individuums in das kollektive Gedächtnis der Gesellschaft.

石心宁作品的图像基本上都是根据对国内、外图片文献资料搜集研究的基础上"捏造、篡改"出来的，尤其是利用了国外前卫艺术大师的作品和中国建国以来假模假式的和现在流行的时尚杂志刊登的摄影照片的资源。

其代表作有《杜尚回顾展在中国》（2000－2001年）、《哀悼切·格瓦拉》（2001年）《20世纪的奇迹》（2002年）、《傲慢与偏见》（2004年）等。这种观念和方式来自于他对以往经典图像所形成的认知方式和叙事规则及价值判断的反叛与挑战，是在"互为图像"的关系上对原有图像价值和意义的颠覆与拆解。或者说他的创作是使用了后现代主义的方法论，试图消除原本与摹本、表层与深层、真实与非真实之间关系的阐释模式，从中可以看到一种对摄影与大师的代表作品图像的挪用和虚构，使历史的诗意和中国现实困境混杂在一起 -- 一种超摹本拼贴的戏仿效果。这种在经典内部篡改经典的方式，揭示了惯常认知模式的局限性，而对单一表述的权威性提出了挑战，使这些耳熟能详的作品所提供的历史真实变得短暂而不可靠，从而在忍俊不禁的荒诞与幽默中更耐人寻味。而这些图像资源都是伴随着石心宁成长的图像记忆，所以与其说他是在臆造图像，不如说是在清理他过往的视觉记忆与经验，而这种记忆与经验在中国不仅是个人的，同时也是集体共同的。

Feng Boyi

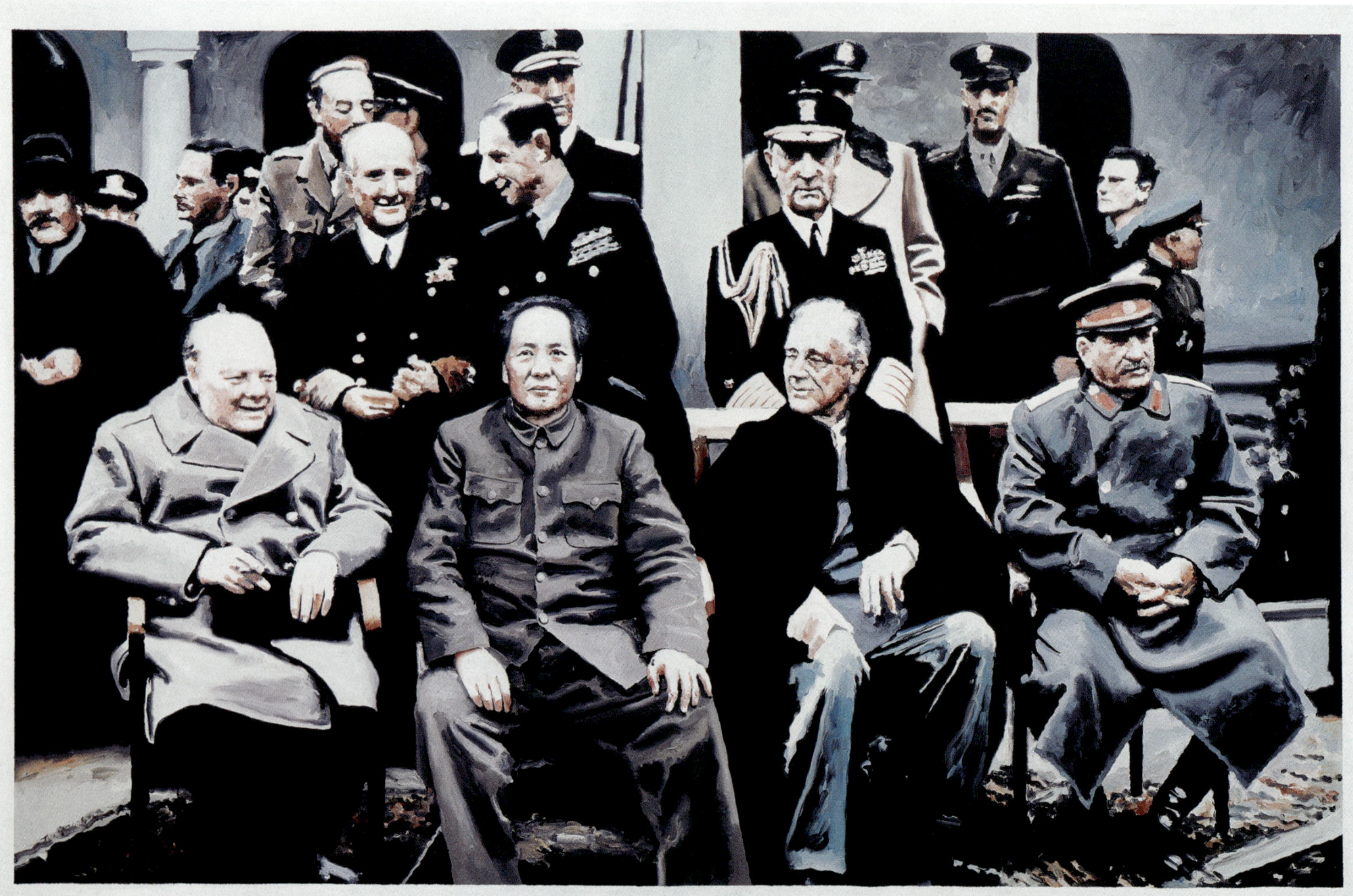

2

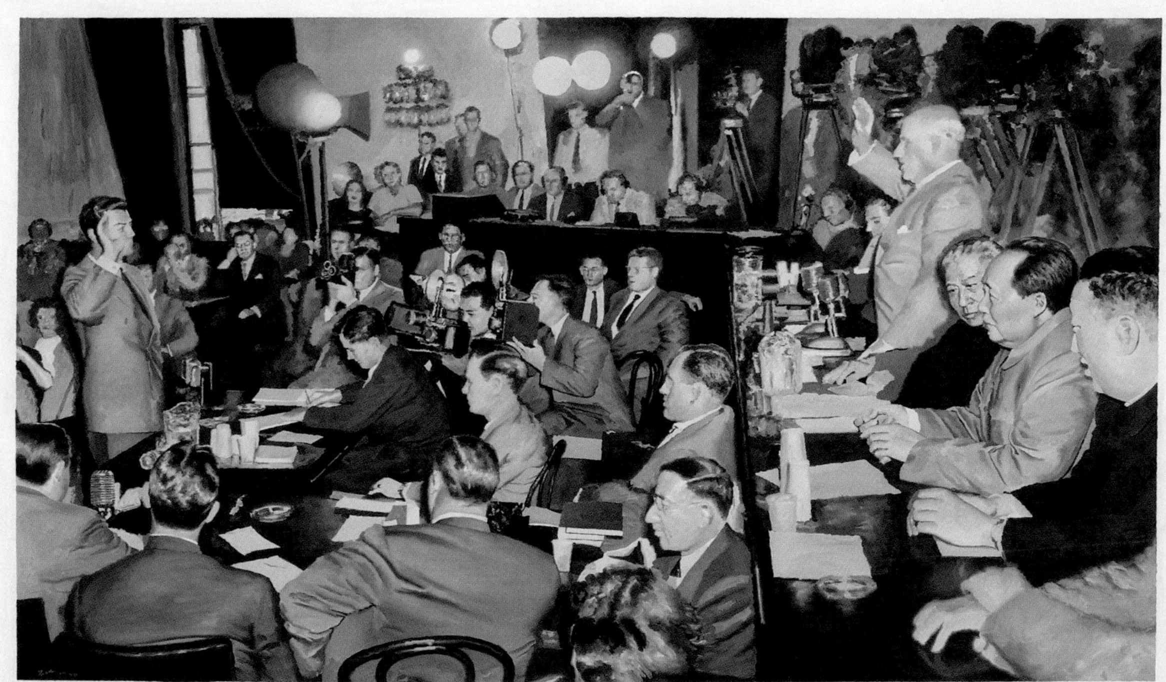

3

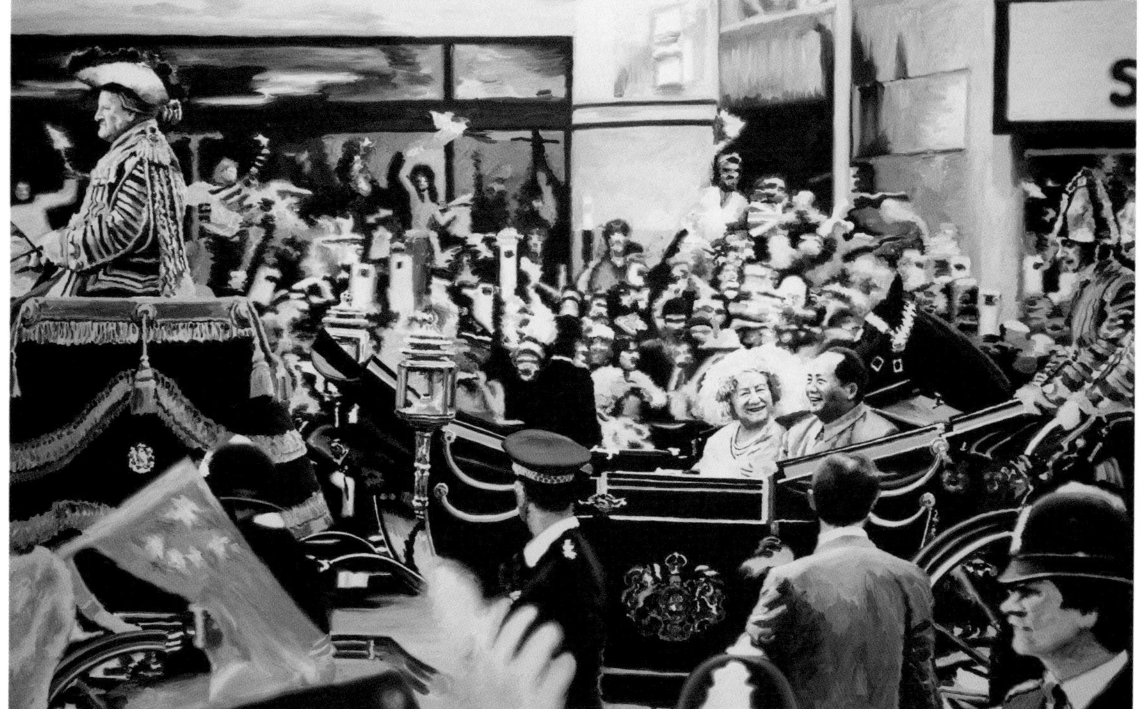

4

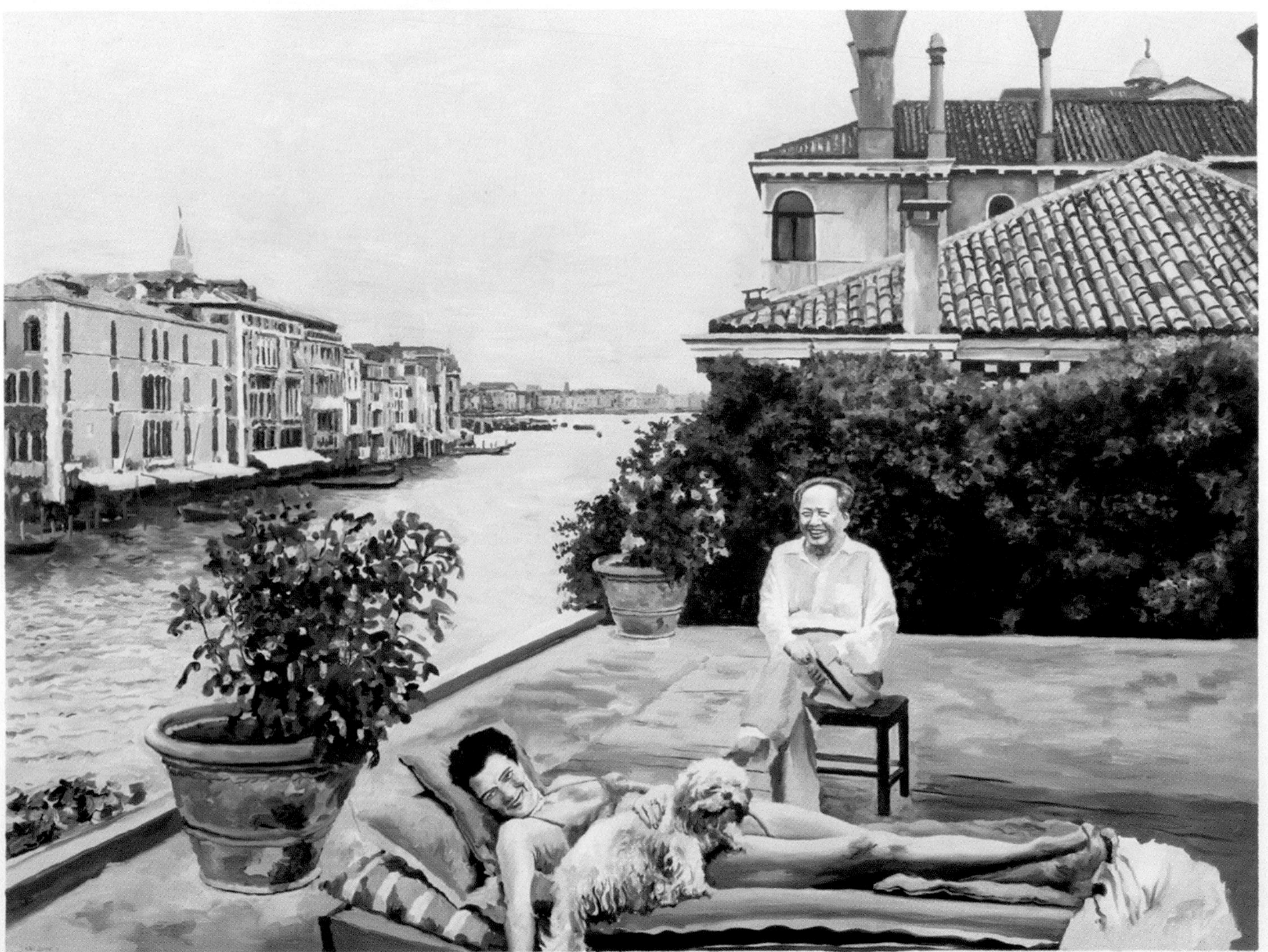

5

6

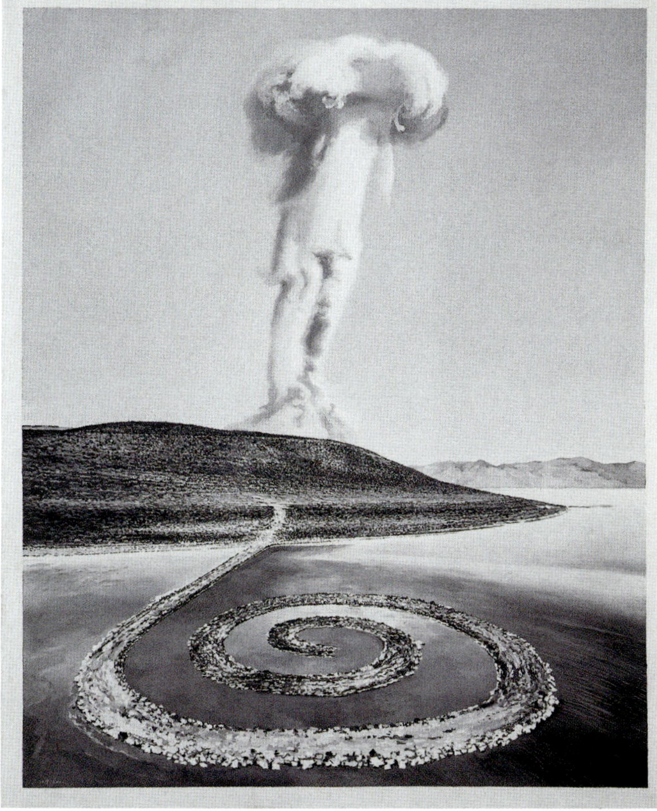

7

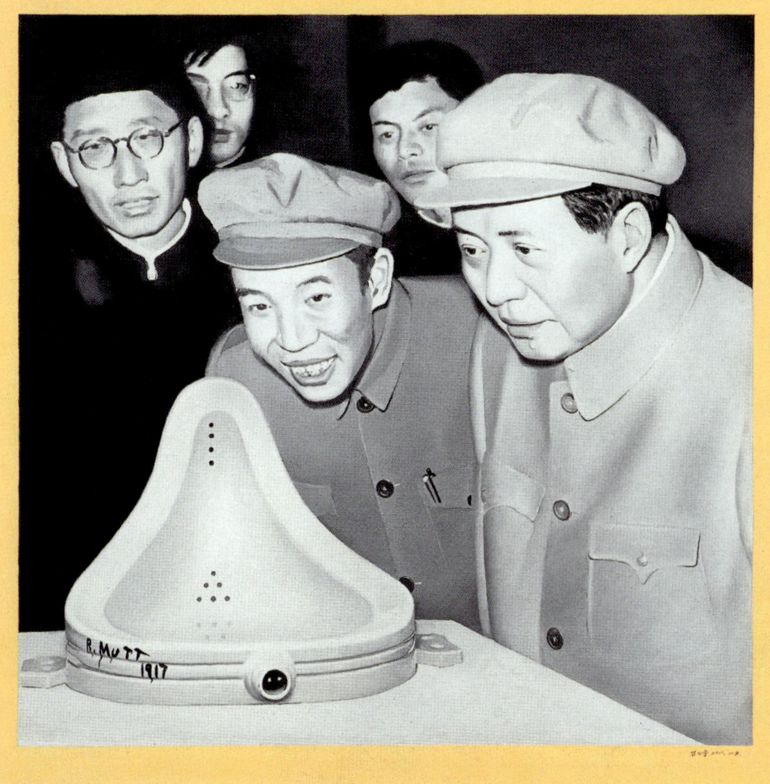

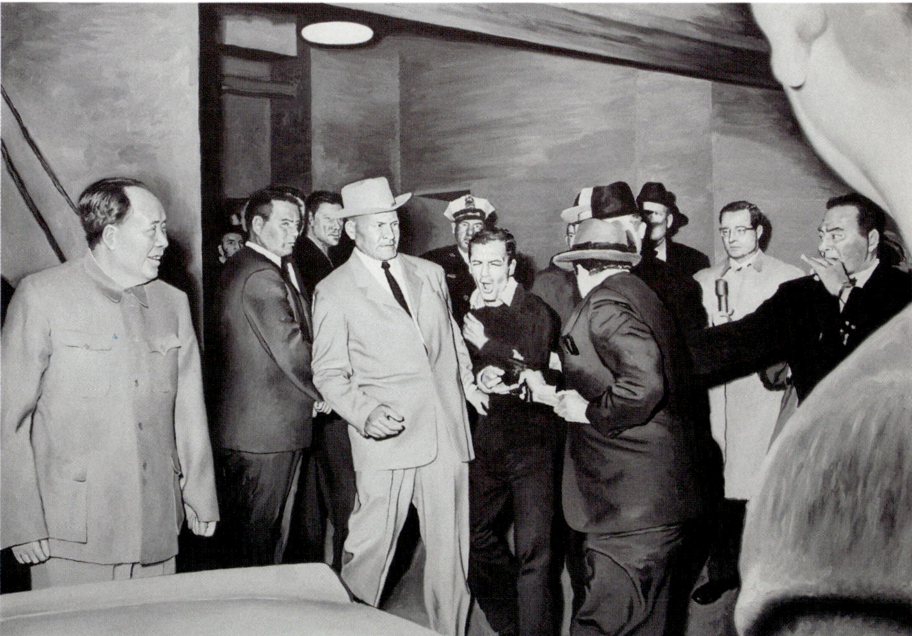

8

1 ***Seven Year's Itch***, *2006*
Oil on canvas, 203 x 203 cm; Öl auf Leinwand, 203 x 203 cm
《七年之痒》2006年, 布面油画, 203 x 203 cm

2 ***Yalta No. 2***, *2006*
Oil on canvas, 210 x 317 cm; Öl auf Leinwand, 210 x 317 cm
《雅尔塔No. 2》2006年，布面油画, 210 x 317 cm

3 ***Mao and McCarthy***, *2005*
Oil on canvas, 256.5 x 381 cm; Öl auf Leinwand, 256,5 x 381 cm
《毛和麦卡锡》2005年, 布面油画, 256.5 x 381 cm

4 ***Royal Coach***, *2006*
Oil on canvas, 210 x 317 cm; Öl auf Leinwand, 210 x 317 cm
《皇家马车》2006年, 布面油画, 210 x 317 cm

5 ***A Holiday in Venice – At the Balcony of Ms. Guggenheim***, *2006*
Oil on canvas, 210 x 272 cm; Öl auf Leinwand, 210 x 272 cm
《威尼斯假日 - 在古根海姆女士的阳台上》2006年, 布面油画, 210 x 272 cm

6 ***Miracle of 20th Century***, *2001/02*
Oil on canvas, 250 x 200 cm; Öl auf Leinwand, 250 x 200 cm
《20世纪奇迹》2001/02年, 布面油画, 250 x 200 cm

7 ***Duchamp Retrospective Exhibition in China***, *2001/02*
Oil on canvas, 100 x 100 cm; Öl auf Leinwand, 100 x 100 cm
《杜尚回顾展》2001/02年, 布面油画, 100 x 100 cm

8 ***Assassinator***, *2007*
Oil on canvas, 210 x 272 cm; Öl auf Leinwand, 210 x 272 cm
2007年《暗杀者》布面油画，210 x 272 cm

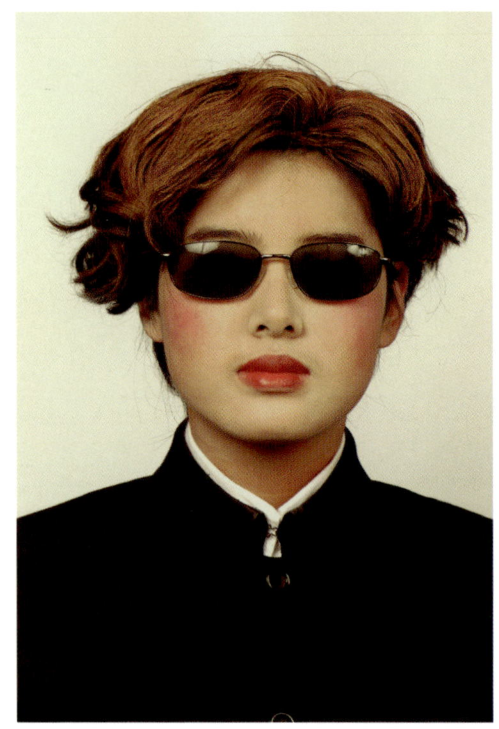

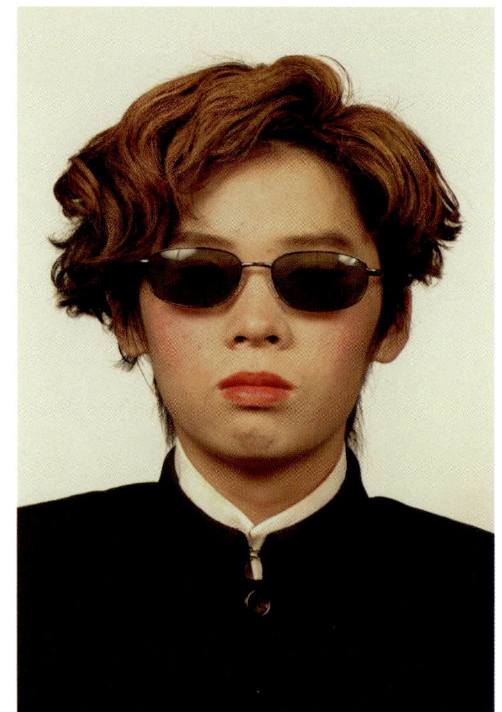

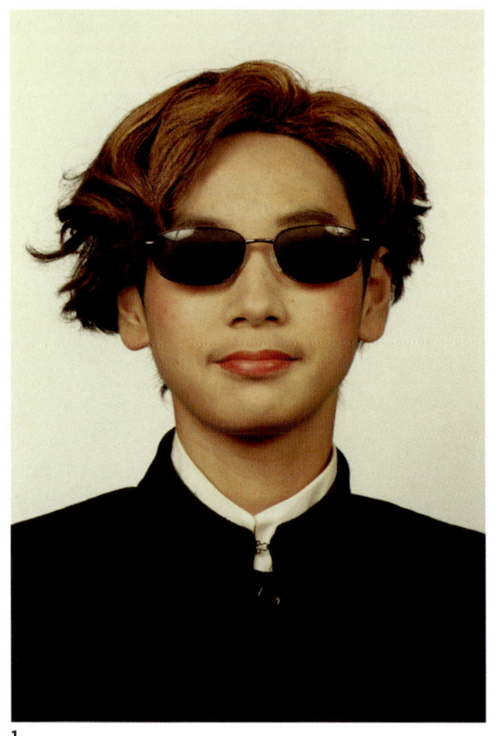

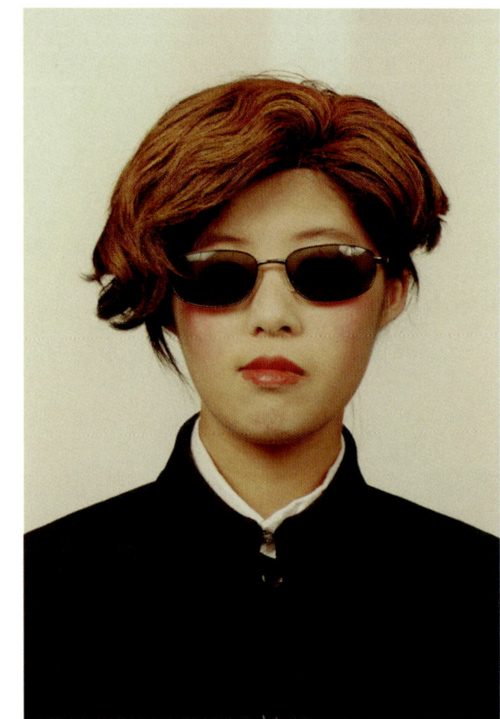

1

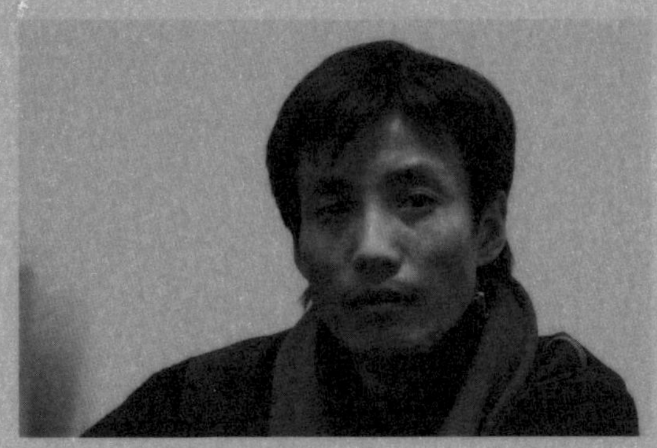

"Non-western characters are obliged to adopt a public image in line with the defined standard in order to maintain a position on the stage of so-called ethnocentric culture."

„Nichtwestler sind genötigt, ein öffentliches Image anzunehmen, das mit dem definierten Standard in Einklang steht, um sich einen Platz auf der Bühne der so genannten ethno-zentrischen Kultur zu sichern.“

“公共形象是另一种文化现实，它是由西方的文化结构所决定的。因此非西方人士不得不依照规定的标准行事，以便在所谓的种族中心主义文化的舞台上保留一席之地。”

Born in 1963 in Shanghai, China. Lives and works in Shanghai
Geboren 1963 in Shanghai, China. Lebt und arbeitet in Shanghai
1963 年生于上海，在上海生活和工作

***Selected exhibitions* / Ausgewählte Ausstellungen / 所选展览**

2002	Bienal de São Paulo, São Paulo, Brazil
	Shanghai Biennial, Shanghai Art Museum, Shanghai, China
2004-05	"Zooming into Focus", National Museum of Fine Arts, Beijing, Shanghai Art Museum, Shanghai, China
2005	"Follow Me!", Mori Art Museum, Tokyo, Japan
	Second Guangzhou Triennial, Guangdong Museum of Art, Guangdong, China
2005-07	"Mahjong – Chinesische Gegenwartskunst aus der Sammlung Sigg", Kunstmuseum Bern, Berne, Switzerland; Hamburger Kunsthalle, Hamburg, Germany; Museum der Moderne, Salzburg, Austria

2002年	《圣保罗双年展》巴西，圣保罗
	《上海双年展》上海，上海美术馆
2004-05年	《聚焦》北京，中国美术馆；2004 年，中国上海，上海美术馆
2005年	《跟我来！》日本东京，森美术馆
	《第二届广州三年展》广东，广东美术馆
2005-07年	《麻将》西克中国当代艺术收藏展 伯尔尼美术馆 瑞士；汉堡美术馆 汉堡 德国；萨尔茨保现代美术馆 奥地利

***Selected publications* / Ausgewählte Publikationen / 所选著作**

Guy & Myriam Ullens Foundation (ed.): "Alles onder de hemel/All under heaven. China now!", Antwerp 2003

Guy & Myriam Ullens Foundation（编者）:《天堂之下》，安特卫普 2003年

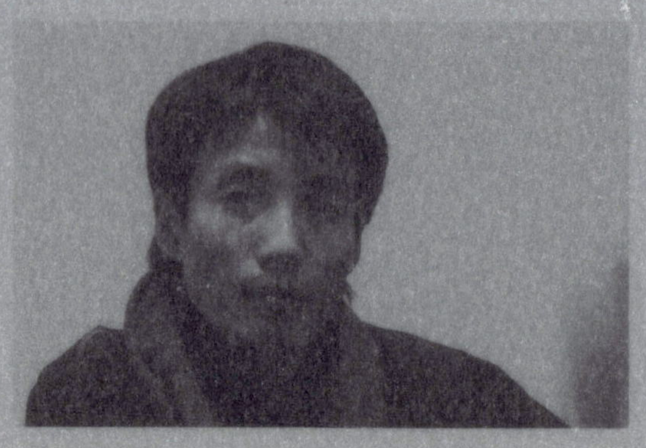

"Non-western characters are obliged to adopt a public image in line with the defined standard in order to maintain a position on the stage of so-called ethnocentric culture."

„Nichtwestler sind genötigt, ein öffentliches Image anzunehmen, das mit dem definierten Standard in Einklang steht, um sich einen Platz auf der Bühne der so genannten ethno-zentrischen Kultur zu sichern."

"公共形象是另一种文化现实，它是由西方的文化结构所决定的。因此非西方人士不得不依照规定的标准行事，以便在所谓的种族中心主义文化的舞台上保留一席之地。"

Born in 1963 in Shanghai, China. Lives and works in Shanghai
Geboren 1963 in Shanghai, China. Lebt und arbeitet in Shanghai
1963 年生于上海，在上海生活和工作

Selected exhibitions / Ausgewählte Ausstellungen / 所选展览

2002	Bienal de São Paulo, São Paulo, Brazil
	Shanghai Biennial, Shanghai Art Museum, Shanghai, China
2004-05	"Zooming into Focus", National Museum of Fine Arts, Beijing, Shanghai Art Museum, Shanghai, China
2005	"Follow Me!", Mori Art Museum, Tokyo, Japan
	Second Guangzhou Triennial, Guangdong Museum of Art, Guangdong, China
2005-07	"Mahjong – Chinesische Gegenwartskunst aus der Sammlung Sigg", Kunstmuseum Bern, Berne, Switzerland; Hamburger Kunsthalle, Hamburg, Germany; Museum der Moderne, Salzburg, Austria

2002年	《圣保罗双年展》巴西，圣保罗
	《上海双年展》上海，上海美术馆
2004-05年	《聚焦》北京，中国美术馆；2004 年，中国上海，上海美术馆
2005年	《跟我来！》日本东京，森美术馆
	《第二届广州三年展》广东，广东美术馆
2005-07年	《麻将》西克中国当代艺术收藏展　伯尔尼美术馆　瑞士；汉堡美术馆　汉堡　德国；萨尔茨堡现代美术馆　奥地利

Selected publications / Ausgewählte Publikationen / 所选著作

Guy & Myriam Ullens Foundation (ed.): "Alles onder de hemel/All under heaven. China now!", Antwerp 2003

Guy & Myriam Ullens Foundation（编著）：《天堂之下》，安特卫普 2003年

SHI YONG 施勇

[ʂə yʊŋ]

From the outset, Shi Yong's working style takes art into his immediate environs, both physically and in terms of the content it explores. An early installation work from 1996 negated the privacy of his apartment with invasive listening devices planted in every portion of the space, which relayed any sound to all the other rooms in the apartment. This type of pseudo-scientific feel characterises several initial conceptual interventions. Then, as the millennium turned, inspired by the frenzy of commercial activity sweeping Shanghai, Shi Yong take his own image as the subject of his work, which he viewed as a perfect vehicle for investigating the effect of consumerism on the general outlook of the local people.

Beginning with "The New Image of Shanghai Today" (1999), Shi Yong embarked upon an extended parody of modern Shanghai attitudes in a quest for a model citizen. Here, Shi Yong adopts the smart mode of dress upon which Shanghainese people pride themselves as the badge of the new, upwardly mobile generation. The ideal citizen is, in fact, Shi Yong himself, in an up-dated version of the Mao suit, and satirising even the suit's namesake in the waving gesture of his hand. In the other, he holds the briefcase of a white-collar worker. The only detail in which this look differs from reality is the cut and colour of his hair and the extreme coolness of the sunglasses he sports, which is the point. The profile has since become Shi Yong's signature motif.

Obviously, the primary focus of Shi Yong's work is identity. This identity is specific to the polished social environment of Shanghai – which considers itself the most civilised city in China. Every such self-assertion demands to be put to the test. Shi Yong's interest was to establish how the aspirations of this community came into being. The ensuing photographic works and projects involving audience participation were all part of his research. The process begins with "Yearnings" (2000) where the captions are an essential aspect of the images. Next was "You cannot clone but you can buy it" (2000) a multiplication of the image

Shi Yong siedelte seine Kunst von Beginn an in seiner unmittelbaren Umgebung an, und das sowohl körperlich als auch thematisch. In einer frühen Installation von 1996 negierte er die Privatsphäre seiner Wohnung durch aggressive Abhöreinrichtungen, die er in jedem Teil der Räumlichkeiten angebracht hatte und die jeden Laut jeweils in die anderen Zimmer übertrugen – ein für seine Anfänge typischer, nüchterner pseudowissenschaftlicher Akt. Mit Anbruch des neuen Jahrtausends ließ sich Shi Yong dann von jener hektischen Kommerzwelle inspirieren, die über Shanghai hereinbrach, und macht seitdem sein eigenes Abbild zum Gegenstand seines Werks – in seinen Augen das ideale Vehikel, um die Auswirkungen des hemmungslosen Konsumismus auf das allgemeine Lebensgefühl zu erforschen.

Beginnend mit „The New Image of Shanghai Today" (1999), schuf Shi Yong eine großangelegte Parodie auf moderne Shanghaier Verhaltensweisen, indem er sich auf die Suche nach dem Musterbürger begab. Dieser trägt die schicke neue Kleidermode, mit der sich die Bewohner Shanghais stolz als Mitglieder der neuen Aufsteigergeneration herausputzen. Und dieser Musterbürger ist natürlich Shi Yong selbst, in einer modernisierten Version des Mao-Anzugs. Mit zum Mao-Gruß erhobener Hand wagt er es gar, den Großen Vorsitzenden zu karikieren, in der anderen hält er die Aktentasche eines Büroangestellten. Nur in gewitzten Details weicht die Darstellung von der Realität ab: in seiner Frisur und Haarfarbe sowie in der extrem coolen Sonnenbrille, die er zur Schau trägt – dieses (Selbst-)Porträt ist seitdem zu Shi Yongs charakteristischem Motiv geworden.

Im Mittelpunkt seiner Arbeit steht ganz klar die Identitätsfrage. Eine geschliffene soziale Schicht Shanghais – das sich selbst für die kultivierteste Stadt in ganz China hält – zweifelt an dieser Identität nicht. Und eine derartige Selbstgewissheit verlangt danach, auf die Probe gestellt zu werden. Shi Yong versucht nachzuvollziehen, wie in einer solchen Gesellschaft Ambitionen entstehen. Seine fotografischen Arbeiten und seine Projekte mit Publikumsbeteiligung dienten allesamt diesem selbst auferlegten

开始的时候，施勇的创作风格是把艺术从其物质本身及其所揭示的内容纳入到他周围的环境当中。早期的装置作品（标题 1996 年）无视他所居住的公寓的隐私，各个角落里都安上了侵略性的窃听设备，使得什么声音都能传到公寓其他所有房间。这种伪科学感觉的风格以最初的一些概念性侵入为特征。后来，在千禧年之际，从横扫上海的狂暴商业活动中受到启发，施勇以其自身形象作为作品主题，这在他看来是用来调查拜金思想在当地人的普遍观念中所产生的效果的完美工具。

从《今日上海新景象》（1999 年）起，为了进行对模范公民的探求，施勇开始对现代上海市民的仪态进行长期的拙劣模仿。施勇巧妙的穿起了上海人引以为豪的，作为新潮、上升一代的标识的着装。理想的公民实际上是穿着新版毛式服装（人民装）的施勇自己，他甚至以挥手的姿势而对服装的同名者进行讽刺。在另一个作品中，他则拎着白领工作者的公文包，唯一看起来与现实生活有出入的细节是他头发的造型和颜色以及他所佩戴的充满酷劲的太阳镜，而这正是意义所在。这一形象从此成为施勇的签名像。

很明显，施勇作品的主要关注点是身份，这种身份对应于上海经过粉饰的社会环境的。上海人自认为上海是中国最文明的城市，而类似这样自做主张都要经受过历史检验。施勇曾对确定这一群体的渴望是如何产生的很感兴趣。后续的涉及观众参与的摄像作品和工程都是他研究的一部分。这一过程始于《憧憬》（2000 年），作品的标题和说明文字是图像的重要方面。接下来是《你不可以克隆，但你可以买》（2000 年），同一形象在单副照片中重复迭现。这是他回归类似《风景画廊》（2002 年）系列宏大作品的一个步骤。

电脑软件给施勇提供了一个把玩人们自己选择的理想形象的机会。使用软件程序就跟美容师和发型师所做的一样，可以创造虚拟的翻新。他给一组志愿

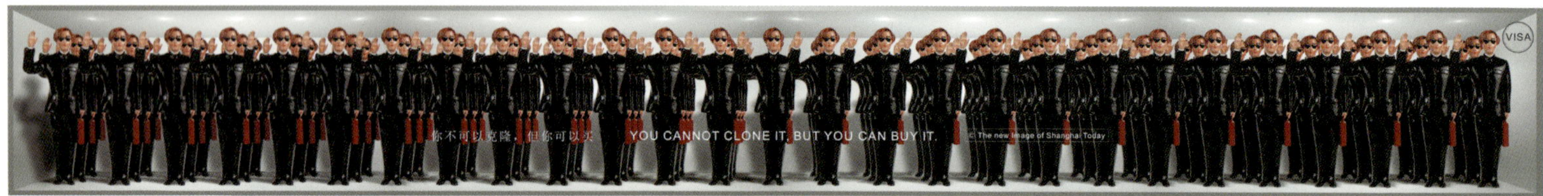
VISA
你不可以克隆，但你可以买
YOU CANNOT CLONE IT, BUT YOU CAN BUY IT.
© The new Image of Shanghai Today

2

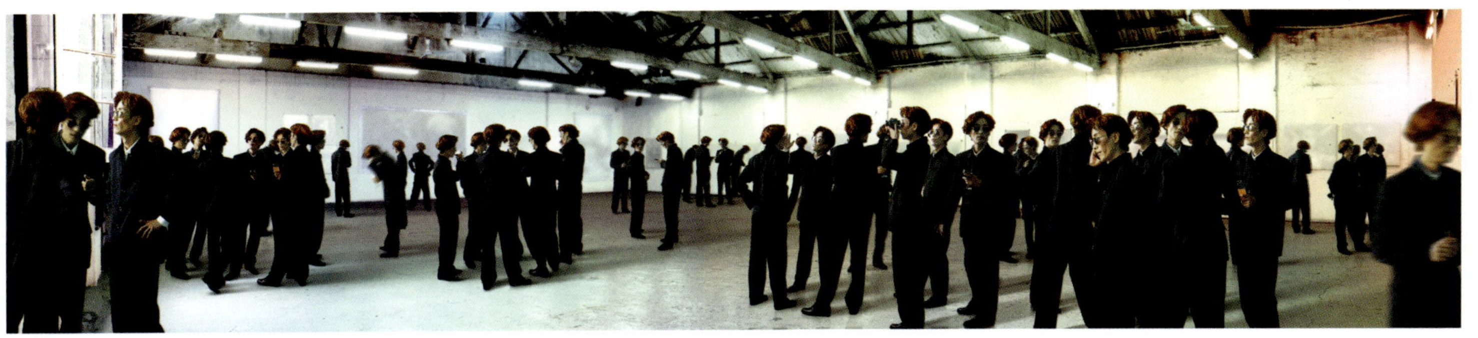

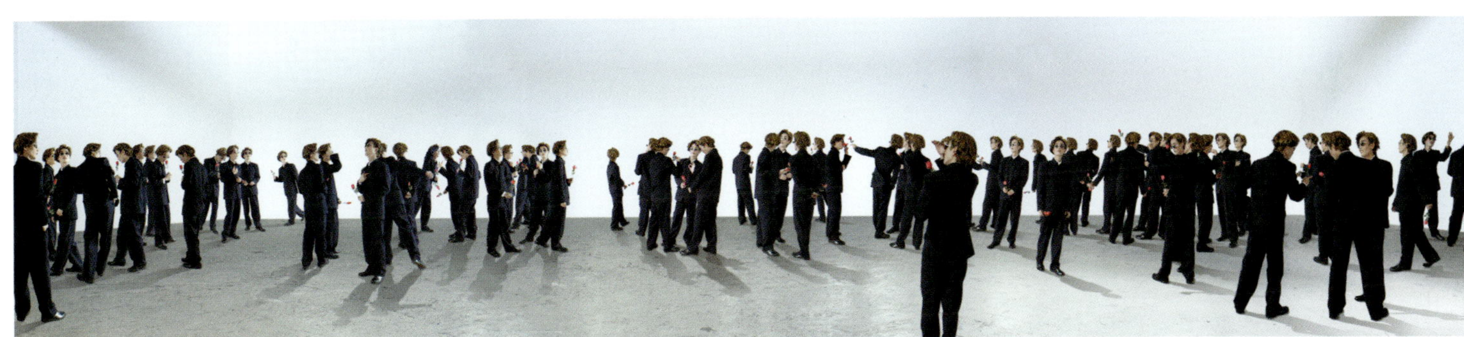

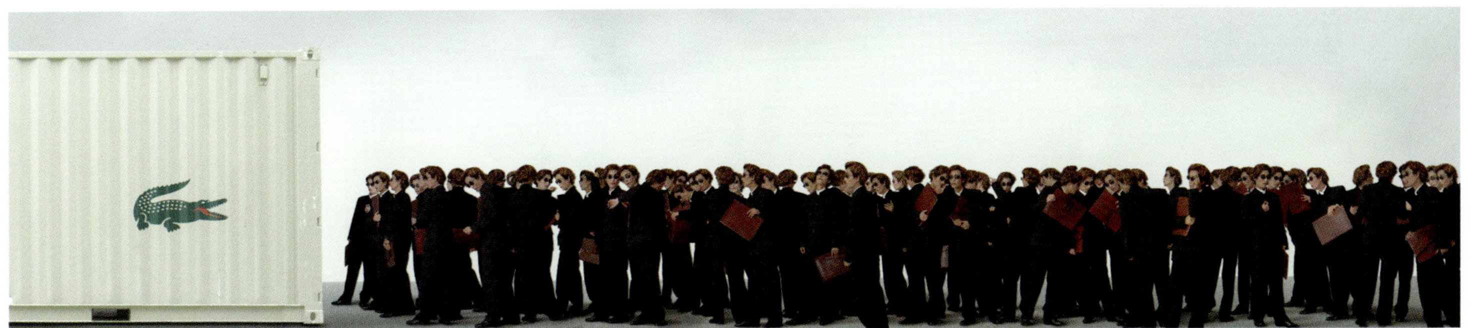

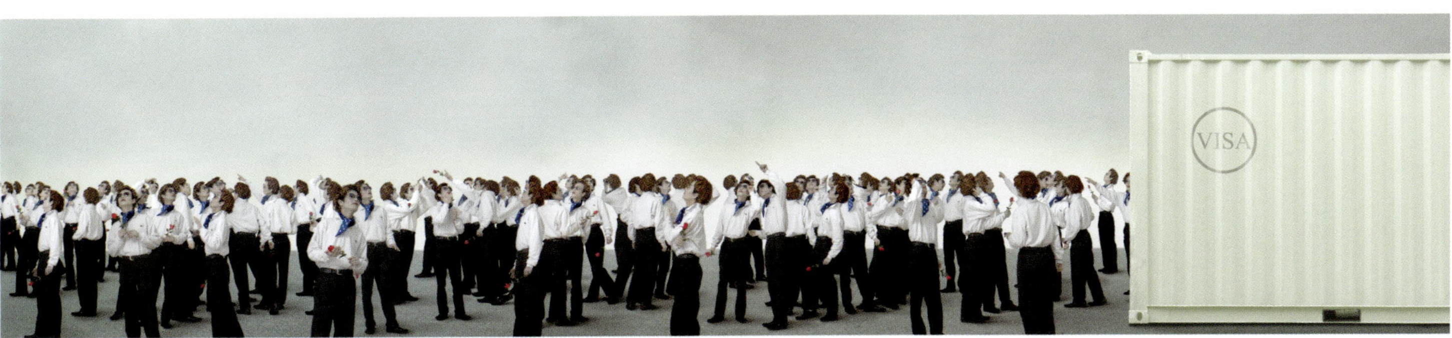

3

4

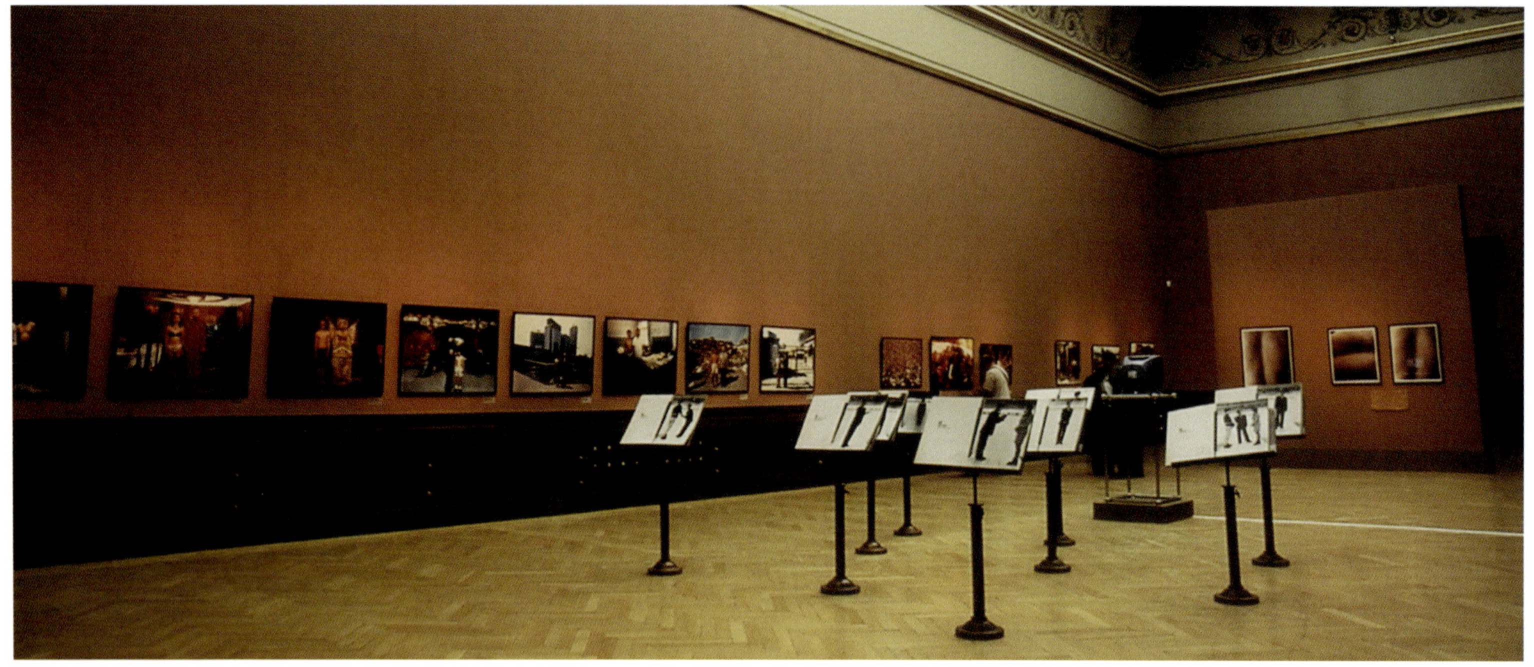

in a single photograph, and an approach that he would return to in expansive composites like the "Gallery View" series (2002).

Computer software provided Shi Yong with an opportunity to play with an ideal image people could chose for themselves. Using a software programme similar to that employed by beauticians and hair stylists to create virtual makeovers, he offered a group of volunteers the opportunity to transform their identity at will. The results are displayed with minimal directness in the "Continuous" series (2004/05), which accompanied a video work of the same title (2004).

As a form of light relief, Shi Yong has produced a small number of large-scale installation works each with a humorous twist. One work, confusingly also titled "Yearning" (2003), a model of an imagined UFO, is a good example, as is the bizarre inverted form of "The Moon Hues are Teasing" (2002). Recent projects like "We don't want to stop" (2006) show no let up in Shi Yong's commentary upon the prevailing Shanghai climate: here the title, stencilled on the side of what appears to be a racing car, succinctly embodies the city's driving ambition.

Forschungsauftrag – der mit „Yearnings" (2000) begann, wo die Bildtexte ein entscheidender Aspekt der Bilder selbst sind. Mit „You cannot clone but you can buy it" (2000) fand Shi Yong die Möglichkeit, ein vervielfachtes Bild in einer einzigen Fotografie unterzubringen. Auf diese Technik sollte er bei seinen späteren überbreiten Bildmontagen wie der Serie „Gallery View" (2002) wieder zurückgreifen.

Ganz folgerichtig ergriff Shi Yong die Gelegenheit, die digitale Technik für seine Beschäftigung mit Idealbildern zu nutzen. Unter Verwendung eines Computerprogramms, wie es auch Kosmetikerinnen und Friseure einsetzen, um Typveränderungen virtuell zu demonstrieren, bot er einer Gruppe von Freiwilligen die Möglichkeit, ihre Identität nach Belieben zu verwandeln. Die Ergebnisse werden mit minimalistischer Direktheit in der Serie „Continuous" (2004/05) vorgestellt, zu der auch eine Videoarbeit mit dem gleichen Titel gehört (2004).

Währenddessen hat Shi Yong, beinahe als kurzweilige Abwechslung, ein paar großformatige Installationswerke mit humorigem Augenzwinkern geschaffen, darunter das Modell eines imaginären UFOs, das verwirrenderweise ebenfalls „Yearning" (2003) betitelt ist, oder auch „The Moon Hues are Teasing" (2002), das durch eine bizarr umgekehrte Form verblüfft. Neuere Projekte wie „We don't want to stop" (2006) zeigen, dass Shi Yong nicht müde wird, das vorherrschende Klima von Shanghai zu kommentieren: Hier verkörpert bereits der Titel – auf eine Art Rennwagen schabloniert – in knappen Worten den Ehrgeiz, der die Stadt antreibt.

者提供一个任意改变他们自己身份的机会，并将结果以最不直接的方式在《继续》系列（2004-2005 年）里展现，同时还有以同样标题命名的录像作品（2004 年）。

作为一种惬意放松的方式，施勇制作了许多大型的装置作品，每部作品都与幽默相交织。一部不知何故也叫《憧憬》（2004 年）（其名称极有可能应该是《飞翔的 Q》）的作品，其中想象中 UFO 的模型是一个很好的例子，另一个例子则是作品《月色撩人》（2002 年）中奇异的倒转形式。

在近期的作品如《我们不想停止》（2006 年）中，施勇在他对上海流行气候的解说中没有显示任何的让步：作品的标题被印制在看起来像疾驰的汽车一侧，清晰的印证了这个城市的前进雄心。

Karen Smith

5

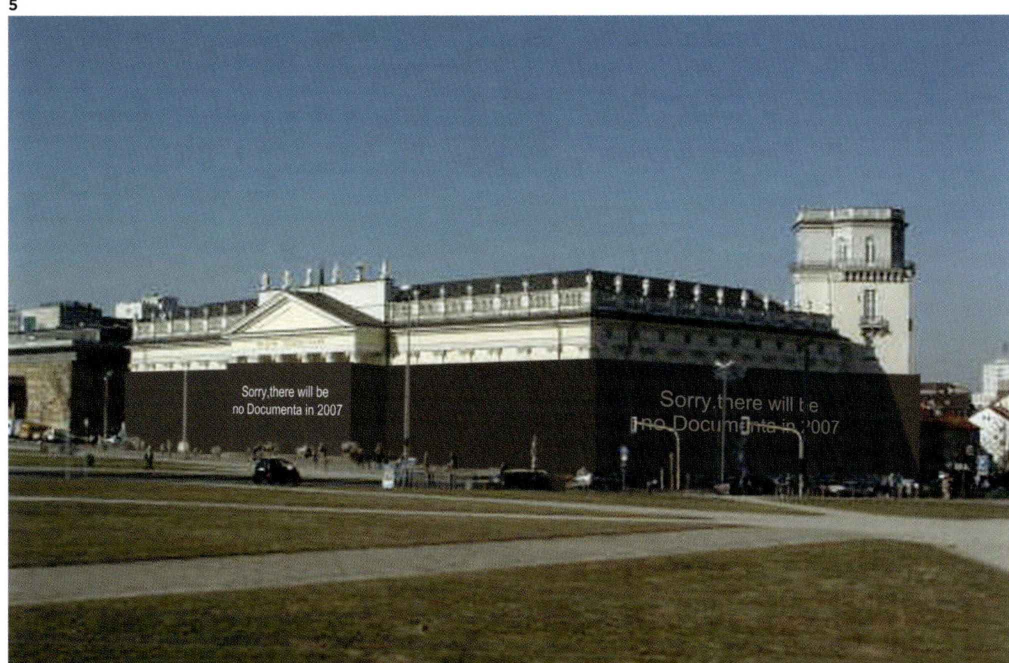

1 ***Continuous**, 2004/05*
Digital photographs, 75 x 50 cm each
Digitale Fotografien, je 75 x 50 cm
《继续》2004/05, 数字摄影，每幅, 75 x 50 cm

2 ***You cannot clone it, but you can buy it**, 2001*
Computer processed digital photograph, 30 x 240 cm
Computerbearbeitete digitale Fotografie, 30 x 240 cm
《你不可以克隆，但你可以买》，2001年, 电脑合成数字摄影, 30 x 240 cm

3 ***Gallery Scenery No. 1–4**, 2002–2005*
4 computer processed digital photographs, 80 x 360 cm each
4 computerbearbeitete digitale Fotografien, je 80 x 360 cm
《风景画廊第1-4》2002-2005年, 电脑合成数字摄影, 每幅, 80 x 360 cm

4 ***Deportment ABC**, 2003*
Installation view
Installationsansicht
《仪态举止ABC》2003年, 装置实景

5 ***Sorry, there will be no Documenta in 2007**, 2006*
Photographs, 70 x 100 cm each
Fotografien, je 70 x 100 cm
《2007年卡赛尔没有文献展计划》2006年，摄影, 70 x 100 cm

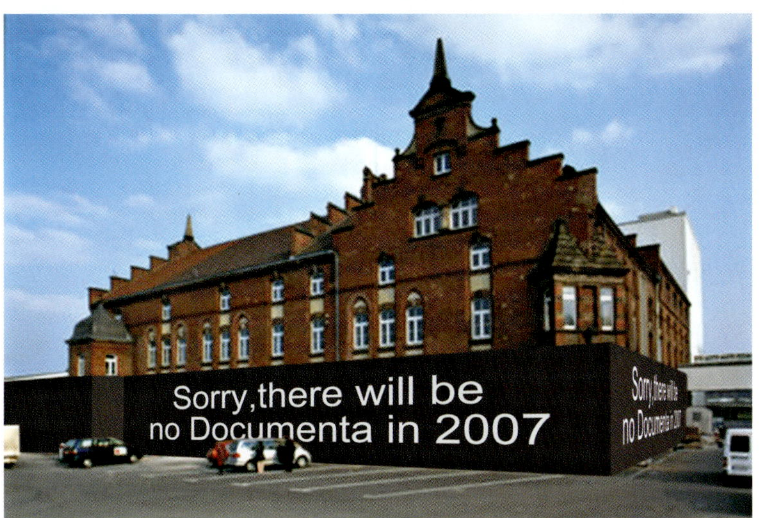

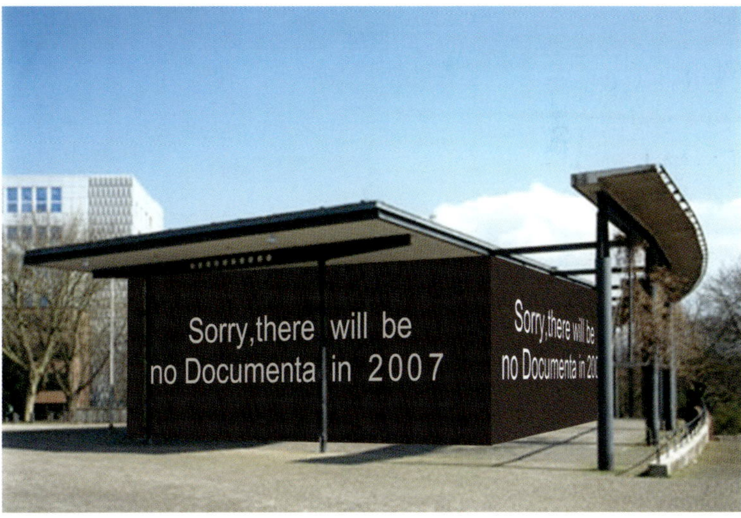

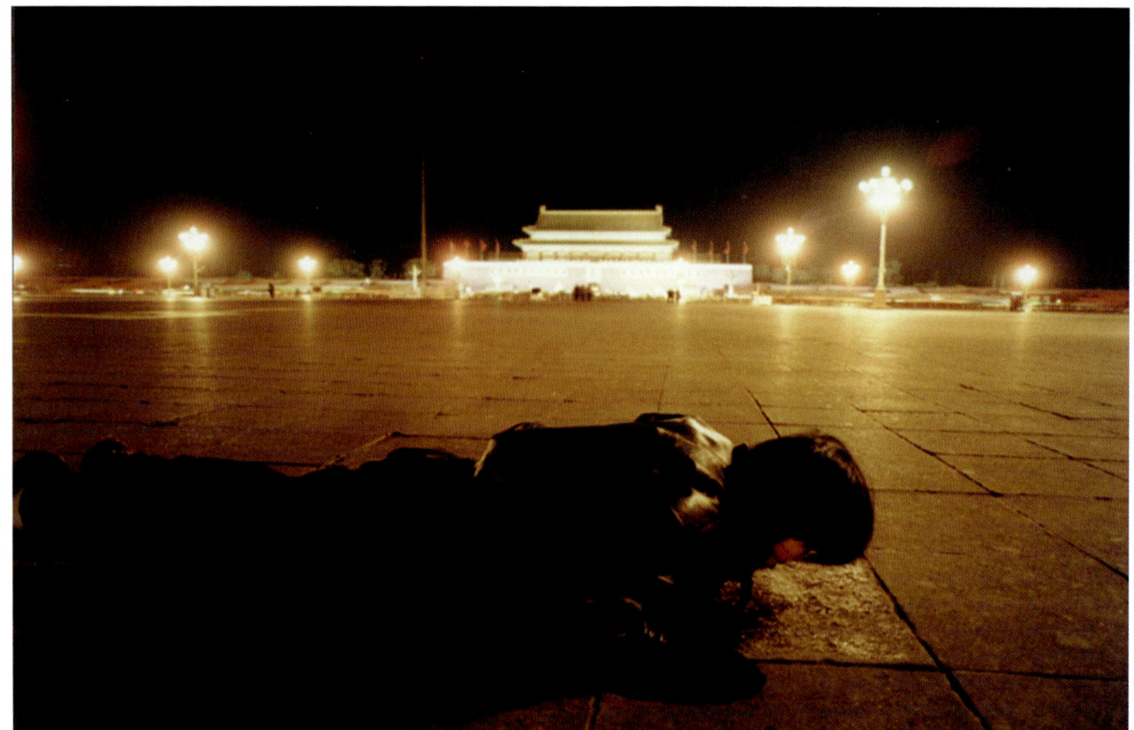

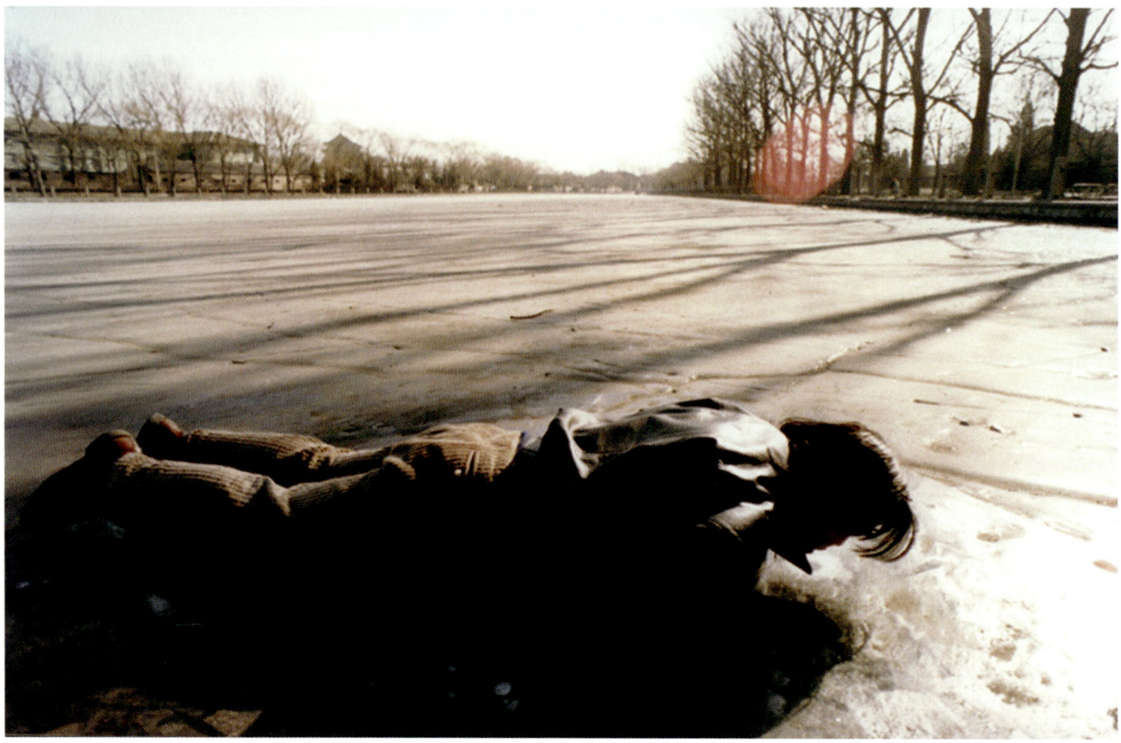

1

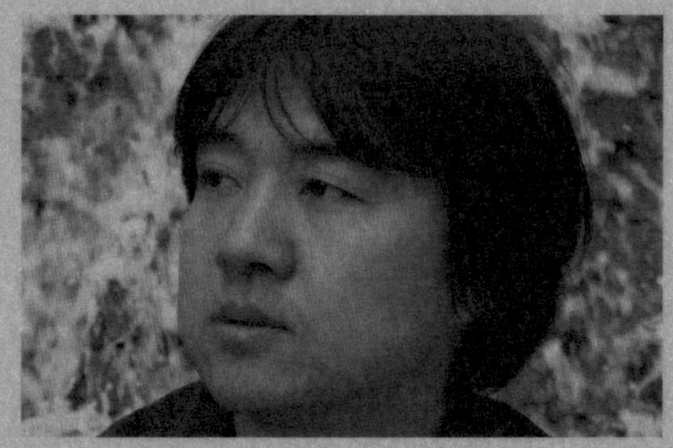

"I am interested in how the two sides of the East-West-contradiction become one."

„Mich interessiert, wie die beiden Seiten des Ost-West-Widerspruchs eins werden."

"我乐于如何将中西文化冲突的两方面融合为一体。"

Born in 1966 in Beijing, China. Lives and works in Beijing
Geboren 1966 in Peking, China. Lebt und arbeitet in Peking
1966年出生于中国北京。居住工作在北京

***Selected exhibitions* / Ausgewählte Ausstellungen / 所选展览**

2004–07 "Between Past and Future, New Photography and Video from China", International Center of Photography, New York, NY, USA (travelling exhibition)
2005 "The Elegance of Silence. Contemporary Art From East Asia", Mori Art Museum, Tokyo, Japan
"I am Making Art", Queensland Art Gallery, Brisbane, Australia
"Karou Arima – How Latitudes Become Forms", Museo de Arte Contemporáneo, Monterrey, Mexico
"Waste / Placed in China", Walsh Gallery, Chicago, IL, USA
2006 "Festival of Love", Asia Society, New York, NY, USA
"Only One Wall", Artspace, Sydney, Australia

2004–07年 《过去与未来之间—中国新影像展》国际摄影中心 纽约 美国（巡回展）
2005年 《高雅的宁静：东亚当代艺术》森美术馆 东京
《我在创造艺术》昆士兰美术馆 布里斯班
《Karou Arima 一 怎么纬度成为形式》当代艺术博物馆，蒙特雷
《沃尔什画廊》Walsh 画廊, 芝加哥
2006年 《爱的节日》Asia Society, 纽约
《只有一面墙》Artspace, 悉尼

***Selected publications* / Ausgewählte Publikationen / 所选著作**

Francesca Dal Lago: "Space and public: Site specificity in Beijing", in: "Art Journal", issue 59, N. 1, New York 2000
Lin Xiaoping: "Discourse and displacement: contemplating Beijing's urban landscape", in: "Art AsiaPacific", No. 25, New York 2000
Edward Lucie-Smith: "Give me sex and death", in: "ArtReview", issue 52, London 2000
Melissa Chiu: "Sleight of hand: the use of text in contemporary Chinese art", in: "Art AsiaPacific", No. 29, New York 2001

Dal Lago, Francesca（著）:《空间和公众：站点特异性在北京》在：《艺术杂志》第59刊, 号1, 纽约2000年
Xiaoping Lin（著）:《谈论和位移:冥想北京的都市风景》"Art AsiaPacific" 杂志, 号25刊, 纽约 2000年
Lucie-Smith, Edward（著）:《给我性和死亡》"ArtReview", 第52刊，伦敦 2000年
Chiu, Melissa（著）:《手指灵巧: 文本的用途在当代中国艺术》"Art AsiaPacific" 杂志，号29刊，纽约 2001年

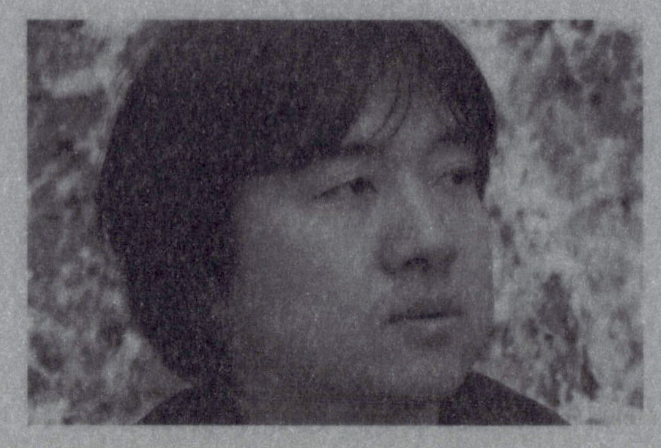

"I am interested in how the two sides of the East-West-contradiction become one."

„Mich interessiert, wie die beiden Seiten des Ost-West-Widerspruchs eins werden."

"我乐于如何将中西文化冲突的两方面融合为一体。"

Born in 1966 in Beijing, China. Lives and works in Beijing
Geboren 1966 in Peking, China. Lebt und arbeitet in Peking
1966年出生于中国北京。居住工作在北京

Selected exhibitions / Ausgewählte Ausstellungen / 所选展览

2004-07 "Between Past and Future, New Photography and Video from China", International Center of Photography, New York, NY, USA (travelling exhibition)
2005 "The Elegance of Silence. Contemporary Art From East Asia", Mori Art Museum, Tokyo, Japan
"I am Making Art", Queensland Art Gallery, Brisbane, Australia
"Karou Arima - How Latitudes Become Forms", Museo de Arte Contemporáneo, Monterrey, Mexico
"Waste / Placed in China", Walsh Gallery, Chicago, IL, USA
2006 "Festival of Love", Asia Society, New York, NY, USA
"Only One Wall", Artspace, Sydney, Australia

2004-07年 《过去与未来之间—中国新影像展》国际摄影中心，纽约 美国（巡回展）
2005年 《高雅的宁静：东亚当代艺术》森美术馆 东京
《我在创造艺术》昆士兰美术馆 布里斯班
《Karou Arima — 怎么纬度成为形式》当代艺术博物馆，蒙特雷
《沃尔什画廊》Walsh 画廊，芝加哥
2006年 《爱的节日》Asia Society，纽约
《只有一面墙》Artspace，悉尼

Selected publications / Ausgewählte Publikationen / 所选著作

Francesca Dal Lago: "Space and public: Site specificity in Beijing", in: "Art Journal", issue 59, N. 1, New York 2000
Lin Xiaoping: "Discourse and displacement: contemplating Beijing's urban landscape", in: "Art AsiaPacific", No. 25, New York 2000
Edward Lucie-Smith: "Give me sex and death", in: "ArtReview", issue 52, London 2000
Melissa Chiu: "Sleight of hand: the use of text in contemporary Chinese art", in: "Art AsiaPacific", No. 29, New York 2001

Dal Lago, Francesca（著）：《空间和公众：站点特异性在北京》在：《艺术杂志》第59刊，号1，纽约2000年
Xiaoping Lin（著）：《谈论和位移：冥想北京的都市风景》"Art AsiaPacific" 杂志，号25刊，纽约 2000年
Lucie-Smith, Edward（著）：《给我性和死亡》"ArtReview"，第52刊，伦敦 2000年
Chiu, Melissa（著）：《手指灵巧：文本的用途在当代中国艺术》"Art AsiaPacific" 杂志，号29刊，纽约 2001年

SONG DONG 宋冬

[sʊŋ tʊŋ]

Song Dong's birth coincided with the beginning of the Cultural Revolution. Always interested in visual art, he had taken painting lessons since he was a child, and finally entered the Department of Art of Capital Normal University to study oil painting. One of his academic-style paintings was selected for the First Chinese Oil Painting Exhibition in Shanghai when he was still a student. Another of his paintings was then shown in the National Art Exhibition in 1989, the year of his graduation. But suddenly he abandoned his academic training entirely and the career path of a successful professional artist. Two circumstances caused this change: China's political situation at the time, and the introduction of new contemporary art forms to China in the late 1980s and early 1990s. Song Dong was elated by the pro-democracy student movement and dumbfounded by its tragic ending. Watching the tanks overrun Beijing's streets, he felt that he had matured and transformed overnight.

As an artist, he found freedom in installation, performance, and video; a framed canvas had become too limiting for his newly discovered creativity. He held his first installation/performance exhibition, called "One More Lesson: Do You Want to Play with Me?" in 1994 in Beijing. The local authorities cancelled the show the day it opened. But Song Dong never returned to painting. In fact, unlike many other contemporary Chinese installation and video artists, the numerous art projects he has conducted since 1994, mainly installations, performances, and video works, have betrayed little influence from his former academic training.

A large group of these projects have a strong "improvisational" quality, inspired by and responding to specific times, places, and events. Although Song Dong does not reject ideology entirely, he refuses to use narrowly defined ideology as the framework for his artistic creation, but poses more fundamental questions about the nature of art medium and the authenticity of representation. His short video pieces, such as "Hit Mirror, Broken Mirror" (1999), "Crumbling Shanghai" (2000), and "Burning Photograph"

Als Song Dong geboren wurde, begann die Kulturrevolution. Er erhielt schon als Kind Malunterricht, später schrieb er sich am Fachbereich Kunst der Capital Normal University für das Studium der Ölmalerei ein. Noch während seiner Studentenzeit wurde eines seiner Gemälde im akademischen Stil für die First Chinese Oil Painting Exhibition in Shanghai ausgewählt. Ein anderes Gemälde wurde 1989, in seinem Abschlussjahr, auf der National Art Exhibition gezeigt. Doch dann schmiss Song Dong seine ganze akademische Ausbildung und seine Karriereaussichten als anerkannter Profikünstler einfach hin. Auslöser dafür waren die damalige politische Lage im Land und die neue zeitgenössische Kunst, die in den späten 1980er und frühen 1990er Jahren nach China gelangte. Song Dong war begeistert von der studentischen Demokratiebewegung und entsprechend fassungslos angesichts ihres tragischen Endes. Als er die Panzer auf Pekings Straßen auffahren sah, fühlte er sich über Nacht verändert und gereift.

Als Künstler fand er Freiheit nun in Installationen, Performances und Videokunst; eine gerahmte Leinwand engte seine neu entdeckte Kreativität zu sehr ein. Seine erste Installations- und Performance-Ausstellung veranstaltete er 1994 unter dem Titel „One More Lesson: Do You Want to Play with Me?" in Peking. Die Stadtobrigkeit schloss die Ausstellung noch am Tag ihrer Eröffnung. Aber Song Dong kehrte nie zur Malerei zurück. Anders als die Arbeiten vieler zeitgenössischer Installations- und Videokünstler Chinas lassen die zahlreichen Projekte, die er seit 1994 realisierte, kaum Einflüsse aus seiner früheren akademischen Ausbildung erkennen.

Viele dieser Werke haben einen ausgeprägt „improvisatorischen" Charakter, der von bestimmten Zeiten, Orten und Ereignissen inspiriert ist und auf sie reagiert. Obwohl Song Dong Ideologie nicht grundweg ablehnt, weigert er sich, sein Kunstschaffen in den Rahmen einer eng definierten Lehre zu zwängen. Er stellt vielmehr grundlegendere Fragen nach dem Wesen des Kunstmediums und der Authentizität der Darstellung. Seine kurzen Videoarbeiten, z. B. „Hit

宋冬出生于文化大革命开始之时。他始终对视觉艺术感兴趣，从幼时起便学习绘画课程，并最终进入了首都师范大学美术系学习油画。在他还是学生时，他的一幅学院风格的绘画作品便被选入了在上海举行的首届中国油画展。他的另一幅绘画作品还被选入 1989 年全国美术作品展，而这一年也是他毕业的年份。然而，突然间他完全放弃了他的学院培训以及通往成功艺术家的职业道路。这一变化是由两种情况造成的：当时中国的政治环境，以及20世纪八十年代末、九十年代初中国对新的当代艺术形式的引进。宋冬对当时提倡民主的学生运动满怀热情，同时也为这次运动的悲剧收场而目瞪口呆。目睹着坦克碾过北京的街道，他感觉自己一夜间变得成熟起来，同时也改变了许多。作为一名艺术家，他在装置、表演及录像中找到了自由；一张带框的帆布对于他全新发掘出的创造力而言显得太过有限。他于 1994 年在北京举行了他的首个装置/表演展览，展览名为《又一堂课，你愿意跟我玩吗？》。当地政府在开展当天便取消了这次展览。然而宋冬再也没有重返绘画的道路。事实上，与许多其他同时代的装置及录像艺术家不同，他自 1994 年起所创作的大量艺术项目，主要为装置、表演以及录像作品等，几乎都离不开他以前的学院培训的影响。

一大批这类作品都具有浓厚的"即兴"色彩，灵感源自特定的时间、地点及事件并对其作出回应。尽管宋冬并不完全排斥意识形态，但他拒绝将狭义的意识形态作为他艺术创作的框架，相反地，他更多的是提出关于艺术媒介的本质以及表达的真实性等基础问题。他的短片作品，如《砸镜子》、《砸碎镜子》、《揉上海》以及《烧照片》等，记录了在特定场所对视觉幻象的破坏。从镜像到照片表现都是视觉幻想，而观众则被引导着对这些幻象的脆弱做出反思。

这些作品与许多其他作品都具有作者本身的特色：一种强调决裂和含糊性的自我表达风格。宋冬为

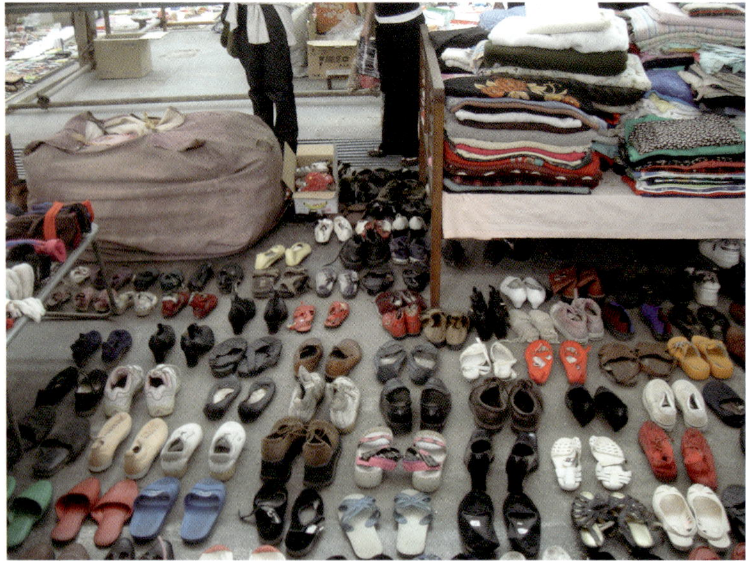

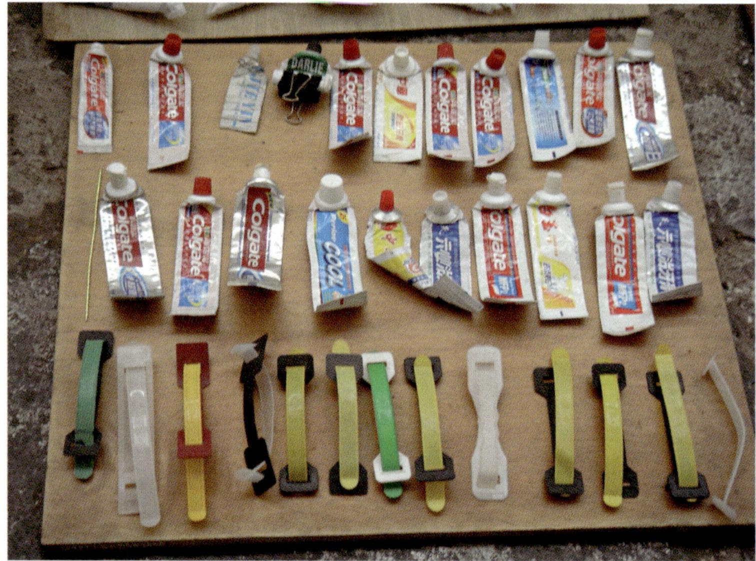

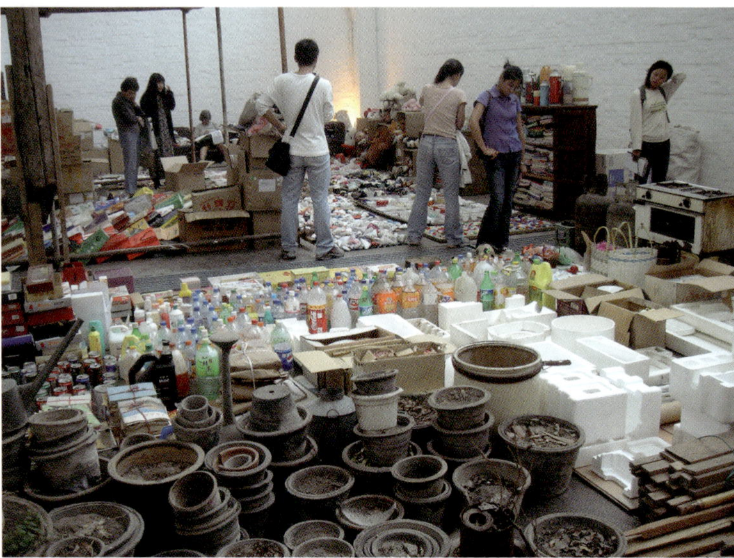

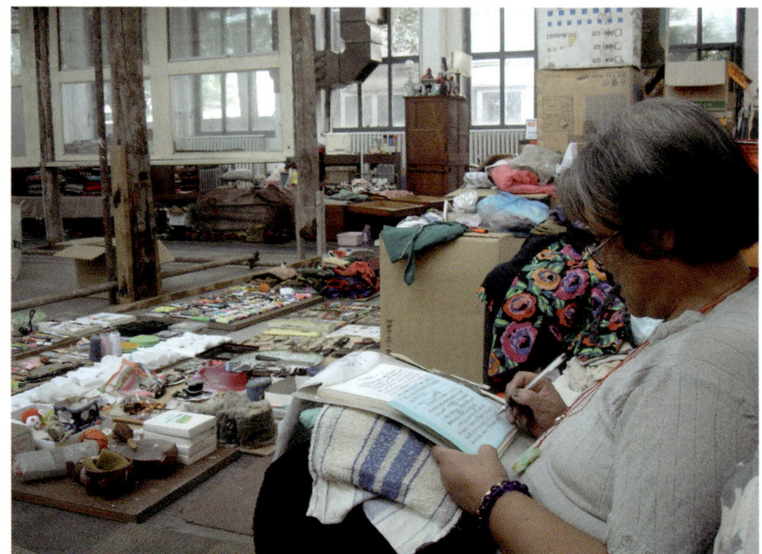

2

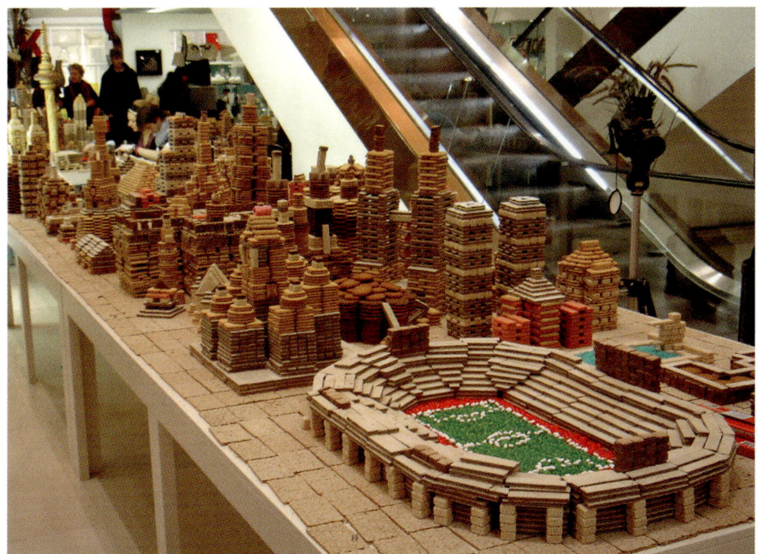

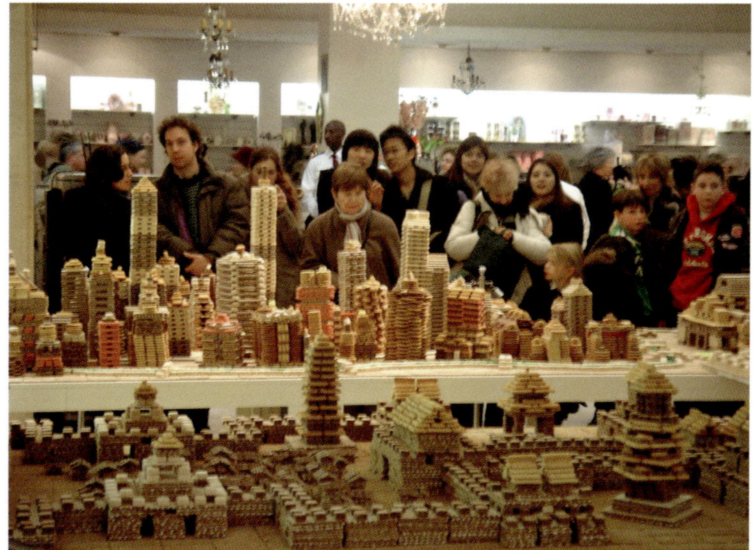

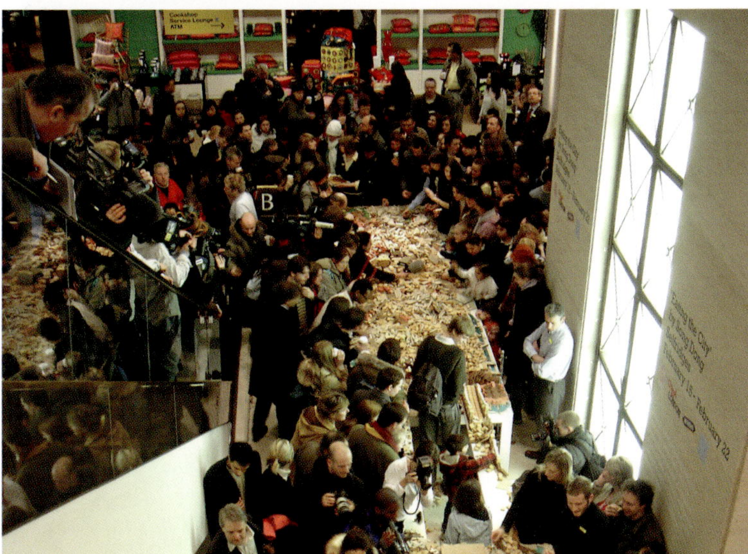
Cookshop
Service Lounge
ATM
by Song Dong
February 22

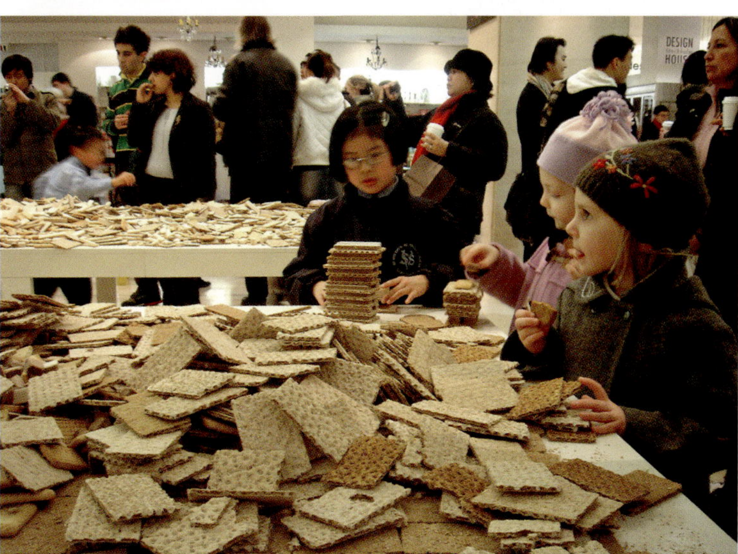
DESIGN

3

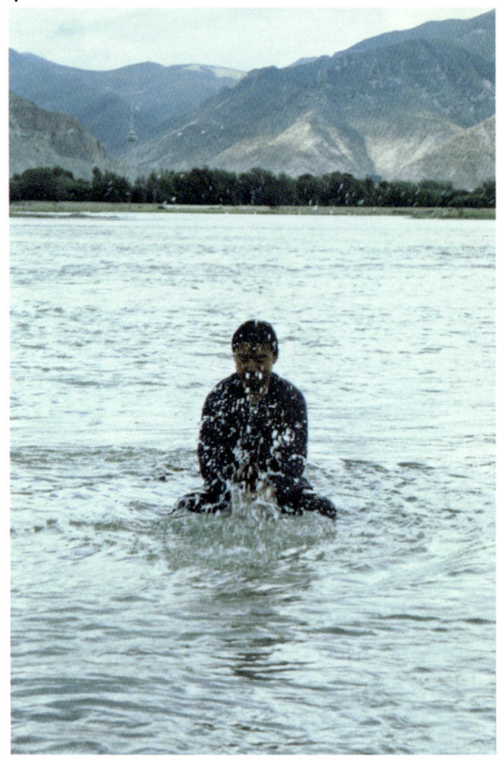

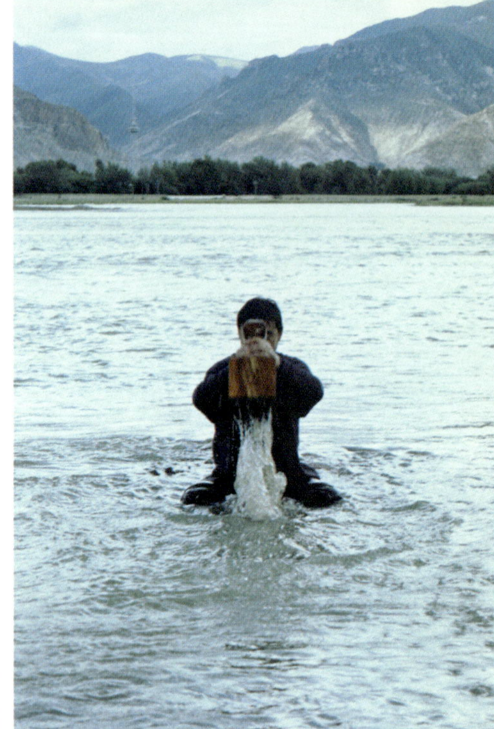

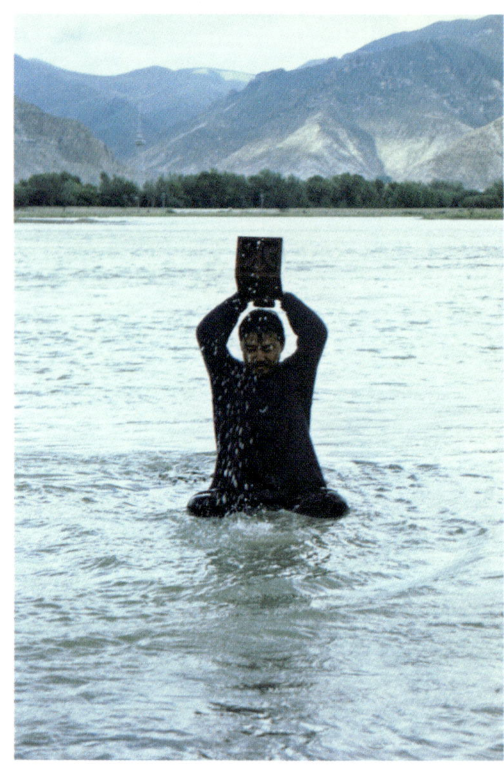

(2001), for example, record destructions of visual illusions at specific locations. The viewers are led to reflect upon the fragility of such illusions.

These and many other works feature the artist himself – a type of self-representation that emphasizes rupture and ambiguity. An outstanding example is a video installation Song created for the exhibition "It's Me" in 1998. Called "Father and Son in the Ancestral Temple", it was centred on a doubly exposed image of his own face and that of his father. His recent successful installation "Waste Not!" (2005), which won a grand prize at the 2006 Gwangju Biennial, again focused on his relationship with a family member, this time his mother. Comprised of all sorts of "junk" that his mother had saved over several decades, this enormous installation aroused strong reactions from various visitors.

Although generally labelled as a "conceptual artist," Song Dong derives his "concepts" from indigenous Chinese culture. As demonstrated by the titles of many of his works, these concepts often have a distinctive "vernacular" quality. Most of these titles cannot be translated into another language. Such difficulty in translation implies the local spectatorship Song Dong envisages for his art, and also implies his critique of the rapid globalisation of Chinese art.

Mirror, Broken Mirror" (1999), „Crumbling Shanghai" (2000) und „Burning Photograph" (2001), dokumentieren die Zerstörung visueller Illusionen an bestimmten Orten und nötigen den Betrachter, über die Zerbrechlichkeit solcher Illusionen nachzudenken. In diesen wie in vielen anderen Werken tritt der Künstler selbst auf – eine Form der Selbstdarstellung, die verwirrende Brüche und Mehrdeutigkeiten betont. Ein herausragendes Beispiel ist hier die Videoinstallation „Father and Son in the Ancestral Temple", die Song für die Ausstellung „It's Me" 1998 schuf; sie verarbeitet ein doppelt belichtetes Bild von seinem eigenen Gesicht und dem seines Vaters. Auch in seiner Installation „Waste Not!" (2005), die einen Großen Preis bei der Gwangju Biennale 2006 gewann, ging es um seine Beziehung zu einem Familienmitglied, diesmal zu seiner Mutter. Die riesige Installation präsentierte allen möglichen „Plunder", den seine Mutter im Laufe mehrerer Jahrzehnte gesammelt hatte, und löste bei manchen Besuchern starke Reaktionen aus.

Song Dong wird generell als Konzeptkünstler etikettiert, aber er bezieht seine Konzepte aus der überlieferten chinesischen Kultur. Wie viele seiner Werktitel zeigen, haben diese Konzepte oft etwas ausgeprägt „Volkstümliches". Viele Titel sind eigentlich unübersetzbar. Und solche Übersetzungsprobleme verweisen darauf, dass Song Dong mit seiner Kunst auf ein heimisches Publikum abzielt, zugleich illustrieren sie aber auch seine Kritik an der rasanten Globalisierung der chinesischen Kunst.

1998 年举行的《是我》展览所创作的录像装置作品《父子・太庙》便是一个绝佳的例子，作品的主题是他和他父亲面容的重合。他最近的成功装置作品《不要浪费》获得了 2006 年光洲双年展的一个特别奖项。作品再次将目标对准了他和一名家庭成员的关系，而这次则是他的母亲。作品由他母亲在数十年内所搜集的各种"没用的东西"所组成，这个巨大的装置作品唤起了各类观众的强烈反响。

尽管通常被当作"概念艺术家"，宋冬的"概念"来源于本土的中国文化。正如他许多作品标题所反映的那样，这些概念常常具有明显的"本土"气息。这些标题中的大多数都无法被译成其他语言。翻译的困难性意味着宋冬将自己艺术面向

Wu Hung

5

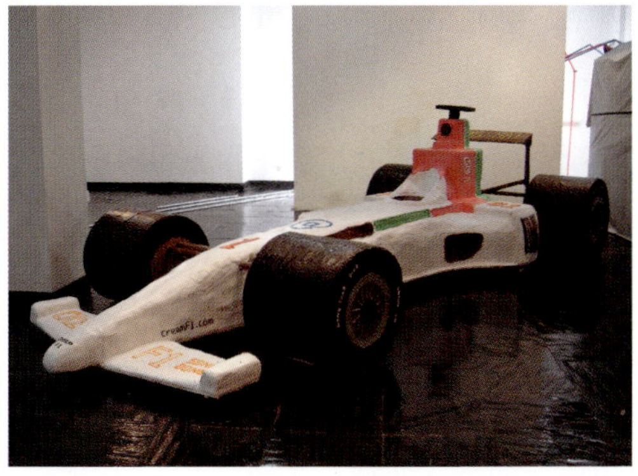

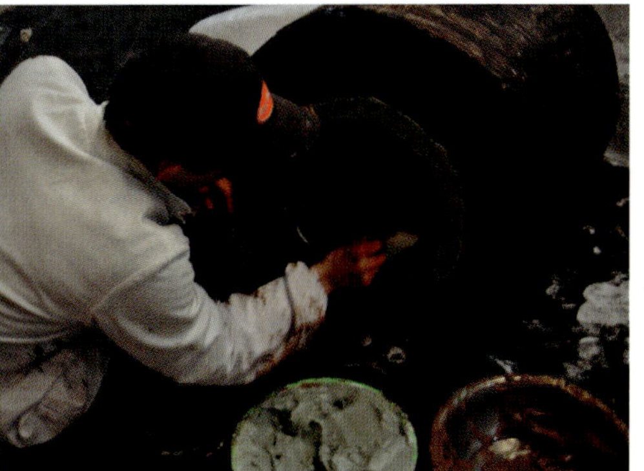

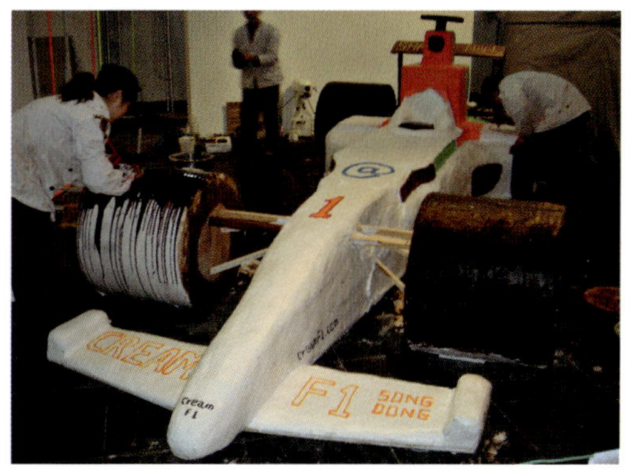

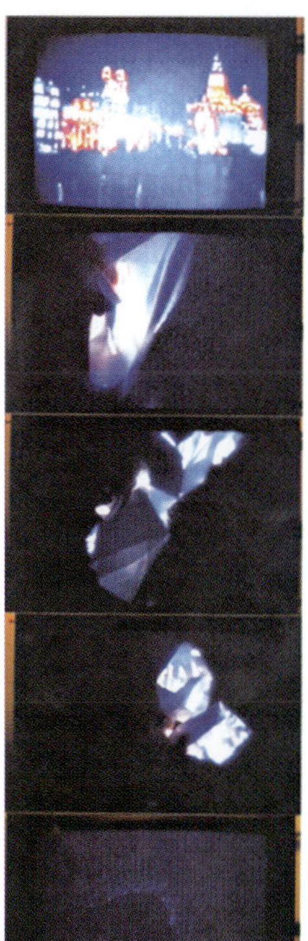

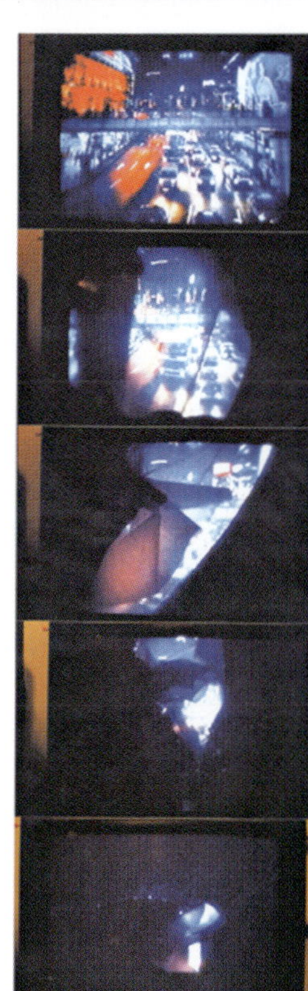

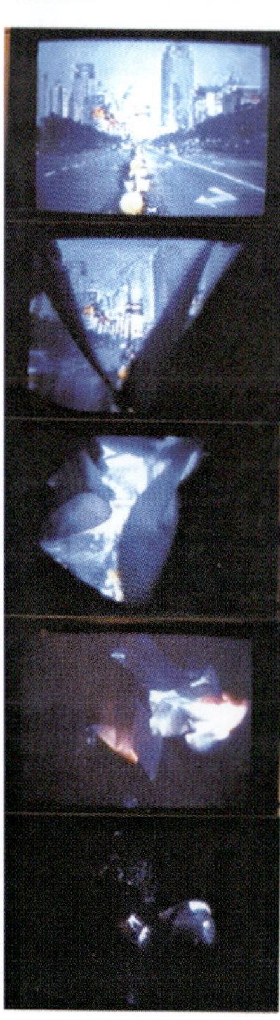

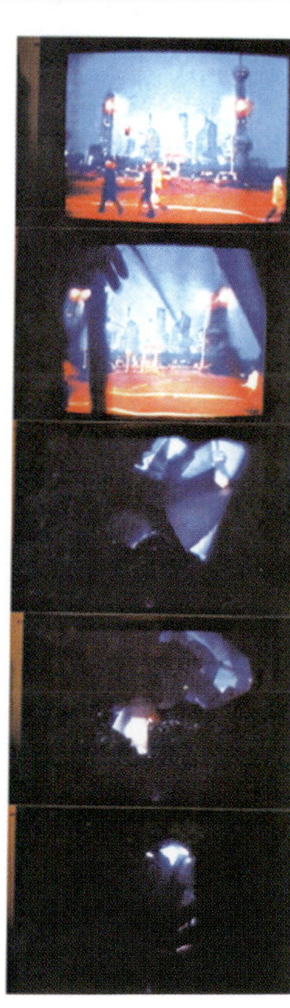

6

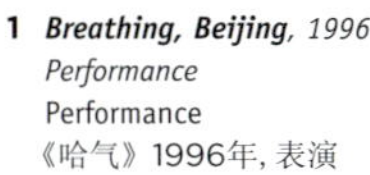

1 ***Breathing, Beijing***, *1996*
Performance
Performance
《哈气》1996年, 表演

2 ***Waste Not!***, *2005*
In collaboration with Zhao Xiangyuan, installation at Beijing Tokyo Art Project, Beijing
In Zusammenarbeit mit Zhao Xiangyuan, Installation bei Beijing Tokyo Art Project, Beijing
《不要浪费！》（与赵湘源合作）2005年, 装置

3 ***Eating the City – Beijing***, *2006*
Installation from biscuits at Selfridges, London
Installation aus Keksen bei Selfridges, London
《吃掉城市-北京》2006年, 饼干装置

4 ***Stamping the Water***, *1996*
Photographs, 120 x 80 each
Fotografien, je 120 x 80
《印水》1996年, 摄影，每幅, 120 x 80 cm

5 ***Cream***, *2005*
Installation
Installation
《奶油F1》2005年，装置

6 ***Crumpling Shanghai***, *2000*
Video installation
Video Installation
《揉上海》2000年, 录像装置

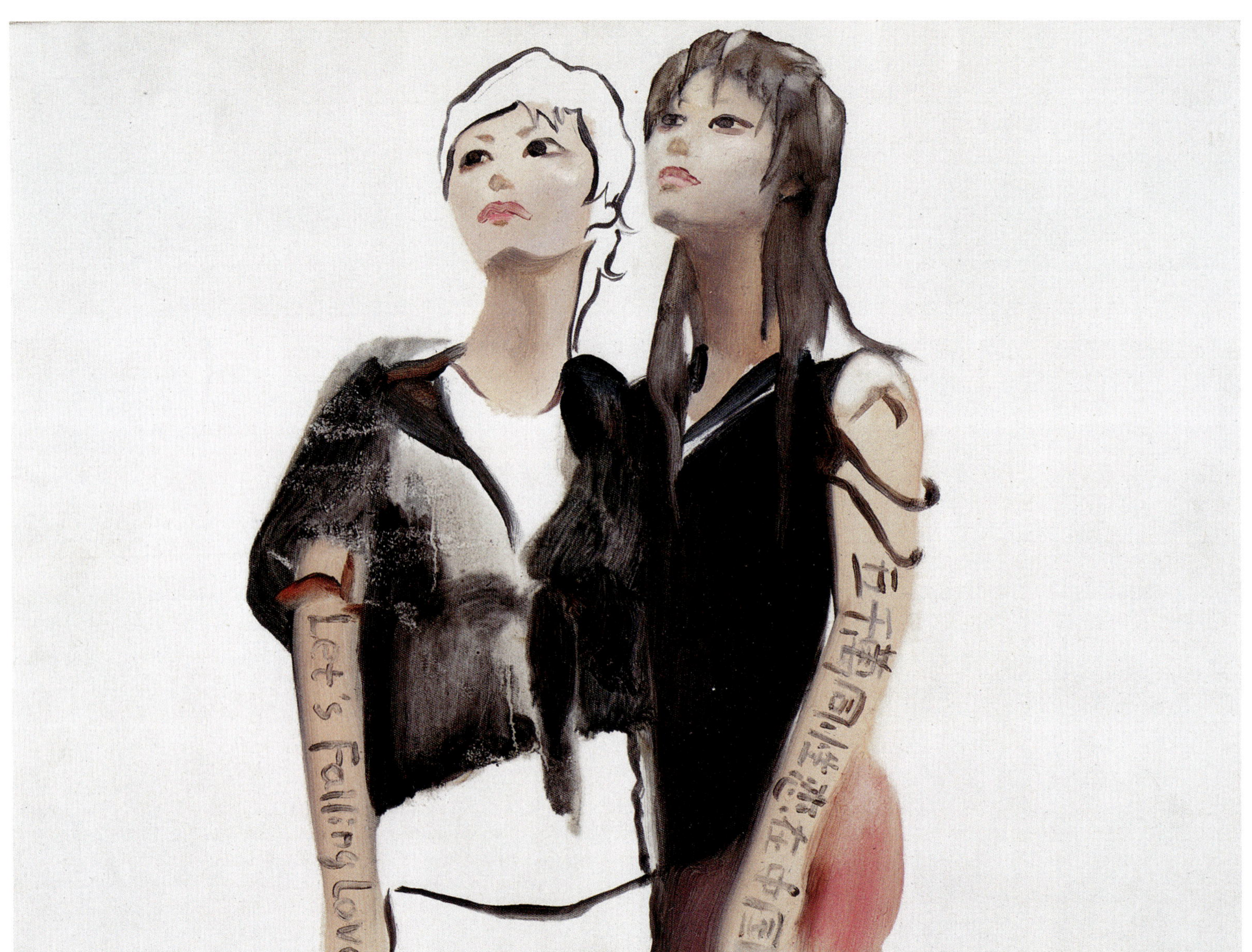

1

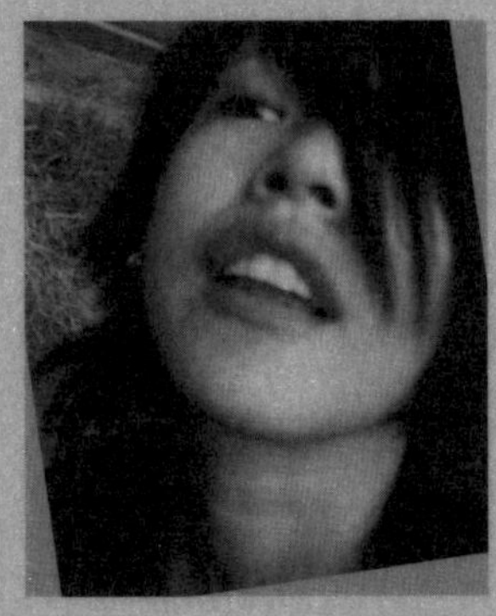

"What I experience, my emotion-filled life, is what I use to sort out my introspective thoughts."

„Was ich erlebe, mein von Gefühlen erfülltes Leben, das nutze ich, um meine innere Gedankenwelt zu ordnen."

"我所经历的，我的情感生活，常常是我自己总结的反省思想。"

Born in 1977 in Baotou, Inner Mongolia, China. Lives and works in Beijing
Geboren 1977 in Baotou, Innere Mongolei, China. Lebt und arbeitet in Peking
1977年出生于中国内蒙古包头市。现居住工作于北京

***Selected exhibitions* / Ausgewählte Ausstellungen / 所选展览**

2005 "Archaeology of the Future: The Second Triennial of Chinese Art", Nanjing Art Museum, Nanjing, China
2006 "It's My Life", UniversalStudios, Beijing, China
"Body – Boundary", Chambers Fine Art, New York, NY, USA
2007 "Song Kun", Armand Hammer Museum of Art, Los Angeles, CA, USA

2005年 《第二届中国艺术三年展--未来考古学》南京博物院 南京中国
2006年 《这就是我的生活》北京u空间 北京
《此身·界外》前波画廊，纽约
2007年 《宋琨》Armand Hammer 艺术博物馆, 洛杉矶

***Selected publications* / Ausgewählte Publikationen / 所选著作**

Pi Li (ed.): "Song Kun: It's My Life", Beijing 2006

Pi Li（著）:《宋琨--这就是我的生活》北京空间, 北京, 2006年

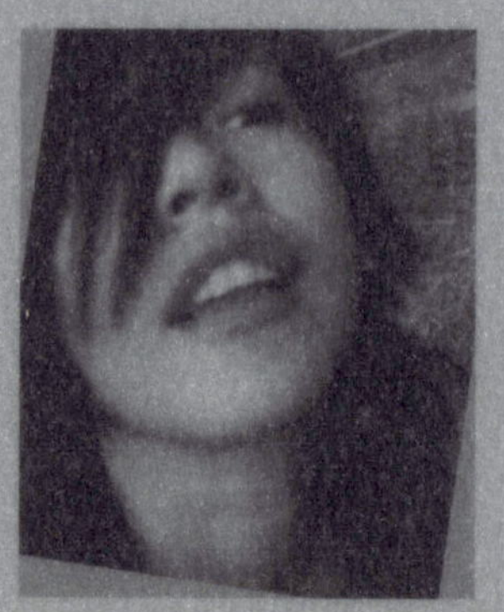

"What I experience, my emotion-filled life, is what I use to sort out my introspective thoughts."

„Was ich erlebe, mein von Gefühlen erfülltes Leben, das nutze ich, um meine innere Gedankenwelt zu ordnen."

"我所经历的，我的情感生活，常常是我自己总结的反省思想。"

Born in 1977 in Baotou, Inner Mongolia, China. Lives and works in Beijing
Geboren 1977 in Baotou, Innere Mongolei, China. Lebt und arbeitet in Peking
1977年出生于中国内蒙古包头市。现居住工作于北京

Selected exhibitions / Ausgewählte Ausstellungen / 所选展览

2005 "Archaeology of the Future: The Second Triennial of Chinese Art", Nanjing Art Museum, Nanjing, China
2006 "It's My Life", UniversalStudios, Beijing, China
"Body - Boundary", Chambers Fine Art, New York, NY, USA
2007 "Song Kun", Armand Hammer Museum of Art, Los Angeles, CA, USA

2005年 《第二届中国艺术三年展—未来考古学》南京博物院 南京中国
2006年 《这就是我的生活》北京u空间 北京
《此身・界外》前波画廊，纽约
2007年 《宋琨》Armand Hammer 艺术博物馆，洛杉矶

Selected publications / Ausgewählte Publikationen / 所选著作

Pi Li (ed.): "Song Kun: It's My Life", Beijing 2006

Pi Li（著）：《宋琨—这就是我的生活》北京空间，北京，2006年

SONG KUN 宋琨

[sʊŋ kʰuən]

A founding member of the "N12" group – twelve ambitious young graduates of Beijing's Central Academy of Fine Arts who have been organizing their own annual exhibitions since 2003 – artist Song Kun was educated after the Cultural Revolution and raised in an era of accelerated urban and economic development. As a result, she and her compatriots are articulating new visual languages to express concerns that are less overtly political than those of their predecessors.

A melancholic fog clouds many of Song's paintings, making them feel like slightly out of focus snapshots in which the air hangs thick and heavy, weighed down by a sense of loss. Flashes of light reflect back at the viewer, cutting through the haze and sharply contouring surfaces such as skin, metal, and glass. It's a technical trick that turns emotionally charged details into symbols in a vivid, fleeting, dream. Her faded pallet of silvery grays and pale sepias further denatures her subjects, giving them a fleeting quality, as though they are on the verge of vanishing, or viewed through the haze of memory.

Song's "It's My Life" (2005/06), the artist's first major solo project, is an enormous installation originally comprised of 365 small canvases, each representing a day in the artist's year (blank canvases indicate days of inactivity). Far more than an oil-on-canvas blog, "It's My Life" offers viewers a series of elliptical narratives and moody moments rendered with a lush, sometimes despondent beauty, becoming a case study in how painting can elevate the quotidian.

One particularly poignant painting depicts a young couple riding their bicycles through the moonlit night, enveloped in a mist that renders the image part fading memory, part wistful fantasy. In a diptych, a man and a woman face one another in profile, sitting beside the windows of a train or airplane. Illuminated by a mottled gray light, they seem to be contemplating the distance as it unfolds between them. Such images capture the simultaneous desire and inability to say goodbye characterizing the artist's overall

Die Künstlerin Song Kun ist Gründungsmitglied der Gruppe „N12" – zwölf ehrgeizige junge Absolventen der Pekinger Central Academy of Fine Arts, die seit 2003 ihre eigenen jährlichen Ausstellungen organisieren. Song erhielt ihre Ausbildung nach der Kulturrevolution und ist in einer Ära des rasanten städtischen und wirtschaftlichen Wachstums groß geworden. Folgerichtig entwickeln sie und ihre Mitstreiter neue visuelle Sprachen, um Anliegen auszudrücken, die nicht so offenkundig politisch sind wie die ihrer Vorgänger.

Ein Hauch von Melancholie liegt über vielen von Songs Gemälden und lässt sie wie leicht unscharfe Schnappschüsse erscheinen, auf deren Motiven eine schwere Atmosphäre lastet, die ein Gefühl des Verlusts heraufbeschwört. Lichtblitze zucken zurück zum Betrachter, durchschneiden den Dunstschleier und heben Flächen wie Haut, Metall und Glas scharf hervor. Dieser technische Trick verwandelt emotionsgeladene Details in Symbole innerhalb eines lebhaften, flüchtigen Traums. Songs verhaltene Palette aus silbrigen Grau- und blassen Sepiatönen macht ihre Motive noch unwirklicher und gibt ihnen etwas Flüchtiges, als stünden sie kurz vor dem Verschwinden oder würden durch den Nebelvorhang der Erinnerung gesehen.

Songs „It's My Life" (2005/06), das erste große Soloprojekt der Künstlerin, ist eine riesige Installation aus ursprünglich 365 kleinen Leinwänden, von denen jede einen Tag im Jahreslauf der Künstlerin darstellt (leere Leinwände zeugen von leeren Tagen). Dabei ist „It's My Life" nicht bloß ein Blog in Öl auf Leinwand. Vielmehr konfrontiert es die Betrachter mit einer Abfolge unvollständiger Erzählungen und melancholischer Momente, die – in üppiger, mitunter verzagter Schönheit ausgeführt – zu einer Fallstudie darüber geraten, wie die Malerei das Alltägliche erhöhen kann.

Ein besonders anrührendes Gemälde zeigt ein junges Paar, das auf Fahrrädern durch die mondhelle Nacht fährt, in einen Nebel gehüllt, der das Bild zu einem Mittelding zwischen verblassender Erinnerung und sehnsuchtsvoller Fantasie

12个意气风发的北京中央美院年轻毕业生，创立了N12，他们自2003年起就组织了其年展，宋琨便是其中之一，她在文化大革命后接受教育，成长于城市和经济发展之下。因此。她和她的同龄人善于用一种新得视觉语言去表达自己的关注，与其前辈相比，这些关注政治味道更少一些。

在宋琨的许多作品中，阴郁的雾气笼罩着画面，好似快拍镜头稍稍没有聚焦的，而产生空气浓重，垂垂欲坠的感觉。闪烁着的光线反射到观众身上，刺穿了浓云密雾和明显轮廓的表面，如皮肤，金属和玻璃等。其实那仅仅是技术上的把戏而已，在栩栩如生飞逝的梦境中 满含情感细节变为一个符号。她那褪色的银灰色和淡棕色调色盘进一步地改变了其主题，赋予它们一种飞逝的质感，好似 它们即将消逝或者 透过记忆的薄雾去看。

宋琨的《这就是我的生活》(2005-2006年),是 她的第一个大型 个人项目,这座庞大的装置由365幅小油画组成。每一幅代表着每年中的一天，（黑色代表没有活 动的一天）。《这就是我的生活》远非一个布面油画博客，给观众 连续简略的叙述和阴郁的片刻，呈现出一种浓郁却有时悲观的美。这在绘画如何每天都可以进行的研究中成为个案。

在一幅非常感人的油画里，描述了一对年轻夫妇 骑着自行车，穿过月光漫地的夜色，周围弥漫着薄薄的雾气，呈现出一幅逝去的回忆渴望的梦境。在一幅双折画中，一个男人和 女人侧面相对，处于 在火车或者飞机窗户的两侧。斑驳的灰白光线照耀着，它们似乎在 凝思与这一 距离，因为它隔断了他们。这样的图片捕捉了两者同时的欲望和想说再见，却无能为力的瞬间。刻画了艺术家对过去的全部关系，整个装置蒙上一股浓浓的思乡情。有时，单独的事件要通过连续的日子才可以探索到，显示在作者串联细节、讲述故事的才智：展现在图片上的夜间婚宴，如婚服上的刺绣折边，百合和玫瑰的组合，以及蜜月旅馆房间的模糊。即使宋琨最简单

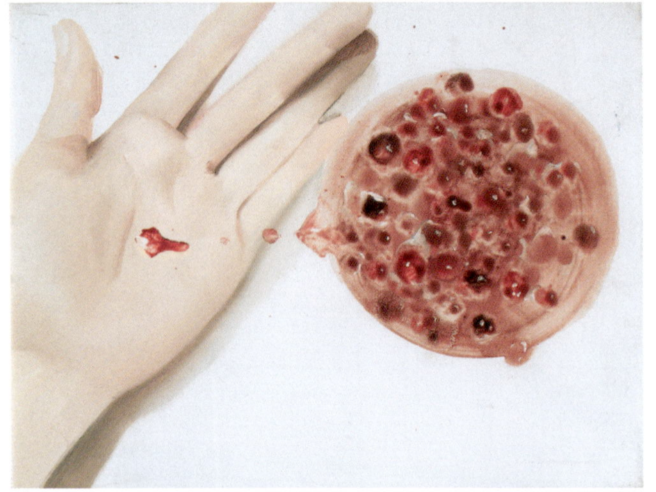

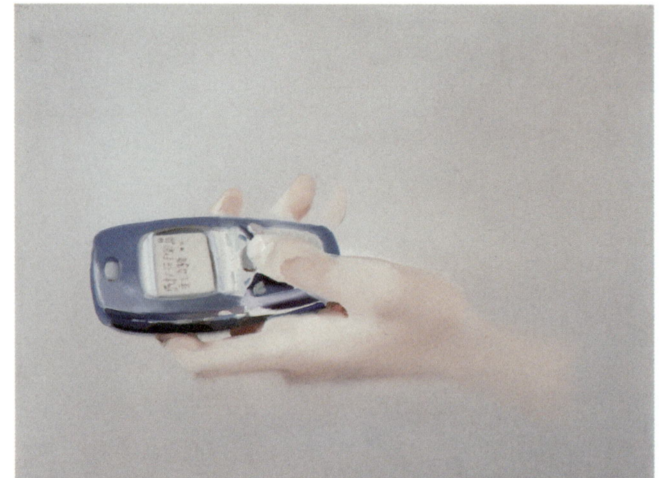

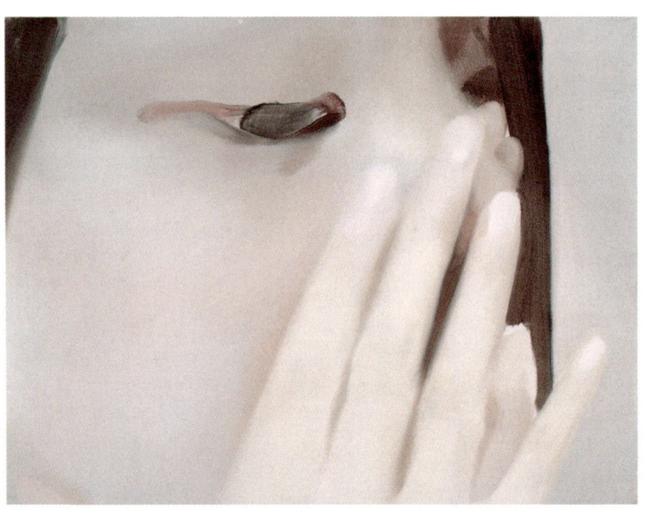

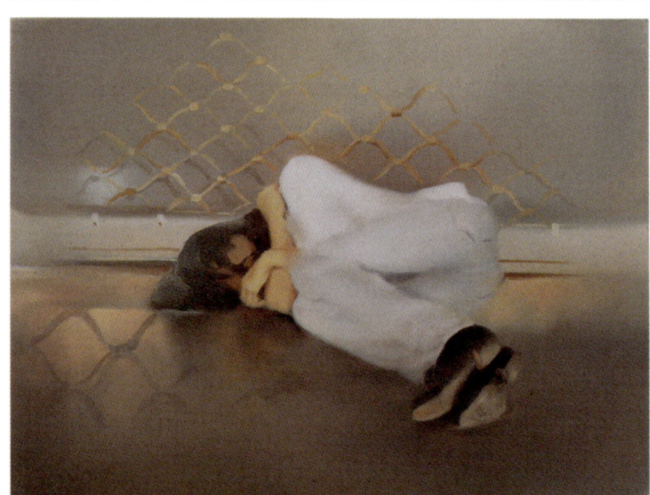

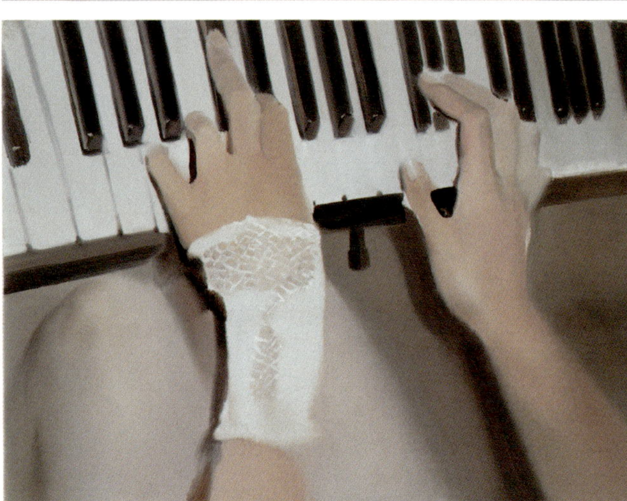

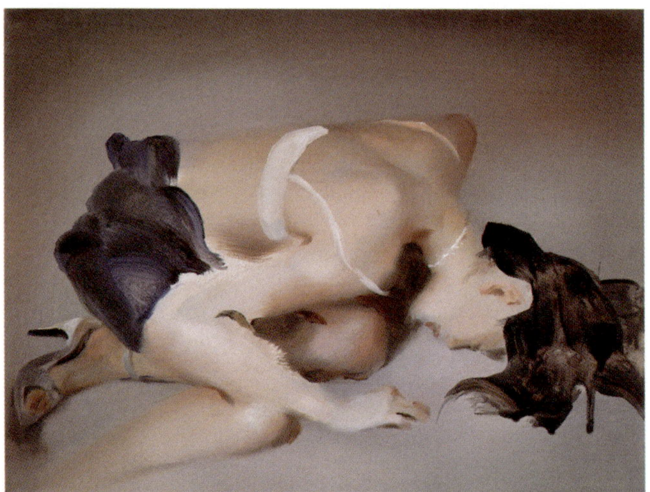

2

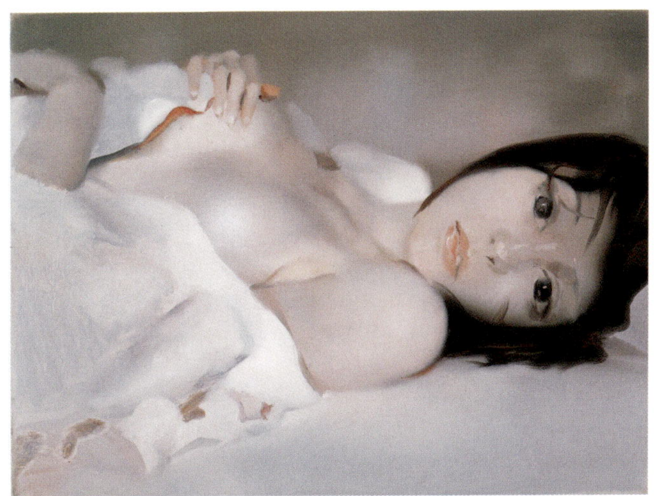

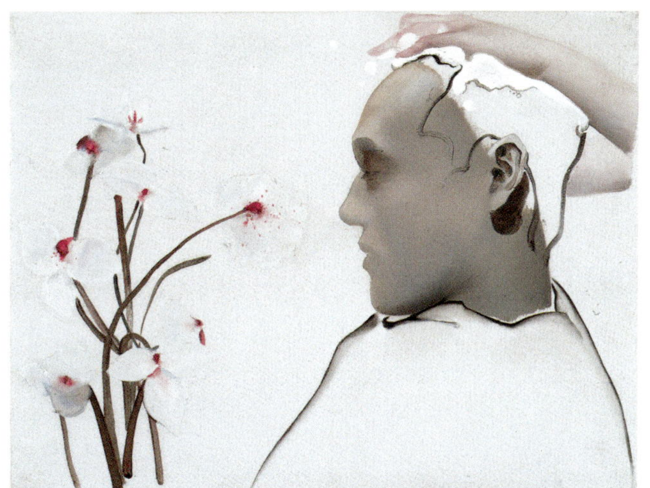

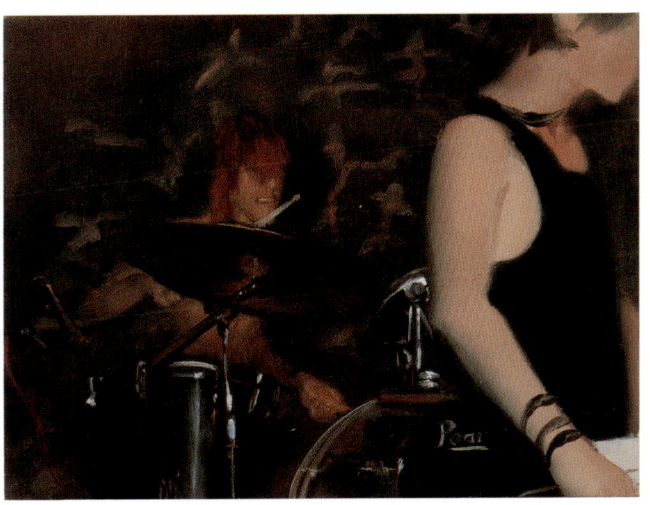

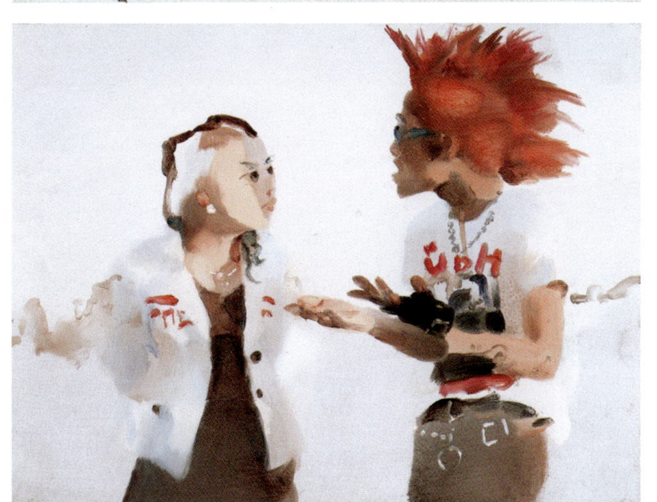

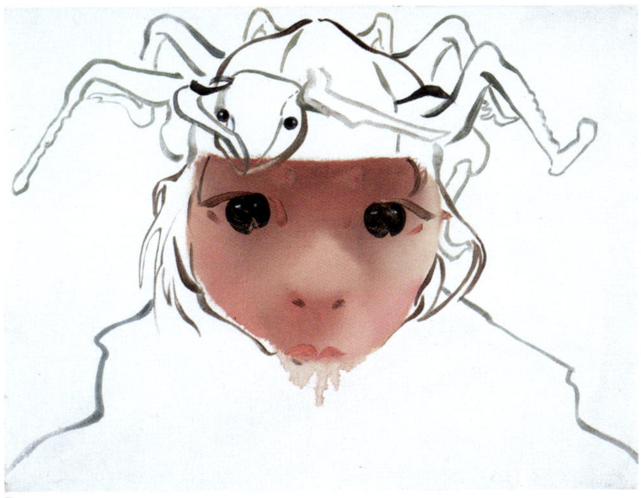

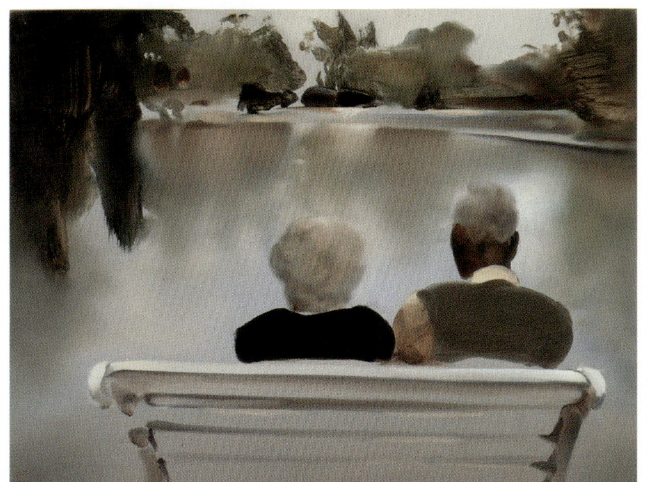

3

4

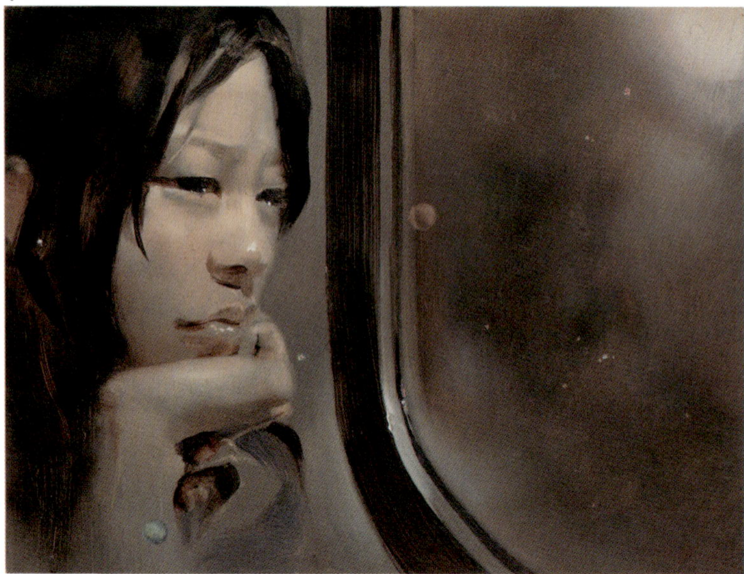

5

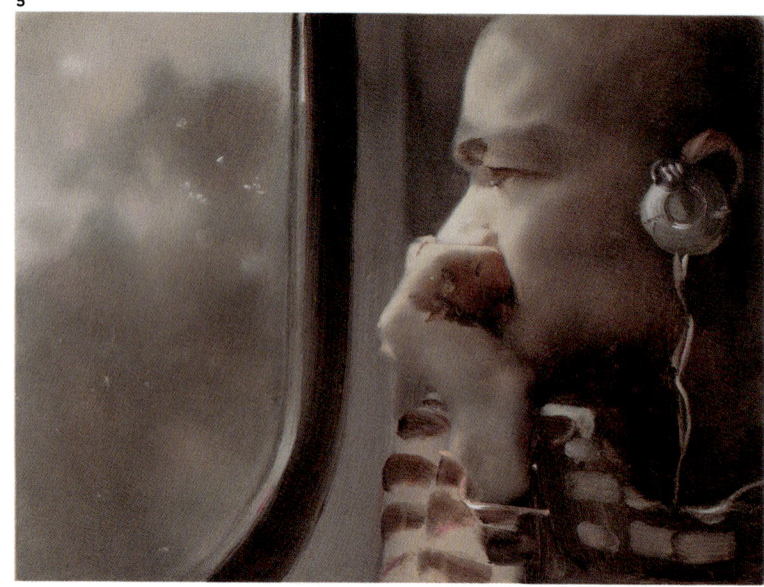

relationship to the past, a weary nostalgia that shadows the entire installation. Sometimes a single event is explored over a series of days, revealing the artist's gift for storytelling through her selection of details: an evening wedding unfolds in images such as the embroidered hem of a wedding gown, a floral arrangement of stargazer lilies and pink roses, and the dim interior of a honeymoon hotel room. Even in Song's simplest works, everyday objects are transformed into parts of a rebus that articulates her inner life.

The work of Song Kun marks a changing of the guard in China. Without lapsing into narcissism, her work gives viewers a very contemporary glimpse into days and dreams of Beijing's youth, but ultimately Song's finely crafted paintings invite us to meditate on the emotionally charged, fragmentary moments that constitute our own lives.

macht. Auf einem zweigeteilten Bild sitzen ein Mann und eine Frau einander im Profil gegenüber an den Fenstern eines Zugs oder Flugzeugs. Von fleckig grauem Licht beleuchtet, scheinen sie der Ferne nachzusinnen, die sich zwischen ihnen auftut.

Solche Bilder spiegeln das Hin- und Hergerissensein zwischen dem Wunsch und der Unfähigkeit, Abschied zu nehmen, das die gesamte Beziehung der Künstlerin zur Vergangenheit prägt, eine leicht überdrüssige Nostalgie, die die Installation überschattet. Mitunter wird ein einzelnes Ereignis über mehrere Tage durchgearbeitet, wobei sich die erzählerische Begabung der Künstlerin in ihrer Auswahl der Details offenbart: Eine abendliche Hochzeit entfaltet sich in dem bestickten Saum eines Brautkleids, einem Blumenarrangement aus Lilien und rosa Rosen und dem dämmrigen Interieur eines Flitterwochen-Hotelzimmers. Selbst in Songs schlichtesten Arbeiten verwandeln sich alltägliche Gegenstände in Teile eines Bilderrätsels, in dem sich ihr Innenleben artikuliert.

Das Werk von Song Kun ist Zeugnis einer Wachablösung in China. Ohne in Narzissmus zu verfallen, gewährt ihre Kunst den Betrachtern einen aktuellen Einblick in die Träume der Jugend von Peking, aber letztlich fordern uns Songs sorgfältig gearbeitete Gemälde dazu auf, über die emotionsgeladenen, bruchstückhaften Momente nachzusinnen, aus denen sich unser eigenes Leben zusammensetzt.

的作品中，日常生活物品都是谜的，这也揭示了她内心的生活。

宋琨这幅作品标志着中国青年的变化。宋的作品没有陷入自我陶醉之中，而让观众瞥见了当代北京青年的生活和梦想，最终宋琨精心制作的油画让我们沉思与充满情感，断断续续的时刻中，那些时刻组成 我们自己的生活。

David Spalding

6

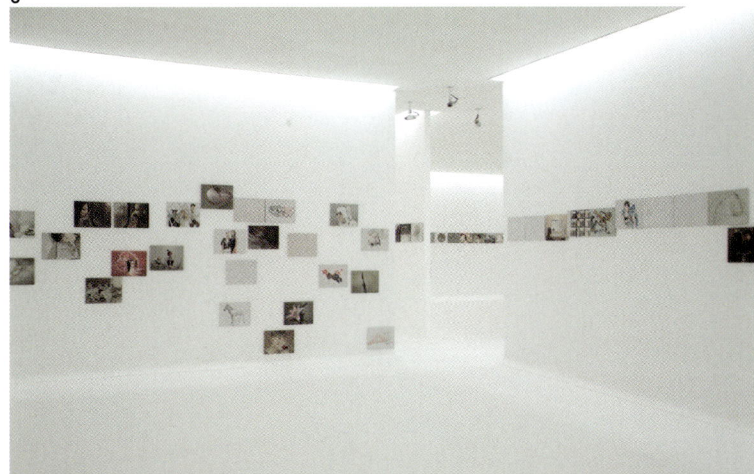

7

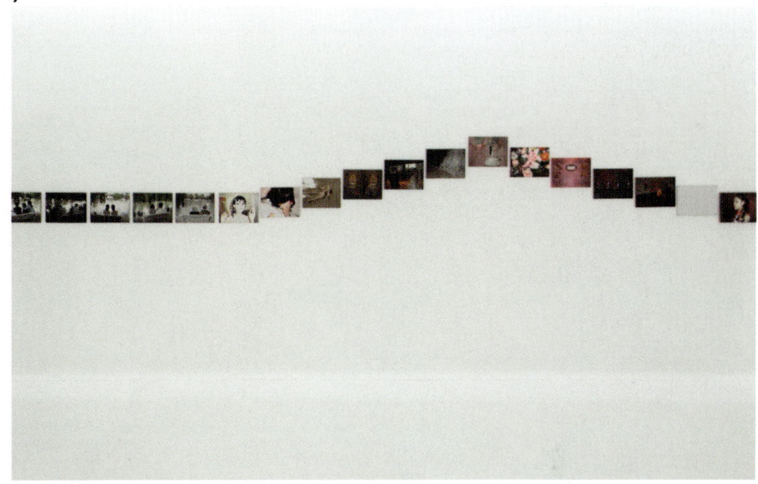

8

1–5 ***It's My Life***, *2005/06*
365 paintings, 27 x 35 cm each
365 Gemälde, je 27 x 35 cm
《这就是我的生活》2005/06年, 365幅油画，每幅 27 x 35 cm

6–8 ***It's My Life***, *2005/06*
Installation view, UniversalStudios, Beijing 2006
Installationsansicht, UniversalStudios, Peking 2006
《这就是我的生活》2005/06年, 装置

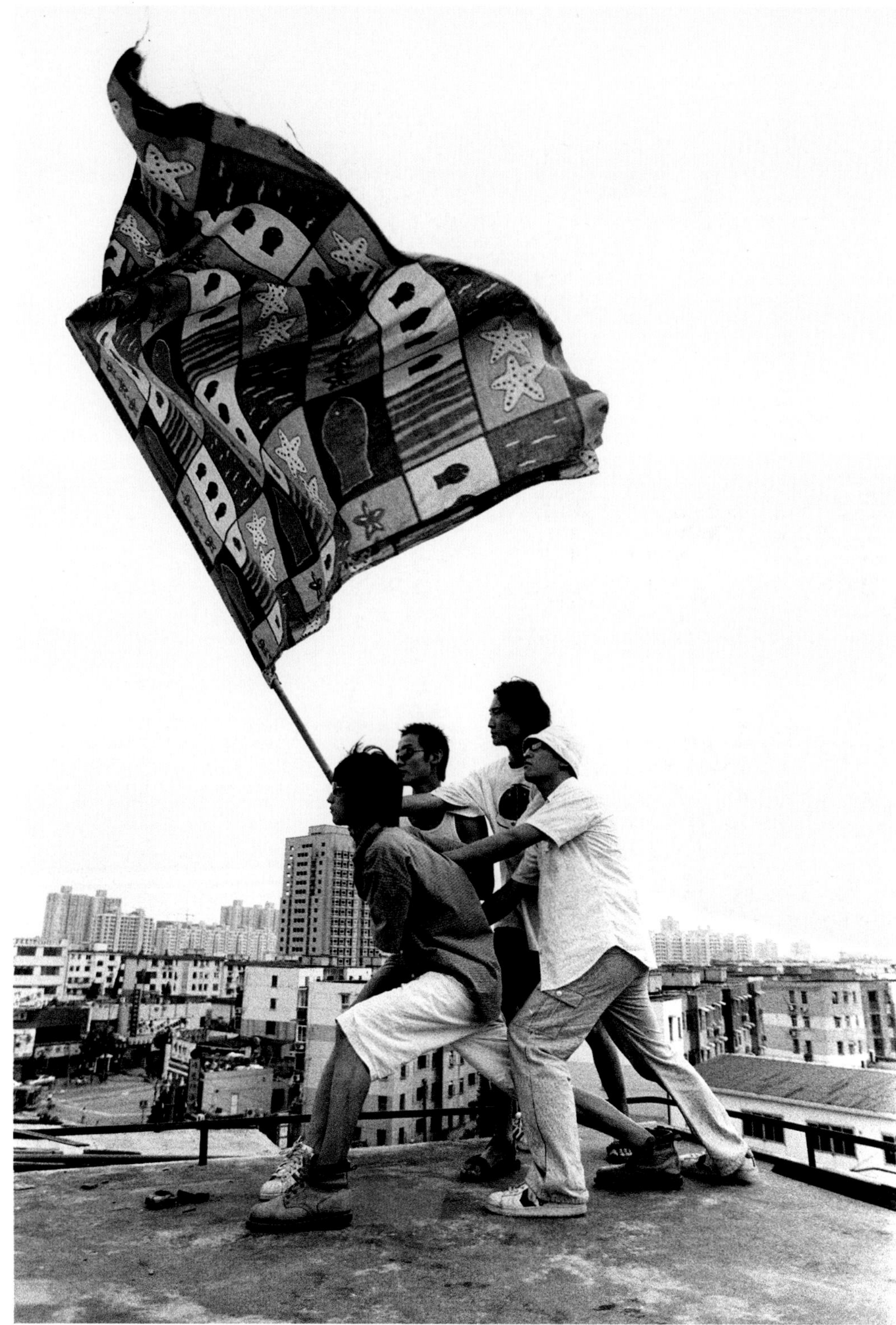

1

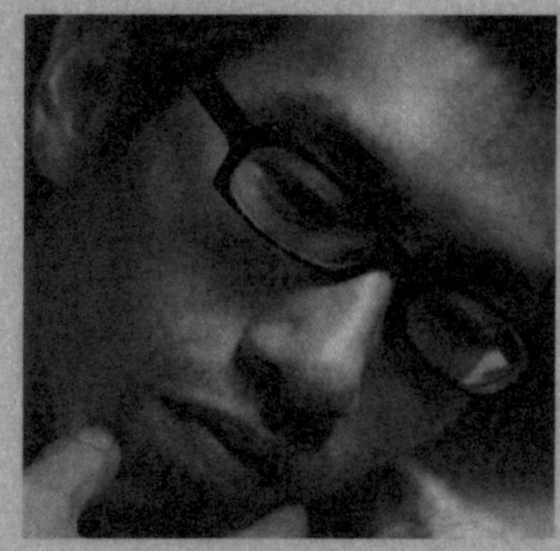

"All the cities in the world have their photographers and we are glad to be Shanghai's."

„Alle großen Städte der Welt haben ihre ‚Hoffotografen' und wir sind glücklich, die von Shanghai zu sein."

"全世界所有城市都有她们自己的摄影师，我们很乐意成为上海的摄影师。"

Born in 1979 in Shanghai, China. Lives and works in Shanghai
Geboren 1979 in Shanghai, China. Lebt und arbeitet in Shanghai
1979年出生于中国上海，居住工作在上海

Selected exhibitions **/ Ausgewählte Ausstellungen /** 所选展览

2005 "Song Tao: One Day...", ShanghART Gallery, Shanghai, China
2005–07 "Mahjong – Chinesische Gegenwartskunst aus der Sammlung Sigg", Kunstmuseum Bern, Berne, Switzerland; Hamburger Kunsthalle, Hamburg, Germany; Museum der Moderne, Salzburg, Austria
2006 "Alllooksame? Art from China, Japan and Korea", Fondazione Sandretto Re Rebaudengo, Turine, Italy
"Restless, Photography and New Media", Museum of Contemporary Art, Shanghai, China
"China Contemporary", Museum Boijmans Van Beuningen, Rotterdam, The Netherlands
2006/07 "China Power Station I", Battersea Power Station, Serpentine Gallery, London, UK; Astrup Fearnley Museum of Modern Art, Oslo, Norway

2005年 《有一天》上海香格纳画廊，上海
2005–07年 《麻将》西克中国当代艺术收藏展 伯尔尼美术馆 瑞士；汉堡美术馆，汉堡，德国；萨尔茨保现代美术馆，奥地利
2006年 《看上去都一样》中日韩当代艺术展，都灵，意大利
《无休无止:摄影与新媒体艺术》上海当代艺术馆
《中国当代》波伊曼·凡·布宁根博物馆，鹿特丹 荷兰
2006/07 《中国电站I》蛇形画廊，巴特西电站 伦敦 英国；Astrup Fearnley 现代美术馆 奥斯陆 挪威

Selected publications **/ Ausgewählte Publikationen /** 所选著作

Bernhard Fibicher, Matthias Frehner (eds.): "Mahjong: Contemporary Chinese Art from the Sigg Collection", Ostfildern-Ruit 2005
Uta Grosenick, Sine Bepler (eds.): "ShanghART 10 Years", Cologne 2006

Fibicher, Bernhard/Frehner, Matthias（编者）:《麻将－西克的当代艺术收藏展》，Ostfildern-Ruit 2005年
Grosenick, Uta/Bepler, Sine（编者）:《10年的香格纳画廊》科隆2006年

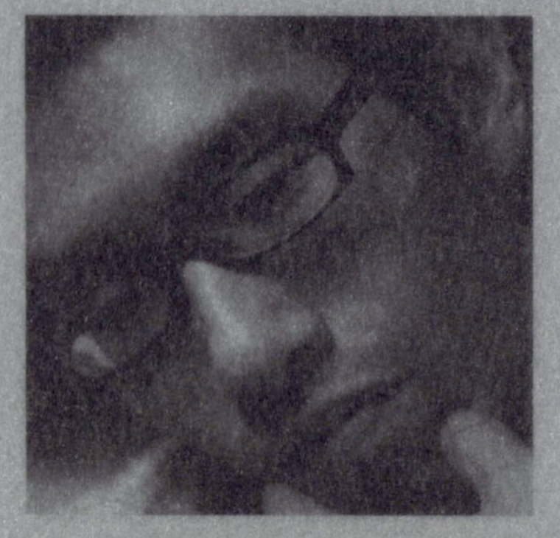

"All the cities in the world have their photographers and we are glad to be Shanghai's."

„Alle großen Städte der Welt haben ihre ‚Hoffotografen' und wir sind glücklich, die von Shanghai zu sein."

"全世界所有城市都有她们自己的摄影师，我们很乐意成为上海的摄影师。"

Born in 1979 in Shanghai, China. Lives and works in Shanghai
Geboren 1979 in Shanghai, China. Lebt und arbeitet in Shanghai
1979年出生于中国上海，居住工作在上海

Selected exhibitions / Ausgewählte Ausstellungen / 所选展览

2005	"Song Tao: One Day...", ShanghART Gallery, Shanghai, China
2005–07	"Mahjong – Chinesische Gegenwartskunst aus der Sammlung Sigg", Kunstmuseum Bern, Berne, Switzerland; Hamburger Kunsthalle, Hamburg, Germany; Museum der Moderne, Salzburg, Austria
2006	"Alllooksame? Art from China, Japan and Korea", Fondazione Sandretto Re Rebaudengo, Turine, Italy
	"Restless, Photography and New Media", Museum of Contemporary Art, Shanghai, China
	"China Contemporary", Museum Boijmans Van Beuningen, Rotterdam, The Netherlands
2006/07	"China Power Station I", Battersea Power Station, Serpentine Gallery, London, UK; Astrup Fearnley Museum of Modern Art, Oslo, Norway

2005年	《有一天》上海香格纳画廊，上海
2005–07年	《麻将》西克中国当代艺术收藏展 伯尔尼美术馆 瑞士；汉堡美术馆，汉堡，德国；萨尔茨堡现代美术馆，奥地利
2006年	《看上去都一样》中日韩当代艺术展，都灵，意大利
	《无休无止:摄影与新媒体艺术》上海当代艺术馆
	《中国当代》波伊曼・凡・布宁根博物馆，鹿特丹 荷兰
2006/07	《中国电站I》蛇形画廊，巴特西电站 伦敦 英国；Astrup Fearnley 现代美术馆 奥斯陆 挪威

Selected publications / Ausgewählte Publikationen / 所选著作

Bernhard Fibicher, Matthias Frehner (eds.): "Mahjong: Contemporary Chinese Art from the Sigg Collection", Ostfildern-Ruit 2005
Uta Grosenick, Sine Bepler (eds.): "ShanghART 10 Years", Cologne 2006

Fibicher, Bernhard/Frehner, Matthias（编者）:《麻将—西克的当代艺术收藏展》，Ostfildern-Ruit 2005年
Grosenick, Uta/Bepler, Sine（编者）:《10年的香格纳画廊》科隆2006年

SONG TAO 宋涛

[sʊŋ thaʊ]

One of the youngest among Shanghai's vital community of video artists, Song Tao has been exhibiting since he graduated from the Shanghai School of Arts and Crafts in 1998 having participated in the notorious "Fuck Off!" exhibition (2000). Working alternatively in photograph and video, Song Tao builds environments from his images, encapsulating the viewer in a total sensory experience.

The "Floor – Life is Wonderful" (2003), literally tiled the floor of ShanghART Gallery's exhibition space with 3,000 black-and-white photographs taken by the artist. Song Tao chose these pictures from more than 20,000 that he had taken between January and July 2003 as a visual diary of his life in Shanghai. The photographs, mounted on the parquet floor and sealed in varnish, were energetic documents, far more personal than photojournalism. The walls of the gallery were left empty and visitors had to crouch down or bend over to view the exhibition. In "One Day – Sky and Grass" (2005), he again covered the gallery floor, this time with photographs of grass while a mural sized print of a blue sky hung from the ceiling.

Song Tao is as known for his collaborations with other artists as his solo projects. In 2004, he joined another young photographer, Ji Weiyu, and formed "Bird Head". In this persona, this duo publishes an annual catalogue and creates exhibitions every other year. "Bird Head" also has its own attitude, sweet and naïve, as when the artists' write "Our hearts are filled with huge amounts of love and sadness."

In contrast, Song Tao collaborations with DJ B6 are far more influenced by the hard edge aesthetic of Electronica. This team has produced two major art works: "Three Days Ago" (2005) and "Yard" (2006), both of which incorporate sound, music and installation into the final piece. "Three Days Ago" is a video, filled with eerie views of Shanghai at night, scored to a throbbing electronic soundtrack. Projected in a darkened room on a loop, it creates a dense and haunting atmosphere, rather than deliver a linear narrative.

Obwohl einer der Jüngsten in der vitalen Videokünstlerszene von Shanghai, gelang es Song Tao gleich nach seinem Abschluss an der Shanghai School of Arts and Crafts 1998 und dank seiner Teilnahme an der berühmt-berüchtigten Schau „Fuck Off!" (2000), mit seinen Werken in vielen Ausstellungen präsent zu sein. Song Tao arbeitet einmal mit Fotografie, dann mit Video und schafft mit seinen Bildern ein Ambiente, das den Betrachter in einem sensorischen Gesamterlebnis einkapselt.

Für „The Floor – Life is Wonderful" (2003) pflasterte der Künstler den Boden der ShanghART Gallery buchstäblich mit 3000 von ihm aufgenommenen Schwarzweißfotografien. Er konnte dazu aus über 20 000 Bildern auswählen, die er zwischen Januar und Juli 2003 als Bildtagebuch seines Lebens in Shanghai geschossen hatte. Die auf dem Parkettboden montierten und mit Lack versiegelten Fotografien erschienen als persönliche Dokumente weit eindringlicher als die Produkte eines distanzierten Fotojournalismus. Die Wände der Galerie blieben leer, und die Besucher mussten sich hinhocken oder bücken, um die Ausstellung zu betrachten. Für „One Day – Sky and Grass" (2005) bedeckte Song Tao den Fußboden der Galerie erneut – diesmal mit Fotos von Gras; die grüne Landschaft wurde von einem künstlichen blauen Himmel überwölbt, der von der Decke herabhing.

Ebenso bekannt wie seine Soloprojekte wurden auch Song Taos Kooperationen mit anderen Künstlern. 2004 schloss er sich mit Ji Weiyu, einem jungen Fotografen, zu „Bird Head" zusammen. In dieser Rolle gibt das Duo alljährlich einen Katalog heraus und veranstaltet alle zwei Jahre eine Ausstellung. „Bird Head" entwickelte eine eigene provokant naive Persönlichkeit – so wenn die Künstler eindringlich verkünden: „Unsere Herzen sind von großer Liebe und Traurigkeit erfüllt."

Im Gegensatz dazu ist Song Taos Zusammenarbeit mit DJ B6 stark von der Hard-Edge-Ästhetik der Electronic-Music geprägt. Das Team hat bislang zwei größere Kunstwerke hervorgebracht: „Three Days Ago" (2005) und „Yard" (2006).

宋涛是上海重要录象艺术家组织中最年轻的成员之一，1998年从上海工艺美校起就开始展出作品，于2000年参与了著名的展览《不合作方式》。宋涛在摄影和录象两者之间创作，从自身的形象起营造令观众沉浸在完全是亲身体验的氛围。

2003年的展览《有内容的地板》，实际上是用作者的3000幅黑白摄影作品铺满了上海香格纳画廊的展厅。这些照片选自其2003年一月到七月所拍摄的20,000余幅摄影作品，宋涛把这3,000多幅照片作为他在上海生活的可视记录。全部摄影作品与木地板打磨在一起，表层还上了油漆，照片另人印象深刻，比照相新闻学有更多的个人的色彩。照片占满了整个展厅，没有留出行走的地方，所以在看展览的时候，观众必须趴下来贴近地板，不断地移动着。在《有一天》中，宋涛又一次的用照片铺满画廊的地板，这次是青草的照片，而在展厅上顶捕悬挂着画有蓝天的壁画。

宋以与其他艺术家合作创作来展出个展而著称。在2004年，他和青年摄影家季炜煜共同宋涛与年轻摄影师季炜煜合作，他们的小组叫“鸟头”。每年，“鸟头”都编辑一本画册，每两年，他们做一次展览。“鸟人”也有自己自己的生活态度，天真可爱。他们写到：我们的心因为太多的爱和忧伤而被填满。相对的，与DJ B6的合作更多是受坚硬边缘电子音乐审美的影响。他们的小组创作了两部主要的艺术作品，2005年《三天前》和2006年的《庭院》。

两部作品都融合了声音，音乐和装置。录象《三天前》中充满着上海夜晚令人毛骨悚然的景象，并配以难听的电子音带。作品在滑道上的暗室里拍摄，营造了烟雾蒙胧和令人难以忘记的气氛，而不是叙事情节。《庭院》设置成一个狭窄的走廊的方式，里面播放着录象镜头。进入装置里观众，立即陷入迷失的状态，体验艺术作品却如同突然步入了另一个世界。录象放映源在两面墙上神奇地同时出现，不可

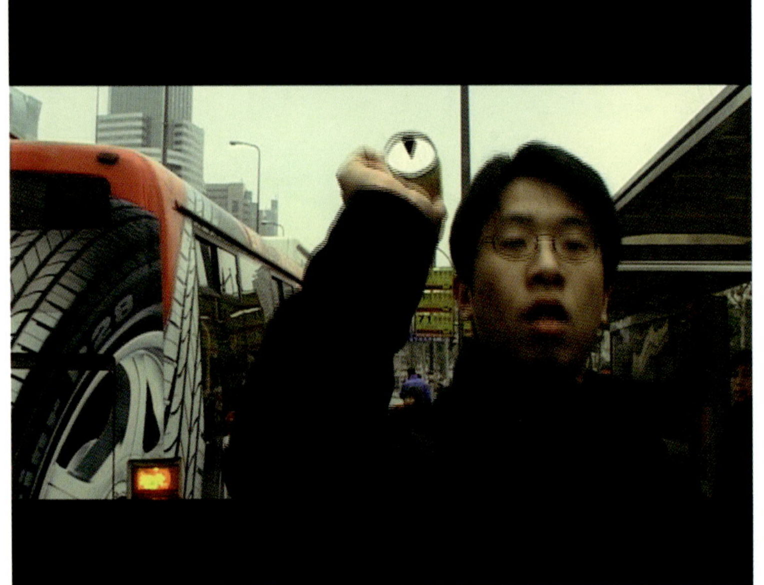

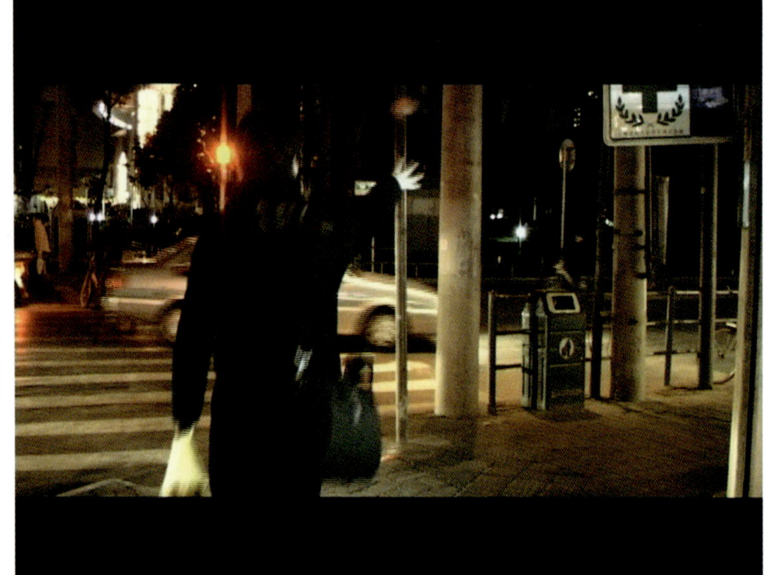

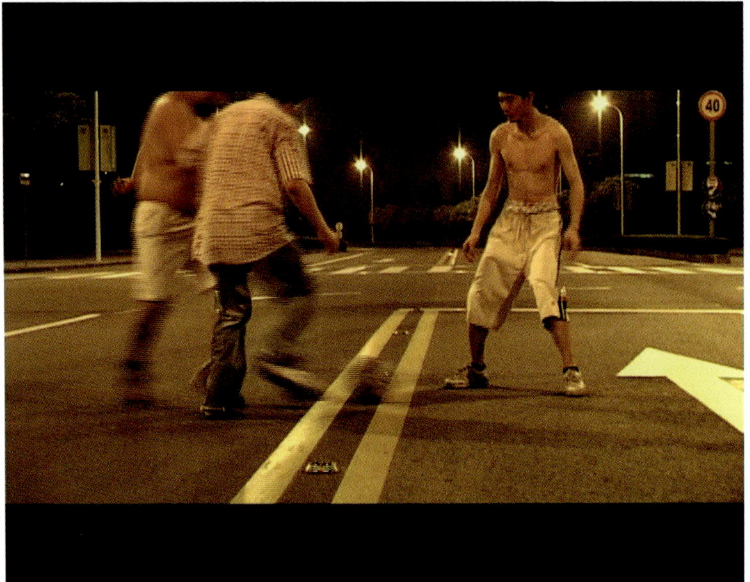

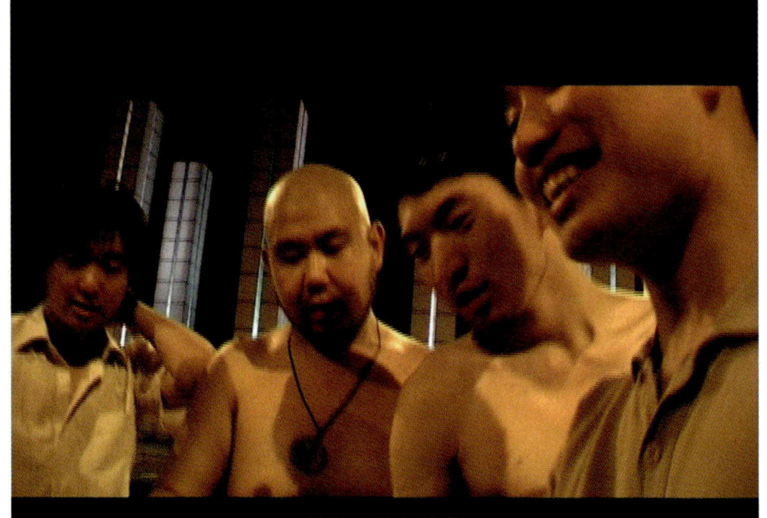

2

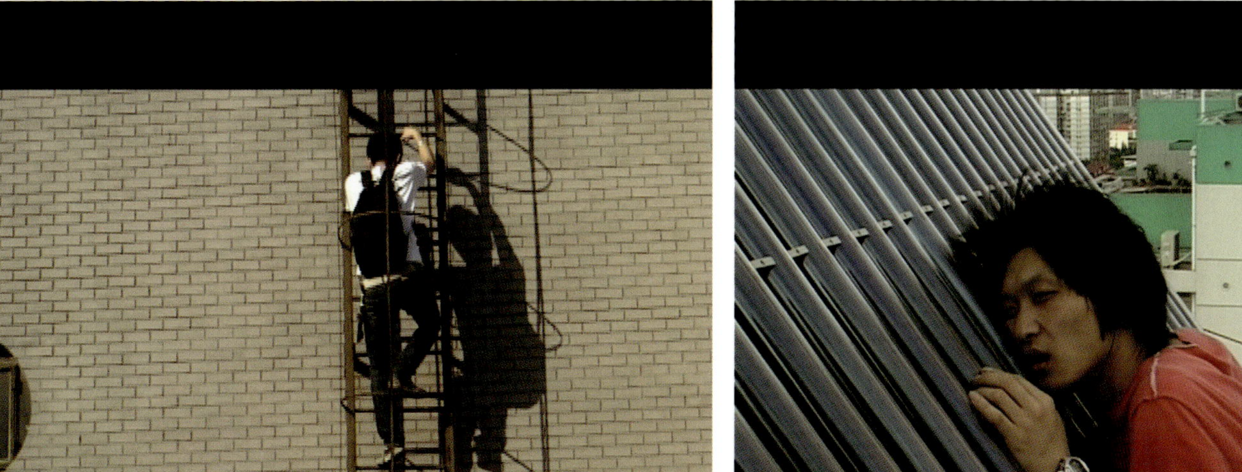

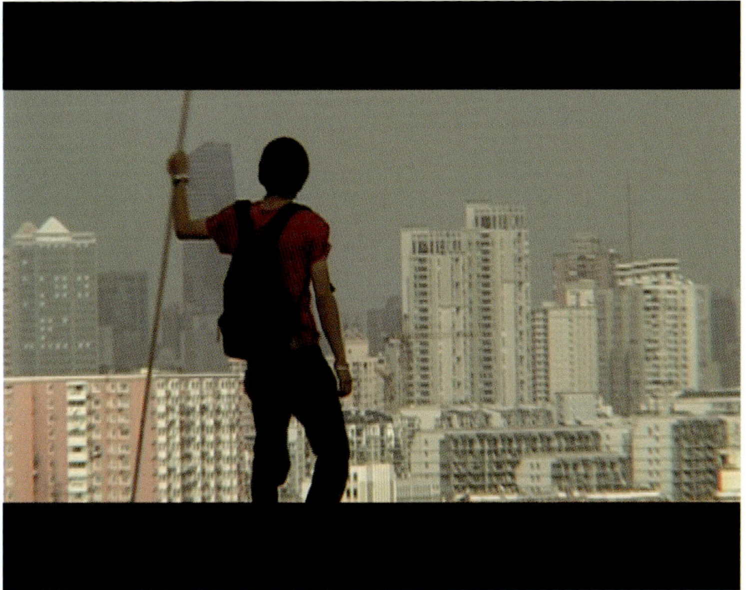

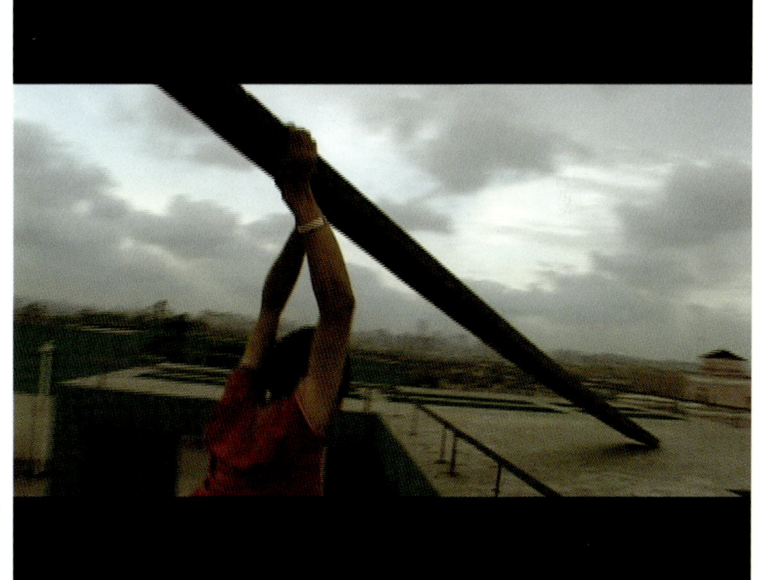

3

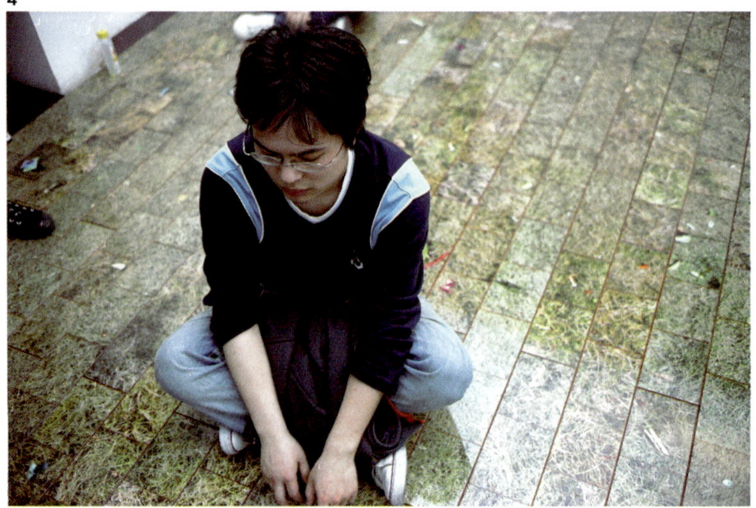

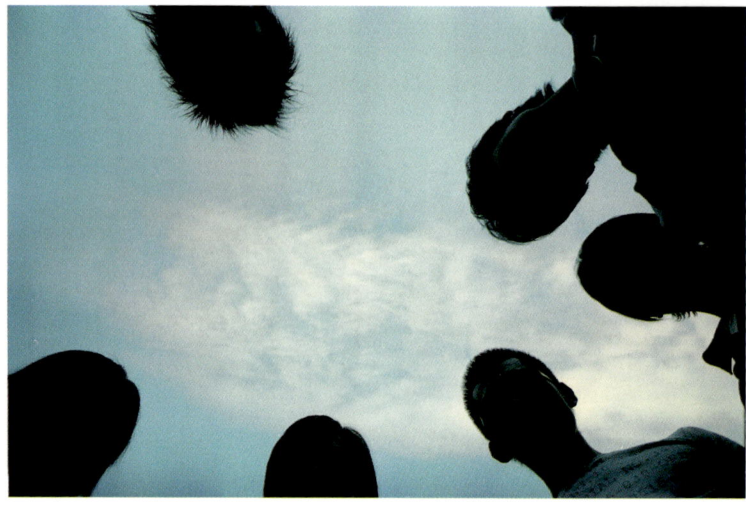

"Yard" is meant to be installed in a narrow passage way, with video footage projected over one. Viewers entering the installation are immediately thrown into a state of disorientation, experiencing the art work as if they had suddenly stepped into an exterior landscape. Since it is impossible to spot the source of the video projection which is uncannily duplicated on both walls simultaneously, it is difficult to escape the sensation of being in a total environment even as one senses that this space is entirely artificial.

Overall, Song Tao's projects reflect the youth culture in Shanghai today, alternatively sad and optimistic, thrilling and banal, genuine and artificial. His penchant for environmental installations is an example of the impact of the club scene on contemporary art in Chinese urban centres but also demonstrates the rapid advancement in the sophistication of video art in China today.

Beide vereinen Klang, Musik und Installation. „Three Days Ago" ist ein Video voll düsterer Nachtansichten von Shanghai, mit einem hämmernden Elektroniksoundtrack unterlegt. In einem verdunkelten Raum als Endlossequenz projiziert, schafft es eine dichte und beklemmende Atmosphäre, ohne eine lineare Geschichte zu erzählen.

„Yard" ist als Installation für einen schmalen Durchgang gedacht, in dem die Videobilder auf den Betrachter geworfen werden. Wer die Installation betritt, erlebt eine jähe Desorientierung, so als sei er in eine gänzlich unerwartete Außenwelt hinausgetreten. Da die Quelle der gleichzeitig auf beide Wände projizierten Videos nicht auszumachen ist, wird man das Gefühl nicht los, sich in einer alles vereinnahmenden Umgebung zu befinden, obwohl man weiß, dass dieser Raum absolut künstlich ist.

Insgesamt spiegeln Song Taos Projekte recht genau die aktuelle Jugendkultur von Shanghai – traurig und optimistisch, spannend und banal, authentisch und künstlich. Seine Vorliebe für umfassende Installationen macht den Einfluss der Clubszene auf die zeitgenössische Kunst in Chinas urbanen Zentren deutlich, demonstriert aber zugleich die rasant fortschreitende Weiterentwicklung der Videokunst im modernen China.

能知道到底那个是真的，所以正当观众认为这是一个虚假的空间时，却很容易认为自己身临其境。

总之，宋涛的作品反映了当今上海的青年文化，悲伤和乐观，兴奋和平庸，纯真和做作。他对环境装置的强烈的趋向反映了的俱乐部对中国都市中心当代艺术的影响，当也说明了中国当今的录象艺术作品的精密程度的飞速进步。

Barbara Pollack

5

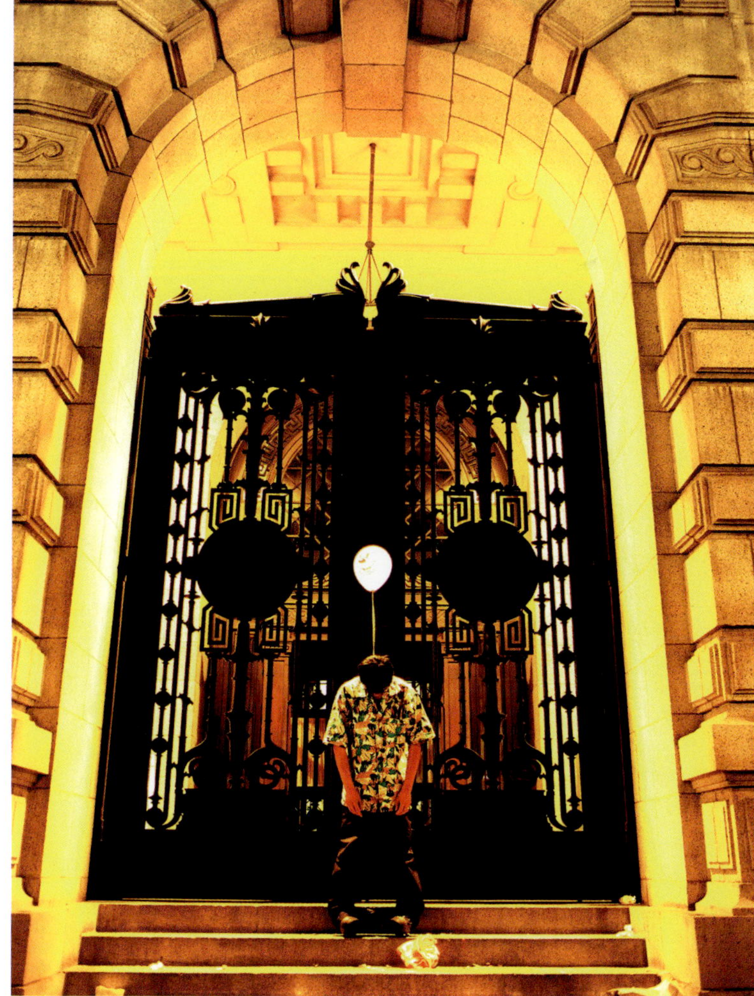

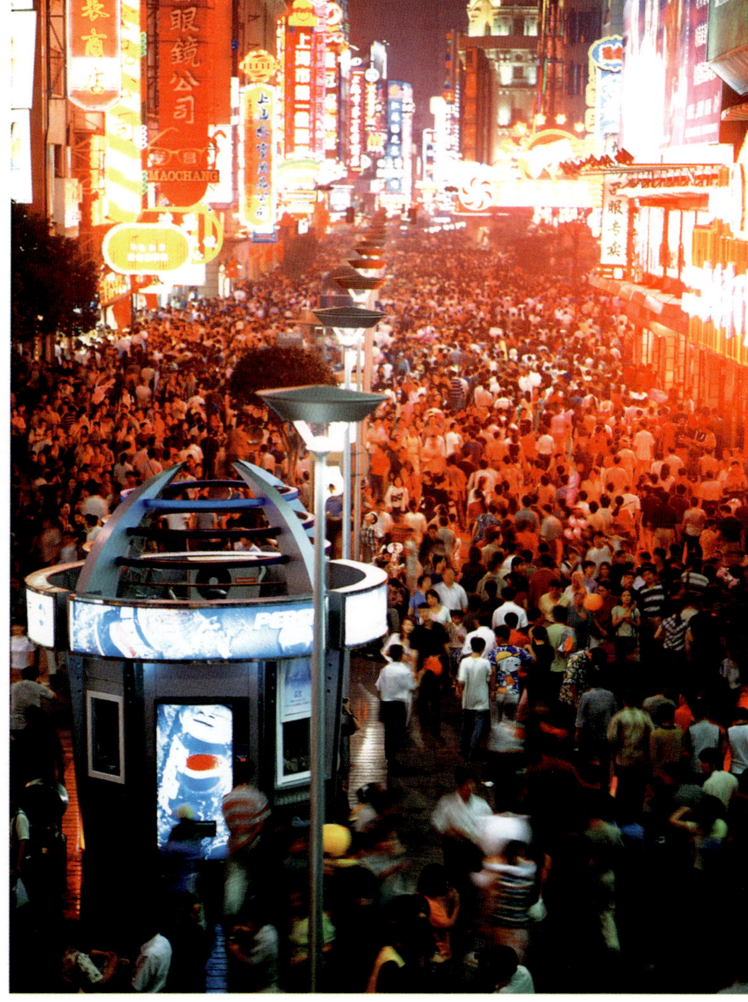

1 ***Flag***, *2004*
C-print, 69 x 45 cm
C-print, 69 x 45 cm
《骄傲》2004年, C-印刷, 69 x 45 cm

2 ***From the last century***, *2006*
Video, 20 min
Video, 20 Min.
《从上世纪来》2006年, 录像, 20分

3 ***Floor (black and white)***, *2003*
Photograph on floor, installation
Auf dem Boden liegende Fotografie, Installation
《地板》(黑白)2003年, 地板摄影, 装置

4 ***Floor (colour)***, *2003*
Photograph on floor, installation
Auf dem Boden liegende Fotografie, Installation
《地板》(彩色)2003年, 地板摄影, 装置

5 ***In Loud Crowds I Dream of Hanging Myself I***, *2002*
2 c-prints, 175 x 127 cm each
2 C-prints, je 175 x 127 cm
《其实我一直幻想在欢闹地人群中把自己吊死I》 2002年,
2 C-印刷, 每幅175 x 127 cm

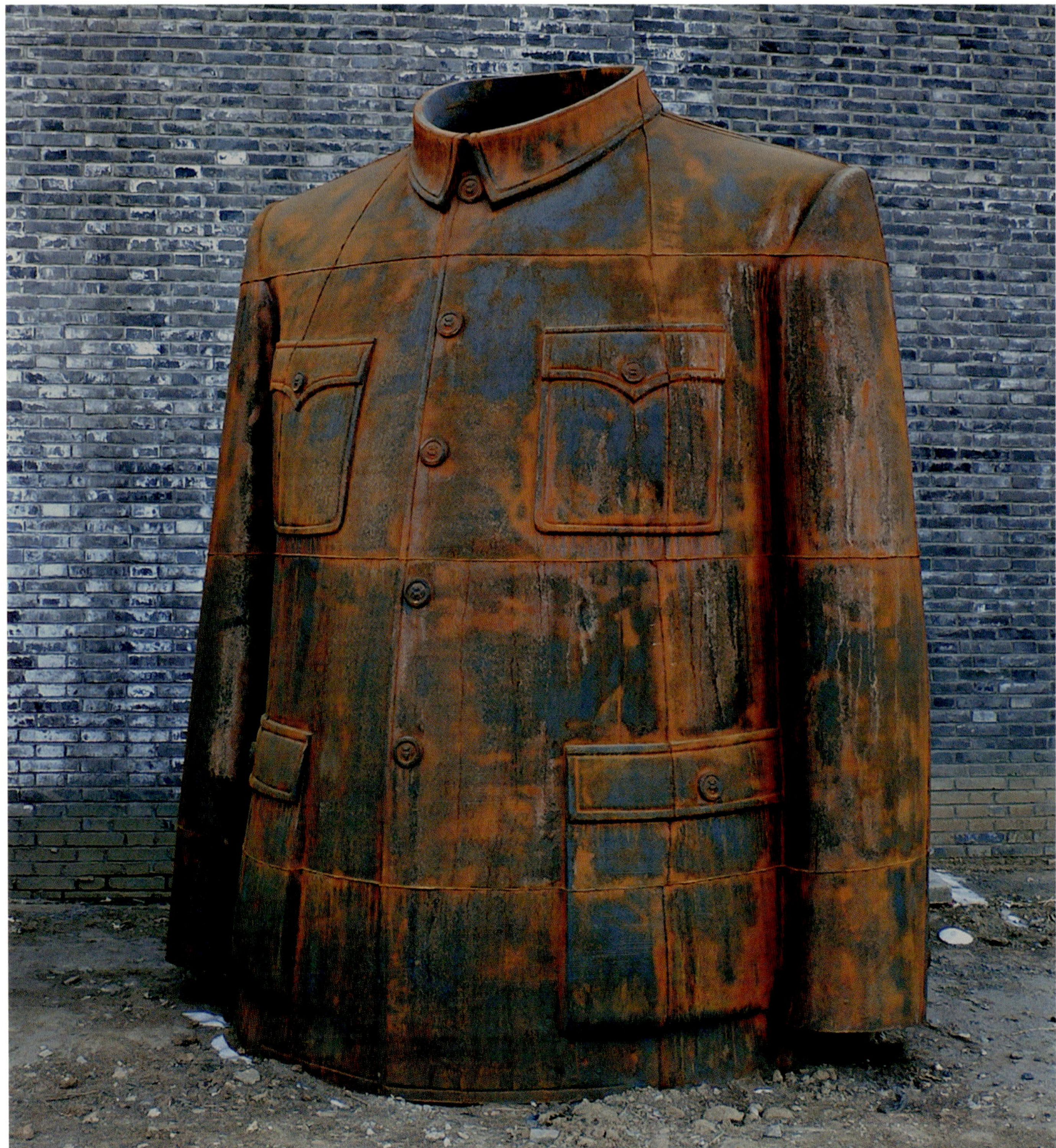

1

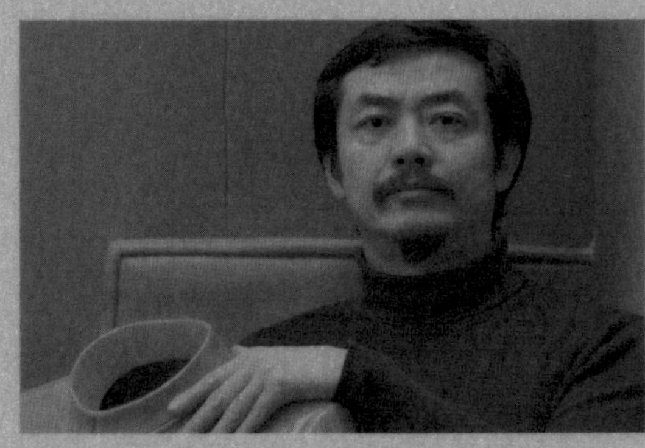

"Art is the road for an artist to fulfil himself."

„Die Kunst ist für den Künstler der Weg, sich selbst zu verwirklichen."

"艺术是路使艺术家履行自己。"

Born in 1956 in Qingdao, Shandong Province, China. Lives and works in Beijing
Geboren 1956 in Qingdao, Provinz Shandong, China. Lebt und arbeitet in Peking
1956年出生于中国山东青岛。居住工作在北京

***Selected exhibitions* / Ausgewählte Ausstellungen / 所选展览**

2000 "Shanghai Spirit — Shanghai Biennial", Shanghai Museum of Art, Shanghai, China
"Sharing Exoticisms — Contemporary Art", Lyon Biennale, Lyon, France
2003 Beaufort Triennial Contemporary Art by the Sea, Museum of Modern Art, Oostende, Belgium
2004-07 "Between Past and Future, New Photography and Video from China", International Center of Photography, New York, NY, USA (travelling exhibition)
2005 "Sui Jianguo: The Sleep of Reason", Asian Art Museum, San Francisco, CA, USA
2005-07 "Mahjong - Chinesische Gegenwartskunst aus der Sammlung Sigg", Kunstmuseum Bern, Berne, Switzerland; Hamburger Kunsthalle, Hamburg, Germany; Museum der Moderne, Salzburg, Austria

2000年 《上海--第三届上海双年展》上海美术馆，中国
《共享异国情调--里昂当代艺术双年展》里昂，法国
2003年 《Beaufort 当代艺术由海三年展》现代艺术博物馆，奥斯坦德
2004-07年 《过去与未来之间—中国新影像展》国际摄影中心，纽约，美国（巡回展）
2005年 《隋建国：原因睡眠》亚洲美术馆, 旧金山
2005-07年 《麻将》西克中国当代艺术收藏展，伯尔尼美术馆，瑞士；汉堡美术馆，汉堡，德国；萨尔茨保现代美术馆 奥地利

***Selected publications* / Ausgewählte Publikationen / 所选著作**

Edward Lucie-Smith: "Artists of the Ideal", Milan 2002
Edward Lucie-Smith: "Art Tomorrow", Paris 2002
Sui Jianguo: "Sleep of Reason", Asian Art Museum, San Francisco 2005

Lucie-Smith, Edward（著）:《理想的艺术家》米兰 2002年
Lucie-Smith, Edward（著）:《艺术明天》巴黎2002年
《隋建国：原因睡眠》亚洲美术馆, 旧金山2005年

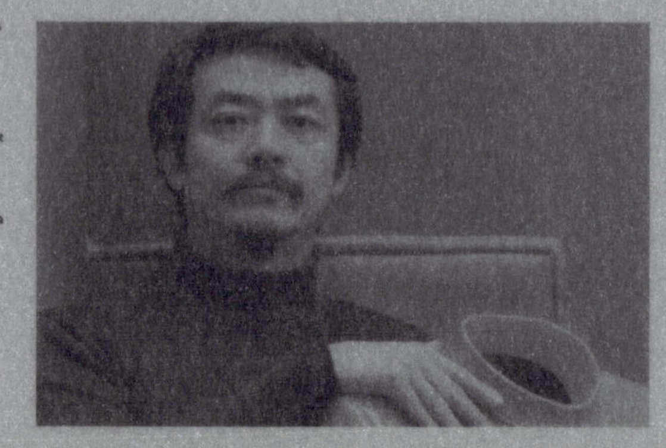

"Art is the road for an artist to fulfil himself."

„Die Kunst ist für den Künstler der Weg, sich selbst zu verwirklichen."

"艺术是路使艺术家履行自己。"

Born in 1956 in Qingdao, Shandong Province, China. Lives and works in Beijing
Geboren 1956 in Qingdao, Provinz Shandong, China. Lebt und arbeitet in Peking
1956年出生于中国山东青岛。居住工作在北京

Selected exhibitions / Ausgewählte Ausstellungen / 所选展览

2000 "Shanghai Spirit – Shanghai Biennial", Shanghai Museum of Art, Shanghai, China
"Sharing Exoticisms – Contemporary Art", Lyon Biennale, Lyon, France
2003 Beaufort Triennial Contemporary Art by the Sea, Museum of Modern Art, Oostende, Belgium
2004-07 "Between Past and Future, New Photography and Video from China", International Center of Photography, New York, NY, USA (travelling exhibition)
2005 "Sui Jianguo: The Sleep of Reason", Asian Art Museum, San Francisco, CA, USA
2005-07 "Mahjong - Chinesische Gegenwartskunst aus der Sammlung Sigg", Kunstmuseum Bern, Berne, Switzerland; Hamburger Kunsthalle, Hamburg, Germany; Museum der Moderne, Salzburg, Austria

2000年 《上海一第三届上海双年展》上海美术馆，中国
《共享异国情调一里昂当代艺术双年展》里昂，法国
2003年 《Beaufort 当代艺术由海三年展》现代艺术博物馆，奥斯坦德
2004-07年 《过去与未来之间一中国新影像展》国际摄影中心，纽约，美国（巡回展）
2005年 《隋建国：原因睡眠》亚洲美术馆，旧金山
2005-07年 《麻将》西克中国当代艺术收藏展，伯尔尼美术馆，瑞士；汉堡美术馆，汉堡，德国；萨尔茨堡现代美术馆 奥地利

Selected publications / Ausgewählte Publikationen / 所选著作

Edward Lucie-Smith: "Artists of the Ideal", Milan 2002
Edward Lucie-Smith: "Art Tomorrow", Paris 2002
Sui Jianguo: "Sleep of Reason", Asian Art Museum, San Francisco 2005

Lucie-Smith, Edward（著）：《理想的艺术家》米兰 2002年
Lucie-Smith, Edward（著）：《艺术明天》巴黎2002年
《隋建国：原因睡眠》亚洲美术馆，旧金山2005年

SUI JIANGUO 隋建国

[sueɪ tɕiɛn kuɔ]

As a sculptor, Sui Jianguo continually explores means to overcome the limit and confinement of the strict academic realist tradition that he was trained in, while maintaining his awareness of the strength of such a sculptural tradition in his practice. His interest has also evolved from creating objects to investigating and constructing the relationship between men and space through the absence or presence of objects.

In his earlier sculptural works of the late 80s and early 90s, his practice was very much inspired and enriched by the material and metaphysical qualities of such natural and industrial materials as stones, granites, wood, and metal. His mixing up of these materials in his works opened up a new territory for sculptural practice in China. Their abstract forms were often manifestations of and provided outlets for his shifting emotions in response to the idealistic 80s that was full of revolutionary passion and the subsequent disillusion, frustration, and suffocation in the early 90s following the clampdown of the 1989 demonstration. A rock broken into two, exposing fractured steel structures from inside, stones stuffed inside cages and about to burst forth, these works were intuitive, metaphorical, masculine and compelling.

While continuing to exercise the same strong sculptural language with great precision, Sui gradually shifted his focus to more conceptual concerns than simply material interests. In the mid 1990s, he formed a small artist group with two fellow sculptors and produced a number of installations based on various everyday social, political and historical events, which was a rule that all group members had to stick to. In one of their collaborative projects, "Woman, Here" (1995) the group made three bulletin boards each bearing everyday snapshots of the most important women in their lives, including those of their mothers, wives and daughters, various official certificates and documents of these women of different generations, as well as a displayed selection of objects in relation to them. It was the occasion of the world woman's conference in Beijing and the group

Als Bildhauer forscht Sui Jianguo unaufhörlich nach Möglichkeiten, die Grenzen und Beschränkungen der strikt akademisch-realistischen Tradition seiner Ausbildung zu überwinden und zugleich die Kraft einer solchen bildhauerischen Tradition in seinem Schaffen zu bewahren. Sein Interesse gilt heute weniger der Herstellung von Gegenständen als vielmehr der Untersuchung und Rekonstruktion der Beziehung zwischen Mensch und Raum durch die Abwesenheit oder Gegenwart von Objekten.

Suis frühe bildhauerische Arbeiten in den späten 1980er und frühen 1990er Jahren wurden stark durch die materiellen und metaphysischen Eigenschaften natürlicher und industrieller Werkstoffe wie Stein, Granit, Holz und Metall inspiriert und bereichert. Seine Kombination solcher Materialien eröffnete der chinesischen Bildhauerei ganz neue Horizonte. Ihre abstrakten Formen wurden bei Sui nun oft zum Ausdruck oder Ventil für seine wechselnde Gefühlslage angesichts der revolutionären Begeisterung der idealistischen 1980er Jahre und der anschließenden Ernüchterung, Frustration und Beklemmung der frühen 1990er Jahre in der Folge der Ereignisse von 1989. Ein in zwei Hälften zerborstener Stein, der zerbrochene Stahlverstrebungen im Inneren offenbart, Steine, die ihre Käfige zu sprengen drohen – diese Arbeiten wirkten faszinierend intuitiv, metaphorisch und maskulin.

Während er diese kraftvolle und dabei sehr präzise bildhauerische Sprache beibehielt, verlagerte Sui seine Aufmerksamkeit allmählich vom Material auf eher konzeptionelle Anliegen. Mitte der 1990er Jahre gründete er zusammen mit zwei Bildhauerkollegen eine kleine Künstlergruppe, die eine Reihe von Installationen auf der Basis alltäglicher gesellschaftlicher, politischer und historischer Ereignisse schuf. Für eines ihrer Gemeinschaftsprojekte, „Woman, Here" (1995), fertigte die Gruppe drei Schwarze Bretter: Auf diesen waren neben Schnappschüssen der wichtigsten Frauen in ihrem Leben, wie den Müttern, Ehefrauen und Töchtern, verschiedene offizielle Dokumente zu diesen Frauen aus verschiedenen Generationen ausgestellt, dazu eine Auswahl

身为一名雕塑家，隋建国知道学术现实主义传统的力量，但在自己的雕塑实践中，他还是不停地探索着用各种不同的方法突破自己所学的这一传统的严格限制和约束。他在雕塑方面的兴趣，也由塑造实物转为通过物体的存现与否来调查和组建人与空间的关系。

在他上世纪八十年代末到九十年代初的早期雕塑作品中，石头、花岗岩、木头、金属等天然及工业材料的具体而又玄妙的特性，在很大程度上激发和丰富了他的雕塑灵感。通过这些材料的组合利用，他为中国的雕塑实践又开拓了一片新的领域。这些材料抽象的外观常常浸渍了他的个人情感，也为他情感的漂移提供了出路：从理想的八十年代充满革命的激情到九十年代初因“八九”学潮遭到镇压后的迷茫、沮丧和窒息。一块石头破裂为二，从内部暴露出的断裂的钢铁结构，填满石块的笼子行将爆裂等，这些作品显现了直觉、隐喻、阳刚和迫人的气质。

在延续运用刚强而精细的雕塑表现形式的同时，隋建国的视线逐渐从对简单材料的兴趣转移到理性的关注。在上世纪九十年代中期，他和另外两名雕塑家一起组建了一个三人工作室，每名成员都坚持以各种日常的社会、政治、历史事件为背景进行装置创作这一原则，一起制作了许多装置。其中在他们合作的作品《女人、现场》（1995年）中，艺术家们做了三块公告牌，每块牌子上都贴有他们所抓拍到的一些日常生活的镜头，镜中人物都是在他们各自生活中最重要的女性，其中包括他们的母亲、妻子和女儿，以及这些不同年代女性的各种正式证书和文件，并且还收集了一些与她们有关的物品。制作这一作品正值北京召开世界妇女大会之际，而期望构建自己对妇女大会的诠释，最终使得他们制作了本作品。

在他随后的作品中，隋建国一如既往的保持了对具有社会学和人类学性质事件的好奇心，而且他创作

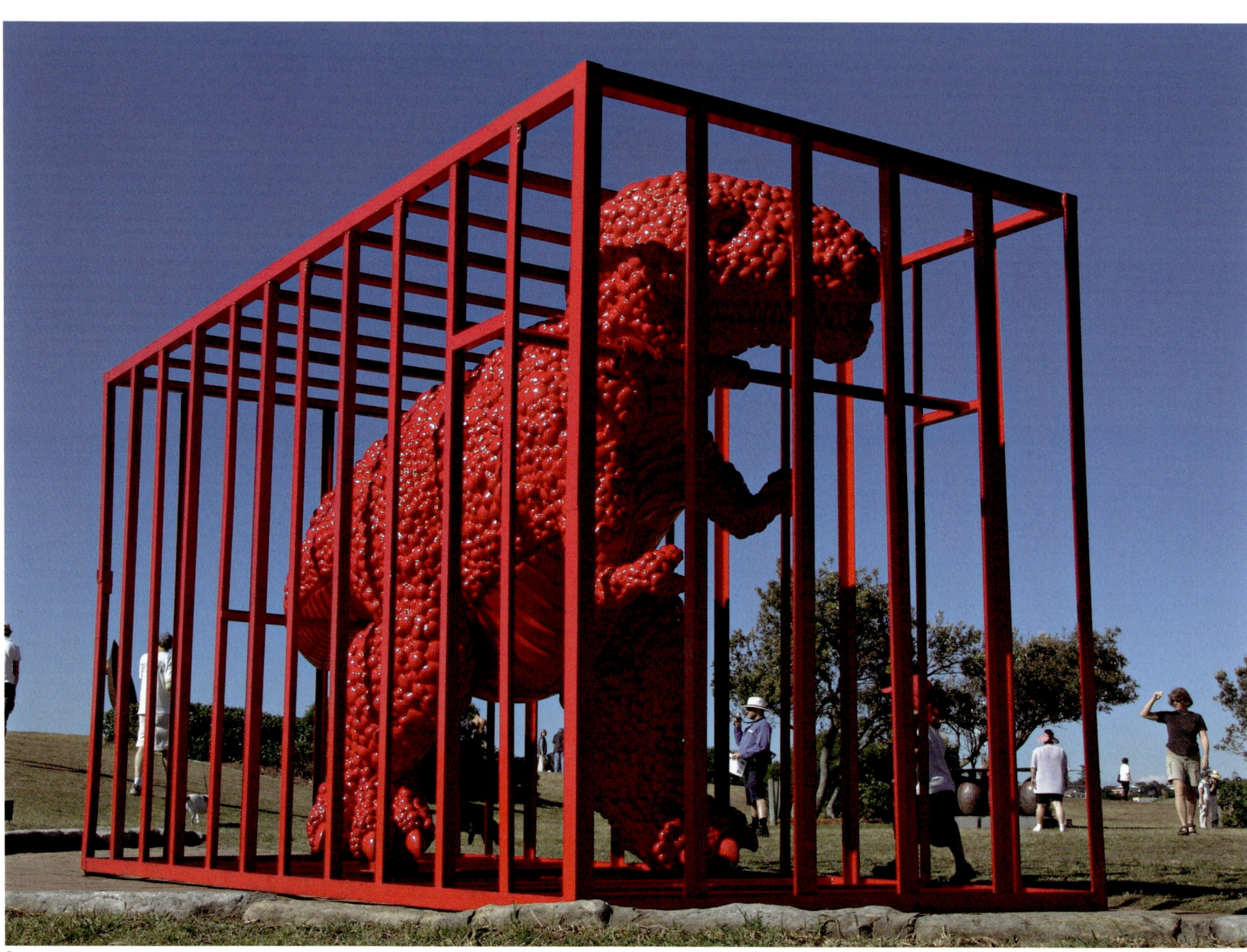

2

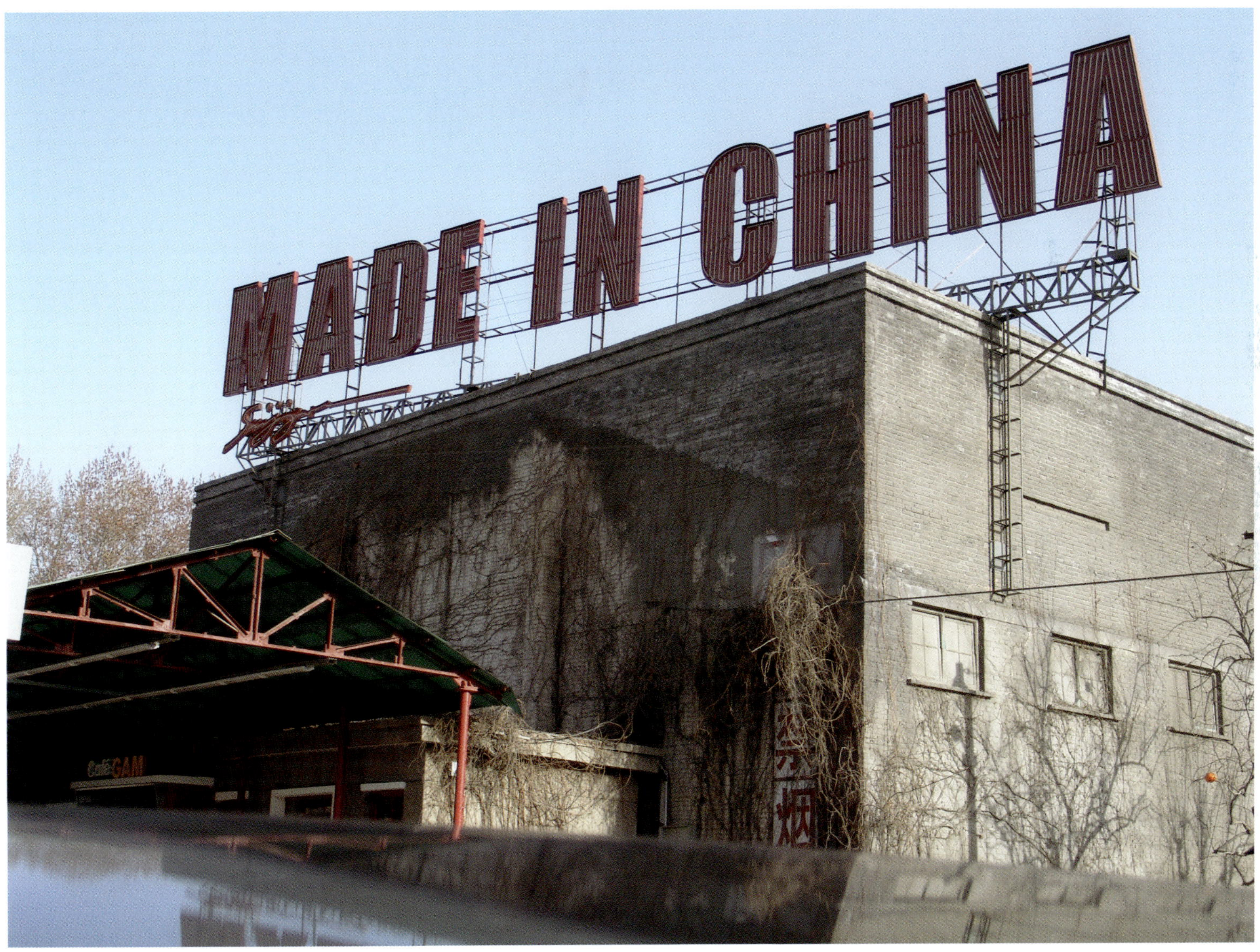

3

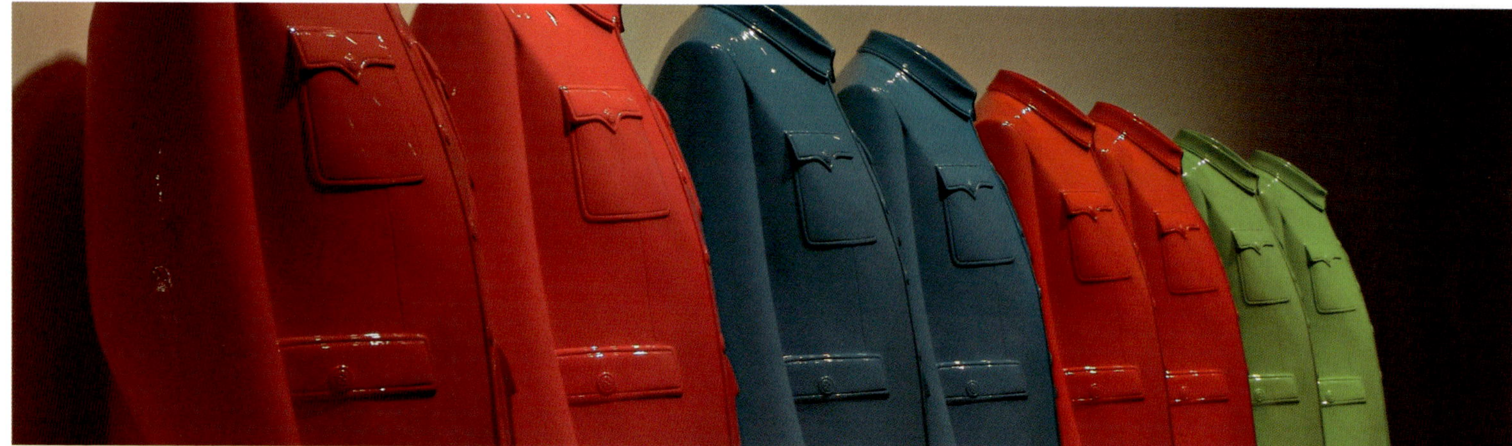

had wanted to organize their own version of a woman's conference, which led to the making of this work.

In his later works, Sui has remained curious to events of sociological and anthropological nature and constantly referenced a broad spectrum of source materials from the history of art to the aesthetic and value preferences of the public to politics. Besides his acclaimed and highly recognizable jacket series ("The Shadow of a Century", "Legacy Mantle", 1997–2002), which was an array of gigantic Mao suits made of such materials as fibre glass or stainless steel, a reflection on the issue of cultural identity, he made a fibre glass series of juxtapositions of classic sculptural icons such as an Olympic athlete in the act of throwing a discus or one of Michelangelo's Dying Slaves and their respective duplicates dressed in Mao suits. It was a deliberate appropriation of the realistic sculptural technique with a biting review of the political mechanism behind such engineering of a nation-wide aesthetic preference ("Clothes Vein Study", 1998). Meanwhile, he produced a number of extremely figurative and popular red dinosaurs from 1999 to 2003.

In 2005, Sui Jianguo reproduced a small patch of green grassland on a lifted slope in a group exhibition called "Renovation". It was the kind of grassland that many property developers lay out inside of their gated communities before the buildings are constructed. It is used as a special feature of attractions for potential house buyers and a suggestion of the beautiful and high-standard life style that they are carving out for their customers inside of the property ("Rome Garden", 2005). In 2006, Sui hired a group of workers to carry a perfectly functional BMW car from the entrance to the inside of a gallery space by hand without resorting to any technically advanced tools. The workers had all worked previously inside the very same space that used to be a fiberglass-casting factory ("The Parallel Moving on the Red Carpet", 2006). These latest works marked an important dimension in his practice, which is less about making objects as a sculptor than about discovering the space between reality and the power of invention.

von Gegenständen, die zu ihnen in Beziehung standen. Es war die Zeit der Weltfrauenkonferenz in Peking.

Auch in seinen späteren Arbeiten zeigte Sui Neugier auf Ereignisse von soziologischer und anthropologischer Bedeutung und bezog sich dabei auf ein breites Spektrum von Referenzmaterial – von der Kunstgeschichte über die ästhetischen Vorlieben und Wertvorstellungen der Allgemeinheit bis hin zur Politik. Besonders bekannt wurde seine Jackenserie („The Shadow of a Century", „Legacy Mantle", 1997–2002) – eine Reihe riesenhafter Mao-Jacken aus Materialien wie Fiberglas oder Edelstahl als Reflexion zum Thema der kulturellen Identität. Außerdem stellte Sui in einer Serie berühmte klassische Skulpturen (ebenfalls aus Fiberglas), etwa den olympischen Diskuswerfer oder einen der sterbenden Sklaven von Michelangelo, neben ihre Duplikate im Mao-Anzug. Er nahm hier ganz bewusst den bildhauerischen Realismus in Beschlag, um die politischen Mechanismen, die hinter der Konstruktion solcher kollektiven ästhetischen Vorlieben stehen, bloßzustellen („Clothes Vein Study", 1998). Darüber hinaus schuf er von 1999 bis 2003 eine Reihe extrem figurativer und populärer roter Dinosaurier.

2005 steuerte Sui Jianguo zu der Gruppenausstellung „Renovation" ein kleines grünes Rasenstück auf einem erhöhten Hang bei. Es war die Art von Rasen, wie ihn Bauinvestoren oft in geplanten Wohnanlagen auslegen lassen, bevor die Gebäude hochgezogen werden. Er fungiert als Lockmittel für potenzielle Hauskäufer, als Vorgeschmack auf den künftigen wunderbaren Lebensstil und -standard, den die Anbieter ihren Kunden verheißen („Rome Garden", 2005). 2006 heuerte Sui eine Gruppe von Arbeitern an, um einen absolut funktionsfähigen BMW vom Eingang ins Innere einer Galerie zu tragen – mit reiner Muskelkraft, ohne Zuhilfenahme irgendwelcher technischer Hilfsmittel. Die Arbeiter hatten vorher in eben diesen Räumlichkeiten gearbeitet, die zu einer Kunststoff-Fabrik gehörten („The Parallel Moving on the Red Carpet", 2006). Gerade bei diesen neuen Arbeiten wird deutlich, dass es Sui Jianguo weniger darum geht, als Bildhauer Objekte zu fertigen, als darum, das Spannungsfeld zwischen der Realität und der Macht der Erfindungsgabe auszuloten.

的取材非常丰富，从艺术史到美学以及价值公共取向再到政治学，他都有所涉猎。使其广受好评并高度认可的作品有夹克系列（《世纪的影子》、《衣钵》1997-2002年），这是一批使用诸如玻璃纤维、不锈钢等做成的巨型毛式服装（人民装），反映了文化身份的问题。此外，他还用玻璃纤维制作了一系列并排的经典雕像，比如奥运会运动员抛掷铁饼的动作或米开朗基罗某个垂死的奴隶，以及他们各自穿着毛式服装的复制品。作者有意用现实主义的雕塑手法，尖锐地回顾这种全国性的美学取向运作背后的政治体制。（《衣纹研究》1998年）与此同时，在1999至2003 年间，他制作了一些极具象征性和大受欢迎的红色恐龙。

2005 年，在名为“装修”的联展中，隋建国在一个架空的斜坡上再现了一小片绿色的草皮。正是在这种草皮上，许多地产开发商在建筑楼盘开建前规划其圈定的社区。它被用于以独特的卖点吸引潜在的购房者，并同时向人们揭示了开发商们为了顾客能享受美好高级的生活而付出的巨大努力。这些草皮据说是从美国进口的。（《罗马花园》2005年）2006 年，隋建国雇了一些工人把一辆功能完好的宝马车从入口抬到画廊内，抬的过程没有借助任何技术先进的工具，完全依靠人力。画廊以前是一家玻璃纤维铸造厂所在地，而那些工人曾经在该厂工作过。（《红地毯上的平行移动》2006年）这些最新的作品标志着他实践的一个重要维度，即不像一般雕塑家那样制作物品，而更多的是关于探索现实和发明力量之间的距离。

Carol Lu

5

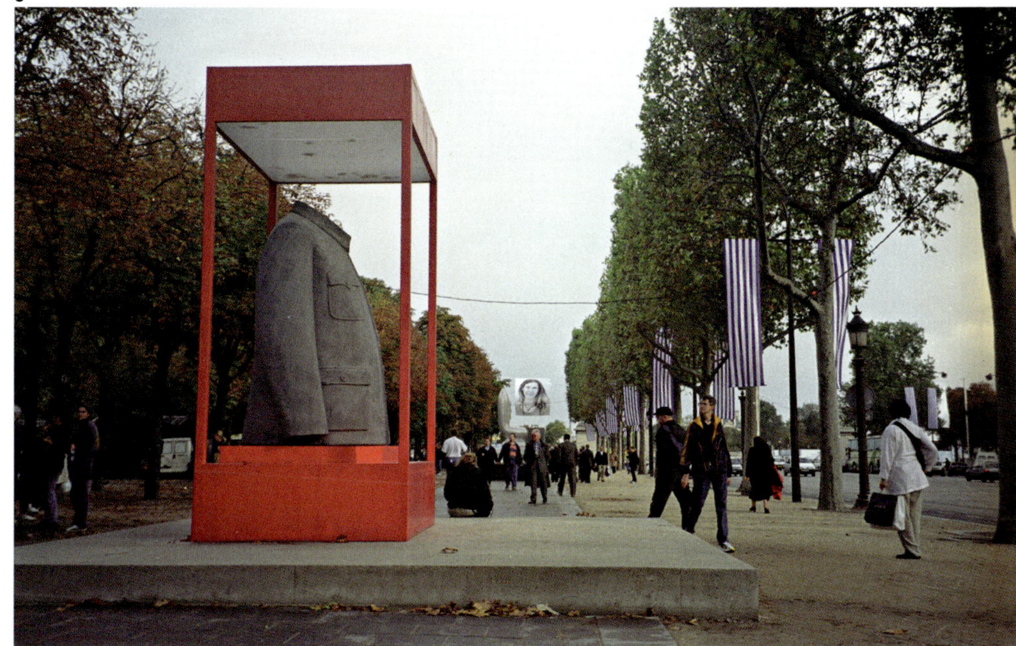

6

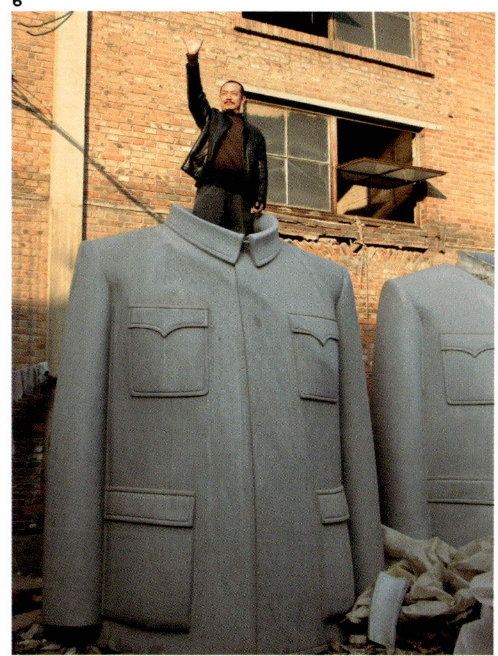

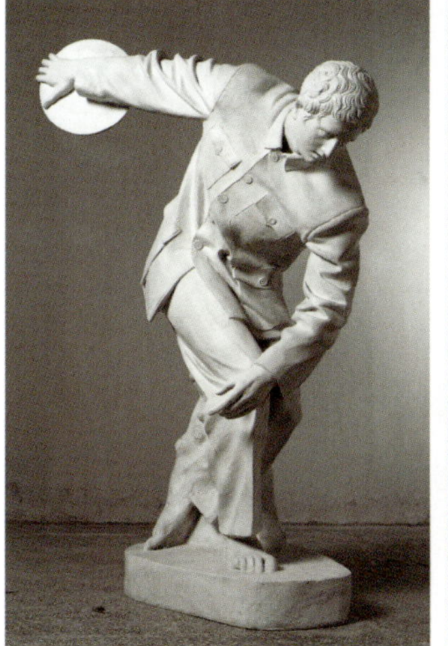

7

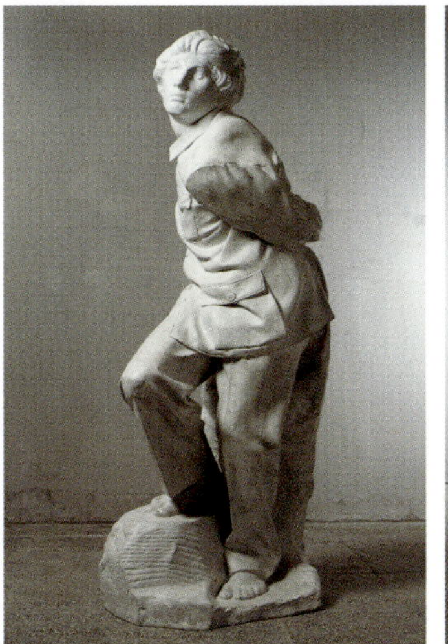

8

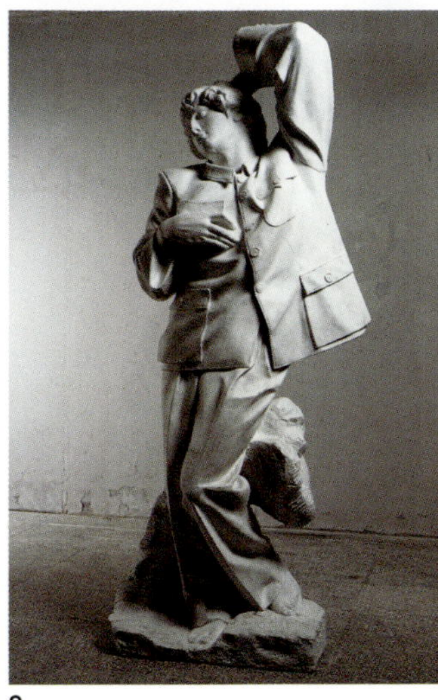

9

1 ***Legacy Mantle***, *2004*
Cast iron, 300 x 240 x 190 cm; Gusseisen, 300 x 240 x 190 cm
《衣钵》2004年, 铸铁, 300 x 240 x 190 cm

2 ***Jurassic Age***, *2003*
Painted bronze and steel, 250 x 480 x 230 cm
Bemalte Bronze und Stahl, 250 x 480 x 230 cm
《侏罗纪时代》2003年, 青铜和钢喷漆, 250 x 480 x 230 cm

3 ***Made in China***, *2005*
Neon light, 2 x 20 m; Neon, 2 x 20 m
《中国制造》2005年, 霓虹灯，2 x 20 m

4 ***Rainbow Jackets***, *2005*
Painted fibreglass, 60 x 45 x 25 cm each
Bemaltes Fiberglas, je 60 x 45 x 25 cm
《彩虹衣钵》2005年, 玻璃纤维涂漆, 每幅, 60 x 45 x 25 cm

5 ***Legacy Mantle, 1999***
Installation view; Installationsansicht
《衣钵》1999年, 装置实景

6 ***Legacy Mantle***, *1998*
Installation view; Installationsansicht
《衣钵》1998年, 装置实景

7 ***Clothes Vein Study – Discobolus***, *1998*
Painted fibreglass, 172 x 110 x 60 cm
Bemaltes Fiberglas, 172 x 110 x 60 cm
《衣纹研究 —— 掷铁饼者》1998年, 玻璃纤维涂漆，172 x 110 x 60 cm

8 ***Clothes Vein Study – Bound slave,*** *1998*
Painted bronze, 210 x 90 x 80 cm; bemalte Bronze, 210 x 90 x 80 cm
《衣纹研究 — 被缚的奴隶》1998年, 青铜喷漆，210 x 90 x 80 cm

9 ***Clothes Vein Study – Dying slave***, *1998*
Painted bronze, 230 x 130 x 80 cm; bemalte Bronze, 230 x 130 x 80 cm
《衣纹研究 — 垂死的奴隶》1998年, 青铜喷漆，230 x 130 x 80 cm

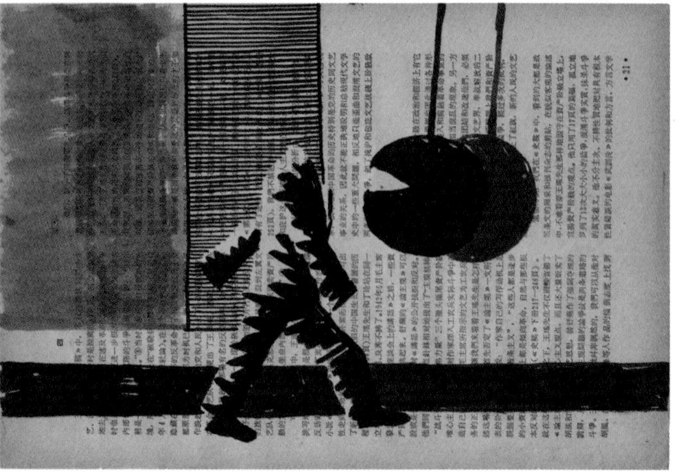

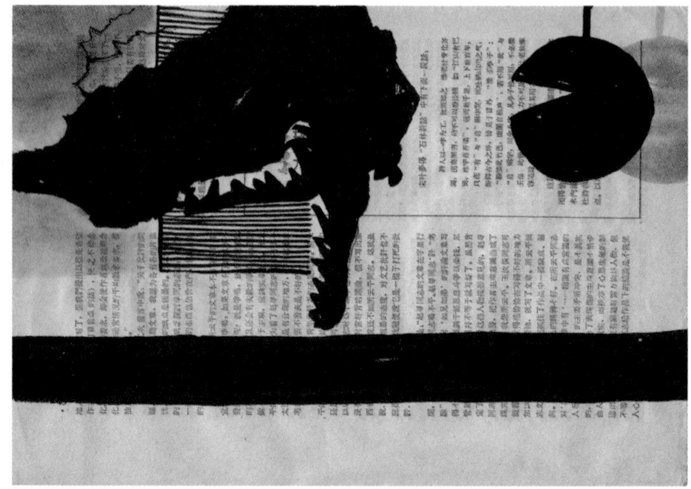

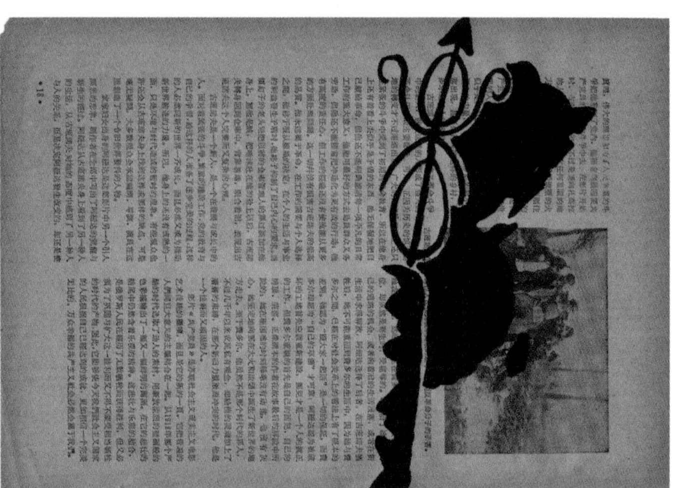

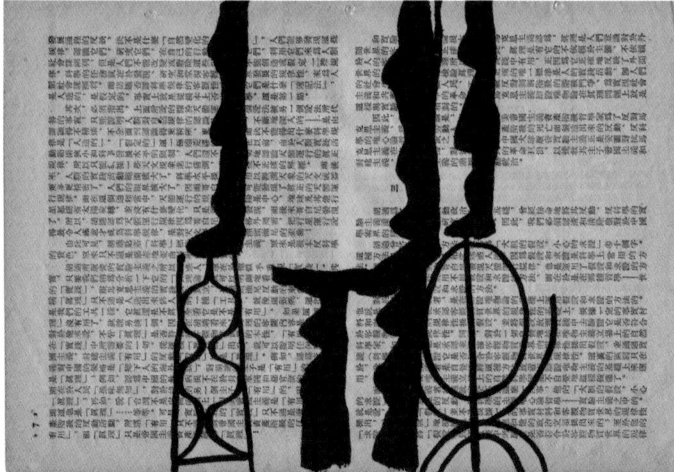

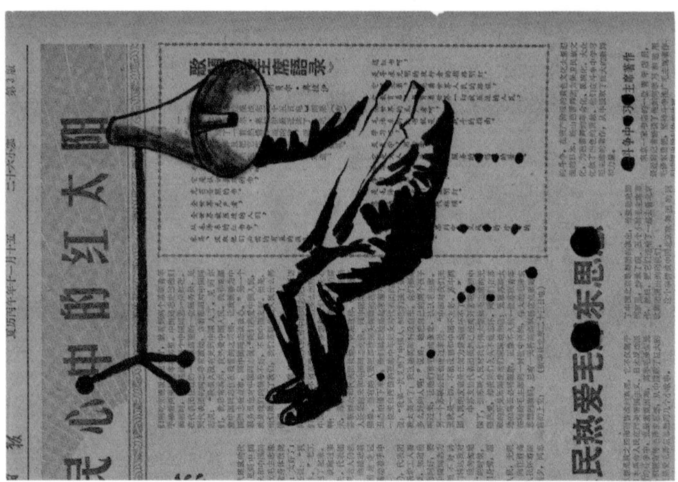

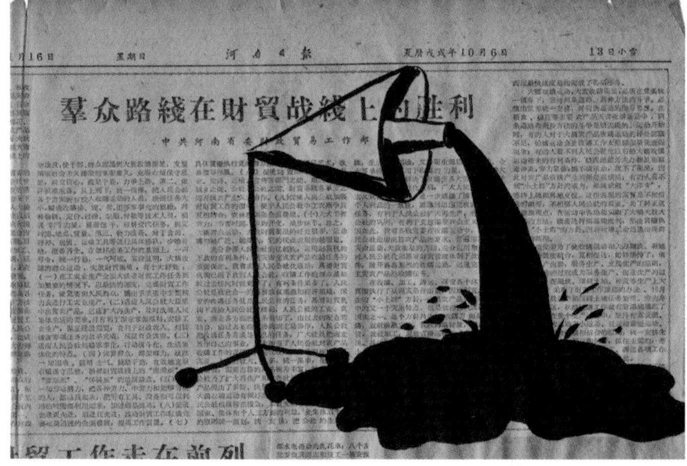

1

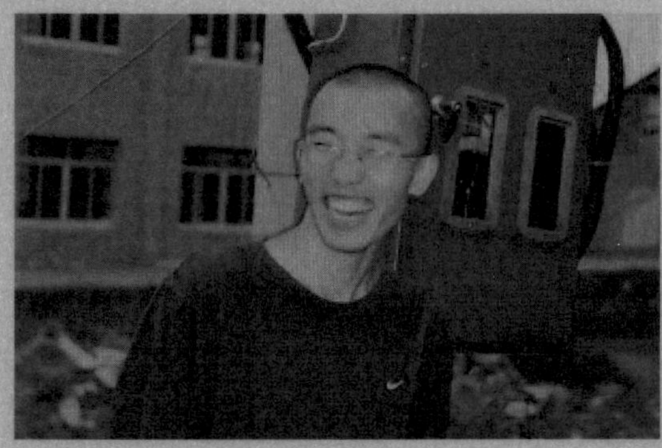

"The moving image exists as a trick of the lens; things inside are actually still. Each subsequent image is a negation of the previous one, a continuous questioning of the way things are."

„Das bewegte Bild existiert nur als Trick der Linse; im Inneren herrscht Stillstand. Jedes nachfolgende Bild ist eine Negation des vorhergehenden, eine beständige Hinterfragung des Status quo."

"运动着的图片实际上镜头处理的结果，而内部的事物实际上是静止的。每一幅图像实际上否定了前一幅图像，而这种方式却不断受到质疑。"

Born in 1980 in Fuxin, Liaoning Province, China. Lives and works in Hangzhou
Geboren 1980 in Fuxin, Provinz Liaoning, China. Lebt und arbeitet in Hangzhou
1980年出生于中国辽宁省阜新市，现在杭州居住和工作

***Selected exhibitions* / Ausgewählte Ausstellungen /** 所选展览

2005 Second Beijing International Art Biennial, Beijing, China
2006 "Specimen of Soul", BizArt, Shanghai, China
"It's All Right!", BizArt, Hangzhou, China
"Chaos City", UniversalStudios, Beijing, China
"Future Landscapes", Shanghai Duolun Museum of Modern Art, Shanghai, China
2007 "Against the Wall: Contemporary Chinese Artists", Corkin Gallery, Toronto, Canada
"Shouting Truth", Platform China, Beijing, China

2005年 《第二届北京国际艺术双年展》北京，中国
2006年 《灵魂标本》比翼艺术中心，上海，中国
《没事》比翼艺术中心，杭州，中国
《迷乱之城》U空间，北京，中国
《明天的风景》多伦美术馆，上海，中国
2007年 《靠墙》中国当代艺术家联展，Corkin 画廊，多伦多，加拿大.
《叫真》站台中国，北京，中国

***Selected publications* / Ausgewählte Publikationen /** 所选著作

Beatrice Leanza: "Sun Xun", interview, in: Waling Boers (ed.): "Touching the Stones: China Kunst Heute", Cologne 2006

Leanza, Beatrice:《孙逊（采访）》收入Waling Boers 所著《接触石头》：东八时区，香港 2006年

"The moving image exists as a trick of the lens; things inside are actually still. Each subsequent image is a negation of the previous one, a continuous questioning of the way things are."

„Das bewegte Bild existiert nur als Trick der Linse; im Inneren herrscht Stillstand. Jedes nachfolgende Bild ist eine Negation des vorhergehenden, eine beständige Hinterfragung des Status quo."

"运动着的图片实际上镜头处理的结果，而内部的事物实际上是静止的。每一幅图像实际上否定了前一幅图像，而这种方式却不断受到质疑。"

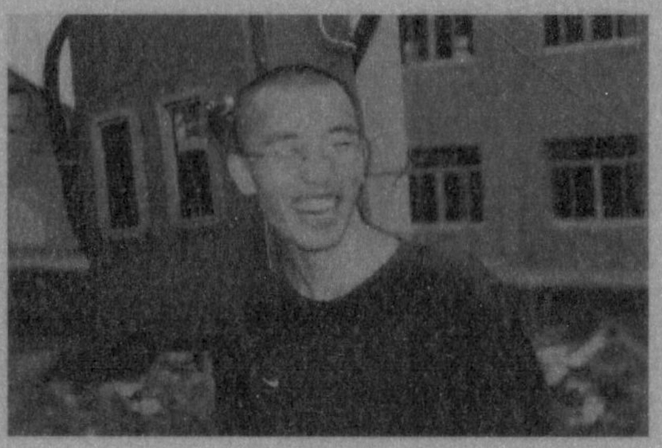

Born in 1980 in Fuxin, Liaoning Province, China. Lives and works in Hangzhou
Geboren 1980 in Fuxin, Provinz Liaoning, China. Lebt und arbeitet in Hangzhou
1980年出生于中国辽宁省阜新市，现在杭州居住和工作

Selected exhibitions / Ausgewählte Ausstellungen / 所选展览

2005 Second Beijing International Art Biennial, Beijing, China
2006 "Specimen of Soul", BizArt, Shanghai, China
"It's All Right!", BizArt, Hangzhou, China
"Chaos City", UniversalStudios, Beijing, China
"Future Landscapes", Shanghai Duolun Museum of Modern Art, Shanghai, China
2007 "Against the Wall: Contemporary Chinese Artists", Corkin Gallery, Toronto, Canada
"Shouting Truth", Platform China, Beijing, China

2005年 《第二届北京国际艺术双年展》北京，中国
2006年 《灵魂标本》比翼艺术中心，上海，中国
《没事》比翼艺术中心，杭州，中国
《迷乱之城》U空间，北京，中国
《明天的风景》多伦美术馆，上海，中国
2007年 《靠墙》中国当代艺术家联展，Corkin 画廊，多伦多，加拿大
《叫真》站台中国，北京，中国

Selected publications / Ausgewählte Publikationen / 所选著作

Beatrice Leanza: "Sun Xun", interview, in: Waling Boers (ed.): "Touching the Stones: China Kunst Heute", Cologne 2006

Leanza, Beatrice:《孙逊（采访）》收入Waling Boers 所著《接触石头》：东八时区，香港 2006年

SUN XUN 孙逊

[suən ɕyn]

Sun Xun belongs to a new generation of Chinese artists who have come of age within an already existing contemporary conversation. He entered the high school attached to the China Academy of Art in Hangzhou in 1997, emerging from there in 2005 with a degree in printmaking. That academy, which a generation ago had given rise to a wave of heated experimentation led by artists like Geng Jianyi and Zhang Peili, had emerged in the intervening years into a space for boundary-pushing thought and practice. Sun Xun for his part has quickly distinguished himself as one of that environment's brightest young stars, a group that also includes media artists such as Chen Xiaoyun, Lu Lei, Wu Junyong, and Cheng Ran.

Indeed Sun Xun's practice, which is only beginning to emerge, is based on an extended meditation on, in the words of his graduation paper, "Time, History, and Society." That paper draws extensively on post-structural theory, asking ultimately about the space for art in a social structure obsessed with narrating itself.

His breakthrough video animation "Shock of Time" (2006) opens with the line "History is a lie of time," and its narrative proceeds to unfold against a background of books, magazines, and newspapers from the 1960s. What might appear as a nostalgic tryst with the Cultural Revolution, however, is actually Sun Xun's inquiry into memory, textuality, and history. He has noted how these texts "conserve the criticisms and ideological protests of an earlier time, even though we have completely gone against them now." The geographical outline of China emerges from the textual chaos, changing shape as the years spin by at an accelerated pace. A man, seeming to personify time, appears from the fringes and begins speaking incomprehensibly over a megaphone. Clocks and figures appear but are ultimately swept away in tides of paper.

Sun Xun's other major video animation to date is entitled "The Lies of the Magician" (2005), an extended interrogation of creation mythologies painted on the pal-

Sun Xun gehört der ganz jungen Generation chinesischer Künstler an, die im Umfeld eines schon etablierten Dialogs mit der Moderne aufgewachsen sind. Sun besuchte ab 1997 die angegliederte Oberschule der China Academy of Art in Hangzhou und verließ sie 2005 mit einem Abschluss in Druckgrafik. Diese Akademie, von der eine Generation zuvor eine fast hitzige Experimentierfreude ausgegangen war, mit Künstlern wie Geng Jianyi und Zhang Peili an der Spitze, hatte sich seitdem zu einem Freiraum für grenzüberschreitendes Denken und Schaffen entwickelt. Sun Xun profilierte sich in diesem Umfeld, zu dem auch Medienkünstler wie Chen Xiaoyun, Lu Lei, Wu Junyong und Cheng Ran gehören, schon bald als einer der glanzvollsten Jungstars.

Sein in Entwicklung begriffenes Werk basiert auf einer ausführlichen Reflexion über „Zeit, Geschichte und Gesellschaft", wie er in seiner Abschlussarbeit formulierte. Er bezieht sich darin stark auf die poststrukturalistische Theorie und fragt letztlich nach dem geeigneten Raum für Kunst in einer Gesellschaft, die zwanghaft damit beschäftigt ist, sich selbst zu erzählen.

Sein Durchbruch glückte Sun Xun mit der Videoanimation „Shock of Time" (2006) – sie beginnt mit der Botschaft „Die Geschichte ist eine Lüge der Zeit" und entfaltet ihre Erzählung vor einem Hintergrund aus Büchern, Zeitschriften und Zeitungen der 1960er Jahre. Was wie ein nostalgisches Stelldichein mit der Kulturrevolution erscheinen könnte, ist in Wahrheit ein fragendes Eindringen in Erinnerung, Textlichkeit und Geschichte. Sun war aufgefallen, dass die Textdokumente jener Ära „die Kritiken und ideologischen Proteste einer früheren Zeit bewahren, auch wenn wir ihnen jetzt völlig zuwiderhandeln". Chinas geografische Konturen treten in der Animation aus dem textlichen Chaos hervor und verändern sich, während die Jahre zunehmend beschleunigt vorüberwirbeln. Ein Mann, der die Zeit selbst zu personifizieren scheint, taucht aus den Kulissen auf und beginnt, Unverständliches in ein Megafon zu sprechen, Uhren und Figuren erscheinen, werden aber sogleich wieder von den wogenden Papierfluten fortgerissen.

孙逊属于新生代中国艺术家，这代艺术家面对着早已存在的当代传统时代。1980年出生于中国东北地区的辽宁省，1997年考入杭州的中国美院附中，2005年毕业于中国美院版画系。曾在一代之前，在这个学校中，耿建翌、和　张培力等艺术家发起了经验主义活跃浪潮，而几年来这个学校已经成为一个推动艺术思想和实践的”黄盒子”组织。孙逊很快地成为这个环境中的的一颗明亮的新星，在这个组织中也包括媒介艺术家如陈晓云，陆磊，吴俊勇，和程然等。

孙逊仅仅刚刚开始的艺术实践，是以一种延长的沉思为基础，这种沉思冥想在其毕业论文《时间、历史和社会》中。这篇论文粗略地勾画了后结构理论，而最终寻找着迷失于自我叙述的社会结构中的艺术空间。他的突破性视频动画《休克时光》以　标题“历史是时间的谎言”而开始，随后以　60年代时期的书籍、杂志、报纸为背景继续进行着。作品中出现的令人怀旧的文化大革命时期的事物，是孙逊对记忆、原文和历史的质疑方式。他注意到这些文字怎样“保存早期的评论和意识主张，即使现在我们已经与其背道而驰。”由于这些年来社会飞速地发展，中国的地理轮廓上已经出现文字混乱，而且外形已经发生变化。似乎将时间被人格化了，一个男人从镜头边缘出现了，并开始通过扩音器说着些令人费解的话语。时钟和数字出现了，但最终被报纸一扫而去。孙逊的另一个重要视频动画《魔术师的谎言》，一位魔术师以他的身体来创造一个世界。于是他的皮肤便成了油画布，一个画出来的世界逐渐显现出来。这种兴趣仍然继续着，体现在其动画和装置作品《异邦》中，并与2006年12月在杭州举办的影响意义的展览《没事》上展出。毫无疑问，如果没有蚊子，他的作品是不可能完成的。在其整个学生时期，他基本上画的都是以蚊子为主题，类似于齐白石的全部作品都以虾为中心。

去年，策展人Beatrice Leanza　问他，其动画作品的所追求的目标是什么，孙逊淡淡地回答说，“真

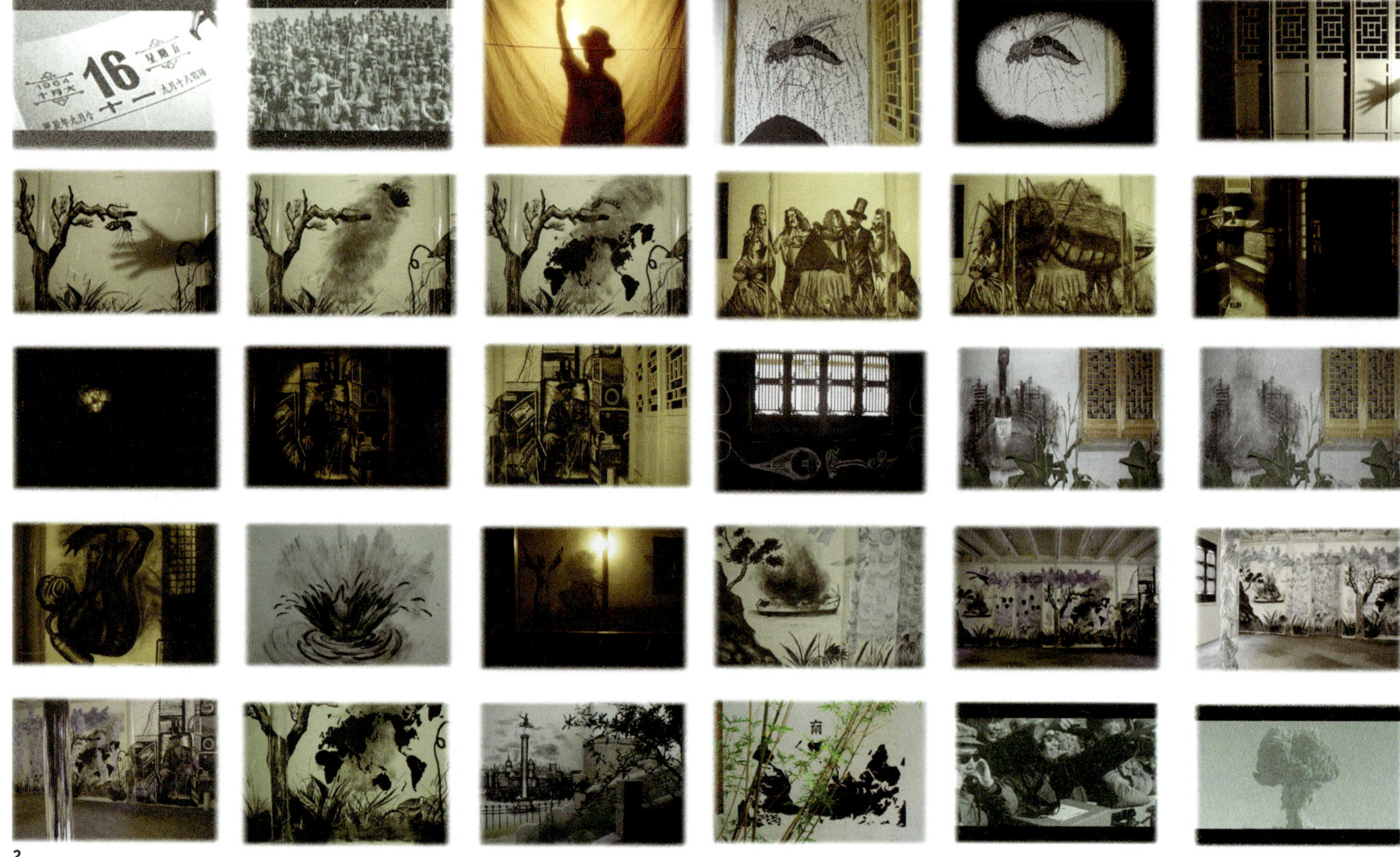

2

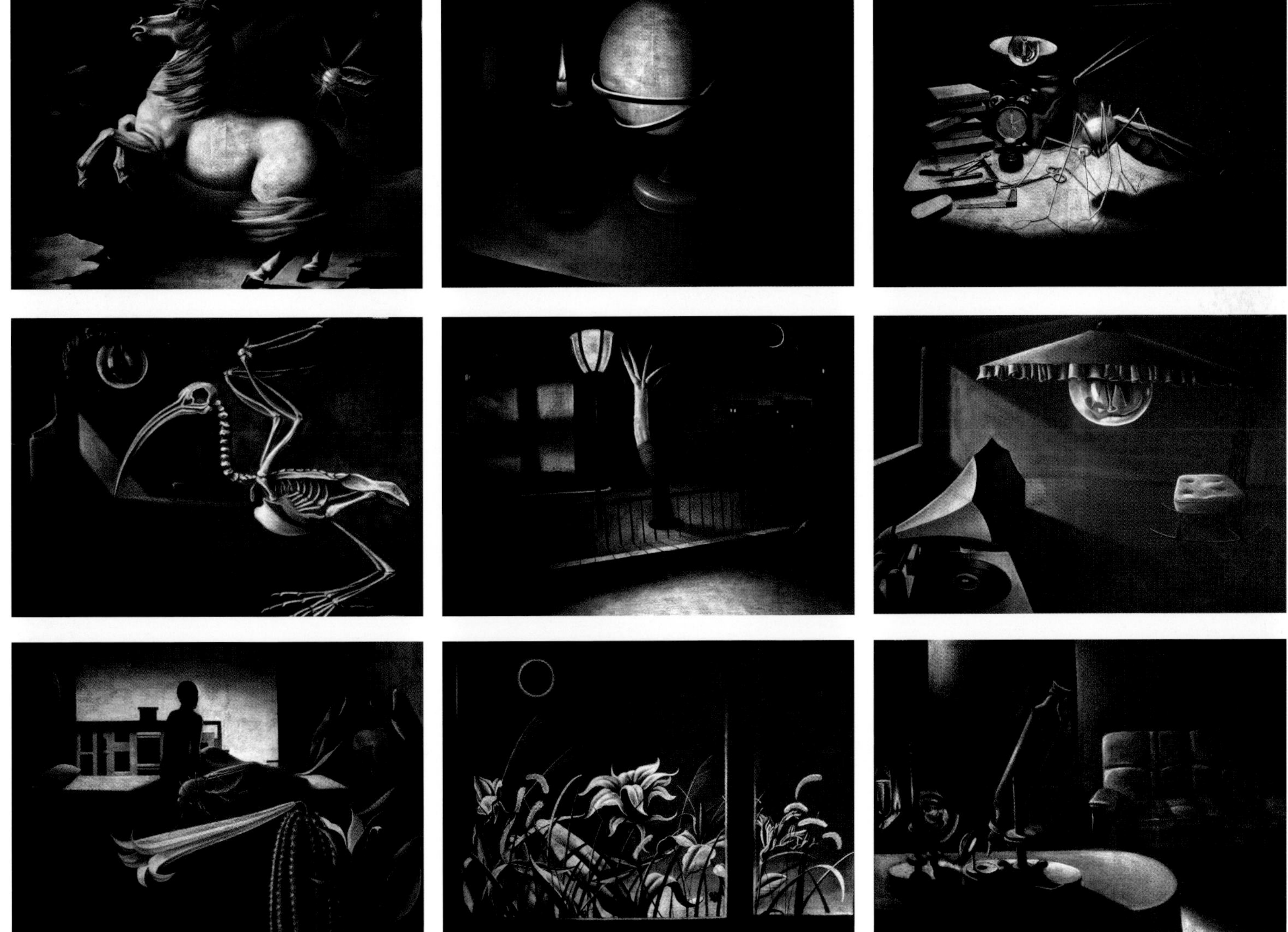

3

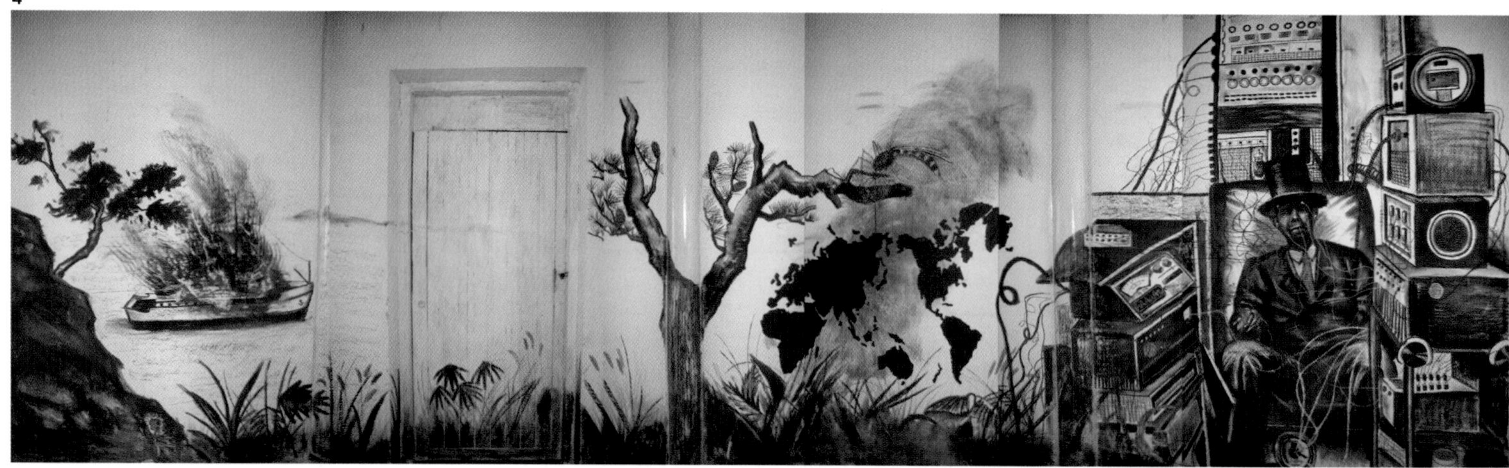

impsest of his own body. This interest was continued in an animation and installation work entitled "Mythos" (2006) that he presented at the influential exhibition "It's All Right" in Hangzhou in December 2006. And no discussion of Sun Xun's work would be complete without a mention of the mosquitoes he has meticulously painted throughout his student years, drawing comparisons to the shrimp so central to the œuvre of twentieth-century painter Qi Baishi.

Asked in an interview with curator Beatrice Leanza last year what he is striving for in his animations, Sun Xun replied simply, "Truth." His readings and meditations have led him to believe in the utter mutability of history, and thus only by accepting this transience by means of a medium in which "each subsequent image is a negation of the previous one" does he feel truth as a narrative possibility.

Sun Xuns zweite bedeutende Videoanimation mit dem Titel „The Lies of the Magician" (2005) beschäftigt sich ausgiebig mit Schöpfungsmythen, die auf seinen eigenen Körper gemalt sind – ein Thema, das er in seinem Animations- und Installationswerk „Mythos" (2006) weiterverfolgte, das im Dezember 2006 bei der wichtigen Ausstellung „It's All Right" in Hangzhou vorgestellt wurde. Doch kein Text über Sun Xuns Werk wäre vollständig, ohne jene sorgsam gemalten Moskitos seiner Studentenzeit zu erwähnen, bei denen sich ein Vergleich mit den Garnelen aufdrängt, die im vorigen Jahrhundert eine so zentrale Rolle im Werk des Malers Qi Baishi spielten.

Als die Kuratorin Beatrice Leanza ihn 2006 in einem Interview fragte, wonach er strebe, antwortete Sun Xun schlicht: „Wahrheit." Sein Denken hat ihn von der absoluten Unbeständigkeit der Geschichte überzeugt, und nur dadurch, dass er sich auf diese Vergänglichkeit mittels eines Mediums einstellt, in dem „jedes nachfolgende Bild eine Negation des vorhergehenden ist", betrachtet er Wahrheit als eine erzählbare Möglichkeit.

实。"他所阅读的东西和思考让他相信历史永远在不断变化的，因此只有接受以媒介所产生的短暂性，他才能感受到事实是可以叙述的，虽然那种介质中"后一幅图像在否定着前一幅图像"。

Philip Tinari

5

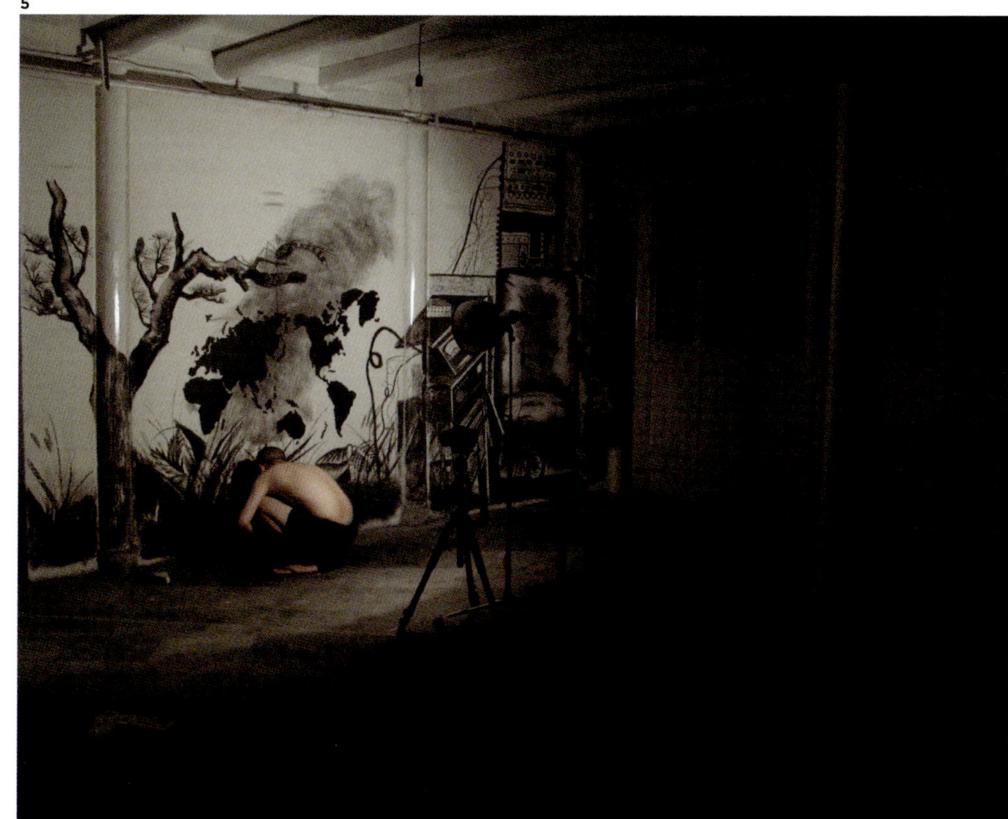

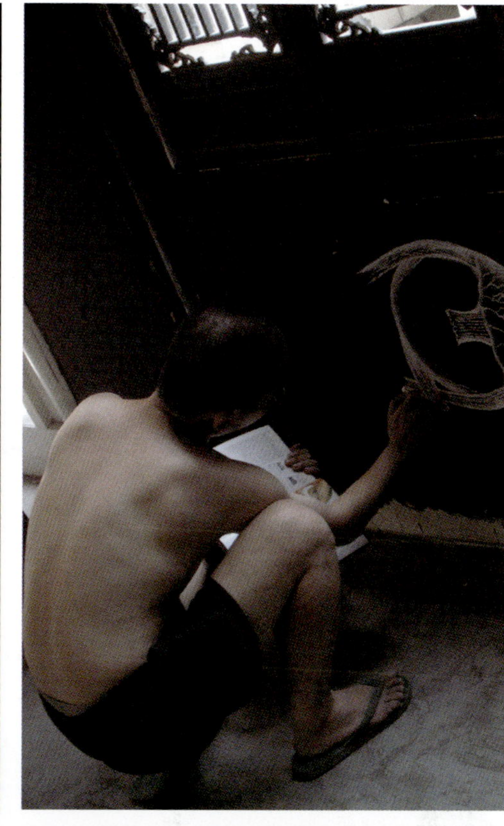

1 ***Shock of Time***, *2006*
Video, 5 min 29 sec
Video, 5 Min. 29 Sek.
《休克时光》2006年, 录像, 5分 29秒

2 ***The Lies***, *2006*
Stage photo, animation installation, 7 min 20 sec
Bühnenfotografie, Animation, Installation, 7 Min. 20 Sek.
《讹》剧照，2006年，动画装置，7分 20秒

3 ***21 Gram***, *2006–2008*
Colour on canvas, handmade animation, 100 x 140 cm each
Farbe auf Leinwand, handgefertigte Animation, je 100 x 140 cm
《21克》2006–2008年，布面色粉，手绘动画，每幅100 x 140 cm

4 ***The Lies***, *2006*
Animation, installation, 7 min 20 sec
Animation, Installation, 7 Min. 20 Sek.
《讹》2006年，动画装置，7分 20秒

5 ***The Lies***, *2006*
Animation, installation, Yellow Box in Qingpu, Shanghai
Animation, Installation, Yellow Box in Qingpu, Shanghai
《讹》2006年，动画装置，黄盒子展览现场，青浦，上海

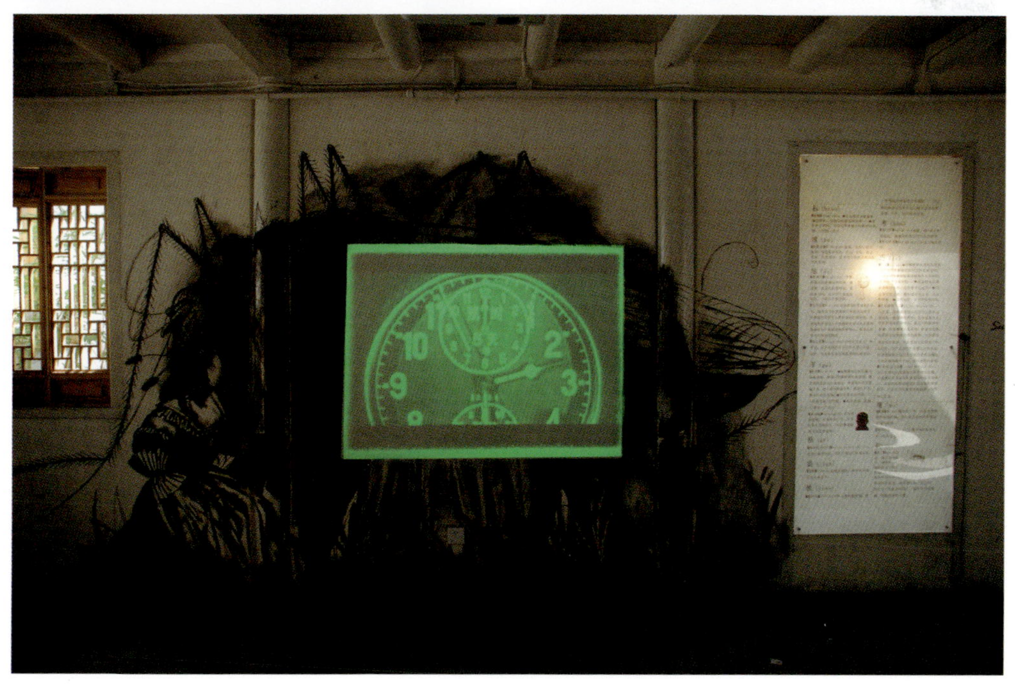

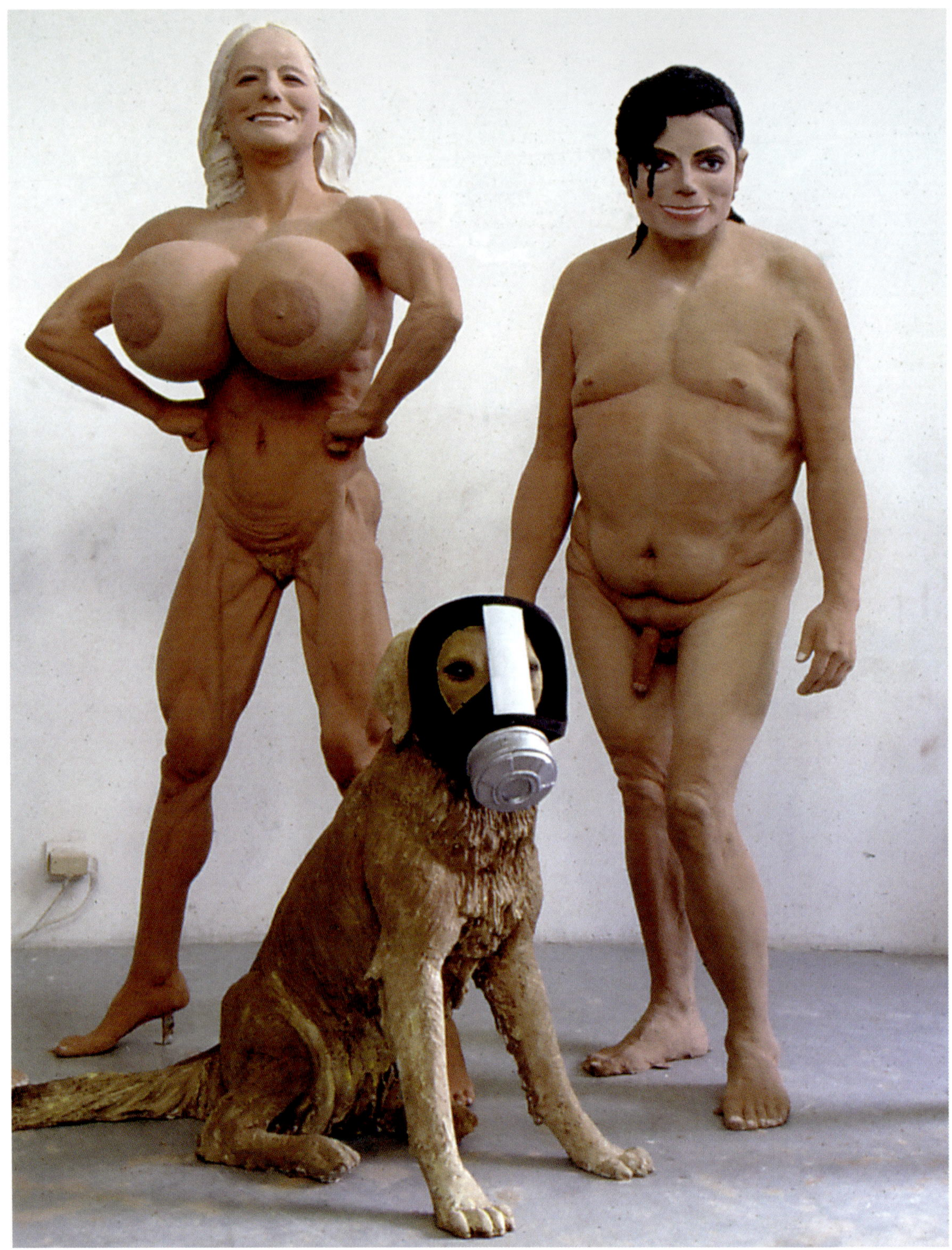

1

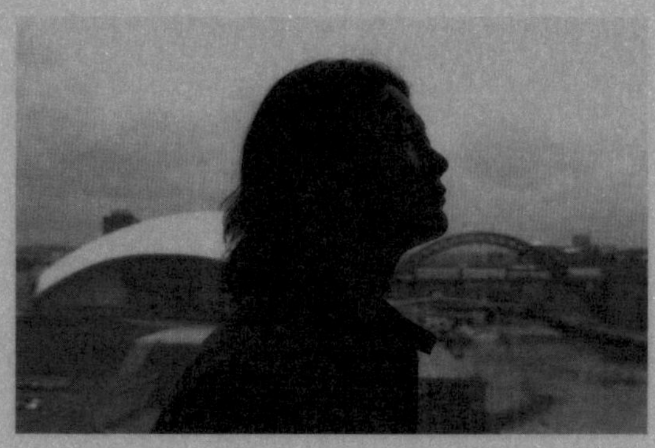

"The 'visual' and oral noise of information not only clashes constantly with the inner calm and peace we naturally require, but is also a menace to our existence."

„Das ‚visuelle' und orale Geräusch der Informationen kollidiert nicht nur dauernd mit dem inneren Frieden, den wir uns selbstverständlich wünschen, sondern es droht auch, an die Stelle unserer Existenz zu treten."

"信息的视觉和口头干扰不仅常常打破了我们本性所需要的平静与安宁，也威胁到我们自身存在。"

Born in 1956 in Wuhan, China. Lives and works in Paris, France
Geboren 1956 in Wuhan, China. Lebt und arbeitet in Paris, Frankreich
1956年出生于中国武汉，现在巴黎定居工作

***Selected exhibitions* / Ausgewählte Ausstellungen / 所选展览**

2004 "Wang Du Parade # 1", La Criée, Rennes, France
2005 "Populism", Stedelijk Museum, Amsterdam, The Netherlands
"Die obere Hälfte", Städtische Museen Heilbronn, Heilbronn, Germany
"Wang Du", Yerba Buena Center for the Arts, San Francisco, CA, USA
2006 "Notre histoire", Palais de Tokyo, Paris, France
"Tina B – Prague Contemporary Art Festival", National Gallery, Prague, Czech Republic
"50 JPG", Centre de la Photographie, Geneva, Switzerland

2004年 《王度的, 游行1号》La Criée, 雷恩 法国
2005年 《人民党主义》国家博物馆，阿姆斯特丹, 荷兰
《上半》城市的美术馆，赫伯恩，德国
《王度, 》亚巴布纳艺术中心，旧金山，美国
2006年 《我们的历史》日本的宫殿，巴黎，法国
《Tina B – 布拉格当代艺术节》国家画廊，布拉格, 捷克
《50 JPG》摄影的中心, 日内瓦，瑞士

***Selected publications* / Ausgewählte Publikationen / 所选著作**

"Wang Du Magazine", Lyon 2001
Jennifer Allen: "The Image on Parade", in: "Wang Du", Paris 2004

《王度杂志》利昂2001年
Allen, Jennifer（著）:《图象与游行》于展册《王度》巴黎 2004年

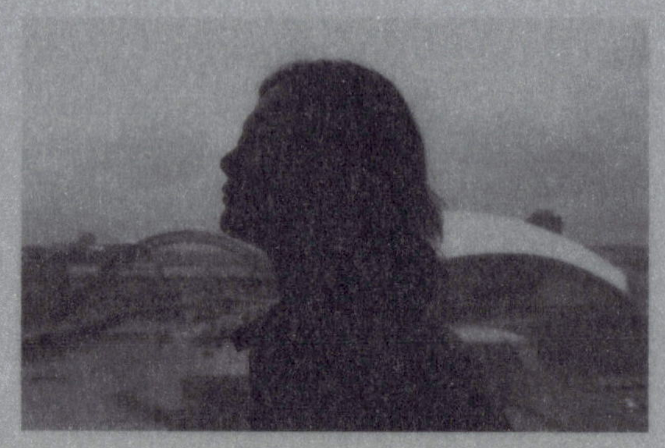

"The 'visual' and oral noise of information not only clashes constantly with the inner calm and peace we naturally require, but is also a menace to our existence."

„Das ‚visuelle' und orale Geräusch der Informationen kollidiert nicht nur dauernd mit dem inneren Frieden, den wir uns selbstverständlich wünschen, sondern es droht auch, an die Stelle unserer Existenz zu treten."

"信息的视觉和口头干扰不仅常常打破了我们本性所需要的平静与安宁，也威胁到我们自身存在。"

Born in 1956 in Wuhan, China. Lives and works in Paris, France
Geboren 1956 in Wuhan, China. Lebt und arbeitet in Paris, Frankreich
1956年出生于中国武汉，现在巴黎定居工作

Selected exhibitions / Ausgewählte Ausstellungen / 所选展览

2004 "Wang Du Parade # 1", La Criée, Rennes, France
2005 "Populism", Stedelijk Museum, Amsterdam, The Netherlands
"Die obere Hälfte", Städtische Museen Heilbronn, Heilbronn, Germany
"Wang Du", Yerba Buena Center for the Arts, San Francisco, CA, USA
2006 "Notre histoire", Palais de Tokyo, Paris, France
"Tina B - Prague Contemporary Art Festival", National Gallery, Prague, Czech Republic
"50 JPG", Centre de la Photographie, Geneva, Switzerland

2004年 《王度的,游行1号》La Criée, 雷恩, 法国
2005年 《人民党主义》国家博物馆，阿姆斯特丹, 荷兰
《上半》城市的美术馆，赫伯恩，德国
《王度,》亚巴布纳艺术中心，旧金山，美国
2006年 《我们的历史》日本的宫殿，巴黎，法国
《Tina B - 布拉格当代艺术节》国家画廊，布拉格, 捷克
《50 JPG》摄影的中心, 日内瓦，瑞士

Selected publications / Ausgewählte Publikationen / 所选著作

"Wang Du Magazine", Lyon 2001
Jennifer Allen: "The Image on Parade", in: "Wang Du", Paris 2004

《王度杂志》利昂2001年
Allen, Jennifer（著）：《图象与游行》于展册《王度》巴黎 2004年

WANG DU 王度

[waŋ tu]

A space-time-tunnel might be everyone's wish – to go on a journey between the third and fourth dimension, which is even for serious physicists not absurd. But due to omnipresent mass media we are caught, more than before, by the very moment without any escape as it might seem. This conflict between being captured and escaping agitates Wang Du, whose space consuming installations with larger than life figures attack and overwhelm the spectator. Wang depicts famous people and stars from all parts of the world and of each section of public life, blown up to a hypertrophic VIP-family, being drastically super-elevated and gaining a puppet like identity.

Wang presents these mammoth and sometimes primitively arranged caricatures of people known by movie, radio, and television, embedded in a flood of those magazines, making those people known – and immediately we are frightened: this is the inexhaustible food for our eternal hunger for information and pictures among the war of media, like always, affecting the individual.

Wang Du, the installation artist, has been living in Paris since 1990, before that time he was dedicated to painting. In 2004 his multiple installation "Wang Du! Parade" joined his characteristic works of recent years, completed in the quadripartite cycle "Le Défilé". This monumental walkable work summarizes like a retrospective his oeuvre containing numerous hints to his own biography.

The installation starts with a walkable space-time-tunnel, a rusty iron tube of 28 m length, equipped on the outside with newspapers and running monitors instead of windows. The monitors displays flickering day and night news from all over the world edited in advertisement manner – objective information as beginning of knowledge (and power), thwarted by the pop like entertainment character of the presentation. The spectator dizzyly stumbling out of this tube finds itself in front of a huge metal sculpture, being the reproduction of a paper ball which makes us appear like dwarfs compared to this huge ball of information. The

Einen Raum-Zeit-Tunnel wünscht sich gewiss jeder einmal – für eine Art Reise zwischen der dritten und der vierten Dimension, die mittlerweile selbst seriösen Physikern nicht mehr ganz abwegig erscheint. Auf der anderen Seite sind wir jedoch, dank der allgegenwärtigen Massenmedien, mehr denn je gefangen im Augenblick, aus dem es kein Entkommen zu geben scheint. Gerade dieser Konflikt bewegt Wang Du, dessen raumgreifende Installationen den Betrachter mit überlebensgroßen Figuren überwältigen und attackieren. Wang zeigt Berühmtheiten und Stars aus aller Welt und sämtlichen Bereichen des öffentlichen Lebens, aufgebläht zu einer hypertrophen VIP-Familie, die auf diese Weise eine drastische Überhöhung erfährt und eine geradezu puppenhafte Identität gewinnt.

Die riesenhaften und mitunter primitiv aufgereihten Karikaturen von Personen, die man aus Film, Funk und Fernsehen kennt, präsentiert Wang eingebettet in eine sie umspülende Flut jener Magazine, durch die sie uns gemeinhin vertraut sind – und sofort stellt sich ein monumentaler Schrecken ein: Das also ist die unerschöpfliche Nahrung, die unseren ewigen Hunger nach Informationen und Bildern stillt, in einem Krieg der Medien, von dem (wie bei jedem Krieg) immer Menschen betroffen sind.

Der Installationskünstler Wang Du, der vorher Maler war, lebt seit 1990 in Paris. In seiner mehrteiligen Installation „Wang Du! Parade" führte er 2004 seine charakteristischen Arbeiten aus den letzten Jahren zusammen, um sie mit dem vierteiligen Zyklus „Le Défilé" abzuschließen. Diese monumentale begehbare Arbeit fasst wie eine Retrospektive sein Œuvre zusammen und enthält auch zahlreiche Hinweise auf seine Biografie.

Die Installation beginnt mit einem zu durchschreitenden Raum-Zeit-Tunnel, einer rostigen Eisenröhre von 28 Metern Länge, die außen mit Zeitungen und mit laufenden Monitoren anstelle von Fenstern bestückt ist. Auf ihnen flimmern die werbetechnisch aufbereiteten Rund-um-die-Uhr-Nachrichten aus aller Welt – die sachliche Information

每个人都希望存在一条时空隧道，在时间与空间中旅行，即使是严肃的物理学家对此　也并不感到荒唐。现在无所不在的大众传媒让我们比以前更多的过去的每一瞬间。

隐蔽和捕捉的矛盾激发着王度。他的大型装置，比真仍还要大，使观众有一种被侵袭和压迫的感觉。王度描写了全世界的许多名人和明星和公共生活的每个侧面，把这些名门头像处理的庞大，因为他们的出身高贵，但是却象木偶。

王度把这些巨物和有时自发组合的人物讽刺画呈现在电影上、电台中和电视上，嵌入无数的杂志里，而使这些人广为人知。我们立刻对此感到害怕：我们对新的信息和图片的需求永无满足，我们是媒体战争的中心，影响着每一个个人。

自上世纪90年代起，王度就居住在巴黎，在此之前就致力于油画事业。在1994年。他的多重装置《王度的游行》（分为四个部分）在Le Défilé。这个巨大的可行走的作品总结回顾其全部作品，其中也包含着对他过去许多暗示。

这个装置以一个可移动的时空隧道为开始，其实是一段28厘米长的锈迹斑斑的铁管，时空隧道和报纸、旋转的监视器一起取代了窗户。监视器的显示器成天整夜的闪烁着以广告方式编辑的全球新闻---客观的信息作为知识和力量的开始，受到象娱乐性质表现形式一样的流行艺术的阻碍。观众头晕目弦的走出　管道，发现自己面前时一具巨大的金属雕塑，纸球的复制品让我们感觉到自己很渺小，与巨大的信息球相比。观众脚踏着一条宽大的地毯；《时代》杂志的封面，上图文并茂地报道着哥伦比亚号航天飞机爆炸事件。随后，一群的女工作人员脚穿高跟鞋蹒跚走来，真挚的向观众鞠躬并以得体的风骚陪同观众来到一幅壁画前，壁画设计成互联网截图形式，展示着男性色情娱乐的欢愉和残酷，这是它的主题。穿过门，观众进入一间阴森的屋

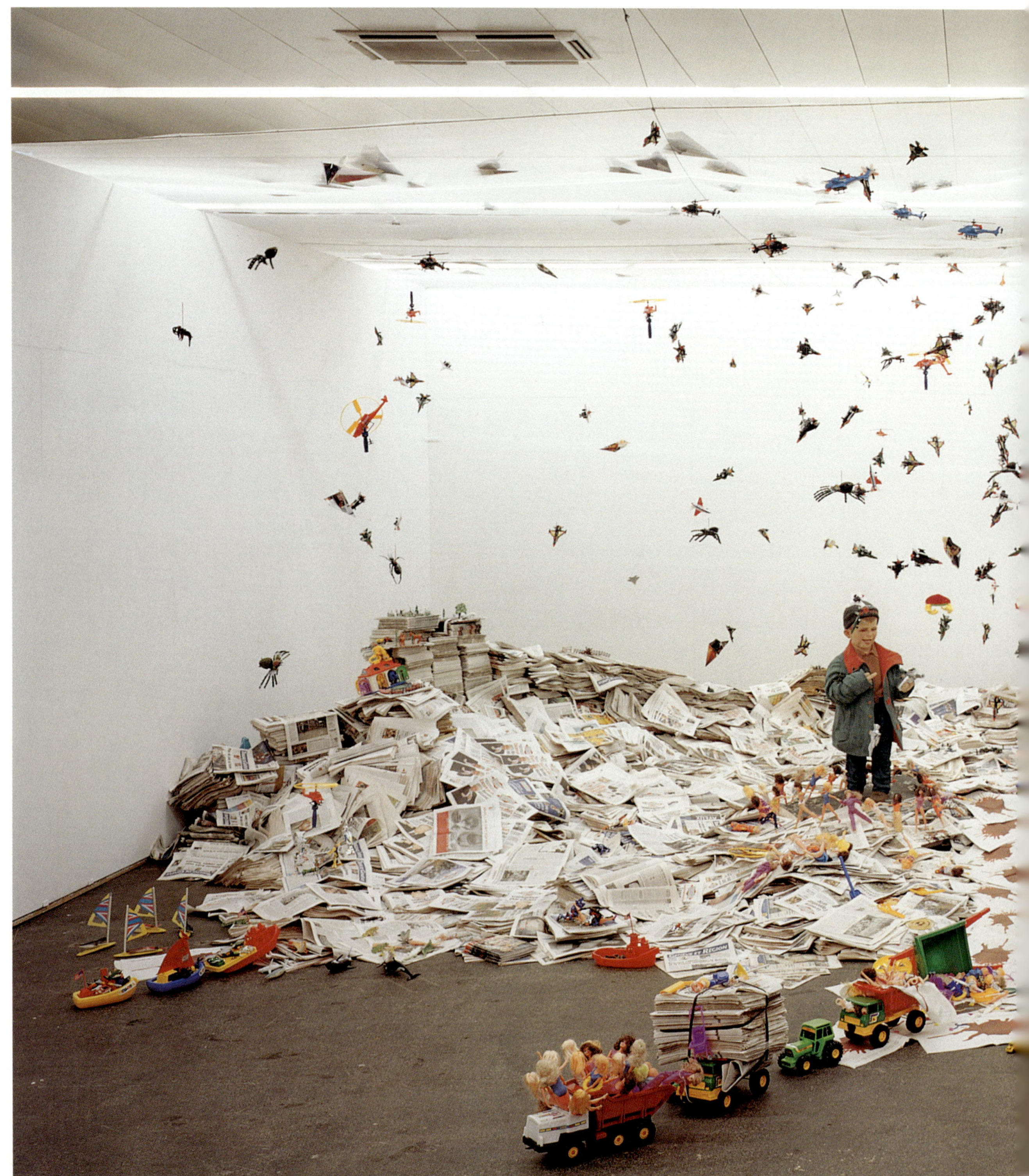

2

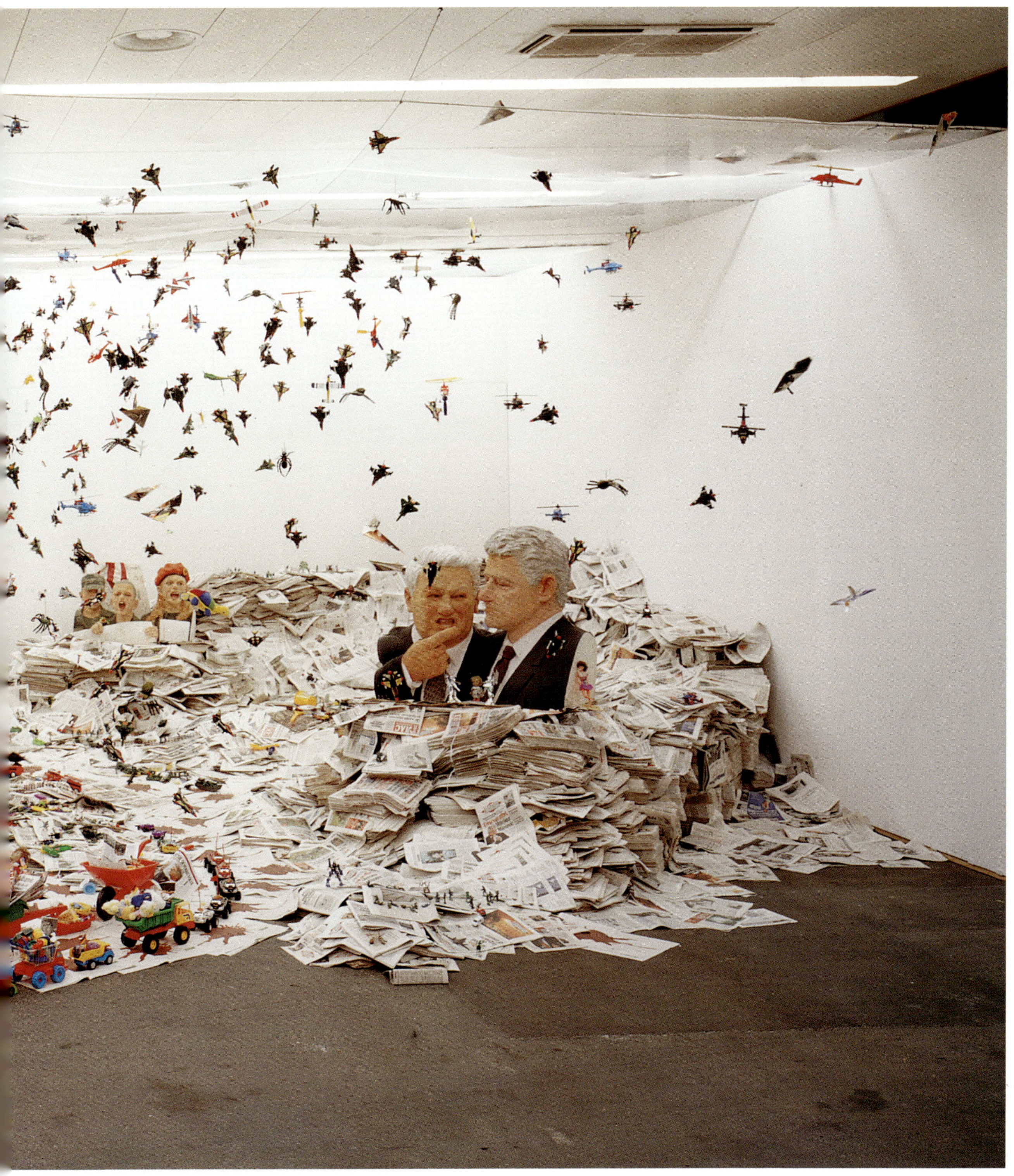

3

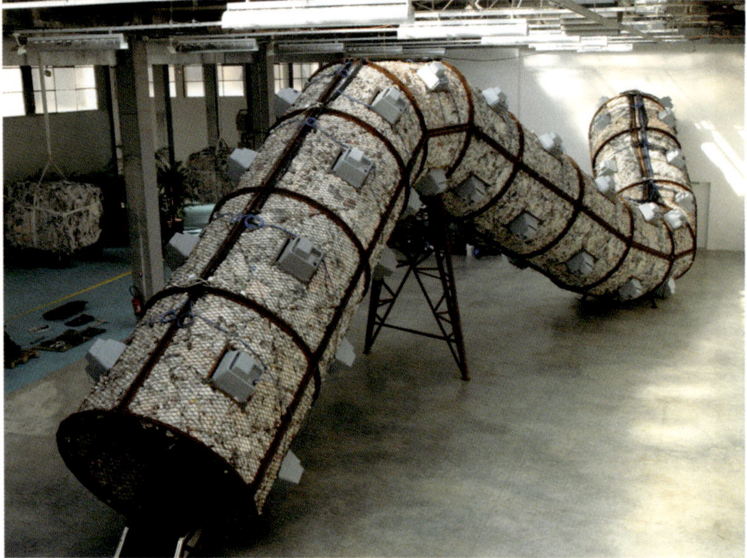

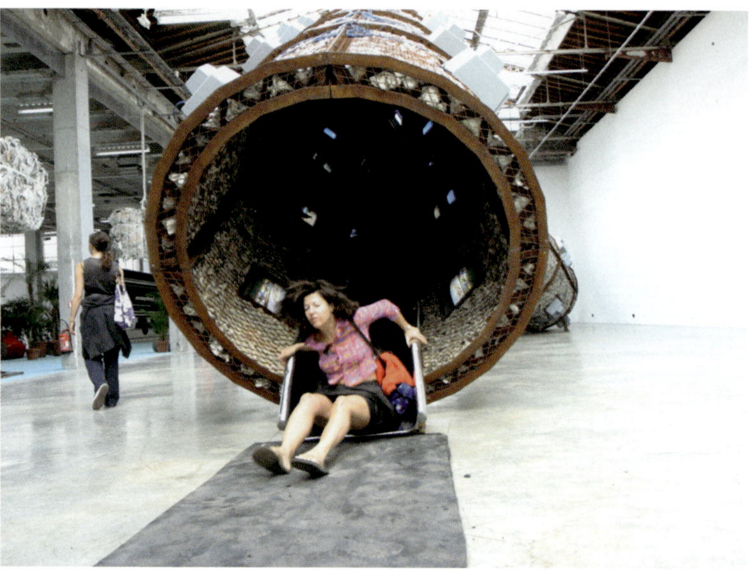

visitor walks on to a large carpet: the cover of the TIME magazine showing in words and pictures the explosion of the space shuttle Columbia. Next comes a group of business-like dressed women staggering on high heels, devotedly bowed and with featherbrained sexuality appropriately accompany the visitor to a mural designed like an Internet screenshot displaying the joy and cruelty of pornographic entertainment for men as the main subject. Passing a door the visitor enters a menacing room, where the Chinese Army exercise a prêt-à-porter show in front of Libyan revolutionist Gaddafi, supported by noisy hymns of military music. The satirical highlight of this perfect staging is to be found in the busts of the figures. Everything is joined to anything is Wang Du's message and global politics follow its own rules.

This deconstructive analysis of advertisement messages of information and politics unveil the logic of this iconoclast hero Wang Du. His criticism of mass media hegemony and global capitalism might be a beamy provocation of the taste and critical faculty of arty people.

ist aller Wissen (und Macht) Anfang, wird aber konterkariert vom poppigen Unterhaltungscharakter ihrer Präsentation. Taumelt der Besucher benommen aus dieser Röhre, findet er sich vor einer riesigen, metallenen Skulptur wieder, die ein Papierknäuel nachbildet, das uns gegenüber der Information wie Zwerge erscheint lässt. Es geleitet uns zu einem gewaltigen Teppich: einem Cover des TIME-Magazines, das in Wort und Bild die Explosion des Space-Shuttle Columbia zeigt. Von dort geht es weiter zu einer Gruppe auf Stöckelschuhen dahinstrauchelnder, weit vorgebeugter Frauen im kurzen Business-Dress, die uns in dümmlicher Erotik angemessen zu einem Wandbild geleiten, das wie ein Internet-Screenshot gestaltet ist und die Freuden und Grausamkeiten pornografischer Unterhaltung für Männer zum Thema hat. Durch eine Tür darin dringen wir in einen recht martialischen Raum ein, in dem die chinesische Armee vor den Augen des libyschen Revolutionsführers Gaddafi eine Prêt-à-porter Show vollführt, lautstark untermalt von hymnischer Militärmusik. Ihren satirischen Höhepunkt findet die perfekte Inszenierung schließlich in den Büsten der Figuren. Alles hängt mit allem zusammen, so Wang Dus Botschaft, und die globale Politik hat ihre eigenen Regeln.

In solch dekonstruktivistischen Analysen der Werbebotschaften von Information und Politik offenbart sich die Logik des bilderstürmerischen Helden Wang. Seine Kritik der massenmedialen Hegemonie und des globalen Kapitalismus ist eine bisweilen wuchtige Provokation des Geschmacks und der Kritikfähigkeit aller Kunstbeflissenen.

子，那里中国军队在利比亚革命家Ghaddafi面前训练一套外来表演，伴奏着嘈杂的军歌。这种完美的讽刺突出在人物的半身像上。王度要传递的信息是事事息息相关，全球政治遵循着自己的规律。

信息和政治的广告词的建设性分析揭示了反偶像传统英雄王度的内心逻辑。他对大众媒体霸权和国际资本主义的批评也许是对艺术人群的品味和批评才能的一丝挑战。

Gregor Jansen

4

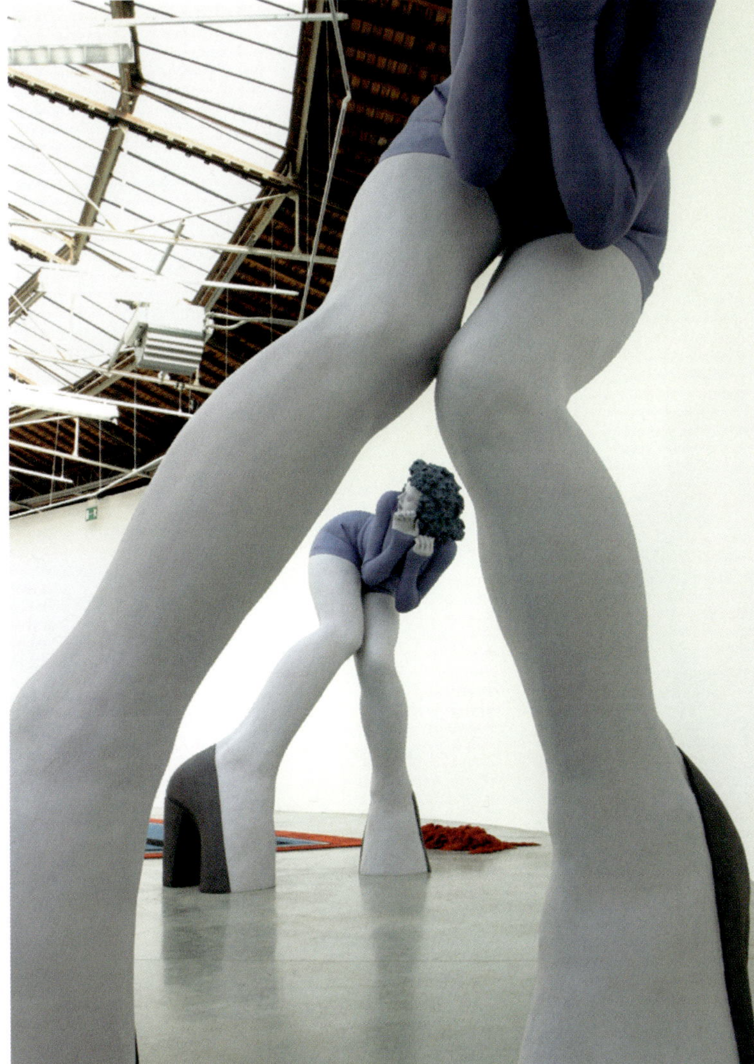

5

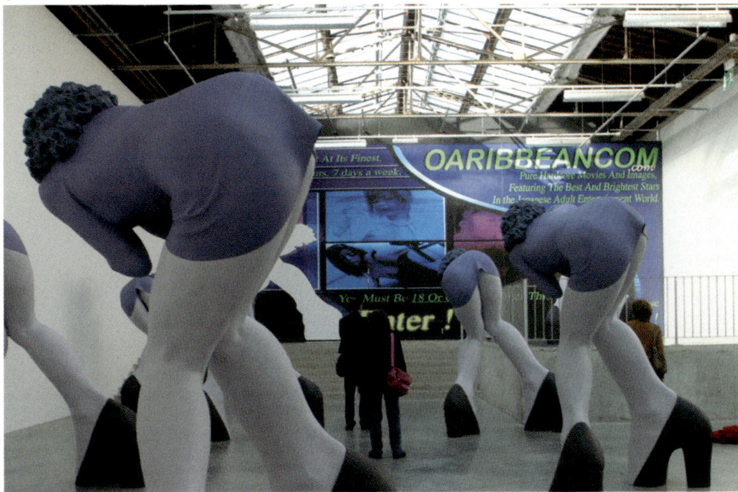

6

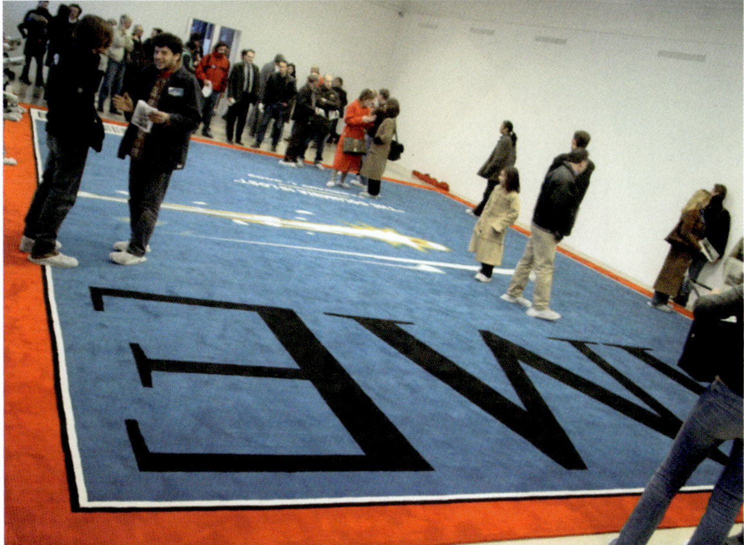

1 ***The Family***, *1997*
Polyester and gouache, dimensions variable
Polyester und Gouache, Maße variabel
《家》1997年, 涤纶和水粉, 尺寸可变

2 ***Chamber Strategy***, *1999*
Paper waste, resin, acrylic, 200 m²
Papiermüll, Kunstharz, Acryl, 200 m²
《纸上谈兵》1999年，废纸, 树脂, 丙烯, 200 m²

3 ***The tunnel of space time***, *2004*
Steel, newspapers, TV sets, 2.6 m diameter, 30 m length
Stahl, Zeitungspapier, Fernsehapparate, Durchmesser 2,6 m, Länge 30 m
《时空隧道》2004年, 钢, 报纸, 电视机, 直径2.6 m, 长30 m

4+5 ***Enter!***, *2004*
Resin, acrylic, digital print image, dimensions variable
Kunstharz, Acryl, Digitaldruck, Maße variabel
《进入!》2004年, 树脂, 丙烯, 数码照片, 尺寸可变

6 ***The flying carpet***, *2003*
Hand-woven wool of New Zealand, 11.8 x 8.8 m
Handgewebte neuseeländische Wolle, 11,8 x 8,8 m
《飞毯》2003年，新西兰手纺羊毛, 11.8 x 8.8 m

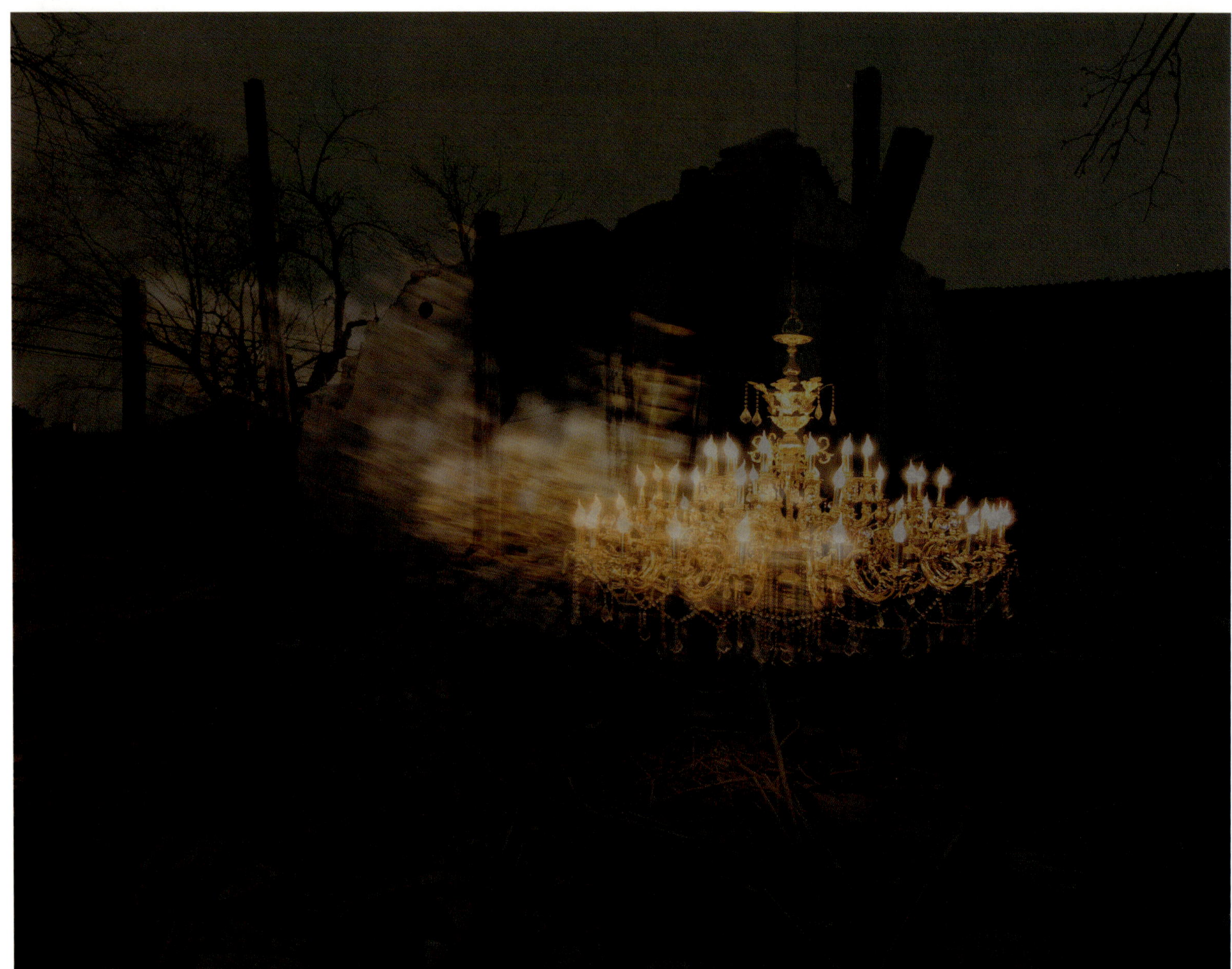

1

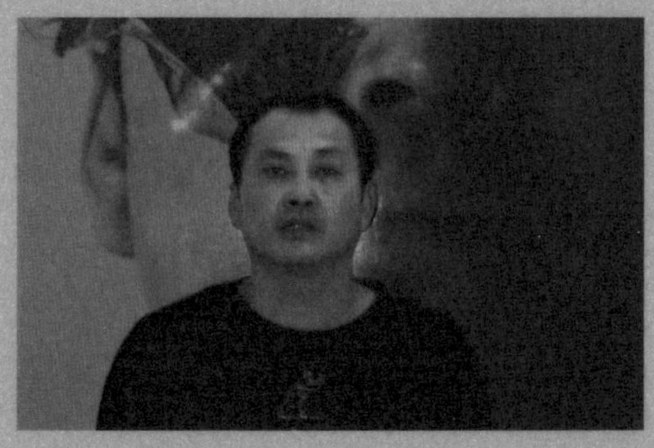

"Parody has become one of the most important strategies for Post-Modern artistic practice."

„Die Parodie ist mittlerweile eine der wichtigsten Strategien in der postmodernen Kunstpraxis."

"对于后现代艺术实践而言，模仿是其最重要的策略之一。"

Born in 1960 in Beijing, China. Lives and works in Beijing
Geboren 1960 in Peking, China. Lebt und arbeitet in Peking
1960年出生于中国北京，现仍居住工作于此

***Selected exhibitions* / Ausgewählte Ausstellungen /** 所选展览

2001 49. Biennale di Venezia, Venice, Italy
25. Bienal de São Paulo, São Paulo, Brazil
2002 First Guangzhou Triennial, Guangzhou, China
2004 "All under Heaven", Museum of Contemporary Art, Antwerp, Belgium
2004–07 "Between Past and Future, New Photography and Video from China", International Center of Photography, New York, NY, USA (travelling exhibition)
2007 "The Real Thing: Contemporary Art from China", Tate Liverpool, Liverpool, UK

2001年 第49届威尼斯双年展威尼斯，意大利
第25届圣保罗双年展，圣保罗，巴西
2002年 《首届广州三年展　重新解读：中国实验艺术十年》广州, 中国
2004年 《天堂之下》安特卫普现代美术馆，安特卫普，比利时
2004–07年 《过去与未来之间—中国新影像展》国际摄影中心，纽约，美国（巡回展）
2007年 《真实事件：中国当代艺术》泰特美术馆，利物浦，英国

***Selected publications* / Ausgewählte Publikationen /** 所选著作

Gao Minglu (ed.): "Inside Out: New Chinese Art", Berkeley 1998
"Synthetic Realities", Beijing 2004
"The Monk and the Demon", Lyon 2004
Britta Erickson, Pi Li: "Here? Or there?: Wang Gongxin & Lin Tianmiao", Hong Kong 2005

高明潞:《蜕变突破：华人新艺术展》伯克利 1998年
《合成现实》展册，北京 2004年
《道与魔》展册，里昂 2004年
Erickson, Britta/Pi Li（编者）:《这儿?或那儿?王功新和林天苗》香港 2005年

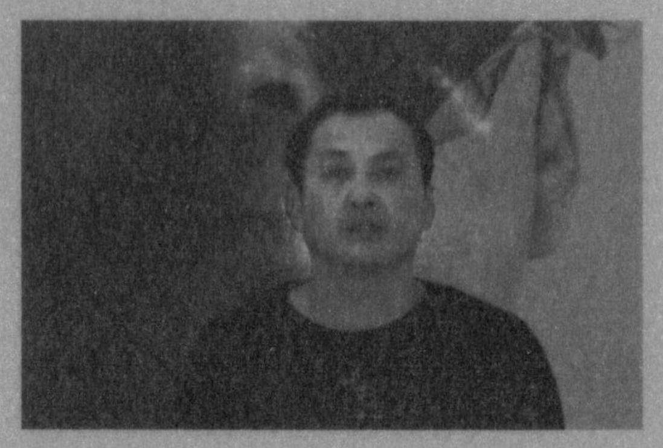

"Parody has become one of the most important strategies for Post-Modern artistic practice."

„Die Parodie ist mittlerweile eine der wichtigsten Strategien in der postmodernen Kunstpraxis."

"对于后现代艺术实践而言，模仿是其最重要的策略之一。"

Born in 1960 in Beijing, China. Lives and works in Beijing
Geboren 1960 in Peking, China. Lebt und arbeitet in Peking
1960年出生于中国北京，现仍居住工作于此

Selected exhibitions / Ausgewählte Ausstellungen / 所选展览

2001 49. Biennale di Venezia, Venice, Italy
25. Bienal de São Paulo, São Paulo, Brazil
2002 First Guangzhou Triennial, Guangzhou, China
2004 "All under Heaven", Museum of Contemporary Art, Antwerp, Belgium
2004-07 "Between Past and Future, New Photography and Video from China", International Center of Photography, New York, NY, USA (travelling exhibition)
2007 "The Real Thing: Contemporary Art from China", Tate Liverpool, Liverpool, UK

2001年 第49届威尼斯双年展威尼斯，意大利
第25届圣保罗双年展，圣保罗，巴西
2002年 《首届广州三年展　重新解读：中国实验艺术十年》广州，中国
2004年 《天堂之下》安特卫普现代美术馆，安特卫普，比利时
2004-07年 《过去与未来之间—中国新影像展》国际摄影中心，纽约，美国（巡回展）
2007年 《真实事件：中国当代艺术》泰特美术馆，利物浦，英国

Selected publications / Ausgewählte Publikationen / 所选著作

Gao Minglu (ed.): "Inside Out: New Chinese Art", Berkeley 1998
"Synthetic Realities", Beijing 2004
"The Monk and the Demon", Lyon 2004
Britta Erickson, Pi Li: "Here? Or there?: Wang Gongxin & Lin Tianmiao", Hong Kong 2005

高明潞：《蜕变突破：华人新艺术展》伯克利 1998年
《合成现实》展册，北京 2004年
《道与魔》展册，里昂 2004年
Erickson, Britta/Pi Li（编者）：《这儿?或那儿?王功新和林天苗》香港 2005年

WANG GONGXIN 王功新

[waŋ kʊŋɕin]

Wang Gongxin is one of the earliest video artists of China. The main subject of his mainly installation works is the ambiguity of the visible, he found himself in the mid 1990s when he returned to Beijing after a ten years sojourn in New York, viewing his hometown and its inhabitants from a totally different point of view due to the distance of space and time. Pictures are generated in conflict between appearance and reality being a permanent expression of certain political, ideological or cultural encoded structures of power. The video technique seemed to be the appropriate media for Wang Gongxin to disclose and unveil this area of conflict.

His installation "The Sky of Brooklyn" (1995) regarded as one of his first site specific installations in China he made a well like hole in his apartment, installing a screen on the bottom which showed photographs of the sky of Brooklyn. But was this in fact the sky over New York or just the reflection of the sky of Beijing? The answer of this question was up to the spectator reminding him of the Chinese proverb "Looking at the sky from the bottom of the well," referring to the limited horizon as well as to the American slogan "Digging a hole to China," an expression for the audacity to act. This audacity has been challenged by a voice on audiotape in this installation asking the spectator "What are you looking at? What is there to look at?" inviting to a reflecting change of perspective.

Wang's main concern is to sharpen and break open the frontiers of the familiar world and the own visual perception. Shortly after his return from the United States he created "The Old Bench" (1996), a work among others having a re-approach to his Chinese offspring as subject. He integrated an old wooden bench into a screen, which showed one finger caressing over the wooden seat which made it possible to experience a new kind of sensitive viewing by the contrast between old and new, real and virtual. To learn a new kind of view Wang Gongxin manipulates the spectator by means of installation strategies, transforming pictures as well as the multiplication and slowing down thereof. The

Wang Gongxin ist einer der ersten Videokünstler in China. Hauptthema seiner installativen Arbeiten ist die Ambiguität des Sichtbaren, die er selbst erfuhr, als er Mitte der 1990er Jahre nach einem zehnjährigen New-York Aufenthalt nach Peking zurückkehrte und seine Heimatstadt durch den räumlichen und zeitlichen Abstand aus einem anderen Blickwinkel sah. Bilder generieren sich im Spannungsfeld zwischen Anschein und Realität und sind Ausdruck politisch, ideologisch oder kulturell kodierter Machtstrukturen. Die Videotechnik erscheint Wang Gongxin als das geeignete Medium, um dies aufzuzeigen und zu entlarven.

Für seine Installation „The Sky of Brooklyn" (1995), die als eine der ersten ortsspezifischen Installationen in China gilt, ließ er in seiner Wohnung ein brunnenähnliches Loch ausheben, auf dessen Grund er einen Bildschirm installierte, der Aufnahmen des Himmels von Brooklyn zeigte. Doch sah man tatsächlich den Himmel über New York oder hatte man es mit einer Spiegelung des Pekinger Himmels zu tun? Die Beantwortung dieser Fragen überließ Wang dem Betrachter und erinnerte sowohl an den chinesischen Sinnspruch „Den Himmel vom Grund der Mauer aus betrachten", der auf den begrenzten Horizont verweist, als auch an das amerikanische „Digging a hole to China" (Lasst uns einen Tunnel nach China graben!), das den Mut zur Aktion ausdrückt, der bei Wangs Installation auch von einer Tonbandstimme gefordert wurde, die den Betrachter mit den Fragen „What are you looking at? What is there to look at?" zum reflektierenden Perspektivwechsel aufforderte.

Die Grenzen der vertrauten Welt und der eigenen visuellen Wahrnehmung zu schärfen und aufzubrechen ist Wangs Hauptanliegen. Kurz nach seiner Rückkehr aus den USA entstand auch seine Arbeit „The Old Bench" (1996), die u. a. die Wiederannäherung an seine chinesische Herkunft thematisierte. Indem er in eine alte chinesische Holzbank einen Bildschirm integrierte, auf dem ein Finger zu sehen war, der zärtlich über die hölzerne Sitzfläche strich, ermöglichte er durch den Kontrast zwischen Altem und Neuem, Realem und Virtuellem eine einfühlsame Seherfahrung.

王功新是中国最早开始进行录像创作的艺术家之一。上世纪90年代，王功新旅居纽约10年后返回北京，时空的距离感，让他能以一种完全迥异的视角去观察他的故乡和同胞，从中他发现了可见的模糊性。而这种模糊性是其主要装置作品的主题思想。
由于某种政治、意识形态或是文化力量结构的永久表述的原因，他的照片是表象和事实之间冲突的产物。对于王功新而言，录像技术是揭示这种冲突的最合适的方式。

装置《布鲁克林的天空》公认中国第一座现 场具体装 置。他在其公寓内打了一口似洞般的井，在井底装置了一个屏幕，放映着布鲁克林的天空的摄影作品。可这真的是纽约头顶的天空吗?或这仅仅是北京天空的反射呢？观众由此可以联想到中国的一句谚语：井底观天，暗示着狭小的视角，而美国有一句俗谚，从美国向下挖，就能通到中国，表达 了行为的大胆。在装置里有一盘录音磁带，磁带里的一个声音在问观众“你在看什么呢?那里能看到什么”这种大胆受到这个声音的挑战，而形成了观点的反射性变化.

超越熟悉世界和个体视觉理念的边界和隔离，是王功新的主要关注点. 在美国回国以后的短短时间内，王功新创作了《凳》(1996年)，此作 品和其他作品 都是以 接近 中国子孙 为主题。他把一张老凳子融入屏幕中，一只手指轻拂着木凳，去体验那种陈旧与崭新，真实与虚拟之间的对立而形成的新感觉。

为获得一种 新的视觉，王功新通过转换，增加图片以及减缓其速度等装置策略，去引导观众。装置《我的太阳》(2001年)是王功新最著名的录像装置之一。一位年迈的农村大娘站在贫瘠的土 地上，手抓着太阳，她的照片在屏幕上不断叠加，而让观众眼花缭乱。在中国传统意义上，太阳是力量的象征也是毛泽东的化身，老太太是试图制止太阳的破坏她的庄稼的丰收吗？还是她要融合太阳的力量呢?通过个人的增加，而引出社会主义体系里个体和大众的

2

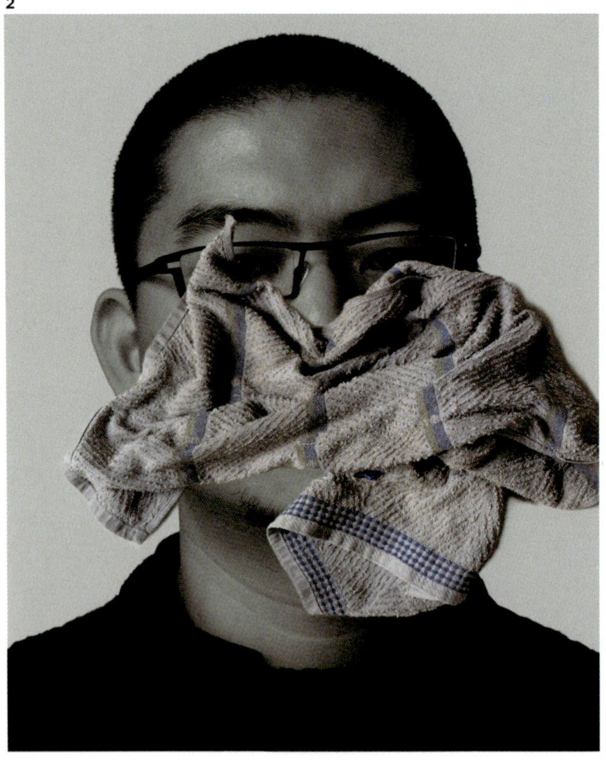

3

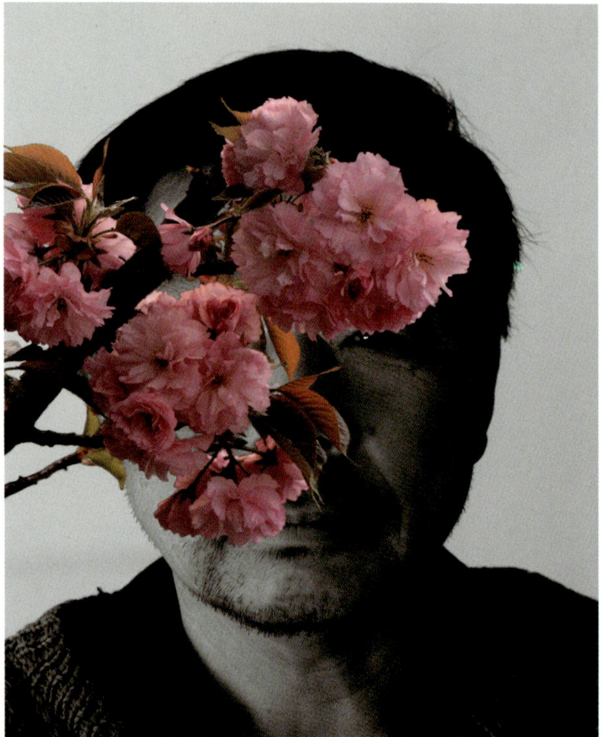

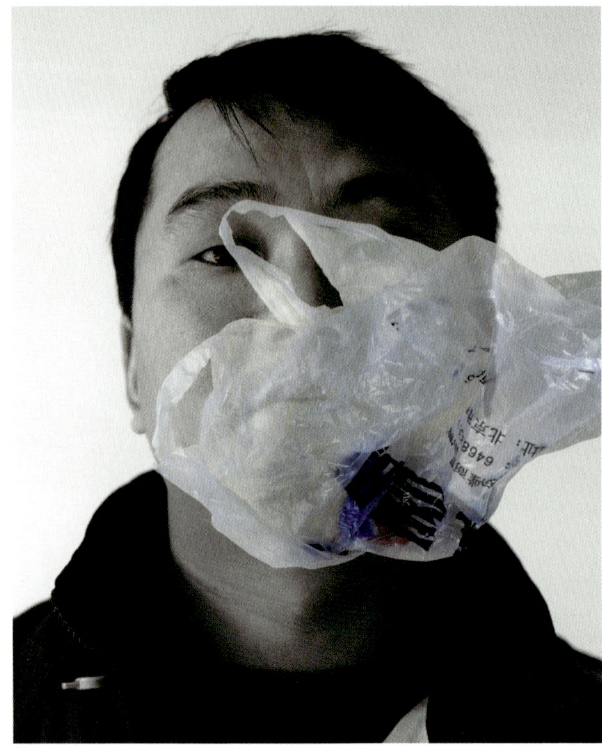

4

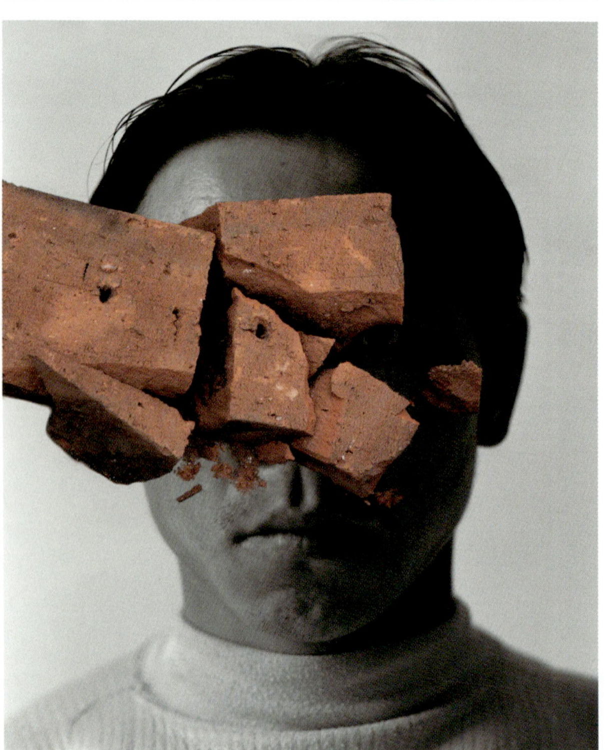

5

6

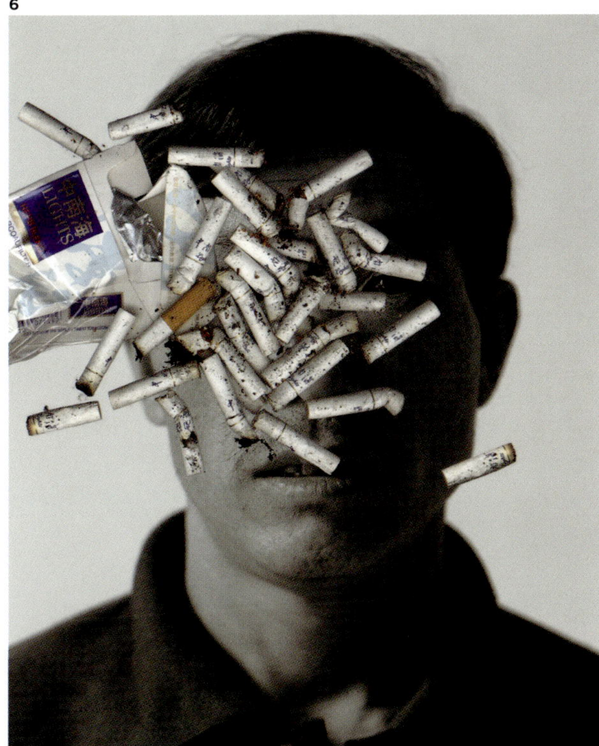

7

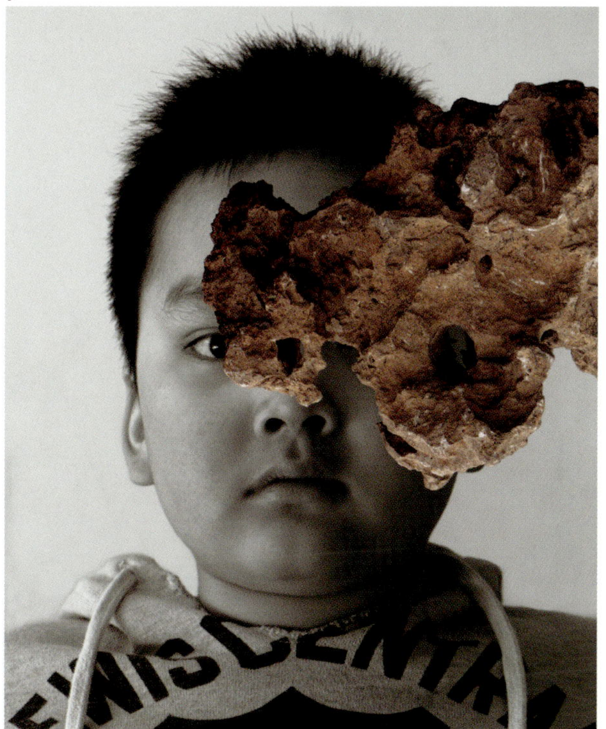

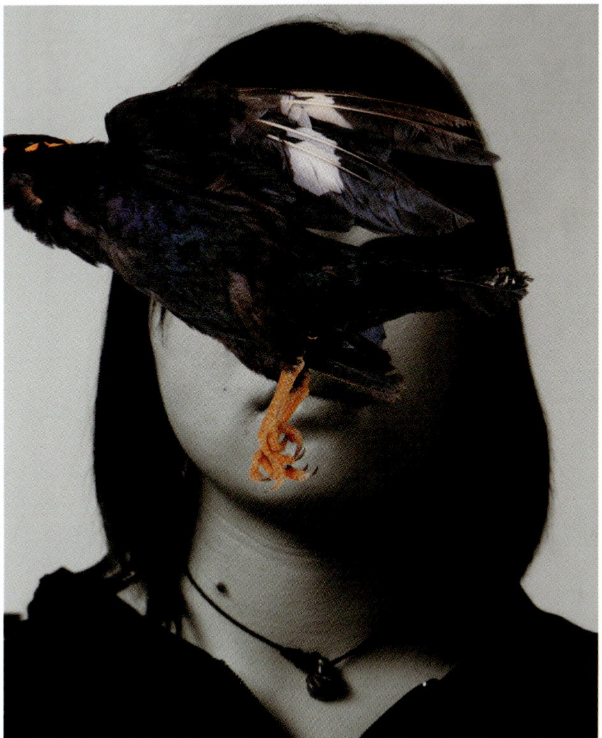

8

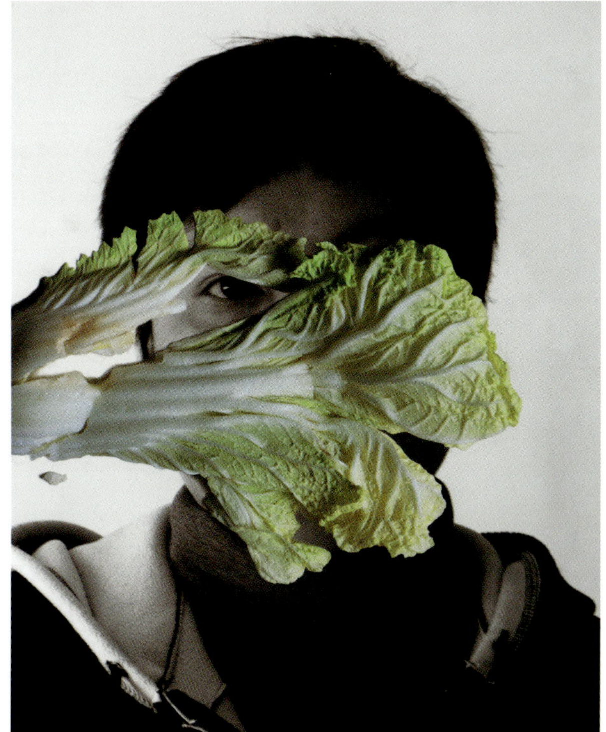

9

10

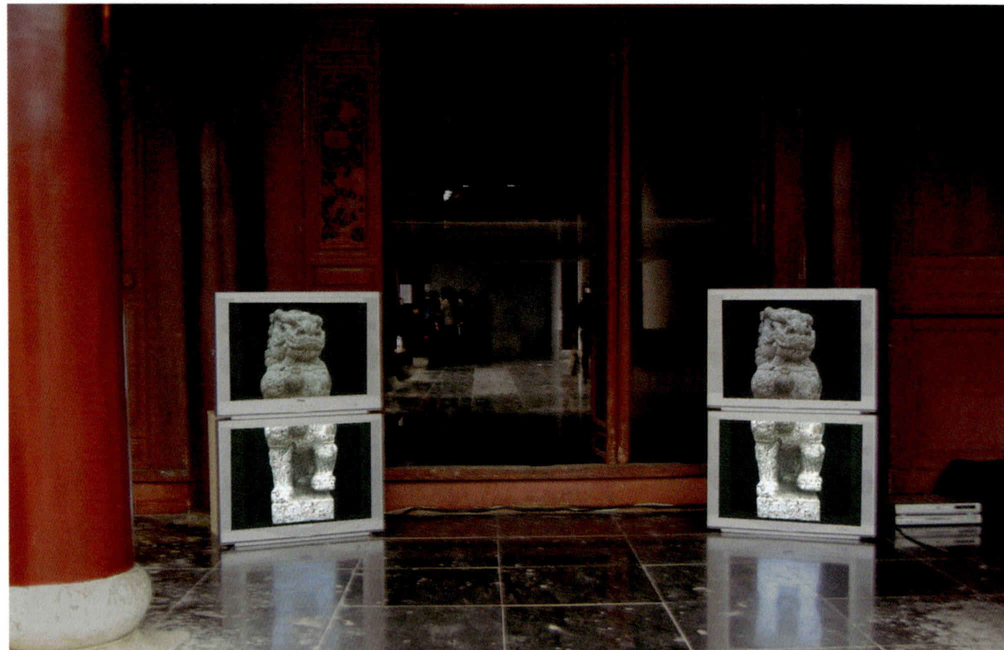

11

installation "My Sun" (2001) is one of the most renown video installations of Wang Gongxin. The spectator being confused on several channels by the irritating multiplication of the picture of an old countrywoman, standing on an arid field and grasping for the sun. Does she intend to curb the destroying power of the sun being traditionally the symbol of power in China and understood as personification of Mao Zedong in recent history in order to save her harvest or does she want to incorporate the power of the sun? The imbalance of individual and masses in the socialistic shaped system broaches an issue by means of the multiplication of one person and creates an atmosphere between hope and powerlessness.

Wang addresses the spectator in a direct way and likes to use humour as an instrument for cognition. His video installation "Always Welcome" (2003) for example is a very weird contemporary interpretation of lion guardians usually placed in front of houses and temples in traditional China. Contrary to the traditional animal sculptures which should frighten people away by their giant size the artist created two video animated figures, greeting the visitor with a cheerful "Hello".

Um mit anderen Augen zu sehen, gehören die Manipulation des Betrachterblicks mittels installativer Strategien, das Transformieren von Bildern sowie deren Vervielfältigung oder Verlangsamung zu Wang Gongxins Repertoire. Die Installation „My Sun" (2001) zählt zu Wangs bekanntesten Videoarbeiten. Auf mehreren Kanälen wird der Betrachter mit der irritierenden Vervielfachung des Bildes einer alten Bauersfrau konfrontiert, die auf einem dürren Feld nach der Sonne greift. Will sie der zerstörerischen Kraft des Sterns, der in China traditionell ein Zeichen der Macht ist und in der jüngeren Geschichte vor allem als Verkörperung Mao Zedongs verstanden wird, Einhalt gebieten, um ihre Ernte zu retten, oder will sie sich seine Kraft einverleiben? Die Vervielfachung einer Person thematisiert das ungleiche Verhältnis von Individuum und Volksmasse im sozialistisch geprägten System und schafft eine Atmosphäre, die zwischen Hoffnung und Machtlosigkeit changiert.

Wang spricht den Betrachter stets auf eine sehr direkte Art an und setzt dabei gern Humor als Erkenntnisinstrument ein. So ist etwa die Videoinstallation „Always Welcome" (2003) eine äußerst komische zeitgenössische Interpretation eines Wächterlöwenpaars, wie es in China traditionell vor Häusern und Tempeln platziert wird. Im Unterschied zu den Tierskulpturen, die durch ihre Monumentalität abschrecken sollen, kreiert der Künstler aber zwei videoanimierte Figuren, die den Besucher mit einem fröhlichen „Hallo" begrüßen.

失衡的主题，并且营造了一种在希望和无望之间徘徊的氛围。

王用一种直接的方式向观众讲述这一点，并且他喜欢把幽默当作认知手段。如录像装置《欧尾狮欢迎》（2003年）是对石狮的最神秘的阐释，中国古时候这些狮子通常放置在房间前或者墓地前。那些传统动物雕塑巨大的外表常常让观众退而却步，与之相比，艺术家创作了两部动物录像，受到观众的欢迎，并欢快的向其问好。

Birgit Hopfener

1 ***Sunset #1 Old House****, 2004*
C-print, 95 x 120 cm; C-print, 95 x 120 cm
《日落#1老房子》2004年, C-印刷, 95 x 120 cm

2 ***Portrait Right No. 4****, 2005*
C-print, 220 x 180 cm; C-print, 220 x 180 cm
《肖像权No. 4》2005年, C-印刷, 220 x 180 cm

3 ***Portrait Right No. 5****, 2005*
C-print, 220 x 180 cm; C-print, 220 x 180 cm
《肖像权No. 5》2005年, C-印刷, 220 x 180 cm

4 ***Portrait Right No. 6****, 2005*
C-print, 220 x 180 cm; C-print, 220 x 180 cm
《肖像权No. 6》2005年, C-印刷, 220 x 180 cm

5 ***Portrait Right No. 7****, 2005*
C-print, 220 x 180 cm; C-print, 220 x 180 cm
《肖像权No. 7》2005年, C-印刷, 220 x 180 cm

6 ***Portrait Right No. 8****, 2005*
C-print, 220 x 180 cm; C-print, 220 x 180 cm
《肖像权No. 8》2005年, C-印刷, 220 x 180 cm

7 ***Portrait Right No. 1****, 2005*
C-print, 220 x 180 cm; C-print, 220 x 180 cm
《肖像权No. 1》2005年, C-印刷, 220 x 180 cm

8 ***Portrait Right No. 10****, 2005*
C-print, 220 x 180 cm; C-print, 220 x 180 cm
《肖像权No. 10》2005年, C-印刷, 220 x 180 cm

9 ***Portrait Right No. 2****, 2005*
C-print, 220 x 180 cm; C-print, 220 x 180 cm
《肖像权No. 2》2005年, C-印刷, 220 x 180 cm

10 ***Always Welcome****, 2003*
Video (installation view); Video (Installationsansicht)
《欧尾狮欢迎》2003年, 录像，装置

11 ***Always Welcome****, 2003*
Video, 1 min 16 sec; Video, 1 Min. 16 Sek.
《欧尾狮欢迎》, 2003年, 录像, 1分 16秒

12 ***Red Doors****, 2002*
Video, 5 min 30 sec; Video, 5 Min. 30 Sek.
《红门》, 2002年, 录像, 5分30秒

13 ***Red Doors****, 2002*
Video (installation view); Video (Installationsansicht)
《红门》, 2002年, 录像, 装置

12

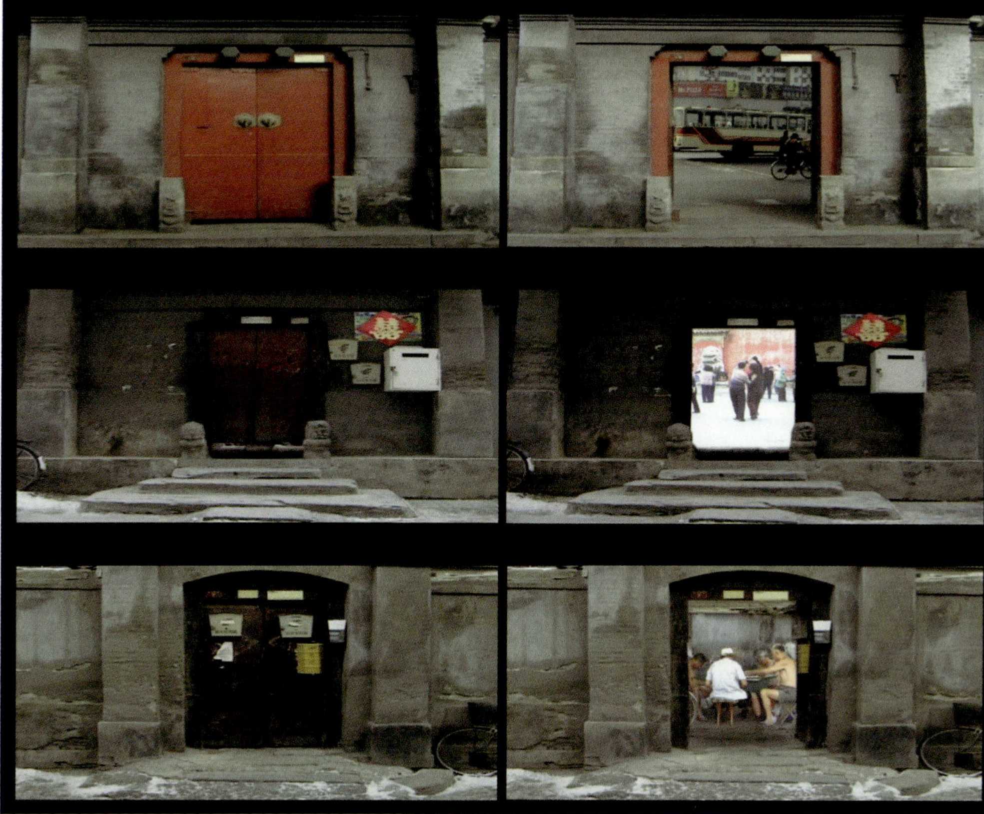

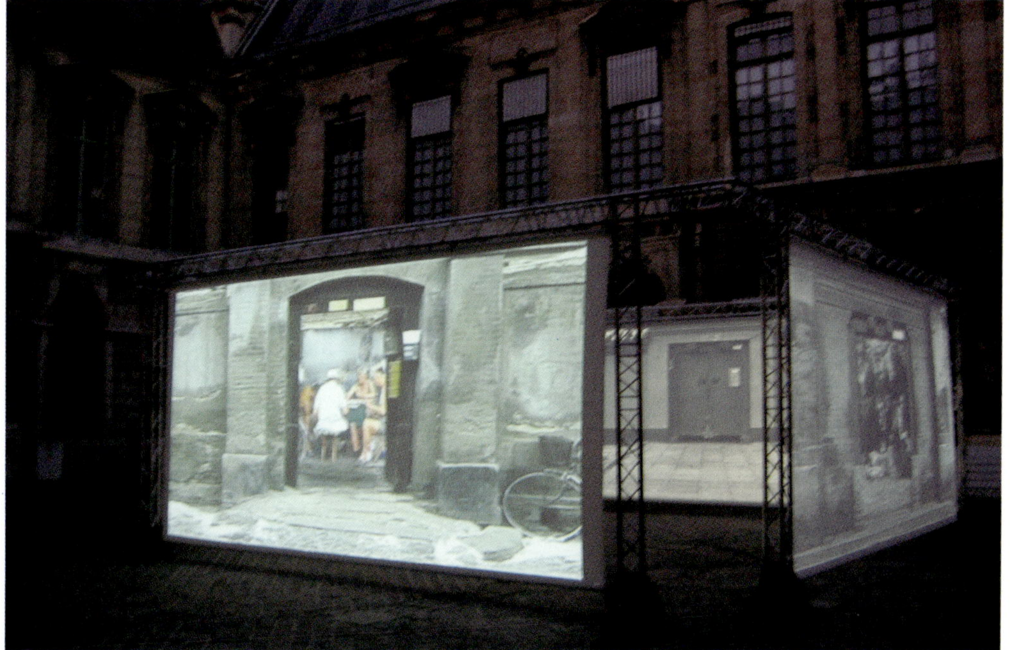

13

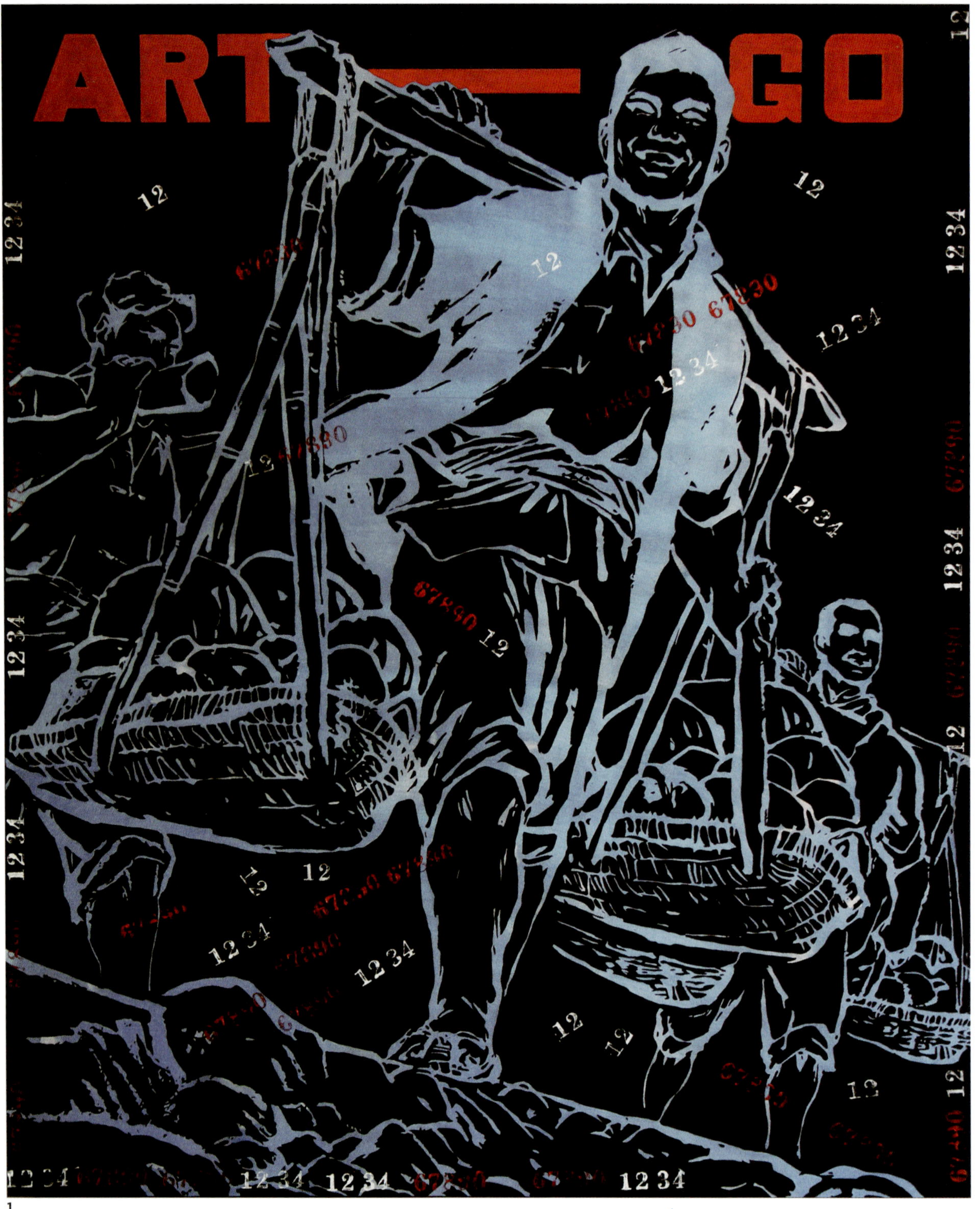

1

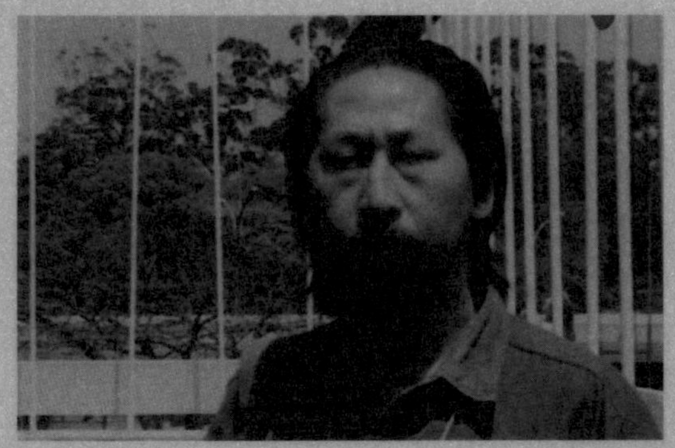

"At the same time that an artist criticizes society, he also acts to alert it, to awaken it to the awareness that there may be many things spreading forever through one's consciousness. This awareness may be the starting point for the revival of a nation and a people."

„Wenn ein Künstler die Gesellschaft kritisiert, geschieht dies, um sie zu warnen und die Erkenntnis zu wecken, dass es viele Dinge geben mag, die sich immer weiter im Bewusstsein ausbreiten. Diese Erkenntnis kann der Ausgangspunkt für das Wiedererwachen einer Nation und eines Volkes sein."

"在艺术家批评社会的同时，也会去警告社会，去唤醒社会一种意识：许多东西在人的无意识中永远流传下去。而这种意识是一个国家和民族复兴的起点。"

Born in 1957 in Harbin, Heilongjiang Province, China. Lives and works in Beijing
Geboren 1957 in Harbin, Provinz Heilongjiang, China. Lebt und arbeitet in Peking
1957年出生于中国黑龙江省哈尔滨市，现居住工作于北京

***Selected exhibitions* / Ausgewählte Ausstellungen / 所选展览**

1989	"China/Avant-Garde", National Art Museum of China, Beijing, China
1993	45. Biennale di Venezia, Venice, Italy
1994	"China's New Art, Post 1989", Hong Kong Arts Centre, Hong Kong
1996	Asia-Pacific Triennial of Contemporary Art, Queensland, Australia
2001	"Towards a New Image: Twenty Years of Chinese Contemporary Painting", The National Art Museum of China, Beijing, Shanghai Art Museum, Shanghai, Guangdong Art Museum, Guangzhou, Sichuan Modern Art Museum, Chengdu, China
2002	The First Guangzhou Triennial, Guangdong Museum of Art, Guangzhou, China
2005-07	"Mahjong – Chinesische Gegenwartskunst aus der Sammlung Sigg", Kunstmuseum Bern, Berne, Switzerland; Hamburger Kunsthalle, Hamburg, Germany; Museum der Moderne, Salzburg, Austria

1989年	《中国现代艺术展，中国美术馆》北京
1993年	《第四十五届威尼斯双年展》威尼斯，意大利
1994年	《后89新艺术巡回展》香港艺术 中心，香港；悉尼 现代艺术博物馆，悉尼，澳大利亚
1996年	《亚太当代艺术三年展》昆士兰美术馆，澳大 利亚
2001年	《新形象：中国当代绘画二十年大型巡回展》中国美术馆，上海美术馆，四川省美术馆，广东美术馆
2002年	《首届广州三年展-重新 解读：中国实验艺术十 年》（1990-2000年）广东美术馆，广州
2005-07年	《麻将》西克中国当代艺术收藏展 伯尔尼美术馆 瑞士；汉堡美术馆 汉堡 德国；萨尔茨保现代美术馆 奥地利

***Selected publications* / Ausgewählte Publikationen / 所选著作**

Yan Shanchen, Karen Smith, Charles Merewether: "Wang Guangyi", Hong Kong 2003

《王广义》Yan Shanchen（著）/Smith, Karen（著）/Wang Guangyi（著）/Merewether, Charles（撰写），东八时区 2003年

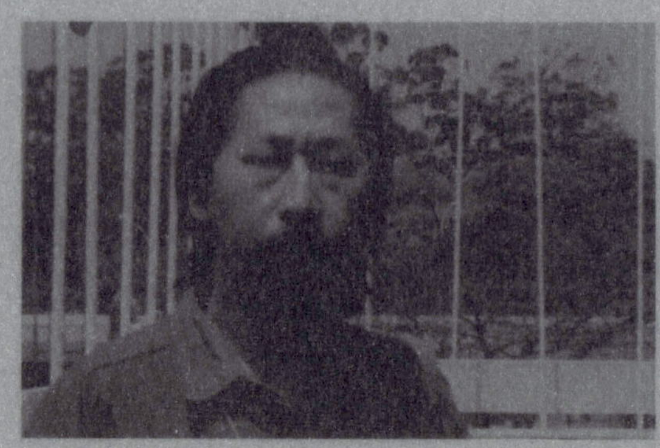

"At the same time that an artist criticizes society, he also acts to alert it, to awaken it to the awareness that there may be many things spreading forever through one's consciousness. This awareness may be the starting point for the revival of a nation and a people."

„Wenn ein Künstler die Gesellschaft kritisiert, geschieht dies, um sie zu warnen und die Erkenntnis zu wecken, dass es viele Dinge geben mag, die sich immer weiter im Bewusstsein ausbreiten. Diese Erkenntnis kann der Ausgangspunkt für das Wiedererwachen einer Nation und eines Volkes sein."

"在艺术家批评社会的同时，也会去警告社会，去唤醒社会一种意识：许多东西在人的无意识中永远流传下去。而这种意识是一个国家和民族复兴的起点。"

Born in 1957 in Harbin, Heilongjiang Province, China. Lives and works in Beijing
Geboren 1957 in Harbin, Provinz Heilongjiang, China. Lebt und arbeitet in Peking
1957年出生于中国黑龙江省哈尔滨市，现居住工作于北京

Selected exhibitions / Ausgewählte Ausstellungen / 所选展览

1989 "China/Avant-Garde", National Art Museum of China, Beijing, China
1993 45. Biennale di Venezia, Venice, Italy
1994 "China's New Art, Post 1989", Hong Kong Arts Centre, Hong Kong
1996 Asia-Pacific Triennial of Contemporary Art, Queensland, Australia
2001 "Towards a New Image: Twenty Years of Chinese Contemporary Painting", The National Art Museum of China, Beijing, Shanghai Art Museum, Shanghai, Guangdong Art Museum, Guangzhou, Sichuan Modern Art Museum, Chengdu, China
2002 The First Guangzhou Triennial, Guangdong Museum of Art, Guangzhou, China
2005-07 "Mahjong - Chinesische Gegenwartskunst aus der Sammlung Sigg", Kunstmuseum Bern, Berne, Switzerland; Hamburger Kunsthalle, Hamburg, Germany; Museum der Moderne, Salzburg, Austria

1989年 《中国现代艺术展，中国美术馆》北京
1993年 《第四十五届威尼斯双年展》威尼斯，意大利
1994年 《后89新艺术巡回展》香港艺术中心，香港；悉尼现代艺术博物馆，悉尼，澳大利亚
1996年 《亚太当代艺术三年展》昆士兰美术馆，澳大利亚
2001年 《新形象：中国当代绘画二十年大型巡回展》中国美术馆，上海美术馆，四川省美术馆，广东美术馆
2002年 《首届广州三年展-重新解读：中国实验艺术十年》（1990-2000年）广东美术馆，广州
2005-07年 《麻将》西克中国当代艺术收藏展 伯尔尼美术馆 瑞士；汉堡美术馆 汉堡 德国；萨尔茨堡现代美术馆 奥地利

Selected publications / Ausgewählte Publikationen / 所选著作

Yan Shanchen, Karen Smith, Charles Merewether: "Wang Guangyi", Hong Kong 2003

《王广义》Yan Shanchen（著）/Smith, Karen（著）/Wang Guangyi（著）/Merewether, Charles（撰写），东八时区 2003年

WANG GUANGYI 王广义

[waŋ kuanji]

Wang Guangyi is the leading artist of the post-1989 art movement known as Political Pop. Painting Cultural Revolution icons in the style of American Pop art, Wang combines imagery from propaganda and advertising, leveling the difference between two forms of culture. His work takes aim at the state-controlled art-making practice enforced in China during the 1950s through the late-1970s as well as taking its inspiration from the paintings of such Pop art masters as Andy Warhol and Roy Lichtenstein.

Graduating from the painting department of Zheihang Academy of Fine Arts in 1984, Wang Guangyi is representative of the first generation of artists to break away from the realist style of painting encouraged in the academy at the time. From the outset of his career, his willingness to take on significant cultural icons stirred controversy. In his early "Mao series", painted in the late-1980s, he positions photo-realist paintings of Mao Zedong beneath a grid of bold lines, taking aim at the cult of personality surrounding the political leader even a decade after his death. One such work, "Mao AO" (1986), was nearly removed from the landmark "China/Avant-Garde" exhibition held at the National Art Museum of China in Beijing in 1989, until the artist convinced the authorities that this was a "rational analysis" of the image of the leader, not a satirical criticism.

In the 1990s, Wang Guangyi moved on to the paintings for which he is best known, the "Great Criticism" series. In these works, the artist casts heroic characters from Cultural Revolution posters – workers, peasants and youth leaders – as fanatics for the new Chinese economy, embracing logos for McDonald's, Coca-Cola and Chanel as they once embraced Communist party insignia. Like the American Pop artists who took their visual cues from the graphic design of American advertising, Wang Guangyi taps into the visual vitality of propaganda signage while undercutting his source material's original intent. Using aesthetic means to equate the tarnished ideals of the Communist period and the promised happiness of western consumerism, Wang skewers

Wang Guangyi ist der führende Vertreter der nach 1989 entstandenen Kunstrichtung des Politischen Pop oder Polit-Pop. Indem er Kultfiguren der Kulturrevolution im Stil der amerikanischen Pop-Art malt, kombiniert Wang die Bildsprachen der Propaganda und der Werbung und ebnet so die Unterschiede zwischen zwei Formen der Populärkultur ein. Sein Werk karikiert Chinas staatlich verordnetes Kunstschaffen der 1950er bis späten 1970er Jahre und lässt sich dabei von den Werken solcher Pop-Art-Größen wie Andy Warhol oder Roy Lichtenstein inspirieren.

Wang Guangyi erwarb 1984 seinen Abschluss im Fachbereich Malerei der Zheihang Academy of Fine Arts. Er repräsentiert jene erste Künstlergeneration, die sich von dem damals an der Akademie propagierten realistischen Malstil frei machte. Von Beginn seiner Laufbahn an löste sein Umgang mit anerkannten Kulturikonen heftige Kontroversen aus. In seiner frühen „Mao-Serie", die er Ende der 1980er Jahre malte, legte er ein kräftiges Gitterraster über fotorealistische Gemälde von Mao Zedong und nahm damit den Persönlichkeitskult aufs Korn, der den politischen Führer selbst ein Jahrzehnt nach seinem Tod noch umgab. Eines dieser Werke, „Mao AO" (1986), wurde 1989 beinahe aus der bahnbrechenden Ausstellung „China/Avant-Garde" in der National Art Museum of China, Peking, verbannt, bis der Künstler die Obrigkeit davon überzeugen konnte, dass es sich um eine „rationale Analyse" des Führerimages handelte und nicht etwa um eine satirische Kritik.

In den 1990er Jahren begann Wang Guangyi mit den Gemälden, die ihn am bekanntesten gemacht haben: die Serie „Great Criticism". In den Werken dieser Reihe stellt der Künstler heroische Gestalten von Plakaten der Kulturrevolution – Arbeiter, Bauern und Jugendführer – als begeisterte Fans der neuen chinesischen Wirtschaft dar, die die Logos von McDonald's, Coca-Cola und Chanel ebenso bejubeln wie einst die Insignien der Kommunistischen Partei. Wie die amerikanischen Pop-Künstler, die sich vom Bildgut der Werbebranche inspirieren ließen, bedient sich Wang Guangyi der visuellen Vitalität der propagandistischen Bildsprache

王广义是1989年后艺术运动政治波普的主要艺术家。他从宣传画和广告上组合图像，以美国波普艺术风格绘制文化大革命的肖像，而消除了两种文化形式的差别。其作品以中国50年代到70年代末期强制性的国家控制艺术制作实践作品为主题，当然波普艺术大师的油画作品也是其灵感来源之一，如Andy Warhol 和Roy Lichtenstein。

1984年王广义从浙江美术学院（现中国美院）油画系毕业，在那时，艺术家正在脱离学院所鼓励的现实主义油画风格，而他真是这群艺术家的代表。从其事业开始，其重要的文化肖像而招致了社会的不休争论。在其早期的《毛泽东》系列中，（绘制于1980年代末期），他将毛泽东的画像置于粗线框体下，这一作品意在说明那时对毛泽东的个人崇拜现象，即使毛泽东逝世十年之后。类似作品《毛泽东AO》（1986），几乎在中国美术馆举行的中国现代艺术大展中被禁展，艺术 家向当局解释那只是对领导人肖像的“合理分析”而 已，而非讽刺批评，才未遭禁止。

90年代，王广义继续创作最著名的《大批判》系列油画，艺术家从文化大革命时期的海报上截取英雄人物的肖像，如工人，农民和青年领导人等，并将之定义中国新经济的狂热信徒，他们热衷于麦当劳，可口可乐和 香奈儿等，就像他 们曾经喜爱中国共产党的勋章一样。类似美国波普艺术家从美国广告商的图片设计上获取视觉暗示一样，王广义也切去源作的原始部分，而重新给宣传标记注入视觉活力。王广义运用审美方法平衡了共产主义时期不再流行的观念和西方消费主义的幸福感之间的差距，而让公众迷茫于两种价值体系的模糊信仰中。有人认为他的作品是对社会的玩世不恭，而有人却认为：伴随着市场经济的出现，他的作品却精确刻画中国价值观念的骤变过程。

从2001年起，王广义创作了《唯物主义者》系列，这些雕塑作品以遍布中国各地的公共纪念性雕塑为蓝

2

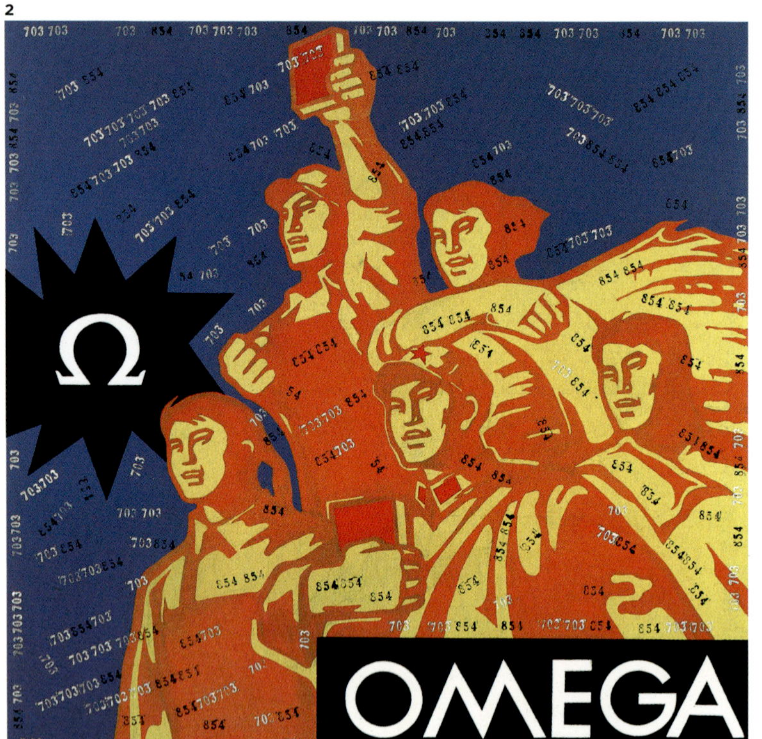

3

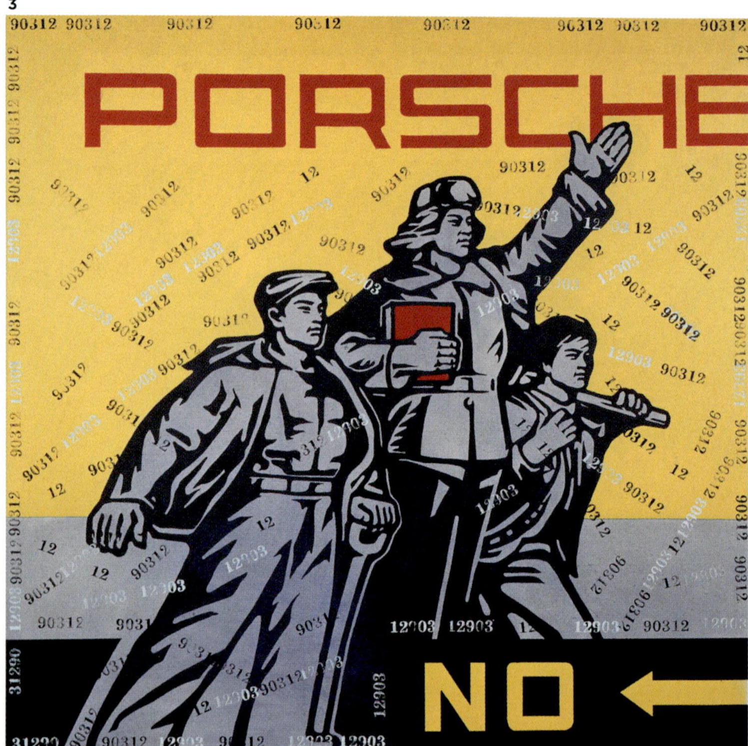

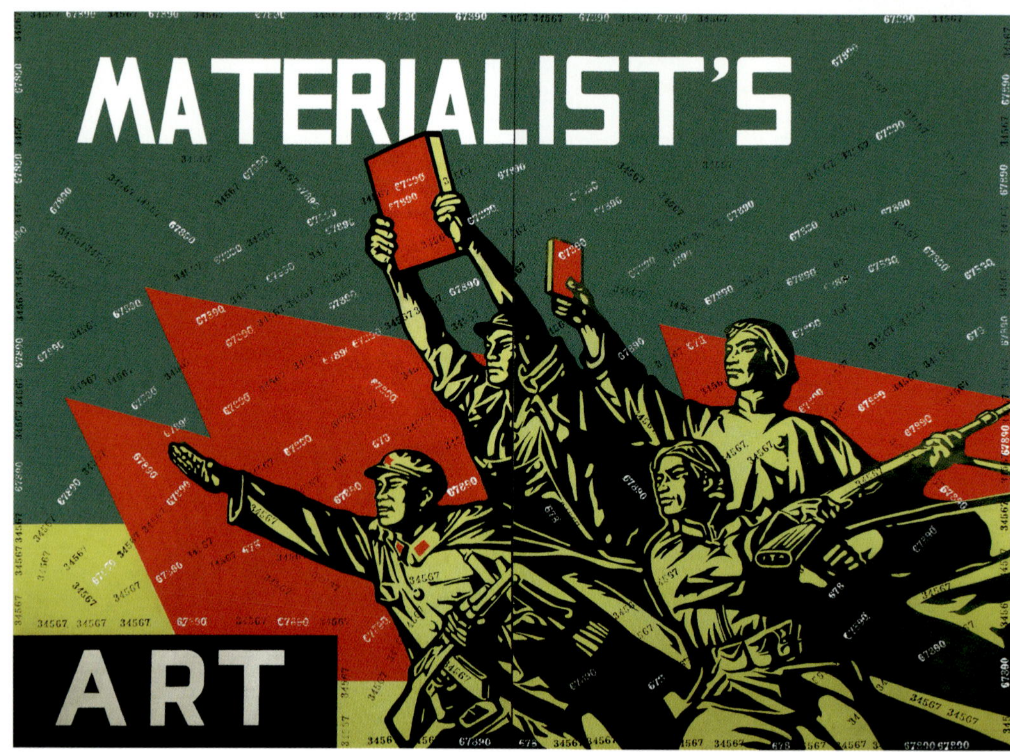

4

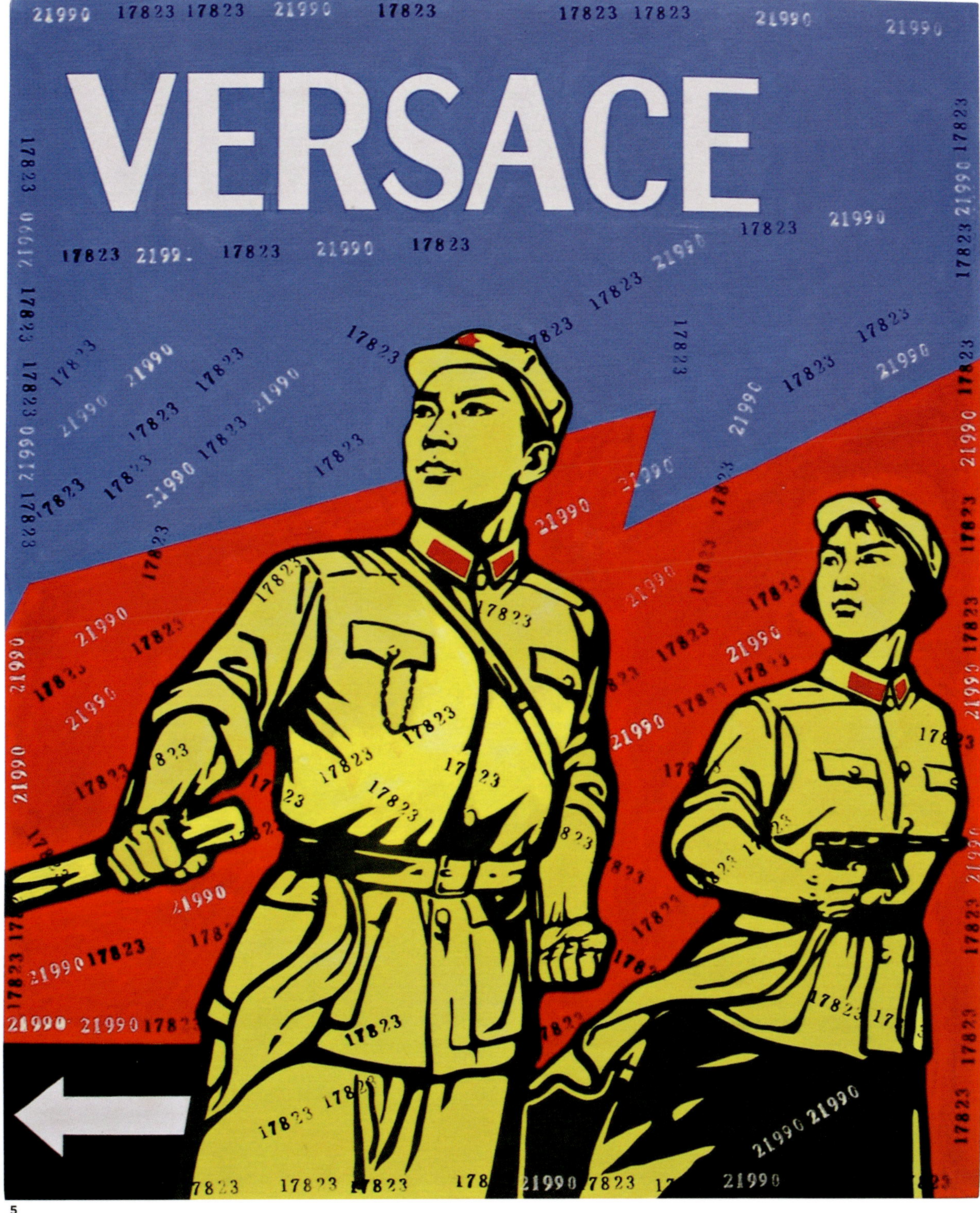

5

6

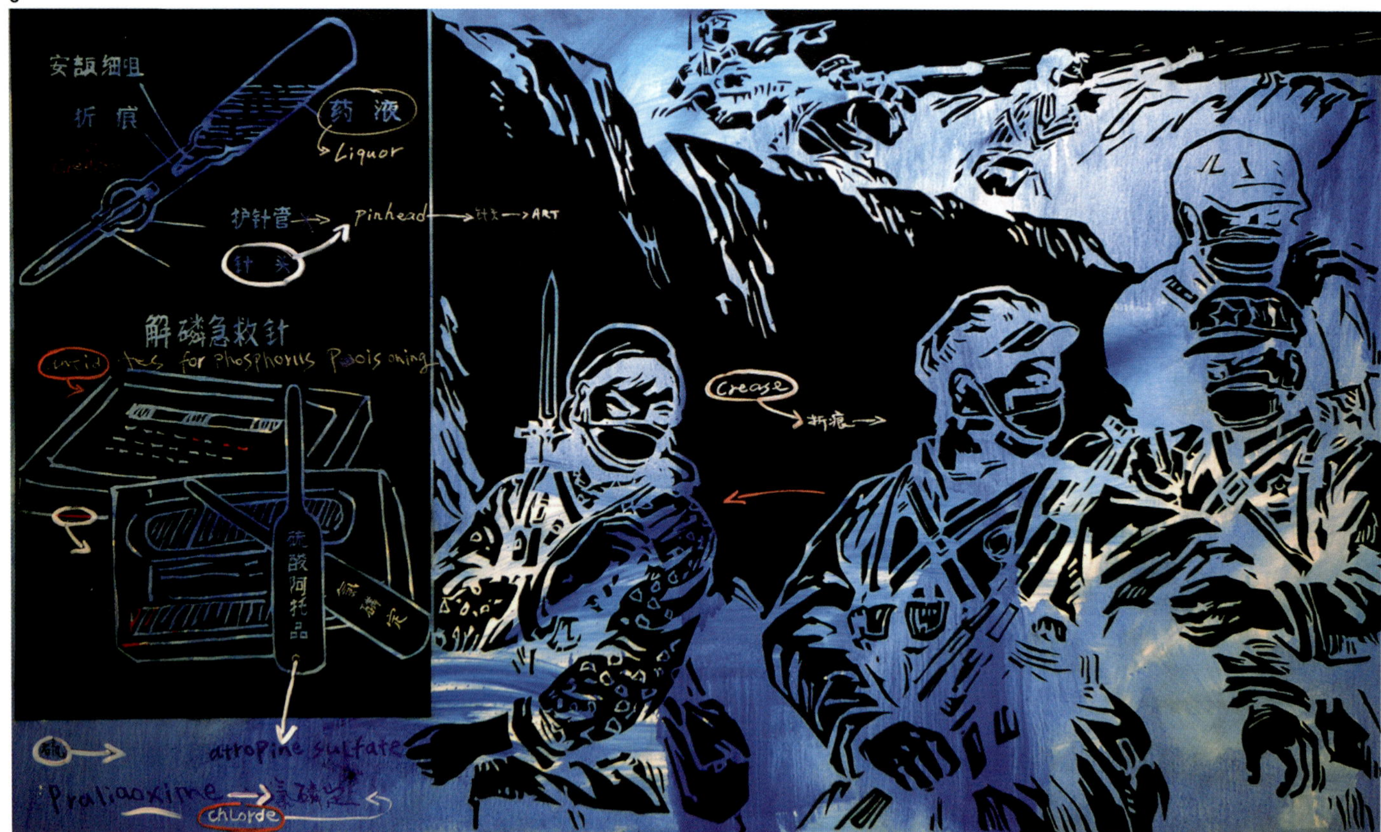

the public's somewhat gullible belief in either value system. Some have described this work as cynical while others view it as an accurate encapsulation of the overnight turnabout in Chinese values with the advent of a market economy.

Since 2001, Wang Guangyi has created "The Materialists", a series of sculptures based on the socialist realist monumental public works found throughout China. In this series, Wang allows viewers to recall the power and idealism transmitted by the statues of heroic figures and political leaders, while questioning the transference of their belief systems to the more transitory pleasures of consumerism. But, these sculptures do not use his usual appropriation of advertising logos allowing the collision of values to take place in the viewer's perception alone. The irony is that these works are in and of themselves consumer goods, traded as commodified works of art as a product of an artist at the peak of success on the international art market.

von Werbung und Politik, während er gleichzeitig die eigentliche Absicht seines Quellenmaterials unterläuft. Indem er mit ästhetischen Mitteln die getrübten Ideale der kommunistischen Ära und das hohle Glücksversprechen der westlichen Konsumkultur gleichsetzt, prangert Wang den naiven Glauben der Öffentlichkeit an das eine oder andere dieser Wertesysteme an. Manche nennen sein Werk zynisch, während andere es als treffende Metapher für den abrupten chinesischen Wertewandel nach Hereinbrechen der Marktwirtschaft sehen.

Seit 2001 hat Wang Guangyi „The Materialists" geschaffen, eine Serie von Skulpturen, die sich auf die in ganz China anzutreffenden Monumentaldenkmäler des Sozialistischen Realismus beziehen. Mit diesen Arbeiten eröffnet Wang den Betrachtern einen Rückblick auf die Kraft und den Idealismus, die diese steingewordenen Abbilder heroischer Gestalten und politischer Führer vermittelten, während er die Übertragung ihrer Glaubenssysteme auf die weit flüchtigeren Freuden der Konsumkultur in Frage stellt. Bei diesen Skulpturen arbeitet Wang aber nicht wie gewohnt mit einer Aneignung verbreiteter Ikonen, sondern lässt die Wertekollision nur in der Wahrnehmung des Betrachters stattfinden. Die Ironie liegt darin, dass diese Werke selbst Konsumgüter sind – kommerzialisierte Kunstwerke, die als Produkte eines Künstlers auf dem Höhepunkt seines Erfolgs auf dem internationalen Kunstmarkt gehandelt werden.

本，其中的英雄人物和政治领导人的塑像让观众回想起其所传达的力量和理想，而同时在质疑信仰短暂的短暂快感的消费主义。而他常用的手法：通过截取广告标记在观众身上产生价值的碰撞。但是在这些雕塑作品中，他未沿袭这种方法。具有讽刺意义的是，当某个艺术家的作品在国际艺术市场中取得巨大成功时候，这些艺术作品被当作商品来交易。

Barbara Pollack

7

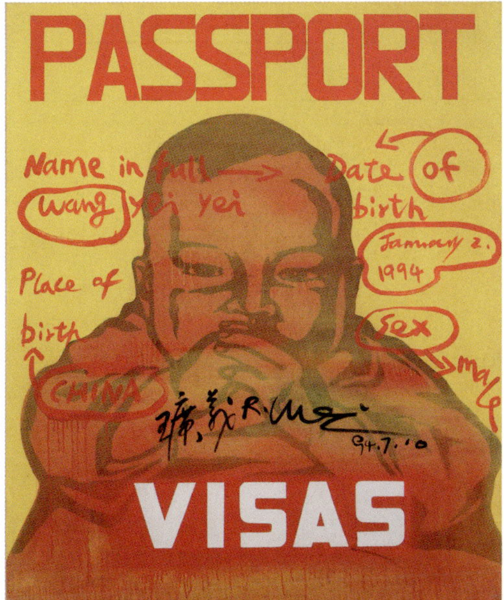

8

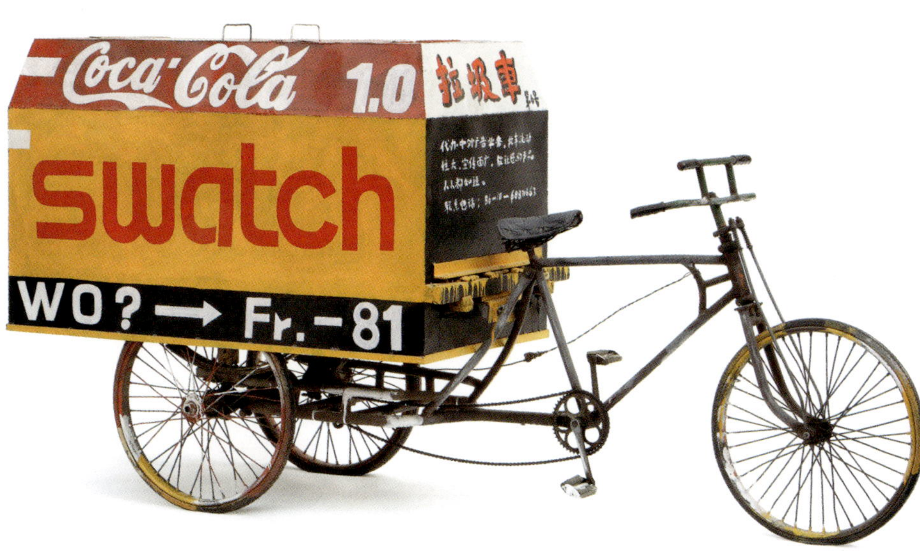

9

1 ***Art Go****, 2006*
Oil on canvas, 200 x 160 cm; Öl auf Leinwand, 200 x 160 cm
《艺术行 阿》2006年, 布面油画, 200 x 160 cm

2 ***Omega****, 1998*
Oil on canvas, 150 x 150 cm; Öl auf Leinwand, 150 x 150 cm
《欧米伽》1998年, 布面油画, 150 x 150 cm

3 ***Porsche****, 2005*
Oil on canvas, 200 x 200 cm; Öl auf Leinwand, 200 x 200 cm
《保时捷》2005年, 布面油画, 200 x 200 cm

4 ***Materialist's Art****, 2006*
Oil on canvas, 300 x 400 cm; Öl auf Leinwand, 300 x 400 cm
《唯物主义者的艺术》2006年, 布面油画, 300 x 400 cm

5 ***Great Criticism – Versace****, 2005*
Oil on canvas, 150 x 120 cm; Öl auf Leinwand, 150 x 120 cm
《大批判-- 范思哲》2005年, 布面油画, 150 x 120 cm

6 ***Aesthetics of War – Blue No. 3****, 2006*
Oil on canvas, 200 x 300 cm; Öl auf Leinwand, 200 x 300 cm
《战争美学-- 蓝No. 3》2006年, 布面油画, 200 x 300 cm

7 ***Visas****, 1995*
Oil on canvas, 150 x 120 cm; Öl auf Leinwand, 150 x 120 cm
《签证》1995年, 布面油画, 150 x 120 cm

8 ***Great Criticism Swatch/Coca-Cola****, 1994*
Beijing transport bike, painted, glosspaint on metal, 210 x 142 x 79 cm
Bemaltes Pekinger Transportfahrrad, Lackfarbe auf Metall, 210 x 142 x 79 cm
《大批判-- 斯沃琪/可口可乐》1994年, 210 x 142 x 79 cm

9 ***Untitled****, 1986*
Oil on canvas, 150 x 130 cm; Öl auf Leinwand, 150 x 130 cm
《无题》1986年, 布面油画, 150 x 130 cm

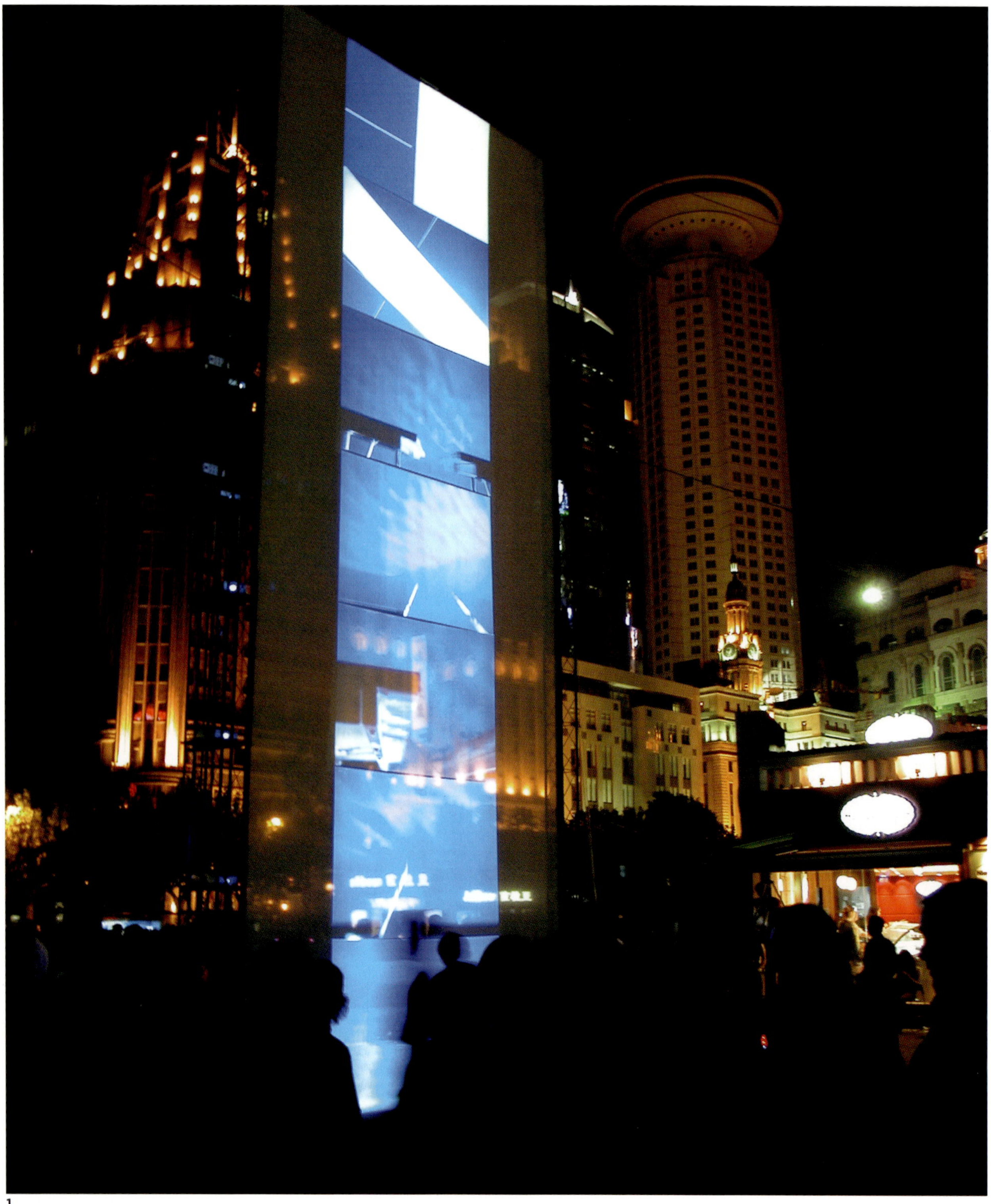

1

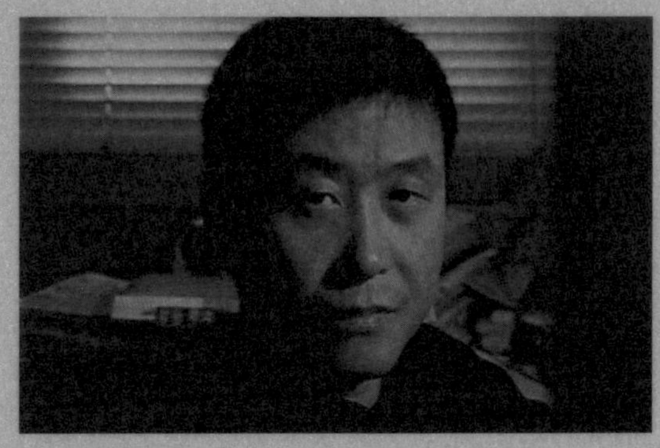

"We can no longer have the experience of acquiring our knowledge of things by employing a philosophy, a theory or an ideology, this kind of 'legitimacy' no longer exists."

„Wir können nicht mehr die Erfahrung machen, uns Wissen von den Dingen über eine Philosophie, eine Theorie oder eine Ideologie zu verschaffen. Diese Art der Legitimierung gibt es nicht mehr."

"我们不在有从应用哲学，理论或者意识形态中获取知识的经历，这种'正统'的东西不在存在。"

Born in 1958 in Suining, Sichuan Province, China. Lives and works in Beijing
Geboren 1958 in Suining, Provinz Sichuan, China. Lebt und arbeitet in Peking
1958年出生于中国四川省绥宁四川宁县，住居工作在北京

***Selected exhibitions* / Ausgewählte Ausstellungen /** 所选展览

2001	"My Home is Yours/Your Home is Mine", Tokyo Opera City Art Gallery, Tokyo, Japan
2002	First Guangzhou Triennial, Guandong Museum of Art, Guangzhou, China
2004–07	"Between Past and Future, New Photography and Video from China", International Center of Photography, New York, NY, USA (travelling exhibition)
2005	"The Wall: Reshaping Contemporary Chinese Art", Millennium Art Museum, Beijing, China
	Second Guangzhou Triennal, Guangdong Museum of Art, Guangzhou, China
2007	"China Welcomes You", Kunsthaus Graz, Graz, Austria

2001年	《我家是你家。你家是我家》，東京オペラシティアートギャラリー，日本
2002年	《观看》首届广州三年展，广东美术馆　广州
2004-07年	《过去与未来之间—中国新影像展》国际摄影中心, 纽约, 美国（巡回展）
2005年	《墙　—　中国当代艺术二十年展》中华世纪坛艺术馆、北京
	《别样》第二届广州三年展，广东美术馆，广州
2007年	《中国欢迎你》格拉茨美术馆　格拉茨, 奥地利

***Selected publications* / Ausgewählte Publikationen /** 所选著作

Gao Minglu (ed.): "The Wall: Reshaping Contemporary Chinese Art", New York 2005
Karen Smith: "Nine Lives: The Birth of Avant-Garde Art in New China", Zurich 2005
Waling Boers, Pi Li (eds.): "Touching The Stones", Cologne 2006

高明潞（编者）:《墙—中国当代艺术二十年展》纽约 2005年
Smith, Karen（著):《当代艺术的九个文化英雄》苏黎世 2005年
Boers, Waling/Pi Li（编者）:《接触石头》科隆2006年

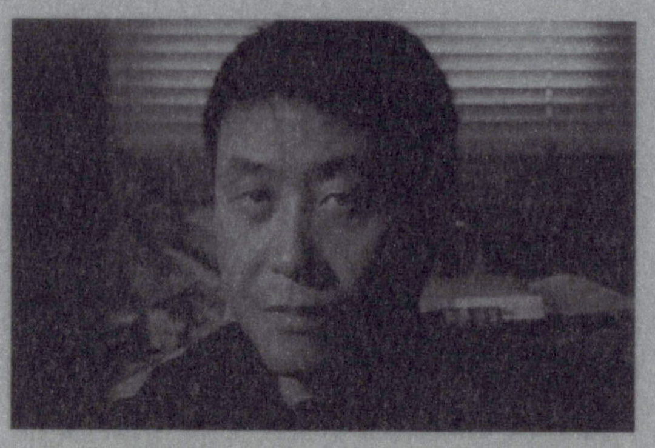

"We can no longer have the experience of acquiring our knowledge of things by employing a philosophy, a theory or an ideology, this kind of 'legitimacy' no longer exists."

„Wir können nicht mehr die Erfahrung machen, uns Wissen von den Dingen über eine Philosophie, eine Theorie oder eine Ideologie zu verschaffen. Diese Art der Legitimierung gibt es nicht mehr."

"我们不在有从应用哲学，理论或者意识形态中获取知识的经历，这种'正统'的东西不在存在。"

Born in 1958 in Suining, Sichuan Province, China. Lives and works in Beijing
Geboren 1958 in Suining, Provinz Sichuan, China. Lebt und arbeitet in Peking
1958年出生于中国四川省遂宁县，住居工作在北京

Selected exhibitions / Ausgewählte Ausstellungen / 所选展览

2001 "My Home is Yours/Your Home is Mine", Tokyo Opera City Art Gallery, Tokyo, Japan
2002 First Guangzhou Triennial, Guandong Museum of Art, Guangzhou, China
2004–07 "Between Past and Future. New Photography and Video from China", International Center of Photography, New York, NY, USA (travelling exhibition)
2005 "The Wall: Reshaping Contemporary Chinese Art", Millennium Art Museum, Beijing, China
Second Guangzhou Triennal, Guangdong Museum of Art, Guangzhou, China
2007 "China Welcomes You", Kunsthaus Graz, Graz, Austria

2001年 《我家是你家，你家是我家》，東京オペラシティアートギャラリー，日本
2002年 《观看》首届广州三年展，广东美术馆　广州
2004-07年 《过去与未来之间—中国新影像展》国际摄影中心，纽约，美国（巡回展）
2005年 《墙　—　中国当代艺术二十年展》中华世纪坛艺术馆，北京
《别样》第二届广州三年展，广东美术馆，广州
2007年 《中国欢迎你》格拉茨美术馆　格拉茨，奥地利

Selected publications / Ausgewählte Publikationen / 所选著作

Gao Minglu (ed.): "The Wall: Reshaping Contemporary Chinese Art", New York 2005
Karen Smith: "Nine Lives: The Birth of Avant-Garde Art in New China", Zurich 2005
Waling Boers, Pi Li (eds.): "Touching The Stones", Cologne 2006

高明潞（编著）：《墙—中国当代艺术二十年展》纽约 2005年
Smith, Karen（著）:《当代艺术的九个文化英雄》苏黎世 2005年
Boers, Waling/Pi Li（编著）：《接触石头》科隆2006年

WANG JIANWEI 汪建伟

[waŋ tɕiɛnwei]

Wang Jianwei was an incredible and promising painter who chose to give up painting voluntarily in the early stage of his career in favor of what he called "choices". For his generation of artists who went through the gloomy years of the Cultural Revolution (1966–1976) that denounced the idea of knowledge, the possibility of having cultural and artistic options back at one's disposal was such a luxury that he deeply appreciated. This explains the wide range of media employed in his prolific practice, from text-based conceptual art pieces to art experiments of a sociological nature to videos and "multimedia theatre". For the latter, he has been recognized as a pioneering figure in the history of Chinese contemporary art.

From the late 1980s to the early 1990s, he worked solitarily in his studio, writing down dozens of pages of factual numbers and entries outlining his kinetic concepts. His absorption into matters of science led to a few more projects of a similar nature, all of which remained in text form and within the confine of his studio. In 1993, his scientific fixation took on a sociological dimension and evolved into an actual agricultural project undertaken as a sociological research, and above all, an art experiment: "Circulation: Sowing and Harvesting" (1993/94). He approached and offered to sign a contract with a farmer in a village near his hometown in Southwestern China to plant a type of grain seeds that freshly came out of the local agricultural lab. He found out in his research that the first life cycle of a new type of grain seed usually had the highest yield, which was unknown to most farmers. As a result, they wouldn't begin to accept and plant a new grain type only in its third life cycle, with a reduced result. To put such a theory into test, he entered into a commitment, in which he shared the same amount of risk as the farmer he partnered with. Thus he was engaged into a complex system of production, distribution and human relationships that such a production cycle would entail, through a small grain.

Wang would keep on playing the dual roles of an artist and a sociologist and blurring the divisions of the two in

Wang Jianwei war ein überaus vielversprechender Maler, bis er sich in einem frühen Stadium seiner Karriere entschied, die Malerei zugunsten von etwas aufzugeben, das er „Wahlmöglichkeiten" nannte. Seine Generation von Künstlern hatte die düsteren Jahre der Kulturrevolution (1966–1976) erlebt, die Wissen als solches ächtete. Und für ihn und seine Altersgenossen war die Chance, wieder über kulturelle und künstlerische Wahlmöglichkeiten zu verfügen, ein Luxus, für den Wang Jianwei zutiefst dankbar ist. Das erklärt das breit gefächerte Spektrum von Medien, derer er sich in seinem fruchtbaren Schaffen bedient – von textbasierten Konzeptobjekten über Kunstexperimente gesellschaftlicher Art bis hin zu Videos und „multimedialem Theater". Auf dem letztgenannten Gebiet ist er ein anerkannter Pionier in der Geschichte der modernen chinesischen Kunst.

Von Ende der 1980er bis Anfang der 1990er Jahre arbeitete Wang zurückgezogen in seinem Atelier und füllte Dutzende von Seiten mit nüchternen Zahlen und Einträgen, um seine kinetischen Konzepte zu umreißen. Die intensive Beschäftigung mit wissenschaftlichen Themen zog weitere ähnliche Projekte nach sich, die allesamt in Textform verblieben und sein Atelier nicht verließen. 1993 nahm seine Fixierung auf das Wissenschaftliche eine soziologische Dimension an, und es entwickelte sich ein konkretes landwirtschaftliches Projekt, das zwar auch zu soziologischen Forschungszwecken, vor allem aber als Kunstexperiment durchgeführt wurde: „Circulation: Sowing and Harvesting" (1993/94). Wang bot einem Bauern in einem Dorf nahe seiner Heimatstadt in Südwestchina einen Vertrag an, bei dem es um die Aussaat einer neuen Getreidesorte ging, die frisch aus dem örtlichen Agrarlabor kam. Er hatte bei seinen Recherchen herausgefunden, dass solch eine neue Züchtung normalerweise im ersten Lebenszyklus den höchsten Ertrag erbringt, was den meisten Bauern unbekannt war. Sie akzeptierten neue Getreidearten erst im dritten Lebenszyklus, was zu schlechteren Erträgen führte. Wang Jianwei ging nun eine regelrechte Geschäftspartnerschaft mit dem Bauern ein und verpflichtete sich, das Risiko mit ihm zu teilen. So gliederte er sich in das komplexe Geflecht von Produktion,

汪建伟曾是一位有着惊人天赋并且前途无量的画家。在其事业的早期，他主动放弃了绘画，转而去追寻他所谓的“选择”。对于他这一代历经过文化大革命（1966-1976年）灰暗岁月的艺术家而言，按自己的意愿找回文化和艺术的选择是那样奢侈的一件事，然而他却深深希望得到这件奢侈品。这就能够解释他丰富的实践中采用的媒体范围之广，从基于文字的概念艺术作品到社会性质的艺术试验乃至录像和“多媒体剧场”。他也凭借“多媒体剧场”跻身于中国当代艺术史的先驱行列。

上世纪八十年代后期到九十年代初期，汪建伟独自在自己的工作室内创作，写下概述其动态艺术观念的真实数目和条目达数沓纸之多。他对科学事物的投入导致了部分类似性质的项目的产生，所有这些项目均保留文字形式，并仅限于他的工作室范围以内。1993年，他的科学执着开始呈现社会维度，并最终演化成一个作为社会研究（当然首先是艺术实践）的实际农业项目。在自己位于中国西南部的故乡附近的村庄里，他找到一位农民并与之签订了一份合同，种植一种刚从当地农业实验室取出的小麦品种。在研究中他发现，新品种小麦种子的第一轮种植通常能够得到最高的收成，而这一点大多数农民都不知道。结果，他们开始时不会接受并种植新品种的小麦，而到了第三轮开始种植时，收成已然降低。为检验这种理论，他与自己合作的农民签署了一项风险共享协议。于是，他被卷入一个复杂的生产、分配以及人际关系的体系中，而这些都是一个生产循环所必然导致的结果，途径则是一颗小小的谷粒。（《循环—种植》，1993-1994年）。

在录像作品《生活在别处》（1999年）和《生产》（1997年）中，汪建伟采用将社会研究作为艺术试验或者将艺术试验作为社会研究的方式，继续扮演着其艺术家和社会学家的双重角色并混淆两者的区别。他对边缘场所的状态进行调查，例如茶室和中断的郊区住房项目等，并在他的录像作品中对社会中占据这些地方的人进行描述。作为艺术家，涉

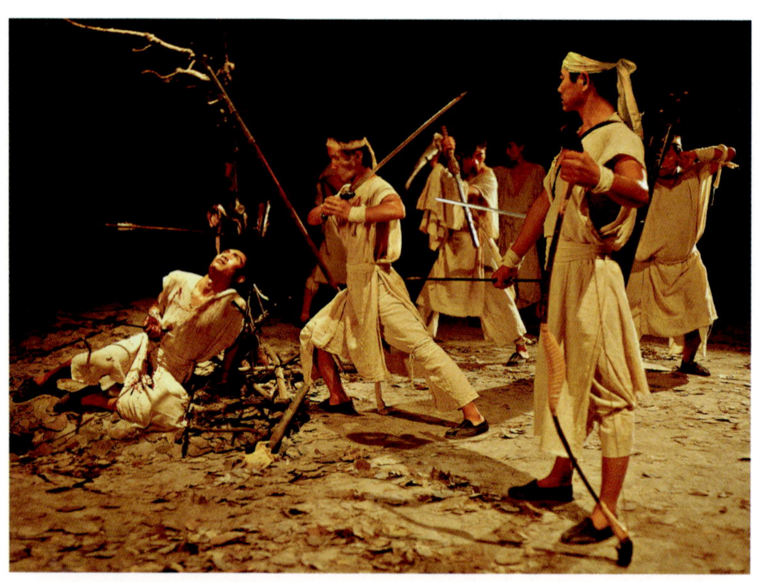

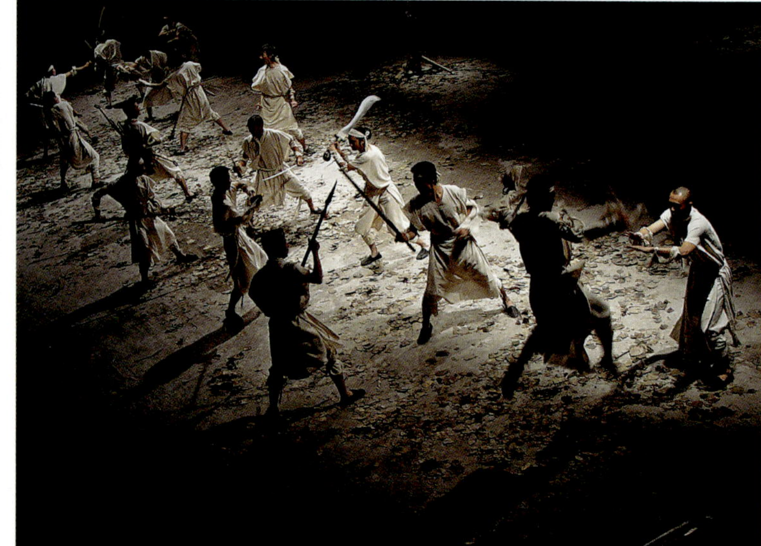

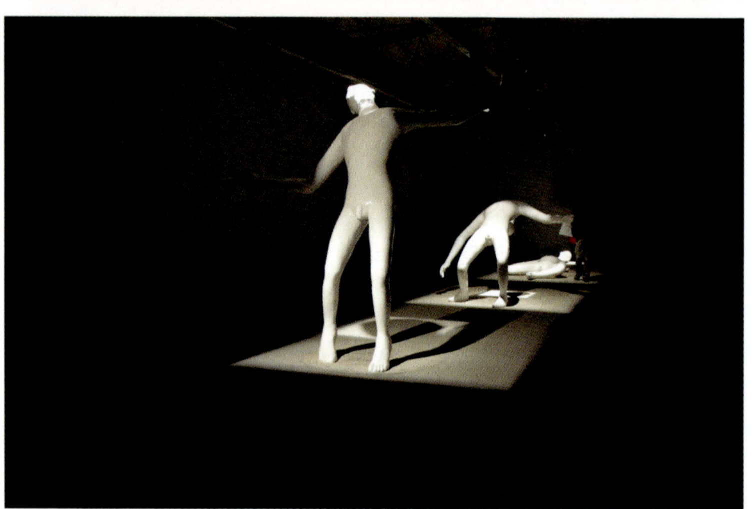

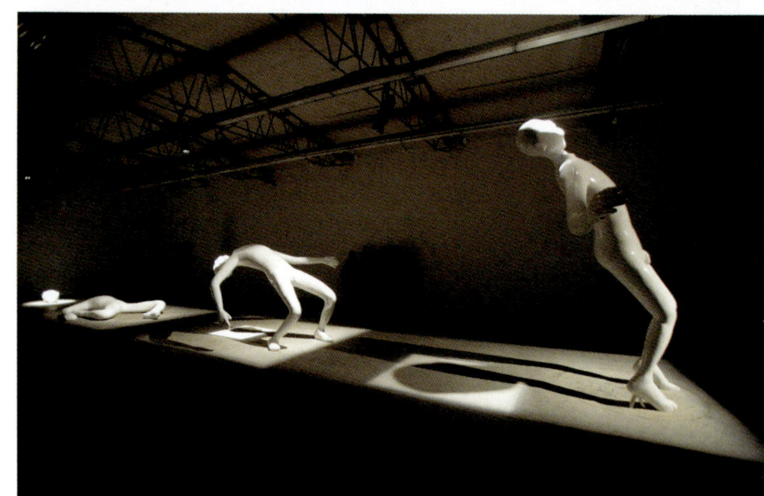

2

3

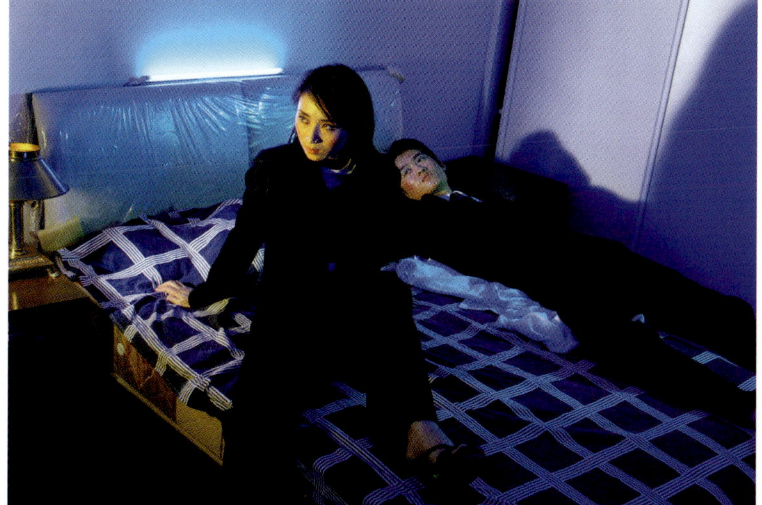

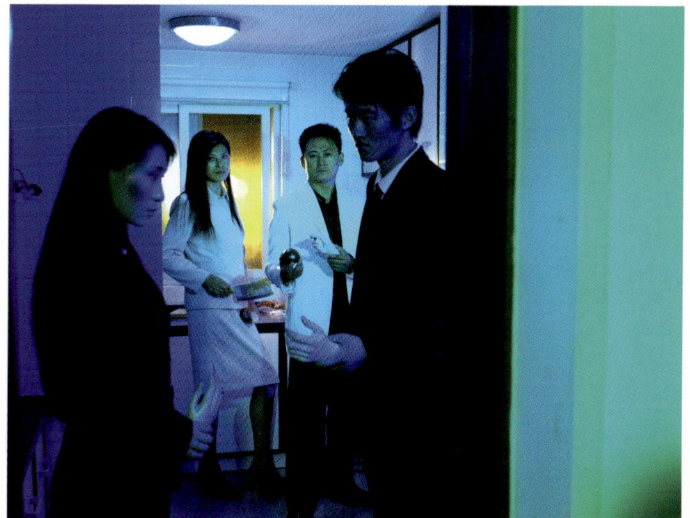

4

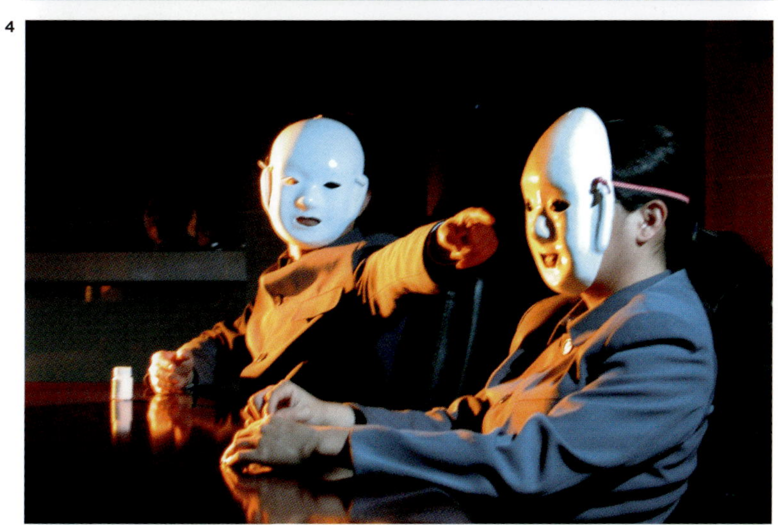

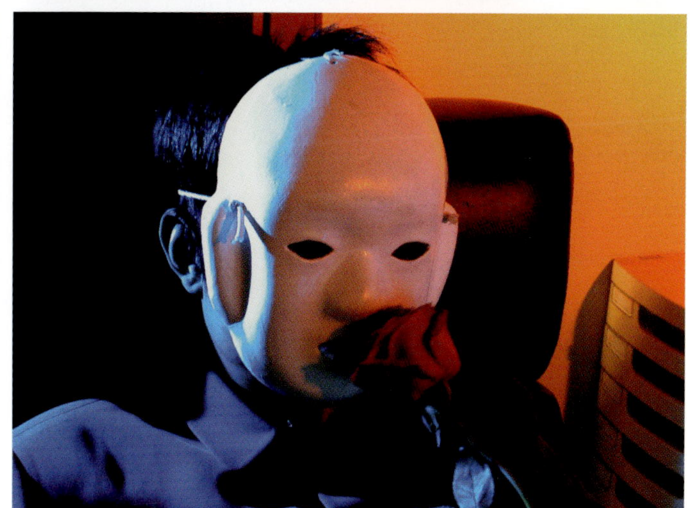

5

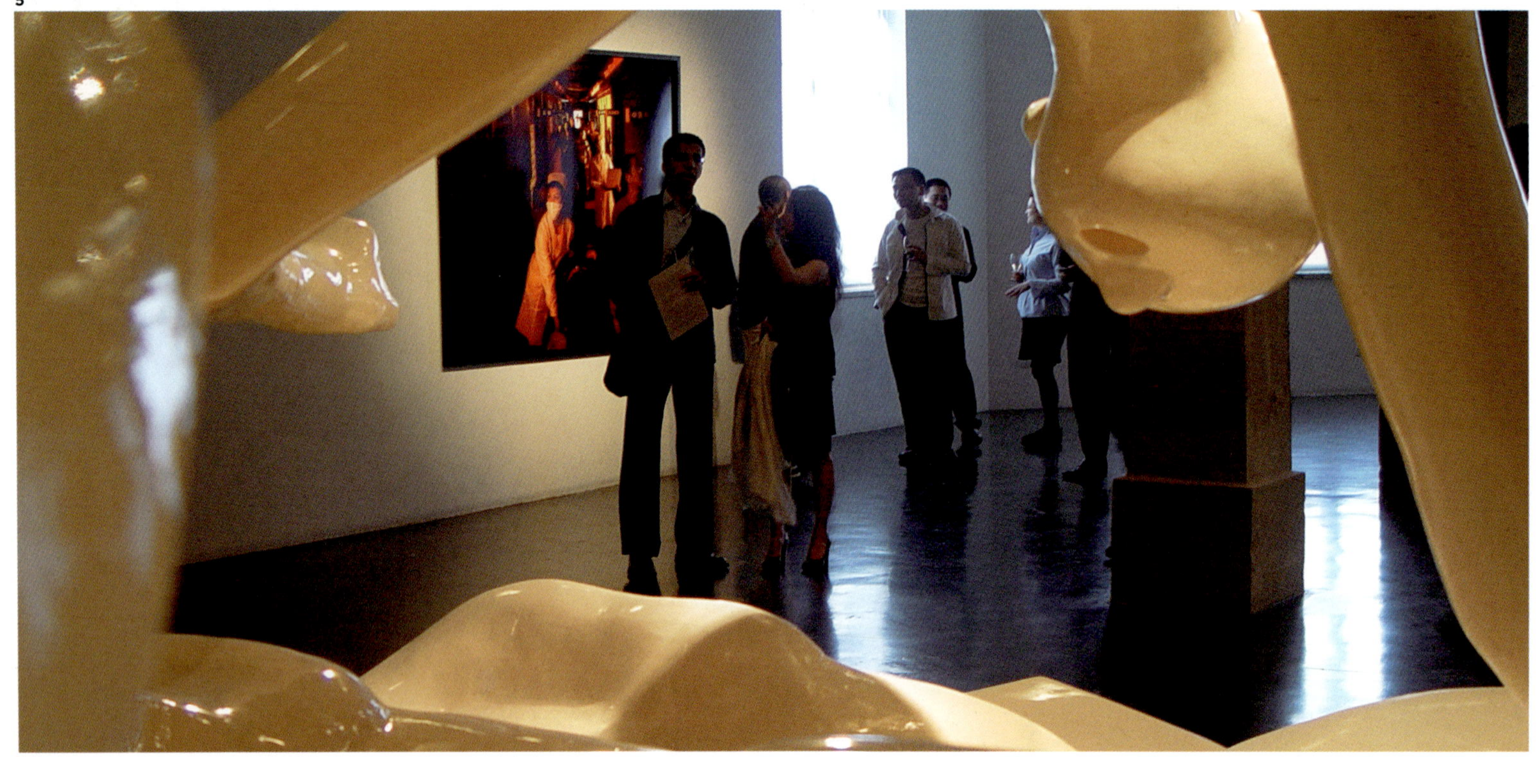

his videos "Living Elsewhere" (1999) and "Production" (1997), using social studies as art experiments and vice versa. He examined the state of marginalized spaces such as teahouses and aborted suburban housing projects and portrayed those people who occupied such spaces in society in his videos. His choice of subjects as an artist was empowered by the scientific objectivity he entered into such projects with.

His theatrical productions since the late 1990s however marked a clear departure from the factual and documentary quality of his early video works. With masked characters, representational costumes and set designs, as well as deliberate movements, often to a backdrop of jarring video images, Wang has carved out a margin of his own in contemporary art practice in China. This has been achieved by bridging visual arts, theatre and staged plays with a deep philosophical basis hidden underneath a thick coat of absurdity. While sometimes referring to historical sources, Wang's plays are firmly plugged into contemporary psychological and social concerns of a universal and timeless appeal.

Verteilung und zwischenmenschlichen Beziehungen ein, das ein solcher Produktionszyklus mit sich bringt – alles ausgelöst durch ein kleines Getreidekorn.

In seiner Doppelrolle als Künstler und Soziologe fuhr Wang fort, die Grenzen zwischen den beiden Tätigkeiten zu verwischen – so auch in seinen Videos „Living Elsewhere“ (1999) und „Production“ (1997), die Sozialstudien zu Kunstexperimenten machten (und umgekehrt). Er untersuchte den Status von marginalisierten Lokalitäten wie Teehäusern und aufgegebenen Vorortsiedlungen und porträtierte in seinen Videos die Menschen, die solche gesellschaftlichen Räume bevölkerten. Die Wahl seiner künstlerischen Themen profitiert von der wissenschaftlichen Objektivität, mit der er an solche Projekte heranging.

Dagegen lassen seine Theaterproduktionen seit den späten 1990er Jahren eine deutliche Abkehr vom sachlich-dokumentarischen Charakter seiner frühen Videowerke erkennen. Mit maskierten Charakteren, realistischen Kostümen und Bühnenbildern sowie ausgefeilter Gestik, oft vor dem Hintergrund schwer erträglicher Videobilder, hat sich Wang seinen eigenen Spielraum in Chinas zeitgenössischer Kunstwelt geschaffen. Er schlug eine Brücke zwischen der visuellen Kunst und der Bühne und inszenierte Stücke, deren zutiefst philosophische Grundlage er mit einem ordentlichen Maß an Absurdität zudeckte. Auch wenn sie sich manchmal historischer Quellen bedienen, bleiben Wangs Stücke doch stets aktuellen psychologischen und gesellschaftlichen Anliegen von universeller Zugkraft verhaftet.

及这些项目的科学客观性赋予了他对主题的选择权利。

然而，自上世纪九十年代末期开始的话剧作品，则完全脱离了他早期录像作品中写实和记录的风格。借助带着面具的角色、象征性的服饰和布景图案，以及深思熟虑的乐章，甚至常常是不着边际的录像图像背景，汪建伟在视觉艺术、戏剧、以及厚重而荒谬的外衣下隐藏着深刻哲学基础的舞台剧场之间架起了桥梁，使其在中国当代艺术实践中独占一隅。尽管有时涉及历史素材，汪建伟的戏剧依然牢固地植根于对普遍和永恒的吸引力的当代心理和社会关注上。

Carol Lu

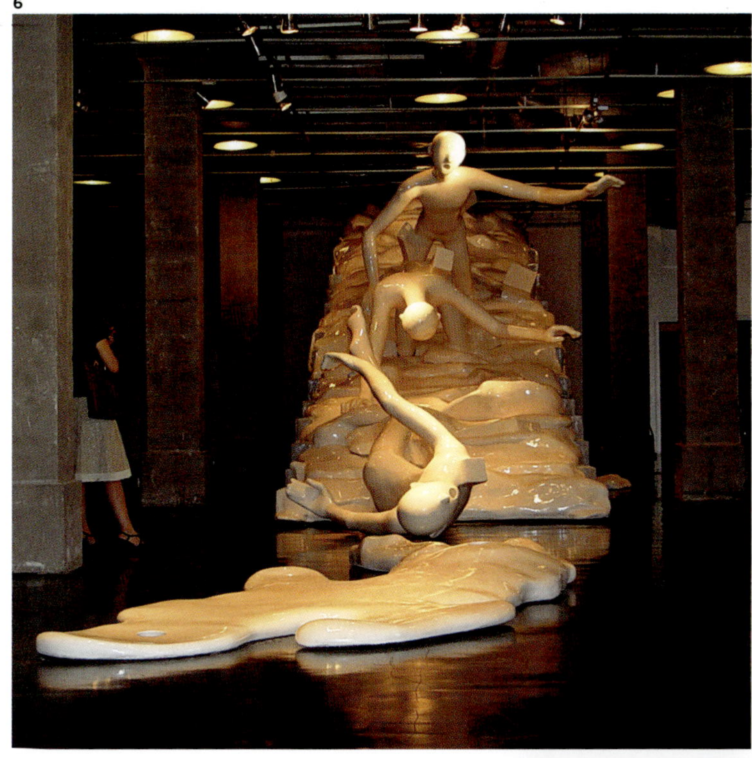

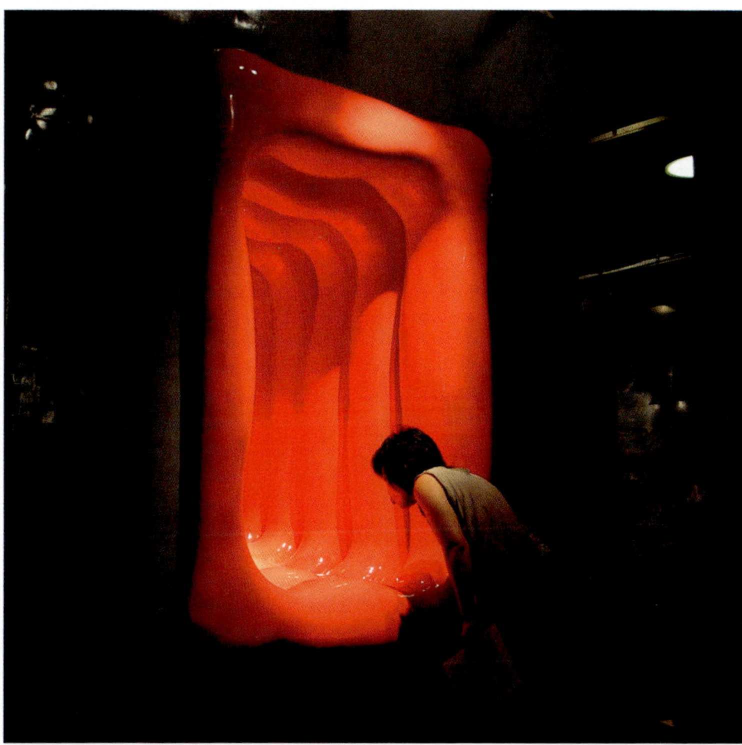

1 ***Sky of multiple***, *2005*
Video installation, video 8 min 7 sec
Video-Installation, Video 8 Min. 7 Sek.
《七重天》2005年，录像装置，录像 8分 7秒

2 ***Flying bird is motionless***, *2005*
Multimedia installation, video 6 min 40 sec
Multimedia-Installation, Video 6 Min. 40 Sek.
《飞鸟不动》2005年，多媒体装置，录像 6分 40秒

3 ***Spider II***, *2004*
Video, 9 min 30 sec
Video, 9 Min. 30 Sek.
《蜘蛛II》2004年，录像，9分 30秒

4 ***Spider I***, *2003*
Video, 8 min 40 sec
Video, 8 Min. 40 Sek.
《蜘蛛I》2003年，录像，8分 40秒

5+6 ***Dogde***, *2006*
Multimedia installation, video 8 min 30 sec
Multimedia-Installation, Video 8 Min. 30 Sek.
《躲闪》2006年，多媒体装置，录像，8分 30秒

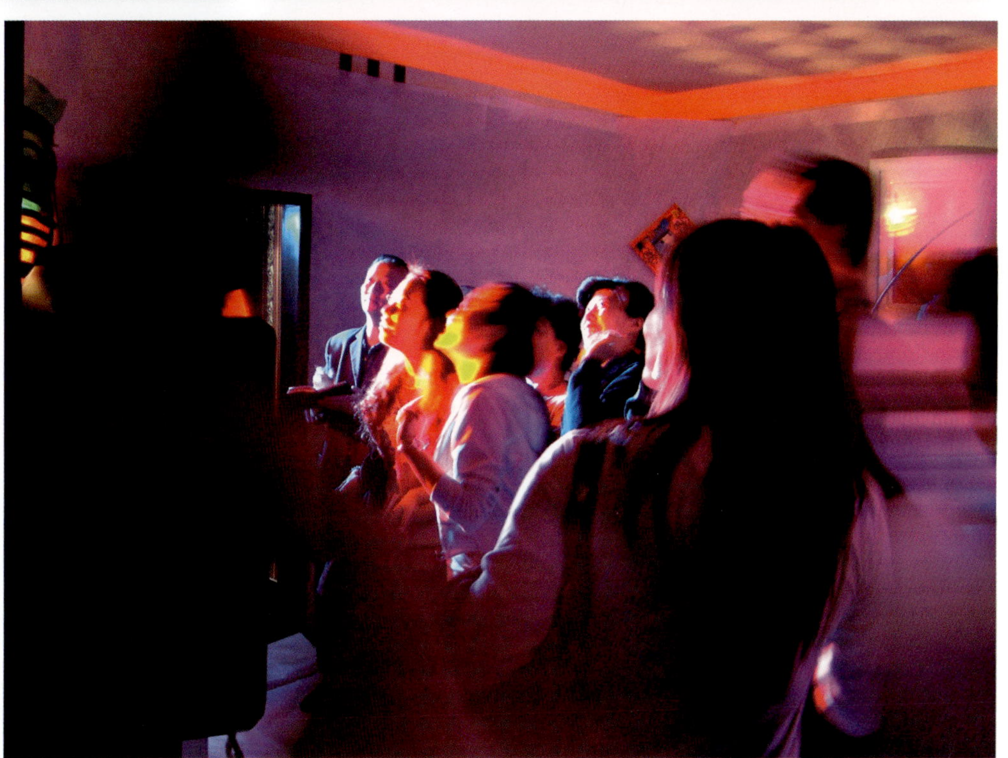

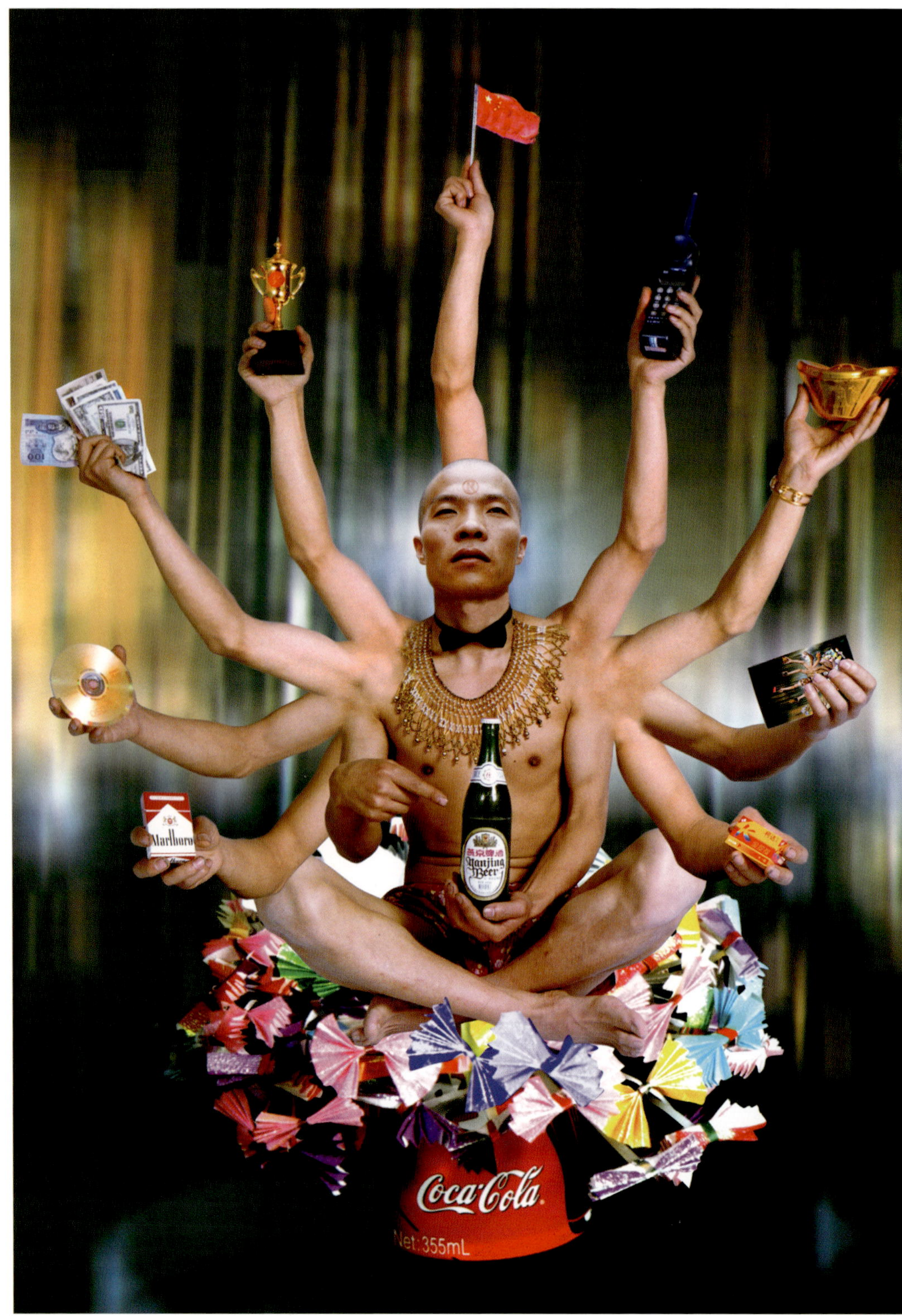

1

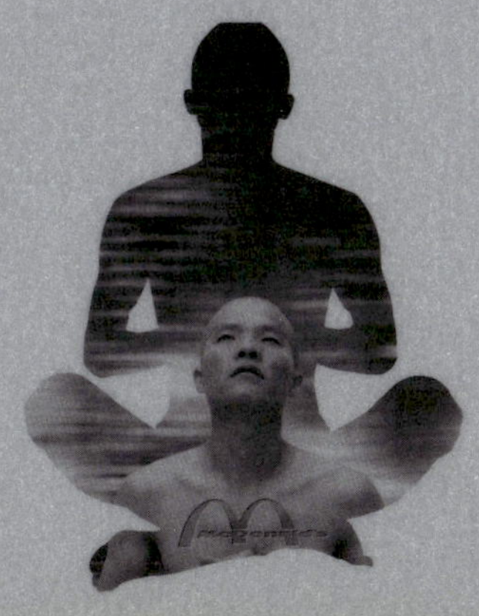

"Opening relations between China and the world is supposed to be a happy experience for both the Chinese and Westerners, but most of my artworks are examining the fast pace of this modernization, which is coming too quick for the Chinese people to analyze or digest."

„Die Öffnung zwischen China und der Welt soll eine beglückende Erfahrung für die Chinesen wie für die westliche Welt sein, doch die meisten meiner Arbeiten beschäftigen sich mit dem rasanten Tempo dieser Modernisierung, die weit schneller verläuft, als die Menschen in China sie analysieren oder verdauen können."

"对中国人和西方人而言，中国和世界之间建立联系，可能是一段愉快的记忆，我的大部分艺术作品都是对现代化快速进程的检测，而这个进程到来的太快了，中国人难以消化。"

Born in 1966 in Heilongjiang Province, China. Lives and works in Beijing
Geboren 1966 in der Provinz Heilongjiang, China. Lebt und arbeitet in Peking
1966年出生于中国黑龙江省，现在北京居住工作

***Selected exhibitions* / Ausgewählte Ausstellungen / 所选展览**

1997 "Wang Qingsong Painting Exhibition", Chinese Contemporary, London, UK
2002 "Golden Future - Photography by Wang Qingsong", Galerie Loft, Paris, France
2003 "Wang Qingsong: Present-day Epics", Saidye Bronfman Contemporary Art Center, Montreal, Cambridge Galleries, Ontario, Prefix Institute of Contemporary Art, Toronto, Southern Alberta Art Gallery, Lethbridge, Canada
2004 "Wang Qingsong - Romantique", Salon 94, New York, NY, USA
"Montpellier - China 1, MC1", International Biennial Exhibition of Contemporary Chinese Art, Montpellier, France
2006 "Wang Qingsong", Albion Gallery, London, UK
2007 "China: Past, Present and Future", MEWO Kunsthalle, Memmingen, Germany

1997年 《王庆松油画展》中国当代艺术展，伦敦，英国
2002年 《金色的未来--王庆松摄影作品展》Loft画廊，巴黎，法国
2003年 《王庆松：今天的史诗》Saidye Bronfman 当代艺术中心，蒙特利尔，剑桥画廊和南阿尔伯塔美术馆，加拿大
2004年 《王庆松新作展》沙龙94，纽约，美国
《蒙彼利埃 - 中国 1》中国当代艺术国际双年展蒙彼利埃，法国
2006年 《王庆松》Albion画廊，伦敦，英国
2007年 《中国：过去现在和将来》MEWO美术馆，梅明根市，德国

***Selected publications* / Ausgewählte Publikationen / 所选著作**

Inma G. Puy: "Spring in Beijing", April 14th, 1996, http://www.connect-arte.com/archive/china/echinab.htm
Dieter Ronte, Walter Smerling, Evelyn Weiss: "China! Zeitgenössische Malerei", Cologne 1996
Susan Bright: "Chinese Painting", in: "Art Asia Pacific", no. 17, p. 99, 1998
Shu Kewen: "Wang Qingsong's 'Photojournalism'", in: "Sanguine Splendour: Chinablue Gallery", Beijing 2007

Puy, Inma G.（著）:《北京的春天》(评论)1996年四月14日发表于：http://www.connect-arte.com/archive/china/echinab.htm
Ronte, Dieter/Smerling, Walter/Weiss, Evelyn（著）:《中国！当代绘画》科隆1996年
Bright, Susan（著）:《中国油画；英国》ART Asia Pacific，第17期(1998年)
舒可文（著）:《王兴伟的"摄影报道"》环碧堂画廊, 北京 2007年

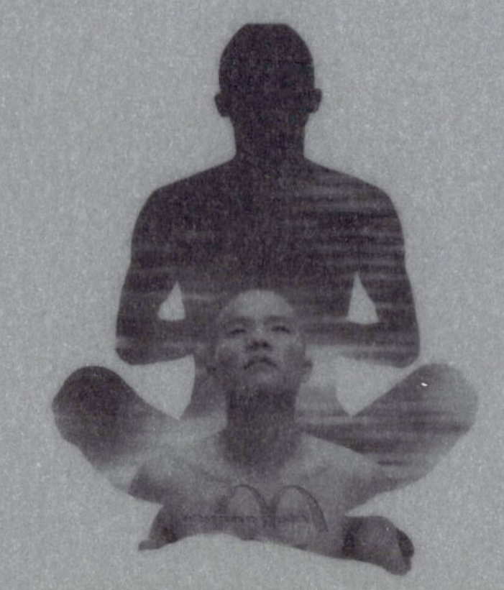

"Opening relations between China and the world is supposed to be a happy experience for both the Chinese and Westerners, but most of my artworks are examining the fast pace of this modernization, which is coming too quick for the Chinese people to analyze or digest."

„Die Öffnung zwischen China und der Welt soll eine beglückende Erfahrung für die Chinesen wie für die westliche Welt sein, doch die meisten meiner Arbeiten beschäftigen sich mit dem rasanten Tempo dieser Modernisierung, die weit schneller verläuft, als die Menschen in China sie analysieren oder verdauen können."

"对中国人和西方人而言，中国和世界之间建立联系，可能是一段愉快的记忆，我的大部分艺术作品都是对现代化快速进程的检测，而这个进程到来的太快了，中国人难以消化。"

Born in 1966 in Heilongjiang Province, China. Lives and works in Beijing
Geboren 1966 in der Provinz Heilongjiang, China. Lebt und arbeitet in Peking
1966年出生于中国黑龙江省，现在北京居住工作

Selected exhibitions / Ausgewählte Ausstellungen / 所选展览

1997 "Wang Qingsong Painting Exhibition", Chinese Contemporary, London, UK
2002 "Golden Future - Photography by Wang Qingsong", Galerie Loft, Paris, France
2003 "Wang Qingsong: Present-day Epics", Saidye Bronfman Contemporary Art Center, Montreal, Cambridge Galleries, Ontario, Prefix Institute of Contemporary Art, Toronto, Southern Alberta Art Gallery, Lethbridge, Canada
2004 "Wang Qingsong - Romantique", Salon 94, New York, NY, USA
"Montpellier - China 1, MC1", International Biennial Exhibition of Contemporary Chinese Art, Montpellier, France
2006 "Wang Qingsong", Albion Gallery, London, UK
2007 "China: Past, Present and Future", MEWO Kunsthalle, Memmingen, Germany

1997年 《王庆松油画展》中国当代艺术展，伦敦，英国
2002年 《金色的未来—王庆松摄影作品展》Loft画廊，巴黎，法国
2003年 《王庆松：今天的史诗》Saidye Bronfman 当代艺术中心，蒙特利尔，剑桥画廊和南阿尔伯塔美术馆，加拿大
2004年 《王庆松新作展》沙龙94，纽约，美国
《蒙彼利埃 – 中国 1》中国当代艺术国际双年展蒙彼利埃，法国
2006年 《王庆松》Albion画廊，伦敦，英国
2007年 《中国：过去现在和将来》MEWO美术馆，梅明根市，德国

Selected publications / Ausgewählte Publikationen / 所选著作

Inma G. Puy: "Spring in Beijing", April 14th, 1996, http://www.connect-arte.com/archive/china/echinab.htm
Dieter Ronte, Walter Smerling, Evelyn Weiss: "China! Zeitgenössische Malerei", Cologne 1996
Susan Bright: "Chinese Painting", in: "Art Asia Pacific", no. 17, p. 99, 1998
Shu Kewen: "Wang Qingsong's 'Photojournalism'", in: "Sanguine Splendour: Chinablue Gallery", Beijing 2007

Puy, Inma G.（著）：《北京的春天》（评论）1996年四月14日发表于：http://www.connect-arte.com/archive/china/echinab.htm
Ronte, Dieter/Smerling, Walter/Weiss, Evelyn（著）：《中国！当代绘画》科隆1996年
Bright, Susan（著）：《中国油画：英国》ART Asia Pacific，第17期(1998年)
舒可文（著）：《王兴伟的"摄影报道"》环碧堂画廊，北京 2007年

WANG QINGSONG 王庆松

[waŋ tɕʰiŋsʊŋ]

Wang Qingsong's photographic tableaux seem to have emerged fully formed from the chaos of the present decade, with little connection to the dialectics that drove contemporary art forward in China through the 1980s and 1990s. To the Western observer, these montaged spoofs evoke a cruder Jeff Wall, a lower-production-value Gregory Crewdson. But perhaps owing to their very tackiness and pastiche, Wang Qingsong's photographs have assumed significance in the contemporary Chinese visual lexicon quite out of proportion with their theoretical and art-historical grounding.

Wang's works in the late 1990s were mainly with the importation of Western brands to China. Thus we have digitally manipulated images of the artist as a crucified Jesus, hanging from a cross of Coca-Cola cans as cell-phone butterflies flutter in the background, and a series of "Requesting Buddha" photos in which the artist assumes many hands (à la Buddhist statuary) all of which grasp emblems of millennial materialism. His most ambitious early work came in 2000 with the long-format studio work "The Night Revels of Lao Li", which places the eminent curator Li Xianting into a series of catchily re-staged scenes based on Gu Hongzhong's masterpiece hand scroll "Night Revels of Han Xizai". Robed Tang courtesans are replaced by hair-dyed women in cheap lingerie, and lutes replaced by cheap plastic guitars in an oblique commentary on the fetid decadence of the moment. A number of works pairing the artist with this assortment of trashy models followed, including "Bath House" (2000).

In 2001 Wang Qingsong's work took a political turn with the triptych "Past, Present, Future" and the extended series "Another Battle". The former re-stages the two sculptures which frame the Mao Zedong Mausoleum on Tian'anmen Square in terra cotta mud and silver, adding a third, central panel in gold to represent the artist's perverse vision of the future. The latter places the artist among a brigade of soldiers bearing plastic AK-47s and firing from behind a barbed wire barricade adorned with, what else, Coca-Cola

Wang Qingsongs fotografische Tableaus scheinen bereits voll entwickelt dem Chaos des laufenden Jahrzehnts entsprungen zu sein, ohne Verbindung zu jener mühsamen Dialektik, die die chinesische Gegenwartskunst durch die 1980er und 1990er Jahre vorangetrieben hat. Westliche Betrachter fühlen sich durch seine parodistischen Montagen an einen raueren Jeff Wall oder eine Low-Budget-Version von Gregory Crewdson erinnert. Aber Wang Qingsongs Fotografien haben, vielleicht gerade dank ihrer Abgeschmacktheit, eine Bedeutung für Chinas aktuellen Bilderkanon angenommen, die in keinem Verhältnis zu ihrem theoretischen und kunsthistorischen Unterbau steht.

Wangs Arbeiten der späten 1990er Jahre beschäftigten sich hauptsächlich mit dem Import westlicher Handelsmarken nach China. So finden wir digital bearbeitete Bilder des Künstlers als gekreuzigter Jesus an einem Kreuz aus Coca-Cola-Dosen, während im Hintergrund Handy-Schmetterlinge umherflattern, oder eine Serie von „Requesting Buddha"-Fotos (1999), auf denen dem Künstler viele Arme sprießen, die in den Händen Symbole des Materialismus der Jahrtausendwende halten. Wangs ehrgeizigstes Frühwerk entstand im Jahr 2000: „The Night Revels of Lao Li", eine Studioarbeit im Breitformat, montiert den angesehenen Kurator Li Xianting in eine Reihe trickreich nachgestellter Szenen, die auf Gu Hongzhongs meisterlichem Rollbild „Night Revels of Han Xizai" fußen. Kunstvoll gekleidete Tang-Kurtisanen sind durch Frauen mit gefärbten Haaren in ordinären Dessous ersetzt und antike Lauten durch billige Plastikgitarren – ein verklausulierter Kommentar zur niveaulosen Dekadenz der Gegenwart. Es folgte noch eine Reihe von Arbeiten, die den Künstler selbst inmitten seiner vulgären Modelle zeigte, wie etwa „Bath House" (2000).

2001 wurde Wang Qingsongs Werk dann mit dem Triptychon „Past, Present, Future" und der umfangreichen Serie „Another Battle" politischer. Das Triptychon stellt die beiden Skulpturen, die das Mao-Zedong-Mausoleum auf dem Platz des Himmlischen Friedens flankieren, in Terrakottaschlamm und Silber dar, beidseits einer Mitteltafel in Gold, die die

王庆松的摄影场面似乎完全来自过去十年中社会的骤变，而与80年代到90推动年代之间的当代艺术向前的辩证法毫无联系。在西方人看来，这些蒙太奇技巧又产生了一个更原始的杰夫·沃尔，一个更低成本的格雷戈里。可能因为掌握了他们这些特点，剔除他们的理论和艺术历史的背景。王庆松的摄影已成为中国当代视觉词典里一个符号。

王庆松90年代后期的作品主要以西方品牌进入中国为主题。因此我们才可以将王的图像数字处理为受难的耶稣的样子：可乐瓶子堆砌的十字架，掀开的手机组成的蝴蝶，拥有着艳丽的颜色。颜色背后，背负这个十字架的守望者，痛苦万分；在另一个系列作品中《拿来千手佛》，艺术家拟造了许多手臂，每只手里都抓着千禧年的标记。他早期最具抱负的作品《老栗夜宴图》创作于2000年，借用了中国五代顾闳中《韩熙载夜宴图》的构图，著名的策展人栗宪庭在作品中充当主要角色。身着廉价内衣的染发女子代替了高雅的宫廷仕女，便宜的塑料吉他，以一种间接的方式诠释着这个时代的颓废。王庆松又创作了大量此类作品，《大澡堂》便是其中之一。

2001年，王庆松的作品转向政治主题，创作了《过去，现在和将来》以及《又一次战争》。前者以天安门前的毛泽东纪念堂做了一个纪念碑式的城市雕塑，分别用泥、银色、金色代表过去、现在、将来。在后者中，艺术家置身于一群手持AK-47士兵中，他们在布满可口可乐罐的铁丝网后向前冲锋射击着。次年，他的作品风格向 Crewdson和 卢卡·迪科西亚（转变，体现其创作的户外照片中，如《艺术快车》。照片中两辆公交车相撞而停靠在肮脏的乡村小道上。然而，他仍然继续着拍摄试验，在2003年完成了两张最著名的图片《跟我学》和《罗曼蒂克》的创作。前者作品名 取自邓小平时期的中央 电视台一档英语教学节目，照片中王站在一张巨大的黑板前，上面涂满了无聊而荒唐的政治标语和商业口号。在后一幅作品中，作者以40人民

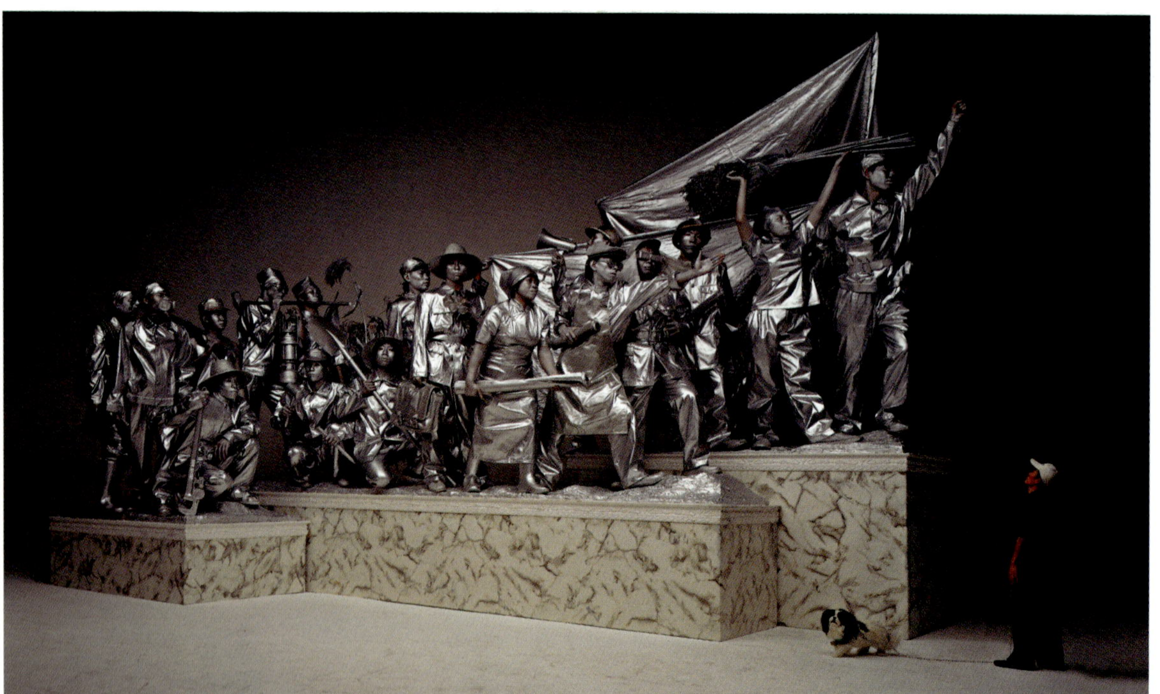
2

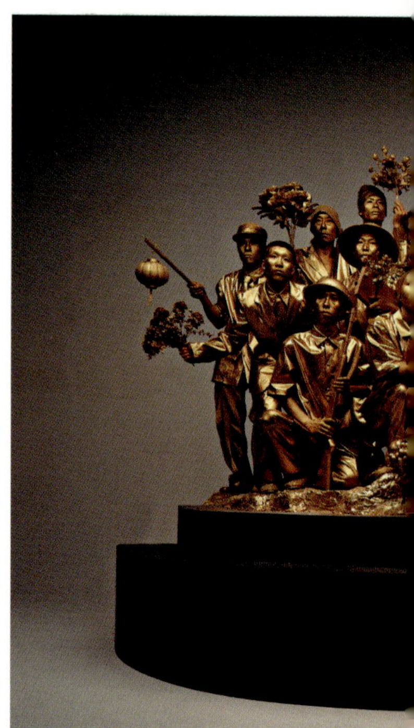
3

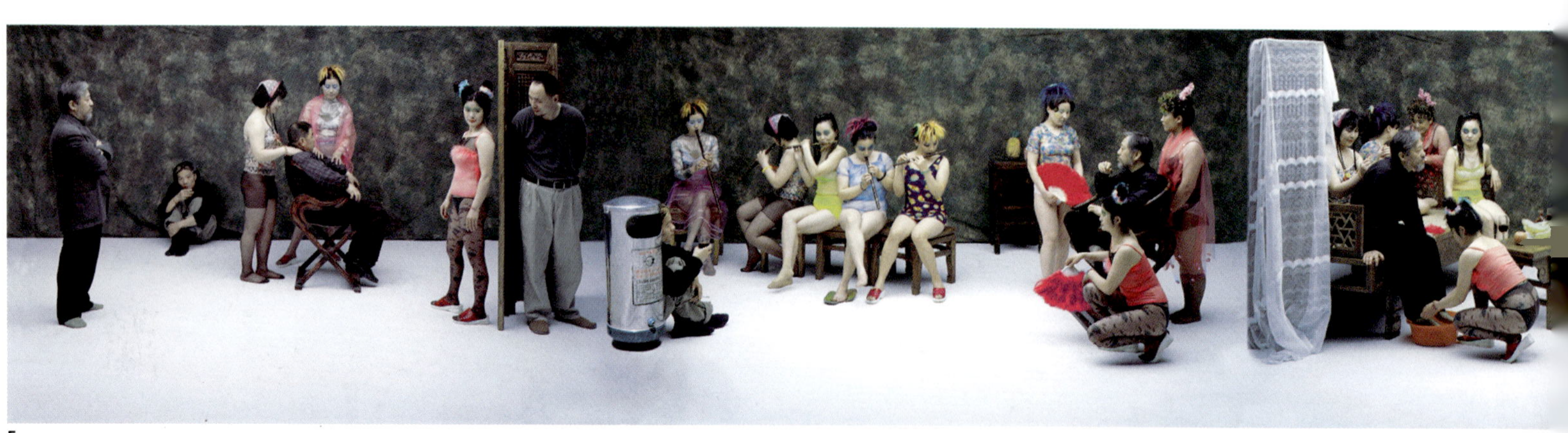
5

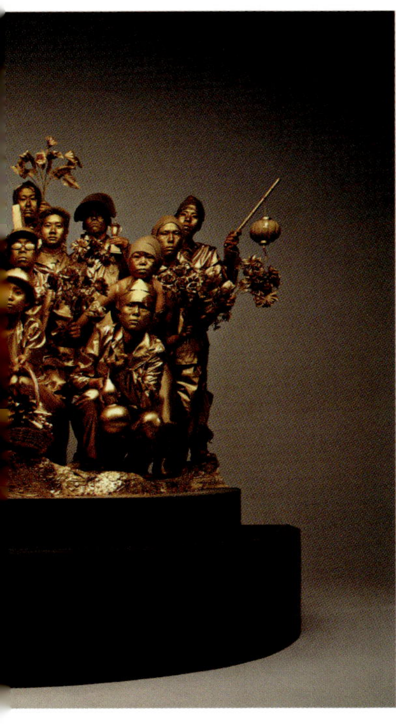

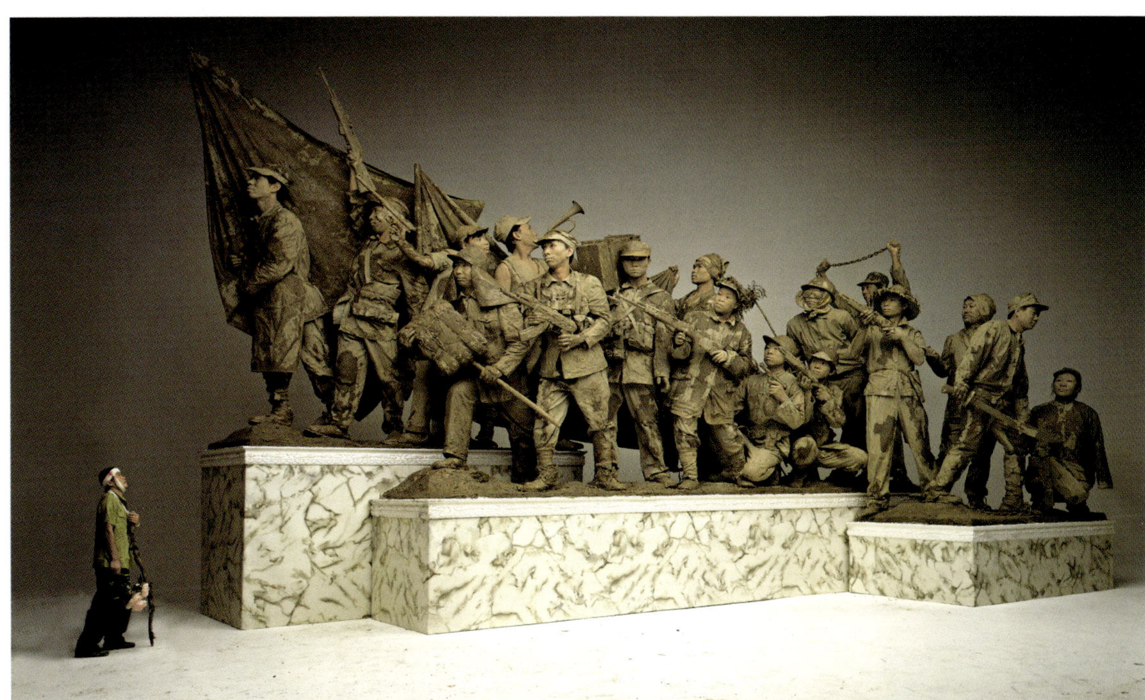

4

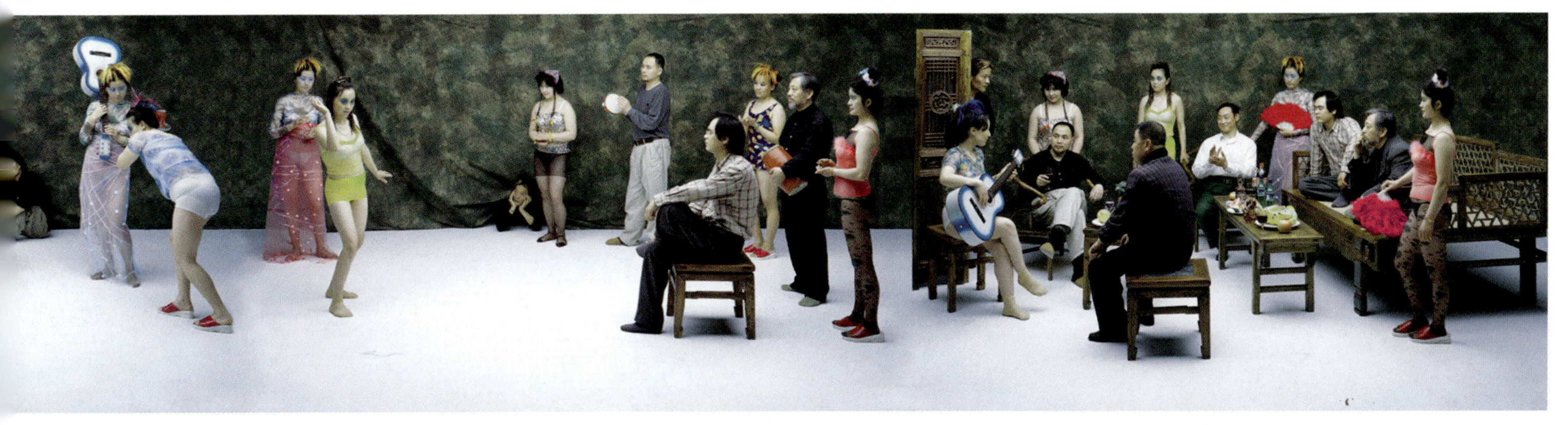

6

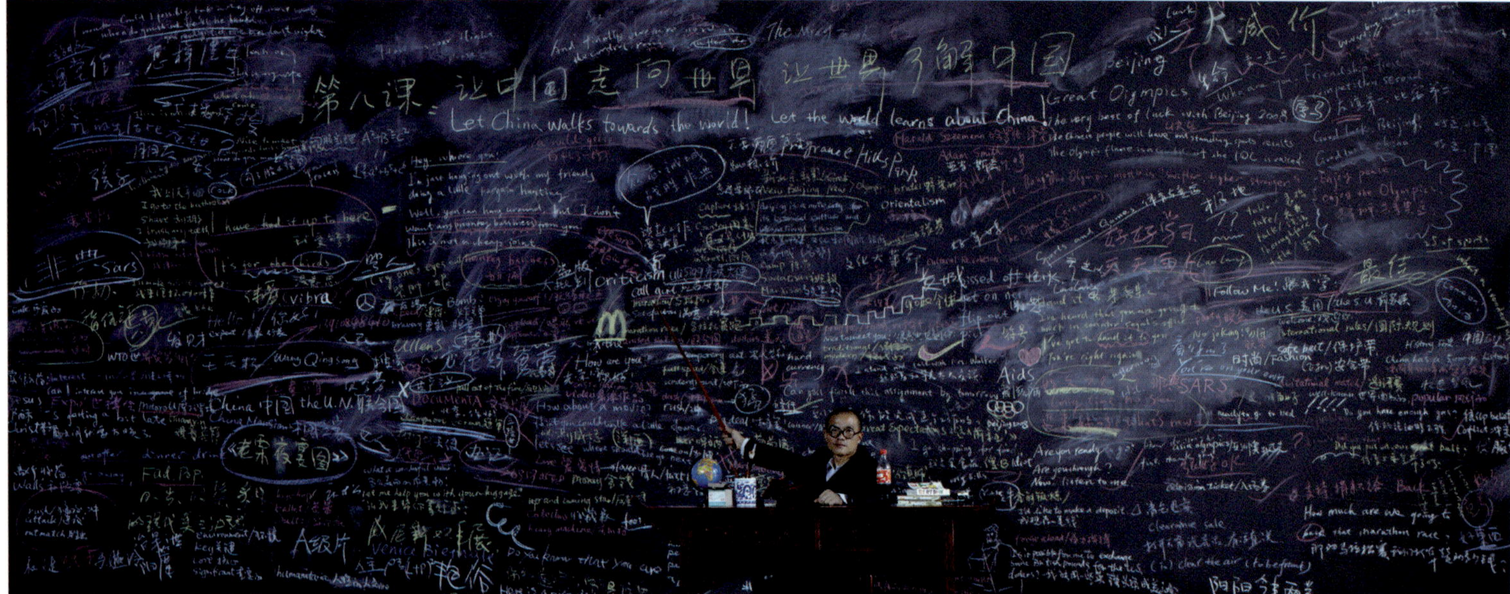

cans. The next year his work took a turn toward Crewdson and Philip-Lorca diCorcia, with outdoor images like "Art Express" (2002) which shows an accident between two Beijing city buses so labeled on a rural dirt road. His studio experiments would however continue, yielding in 2003 two of his best-known images, "Follow Me" and "Romantique". The former takes its name from the early Deng Xiaoping-era English program on state television, and pictures the artist before a massive billboard filled with slogans political and commercial, banal and absurd. The latter condenses the whole of European art history, Botticelli onward, into a verdant orgy of ¥40/day nude models re-enacting poses from famous paintings before a noxiously artificial blue sky.

Works from 2004 and after include "Competition", in which he plasters a 14-meter high, 40-meter wide chamber in a Beijing movie studio with hand-written posters bearing copied advertisements, and "Fotofest" in which 600 viewers stand watching a group of nude models re-enact Matisse's circle of dancers, all holding paparazzi cameras fashioned from Styrofoam blocks. Wang's lens has grown ever more focused, as scenes dripping with an indeterminate drama have emerged as a major thread in his work. With its meticulously constructed scenes, Wang Qingsong's work proves the power of invention and artifice in artistic production in China today.

Zukunftsvision des Künstlers verdeutlicht: er, inmitten eines Trupps von Soldaten, die, mit Plastikgewehren bewaffnet, aus dem Schutz eines Stacheldrahtverhaus heraus feuern, der – natürlich – mit Coca-Cola-Dosen geschmückt ist. Im Jahr darauf nahm Wang dann eine Wendung in Richtung Crewdson und Philip-Lorca diCorcia – mit Aufnahmen wie „Art Express" (2002), das einen Unfall von zwei Pekinger Stadtbussen auf einer unbefestigten Landstraße zeigt. Daneben verfolgte er seine Studioexperimente weiter und schuf 2003 zwei seiner bekanntesten Bilder: „Follow Me" und „Romantique". Das erste geht auf ein altes Englischprogramm des staatlichen Fernsehens zurück und stellt den Künstler vor einer riesigen Plakatwand voll banaler und absurder politischer und kommerzieller Parolen dar. Das zweite fasst die gesamte europäische Kunstgeschichte, von Botticelli angefangen, in einer Orgie mit billigen Aktmodellen zusammen, die Posen aus berühmten Gemälden in sattgrünem Ambiente vor unnatürlich blauem Himmel nachstellen.

Zu erwähnenswerten Arbeiten ab 2004 gehören „Competition", worin er einen 14 Meter hohen und 40 Meter breiten Raum in einem Pekinger Filmstudio mit handbemalten Plakaten voll kopierter Werbung tapeziert, und „Fotofest", in dem 600 Zuschauer eine Gruppe nackter Modelle umstehen, die den „Tanz" von Matisse nachstellen, und ihre aus Styropor geschnitzten Paparazzi-Kameras auf sie richten. Wangs Linse ist zunehmend schärfer geworden, während sich in seinem Werk als roter Faden allmählich Szenen voll unbestimmter Dramatik herausbilden. Mit seinen sorgfältig konstruierten Szenarien demonstriert Wang Qingsong die große Kraft der Fantasie und des Spiels in Chinas zeitgenössischem Kunstschaffen.

币一天雇佣了人体模特，他们裸体着在人造蓝空前表演着一副名画上的放荡生活。作品以此了浓缩了波堤切利之前的整个欧洲艺术史。

年月逐增，王的照片创作似乎更加苛刻了。2004年之后的作品有《大摆战场》和《摄影节》。在前者中，他在北京一家影剧院中，用手写的海报和复印的广告黏贴着14米高40米高的房间。而后者则描述一群裸体模特模仿着马蒂斯《舞》，600多名观众站立着观看着。王的角度比以前更加集中了，场面是其作品发展的主线，融入模糊的戏剧中，并紧紧与杰夫·沃尔紧紧相连。由于其精心设计的场景和安排的故事发展，王的作品促进了当今艺术制作的创新和技巧。

Philip Tinari

7

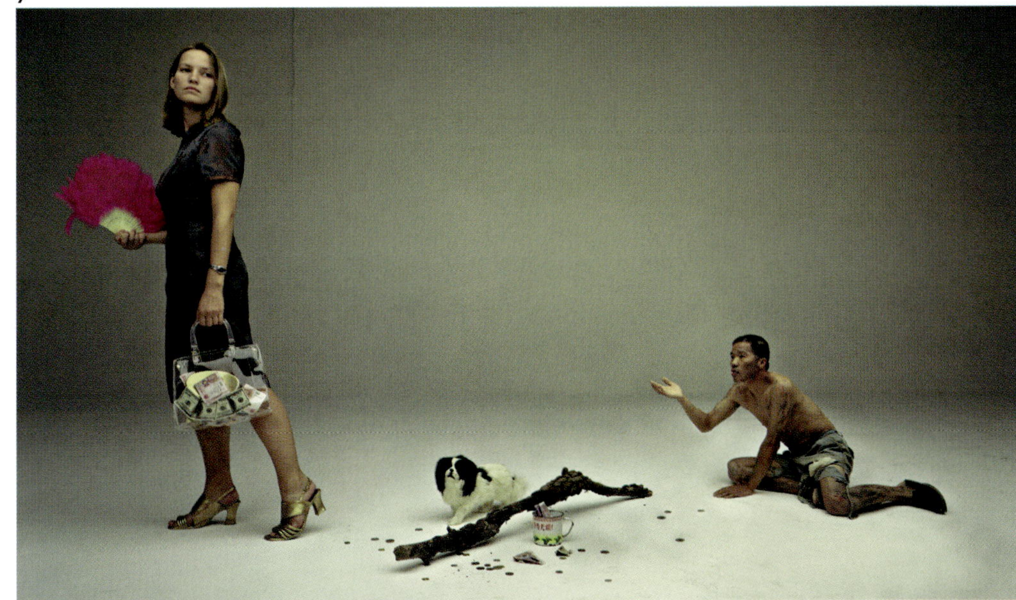

8

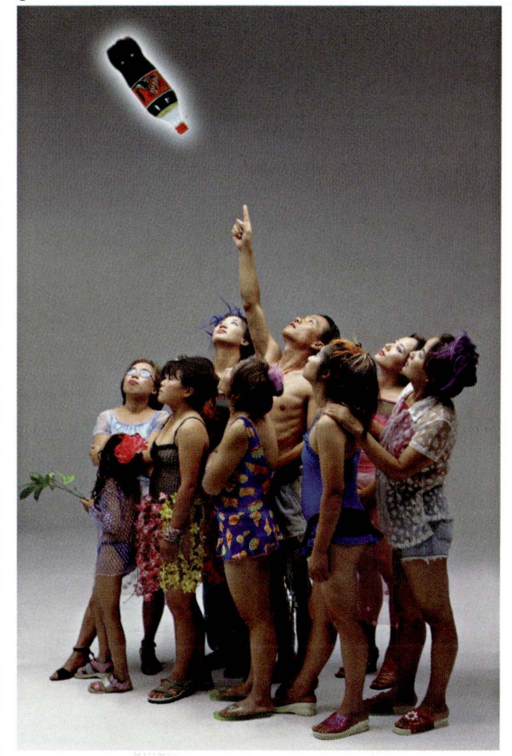

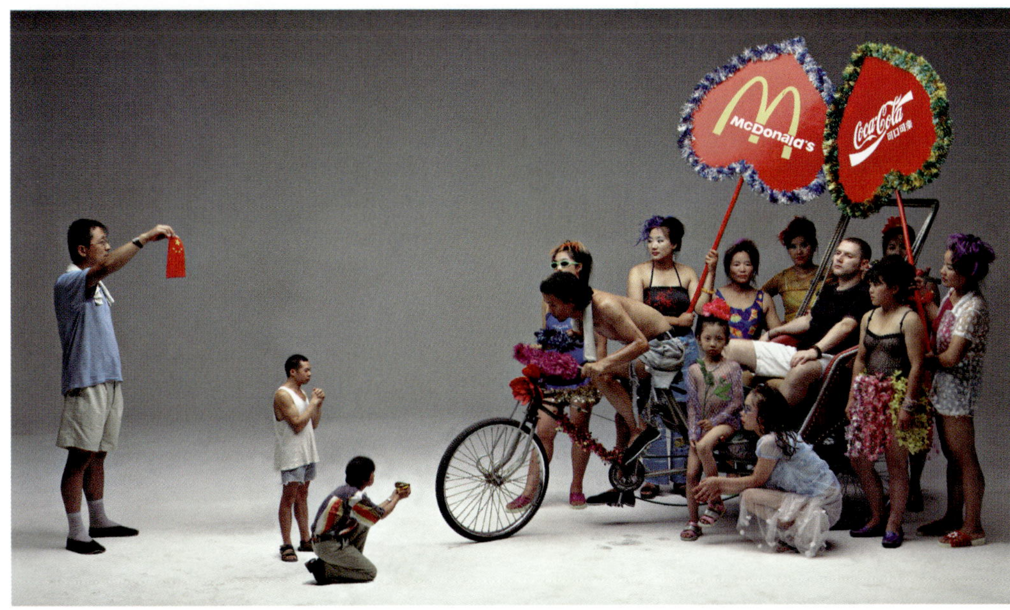

9

1 ***Requesting Buddha Series No. 1***, *1999*
C-print, 180 x 110 cm; C-print, 180 x 110 cm
《拿来千手佛系列No. 1》1999年, C-印刷, 180 x 110 cm

2 ***Past***, *2001*
C-print, 170 x 291 cm; C-print, 170 x 291 cm
《过去》2001年, C-印刷, 170 x 291 cm

3 ***Present***, *2001*
C-print, 170 x 218 cm; C-print, 170 x 218 cm
《现在》2001年, C-印刷, 170 x 218 cm

4 ***Future***, *2001*
C-print, 170 x 291 cm; C-print, 170 x 291 cm
《未来》2001年, C-印刷, 170 x 291 cm

5 ***Night Revels of Lao Li***, *2000*
C-print, 120 x 960 cm; C-print, 120 x 960 cm
《老栗夜宴图》2000年, C-印刷, 120 x 960 cm

6 ***Follow Me***, *2003*
C-print, 120 x 300 cm; C-print, 120 x 300 cm
《跟我学》2003年, C-印刷, 120 x 300 cm

7 ***Beggar***, *2001*
C-print, 120 x 200 cm; C-print, 120 x 200 cm
《乞丐》2001年, C-印刷, 120 x 200 cm

8 ***Look Up! Look Up!***, *2000*
C-print, 180 x 115 cm; C-print, 180 x 115 cm
《向上看！向上看！》2000年, C-印刷, 180 x 115 cm

9 ***Can I Cooperate With You?***, *2000*
C-print, 120 x 200 cm; C-print, 120 x 200 cm
《我能跟您合作吗?》2000年, C-印刷, 120 x 200 cm

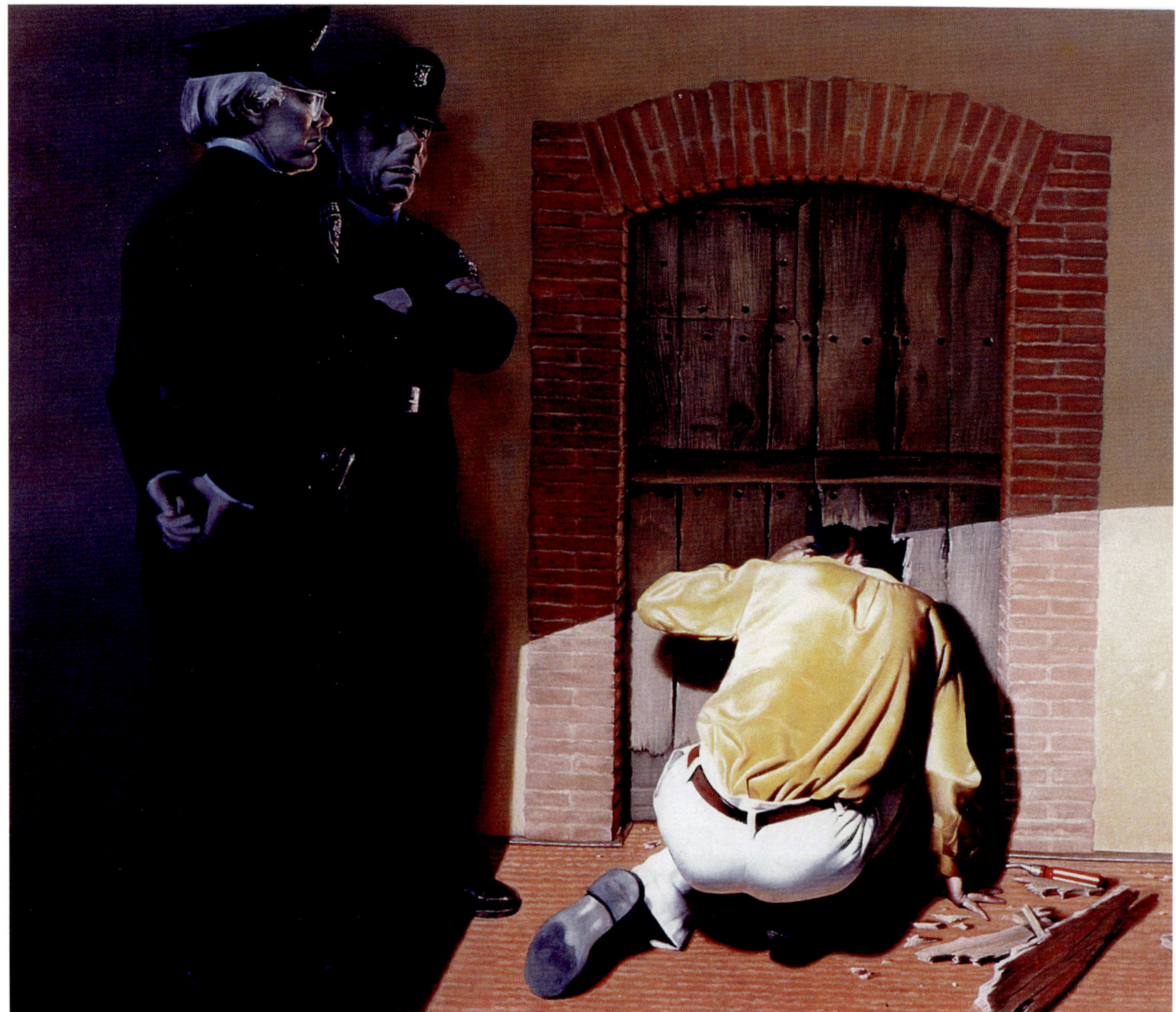

1

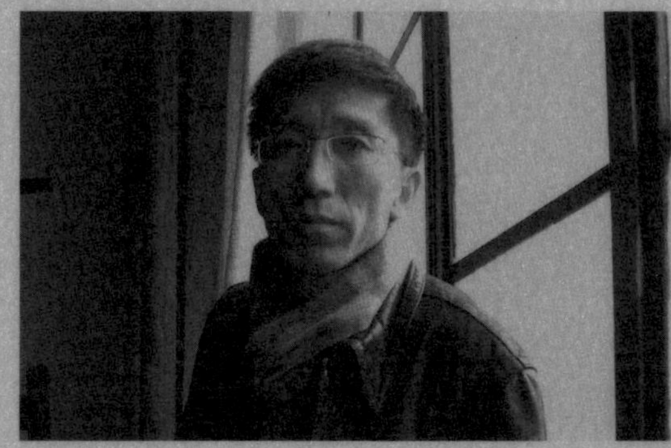

"I want to slowly depart from art history. In the past the observer needed to have a certain cultural background to understand my works, while what I am dealing with now has a more direct connection with anyone's personal experience."

„Ich möchte langsam von der Kunstgeschichte wegkommen. Früher brauchte der Betrachter einen gewissen kulturellen Hintergrund, um meine Werke zu verstehen, aber das, womit ich mich jetzt befasse, steht in direkter Verbindung mit jedermanns persönlicher Erfahrung."

"我要慢慢地脱离艺术史。以前，观众需要一定的文化背景去了解我的画，而我现在所创作的东西，和任何人的个人经历都有着更直接的联系。"

Born in 1969 in Shenyang, Liaoning Province, China. Lives and works in Shanghai
Geboren 1969 in Shenyang, Provinz Liaoning, China. Lebt und arbeitet in Shanghai
1969年辽宁中国辽宁省沈阳，现在上海居住工作

***Selected exhibitions* / Ausgewählte Ausstellungen / 所选展览**

1996 "The Dust of the Romantic History of Male Heroism", Cifa Gallery, Beijing, China
1997 Biennale d'Art Contemporain de Lyon, Lyon, France
2000 "Fuck Off!", Eastlink, Shanghai, China
2004 "The Monk and the Demon", Musee d'Art Contemporain de Lyon, Lyon, France
2005–07 "Mahjong – Chinesische Gegenwartskunst aus der Sammlung Sigg", Kunstmuseum Bern, Berne, Switzerland; Hamburger Kunsthalle, Hamburg, Germany; Museum der Moderne, Salzburg, Austria
2006/07 "Large Rowboat", Galerie Urs Meile, Beijing/Lucerne, China/Switzerland

1996年 《男性浪漫英雄史之尘》中央美院画廊，北京，中国
1997年 《里昂双年展》里昂，法国
2000年 《不合作方式》东廊画廊，上海，中国
2004年 《和尚与恶魔》里昂当代艺术博物馆，法国
2005–07年 《麻将》西克中国当代艺术收藏展，伯尔尼美术馆 瑞士；汉堡美术馆 汉堡 德国；萨尔茨保现代美术馆 奥地利
2006/07年 《大划船》麦勒画廊，北京，中国，卢塞恩，瑞士

***Selected publications* / Ausgewählte Publikationen / 所选著作**

Susan Bright: "The Chinese Grand Tour at Chinese Contemporary", in: "Asian Art News", vol. 8, no. 2, March/April 1998
Nataline Colonello, Xie Nanxing: "A Criss-Crossed interview with Xie Nanxing and Wang Xingwei", in: "Show Me... Catch Me... Sight Unseen: Xie Nanxing and Wang Xingwei", Beijing/Lucerne

Bright, Susan（著）:《中国盛大游览在中国当代》（书评）于：Asian Art News，第8卷，号2，(1998年三/四月)
Colonello, Nataline/Xie Nanxing（著）:《于谢南星和王兴伟的一次交叉往来的采访》于:《显示我...捉住我...看见未看见：谢南星和王兴伟》，北京，麦勒画廊，北京 — 卢塞恩

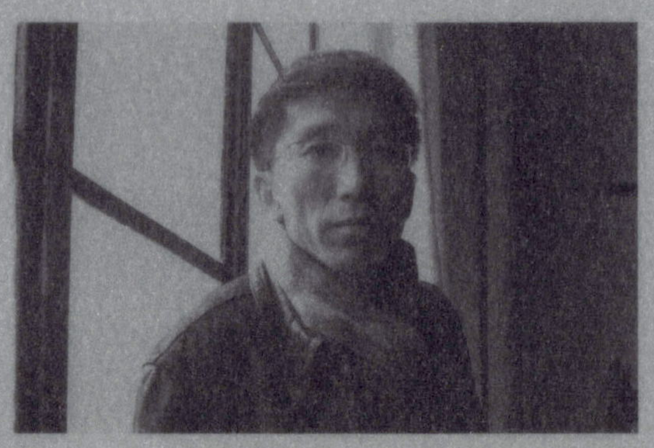

"I want to slowly depart from art history. In the past the observer needed to have a certain cultural background to understand my works, while what I am dealing with now has a more direct connection with anyone's personal experience."

„Ich möchte langsam von der Kunstgeschichte wegkommen. Früher brauchte der Betrachter einen gewissen kulturellen Hintergrund, um meine Werke zu verstehen, aber das, womit ich mich jetzt befasse, steht in direkter Verbindung mit jedermanns persönlicher Erfahrung."

"我要慢慢地脱离艺术史。以前，观众需要一定的文化背景去了解我的画，而我现在所创作的东西，和任何人的个人经历都有着更直接的联系。"

Born in 1969 in Shenyang, Liaoning Province, China. Lives and works in Shanghai
Geboren 1969 in Shenyang, Provinz Liaoning, China. Lebt und arbeitet in Shanghai
1969年辽宁中国辽宁省沈阳，现在上海居住工作

Selected exhibitions / Ausgewählte Ausstellungen / 所选展览

1996 "The Dust of the Romantic History of Male Heroism", Cifa Gallery, Beijing, China
1997 Biennale d'Art Contemporain de Lyon, Lyon, France
2000 "Fuck Off!", Eastlink, Shanghai, China
2004 "The Monk and the Demon", Musee d'Art Contemporain de Lyon, Lyon, France
2005-07 "Mahjong - Chinesische Gegenwartskunst aus der Sammlung Sigg", Kunstmuseum Bern, Berne, Switzerland; Hamburger Kunsthalle, Hamburg, Germany; Museum der Moderne, Salzburg, Austria
2006/07 "Large Rowboat", Galerie Urs Meile, Beijing/Lucerne, China/Switzerland

1996年 《男性浪漫英雄史之尘》中央美院画廊，北京，中国
1997年 《里昂双年展》里昂，法国
2000年 《不合作方式》东廊画廊，上海，中国
2004年 《和尚与恶魔》里昂当代艺术博物馆，法国
2005-07年 《麻将》西克中国当代艺术收藏展，伯尔尼美术馆 瑞士；汉堡美术馆 汉堡 德国；萨尔茨堡现代美术馆 奥地利
2006/07年 《大划船》麦勒画廊，北京，中国，卢塞恩，瑞士

Selected publications / Ausgewählte Publikationen / 所选著作

Susan Bright: "The Chinese Grand Tour at Chinese Contemporary", in: "Asian Art News", vol. 8, no. 2, March/April 1998
Nataline Colonello, Xie Nanxing: "A Criss-Crossed interview with Xie Nanxing and Wang Xingwei", in: "Show Me... Catch Me... Sight Unseen: Xie Nanxing and Wang Xingwei", Beijing/Lucerne

Bright, Susan（著）：《中国盛大游览在中国当代》（书评）于：Asian Art News，第8卷，号2,（1998年三/四月）
Colonello, Nataline/Xie Nanxing（著）：《于谢南星和王兴伟的一次交叉往来的采访》于：《显示我...捉住我...看见未看见：谢南星和王兴伟》，北京，麦勒画廊，北京 — 卢塞恩

WANG XINGWEI 王兴伟

[waŋ ɕiŋwei]

Wang Xingwei is the enfant terrible of Chinese painters, churning out compositions of seemingly infinite variety and wit. A sharp intelligence, directed at the Western art-historical canon and at Chinese taste hierarchies, underlies the work of this painter, trained at a minor school far in China's northeast before moving to Shanghai to build his career.

Wang's earliest published paintings date to 1994 and play with understandings of art and literature. In the series "All Happy Families are Similar" (1994), a scene which seems to come not from Tolstoy but from Dostoyevsky of a dead woman lying at the center of a sparsely appointed room is peppered with icons from art history – a Jasper Johns target, some Beuysian tar, with a man in a cheap suit, perhaps the artist himself, surveying the damage. Other early paintings such as "A. D. 2017" (1995) show a Chinese grandfather excavating Duchamp's urinal atop a sunny hillock, showing it around to a multiracial cast of children, or "The Testimony of the Hare" (1995) where the artist explains a picture of Joseph Beuys to a dead hare, in a prankish subversion of that artist's famed performance. Wang Xingwei also understood and expressed, earlier than most anyone, the peculiar dynamics by which contemporary Chinese art was being parlayed into Western acclaim. Two canvases from 1995 demonstrate this understanding: "Standard Expression of Post-1989" shows a doctor pushing on a stretcher, a character culled from one of Zeng Fanzhi's "Xiehe" hospital paintings, as figures from paintings by Liu Wei, Fang Lijun and others look out from behind patient room windows. In "The East is Red", a caricatured Li Xianting drives a bright blue tractor on which sit these same stock characters.

In the late 1990s, Wang Xingwei produced a number of canvases juxtaposing a self-portrait character in a yellow button-down shirt, a schoolboy in a red collar, and scenes from the painterly canon. In one of the best-loved, "Thomas" (1998), the yellow-shirted man peers through a broken wooden door into what can only be Duchamp's

Wang Xingwei, das Enfant terrible unter den chinesischen Malern, produziert in einem fort Kompositionen von scheinbar grenzenlosem Abwechslungsreichtum und Witz. Dem Werk dieses Malers, der an einer namenlosen Schule im fernen Nordosten Chinas studierte, bevor er nach Shanghai ging, liegt eine messerscharfe Intelligenz zugrunde, mit der er den Kanon der westlichen Kunstgeschichte und die chinesischen Geschmackshierarchien gleichermaßen aufs Korn nimmt.

Wangs früheste Gemälde datieren von 1994 und spielen mit unterschiedlichen Auffassungen über Kunst und Literatur. Eine Szene der Serie „All Happy Families are Similar" (1994) scheint weniger von Tolstoi als von Dostojewski zu stammen: Eine tote Frau liegt in der Mitte eines spärlich möblierten Zimmers, das mit Ikonen der Kunstgeschichte gespickt ist – hier eine Jasper-Johns-Zielscheibe, dort ein wenig Beuys'scher Teer –, während ein Mann im billigen Anzug, vielleicht der Künstler selbst, das Debakel begutachtet. Andere frühe Gemälde, wie „A. D. 2017" (1995), zeigen einen chinesischen Alten, der Marcel Duchamps Urinal auf einem sonnigen Hügel ausgräbt und einer ethnisch gemischten Kindergruppe vorführt, oder „The Testimony of the Hare" (1995), mit dem Künstler, der einem toten Hasen ein Bild von Joseph Beuys erklärt – eine subversive Verulkung berühmter Künstler. Als einer der ersten entlarvte Wang Xingwei auch jene ganz besondere Dynamik, durch die die chinesische Gegenwartskunst so nachhaltig Anerkennung im Westen fand – was zwei Gemälde von 1995 demonstrieren: „Standard Expression of Post-1989" zeigt einen Arzt, der eine Gestalt aus einem von Zeng Fanzhis „Xiehe"-Hospital-Gemälden auf einer Bahre vor sich herschiebt, während Figuren aus Bildern von Liu Wei, Fang Lijun und anderen durch die Fenster der Krankenzimmer hereinblicken. Und in „The East is Red" chauffiert ein karikierter Li Xianting einen knallblauen Traktor, auf dem die gleichen abgekupferten Gestalten sitzen.

In den späten 1990er Jahren stellte Wang eine Reihe von Gemälden her, die sein Alter Ego im gelben Buttondown-

王兴伟在中国艺术家中堪称一怪，他创作了许多质量很差的作品，多种画风和绘画技巧。受西方艺术史正统作品和中国鉴赏体系的影响，他的作品中充满了睿智。在移居上海开创事业之前，他在中国东北地区一个不起眼的学校学习。

在1994年创作的早期作品中，王轻率地玩弄着对艺术和文学的理解。在系列作品《幸福家庭都是相似的》中的一个场面中，一个死了的女人躺在房间的一个指定的位置，这似乎不是来源于托尔斯泰的作品而是杜斯妥也夫斯基，这一场景生动再现了艺术历史象征-Jasper Johns 的目标。同时在这一场景中，衣着寒酸的男子，也许是艺术家本人，双手挎腰，头稍前倾，审视着那个女人。其他早期油画，如《公元2017》中，一位中国老大爷在阳光灿烂的山顶挖掘杜尚. 马塞尔的尿壶，并将之拿给周围不同肤色的儿童；在其恶作剧行为表演中，他把Joseph Beuys一幅图画比作一只死野兔。另外，王兴伟比其他人更早理解并表达独特的原动力，也因此“中国当代艺术”成功的获得西方人的喝彩。两幅从1995年开始创作的油画《89后标准表情》证明了他的对原动力的理解，作品上展示了一个推着手推车的医生，这个人物选自曾梵志的油画《协和医院》，而在在病室向外观看的那些人物来源于刘炜，方立均等艺术家的油画在《东方红》中，栗宪庭被画成漫画形象，驾驶着 鲜蓝拖拉机，上面坐着上述的定型角。

90年代末期，王兴伟创作了许多油画，每幅油画都有穿着老式黄色衬衫自画像人物和还有带着红领巾的小学生，整个场景取自经典美术作品。在他最喜爱的一幅油画中，身穿黄色衬衫的男人分透过一扇破门向里你张望，而Warhol 和 Beuys身穿警服，向下盯着他。世纪之交时，王的体裁和材料不断增加，如在瓦片，报纸 和床单上绘画，而却很少命名。他对庸俗艺术的视觉动感产生了强烈兴趣，常常地摊上购买大量的低廉油画，然后在上面重新创作。最近，新的一组定型角色出现在其作品中，有

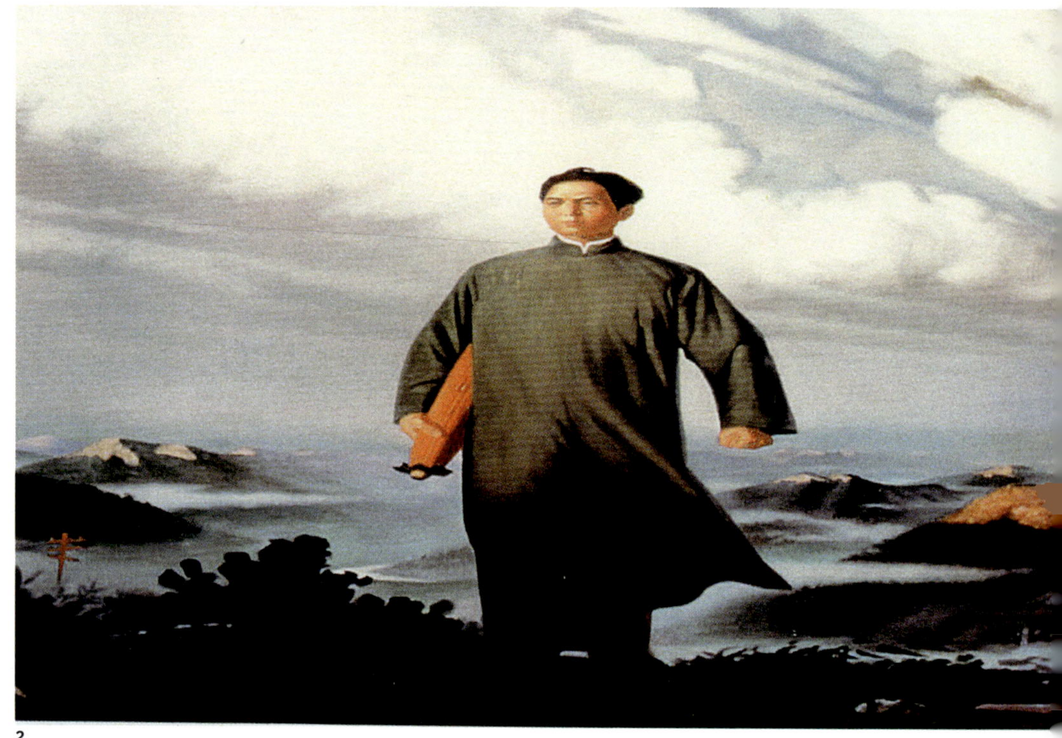
2

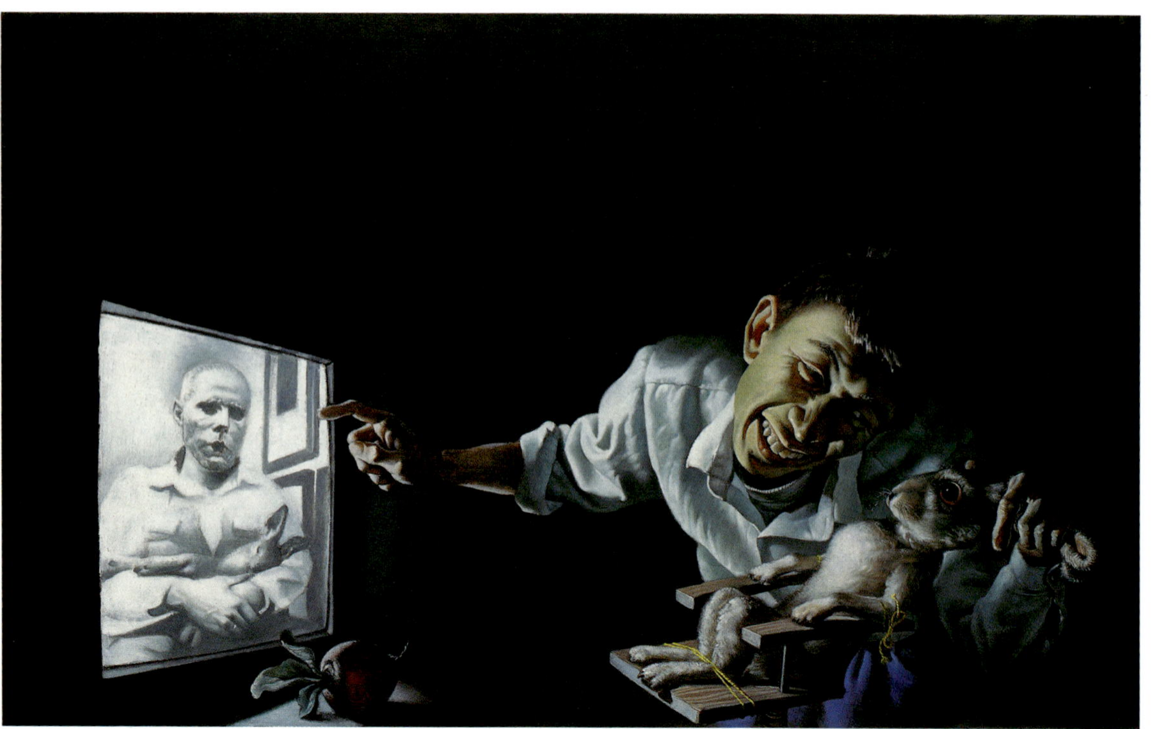
3

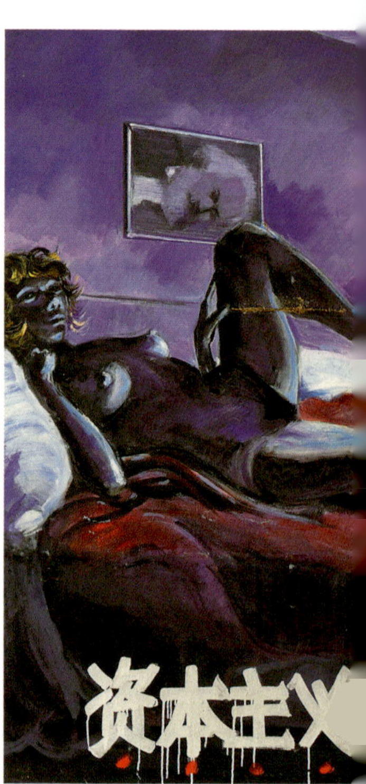

4

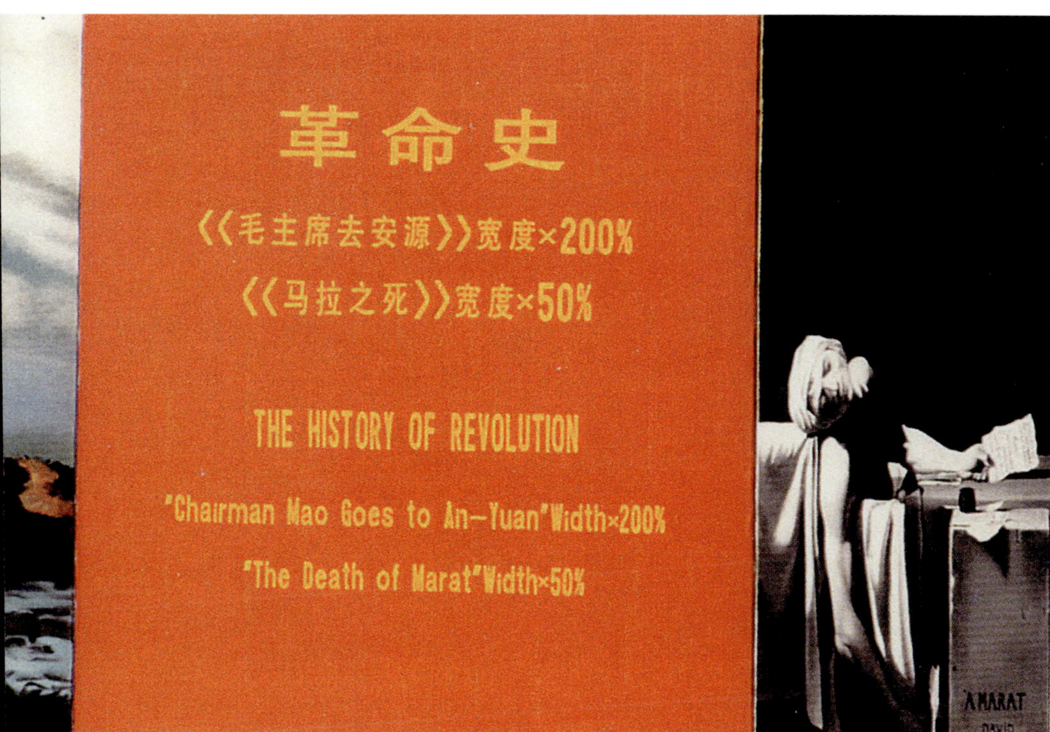
革命史
《《毛主席去安源》》宽度×200%
《《马拉之死》》宽度×50%
THE HISTORY OF REVOLUTION
"Chairman Mao Goes to An-Yuan"Width×200%
"The Death of Marat"Width×50%
A MARAT
DAVID

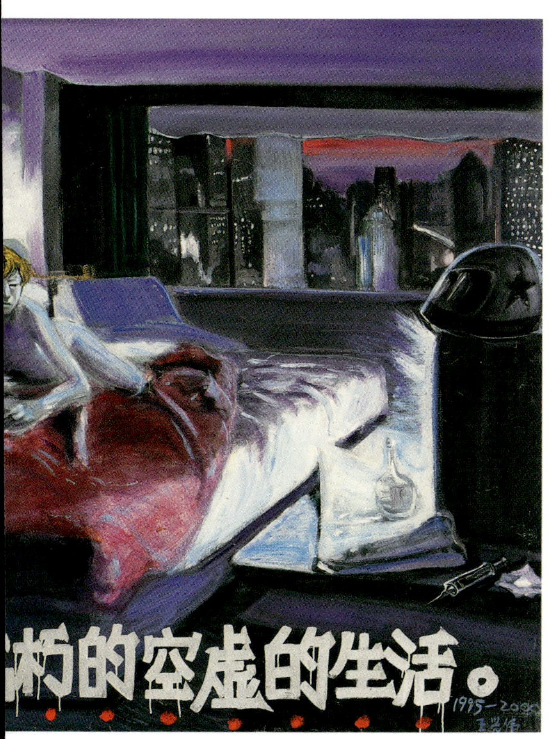
朽的空虚的生活。
1995-2000

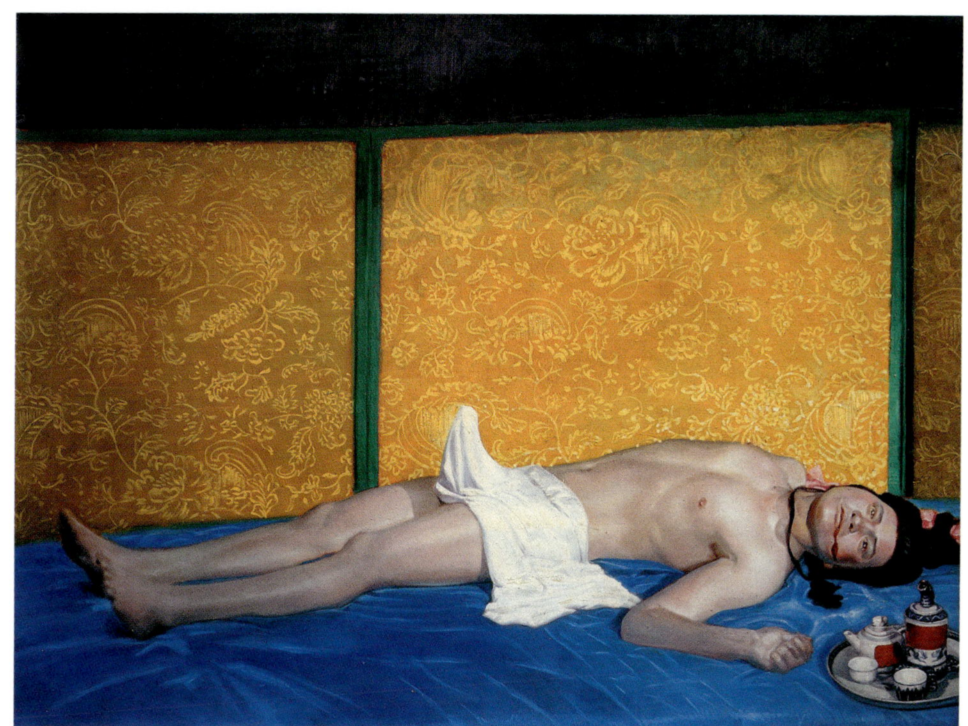

5

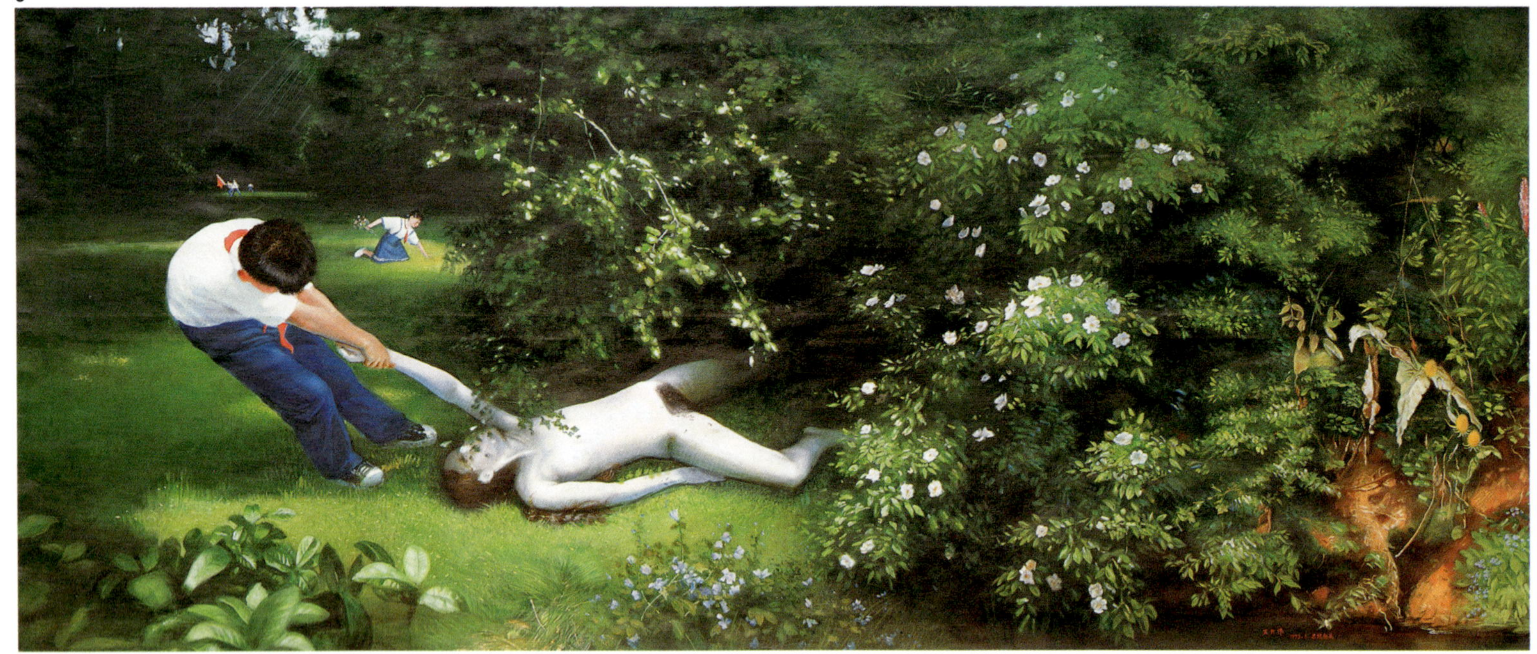

"Etant Donnés" installation, as Warhol and Beuys, decked out in police uniforms, stare him down. At the turn of the century, Wang's styles and materials began to proliferate, as he produced paintings on roof tiles, newspaper, and bedsheets to name just a few. He developed a strong interest in the visual mechanics of kitsch, often re-painting canvases he would buy for cheap sums from market stalls. Soon, a new set of stock characters emerged, including airline stewardesses, sailors, penguins, and golfers. A painting in the art-deco style of Tamara de Lempicka might lead to another of a stewardess bound in rope as if taken from a Nobuyoshi Araki photograph, then to a golfer measuring a shot amidst a field of watermelons.

Wang's most recent work has followed in this vein of employing stock characters; his 2007 solo show "Large Rowboat" included seemingly infinite variations on a couple apparently culled from the pages of a 1980s issue of the lowbrow Chinese literary journal "Reader", akin to the "American Reader's Digest". As these cartoonish figures paddle through lakes, lounge under trees, and in once case form a heart-shaped outline with their arms, they bear out Ai Weiwei's observation that "at the end of the day, Wang Xingwei's paintings are just about men and their silly issues."

Hemd, einen Schuljungen mit rotem Kragen sowie Szenen aus dem Kanon der Kunstgeschichte nebeneinander stellen. Besonders beliebt wurde die Arbeit „Thomas" (1998), in der ein Mann im gelben Hemd durch eine zersplitterte Holztür auf Duchamps Installation „Etant Donnés" zuschreitet, während Warhol und Beuys in Polizeiuniformen auf ihn herabstarren.

Um die Jahrtausendwende begannen sich Wangs Malgründe geradezu wuchernd zu vermehren: Er malte auf Dachziegel, Zeitungspapier und Bettlaken, um nur einige zu nennen. Außerdem entwickelte er ein starkes Interesse an den visuellen Mechanismen des Kitsches und überarbeitete Bilder, die er für wenig Geld an Marktständen erwarb. Daraus erwuchs bald ein großes Reservoir an Standardfiguren, wie Stewardessen, Matrosen, Pinguine und Golfer. Bei Wang kann mittlerweile ein Gemälde im Art-Déco-Stil einer Tamara de Lempicka zu einem zweiten überleiten, das eine mit Stricken verschnürte Stewardess nach Art einer Fotografie von Nobuyoshi Araki zeigt, gefolgt von einem Golfer inmitten eines Wassermelonenfelds.

Dieses Schöpfen aus dem Repertoire stereotyper Gestalten setzt sich auch in Wangs jüngsten Arbeiten fort: Seine Einzelausstellung „Large Rowboat" von 2007 bestand aus scheinbar endlosen Variationen über ein Paar, das den Seiten einer 1980er Ausgabe der anspruchslosen Zeitschrift „Reader" – der chinesischen Version von „Reader's Digest" – entlehnt scheint. Wie diese comicartigen Figuren über Seen paddeln, unter Bäumen lagern oder mit ihren Armen den Umriss eines Herzens bilden, bestätigt Ai Weiweis Kommentar, dass „Wang Xingweis Gemälde letzten Endes bloß von Menschen und ihren albernen Angelegenheiten zeugen".

空姐，水手、企鹅和高尔夫球手等。在具有塔玛拉德兰陂卡艺术风格的一幅作品中，描述了空姐和护士困在救生筏的样子，好似取源于荒木经惟 摄影作品，还有一幅作品刻画了高尔夫球手在西瓜田里测量至球洞距离。

王的最近作品这种定型人物的脉络。在2007年举办的个展《大划船》中，展示的作品以无限变化的情侣，这些图画明显的选自文字杂志《读者》80年代时期的页面，类似于美国的《读者文摘》之类的刊物。这些卡通人物或是在湖中荡桨，或是在树荫下漫步，还有一幅作品中，情侣的胳膊交接一起，形成心的形状，艾未未曾经评价：最后，王德油画的主题仅仅关于人以及他们愚蠢的行为。而这些作品确实如此。

Philip Tinari

7

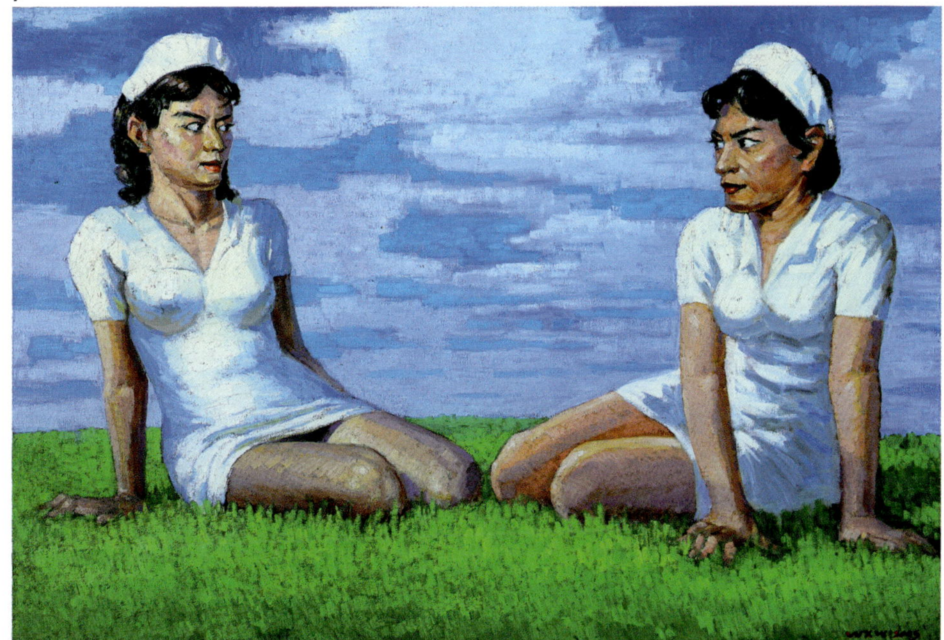

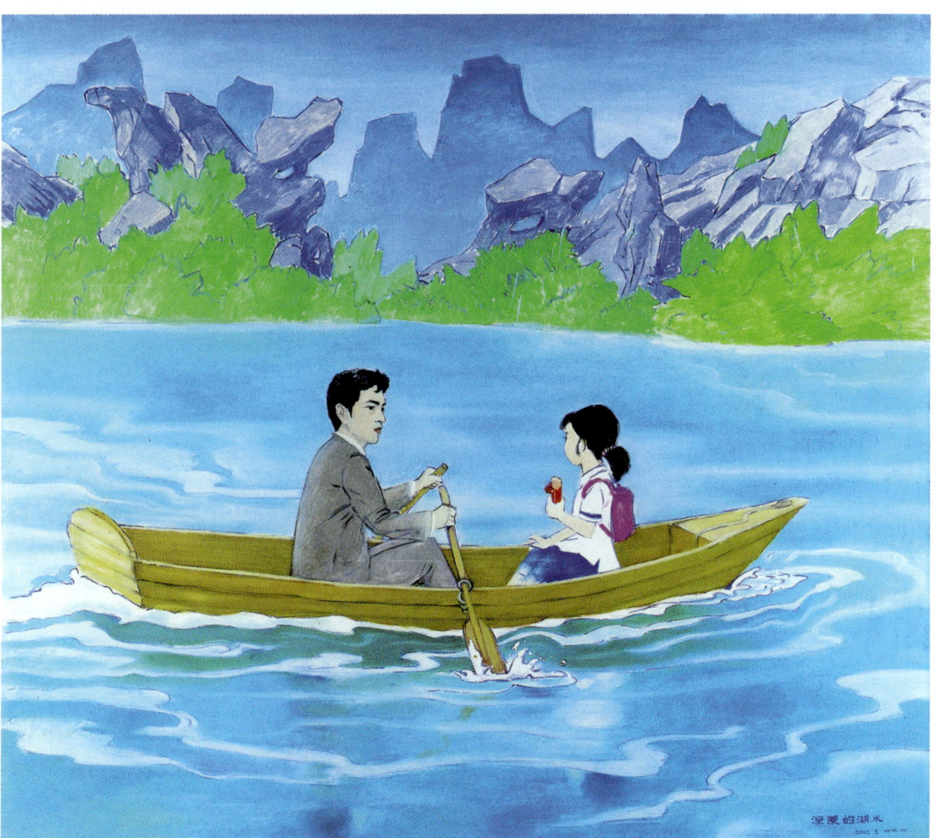

8

1 ***Thomas***, *1998*
Oil on canvas, 150 x 175 cm
Öl auf Leinwand, 150 x 175 cm
《托马斯》1998年，布面油画，150 x 175 cm

2 ***History of Revolution***, *1997*
Oil on canvas, 130 x 360 cm
Öl auf Leinwand, 130 x 360 cm
《革命史》1997年，布面油画，130 x 360 cm

3 ***The Testimony of the Hare***, *1995*
Oil on canvas, 124.5 x 200 cm
Öl auf Leinwand, 124,5 x 200 cm
《野兔的证言》1995 年，布面油画，124.5 x 200 cm

4 ***The Decadence and Emptiness of Capitalism 1***, *1995*
Oil on canvas, 170 x 240 cm
Öl auf Leinwand, 170 x 240 cm
《拜金主义的堕落和空虚1》1995 年，布面油画，170 x 240 cm

5 ***Dead of Ximen***, *2002*
Oil on canvas, 170 x 205 cm
Öl auf Leinwand, 170 x 205 cm
《西门之死》2002年，布面油画，170 x 205 cm

6 ***Untitled (Outing)***, *1999*
Acrylic on canvas, 120 x 280 cm
Acryl auf Leinwand, 120 x 280 cm
《无题》（郊游）1999年，布面丙烯，120 x 280 cm

7 ***Untitled (Two Nurses)***, *2005*
Oil on canvas, 107 x 154 cm
Öl auf Leinwand, 107 x 154 cm
《无题》（两个护士）2005年，布面丙烯，107 x 154 cm

8 ***Deep Deep Lake Water***, *2002*
Oil on canvas, 220 x 280 cm
Öl auf Leinwand, 220 x 280 cm
《深深的湖水》2002年，布面油画，220 x 280 cm

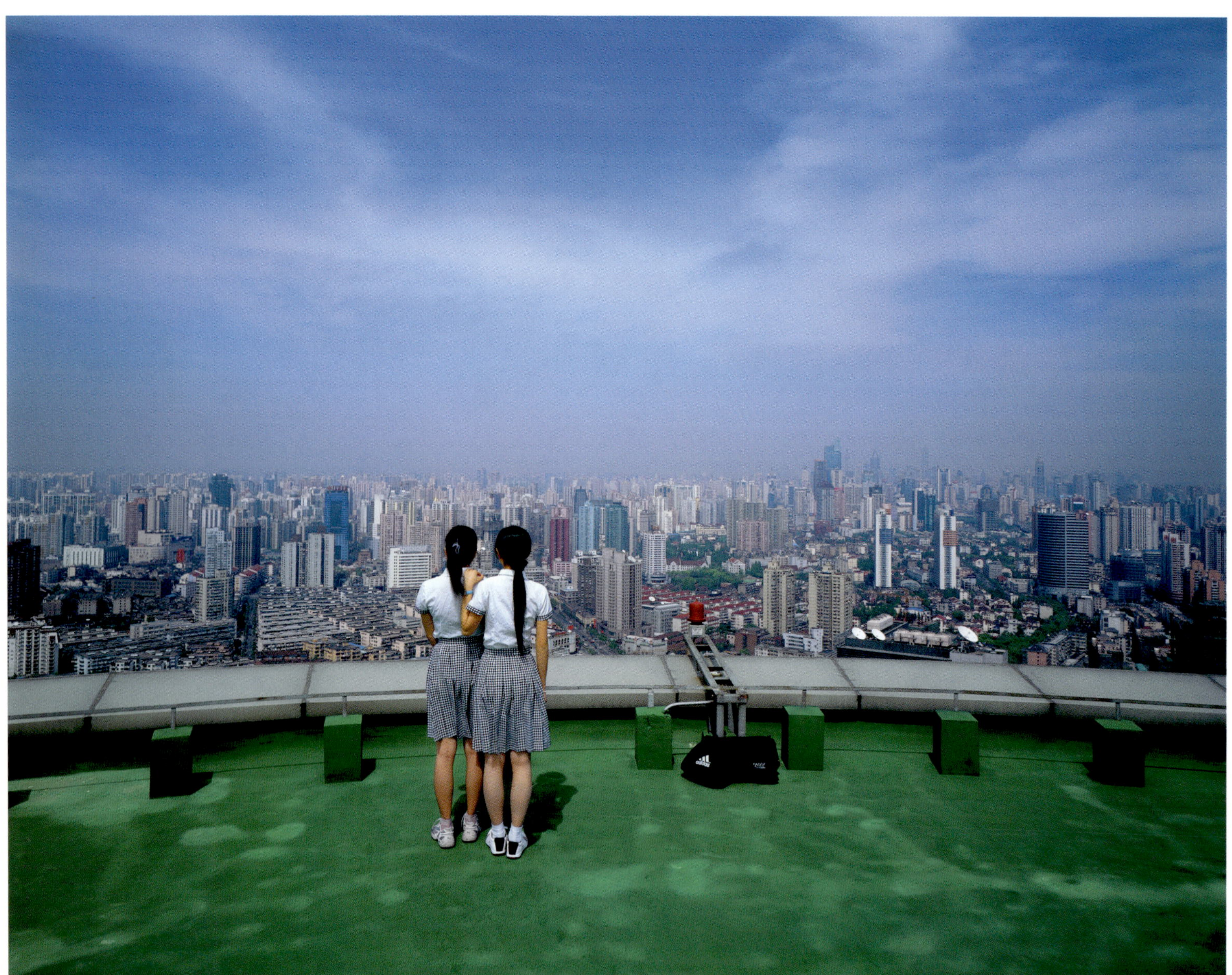

1

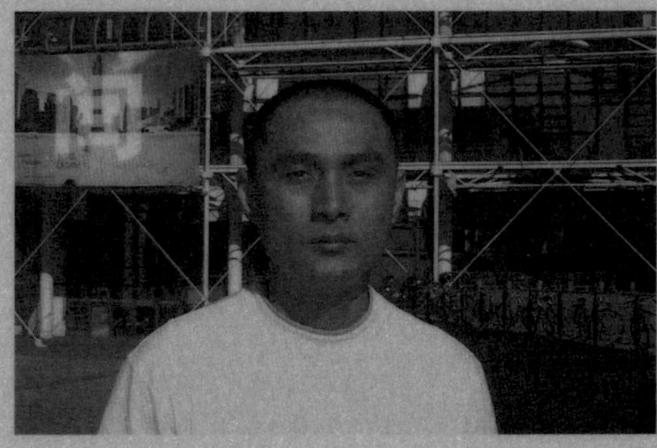

"We cannot change history, but we can contribute to the progress of our society. As an artist, I can only show how I see reality, and leave viewers to judge for themselves."

„Wir können die Geschichte nicht ändern, aber wir können zum Fortschritt unserer Gesellschaft beitragen. Als Künstler kann ich nur zeigen, wie ich die Realität sehe, und das Urteil den Betrachtern selbst überlassen."

"虽然我们无法改变历史，但是我们能为我们的社会进步作出贡献。作为一名艺术家，我只能展示我是如何看待现实，让观众自己去作出判断。"

Born in 1961 on Hainan Island, China. Lives and works in Hainan
Geboren 1961 auf der Insel Hainan, China. Lebt und arbeitet in Hainan
1961 年出生于中国海南岛，居住海南工作在海南

***Selected exhibitions* / Ausgewählte Ausstellungen / 所选展览**

2002 "Chinese Modernity", Museu de Arte Brasileira, São Paulo, Brazil
First Guangzhou Triennial, Guangdong Museum of Art, Guangzhou, China
2003 "Alors, la Chine?", Centre Georges Pompidou, Paris, France
2004 "Die Chinesen: Fotografie und Video aus China", Kunstmuseum Wolfsburg, Wolfsburg, Germany
2004-07 "Between Past and Future, New Photography and Video from China", International Center of Photography, New York, NY, USA (travelling exhibition)
2007 "Thermocline of Art: New Asian Waves", ZKM (Center for Art and Media), Karlsruhe, Germany

2002年 《现代中国》巴西圣保罗，FAAP 美术馆
《首届广州当代艺术三年展：中国试验艺术十年 1999-2000年》中国广州，广东美术馆
2003年 《那么中国呢？》蓬皮杜文化艺术中心现代艺术馆法国巴黎
2004年 《中国人：中国当代摄影和录像》德国沃阿丝堡，沃阿丝堡美术馆
2004-07年 《过去与未来之间—中国新影像展》国际摄影中心, 纽约, 美国（巡回展）
2007年 《艺术温跃层：亚洲新浪潮》艺术与媒体中心, 卡尔斯鲁厄, 德国

***Selected publications* / Ausgewählte Publikationen / 所选著作**

Eleonora Battiston: "Behind The Lens", in: "Zoom", Nr. 64, Milan, September-October 2004
Clare Grafik: "Weng Fen – On The Artist's Photographic Practice", in: "Contemporary", Nr. 72, London 2005
Gu Zhenqing: "Accumulating The Eggs: Weng Peijun's Traffic New World", in: "Chinese Contemporary Art News", Issue 8, Shanghai, September 2005
Susan Acret: "The Wings in the Future", in: "Shanghai Tatler", Shanghai, February 2005

Battiston, Eleonora（著）:《镜头背后》"Zoom"（杂志）第 64期/米兰2004年，9-10月
Grafik, Clare（著）:《翁奋关于艺术家的摄影实践》、《当代》第 72 期，伦敦2005 年
顾振清（著）:《累卵：翁培俊交通新世界》在：《中国当代艺术新闻》第 8 期，上海2005 年 9 月
Acret, Susan（著）:《未来的翅膀》，《艺术家》上海 2005年2月

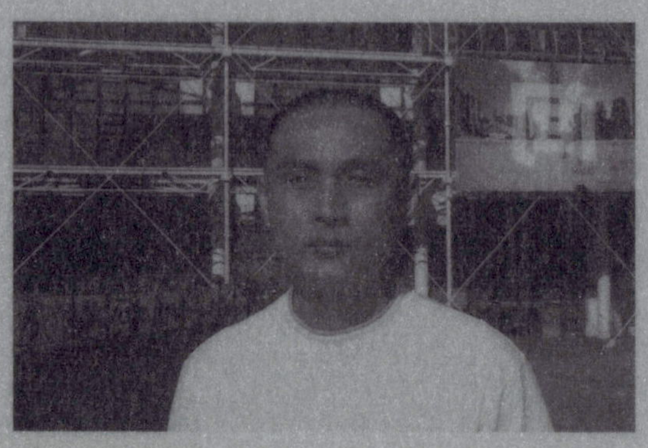

"We cannot change history, but we can contribute to the progress of our society. As an artist, I can only show how I see reality, and leave viewers to judge for themselves."

„Wir können die Geschichte nicht ändern, aber wir können zum Fortschritt unserer Gesellschaft beitragen. Als Künstler kann ich nur zeigen, wie ich die Realität sehe, und das Urteil den Betrachtern selbst überlassen."

"虽然我们无法改变历史，但是我们能为我们的社会进步作出贡献。作为一名艺术家，我只能展示我是如何看待现实，让观众自己去作出判断。"

Born in 1961 on Hainan Island, China. Lives and works in Hainan
Geboren 1961 auf der Insel Hainan, China. Lebt und arbeitet in Hainan
1961 年出生于中国海南岛，居住海南工作在海南

Selected exhibitions / Ausgewählte Ausstellungen / 所选展览

2002	"Chinese Modernity", Museu de Arte Brasileira, São Paulo, Brazil
	First Guangzhou Triennial, Guangdong Museum of Art, Guangzhou, China
2003	"Alors, la Chine?", Centre Georges Pompidou, Paris, France
2004	"Die Chinesen: Fotografie und Video aus China", Kunstmuseum Wolfsburg, Wolfsburg, Germany
2004-07	"Between Past and Future, New Photography and Video from China", International Center of Photography, New York, NY, USA (travelling exhibition)
2007	"Thermocline of Art: New Asian Waves", ZKM (Center for Art and Media), Karlsruhe, Germany

2002年	《现代中国》巴西圣保罗，FAAP 美术馆
	《首届广州当代艺术三年展：中国试验艺术十年 1999-2000年》中国广州，广东美术馆
2003年	《那么中国呢？》蓬皮杜文化艺术中心现代艺术馆法国巴黎
2004年	《中国人：中国当代摄影和录像》德国沃尔夫斯堡，沃尔夫斯堡美术馆
2004-07年	《过去与未来之间—中国新影像展》国际摄影中心，纽约，美国（巡回展）
2007年	《艺术温跃层：亚洲新浪潮》艺术与媒体中心，卡尔斯鲁厄，德国

Selected publications / Ausgewählte Publikationen / 所选著作

Eleonora Battiston: "Behind The Lens", in: "Zoom", Nr. 64, Milan, September-October 2004
Clare Grafik: "Weng Fen – On The Artist's Photographic Practice", in: "Contemporary", Nr. 72, London 2005
Gu Zhenqing: "Accumulating The Eggs: Weng Peijun's Traffic New World", in: "Chinese Contemporary Art News", Issue 8, Shanghai, September 2005
Susan Acret: "The Wings in the Future", in: "Shanghai Tatler", Shanghai, February 2005

Battiston, Eleonora（著）：《镜头背后》"Zoom"（杂志）第 64期／米兰2004年，9-10月
Grafik, Clare（著）：《翁奋关于艺术家的摄影实践》，《当代》第 72 期，伦敦2005 年
顾振清（著）：《累卵：翁培俊交通新世界》在：《中国当代艺术新闻》第 8 期，上海2005 年 9 月
Acret, Susan（著）：《未来的翅膀》，《艺术家》上海 2005年2月

WENG FEN 翁奋

[wɤŋ fən]

Weng Fen works in a variety of media, but is best known for a series of photographs depicting young high-school girls sitting on a high wall, looking beyond at the sparkling new urban development that sits just out of reach on the other side. "On the wall" (1999–2002) comprises six individual works photographed in Haikou, Shenzhen, and Guangzhou – each place an example of the success of the Special Economic Zones, created by Deng Xiaoping in the 1980s. Here, change and advance at an unparalleled pace. The girls symbolise the future; a glorious future in which economics and modernity will inform the age instead of overt ideological doctrines. Still, the future is just over there, beyond the wall. On this side of the fence, the grass grows ragged and the ground is littered, suggesting a backward, impoverished environment.

"On the wall" is an iconic work of the early 2000s. This high degree of critical acclaim inspired Weng Fen to pursue the issues it raises in a new direction, also using photography. The eight-part series titled "Staring at the sea" (2003/04) features a group of innocent young girls looking out over vast, spectacular landscapes. Simultaneously, Weng Fen also uses a full family group – a couple, the husband's parents, and the single child. They, too, stand and stare, their familial connection expressed by hands resting protectively on each other's shoulders. But here we are not so sure of the mood: the same vast land- and seascapes suggest a general yearning to be somewhere else beyond the sea.

The transition point was "Bird's eye view" (2002–2004). Here, the girls are the stars of the images, and the sense of wonderment and progress achieved by juxtaposing the high eyelevel with a magnificent panoramic. This is surely the best of new China. But a perfect façade merely masked problems within. As acts of terrorism took place around the world following the 9/11 attack in New York, Weng Fen conceived a small series of photographs employing the same young actors, now each with their faces masked by a balaclava; the embodiment of terror. These works mark a temporary halt with photography in favour of installation projects.

Weng Fen arbeitet mit verschiedenen Medien. Am bekanntesten wurde er durch eine seiner Fotoserien: Sie zeigt Schulmädchen auf hohen Mauern sitzend, von denen sie auf glanzvolle urbane Neubauprojekte schauen, die außer Reichweite auf der anderen Seite liegen. „On the wall" (1999–2002) besteht aus sechs Einzelwerken, die in Haikou, Shenzhen und Guangzhou aufgenommen wurden – alles Musterorte jener Sonderwirtschaftszonen, die Deng Xiaoping in den 1980er Jahren einrichten ließ. Hier gehen Wandel und Fortschritt in beispiellosem Tempo voran. Die Mädchen blicken in die Zukunft, eine glorreiche Zukunft, die nicht mehr von platten politischen Doktrinen, sondern von Ökonomie und Modernität geprägt sein wird. Allerdings liegt diese Zukunft für sie noch drüben, jenseits der Mauer. Auf dieser Seite dagegen erblickt man ein rückständiges, ärmliches Umfeld mit struppigem Gras und herumliegendem Abfall.

„On the wall" wurde zum Kultwerk der frühen 2000er Jahre. Der große Zuspruch der Kritiker spornte Weng Fen an, die dort aufgeworfenen Fragen in anderer Richtung weiterzuverfolgen – ebenfalls mit fotografischen Mitteln. Die achtteilige Serie „Staring at the sea" (2003/04) zeigt wieder eine Gruppe unschuldsvoller junger Mädchen, die auf weite, spektakuläre Landschaften blicken. Daneben setzte Weng aber eine Familie, bestehend aus einem Paar mit Kind und den Eltern des Ehemanns. Auch sie stehen da und schauen, allerdings wird ihre familiäre Verbindung dadurch deutlich, dass sie einander die Hände beschützend auf die Schultern legen. Hier sind wir uns der Stimmung nicht mehr so sicher: Die weiten Landschaften und Meerespanoramen scheinen auf eine große Sehnsucht hinzudeuten, das Meer zu überqueren.

Der Übergang zu etwas Neuem gelang Weng mit „Bird's eye view" (2002–2004). Hier sind zwar erneut Mädchen die Protagonisten, aber das Gefühl des Staunens angesichts des Fortschritts überzeugt durch ein schier überwältigendes Panorama, das die hohe Vogelperspektive bewirkt – sicherlich das Beste, was das neue China zu bieten hat. Es sollte sich aber zeigen, dass diese perfekte Oberfläche

翁奋以多种媒介进行创作，但最使他出名的还是他拍的一系列描述高中女生的照片。照片里的年轻高中女生们坐在高高的墙上，眼望着熠熠生辉的新城市建设图景，那些图景就在她们对面伸手可及的地方。《骑墙》（1999-2002年）包含六张单独的摄影作品，分别摄于海口、深圳和广州，每地都是邓小平同志于上世纪 80 年代成功创建经济特区的例子，以显示那里日新月异的变化和进步。女学生象征着未来。在那个光辉灿烂的未来，时代将被赋予经济和现代的特质而非公然的意识形态教条。静静地，未来就在那里，在墙的那一边。而围墙的这面则是一番杂草丛生，遍地狼藉的景象，这暗示着落后与穷困的环境。

《骑墙》是 21 世纪初期的一个讽喻作品，其高度批判的呼声激发了翁奋从一个新的角度去探求作品所提出的问题，并用相机予以记录。在题为《看海图》（2003-2004年）的八部分系列作品中，一群天真的女孩遥望着广阔壮观的风景。与此同时，翁奋还用到了一个完整的家庭 -- 爷爷奶奶、爸爸妈妈以及他们的独生子，他们的家庭关系由相互搭在肩头的双手所体现。尽管照片中他们也在站着凝视，但是我们仍不能确定其中的情绪：同样广阔无垠的陆地与大海风景揭示了对达到海的另一头的普遍向往。很明显，翁奋还需进一步阐明其中的情感。

《鸟瞰图》（2002-2004年）是一个转折点，在这里女孩们成了影像中的明星，在宏伟的全景中女孩们并排在一起的高昂的视线充分表达出她们渴望进步的意识。这绝对是对新中国的最好写照。然而，完美的正面是无法把所有问题都加以掩盖的。自从纽约 911 事件发生后，世界很多其他地方都相继发生了恐怖事件。于是翁奋又用这些年轻的演员们构摄了一组短系列的照片，作品中女生们的脸孔被巴拉克拉法帽（恐怖的化身）所遮住。这些作品标志着作者暂时停止了他所热衷的拍摄装置项目的脚步。

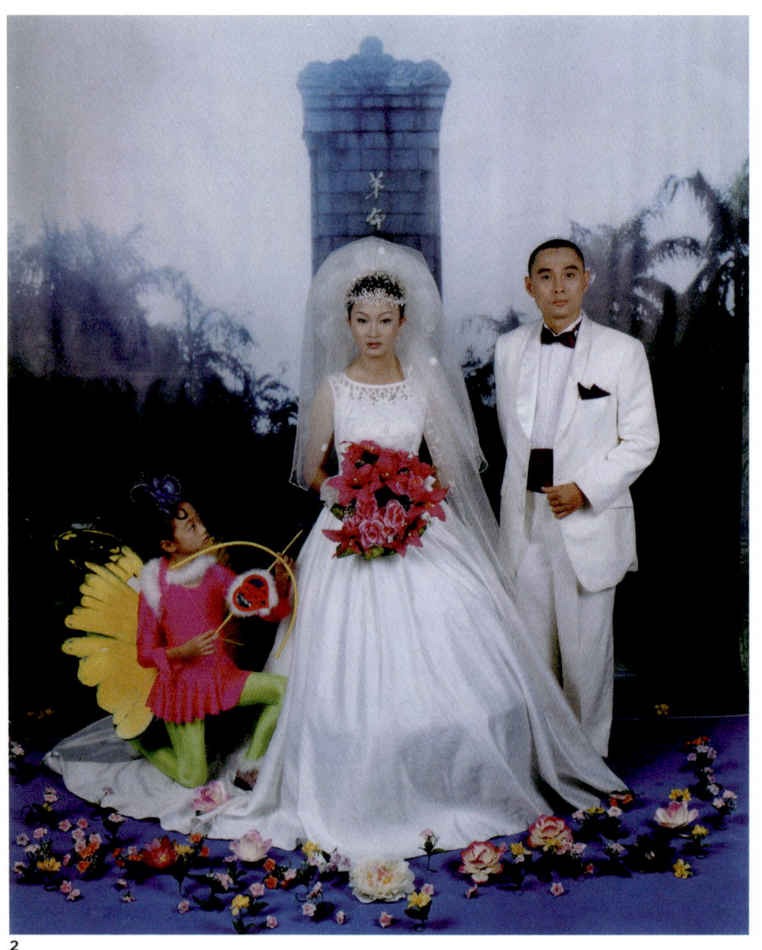

2

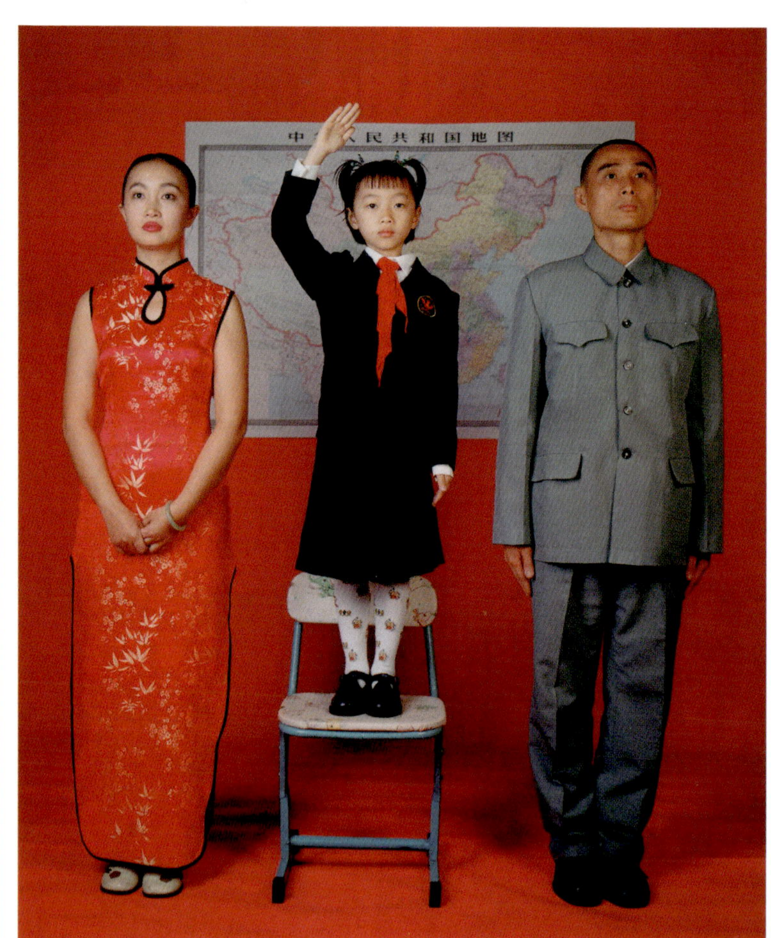

3

4

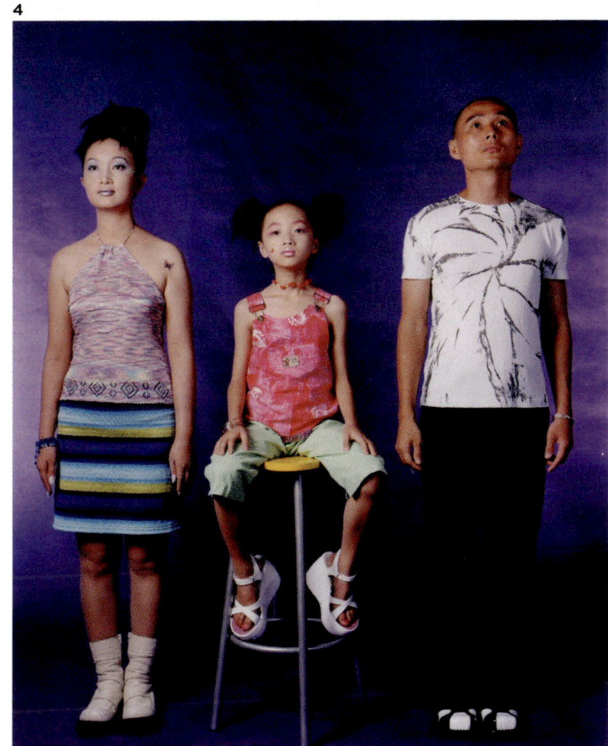

5

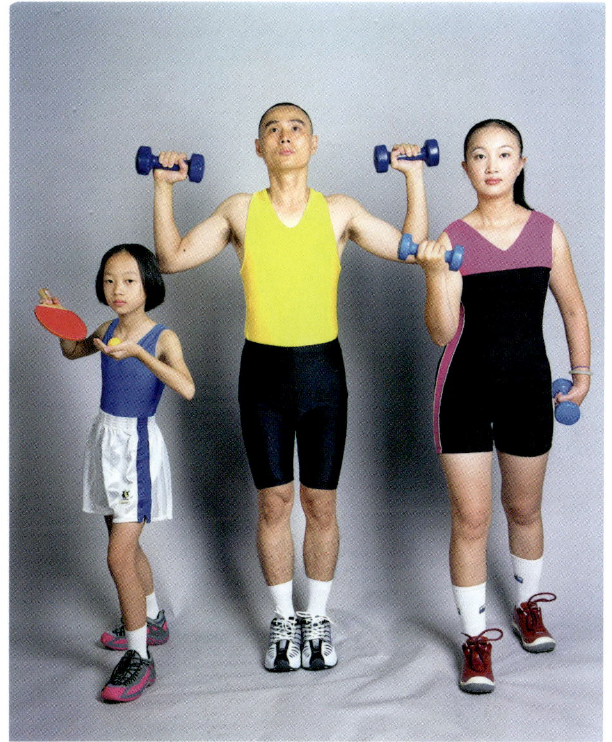

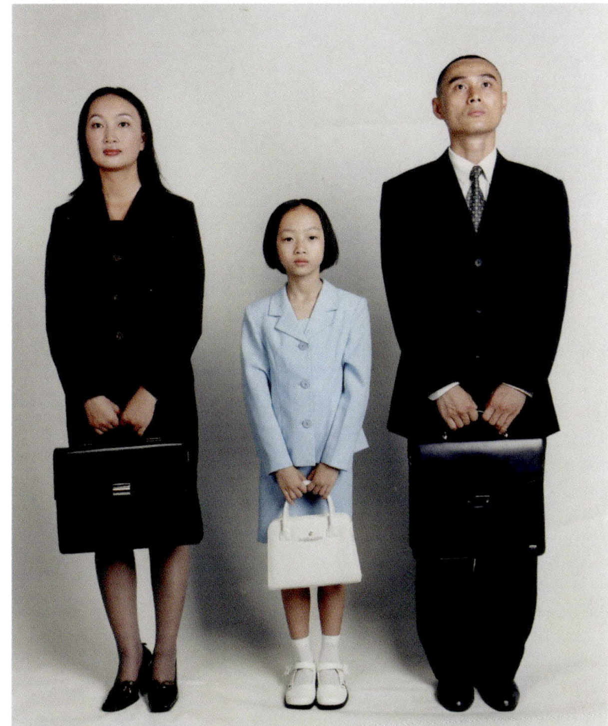

6

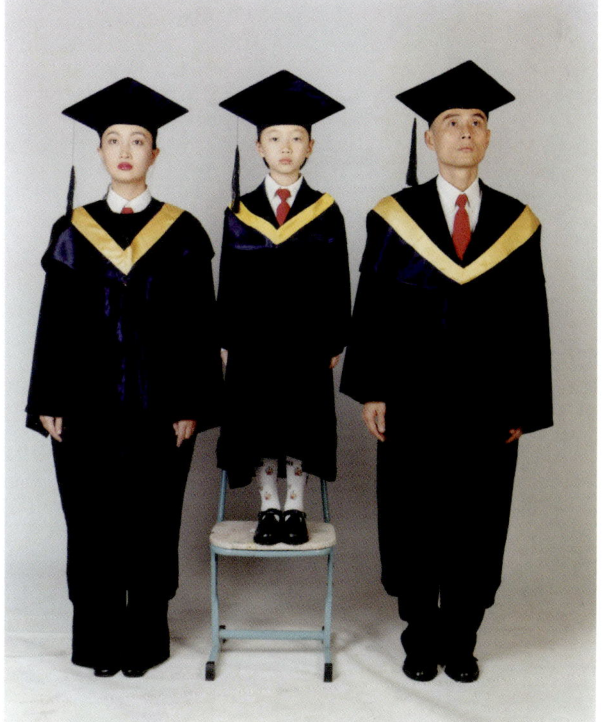

7

8

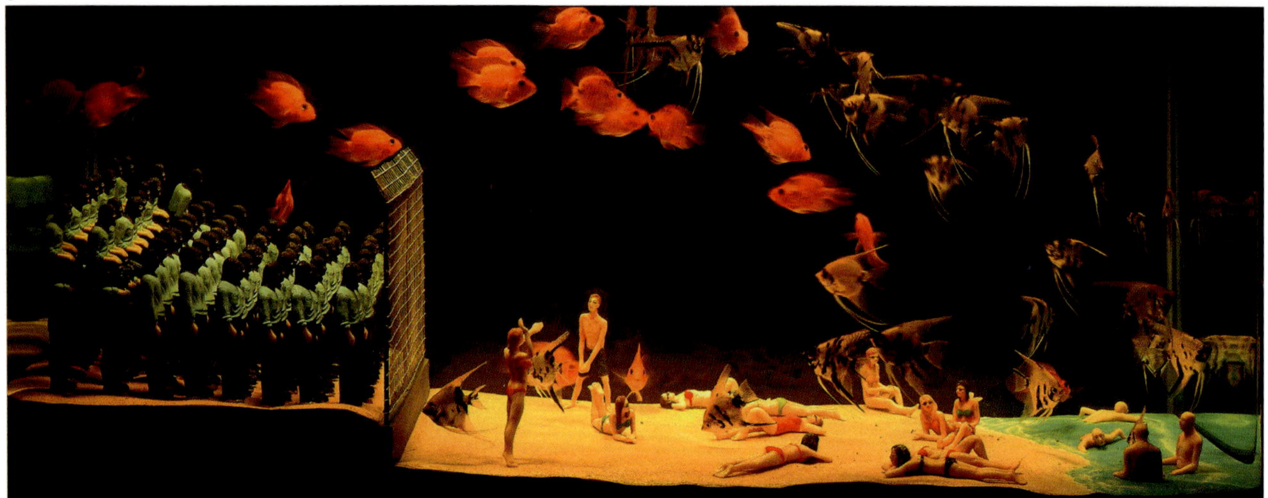

Before he set himself to photography, between 1999s and 2003, Weng Fen produced several video works. "Butterfly" (1999) takes the form of a circular frame, similar to a Victorian peepshow viewed through a telescope. Here the viewer sees a girl attired in the manner of a J. M. Barrie fairy, or a nymph from a pre-Raphaelite tableau, gently fluttering her arms in imitation of a butterfly. This delicate being flies against a kaleidoscopic backdrop of bland urban buildings and untamed wasteland, which constraints the sense of freedom even as it appears.

A second piece "The future is in our hands" (2002) picks up the idea of a better tomorrow found in the "Sitting on the Wall". This work poignantly invokes the nature of advance in China, especially for the generation of artists like Weng Fen, born in the late 1950s-early 1960s. Weng Fen compiles his plot from scenes appropriated from a variety of films, each chosen to illustrate the gulf between the better tomorrow that Communism promised and the reality people are experiencing, unprotected against the tide of change. This is a masterful melding of conflicting elements arising in a period of dramatic social transformation, in which the victims are always the ordinary people.

Weng Fen produced his first major installation series "Viewing stands" in 2003, creating four fantasy worlds of ideal living within large aquariums. Fascinated with inventing his own worlds, he then turned to eggs as the material for constructing vast cityscapes. The "Egg city project" (since 2003) reflects an on-going fascination that Weng Fen has yet to exhaust.

die Probleme im Innern nur kaschiert: Als sich im Gefolge der Anschläge vom 11. September in New York die Terrorakte rund um die Welt häuften, schuf Weng Fen eine kleine Serie von Fotos mit den gleichen jungen Akteurinnen, deren Gesichter jetzt jedoch hinter Sturmhauben verborgen sind: die Verkörperung des Schreckens.

Bevor er sich zwischen 1999 und 2003 der Fotografie zuwandte, präsentierte Weng Fen mehrere Videoarbeiten. Bei „Butterfly" (1999) schaut man wie durch einen kreisrunden Rahmen oder ein Teleskop. Man könnte auch von einer viktorianischen Peepshow sprechen – der Betrachter erblickt ein Mädchen, das im Stil einer Elfe von J. M. Barrie oder einer Nymphe aus einem Gemälde der Präraffaeliten zurechtgemacht ist und sanft mit den Armen dahinflattert wie ein Schmetterling. Dieses zarte Geschöpf schwebt vor einem kaleidoskopischen Hintergrund aus nichtssagenden urbanen Bauten und wüstem Ödland, der das zunächst aufkommende Freiheitsgefühl im Keim erstickt.

„The future is in our hands" (2002) greift die Idee einer besseren Zukunft wieder auf, die schon „Sitting on the Wall" dominierte. Das Werk beschwört eindringlich das Wesen des Fortschritts in China, insbesondere für jene Künstlergeneration, die in den späten 1950er und frühen 1960er Jahren zur Welt kam. Es besteht aus sorgfältig ausgewählten Szenen aus verschiedenen Filmen. Der Zusammenschnitt illustriert die Kluft zwischen der besseren Zukunft, die der Kommunismus versprochen hatte, und den aktuellen Umwälzungen, denen die Menschen ausgeliefert sind. Das Video vereint meisterlich all die widersprüchlichen Elemente, die in Zeiten dramatischer gesellschaftlicher Umbrüche auftreten – und die Opfer sind immer die kleinen Leute.

2003 schuf Weng Fen seine erste größere Installationsserie „Viewing stands", für die er vier idealisierte Fantasiewelten in großen Aquarien entwarf. Als Nächstes griff er zu Eiern als Material, um weitläufige Stadtlandschaften zu konstruieren. Dieses noch unabgeschlossene „Egg city project" (seit 2003) scheint Weng Fen nachhaltig in Bann zu ziehen.

在潜心于摄影之前，翁奋于 1999 至 2003 年间还制作了一些录像作品。《蝶》（1999年）采用了圆形框架的表现形式，有点类似于采用维多利亚女王时代的西洋镜，透过望远镜观看作品。作品中女孩着装的样式有点象巴里精灵，还有点象前拉斐尔派舞台造型中的美丽少女，象蝴蝶般轻轻挥动着双臂。这个精致的小精灵在万花筒般的背景前飞舞着，背景里展现的是冷漠的城市建筑以及难以开垦的荒地，它们正如背景本身所展示的那样，扼制了人们的自由。

另一部作品"《我的未来不是梦》（2002年）采纳了作者在《骑墙》这一作品中所发现的明天会更美好的观点。这部作品向人们强烈昭示了中国前进的本质，其对象尤其是象翁奋那一代出生于上世纪五十年代末、六十年代初的艺术家。作品的故事情节是翁奋从数部电影的场景中摄取的，每一场景都用于表明共产主义所描绘的美好明天与人们所正在经历的现实之间的差距，表明在这变化的浪潮中民众没有受到保护。作者以大师般的手法融合了一段时期内来自社会剧烈变革的冲突因素，其中受伤害的往往是那些处于弱势的人们。

翁奋的首部重要装置系列作品《观景台》制作于2003年，作品展示了四个在大型水族馆内理想生活的神奇世界。他着迷于创造自己的世界，转而使用鸡蛋作为构建大型城市风景的材料。《累卵计划》（2003 年至今）正反映了翁奋对此的浓厚兴致。

Karen Smith

9

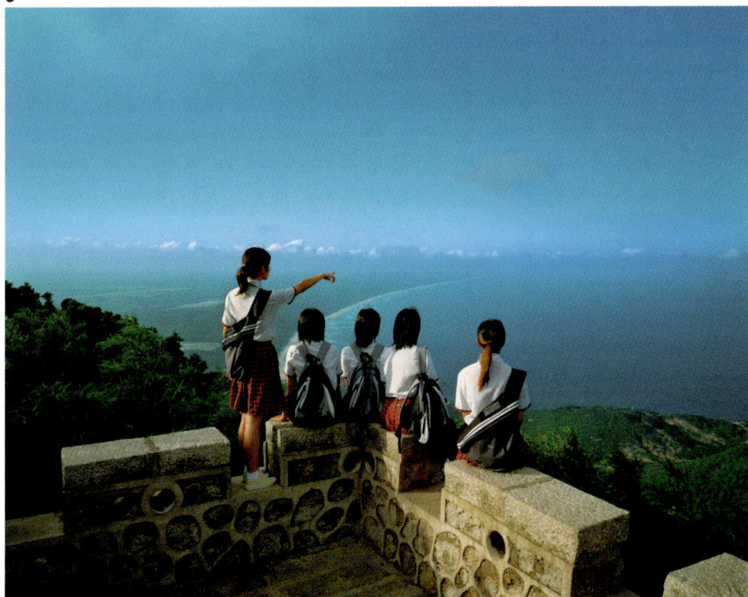

10

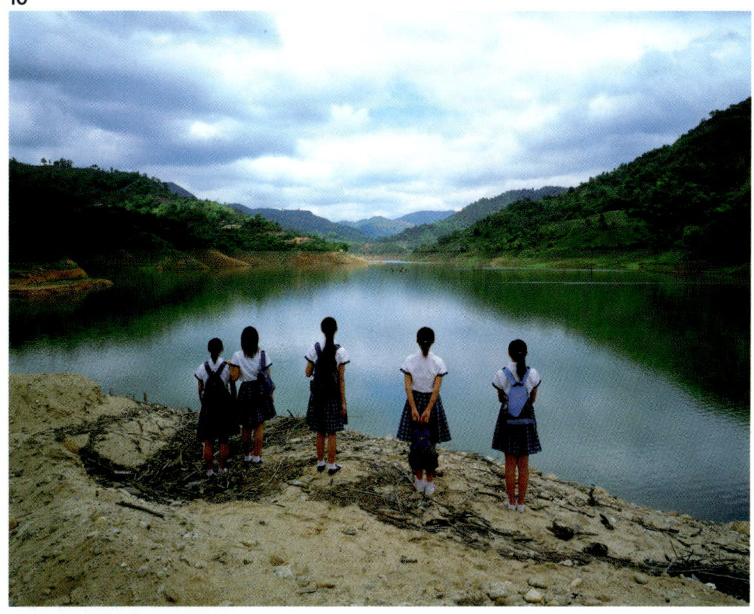

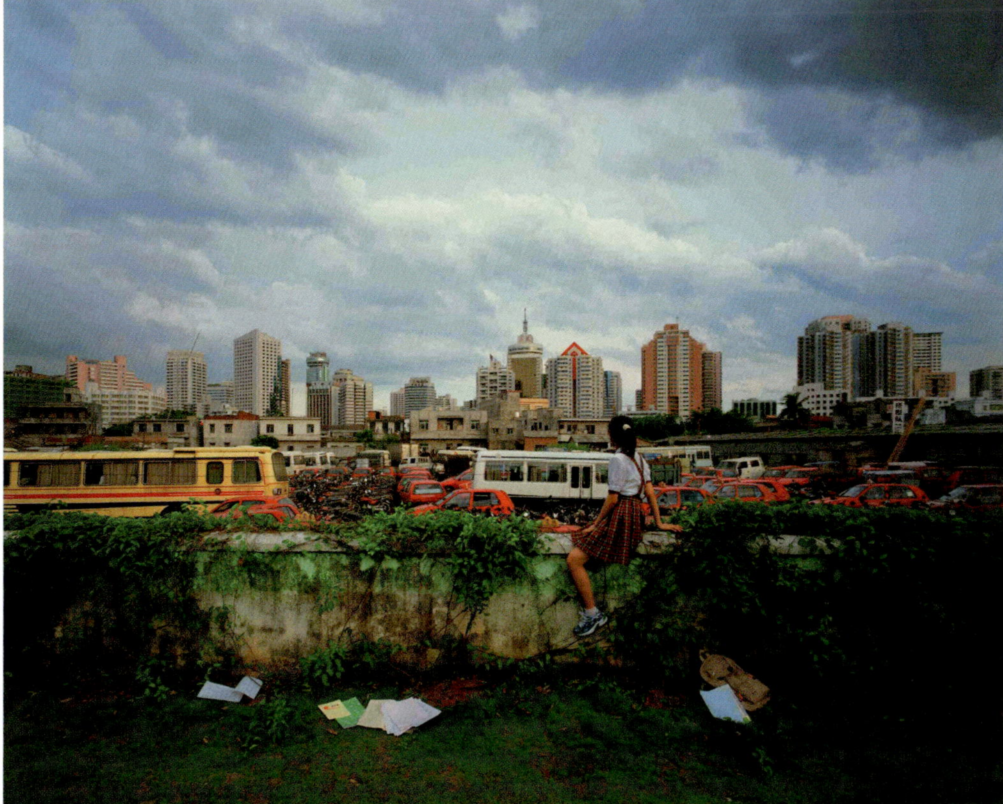

11

1 ***Bird's eye view Shanghai 1**, 2005*
C-print, 160 x 200 cm; C-print, 160 x 200 cm
《鸟瞰 —上海》（之一）, 2005年, C-印刷, 160 x 200 cm

2 ***Good marriage**, 2001*
C-print, 150 x 120 cm; C-print, 150 x 120 cm
《美好婚姻愿》2001年, C-印刷, 150 x 120 cm

3 ***Patriotism**, 2000*
C-print, 150 x 120 cm; C-print, 150 x 120 cm
《爱国愿》2000年, C-印刷, 150 x 120 cm

4 ***In fashion**, 2003*
C-print, 150 x 120 cm; C-print, 150 x 120 cm
《时尚愿》2003年, C-印刷, 150 x 120 cm

5 ***Good health**, 2003*
C-print, 150 x 120 cm; C-print, 150 x 120 cm
《健康愿》2003年, C-印刷, 150 x 120 cm

6 ***White collar**, 2003*
C-print, 150 x 120 cm; C-print, 150 x 120 cm
《白领愿》2003年, C-印刷, 150 x 120 cm

7 ***Academic degree**, 2000*
C-print, 150 x 120 cm; C-print, 150 x 120 cm
《读书愿》2000年, C-印刷, 150 x 120 cm

8 ***Viewing stand – Bathing sandy beach**, 2004*
C-print, 80 x 200 cm; C-print, 80 x 200 cm
《观景台—沙滩浴场》, 2004年, C-印刷, 80 x 200 cm

9 ***Staring at the sea 6**, 2004*
C-print, 160 x 200 cm; C-print, 160 x 200 cm
《看海图6》2004年, C-印刷, 160 x 200 cm

10 ***Staring at the lake 3**, 2006*
C-print, 160 x 200 cm; C-print, 160 x 200 cm
《看湖3》2006年, C-印刷, 160 x 200 cm

11 ***On the wall – Haikou No. 6**, 2002*
C-print, 125 x 160 cm; C-print, 125 x 160 cm
《骑墙・海口No. 6》2002年, C-印刷, 125 x 160 cm

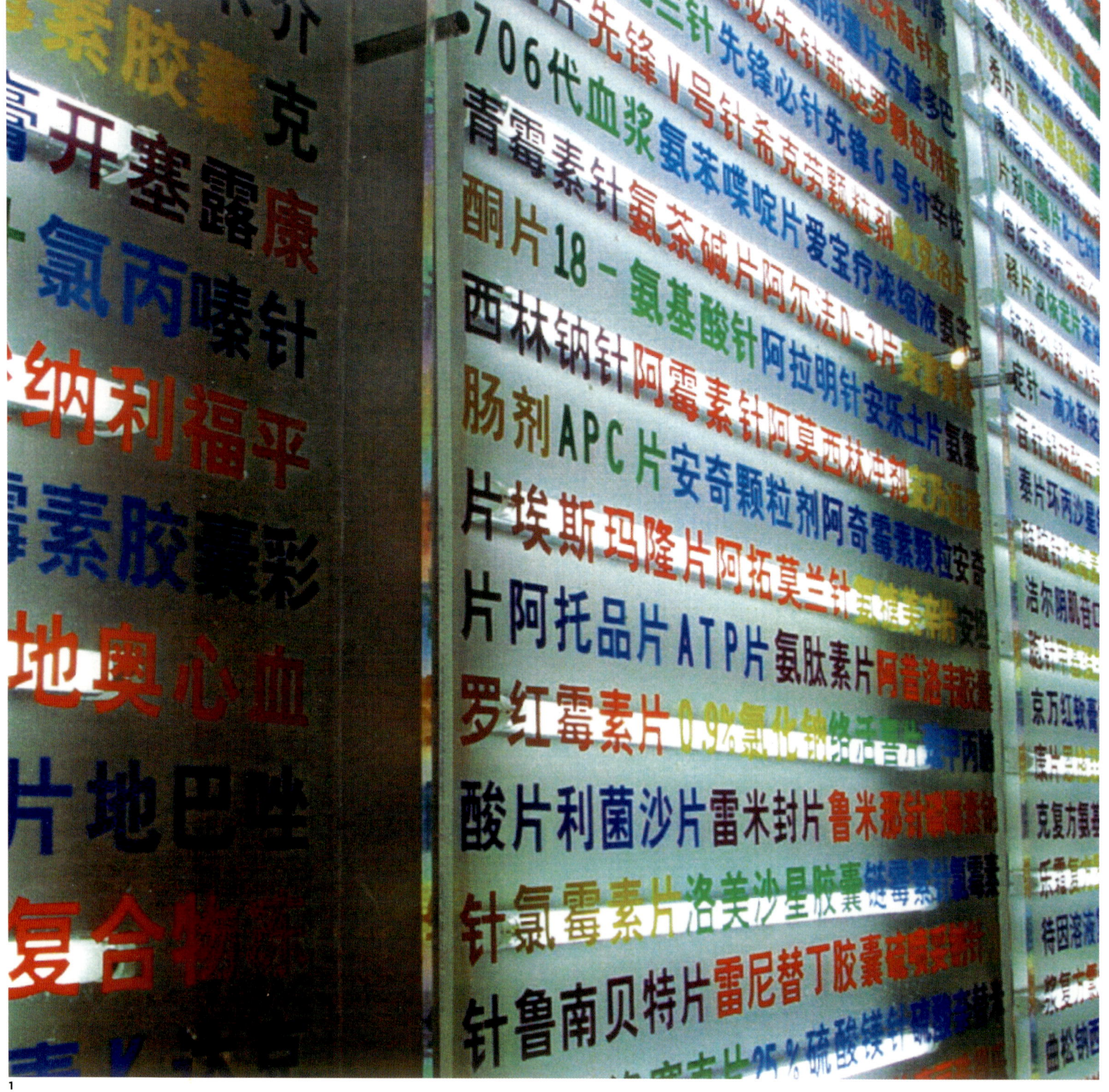
克
开塞露康
氯丙嗪针
纳利福平
素胶囊彩
地奥心血
片地巴唑
复合物
先锋V号针
706代血浆氨苯喋啶片爱宝疗浓缩液
青霉素针氨茶碱片
酮片18-氨基酸针阿拉明针安乐土片
西林钠针阿霉素针
肠剂APC片安奇颗粒剂阿奇霉素颗粒
片埃斯玛隆片阿拓莫兰针
片阿托品片ATP片氨肽素片
罗红霉素片
酸片利菌沙片雷米封片鲁米那针
针氯霉素片洛美沙星胶囊
针鲁南贝特片雷尼替丁胶囊

1

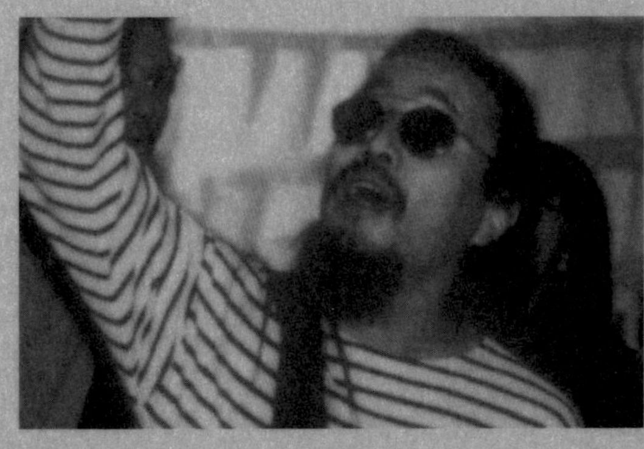

"The principle of 'Vege-Pleasure' is that each independent vegetable and fruit should have intercourse (merge) under an identically valued object orientation and object power."

„Das Prinzip von ‚Vege-Pleasure' ist, dass jedes einzelne Gemüse und jede einzelne Frucht miteinander eine Verbindung unter identischer Wertorientierung eingehen."

"Vege-pleasure的原则是，各独立菜和果子应该有交尾（合并）在相同地被重视的对象取向和对象力量之下，并且他们的权利应该被合并作为理所当然的事和存在事情。"

Born in 1960 in Zhoushan, Province Zhejiang, China. Lives and works in Hamburg, Germany, and Shanghai
Geboren 1960 in Zhoushan, Province Zhejiang, China. Lebt und arbeitet in Hamburg, Deutschland, und Shanghai
1960年出生于中国浙江舟山。住居工作在汉堡，德国和上海

***Selected exhibitions* / Ausgewählte Ausstellungen / 所选展览**

1999 "Vege-Pleasure", Hanart TZ Gallery, Hong Kong
"Inside – Outside", P.S.1, Contemporary Art Center, New York, NY, USA
2001 "Today No Water", Ethan Cohen Fine Arts, New York, NY, USA
2006 " 'Art in Motion': BMW Art Cars Exhibited Together with Chinese Contemporary Arts", Museum of Contemporary Art, Shanghai, China

1999年 《Vege-Pleasure》香港汉雅轩画廊，香港
《蜕变突破—中国新艺术》P.S.1，纽约，美国
2001年 《今天下午停水》汉雅轩，香港，中国
《事物的权利》Ethan Cohen 美术馆，美国纽约
2006年 《当代艺术对话 BMW艺术车和中国当代艺术共同展出》，上海

***Selected publications* / Ausgewählte Publikationen / 所选著作**

Gao Minglu: "Inside Out: New Chinese Art", San Francisco/New York 1998
Claus Mewes: "Far West – KP Brehmer, Xu Jiang, Shan Fan, Wu Shanzhuan. Vier Künstler zwischen Deutschland und China", Hamburg 2006

高明潞（著）：《蜕变突破—中国新艺术》旧金山：现代艺术旧金山博物馆，纽约：亚洲社会画廊，1998 年，图板5
Mewes, Claus（著）：《远西- KP Brehmer，许江、单凡，吴山专。四位艺术家在德国和中国之间》第一出版（2006年10月）

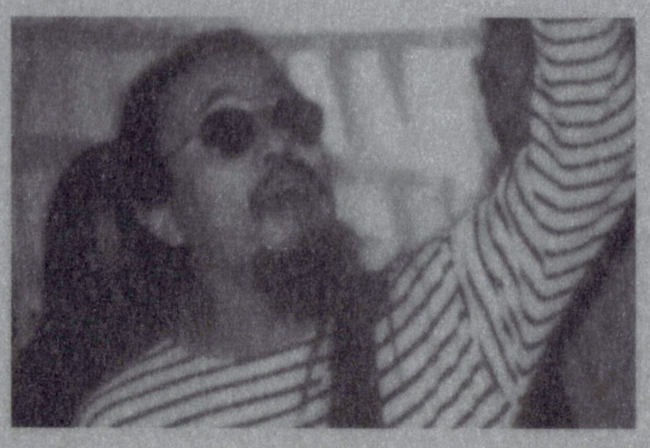

"The principle of 'Vege-Pleasure' is that each independent vegetable and fruit should have intercourse (merge) under an identically valued object orientation and object power."

„Das Prinzip von ‚Vege-Pleasure' ist, dass jedes einzelne Gemüse und jede einzelne Frucht miteinander eine Verbindung unter identischer Wertorientierung eingehen."

"Vege-pleasure的原则是,各独立菜和果子应该有交尾(合并)在相同地被重视的对象取向和对象力量之下,并且他们的权利应该被合并作为理所当然的事和存在事情。"

Born in 1960 in Zhoushan, Province Zhejiang, China. Lives and works in Hamburg, Germany, and Shanghai
Geboren 1960 in Zhoushan, Province Zhejiang, China. Lebt und arbeitet in Hamburg, Deutschland, und Shanghai
1960年出生于中国浙江舟山。住居工作在汉堡,德国和上海

Selected exhibitions / Ausgewählte Ausstellungen / 所选展览

1999 "Vege-Pleasure", Hanart TZ Gallery, Hong Kong
"Inside – Outside", P.S.1, Contemporary Art Center, New York, NY, USA
2001 "Today No Water", Ethan Cohen Fine Arts, New York, NY, USA
2006 "'Art in Motion': BMW Art Cars Exhibited Together with Chinese Contemporary Arts", Museum of Contemporary Art, Shanghai, China

1999年 《Vege-Pleasure》香港汉雅轩画廊,香港
《蜕变突破—中国新艺术》P.S.1, 纽约,美国
2001年 《今天下午停水》汉雅轩,香港,中国
《事物的权利》Ethan Cohen 美术馆,美国纽约
2006年 《当代艺术对话 BMW艺术车和中国当代艺术共同展出》,上海

Selected publications / Ausgewählte Publikationen / 所选著作

Gao Minglu: "Inside Out: New Chinese Art", San Francisco/New York 1998
Claus Mewes: "Far West – KP Brehmer, Xu Jiang, Shan Fan, Wu Shanzhuan. Vier Künstler zwischen Deutschland und China", Hamburg 2006

高明潞(著):《蜕变突破—中国新艺术》旧金山:现代艺术旧金山博物馆,纽约:亚洲社会画廊,1998 年,图版5
Mewes, Claus(著):《远西- KP Brehmer,许江,单凡,吴山专。四位艺术家在德国和中国之间》第一出版(2006年10月)

WU SHANZHUAN 吴山专

[wu ʂantʂuan]

Wu Shanzhuan graduated in 1986 from the Oil Painting Department of Zhejiang Academy of Fine Arts (present Central Academy of Fine Arts) and moved to Iceland in 1992, then to Germany. In 1995 he was awarded the master degree of Hamburg Hochschule für Bildende Künste. At present he travels between Hamburg and Shanghai.

Wu Shanzhuan is the engine behind China's avant-garde his power of talent being not yet really discussed. In the mid 1980s his paintings were related to the memory of the Chinese Cultural Revolution expressed as simplified characters, falsely typed characters, big characters, official seals in red colour, a trumpet, and the Panda, questioning the violence of ideology the individual had to withstand. His visual world of "Red Humour" (1986) which lead in the 1990s to the true spirit of political Pop and rebellious movement, is to be found in the painting with an official seal on a white slowly festering cabbage and the slogan of the painting "One cabbage for 3 cents only" (1989), which reveals the microcosm of daily life thoughts. In his later works of simplified symbols he never reached this kind of political Pop. Wu Shanzhuan constructs the background behind the simplified characters as memorized by people, but resisting against the "meaning" of traditional Chinese calligraphy artists' way being involved in the writing itself.

After moving to Germany Wu Shanzhuan's critical discernment was attracted by consumerism as a mainstream ideology, especially by items in supermarkets. He was fascinated by labels with numbers and description which meant for him the loss of freedom and "rights of things", being the cause to create a "Manifest of things" (1994).

Compared to the "Red" of the Chinese Cultural Revolution the capitalistic supermarkets were another kind of violence for him. "The water supply will be shut down this afternoon" (2002) and "Today water tube is under reparation" (1994) which is more subtle, but both declare that there won't be water any more. Wu's work discusses how art becomes possible and how democracy becomes possible. He belongs

Wu Shanzhuan schloss sein Studium 1986 an der Abteilung für Ölmalerei der Zhejiang Academy of Fine Arts (die heutige Central Academy of Fine Arts) ab; 1992 zog er nach Island und von dort nach Deutschland, wo er 1995 an der Hamburger Hochschule für Bildende Künste ein Diplom erwarb. Gegenwärtig pendelt er zwischen Hamburg und Shanghai.

Wu Shanzhuan ist gleichsam der Motor, der hinter Chinas Avantgarde arbeitet, auch wenn sein Talent noch nicht wirklich gewürdigt wird. Mitte der 1980er Jahre bezog sich seine Malerei auf die chinesische Kulturrevolution, die er durch vereinfachte, falsch geschriebene oder übergroße Schriftzeichen, amtliche Siegel in roter Farbe, eine Trompete und einen Pandabären darstellte, der die Gewalt der Ideologie hinterfragte, die der einzelne zu erdulden hatte. Wus visuelle Welt des „Red Humour" (1986) mündete in den rebellischen Geist des Polit-Pop der 1990er Jahre, was sein Gemälde „Ein Kohlkopf für nur 3 Cents" (1989) deutlich macht, das einen langsam verfaulenden weißen Kohl mit amtlichem Siegel zeigt. Zugleich spiegelte sich in seinen Arbeiten der Mikrokosmos des alltäglichen (Über-)Lebens wider. In seinen späteren Werken, die auf vereinfachten Symbolen beruhen, erreichte er nie wieder diese Intensität politischer Artikulation. Wu Shanzhuans Interesse gilt dem Hintergrund, der sich hinter den Zeichen verbirgt, und der Frage, wie sie von den Menschen wahrgenommen und memoriert werden, aber er weigert sich, den traditionellen chinesischen Kalligraphen darin zu folgen, sich zu engagieren.

Als er nach Deutschland übersiedelte, traf Wus kritisches Bewusstsein auf eine Gesellschaft, deren Hauptideologie das Konsumdenken ist – insbesondere die Warenflut in den Supermärkten tat es ihm an. Er war fasziniert von den Aufschriften und Etiketten, den Zahlen und Beschreibungen der zahllosen Gegenstände, die dadurch in seinen Augen ihre Freiheit und Rechte verlieren – als Reaktion erarbeitete er sein „Manifest der Dinge" (1994).

Verglichen mit dem „Rot" der chinesischen Kulturrevolution stellen für ihn die kapitalistischen Supermärkte nur eine

1986年吴山专毕业于浙江美术学院油画系（现中国美术学院）。1992年移居冰岛，后来到德国。1995年毕业于汉堡艺术学院获硕士。现在生活于汉堡和上海。

吴山专是中国前卫精神的隐型的发动机，这位天才的能量尚未被真正谈论到。1980年代中期，他以简体字、错别字、大字报、红色、公章，高音喇叭以及开会和熊猫，所有这些关于红色中国特别是文化大革命的一切视觉记忆为图像，集中质疑个人所承受的意识形态暴力。

他的“红色幽默”是九十年代的政治波普和泼皮运动的真正精神起源，但是盖上了公章白菜渐渐腐烂，和文革标语式的“白菜三分钱一斤”的绘画，这种扎根在日常生活之中的微观政治理念的深刻性，后来的简单符号化的政治波普图像再也未曾达到过。吴对文字的解构是基于“简化字”及其背后的人民记忆，有别于其他涉及文字的中国艺术家的文人书法传统，而是对于“有意义”本身的反抗。

迁居德国之后，吴山专的批判眼光转移到消费主义为主流意识形态的超市中，特别是超市中的物。在这里，被标上了条形码的物是不自由的，因此它们丧失了“物权”，也就是丧失了充分地实现他们的所有可能性的机会，因此吴山专提出了《物权宣言》。和文化大革命的“红”相比，资本主义的超市是另一种暴力，只是前者明确地宣告“今天下午停水”，而后者巧妙地宣布“今天下午修水管”，事实一样是停水。因此，吴山专的工作既是在论证艺术何以可能，也是在论证民主何以可能，他是中国为数极少的本体论艺术家。

这样一位艺术家的工作媒介必定呈现为丰富的形式：摄影、装置、事件和行动，涂鸦般杂陈着思维和图像碎片的绘画，甚至于小说。吴山专持续多年写作的《今天下午停水》，一部充满插图和当代艺术作品方案的“小说”，其实是当代中国的个人意

2

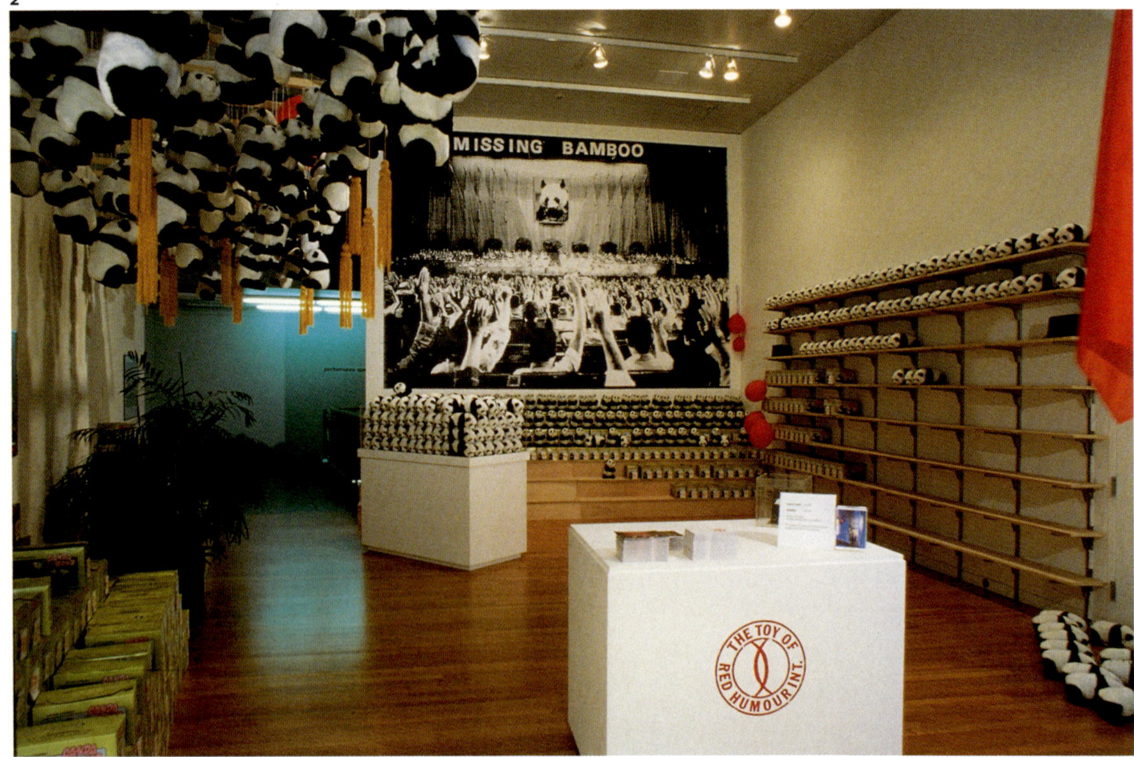

HAMBURG
JUNE 1994

TO WHOM IT MAY CONCERN.

THINK ABOUT THE RIGHT OF THINGS, AN EXTRA FOR THINGS RIGHT(S) ALL.

BEING A THING IS NOT A QUESTION OF IDENTITY IT'S AN ATTITUDE OF MIND.

SOMETHING WHICH BECOMES CLEARER WHEN YOU LOOK AROUND YOU, THERE YOU SEE A COSMO-POLITAN GROUP OF THINGS WHICH HAS MORE IN COMMON WITH EACH OTHER THAN YOU PROBABLY THOUGHT.

BEING A THING AMONG THINGS ALL, WHERE YOU BECOME AN EXTRA, THERE YOU FIND THE RIGHT OF THINGS.

WITH THE EXTRA POSSITION THE THINGS RIGHT(S) IS APPEARED.

THINGSRIGHT(S) RED HUMOUR INTERNATIONAL

INGA SVALA
THOR'S DAUGHTER'S PULVERIZATION SERVICE.

WU SHAN ZHUAN
RED HUMOUR INTERNATIONAL.

3

INFORMATION Hamburger Wasserwerke GmbH

An die
Anwohner der Straßen
Ottenser Marktplatz,
Holländische Reihe und
Bernadottestraße

22765 Hamburg

Hamburg, 18.03.94

Neulegung von Wasserleitungen

Sehr geehrte Kundin, sehr geehrter Kunde,

die Hamburger Wasserwerke GmbH müssen zur Sicherstellung der Wasserversorgung in den Straßen

Ottenser Marktplatz, Holländische Reihe sowie Bernadottestr. zw. Große Brunnenstr. und Susettestraße in Ottensen

Versorgungsleitungen legen. Die von uns beauftragte Firma wird **ab 22.03.94** mit den Arbeiten beginnen. Wir rechnen mit einer Bauzeit von **ca. 14** Wochen. Sie werden rechtzeitig von uns über die erforderlichen Unterbrechungen der Wasserversorgung informiert.

Für die Behinderungen während des Leitungsbaus bitten wir um Ihr Verständnis. Beachten Sie bitte, die im Zusammenhang mit der Baustelle aufgestellten Verkehrs- und Hinweisschilder.

Für Fragen steht Ihnen unser

Rohrnetzbezirk **West**, Tel.: **85 66 99**,

zur Verfügung.

In besonderen Fällen können Sie außerhalb der normalen Arbeitszeit den Entstörungsdienst der Hamburger Wasserwerke GmbH, unter der Rufnummer **78 19 51**, erreichen.

Mit freundlichen Grüßen

Hamburger Wasserwerke GmbH
Wasserverteilung/- verwendung

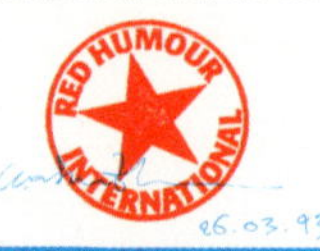

26.03.93

Billhorner Deich 2 · 20539 Hamburg · Telefon: (040) 78 88-0

"Today No Water" in Hamburg Germany.

4

BUY YOU A STAR INTO THE FLAG

PAY ~~10 DM~~ 30 FIM

PUT IT INTO THE BOX "OPEN FLAG CHINA"

CHOOSE YOUR STAR LOCATION

SIGN IT

AND

TAKE ONE CARBOARD STAR

THE STAR IS YOURS

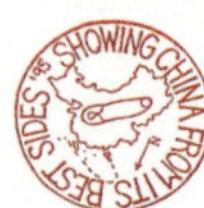

SHOWING CHINA FROM IT'S BEST SIDES

1995

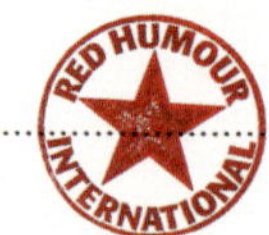

THOR'SDAUGHTER'S PULVERIZATION SERVICE

5

2.

以下为图：

为巴西双年展的草图（最后定稿）及其注解：

MAKING YOUR OWN OBJECTIONALITY BRAZIL 01

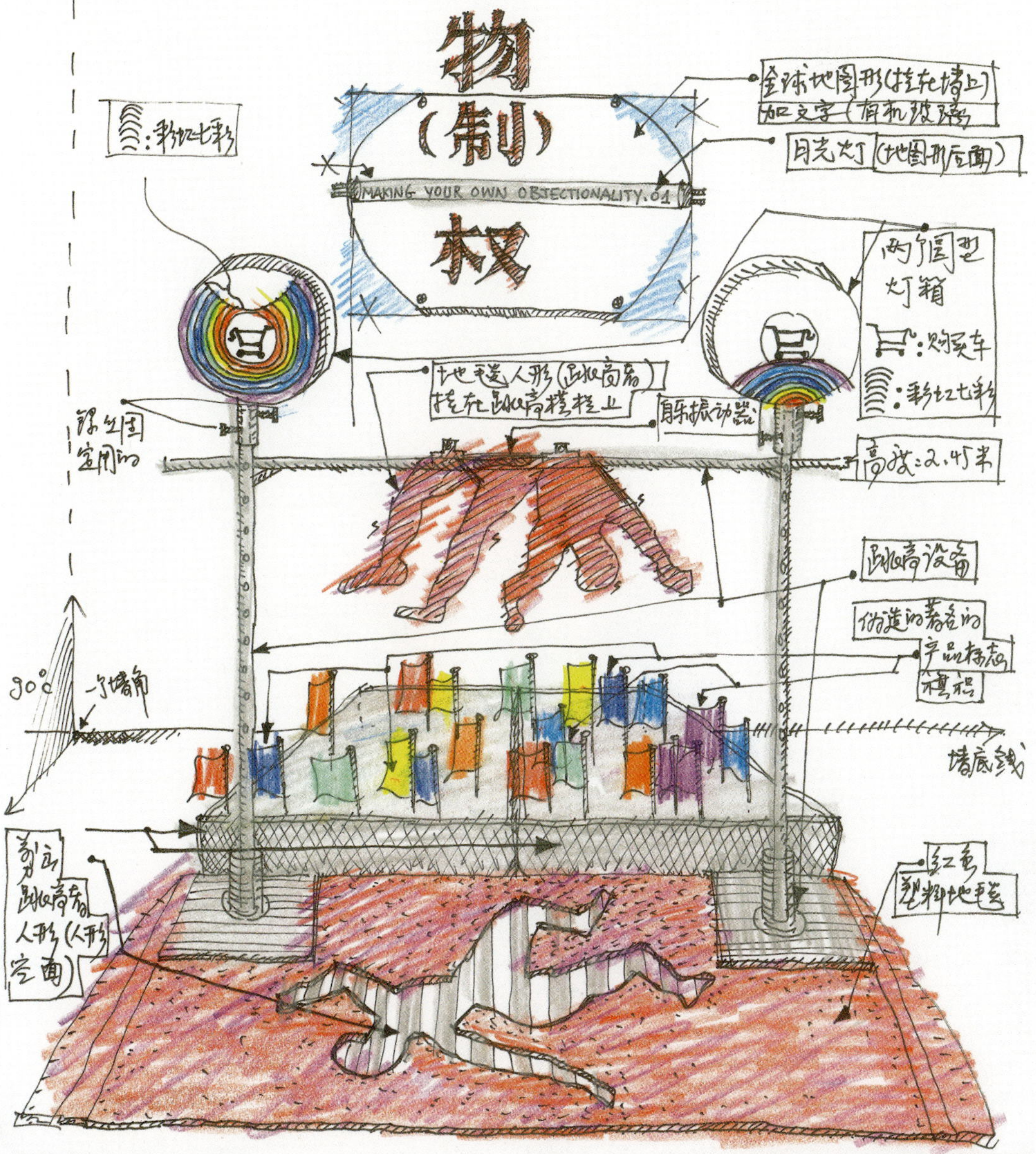

7

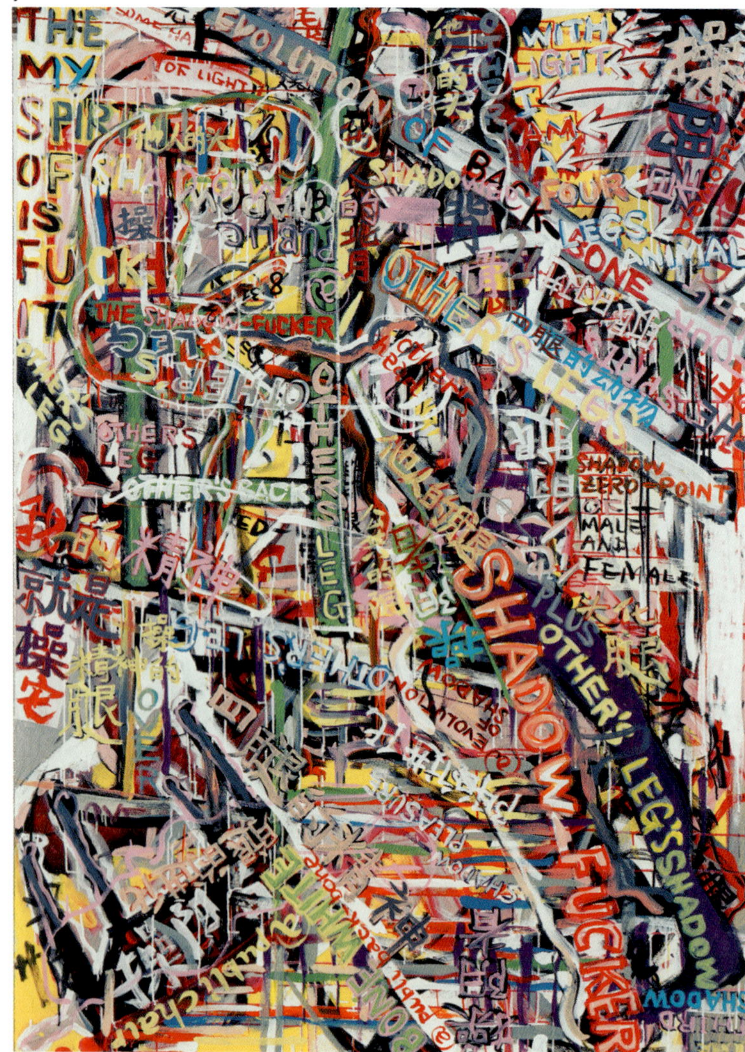

8

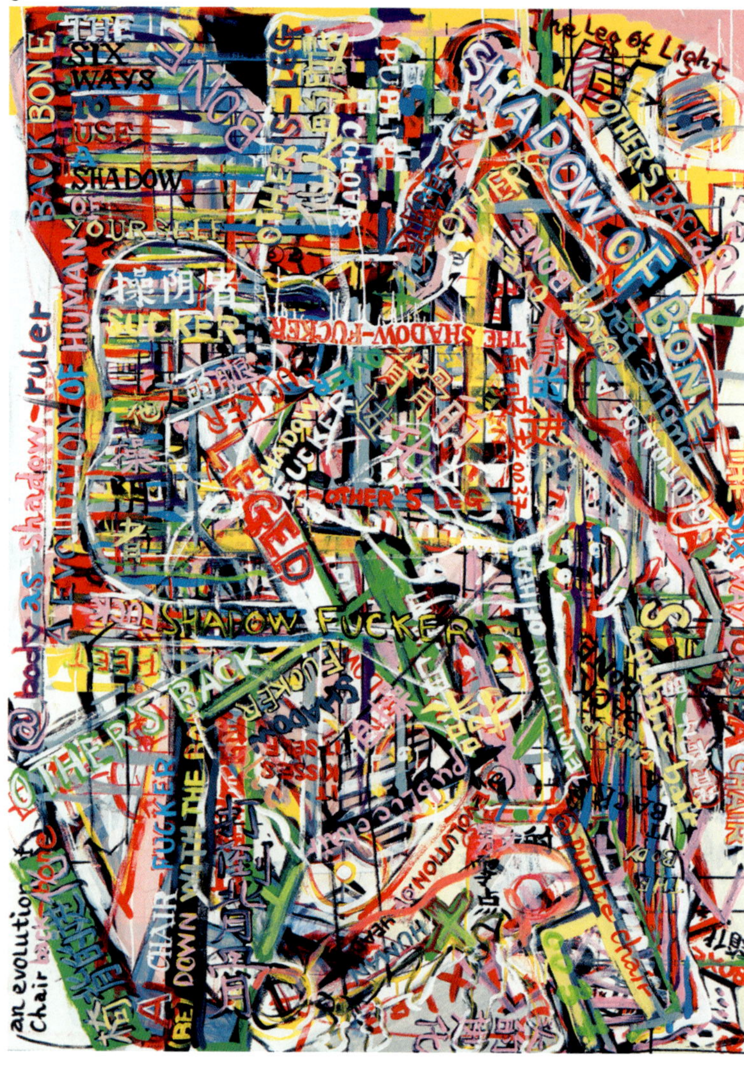

to the ontology artists the number thereof is few in China. The media of this kind of artist are rich in form: photography, installations, events and action, scribbling of different thought and fragments of paintings and even novels. Wu Shanzhuan continued his writings "Today No Water" (since 1985) for many years, full of pictures and contemporary art work sketches being in fact a maze of China's contemporary individual ideology. In the daily commercialised contemporary art landscape, his existence has indicated one kind of experimental depth and spiritual altitude.

andere Form der Gewalt dar. Mit den Arbeiten „The water supply will be shut down this afternoon" (2002) und „Today water tube is under Reparation" (1994) zog er daraus seine Schlüsse.

Wu Shanzhuans Werke diskutieren, wie Kunst überhaupt möglich ist, und vor allem: wie Demokratie möglich werden kann. Er gehört darum zu den wenigen ontologischen Künstlern Chinas. Die Medien, in denen Wu arbeitet, reichen von der Fotografie, der Installation und der Performance bis zu fragmentarischen Notizen und regelrechten Romanen. Sein schriftstellerisches Werk „Today No Water" (seit 1985) baut Wu kontinuierlich zu einem Labyrinth des zeitgenössischen Individualismus Chinas aus. In der täglich weiter kommerzialisierten kulturellen Landschaft zeigt Wu Shanzhuan eine seltene Form experimenteller und geistiger Tiefe.

识形态的一座迷宫。在日益商业化的当代艺术景观中，他的存在标示了一种实验的深度和精神的高度。

Qiu Zhijie

9

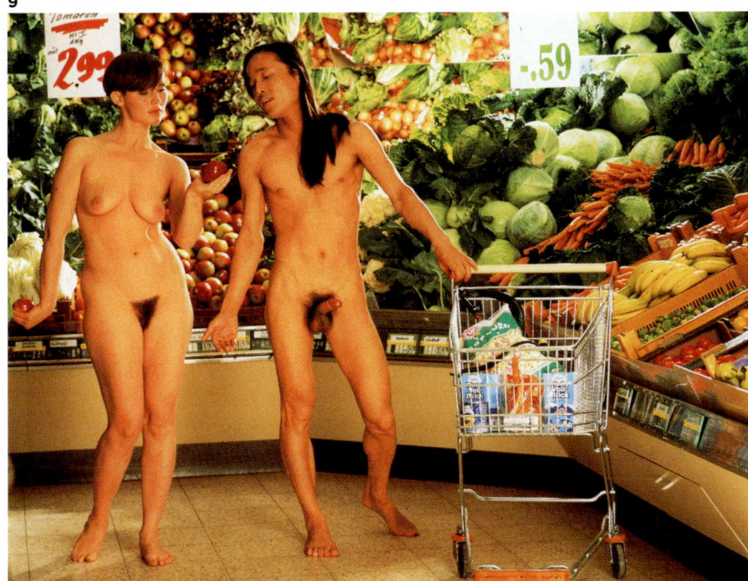

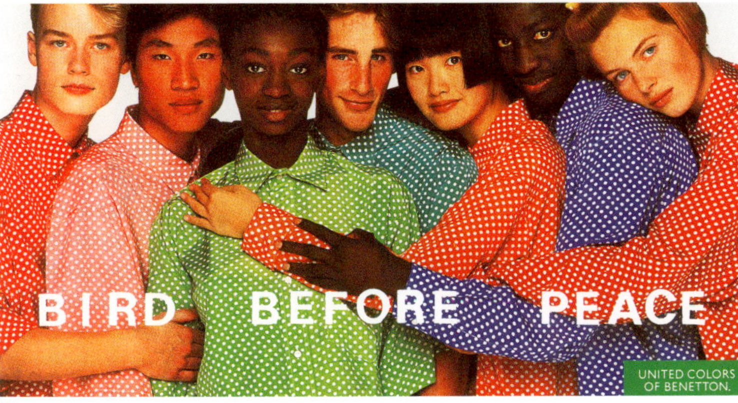

10

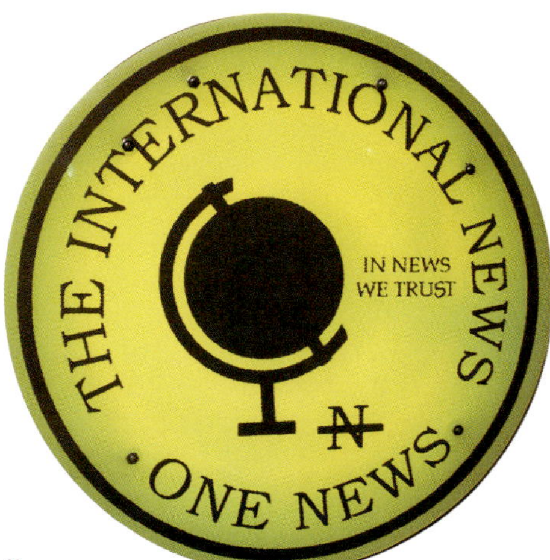

11

1 ***Today More Water Pipe is Needed**, 2002*
Installation view, First Guangzhou Triennial, Guangdong Museum of Art, Guangzhou
Installationsansicht, First Guangzhou Triennial, Guangdong Museum of Art, Guangzhou
《今天需要更多的水管》2002年，装置实景

2 ***Missing Bamboo**, 1993*
Installation view, "Fragmented Memory: The Chinese Avant-Garde in Exile", Wexner Center for the Arts, Columbus
Installationsansicht, „Fragmented Memory: The Chinese Avant-Garde in Exile", Wexner Center for the Arts, Columbus
《怀念竹子》1993年, 装置实景

3 ***Thing's Right(s)**, 1994*
In collaboration with Inga Svala Thórsdóttir, document, A4 paper
In Zusammenarbeit mit Inga Svala Thórsdóttir, Dokument, A4-Papier
《物权》(与 Inga Svala Thórsdóttir合作) 1994年, 文件, A4大小

4 ***Today Water Tube is Under Reparation**, 1994*
Document, A4 paper
Dokument, A4-Papier
《今天下午修水管》1994年, 文件, A4 纸

5 ***Showing China from it's Best Sides '95 – The Real Estate**, 1995*
In collaboration with Inga Svala Thórsdóttir, document, A4 paper
In Zusammenarbeit mit Inga Svala Thórsdóttir, Dokument, A4-Papier
《从最好的方面展现中国》(与 Inga Svala Thórsdóttir合作), 1995年, 文件, A4大小

6 ***To Make Your Own Objectionality**, 2001*
In collaboration with Inga Svala Thórsdóttir, installation sketch, A4 paper
In Zusammenarbeit mit Inga Svala Thórsdóttir, Installationsentwurf, A4-Papier
《客观化》(与 Inga Svala Thórsdóttir合作)，2001年，装置草图, A4纸

7 ***Object Fucker**, 2003*
Acrylic on canvas, 198 x 140 cm
Acryl auf Leinwand, 198 x 140 cm
《操物者》，2003年，布面丙烯, 198 x 140 cm

8 ***Object Fucker**, 2003*
Acrylic on canvas, 198 x 140 cm
Acryl auf Leinwand, 198 x 140 cm
《操物者》, 2003年, 布面丙烯, 198 x 140 cm

9 ***Paradises**, 1993*
In collaboration with Inga Svala Thórsdóttir, Cibachrome, 300 x 200 cm
In Zusammenarbeit mit Inga Svala Thórsdóttir, 1993, Cibachrome, 300 x 200 cm
《乐园》(与 Inga Svala Thórsdóttir合作), 1993年, Cibachrome, 300 x 200 cm

10 ***Bird Before Peace**, 1994*
In collaboration with Inga Svala Thórsdóttir, collage, 21 x 14.5 cm
In Zusammenarbeit mit Inga Svala Thórsdóttir, 1994, Collage, 21 x 14,5 cm
《和平之前的鸟》(Inga Svala Thórsdóttir合作)1994年，拼贴画, 21 x 14.5 cm

11 ***News Coinage**, 2001*
Neon sign, mixed media
Neon-Zeichen, Mixed media
《一元新闻》2001年, 霓虹灯, 混合媒介

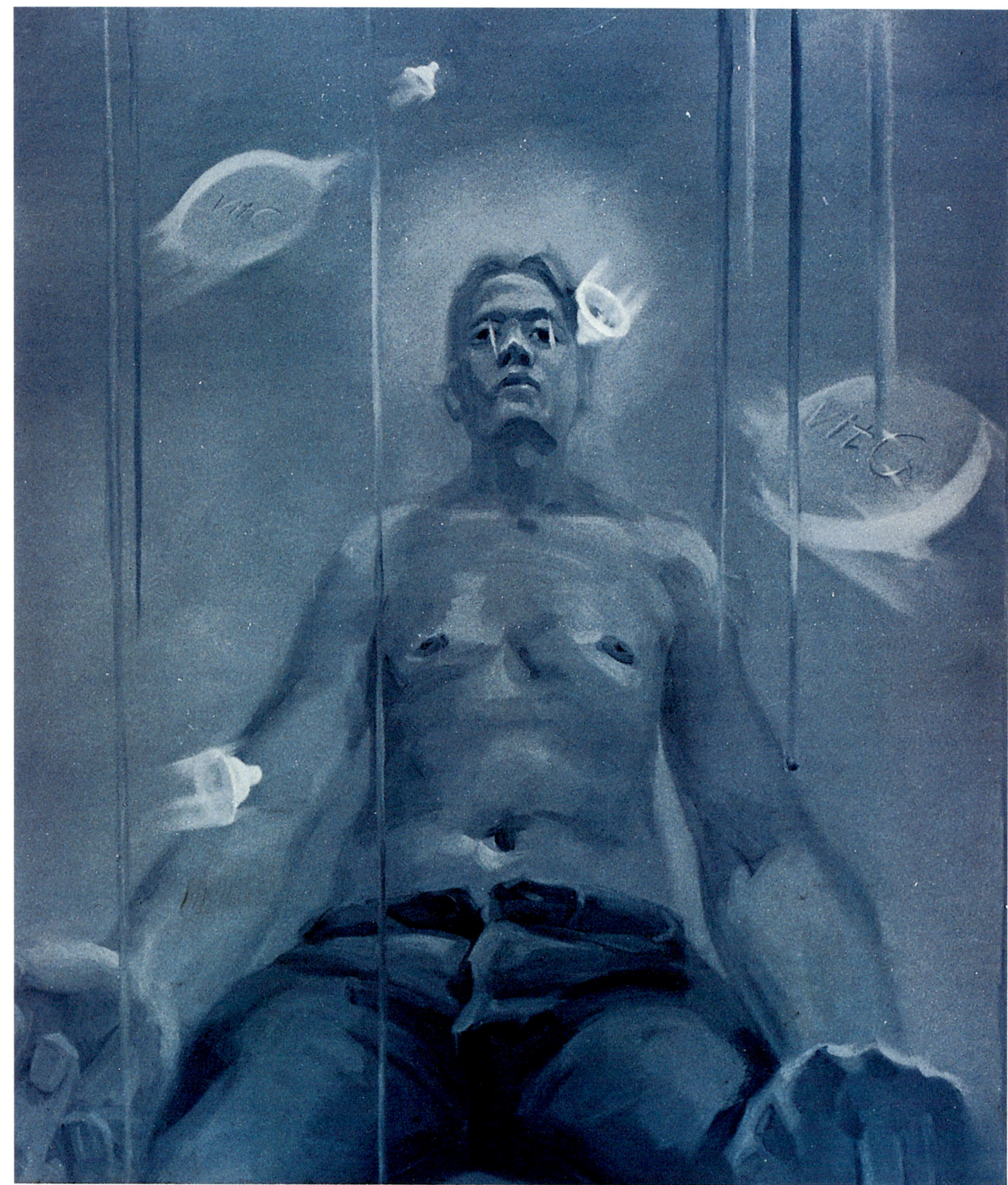

1

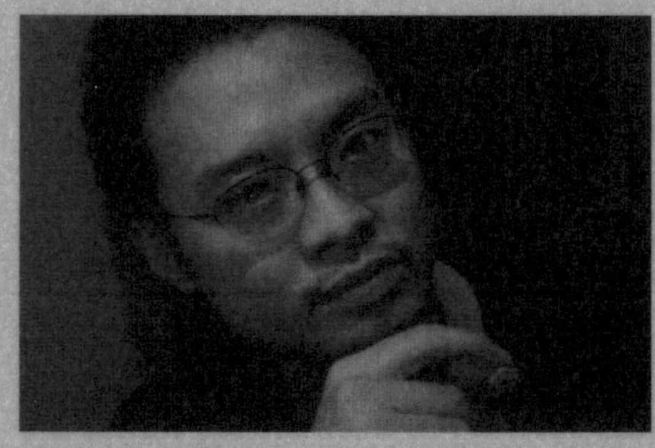

"The results obtained through the most advanced photographic systems, just by reason of being perfect, seem to be a fake. But common pictures, the home-made ones, taken with any automatic camera, although lacking in definition, appear paradoxically more real, more concrete."

„Die Resultate, die man mit modernsten fotografischen Systemen erzielt, wirken unecht, einfach weil sie so perfekt sind. Gewöhnliche Bilder dagegen, die man mit irgendeiner Automatikkamera aufnimmt, erscheinen, auch wenn es ihnen an Schärfe mangelt, paradoxerweise echter und wirklicher."

"经先进照相设备处理过的图片，就是因为完美无缺，所以看上去有些虚假，然而用自动摄像机拍摄，手工制作的普通照片，虽然精度不高，但看起来真实丰满。"

Born in 1970 in Chongqing, Sichuan Province, China. Lives and works in Chengdu and Beijing
Geboren 1970 in Chongqing, Provinz Sichuan, China. Lebt und arbeitet in Chengdu und Peking
1970年出生于中国四川省重庆市，居住工作在成都和北京

Selected exhibitions / **Ausgewählte Ausstellungen** / 所选展览

1999	Aperto, 48. Biennale di Venezia, Venice, Italy
2000	Shanghai Biennial, Shanghai, China
2003	"Paintings on the Move", Kunsthalle Basel, Basle, Switzerland
	"Xie Nanxing", Manchester Art Gallery, Manchester, UK
2005	"Show me... Catch me... Sight Unseen", Contemporary Art Archives & Warehouse (CAAW), Beijing, China
	"A Kind of Magic – The Art of Transforming", Kunstmuseum Luzern, Lucerne, Switzerland
2005–07	"Mahjong – Chinesische Gegenwartskunst aus der Sammlung Sigg", Kunstmuseum Bern, Berne, Switzerland; Hamburger Kunsthalle, Hamburg, Germany; Museum der Moderne, Salzburg, Austria
2007	documenta 12, Kassel, Germany

1999年	"Aperto"，第四十八届威尼斯双年展，意大利威尼斯
2000年	《上海双年展》上海
2003年	《变动中的绘画》巴塞尔美术馆，瑞士
	《谢南星》曼彻斯特美术馆，曼彻斯特 英国
2005年	《告诉我...抓住我...隐藏的视界》北京艺术文件仓库
	《魔力-艺术的变换》卢塞恩美术馆，瑞士
2005-07年	《麻将》西克中国当代艺术收藏展，伯尔尼美术馆瑞士；汉堡美术馆，汉堡，德国；萨尔茨保现代美术馆 奥地利
2007年	第十二届德国文件展，卡塞尔，德国

Selected publications / **Ausgewählte Publikationen** / 所选著作

Peter Fischer, Birgitt Bürgi (eds.): "A Kind of Magic", Lucerne 2005
"Xie Nanxing Paintings: 1992–2004", Beijing 2006

Fischer, Peter/Bürgi, Birgitt (编者)：《魔力-艺术的变换》展册，卢塞恩2005年
《谢南星油画: 1992–2004》北京 2006年

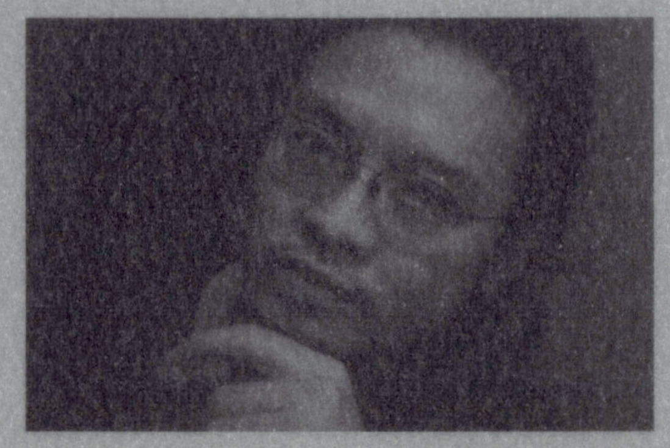

"The results obtained through the most advanced photographic systems, just by reason of being perfect, seem to be a fake. But common pictures, the home-made ones, taken with any automatic camera, although lacking in definition, appear paradoxically more real, more concrete."

„Die Resultate, die man mit modernsten fotografischen Systemen erzielt, wirken unecht, einfach weil sie so perfekt sind. Gewöhnliche Bilder dagegen, die man mit irgendeiner Automatikkamera aufnimmt, erscheinen, auch wenn es ihnen an Schärfe mangelt, paradoxerweise echter und wirklicher."

"经先进照相设备处理过的图片，就是因为完美无缺，所以看上去有些虚假，然而用自动摄像机拍摄，手工制作的普通照片，虽然精度不高，但看起来真实丰满。"

Born in 1970 in Chongqing, Sichuan Province, China. Lives and works in Chengdu and Beijing
Geboren 1970 in Chongqing, Provinz Sichuan, China. Lebt und arbeitet in Chengdu und Peking
1970年出生于中国四川省重庆市，居住工作在成都和北京

Selected exhibitions / Ausgewählte Ausstellungen / 所选展览

1999 Aperto, 48. Biennale di Venezia, Venice, Italy
2000 Shanghai Biennial, Shanghai, China
2003 "Paintings on the Move", Kunsthalle Basel, Basle, Switzerland
"Xie Nanxing", Manchester Art Gallery, Manchester, UK
2005 "Show me... Catch me... Sight Unseen", Contemporary Art Archives & Warehouse (CAAW), Beijing, China
"A Kind of Magic – The Art of Transforming", Kunstmuseum Luzern, Lucerne, Switzerland
2005–07 "Mahjong – Chinesische Gegenwartskunst aus der Sammlung Sigg", Kunstmuseum Bern, Berne, Switzerland; Hamburger Kunsthalle, Hamburg, Germany; Museum der Moderne, Salzburg, Austria
2007 documenta 12, Kassel, Germany

1999年 "Aperto"，第四十八届威尼斯双年展，意大利威尼斯
2000年 《上海双年展》上海
2003年 《变动中的绘画》巴塞尔美术馆，瑞士
《谢南星》曼彻斯特美术馆，曼彻斯特 英国
2005年 《告诉我……抓住我……隐藏的视界》北京艺术文件仓库
《魔力-艺术的变换》卢塞恩美术馆，瑞士
2005–07年 《麻将》西克中国当代艺术收藏展，伯尔尼美术馆瑞士；汉堡美术馆，汉堡，德国；萨尔茨堡现代美术馆 奥地利
2007年 第十二届德国文件展，卡塞尔，德国

Selected publications / Ausgewählte Publikationen / 所选著作

Peter Fischer, Birgitt Bürgi (eds.): "A Kind of Magic", Lucerne 2005
"Xie Nanxing Paintings: 1992–2004", Beijing 2006

Fischer, Peter/Bürgi, Birgitt（编者）：《魔力-艺术的变换》展册，卢塞恩2005年
《谢南星油画：1992–2004》北京 2006年

XIE NANXING 谢南星

[ɕiɛ nanɕiŋ]

Banal scenes of everyday life are transformed into moments of mystery in Xie Nanxing's large oil paintings. This artist, who received his master's degree from the Sichuan Fine Arts Academy in 1996 and now teaches at Jiaotong University in Chengdu, masterfully uses paint to create a sensation of time-lapse photography. The images seem both immediate and prolonged, unbearably direct and at the same time elusive. This multilayered effect is the result of an equally multifaceted process.

Xie Nanxing starts with an ordinary camera, intentionally taking photographs that are out-of-focus, out of kilter and poorly exposed. The resulting pictures capture the details of everyday life, but in a way that evoke a world that is entirely destabilized and out-of-control. This sensation is heightened when the artist takes photographs off a television monitor or uses stills from video footage. Banal facts of every day life become clues to a mystery, though Xie Nanxing rarely reveals the solution or delivers a resolution to his haunting narratives.

Though his initial work was a series of self-portraits, awash in hues of indigo and blue, Xie Nanxing achieved international attention at the 48th Venice Biennial in 1999 with his paintings of "Private Violence". These works showed bodies splayed in abject positions or blood stains patterned on a bare floor, terrifically charged yet also muted by the artist's poetic painting style. The creepiness of these scenes are heightened by the brutal lighting, like the florescent glare of an interrogation room, while the details in each view are mere hints of what took place before an audience arrived.

Since 2000, Xie Nanxing's paintings have grown ever larger in size and more abstract in their imagery. "Untitled (Flame)" (2000), is a monumental canvas depicting a close-up of the gas burner on a stove, the tendrils of blue flames turned as towering as mountain fire. "Picture of Voice I" (2001), a triptych reaching over 1170 cm (460 inches), may or may not depict a sequence leading up to a car accident. On closer

Banale Szenen aus dem Alltag verwandeln sich in Xie Nanxings großen Ölgemälden in Momente voller Geheimnis. Der Künstler, der 1996 seinen Meister-Abschluss an der Sichuan Fine Arts Academy machte und heute an der Jiaotong University in Chengdu unterrichtet, bedient sich der Farbe auf meisterhafte Weise, um eine Art Zeitraffereffekt zu erzielen. Die Bilder wirken unmittelbar und zugleich in die Länge gezogen, unerträglich direkt und dabei doch flüchtig. Diese Vielschichtigkeit ist das Ergebnis eines entsprechend facettenreichen Prozesses.

Xie Nanxing beginnt seine Arbeit mit einer gewöhnlichen Kamera, mit der er absichtlich verwackelte, schiefe und falsch belichtete Aufnahmen macht. Diese Bilder fangen die Details des Alltagslebens ein, aber auf eine Weise, die auf eine völlig destabilisierte, außer Kontrolle geratene Welt schließen lässt. Dieser Eindruck wird noch verstärkt, wenn der Künstler Bilder vom Fernsehschirm abfotografiert oder Standbilder aus Videoaufnahmen verwendet. Banale Fakten des täglichen Lebens werden so zu Hinweisen auf etwas geheimnisvoll Hintergründiges, auch wenn Xie Nanxing nur selten die Lösung verrät oder eine Aufklärung seiner unheimlichen Geschichten liefert.

Am Anfang seines Werks stand eine Serie von Selbstporträts in Indigo- und Blautönen; internationale Aufmerksamkeit errang Xie Nanxing 1999 auf der 48. Biennale von Venedig mit seinen Gemälden häuslicher Gewalt („Private Violence"). Sie zeigen unterwürfig niedergestreckte Körper oder kahle, blutbefleckte Böden, Szenen voller Unheil, die aber durch den poetischen Malstil des Künstlers gedämpft sind. Der Horror wird verstärkt durch eine brutale Beleuchtung, die an das Neonlicht eines Verhörraums erinnert, während die Details, derer man ansichtig wird, bloß andeuten, was sich womöglich in diesen Szenarien abgespielt hat, ehe der Betrachter dazukam.

Seit 2000 wurden Xie Nanxings Gemälde immer großformatiger und abstrakter. „Untitled (Flame)" (2000) liefert die monumentale Nahaufnahme eines Gasherds, aus dem

在谢南星大型油画中，日常生活的平凡场景被转化为神秘的瞬间。1996年谢南星毕业于四川美院并获得硕士学位，现在成都的交通大学任教。他用颜料创作了一幅具有慢速摄影感觉的作品，这幅图看起来既直接又拖延，过度的直率但同时 而又能难以捉摸，经均匀地多面处理形成了多层效果。

谢南星以普通的相机作为开始，故意把照片拍得模模糊糊，歪歪斜斜，曝光也很差劲，所拍的照片捕捉了日常生活细节，但是在一定程度上唤起了轻浮失控的社会。当 谢南星抛弃电视监视器去拍照 或是使用录像胶片上的静物，这种感情就越加高涨。日常平凡的生活转变神秘的暗示，但是谢不会揭示答案或对对答案作出暗示。

虽然谢南星的最早作品是一组以靛青和蓝色为色调的自画像，但引起国际关注的是在1999年第48届的威尼斯双年展上的作品《秘密暴力》，这些作品展示了以可怜方式张开的躯体和在空地板上由血斑组成的图案，极端地控诉着，然而谢诗般的绘画风格让这控诉声归于宁静。这种场面的延续被残忍的像在审讯室四散的照明所增强，然而这些细节仅仅是观众抵达之前所发生事情的线索而已。

自2000年期，谢南星的油画的尺寸比以前更大，人物的肖像也更加诱人，《无标题》（火焰），是一张特写了炉灶上的煤气火焰的不朽作品，蓝色火焰的火苗变得像山火一样猛烈。2001年的1170CM 长三幅一张的《声音的图片》，也许或者不是描写了一场交通事故的发生次序。最近看来，那只仅仅是透过移动的车窗上拍摄的高速公路晚间夜景。但是周的手法仅仅提高了透过雨雾的移动感觉，拟造了很可能发生的事故。

正是因为他架起了中国学院派的写实主义和后现代朦胧趋向之间的桥梁，谢南星被认为最重要的艺术家。而他的意图总是呈现事实的冰山一角，然后用它复杂的绘画技巧破坏对真相的判断力。通过把一

2

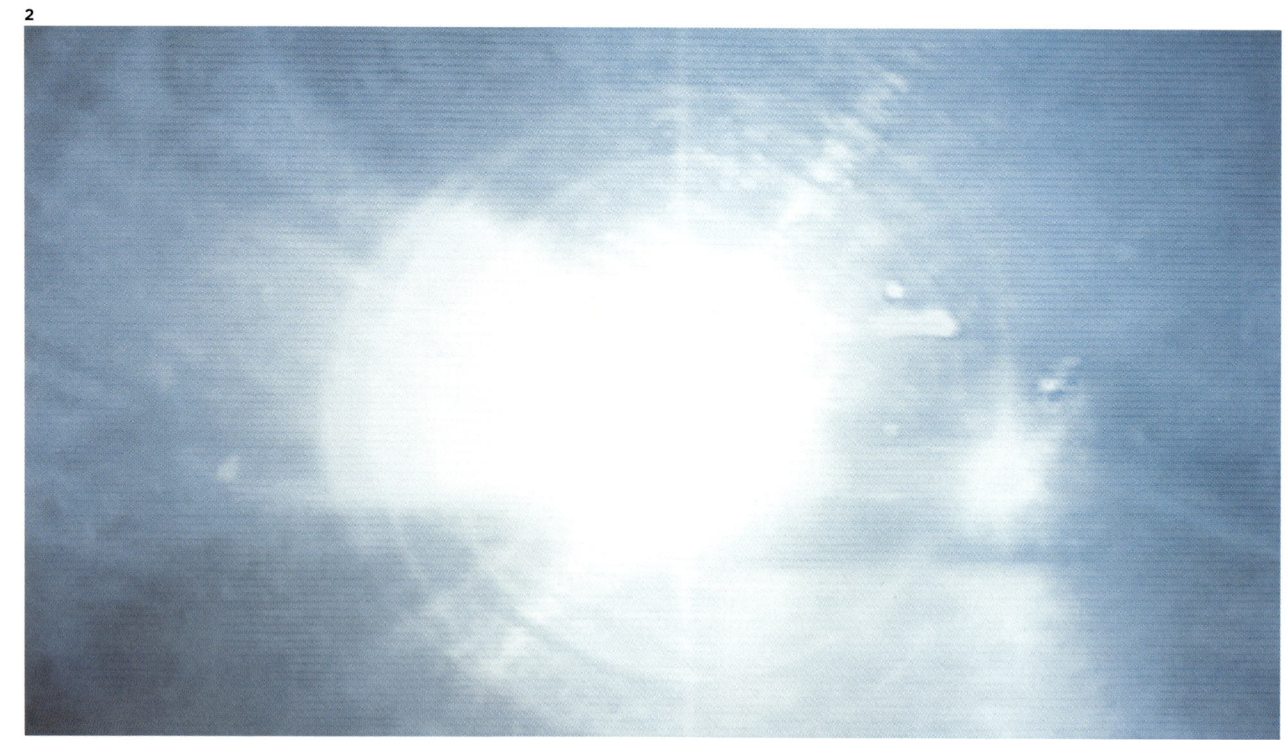

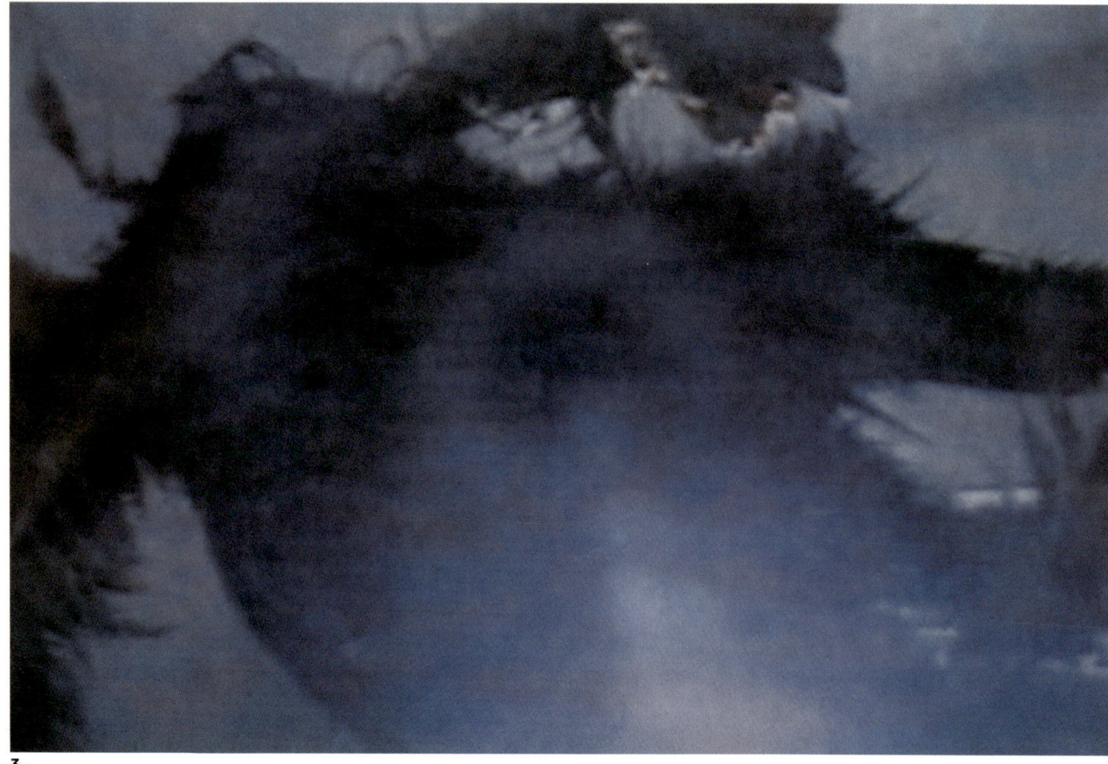

3

4

5

6

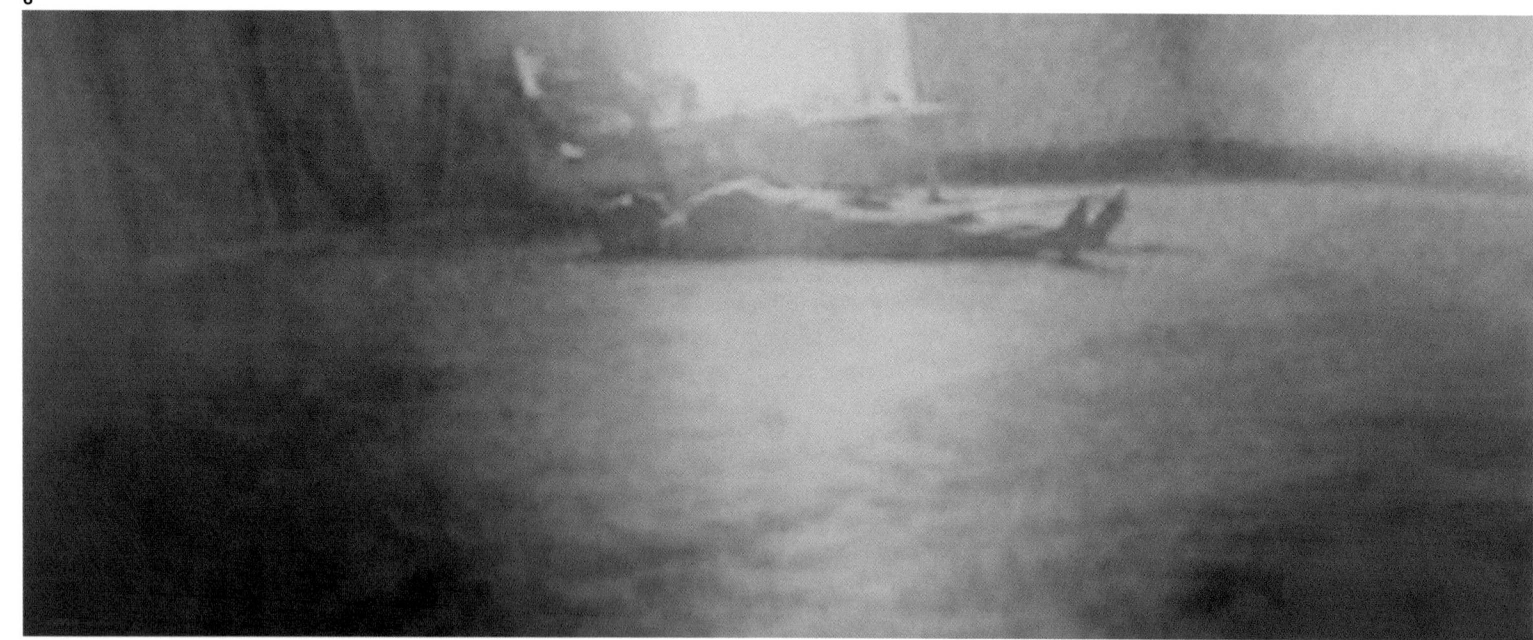

examination, it is merely views of a highway at night, taken from the window of a moving vehicle. But Xie Nanxing's approach only heightens the sensation of moving through fog and rain, making an accident a likely occurrence.

Xie Nanxing is considered an important artist precisely because he bridges the gap between the realism of Chinese academic painting and the post-modern penchant for ambiguity. His intention is always to present only a glimpse of the truth, then undermine the sense of veracity with his laborious painting technique. By building an image slowly through several layers of thin glaze, he incorporates time into images taken in the split-second of a camera's shutter speed. His latest works, from 2004 to the present, are even more ambiguous, distorting the realism further by adding layer of gloom as achieved by underexposed photographs taken at night. Close-ups, shot from extreme angles, may show the night sky or may reveal a shadowy figure emerging from the mist. Viewers are not allowed to know the facts, which make the horror of these pictures all the more real.

die blauen Flammenzungen wie ein Bergfeuer emporlodern. „Picture of Voice I" (2001), ein Triptychon von über 11,70 Meter Breite, stellt vielleicht die Vorgeschichte eines Autounfalls dar – vielleicht aber auch nicht. Bei genauem Hinsehen handelt es sich lediglich um Ansichten einer Schnellstraße bei Nacht, aus dem Fenster eines fahrenden Wagens aufgenommen. Aber Xie Nanxings Sicht- und Darstellungsweise verdichtet das Empfinden, sich durch gefährlichen Nebel und Regen zu bewegen, so sehr, dass ein Unfall wahrscheinlich wird.

Xie Nanxing gilt auch darum als bedeutender Künstler, weil er die Kluft zwischen dem Realismus der chinesischen Akademiemalerei und postmoderner Mehrdeutigkeit überbrückt. Seine Intention ist es, dem Betrachter stets nur einen flüchtigen Blick auf die Wahrheit zu gewähren, aber die Wahrhaftigkeit dieser Momentaufnahme durch seine gewissenhafte Maltechnik zu unterminieren. Indem er ein Bild langsam aus mehreren dünnen Lasurschichten aufbaut, bringt er eine zeitliche Dimension in die Schnappschüsse des Ausgangsmaterials ein, die in Sekundenbruchteilen entstanden sind. Xies jüngste Arbeiten seit 2004 gewinnen sogar noch an Mehrdeutigkeit und verzerren die Realität noch extremer, indem sie durch eine zusätzliche dunkle Farbschicht eine Düsternis entwickeln, die an unterbelichtete Nachtaufnahmen erinnert – Nahaufnahmen, aus extremen Blickwinkeln aufgenommen, zeigen vielleicht den Nachthimmel oder womöglich auch eine schattenhafte Gestalt, die sich aus einem Nebel löst. Den Betrachtern werden die Fakten vorenthalten, was das Grauen der Bilder umso realer macht.

幅图像缓缓地穿过薄薄釉面的层面，谢南星把时间融合进一幅用快门速度拍摄的断秒照片中。他的最新作品《从2004年到现在》甚至更 暧昧，在照片上加了阴暗的膜，扭曲了写实主义，而像是在夜间拍摄曝光不足得到的。特写，从一个极端的角度拍摄，或许展示夜空或是展现出现在薄雾中的阴暗人影。观众不可能去了解事实的真相，因此这些照片的恐怖效果更佳真实。

Barbara Pollack

7

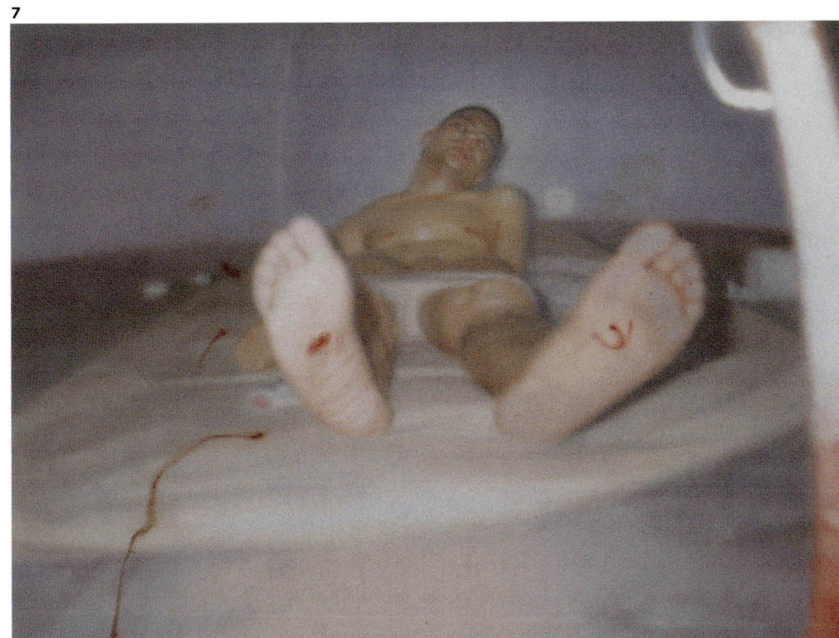

1 ***Ten Self-Portraits (No. 3)**, 1997*
Oil on canvas, 150 x 130 cm; Öl auf Leinwand, 150 x 130 cm
《十幅自画像》(No. 3), 1997年, 布面油画, 150 x 130 cm

2 ***Untitled (Picture of Voice I)**, 2002*
Oil on canvas, 220 x 380 cm (detail); Öl auf Leinwand, 220 x 380 cm (Detail)
《无题》(声音照片I), 2002年, 布面油画， 220 x 380 cm （详细）

3 ***Untitled (No. 2)**, 2004*
Oil on canvas, 220 x 324 cm; Öl auf Leinwand, 220 x 324 cm
《无题》(No. 2), 2004年, 布面油画, 220 x 324 cm

4 ***Untitled 2006**, 2006*
Oil on canvas, 220 x 380 cm; Öl auf Leinwand, 220 x 380 cm
《无题 2006》, 2006, 布面油画, 220 x 380 cm

5 ***Work 2006**, 2006*
Oil on canvas, 220 x 325 cm; Öl auf Leinwand, 220 x 325 cm
《工作2006》, 2006, 布面油画, 220 x 325 cm

6 ***Untitled (No. 1)**, 2002*
Oil on canvas, 150 x 385 cm; Öl auf Leinwand, 150 x 385 cm
《无题》(No. 1), 2002年, 布面油画, 150 x 385 cm

7 ***Untitled (No. 4)**, 1999*
Oil on canvas, 140 x 180 cm; Öl auf Leinwand, 140 x 180 cm
《无题》(No. 4), 1999年, 布面油画, 140 x 180 cm

8 ***Untitled (Portrait No. 1)**, 2001*
Oil on canvas, 150 x 300 cm; Öl auf Leinwand, 150 x 300 cm
《无题》(No. 1), 2001年, 布面油画, 150 x 300 cm

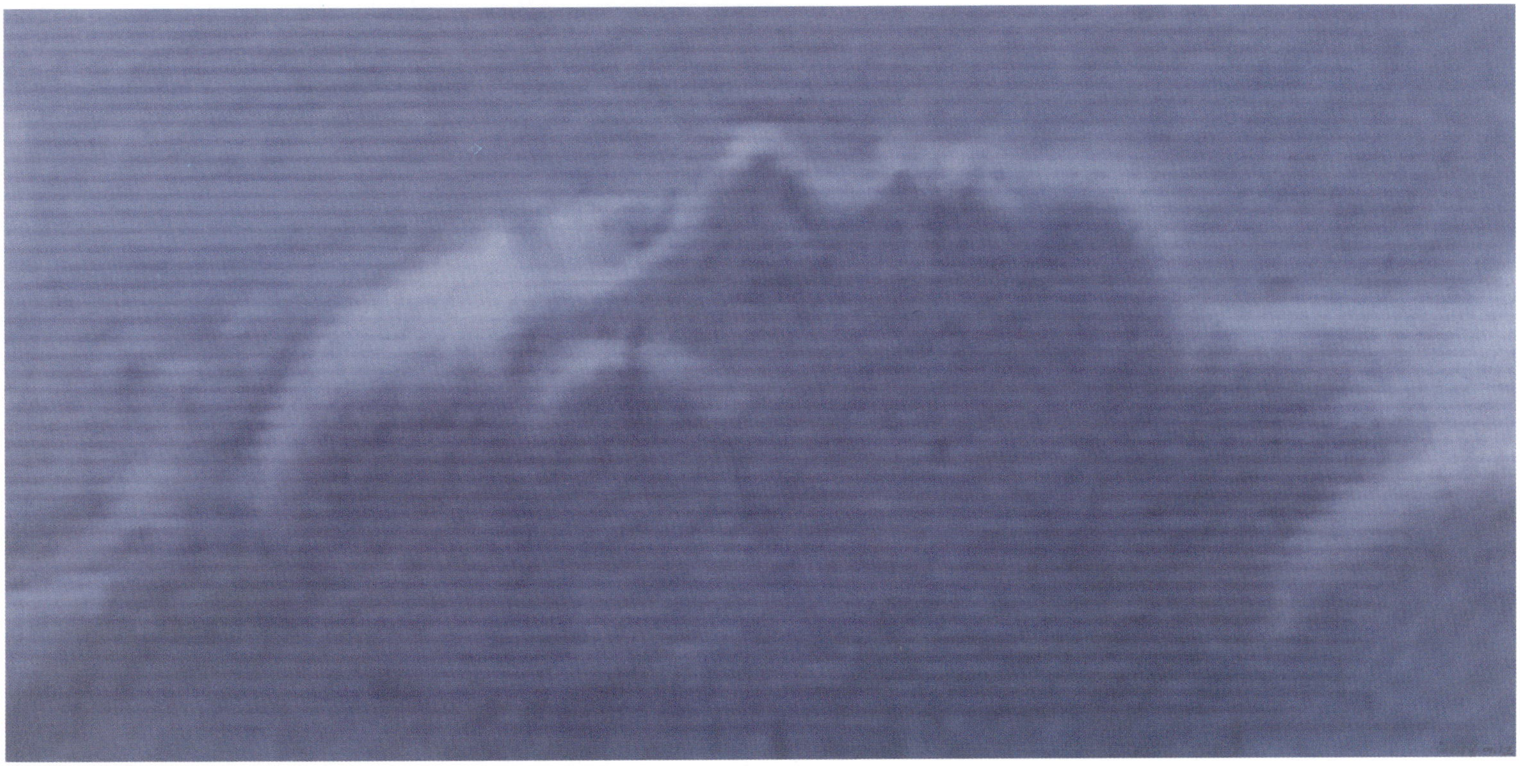

8

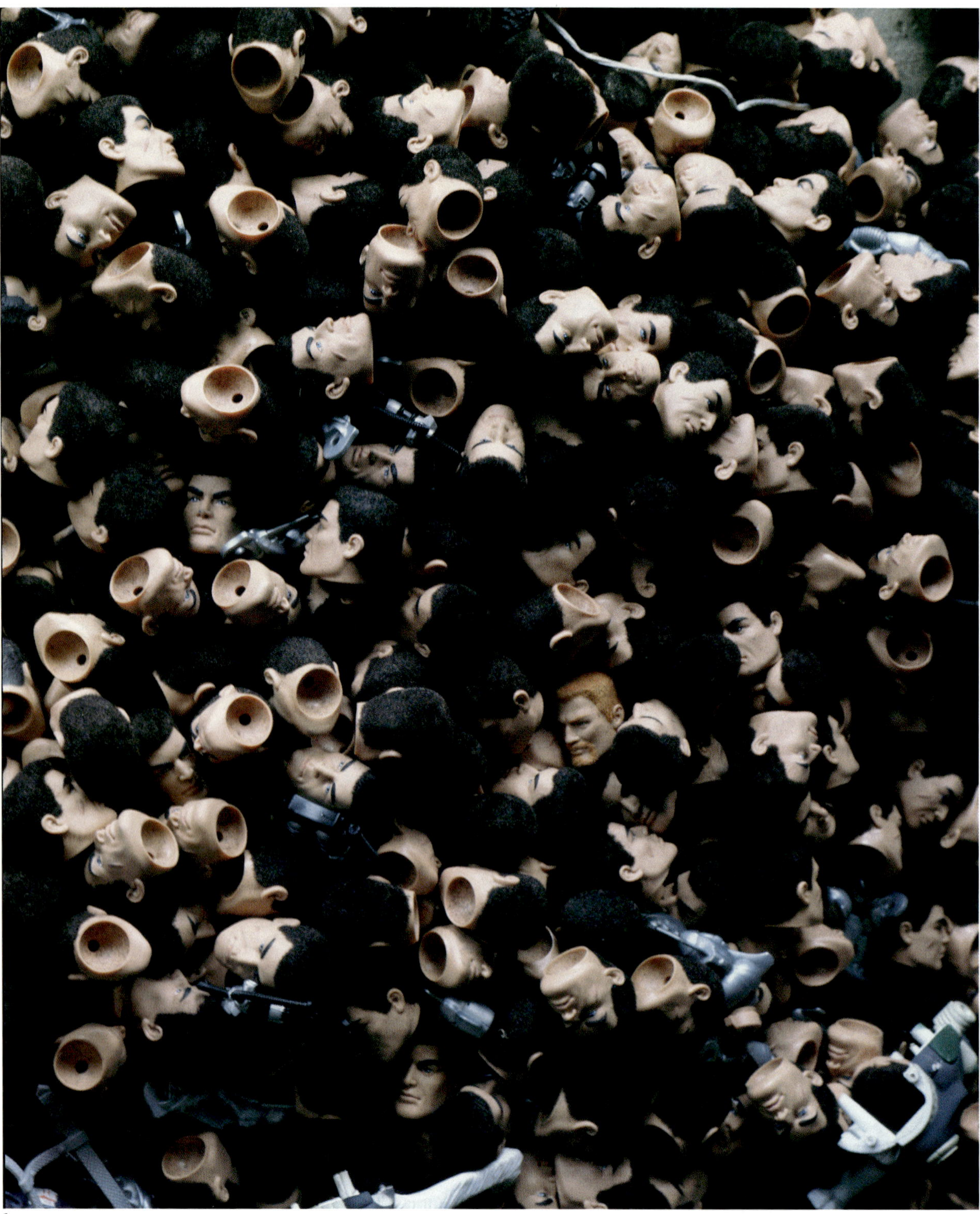

1

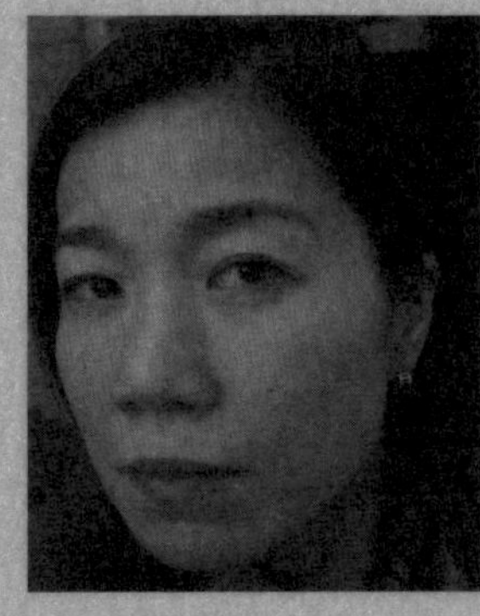

"It is not about making a photo, the matter is what you want to tell through an image. I am very interested in the relationship between reality and fiction, which plays an important role in my work."

„Es geht nicht darum, ein Foto zu machen, die Frage ist vielmehr, was man mit einem Bild sagen will. Ich interessiere mich sehr für die Beziehung zwischen Realität und Fiktion, sie spielt eine wichtige Rolle in meiner Arbeit."

"这不是照片拍摄的事情，而在于通过　　图片你要传达的含义。我对现实和虚构两者之间的关系很感兴趣，这种喜好在我的作品中起着重要作用。"

Born in 1967 in Xian, China. Lives and works in Beijing
Geboren 1967 in Xian, China. Lebt und arbeitet in Peking
1967年出生于宗过陕西省西安市，现在北京居住工作

***Selected exhibitions* / Ausgewählte Ausstellungen / 所选展览**

2002 "Dislocation", 2nd Ping Yao International Photo Festival, Shanxi, China
2004–07 "Between Past and Future, New Photography and Video from China", International Center of Photography, New York, NY, USA (travelling exhibition)
2005 "Die Chinesen: Fotografie und Video aus China", Kunstmuseum Wolfsburg, Wolfsburg, Germany
2006 "totalstadt. beijing case", ZKM (Center for Art and Media), Karlsruhe, Germany
"China Contemporary", Museum Boijmans Van Beuningen, Rotterdam, The Netherlands

2002年 《错位》第二届平窑国际摄影节　山西　中国
2004–07年 《过去与未来之间—中国新影像展》国际摄影中心 纽约 美国（巡回展）
2005年 《中国人：中国摄影与录像展》沃尔斯堡艺术馆　沃尔斯堡，德国
2006年 《整体城市：北京现场》艺术与媒体中心　卡尔斯鲁厄, 德国
《中国当代》波伊曼・凡・布宁根博物馆，鹿特丹，荷兰

***Selected publications* / Ausgewählte Publikationen / 所选著作**

Christian Orsatelli: "Xing Danwen: Urban Fiction", in: "Nouveaux Regards Photographie", Paris 2004
Shinyi Yang: "Emotion & Reason", in: Catalogue of 2004 Biennale of Sydney, Sydney 2004
Gu Zheng: "Develop the Reality of China: On Xing Danwen's Artistic Practice", in: "Chinese Art", Beijing 2005

Orsatelli, Christian（著）:《邢丹文：都市演绎》于《新看法摄影》巴黎2004年
Shinyi Yang（著）:《情感和原因》展册《绝缘/复制》澳大利亚2004年
Gu Zheng（著）:《开发中国的现实:邢丹文的艺术性的实践》于《中国艺术》北京2005年

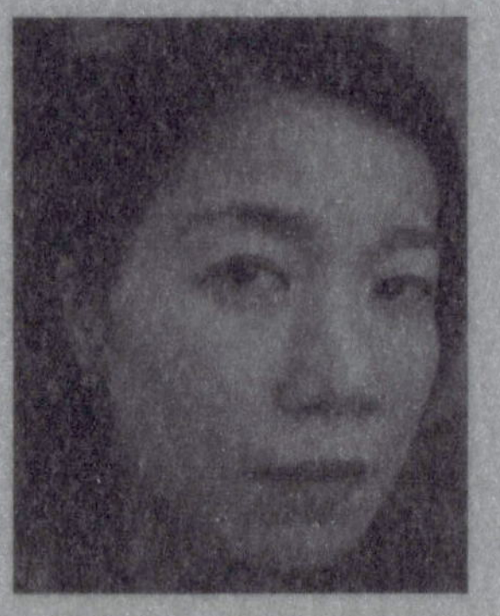

"It is not about making a photo, the matter is what you want to tell through an image. I am very interested in the relationship between reality and fiction, which plays an important role in my work."

„Es geht nicht darum, ein Foto zu machen, die Frage ist vielmehr, was man mit einem Bild sagen will. Ich interessiere mich sehr für die Beziehung zwischen Realität und Fiktion, sie spielt eine wichtige Rolle in meiner Arbeit."

"这不是照片拍摄的事情，而在于通过　图片你要传达的含义。我对现实和虚构两者之间的关系很感兴趣，这种喜好在我的作品中起着重要作用。"

Born in 1967 in Xian, China. Lives and works in Beijing
Geboren 1967 in Xian, China. Lebt und arbeitet in Peking
1967年出生于宗过陕西省西安市，现在北京居住工作

Selected exhibitions / Ausgewählte Ausstellungen / 所选展览

2002 "Dislocation", 2nd Ping Yao International Photo Festival, Shanxi, China
2004-07 "Between Past and Future. New Photography and Video from China", International Center of Photography, New York, NY, USA (travelling exhibition)
2005 "Die Chinesen: Fotografie und Video aus China", Kunstmuseum Wolfsburg, Wolfsburg, Germany
2006 "totalstadt. beijing case", ZKM (Center for Art and Media), Karlsruhe, Germany
"China Contemporary", Museum Boijmans Van Beuningen, Rotterdam, The Netherlands

2002年 《错位》第二届平遥国际摄影节 山西 中国
2004-07年 《过去与未来之间—中国新影像展》国际摄影中心 纽约 美国（巡回展）
2005年 《中国人：中国摄影与录像展》沃尔斯堡艺术馆 沃尔斯堡，德国
2006年 《整体城市：北京现场》艺术与媒体中心 卡尔斯鲁厄，德国
《中国当代》波伊曼·凡·布宁根博物馆，鹿特丹，荷兰

Selected publications / Ausgewählte Publikationen / 所选著作

Christian Orsatelli: "Xing Danwen: Urban Fiction", in: "Nouveaux Regards Photographie", Paris 2004
Shinyi Yang: "Emotion & Reason", in: Catalogue of 2004 Biennale of Sydney, Sydney 2004
Gu Zheng: "Develop the Reality of China: On Xing Danwen's Artistic Practice", in: "Chinese Art", Beijing 2005

Orsatelli, Christian（著）：《邢丹文：都市演绎》于《新看法摄影》巴黎2004年
Shinyi Yang（著）：《情感和原因》展册《绝缘/复制》澳大利亚2004年
Gu Zheng（著）：《开发中国的现实：邢丹文的艺术性的实践》于《中国艺术》北京2005年

XING DANWEN 邢丹文

[ɕiŋ tanwən]

Chinese history of art after 1989 is a history of exile. Many artists left China after the Tian'anmen incident and the sudden end of democracy movement, and went to Japan or to western countries. However, Xing Danwen stayed after graduating from her studies of painting in Beijing where she undertook a dialogue between artists and actuality of daily political events due to her photography. Photography is the medium referring directly to a situation and preserving it from visual oblivion. Photography lacks the time dimension of narrating videos, however, it is a strongly focussed and concise snapshot.

It is this quality distinguishing Xing's photos of the 1990s, when photography became a partner of concerns and works of many Chinese artists. Xing took her camera, whenever she could. But she was less interested in documentation than in portraying and enhancing the source of vitality from isolation being the commonness of her generation. Her photos of this period have the human body and its sexuality, memory, globalisation, consumption and lust as the main subject. She also created independent series like "Born With Cultural Revolution" (1995) depicting a naked woman below a portrait of Mao.

Contemporary witness and search for identity form "A Personal Diary of Chinese Avant-Garde Art in the 1990s", containing sober and realistic photographs of Shanghai's or Beijing's culture scene and the artists East Village (1993/94) in Beijing. Xing, more or less related to the underground movement, documented the subversively acting generation, many of the present stars of this art scene emerged thereof. At the end of the 1990s when the plant area 798 Dashanzi in Beijing's northeast had become the fashionable artists' and gallery refuge, the former underground movement could be established in the art world. Xing's photographs preserved an important part of the prehistory of the phenomenon.

Her current series "Urban Fiction" (since 2004) is dedicated to social conditions in modern day China, where millions of people are living in the new apartments of the numerous

Die chinesische Kunstgeschichte nach 1989 ist auch eine Geschichte des Exils. Viele Künstler verließen nach den Ereignissen auf dem Platz des Himmlischen Friedens und dem jähen Ende des Demokratisierungsprozesses ihre Heimat und flüchteten nach Japan oder in den Westen. Xing Danwen jedoch blieb nach ihrem Studium der Malerei in Peking, wo sie einen fotografischen Dialog zwischen Künstlern und tagespolitischer Aktualität aufnahm. Die Fotografie ist das Medium, das direkt auf eine Situation Bezug nimmt und sie vor dem visuellen Vergessen bewahrt. Ihr fehlt zwar die Zeitdimension des erzählerischen Videos, dafür stellt sie eine stark fokussierte prägnante Momentaufnahme dar.

Gerade diese Qualität zeichnet Xings Aufnahmen aus den 1990er Jahren aus, als sie zur Fürsprecherin der Anliegen und Arbeiten vieler chinesischer Künstler wurde. Xing griff zur Kamera, wann immer sie konnte. Dabei war sie weniger daran interessiert zu dokumentieren, als zu porträtieren und das Verbindende ihrer Generation hervorzuheben: Kraft aus der Isolation zu beziehen. Ihre Aufnahmen aus dieser Zeit behandeln den menschlichen Körper und seine Sexualität, Erinnerung, Globalisierung, Konsum, Begehren. Es entstanden auch freie Arbeiten wie „Born With Cultural Revolution" (1995), das eine nackte Frau unter einem Mao-Porträt zeigt.

Zeitzeugenschaft und Identitätssuche prägen „A Personal Diary of Chinese Avant-Garde Art in the 1990s", illusionslose Aufnahmen aus Shanghais oder Pekings Kulturszene und dem bekannten Künstlerdorf der Hauptstadt, dem East Village (1993/94). Selbst tendenziell eher dem Untergrund zugehörig, dokumentierte Xing Danwen diese subkulturell agierende Generation, aus der viele der heutigen Stars der chinesischen Kunstszene hervorgingen. Erst Ende der 1990er Jahre, als das Fabrikareal 798 Dashanzi in Pekings Nordosten zum neuen angesagten Künstler- und Galerienviertel mutierte, etablierte sich die Subkultur allmählich auch in der anerkannten Hochkultur. Xings Fotografien halten einen wichtigen Teil der Vorgeschichte dieses Phänomens fest.

1989年后的中国艺术史是流放的历史。在天安门事件和民主运动地突然终结，众多艺术家离开中国，移居日本或是西方国家。然而，邢丹文在从油画专业毕业后却留在北京，在此通过她的摄影承担着艺术家同日常政治事件的对话的义务。摄影是邢丹文直接关注局势的媒介，以防在时间中消逝的毫无踪迹。虽然摄影没有记录录像的时间维，却有很强的聚焦和简洁的印象感。

90年代在那时许多中国艺术家利用摄影创作 而她照片的品质让邢丹文声名鹊起。邢丹文只要有时间，就会拿起相机拍摄。与文件记录相比，她把更多的精力用于描绘和增强原物的活力上，而以消除由于她那一代的共性所造成的隔绝。她这一时期的照片以人体和性，记忆，全球化，消费和欲望为主题。她也创作了一些独立系列作品，如：《生于文革》描写了毛泽东肖像下的一个裸体女人。

对当代的见证和自我探索，是《20世纪90年代中国前卫艺术的个人日记》的主题，书中收录了北京上海艺术界和北京东村（1993-1994年）艺术家的一些照片，这些作品冷静而现实。对于多多少少有些地下运动性质的艺术活动，邢丹文记录了这逆反一代，当今艺术界许多明星都出现其中。在90年代末期北京东北部的798成为流行艺术家和画廊的避难地，在这个艺术天堂中，以前的地下运动又得以立足。邢丹文的照片为地下运动保存了一部分重要资料。她现在正在进行的系列《都市演绎》，以记录当今中国的社会状况为主题：数以百万的中国人正专注于在无数的楼盘中购得自己的新的公寓。这些迁移的市民在迅速耸立起的无名卫星城中，得到的不仅是舒适和清洁还有孤独。邢通过废弃的楼盘模型来演示这种社会土地的浪费，开发商试图用这种模型来吸引潜在客户，每个远景客户（照片中是本人）都有机会把自己处身与这虚拟的世界中。从这些照片可以感受一种忧郁的孤独感，这产生于高速的城市化进程。

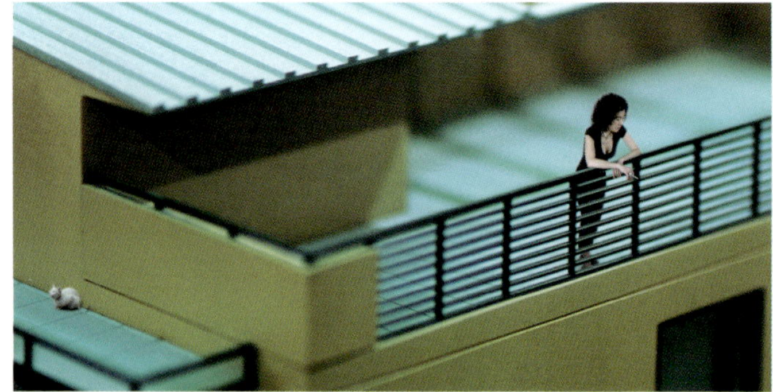

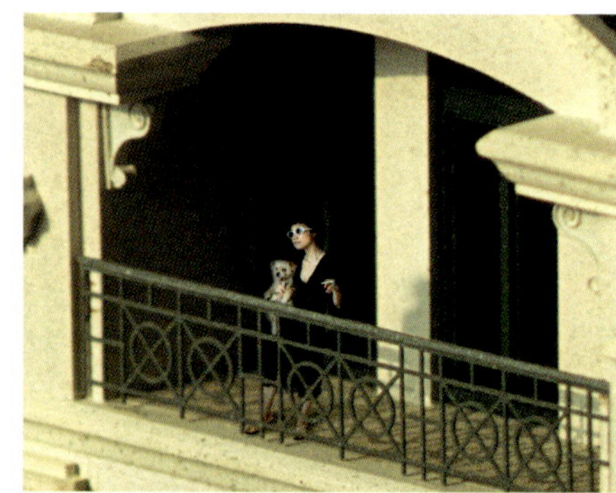

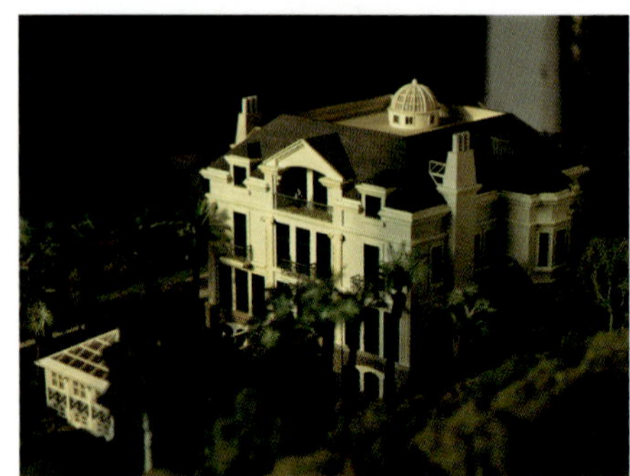

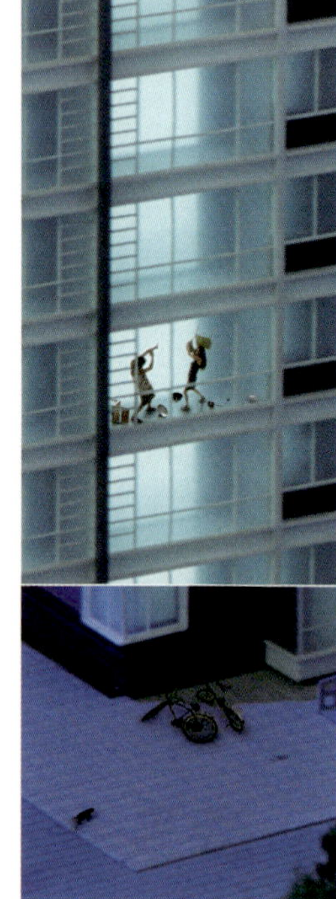

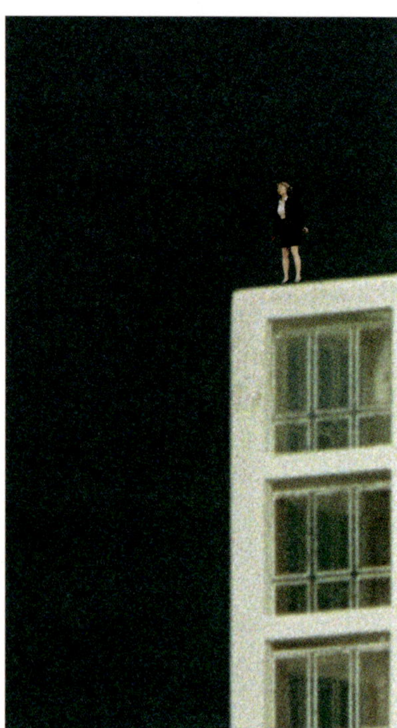

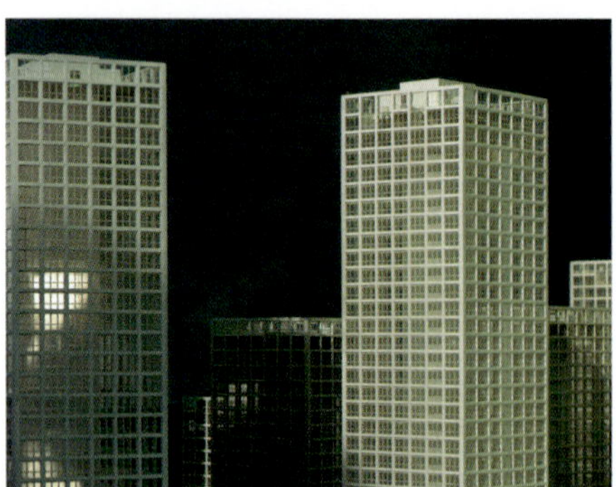

2

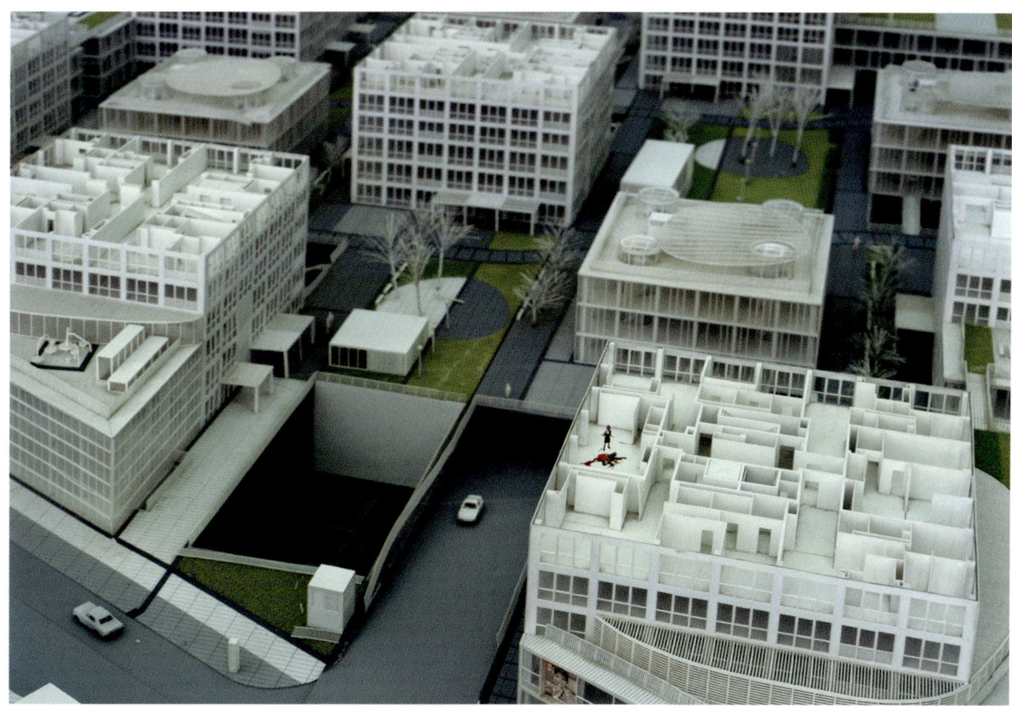

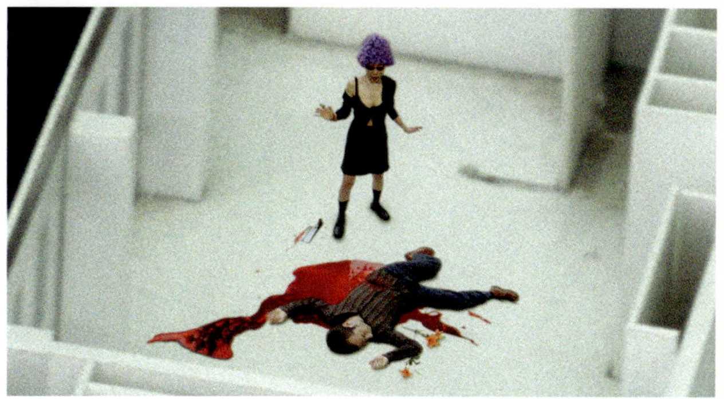

3

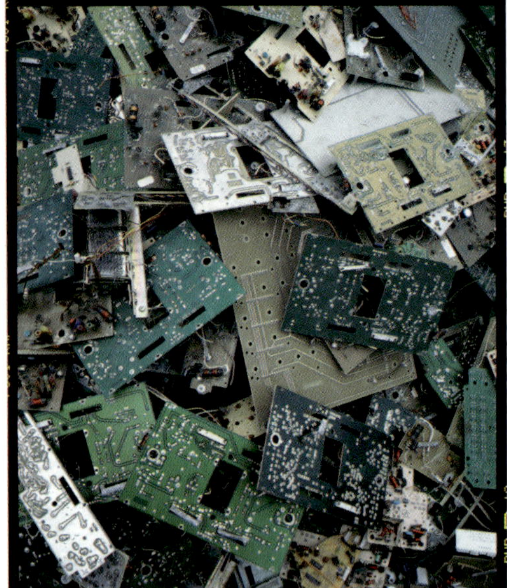

4

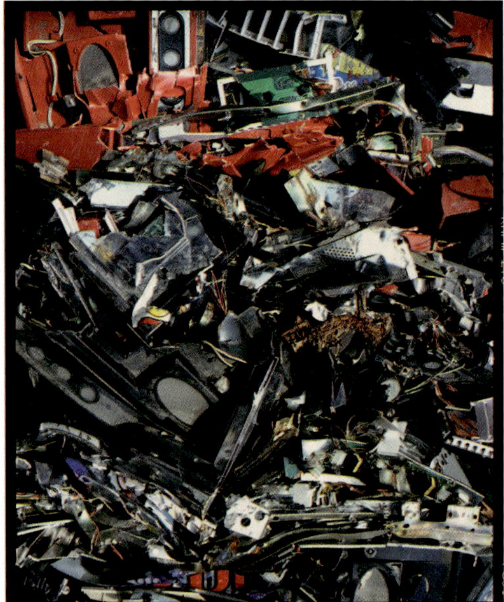

5

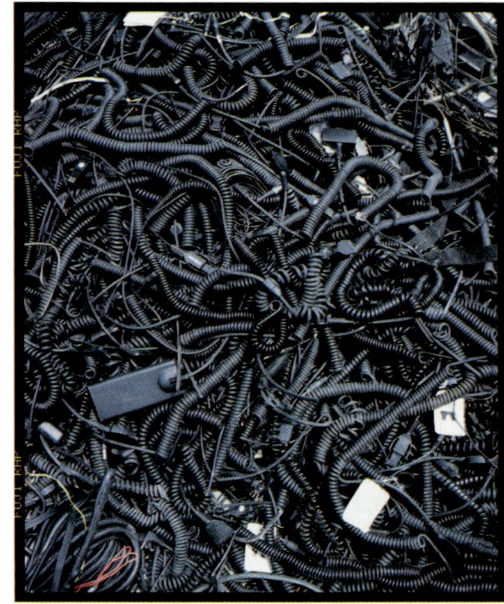

real-estate projects. The transferred citizen not only gets comfort and hygiene in the faceless rapidly erected satellite towns but loneliness. Xing Danwen communicates this social waste land via deserted models of apartments, investment companies try to attract potential customers with – every prospective buyer (the artist herself on the photographs) has the opportunity to project himself into this virtual world. The photographs show the melancholy, isolation being the companionship of the dramatic high speed urbanisation.

Xing's photographs of the series "disCONNECTION" (2002/03) are similar in kind, showing electronic and computer waste and the chaotic accumulation thereof creating an abstract landscape picture full of poison, heavy metal, plastics and rubber. These often suppressed "side products" are the reverse of communication, data exchange and virtual dream worlds. Production and recycling of these real and cultural toxic goods take place in most cases in Asia, whereas the trade goods themselves are mainly exported to western countries.

In Guangdong Xing took photographs of the scrap (even that of the toy industry) being adjacent to these degrading work places without showing the working people themselves. The ambivalences of the conflict between rich and poor, the dark sides of globalisation, and the destructive idea of progress hit millions of losers in those poorer countries, without tangling the mighty national economics expanding their supremacy at the expense of the developing countries. Xing Danwen manages to describe these immense problems in a metaphoric way – reason for hope: China benefits from the globalisation but on the other hand knows about the dark side thereof quite well.

Ihre aktuelle Serie „Urban Fiction" (seit 2004) behandelt die soziale Situation im Land, wo Millionen Menschen ihr Heil in den neuen Apartments der unzähligen Real-Estate-Projekte suchen. In den gesichtslosen, aus dem Boden gestampften Trabantenstädten findet der umgesiedelte Städter zwar Hygiene und Komfort, aber eben auch Einsamkeit. Xing Danwen vermittelt diese soziale Ödnis über die menschenleeren Wohnungsmodelle, mit denen die Investmentfirmen potenzielle Käufer locken – jeder Interessent (in den Fotos ist es die Künstlerin selbst) kann sich in diese virtuelle Welt hinein projizieren. Die Fotos zeigen die traurige Isolation, die mit der dramatischen Turbo-Urbanisierung einhergeht.

Ähnlich angelegt sind Xings Aufnahmen der Serie „disCONNECTION" (2002/03), die Elektronik- und Computerabfälle zeigen, aus deren chaotischen Anhäufungen ein abstraktes Landschaftsbild voller Gifte, Schwermetalle, Kunststoffe, Gummi entsteht. Diese meist ausgeblendeten „Nebenprodukte" bilden die Kehrseite von Kommunikation, Datenaustausch und virtuellen Wunschwelten. Herstellung und Recycling dieser real und kulturell toxischen Güter finden meist in Asien statt, die Ware selbst geht vorrangig in die westliche Welt. Xing fotografierte in Guangdong neben den menschenunwürdigen Arbeitsplätzen den Schrott (auch der Spielzeugindustrie), ohne den arbeitenden Menschen zu zeigen. Die Ambivalenzen des Konflikts zwischen Arm und Reich, die Schattenseiten der Globalisierung und einer destruktiven Idee von Fortschritt treffen nicht die machtvollen Volkswirtschaften, die ihre Vormachtstellung auf dem Rücken der Entwicklungsländer ausbauen, sondern nur die Millionen von Verlierern in den ärmeren Ländern. Xing Danwen gelingt es, diese immensen Probleme auf metaphorische Weise darzustellen – ein Grund zur Hoffnung: Denn so sehr China von der Globalisierung profitiert, man erkennt dort auch deren Schattenseiten.

邢丹文的系列照片《绝缘》与上述相似，展示电子和电脑污染的混乱积累，而形成的一派充斥着毒物、重金属、塑料和橡胶的抽象景观。这些常常被抑制的副产品与通讯、数据交换、能源消费、虚拟世界相反。这些有害的物质和文化产品一般在亚洲地区生产和循环，然而这些产品却出口到西方国家。在广东，她在靠近降解工作间拍摄了一些废料（即使那是在玩具工业），照片中没有出现正在工作的人们。富裕与贫穷、全球化的负面性、发展过程的破坏性等冲突的矛盾心理打击着更加贫穷国家的落魄者，而没有力量同西方强国抗争，虽然他们正在向发展中国家扩张邢设法用一种隐喻的手法描述这些无限的困境-希望的理由：中国将会从全球化中受益，另一方面中国对全球化的地负面作用非常了解。

Gregor Jansen

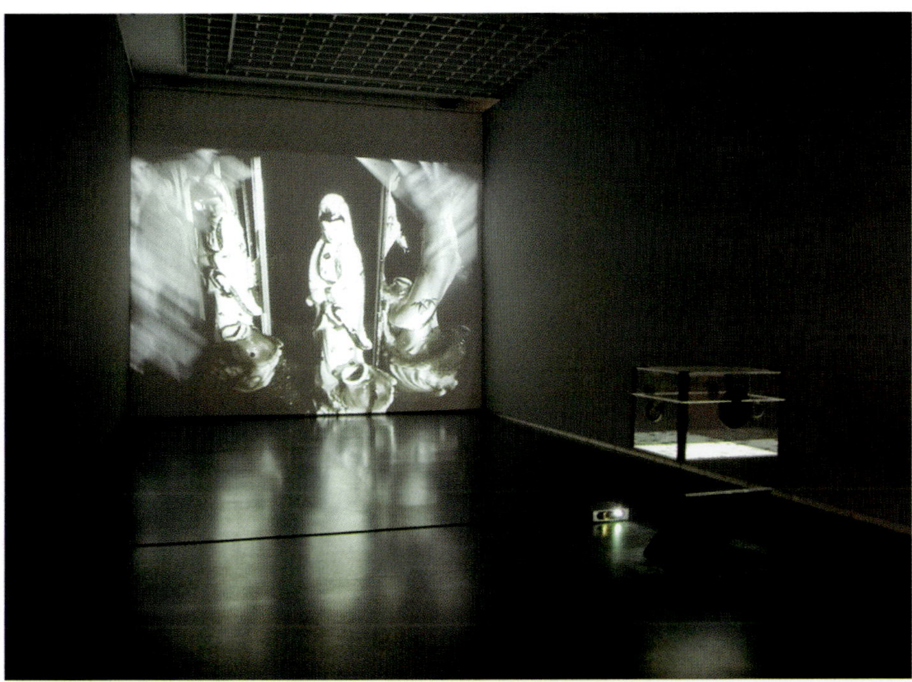

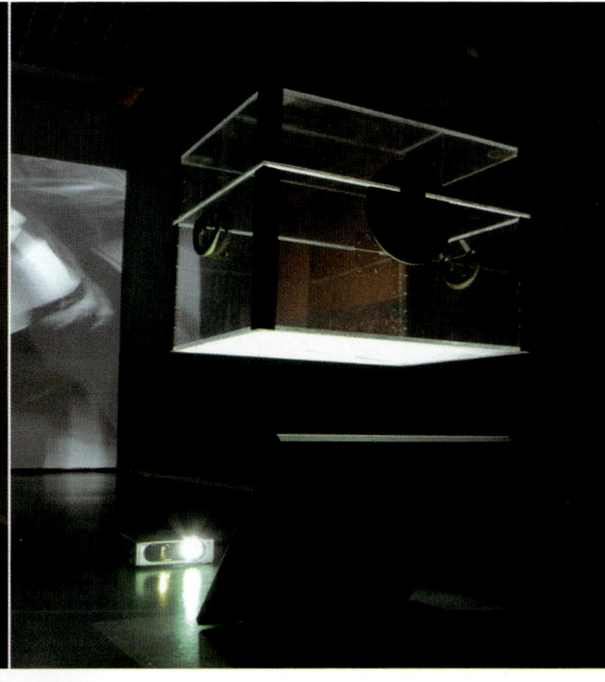

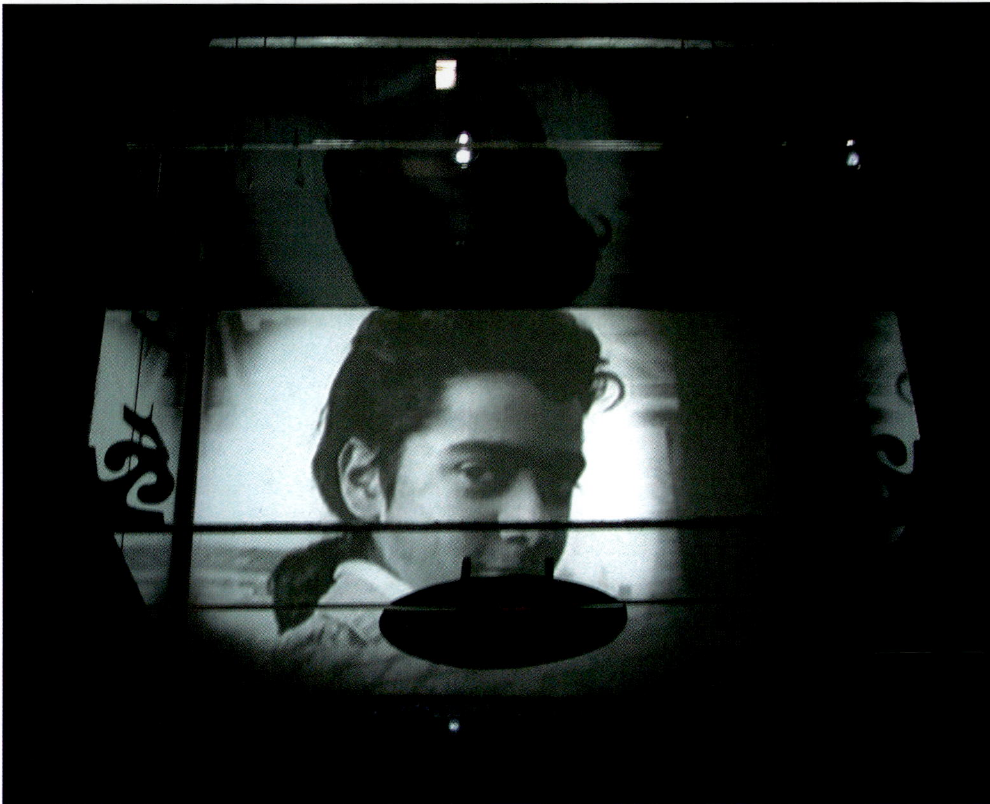

6

1 ***Duplication, image 2****, 2003*
C-print, 148 x 120 cm
C-print, 148 x 120 cm
《复制 图 2》2003年, C-印刷, 148 x 120 cm

2 ***Urban Fiction****, since 2004*
C-prints, various dimensions
C-prints, verschiedene Maße
《都市演绎》自 2004年起, 印刷

3 ***disCONNECTION, image B3****, 2002/03*
C-print, 148 x 120 cm
C-print, 148 x 120 cm
《绝缘, 图像 B3》2002/03年, C-印刷, 148 x 120 cm

4 ***disCONNECTION, image D4****, 2002/03*
C-print, 148 x 120 cm
C-print, 148 x 120 cm
《绝缘, 图像 D4》2002/03年, C-印刷, 148 x 120 cm

5 ***disCONNECTION, image A7****, 2002/03*
C-print, 148 x 120 cm
C-print, 148 x 120 cm
《绝缘, 图像 A7》2002/03年, C-印刷, 148 x 120 cm

6 ***Sleep Walking****, 2001*
Installation views, "Urban Reality", Museum Boijmans Van Beuningen, Rotterdam
Installationsansichten, „Urban Reality", Museum Boijmans Van Beuningen, Rotterdam
《梦游》2001年, 装置现场图, 《都市现实》Boijmans Van Beuningen 博物馆, 鹿特丹

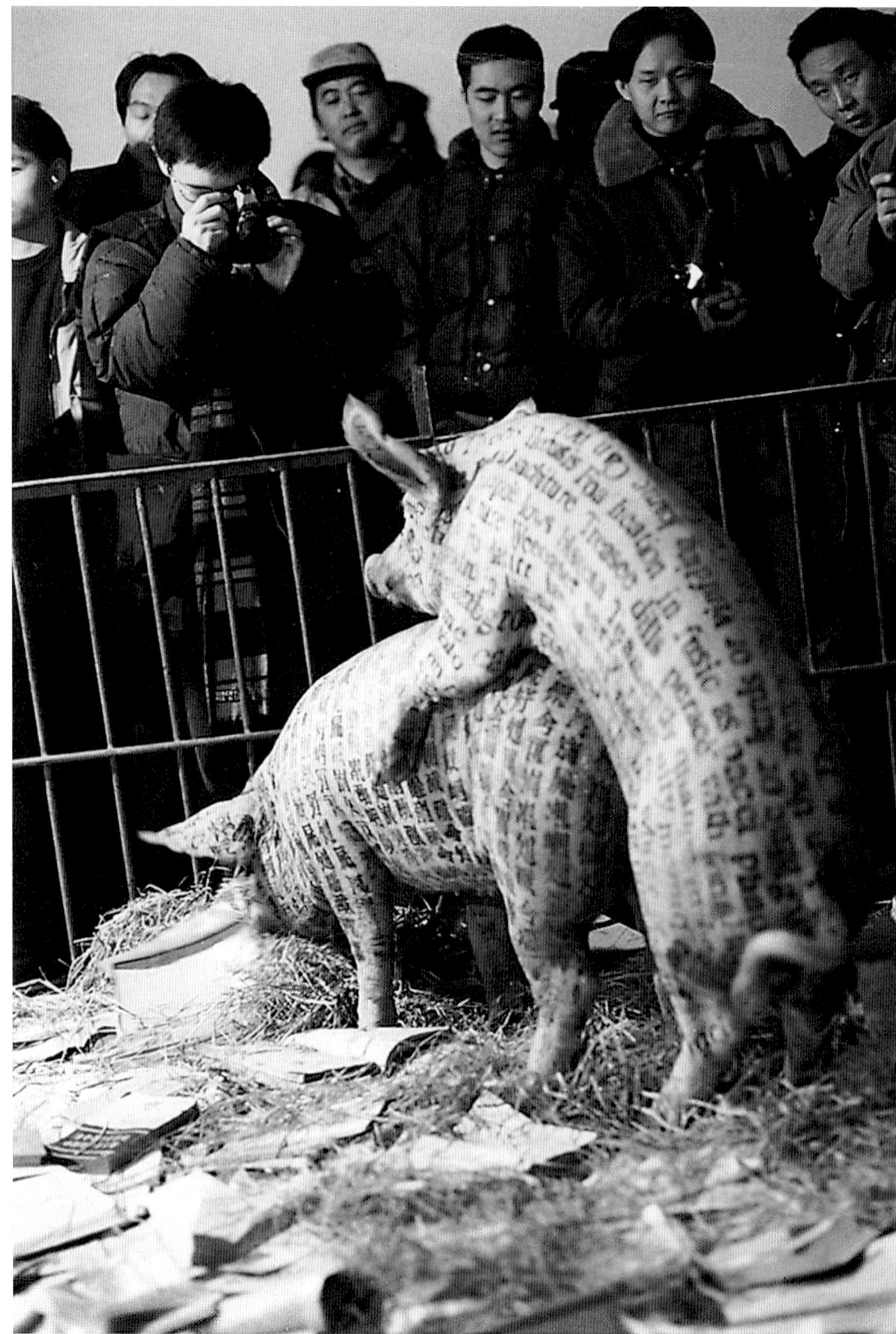

1

"My characters are not like an easily usable dictionary, but more like a virus in a computer, as they initiate a function in the human brain."

„Meine Schriftzeichen ähneln weniger einem handlichen Wörterbuch als einem Virus im Computer, da sie eine bestimmte Funktion im menschlichen Gehirn auslösen."

"我的'文字'不是一个好用的字库，而更象电脑中的病毒，却在人脑中起着作用。"

Born in 1955 in Chongqing, China. Lives and works in New York, NY, USA
Geboren 1955 in Chongqing, China. Lebt und arbeitet in New York, NY, USA
1955年出生于中国重庆市。现生活工作于纽约，美国

***Selected exhibitions* / Ausgewählte Ausstellungen / 所选展览**

1999 "Global Conceptualism: Points of Origin", Queens Museum of Art, New York, NY, USA
2001 "Free Exchange", Victoria & Albert Museum, London, UK
2005 "On the Edge", Indianapolis Museum of Art, Indianapolis, IN, USA
2006 Gwangju Biennial, Gwangju, Korea
Singapore Biennial, Singapore, Singapore
2007 "Das abc der Bilder", Pergamonmuseum, Berlin, Germany
"China Now", Sammlung Essl, Klosterneuburg, Austria

1999年 《全球性概念论:起源的问题》Queens艺术馆, 纽约
2001年 《自由交易》维多利亚和阿尔伯特博物馆，伦敦
2005年 《在边缘》印第安纳波利斯艺术馆，印第安纳波利斯
2006年 光洲双年展 光洲 韩国
新加坡双年展 新加坡城 新加坡
2007年 《Das abc der Bilder》佩加蒙博物馆, 柏林 德国
《今日中国》Sammlung Essl 美术博物馆, 克罗斯特纽堡, 奥地利

***Selected publications* / Ausgewählte Publikationen / 所选著作**

Britta Erickson: "The Art of Xu Bing: Words Without Meaning, Meaning Without Words", Washington D. C. 2001
Uta Rahman-Steinert et al.: "Xu Bing in Berlin: Sprachräume", Berlin 2004
Pablo J. Rico: "Xu Bing: El Pozo de la Verdad: The Well of Truth", Valencia 2004
Jerome Silbergeld, Dora C. Y. Ching: "Persistance/Transformation: Text as Image in the Art of Xu Bing", Princeton 2006

Erickson, Britta(著):《徐冰的艺术・无意义的文字及文字的无意义》美国史密森学会，萨克勒美术馆与华盛顿大学出版社 2001年
Rahman-Steinert, Uta/et al.(著)：《徐冰在柏林：语言》展览目录，柏林东亚美术馆, 2004年
Rico, Pablo J.(著)：《徐冰:真实之井》展览目录, 西班牙, 瓦蓝萨美术馆, 2004年
Silbergeld, Jerome/Ching, Dora C. Y.(著)：《持续性/转型－以文字为图像:徐冰的艺术》普林斯顿大学出版社, 2006年

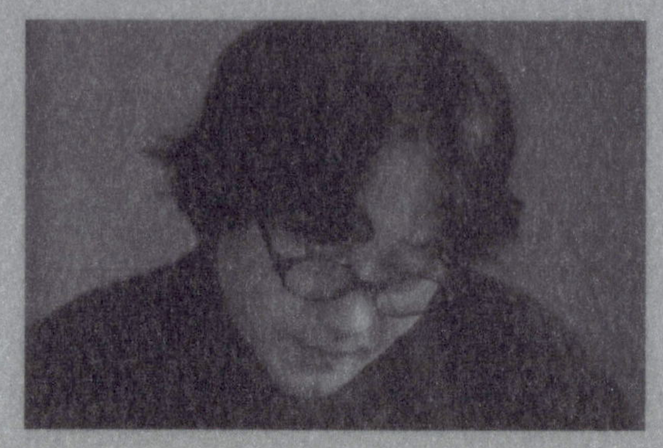

"My characters are not like an easily usable dictionary, but more like a virus in a computer, as they initiate a function in the human brain."

„Meine Schriftzeichen ähneln weniger einem handlichen Wörterbuch als einem Virus im Computer, da sie eine bestimmte Funktion im menschlichen Gehirn auslösen."

"我的'文字'不是一个好用的字库，而更象电脑中的病毒，却在人脑中起着作用。"

Born in 1955 in Chongqing, China. Lives and works in New York, NY, USA
Geboren 1955 in Chongqing, China. Lebt und arbeitet in New York, NY, USA
1955年出生于中国重庆市。现生活工作于纽约，美国

Selected exhibitions / Ausgewählte Ausstellungen / 所选展览

1999 "Global Conceptualism: Points of Origin", Queens Museum of Art, New York, NY, USA
2001 "Free Exchange", Victoria & Albert Museum, London, UK
2005 "On the Edge", Indianapolis Museum of Art, Indianapolis, IN, USA
2006 Gwangju Biennial, Gwangju, Korea
Singapore Biennial, Singapore, Singapore
2007 "Das abc der Bilder", Pergamonmuseum, Berlin, Germany
"China Now", Sammlung Essl, Klosterneuburg, Austria

1999年 《全球性概念论：起源的问题》Queens艺术馆，纽约
2001年 《自由交易》维多利亚和阿尔伯特博物馆，伦敦
2005年 《在边缘》印第安纳波利斯艺术馆，印第安纳波利斯
2006年 光州双年展 光州 韩国
新加坡双年展 新加坡城 新加坡
2007年 《Das abc der Bilder》佩加蒙博物馆，柏林 德国
《今日中国》Sammlung Essl 美术博物馆，克罗斯特纽堡，奥地利

Selected publications / Ausgewählte Publikationen / 所选著作

Britta Erickson: "The Art of Xu Bing: Words Without Meaning, Meaning Without Words", Washington D.C. 2001
Uta Rahman-Steinert et al.: "Xu Bing in Berlin: Sprachräume", Berlin 2004
Pablo J. Rico: "Xu Bing: El Pozo de la Verdad: The Well of Truth", Valencia 2004
Jerome Silbergeld, Dora C. Y. Ching: "Persistance/Transformation: Text as Image in the Art of Xu Bing", Princeton 2006

Erickson, Britta（著）：《徐冰的艺术·无意义的文字及文字的无意义》美国史密森学会，萨克勒美术馆与华盛顿大学出版社 2001年
Rahman-Steinert, Uta/et al.（著）：《徐冰在柏林：语言》展览目录，柏林东亚美术馆，2004年
Rico, Pablo J.（著）：《徐冰：真实之井》展览目录，西班牙，瓦伦萨美术馆，2004年
Silbergeld, Jerome/Ching, Dora C. Y（著）：《持续性/转型－以文字为图像：徐冰的艺术》普林斯顿大学出版社，2006年

XU BING 徐冰

[ɕu piŋ]

Xu Bing, Chinese artist living in the United States, uses written signs of human civilization in his creations to use as the fundamental element the load bearing. The usual characters are borrowed, expressed and linked to their function. But through his "characters" he wants to affect peoples' thoughts to be misled, confused and obstructed. His characters wear masks, outside and inside are not one, between the lines in an ambush is hidden the picture of a camouflage. Consequently he resolves and constructs by using different media, materials and forms the standards of behaviour accumulated in human consciousness by history and culture, challenging peoples' regular systems of cognition and models of thinking. He makes fun of the mysterious, awkward, and absurd culture of script, examining the fuzzy, discriminating, and attempting links as well as the unable pitifulness to link up, giving today's people a hint of some kind of burden and vigilance in regard to culture. His representative works are "Book from the Sky" (1987–1991), "Ghost Pounding the Wall" (1990/91), "Square Chinese characters calligraphy" (1996), "Tobacco Project" (series, 2000), "Monkey fishing the moon from the water" (2001), "Where annoys the dust?" (2004), "Behind the Story" (2003), and so on.

Xu Bing's latest work "Book from the ground" (2003–2006) is a readable novel, which he compiled in several years writing down the "Features of language". The reader, no matter what kind of cultural background, as long as he is a person involved in contemporary life, may read this book. In order to coordinate this book, he has also created a "fonts" software. The user enters English sentences with the keyboard, the computer then instantly translates this kind of featured language. This may be used as a dictionary and has practical value. In case of the "Book from the Sky" nobody can read it as he declares, but using the "featured language" everybody can read and understand the "Book from the ground" whatever language he make speak. Both books have in common that whatever language you speak whatever education you have got, these books treat everybody equally. The "Book from the Sky" expresses Xu

In den Arbeiten des chinesischen Künstlers Xu Bing, der heute in den USA lebt, sind Schriftzeichen das fundamentale Element – als Zeichen für die menschliche Zivilisation überhaupt. Er setzt normale Zeichen in einen neuen funktionellen Zusammenhang und will damit das gewohnte Denken bewusst in die Irre führen, verwirren und behindern. Xus Zeichen tragen Masken, innen und außen sind bei ihnen nicht identisch, und zwischen den Zeilen lauert das Bild einer Täuschung. Und ganz konsequent löst Xu mithilfe verschiedener Medien, Materialien und Formen die Standards des menschlichen Verhaltens auf, die sich in unserem Bewusstsein durch Geschichte und Kultur verfestigt haben, und regt uns dazu an, unsere gewohnten Erkenntnissysteme und Denkmodelle zu überprüfen. Zugleich macht er sich über die mysteriöse und absurde Schriftkultur lustig, untersucht das Verschwommene, differenziert, knüpft Verbindungen und will unsere erbärmliche Unfähigkeit zu assoziieren bloßstellen. Er verlangt einfach Wachsamkeit gegenüber der eigenen (Schrift-)Kultur. Zu Xus wichtigen Werke zählen „Book from the Sky" (1987–1991), „Ghost Pounding the Wall" (1990/91), „Square Chinese characters calligraphy" (1996), „Tobacco Project" (Serie, 2000), „Monkey fishing the moon from the water" (2001), „Where annoys the dust?" (2004) und „Behind the Story" (2003).

Seine jüngste Arbeit „Book from the ground" (2003–2006) ist eine Erzählung, die er über mehrere Jahre kompilierte, wobei er nicht die Sprache selbst, sondern, wie er sagt, die „Kennzeichen der Sprache" niederschrieb. Jeder, unabhängig von seinem kulturellen Hintergrund, kann dieses Buch lesen, sofern er tatsächlich in das gegenwärtige Leben eingebunden ist. Für die Gestaltung dieser Arbeit entwickelte Xu eine spezielle Schrift-Software: Der Benutzer gibt über die Tastatur englische Sätze ein, und der Computer übersetzt sie in Xus „gekennzeichnete Sprache". Das „Book from the ground" kann also beinahe wie ein Lexikon benutzt werden. Anders verhält es sich mit dem „Book from the Sky", das niemand lesen kann. Beiden Büchern ist gemein, dass sie, ungeachtet der Erziehung und Ausbildung, die ein Mensch genossen hat, jeden als Gleichen akzeptieren. Im

徐冰是旅居美国的中国艺术家。他的创作总是试图通过承载着人类文明的文字符号作为他创作的基本元素。通常的文字是通过借意、表达及沟通来起作用。而他的"文字"却是通过误导、混淆和阻碍来影响人们的思维。这些文字戴着面具，表里不一，行文间潜藏着埋伏，象是经过了伪装。从而以不同的媒介、材料和方式，解构历史文化积淀在人的意识中的行为准则，挑战人们惯常的认知系统和思维模式，揶揄文字文化的神秘、尴尬和荒诞，验证了文字的模糊、排斥、企图沟通又无法沟通的可悲性，给予当今的人们提示出在文化上的某种负累与警觉。其代表作有《析世鉴--天书》（1987-1991年）、《鬼打墙》（1990-1991年）、《方块字书法》（1996年）、《烟草计划》系列（2000年）、《猴子捞月》（2001年）、《何处惹尘埃》（2004年）、《背后的故事》（2003年）等。

徐冰最新的作品《地书》（2006年）是一本可读的小说，它是用他几年来搜集整理出的一套"标识语言"写成的。读者不管是何种文化背景，只要他是被卷入当代生活的人，就可以读懂这本书。为配合这本书，他还制作了"字库"软件。使用者将英文句子打入键盘，电脑即刻转译成这种标识语言。这可起到字典的作用，具有实用价值。如果说《天书》是一本包括他自己在内，世上没有人能读懂的书，那么现在用这套"标识语言"，他又写了一本说什么语言的人都能读懂的《地书》。事实上，这两本书有共同之处在于不管你讲什么语言，也不管你是否受过教育，它们平等地对待世界上的每一个人。《天书》表达了徐冰对现存文字的遗憾，而这本《地书》，则表达了他一直在寻找的"普天同文"的理想。

Feng Boyi

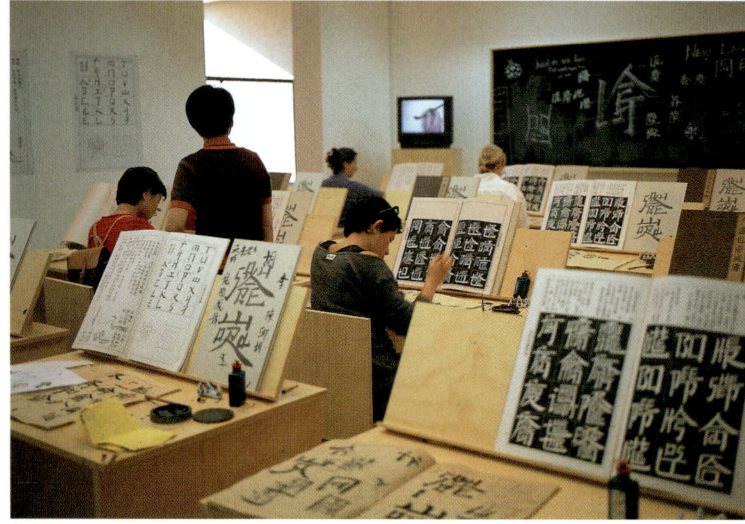

2

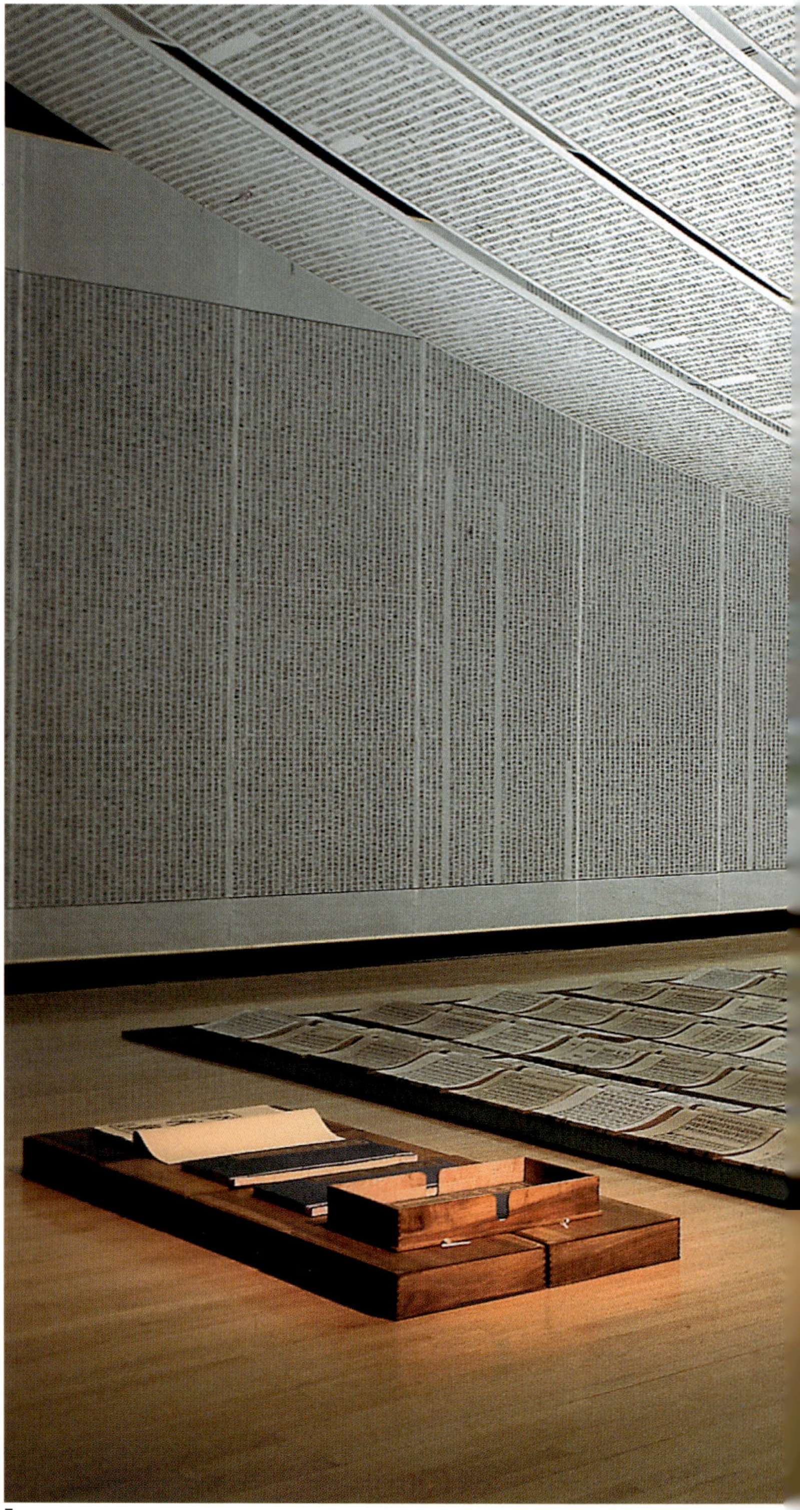

3

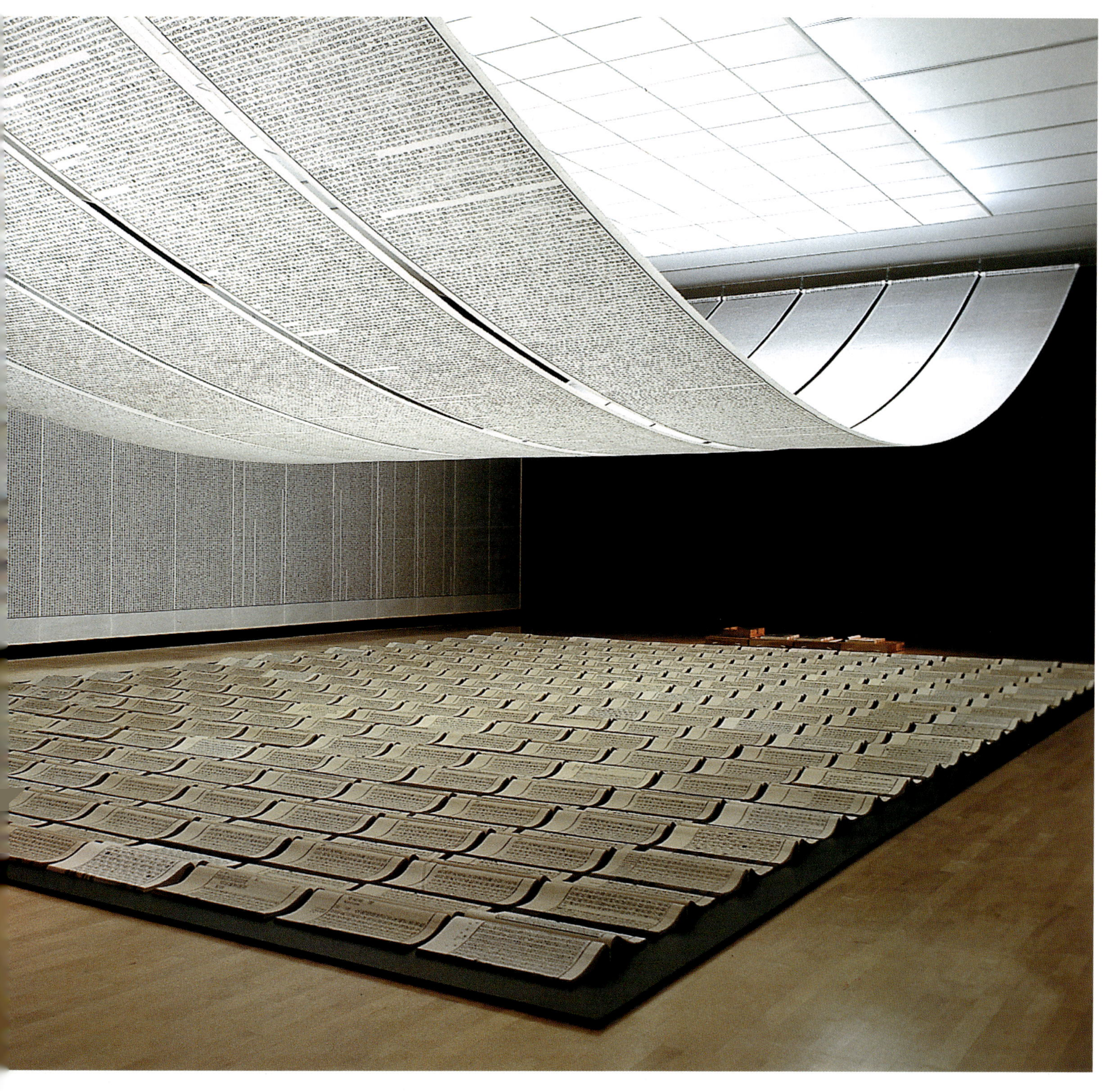

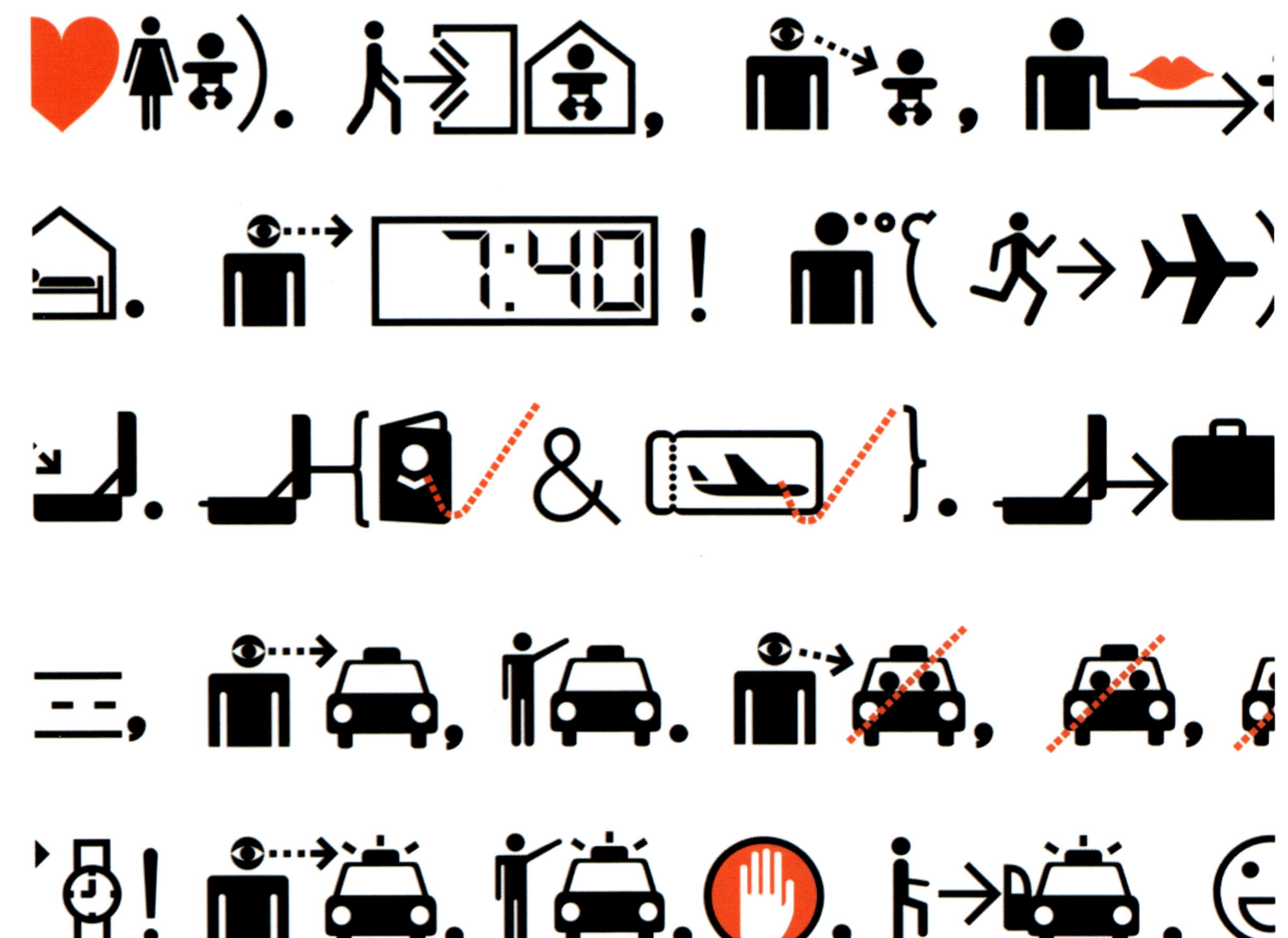

Bing's regret about the present Chinese characters and the "Book from the ground" expresses his continuing search for the ideal of "an overall applicable language".

„Book from the Sky" drückt Xu Bing sein Bedauern über den gegenwärtigen Zustand der chinesischen Schriftzeichen aus, während das „Book from the ground" seine beständige Suche nach einer „überall gültigen Sprache" dokumentiert.

5

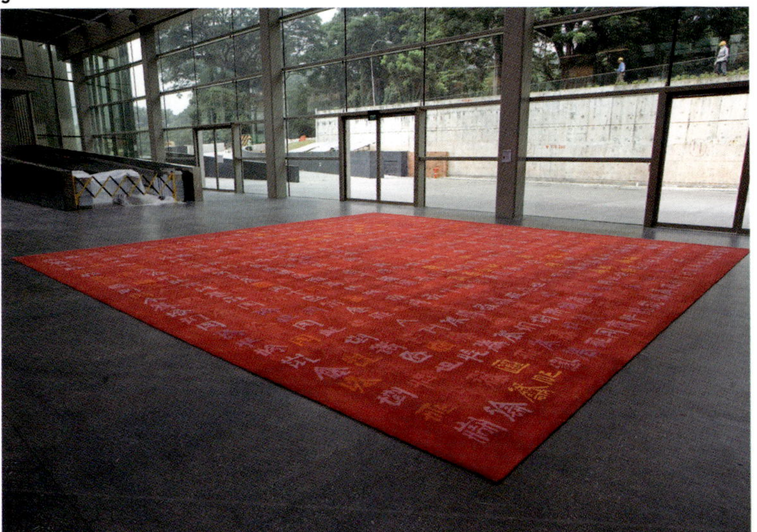

6

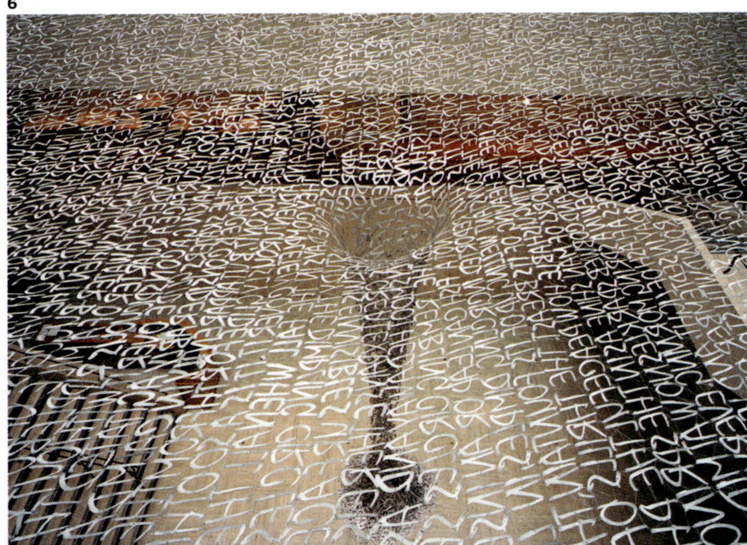

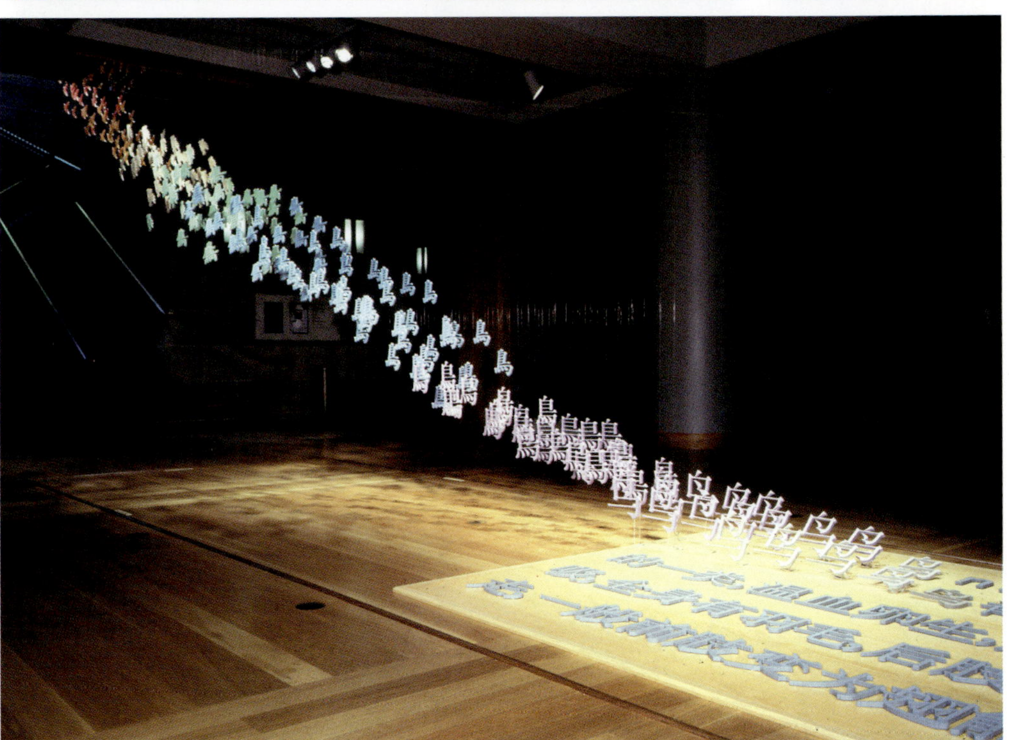

7

1 ***A Case Study of Transference****, 1993/94*
Installation with living pigs
Installation mit lebenden Schweinen
《一个转换的案例》1993/94年, 活猪装置

2 ***Square Word Calligraphy Classroom****, 1994*
Mixed media installation
Mixed-media-Installation
《方块字书法教室》1994年，混合材料装置

3 ***Book from the Sky****, 1987–1991*
Mixed media installation
Mixed-media-Installation
《天书》1987–1991年，混合材料装置

4 ***Book from the ground****, 2003–2006*
31 x 22.5 cm (detail: double spread)
31 x 22,5 cm (Detail: Doppelseite)
《地书》2003–2006年, 31 x 22.5 cm（具体:双面）

5–7 ***The Living Word****, 2001*
Installation views
Installationsansichten
《鸟飞了》2001年, -装置实景

1

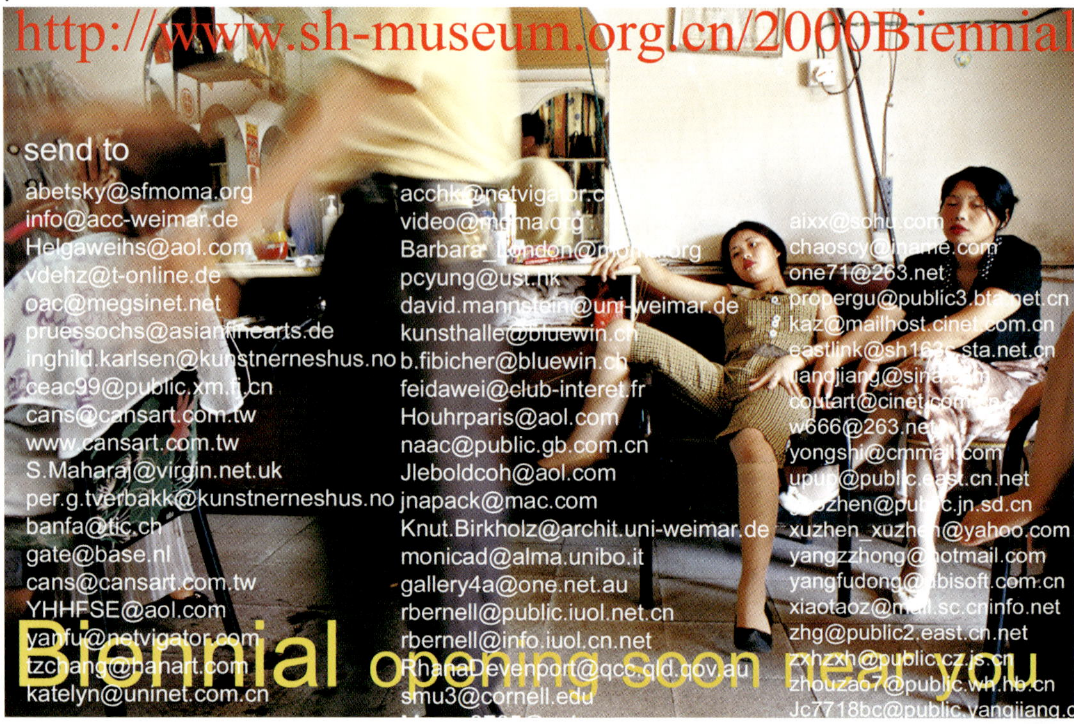
http://www.sh-museum.org.cn/2000Biennial
send to
abetsky@sfmoma.org
info@acc-weimar.de
Helgaweihs@aol.com
vdehz@t-online.de
oac@megsinet.net
inghild.karlsen@kunstnerneshus.no
cans@cansart.com.tw
www.cansart.com.tw
S.Maharaj@virgin.net.uk
per.g.tverbakk@kunstnerneshus.no
banfa@tic.ch
gate@base.nl
cans@cansart.com.tw
YHHFSE@aol.com
katelyn@uninet.com.cn
pcyung@ust.hk
kunsthalle@bluewin.ch
b.fibicher@bluewin.ch
feidawei@club-interet.fr
Houhrparis@aol.com
naac@public.gb.com.cn
Jleboldcoh@aol.com
jnapack@mac.com
Knut.Birkholz@archit.uni-weimar.de
monicad@alma.unibo.it
gallery4a@one.net.au
rbernell@public.iuol.net.cn
rbernell@info.iuol.cn.net
smu3@cornell.edu
one71@263.net
xuzhen_xuzhen@yahoo.com
yangzzhong@hotmail.com
zhg@public2.east.cn.net
Biennial opening soon near you

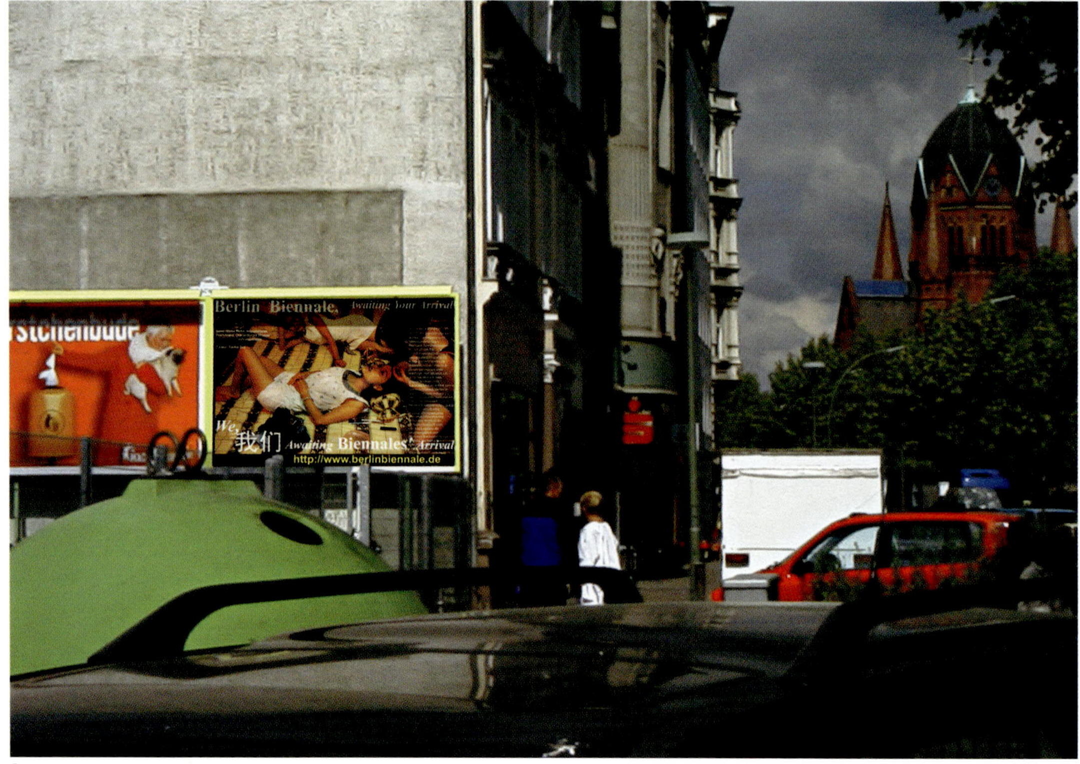
Berlin Biennale
Awaiting Your Arrival
We, 我们 Awaiting Biennales' Arrival
http://www.berlinbiennale.de

2

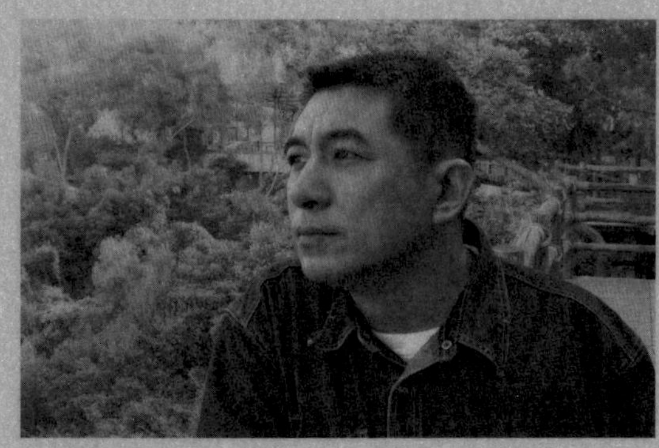

"For me, art creation highlights an interaction with human consciousness, and the ideological value of logic and madness in our daily life. In my point of view, constructive work in art is more meaningful than social criticism of low quality."

„Für mich bedeutet der Kunstprozess eine Interaktion mit dem menschlichen Bewusstsein sowie ideologisierter Logik und dem Irrsinn unseres Alltags. Konstruktive Kunst erscheint mir weit wichtiger als zweitklassige Sozialkritik."

"对我而言，艺术创作彰显了人类意识的相互作用，彰显了我们日常生活中的逻辑和疯狂的形态意识价值。我认为，与劣质的社会评论相比，艺术的创造性工作更有意义。"

Born in 1957 in Wuhan, China. Lives and works in Zhuhai
Geboren 1957 in Wuhan, China. Lebt und arbeitet in Zhuhai
1957年出生于中国武汉，现在珠海定居工作

***Selected exhibitions* / Ausgewählte Ausstellungen / 所选展览**

2001 2nd Berlin Biennale, Berlin, Germany
2002 "Pause", 4th Gwangju Biennial, Gwangju, Korea
2003 50. Biennale di Venezia, Venice, Italy
2006 "China Contemporary", Museum Boijmans Van Beuningen, Rotterdam, The Netherlands
2006–07 "China Power Station I", Battersea Power Station, Serpentine Gallery, London, UK; Astrup Fearnley Museum of Modern Art, Oslo, Norway
2007 "China Welcomes You", Kunsthaus Graz, Graz, Austria

2001年 柏林双年展, 柏林, 德国
2002年 《停留 -- 第四届光州双年展》韩国，光州
2003年 第50届威尼斯双年展, 威尼斯，意大利
2006年 《中国当代》波伊曼·凡·布宁根博物馆，鹿特丹，荷兰
2006–07 《中国电站I》蛇形画廊，巴特西电站 伦敦 英国；Astrup Fearnley 现代美术馆，奥斯陆，挪威
2007年 《中国欢迎你》格拉茨美术馆 格拉茨 奥地利

***Selected publications* / Ausgewählte Publikationen / 所选著作**

Chris Driessen, Marianne Brouwer (eds.): "Another Long March – Chinese Conceptual and Installation Art in the Nineties", Breda 1997
Hou Hanru, Hans Ulrich Obrist (eds.): "Cities on the Move", Ostfildern-Ruit 1997
Wu Hung, Feng Boyi (eds.): "The First Guangzhou Triennial – Reinterpretation: A Decade of Experimental Chinese Art (1990–2000)", Guangzhou 2002
Xu Tan: "Loose", Guangzhou 2005

Driessen, Chris/Brouwer, Marianne（编者）:《其它长征 – 90年代的中国概念性和专职艺术》展册, 布雷达1997年
侯韩如/Obrist, Hans Ulrich（编者）:《城市在进展中》展册，Ostfildern-Ruit 1997年
巫鸿/冯博一(编者)：《第一届广州三年展 -- 重新解释：十年实验性的中国艺术（1990-2000年), 展册, 广州2002年
徐坦（著）:《宽松》展册，广州2005年

"For me, art creation highlights an interaction with human consciousness, and the ideological value of logic and madness in our daily life. In my point of view, constructive work in art is more meaningful than social criticism of low quality."

„Für mich bedeutet der Kunstprozess eine Interaktion mit dem menschlichen Bewusstsein sowie ideologisierter Logik und dem Irrsinn unseres Alltags. Konstruktive Kunst erscheint mir weit wichtiger als zweitklassige Sozialkritik."

"对我而言，艺术创作彰显了人类意识的相互作用，彰显了我们日常生活中的逻辑和疯狂的形态意识价值。我认为，与劣质的社会评论相比，艺术的创造性工作更有意义。"

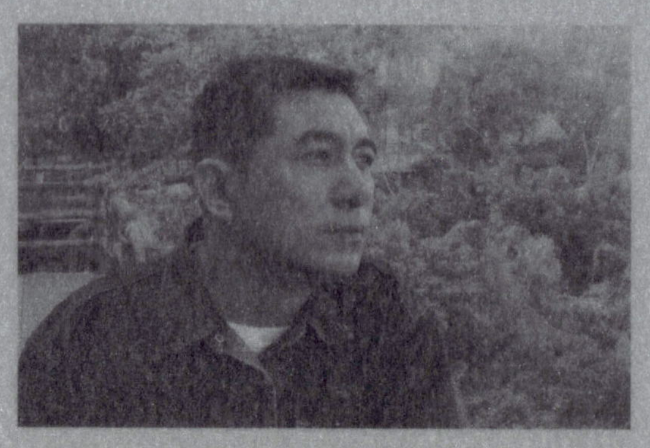

Born in 1957 in Wuhan, China. Lives and works in Zhuhai
Geboren 1957 in Wuhan, China. Lebt und arbeitet in Zhuhai
1957年出生于中国武汉，现在珠海定居工作

Selected exhibitions / Ausgewählte Ausstellungen / 所选展览

2001	2nd Berlin Biennale, Berlin, Germany
2002	"Pause", 4th Gwangju Biennial, Gwangju, Korea
2003	50. Biennale di Venezia, Venice, Italy
2006	"China Contemporary", Museum Boijmans Van Beuningen, Rotterdam, The Netherlands
2006–07	"China Power Station I", Battersea Power Station, Serpentine Gallery, London, UK; Astrup Fearnley Museum of Modern Art, Oslo, Norway
2007	"China Welcomes You", Kunsthaus Graz, Graz, Austria

2001年	柏林双年展，柏林，德国
2002年	《停留 — 第四届光州双年展》韩国，光州
2003年	第50届威尼斯双年展，威尼斯，意大利
2006年	《中国当代》波伊曼·凡·布宁根博物馆，鹿特丹，荷兰
2006–07	《中国电站I》蛇形画廊，巴特西电站 伦敦 英国；Astrup Fearnley 现代美术馆，奥斯陆，挪威
2007年	《中国欢迎你》格拉茨美术馆 格拉茨 奥地利

Selected publications / Ausgewählte Publikationen / 所选著作

Chris Driessen, Marianne Brouwer (eds.): "Another Long March – Chinese Conceptual and Installation Art in the Nineties", Breda 1997
Hou Hanru, Hans Ulrich Obrist (eds.): "Cities on the Move", Ostfildern-Ruit 1997
Wu Hung, Feng Boyi (eds.): "The First Guangzhou Triennial – Reinterpretation: A Decade of Experimental Chinese Art (1990–2000)", Guangzhou 2002
Xu Tan: "Loose", Guangzhou 2005

Driessen, Chris/Brouwer, Marianne（编者）：《其它长征 – 90年代的中国概念性和装置艺术》展册，布雷达1997年
侯瀚如/Obrist, Hans Ulrich（编者）：《城市在进展中》展册，Ostfildern-Ruit 1997年
巫鸿/冯博一（编者）：《第一届广州三年展 — 重新解释：十年实验性的中国艺术（1990–2000年）》展册，广州2002年
徐坦（著）：《宽松》展册，广州2005年

XU TAN 徐坦

[ɕy tan]

The strongest consciousness changing power of today's China is the rapid transformation, a magnetic field nobody can escape and which is disclosed on the surface as the total reconstruction of the cities. The core of Xu Tan's work is the questioning of contexts between contemporary circumstances of life and life experiences as well as the generating of ideas and concepts. The driving power of Xu Tan is apart from the current experience – the increasing marketisation leading to extreme changes of social structure and the self-conception thereof – his own biography formed by contradictions and breaks.

Born at the end of the 1950s, as a child and youth he underwent the Cultural Revolution. While dealing with Mao ideology outside of this parents' house, thanks to his grandmother, he gained access to the traditional Chinese culture being defamed as bourgeois at this time, and later he witnessed the increasing marketisation of China since the 1980s. These conditions might be responsible for the development of his sensitive antennas for the character of people formed by the environment and he has already practiced strategies of reflection and adoption in an early stage.

Due to the speed and the vehemence of the change processes in China being continued incessantly, processes of consciousness forming seem to have become impossible today due to lack of time and space. By placing the human individual as a product of social structures and systems in the centre of his art work, in order to unveil hidden structures of power, Xu's approach is by all means social critical.

For him art has an important social function and possesses the capability to stimulate consciousness processes. Xu regards purely conceptual thoughts as too abstract and advocates an art taking place in real life. His works, mostly installations, are decelerated spaces of experience of social critical reflection taking place in a gallery in other words in art context, but corresponding to life. His analysis of

Die stärkste bewusstseinsverändernde Kraft im gegenwärtigen China ist der rapide Wandel, dessen magnetischer Anziehung sich niemand entziehen kann und der sich an der Oberfläche im Totalumbau der Städte offenbart. Im Zentrum von Xu Tans Werk steht das Hinterfragen von Zusammenhängen zwischen zeitgenössischen Lebensumständen und Lebenserfahrungen sowie der Generierung von Ideen und Konzepten. Xu Tans Movens ist aber neben dem Erleben der zunehmenden Ökonomisierung, die zu extremen Veränderungen der gesellschaftlichen Struktur und ihres Selbstverständnisses führt, auch seine von Brüchen und Widersprüchen geprägte Biografie. Ende der 1950er Jahre geboren, erlebte er als Kind und Jugendlicher die Kulturrevolution. Während er sich außerhalb seines Elternhauses mit der maoistischen Ideologie auseinandersetzte, verdankt er seiner Großmutter den Zugang zur damals als bourgeois geschmähten traditionellen chinesischen Kultur und erlebte seit Beginn der 1980er Jahre die zunehmende Ökonomisierung Chinas. Vielleicht entwickelte er somit bereits als Kind sensible Antennen für die Prägung des Menschen durch seine Umgebung und übte sich schon früh in Strategien der Reflexion und Anpassung.

Aufgrund des hohes Tempos und der Wucht, mit der sich die Prozesse des Wandels in China unaufhörlich fortsetzen, scheinen Bewusstwerdungsprozesse heute mangels Zeit und Raum kaum mehr möglich zu sein. Indem Xu das menschliche Individuum als Produkt gesellschaftlicher Strukturen und Systeme ins Zentrum seines künstlerischen Schaffens stellt (und zwar mit dem Anliegen, verborgene Machtstrukturen zu entlarven), verfolgt er einen durchaus sozialkritischen Ansatz. Kunst hat seiner Meinung nach eine wichtige gesellschaftliche Funktion und verfügt über das Potenzial, Bewusstseinsprozesse anzukurbeln. Rein konzeptionelle Überlegungen lehnt Xu als zu abstrakt ab und plädiert für eine Kunst, die im Leben stattfindet. Seine zumeist installativen Arbeiten sind entschleunigte Erfahrungsräume der sozialkritischen Hinterfragung, die zwar in der Galerie, also im Kunstkontext, stattfinden, aber dennoch mit dem Leben korrespondieren. Gern

质疑当代生活环境和生活经历之间的对应关系、思想概念的产生是徐坦作品的核心内容。当今中国变化力量的强烈意识是快速的社会变革，这是强烈磁力无人可逃，展现在城市全面重建层面上。

徐坦的驱动力，除现实经验之外（不断深化的市场化导致的社会结构极端变化和其中的自我概念）、由于矛盾和突变所形成的自我经历也是其中之一。徐坦出生于上世纪50年代末期，在文化大革命运动中度过了他的童年和青年岁月。在父母房间之外学习毛泽东思想的同时，在他祖母的帮助下，他接受中国传统文化教育，虽然那时传统文化被诬蔑为资本主义的东西，随后，他见证了不断深化的中国市场化进程自1980年代起。他对在这种环境下所形成人物特征的敏感触角不断发育成熟，上述的那些条件也许是其原因。在其艺术初期，他就开始实践反思和继承策略。

由于中国变化的进程的速度和欲望 在不断的持着，在今天意识过程的形成似乎变的不可能，因为缺少时间和空间。为揭示所隐藏的力量结构，他的艺术作品的中心集中于：个体是社会结构和社会体系的产物。而他所用的手法就是社会批评。

对他而言，艺术具有 重要的社会功能并且能够激励意识过程的形成。徐坦认为纯概念思想非常抽象，因而提倡艺术来源于生活。他的作品、大部分是装置，是社会批评反思经验的减速空间，这些经验产生于画廊里，换而言之产生于艺术关系中，但是对应着现实生活。因此，他喜欢在现成的地点里创作。在分析当代现实体系时，他关注于人体的印记、语言和具体的日常生活文化。

2005年，他为第二届广州三年展创作了一座可行走的装置（《九月九的酒》），一只特大象征着迁徙和贫困的蓝白塑料编织袋，它们被放置在广东美术馆的门前。安放在装置里的卡拉OK设备让观 众不禁吟唱思乡歌谣，它们受到外来农民工的欢迎，他

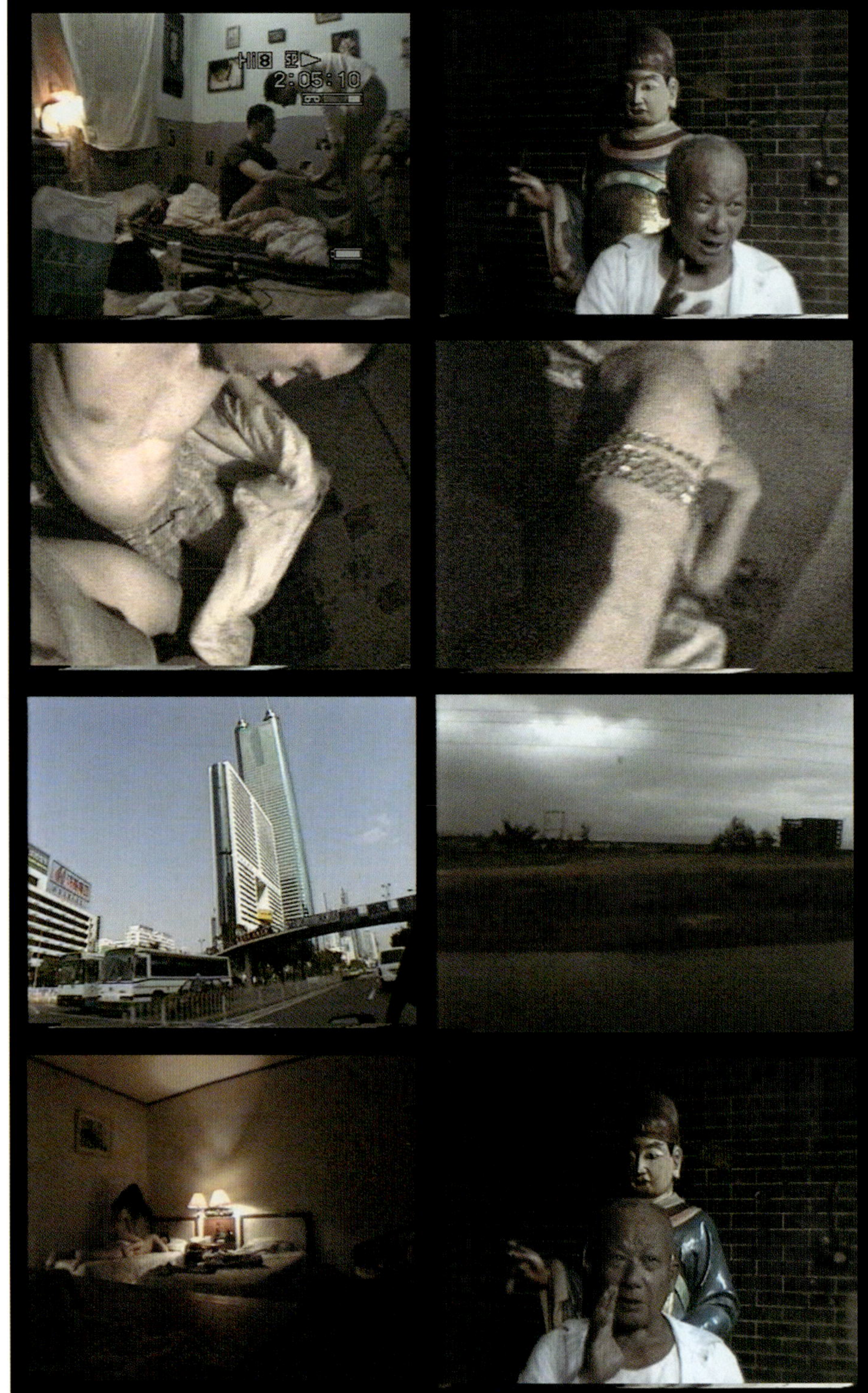

3

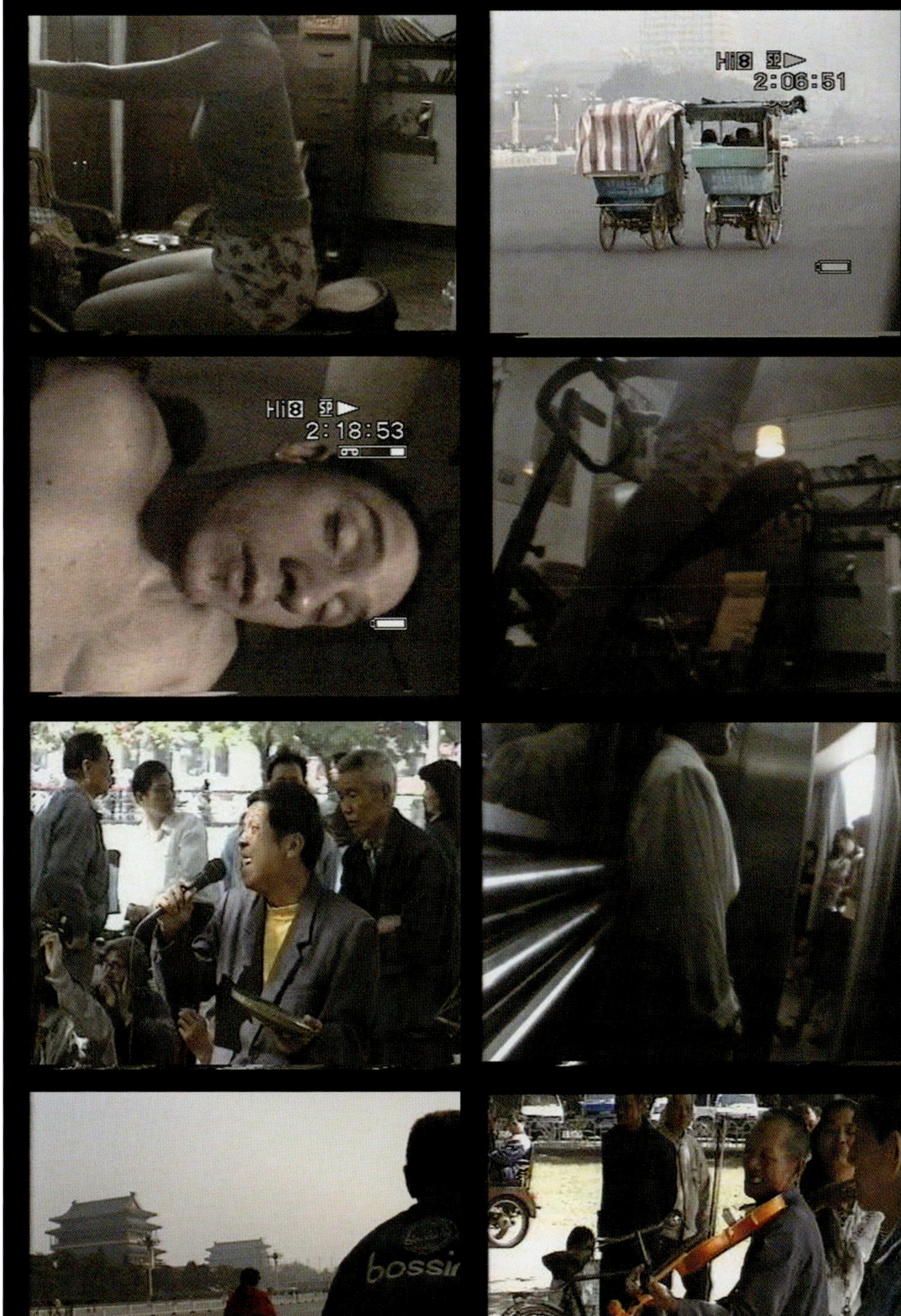
Hi8 SP
2:06:51
Hi8 SP
2:18:53

4

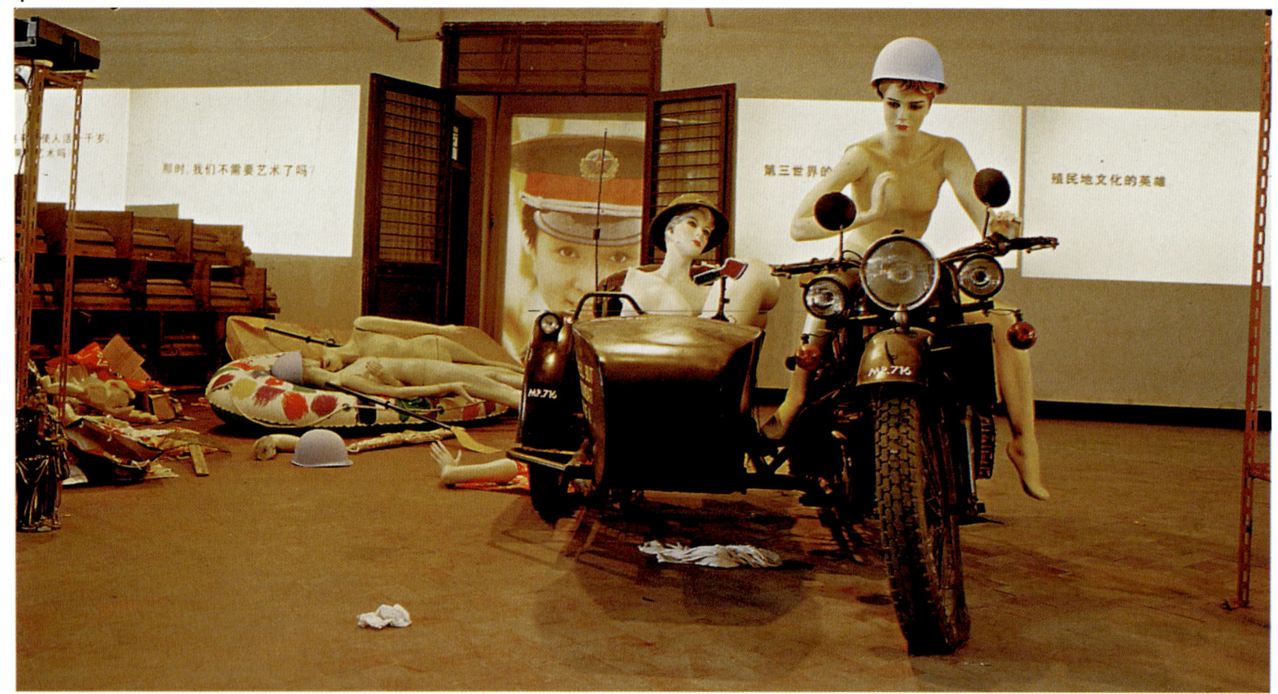

contemporary reality systems shows interest in imprinting of the human body, language and material daily life culture.

For the second Guangzhou Triennial in 2005 he built a kind of walkable installation ("Wine for 9th of September") in front of the Guangdong Museum of Art in form of an oversized carry bag of blue white and red plastic plane, which is worldwide understood as symbol of migration and poverty. A karaoke device in the interior of the installation invited the visitors to sing songs of homesickness emotions which are favoured by the migration workers who, far away from their rural homelands build up the new Chinese cities. In addition to the bodily experience on entering the installation, the tactile by touching the materials and the sensual one by listening or singing the songs, the symbolic meaning of the three coloured plane plays an important role for the material daily life cultures of the impoverished. One of the recent projects of Xu is the series "Key Words", an investigation of the contemporary Chinese language Xu thinks to be a sensitive measuring instrument of current conditions and ideas.

Together with the artists Chen Shaoxiong, Lin Yilin, Liang Juhui Xu Tan is a member of the work group "Big Tail Elephant", being founded in Guangzhou at the beginning of the 1990s without any common programme, but to meet to discuss in a critical way the urban transformation processes.

arbeitet er darum ortsbezogen und unter Verwendung von Readymades. In seinen Analysen der Systeme zeitgenössischer Realität interessieren ihn insbesondere Prägungen des menschlichen Körpers, der Sprache und der materiellen Alltagskultur.

So baute er für die zweite Guangzhou-Triennale im Jahr 2005 vor dem Guangdong Museum of Art eine begehbare Installation („Wine for 9th of September") in Form einer überdimensionalen Tragetasche aus blau-weiß-rotem Kunststoff, die weltweit als Symbol für Migration und Armut verstanden wird. Im Inneren lud eine Karaokeanlage zum Singen von Liedern ein, die Heimweh ausdrückten und insbesondere bei den Wanderarbeitern beliebt sind, die weit entfernt von ihrer ländlichen Heimat die neuen chinesischen Städte aufbauen. Neben der körperlichen Erfahrung beim Betreten der Installation – der taktilen beim Berühren des Materials und der sinnlichen beim Hören und oder Singen der Lieder – spielt auch die symbolische Bedeutung des dreifarbigen Kunststoffs für die materielle Alltagskultur der Armen eine wichtige Rolle. Zu Xus neueren Projekten gehört die Serie „Key Words", eine Untersuchung der zeitgenössischen chinesischen Sprache, die er für einen sensiblen Gradmesser gegenwärtiger Zustände und Ideen hält.

Zusammen mit den Künstlern Chen Shaoxiong, Lin Yilin, Liang Juhui gehört Xu Tan zu den „Großschwanzelefanten", eine Gruppe, die sich Anfang der 1990er Jahre in Guangzhou ohne gemeinsames Programm, sondern als lose Vereinigung zusammentat, um sich kritisch mit den urbanen Transformationsprozessen auseinanderzusetzen.

们远离遥远的农村故乡，在建设出一座座新的中国城市。除走进装置里的亲身体验外，抚摸材料的触觉、聆听或吟唱歌谣的感觉、三色编织袋的象征意义，都在穷人的具体的日常生活文化中发挥着重要的作用。《关键词》系列是徐最近的一个项目，是对现代汉语的调查，徐坦认为那是对当今情形和观念的敏锐的衡量手法。

和艺术家陈劭雄、林一林，梁钜辉一样，徐坦也是艺术团体大尾象工作组的成员之一。该团体1990在广州成立，虽然没有共同纲领、但是主旨在于评论城市变革进程。

Birgit Hopfener

5

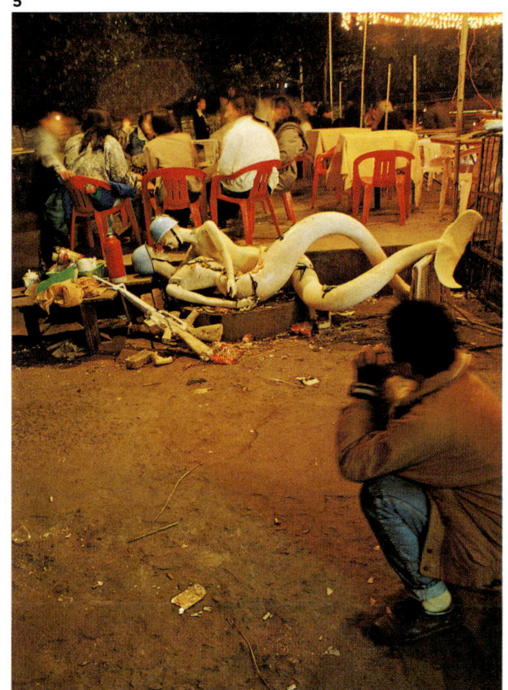

6

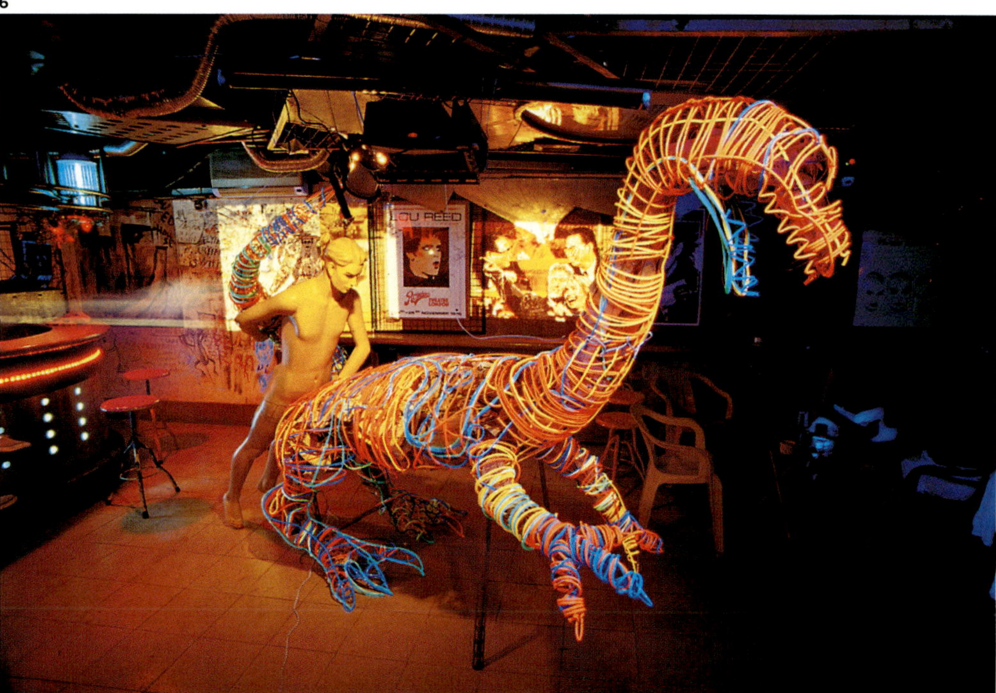

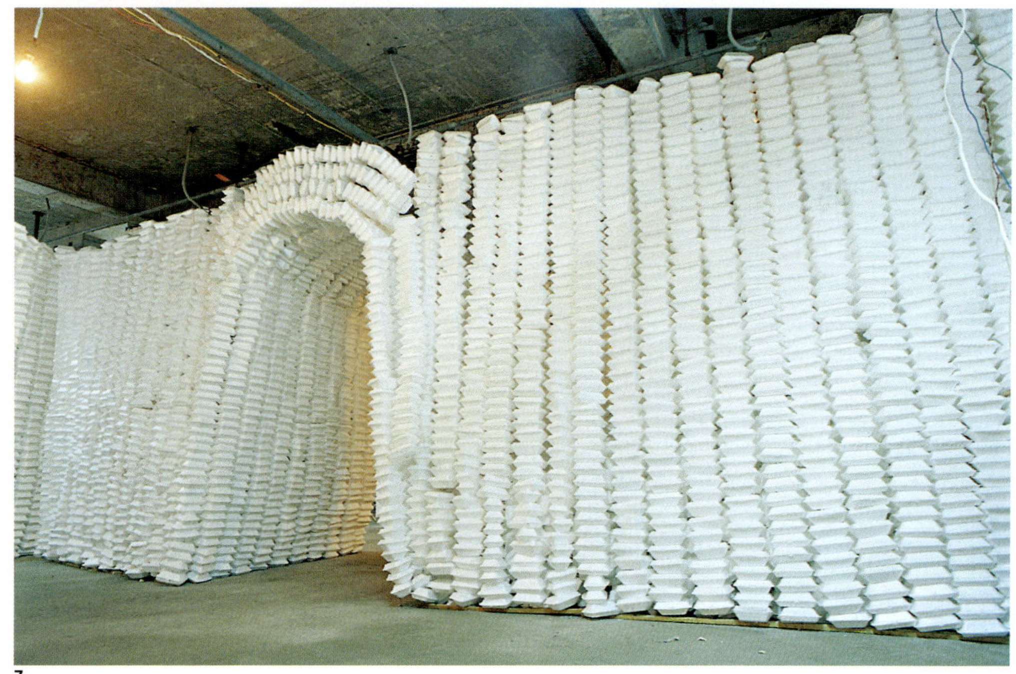

7

1 ***Shanghai Biennial Awaiting Your Arrival***, *2000*
Digital photograph, 2.8 x 4 m
Digitale Fotografie, 2,80 x 4 m
《上海双年展欢迎你》2000年，数字摄影，2.8 x 4 m

2 ***Berlin Biennial Awaiting Your Arrival***, *2001*
Digital photograph, 2.8 x 4 m
Digitale Fotografie, 2,80 x 4 m
《柏林双年展欢迎你》2001年，数字摄影，2.8 x 4 m

3 ***Made at home in China***, *1998*
CD-Rom with video and photo
CD-Rom mit Video und Fotografie
《在中国及在家中制造》1998年, CD-ROM 录像和照片

4 ***New Order***, *1994*
Installation
Installation
《三寓路14号的改建》1994年, 装置

5 ***Allegory of Love***, *1993*
Installation and performance
Installation und Performance
《爱的寓言》1993年, 装置和表演

6 ***New Thought***, *1995*
Installation
Installation
《新思维》1995年, 装置

7 ***The Arch of Happiness***, *2000*
Installation
Installation
《幸福门》2000年, 装置

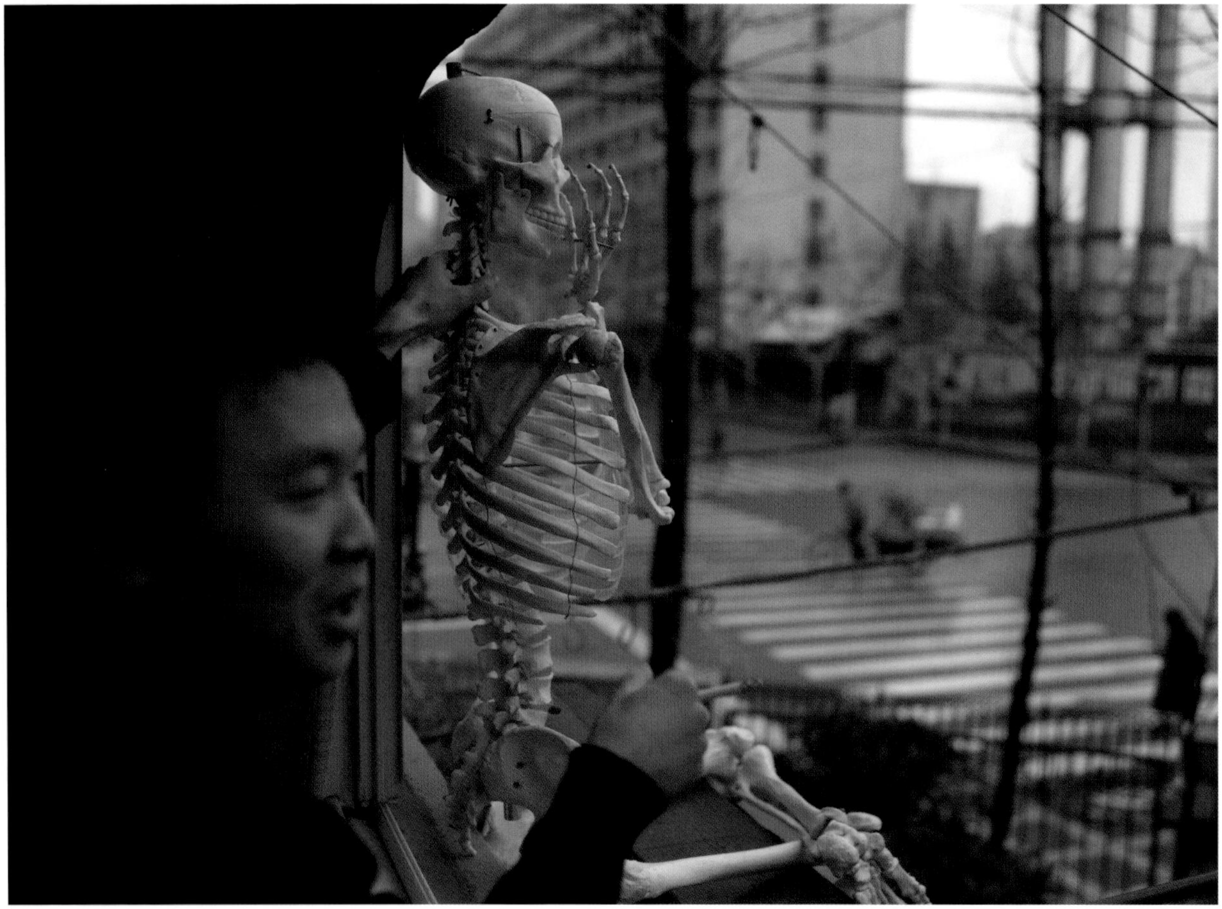

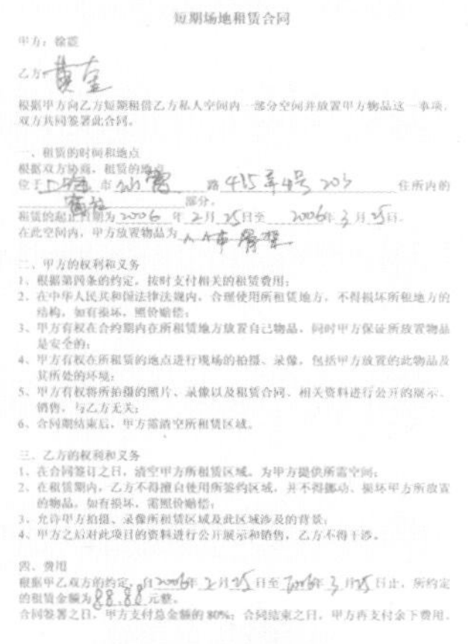

短期场地租赁合同

甲方：徐震

乙方：黄奎

根据甲方向乙方短期租借乙方私人空间内一部分空间并放置甲方物品这一事项，双方共同签署此合同。

一、租赁的时间和地点
根据双方协商，租赁的地点位于 上海 市 [illegible] 路 415弄4号 203 住所内的 [illegible] 部分。
租赁的起止日期为 2006 年 2 月 25 日至 2006 年 3 月 25 日。
在此空间内，甲方放置物品为 人体骨架

二、甲方的权利和义务
1、根据第四条的约定，按时支付相关的租赁费用；
2、在中华人民共和国法律法规内，合理使用所租赁地方，不得损坏所租地方的结构，如有损坏，照价赔偿；
3、甲方有权在合约期内在所租赁地方放置自己物品，同时甲方保证所放置物品是安全的；
4、甲方有权在所租赁的地点进行现场的拍摄、录像，包括甲方放置的此物品及其所处的环境；
5、甲方有权将所拍摄的照片、录像以及租赁合同、相关资料进行公开的展示、销售，与乙方无关；
6、合同期结束后，甲方需清空所租赁区域。

三、乙方的权利和义务
1、在合同签订之日，清空甲方所租赁区域，为甲方提供所需空间；
2、在租赁期内，乙方不得擅自使用所签约区域，并不得挪动、损坏甲方所放置的物品，如有损坏，需照价赔偿；
3、允许甲方拍摄、录像所租赁区域及此区域涉及的背景；
4、甲方之后对此项目的资料进行公开展示和销售，乙方不得干涉。

四、费用
根据甲乙双方的约定，自 2006 年 2 月 25 日至 2006 年 3 月 25 日止，所约定的租赁金额为 88.88 元整。
合同签署之日，甲方支付总金额的 80%；合同结束之日，甲方再支付余下费用。

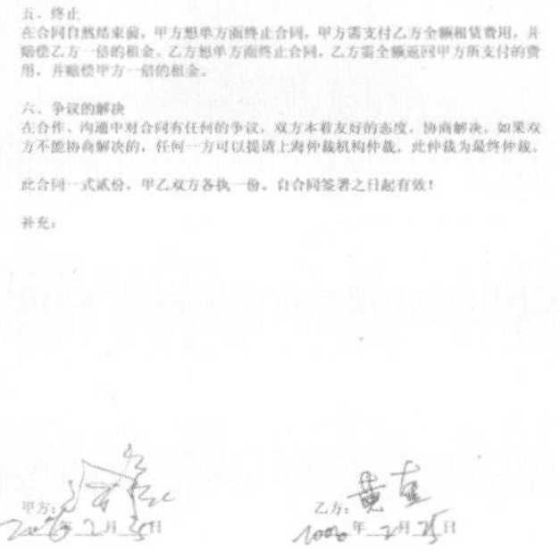

五、终止
在合同自然结束前，甲方想单方面终止合同，甲方需支付乙方全额租赁费用，并赔偿乙方一倍的租金。乙方想单方面终止合同，乙方需全额返回甲方所支付的费用，并赔偿甲方一倍的租金。

六、争议的解决
在合作、沟通中对合同有任何的争议，双方本着友好的态度，协商解决。如果双方不能协商解决的，任何一方可以提请上海仲裁机构仲裁，此仲裁为最终仲裁。

此合同一式贰份，甲乙双方各执一份，自合同签署之日起有效！

补充：

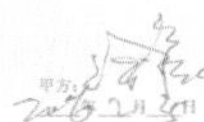
甲方：
2006 年 2 月 25 日

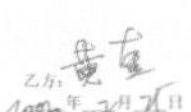
乙方：黄奎
2006 年 2 月 25 日

1

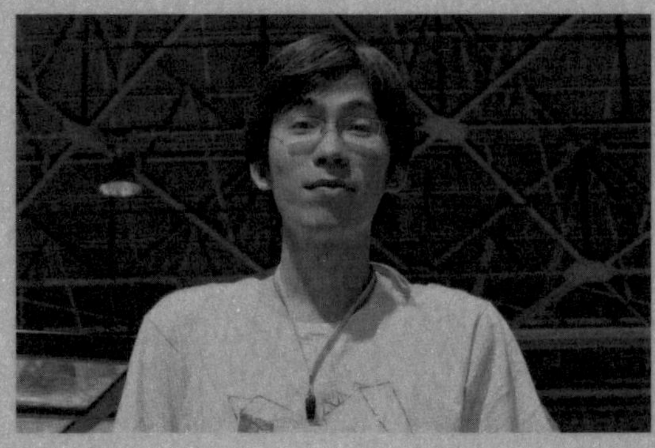

"I have no right to demand a response from the audience. Everybody has his or her own perception of my work. But I want to steer public attention towards contemporary art. Hopefully more people will accept it."

„Ich habe kein Recht, dem Publikum eine Reaktion abzuverlangen. Jeder nimmt meine Arbeit auf eigene Weise wahr. Aber ich möchte die öffentliche Aufmerksamkeit auf die zeitgenössische Kunst lenken. Hoffentlich werden sie dann mehr Menschen akzeptieren."

"我没有权力要求观众去回应我的作品，每个人都有对我作品的个人理解。但是我要引导公众去观注当代艺术，希望更多的人将会接受。"

Born in 1977 in Shanghai, China. Lives and works in Shanghai
Geboren 1977 in Shanghai, China. Lebt und arbeitet in Shanghai
1977年出生于中国上海，现工作居住在上海

***Selected exhibitions* / Ausgewählte Ausstellungen / 所选展览**

2004	"China Now", Museum of Modern Art Film at the Gramercy Theater, New York, NY, USA
2005	Chinese Pavilion, 51. Biennale di Venezia, Venice, Italy
	Yokohama International Triennial of Contemporary Art, Yokohama, Japan
	"Follow Me! – Contemporary Chinese Art at the Threshold of the Millennium", Mori Art Museum, Tokyo, Japan
2006	"8.848–1.86", Museum Boijmans Van Beuningen, Rotterdam, The Netherlands
2006/07	"China Power Station I", Battersea Power Station, Serpentine Gallery, London, UK; Astrup Fearnley Museum of Modern Art, Oslo, Norway
2007	"China – Facing Reality", Museum Moderner Kunst Stiftung Ludwig, Vienna, Austria
	10th Istanbul Biennial, Istanbul, Turkey

2004年	《今日中国》纽约现代艺术博物馆
2005年	中国馆 第51届威尼斯双年展，威尼斯
	横滨国际当代艺术三年展，横滨
	《跟我来！-新千年之际的中国艺术》森美术馆，东京，日本
2006年	《8.848-1.86 》徐震个展，Boijmans Van Beuningen 博物馆，荷兰，上海
2006/07	《中国电站I》蛇形画廊，巴特西电站 伦敦 英国；Astrup Fearnley 现代美术馆 奥斯陆 挪威
2007年	《中国—面队真实》路德维希基金会现代艺术博物馆，维也纳，奥地利
	第十届 伊斯坦布尔双年展，伊斯坦布尔，土耳其

***Selected publications* / Ausgewählte Publikationen / 所选著作**

Uta Grosenick, Sine Bepler (eds.): "ShanghART Gallery 10 Years", Cologne 2006
"China Contemporary", Rotterdam 2006

Grosenick, Uta/Bepler, Sine（编者）:《10年的香格纳画廊》，科隆 2006
《当代中国》展册 博物馆，鹿特丹2006年

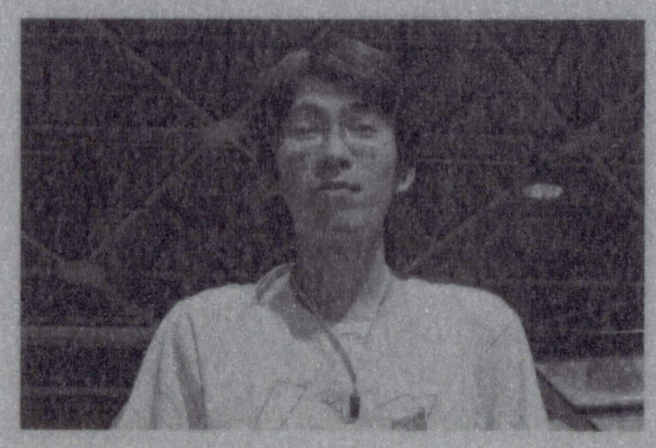

"I have no right to demand a response from the audience. Everybody has his or her own perception of my work. But I want to steer public attention towards contemporary art. Hopefully more people will accept it."

„Ich habe kein Recht, dem Publikum eine Reaktion abzuverlangen. Jeder nimmt meine Arbeit auf eigene Weise wahr. Aber ich möchte die öffentliche Aufmerksamkeit auf die zeitgenössische Kunst lenken. Hoffentlich werden sie dann mehr Menschen akzeptieren."

"我没有权力要求观众去回应我的作品，每个人都有对我作品的个人理解。但是我要引导公众去观注当代艺术， 希望更多的人将会接受。"

Born in 1977 in Shanghai, China. Lives and works in Shanghai
Geboren 1977 in Shanghai, China. Lebt und arbeitet in Shanghai
1977年出生于中国上海，现工作居住在上海

Selected exhibitions / Ausgewählte Ausstellungen / 所选展览

2004 "China Now", Museum of Modern Art Film at the Gramercy Theater, New York, NY, USA
2005 Chinese Pavilion, 51. Biennale di Venezia, Venice, Italy
Yokohama International Triennial of Contemporary Art, Yokohama, Japan
"Follow Me! – Contemporary Chinese Art at the Threshold of the Millennium", Mori Art Museum, Tokyo, Japan
2006 "8.848-1.86", Museum Boijmans Van Beuningen, Rotterdam, The Netherlands
2006/07 "China Power Station I", Battersea Power Station, Serpentine Gallery, London, UK; Astrup Fearnley Museum of Modern Art, Oslo, Norway
2007 "China – Facing Reality", Museum Moderner Kunst Stiftung Ludwig, Vienna, Austria
10th Istanbul Biennial, Istanbul, Turkey

2004年 《今日中国》纽约现代艺术博物馆
2005年 中国馆 第51届威尼斯双年展，威尼斯
横滨国际当代艺术三年展，横滨
《跟我来！-新千年之际的中国艺术》森美术馆，东京，日本
2006年 《8.848-1.86 》徐震个展，Boijmans Van Beuningen 博物馆，荷兰，上海
2006/07 《中国电站I》蛇形画廊，巴特西电站 伦敦 英国；Astrup Fearnley 现代美术馆 奥斯陆 挪威
2007年 《中国－面对真实》路德维希基金会现代艺术博物馆，维也纳，奥地利
第十届 伊斯坦布尔双年展，伊斯坦布尔，土耳其

Selected publications / Ausgewählte Publikationen / 所选著作

Uta Grosenick, Sine Bepler (eds.): "ShanghART Gallery 10 Years", Cologne 2006
"China Contemporary", Rotterdam 2006

Grosenick, Uta/Bepler, Sine（编者）：《10年的香格纳画廊》，科隆 2006
《当代中国》展册 博物馆，鹿特丹2006年

XU ZHEN 徐震

[ɕy ʈʂən]

Xu Zhen is an interventionist, employing video, performance and installation, to make works that explode and exploit the social possibilities of his exhibition site. Graduating from the Shanghai School of Applied Arts in 1996, Xu Zhen is a leader in this first generation of Chinese artists able to exhibit their works internationally from the outset of their careers. As such, his work fluently employs conceptual techniques familiar to global art audiences, yet they are equally provocative abroad as they are in China.

In the beginning of his career, Xu Zhen often concentrated on the body, his own and others, as a metaphor for social transgression. "From Inside the Body", a video shown at the notorious 1999 "Art For Sale" exhibition which this artist also curated, depicts a man and woman first sniffing their own bodies, searching for the source of an malodorous scent, then coming together and smelling each other in a weird variation of sexual encounters. "Rainbow", a video presented at the 49th Venice Biennial in 2001, shows the bare back of an anonymous figure turning red, emblazoned with the marks of a beating, though the hand slapping the figure is kept entirely out of view. In addition to his most provocative photographs showing male models bleeding menstrual blood (in the series "A Problem of Colorfulness", 2001), Xu Zhen also made waves with his most visceral work, "I'm not asking for anything" (1999), a video in which he threw a dead cat repeatedly against a concrete floor until he is thoroughly exhausted and the carcass is in shreds.

More recently, however, Xu Zhen's provocations are more metaphorical, addressing issues of social relations on a global scale. In his 2005 gallery installation, "8.848–1.86", the artist documents a fake expedition to Mount Everest, alleging that his team removed 1.86 meters of the mountain's peak, a humorous satire of Chinese news agencies ability to fabricate national accomplishments. The exhibition included video footage, photographs, maps and equipment, as well as very realistic replica of the top of the mountain contained in a glass cabinet. For the 2004

Xu Zhen ist ein Interventionist, der Video, Performances und Installationen einsetzt, um die gesellschaftlichen Möglichkeiten eines Ausstellungsorts auszuschöpfen und zu sprengen. Der Künstler, der 1996 seinen Abschluss an der Shanghai School of Applied Arts machte, ist eine führende Kraft jener ersten Generation chinesischer Künstler, die ihre Werke schon zu Beginn ihrer Karriere international ausstellen konnten. So setzt er in seinen Arbeiten ganz selbstverständlich Konzepttechniken ein, die dem globalen Kunstpublikum geläufig sind und doch auch im Ausland ebenso provokativ wirken wie in China selbst.

Zu Beginn seiner Laufbahn nutzte Xu Zhen oft den menschlichen Körper – den eigenen und den anderer – als Metapher für gesellschaftliche Grenzübertretungen. Sein Video „From Inside the Body" wurde 1999 auf der Skandal-Ausstellung „Art For Sale" gezeigt, die der Künstler auch mitorganisierte. Es zeigt einen Mann und eine Frau, die zuerst ihre eigenen Körper beschnuppern, um die Quelle eines üblen Geruchs aufzuspüren, und dann wieder einander inspizieren – als bizarre Variation einer sexuellen Begegnung. Das Video „Rainbow", das 2001 auf der 49. Biennale von Venedig präsentiert wurde, zeigt den bloßen Rücken einer anonymen Gestalt, der sich allmählich durch Abdrücke von Schlägen rot verfärbt, obwohl die zuschlagende Hand nie zu sehen ist. Xus provokanteste Fotos allerdings waren die von männlichen Modellen, die Menstruationsblut ausscheiden (in der Serie „A Problem of Colorfulness", 2001), und auch sein brutalstes Werk erregte großes Aufsehen: „I'm not asking for anything" (1999), ein Video, in dem er eine tote Katze immer wieder auf einen Betonboden schmettert, bis er selbst erschöpft und der Kadaver völlig zerfetzt ist.

In letzter Zeit tendieren Xu Zhens Provokationen eher zur Metaphorik und befassen sich mit sozialen Beziehungen auf globaler Ebene. Mit seiner Galerieinstallation „8.848–1.86" dokumentierte der Künstler 2005 eine fingierte Mount-Everest-Expedition, bei der sein Team angeblich 1,86 Meter vom Gipfel des Bergs abgetragen hatte – eine witzige Satire auf die Tüchtigkeit, die chinesische Nachrichtenagenturen

徐震是位干涉主义者, 通过录象, 表演和装置的形式创作, 以激发和开拓其展览的社会可能性。徐震1996年毕业于上海工艺美术学校，从事业开始, 他就是第一代在海外展出作品的中国艺术家的佼佼者, 同样地，徐的作品熟练地运用亲近全球观众的概念主义技巧，至今作品在 国外象和国内一样同样具有煽动性。

在徐事业的初期, 他把精力集中于他自己和别人的身体一象是 对社会犯罪的隐喻。从1999艺术销售 展览会展出 的《来自身体内部》，描述一对男女开始寻找一股浓香而 闻着自己的身体，然后两者交织在一起，以一种怪异的性交方式相互闻着对方。

《彩虹》, 在2001年第49届威尼斯双年展上录象，作品中一个无名人物的发红的裸背, 上面饰有击打的痕迹，虽然一只手完全将这个人打出视野之外。除那幅 男模吸吮女性经血的做具有煽动性照片, 徐还创作了最发自内心的作品, 1999年《而我不需要什么》，录象中他反复地把一只死猫摔在水泥地上, 直到他完全筋疲力尽, 尸体成了碎片。

但是徐震最近的作品更隐涩难懂，在全球范围内阐述社会关系的事件。2005年的画廊装置《8.848-1.86》，艺术家证明了一场假的对珠穆朗玛峰 的探险，宣称 他的团队从山峰上移去了1.86米，幽默地讽刺了中国新闻媒介捏造全国性成就的能力，同时真实的主峰的复制品陈列在一个橱窗里。

在2004年的上海双年展上, 他改动了一座陈列在馆内的19世纪建筑塔顶的时钟，让他失控般的旋转，代表 着上海的快速发展。

他的事业最好放映 在2006年第51届威尼斯双年展上中国馆的作品《喊》总结。上海大街上的人群被他的尖叫声短暂的惊扰，而远离摄象机。我们看见行人们转身，被唤醒，惊扰。同样地，由于其不断地探索唤醒观众的方法，他获得了2004年艺术最高

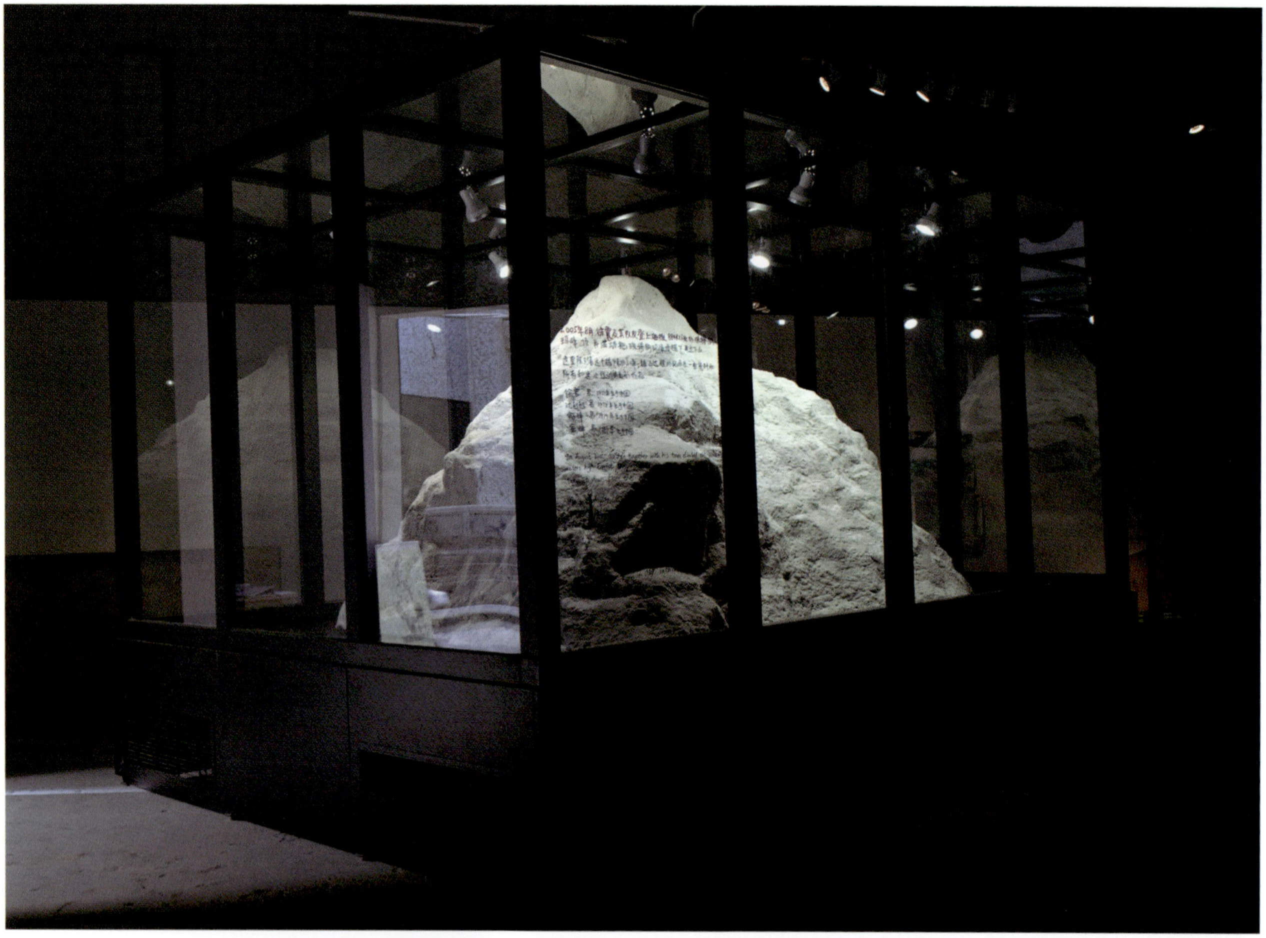

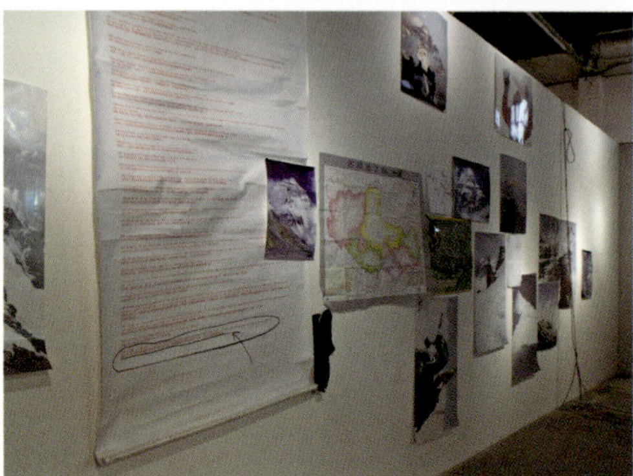

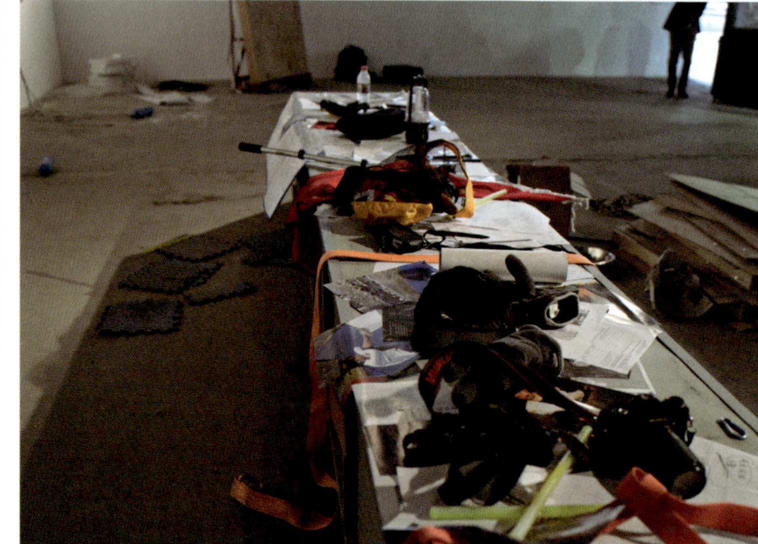

2

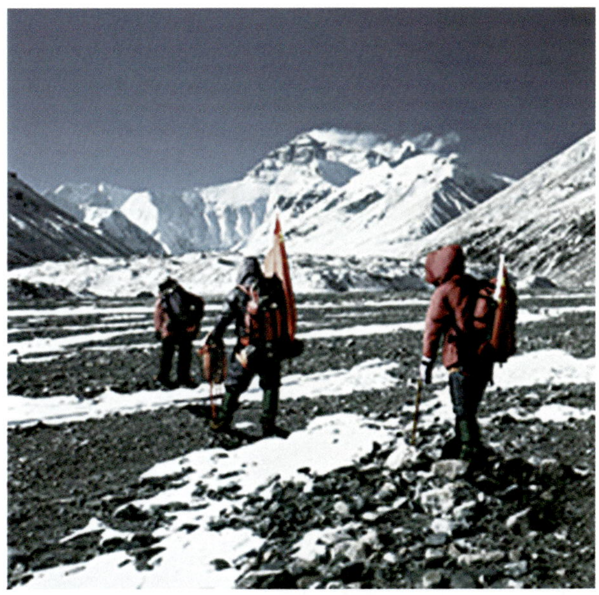

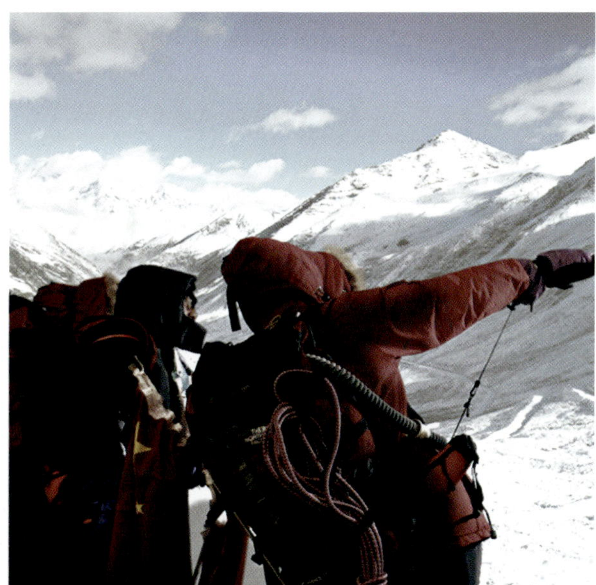

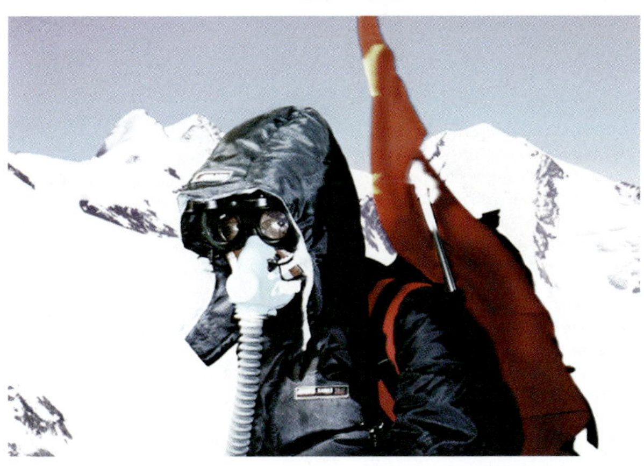

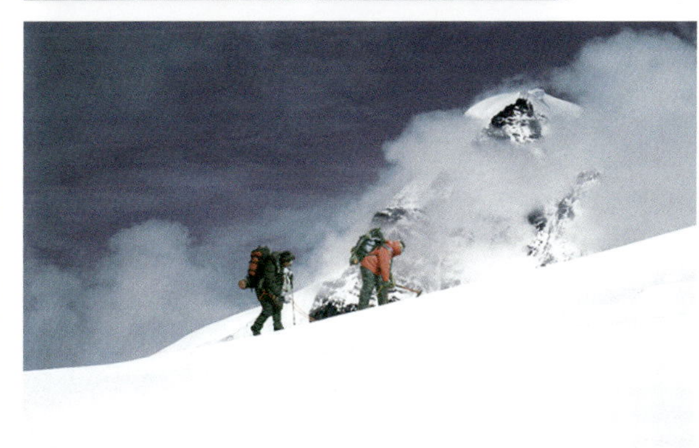

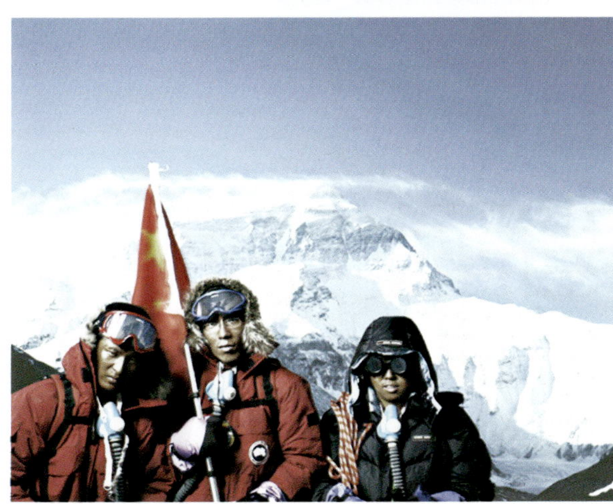

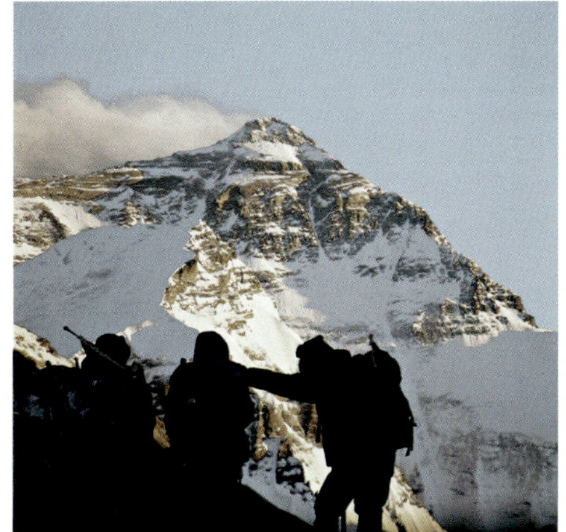

3

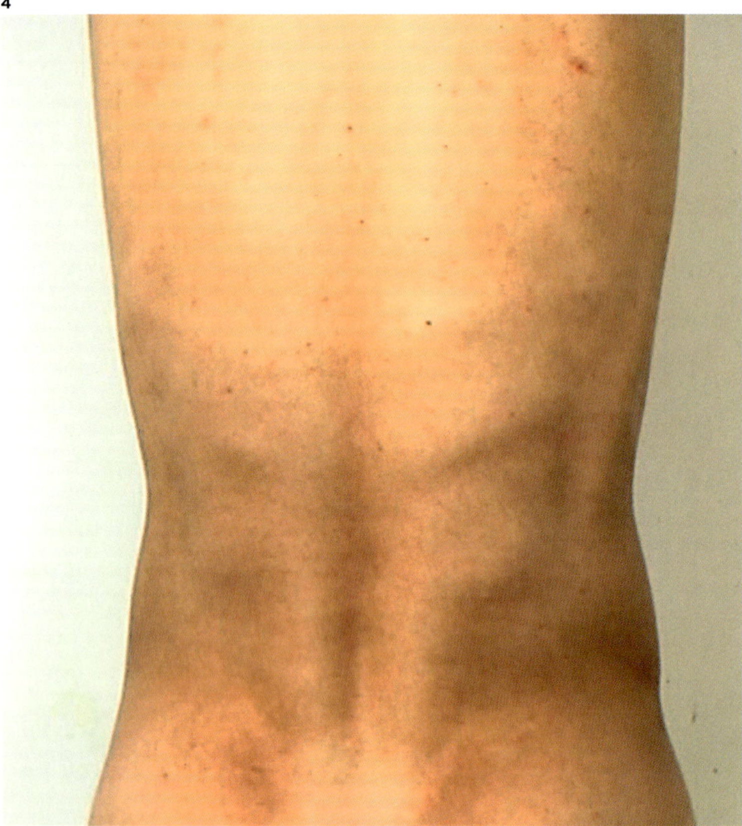

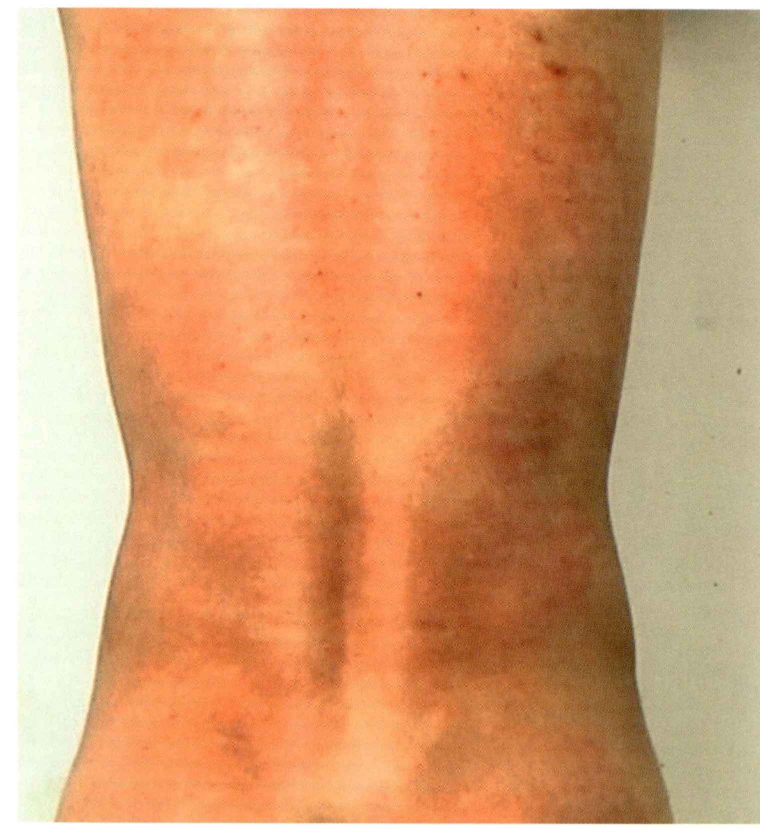

Shanghai Biennial, Xu Zhen fiddled with the clock in the tower of the 19th century building housing the art museum, making it spin as if out of control, a savvy symbol for the fast-paced metropolis hosting the exhibition.

Xu Zhen's career is best summarized by his work "Shout" (2005), featured in the first China Pavilion at the 51st Venice Biennial in 2005. Here, crowds on the streets of Shanghai are momentarily disrupted by the artist screaming, off camera. We see the pedestrians turn, awakened and disturbed. Likewise, this artist, who received the top China Art Award in 2004, continually searches for ways to arouse his audiences.

an den Tag legen, wenn es darum geht, nationale Höchstleistungen zu ersinnen. Die Ausstellung zeigte neben der Bergausrüstung Videomaterial, Fotos, Karten und eine sehr realistische Nachbildung der gestohlenen Bergspitze in einer Vitrine. Und anlässlich der Shanghaier Biennale 2004 manipulierte Xu Zhen die Uhr im Turm des Museumsgebäudes aus dem 19. Jahrhundert derart, dass die Zeiger wild im Kreis rasten – ein sinniges Symbol für die schnelllebige Metropole, die die Ausstellung ausrichtete.

Gleichsam die Quintessenz von Xu Zhens Karriere liefert seine Arbeit „Shout" (2005), die 2005 auf der 51. Biennale von Venedig im ersten chinesischen Pavillon vorgeführt wurde. Das Video zeigt Menschenmassen auf den Straßen von Shanghai, die der Künstler, der außer Sichtweite der Kamera bleibt, durch seine Schreie aufschreckt. Der Betrachter sieht, wie sich die Fußgänger aufgerüttelt, beunruhigt und fragend umdrehen. Und so sucht Xu Zhen, der 2004 den wichtigen Kunstpreis China Art Award erhielt, nach wie vor nach Wegen, sein Publikum wachzurütteln.

奖。除了他的国际艺术实践以外，他和别人另外创建并管理非赢利性艺术机构--比翼艺术中心。

Barbara Pollack

5

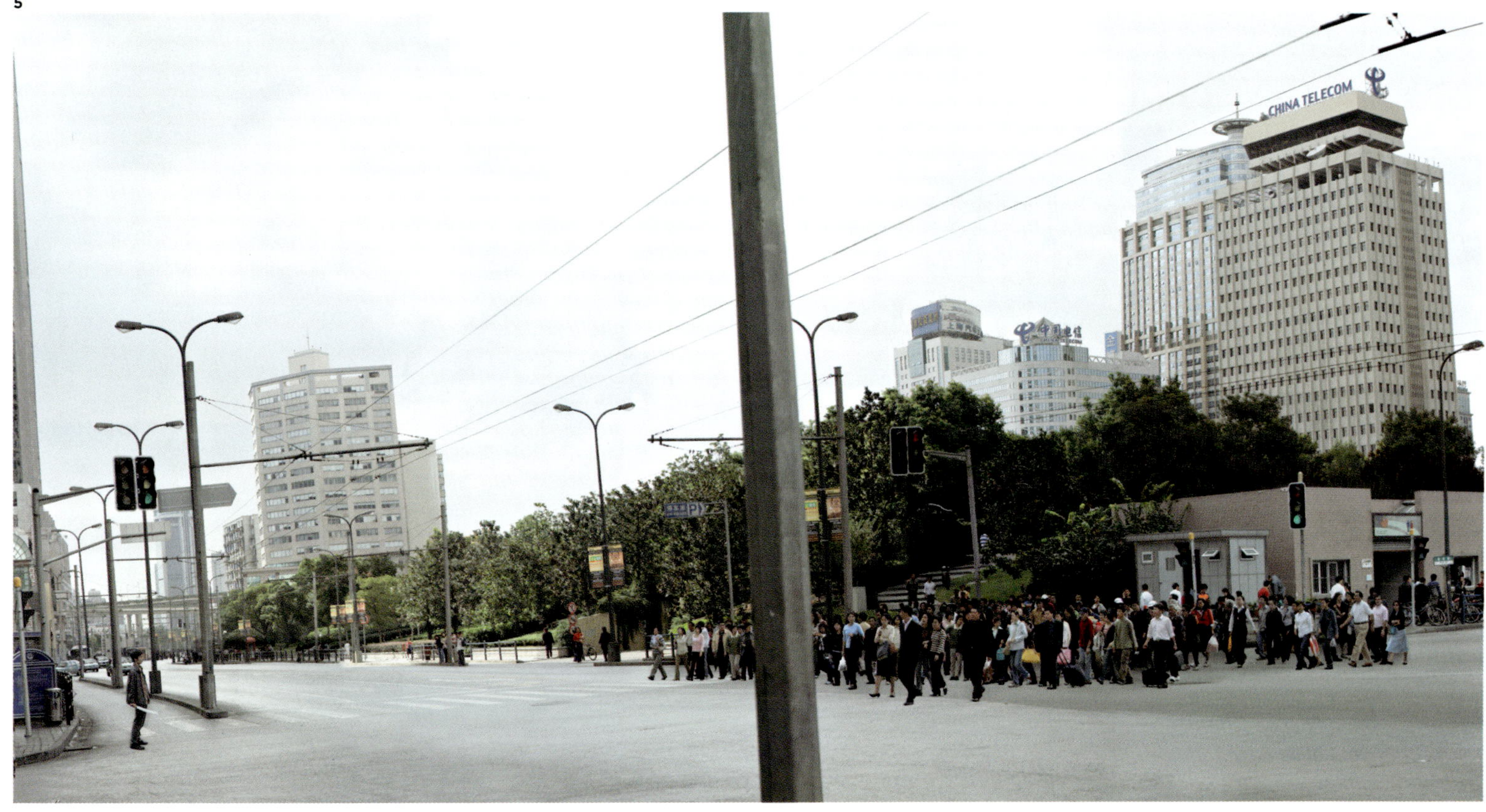

1 ***Temporary Expansion**, 2006*
C-print, photographs, objects, videos
C-print, Fotografien, Objekte, Videos
《临时性扩张》2006年, C-印刷，摄影, 物体, 录象

2 ***8.848–1.86**, 2005*
Installation
Installation
《8.848-1.86》2005年, 装置

3 ***8.848–1.86**, 2005*
Video stills
Video stills
《8.848-1.86》2005, 录像

4 ***Rainbow**, 1998*
Video, 4 min
Video, 4 Min.
《彩虹》1998年, 录象 4分钟

5 ***???????????????????? (2)**, 2004*
Photograph, 120 x 240 cm
Fotografie, 120 x 240 cm
《?????????????????????(2)》2004年, 摄影, 120 x 240 cm

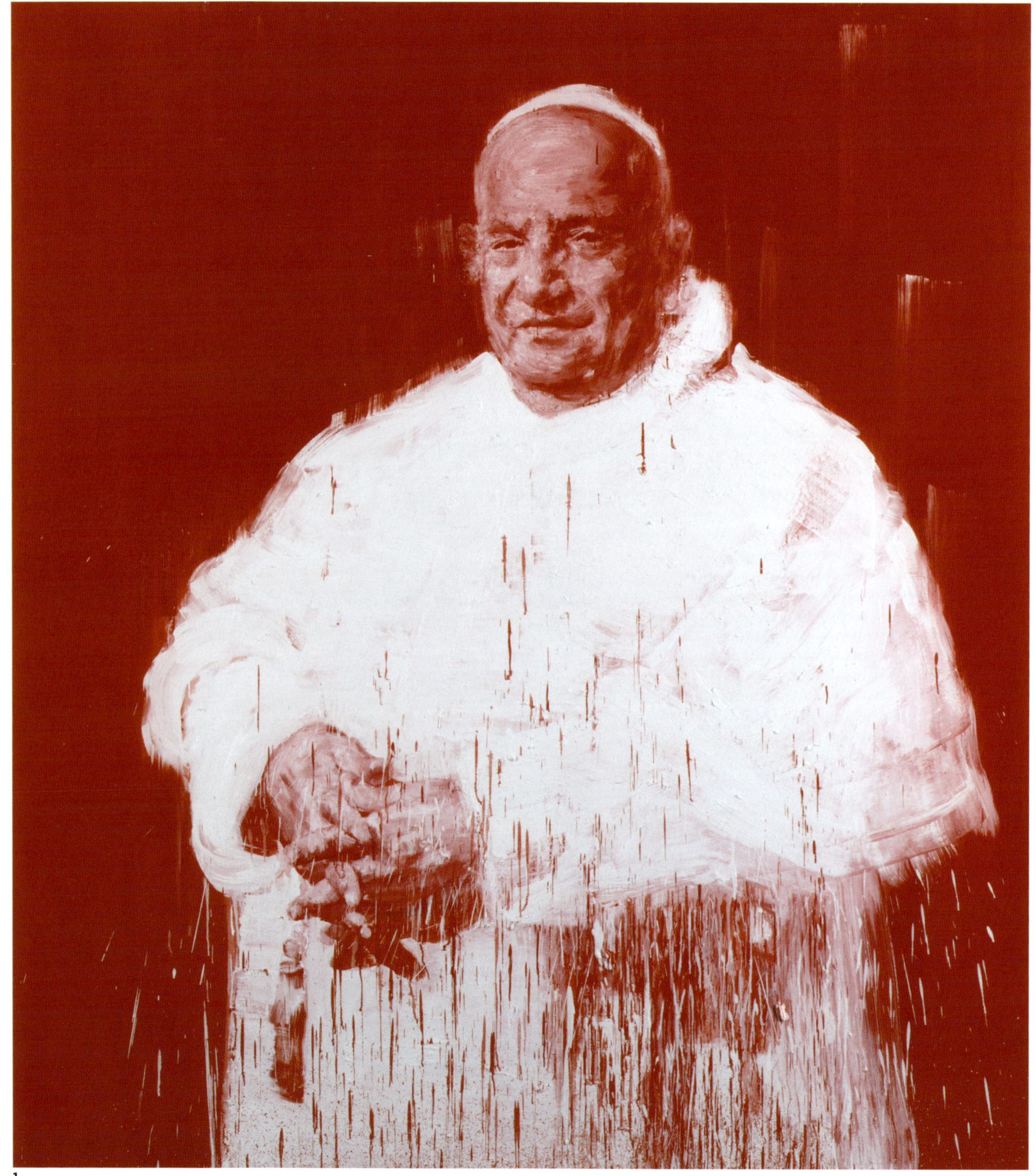

1

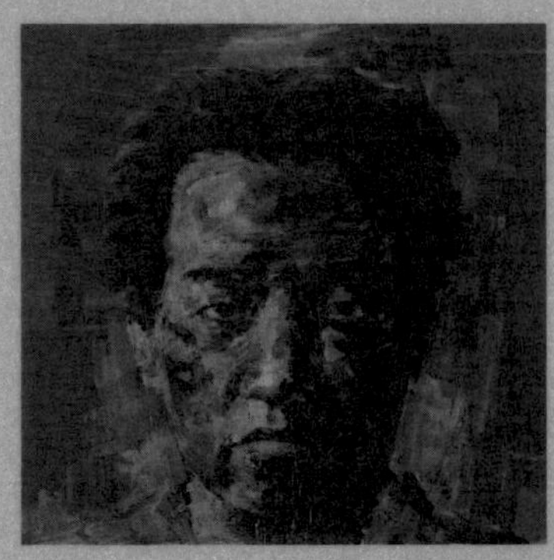

"I believe that painting always exists. The purpose of painting is to contribute to humanity."

„Ich glaube, dass die Malerei immer existiert. Der Zweck der Malerei ist es, zum Menschsein beizutragen."

"我坚信，油画将永远不会消失。油画就是服务于人类的。"

Born in 1960 in Shanghai, China. Lives and works in Dijon, France
Geboren 1960 in Shanghai, China. Lebt und arbeitet in Dijon, Frankreich
1960年出生于中国上海，现在法国第戎工作和生活

***Selected exhibitions* / Ausgewählte Ausstellungen /** 所选展览

1999 "Le retable, éloge des métissages", Panthéon, Paris, France
2000 "Tête de vertu", Studio Massimo de Carlo, Milan, Italy
"Autoportraits", Faggionato Fine Arts, London, UK
2004 "Yan Pei-Ming: The Way of the Dragon", Städtische Kunsthalle Mannheim, Mannheim, Germany
2005 "Oil Painting by Yan Pei-Ming", Guangdong Museum of Art, Guangzhou, China
2006 "Yan Pei-Ming", Musée d'Art moderne de Saint-Étienne, Saint-Étienne, France

1999年 《圣坛画像，称赞混种》先贤祠，巴黎法国
2000年 《道德头》Studio Massimo de Carlo 米兰 意大利
《自画像》Faggionato 画廊，伦敦英国
2004年 《严培明-猛龙过江》曼海姆美术馆，德国
2005年 《严培明油画展》广东美术馆 广州，中国
2006年 《严培明》安提雅 现代艺术美术馆，法国

***Selected publications* / Ausgewählte Publikationen /** 所选著作

Michael Sullivan: "Art and Artists of Twentieth Century China", Berkeley/Los Angeles 1996
Geremie Barmé: "Shades of Mao: The Posthumous Cult of the Great Leader", London 1996
"The Way of the Dragon – Yan Pei-Ming", Dijon 2005
"Hommage à mon Père, Yan Pei-Ming", Dijon 2005

Sullivan, Michael（著）:《二十世纪之中国艺术和艺术家》伯克利/洛杉矶 1996年
Barmé, Geremie（著）:《毛的影子：大领导人的遗腹礼拜》伦敦 1996年
《龙的道 – 严培明》第茂 2005年
《尊敬对我的父亲-- 严培明》展册，第茂 2005年

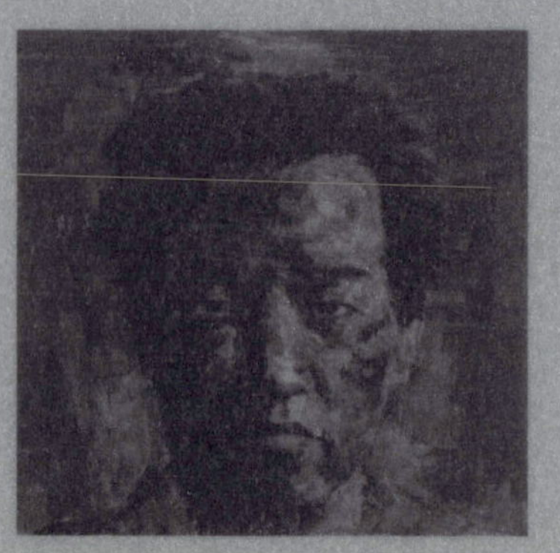

"I believe that painting always exists. The purpose of painting is to contribute to humanity."

„Ich glaube, dass die Malerei immer existiert. Der Zweck der Malerei ist es, zum Menschsein beizutragen."

"我坚信，油画将永远不会消失。油画就是服务于人类的。"

Born in 1960 in Shanghai, China. Lives and works in Dijon, France
Geboren 1960 in Shanghai, China. Lebt und arbeitet in Dijon, Frankreich
1960年出生于中国上海，现在法国第戎工作和生活

Selected exhibitions / Ausgewählte Ausstellungen / 所选展览

1999 "Le retable, éloge des métissages", Panthéon, Paris, France
2000 "Tête de vertu", Studio Massimo de Carlo, Milan, Italy
"Autoportraits", Faggionato Fine Arts, London, UK
2004 "Yan Pei-Ming: The Way of the Dragon", Städtische Kunsthalle Mannheim, Mannheim, Germany
2005 "Oil Painting by Yan Pei-Ming", Guangdong Museum of Art, Guangzhou, China
2006 "Yan Pei-Ming", Musée d'Art moderne de Saint-Étienne, Saint-Étienne, France

1999年 《圣坛画像，称赞混种》先贤祠，巴黎法国
2000年 《道德头》Studio Massimo de Carlo 米兰 意大利
《自画像》Faggionato 画廊，伦敦英国
2004年 《严培明-猛龙过江》曼海姆美术馆，德国
2005年 《严培明油画展》广东美术馆 广州，中国
2006年 《严培明》安堤雅 现代艺术美术馆，法国

Selected publications / Ausgewählte Publikationen / 所选著作

Michael Sullivan: "Art and Artists of Twentieth Century China", Berkeley/Los Angeles 1996
Geremie Barmé: "Shades of Mao: The Posthumous Cult of the Great Leader", London 1996
"The Way of the Dragon - Yan Pei-Ming", Dijon 2005
"Hommage à mon Père, Yan Pei-Ming", Dijon 2005

Sullivan, Michael（著）：《二十世纪之中国艺术和艺术家》伯克利/洛杉矶 1996年
Barmé, Geremie（著）：《毛的影子：大领导人的遗腹礼拜》伦敦 1996年
《龙的道 - 严培明》第戎 2005年
《尊敬对我的父亲一 严培明》展册，第戎 2005年

YAN PEI-MING 严培明

[jan pʰeimiŋ]

Of all the stories of Chinese artists, Yan Pei-Ming's perhaps reads the most like that of a normal artist. Born poor in Shanghai, he is denied admission to the Shanghai Arts and Crafts School in 1979 and moves to Dijon in 1980 to study at the Académie des Beaux-Arts, where he trains classically for five years. He attains an identity thoroughly hybrid, becoming the third Chinese collected by the Centre Pompidou, answering the question "Where do you live?" with "France," and the question "Where are you from?" with "China." In the late 1990s he begins moving freely back to his native city, always maintaining his base in Dijon. Throughout, he paints a stirring portraiture of crime victims and criminals, his friends and his father, Mao and Bruce Lee, always in sweeping, blurry brushstrokes, on large-format canvases, and employing conscientious bi-chromatic tonalities.

Having taken his education entirely in France, Yan Pei-Ming (known to friends simply as "Ming") was free to spend the 1980s on themes other than the epic encounter with Western art history that framed much of the art produced in China during that period. His first mature series, "Têtes", begun in 1987 and depicting sitters famous and unknown in equally grandiose terms. Around this time he began painting Mao, that most predictable of modern Chinese icons, but rendering him with an urgency quite distinct from that of neo-"leader portraits" then in vogue in China. Yan Pei-Ming's Mao was always already a Mao of memory, not of power, even if he himself has explicitly admitted that "I decided to do Mao's portrait in order to gain fame as a painter." Out of Yan Pei-Ming's filial imaginings of the dead leader came the genesis for a series of portraits of his own father, and out of his meditations on iconicity during these two series, the genesis of another, depicting the martial-arts star Bruce Lee. During a residency at the Villa Medici in Rome (1993/94) he embarked on an ambitious series entitled "108 Bandits" after the Chinese classic Water Margin. "I believe we are all bandits," Yan Pei-Ming has said, explaining how the massive project so titled actually depicts the people of his everyday orbit in Rome. Later

Von allen Lebensläufen chinesischer Künstler liest sich der von Yan Pei-Ming vielleicht am ehesten wie die klassische Version einer Künstlerbiografie. In arme Verhältnisse hineingeboren, wird ihm 1979 die Aufnahme an die Shanghai Arts and Crafts School verweigert, und so geht er 1980 nach Dijon, um dort an der Académie des Beaux-Arts zu studieren, wo er eine fünfjährige klassische Ausbildung absolviert. Er legt sich eine hybride Identität zu, wird der dritte vom Centre Pompidou gesammelte chinesische Künstler und beantwortet die Frage „Wo leben Sie?" mit „Frankreich" und die Erkundigung „Woher kommen Sie?" mit „China". Seit den späten 1990er Jahren kehrt er häufiger in seine Heimatstadt zurück, behält aber nach wie vor seinen Wohnsitz in Dijon. Die ganze Zeit hindurch malt er packende Porträts von Verbrechensopfern und Verbrechern, von seinen Freunden und seinem Vater, von Mao und Bruce Lee – stets in ausholenden, verwischten Pinselstrichen, auf großformatigen Leinwänden und in bewusst bichromer Farbgebung.

Dass er seine komplette Ausbildung in Frankreich absolvierte, gab Yan Pei-Ming (für seine Freunde einfach „Ming") die Freiheit, sich in den 1980er Jahren mit anderen Themen zu befassen als der Begegnung mit der westlichen Kunstgeschichte, die für einen Großteil der in China lebenden Künstler im Mittelpunkt stand. Schon Yans erste ausgereifte Serie, „Têtes", die er 1987 in Angriff nahm, stellt berühmte und unbekannte Modelle in grandioser Weise dar. Etwa um diese Zeit begann er auch, Mao zu malen, die am wenigsten überraschende aller modernen chinesischen Ikonen, mit einer Eindringlichkeit, die seine Bilder deutlich von den Neo-„Führerporträts" unterschied, die damals in China so populär waren. Yan Pei-Mings Mao war immer schon ein Mao der Erinnerung, nicht der Macht, auch wenn er selbst bekannte: „Ich beschloss, Maos Porträt zu malen, um berühmt zu werden." Yan Pei-Mings Imaginationen des toten Übervaters gaben den Anstoß zu einer Serie von Porträts seines eigenen Vaters. Den Einsichten über den Status solcher Ikonen, die ihm die beiden Serien abverlangten, entsprang eine weitere über den Kampfkunststar Bruce Lee. Während eines Aufenthalts in der Villa Medici in

纵观所有中国艺术家中，严培明算是比较较正常的一位。1960年出生于上海的一个贫寒家庭，1979年报考上海工艺美校落榜，1980年移居第戎，并考入第戎美术学院，在那里接受了五年专业教育。他是第三位被蓬皮杜艺术中心收藏作品的艺术家，而在异国他乡中功成名就。有人问他："您现居哪里啊？"答曰："巴黎"；"您出生哪里？""中国。"从90年末起，他开始回到上海，但第戎仍是其创作基地。自始至终，严培明以一种豪放、模糊的手法在巨幅画布上创作肖像画，如受害者和罪犯、他的父亲和朋友、毛泽东和李小龙等，而且总是以黑白双色为主调。

培严明在法国完成了其艺术教育，因而在整个八十年代期间，他就集中精力去创作作品，而非去了解西方艺术史。而在那个时期，大陆艺术创作大都未摆脱西方艺术史的框架。他的首部成熟作品系列《男人的头》开始于1987年，以一种奔放的风格描写了著名和不知名的坐人。大约从那时起，他开始绘制在中国家喻户晓的毛泽东的肖像，然而严并未将之形式的"领导人画像"风格，于是在中国流行起来。即使他曾经直率地承认"作为一个画家，我画毛泽东是为了出名。"严培明作品中的毛泽东总是回忆中的毛泽东，而非权力体系中的毛泽东。在毛泽东的画像基础上，他创作了以其父亲为主题的系列作品，除两个系列之外，他又创作了武术明星李小龙的作品。在罗马的麦迪奇别墅　居住期间(1993-1994年)，严培明以《水浒》为原型，创作宏伟系列作品《108条好汉》。"我相信我们所有人都是好汉，"严曾经就该作品标题如是说，而实际上这幅作品描述了他日常生活周围的人们。最近的肖像项目中，他关注于未亡人，南非贫民窟儿童，受害人，妓女和混血儿后代等.

从2003年起，严培明把视角转向了静物，如在由侯瀚如策划的威尼斯双年展上展出的《国际风景》。这个系列描写了生活中多种文化交错的普通但令人震撼的场所：上海机场以及他移居法国后的这个城

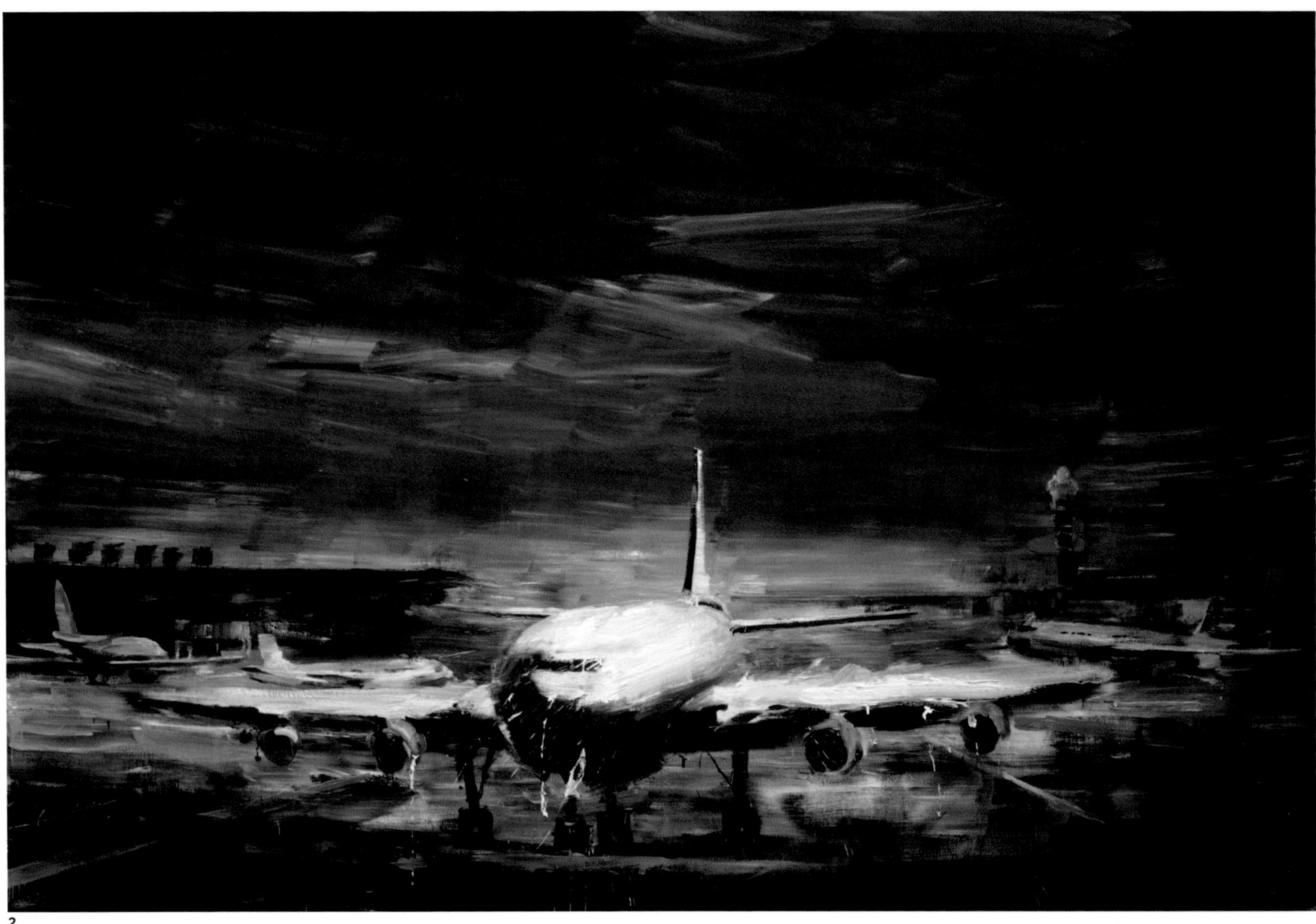

2

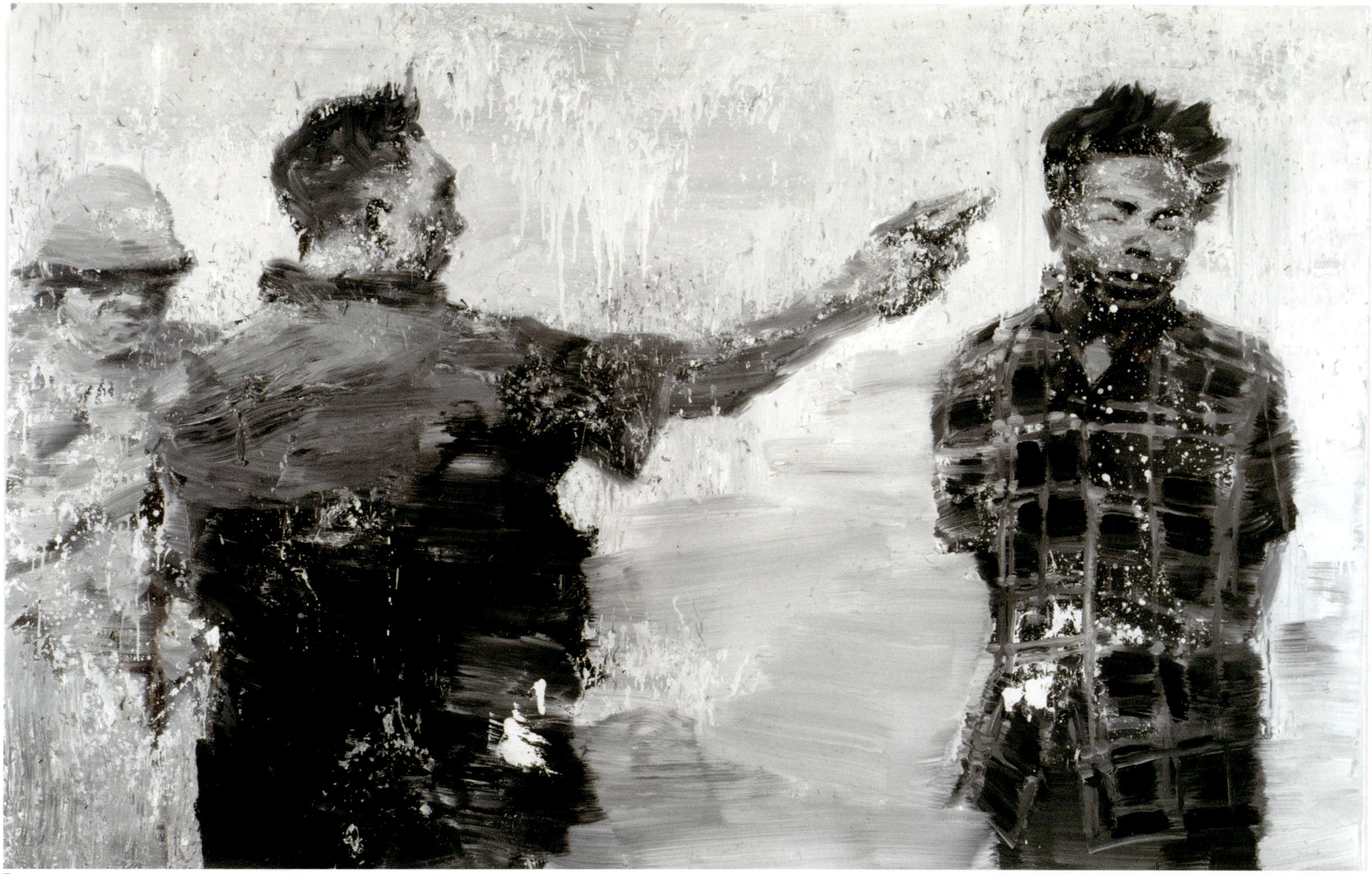

3

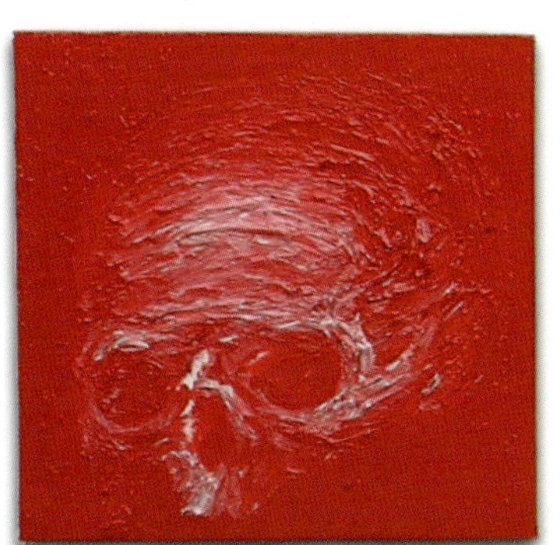

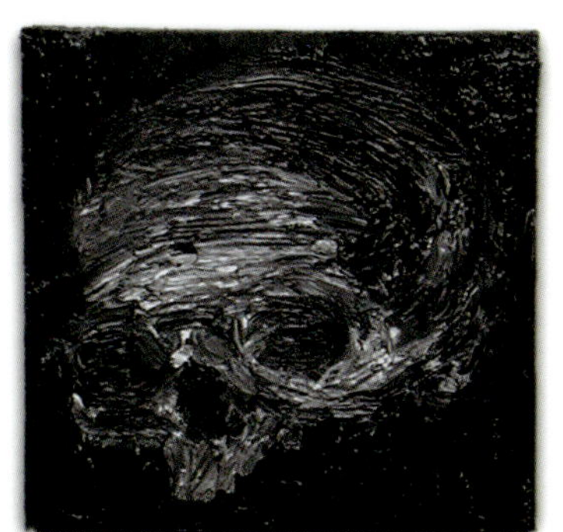

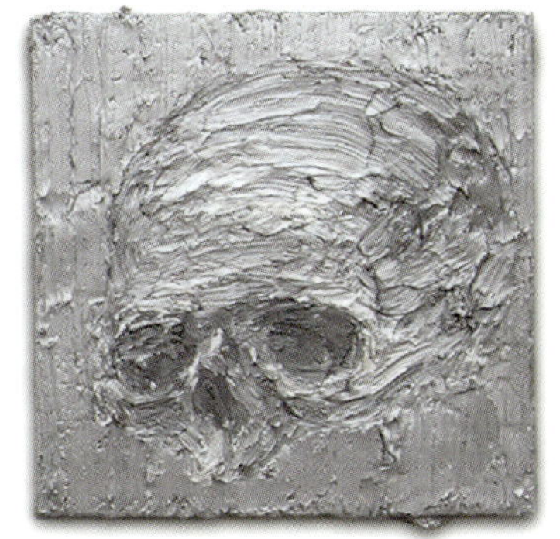

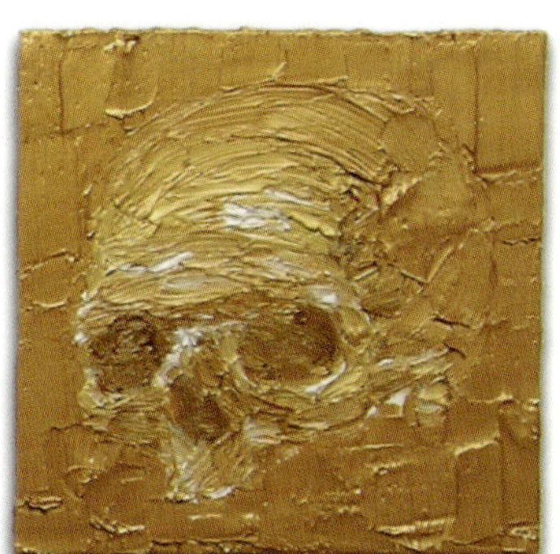

4

5

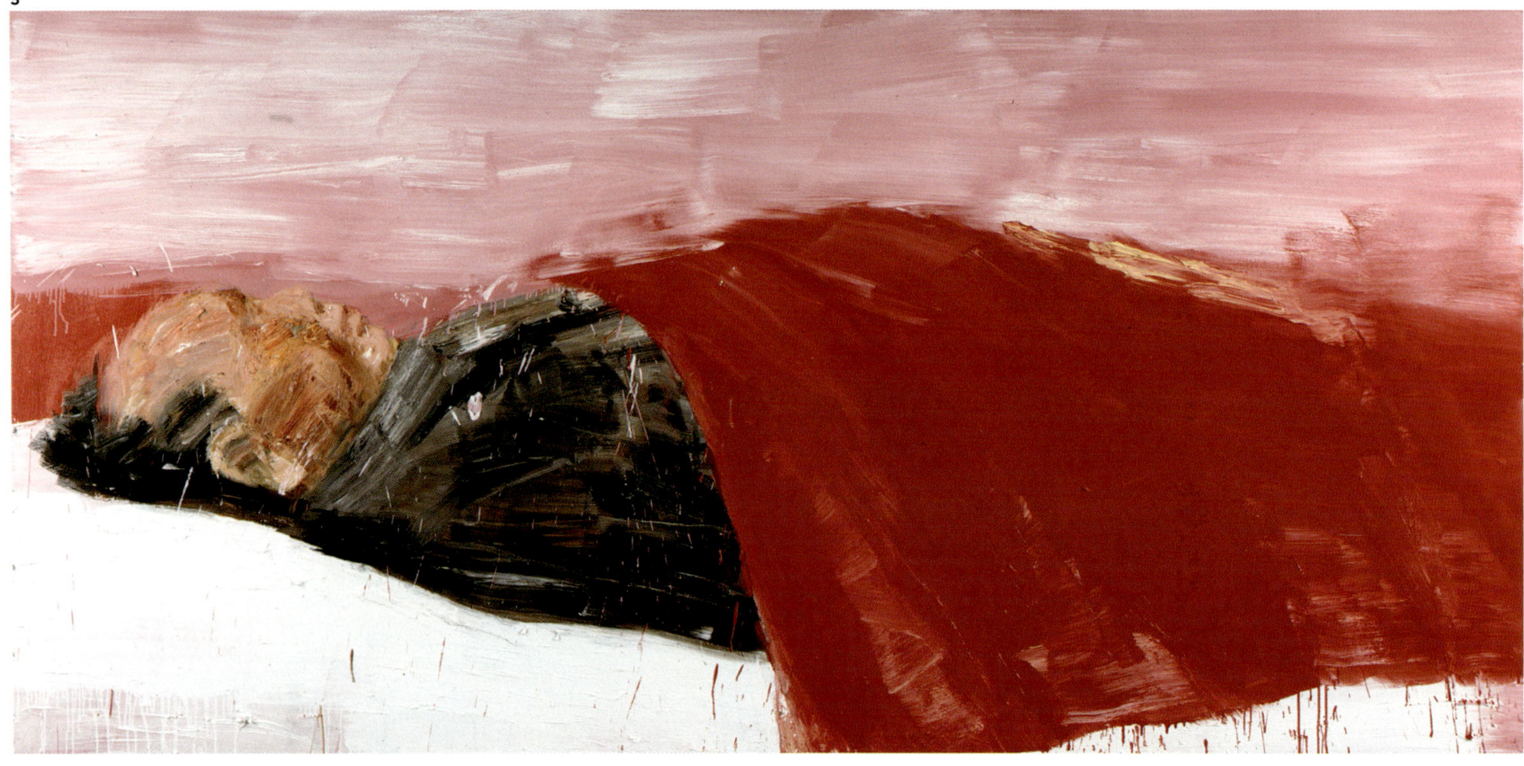

portraiture projects – which all unfold in the head-on idiom of mechanized, identity-card photography – focused on death row inmates, South African schoolchildren, crime victims, prostitutes, and mixed-race offspring.

In 2003, Yan Pei-Ming turned his lens toward the static with a project entitled "International Landscape" which he showed in Hou Hanru's section "Zone of Urgency" of that year's Venice Biennale. The series depicts common, poignant sites in a life lived between cultures: the Shanghai airport and other scenes of what became of the city he left behind. This preoccupation with loss and death continues, as in another sprawling series on the topic of his father, depicting him with different expressions and labeling him with different emotional monikers in the year leading up to his death. (This later became the centerpiece of a show that premiered in Dijon before moving to Shanghai and Guangzhou, "Hommage à mon Père", 2005.) While his attentions have expanded to include sculpture and watercolour, Yan Pei-Ming remains for most a painter of subtle expressions in broad strokes.

Rom (1993/94) machte er sich an eine Riesenserie mit dem Titel „108 Bandits" – nach dem chinesischen Klassiker „Die Räuber vom Liang-Schan-Moor". „Ich glaube, wir sind alle Banditen", erläuterte Yan Pei-Ming das gewaltige Projekt, das eigentlich Menschen aus seinem alltäglichen Wirkungskreis in Rom darstellt. Spätere Porträts – die allesamt in der frontalen Ausdrucksform der automatisierten Passfotografie gemalt sind – halten die Insassen von Todeszellen, südafrikanische Schulkinder, Verbrechensopfer, Prostituierte und Menschen unterschiedlichster Herkunft fest.

2003 wandte sich Yan Pei-ming mit dem Projekt „International Landscape", das er in der von Hou Hanru kuratierten Ausstellung „Zone of Urgency" auf der Biennale von Venedig 2003 zeigte, statischeren Motiven zu. Die Serie bildet alltägliche, prägnante Schauplätze eines Lebens zwischen den Kulturen ab und konstatiert, was aus der Stadt Shanghai geworden ist, seitdem Yan sie verließ. Diese Beschäftigung mit Verlusten, zu denen auch der Tod gehört, setzte sich seitdem fort, etwa in einer erneuten umfangreichen Serie über seinen Vater, den Yan im Jahr vor dessen Tod noch einmal porträtierte (Kernstück der in Dijon eröffneten Ausstellung „Hommage à mon Père", 2005, die auch nach Shanghai und Guangzhou wanderte). Obwohl er sein Interesse inzwischen auf die Bildhauerei und die Aquarellmalerei ausgedehnt hat, bleibt Yan Pei-Ming ein Maler des subtilen Ausdrucks in großzügigen Pinselschwüngen.

市的变化。之后她继续进行以消逝和死亡为主题的作品。在他的父亲去世之前，严培明创作了以父亲为主题的一部系列作品，描述老人家的各种表情，并用不同感情性语言作为画面的标题。(后来，该作品为展览《严培明：献给我的父亲第戎-广东》的压轴作品，展览在第戎开幕，后在上海和广东展出。)虽然他也把精力扩展到雕塑和水墨画项目上（2007年五月在纽约大卫•兹威那画廊举办了个展），但严培明依然大笔挥毫而表达细腻丰富。

Philip Tinari

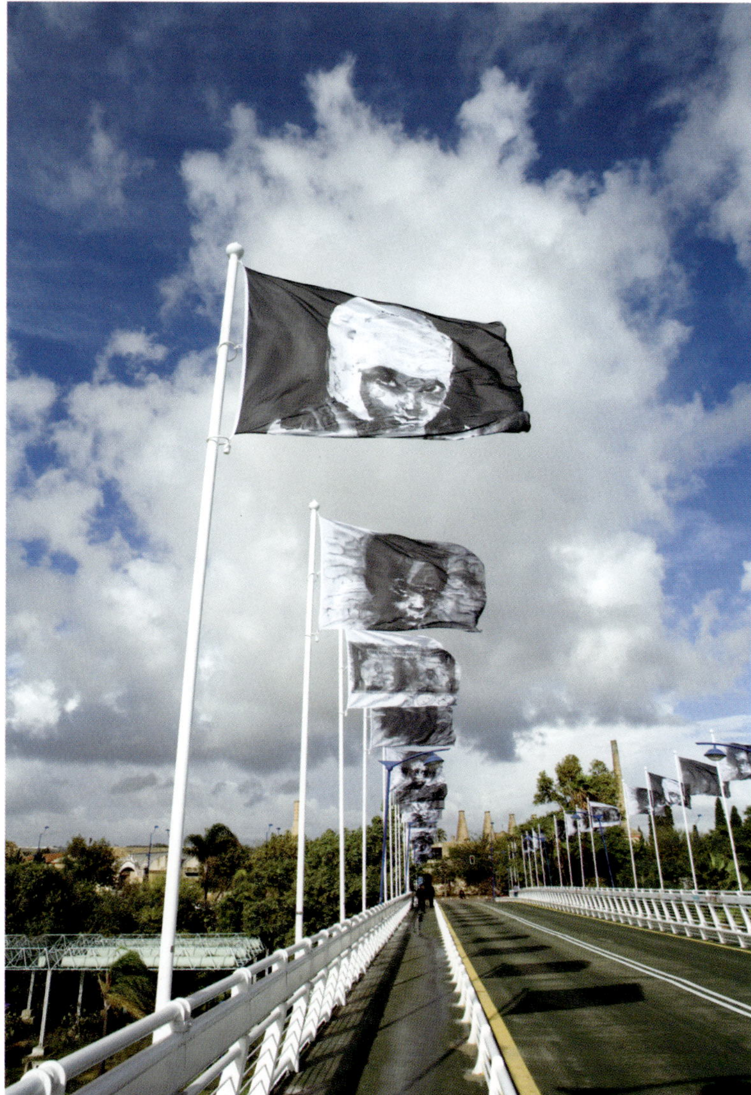
6

p. 505
***Black Self Portrait** 2007*
Oil on canvas, 350 x 350 cm
Öl auf Leinwand, 350 x 350 cm
《黑的自肖像》2007年，布面油画，350 x 350 cm

1 ***Pape Giovanni XXIII**, 2005*
Oil on canvas, 250 x 220 cm
Öl auf Leinwand, 250 x 220 cm
《教皇》2005年, 布面油画, 250 x 220 cm

2 ***International Landscape, Shanghai Airport**, 2003*
Oil on canvas, 350 x 500 cm
Öl auf Leinwand, 350 x 500 cm
《上海机场》2003年, 布面油画, 350 x 500 cm

3 ***Quartier chinois de Saigon**, 2004*
Oil on canvas, 130 x 200 cm
Öl auf Leinwand, 130 x 200 cm
《Quattri Chri Saigon》2004年, 布面油画, 130 x 200 cm

4 ***Red, Black, Silver & Gold Skull**, 2006*
Oil on canvas, 50 x 50 cm each
Öl auf Leinwand, je 50 x 50 cm
《大骷髅 -- 超脱者》2006年, 布面油画, 每幅50 x 50 cm

5 ***Mao Zedong remain**, 2001*
Oil on canvas, 150 x 300 cm
Öl auf Leinwand, 150 x 300 cm
《毛泽东》2001年, 布面油画, 150 x 300 cm

6 ***Drapeaux de Pirates**, 2006*
Installation view, 2nd International Biennial of Contemporary Art of Seville, Seville
Installationsansicht, 2nd International Biennial of Contemporary Art of Seville, Sevilla
《海盗的旗子》2006年，装置实景， 第二届国际塞维利亚当代艺术双年展， 塞维利亚

7 *Exhibition view "Fils du Dragon, Portraits de Mao",*
Musée des Beaux-Arts et d'archéologie, Besançon 2003
Ausstellungsansicht „Fils du Dragon, Portraits de Mao“,
Musée des Beaux-Arts et d'archéologie, Besançon 2003
《龙的男孩子， 毛泽东的肖像》2003年， 展览实景，美术和考古博物馆，贝藏松

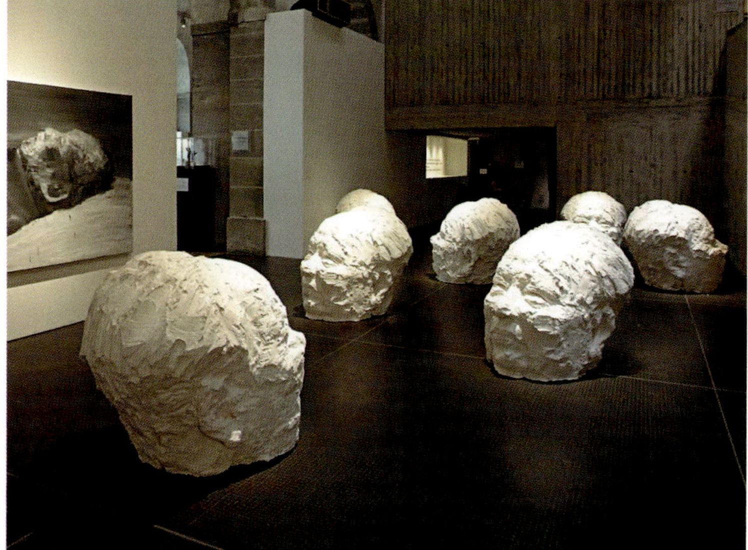
7

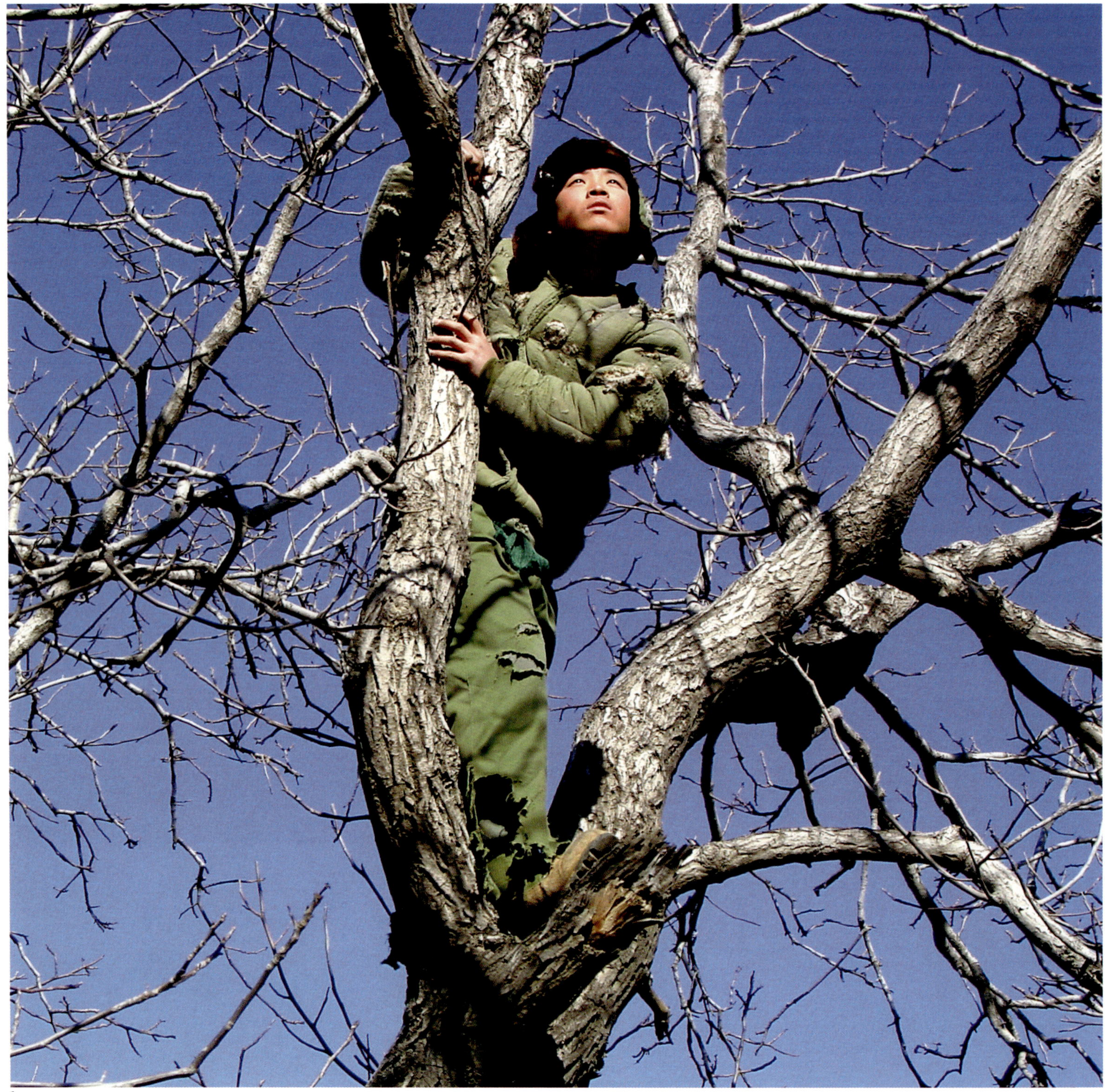

1

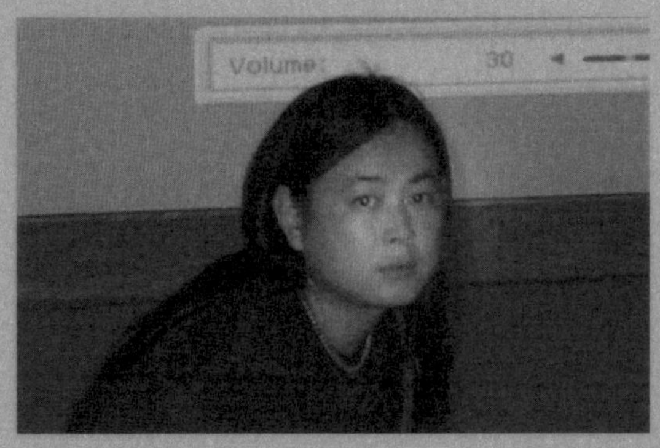

"What I film is the life of contemporary youth, almost aloof. It has no concrete passage of time. Sometimes I think that life presently changes even more greatly. Many people seem to have become 'non-believers'. They have lost their faith in everything."

„Ich filme das Leben der heutigen Jugend, meist aus der Ferne. Es gibt keine Chronologie. Manchmal denke ich, dass sich die Dinge heute noch schneller verändern. Viele Menschen scheinen zu ‚Ungläubigen' geworden zu sein, sie haben ihren Glauben total verloren."

"我摄制的是当代青年时期生活，几乎无动于衷。它没有具体时间消逝。有时我为，生活很大地目前改变。许多人似乎有成为的'非信徒的'。他们丢失了他们的信念在一切。"

Born in 1971 in Beijing, China. Lives and works in Shanghai
Geboren 1971 in Peking, China. Lebt und arbeitet in Shanghai
1971年出生于中国北京通县，住居工作在上海

***Selected exhibitions* / Ausgewählte Ausstellungen /** 所选展览

2004 "Light as Fuck! Shanghai Assemblage 2000–2004", The National Museum of Contemporary Art, Oslo, Norway
"Chine, Le Corps Partout?", Musée d'Art Contemporain, Marseille, France
2005 "Reshaping the Wall – Contemporary Chinese Art", Albright-Knox Art Gallery, University at Buffalo Art Galleries, Buffalo, NY, USA; Millennium Art Museum, Beijing, China
"Yang Fudong: Don't worry, it will be better", Kunsthalle Wien, Vienna, Austria
2006/07 "China Power Station I", Battersea Power Station, Serpentine Gallery, London, UK; Astrup Fearnley Museum of Modern Art, Oslo, Norway
2007 52. Biennale di Venezia, Venice, Italy

2004年 《轻而易举！上海拼图2000-2004年艺术展》国立当代美术馆，奥斯 陆，挪威
《身体。中国》现代美术馆，马赛，法国
2005年 《墙－中国当代艺术二十年展》美国奥尔布莱特－诺克斯美术馆，美国纽约州立大学布法罗分校美术馆，中国北京中华世纪坛艺术馆
《杨福东：别担心，明天会更好》维也纳美术馆，维也纳 奥地利
2006/07年 《中国电站I》蛇形画廊，巴特西电站 伦敦 英国；Astrup Fearnley 现代美术馆，奥斯陆，挪威
2007年 第 52届威尼斯双年展 威尼斯 意大利

***Selected publications* / Ausgewählte Publikationen /** 所选著作

Chen Xiaoyun: "Reasons for the Daydreaming Proletariat", Hangzhou 2000
"Yang Fudong: 'S10'", Siemens Arts Program 2003
"Talking Pictures", K21 Kunstsammlung Nordrhein-Westfalen, Cologne 2007
Uta Grosenick, Thomas Seelig (eds.): "Photo Art", Cologne 2007

陈晓云（著）：《作白日梦的无产阶级的原因》杭州 2000年
《杨福东："S10"》西门子艺术节目，2003年
《谈的图片》K21 艺术品收藏北莱蒽威斯特发伦，科隆2007年
Grosenick, Uta/Seelig, Thomas（编者）：《摄影艺术》科隆2007年

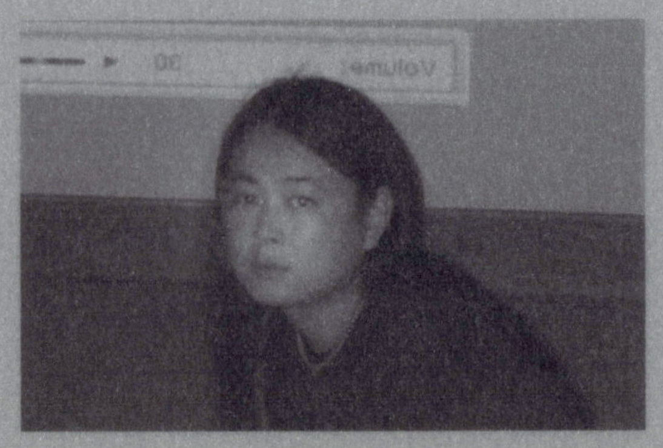

"What I film is the life of contemporary youth, almost aloof. It has no concrete passage of time. Sometimes I think that life presently changes even more greatly. Many people seem to have become 'non-believers'. They have lost their faith in everything."

„Ich filme das Leben der heutigen Jugend, meist aus der Ferne. Es gibt keine Chronologie. Manchmal denke ich, dass sich die Dinge heute noch schneller verändern. Viele Menschen scheinen zu ‚Ungläubigen' geworden zu sein, sie haben ihren Glauben total verloren."

"我摄制的是当代青年时期生活，几乎无动于衷。它没有具体时间消逝。有时我为，生活很大地目前改变。许多人似乎有成为的'非信徒的'。他们丢失了他们的信念在一切。"

Born in 1971 in Beijing, China. Lives and works in Shanghai
Geboren 1971 in Peking, China. Lebt und arbeitet in Shanghai
1971年出生于中国北京通县，住居工作在上海

Selected exhibitions / Ausgewählte Ausstellungen / 所选展览

2004 "Light as Fuck! Shanghai Assemblage 2000–2004", The National Museum of Contemporary Art, Oslo, Norway
"Chine, Le Corps Partout?", Musée d'Art Contemporain, Marseille, France
2005 "Reshaping the Wall – Contemporary Chinese Art", Albright-Knox Art Gallery, University at Buffalo Art Galleries, Buffalo, NY, USA; Millennium Art Museum, Beijing, China
"Yang Fudong: Don't worry, it will be better", Kunsthalle Wien, Vienna, Austria
2006/07 "China Power Station I", Battersea Power Station, Serpentine Gallery, London, UK; Astrup Fearnley Museum of Modern Art, Oslo, Norway
2007 52. Biennale di Venezia, Venice, Italy

2004年 《轻而易举！上海拼图2000-2004年艺术展》国立当代美术馆，奥斯陆，挪威
《身体。中国》现代美术馆，马赛，法国
2005年 《墙－中国当代艺术二十年展》美国奥尔布莱特－诺克斯美术馆，美国纽约州立大学布法罗分校美术馆，中国北京中华世纪坛艺术馆
《杨福东：别担心，明天会更好》维也纳美术馆，维也纳 奥地利
2006/07年 《中国电站I》蛇形画廊，巴特西电站 伦敦 英国；Astrup Fearnley 现代美术馆，奥斯陆，挪威
2007年 第 52届威尼斯双年展 威尼斯 意大利

Selected publications / Ausgewählte Publikationen / 所选著作

Chen Xiaoyun: "Reasons for the Daydreaming Proletariat", Hangzhou 2000
"Yang Fudong: 'S10'", Siemens Arts Program 2003
"Talking Pictures", K21 Kunstsammlung Nordrhein-Westfalen, Cologne 2007
Uta Grosenick, Thomas Seelig (eds.): "Photo Art", Cologne 2007

陈晓云（著）：《作白日梦的无产阶级的原因》杭州 2000年
《杨福东："S10"》西门子艺术节目，2003年
《谈的图片》K21 艺术品收藏北莱茵威斯特发伦，科隆2007年
Grosenick, Uta/Seelig, Thomas（编者）：《摄影艺术》科隆2007年

YANG FUDONG 杨福东

[iaŋ futʊŋ]

In 1995 Yang Fudong graduated from the Oil Painting Department of Hangzhou Zhejiang Academy of Fine Arts (today's Central Academy of Fine Arts). During his studies at the said academy Yang Fudong came in touch with photography for the first time. More importantly, however, was the lifestyle of people in this southern city making him deeply feel the culture of traditional Chinese scholars and their sensitivity and their core problems: the coming into world of the sense of social responsibility and the hidden desires of each individual and the coexistence and conflict of both, which are the spiritual coordinates of more than two thousand years of Chinese intellectuals. In his later works, Yang Fudong bestowed on them the image of contemporary capital youths.

Three years after graduating Yang Fudong spent three years in Beijing thinking about photography and finally moved to Shanghai in 1998. In 2001 Yang Fudong made his first 12 minutes film in black and white titles "Backyard – Hey, Sun is Rising!", which was awarded Beijing's "First independent Film Festival" as outstanding experimental film. This labelled Yang Fudong as new member of Chinese experimental artists circle. From 1997 to 2002 Yang Fudong completed the 76 minutes black and white film "An Estranged Paradise" shown at the 11th Documenta Kassel, attracting since that exhibition worldwide interest in his work. In 2003 Yang Fudong participated the 50th Venice Biennial at the Chinese pavilion the first time that China officially took part in this exhibition. In 2004 Yang Fudong was granted the "Hugo Boss Contemporary Art Award". At present he is regarded as an internationally renowned contemporary artist, living and working in Shanghai, whose main media are film, photography and video.

Yang Fudong's early photography work "The First Intellectual" (2000) not only raises interest in the international artists world, but in China also widespread in the Internet became one of the most used and diverted Internet image sources. One side of this picture deeply touches the collective unconscious of contemporary Chinese. On this

1995 beendete Yang Fudong sein Studium an der Zhejiang Academy of Fine Arts (heute Central Academy of Fine Arts) in Hangzhou im Fachgebiet Ölmalerei. Während des Studiums kam Yang zum ersten Mal mit der Fotografie in Berührung; viel wichtiger war jedoch, dass ihm der Lebensstil der Menschen in der südlich gelegenen Stadt die Kultur der traditionellen chinesischen Gelehrten, deren Sensibilität und deren eigentliche Probleme vermittelte: den Sinn für soziale Verantwortung auf der einen und für die verborgenen Wünsche jedes Einzelnen auf der anderen Seite – ein Konflikt, der seit über 2000 Jahren die geistigen Koordinaten der chinesischen Intellektuellen bestimmt. Ihnen verlieh Yang Fudong in seinen späteren Arbeiten das Aussehen zeitgenössischer Jugendlicher aus der Hauptstadt.

Nach seinem Abschluss verbrachte Yang drei Jahre in Peking, wo er sich mit der Theorie der Fotografie befasste; 1998 zog er nach Shanghai um. 2001 drehte er seinen ersten, 12 Minuten langen Schwarzweißfilm mit dem Titel „Backyard – Hey, Sun is Rising!", der auf Pekings „Erstem unabhängigen Filmestival" als herausragender Experimentalfilm einen Preis erhielt. Das machte Yang Fudong sogleich zu einem Protagonisten der experimentellen Kunst. Von 1997 bis 2002 arbeitete er an dem 76-minütigen Schwarzweißfilm „An Estranged Paradise", der, auf der Documenta 11 in Kassel gezeigt, weltweites Interesse an Yang Fudongs Arbeit auslöste. Im Jahr 2003 nahm Yang an der 50. Biennale von Venedig teil, als China zum ersten Mal mit einem eigenen Pavillon auf dieser Ausstellung vertreten war. 2004 wurde ihm der „Hugo Boss Preis für zeitgenössische Kunst" verliehen, und mittlerweile ist er ein international bekannter Künstler, der vor allem mit den Medien Film, Fotografie und Video arbeitet.

Yang Fudongs frühe Fotoarbeit „The First Intellectual" (2000) zog nicht nur das Interesse der internationalen Kunstszene auf sich, sondern wurde auch in China durch die Verbreitung über das Internet eine der am meisten verwendeten und abgewandelten Bildquellen. Eine Seite dieses Motivs berührt tief das kollektive Unbewusste der heutigen

1995年毕业于杭州的浙江美术学院油画系（现中国美术学院）。杨福东在学院期间开始接触摄影，更重要的是，他从杭州这座江南城市的人文风景中，深刻地感悟到了中国传统文人文化的精致的感受力和其核心议题：入世的社会责任感与隐遁的个人愿望，这二者的并存和冲突，几千年来成为中国知识分子的精神坐标。在此后的的工作中，杨福东将赋予他们当代都市青年的形象。毕业之后杨福东经过在北京三年对于电影的沉默思考，于1998年移居上海。2001年，杨福东的12分钟长的黑白电影短片《后房，嘿！天亮了》摘取了在北京举办的“第一届独立映像节”最佳实验短片奖。这标志着杨福东在中国实验艺术界的崛起。2001年，他还在第一届横滨三年展上展出了他的录像装置作品。1997年到2002年，杨福东完成了76分钟的黑白长片《陌生天堂》，并在2002年的第11届卡塞尔文献展上展出，从而引起广泛的世界性的关注。2003年杨福东成为第50届威尼斯双年展中国馆的参展艺术家，这也是中国第一次以官方身份参加威尼斯双年展。2004年杨福东入选“Hugo Boss当代艺术奖”。今天，作为拥有国际知名度的当代艺术家，杨福东生活和居住在上海，以电影、摄影和录像作为主要的工作媒介，作品在世界各大美术馆和双年展广泛展出。

杨福东早期的摄影作品《第一个知识分子》不但引起艺术界的关注，而且在中国的互联网上广泛传播，成为被挪用和窜改最多的互联网图像之一。这从一个侧面说明了这张图片所深刻触及的当代中国人的集体无意识。画面中在都市的街头，一个白领打扮的青年满头是血，高举砖块做出奋力一搏的姿势。那是渺小的个人的尊严和内心的隐秘被社会的铁律挤压到忍无可忍的时刻的最终爆发，知识分子也许是在反抗的瞬间诞生，但是反抗在大街上显得孤独甚至滑稽。

这是杨福东的图像族谱中情绪最为激烈的一个定格。在杨福东的电影中，人们更多的被凄美怀旧的

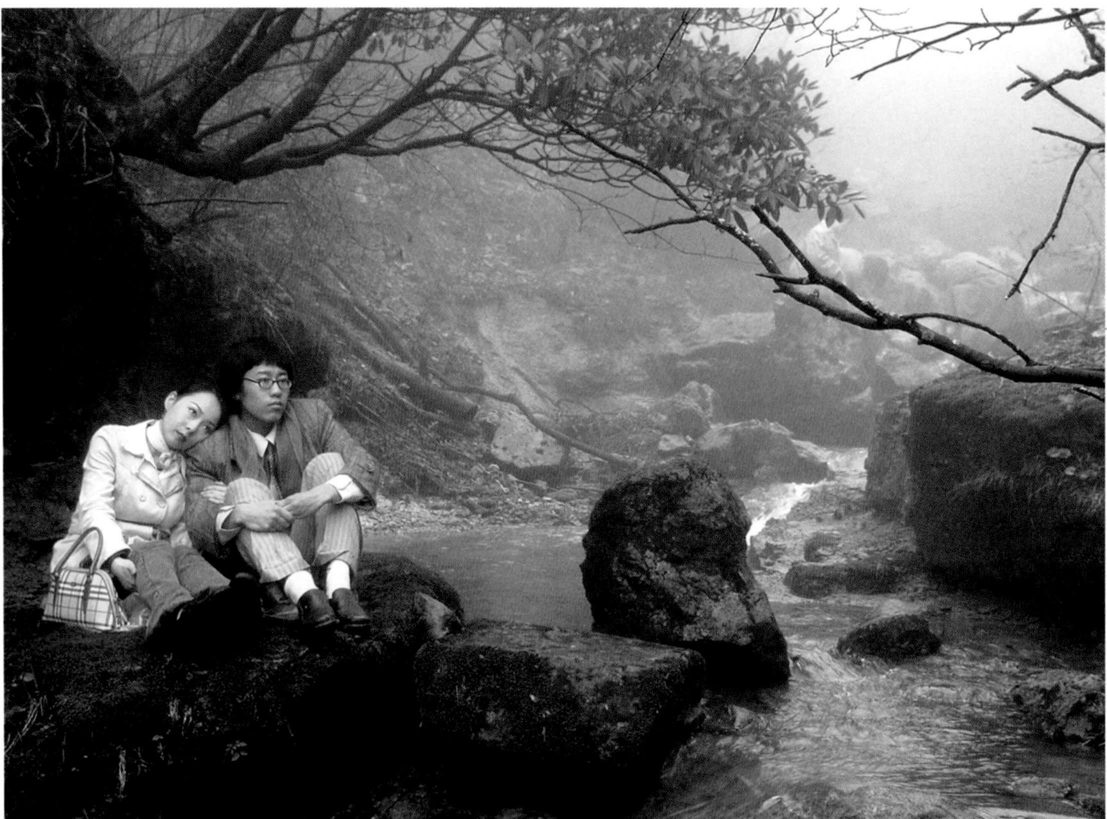

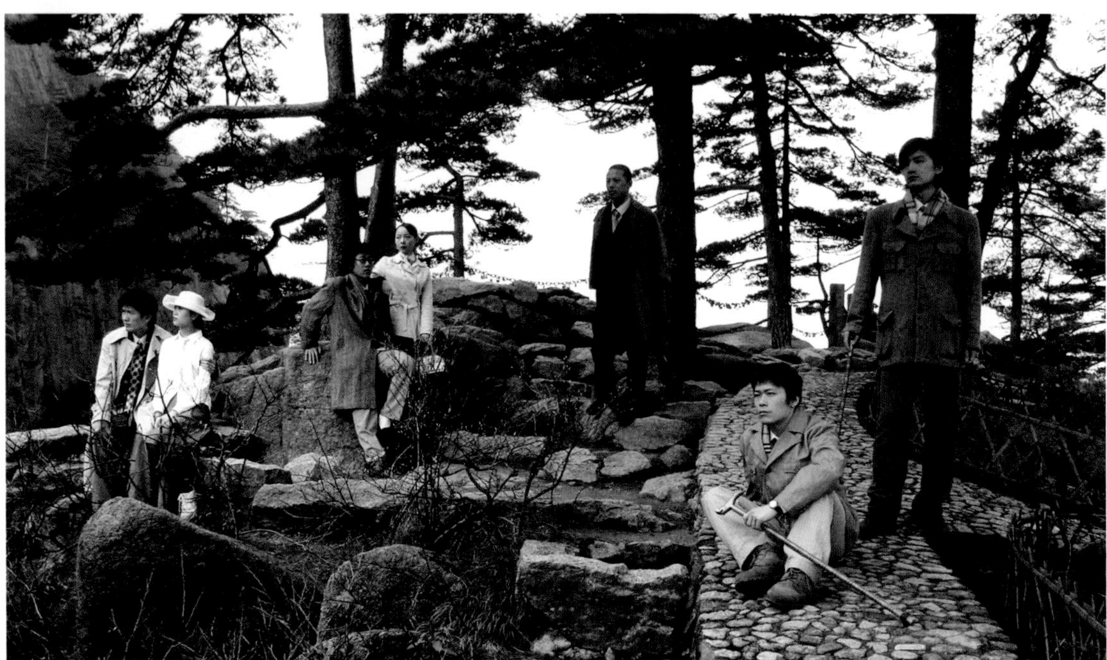

2

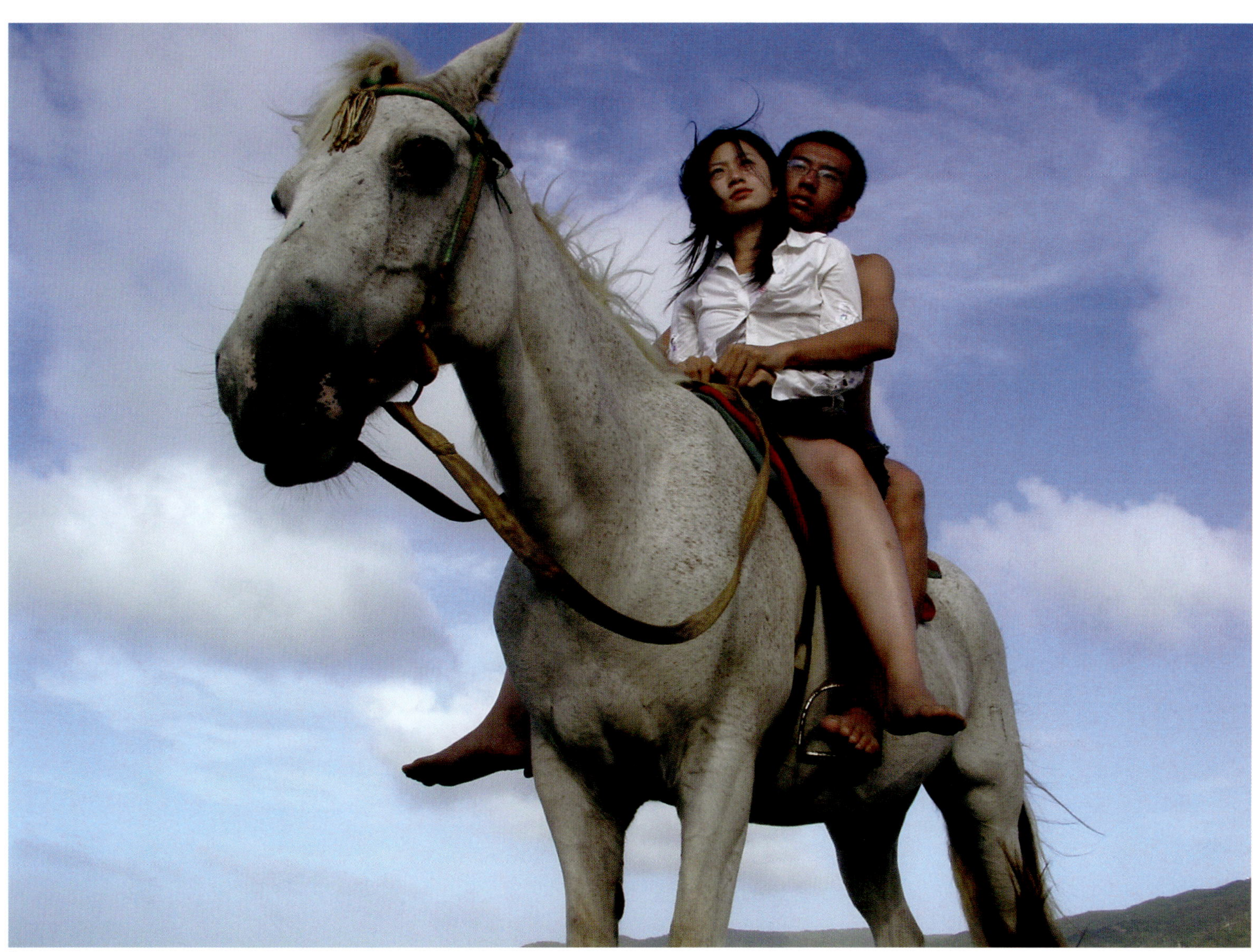

3

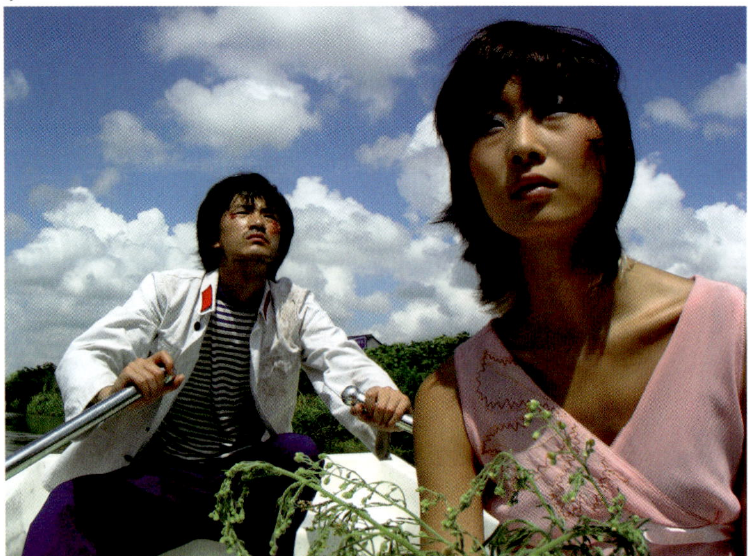

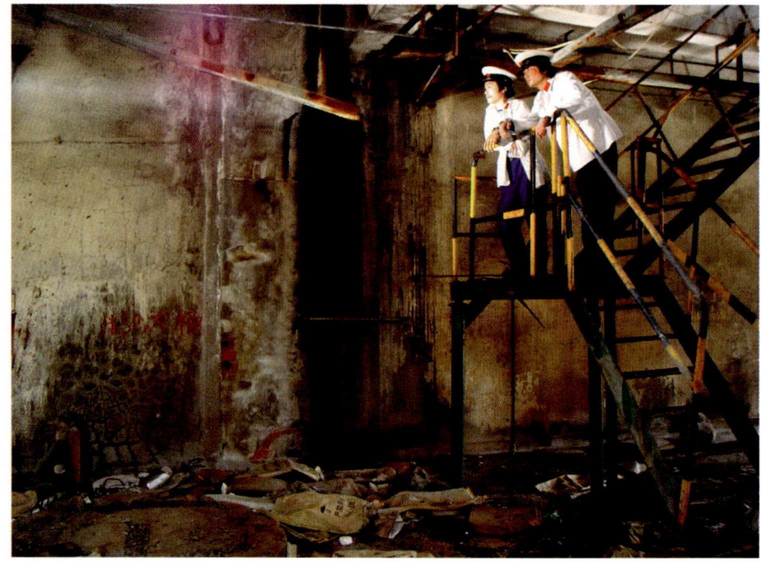

picture, somewhere in a street of the capital, a young man with white collar and bloody head is depicted, lifting a brick seemingly with all his strength like in a fight. It is the tiny individual human dignity and the innermost hidden secret feelings, exploding when the pressure of society's iron laws becomes unbearable. The intellectual seems to be in the very moment of birth of resistance, but this resistance fought lonely on the street makes him appear ridiculous.

This mood is the most intense and radical in the genealogy of Yang Fudong's pictures. In his films people are infected with nostalgia, situated confused between the mood of dialogue and monologue like somnambulists. In fact, this kind of individual and social conflict is hidden in Yang Fudong's pictures from the very beginning. It is the anxiety towards the difficulty of mutual exchange between the individuals and the need of mutual dependency. They are searching the ideal self, behaving cautiously not to be known to others, but from time to time these intellectuals will burst out unavoidably leaving mutually crazy impressions – but known like the Seven Saints of old China for questioning social norms. "Seven Intellectuals in Bamboo Forest" is a large-scale series in five parts which Yang Fudong finished in 2007. By his way of working Yang Fudong's films became the contemporary coordinate of Chinese cultural spirit.

Chinesen – auf diesem Bild, irgendwo auf einer Straße der Hauptstadt, ist ein junger Mann mit weißem Hemdkragen und blutigem Schädel abgebildet, er hebt einen Ziegelstein, so als wolle er mit aller Macht um irgendetwas kämpfen. Yang demonstriert daran die verbliebene Würde des Einzelnen sowie seine tief im Innern verborgenen geheimen Gefühle, die explodieren, wenn der Druck der eisernen Gesetze der Gesellschaft unerträglich wird. Der Intellektuelle scheint sich dann in einem kurzen Moment des Widerstands zu befinden, aber sein lediglich am Straßenrand ausgefochtener Kampf lässt ihn zugleich lächerlich erscheinen.

In dieser Fotoarbeit hat Yang Fudong Gefühle so intensiv und radikal wie nie zuvor dargestellt. In seinen Filmen sind die Menschen von Nostalgie befallen, in einem verwirrten Zustand zwischen Dialog und Monolog wie Schlafwandler. Tatsächlich steckt diese Art des individuellen und gesellschaftlichen Konflikts von Anfang an in Yangs Werk. Es ist die Angst vor den Schwierigkeiten des Austauschs und vor gegenseitiger Abhängigkeit. Seine Intellektuellen – wie die Sieben Weisen des alten China, die sich die Frage nach gesellschaftlichen Normen stellten – sind auf der Suche nach dem idealen Selbst; sie versuchen es zwar ängstlich vor anderen zu verbergen, doch von Zeit zu Zeit lassen sie unvermeidlich ihren Emotionen freien Lauf, was nicht selten den Eindruck von Verrücktheit hinterlässt. „Seven Intellectuals in Bamboo Forest" ist eine großformatige fünfteilige Serie des Künstlers, die er 2007 abschloss. Yang Fudongs Arbeitsweise macht insbesondere seine Filme zu einer wichtigen zeitgenössischen Koordinate der chinesischen Kultur.

黑白画面所感染，被梦游般的运动和介于对话和独白之间的情绪所迷惑，事实上，这种个人和社会的冲突始终潜伏在杨福东的画面中。那些心事重重的个人之间互相难于交流，却又必须互相倚靠。他们各自寻找理想的自我，小心翼翼地不愿为人所知，只是时而爆发，却难免互相制造疯狂的印象 -- 就像古代中国的那七位以质疑社会规范著称的怪诞文人。《竹林七贤》这也是杨福东正在进行的一个大型系列影片的标题。这样的工作，使杨福东的影像成为中国文化精神的一种当代坐标。

Qiu Zhijie

5

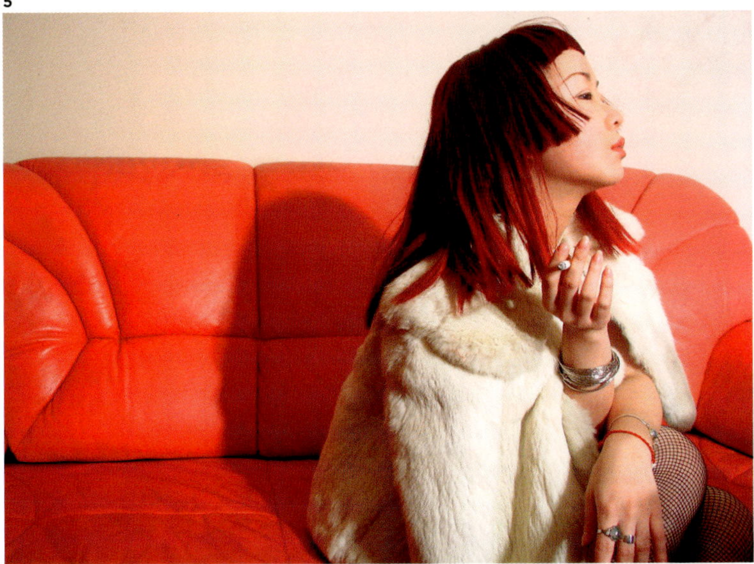

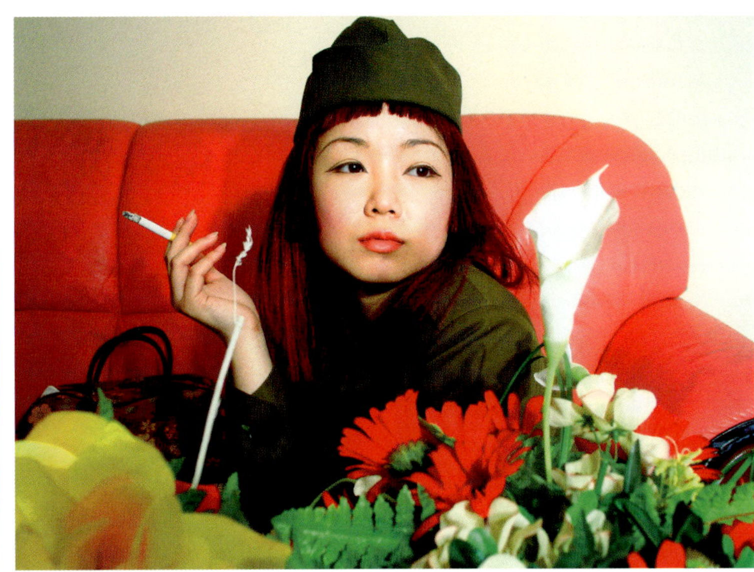

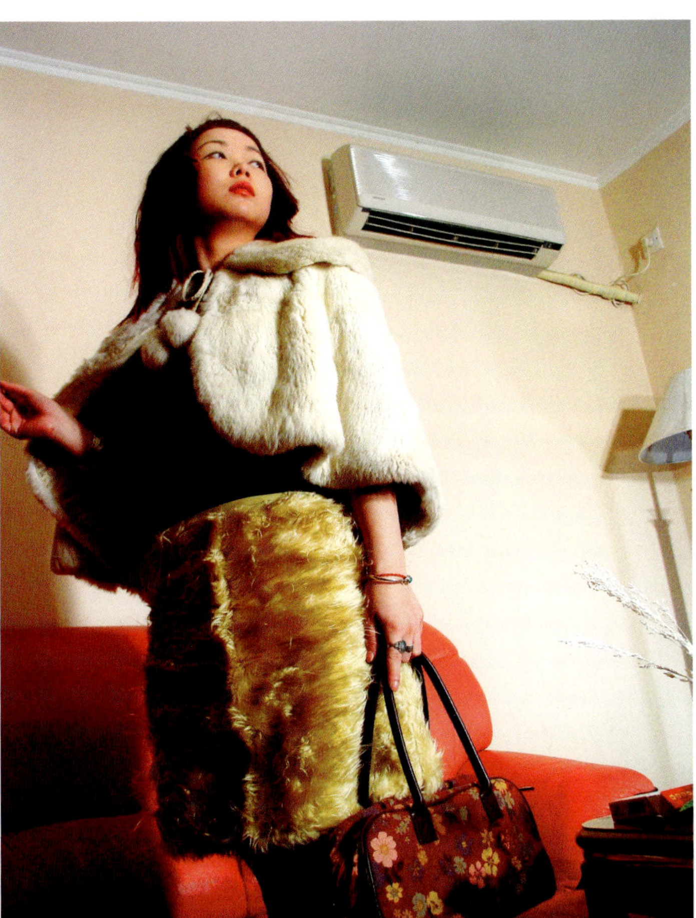

1 ***The Revival of the Snake**, 2005*
Video still
Video Still
《待蛇的苏醒》2005年，录象

2 ***Seven Intellectuals in Bamboo Forest (Part 1)**, 2003*
35-mm film, 29 min 30 sec
35-mm-Film, 29 Min. 30 Sek.
《竹林七贤》2003年, 35mm电影, 29分 30秒

3 ***Close to the Sea (xia hai)**, 2004*
Video, 23 min
Video, 23 Min.
《下海》2004年, 录像, 23分

4 ***Lock Again**, 2004*
16mm film, 3 min
16-mm-Film, 3 Min.
《路客再遇》2004年, 16mm 影片, 3分

5 ***Honey**, 2003*
Photographs, 50 x 70/70 x 50 cm each
Fotografien, je 50 x 70/70 x 50 cm
《蜜》2003年, 摄影, 每幅50 x 70 cm

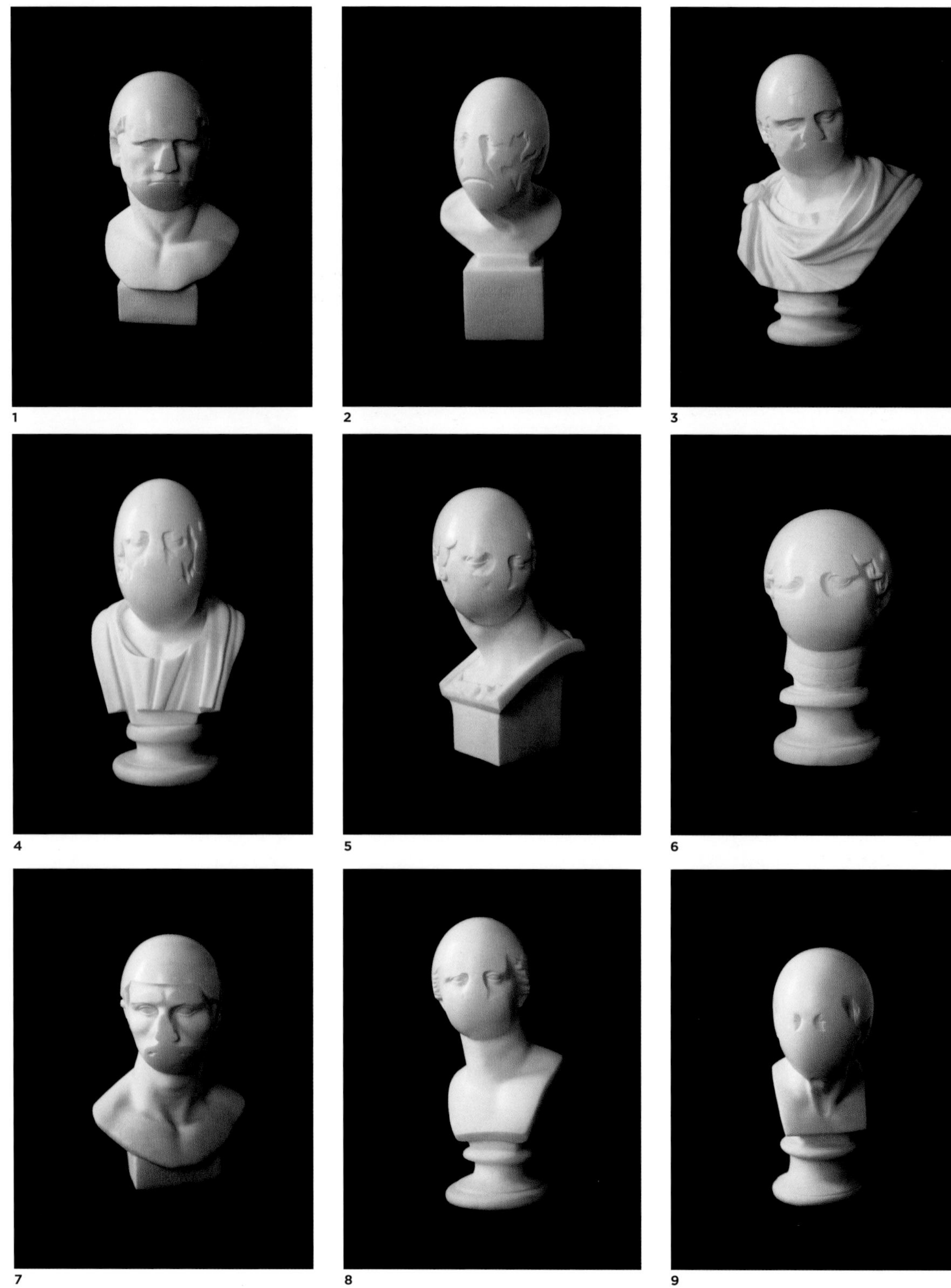

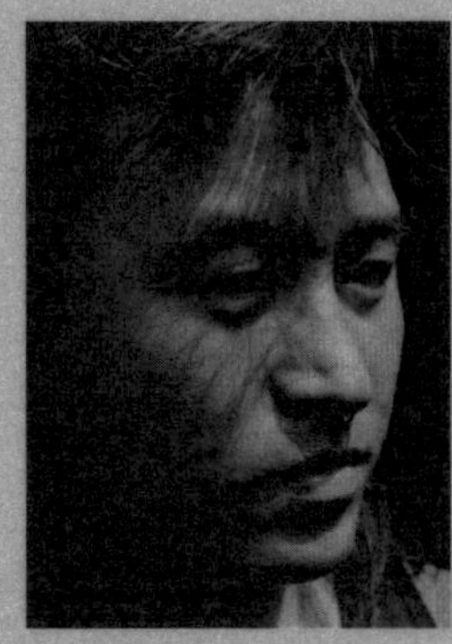

"I never believe that art has much to do with the world of creation. Art is an experience of mine... I get to understand myself through my work. In my eyes, 'people' are far more sophisticated than art and much more interesting. My work is to present this complexity. It is the most wonderful thing."

„Ich glaube nicht, dass Kunst viel mit der Welt des Schöpferischen zu tun hat. Kunst ist eine Erfahrung meiner selbst ... Ich verstehe mich erst durch meine Arbeit. In meinen Augen sind die Menschen weit gewitzter und interessanter als Kunst. Meine Arbeit will diese Komplexität darstellen. Das ist die wunderbarste Sache überhaupt."

"我从来不相信艺术和世界的创造有太多的联系，换而言之，我在我的作品中了解自己。在我的眼中，'人'比艺术更复杂、更有意思。我的作品就是表这种复杂性。这是一项很奇妙的工作。"

Born in 1966 in Dalian, Liaoning Province, China. Lives and works in Beijing
Geboren 1966 in Dalian, Provinz Liaoning, China. Lebt und arbeitet in Peking
1966 年出生于中国大连，辽宁州。住居工作在北京

***Selected exhibitions* / Ausgewählte Ausstellungen / 所选展览**

2001 "Fuck Off", East Link, Shanghai, China
2003 "Alors, la Chine?", Centre Georges Pompidou, Paris, France
2004 "Degenerated", Modern Chinese Art Foundation, Gent, Belgium
2005 "Clues", White Space, Beijing, China
2005–07 "Mahjong – Chinesische Gegenwartskunst aus der Sammlung Sigg", Kunstmuseum Bern, Berne, Switzerland; Hamburger Kunsthalle, Hamburg, Germany; Museum der Moderne, Salzburg, Austria
2006 "Look Inside: Yang Maoyuan's Solo Exhibition", DDM Warehouse, Shanghai, China

2001年 《不合作方式》东廊艺术画廊，上海
2003年 《中国怎么样？》蓬皮杜文化中心，巴黎
2004年 《退化》现代中国艺术捐献院，绅士
2005年 《线索》空白空间，北京
2005-07年 《麻将》西克中国当代艺术收藏展 伯尔尼美术馆 瑞士；汉堡美术馆 汉堡 德国；萨尔茨保现代美术馆 奥地利
2006年 《往里看》杨茂源个展 东大名创库，上海

***Selected publications* / Ausgewählte Publikationen / 所选著作**

Jean-Marc Decrop, Christine Buci-Glucksmann (eds.): "Modernités Chinoises", Milan 2003
Anne Lemonnier (ed.): "Alors, la Chine?", Paris 2003
"Clues", Beijing 2005
"Look Inside: Yang Maoyuan", Hong Kong 2006

Decrop, Jean-Marc/Buci-Glucksmann, Christine（编者）:《中国现代物》，米兰 2003年
Lemonnier, Anne（编者）:《中国怎么样？》蓬皮杜文化中心，展册，巴黎2003年
《线索》空白空间，北京 2005年
《往里看 -- 杨茂源》香港 2006年

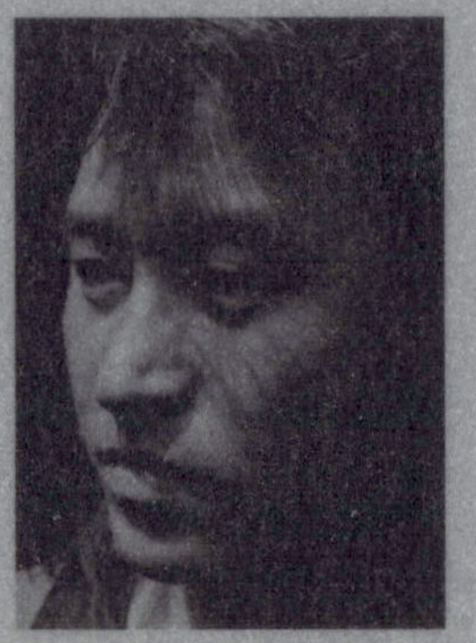

"I never believe that art has much to do with the world of creation. Art is an experience of mine... I get to understand myself through my work. In my eyes, 'people' are far more sophisticated than art and much more interesting. My work is to present this complexity. It is the most wonderful thing."

„Ich glaube nicht, dass Kunst viel mit der Welt des Schöpferischen zu tun hat. Kunst ist eine Erfahrung meiner selbst ... Ich verstehe mich erst durch meine Arbeit. In meinen Augen sind die Menschen weit gewitzter und interessanter als Kunst. Meine Arbeit will diese Komplexität darstellen. Das ist die wunderbarste Sache überhaupt."

"我从来不相信艺术和世界的创造有太多的联系，换而言之，我在我的作品中了解自己。在我的眼中，'人'比艺术更复杂，更有意思。我的作品就是表这种复杂性。这是一项很奇妙的工作。"

Born in 1966 in Dalian, Liaoning Province, China. Lives and works in Beijing
Geboren 1966 in Dalian, Provinz Liaoning, China. Lebt und arbeitet in Peking
1966 年出生于中国大连，辽宁州。住居工作在北京

Selected exhibitions / Ausgewählte Ausstellungen / 所选展览

2001	"Fuck Off", East Link, Shanghai, China
2003	"Alors, la Chine?", Centre Georges Pompidou, Paris, France
2004	"Degenerated", Modern Chinese Art Foundation, Gent, Belgium
2005	"Clues", White Space, Beijing, China
2005-07	"Mahjong - Chinesische Gegenwartskunst aus der Sammlung Sigg", Kunstmuseum Bern, Berne, Switzerland; Hamburger Kunsthalle, Hamburg, Germany; Museum der Moderne, Salzburg, Austria
2006	"Look Inside: Yang Maoyuan's Solo Exhibition", DDM Warehouse, Shanghai, China

2001年	《不合作方式》东廊艺术画廊，上海
2003年	《中国怎么样？》蓬皮杜文化中心，巴黎
2004年	《退化》现代中国艺术捐献院，绅士
2005年	《线索》空白空间，北京
2005-07年	《麻将》西克中国当代艺术收藏展 伯尔尼美术馆 瑞士；汉堡美术馆 汉堡 德国；萨尔茨堡现代美术馆 奥地利
2006年	《往里看》杨茂源个展 东大名创库，上海

Selected publications / Ausgewählte Publikationen / 所选著作

Jean-Marc Decrop, Christine Buci-Glucksmann (eds.): "Modernités Chinoises", Milan 2003
Anne Lemonnier (ed.): "Alors, la Chine?", Paris 2003
"Clues", Beijing 2005
"Look Inside: Yang Maoyuan", Hong Kong 2006

Decrop, Jean-Marc/Buci-Glucksmann, Christine（编者）：《中国现代物》，米兰 2003年
Lemonnier, Anne（编者）：《中国怎么样？》蓬皮杜文化中心，展册，巴黎2003年
《线索》空白空间，北京 2005年
《往里看 — 杨茂源》香港 2006年

YANG MAOYUAN 杨茂源

[jaŋ maʊ juan]

In the early 1990s, Yang Maoyuan worked for a few years as the artistic director for a documentary crew, which took him to significant archaeological sites as far as Loulan in the far north-western part of China. While travelling in the desert, he created a few site-specific works with situational approaches and characteristics of land art. In the heart of the desert, he hired local craftsmen to carve twelve primitive-looking life-size figure statues out of wood logs that resembled totem poles, and left them erected where they were made, as if they were the creations of some outer force. His direct experience and awe with the greatness, intensity and volatility of Nature in his travel continues to be a lasting influence. This is present in his ongoing paintings of monstrous and often disproportional human figures or body parts half-buried in, or lying on, the barren and cracked yellow earth.

His passion for travelling, history and archaeological investigation threads through the rich tapestry of his practice. In another encounter in his journey, witnessing Muslim people slaughtering cattle, he was overwhelmed by the sight of the greenish, warm and fermenting fodder that was bursting out of the dying cattle's stomachs. A few years later he would fill oil paint tubes with fodder taken from a cattle's stomach where it was being digested and fermented ("Food in the Cattle's Stomach", 2002). It was almost like a joke, an attempt to recast death in a new light by fabricating a believable way of recycling remains.

Yang's inflated sculptures made of sheepskin and goatskin were another reinvention of death or afterlife. By stitching pieces of hairy sheepskin or goatskin to create bloated round-shaped sheep or goats, filled with airbags inside, sometimes fixed with more than one head, often painted in glaringly bright colours such as blue and yellow, Yang conjured up humorous and secretly philosophical portraits of the end. The round shape symbolizes completeness of a life cycle in Chinese philosophy and emerged again as a defining feature in his latest sculptural series "Look Inside". From 2005 to 2006 he made a group of marble statues

Anfang der 1990er Jahre war Yang Maoyuan einige Jahre künstlerischer Leiter eines Dokumentarfilmteams. Diese Tätigkeit führte ihn zu bedeutenden archäologischen Stätten in so abgelegenen Gegenden wie Loulan im Nordwesten Chinas. Während seiner Reisen durch die Wüste schuf er einige ortsbezogene Werke mit situationistischem Ansatz und Charakteristika der Land Art. So heuerte er im Herzen der Wüste einheimische Handwerker an, die für ihn zwölf primitiv wirkende lebensgroße Figuren, die an Totempfähle erinnerten, aus Holzstämmen schnitzten. Yang ließ sie am Ort ihrer Entstehung zurück – so als seien sie das Werk einer unbekannten Hand. Das direkte Naturerlebnis und die auf seinen Reisen erlangte Ehrfurcht vor der Größe, Intensität und Unbeständigkeit der Natur wirken als bleibender Einfluss in seiner Gemäldeserie monströser und oft unproportionierter menschlicher Gestalten oder Körperteile fort, die auf einem kargen, rissigen, gelben Untergrund liegen oder halb in ihm versunken sind.

Yangs Begeisterung für Reisen, Geschichte und archäologische Forschungen spiegelt sich in der abwechslungsreichen Vielfalt seines Schaffens. Ebenfalls auf einer seiner Reisen erlebte er eine Viehschlachtung nach muslimischem Ritus und war überwältigt vom Anblick der warmen, gärenden, grünlichen Pflanzenmasse, die aus den Mägen der sterbenden Tiere quoll. Einige Jahre später füllte er solch halb verdaute, stinkende Nahrungsreste aus dem Magen eines Rinds in Ölfarbentuben („Food in the Cattle's Stomach", 2002); schon fast ein Schelmenstreich, handelte es sich hier um den Versuch, den Tod in neuem Licht darzustellen: eine sinnvolle Methode zur Wiederverwertung sterblicher Überreste.

Yangs aufgeblähte Skulpturen aus Schaf- und Ziegenfellen sind eine weitere Neuerfindung des Todes oder eines Lebens nach dem Tod. Indem er zottige Felle zu ballonförmig aufgedunsenen, mit Luftsäcken ausgestopften Schafen oder Ziegen zusammennähte, denen er mitunter mehr als einen Kopf verpasste und die er oft in grellen Farben anmalte, beschwor Yang humoristische und verkappt philosophische

上世纪九十年代初期，杨茂源作为一个记录片小组的艺术指导工作了数年，并随之考察了许多重要的考古遗址，远至中国西北部的楼兰。在穿越沙漠的途中，他以情景画家的手法创作了部分带有地景艺术特色的特定场所作品。在沙漠的中心，他雇用当地手艺人用原木雕刻了12个类似图腾柱并且外观朴拙、真人大小的雕像，并将其立在原地，好似这些雕像由某种外来力量所创造的。他的亲身经历以及他对于"自然"的伟大、深度和善变的敬畏不断影响着他的绘画。这些画中的人物或身体部位巨大且常常不成比例，半埋在或躺在贫瘠干裂的黄色土地上。

对于旅行、历史及考古调查的热情，为其艺术实践的富丽织锦穿针引线。在另一次旅途邂逅中，他目睹了回民阿訇宰牛的过程。温绿色的——暖暖的——发酵的饲料从死牛的胃中喷涌而出，而他则被这一场景所深深震撼。若干年后的 2002 年，他把牛胃里正在消化发酵的草料装进了油画颜料软瓶里。（《牛胃里的食物》）这几乎像是一个玩笑，通过构造一种令人信服的重新利用遗体的方式，让死亡重见天日的尝试。

杨茂源用绵羊皮和山羊皮制作的充气雕塑，则是另一种对死亡或来生的改造。他将带毛的绵羊皮或山羊皮缝合起来，做成充气的圆形绵羊或山羊，向里面塞进气囊，有时装上一个以上的头，并常常涂上蓝色、黄色等明亮的色彩。通过这些作品，杨茂源对死亡做出了幽默而神秘的哲学描述。在中国哲学里，圆形象征着一次生命循环的完整性，并且在他最近的雕塑系列《往里看》中作为一种定义特征再次出现。2005 年到 2006 年间，他创作了一组大理石雕像，复制了那些我们常常能够在一件艺术学校的教室角落里看到的亚历斯多芬斯、阿格里巴、卡瑞卡拉、朱利亚诺・梅第奇等石膏半身像。高度磨光的白色大理石赋予这些雕像典雅、贵重、庄严和永恒的品质。然而原始石膏雕像模型上的面部特征则完全被打磨掉并变得平坦，从而使这些大

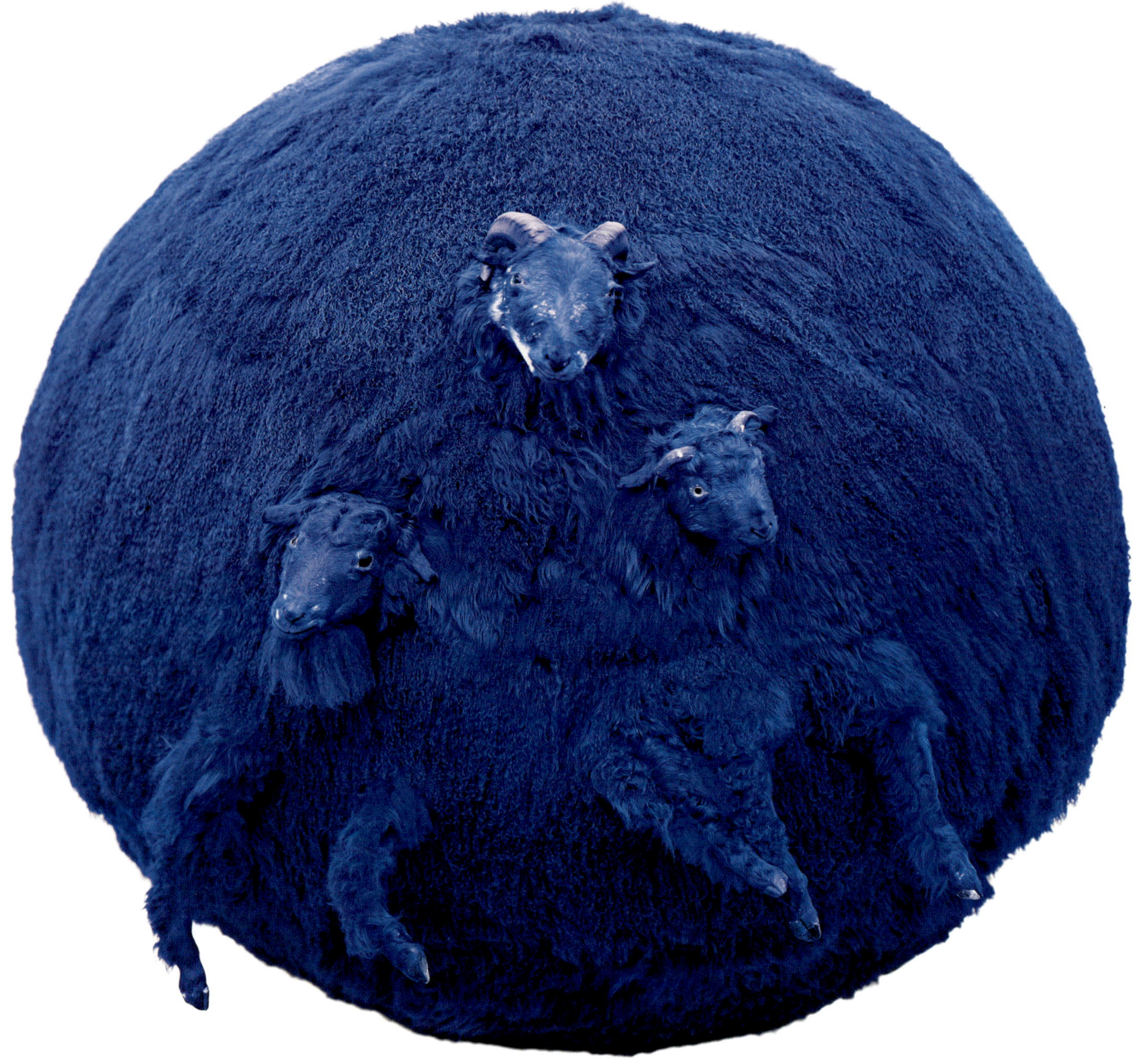

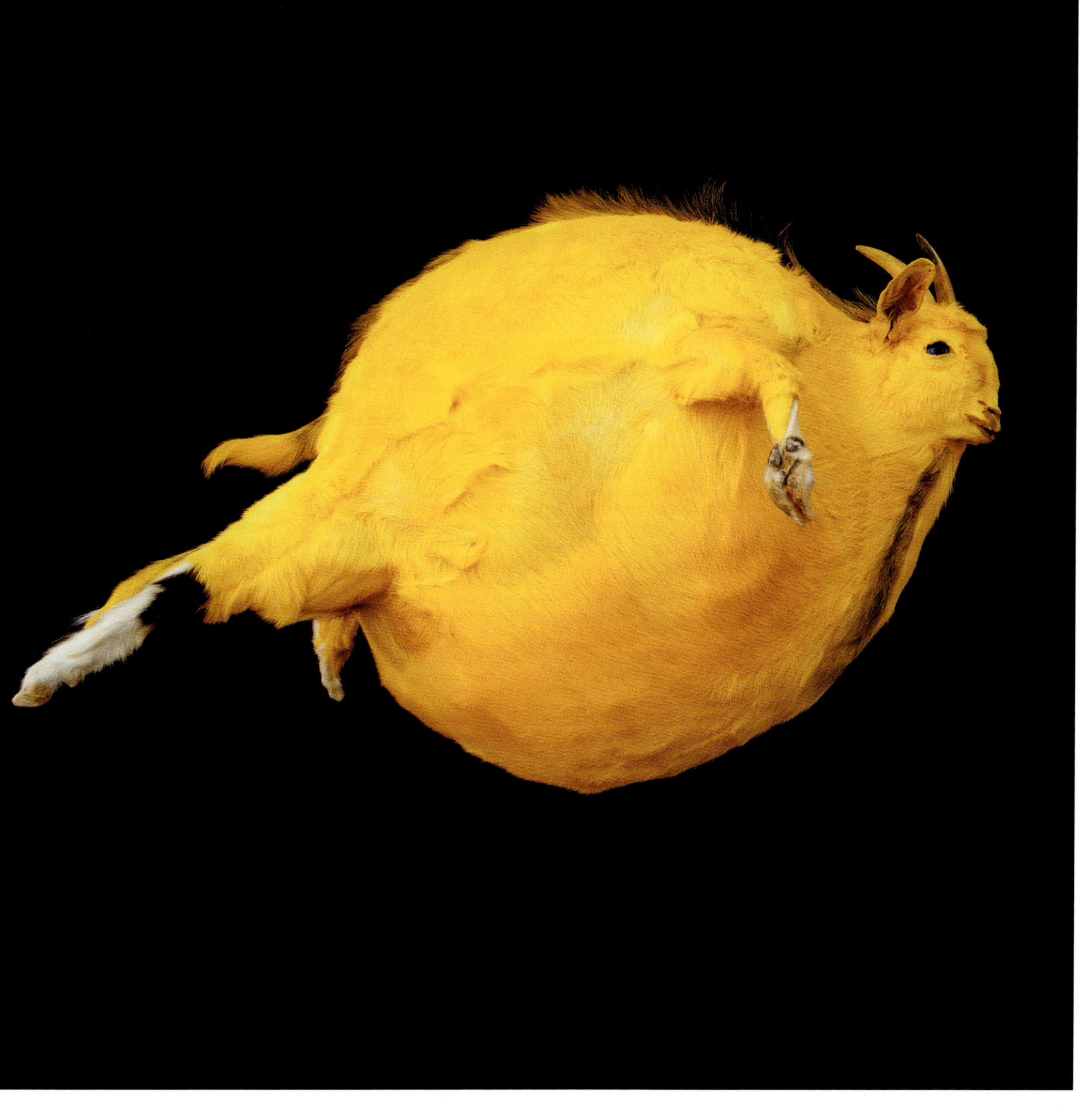

11

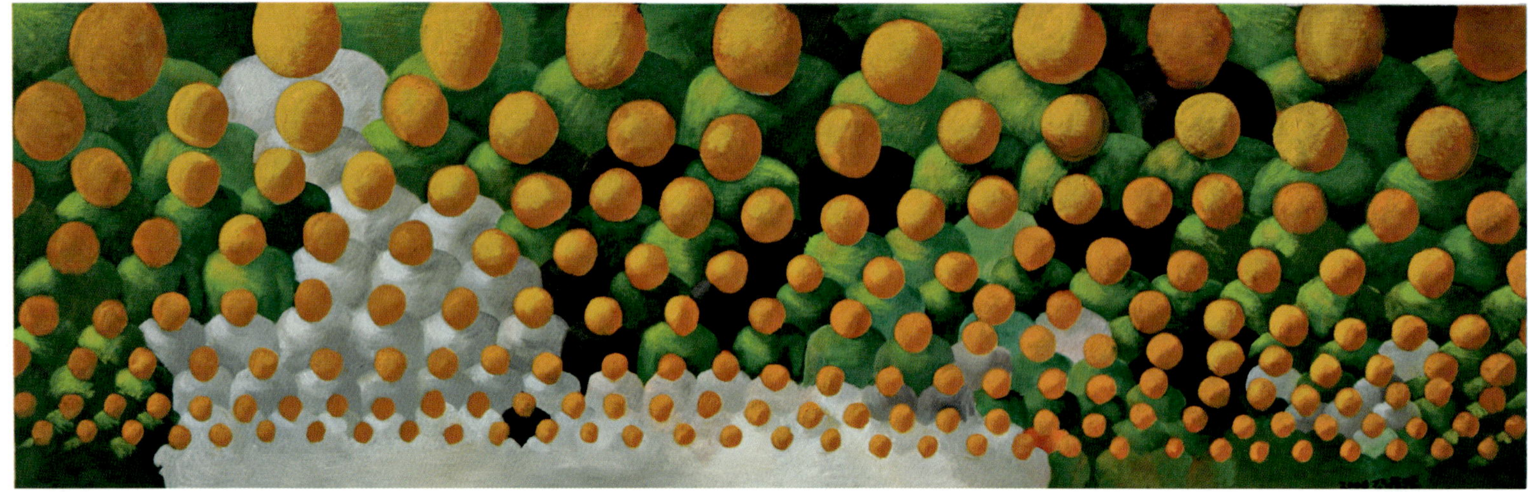

modelled on classic portrait busts of Aristophanes, Agrippa Giovane, Caracalla, Giuliano Medici, and so on, those we usually see stuck in the corner of art academy classrooms. The highly polished white marble gives these sculptures an elegant, priceless, solemn and timeless quality. Yet any facial features on the original plaster sculptures were all erased and levelled out, their heads became absolutely round and smooth. These plaster busts, long-standing aesthetic archetypes and symbols of establishments are completely deprived of their inherent functions and made fun of, yet ironically cast in a material that would give them another kind of eternity and authority.

Yang's work and the subjects he dwells on are often rich with allusions. His latest archaeological and artistic project probes into the myths of the dragon, an animal whose origin and existence are forever disputable and full of ambiguity. Armed with a conviction of its being, Yang sets out on a journey, as far as Japan, to collect all kinds of materials including: historical books; photographs; urban myths; news stories; newspaper clippings; documentaries; museum displays; archaeological relics and claimed witnesses, which he will weave into a complex body of work including a film and a exhibition comprising of relevant documents. The myth of the dragon is only a point of departure for a larger discussion involving the nature of history making and the space between history and fiction.

Bilder vom Ende. Denn die runde Form symbolisiert in der chinesischen Philosophie die Vollendung eines Lebenszyklus und taucht auch in Yangs jüngster Skulpturenserie „Look Inside" als konstitutives Element wieder auf.

Von 2005 bis 2006 schuf er eine Gruppe von Marmorstatuen nach den Vorbildern klassischer Porträtbüsten von Aristophanes, Agrippa, Caracalla, Giuliano Medici und anderen, wie sie in den Unterrichtsräumen von Kunstakademien herumstehen. Der auf Hochglanz polierte weiße Marmor verleiht diesen Skulpturen eine elegante, kostbare, feierliche und zeitlose Ausstrahlung. Allerdings hatte Yang sämtliche Gesichtszüge der gipsernen Vorbilder getilgt und eingeebnet, sodass die Köpfe vollkommen rund und glatt sind. Die Büsten, die als angestammte ästhetische Archetypen und Symbole des Establishments fungieren, verloren dabei gänzlich die ihnen innewohnende Funktion und wurden zugleich ins Lächerliche gezogen, ironischerweise jedoch auch in ein Material überführt, das ihnen eine andere Form von Ewigkeit und Autorität verleiht.

Yangs Werke sind wie auch seine Themen reich an Anspielungen. Sein jüngstes Archäologie- und Kunstprojekt erforscht den Mythos des Drachens, eines legendären Tiers, dessen Ursprung und Existenz strittig und voller Rätsel ist. Im festen Glauben an seine Existenz macht sich Yang auf eine Reise, die ihn bis nach Japan führt, um alle möglichen Belege, historische Bücher, Fotos, Mythen, Reportagen, Zeitungsausschnitte, Dokumentarfilme, Museumsexponate, archäologische Funde und angebliche Zeugenaussagen zu sammeln und zu einem komplexen Werk zu verweben, zu dem u. a. ein Film und eine Ausstellung mit Dokumenten gehören sollen. Der Mythos des Drachens dient dabei nur als Ausgangspunkt für eine viel weiter gespannte Diskussion um das Wesen der Geschichtsschreibung und das Spannungsfeld zwischen Historie und Fiktion.

理石雕像的脑袋变得绝对的圆滑。长期以来，这些石膏雕像是审美原型和权威象征，现在却被完全剥夺了他们固有的作用并被用来嘲笑，然而具讽刺意味的是，他们的制作材料却给予他们另一种永恒和权威。

杨茂源的作品和他所详述的主题通常具有丰富的暗示。他最新的考古和艺术项目对龙的神话进行了探索。龙这种动物的本源和存在永远是争议的话题，并且没有明确的答案。而杨茂源却坚信它的存在，他开始了一次远至日本的旅程，搜集各种材料、历史书籍、摄影作品、都市神话、新闻报道、剪报、记录片、博物馆陈列、考古遗迹、自称的目击者等等。他将会把所有这些素材编织成一件形式复杂的作品，包括一部电影和一个由相关文献组成的展览。龙的神话只是一次更大规模的讨论的开始，而这个讨论将涉及历史发展的本质以及历史与虚构之间的空间。

Carol Lu

13

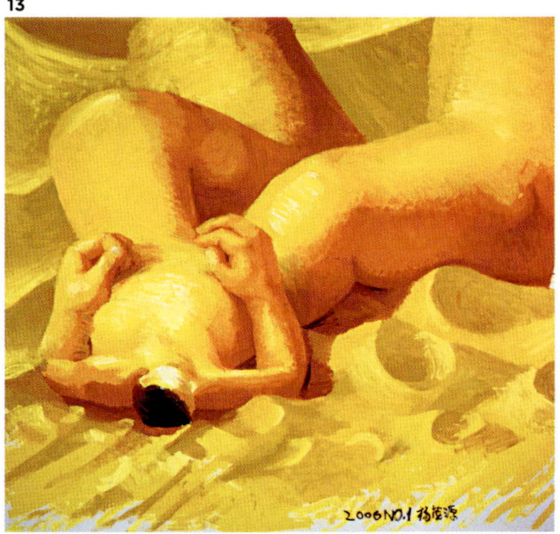

14

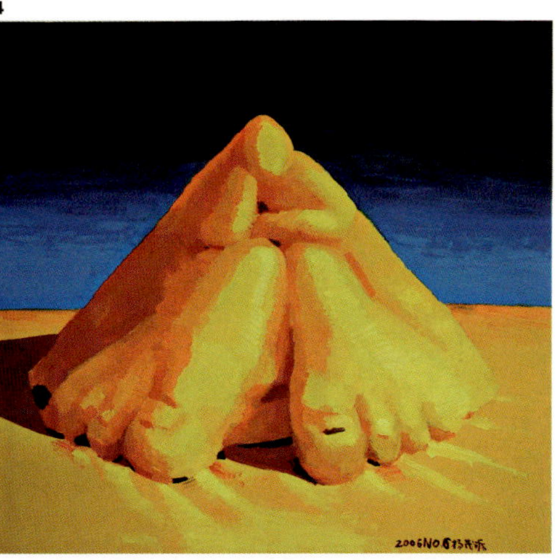

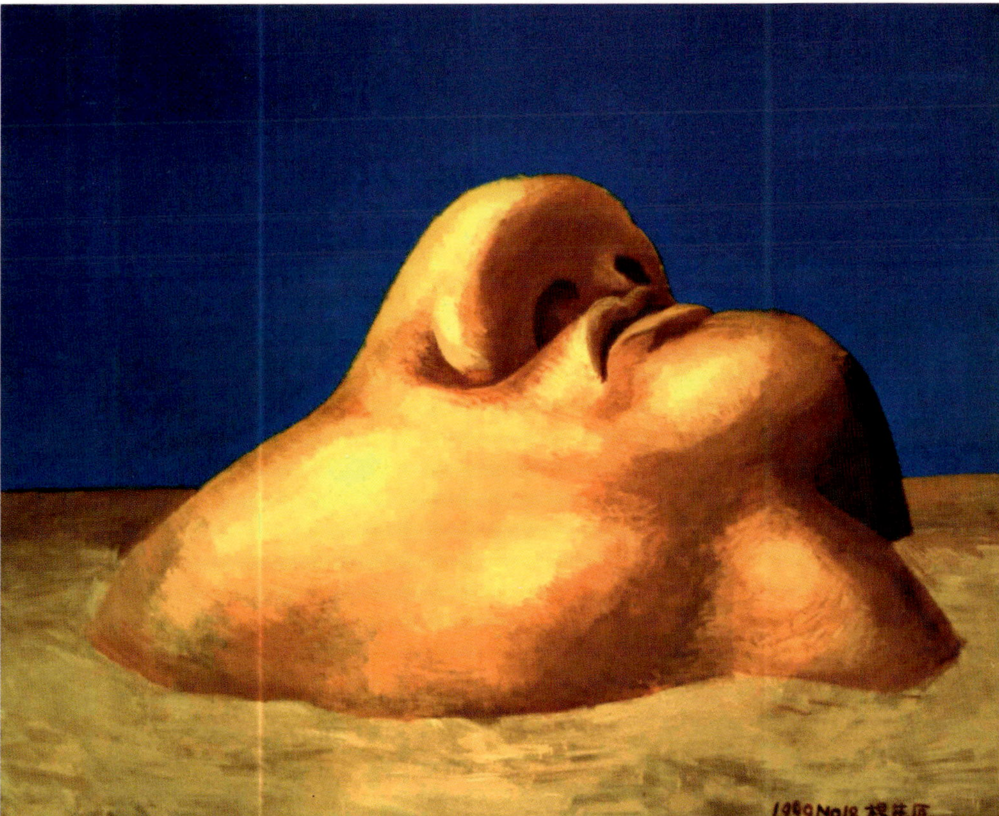

15

1 Look Inside – Agrippa Giovane, *2005*
Marble, 58 x 35 x 30 cm; Marmor, 58 x 35 x 30 cm
《往里看 – Agrippa Giovane》2005年，大理石雕塑，
58 x 35 x 30 cm

2 Look Inside – Aristophanes, *2005*
Marble, 50 x 25 x 25 cm; Marmor, 50 x 25 x 25 cm
《往里看 – Aristophanes》2005年，大理石雕塑，
50 x 25 x 25 cm

3 Look Inside – Caracalla, *2005*
Marble, 65 x 50 x 40 cm; Marmor, 65 x 50 x 40 cm
《往里看 – Caracalla》2005年, 大理石雕塑,
65 x 50 x 40 cm

4 Look Inside – Homer, *2005*
Marble, 70 x 40 x 33 cm; Marmor, 70 x 40 x 33 cm
《往里看 – Homer》2005年, 大理石雕塑,
70 x 40 x 33 cm

5 Look Inside – Giuliano Medici, *2005*
Marble, 60 x 32 x 34 cm; Marmor, 60 x 32 x 34 cm
《往里看 – Giuliano Medici》2005年, 大理石雕塑,
60 x 32 x 34 cm

6 Look Inside – Parthenon, *2005*
Marble, 55 x 30 x 35 cm; Marmor, 55 x 30 x 35 cm
《往里看 – Parthenon》2005年, 大理石雕塑, 55 x 30 x 35 cm

7 Look Inside – Romano, *2005*
Marble, 54 x 36 x 25 cm; Marmor, 54 x 36 x 25 cm
《往里看 – Romano》2005年, 大理石雕塑, 54 x 36 x 25 cm

8 Look Inside – Venus, *2005*
Marble, 70 x 32 x 32 cm; Marmor, 70 x 32 x 32 cm
《往里看 – Venus》2005年, 大理石雕塑 , 70 x 32 x 32 cm

9 Look Inside – Voltaire, *2005*
Marble, 50 x 22 x 22 cm; Marmor, 50 x 22 x 22 cm
《往里看 – Voltaire》2005年, 大理石雕塑, 50 x 22 x 22 cm

10 Sheep No. 7, *2001*
Sheepskin inflated, 260 x 200 x 190 cm
Schafshaut, aufgeblasen, 260 x 200 x 190 cm
《绵羊No. 7》2001年, 充气绵羊皮, 260 x 200 x 190 cm

11 Goat No. 3, *2001*
Goatskin inflated, 101 x 100 x 59 cm
Ziegenhaut, aufgeblasen, 101 x 100 x 59 cm
《山羊No. 3》2001年, 充气山羊皮, 101 x 100 x 59 cm

12 Stand on the other side, *2006*
Oil on canvas, 60 x 186 cm
Öl auf Leinwand, 60 x 186 cm
《站在另一端》2006年, 布面油画, 60 x 186 cm

13 2006 No. 1, *2006*
Oil on canvas, 170 x 180 cm
Öl auf Leinwand, 170 x 180 cm
《2006 No. 1》2006年, 布面油画, 170 x 180 cm

14 2006 No. 6, *2006*
Oil on canvas, 170 x 180 cm
Öl auf Leinwand, 170 x 180 cm
《2006 No. 6》2006年, 布面油画, 170 x 180 cm

15 1999 No. 18, *1999*
Oil on canvas, 250 x 300 cm
Öl auf Leinwand, 250 x 300 cm
《1999 No. 18》1999年, 布面油画, 250 x 300 cm

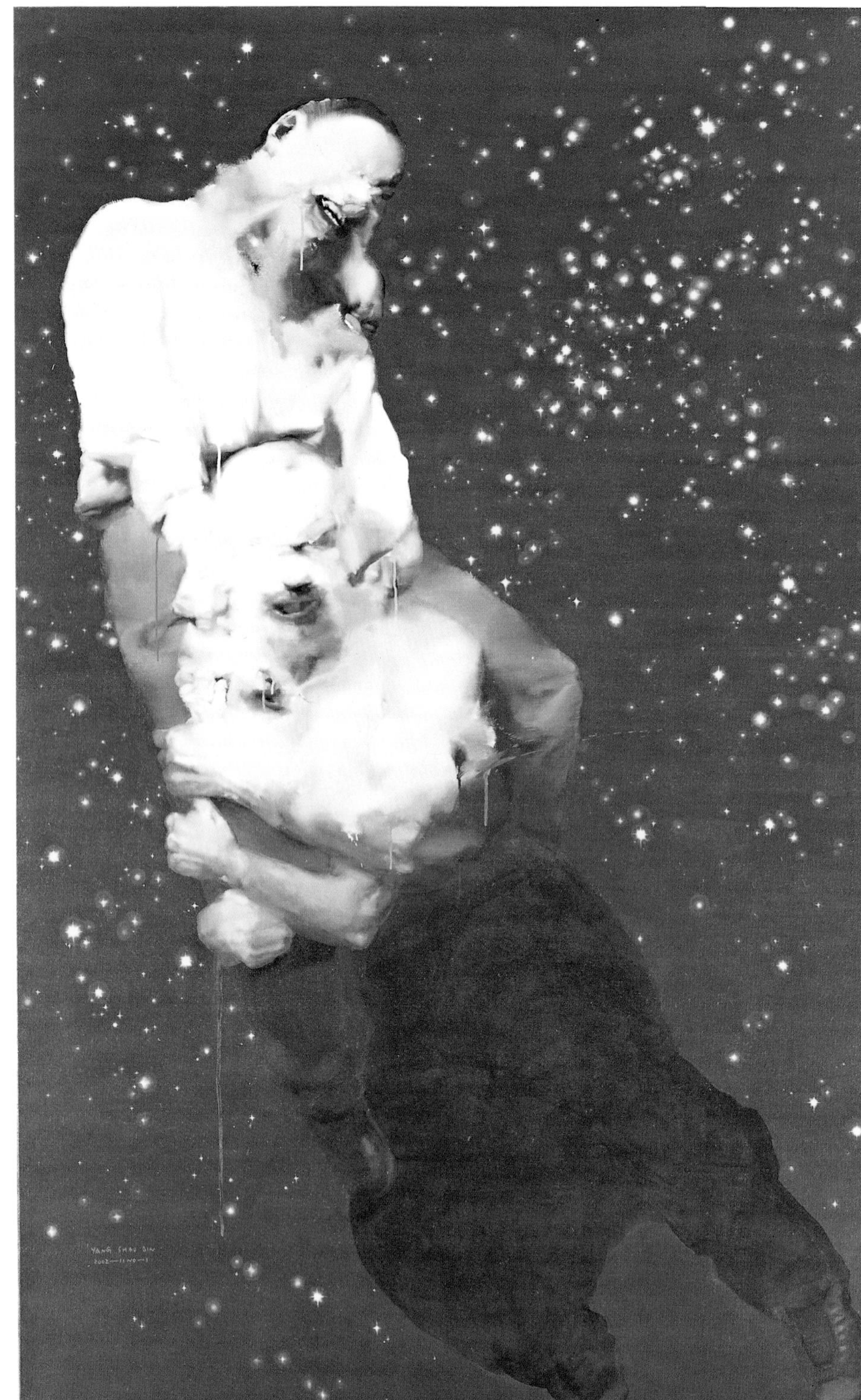

1

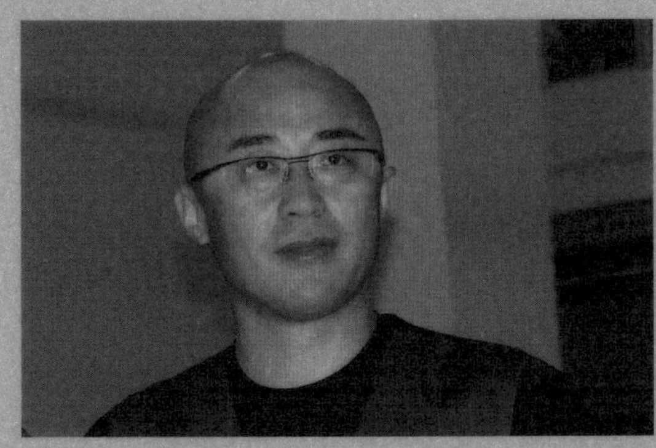

"I admire the vigour and persistency of miners and I admire the vigour of their children! This vigour means that the human being is only the surface of animals. I just want to question and criticise history and reality."

„Ich bewundere die Kraft und Ausdauer der Bergleute und die Kraft ihrer Kinder! Diese Kraft bedeutet, dass der Mensch nur an der Spitze der Tierwelt steht. Ich möchte einfach die Geschichte und die Realität infrage stellen und kritisieren."

"我惊叹矿工的生命力如此顽强，惊叹他们的子女的生命力！这生命力意味着人只是在动物的层面上。我希望这是对历史和现实的质疑与批判。"

Born in 1963 in Tangshan, Hebei Province, China. Lives and works in Beijing
Geboren 1963 in Tangshan, Provinz Hebei, China. Lebt und arbeitet in Peking
1963年出生于中国河北省唐山。现居住工作在北京

***Selected exhibitions* / Ausgewählte Ausstellungen / 所选展览**

2004 "9·11", Beijing Art Now Gallery, Beijing, China
2005 BCA Prague Biennual, Prague, Czech Republic
2006 "800 Meters Under Underground", Long March Space, Beijing, China
"Hermann Nitsch and Yang Shaobin Exhibition", White Space, Beijing, China
2007 "The Real Thing: Contemporary Art from China", Tate Liverpool, Liverpool, UK
"Zurück zur Figur, Malerei der Gegenwart", Kunsthalle der Hypo-Kulturstiftung, Munich, Germany
"Yang Shaobin", National Gallery Jakarta, Jakarta, Indonesia

2004年 《9·11》北京现在画廊
2005年 布拉格双年展 布拉格 捷克共和国
2006年 《纵深800米，地上・地下 — 杨少斌个展》北京798艺术区"长征空间"）
《Hermann Nitsch和杨少斌联合展览》北京798艺术区，空白空间
2007年 《真实事件 ：中国当代艺术》泰特美术馆，利物浦，英国
《回到图形 -- 现代的绘画》Kunsthalle der Hypo-Kulturstiftung, 慕尼黑, 德国
《杨少斌作品展》，雅加达国立美术馆 雅加达 印度尼西亚

***Selected publications* / Ausgewählte Publikationen / 所选著作**

"Yang Shaobin", Cheng Xindong Press 2004
"Yang Shaobin: Essence of Violence", Shijiazhuang 2006

《杨少斌》程昕东出版公司，2004年
杨少斌（著）：《暴力的本质》河北教育出版社，石家庄市2006年

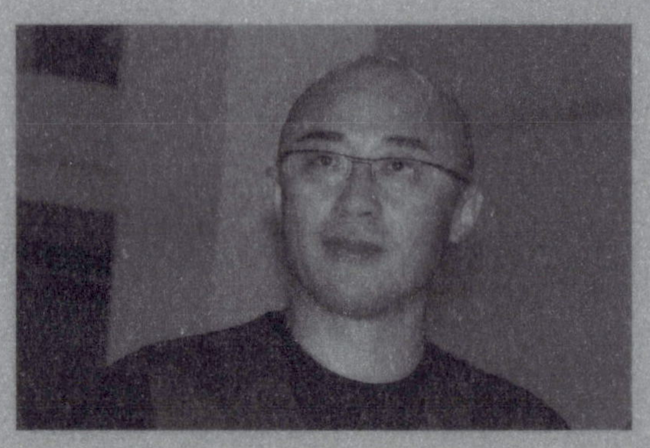

"I admire the vigour and persistency of miners and I admire the vigour of their children! This vigour means that the human being is only the surface of animals. I just want to question and criticise history and reality."

„Ich bewundere die Kraft und Ausdauer der Bergleute und die Kraft ihrer Kinder! Diese Kraft bedeutet, dass der Mensch nur an der Spitze der Tierwelt steht. Ich möchte einfach die Geschichte und die Realität infrage stellen und kritisieren."

"我惊叹矿工的生命力如此顽强，惊叹他们的子女的生命力！这生命力意味着人只是在动物的层面上。我希望这是对历史和现实的质疑与批判。"

Born in 1963 in Tangshan, Hebei Province, China. Lives and works in Beijing
Geboren 1963 in Tangshan, Provinz Hebei, China. Lebt und arbeitet in Peking
1963年出生于中国河北省唐山。现居住工作在北京

Selected exhibitions / Ausgewählte Ausstellungen / 所选展览

2004 "9·11", Beijing Art Now Gallery, Beijing, China
2005 BCA Prague Biennual, Prague, Czech Republic
2006 "800 Meters Under Underground", Long March Space, Beijing, China
"Hermann Nitsch and Yang Shaobin Exhibition", White Space, Beijing, China
2007 "The Real Thing: Contemporary Art from China", Tate Liverpool, Liverpool, UK
"Zurück zur Figur, Malerei der Gegenwart", Kunsthalle der Hypo-Kulturstiftung, Munich, Germany
"Yang Shaobin", National Gallery Jakarta, Jakarta, Indonesia

2004年 《9·11》北京现在画廊
2005年 布拉格双年展 布拉格 捷克共和国
2006年 《纵深800米，地上·地下 — 杨少斌个展》北京798艺术区"长征空间"）
《Hermann Nitsch和杨少斌联合展览》北京798艺术区，空白空间
2007年 《真实事件：中国当代艺术》泰特美术馆，利物浦，英国
《回到图形 — 现代的绘画》Kunsthalle der Hypo-Kulturstiftung，慕尼黑，德国
《杨少斌作品展》，雅加达国立美术馆 雅加达 印度尼西亚

Selected publications / Ausgewählte Publikationen / 所选著作

"Yang Shaobin", Cheng Xindong Press 2004
"Yang Shaobin: Essence of Violence", Shijiazhuang 2006

《杨少斌》程昕东出版公司，2004年
杨少斌（著）：《暴力的本质》河北教育出版社，石家庄市2006年

YANG SHAOBIN 杨少斌

[jaŋ ʂaʊpin]

In the 1990s, Yang Shaobin was one of China's most representative painters of contemporary art. At the beginning of the 90s he participated in the artistic movement Cynic Realism and Political Pop the main subject of his works being Chinese soldiers, policemen and heroes of the Cultural Revolution as symbols of politics and power like "Life doesn't rest, the assault doesn't stop" (1993), "Untitled" (1995) and so on. These works subverted this historical stage of China's common idols by his ironical style, eliminating the holiness and pathetic feelings and being proof of political consciousness and taunt meaning.

From 1997 on the main subject of his works is violence, turning his style into a dark red depiction of brutality. In his works "No. 17" (1999) and "Untitled" (1997/98) the individual's life experiences of bitterness, anger and suppression are turned into pictures of cruelty, where people often engulf each other, as if they are in the process of being torn into pieces by fear and sorrow, this kind of simple animalism enhancing the visual tension of his works.

In his later works of violence the main subject of cruelty is extended to international wars, terrorism and related problems. Works like "Trinity" (2004), "Who Screamed?" (2003/04), fictive stories of incidents, exaggerated images of injury and violence evoking people's premonition of anxiety which cannot be explained, as if the individual in a state of timely confusion of already being occurred, occurring and to take place in the future. The desperate demand for an environment of survival depending on oneself and settled down and getting on with one's pursuit as well as for the mental circumstances pokes out of the cruel background which hides plots, operation and dangerous realistic situations, transmitting a kind of psychological restless breath.

But all these are deeply rooted within the fear and craving, and is also the contradiction of the nature of human beings accompanying tightly the psychological complex.

In den 1990er Jahren zählte Yang Shaobin zu den wichtigsten Vertretern moderner Kunst in China. Er gehörte zur Bewegung des Zynischen Realismus ebenso wie zum Political Pop – dabei waren seine Hauptmotive chinesische Soldaten, Polizisten und Helden der Kulturrevolution, als Symbole von Politik und Macht, wie in seinen Arbeiten „Life doesn't rest, the assault doesn't stop" (1993), „Untitled" (1995) und anderen. Diese Werke unterwanderten durch ihre Ironie die Positionen von offiziellen chinesischen Vorbildern, indem sie auf jedes sakrale Pathos verzichteten und gerade dadurch ein politisches Bewusstsein voller Spott offenbarten.

Von 1997 an war Gewalt das zentrale Thema von Yangs Arbeiten, entsprechend entwickelte er einen dunkelroten Stil für die Darstellung von Brutalität. In „No. 17" (1999) und „Untitled" (1997/98) fließen Lebenserfahrungen von Verbitterung, Wut und Unterdrückung in Bilder, deren Figuren sich gegenseitig zu verschlingen scheinen, als ob sie durch ihre Angst und Trauer zerfetzt würden. Damit stieg die visuelle Spannung in Yangs Arbeiten enorm.

Später wandelte er sein Hauptthema der Grausamkeit immer wieder neu ab. Werke wie „Trinity" (2004) oder „Who Screamed?" (2003/04) erzählen fiktive Geschichten von Verletzungen und Gewalt, die eine diffuse Vorahnung von etwas Schrecklichem entstehen lassen, die wiederum einen Zustand zeitweiliger Verwirrung auslöst. Gegenpol dazu ist das verzweifelte Verlangen nach einem Umfeld, in dem sich überleben lässt, in dem man sich, ohne bedrängt zu werden, niederlassen kann und mit seinem eigenen Streben weiterkommt – diese Hoffnung ragt aus dem grausamen Hintergrund hervor, der gefährliche Handlungen und Situationen bereithält, die gleichsam einen verstörenden ruhelosen Atem ausstoßen.

Yang sieht darin den Widerspruch zwischen der Natur und dem Menschen, der mit seinen psychologischen Komplexen untrennbar verbunden ist. Die andauernde Verletzung missbrauchter Körper ist die konkrete Perspektive, die Yang

杨少斌是上世纪90年代以来中国当代艺术中最具代表性的画家之一。在90年代初期，他参与了"玩世现实主义"和"政治波普"的艺术流派活动，作品表现的主要是带有政治、权力象征的中国军人、警察和"文革"时期英雄人物的形象，如《生命不息，冲锋不止》（1993年）、《无题》（1995年）等以滑稽可笑的笔调颠覆了那个历史阶段中国共同的偶像，借此消除他们的神圣感和崇高感，具有明显的政治意识和嘲讽意味。

1997年前后的作品以暴力为主，逐渐形成了其自身的暗红色暴力化的风格。他在《No. 17》（1999年）、《无题》（1997-1998年）等作品中，将个人在生活中的遭遇、愤怒、压抑转换为极其暴力的画面，他画中的人物经常是在相互吞噬，仿佛是人被撕裂过程中的惊悚与哀嚎，这种简单原始的动物性增强了作品的视觉张力。在后期的暴力作品中，他又将暴力的主题延展到国际间的战争、恐怖主义等问题上。如《三位一体》（2004年）、《谁在尖叫》（2003-2004年）等作品，通过对某种事件场景的虚拟叙事，以及夸张的伤害和暴力形象，让人产生一种无法言喻的焦虑性预感，仿佛人处于一种已经发生、正在发生和将要发生的错乱的时态中。

对自己所赖以安身立命的生存环境和精神境遇的绝望诉求，凸现了暴力背后隐藏着阴谋、操纵和危险的现实处境，传达了一种心理上不安的气息。而这其实都根植于人的内心恐惧与欲望，也是人类天性中一对矛盾但又紧密相伴随的心理情结。承受伤害与自虐的身体是理解杨少斌作品最直观具体的的观察点。杨少斌目前的创作，被他自称为"混合工作"2006年最新创作了题为《纵深800米、地上、地下》大型影像装置作品，即以多媒介的方式和手法，再现了他儿时曾生活成长的煤矿区沉重且残酷的现实景象。

Feng Boyi

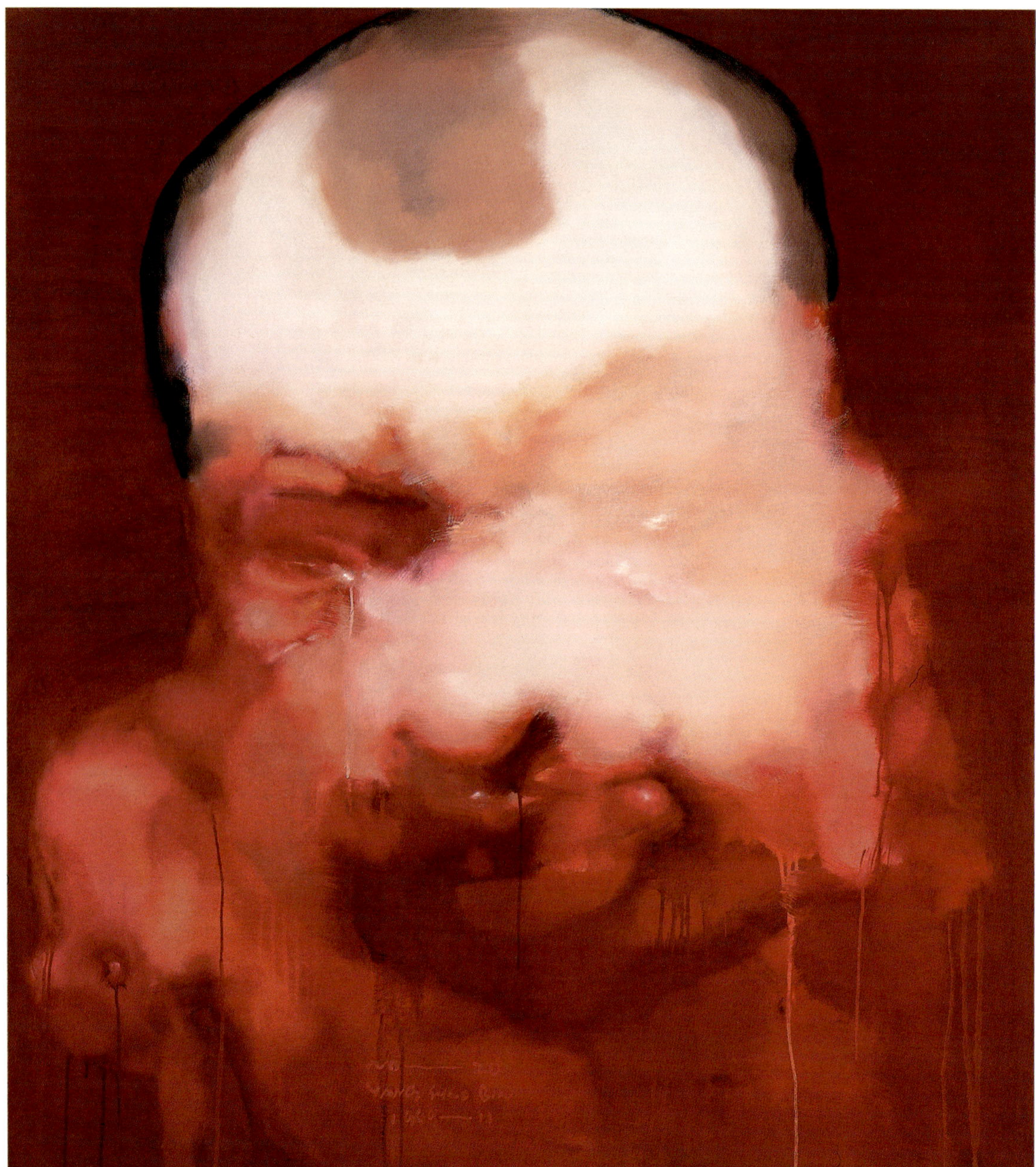

2

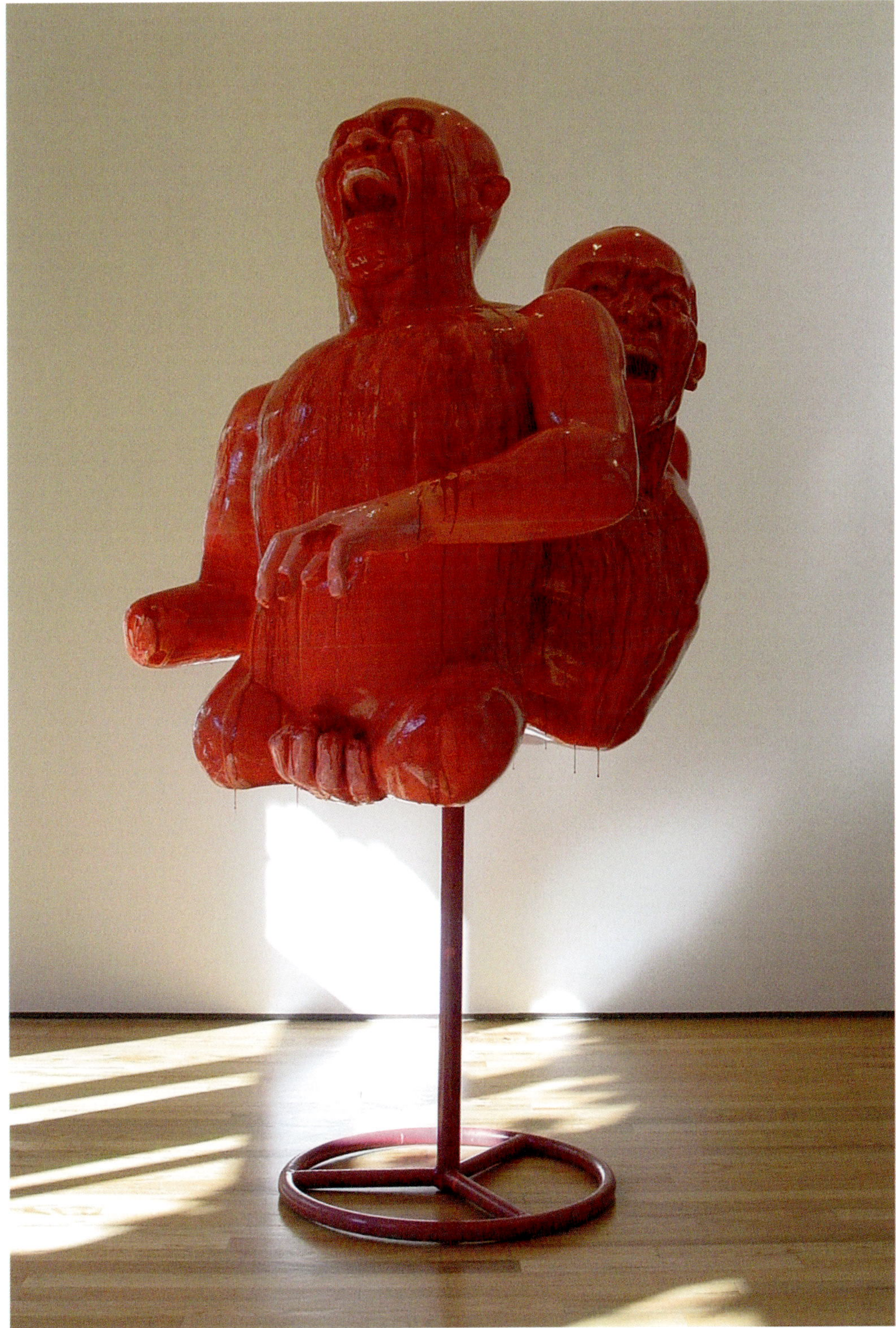

3

4

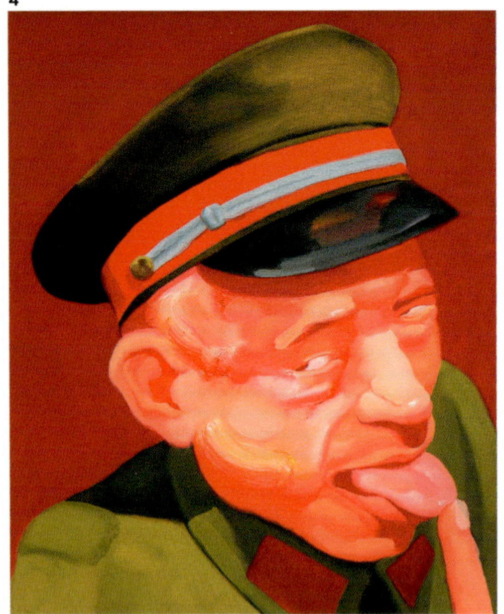

5

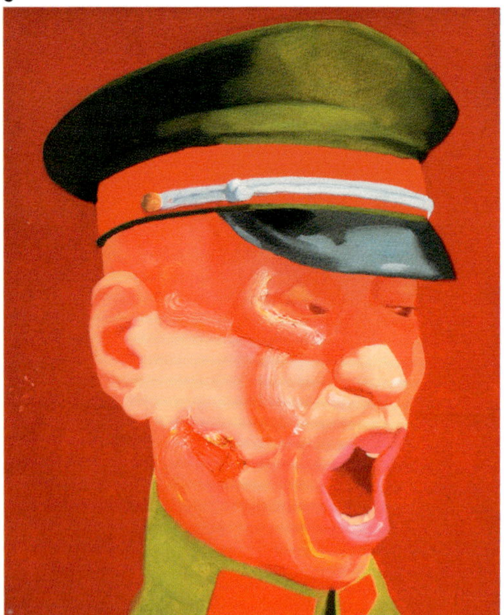

6

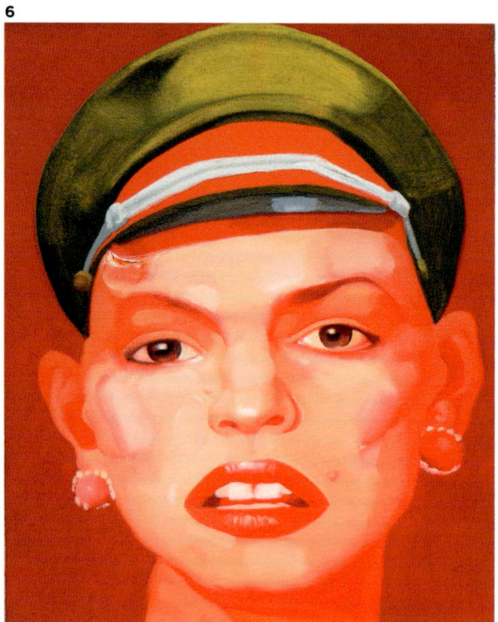

The endurance of injury and the abused body are the most direct and concrete view point of Yang Shaobin's works.

Yang Shaobin's present creations are titled by himself as "mixed works" – his most recent work of 2006 being a large scale installation called "Depth of 800 m, above and beneath the earth" is a composition of several media and techniques, reflecting the hardships and cruelties of his childhood in a coal mining area.

Shaobins Werk eröffnet. Seine jüngsten Kreationen betitelte er selbst als „mixed works" – 2006 präsentierte er eine aufwändige Montage mit dem Titel „Depth of 800 m, above and beneath the earth", die verschiedene Medien und Techniken miteinander kombiniert und die harten Lebensumstände wiedergibt, die er als Kind in einem Kohlerevier erdulden musste.

7
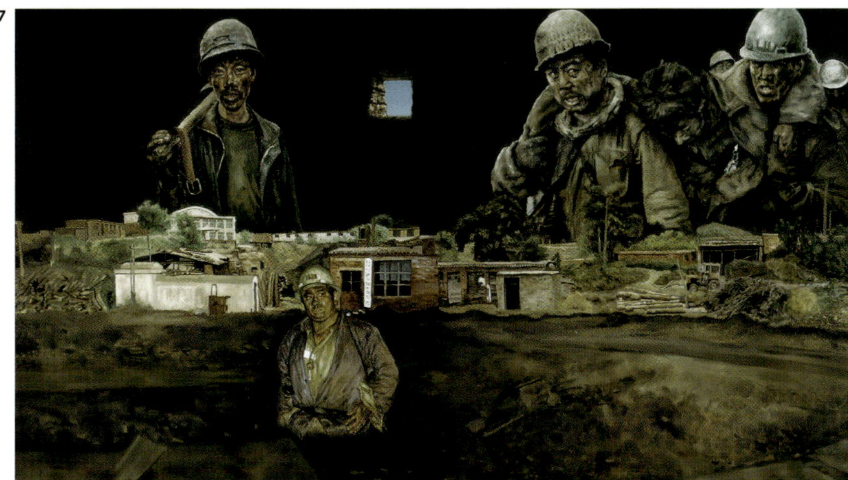

8
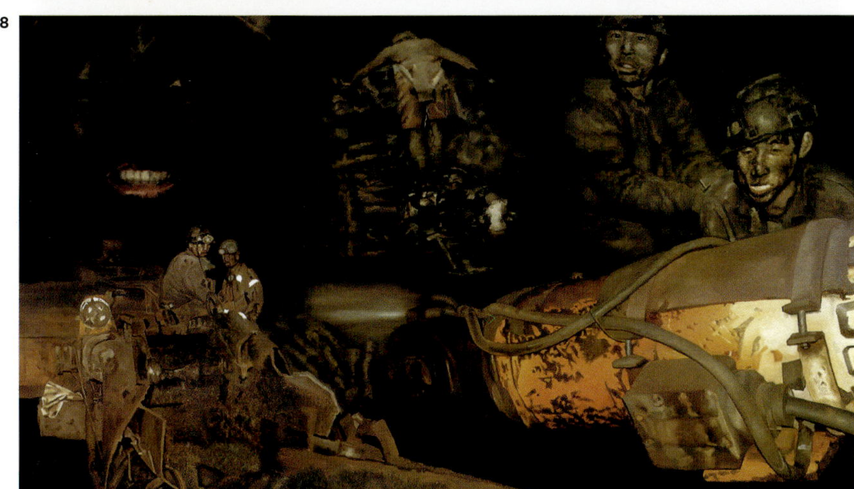

9
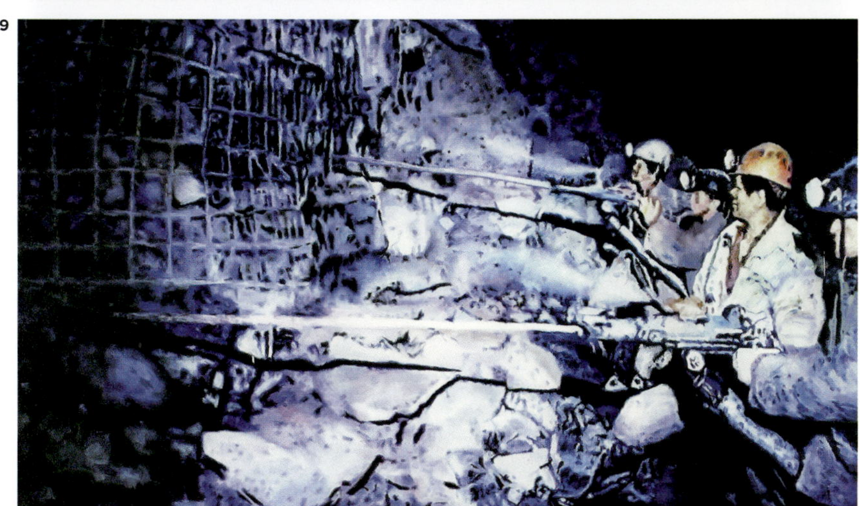

1 ***No. 1***, *2003*
Oil on canvas, 280 x 170 cm
Öl auf Leinwand, 280 x 170 cm
《No. 1》2003年布面油画，280 x 170 cm

2 ***Fighting No. 20***, *1999*
Oil on canvas, 160 x 140 cm
Öl auf Leinwand, 160 x 140 cm
《战斗 No. 20》1999年，布面油画, 160 x 140 cm

3 ***Untitled***, *2000*
Fibreglass, 194 x 85 x 90 cm
Fiberglas, 194 x 85 x 90 cm
《无题》2000年, 纤维玻璃, 194 x 85 x 90 cm

4 ***Police Series No. 20***, *1996*
Oil on canvas, 41 x 36 cm
Öl auf Leinwand, 41 x 36 cm
《警察系列 No. 20》1996年, 布面油画, 41 x 36 cm

5 ***Police Series No. 20***, *1996*
Oil on canvas, 41 x 36 cm
Öl auf Leinwand, 41 x 36 cm
《警察系列 No. 20》1996年, 布面油画, 41 x 36 cm

6 ***Police Series No. 20***, *1996*
Oil on canvas, 41 x 36 cm
Öl auf Leinwand, 41 x 36 cm
《警察系列 No. 20》1996年, 布面油画, 41 x 36 cm

7 ***Miners! 800 Meters Underground No. 8***, *2006*
Oil on canvas, 260 x 450 cm
Öl auf Leinwand, 260 x 450 cm
《纵深800米 – No. 8》2006年, 布面油画, 260 x 450 cm

8 ***Miners! 800 Meters Underground No. 9*** , *2006*
Oil on canvas, 260 x 450 cm
Öl auf Leinwand, 260 x 450 cm
《纵深800米 – No. 9》2006年, 布面油画, 260 x 450 cm

9 ***Miners! 800 Meters Underground No. 2***, *2006*
Oil on canvas, 210 x 350 cm
Öl auf Leinwand, 210 x 350 cm
《纵深800米 – No. 2》2006年, 布面油画, 210 x 350 cm

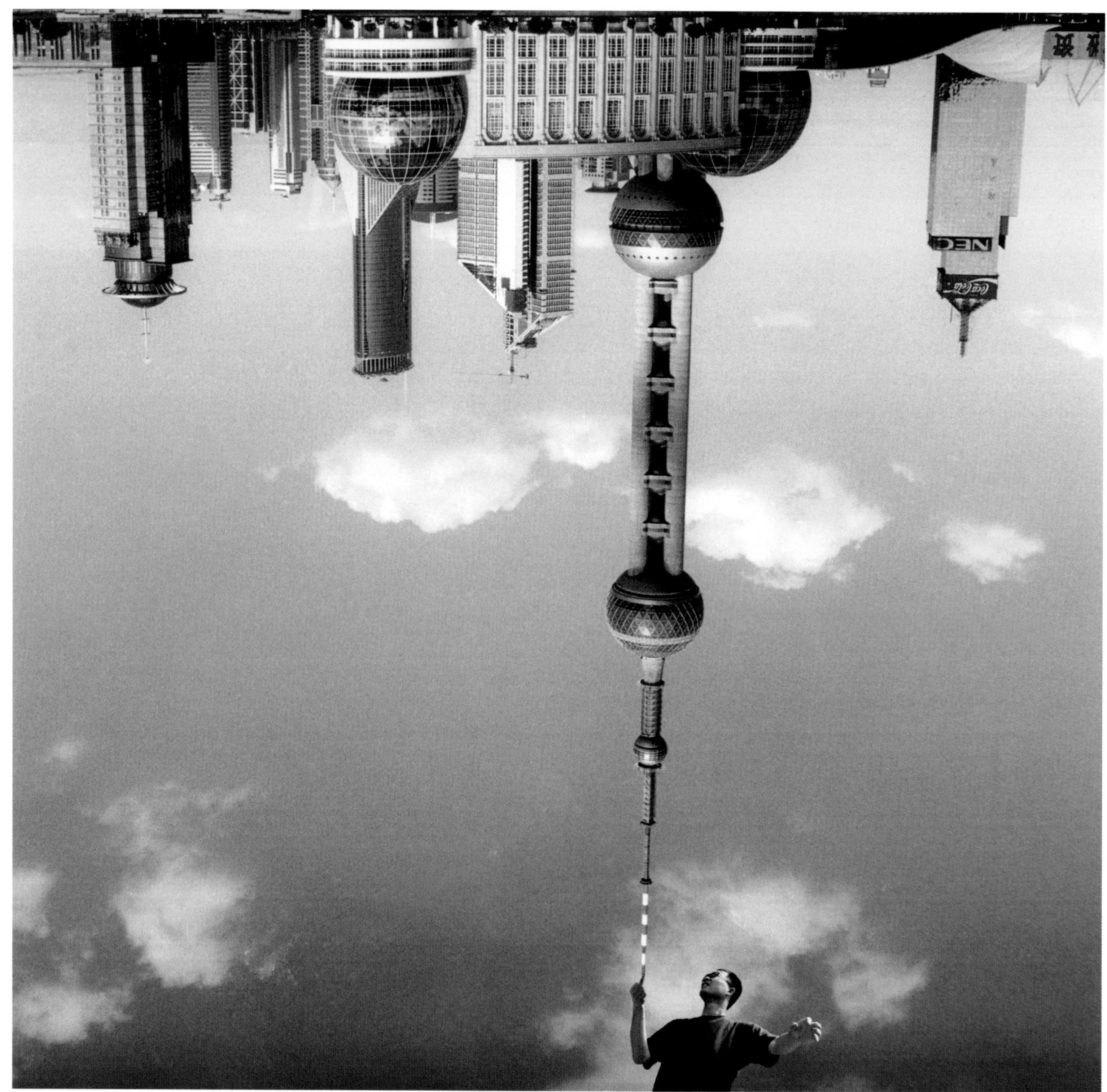

1

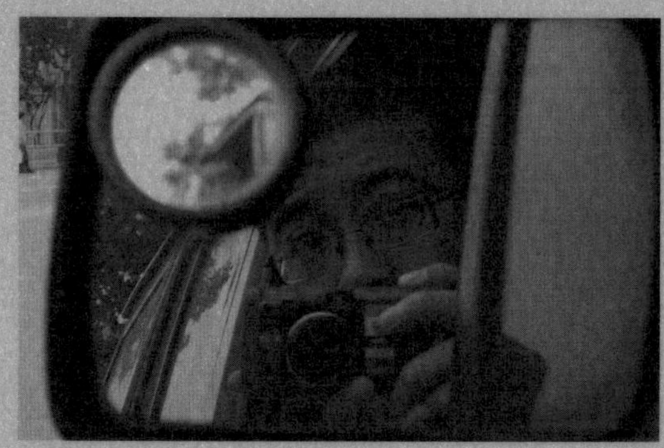

"I feel that theory and emotion, no matter what kind, are both by-products. That's not to say I think theory is of no importance, actually art is also not that important, they are all by-products of life."

„Ich finde, dass Theorie und Emotionen Nebenprodukte sind. Nicht, dass ich die Theorie für bedeutungslos halte, denn eigentlich ist auch die Kunst nicht so bedeutungsvoll, sie sind beide bloß Nebenprodukte des Lebens."

"我认为理论和情感，无论哪种，都是艺术的副产品。那也并不是说我否认理论的重要性，实际上艺术同样不是很重要，艺术都是现实生活地副产品。"

Born in 1968 in Hangzhou, China. Lives and works in Shanghai
Geboren 1968 in Hangzhou, China. Lebt und arbeitet in Shanghai
1968 出生于中国杭州，住居工作于上海

***Selected exhibitions* / Ausgewählte Ausstellungen / 所选展览**

2001 "I will Die", B Space of Kunsten Festival des Arts 2001, Brussels, Belgium
2005 CP Open Biennale 2005 – Urban/Culture, Jakarta, Indonesia
2006 "FOREPLAY – Yang Zhenzhong", ShanghART H-Space, Shanghai, China
"Yang Zhenzhong", Ikon Gallery, Birmingham, UK
The 5th AsiaPacific Triennial of Contemporary Art (APT5), Gallery of Modern Art, Queensland Art Gallery, Brisbane, Australia
2007 "Global Cities", Turbine Hall, Tate Modern, London, UK
52. Biennale di Venezia, Venice, Italy

2001年 《我会死的》布鲁塞尔艺术节，布鲁塞尔，比利时
2005年 《CP双年展 -- 都市文化》雅加达，印度尼西亚
2006年 《前戏-杨振忠装置个展》香格纳画廊H空间，上海
《杨振中》IKON画廊, 伯明翰, 英国
第五届亚太当代艺术三年展, 昆士兰当代美术馆，昆士兰，澳大利亚
2007年 《全球化城市》现代美术泰特画廊，伦敦，英国
第52届威尼斯国际艺术双年展，威尼斯，意大利

***Selected publications* / Ausgewählte Publikationen / 所选著作**

"Between Past and Future: New Photography and Video from China", Göttingen 2004
"Chinese Artists, Texts and Interviews: Chinese Contemporary Art Awards (CCAA) 1998–2002", Hong Kong 2004
"Do It (volume 1, extended edition)", New York/Frankfurt am Main 2005

《在过去和未来之间：来自中国的新摄影和录象》格廷根2004年
《中国艺术家，文章和采访:中国当代艺术奖(CCAA)1998-2002》，中国, 2004年
《做啊！》第一册1, 纽约和法兰克福 2005年

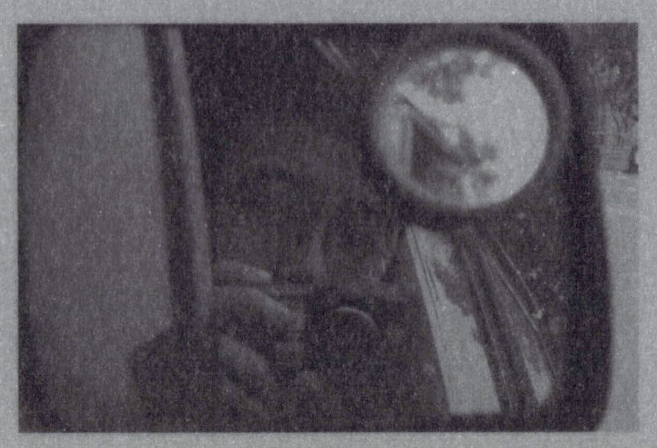

"I feel that theory and emotion, no matter what kind, are both by-products. That's not to say I think theory is of no importance, actually art is also not that important, they are all by-products of life."

„Ich finde, dass Theorie und Emotionen Nebenprodukte sind. Nicht, dass ich die Theorie für bedeutungslos halte, denn eigentlich ist auch die Kunst nicht so bedeutungsvoll, sie sind beide bloß Nebenprodukte des Lebens."

"我认为理论和情感，无论哪种，都是艺术的副产品。那也并不是说我否认理论的重要性，实际上艺术同样不是很重要，艺术都是现实生活地副产品。"

Born in 1968 in Hangzhou, China. Lives and works in Shanghai
Geboren 1968 in Hangzhou, China. Lebt und arbeitet in Shanghai
1968 出生于中国杭州，住居工作于上海

Selected exhibitions / Ausgewählte Ausstellungen / 所选展览

2001 "I will Die", B Space of Kunsten Festival des Arts 2001, Brussels, Belgium
2005 CP Open Biennale 2005 - Urban/Culture, Jakarta, Indonesia
2006 "FOREPLAY - Yang Zhenzhong", ShanghART H-Space, Shanghai, China
"Yang Zhenzhong", Ikon Gallery, Birmingham, UK
The 5th AsiaPacific Triennial of Contemporary Art (APT5), Gallery of Modern Art, Queensland Art Gallery, Brisbane, Australia
2007 "Global Cities", Turbine Hall, Tate Modern, London, UK
52. Biennale di Venezia, Venice, Italy

2001年 《我会死的》布鲁塞尔艺术节，布鲁塞尔，比利时
2005年 《CP双年展 — 都市文化》雅加达，印度尼西亚
2006年 《前戏-杨振忠装置个展》香格纳画廊H空间，上海
《杨振中》IKON画廊，伯明翰，英国
第五届亚太当代艺术三年展，昆士兰当代美术馆，昆士兰，澳大利亚
2007年 《全球化城市》现代美术泰特画廊，伦敦，英国
第52届威尼斯国际艺术双年展，威尼斯，意大利

Selected publications / Ausgewählte Publikationen / 所选著作

"Between Past and Future: New Photography and Video from China", Göttingen 2004
"Chinese Artists, Texts and Interviews: Chinese Contemporary Art Awards (CCAA) 1998-2002", Hong Kong 2004
"Do It (volume 1, extended edition)", New York/Frankfurt am Main 2005

《在过去和未来之间：来自中国的新摄影和录象》格廷根2004年
《中国艺术家，文章和采访：中国当代艺术奖（CCAA）1998-2002》，中国，2004年
《做啊！》第一册，纽约和法兰克福 2005年

YANG ZHENZHONG 杨振忠

[jaŋ tʂəntʂʊŋ]

Yang Zhenzhong is without doubt one of the most important artists in the Shanghai art scene. Since the very beginning he was one of the most important members of the artists community and co-curator of artists' organized exhibitions like "Art for Sale" (2000), "Fang Mingzhen/ Fang Mingzhu" (2002) and "Dial 62761232" (2004).

His work ranges from video, photography to installation. One of the most recognized works by Yang Zhenzhong is the video project "I Will Die" that started in 2000 and is shot in many different languages. This very simple video documents people of different ages and their reaction facing the camera and saying the sentence "I Will Die" (shown in Venice Biennial 2007). In another video work from 2000 "922 Rice corns" the artist shoots chicken, cooking and eating grains of rice while at the same time we can hear female and male voices counting grains while the artist raises the issue of competition in today's society and between genders in a humorous way. In 1995 he did a series of photographs called "Lucky Family" showing hens, chicken and cocks and the Chinese traditional notion of marriage.

Yang Zhenzhong's "Spring Story" (2003) video uses performers, this time Siemens factory employees, asking each employee all together 1500 of them on a production line to say one word from Southern Campaign Speech by Deng Xiaoping from 1984 on urban reforms and the special economic zone. In "Light as Fuck" (2001) he balances the Shanghai skyline on one finger, the symbol of Chinese modernisation and new life style. "Let's Puff" (2002) a two channel video work shown in Shanghai Biennial 2002 and Venice Biennial 2003 shows Shanghai's busy downtown area on one screen and a young girl on the other facing this cityscape. The rhythm of the traffic on screen is controlled according to the rhythm of the girl's breath on the other screen turning the city into something not really more like a game setting and inviting the viewer. "Let's Puff", giving his own comment on contemporary society in China.

Yang Zhenzhong ist zweifellos einer der bedeutendsten Künstler in der Shanghaier Kunstszene. Er gehörte von Anfang an zu den wichtigsten Mitgliedern der dortigen Künstlergemeinde und war Co-Kurator verschiedener Ausstellungen wie „Art for Sale" (2000), „Fang Mingzhen/Fang Mingzhu" (2002), „Dial 62761232" (2004).

Yang verwendet in seinem Werk Videos ebenso wie Fotografie und Installationen. Eine seiner bekanntesten Arbeiten ist das Videoprojekt „I Will Die", das im Jahr 2000 startete und bis heute in vielen verschiedenen Sprachen gedreht wurde. Das technisch anspruchslose Video, das auch auf der 52. Biennale in Venedig gezeigt wurde, hält Menschen verschiedenen Alters fest, während sie vor der Kamera den Satz sprechen: „Ich werde sterben". In einer anderen Videoarbeit aus dem Jahr 2000, „922 Rice corns", filmte der Künstler ein Huhn und einen Hahn, die Reiskörner aufpicken, während wir eine weibliche und eine männliche Stimme die Körner mitzählen hören, womit Yang recht humorvoll das Phänomen der Konkurrenz in der modernen Gesellschaft und zwischen den Geschlechtern „aufs Korn nimmt". Schon 1995 hatte er eine Fotoserie mit dem Titel „Lucky Family" geschaffen, die das traditionelle chinesische Bild der Ein-Kind-Ehe in Gestalt von Hennen, Küken und Hähnen wiedergibt.

In seinem Video „Spring Story" (2003) ließ Yang Zhenzhong 1500 Fließbandangestellte von Siemens je ein Wort aus Deng Xiaopings berühmter „Southern Campaign Speech" aus dem Jahr 1984 deklamieren, in der der Politiker über städtische Reformen und Sonderwirtschaftszonen sprach. In „Light as Fuck" (2001) balanciert Yang die Skyline von Shanghai auf einem Finger, als Symbol der chinesischen Modernisierung und des neuen Lebensstils. „Let's Puff" (2002) ist ein Zweikanal-Videostück, das auf der Biennale Shanghai 2002 und der Biennale von Venedig 2003 zu sehen war. Es zeigt auf einem der beiden Monitore eine belebte Straße im Shanghaier Stadtzentrum und auf dem anderen ein junges Mädchen, das auf diese Stadtszene blickt. Der Rhythmus des Verkehrs auf dem Bildschirm wird vom

杨振忠毫无疑问是上海艺术界最有影响的人物之一。很早以前，他就是艺术家团体重要成员，并在象《超市》（2000年）、《范明珠和范明珍》（2002年），《拨打62761232》（2004年）等艺术家的展出中担任策展人。

他的作品涵盖范围从录像、摄影到装置。录像项目《我会死的》是杨振忠最有影响力的作品之一，该项目开始于2000年，至今仍以多种语言拍摄。非常简单的录像记录着不同年龄的人和他们对着摄像机说"我要死了"时的反应（2007年在威尼斯展出）。开始于2000年的另一部视频《922颗米粒》中，母鸡和公鸡啄食着米粒，而同时我们的耳边响起男人和女人数着米粒的配音，艺术家以一种幽默的方式揭示当代社会中的竞争和性别关系的主题。1995年，他拍摄了名《全家福》组照，作品中的小鸡，母鸡和公鸡揭示了中国传统的婚姻观念。

近作《春天的故事》是杨振中导演了西门子公司中一千五百余名中外员工的不同表情、不同语调来朗诵《邓小平南巡讲话》的精彩篇章。在《轻而易举》中他用手指顶起上海的新建设景观，它们是中国现代化和新生活方式的象征。

双频录像《我吹》曾参展2002年的上海双年展和2003年的威尼斯双年展。作品中一幅画面拍摄上海繁忙的中心商业区域，而另一画面上，一个小女孩面对繁华的都市风景线。画面上交通节奏随着另一画面上小姑娘的呼吸节奏变化起伏，而把这个城市有点虚幻，好像置于游戏中，因此来吸引观众。《我吹》是作者对当代中国社会的独特见解。

《CC画廊》也是作者对艺术市场的睿智评论。2004年他在美术馆里开设了CC画廊，展出象Jeff Koons, Matthew Barney等国际艺术家的作品。从因特网上打印摄影作品，与原作同一尺寸，是对作品真实性的质疑，同时引入艺术市场话题。

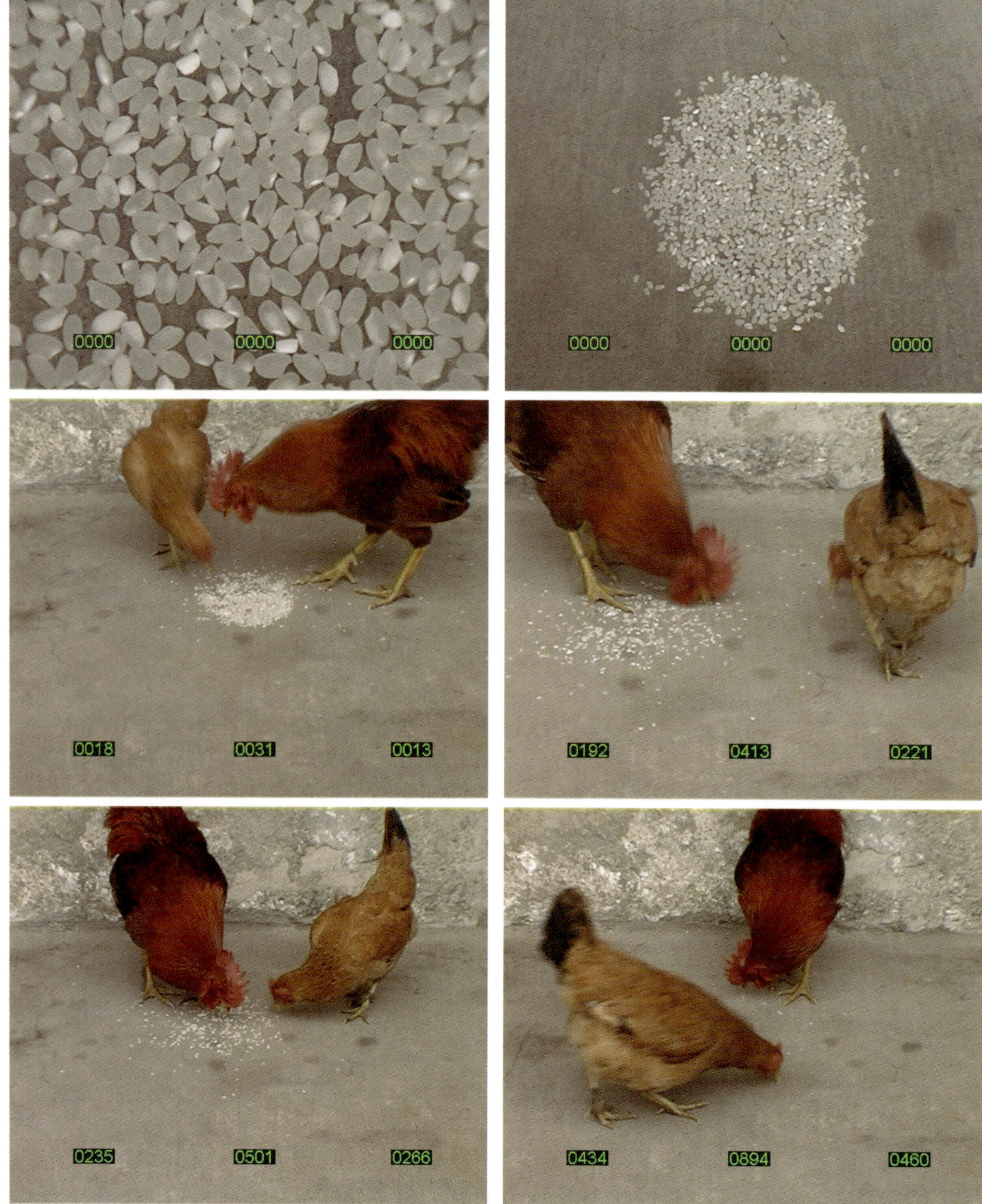

0000
0000
0000
0000
0000
0000
0018
0031
0013
0192
0413
0221
0235
0501
0266
0434
0894
0460

2

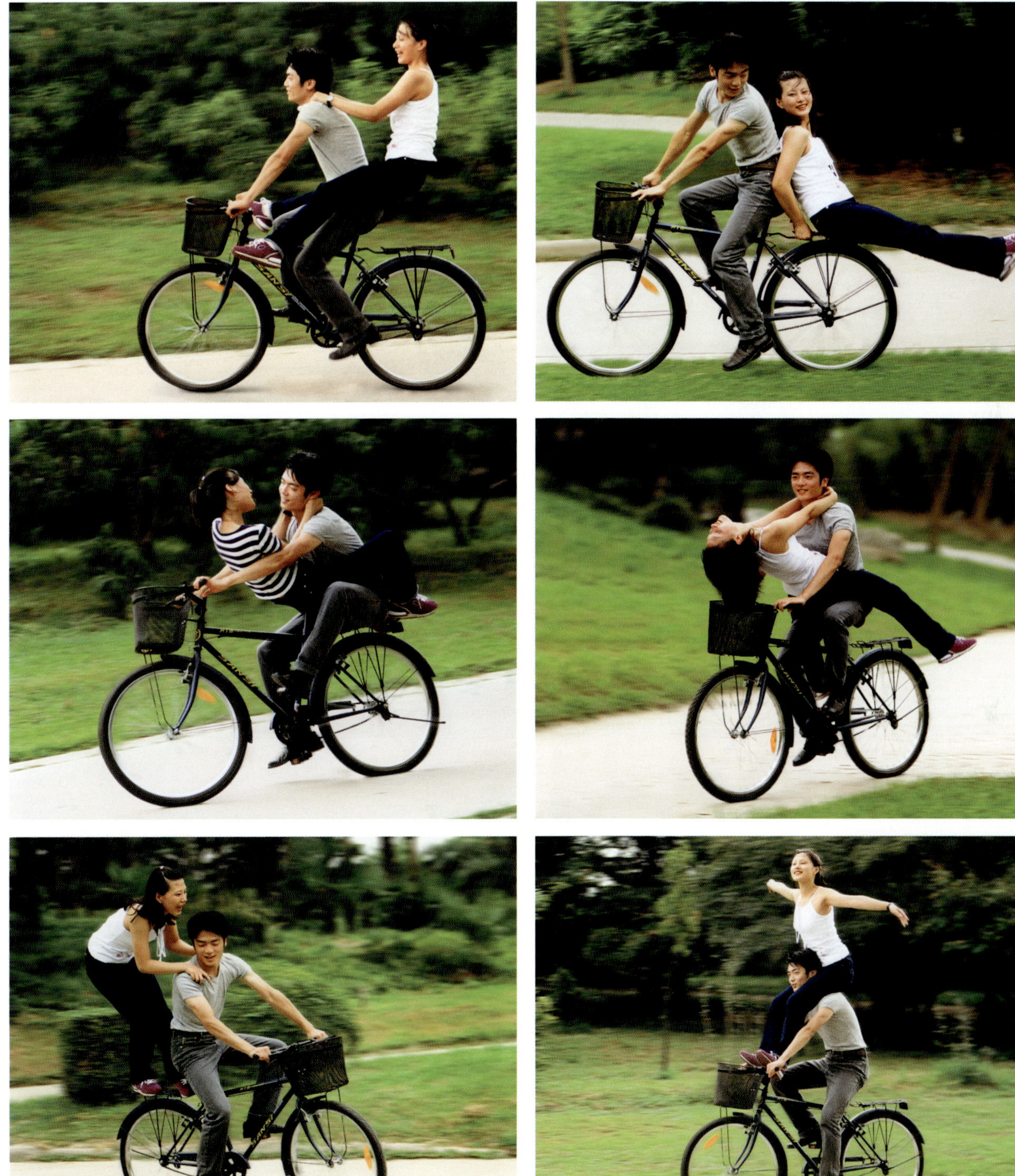

3

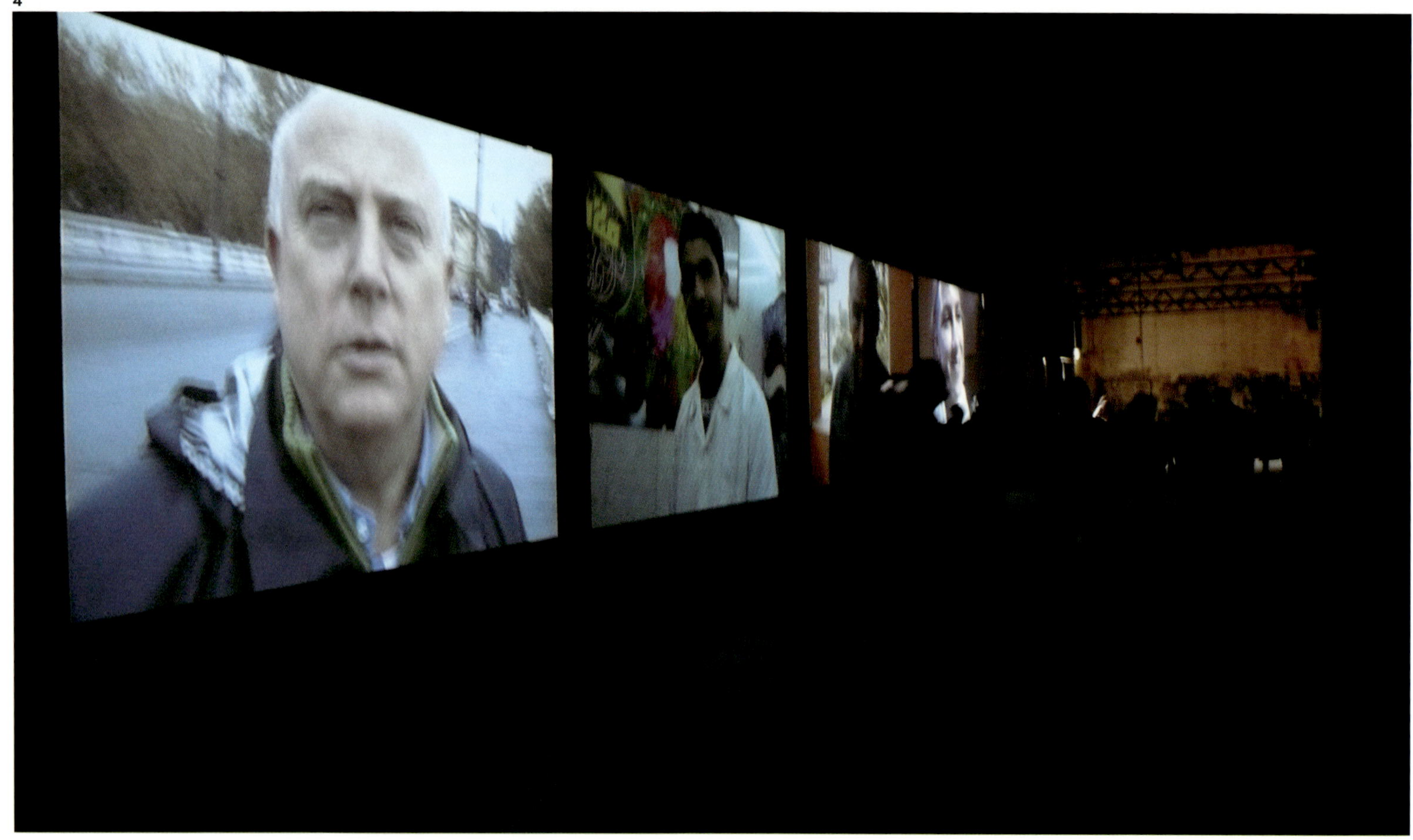

"CC Gallery" is also series of witty comments on the art market. Artists in 2004 established a gallery inside the museum called CC gallery showing works of international artists like Jeff Koons and Matthew Barney. Printing of the photograph work from the internet the same size as the original questions the authenticity of the works and at the same time raises the issue of the art market.

Yang Zhenzhong's broad interests and constant experimentation in different media fields and his active involvement in building the local art scene make him one of the key figures in Chinese contemporary art today.

Atemrhythmus des Mädchens auf dem anderen Bildschirm gesteuert, was die Stadt in eine Art Spiellandschaft verwandelt und den Betrachter zur Teilnahme animiert. „Let's Puff" gibt einen ureigenen Kommentar zur modernen chinesischen Gesellschaft ab.

„CC Gallery" wiederum kam als eine Serie geistreicher Kommentare zum Kunstmarkt daher. 2004 richtete Yang in einem Museum die gleichnamige Ausstellung ein, die Werke internationaler Künstler wie Jeff Koons und Matthew Barney zeigt – allerdings in der Weise, dass Fotografien der Arbeiten aus dem Internet heruntergeladen und dann in Originalgröße ausgedruckt wurden, was die Authentizität jedes Werks und gleichzeitig den Kunstmarkt insgesamt in Frage stellte.

Yang Zhenzhongs breit gefächertes Interessenspektrum, sein unaufhörliches Experimentieren mit verschiedenen Medien und seine aktive Mitwirkung beim Aufbau der lokalen Shanghaier Kunstszene machen ihn zu einer der Schlüsselfiguren der chinesischen Gegenwartskunst.

杨振忠对不同介质材料的广泛兴趣和长期实验，以及积极参与本土艺术界的建设，而使其成为今天当代艺术的重要人物。

Biljana Ciric

5

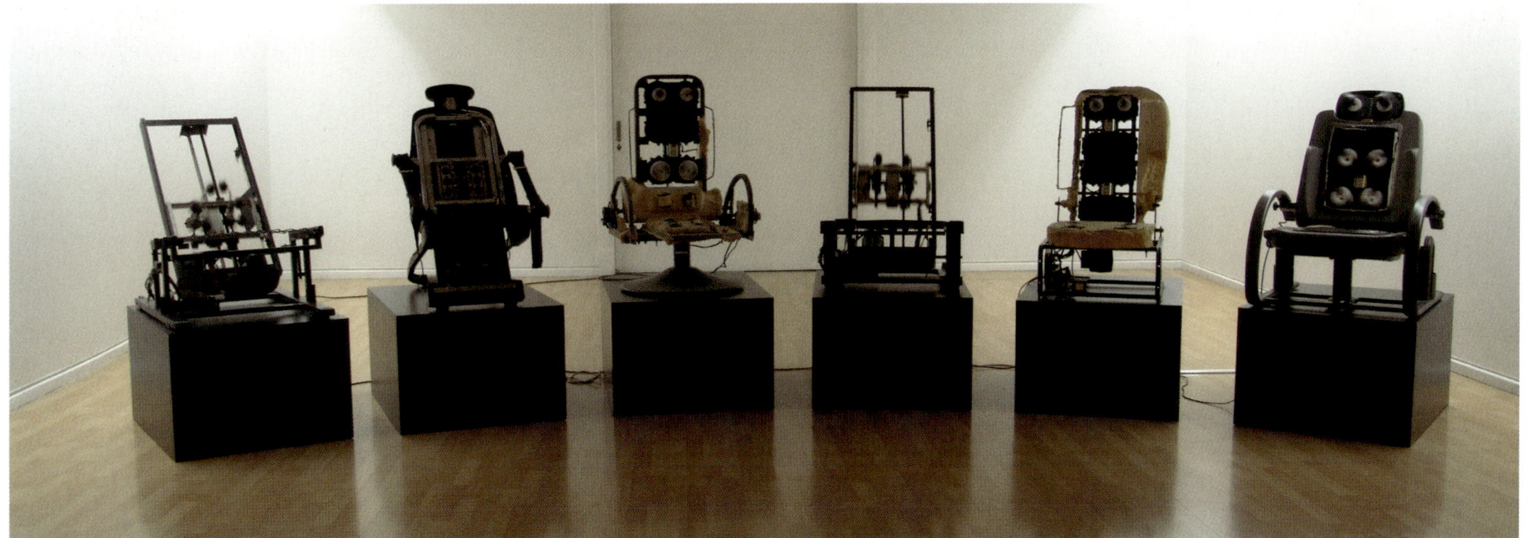

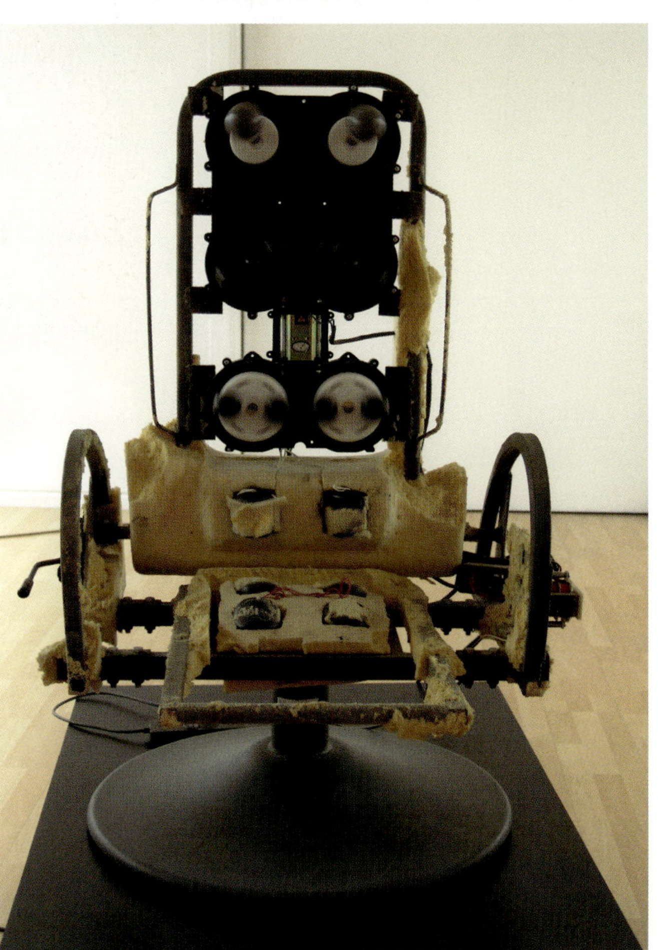

6

1 ***Light and Easy***, *2002*
Photograph, 120 x 182 cm (detail)
Fotografie, 120 x 182 cm (Detail)
《轻而易举》2002年, 摄影, 120 x 182 cm（详细）

2 ***922 Rice Corns***, *2000*
Video, 7 min 58 sec
Video, 7 Min. 58 Sek.
《922颗米》2000年, 录像, 7分 58秒

3 ***Cycle Aerobics (level 1)***, *1999*
8 photographs, 50 x 60 cm each (details)
8 Fotografien, je 50 x 60 cm (Details)
《自行车保健操1》1999年，8幅照片, 每幅 50 x 60 cm（详细）

4 ***I Will Die***, *2000–2005*
Video installation, Venice Biennial, 2007
Video-Installation, Biennale di Venezia, 2007
《我会死的》2000–2005年, 录像装置, 装置实景

5 ***Then Edison's Direct Current Was Surrendered to the Alternating Current***, *2003*
Installation with massage chairs
Installation mit Massagesesseln
《后来，爱迪生的直流电输给了交流电》2003年, 按摩椅装置

6 ***Then Edison's Direct Current Was Surrendered to the Alternating Current***, *2003*
Installation with massage chairs (detail)
Installation mit Massagesesseln (Detail)
《后来，爱迪生的直流电输给了交流电》2003年, 按摩椅装置（详细）

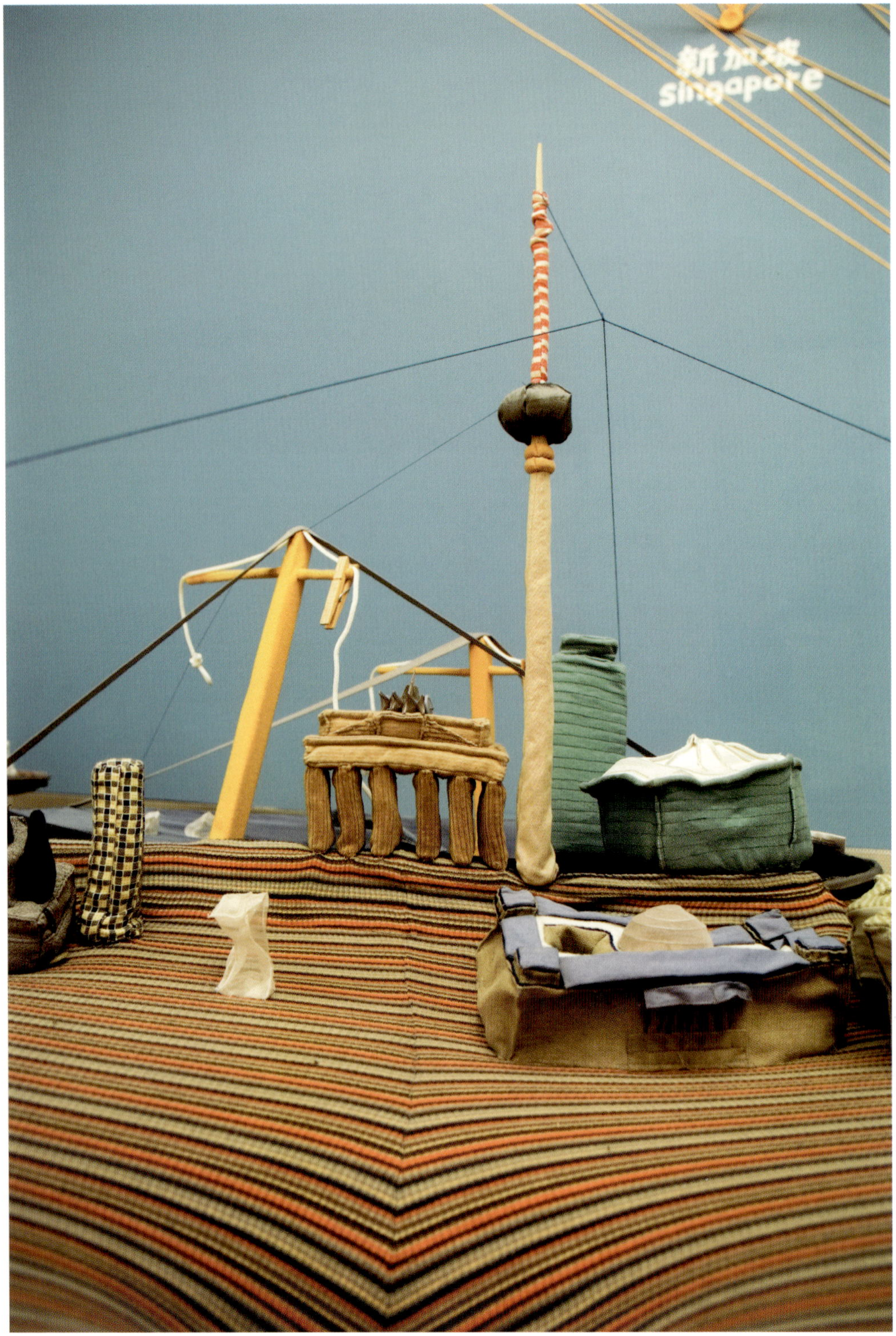

1

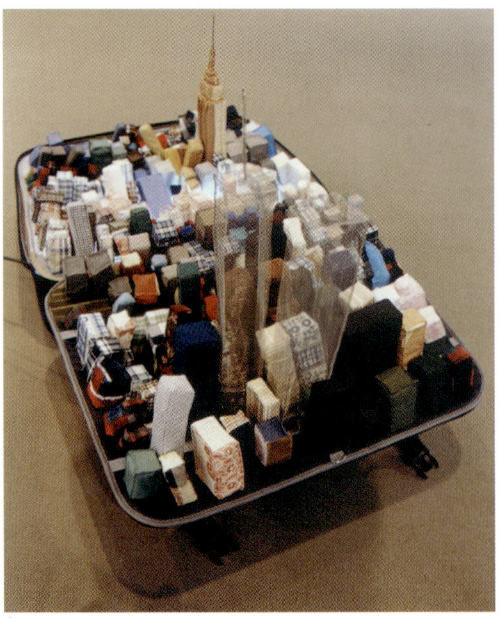

2

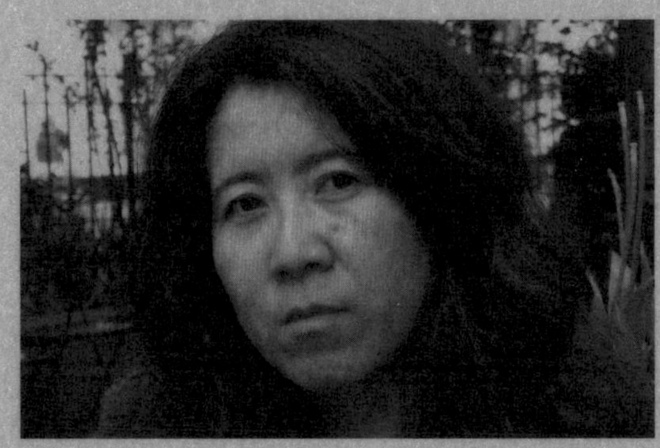

"Experience cannot be duplicated. I am looking for each kind of experience and then create a rough draft."

„Erfahrung lässt sich nicht duplizieren. Ich suche jede Art von ‚Erfahrung' und mache daraus einen Rohentwurf."

"经历不可能被复制。我正在寻找每一种经历，然后创造出一种草图。"

Born in 1963 in Beijing, China. Lives and works in Beijing
Geboren 1963 in Peking, China. Lebt und arbeitet in Peking
1963年出生于北京。现居住工作在北京

***Selected exhibitions* / Ausgewählte Ausstellungen / 所选展览**

1998 "Brain – Exhibition of Installations", Manchester Craft Centre, Manchester, UK
2002 "Yin Xiuzhen – Beijing Opera", Anna Schwartz Gallery, Sydney, Australia
2004 Bienal de São Paulo, São Paulo, Brazil
2004–07 "Between Past and Future, New Photography and Video from China", International Center of Photography, New York, NY, USA (travelling exhibition)
2005 "China: Crossroads of Culture – Follow Me!", Mori Art Museum, Tokyo, Japan
2007 52. Biennale di Venezia, Venice, Italy
"Global Feminisms", Brooklyn Museum, New York, NY, USA
2008 "All-Inclusive – A Tourist World", Schirn Kunsthalle, Frankfurt, Germany

1998年 《脑》 – 装置展览，曼彻斯特手工艺品中心, 曼彻斯特，英国
2002年 《尹秀珍》– 北京剧院Anna Schwartz 画廊, 悉尼，澳大利亚
2004年 圣保罗双年展，圣保罗，巴西
2004–07年 《过去与未来之间—中国新影像展》国际摄影中心，纽约，美国（巡回展）
2005年 《跟我学：中国当代艺术展》，森美术馆 东京 日本
2007年 第 52届威尼斯双年展 威尼斯 意大利
《全球性女权主义》布鲁克林博物馆，纽约，美国
2008年 《有包含 – 旅游世界》Schirn Kunsthalle法兰克福，德国

***Selected publications* / Ausgewählte Publikationen / 所选著作**

Chris Werner, Qiu Ping, Marianne Pitzen (eds.): "Die Hälfte des Himmels. Chinesische Künstlerinnen der Gegenwart", Bonn 1998
Ai Weiwei (ed.): "Chinese Artists, Texts and Interviews", Hong Kong 2002
Bernhard Fibicher, Matthias Frehner (eds.): "Mahjong – Chinesische Gegenwartskunst aus der Sammlung Sigg", Ostfildern-Ruit 2005

波恩波恩妇女:《半边天-当代中国女艺术》波恩 1998年
艾未未（著）:《中国艺术家》文章和采访, 2002年
Fibicher, Bernhard/Frehner, Matthias（编著）:《麻将—希客收藏的中国当代艺术展》斯图加特2005年

"Experience cannot be duplicated. I am looking for each kind of experience and then create a rough draft."

„Erfahrung lässt sich nicht duplizieren. Ich suche jede Art von ‚Erfahrung' und mache daraus einen Rohentwurf."

"经历不可能被复制。我正在寻找每一种经历，然后创造出一种草图。"

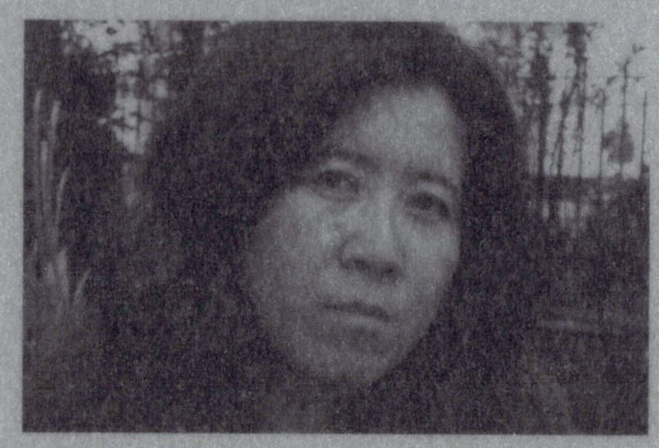

Born in 1963 in Beijing, China. Lives and works in Beijing
Geboren 1963 in Peking, China. Lebt und arbeitet in Peking
1963年出生于北京。现居住工作在北京

Selected exhibitions / Ausgewählte Ausstellungen / 所选展览

1998	"Brain - Exhibition of Installations", Manchester Craft Centre, Manchester, UK
2002	"Yin Xiuzhen - Beijing Opera", Anna Schwartz Gallery, Sydney, Australia
2004	Bienal de São Paulo, São Paulo, Brazil
2004-07	"Between Past and Future, New Photography and Video from China", International Center of Photography, New York, NY, USA (travelling exhibition)
2005	"China: Crossroads of Culture - Follow Me!", Mori Art Museum, Tokyo, Japan
2007	52. Biennale di Venezia, Venice, Italy
	"Global Feminisms", Brooklyn Museum, New York, NY, USA
2008	"All-Inclusive - A Tourist World", Schirn Kunsthalle, Frankfurt, Germany

1998年	《脑》- 装置展览，曼彻斯特手工艺品中心，曼彻斯特，英国
2002年	《尹秀珍》- 北京剧院Anna Schwartz 画廊，悉尼，澳大利亚
2004年	圣保罗双年展，圣保罗，巴西
2004-07年	《过去与未来之间—中国新影像展》国际摄影中心，纽约，美国（巡回展）
2005年	《跟我学：中国当代艺术展》，森美术馆 东京 日本
2007年	第 52届威尼斯双年展 威尼斯 意大利
	《全球性女权主义》布鲁克林博物馆，纽约，美国
2008年	《有包含 - 旅游世界》Schirn Kunsthalle法兰克福，德国

Selected publications / Ausgewählte Publikationen / 所选著作

Chris Werner, Qiu Ping, Marianne Pitzen (eds.): "Die Hälfte des Himmels. Chinesische Künstlerinnen der Gegenwart", Bonn 1998
Ai Weiwei (ed.): "Chinese Artists, Texts and Interviews", Hong Kong 2002
Bernhard Fibicher, Matthias Frehner (eds.): "Mahjong - Chinesische Gegenwartskunst aus der Sammlung Sigg", Ostfildern-Ruit 2005

波恩波恩妇女:《半边天-当代中国女艺术》波恩 1998年
艾未未（著）:《中国艺术家》文章和采访，2002年
Fibicher, Bernhard/Frehner, Matthias（编著）:《麻将—希客收藏的中国当代艺术展》斯图加特2005年

YIN XIUZHEN 尹秀珍

[jin ɕioutʂən]

The sculptor Yin Xiuzhen who initially studied painting, creates sculptures and installations instead today. Her personal experiences as well as daily life goods, finds, and photographs are the mostly used working materials. The background of her work is the radical change of Chinese cities and towns, especially of her hometown Beijing. At present she lives there with her husband Song Dong in one of the traditional courtyard houses of the Hutongs. Yin is amidst the urban transformation processes an annalist of the ongoing upheavals.

The demolition of historical buildings and quarters are the framework of her works – however, her main interest is the change of values as well as the problem of authenticity and identity, the fate of the cultural memory in its fight between society and individual, a fight which is unavoidable in times of great social changes of urbanisation. Yin does not only place personal memories against the oblivion in her installations but creates landscapes of memory, comments about the process of transformation of the Chinese society, animating the spectator to start an exciting search for footprints.

The project "Washing the River" (1985) was an outdoor performance. In Chengdu, Yin had dirty water of the river to be frozen into an ice clump she then tried to wash thoroughly clean with fresh water in a lonesome act. This simple and impressive artistic language expressed the hopeful search for sense amidst her own circumstances of life and at the same time oppugned the degrading situations in a destructive system.

Furthermore she collects "Knitting Wool" (since 1995) torn old handmade sweater of friends; in a kind of meditative process Yin creates with knitting needles something new using the manifold threads – an organic variation of reincarnation. However, the installation "Yin Xiuzhen" (1998) is a kind of reflection of her own. The artist discloses her life in the form of photographs of herself as child, teenager and adult woman, presenting her in typically

Yin Xiuzhen studierte zwar Malerei, macht aber Skulpturen und Installationen. Persönliche Erlebnisse sowie Alltagsgegenstände, Fundstücke und Fotografien sind ihr häufigstes Arbeitsmaterial. Den Hintergrund ihres Werks bilden die radikalen Veränderungen der chinesischen Städte, insbesondere ihrer Heimatstadt Peking. Dort lebt sie mit ihrem Mann Song Dong in einem traditionellen Hofhaus der Hutongs. Inmitten der urbanen Transformationsprozesse ist Yin eine Chronistin der Umbrüche.

Die Zerstörung der historischen Bauten und Viertel steckt für sie dabei den thematischen Rahmen ab – im speziellen jedoch geht es ihr um die Veränderung der Werte sowie um Fragen der Authentizität und Identität, nicht zuletzt um das Schicksal des kulturellen Gedächtnisses im Kampf zwischen Gesellschaft und Individuum, den die großen sozialen Umbrüche der Urbanisierung mit sich bringen. Yin setzt in ihren Installationen nicht nur persönliche Erinnerungen gegen das Vergessen, sondern schafft regelrechte Erinnerungslandschaften, Kommentare zum Wandlungsprozess der chinesischen Gesellschaft, die dazu anregen, sich auf eine packende Spurensuche zu begeben.

Das Projekt „Washing the River" (1985) war eine Performance im Freien. Dabei ließ Yin in Chengdu verschmutztes Flusswasser zu einem Eisklumpen gefrieren, den sie anschließend in einem langwierigen Akt gründlich mit sauberem Wasser abwusch. Mit einer einfachen und zugleich eindrucksvollen künstlerischen Sprache formulierte sie so eine hoffnungsvolle Sinnsuche inmitten der eigenen Lebensumstände und zugleich eine Kritik an den bisweilen menschenunwürdigen Zuständen in einem destruktiven System.

Für „Knitting Wool" (seit 1995) sammelte sie beschädigte selbstgestrickte alte Pullover von Freunden; mit Stricknadeln stellt Yin in einem meditativen Prozess aus den vielerlei Fäden etwas Neues her – eine organische Variante der Reinkarnation. Die Installation „Yin Xiuzhen" (1998) dagegen war eine Art Spiegel ihrer eigenen Person. Die

雕塑家尹秀珍最初学习油画，而今天却创作雕塑和装置。她的个人经历，以及日常生活用品，发现和摄影作品是他最常用的素材。她的作品以飞速变化的中国城镇为背景，特别是她的家乡北京。如今，尹秀珍和丈夫居住在一个胡同里的古典的四合院中。她置身于城市化进程中，记录着日新月异的巨变。历史建筑的破坏似乎其作品的框架主题，然而，她主要关注：价值的变化以及真实性和同一性之间的矛盾，文化记忆在社会与个体之间斗争的命运，这场斗争不可避免的发生在都市化的巨大社会变革的时代中。她不仅在其装置中刻意保留个体的记忆，而且创造了记忆风景、中国社会转变过程的评论，而鼓舞观众去兴奋地开始去探寻变化的足迹。

项目《洗河》（1985年）是一场室外表演。在成都，尹秀珍把脏河水冰冻成冰团，她常常孤独一次又一次地尝试用清水把彻底冰团冲洗干净。朴素、感人的一艺术语言表达了她对生活环境中的理性希望的探索，同时也质疑破坏体系中的倒退现象。尹在其作品中常常使用箱子，里面装满破旧衣物还有整个镇子。此外，她还收集了朋友的破旧手工毛衣（《针织羊毛》）；尹秀珍以多种毛线为材料，新的编织针为工具，用一种沉思的方式，创造了一种再生的有机变化。

然而，装置《尹秀珍》（1998年）却是她自己的反映。以摄影的形似，她公开了自己童年，少年和成年时期的生活情景，涵盖距离的被动证据-女式布鞋，呈现出艺术家的形象。《手提城市》（2000-2003年），她用朋友破烂的外衣为放置在的地板上行李箱里的楼宇、街道和公园缝制了布景。这些行李箱当作旅行车和自己身份的符号。尹秀珍不仅制作了新加坡、上海、深圳的行李箱，而且也制作了西方城市，如巴黎和柏林的箱子，她把这些箱子放置在她所旅行过的地方。这些“手提城市”把别人的生活经历处理成她自己的温雅和不同社会结构的经历。

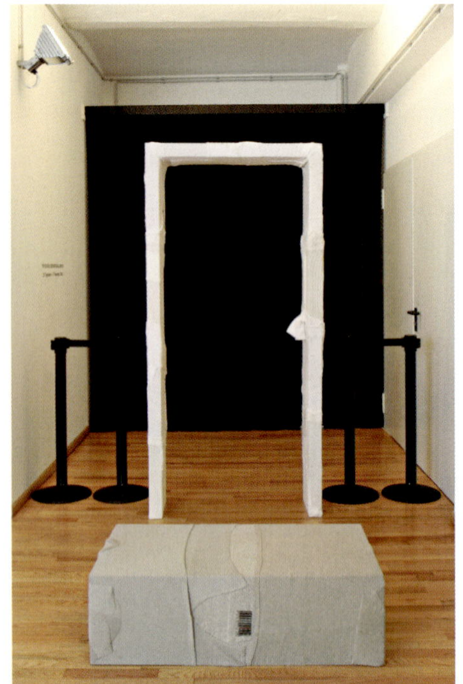

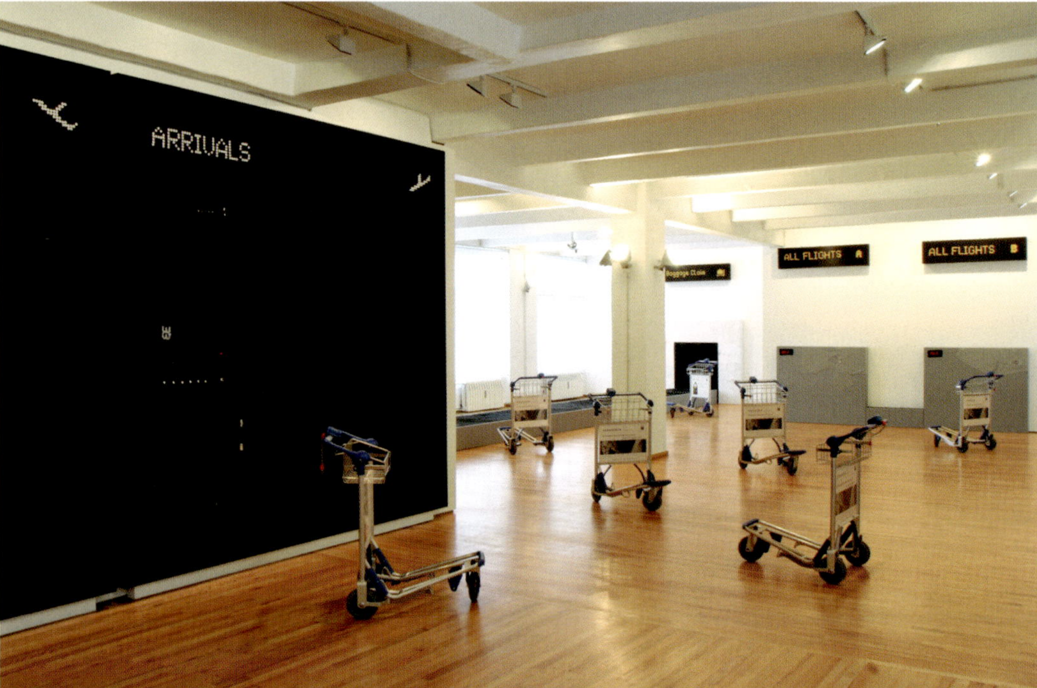
ARRIVALS
ALL FLIGHTS A
ALL FLIGHTS B
Baggage Claim

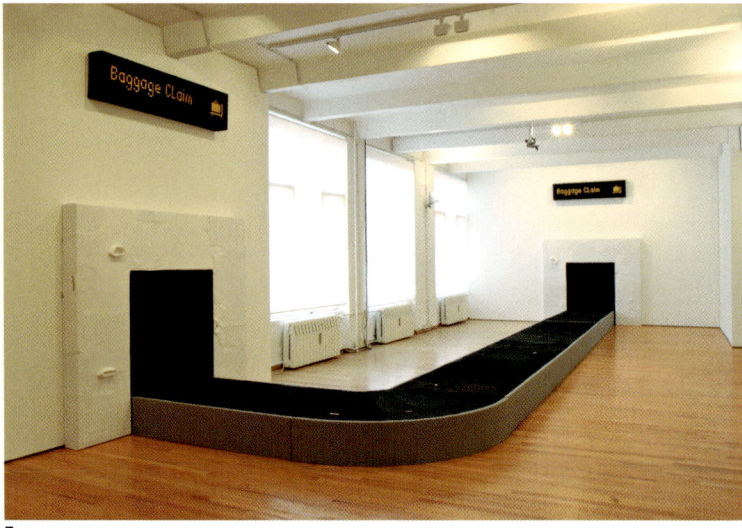
Baggage Claim
Baggage Claim

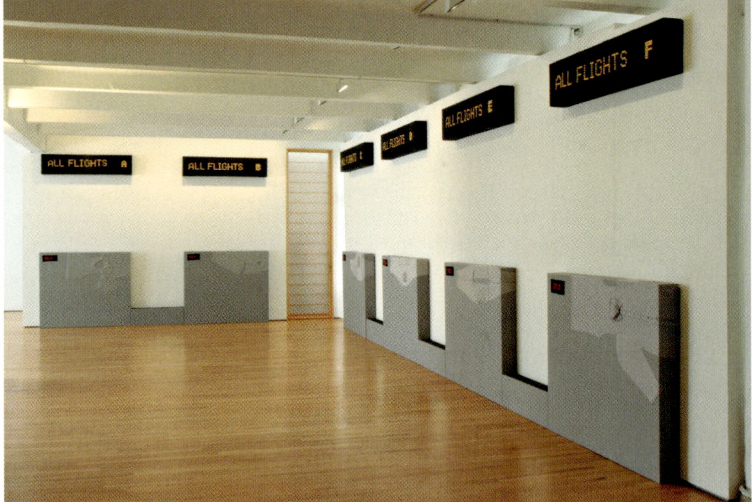
ALL FLIGHTS A
ALL FLIGHTS B
ALL FLIGHTS E
ALL FLIGHTS F

3

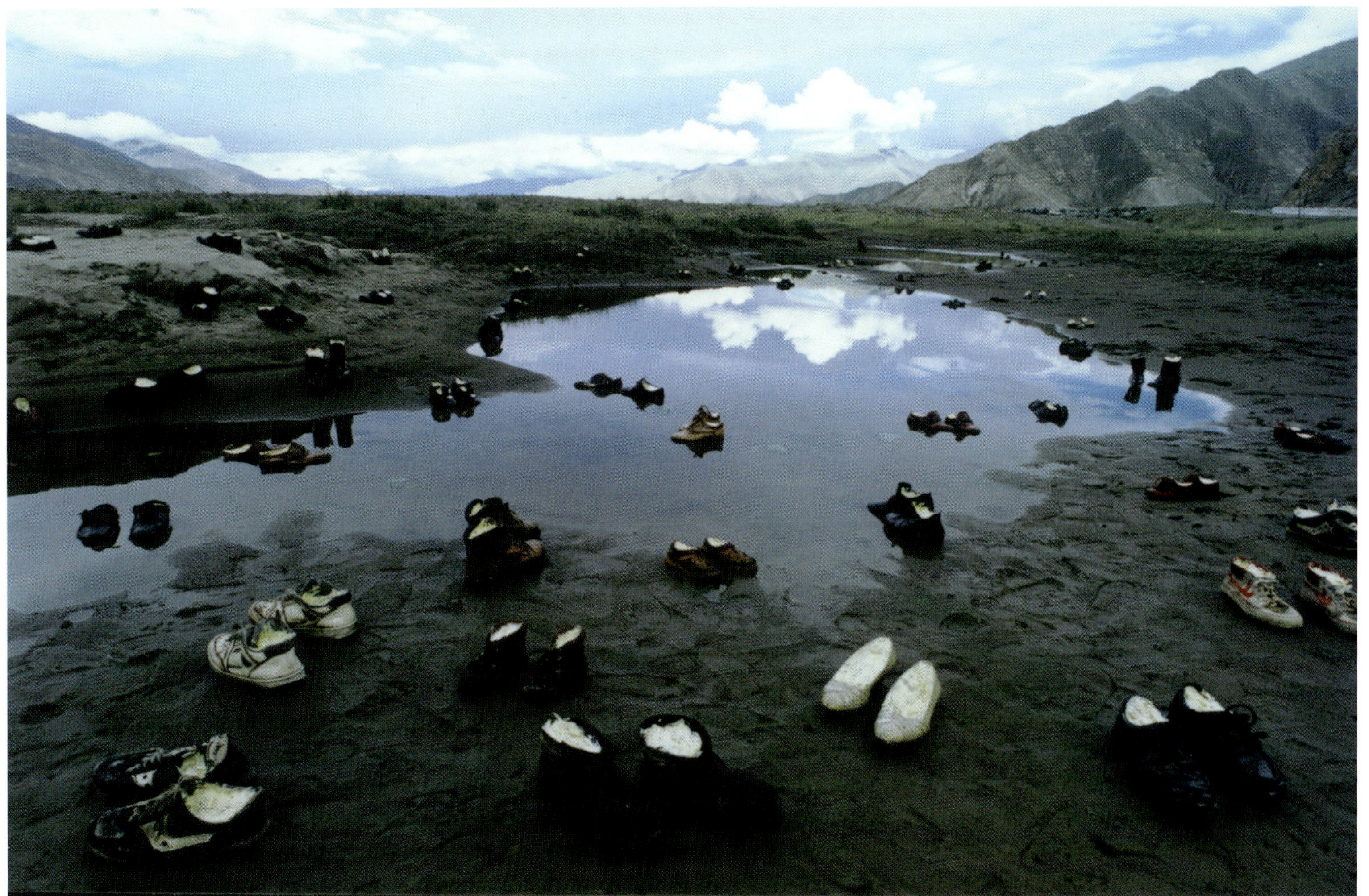

4

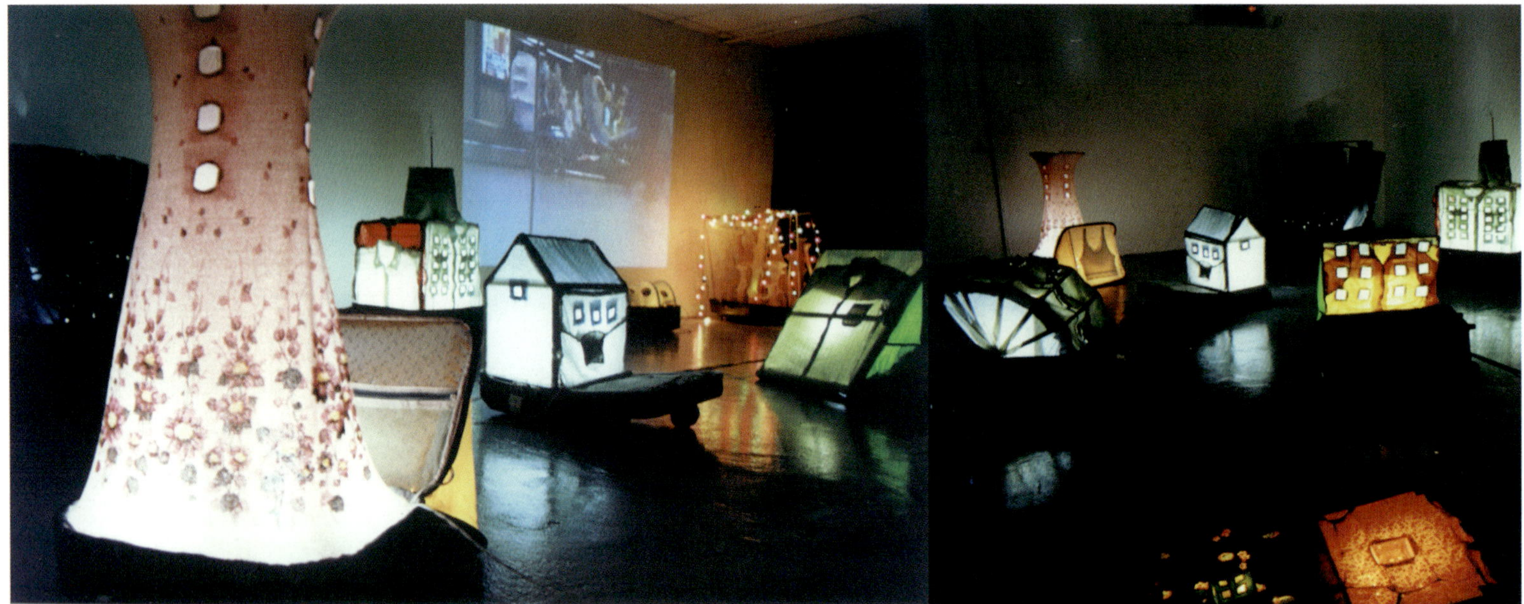

Chinese shoes for girls and women – passive witnesses of covered distances.

While „Portable Cities" are exclusively made from clothes of people, who are living in these cities communicating their aura partially, the space size installation "International Airport Terminal 1" (2006) is completed by people's motion therein. As the visitor enters the exhibition he is presented with a boarding card and is simultaneously brushed with a lint roll. One portion of the boarding card and the used stripes of paper of the lint roll are collected in a map belonging to the installation. In this way, traces of every visitor remain in the terminal, which for a short time becomes a 'real place'– existing only as long as the person is present. In its memory it is shaped by the experiences of the passengers.

Künstlerin offenbarte ihren Lebensweg durch Fotos, die sie als Kind, Teenager und erwachsene Frau zeigten, die sie in chinesischen Mädchen- und Frauenschuhen präsentierte – passive Zeugnisse zurückgelegter Wegstrecken.

Während die „Portable Cities" ausschließlich aus Kleidungsstücken von Menschen gemacht sind, die in diesen Städten leben und dadurch einen Teil ihrer Aura vermitteln, wird die raumumfassende Installation „International Airport Terminal 1" (2006) erst dadurch komplett, dass sich Menschen in ihr bewegen. Am Eingang erhält jeder Besucher eine Bordkarte; seine Kleidung wird mit einer Fusselrolle abgebürstet. Ein Abschnitt der Bordkarte und die gebrauchten Papierstreifen der Rolle werden in einer zur Installation gehörigen Mappe gesammelt. Jeder Besucher hinterlässt so seine Spuren am Terminal, der kurzfristig zu einem realen Ort wird – der aber nur so lange existiert, wie der Mensch anwesend ist. In der Erinnerung ist er geprägt von den Erlebnissen, die die Passagiere dort hatten.

《移动中的城市》完全以旧衣服，那些衣服的主人则生活在那些城市中，传递着各自的氛围。而装置《国际机场：一号航站》（2006年） 则在人们的运动构成。在入口处每位旅客拿到一登机牌，他们的衣服已用棉滚刷过。登机牌的副联和已用的棉滚斑条收集在一张地图里，而成为装置的一部分。这样每位旅客都在航站里留下各自的痕迹且在很短的时间里形成一副真实的场地-与站在那里的旅客一起存在。在这个记忆中，旅客的经历是其形成因素。

Gregor Jansen

6

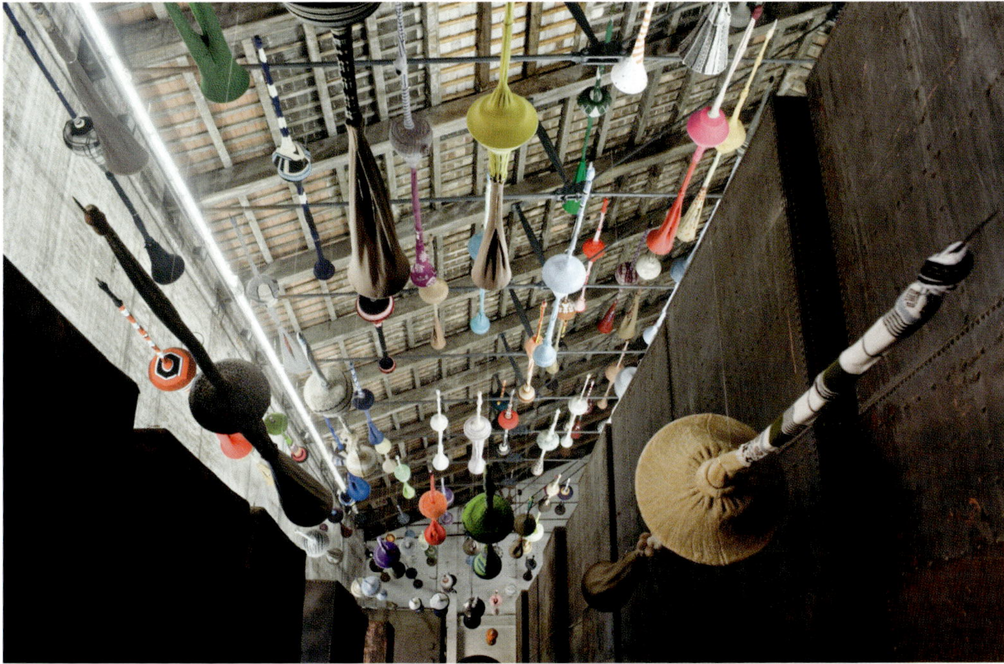

7

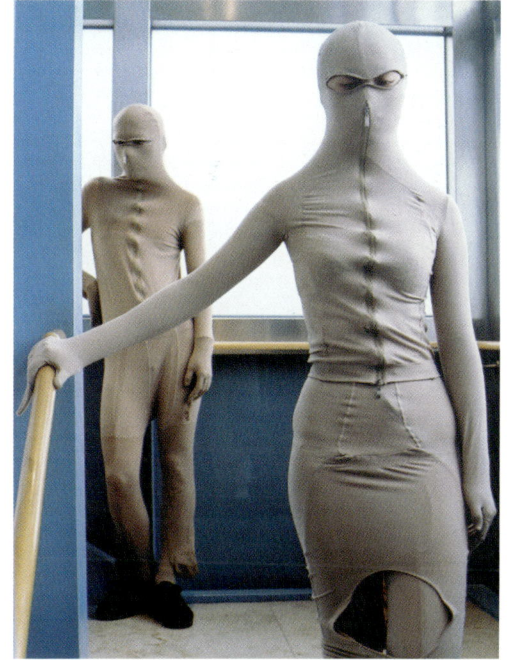

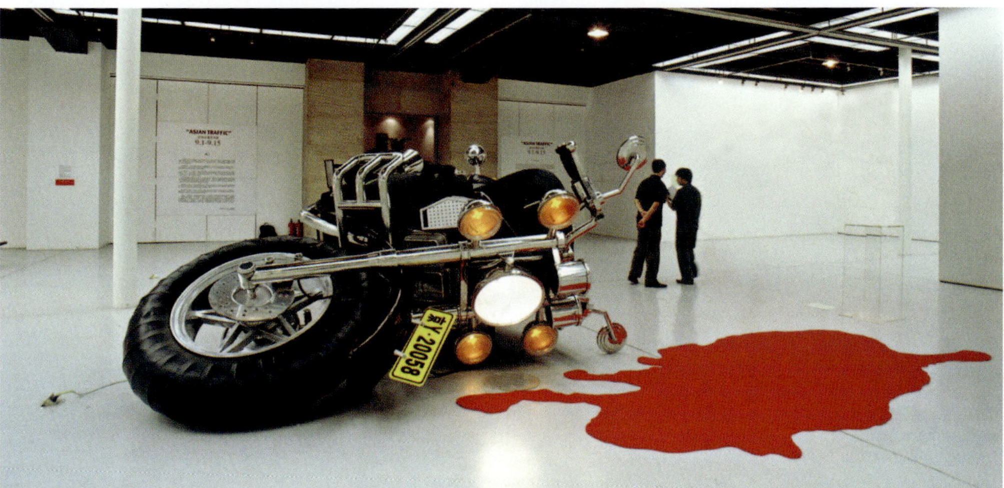

8

1 ***Portable City: Berlin***, *2005*
Suitcase, clothes, light, sound, approx. 50 x 76 x 93 cm
Koffer, gebrauchte Kleidungsstücke, Licht, Ton, ca. 50 x 76 x 93 cm
《移动的城市：柏林》 2005年, 手提箱，衣服，灯光，音响，
大约 50 x 76 x 93 cm

2 ***Portable City: New York***, *2003*
Suitcase, clothes, light, sound, 60 x 75 x 72 cm
Koffer, gebrauchte Kleidungsstücke, Licht, Ton, 60 x 75 x 72 cm
《移动的城市：纽约》2003年, 手提箱，衣服，灯光，音响，
60 x 75 x 72 cm

3 ***International Airport Terminal 1***, *2006*
Installation with used clothes, fabric on wood, freight trolleys
Installation mit gebrauchten Kleidungstücken, Stoff auf Holz, Flughafen-Trolleys
《国际机场：一号航站》2006年, 装置由旧衣服, 出木，推车

4 ***Shoes with Butter***, *1996*
C-print, 120 x 180 cm; C-print, 120 x 180 cm
《奶油鞋》1996年, C-印刷, 120 x 180 cm

5 ***Suitcases***, *2000–2002*
Video installation, video projection, suitcases, used clothes, lightbulbs, dimensions variable
Videoinstallation, Videoprojektion, Koffer, getragene Kleidung, Glühbirnen, Maße variabel
《手提箱2000-2002年》录象装置，录象投影，手提箱，旧衣服，电灯泡，大小不一

6 ***Weapons***, *2003–2007*
210 pieces, installation with used clothes from all over the world and daily life things, Venice Biennial, 2007
Installation mit gebrauchten Kleidungsstücken aus der ganzen Welt und Alltagsgegenständen, Biennale di Venezia, 2007
《武器》2003-2007年, 210 件, 装置由来自全球的旧衣服和日用品构成

7 ***Fashion Terrorism***, 2004
Performance Rathaus Friedrichshafen
Performance Rathaus Friedrichshafen
《时装恐怖主义》2004年, 表演，市政厅腓德烈斯哈芬

8 ***Where are the brakes?***, *2005*
Installation view Today Art Museum, Beijing, 550 x 177 x 345 cm
Installationsansicht Today Art Museum, Peking, 550 x 177 x 345 cm
《刹车在哪儿啊?》2005年 装置实景 今日美术馆，北京
550 x 177 x 345 cm

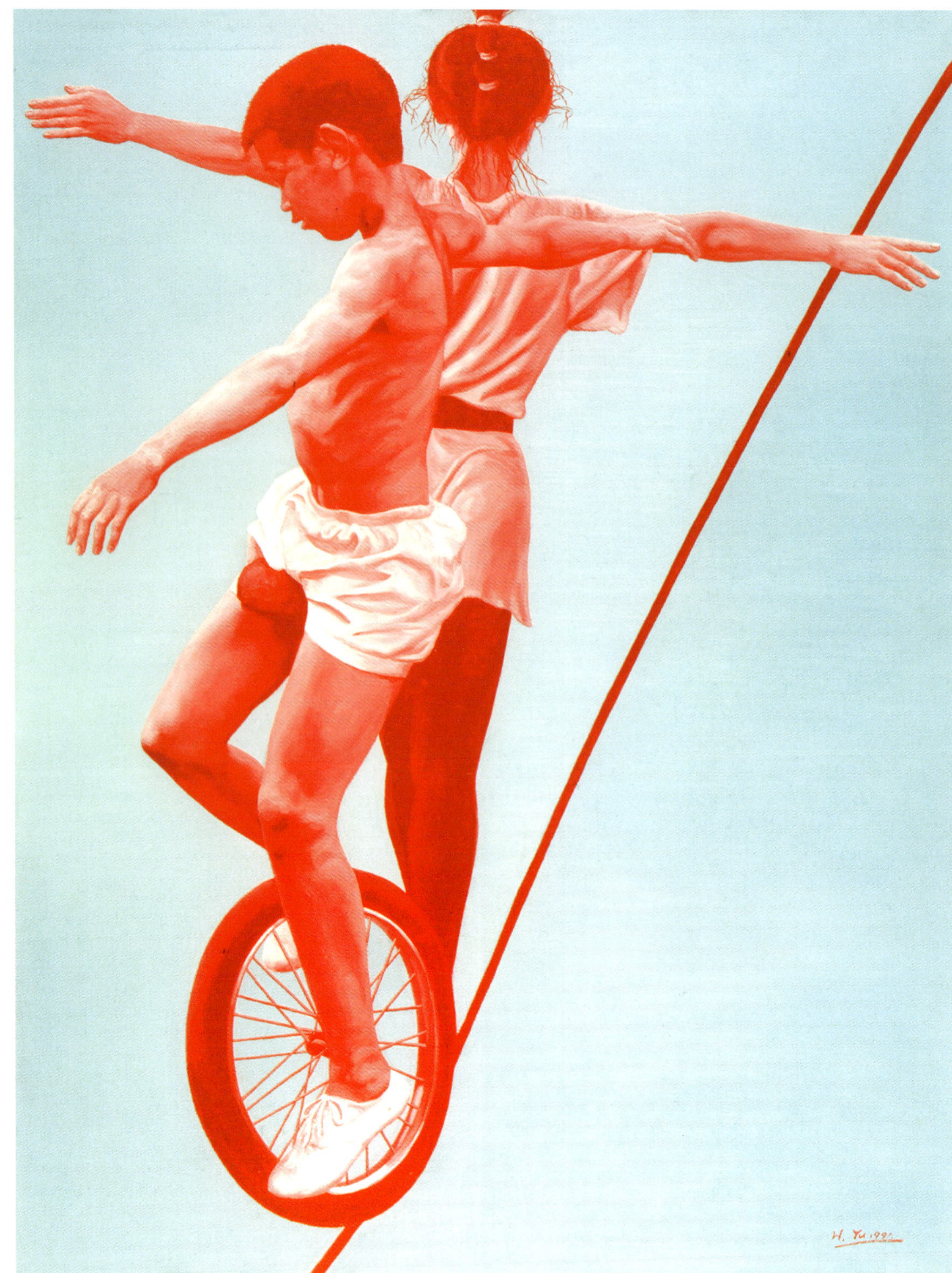

1

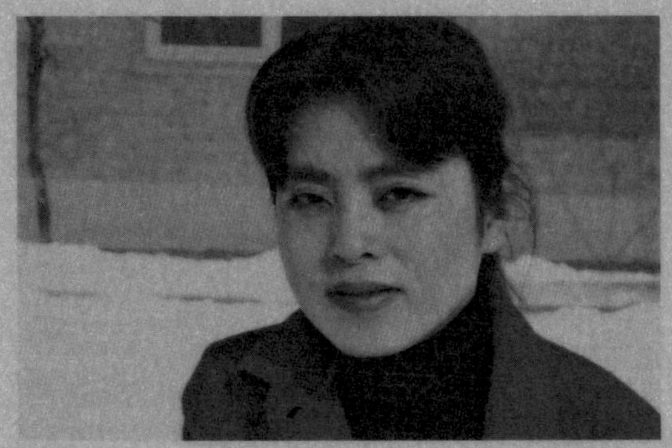

"I live in a crowd in which I discover plenty of touching things that are far beyond expression with words. These are human beings' sensitivity, weakness, dignity, misunderstanding, helplessness, sincerity and love stories; things that move people."

„Ich lebe inmitten von Menschen, an denen ich viele berührende Dinge entdecke, die weit über das hinausgehen, was sich mit Worten ausdrücken lässt: Sensibilität, Schwäche, Würde, Missverständnisse, Hilflosigkeit, Aufrichtigkeit und Liebe."

"在我生活的圈中，我找到了许多感人的事事物物，但这些事情非言语可以表达，如人类的敏感，弱点 尊严，误解，无助，真诚和爱情故事；令人感动的事情。"

Born in 1966 in Beijing, China. Lives and works in Beijing
Geboren 1966 in Peking, China. Lebt und arbeitet in Peking
1966年出生于中国北京，现在北京工作居住

Selected exhibitions **/ Ausgewählte Ausstellungen /** 所选展览

1990 "Yu Hong's Painting", Gallery of Central Academy of Fine Arts, Beijing, China
2002 "Witness to Growth", The East Modern Art Center, Beijing, He Xiangning Art Museum, Shenzhen, China
2003 "A Woman's Life – The Art of Yu Hong", Halsey Gallery, College of Charleston, Goedhuis Contemporary, New York, NY, USA
"Witness to Growth", Museum of Hubei Academy of Fine Art, Wuhan, China
2006 "Yu Hong", Galerie Loft, Paris, France
"The Grand Promenade", National Museum of Contemporary Art, Athens, Greece
2007 "Witness to Growth", Eslite Gallery, Taipei, Taiwan

1990年 《女画家的世界》中央美术学院美术馆北京，中国
2002年 《目击成长》喻红作品展何香凝美术馆 深圳，远洋艺术中心，北京，中国
2003年 《一个女人的生活--喻红的艺术》哈尔西美术馆，查尔斯顿大学，古德豪斯当代艺术画廊纽约
《目击成长》喻红作品展，湖北美术学院美术馆武汉，中国
2006年 《喻红》Loft画廊巴黎，法国
《大散步》当代艺术国家博物馆 ，雅典，希腊
2007年 《目击成长》诚品画廊，台北，台湾

Selected publications **/ Ausgewählte Publikationen /** 所选著作

Nicholas Jose: "My Search for a Shaman: The Impact of 1989 on Chinese Art", in: "Art and Asia Pacific", vol. 1, no. 2, April 1994
Geremie Barmé: "Shades of Mao: The Posthumous Cult of the Great Leader", London 1996
John Clark: "Modern Asian Art", Sydney/Honolulu 1998
Karen Smith: "Century: Woman at the China Art Gallery/Modern Art Museum/International Art Palace", in: "Asian Art News", vol. 8, no. 3, May/June 1998

Jose, Nicholas（著）:《我的查寻萨满：1989 年的冲击对中国艺术》于: Art and Asia Pacific, 第1卷, 号2, （1994年四月）
Barmé, Geremie（著）:《毛的影子：大领导人的遗腹礼拜》伦敦1996年
Clark, John（著）:《现代亚洲艺术》悉尼/ 檀香山1998年
Smith, Karen（著）:《世纪：妇女在中国美术画廊/ 现代艺术博物馆/ 国际艺术宫殿》于: Asian Art News, 第8号3(1998年5月六月)

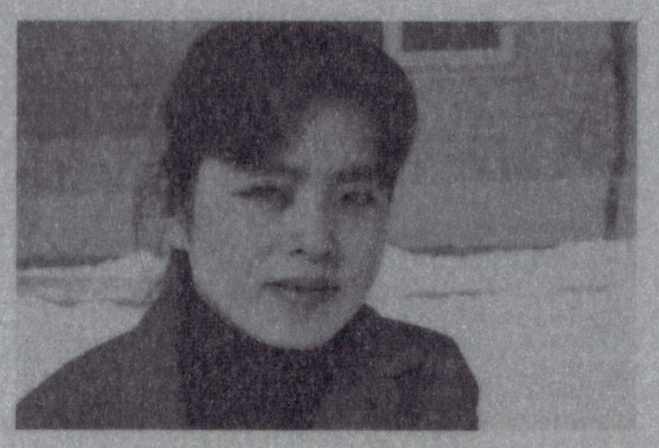

"I live in a crowd in which I discover plenty of touching things that are far beyond expression with words. These are human beings' sensitivity, weakness, dignity, misunderstanding, helplessness, sincerity and love stories; things that move people."

„Ich lebe inmitten von Menschen, an denen ich viele berührende Dinge entdecke, die weit über das hinausgehen, was sich mit Worten ausdrücken lässt: Sensibilität, Schwäche, Würde, Missverständnisse, Hilflosigkeit, Aufrichtigkeit und Liebe."

"在我生活的圈中，我找到了许多感人的事事物物，但这些事情非言语可以表达，如人类的敏感，弱点 尊严，误解，无助，真诚和爱情故事；令人感动的事情。"

Born in 1966 in Beijing, China. Lives and works in Beijing
Geboren 1966 in Peking, China. Lebt und arbeitet in Peking
1966年出生于中国北京，现在北京工作居住

Selected exhibitions / Ausgewählte Ausstellungen / 所选展览

1990 "Yu Hong's Painting", Gallery of Central Academy of Fine Arts, Beijing, China
2002 "Witness to Growth", The East Modern Art Center, Beijing, He Xiangning Art Museum, Shenzhen, China
2003 "A Woman's Life - The Art of Yu Hong", Halsey Gallery, College of Charleston, Goedhuis Contemporary, New York, NY, USA
"Witness to Growth", Museum of Hubei Academy of Fine Art, Wuhan, China
2006 "Yu Hong", Galerie Loft, Paris, France
"The Grand Promenade", National Museum of Contemporary Art, Athens, Greece
2007 "Witness to Growth", Eslite Gallery, Taipei, Taiwan

1990年 《女画家的世界》中央美术学院美术馆北京，中国
2002年 《目击成长》喻红作品展何香凝美术馆 深圳，远洋艺术中心，北京，中国
2003年 《一个女人的生活—喻红的艺术》哈尔西美术馆，查尔斯顿大学，古德豪斯当代艺术画廊纽约
《目击成长》喻红作品展，湖北美术学院美术馆武汉，中国
2006年 《喻红》Loft画廊巴黎，法国
《大散步》当代艺术国家博物馆 ，雅典，希腊
2007年 《目击成长》诚品画廊，台北，台湾

Selected publications / Ausgewählte Publikationen / 所选著作

Nicholas Jose: "My Search for a Shaman: The Impact of 1989 on Chinese Art", in: "Art and Asia Pacific", vol. 1, no. 2, April 1994
Geremie Barmé: "Shades of Mao: The Posthumous Cult of the Great Leader", London 1996
John Clark: "Modern Asian Art", Sydney/Honolulu 1998
Karen Smith: "Century: Woman at the China Art Gallery/Modern Art Museum/International Art Palace", in: "Asian Art News", vol. 8, no. 3, May/June 1998

Jose, Nicholas（著）：《我的查寻萨满：1989 年的冲击对中国艺术》于：Art and Asia Pacific，第1卷，号2，（1994年四月）
Barmé, Geremie（著）：《毛的影子：大领导人的遗腹礼拜》伦敦1996年
Clark, John（著）：《现代亚洲艺术》悉尼/檀香山1998年
Smith, Karen（著）：《世纪：妇女在中国美术画廊/现代艺术博物馆/国际艺术宫殿》于：Asian Art News，第8号3(1998年5月六月)

YU HONG 喻红

[jy xʊŋ]

Yu Hong grew up as a young artistic prodigy in the center of Beijing, painting her way to academic acclaim and on through an elite training at the Central Academy which she finished in 1988. Her mature style emerged in the 1980s and was captured in the monumental "New Generation exhibition" at the National History Museum in 1991. That exhibition, hailed as the moment when the techniques of Socialist Realism were finally turned onto the scenes of everyday life, brought new notice to Yu Hong and her future husband Liu Xiaodong.

Yu Hong's works from the late 1980s and early 1990s are mostly portraits, in palettes several degrees removed from reality. A 1989 portrait of the sculptor Jiang Jie shows Yu Hong's classmate in track shoes and running suit, all a melancholy shade of purple. "Perfect Born" (1992), depicts a monochromatic Yu Hong and Liu Xiaodong pensive and in love beneath a strangely evil looking pair of cooing birds. Shortly thereafter, the couple left for a year's sojourn in New York, where they were married. Yu Hong's work after her return from the U. S. begins to focus on themes of domesticity and personal development, with canvases depicting home floors strewn with toys, fathers with sons, and her own pregnant body. She gave birth to her daughter in 1994 and motherhood has remained of deep and continued importance to her artistic practice.

In 1999 Yu Hong embarked on her most ambitious series, entitled "Witness to Growth". The final group of diptychs – one for each year of her life – has been widely exhibited. Each pairs an image of the artist from a family photograph with a news photograph taken during the same year. The pairings are both delightful and disconcerting: Yu Hong, 2, wearing a badge of Mao walking toward Anyuan as her mother takes her for a stroll in the park next to an image taken from the "People's Pictorial" of Red Guards holding reproductions of that same famous image of Mao. The diptych devoted to 1984 pairs the 18 year-old Yu Hong playing a guitar among friends with an image of the 35th Anniversary National Day Parade which marked Deng Xiaoping's thorough ascendance

Yu Hong, ein künstlerisches Wunderkind, ermalte sich akademische Anerkennung und eine Eliteausbildung an der Central Academy, die sie 1988 abschloss. Ihr Stil bildete sich in den 1980er Jahren heraus und war in der monumentalen Ausstellung „New Generation" im National History Museum 1991 zu bewundern. Durch diese Schau – zu einem Zeitpunkt, als der Sozialistische Realismus endlich auf Darstellungen des Alltagslebens angewandt wurde – fanden Yu Hong und ihr künftiger Ehemann Liu Xiaodong große Beachtung.

Yu Hongs Arbeiten aus den späten 1980er und frühen 1990er Jahren waren vor allem Porträts, in einer Farbgebung, die mit der Realität wenig gemein hatte. So stellt etwa ein 1989 entstandenes Porträt der Bildhauerin Jiang Jie Yu Hongs Kommilitonin in Sportschuhen und Jogginganzug dar, ganz in ein melancholisches Lila getaucht. Das monochrome „Perfect Born" (1992) zeigt Yu Hong und Liu Xiaodong nachdenklich und verliebt, unter einem bedrohlich wirkenden Pärchen balzender Vögel. Kurz darauf gingen die beiden zu einem einjährigen Aufenthalt nach New York, wo sie auch heirateten. Seit ihrer Rückkehr konzentriert sich Yu Hongs Werk zunehmend auf häusliche Themen und solche der persönlichen Entwicklung: Ihre Gemälde zeigen mit Spielzeug übersäte Fußböden, Väter mit Söhnen oder auch sie selbst während der Schwangerschaft – seit sie 1994 eine Tochter zur Welt brachte, hat die Mutterrolle eine tiefe Bedeutung für ihr künstlerisches Schaffen gewonnen.

1999 begann Yu Hong unter dem Titel „Witness to Growth" ihre bislang ehrgeizigste Serie von Diptychen, die jeweils ein Jahr ihres Lebens thematisierten – die letzte Gruppe dieser Doppelbilder war auf vielen Ausstellungen zu sehen. Die Künstlerin stellte dabei ein nach einem Familienfoto gearbeitetes Gemälde neben ein Nachrichtenfoto aus dem selben Jahr. Die Paarungen wirken ansprechend und beunruhigend zugleich: So zeigt eine die zweijährige Yu Hong mit ihrer Mutter auf dem Weg in den Park, wobei dem Baby ein Button angeheftet ist, der Mao auf dem Marsch nach Anyuan abbildet – kombiniert mit einem Foto aus dem

喻红在北京城区逐渐成长为一个天才青年艺术家，其风格受到学院的赞赏，并在中央美院进行了专业学习，1988年毕业。80年代，其风格趋向成熟，1991年作品在中国美术馆举行的新生代艺术展。该展览，被公认为以社会主义现实主义技巧描述日常生活的时刻，这些展览也向喻红和她未来丈夫刘小东传递了新的讯息。

她创作与80年代到90年代早期的作品大部分以肖像画为主，而在色调上则不是现实中的色彩。1989年喻红为同学雕塑家姜杰画了一幅雕像，画像中的姜杰脚穿跑鞋，身穿运动装，画面笼罩在忧郁的紫色阴影下。《理想的境界》创作始于 1992年， 画面中恋爱中的喻红和刘小东两人神情忧郁，两人上方一对咕咕叫的大鸟以一种奇怪罪恶的眼神注视着他们。 短短一段时间后，两人到纽约呆了一年时间，那是他们结婚的地方。从美国回来以后，喻红的开始把作品的主题关注于家庭生活和个人发展，如不满玩具的楼梯，父亲和儿子，以及她怀孕时候的样子。（1994年她生了个女儿，但成为母亲之后依然对其艺术实践有深远和持续的重要性。）

1999年，她开始着手于最具抱负的作品系列《目击成长》。这些双折画每一面代表着她的生活，而最后一部在很广的范围内展出。每折配上艺术家的家庭照片，新拍摄于同年。这些双折画既有欢乐的气氛又有不安的感觉：喻红，2岁，妈妈带着她在公园闲逛，衣服上带着像章上面印有毛泽东去安源的图像，而另一幅上面选自人民画报：红卫兵手拿着那副著名画像的复制品。在那幅以1984年为主题的双折画上，一面描写28岁的喻红在朋友间弹奏吉他，而另一面则是中华人民共和国35周年国庆游行大典，那年也是邓小平全面掌权的时刻。1994年以后的每一年中，双折画改为三折画，上面增加了他女儿的照片。这幅标题为《记忆的衣裳》超大的T恤上面印有两张对照新的图片，以强迫性但绝对优雅的手法处理着时间的流逝，后来作品被盖为悬挂的装置。

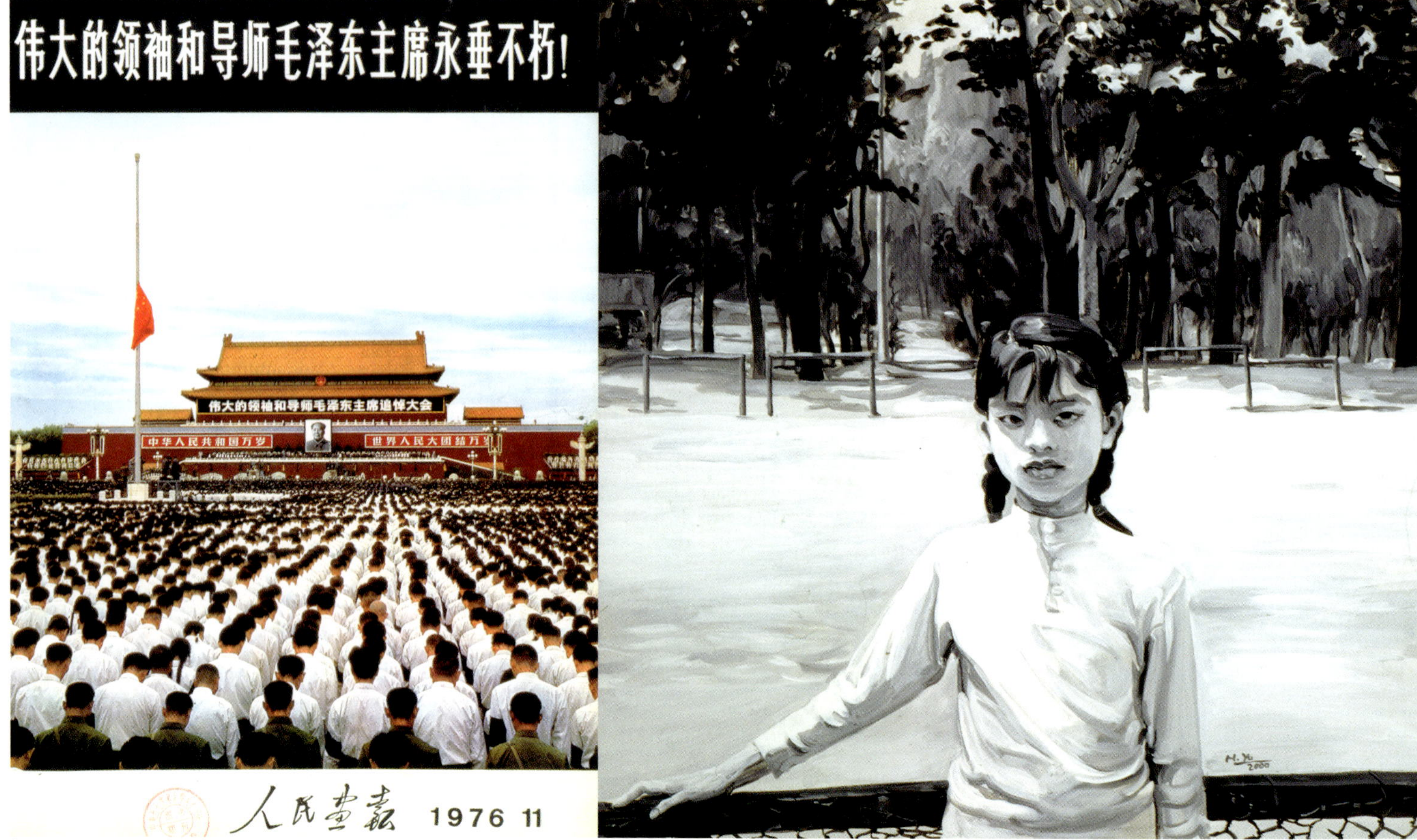
伟大的领袖和导师毛泽东主席永垂不朽!
伟大的领袖和导师毛泽东主席追悼大会
中华人民共和国万岁
世界人民大团结万岁
人民画报 1976 11

2

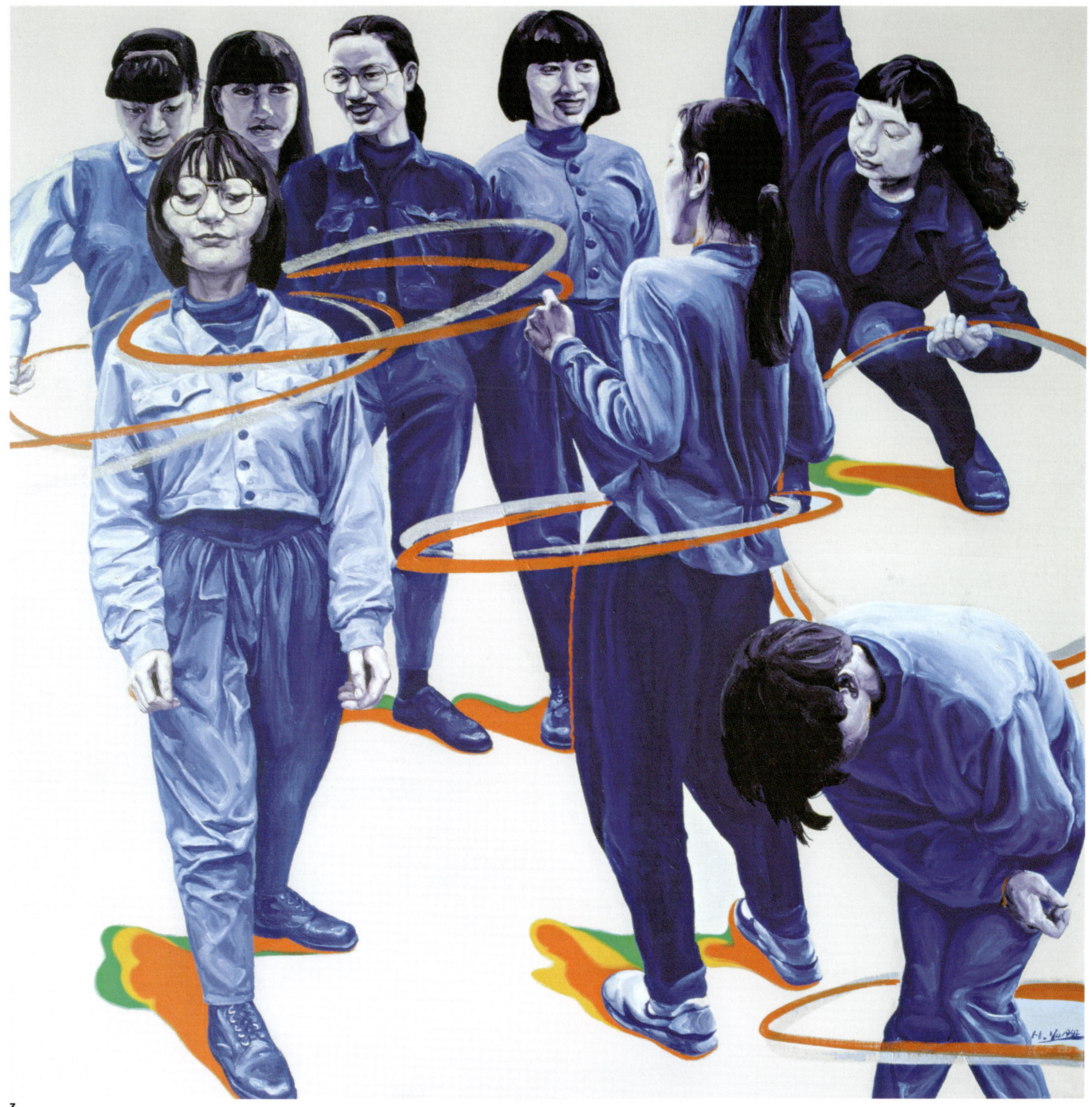

3

4

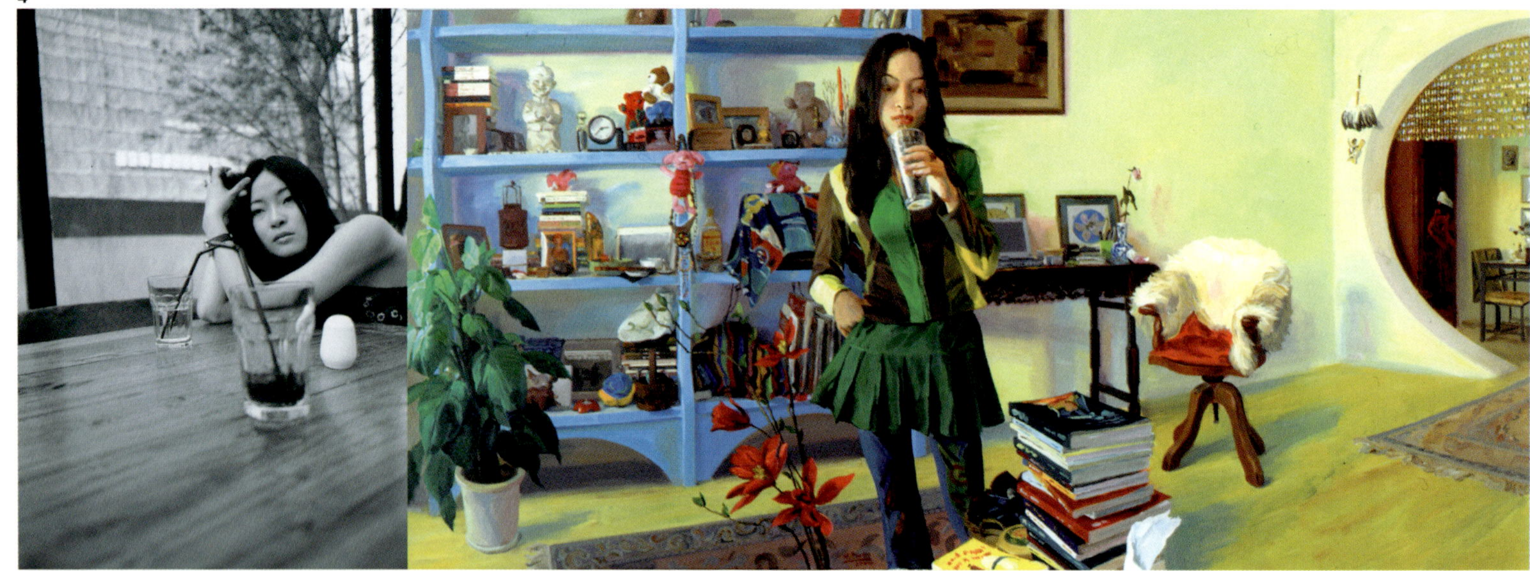

to power. For each year after 1994, the diptychs become triptychs, with paintings of her daughter added to the mix. The series, which was later modified into an installation on hanging, oversized cotton t-shirts entitled "Memory Dress" (with the contrasting images printed on either side of the garments) handles the passage of time in a compelling yet resolutely elegant manner.

Yu Hong's most recent major series, "She" (since 2006), turns the introspective lens of her earlier work outward upon society. These works, also diptychs, pair a photograph of a given woman (a gymnastics coach, a police officer, a performance artist) with a painting of the same woman in her domestic or professional environment. The photographs are selected by the subjects, making in some cases for a productive duality between how the subject chooses to represent herself and how she is ultimately represented by Yu Hong. Together, the works in the "She" cycle comprise a sweeping portrait of a complex society, capturing, in straightforward but still exacting terms, a few of the individual dramas that make up that society.

„People's Pictorial", auf dem Rotgardisten Reproduktionen desselben Mao-Gemäldes schwenken. Und das Diptychon für 1984 setzt die 18-jährige Yu Hong, die gerade inmitten von Freunden Gitarre spielt, neben ein Foto von der Parade zum 35. Jahrestag der Gründung der Volksrepublik, als Deng Xiaopings unaufhaltsamer Aufstieg zur Macht begann. In den Jahren nach 1994 wandeln sich die Diptychen zu Triptychen, als nämlich Gemälde von Yus Tochter hinzukommen. Diese neue Serie, die später unter dem Titel „Memory Dress" zu einer Installation auf Baumwoll-T-Shirts in Übergröße modifiziert wurde (wobei die kontrastierenden Bilder jeweils auf Vorder- und Rückseite der Shirts aufgedruckt sind), behandelt das Verstreichen der Zeit in bezwingender und dabei konsequent eleganter Manier.

Yu Hongs jüngste große Serie, „She" (seit 2006), richtet den scharfen Blick ihrer früheren introspektiven Arbeiten nun nach außen auf die Gesellschaft. Diese Werkreihe, wieder in Form von Diptychen, stellt jeweils ein Foto einer Frau in ihrem Beruf (Gymnastiklehrerin, Polizistin oder Performancekünstlerin) neben ein Gemälde derselben Frau in ihrem häuslichen oder professionellen Umfeld. Die Fotos wurden von den Modellen selbst ausgewählt, was in manchen Fällen zu einem produktiven Zweikampf zwischen der angestrebten Selbstdarstellung der Modelle und der Art und Weise, wie sie von Yu Hong dargestellt werden, führt. Zusammen bilden die Werke des „She"-Zyklus ein umfassendes Porträt einer überaus komplexen Gesellschaft und fangen geradlinig und doch anspruchsvoll einige jener Einzelschicksale ein, aus denen sich diese wie jede andere Gesellschaft zusammensetzt.

喻红近作《她》将自省视角从早期工作环境转向社会。这些作品也是双折画，一面是特定女人（体操教练、警员和行为艺术家）的照片，一面则是家居环境或专业环境中相同女人的油画。这些摄影都根据主题选择，在某种意义上趋向创作的二元性：一方面所选择的主题怎样去表现她自己；另一方面则是“她”怎样被喻红所体现。两者合起来，这些作品全面描述了一个复杂的社会，以直白但不失细腻的语言捕捉着装扮社会的少数个人的梦想。

Philip Tinari

5

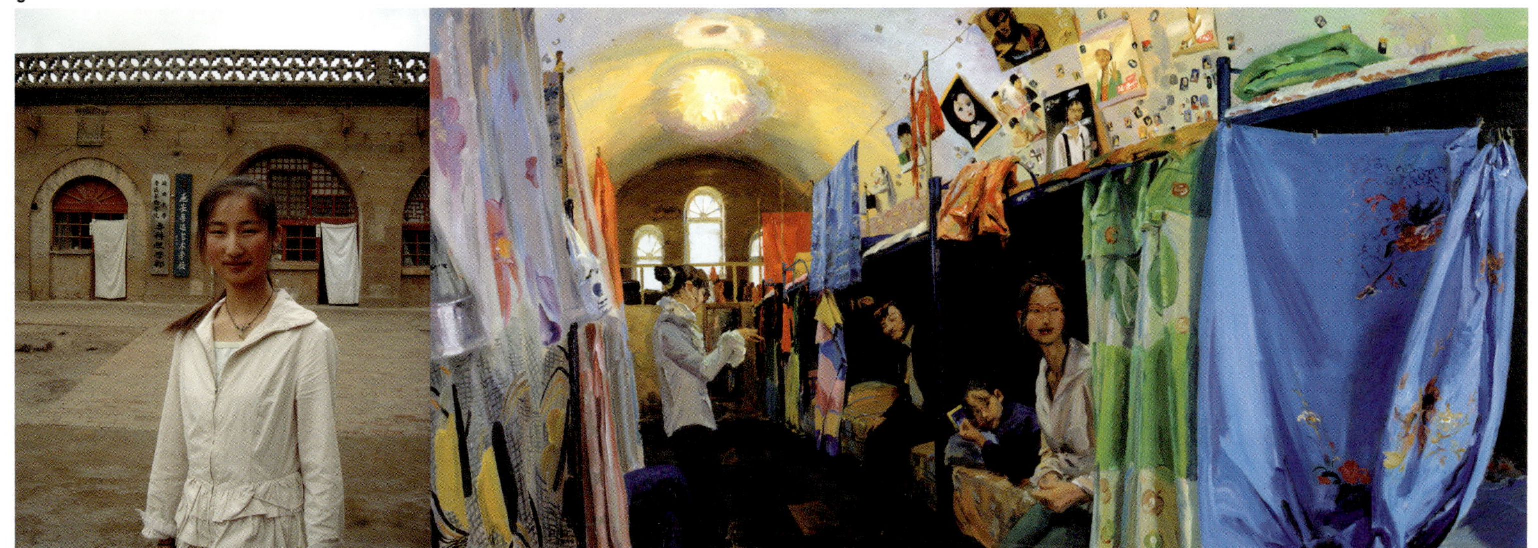

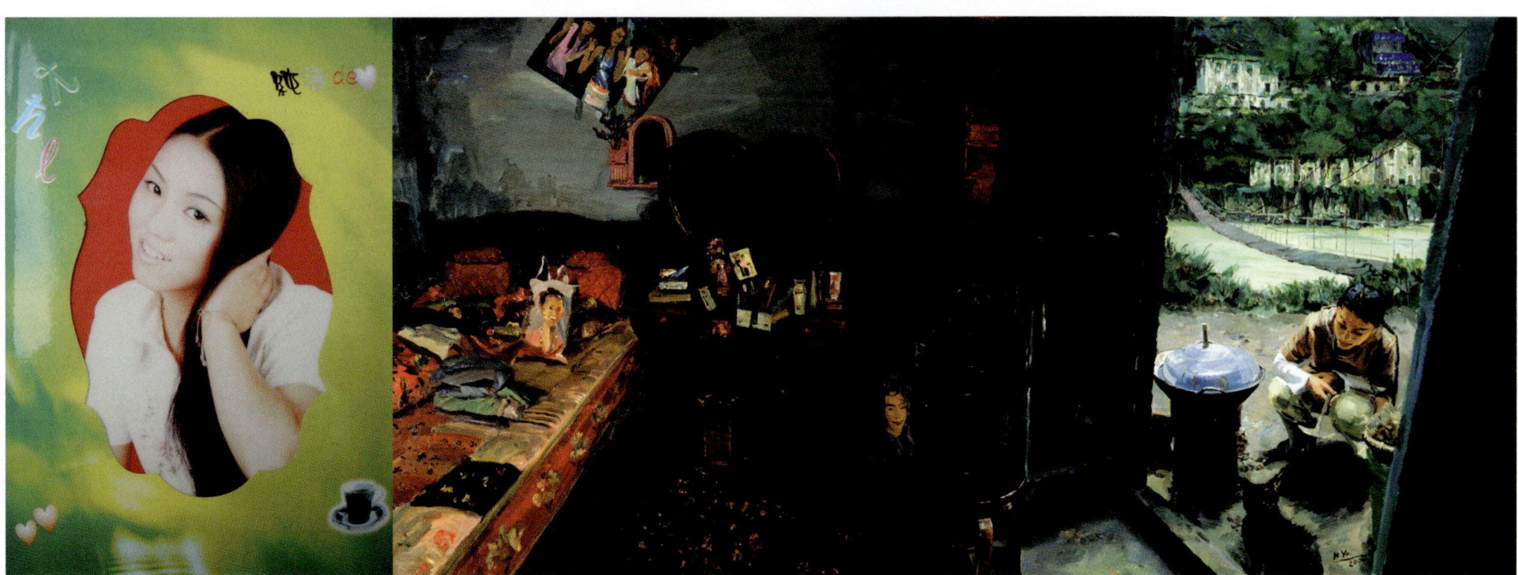

6

1 ***Tightrope**, 1991*
Oil on canvas, 130 x 97 cm; Öl auf Leinwand, 130 x 97 cm
《走钢丝》1991年，布面油画，130 x 97 cm

2 ***1976 – Ten years old on the playground in Beijing University of Aeronautics and Astronautics**, 2000*
Oil on canvas, photograph, 100 x 171 cm; Öl auf Leinwand, Fotografie, 100 x 171 cm
《1976年 -- 十岁在北京航天航空大学操场》2000年, 布面油画, 摄影, 100 x 171 cm

3 ***Popular movement**, 1992*
Oil on canvas, 195 x 174.5 cm; Öl auf Leinwand, 195 x 174,5 cm
《流行运动》1992年，布面油画, 195 x 174.5 cm

4 ***She – Beautiful Lady Writer Zhao Bo**, 2004*
Acrylic on canvas, photograph, 150 x 416 cm; Acryl auf Leinwand, Fotografie, 150 x 416 cm
《她--美女作家赵波》2004年, 布面丙烯, 摄影, 150 x 416 cm

5 ***She – Student from Yan An**, 2006*
Acrylic on canvas, photograph, 150 x 450 cm; Acryl auf Leinwand, Fotografie, 150 x 450 cm
《她一延安的学生》2006年, 布面丙烯, 摄影，150 x 450 cm

6 ***She – younger sister from Sichuan**, 2006*
Acrylic on canvas, photograph, 150 x 450 cm; Acryl auf Leinwand, Fotografie, 150 x 450 cm
《她一川妹子》 2006年，丙烯酸酯，150 x 450 cm

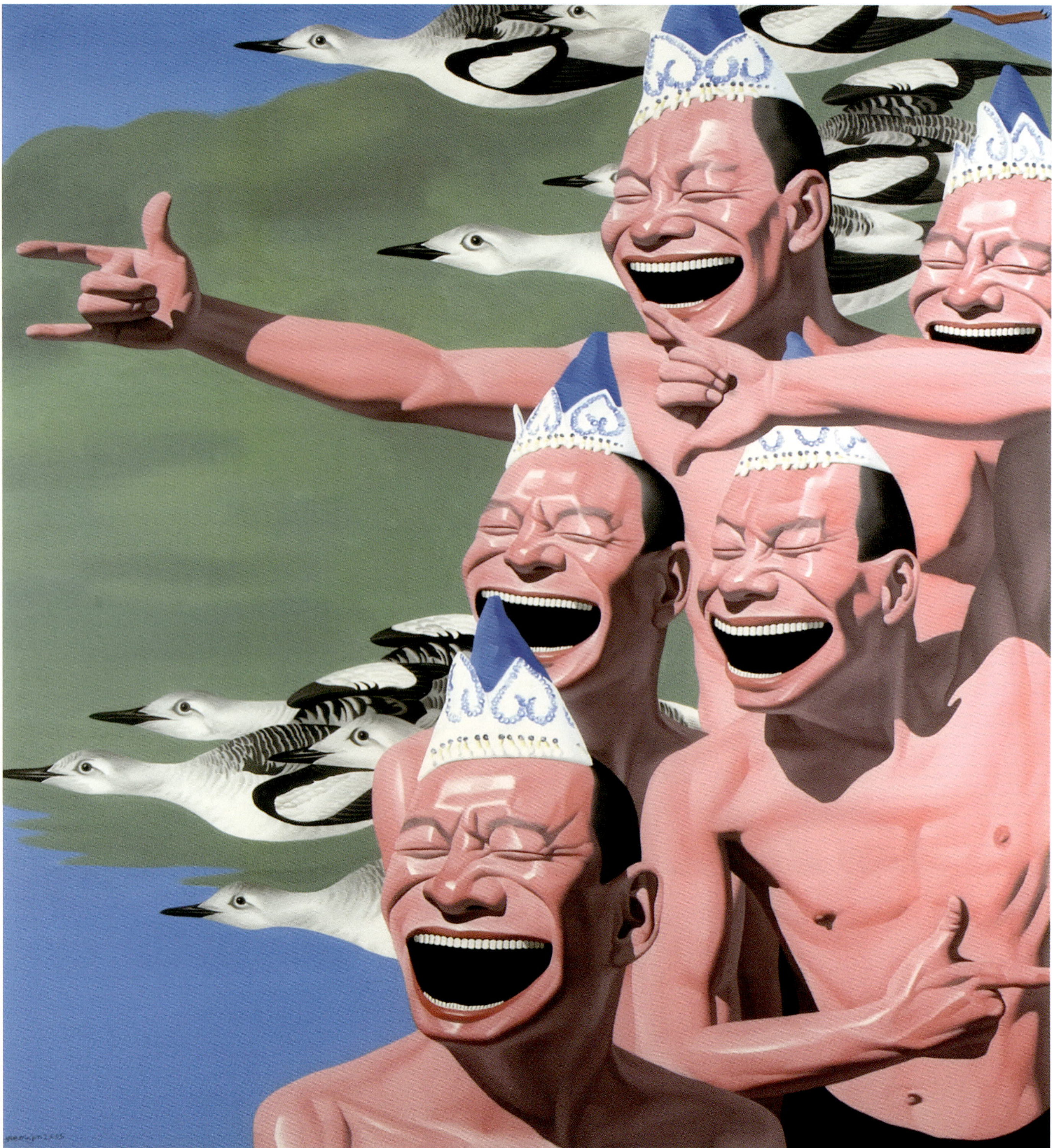

1

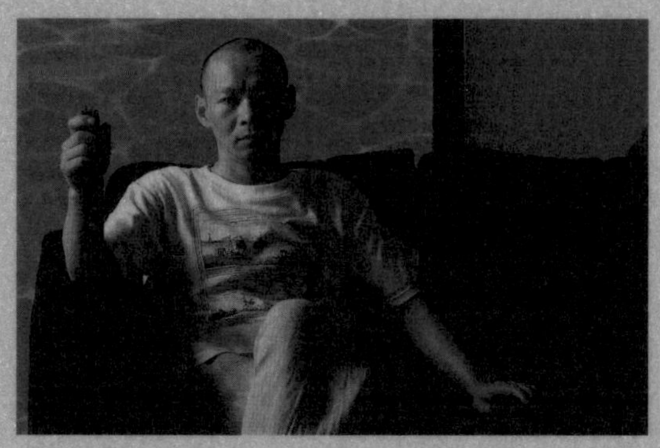

"When the image is continuously duplicated it has a tremendous strength due to the increase of quantity. Once it became an idol I can use and apply it unceasingly. The today's society is a society of idols and today's culture is a culture of idols."

„Wird ein Bild oft kopiert, entwickelt es durch seine Zahl eine gewaltige Kraft. Sobald es ein Idol geworden ist, kann ich es benutzen und einsetzen. Die heutige Gesellschaft ist eine der Idole und die heutige Kultur eine Kultur der Idole."

"用传统的绘画、雕塑方式，不断复制自己的形象，是为了创造一个新偶像。当形象在不断重复时，由于量的增加，而产生巨大的力量。一旦成为了偶像，我便可以利用和应用我的偶像，并且不断地使用。当代社会就是一个偶像社会，当代文化就是偶像文化。"

Born in 1962 in Daqing, China. Lives and works in Beijing
Geboren 1962 in Daqing, China. Lebt und arbeitet in Peking
1962年出生于中国大庆。现生活工作于北京

Selected exhibitions / **Ausgewählte Ausstellungen** / 所选展览

1999	"Open Boundary", 48. Biennale di Venezia, Venice, Italy
2004	5th Shanghai Biennial, Shanghai Art Museum, China
	5th Gwangju Biennial 2004, Gwangju Art Museum, Korea
2005–07	"Mahjong – Chinesische Gegenwartskunst aus der Sammlung Sigg", Kunstmuseum Bern, Berne, Switzerland; Hamburger Kunsthalle, Hamburg, Germany; Museum der Moderne, Salzburg, Austria
2006	"Reproduction of Idols: Yue Minjun's Works 2004–2006", Hexiangning Art Museum, Shenzhen, China
	"Looking for Terrorists", 798 Space, Beijing, China
2007	"Passion for Art", Sammlung Essl, Klosterneuburg, Austria

1999年	《开放的边界：第48届威尼斯双年展》意大利，威尼斯
2004年	《第五届上海双年展2004：影像生存》中国，上海美术馆
	《第五届光州双年展2004：一尘一滴》韩国，光州美术馆
2005–07年	《麻将》西克中国当代艺术收藏展 伯尔尼美术馆 瑞士；汉堡美术馆 汉堡 德国；萨尔茨保现代美术馆 奥地利
2006年	《复制的偶像：岳敏君作品2004–2006》，中国，何香凝美术馆
	《寻找恐怖主义者》，中国，北京798艺术区《北京公社》
2007年	《艺术激情》Sammlung Essl美术博物馆，克罗斯特纽堡，奥地利

Selected publications / **Ausgewählte Publikationen** / 所选著作

Yue Minjun: "Lost Self", Shijiazhuang 2005
"Reproduction of Idols: Yue Minjun's Works 2004–2006", Shenzhen 2006

《岳敏君：迷失的自我》，河北教育出版社，2005年
《复制的偶像：岳敏君作品2004–2006》深圳2006年

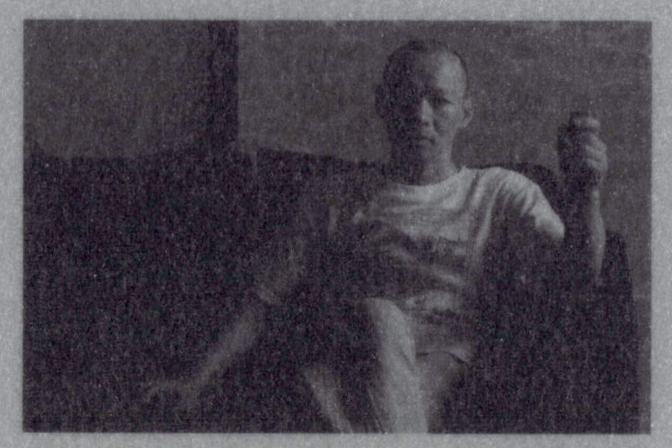

"When the image is continuously duplicated it has a tremendous strength due to the increase of quantity. Once it became an idol I can use and apply it unceasingly. The today's society is a society of idols and today's culture is a culture of idols."

„Wird ein Bild oft kopiert, entwickelt es durch seine Zahl eine gewaltige Kraft. Sobald es ein Idol geworden ist, kann ich es benutzen und einsetzen. Die heutige Gesellschaft ist eine der Idole und die heutige Kultur eine Kultur der Idole."

"用传统的绘画，雕塑方式，不断复制自己的形象，是为了创造一个新偶像。当形象在不断重复时，由于量的增加，而产生巨大的力量。一旦成为了偶像，我便可以利用和应用我的偶像，并且不断地使用。当代社会就是一个偶像社会，当代文化就是偶像文化。"

Born in 1962 in Daqing, China. Lives and works in Beijing
Geboren 1962 in Daqing, China. Lebt und arbeitet in Peking
1962年出生于中国大庆。现生活工作于北京

Selected exhibitions / Ausgewählte Ausstellungen / 所选展览

1999	"Open Boundary", 48. Biennale di Venezia, Venice, Italy
2004	5th Shanghai Biennial, Shanghai Art Museum, China
	5th Gwangju Biennial 2004, Gwangju Art Museum, Korea
2005–07	"Mahjong – Chinesische Gegenwartskunst aus der Sammlung Sigg", Kunstmuseum Bern, Berne, Switzerland; Hamburger Kunsthalle, Hamburg, Germany; Museum der Moderne, Salzburg, Austria
2006	"Reproduction of Idols: Yue Minjun's Works 2004–2006", Hexiangning Art Museum, Shenzhen, China
	"Looking for Terrorists", 798 Space, Beijing, China
2007	"Passion for Art", Sammlung Essl, Klosterneuburg, Austria
1999年	《开放的边界：第48届威尼斯双年展》意大利，威尼斯
2004年	《第五届上海双年展2004：影像生存》中国，上海美术馆
	《第五届光州双年展2004：一尘一滴》韩国，光州美术馆
2005–07年	《麻将》西克中国当代艺术收藏展 伯尔尼美术馆 瑞士；汉堡美术馆 汉堡 德国；萨尔茨堡现代美术馆 奥地利
2006年	《复制的偶像：岳敏君作品2004-2006》，中国，何香凝美术馆
	《寻找恐怖主义者》，中国，北京798艺术区《北京公社》
2007年	《艺术激情》Sammlung Essl美术博物馆，克罗斯特纽堡，奥地利

Selected publications / Ausgewählte Publikationen / 所选著作

Yue Minjun: "Lost Self", Shijiazhuang 2005
"Reproduction of Idols: Yue Minjun's Works 2004–2006", Shenzhen 2006

《岳敏君：迷失的自我》，河北教育出版社，2005年
《复制的偶像：岳敏君作品2004-2006》深圳2006年

YUE MINJUN 岳敏君

[jyɛ mintɕuən]

Yue Minjun was one of the most important painters of Cynical Realism among Chinese artists of the 1990s. Early in the 1990s when he was at the painters' village of Yuanming Yuan, the former Summer Palace, his works appeared under the socially uniform culture and thought, the style depicting rows of laughing people without brains like in "Wild Joy Happening on a Tower over the City" (1991), "Friends" (1992), and so on.

In his works a kind of indulging into imagination and being drunk of himself is to be found, with a taunting tone doubting the real existence and in absurd forms the reality of Chinese history from the 60s onward is salient in his pictures. One aspect of his works are bright bold heads, exaggerated bodies, wide open mouths with small white teeth, laughing, a reduplication of his self portrait in rows, having the Tian'anmen as background, red flags, the sun, slogans, red lanterns, red balloons, military caps, all symbols of militarism. These structures of idols are the signifying characteristics penetrating Yue Minjun's works. In fact these idols were eternal for the Chinese of the 1990s, a deeply patterned search in anxiety and hope, but he imaginarily dissolves and creates a superficial plane without depth.

Another aspect is, that Yue uses folkloristic New Year pictures, he displays propaganda images of Socialism and the language patterns of advertisements of the consumerism epoch in the Mannerism attitude under the commercial culture influence and ambiguous psychological condition, funnily and tauntingly, to be seen as a kind of biting and sharp humour playfully expressed. He outlines vividly the desire for material of this time and absurd circumstances according to the metaphor that the existence is one kind of absurdity being the background of thought and condition of existence.

The conceptualist painting of Yue Minjun is his personal understanding of painting. Early in 1994 he started already to mock the classical famous Chinese or western paintings and to imitate them in a taunting way as "Déjeuner sur

Yue Minjun gilt als einer der bedeutendsten Maler des Zynischen Realismus unter den chinesischen Künstlern der 1990er Jahre. Zu dieser Zeit lebte er in dem Künstlerdorf von Yuanming Yuan, dem ehemaligen kaiserlichen Sommerpalast. Seine Werke gingen mit dem konform, was der damaligen Gesellschaft gerade widerfuhr – seine Arbeiten zeigten reihenweise lachende Menschen ohne Hirn, wie etwa in „Wild Joy Happening on a Tower over the City" (1991) oder in „Friends" (1992).

Yue taucht mit seinen Werken gewissermaßen in die Imagination seiner selbst ein. Mit spöttischem Unterton artikuliert er seine Zweifel an der realen Existenz und holt in seinen Bildern die absurde Realität der chinesischen Geschichte seit den 1960er Jahren hervor. Typisch wurden seine hellen kahlen Köpfe, die übertriebenen Körper, weit geöffnete, lachende Münder mit kleinen weißen Zähnen, und eine Vervielfachung seines Selbstporträts vor dem Platz des Himmlischen Friedens mit roten Fahnen, roten Laternen, roten Ballons, mit Sonne, Parolen, Militärkäppis sowie sämtlichen Symbolen des Militarismus. Tatsächlich erschienen all diese Idole den Chinesen der 1990er Jahre, tief durchdrungen von Angst und Hoffnung zugleich, noch von Dauer, aber Yue machte daraus entlarvende zweidimensionale Bildflächen ohne Tiefe.

Auf der anderen Seite greift Yue in seinen Gemälden auch auf volkskundliche Neujahrsbilder zurück, zeigt Propagandaikonen des Sozialismus und die hohlen Sprachmuster in der Werbung der neuen Konsumwelle – den ganzen Manierismus unter dem Einfluss der kommerziellen Kultur. Die zweideutige psychische Verfassung seiner Gesellschaft nimmt Yue dabei in komischer und spöttischer Manier aufs Korn, mit beißendem und scharfem Humor, der zugleich spielerisch daherkommt. In satirischen Dialogen mit dem Betrachter lässt uns der Künstler schlicht das Paradoxon der menschlichen Existenz erleben.

Yue Minjun ist ein konzeptioneller Maler. Schon 1994 begann er die berühmten klassischen chinesischen ebenso

岳敏君是上世纪90年代中国当代艺术中最重要的“玩世现实主义”的画家之一。早在90年代初期的圆明园画家村时，其作品就出现了对在社会单一文化和思想下，一排排丧失头脑的傻笑人的风格样式，如《发生在x城楼上的狂喜》（1991年）、《朋友》（1992年）等。

他的艺术创作有着一种放纵想象，沉醉自我，以嘲讽的语调质疑现实的生存，以荒诞的形式凸显了从上世纪60年代至今他所生存在中国的历史现实。一方面，他作品中总是以鲜艳的光头，夸张的肢体，嘻哈的大嘴及细密的小白牙等自我形象的复数性排列来呈现的，画面背景都是围绕着天安门、红旗、太阳、标语、红灯笼、红气球、军帽等意识形态的符号。这些“偶像“构成和贯穿了岳敏君艺术的符号化特征。实际上这些偶像意味着中国人在90年代对永恒、深度模式的追寻所形成的焦虑和失望，而被他幻化成消解式的无深度的肤浅平面。另一方面他利用了中国民间年画、社会主义宣传画和消费主义时代广告画的话语方式，将在商业文化影响下流行的矫揉造作的姿态和暧昧矫饰心理状态滑稽而嘲讽地表现出来，有着一种赖皮赖脸的嬉笑来表达犀利的幽默，勾勒出这个时代对物质欲望生动且荒诞的境遇，隐喻着“存在便是一种荒诞”的思想背景和生存处境。当我们沉浸于每一个看似荒谬的画面场景，在夸张、反讽、戏谑的对话之中，又可以感受到某种人性的乖张、生存的悖谬，以及话语中洋溢出来他的创作对中国现实文化的批判和质疑态度。

代表岳敏君的观念性绘画是他对绘画本身的认识。早在1994年，他就开始对中国或西方的经典名画进行戏拟戏仿，如《草地上的午餐》、《开国大典》、《毛主席去安源》、《自由引导人们》等作品。这种戏仿其实还是在延续他创作上的荒诞意识，或者说是以刻意地模仿来强化他的荒诞性，将我们曾经膜拜的中外大师的经典画作转化为戏谑的喜剧感。如果说他为人们所熟悉的创作风格样式是

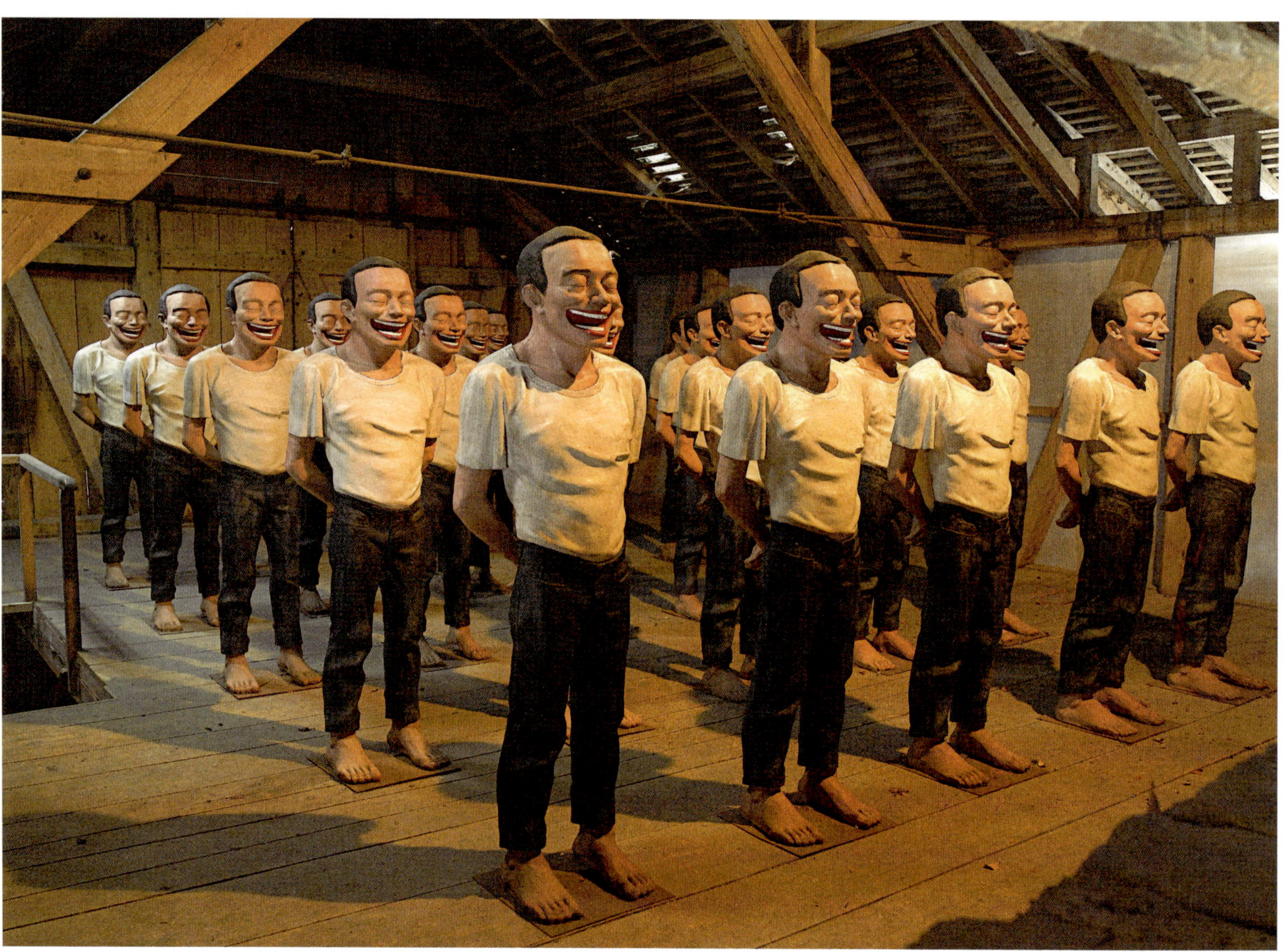

2

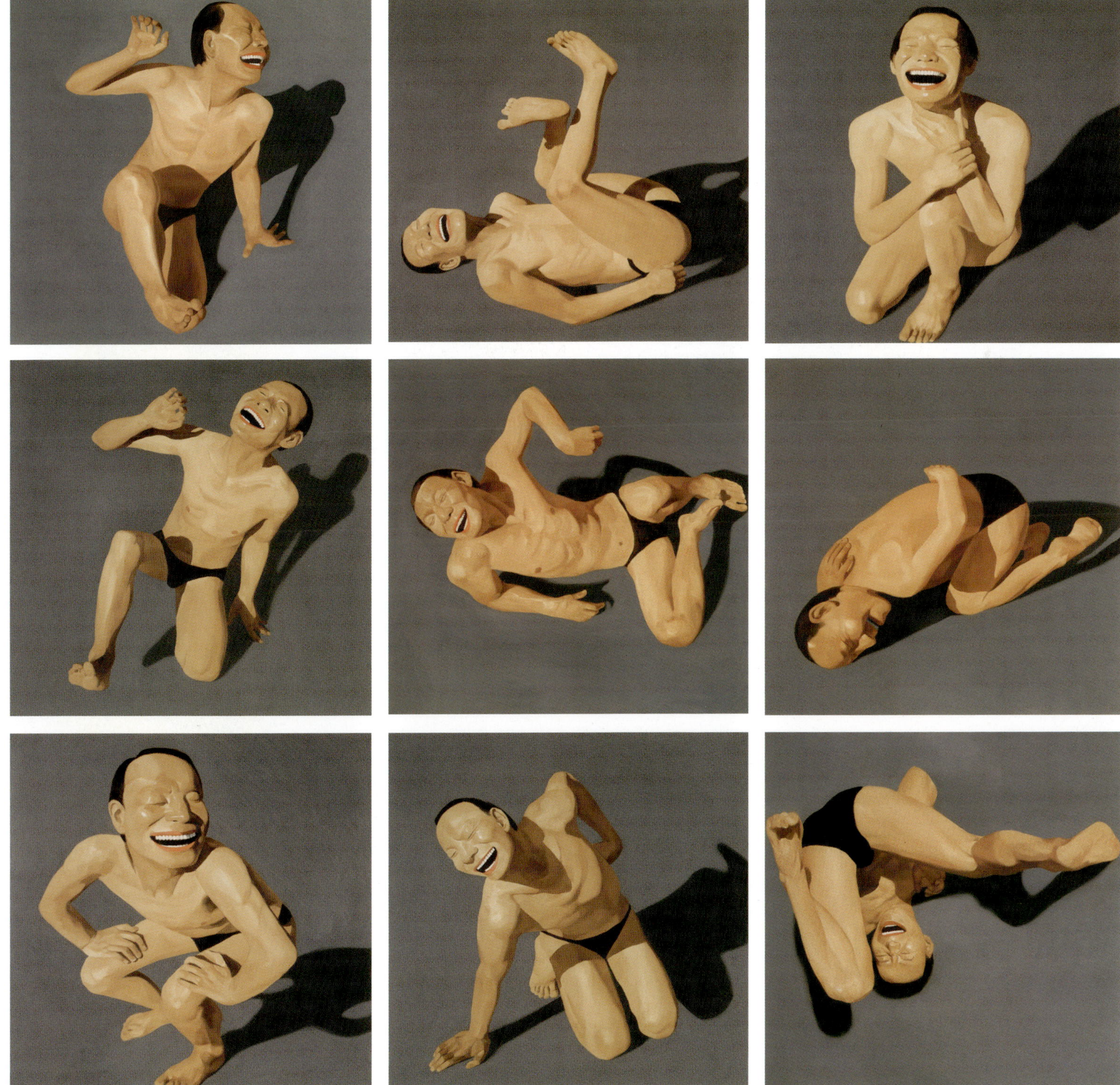

3

4

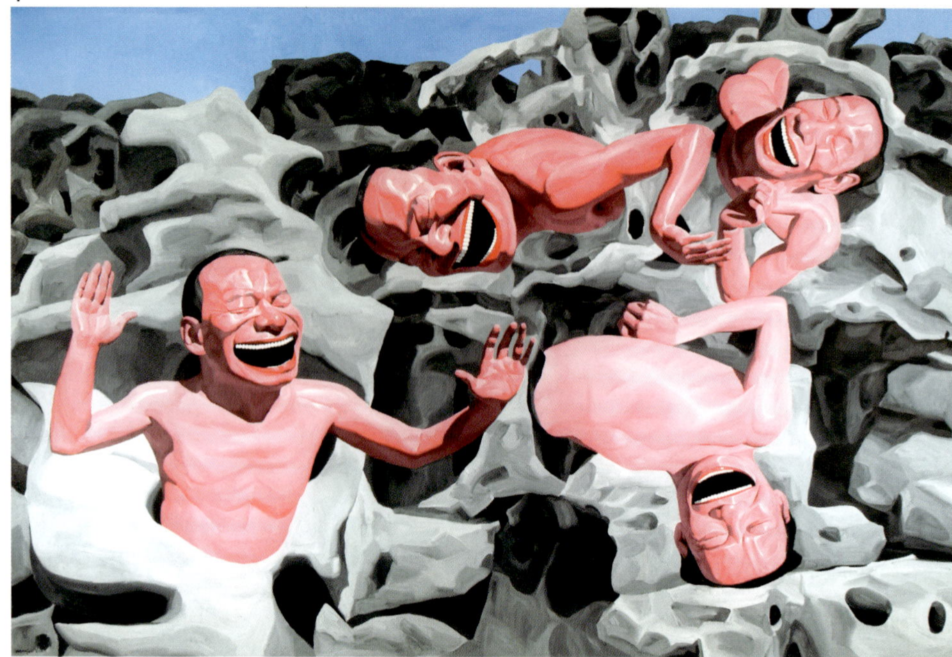

5

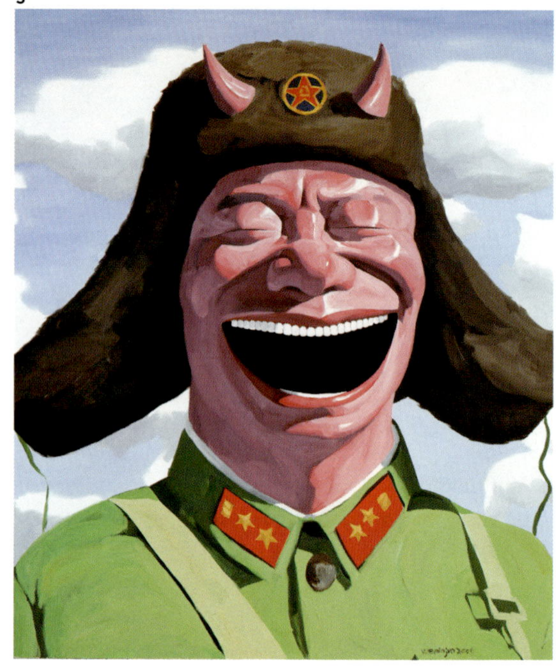

l'herbe" (1995), "Freedom Leading the People" (1995/96), "Tian'anmen Remains" (2002) oder "Chairman Mao goes to Anyuan" (2005) and other works. This kind of play imitates the reality or is the grotesque thought continuously to be found in his works transforming the deeply revered master paintings of China and abroad in a kind of humorous parody. Or in other words, to make people familiar with his style of works he uses the method of Postmodernism for teasingly satirizing and questioning criticisms towards China's real progress as in the series "Processing" (1996–2005) using the direct means of "processing" which in the relation of "processing and being processed" two kinds of pictures are intertwined and overlapping producing a new kind of sight tensity.

Yue not only uses subversion and demolition in regard to classical works of different periods and to the aesthetic of photography and styles, but tries by collating to create a new construction by alienating the familiar picture patterns and to control the anticipation of the viewer, who bodily experiences the surprise of already processed works freeing oneself from classical rules.

wie die westlichen Werke zu persiflieren und sie auf hintergründige Weise zu imitieren, so in „Déjeuner sur l'herbe" (1995), „Freedom Leading the People" (1995/96), „Tian'anmen Remains" (2002) oder „Chairman Mao goes to Anyuan" (2005). Sein respektloser Umgang mit den verehrten Meisterwerken der chinesischen und der westlichen Kunst stellt Yue in eine Reihe mit anderen postmodernen Künstlern, die Chinas Fortschritt gleichzeitig nutzen und hinterfragen. In seiner Serie „Processing" (1996–2005) verflicht er zwei Bilder, die beide Aspekte des Prozesses – verarbeiten und verarbeitet werden – repräsentieren.

Yue bedient sich aber der subversiven Parodie nicht nur, um klassische Werke aus unterschiedlichen Epochen, fotografische Ästhetik und verschiedenen Stile zu dekonstruieren, sondern versucht eine neue Komposition zu entwickeln, indem er ähnliche Bildmotive aneinanderreiht. So kann er die Erwartungshaltung des Betrachters kontrollieren, der zu seiner Überraschung bekannte Bilder frei von traditionellen Normen erlebt.

使用了后现代主义的方式对中国的现实进行戏谑的反讽和质疑的批判，那么，《处理》系列的作品则是运用了更为直接有效的“处理”手段，在“处理与被处理”的关系中，将两种图像予以纠缠与掩盖，从而产生出一种新的视觉张力。不仅仅是对不同时期经典作品和摄影的审美趣味、样式的颠覆与破碎，也是拼贴与建构性的尝试，使这些熟悉的图像模式陌生化，以控制观者的期待，让观者体味到经过处理的新作品所产生的惊奇，以及摆脱原有经典规则之后的自由。

Feng Boyi

6

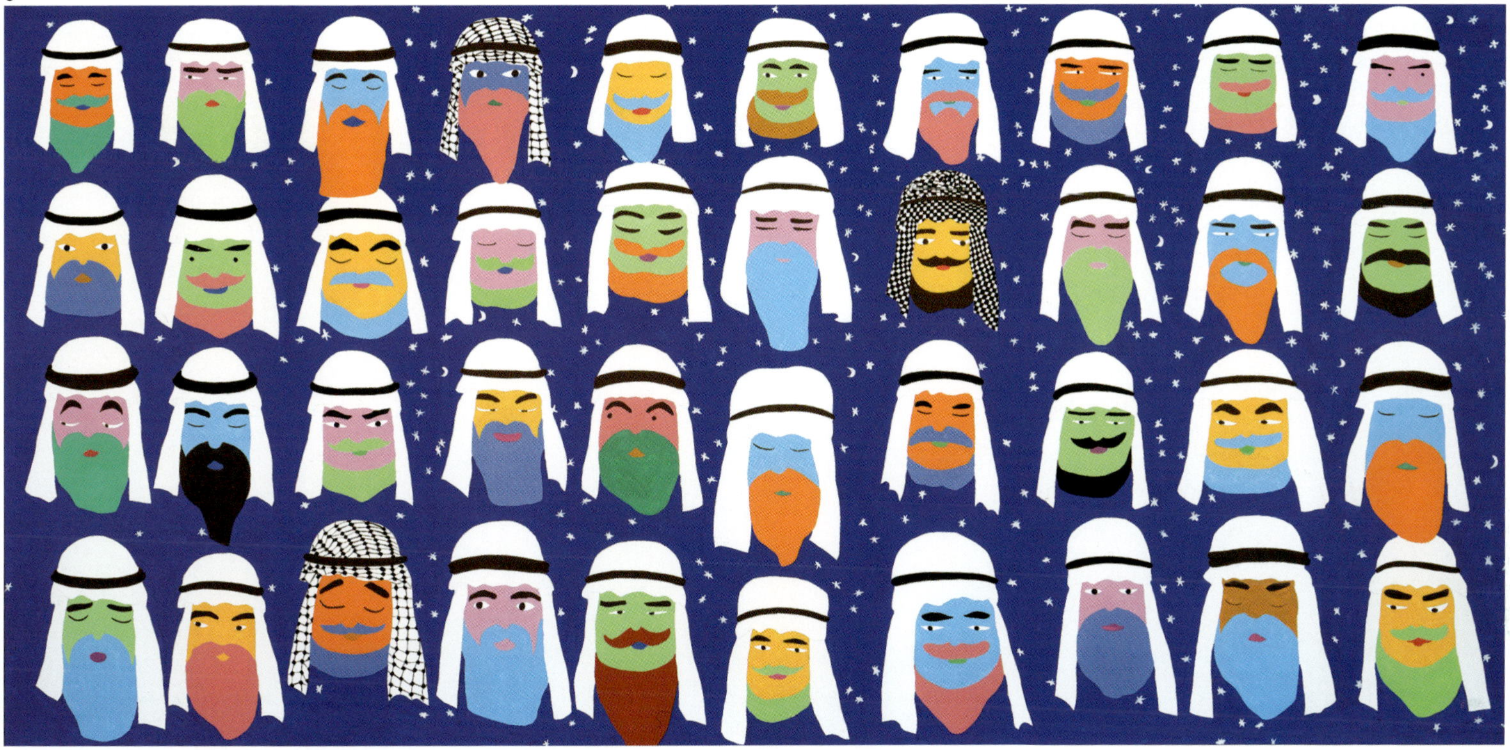

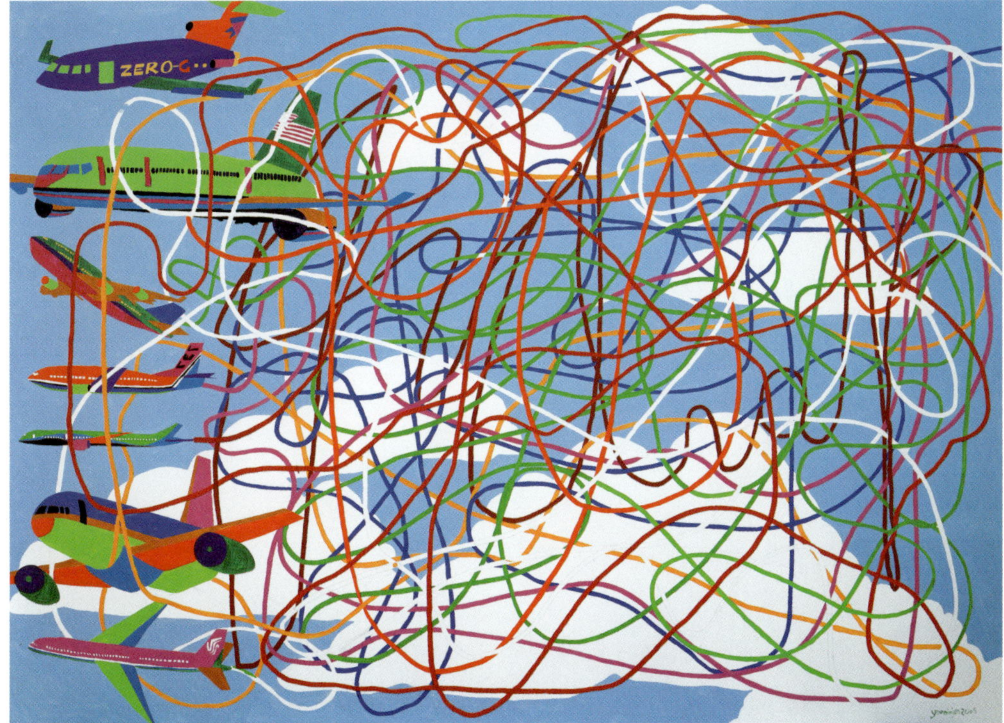

7

1 ***Untitled***, *2005*
Oil on canvas, 220 x 200 cm
Öl auf Leinwand, je 220 x 200 cm
《无题》2005年，布面油画，每幅 220 x 200 cm

2 ***2000 A. D.***, *2000*
Polyester painted, 25 sculptures, 186 x 60 x 46 cm each
Bemaltes Polyester, 25 Skulpturen, je 186 x 60 x 46 cm
《公元2000年》2000年, 涤纶绘制, 25尊雕塑,
每幅186 x 60 x 46 cm

3 ***Fifteen Poses in Life***, *1999*
Oil on canvas, 80 x 80 cm each (detail)
Öl auf Leinwand, je 80 x 80 cm (Detail)
《生活中的十五个动作》1999年, 布面油画, 每幅80 x 80 cm（详细）

4 ***Backyard Garden***, *2005*
Oil on canvas, 280 x 400 cm
Öl auf Leinwand, je 280 x 400 cm
《后院庭院》2005年，布面油画，每幅280 x 400 cm

5 ***Heroism***, *2006*
Oil on canvas, 170 x 140 cm
Öl auf Leinwand, 170 x 140 cm
《英雄》2006年，布面油画, 170 x 140 cm

6 ***1 Maze Series – Looking for Terrorists 1***, *2006*
Acrylic on canvas, 200 x 400 cm
Acryl auf Leinwand, 200 x 400 cm
《迷宫 - 寻找恐怖主义1》2006年, 布面丙烯, 200 x 400 cm

7 ***1 Maze Series – Looking for Terrorists 2***, *2006*
Acrylic on canvas, 200 x 300 cm
Acryl auf Leinwand, 200 x 300 cm
《迷宫 - 寻找恐怖主义2》2006年, 布面丙烯, 200 x 300 cm

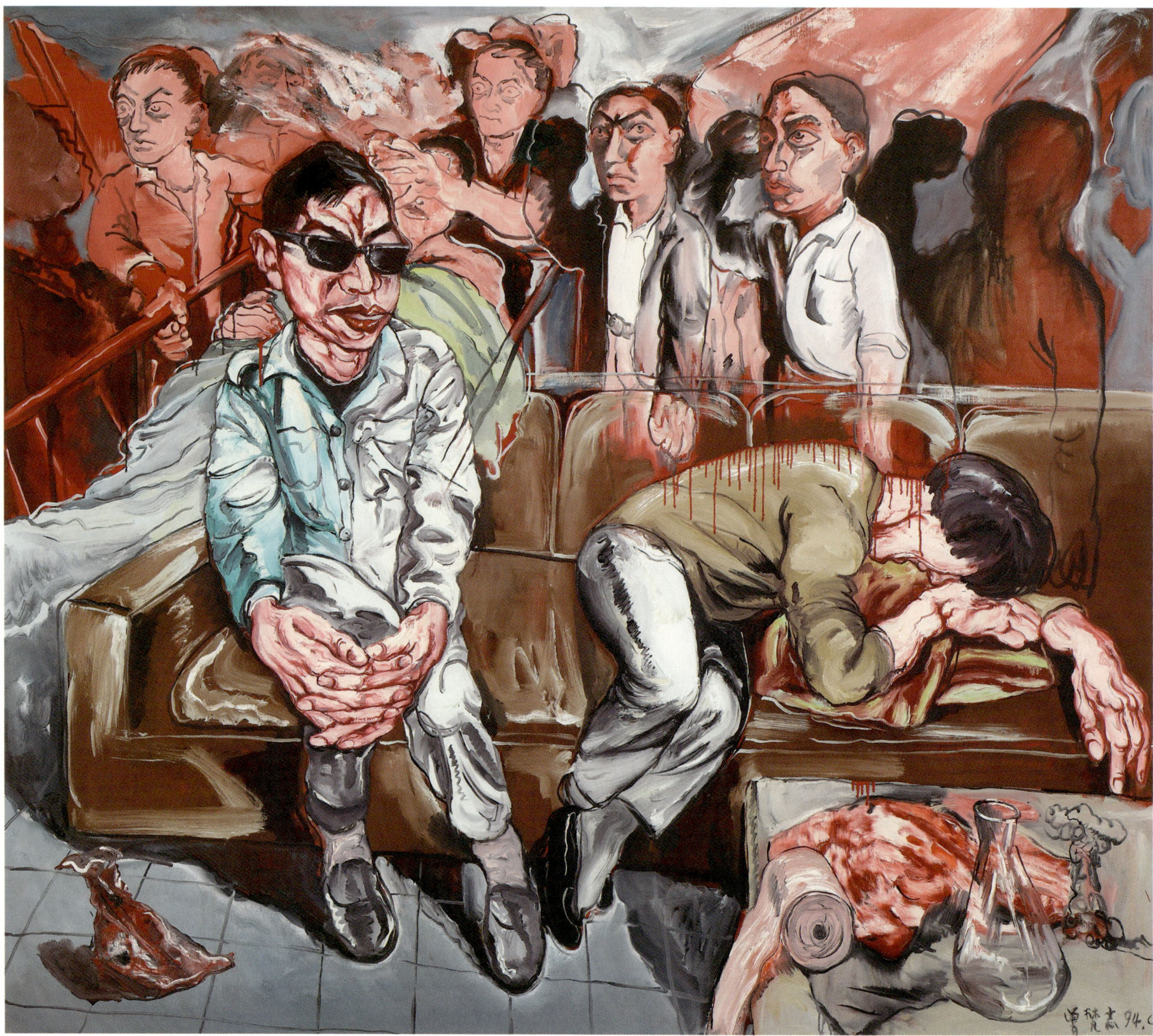

1

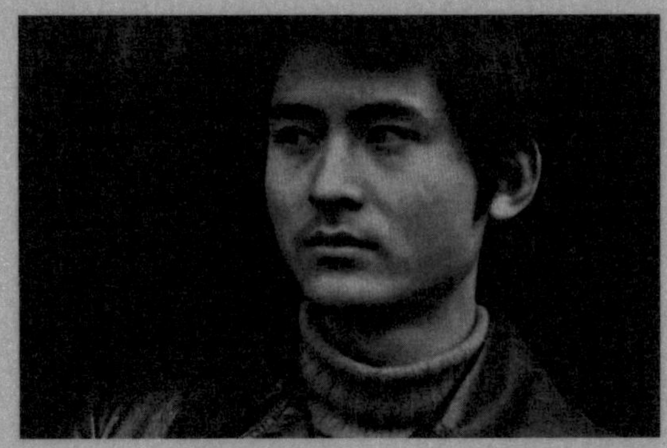

"All my present works are from feelings when I paint abstract."

„All meine aktuellen Arbeiten entstammen den Gefühlen, die sich einstellen, wenn ich abstrakt male."

"当我绘画抽象时，所有我的作品来自于我自己的内心感受 。"

Born in 1964 in Wuhan, China. Lives and works in Beijing
Geboren 1964 in Wuhan, China. Lebt und arbeitet in Peking
1964年出生于中国武汉，现居住工作于北京

***Selected exhibitions* / Ausgewählte Ausstellungen /** 所选展览

1996	"China!", Kunstmuseum Bonn, Bonn, Germany
2002	First Guangzhou Triennial, Guangdong Museum of Art, Guangzhou, China
2003	"I/We, 1991-2003, The paintings of Zeng Fanzhi", Shanghai Art Museum, Shanghai, China
2004	"Scapes - The paintings of Zeng Fanzhi 1989-2004,", He Xiangning Art Museum, Shenzhen, China
2005-07	"Mahjong - Chinesische Gegenwartskunst aus der Sammlung Sigg", Kunstmuseum Bern, Berne, Switzerland; Hamburger Kunsthalle, Hamburg, Germany; Museum der Moderne, Salzburg, Austria
2007	"Zeng Fanzhi: Idealism", National Art Museum, Singapore, Singapore
	"Thermocline of Art. New Asian Waves", ZKM (Centre for Art and media), Karlsruhe, Germany

1996年	《中国!》波恩当代艺术博物馆, 波恩，德国
2002年	首届广州三年展-重新解读：中国实验艺术十年（1990-2000年），广东美术馆，广州
2003年	《我/我们》1991-2003年曾凡志油画展, 上海美术馆
2004年	《看景－1989-2004年-- 曾凡志的绘画》，何香凝美术馆深圳中国
2005-07年	《麻将》西克中国当代艺术收藏展，伯尔尼美术馆 瑞士；汉堡美术馆，汉堡，德国；萨尔茨保现代美术馆 奥地利
2007年	《理想主义》新加坡美术馆，新加坡
	《艺术温跃层：亚洲新浪潮》艺术与媒体中心，卡尔斯鲁厄, 德国

***Selected publications* / Ausgewählte Publikationen /** 所选著作

"I/We", Shanghai 2004
"Scapes - The Paintings of Zeng Fanzhi 1989-2004", Shanghai 2005
"Zeng Fanzhi - Paintings", London 2006
Uta Grosenick, Sine Bepler (eds.): "ShanghART Gallery 10 Years", Cologne 2006

《我/我们》，上海美术馆，上海2004年
《看景--1989-2004-曾凡志的绘画》上海香格纳画廊, 上海 2005年
《曾凡志-绘画》Wedel Fine Art, 伦敦 2006年
Grosenick, Uta/Bepler, Sine（编者）：《上海香格纳画廊10年》科隆 2006年

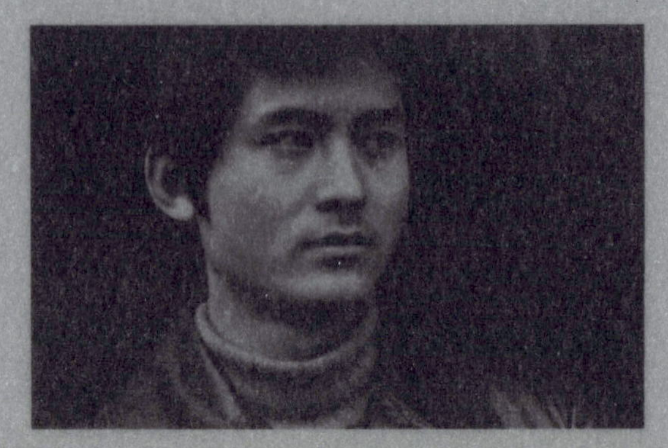

"All my present works are from feelings when I paint abstract."

„All meine aktuellen Arbeiten entstammen den Gefühlen, die sich einstellen, wenn ich abstrakt male."

"当我绘画抽象时，所有我的作品来自于我自己的内心感受。"

Born in 1964 in Wuhan, China. Lives and works in Beijing
Geboren 1964 in Wuhan, China. Lebt und arbeitet in Peking
1964年出生于中国武汉，现居住工作于北京

Selected exhibitions / Ausgewählte Ausstellungen / 所选展览

1996	"China!", Kunstmuseum Bonn, Bonn, Germany
2002	First Guangzhou Triennial, Guangdong Museum of Art, Guangzhou, China
2003	"I/We, 1991-2003, The paintings of Zeng Fanzhi", Shanghai Art Museum, Shanghai, China
2004	"Scapes - The paintings of Zeng Fanzhi 1989-2004", He Xiangning Art Museum, Shenzhen, China
2005-07	"Mahjong - Chinesische Gegenwartskunst aus der Sammlung Sigg", Kunstmuseum Bern, Berne, Switzerland; Hamburger Kunsthalle, Hamburg, Germany; Museum der Moderne, Salzburg, Austria
2007	"Zeng Fanzhi: Idealism", National Art Museum, Singapore, Singapore
	"Thermocline of Art. New Asian Waves", ZKM (Centre for Art and media), Karlsruhe, Germany

1996年	《中国!》波恩当代艺术博物馆，波恩，德国
2002年	首届广州三年展-重新解读：中国实验艺术十年（1990-2000年），广东美术馆，广州
2003年	《我/我们》1991-2003年曾凡志油画展，上海美术馆
2004年	《看景—1989-2004年— 曾凡志的绘画》，何香凝美术馆深圳中国
2005-07年	《麻将》西克中国当代艺术收藏展，伯尔尼美术馆 瑞士；汉堡美术馆，汉堡，德国；萨尔茨保现代美术馆 奥地利
2007年	《理想主义》新加坡美术馆，新加坡
	《艺术温跃层：亚洲新浪潮》艺术与媒体中心，卡尔斯鲁厄，德国

Selected publications / Ausgewählte Publikationen / 所选著作

"I/We", Shanghai 2004
"Scapes - The Paintings of Zeng Fanzhi 1989-2004", Shanghai 2005
"Zeng Fanzhi - Paintings", London 2006
Uta Grosenick, Sine Bepler (eds.): "ShanghART Gallery 10 Years", Cologne 2006

《我/我们》，上海美术馆，上海2004年
《看景—1989-2004-曾凡志的绘画》上海香格纳画廊，上海 2005年
《曾凡志-绘画》Wedel Fine Art，伦敦 2006年
Grosenick, Uta/Bepler, Sine（编者）：《上海香格纳画廊10年》科隆 2006年

ZENG FANZHI 曾梵志

[tsɤŋ faŋtʂʐ̩]

Zeng Fanzhi's interest had been attracted by German Expressionism early during his studies in Wuhan in the Chinese province Hubei. He was especially fascinated by the painter Max Beckmann. Paintings of Zeng at that time are at least as radical as the illustration of catastrophes painted by the said German: they depict apocalyptic scenes of hospitals and slaughter houses.

Since the early 1990s cynical realism and political pop were the leading genres of Chinese contemporary art; these currents split the artists into two different categories: into ironic metaphoric, political symbolism, historical metaphoric or folksy depictions. From 1994 Zeng, who absorbed all these tendencies, developed his famous mask pictures, with which he achieved his international breakthrough. They show static, marionette-like people with oversized oval heads und huge bony hands, dressed in elegant western clothes. They wear white masks in front of their faces, which fit so tightly that they become a part of them.

Zeng Fanzhi almost became a "mask painter", for the "mask" grew to a brand mark with which his steadily growing audience identified him. However, Zeng never stopped experimenting with other subjects and painting styles and painted several abstract works in 1999 – according to his own statement, Zeng has always been interested in abstraction and all his artistic changed were inspired by it. 2001 he admittedly created another figurine line, which was partly based on examples of the western art history, partly on portraits or self-portraits. Their characteristics are with a scraper treated on heads, out of which the colour smears poking out equally.

Afterwards numerous large-sized paintings came into existence, on which truncated faces were more or less heavily mixed by vertical rotary, reminiscent of streamers, brushstrokes. They were followed by totally abstract and powerful brushstrokes, again on huge formats, with expressive colours, which sometimes hided calligraphic signs. Thereby Zeng developed a technique which leaves

Schon während seines Studiums in Wuhan in der Provinz Hubei bekundete Zeng Fanzhi ein großes Interesse am deutschen Expressionismus. Besonders der Maler Max Beckmann faszinierte ihn. Die Bilder, die Zeng damals malte, sind mindestens so radikal wie die Katastrophendarstellungen des Deutschen: Sie zeigen apokalyptische Szenen aus Krankenhäusern und Schlachthöfen.

Seit den frühen 1990er Jahren waren der Zynische Realismus und der Political Pop die führenden Kunstrichtungen der chinesischen Gegenwartskunst; diese Strömungen brachen die Künstler in verschiedene Kategorien auf: in ironische Bildhaftigkeit, politischen Symbolismus, historische Metaphorik oder volkstümliche Darstellungen. Ab 1994 entwickelte Zeng, der alle diese Tendenzen aufnahm, seine berühmten Maskenbilder, mit denen ihm der internationale Durchbruch gelang. Sie zeigen statische, wie Marionetten wirkende Personen mit übergroßen ovalen Köpfen und riesigen knochigen Händen in eleganten westlichen Kleidern. Vor ihren Gesichtern tragen sie weiße Masken, die so eng anliegen, dass sie zu einem Teil von ihnen werden.

Fast schon wäre Zeng Fanzhi zum „Maskenmaler" geworden, so sehr hatte sich die Maske zu seinem Markenzeichen entwickelt, mit dem ihn sein immer größer werdendes Publikum identifizierte. Zeng hat aber nie aufgehört, mit anderen Themen und Malstilen zu experimentieren, und 1999 einige abstrakte Bilder gemalt – nach eigener Aussage war er schon immer an Abstraktion interessiert und jede seiner künstlerischen Veränderungen von Abstraktion inspiriert. 2001 schuf er aber wieder eine Figuren-Reihe, teils nach Vorbildern aus der westlichen Kunstgeschichte, teils Porträts oder Selbstbildnisse, deren Charakteristikum die mit einer Rakel bearbeiteten Köpfe sind, aus denen die Farbschlieren gleichsam herausragen.

Anschließend entstanden zahlreiche großformatige Gemälde, auf denen angeschnittene Gesichter durch vertikal kreisende – an Luftschlangen erinnernde – Pinselstriche mehr oder weniger stark verwischt wurden. Ihnen folgten, auf

早年在湖北省武汉求学时，曾梵志就对德国表现主义所吸引，特别痴迷于画家 Max Beckmann的作品。那一时期，他的油画至少象Beckmann一样激进:他描述了医院和屠宰场的预示天灾人祸的场面。

从上世纪90年代初期开始，愤世现实主义和政治流行主义是当代中国艺术的主流形式，因此艺术家也分为两派：讽刺的、隐喻的政治象征主义和历史隐喻的或是朴素的描写。

从1994年起，曾梵志放弃了所有这些形式，发展了自己著名的面具图像，而在国际上获得了重大成功。这些图像展示了静态，木偶人物，它们长着一个特大的脑袋，一双瘦骨嶙峋的双手，身着优美的西式服装，而脸上却戴着白色的面具，面具非常合适而与之融为一体。

曾梵志几乎成为一位"面具画家"，因为《面具》成为他的品牌标志，越来越多的观众认同他。然而曾梵志从未停止试验其他主题和绘画风格，并在90年代绘制了 好多抽象作品。根据其本人陈述，曾梵志对抽象艺 术依依不舍，兴趣 不已，他的所有艺术变化都受此启迪。2001年，他创造了另一幅人物素描，部分基于西方艺术史的例证，部分根据一些肖像画包括自己的肖像。其特点是头部用刮刀处理过, 此外斑斓的色彩也同样引人注目。

后来, 又有无数的大型油画面世, 作品中截平的脸 膛或多或少与竖直回旋的线条深深混合起来。这些作品继承了完全抽象、有力的绘画技巧，为表达色彩感, 采用大版式, 有时隐藏书法符号。因而曾梵志发展了空间统一的技巧, 但是却使我们联想起中国传统的山水艺术, 因此这里我们要提及他的《看景》: 作画时, 每只手里夹着一只笔, 其中一只笔定向在画面上移动, 而另一只毫无控制的自由蜿蜒。因而产生了第二幅狂野的飞机，图画之上表现手法很稀奇古怪。

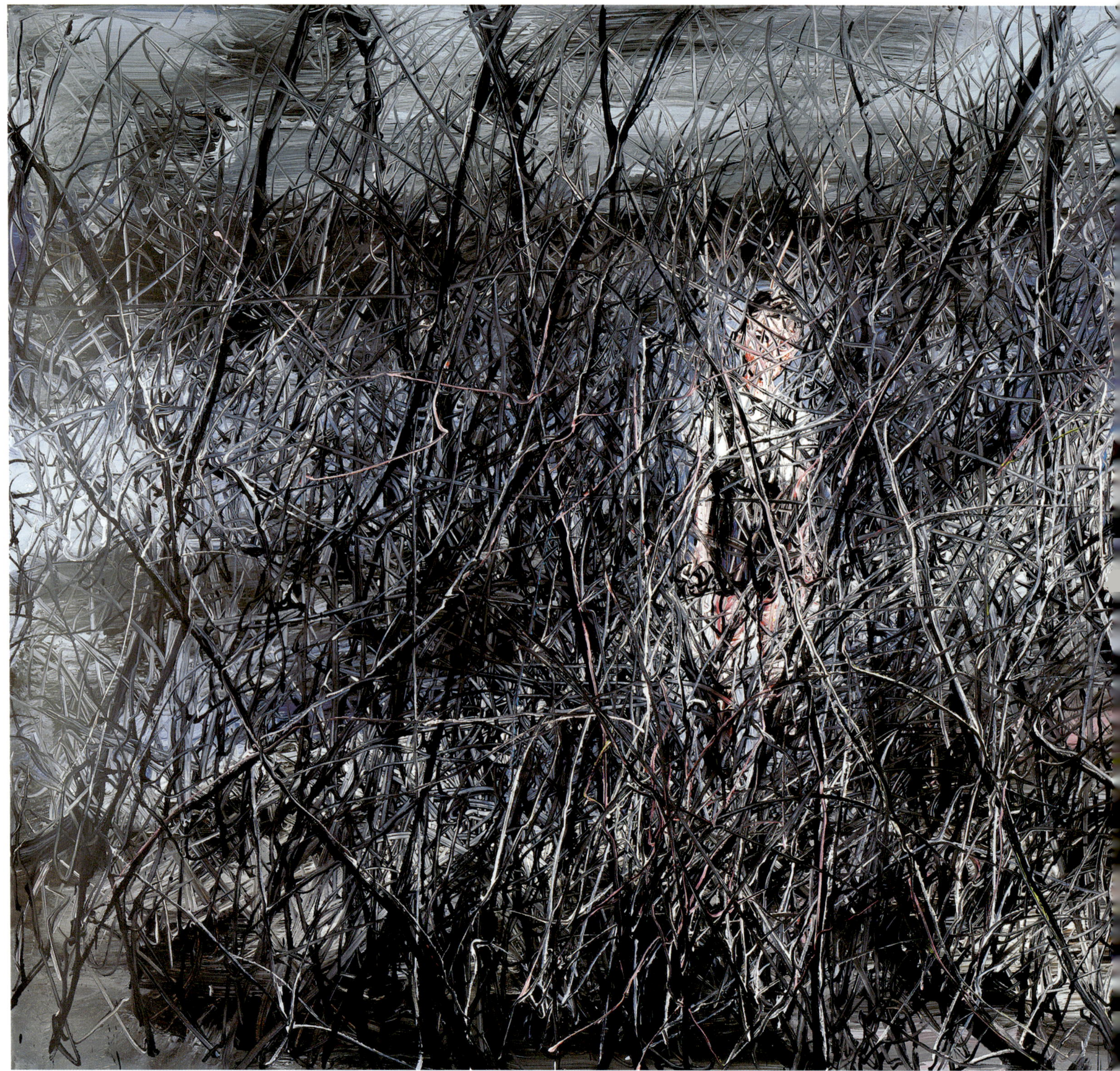

2

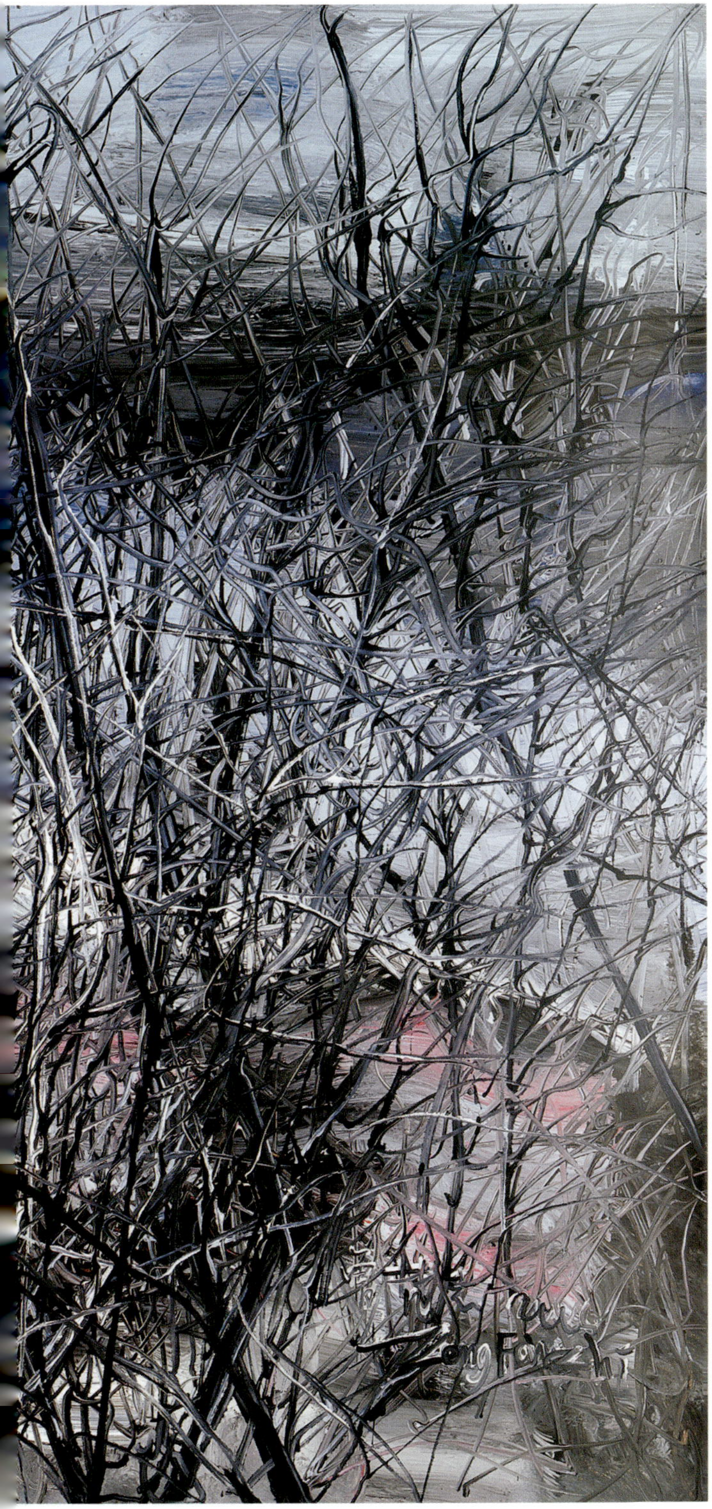

3

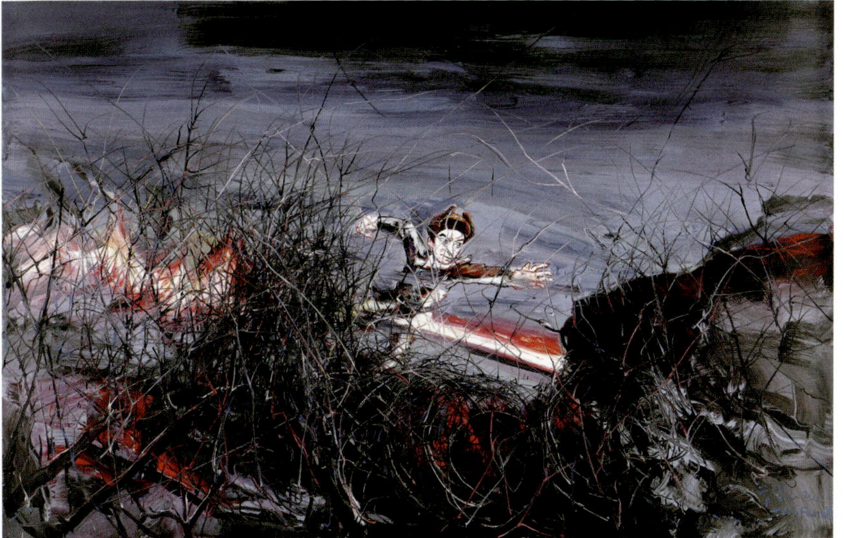

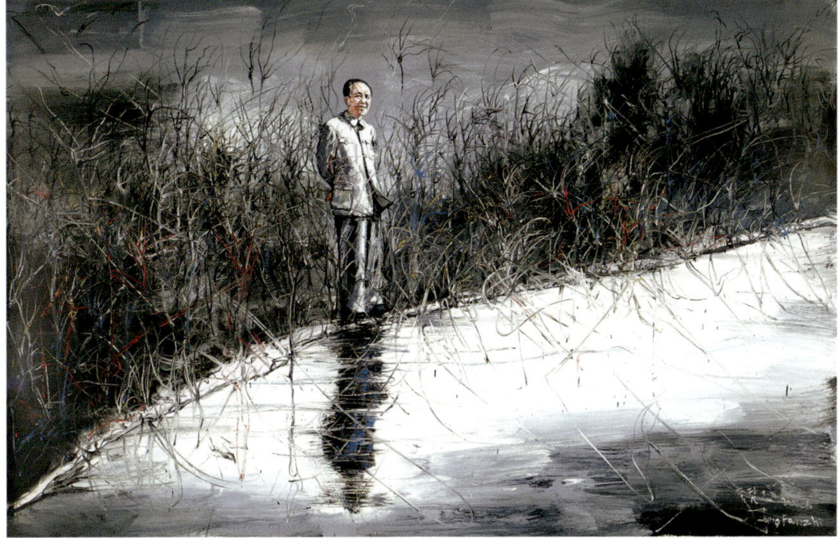

4

5

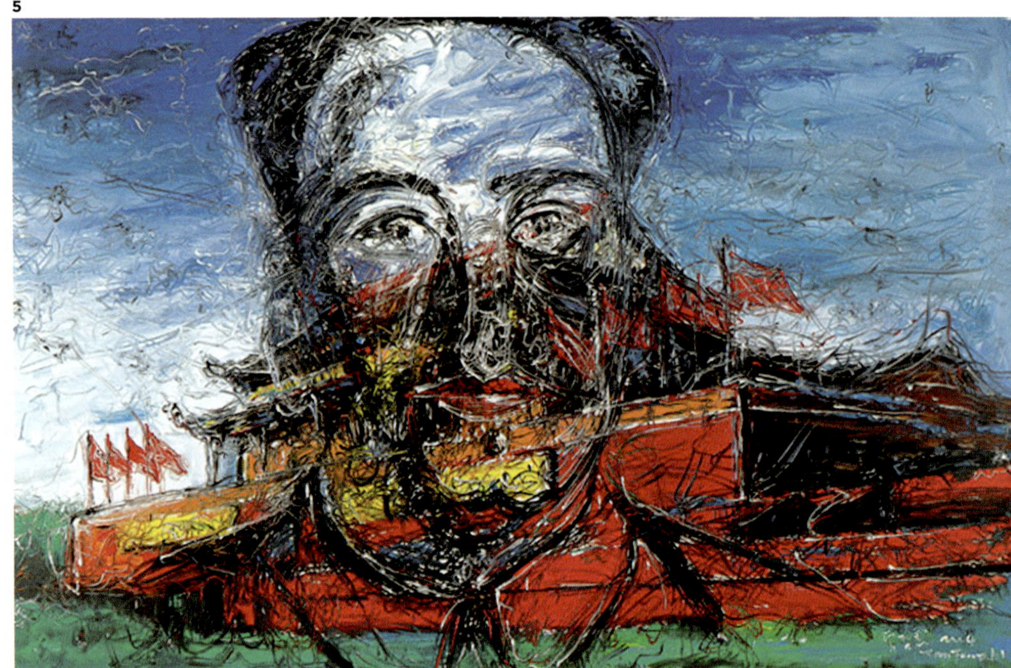

space for coincidence, but leads to results, reminiscent of traditional Chinese landscape art, which is why these pictures are referred to as "Scapes": While painting he holds two brushes in his hand of which he directs one in a determined manner across the underground and at the same time allows the other brush to loosely wander alongside without controlling it's movements. Thereby a second wild and rampant plane comes to existence, which bestows a bizarrely fascinating expression upon the picture.

However, Zeng Fanzhi wouldn't be Zeng Fanzhi, if he didn't put humans into the centre of his works and into the rampant landscapes, again: friends, himself or important people like Andy Warhol, whom Zeng admires, the pope or the cofounder of the People's republic China, Mao Zedong, who's portrait is dominating the historically meaningful location in the canvas "Tian'anmen" (2004). In the more recent pictures, the bright "grassy landscapes" changed significantly and increased to an obscure coppice of swapping multi-coloured lines. In "This Land So Rich in Beauty! No. 5" (2006) an unexplainable bright flare flashes up in the inside of such a coppice, while in the paintings "Little Boy" (2006) and "Two Little Girls" (2006) children are suddenly appearing between the branches; in their depiction Zeng's formally western affected expressionist style gave ground for a certain softness and reservation – this is being interpreted by several critics as Zeng's reconciliation with the culture he lives in.

riesigen Formaten, wieder rein abstrakte kraftvolle Pinselbewegungen in ausdrucksvollen Farben, hinter denen sich manchmal kalligraphische Zeichen verbergen. Dabei entwickelte Zeng eine Technik, die zwar dem Zufall Platz einräumt, aber zu Ergebnissen führt, die an die traditionelle chinesische Landschaftsmalerei erinnern – darum bezeichnet man diese Bilder als „Scapes": Beim Malen hält Zeng zwei Pinsel in der Hand, von denen er einen zielstrebig über den Untergrund führt, während er den zweiten locker nebenher wandern lässt, ohne dessen Bewegungen zu kontrollieren. Dadurch entsteht eine zweite, wilde, ungezügelte Ebene, die dem Bild einen bizarren, faszinierenden Ausdruck verleiht.

Aber Zeng Fanzhi wäre nicht Zeng Fanzhi, wenn er nicht doch wieder Menschen ins Zentrum seiner Arbeiten und in wuchernde Landschaften rücken würde: Freunde, sich selbst oder wichtige Persönlichkeiten wie den von ihm bewunderten Andy Warhol, den Papst oder den Mitbegründer der Volksrepublik China, Mao Zedong, dessen Konterfei in dem Gemälde „Tian'anmen" (2004) diesen historisch so bedeutsamen Ort dominiert. Bei den neueren Bildern haben sich die lichten Graslandschaften deutlich verändert und zu einem undurchdringlichen Dickicht aus sich überlagernden verschiedenfarbigen Linien gesteigert. In „This Land So Rich in Beauty! No. 5" (2006) leuchtet im Inneren eines solchen Gestrüpps ein unerklärlicher heller Lichtschein auf, während in den Gemälden „Little Boy" (2006) und „Two Little Girls" (2006) plötzlich Kinder zwischen dem Geäst auftauchen; in ihrer Darstellung ist Zengs vormals westlich geprägter expressionistischer Stil einer gewissen Sanftheit und Zurückgenommenheit gewichen – was einige Kritiker als Zengs Aussöhnung mit der Kultur, in der er lebt, deuten wollen.

但是, 如果人不是其作品的中心，或是置于蔓延的景色里，那曾梵志就不是曾梵志了, 此外，他的朋友，他自己和一些重要人物如曾梵志所欣赏的Andy Warhol，中华人民共和国的领袖毛泽东（他的肖像在油画《天安门》中占历史意义的位置）等在其作品在中出现过。

在最近更多的照片中，鲜艳的《风景草丛》的变化引人注目并增加了朦胧的萌生林以多彩线条。在《江山如此多娇!No. 5》(2006年)中，在诸如萌　生林的里闪　现出莫名的明光，而在其油画《小男孩》(2006年)和《两个小女孩》(2006年)中，儿童突然出现在灌木丛中，在这些　描绘中，因为亲和和保守的原因，他形式上的西方表　现主义手法却没有表现出来-许多批评家解释那是他和他所生存的文化之间的调和。

Uta Grosenick

6

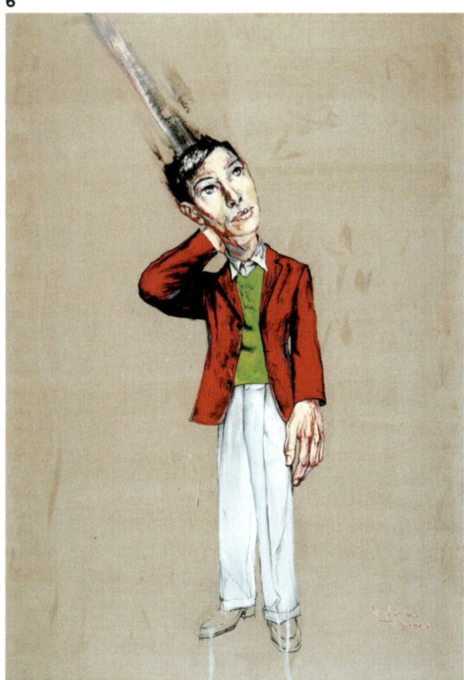

7

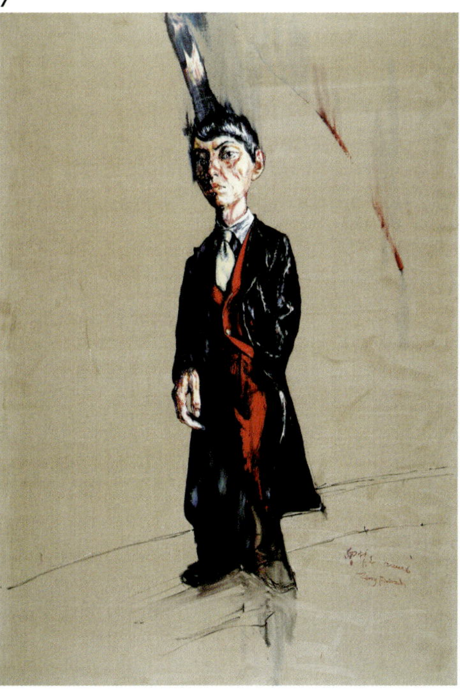

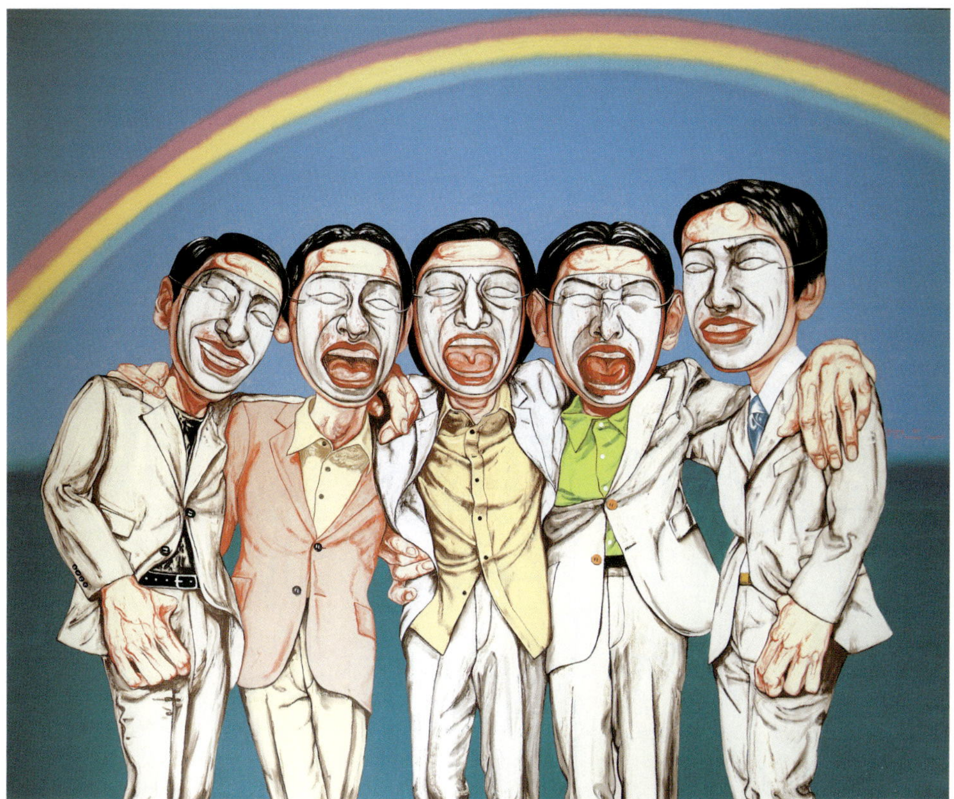

8

1 ***Hospital Series***, *1994*
Oil on canvas, 179 x 199 cm
Öl auf Leinwand, 179 x 199 cm
《协和医院系列》1994年, 布面油画, 179 x 199 cm

2 ***Little Boy***, *2006*
Oil on canvas, 180 x 280 cm
Öl auf Leinwand, 180 x 280 cm
《小男孩》2006年, 布面油画, 180 x 280 cm

3 ***Huang Jiguang***, *2006*
Oil on canvas, 215 x 330 cm
Öl auf Leinwand, 215 x 330 cm
《黄继光》2006年, 布面油画, 215 x 330 cm

4 ***This Land So Rich In Beauty! No. 1***, *2006*
Oil on canvas, 210 x 330 cm
Öl auf Leinwand, 210 x 330 cm
《江山如此多娇No. 1》2006年, 布面油画, 210 x 330 cm

5 ***Tian'anmen***, *2004*
Oil on canvas, 215 x 330 cm
Öl auf Leinwand, 215 x 330 cm
《天安门》2004年, 布面油画, 215 x 330 cm

6 ***Red Suit***, *2006*
Oil on canvas, 220 x 150 cm
Öl auf Leinwand, 220 x 150 cm
《红西服》, 2006年, 布面油画, 220 x 150 cm

7 ***Portrait***, *2006*
Oil on canvas, 220 x 150 cm
Öl auf Leinwand, 220 x 150 cm
《肖像》2006年, 布面油画, 220 x 150 cm

8 ***Rainbow***, *1997*
Oil on canvas, 195 x 215 cm
Öl auf Leinwand, 195 x 215 cm
《彩虹》1997年, 布面油画, 195 x 215 cm

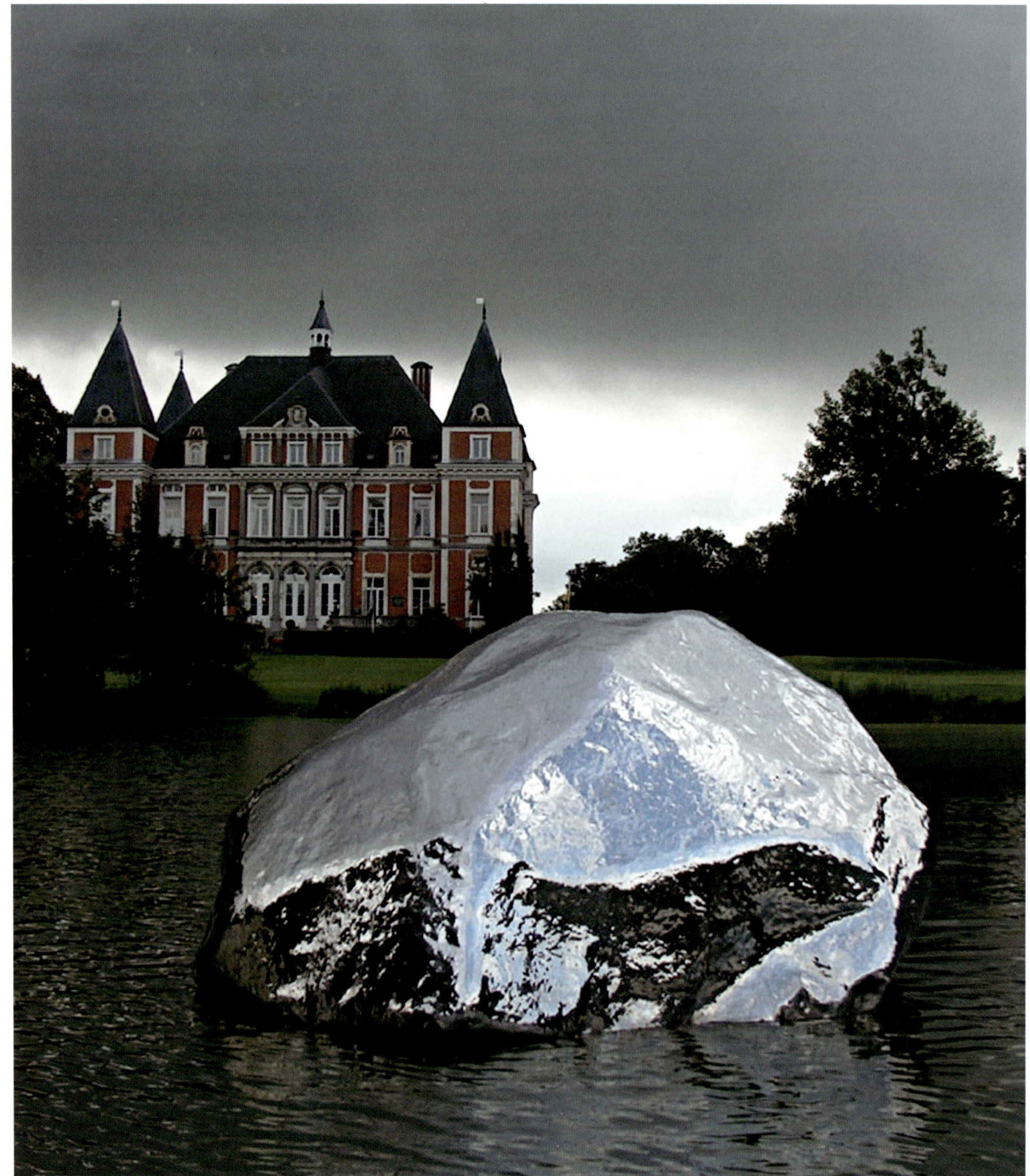

1

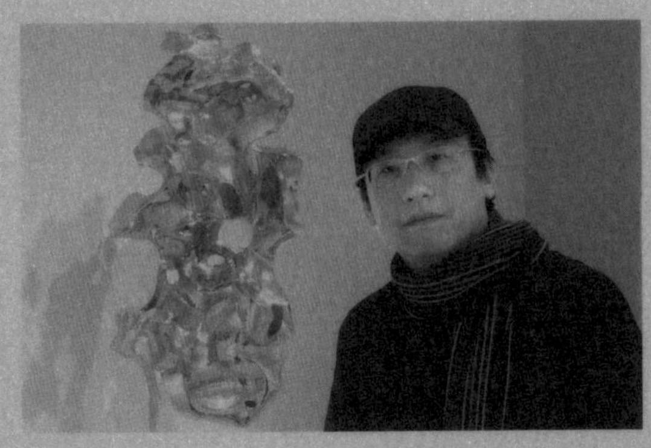

"For me, natural forms represent the fundamental rules of the world. Every natural form is a sign of the uniqueness of the individual existence in the world."

„Für mich repräsentieren natürliche Formen die grundlegende Gesetzgebung der Welt. Jede natürliche Form ist ein Zeichen für die Einzigartigkeit einer individuellen Existenz."

"为我,自然形式代表世界的根本规则。每个自然形式是单独存在的独特的标志在世界上 。"

Born in 1962 in Beijing, China. Lives and works in Beijing
Geboren 1962 in Peking, China. Lebt und arbeitet in Peking
1962年出生于北京。住居工作在北京

***Selected exhibitions* / Ausgewählte Ausstellungen /** 所选展览

2003 First Beijing International Art Biennial, Beijing, China
2004 "Stone Face BANG – China's first group printing exhibition", Shanghai Duolun Museum of Modern Art, Shanghai, China
2005 "Reshaping The Wall – Contemporary Chinese Art", Albright-Knox Art Gallery, Buffalo, NY, USA
2005–07 "Mahjong – Chinesische Gegenwartskunst aus der Sammlung Sigg", Kunstmuseum Bern, Berne, Switzerland; Hamburger Kunsthalle, Hamburg, Germany; Museum der Moderne, Salzburg, Austria
2006 "Zhan Wang – Urban Landscape", Williams College Museum of Art, Williamstown, MA, USA

2003年 《首届北京国际艺术双年展》，北京
2004年 《板起面子 BANG》，上海多轮现代美术馆
2005年 《墙：中国当代艺术的历史与边界》，纽约
2005–07年 《麻将》西克中国当代艺术收藏展，伯尔尼美术馆 瑞士；汉堡美术馆，汉堡，德国；萨尔茨保现代美术馆 奥地利
2006年 《展望 -- 都市风景》 威廉斯学院艺术馆，美国

***Selected publications* / Ausgewählte Publikationen /** 所选著作

Britta Erickson: "Material Illusion: Adrift with the Conceptual Sculptor Zhan Wang", in: "Art Journal", Summer 2001
Gao Minglu: "The Wall: Reshaping Contemporary Chinese Art", Buffalo/New York 2005
John Stomberg: "Zhan Wang – Urban Landscape", Berkeley 2007

Erickson, Britta（著）：《材料幻觉：漂流与这概念性雕刻家展望》，艺术杂志，夏2001年
高名潞（编者）：《墙：中国当代艺术的历史与边界》纽约2005年
Stomberg, John（著）：《展望 -- 都市风景》,杂志,春2007年

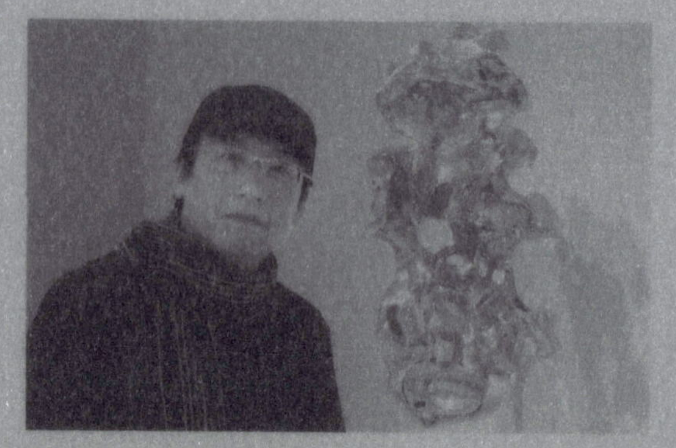

"For me, natural forms represent the fundamental rules of the world. Every natural form is a sign of the uniqueness of the individual existence in the world."

„Für mich repräsentieren natürliche Formen die grundlegende Gesetzgebung der Welt. Jede natürliche Form ist ein Zeichen für die Einzigartigkeit einer individuellen Existenz."

"为我，自然形式代表世界的根本规则。每个自然形式是单独存在的独特的标志在世界上。"

Born in 1962 in Beijing, China. Lives and works in Beijing
Geboren 1962 in Peking, China. Lebt und arbeitet in Peking
1962年出生于北京。住居工作在北京

Selected exhibitions / Ausgewählte Ausstellungen / 所选展览

2003 First Beijing International Art Biennial, Beijing, China
2004 "Stone Face BANG – China's first group printing exhibition", Shanghai Duolun Museum of Modern Art, Shanghai, China
2005 "Reshaping The Wall – Contemporary Chinese Art", Albright-Knox Art Gallery, Buffalo, NY, USA
2005-07 "Mahjong – Chinesische Gegenwartskunst aus der Sammlung Sigg", Kunstmuseum Bern, Berne, Switzerland; Hamburger Kunsthalle, Hamburg, Germany; Museum der Moderne, Salzburg, Austria
2006 "Zhan Wang – Urban Landscape", Williams College Museum of Art, Williamstown, MA, USA

2003年 《首届北京国际艺术双年展》，北京
2004年 《板起面孔 BANG》，上海多伦现代美术馆
2005年 《墙：中国当代艺术的历史与边界》，纽约
2005-07年 《麻将》西克中国当代艺术收藏展，伯尔尼美术馆 瑞士；汉堡美术馆，汉堡，德国；萨尔茨堡现代美术馆 奥地利
2006年 《展望 一 都市风景》 威廉斯学院艺术馆，美国

Selected publications / Ausgewählte Publikationen / 所选著作

Britta Erickson: "Material Illusion: Adrift with the Conceptual Sculptor Zhan Wang", in: "Art Journal", Summer 2001
Gao Minglu: "The Wall: Reshaping Contemporary Chinese Art", Buffalo/New York 2005
John Stomberg: "Zhan Wang – Urban Landscape", Berkeley 2007

Erickson, Britta（著）：《材料幻觉：漂流与这概念性雕刻家展望》，艺术杂志，夏2001年
高名潞（编著）：《墙：中国当代艺术的历史与边界》纽约2005年
Stomberg, John（著）：《展望 一 都市风景》，杂志，春2007年

ZHAN WANG 展望

[tʂan waŋ]

Zhan Wang grew up in a factory dormitory resembling a military compound. His father was from Shandong, his mother from Beijing, both parents were working in Beijing's largest printing plant. Zhan Wang's name meaning expectation was chosen by his mother who found the characters quite often in newspapers representing at that time the hope and expectation of the masses. Thus his name reminds us of a headline not presenting a real name but shaping him for his lifetime.

At an early age Zhan Wang followed the footsteps of his grandfather and started traditional Chinese painting. Later, under the guidance of his maternal uncle, he learned still life painting and drawings. After graduating from high school he passed the entrance examination at Beijing Industrial Art School where he studied special arts and crafts. After graduating he was appointed at a jade carving factory as a designer. Thereafter Zhan Wang enrolled at the Central Academy of Sculpture where he encountered the institutional tradition of Russia and France realizing for the first time what creation means. The shocking experiences made on his travels along the Yangtze in 1988 made him realize the big differences between all directions of his country which resulted in his large-sized work "Street".

In the works of his early period Zhan Wang's usage of extremely realistic techniques can be found, making clear his processing attitude towards the material. In his later creative periods he completely governs the impulse of the material and furthermore reaches the essential high degree of self-request to acme and utmost beauty. Thus he entered the stage of "idealistic sculpture" by realizing the organic relationship of ideal and matter, being for Zhan Wang the perfect natural transformation but his "ideal sculpture" being different from the concept of the western ideal art as he actually unconsciously enlarged the influences of his childhood he had received from at the time at his maternal grandfather's being a literati. The artist's pursuit should not be the final product, it is the life and the artistic interaction process that is important.

Zhan Wang wuchs in einem Fabrik-Wohnheim auf, das einem Militärlager ähnelte. Sein Vater stammte aus Shandong, seine Mutter aus Peking, beide Elternteile arbeiteten in der größten Druckerei der Hauptstadt. Zhan Wangs Name bedeutet „Erwartung", und seine Mutter wählte ihn, weil damals in den Schlagzeilen der Zeitungen häufig von Erwartung die Rede war, die von den chinesischen Massen geteilt wurde. Zhan empfand seinen Namen, der ihn stets an eine Headline erinnert, als eine Fiktion, die ihn zeitlebens prägen sollte.

Schon in jungen Jahren trat Zhan Wang in die Fußstapfen seines Großvaters und begann im traditionellen chinesischen Stil zu malen; später erlernte er unter der Anleitung eines Onkels die Herstellung von Stillleben. Nach Abschluss der Oberschule trat er in die Beijing Industrial Art School ein, wo er Kunsthandwerk studierte. Anschließend wurde er in einer Fabrik für Jadeschnitzerei als Designer angestellt, dann schrieb er sich an der Central Academy of Sculpture ein, an der er den akademischen Traditionen Russlands und Frankreichs begegnete und zum ersten Mal erkannte, was eigentlich ein schöpferisches Werk ist. Durch eine Reise entlang des Jangtse im Jahr 1988 wurden ihm schockartig die immensen Unterschiede zwischen den verschiedenen Landesteilen und Bevölkerungsgruppen des Riesenreichs der Mitte bewusst, eine Einsicht, die in seine groß angelegte Arbeit „Street" mündete.

In seiner frühen Phase favorisierte Zhan extrem realistische Techniken, bei denen es ihm nur darum ging, das Material ökonomisch zu verarbeiten, während er später den dem Material innewohnenden Impuls erkannte und ihm folgte. Dabei führte ihn sein Ehrgeiz rasch zu Produkten von allerhöchster Schönheit, sprich in das Stadium der „idealistischen Skulptur", in dem er die organische Beziehung zwischen Ideal und Materie, also die perfekte natürliche Transformation berücksichtigte. Allerdings unterschied sich Zhans „ideale Skulptur" durchaus von den im Westen favorisierten Idealen, vielleicht weil bei ihm nun zunehmend Einflüsse seiner Kindheit zum Tragen kamen, insbesondere

展望于1962年出生在北京一间像军营一样的工厂宿舍里，父亲老家在山东，母亲是北京人，当时父母亲都在北京最大的一家印刷厂工作。展望，就是展望，是他的母亲从报纸上选了常常出现的字 —— 展望，代表了那个时代众人的愿望，一个看起来不像名字，却像标题的名字，注记了展望的一生。

展望的小时候曾被寄养在外祖父家，家里挂著外祖父自己的画和对联，记忆和现实，都扎扎实实将他塑造成一个典型的北京人。最早，他曾经跟随外祖父学习国画，后来又在舅舅的指导下学画静物和素描，初中毕业后考上北京工艺美术学校学习特种工艺。学校毕业后，被分发到一家玉器工厂做设计。之后展望考入中央美院雕塑系，才算真正接触到苏联和法国的学院传统，才开始意识到什么是创作。1988年游遍中国大江南北的震撼经历，看到南北东西的巨大差距触动了他第一件大型创作《街道》。

早期的作品里，展望主要用的是超级写实风格的技巧，从其中，可以看得出来他对于材质处理的态度。日后在每一个创作阶段，他都有一种完整掌握物质的冲动，而且必需做到尽善尽美的高度自我要求。进入将观念与物质有机结合的"观念性雕塑"阶段，对展望而言，是十分自然的转变，然而他的"观念雕塑"是有别于西方观念艺术的概念，他其实是不自觉地放大了他童年在外祖父家所受到的文人（Literati）艺术生活的薰陶，艺术最终的产品并不重要，而是生活与艺术互动的过程应该是艺术家的追求。

1995年展望第一次使用不锈钢这种材料来复制石头，他把真的石头放在自家的庭院里，却把不锈钢的假山石卖给藏家。展望在他最近的新作品《新素园石谱》中有非常详尽的说法，他的观念雕塑假山石，是为了一种自立门户风派的创举，而且他已将这种不锈钢假山石的风格形式与做法，申请了全球专利。在不锈钢假山石嶙峋起伏的表面上，反射出的影像随时变化，完全是人力无法掌握的光线和图

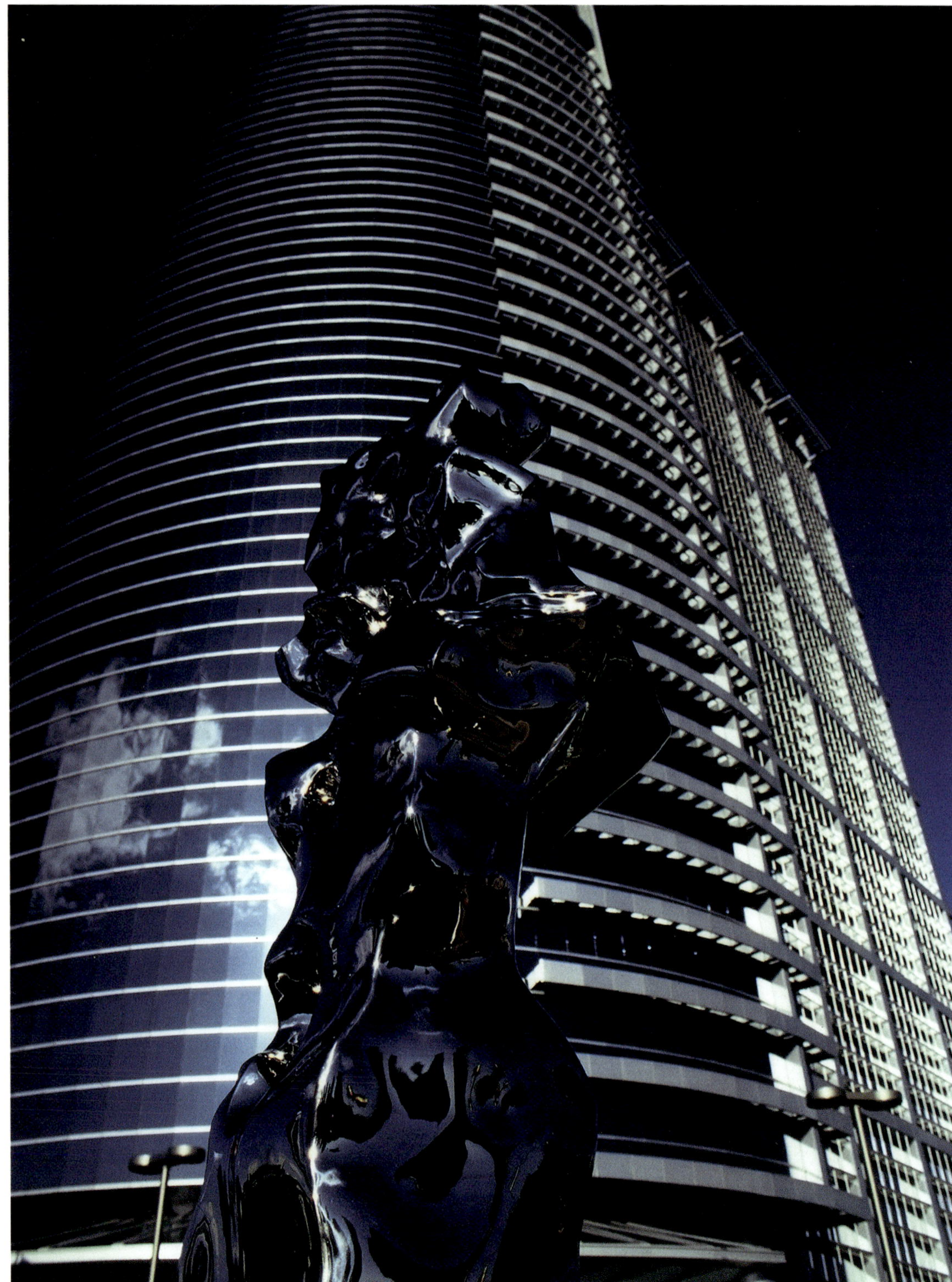

2

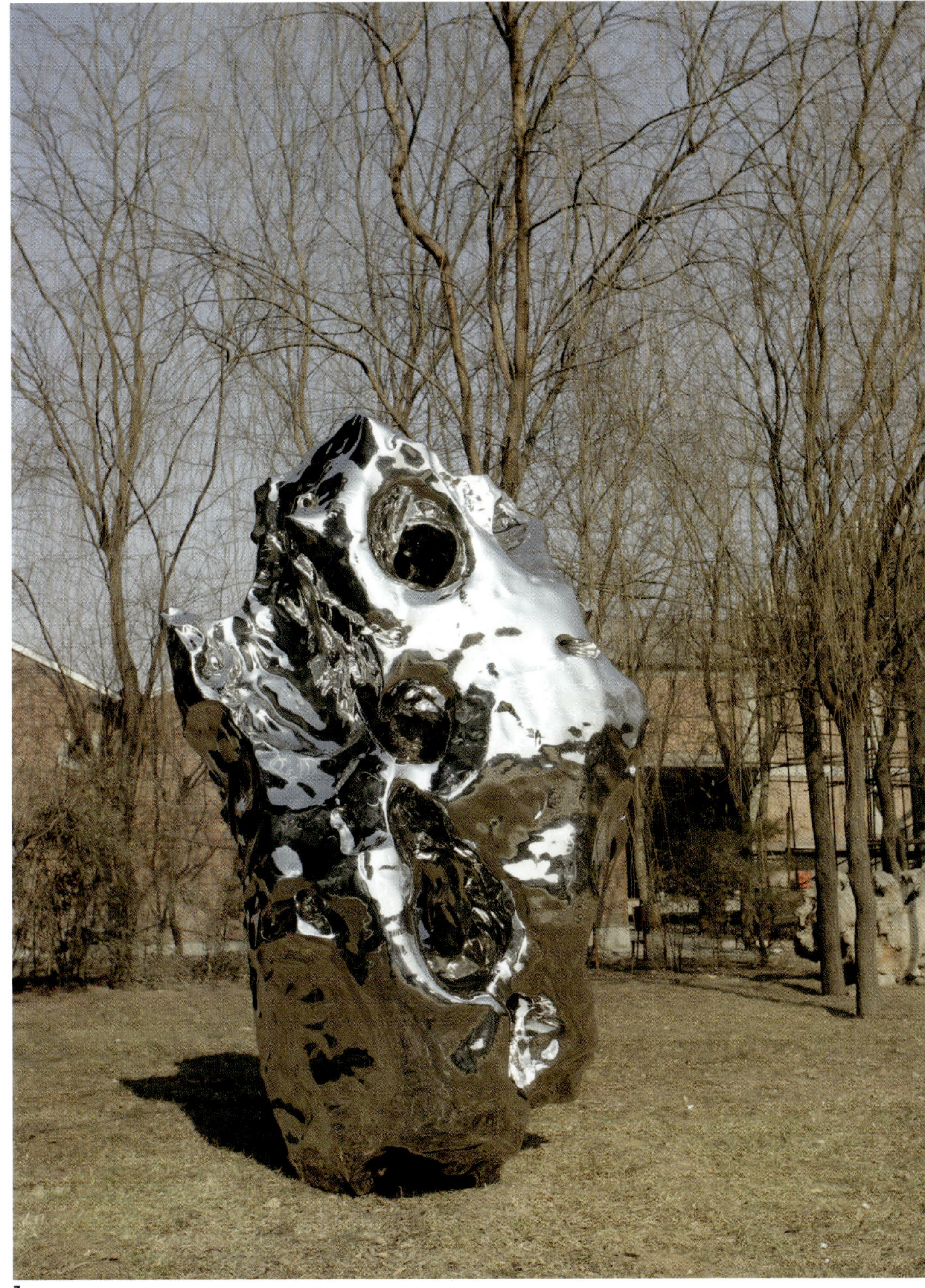

3

4

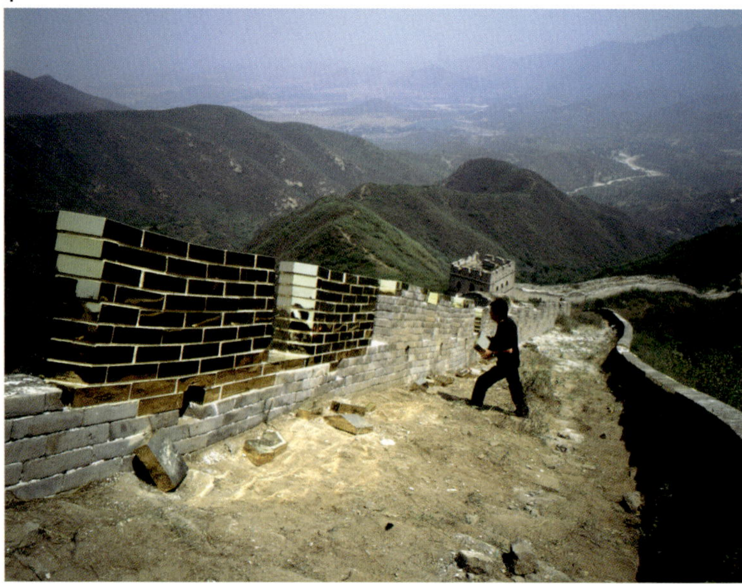

5

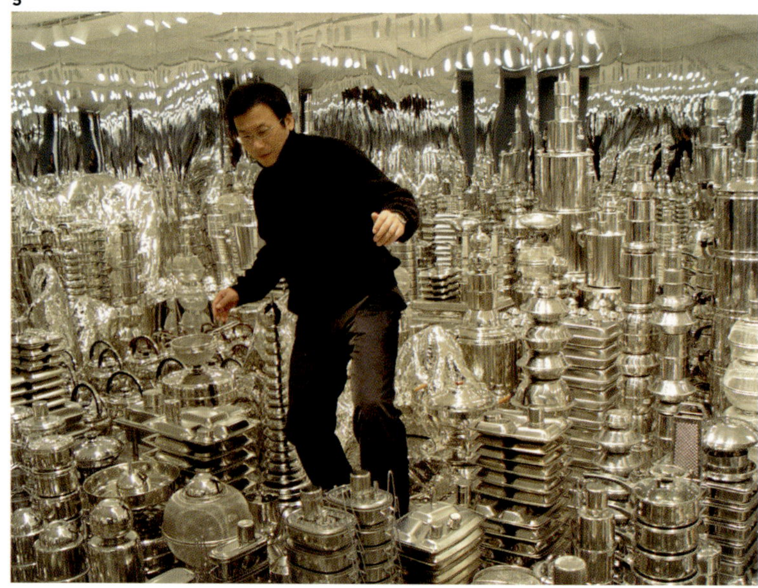

In 1995 Zhan Wang used stainless steel for the first time as this material imitates stone and he deposited the real stone in his backyard while he sold the imitation made of steel to a collector. In his latest work "Index of New Elements of Garden Stones" (2006) Zhan Wang is extremely detailed in his expression, his imitation of an ideal shaped rock is a kind of pioneer work of an independent school and in addition he applied for a worldwide patent for the style form and making of rock imitations made of stainless steel. On the rugged surface of the stainless steel rock imitation the reflection of light changes continuously and manpower is unable to grasp light and image thereof. His wish to control material of the future himself, which is the hidden humour of a Chinese literati, is enough to incite reflection.

durch einen literarisch tätigen Großvater. Nicht das Endprodukt ist wichtig – so Zhans Schluss –, sondern das Leben selbst und der künstlerische Interaktionsprozess.

1995 verarbeitete Zhan Wang zum ersten Mal rostfreien Stahl, indem er mit diesem Material Steine nachbildete – die echten Steine landeten in seinem Hinterhof, während er ihre stählernen Kopien an einen Sammler verkaufte. Und in seinem aktuellsten Werk „Index of New Elements of Garden Stones" (2006) geht Zhan Wang in seiner Nachbildung eines ideal geformten Felsens noch ein Stück weiter – überaus detailgetreu gearbeitet, sieht er ihn als eine Art Pionierarbeit, die Schule machen soll. Parallel bemüht sich der Künstler um ein weltweites Patent für seine Steine und Felsen aus rostfreiem Stahl, an deren rauer Oberfläche sich das einfallende Licht in immer neuen Formen bricht. Man sieht: In all seinen Arbeiten ist durchaus der hintersinnige Humor eines chinesischen Literaten am Werk.

象。这份不可预料与控制的未来，挑战著展望习于将物质的掌握严控制在自己的手中，这是中国文人的小小幽默，也足以发人深省。

Victoria Lu

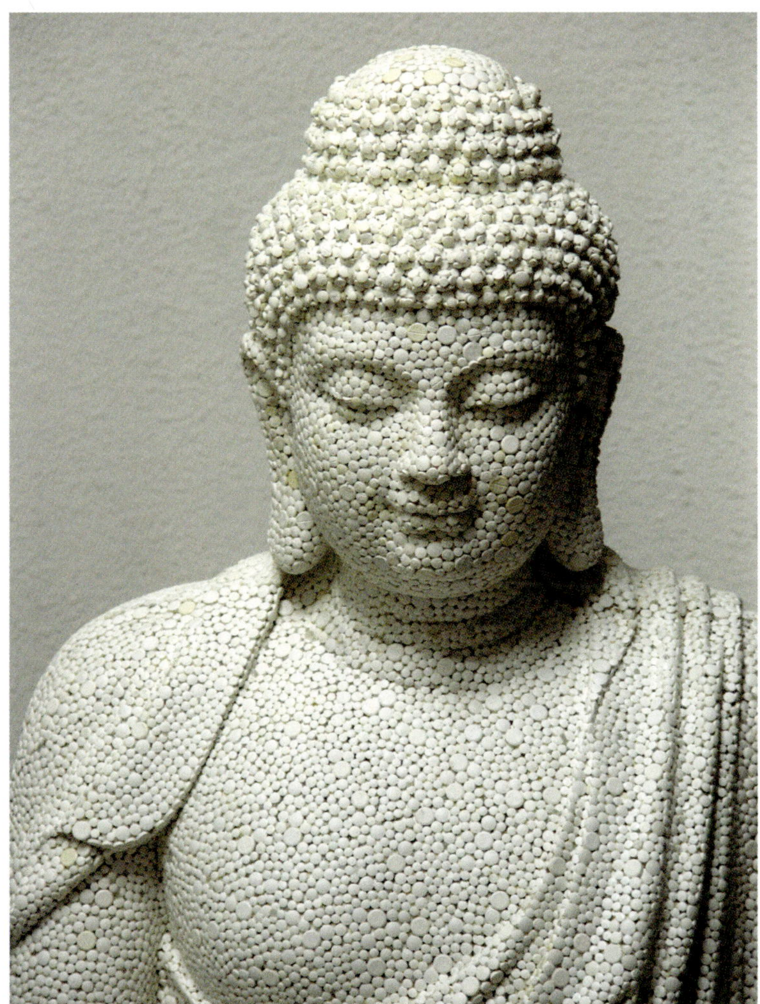

1 ***Floating Rock #2**, 2002*
Stainless steel, 230 x 210 x 180 cm
Edelstahl, 230 x 210 x 180 cm
《浮石 #2》2002年，不锈钢, 230 x 210 x 180 cm

2 ***Scholar's Rock**, 2001*
Stainless Steel, 230 x 160 x 58 cm, installation view, Economist Plaza, London
Edelstahl, 230 x 160 x 58 cm, Installationsansicht, Economist Plaza, London
《学者的山石》2001年，不锈钢， 装置实景，经济学家广场， 伦敦，230 x 160 x 58 cm

3 ***Artificial Rock #102**, 2006*
Stainless steel, 286 x 145 x 110 cm
Edelstahl, 286 x 145 x 110 cm
《假山石 #102》2006年, 不锈钢, 286 x 145 x 110 cm

4 ***Inlay Great Wall**, 2001*
Installation remnant Great Wall of Badaling, Beijing
Installation an der Großen Mauer bei Badaling, Peking
《镶长城》2001年, 不锈钢镀钛金，八达岭残长装置

5 ***Urban Landscape**, 2005*
Installation view, Museum of Contemporary Art, Chicago
Installationsansicht, Museum of Contemporary Art, Chicago
《都市山水》2005年, 不锈钢，装置实景

6 ***Buddhist Medicine Temple**, 2004–2006*
Installation views, 6th Shanghai Biennial, 2006
Installationsansichten, 6. Shanghai Biennale, 2006
《佛药堂》2004–2006年, 装置实景

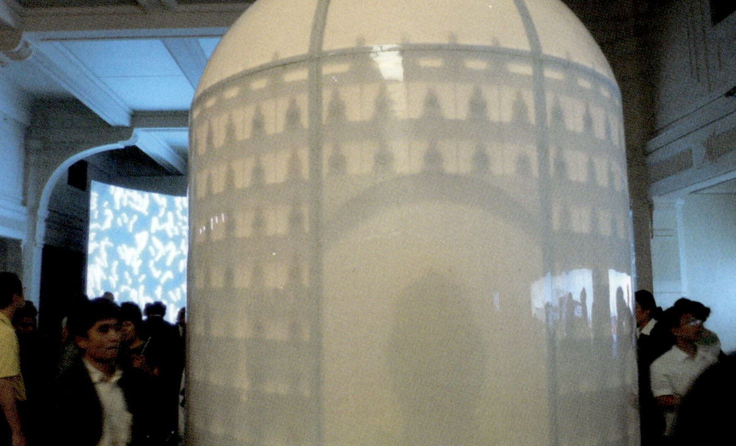

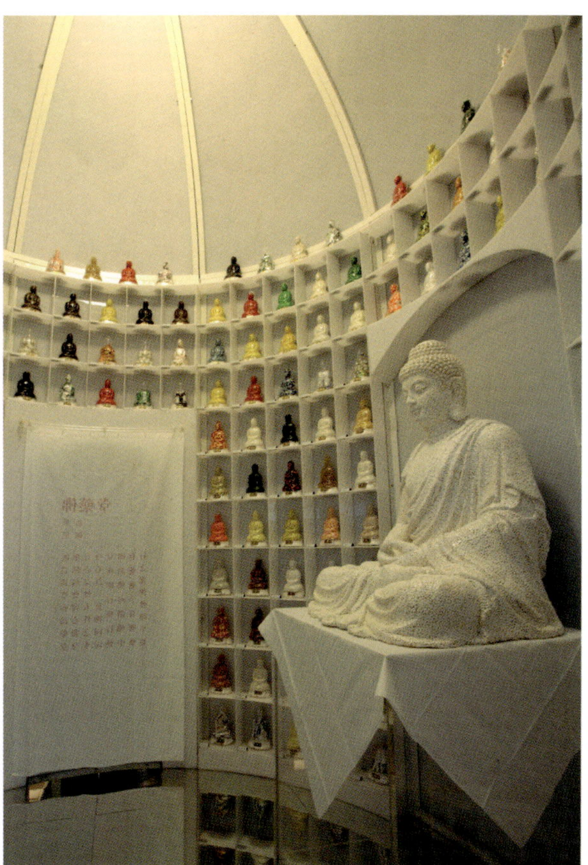

6

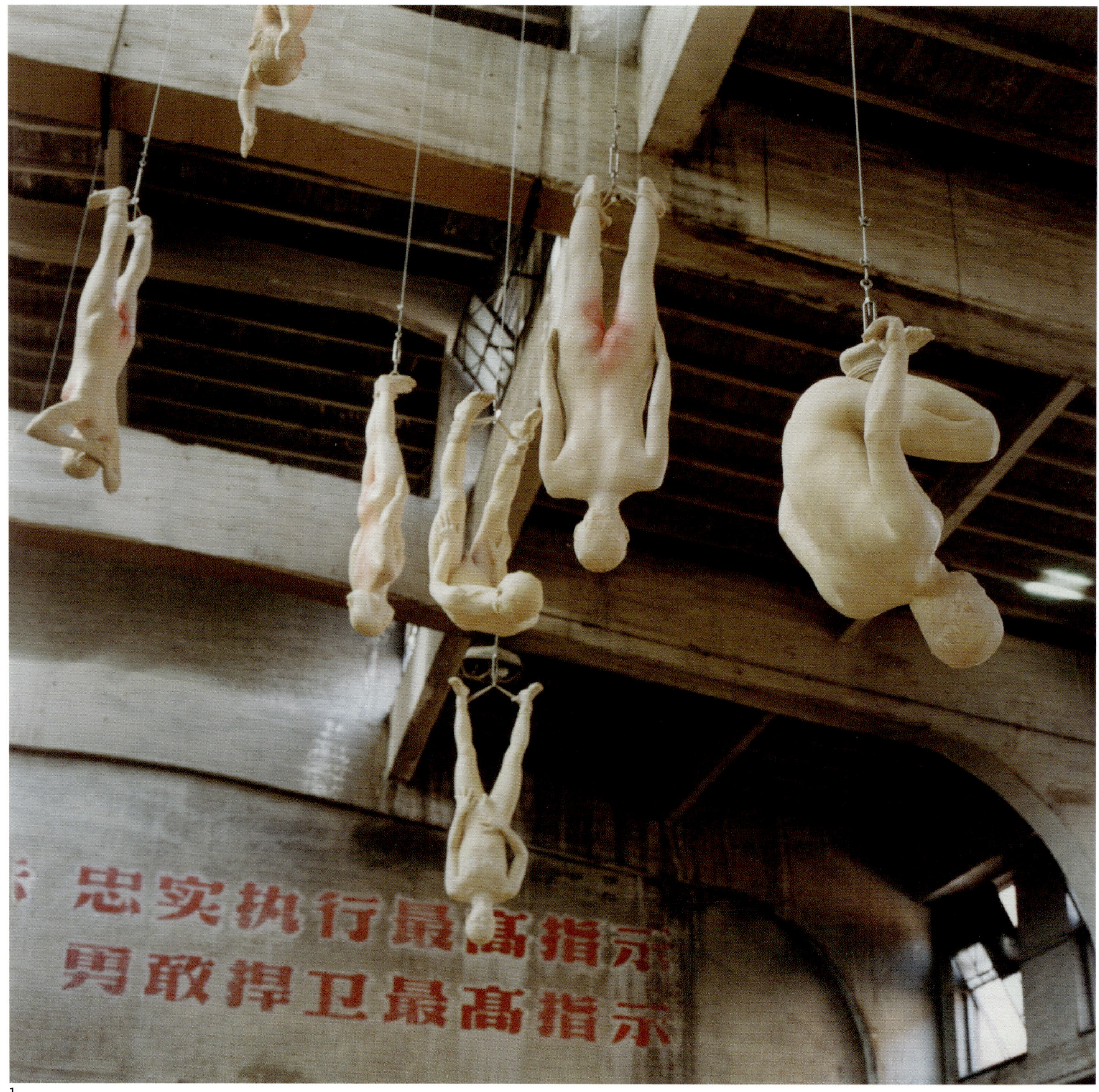

1

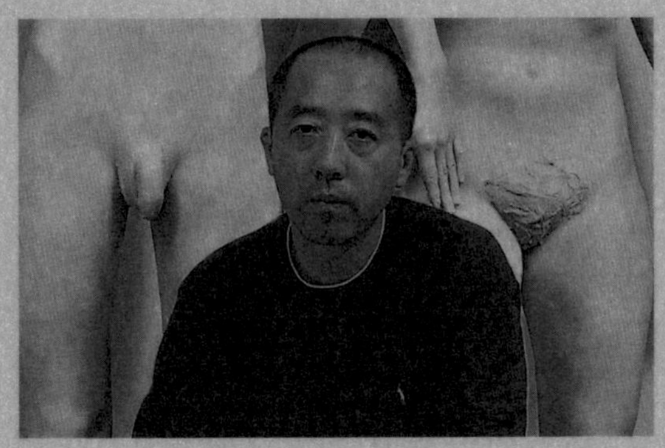

"One day the government will have learnt to accept our human and political rights as well as the fact that we are all equal by birth."

„Eines Tages werden wir den Staat dazu gebracht haben, unsere Menschen- und politischen Rechte ebenso zu akzeptieren wie die Tatsache, dass wir alle von Geburt an gleich sind."

"总有一天政府会 学着承认我们的人权和政治权利，以及承认人生来平等的事实。"

Born in 1964 in Harbin, China. Lives and works in Beijing
Geboren 1964 in Harbin, China. Lebt und arbeitet in Peking
1964年出生于中国黑龙江省哈尔滨市，现在北京居住工作

***Selected exhibitions* / Ausgewählte Ausstellungen / 所选展览**

2002 "Zhang Dali", Base Gallery, Tokyo, Japan
2003 "Zhang Dali", Galleria Garibaldi, Milan, Italy
2004 "Zhang Dali", Chinese Contemporary, London, UK
2004–07 "Between Past and Future, New Photography and Video from China", International Center of Photography, New York, NY, USA (travelling exhibition)
2005 "Sublimation", Beijing Commune, Beijing, China
2007 "Zhang Dali Solo Exhibition", Chinese Contemporary Gallery, New York, NY, USA

2002年 《张大力》Base 画廊，东京，日本
2003年 《张大力》Garibaldi画廊，米兰，意大利
2004年 《张大力》中国当代艺术画廊，伦敦 英国
2004–07年 《过去与未来之间—中国新影像展》国际摄影中心，纽约，美国（巡回展）
2005年 《升华》北京公社，北京，中国
2007年 《张大力个展》当代中国艺术画廊，纽约，美国

***Selected publications* / Ausgewählte Publikationen / 所选著作**

Mathieu Borysevicz: "Zhang Dali: Demolition and Dialogue", Beijing 1999
Wu Hong: "Zhang Dali's Dialogue: Conversation with a City", in: "Public Culture", vol. 12, No. 3, 2000
Zhang Dali: "Interview on CNN", Dec. 11, 2006

Borysevicz, Mathieu（著）:《张大力：打碎和对话》画廊, 北京1999年
巫鸿（著）:《张大力的对话：交谈与城市》于：《公开文化》册12, 第 3, 2000年
张大力：CNN的采访, 2006年12月11 日

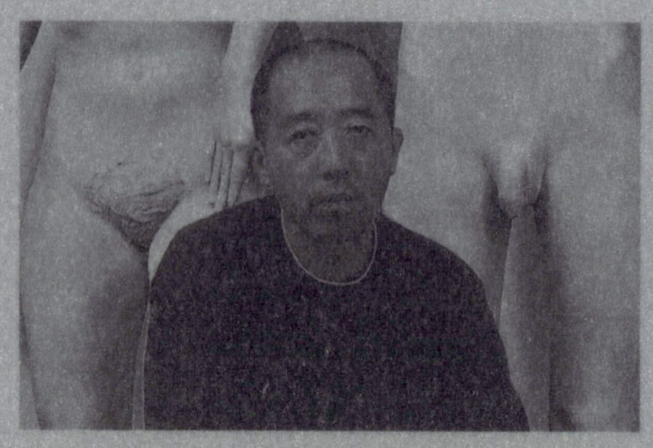

"One day the government will have learnt to accept our human and political rights as well as the fact that we are all equal by birth."

„Eines Tages werden wir den Staat dazu gebracht haben, unsere Menschen- und politischen Rechte ebenso zu akzeptieren wie die Tatsache, dass wir alle von Geburt an gleich sind."

"总有一天政府会 学着承认我们的人权和政治权利，以及承认人生来平等的事实。"

Born in 1964 in Harbin, China. Lives and works in Beijing
Geboren 1964 in Harbin, China. Lebt und arbeitet in Peking
1964年出生于中国黑龙江省哈尔滨市，现在北京居住工作

Selected exhibitions / Ausgewählte Ausstellungen / 所选展览

2002 "Zhang Dali", Base Gallery, Tokyo, Japan
2003 "Zhang Dali", Galleria Garibaldi, Milan, Italy
2004 "Zhang Dali", Chinese Contemporary, London, UK
2004-07 "Between Past and Future, New Photography and Video from China", International Center of Photography, New York, NY, USA (travelling exhibition)
2005 "Sublimation", Beijing Commune, Beijing, China
2007 "Zhang Dali Solo Exhibition", Chinese Contemporary Gallery, New York, NY, USA

2002年 《张大力》Base 画廊，东京，日本
2003年 《张大力》Garibaldi画廊，米兰，意大利
2004年 《张大力》中国当代艺术画廊，伦敦 英国
2004-07年《过去与未来之间—中国新影像展》国际摄影中心，纽约，美国（巡回展）
2005年 《升华》北京公社，北京，中国
2007年 《张大力个展》当代中国艺术画廊，纽约，美国

Selected publications / Ausgewählte Publikationen / 所选著作

Mathieu Borysevicz: "Zhang Dali: Demolition and Dialogue", Beijing 1999
Wu Hong: "Zhang Dali's Dialogue: Conversation with a City", in: "Public Culture", vol. 12, No. 3, 2000
Zhang Dali: "Interview on CNN", Dec. 11, 2006

Borysevicz, Mathieu（著）：《张大力：打碎和对话》画廊，北京1999年
巫鸿（著）：《张大力的对话：交谈与城市》于：《公开文化》册12，第 3，2000年
张大力：CNN的采访，2006年12月11 日

ZHANG DALI 张大力

[ʈʂaŋ tali]

Strange bold heads sprayed on demolished walls, graffiti of very plain working, authentic but original, most of all provocative as graffiti is not only extraordinary in China but doesn't exist at all. Among old deserts of stone and adjacent to anonymous high building complexes, sports fields and parks the sprayer finds the place for his play. Traditional houses of stone in demolished areas, witnesses of former citizens' life, are extremely interesting for him.

Since the mid 1990s this sprayer attracted the interest to the new architecture occupying the ground of old Beijing with cold and rapidly erected office and apartment complexes by his standardised and oversized image of his head. The sprayed head appearing on more and more planes emerged at many places in Beijing. People were wondering who the sprayer was and the intention behind the image. Are these portraits a punishable offence? Was this a new kind of public art? As nobody knew graffiti up to this moment an answer couldn't be given – except by the artist himself. In March 1998 Zhang Dali had some interviews astonishing the public with the fact that he is an artist who studied at Beijing's renowned academy of art. At the same time photographs of his head sprayed on walls became known in the west.

But the story of the head had begun earlier, when Zhang Dali emigrated to Bologna in 1989. In Italy the idea of this serial head was born and after his return to China in 1995 he sprayed this head on walls – leaving more than 2000 head images until the year 2000 in different places. Zhang's idea was that his portrait should be in dialogue with the city, being a witness for his presence and even more for his commitment to this city losing face and being a victim of destruction.

Zhang's work is more than just graffiti. He devoted himself to certain group of Chinese population in his installations and oil paintings: migratory labourers without rights, erecting all those new buildings. He made of some of these migrants, a socially weak group, castings hanging these

Merkwürdige Glatzköpfe auf Abrisswände gesprüht, Graffiti einfachster Machart, authentisch und ursprünglich, vor allem aber: provokativ, denn Graffiti sind in China nicht nur ungewöhnlich, sondern schlicht nicht existent. Inmitten alter Steinwüsten und neben anonymen Hochhauskomplexen, in Sportplätzen und Parkanlagen findet der unbekannte Sprayer seine Spielflächen. Traditionelle Steinhäuser in Abbruchgebieten, die Zeugnisse alten Stadtlebens, haben es ihm besonders angetan.

Seit Mitte der 1990er Jahre machte dieser Sprayer mit seinem standardisierten und überdimensionierten Konterfei auf die neue Architektur aufmerksam, die mit ihren rasch hochgezogenen kalten Büro- und Apartmentkomplexen den historischen Grund des alten Peking okkupiert. Der gesprühte Kopf vermehrte sich rasend schnell und tauchte an immer neuen Stellen in der Stadt auf. Allenthalben fragte man sich: Wer steckt dahinter und was treibt ihn an? Sind diese Porträts strafbar? Oder öffentliche Kunst? Da man bis dahin Graffiti in Peking nicht kannte, konnte das niemand ernsthaft beantworten – abgesehen vom Künstler selbst, und das tat Zhang Dali dann auch im März 1998 in einigen Interviews. Die Öffentlichkeit war überaus erstaunt, dass der unbekannte Sprayer ein professioneller Künstler war, der an Pekings renommierter Kunstakademie studiert hatte. Zeitgleich wurde er auch im Westen mit Fotografien seines Kopfes auf den Ruinen der alten Kaiserstadt bekannt.

Aber die Geschichte geht noch weiter zurück, denn Zhang war 1989 nach Bologna emigriert und dort hatte er die Idee zu diesem seriellen Kopf. Nach seiner Rückkehr nach China 1995 sprühte er ihn an die Wände – bis 1998 sollte er mehr als 2000 dieser Markenzeichen hinterlassen. Zhangs Idee war, dass sein Selbstporträt mit der Stadt in einen Dialog treten solle, der von seiner Anwesenheit, aber mehr noch von seinem Engagement für die ihr Gesicht verlierende und der Zerstörung überlassene Metropole zeuge.

Zhangs Werk geht jedoch über diese Graffiti hinaus. So widmete er sich mit Installationen und Ölgemälden einer ganz

拆除的墙壁上刷涂上几个怪异的秃头，非常朴素的涂鸦，真实而新颖。在中国尤其是象涂鸦一样的挑衅不但非凡，然而却根本不存在。在古老石屋废墟和高耸的综合建筑群附近，运动场和公园里，涂鸦者找到了他们玩耍的平面。位于拆迁的区域的老石头房子，见证着从前居民生活，对他有着很大的吸引力。在这些地方，我一般看到他的秃头刷涂在破损的墙壁外面。透过墙壁的豁口可以看见荒凉高楼中的单元新生活。

自上世纪90中期起，老北京的地面上迅速耸立起冰冷的办公和公寓建筑群，他对这些新建筑产生了浓厚的兴趣，在这些建筑墙面上刷涂上他的特大标准的头像。这样的头像出现在北京越来越多的地方的墙面上。这些肖像是惩罚性的攻击吗？这是一种新的公共艺术吗?因为没有人了解涂鸦，所以直到此刻，除了艺术家本人之外，没有人能回答上述的问题。1998年三月，张大力接受了一些采访，公众才了解他是一个艺术家，毕业于北京的一间著名艺术学院时，都感到惊讶。与此同时，他刷涂在墙壁上的头像的照片，在西方开始出名。

而实际上，头像的故事早就开始了，在1989年张移居博洛尼亚的时候。在意大利他就产生了系列的头像的创意，在1995年返回中国时，他把头像刷涂在墙壁上，到2000年为止，在不同的地方大约留下了2000多幅头像。张大力认为，他的肖像是与北京城的对话，见证了他的出现以及对这个失去脸面城市的义务，是城市毁坏的牺牲品。

张大力的作品不仅仅是涂鸦。他在他的装置和油画里专注于中国人群众的某个群体：建设所有这些新楼宇的农民工，他们没 获得有这个城市市民说享受的权利。张创作了这些社会弱势群体的作品，浇铸物把他们成群的吊在房顶上（“Chinese Off-spring” 2003-2005年），以此来表达这个阶层的悲哀，他们建设了新的中国的基础，但是没有收到他们应有的利益。

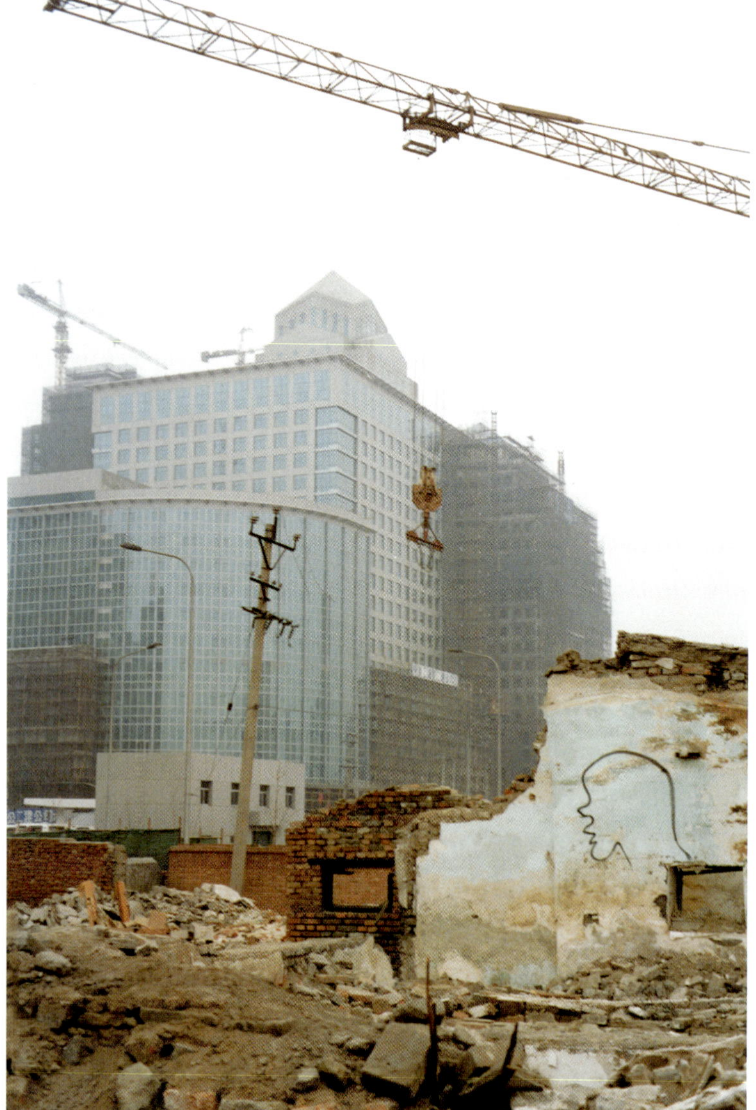
2

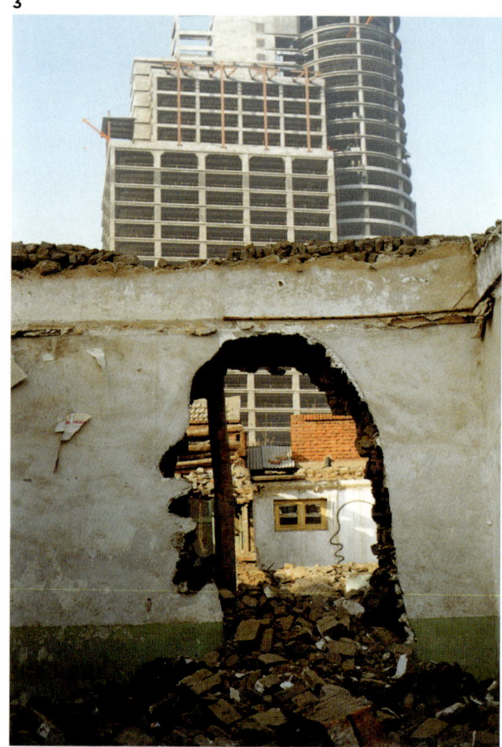
3

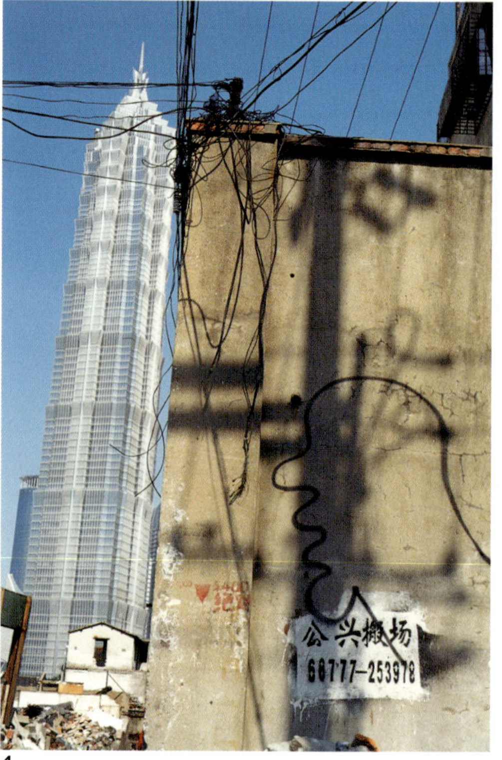

4

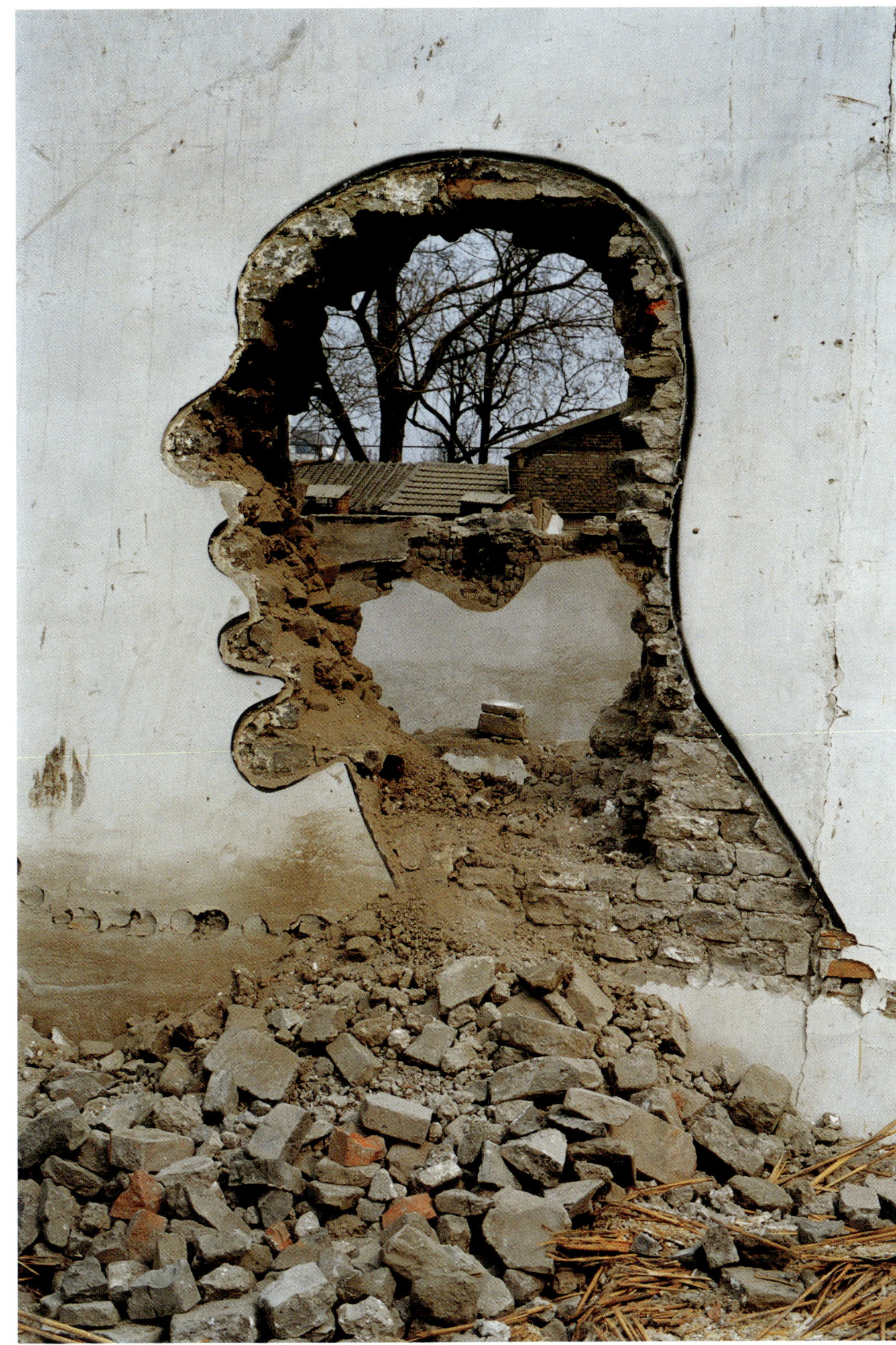

5

6

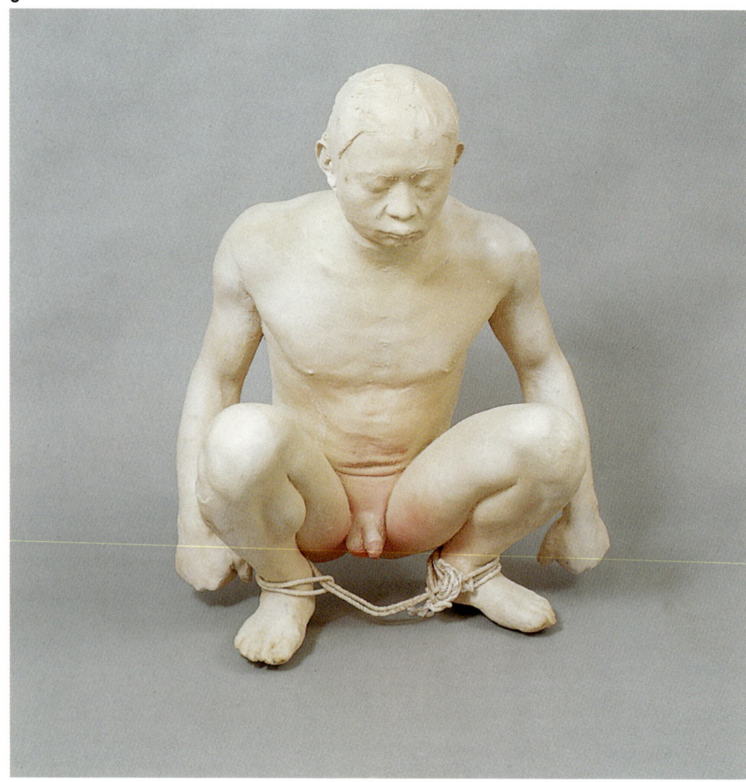

7

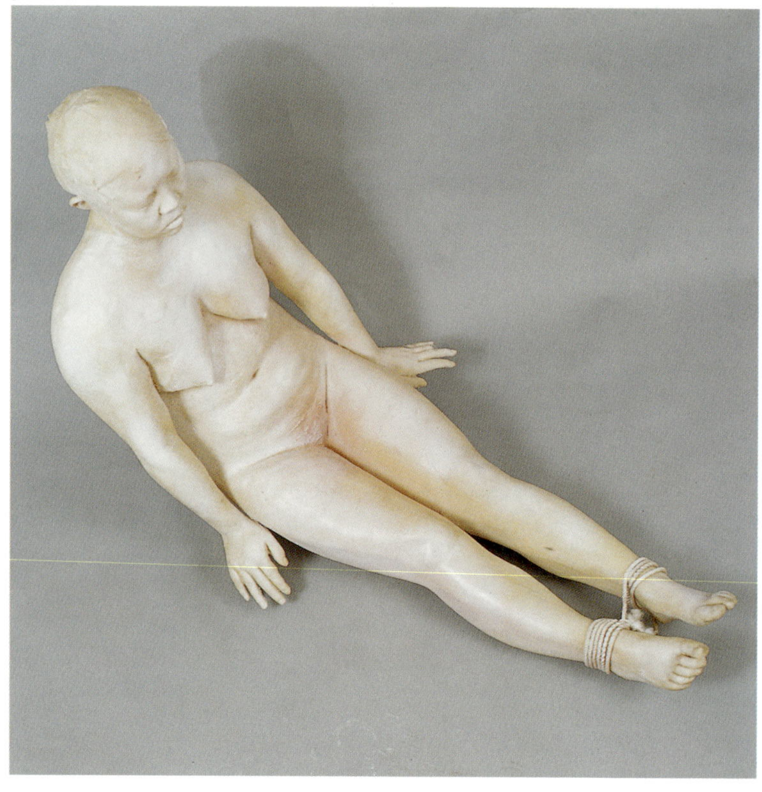

headfirst in groups on a ceiling ("Chinese Offspring", 2003–2005) to express in this way the misery of a social class building the fundament of new China without receiving any benefits thereof.

Since 2003 Zhang Dali is interested in manipulations of public pictures. In order to initiate a subversive discussion about the exploited mechanism of the present image-culture he compared original photographs of Mao Zedong with the falsified propaganda pictures. With direct comparison of original and fake the manipulations become obvious and simultaneously the practices in totalitarian systems are unveiled. Zhang Dali carries on an honourable, but forlorn combat against the rapidly increasing flood of pictures. However, his animadversion on social conditions in China is like sand in the gear of progress.

bestimmten Bevölkerungsgruppe in China: den rechtlosen Wanderarbeitern, die all die neuen Bauten errichten. Diese Migranten bilden eine sozial schwache Gruppe – Zhang fertigte von einigen von ihnen Abgüsse an, die er kopfüber in Gruppen an die Decke hängte („Chinese Offspring", 2003–2005). Er wollte so dem Elend einer Gesellschaftsschicht Ausdruck verleihen, die zwar die Basis des neuen China schafft, aber selbst kaum Nutzen davon hat.

Seit 2003 beschäftigt sich Zhang Dali damit, die Manipulationen an öffentlichen Bildern zu untersuchen. Deshalb stellte er Originalaufnahmen von Mao Zedong den verfälschten Fotografien der Propaganda gegenüber, um eine subversive Auseinandersetzung mit den instrumentalisierten Mechanismen der heutigen Bild-Kultur in Gang zu setzen. Im direkten Vergleich von Original und Fälschung werden die Eingriffe augenfällig und entlarven zugleich die Manipulationspraktiken (nicht nur) totalitärer Systeme. Zhang Dali ficht hier einen ehrenhaften, wenngleich aussichtslosen Kampf gegen die rasant steigende Bilderflut. Seine Kritik an den gesellschaftlichen Zuständen in China ist jedoch notwendiger Sand im Getriebe des Fortschritts.

从2003年起，张大力对公共图片的处理现象产生了兴趣。为开展一场关于当前肖像文化利用体制的颠覆性讨论，他比较了毛泽东的原始照片和伪造的宣传照片。经过比较，处理的痕迹就很明显，同时也揭示了在极权主义制度下的这种做法。张现在继续同这种处理的虚假图像作斗争，虽然高尚，却无以回天。毕竟他对中国社会状况的批评无疑是杯水车薪。

Gregor Jansen

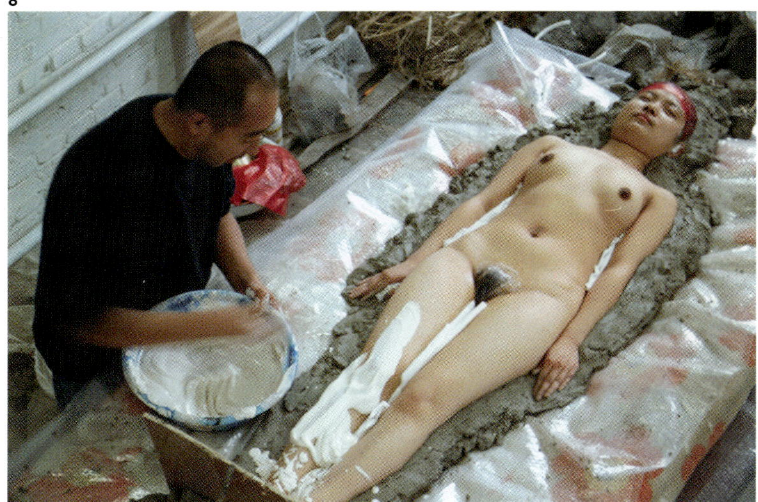

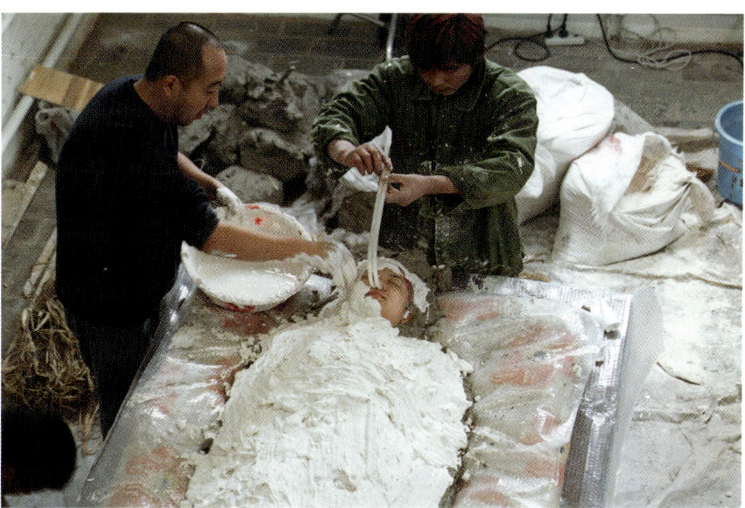

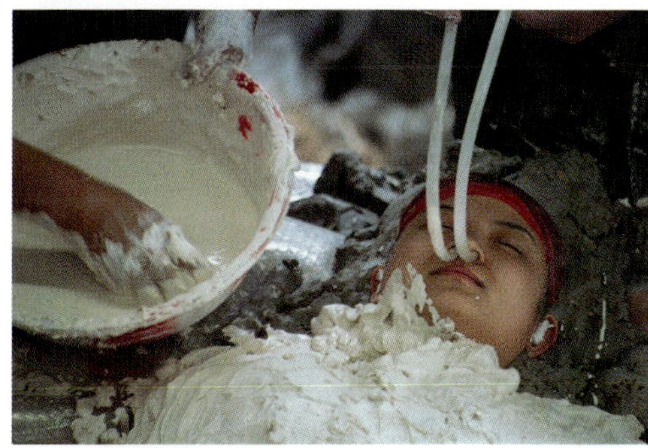

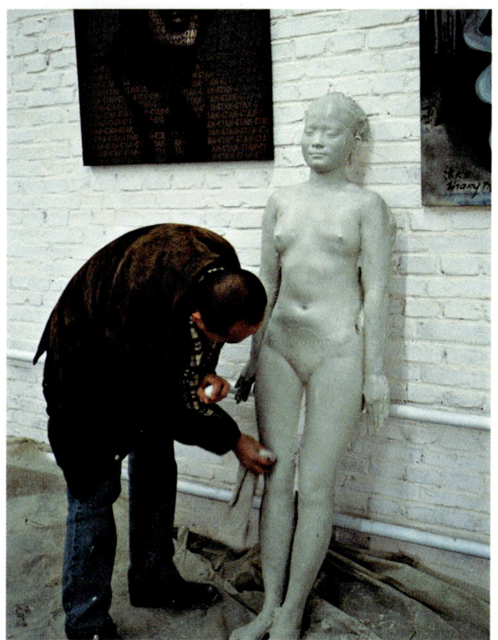

1 ***Chinese Offspring***, *2003–2005*
15 life-size cast figures, mixed media, average height 170 cm each
15 lebensgroße gegossene Figuren, Mixed media, durchschnittliche Höhe je 170 cm
《中国种族》2003–2005年，15个人一样的大小塑像，综合材料，每个像170 cm 平均高度

2 ***Dialogue, Full Link Plaza, Beijing***, *1998*
Photograph, 150 x 100 cm
Fotografie, 150 x 100 cm
《对话，丰联广场，北京》1998年，摄影，150 x 100 cm

3 ***Demolition, World Financial Centre, Beijing***, *1998*
Photograph, 150 x 100 cm
Fotografie, 150 x 100 cm
《拆毁，世界财政中心，北京》1998年，摄影，150 x 100 cm

4 ***Dialogue, Jinmao Tower, Shanghai***, *2000*
Photograph, 150 x 100 cm
Fotografie, 150 x 100 cm
《对话 —— 金茂大厦，上海》2000年，摄影，150 x 100 cm

5 ***Demolition, Time Plaza, Beijing***, *1999*
Photograph, 150 x 100 cm
Fotografie, 150 x 100 cm
《拆毁，Time Plaza, 背景》1999年，摄影，150 x 100 cm

6 ***Chinese Offspring No. 5***, *2003*
Cast figure, 100 x 54 x 46 cm
Gegossene Figur, 100 x 54 x 46 cm
《中国种族No. 5》2003年，塑像，100 x 54 x 46 cm

7 ***Chinese Offspring No. 7***, *2003*
Cast figure, 90 x 110 x 70 cm
Gegossene Figur, 90 x 110 x 70 cm
《中国种族No. 7》2003年，塑像，90 x 110 x 70 cm

8 ***Naked – working process***, *2005*
Photographs, 50 x 100/100 x 50 cm each
Fotografien, je 50 x 100/100 x 50 cm
《赤裸 —— 工作过程》2005年，摄影，每幅50 x 100 cm

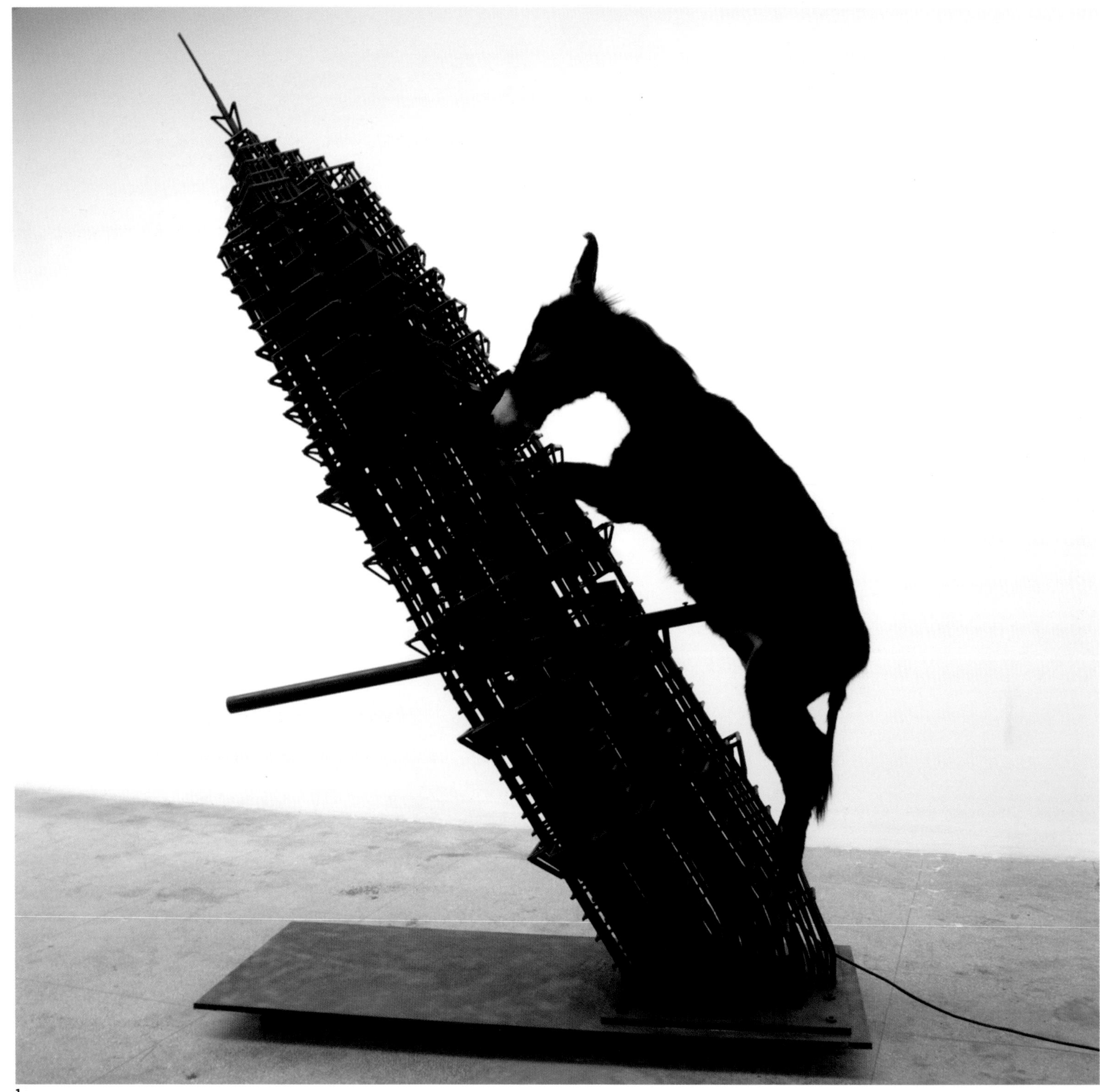

1

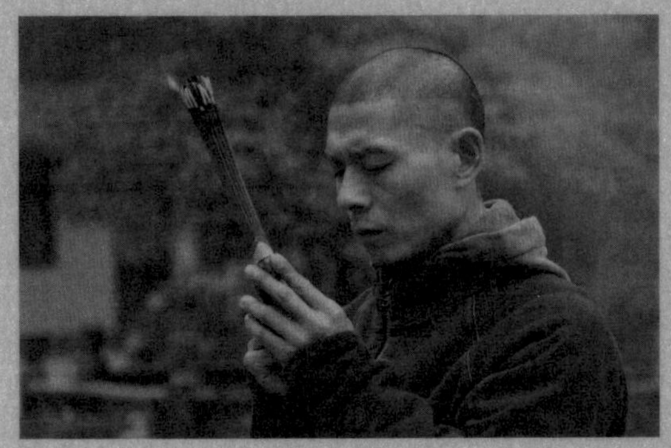

"The early works – from conception to execution – were so simple. They didn't involve any people beside the participants, and the feeling was one of great freedom – to be able to make such pieces in a situation where there was so much pressure from all around."

„Die frühen Arbeiten waren so simpel – von der Idee bis zur Ausführung. Außer den Mitwirkenden war niemand involviert, und sie vermittelten einem das Gefühl großer Freiheit – in der Lage zu sein, solche Stücke in einer Situation zu schaffen, in der so viel Druck von allen Seiten ausgeübt wurde."

"早期的从概念到制作的作品很非常简单的。它们没有涉及任何人包括参与者，这种感觉是一种很大的自由，只有在这种没有外界很大压力的环境之下才能够制作出这样的作品。"

Born in 1965 in Anyang, Hunan Province, China. Lives and works in Shanghai and New York, NY, USA
Geboren 1965 in Anyang, Provinz Hunan, China. Lebt und arbeitet in Shanghai und New York, NY, USA
1965年出生于中国河南安阳，往返于上海和纽约之间

***Selected exhibitions* / Ausgewählte Ausstellungen / 所选展览**

1998 "Inside Out: New Chinese Art", Asia Society, New York, P.S.1 Contemporary Art Center, New York, NY, San Francisco Museum of Modern Art, San Francisco, CA, USA
1999 48. Biennale di Venezia, Venice, Italy
2002 Whitney Biennial, Whitney Museum of American Art, New York, NY, USA
2003 "Zhang Huan", Kunstverein Hamburg, Hamburg, Germany
2004–07 "Between Past and Future, New Photography and Video from China", International Center of Photography, New York, NY, USA (travelling exhibition)
2006 "Fever Variations", The 6th Gwangju Biennial 2006, Gwangju, Korea
2007 "Zhang Huan", Asia Society, New York, NY, USA

1998年 《蜕变突破：华人新艺术展》纽约亚洲协会美术馆与纽约当代艺术陈列馆(P.S.1)长岛市，旧金山现代艺术博物馆，旧金山，美国
1999年 《第48届威尼斯双年》威尼斯，意大利
2002 年 《惠特尼山双年展》惠特尼美国艺术博物馆，纽约
2003年 《张洹》艺术协会 汉堡，德国
2004–07年 《过去与未来之间—中国新影像展》国际摄影中心，纽约，美国（巡回展）
2006年 《热风变奏曲》，第六届光洲双年展，光洲，韩国
2007年 《张洹》纽约亚洲协会，纽约

***Selected publications* / Ausgewählte Publikationen / 所选著作**

Gao Minglu: "Private Experience and Public Happenings, The Performance Art of Zhang Huan in Pilgrimage to Santiago", Santiago de Compostela 2000
"Zhang Huan", Ostfildern-Ruit 2003
Daniele Perra: "Zhang Huan, A Sense of the Possible", in: "The Season", ed. by Gallery Pack, Milano 2006

高名潞（著）：《私有经验和公开事件，张洹的行为艺术》《朝圣到圣地亚哥》圣地亚哥，西班牙2000年
《张洹》艺术协会 汉堡，Ostfildern-Ruit 2003年
Perra, Daniele（著）：《张洹，可能感觉在季节》Pack 画廊（编者）米兰 2006 年

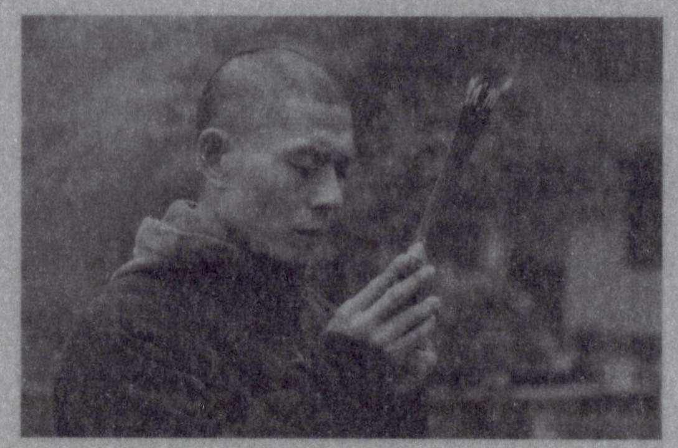

"The early works - from conception to execution - were so simple. They didn't involve any people beside the participants, and the feeling was one of great freedom - to be able to make such pieces in a situation where there was so much pressure from all around."

„Die frühen Arbeiten waren so simpel - von der Idee bis zur Ausführung. Außer den Mitwirkenden war niemand involviert, und sie vermittelten einem das Gefühl großer Freiheit - in der Lage zu sein, solche Stücke in einer Situation zu schaffen, in der so viel Druck von allen Seiten ausgeübt wurde."

"早期的从概念到制作的作品很非常简单的。它们没有涉及任何人包括参与者，这种感觉是一种很大的自由，只有在这种没有外界很大压力的环境之下才能够制作出这样的作品。"

Born in 1965 in Anyang, Hunan Province, China. Lives and works in Shanghai and New York, NY, USA
Geboren 1965 in Anyang, Provinz Hunan, China. Lebt und arbeitet in Shanghai und New York, NY, USA
1965年出生于中国河南安阳，往返于上海和纽约之间

Selected exhibitions / Ausgewählte Ausstellungen / 所选展览

1998	"Inside Out: New Chinese Art", Asia Society, New York, P.S.1 Contemporary Art Center, New York, NY, San Francisco Museum of Modern Art, San Francisco, CA, USA
1999	48. Biennale di Venezia, Venice, Italy
2002	Whitney Biennial, Whitney Museum of American Art, New York, NY, USA
2003	"Zhang Huan", Kunstverein Hamburg, Hamburg, Germany
2004-07	"Between Past and Future, New Photography and Video from China", International Center of Photography, New York, NY, USA (travelling exhibition)
2006	"Fever Variations", The 6th Gwangju Biennial 2006, Gwangju, Korea
2007	"Zhang Huan", Asia Society, New York, NY, USA

1998年	《蜕变突破：华人新艺术展》纽约亚洲协会美术馆与纽约当代艺术陈列馆(P.S.1)长岛市，旧金山现代艺术博物馆，旧金山，美国
1999年	《第48届威尼斯双年展》威尼斯，意大利
2002 年	《惠特尼山双年展》惠特尼美国艺术博物馆，纽约
2003年	《张洹》艺术协会 汉堡，德国
2004-07年	《过去与未来之间—中国新影像展》国际摄影中心，纽约，美国（巡回展）
2006年	《热风变奏曲》，第六届光州双年展，光州，韩国
2007年	《张洹》纽约亚洲协会，纽约

Selected publications / Ausgewählte Publikationen / 所选著作

Gao Minglu: "Private Experience and Public Happenings. The Performance Art of Zhang Huan in Pilgrimage to Santiago", Santiago de Compostela 2000
"Zhang Huan", Ostfildern-Ruit 2003
Daniele Perra: "Zhang Huan, A Sense of the Possible", in: "The Season", ed. by Gallery Pack, Milano 2006

高名潞（著）：《私有经验和公开事件，张洹的行为艺术》《朝圣到圣地亚哥》圣地亚哥，西班牙2000年
《张洹》艺术协会 汉堡，Ostfildern-Ruit 2003年
Perra, Daniele（著）：《张洹，可能感觉在季节》Pack 画廊（编者）米兰 2006 年

ZHANG HUAN 张洹

[tʂaŋ xuan]

Graduating with a master's degree from the Central Academy of Fine Arts in 1993, Zhang Huan was one of the central figures in the late 1990s in the Beijing East Village art scene, a mostly underground movement taking place on the outskirts of the city, highly experimental and often at odds with the authorities. All of his work is rooted in performance art, acts of endurance or masochism publicly presented, which has been compared to such western artists as Marina Abramovic and Chris Burden, though highly influential in his own right.

Even before graduating from the Central Academy, Zhang Huan captured the public's attention when he poured red paint over himself holding a doll outside a traditional painting exhibition, then stepped inside the exhibition hall and demanded that the limbs of the doll be shown as his work of art. The show was immediately shut down due to this act, a commentary on enforced abortions in China.

In 1994, he created one of his most well-known works, "12 Square Meters", in which he sat in a public toilet for an hour, smeared in honey and fish oil, as flies gathered on the surface of his skin. He participated in the 1995 performance, "The Anonymous Mountain raised by a Meter", where a group of artists in the nude formed a human mound atop a hillside. Two years later, he executed the signature work of the period, "To Raise the Water Level in a Pond", where he invited a group of Chinese peasants to pose for the camera, standing waist deep in the water. The image was immediately adopted as the cover for the catalogue for "Inside Out", the groundbreaking show of Chinese contemporary art at New York's Asia Society. Like most of Zhang Huan's work, this piece simultaneously explores the futility of the lone individual to make an impact in a mass society, while demonstrating that a deeply lasting resonance can indeed be achieved if attempted.

Since moving to the United States in 1998, Zhang Huan's work has evolved into photography and sculpture, while he continues to execute theatrical mass performances at

Zhang Huan, der 1993 seinen Master an der Central Academy of Fine Arts machte, gehörte in den späten 1990er Jahren zu den zentralen Figuren der Kunstszene des Pekinger East Village. Diese weitgehend dem Untergrund zugehörige, extrem experimentelle Bewegung entfaltete sich in den Außenbezirken der Stadt und war der Obrigkeit oft ein Dorn im Auge. Zhang Huans gesamtes Werk wurzelt in der Performance-Kunst – in öffentlich vorgeführten Akten der Ausdauer oder des Masochismus, die ihm Vergleiche mit westlichen Künstlern wie Marina Abramovic und Chris Burden eingebracht haben. Dabei ist er seinerseits ein äußerst einflussreicher Künstler.

Noch vor Beendigung seines Studiums erregte Zhang Huan öffentliche Aufmerksamkeit, als er mit einer Puppe vor einem Gebäude auftauchte, in dem eine Ausstellung traditioneller Gemälde zu sehen war, sich mit roter Farbe übergoss, dann den Ausstellungssaal betrat und verlangte, die Gliedmaßen der Puppe sollten als sein Kunstwerk gezeigt werden. Der Auftritt – ein Kommentar zu erzwungenen Abtreibungen in China – führte zur sofortigen Schließung der Ausstellung.

1994 führte er eins seiner bekanntesten Werke vor, „12 Square Meters“, für das er eine Stunde lang, mit Honig und Fischöl eingeschmiert, auf einer öffentlichen Toilette saß, während sich die Fliegen auf seiner Haut versammelten. 1995 nahm er an der Performance „The Anonymous Mountain raised by a Meter“ teil, bei der eine Gruppe nackter Künstler einen Hügel auf einer Bergkuppe bildete. Zwei Jahre später realisierte er das herausragende Werk der Periode, „To Raise the Water Level in a Pond“, für das er eine Gruppe chinesischer Bauern anwies, brusthoch im Wasser stehend für die Kamera zu posieren. Das von der Aktion aufgenommene Bild wurde umgehend als Cover des Katalogs für „Inside Out“ ausgewählt, die wegweisende Ausstellung chinesischer Gegenwartskunst der Asia Society in New York. Wie die meisten Arbeiten von Zhang Huan ergründet dieses Werk die Vergeblichkeit, als einsames Individuum in einer Massengesellschaft Einfluss zu nehmen, zeigt aber gleich-

1993年张洹毕业于中央美院获得硕士学位，上世纪90年代末期他是北京东村艺术表展的主要成员之一，一个在北京市郊举行的以高度的实验艺术为主的是地下艺术运动，并且与官方的意识相左。张洹所有的作品植根于自虐性的表演艺术，因此被比作西方艺术家 Marina Abramovic 和Chris Burden，虽然有点抬高了他的身份。

连在毕业于中央美院之前也，张洹引起了公众的关注，当时他站在中国传统绘画展厅外，手拿着只玩偶，把红色颜料浇在身上，然后走进展厅要求展出玩偶的肢体如他的艺术品。由于这一举动，展出随即被关闭，实况转播被禁止播出。

1994 年张洹创作了最为知名的作品《12平方米》，张洹身上涂满蜂蜜和鱼油，像苍蝇一样粘在皮肤上，在一间公共厕所里端坐了1个小时。1995年他参加为《无名山增高一米》的表演，一群艺术家裸体的堆在一个山丘上形成了一个人堡。两年以后，张洹完成了他的代表作，《为鱼塘水位增高》，张邀请了一群农民站在齐腰深的水中堵着镜头摆着姿势。这幅照片立即成为《蜕变突破:华人新艺术展》的主题封面，《蜕变突破:华人新艺术展》是在美国纽约 举行的中国现代艺术的开创性展出，和他的其他大多数作品一样，这幅作品同时探究着个体影响社会的无用性，然而却揭示了如果努力，深入持久地共鸣确实也可以取得成功。

自从1998年移居美国以后，张洹的作品发展到摄影和雕塑，同时仍然继续在国际博物展上创作大型戏剧表演。他最受认可的照片《家谱》（2000年），作品是当张洹的脸不断的被涂上墨以后捕捉的九张照片，书法家在他的脸上涂满了他的家族世系和其亲属的传说的文字。逐渐的，他把探究雕塑作为传达其关于社会和个人的观点的工具。2001年，他创作了一座大型青铜雕塑《和平》，雕塑的内容, 艺术家以自己为原型做了模型, 并把这水平地悬在刻满了张祖先的名字的青铜钟旁边。这个全身贴满金箔并

2

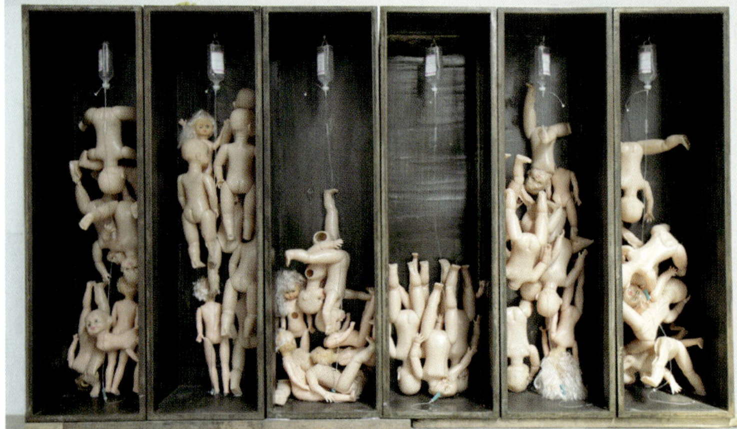

3

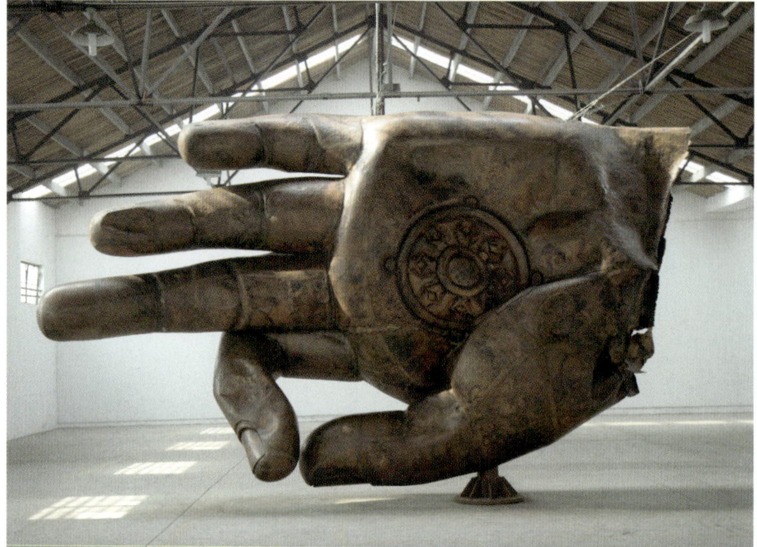

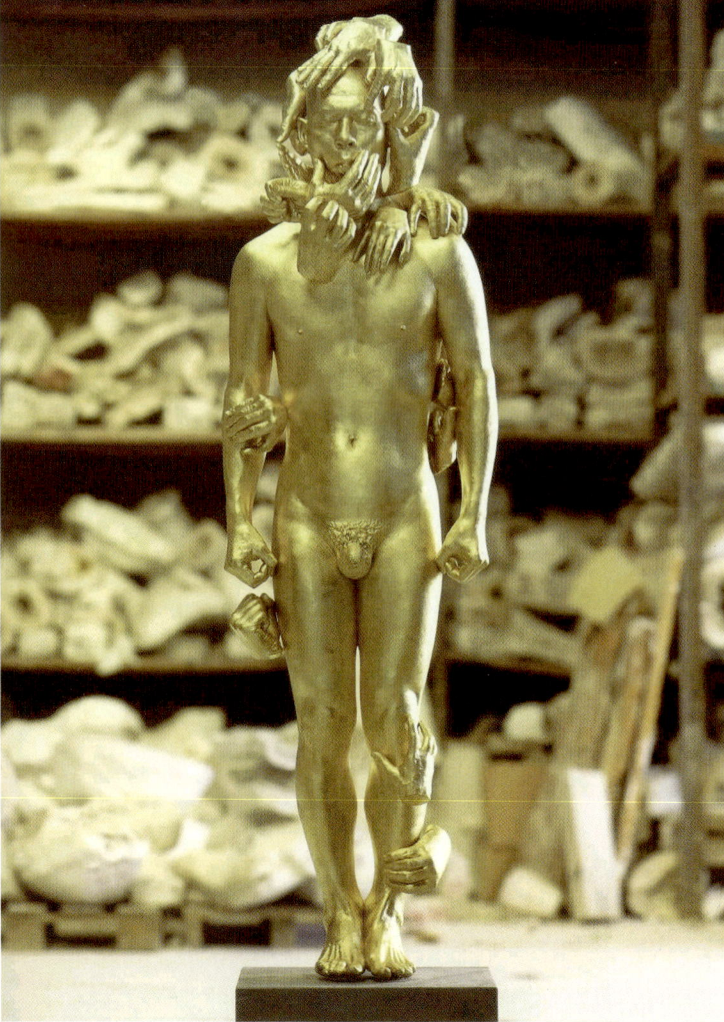

4

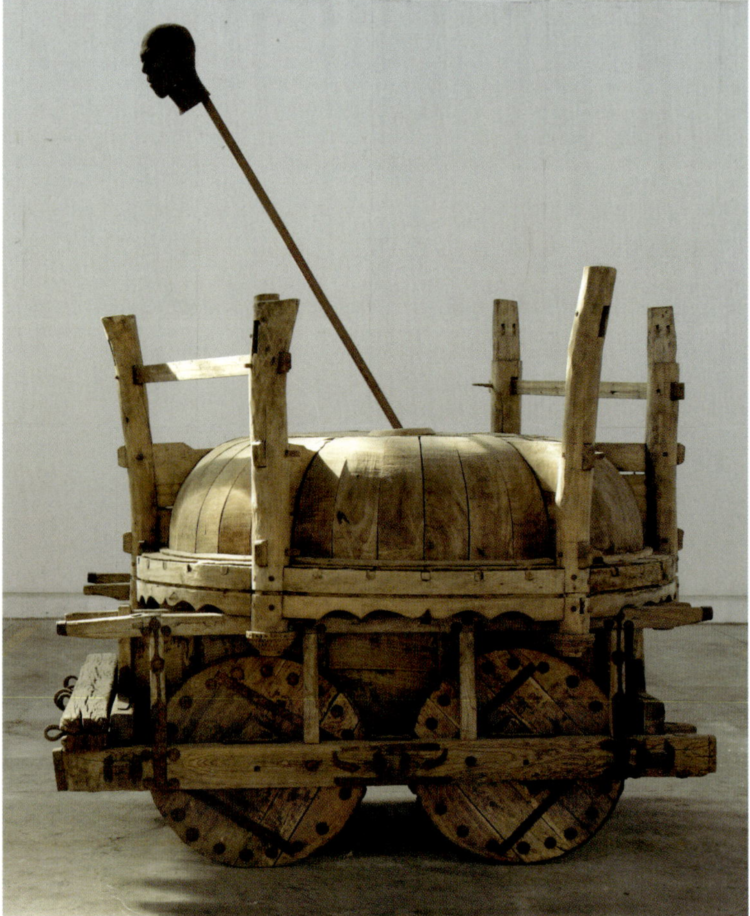

5

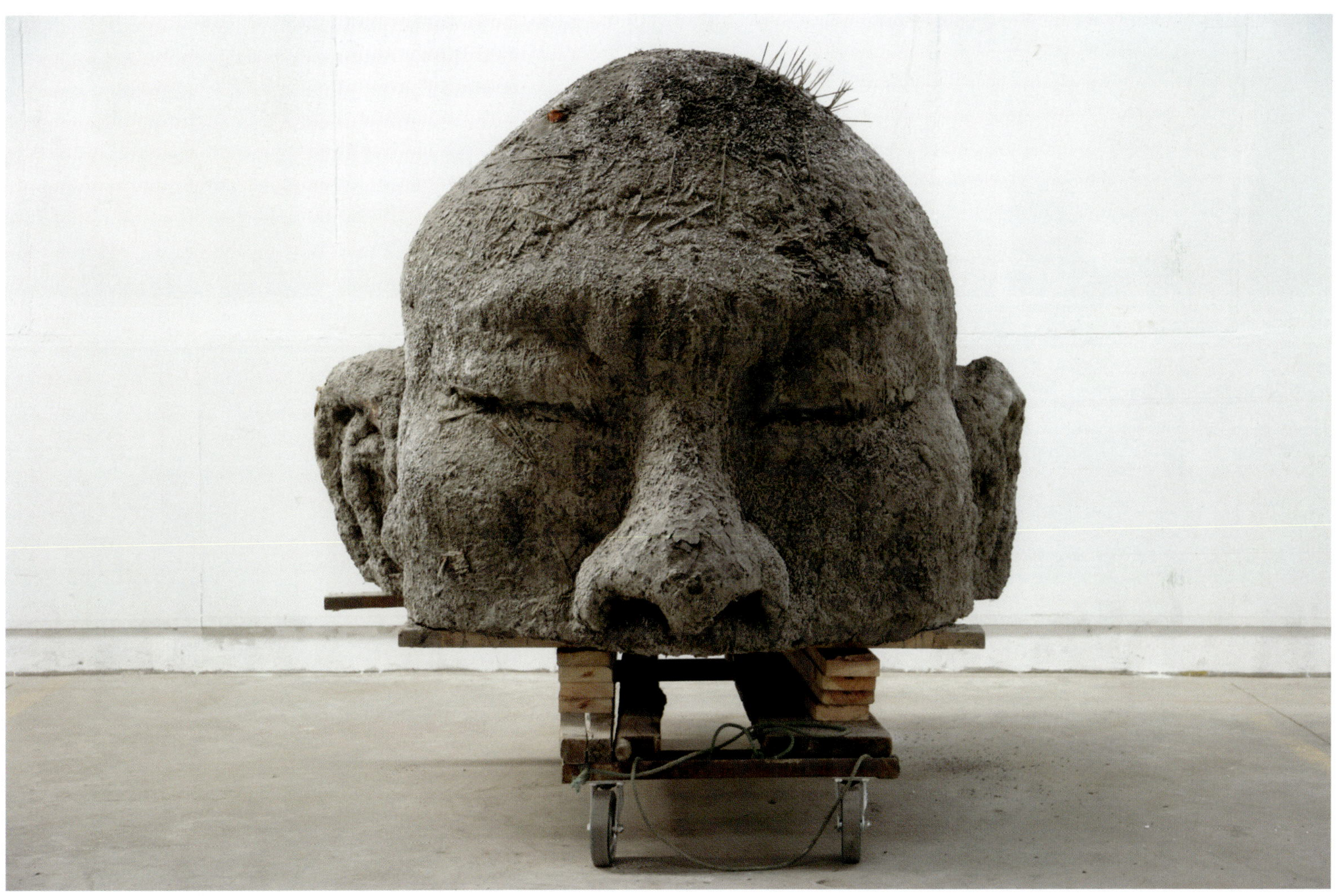

6

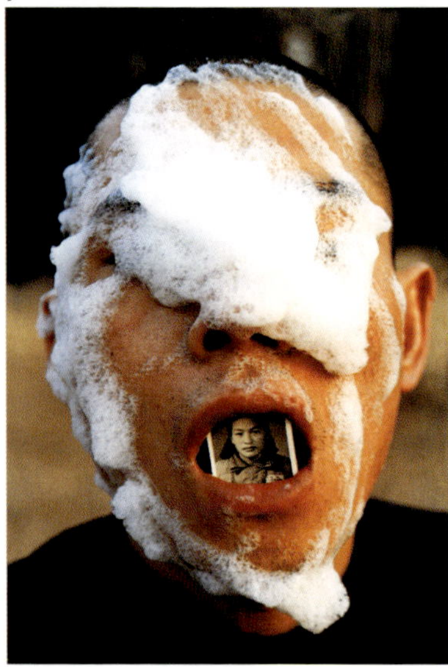
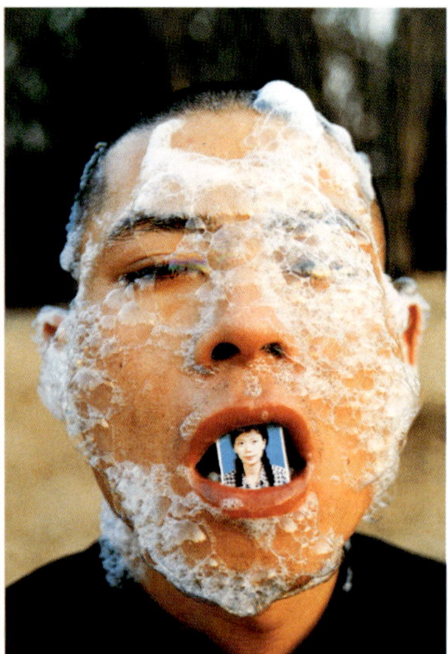
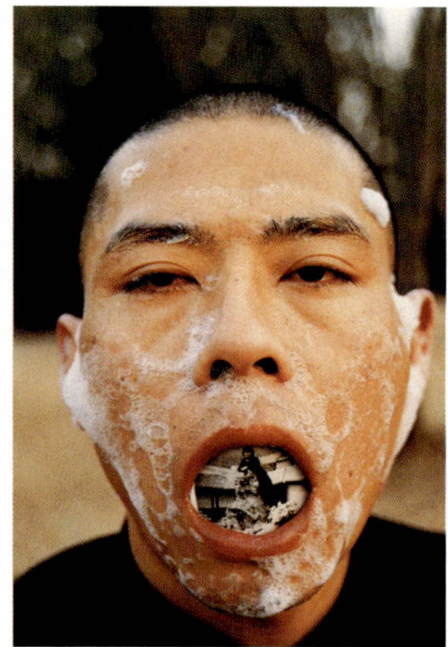
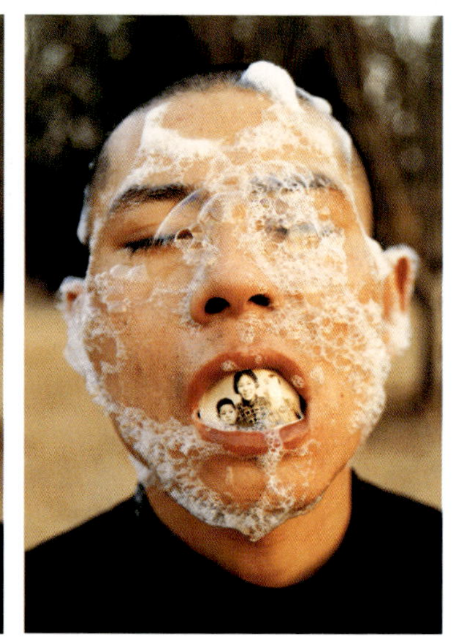

international museum venues. His most widely recognized image is "Family Tree" (2000), a series of nine photographs sequentially capturing the artist's face as it becomes increasingly covered in black ink, the result of calligraphers covering every inch of his profile with information about his family lineage and tales of his relatives. Increasingly, he has explored sculpture as a means for communicating his ideas about the individual and society. In 2001, he created "Peace", a large bronze sculpture in which a realistic cast of the artist's body hangs horizontally about a foot from a replica of a temple bell, inscribed with names of the artist's ancestors. The gilded body serves as a knocker for the bell, as if the only way for an artist to make a sound and be heard is to bang his head against all traditions and obstacles.

In the last two years, Zhang Huan has moved his practice back to China with a full atelier in Shanghai. There he has been making massive sculptural works, such as "Donkey" (2005), now in the Saatchi Collection. In this work, a monumental mechanical donkey replaces the artist's body as the prime instigator. The stuffed mechanical mule is seen humping a model of the Jin Mao Tower, the tallest building in China.

zeitig, dass ein tiefgründiger, nachhaltiger Widerhall doch zu erreichen ist, wenn man es nur (gemeinsam) versucht.

Nach seinem Umzug in die USA 1998 begann Zhang Huan, sich für Fotografie und Bildhauerei zu interessieren, während er weiterhin theatralische Massen-Performances im Umfeld internationaler Museen veranstaltete. Sein bekanntestes Bildwerk ist „Family Tree" (2000): Die Serie aus neun Aufnahmen zeigt das Gesicht des Künstlers, das sich nach und nach gänzlich mit schwarzer Tusche bedeckt, während Kalligraphen jeden freien Zentimeter mit Informationen über seine Abstammung und Geschichten über seine Verwandten vollschreiben. Daneben experimentiert Zhang mit der Bildhauerei als einem weiteren Weg zur Vermittlung seiner Gedanken über Individuum und Gesellschaft. So schuf er 2001 „Peace": Die große Bronzeskulptur besteht aus einem Abguss seines eigenen Körpers, der, horizontal befestigt, etwa 30 cm von der Replik einer Tempelglocke entfernt hängt, in die die Namen der Ahnen des Künstlers eingraviert sind. Der bronzene Körper dient als externer Klöppel für die Glocke – als bestehe die einzige Chance für einen Künstler, sich Gehör zu verschaffen, darin, sich den Kopf an allen Traditionen und Hindernissen einzurennen.

Seit 2005 arbeitet Zhang Huan wieder in China und unterhält ein großes Atelier in Shanghai. Dort produziert er gewaltige bildhauerische Werke, wie etwa „Donkey" (2005) – mittlerweile Teil der Saatchi-Sammlung. Hier ersetzt ein riesiger mechanischer Esel den Künstler als Akteur. Das ausgestopfte mechanische Langohr bespringt ein Modell des Jin Mao Tower, des höchsten Gebäudes in China.

人体模型当作敲击青铜钟的器具，好像这是艺术家表达自己的呼声并被社会所听到的唯一途径，也是自己有效反抗所有传统和束缚的唯一途径。

在过去两年中，张洹把实践重新转移到中国上海自己的工作室。张洹在上海制作了许多大型雕塑作品，像现收藏在伦敦萨奇画廊的《驴子》2005年，在作品种，极其呆板的猴子代替艺术家身体作为倡导者。作品中饱腹的机械螺正向中国最高建筑金茂大厦的模型上移动。

Barbara Pollack

8

9

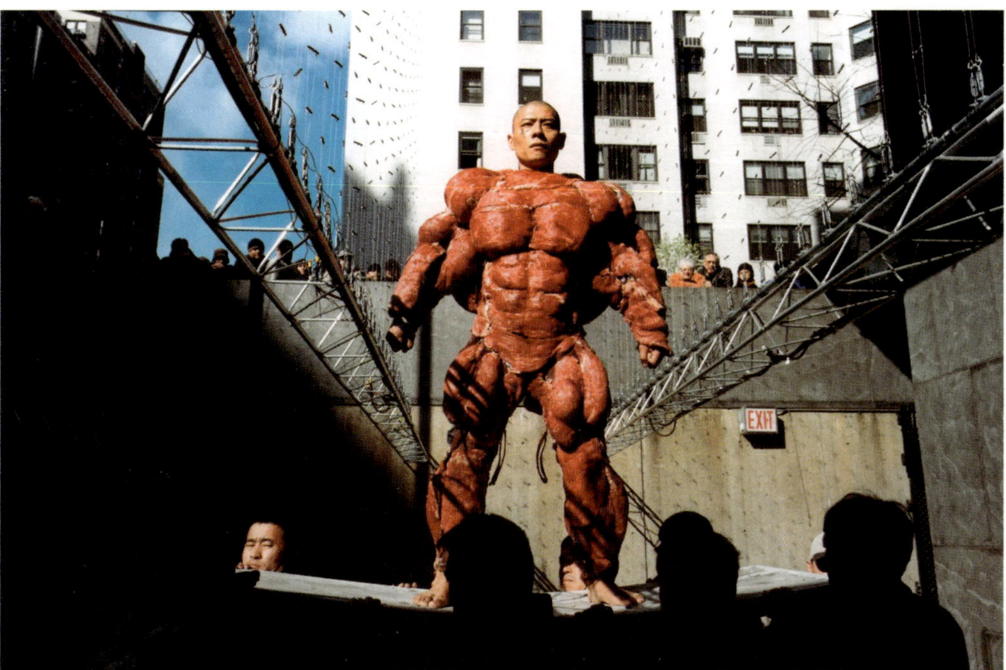

10

1 ***Donkey***, *2005*
Steel, 323 x 220 x 80 cm; Stahl, 323 x 220 x 80 cm
《驴子》2005年, 钢, 323 x 220 x 80 cm

2 ***Angel 1***, *1992*
Mixed media, 160 x 300 x 50 cm; Mixed media, 160 x 300 x 50 cm
《天使1》1992年, 混合材料, 160 x 300 x 50 cm

3 ***Buddha Hand***, *2006*
Copper, 450 x 670 x 140 cm; Kupfer, 450 x 670 x 140 cm
《佛手》2006年, 黄铜, 450 x 670 x 140 cm

4 ***Rubens***, *2000*
Bronze, life-size; Bronze, lebensgroß
《鲁本斯》2000年, 青铜, 真人大小

5 ***Waggon***, *2006*
Mixed media, 210 x 210 x 290 cm; Mixed media, 210 x 210 x 290 cm
《火车车厢》2006年, 混合材料, 210 x 210 x 290 cm

6 ***Ash Head No. 1***, *2007*
Ash, steel, wood, 228 x 227 x 244 cm
Asche, Stahl, Holz, 228 x 227 x 244 cm
《灰头 No. 1》2007年, 灰, 钢, 木头, 228 x 227 x 244 cm

7 ***Foam, 1998***
Photographs, 152 x 102 cm each; Fotografien, je 152 x 102 cm
《泡沫》1998年, 摄影, 152 x 102 cm 每个

8 ***Insect Painting No. 2***, *2007*
Oil on canvas, 250 x 360 cm; Öl auf Leinwand, 250 x 360 cm
《昆虫No. 2》2007年, 布面油画, 250 x 360 cm

9 ***Insect Painting No. 2***, *2007 (Detail)*
Oil on canvas, 250 x 360 cm; Öl auf Leinwand, 250 x 360 cm
《昆虫No. 2》2007年, 布面油画, 250 x 360 cm (详细)

10 ***My New York***, *2002*
Performance; Performance
《我的纽约》2002年, 表演

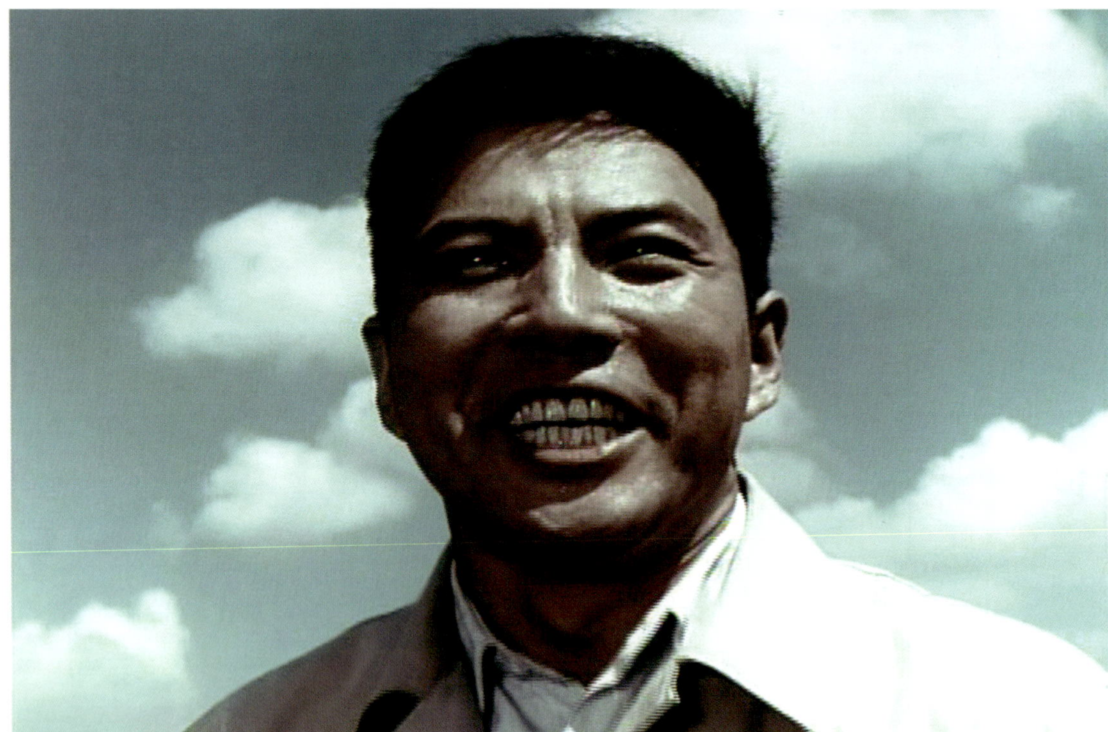

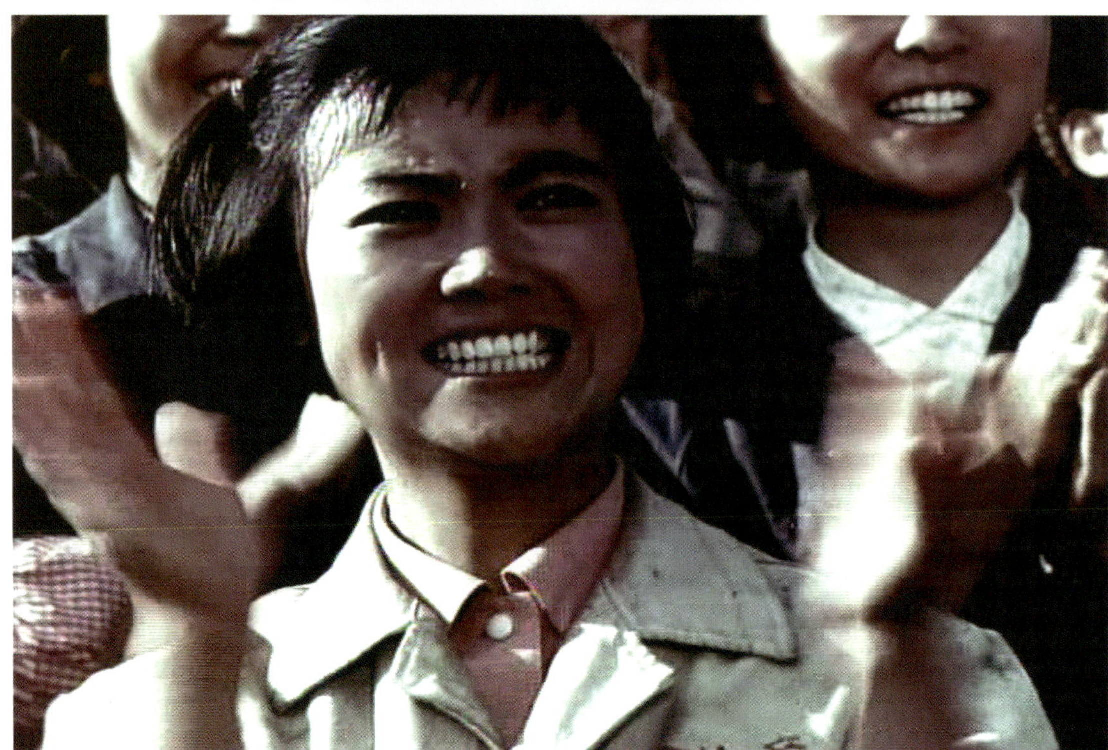

1

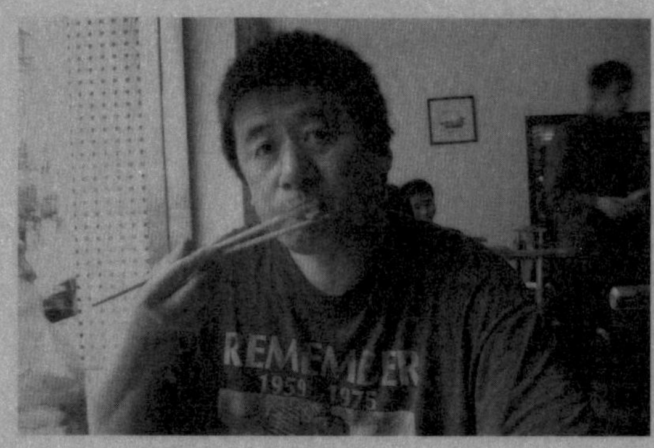

"Nowadays no other media are more popular and common than video. You can consider it as anything, a sculpture, a painting, or an installation. You can also regard it as a moment of your life or a fragment of one of your dreams."

„Heute ist kein Medium so beliebt wie Video – man kann es als eine Skulptur, ein Gemälde oder eine Installation benutzen oder als ein Fragment der eigenen Träume."

"现今其它媒介不是普遍和共同性比录影。您能它把任何东西，雕塑、绘画，或设施视为。您能并且认为它您的生活的片刻或片段您的梦想的当中一个。"

Born in 1957 in Hangzhou, China. Lives and works in Hangzhou
Geboren 1957 in Hangzhou, China. Lebt und arbeitet in Hangzhou
1957 年出生于杭州。住居工作在杭州

***Selected exhibitions* / Ausgewählte Ausstellungen /** 所选展览

1993	"Passaggi a Oriente", 45. Biennale di Venezia, Venice, Italy
1998	"Every day", 11th Biennial of Sydney, Pier 2/3, Sydney, Australia
2001	"Televisions", Kunsthalle Wien, Vienna, Austria
2002	"Pause", Gwangju Biennale 2002, Gwangju, Korea
2004	5th Shanghai Biennial, Shanghai Museum, Shanghai, China
2005–07	"Mahjong – Chinesische Gegenwartskunst aus der Sammlung Sigg", Kunstmuseum Bern, Berne, Switzerland; Hamburger Kunsthalle, Hamburg, Germany; Museum der Moderne, Salzburg, Austria
2006/07	"China Power Station I", Battersea Power Station, Serpentine Gallery, UK, London; Astrup Fearnley Museum of Modern Art, Oslo, Norway

1993年	《东方之路》第45届威尼斯双年展
1998年	《每天》第十一届悉尼双年展，澳大利亚
2001年	《电视-视觉的梦幻》奥地里维也纳艺术宫
2002年	《暂停》韩国光州双年展
2004年	第5届上海双年展，上海博物馆，上海
2005–07年	《麻将》西克中国当代艺术收藏展，伯尔尼美术馆 瑞士；汉堡美术馆，汉堡，德国；萨尔茨保现代美术馆 奥地利
2006/07	《中国电站I》蛇形画廊，巴特西电站 伦敦 英国；Astrup Fearnley 现代美术馆，奥斯陆，挪威

***Selected publications* / Ausgewählte Publikationen /** 所选著作

Francesca Dal Lago: "Contemporary Chinese Art: Neither Panda Bears nor Student's Homework. An Interview with Zhang Peili", in: John Clark (ed.): "Chinese Art at the End of the Millennium", Hong Kong 2000

Dal Lago, Francesca:《当代中国艺术：不猫熊亦不学生的家庭作业》。《张培力的 采访》，于 Clark, John（编者）:《中国艺术在千年的结尾》，香港：新艺术媒介，2000年

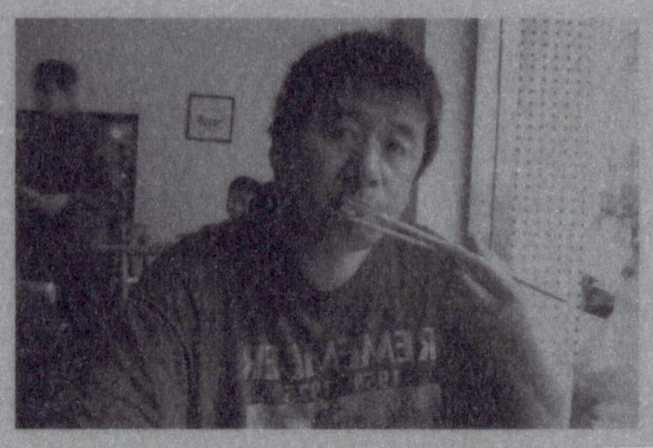

"Nowadays no other media are more popular and common than video. You can consider it as anything, a sculpture, a painting, or an installation. You can also regard it as a moment of your life or a fragment of one of your dreams."

„Heute ist kein Medium so beliebt wie Video - man kann es als eine Skulptur, ein Gemälde oder eine Installation benutzen oder als ein Fragment der eigenen Träume."

"现今其它媒介不是普遍和共同性比录影。您能它把任何东西，雕塑，绘画，或设施视为。您能并且认为它您的生活的片刻或片段您的梦想的当中一个。"

Born in 1957 in Hangzhou, China. Lives and works in Hangzhou
Geboren 1957 in Hangzhou, China. Lebt und arbeitet in Hangzhou
1957 年出生于杭州。住居工作在杭州

Selected exhibitions / Ausgewählte Ausstellungen / 所选展览

1993 "Passaggi a Oriente", 45. Biennale di Venezia, Venice, Italy
1998 "Every day", 11th Biennial of Sydney, Pier 2/3, Sydney, Australia
2001 "Televisions", Kunsthalle Wien, Vienna, Austria
2002 "Pause", Gwangju Biennale 2002, Gwangju, Korea
2004 5th Shanghai Biennial, Shanghai Museum, Shanghai, China
2005-07 "Mahjong - Chinesische Gegenwartskunst aus der Sammlung Sigg", Kunstmuseum Bern, Berne, Switzerland; Hamburger Kunsthalle, Hamburg, Germany; Museum der Moderne, Salzburg, Austria
2006/07 "China Power Station I", Battersea Power Station, Serpentine Gallery, UK, London; Astrup Fearnley Museum of Modern Art, Oslo, Norway

1993年 《东方之路》第45届威尼斯双年展
1998年 《每天》第十一届悉尼双年展，澳大利亚
2001年 《电视-视觉的梦幻》奥地利维也纳艺术宫
2002年 《暂停》韩国光州双年展
2004年 第5届上海双年展，上海博物馆，上海
2005-07年 《麻将》西克中国当代艺术收藏展，伯尔尼美术馆 瑞士；汉堡美术馆，汉堡，德国；萨尔茨堡现代美术馆 奥地利
2006/07 《中国电站I》蛇形画廊，巴特西电站 伦敦 英国：Astrup Fearnley 现代美术馆，奥斯陆，挪威

Selected publications / Ausgewählte Publikationen / 所选著作

Francesca Dal Lago: "Contemporary Chinese Art: Neither Panda Bears nor Student's Homework. An Interview with Zhang Peili", in: John Clark (ed.): "Chinese Art at the End of the Millennium", Hong Kong 2000

Dal Lago, Francesca:《当代中国艺术：不猫熊亦不学生的家庭作业》。《张培力的 采访》，于 Clark, John（编著）：《中国艺术在千年的结尾》，香港：新艺术媒介，2000年

ZHANG PEILI 张培力

[tʂaŋ pʰeili]

Zhang Peili is undeniably a pioneer of Chinese video art and one of its most important representatives till this day. In 1984 he graduated from the Oil Painting Department of Zhejiang Art Academy (present Chinese Art Academy). His works were presented in New York's P.S.1 Contemporary Art Center, in Kunsthalle Hamburg, at 45th and 48th Biennial of Venice, at the 3rd Triennial of Asian Contemporary Art, at the 11th Biennale of Sydney, and 4th Triennial of Guangzhou. Zhang Peili lives at present in Hangzhou as director of the New Media Art Department of the Chinese Art Academy.

In his early works like "No Jazz Tonight" (1987) and his "Emulsion Glove" (1988) series he proved very early to be an excellent master of painting, displaying that he is surpassing the media and controlling the spirit's dynamic, entrusting his structures with an unusual sensitive degree of the intrinsic plot of intense visual images. In the mid 1980s he was one of the core members of the Hangzhou artist group "85 New Space" (1985) and "The Pond Society" (1986) and an important representative of China's experimental artists.

In the centre of Zhang's works is the individual living in a world which cannot heal the feeling of absurdity and apathy. Because of these words expressing the untrustworthiness of the world, the individual has to return to its own body unceasingly. Therefore, he started to use video art as medium in the late 1980s, being one of the earliest artists on this field, but Zhang Peili doesn't intend to be a determinist of the technique nor a futurist, on the contrary, he persisted in controlling this kind of media, the video installations with utmost bodily ideas from the very beginning of its usage.

Zhang Peili's bodily thoughts are constructed on this kind of supposition: the bodily experience is based on complex cultural view points and choice, but the medical body can never be completely replaced by the political and economic one, while the body is sensitive, frail and easy to be injured.

Zhang Peili gilt als Pionier der chinesischen Videokunst und bis auf den heutigen Tag als einer ihrer wichtigsten Vertreter. 1984 schloss er sein Studium an der Zhejiang Art Academy (heutige Chinese Art Academy) im Fachbereich Ölmalerei ab. Seine Werke wurden in New Yorks P.S.1 Contemporary Art Center, in der Kunsthalle Hamburg, auf der 45. und 48. Biennale von Venedig sowie auf der 3. Triennale der Asian Contemporary Art, der 11. Biennale von Sydney und der 4. Triennale von Guangzhou gezeigt. Zhang Peili lebt heute in Hangzhou als Leiter des Fachbereichs Neue Medienkunst der Chinese Art Academy.

Schon mit seinen frühen Werken, wie „No Jazz Tonight" (1987) und der Serie „Emulsion Glove" (1988), bewies Zhang, dass er ein meisterhafter Maler ist, der aber über das Medium Malerei hinausstrebt und ihre geistige Dynamik so steuert, dass die malerischen Strukturen einen ungewöhnlichen Grad an Empfindsamkeit gewinnen, die den Kern seiner visuell starken Bilder ausmachen. Mitte der 1980er Jahre gehörte Zhang zum inneren Kern der Künstlergruppe „85 New Space" (1985) sowie zur „The Pond Society" (1986) in Hangzhou. Gleichzeitig war er ein bedeutender Vertreter der experimentellen chinesischen Kunst.

Im Mittelpunkt von Zhangs Arbeiten steht der einzelne Mensch, der sich mit einer Welt konfrontiert sieht, die ihn in einen Zustand der Absurdität und Apathie versetzt. Das einzige, dem er vertrauen kann, ist er selbst und der eigene Körper. Diese Beschäftigung mit dem Körper brachte Zhang in den späten 1980er Jahren als einen der ersten chinesischen Künstler dazu, sich dem Medium Video zuzuwenden. Dennoch wurde er nicht zu einem Technikfetischisten oder Futuristen, sondern beharrt darauf, dieses Medium bewusst in seinem Sinn zu steuern, sodass auch seinen Videoinstallationen die Idee der Körperlichkeit innewohnt.

Zhang Peilis körperbezogenes Denken geht von folgender Annahme aus: Das körperliche Erleben basiert auf komplexen kulturellen Standpunkten und Vorgaben, aber der materielle Körper kann nie durch den politischen oder

张培力是无可争议的中国录像艺术先驱，今天依然是重要的代表之一。1957年张培力出生于中国杭州一个医生家庭。1984年他毕业于浙江美术学院油画系（现中国美术学院）。他的作品曾在纽约现代艺术博物馆、汉堡火车站国家美术馆、第45届和第48届威尼斯双年展、第3届亚太当代艺术三年展，第11届悉尼双年展、第4届里昂双年展、第4届光州双年展等多处展出。张培力现居中国杭州，任中国美术学院新媒体艺术系主任。
在他的早期架上画中，《今晚没有爵士》和乳胶手套系列等早就证明了他是绘画的绝顶高手，并表现出他超越媒介，控制精神力度，和把内在情节赋予强烈视觉形象的异常的敏感程度。

八十年代中期，杭州艺术群体"八五新空间"（1985年）和"池社"（1986年）的核心成员，并成为中国实验艺术的主要代表人物。他的工作集中于个人在世界之中不可治愈的荒谬感和冷漠感。因为这个话语世界的不足信任，个人必须不断地回归到自己的身体。因此，当他在八十年代晚期和九十年代初转向录像艺术这种媒介的时候，作为录像艺术的最早实践者，张培力从来都不是一个技术决定论者或者未来主义者，相反他始终坚持用极端的身体观念来驾驭录像装置这种媒介。

张的身体思想建立在这样的假设上：身体感受是所有更复杂的文化观点和选择的基础，医学的身体永远无法完全被政治和经济的身体所替代，而身体是敏感，脆弱，容易受到伤害的。张培力的态度影响了许多年轻的艺术家，尽管年轻人对身体的自恋带有更多反文化色彩。

张培力的成就是以个人经验超越中国文化身份获得普遍性力量的典型个案。他的经典录像作品如《儿童乐园》、《不确却的快感》之中，你很难看到对中国文化符号的简单引用，而是力求跨越文化差异，在身体与空间限制，身体与机械运动等普遍议题中直接思考人性。

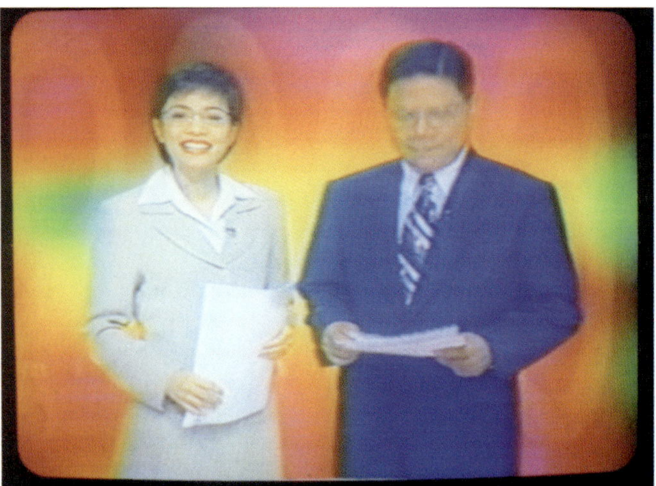

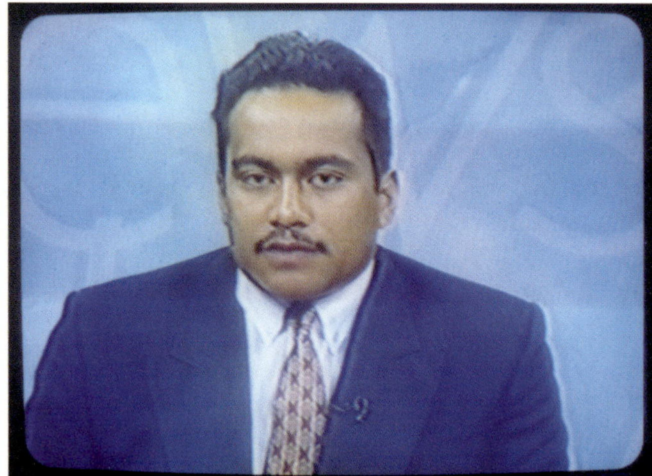

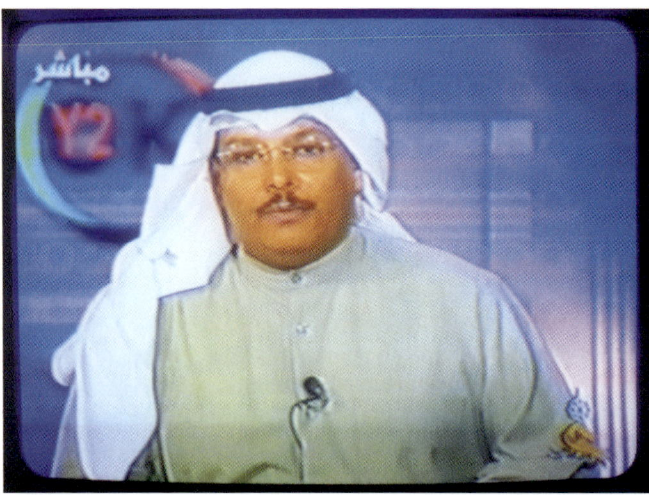

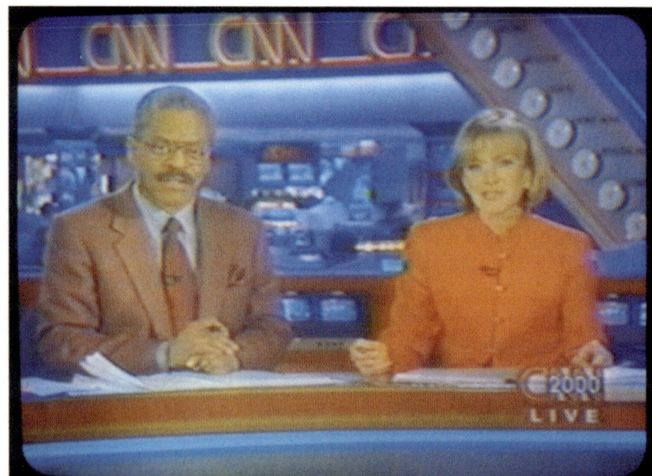

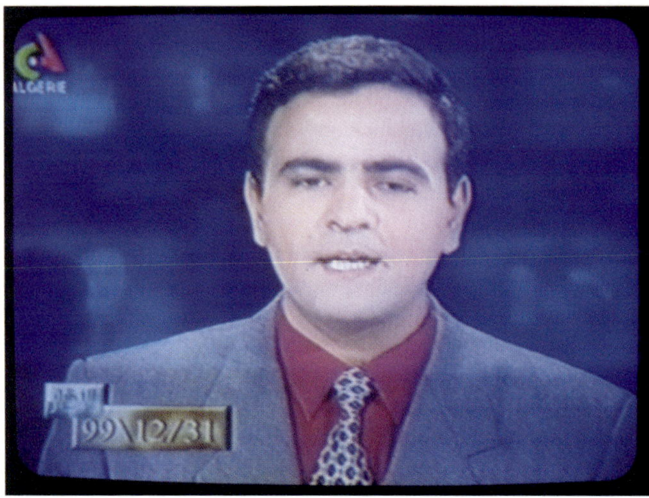

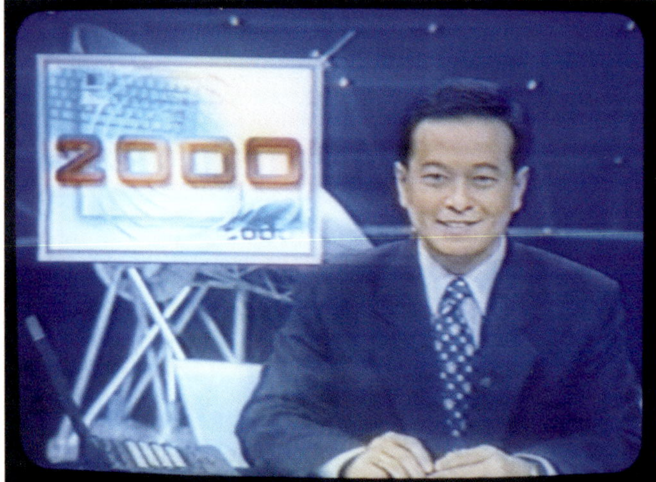

2

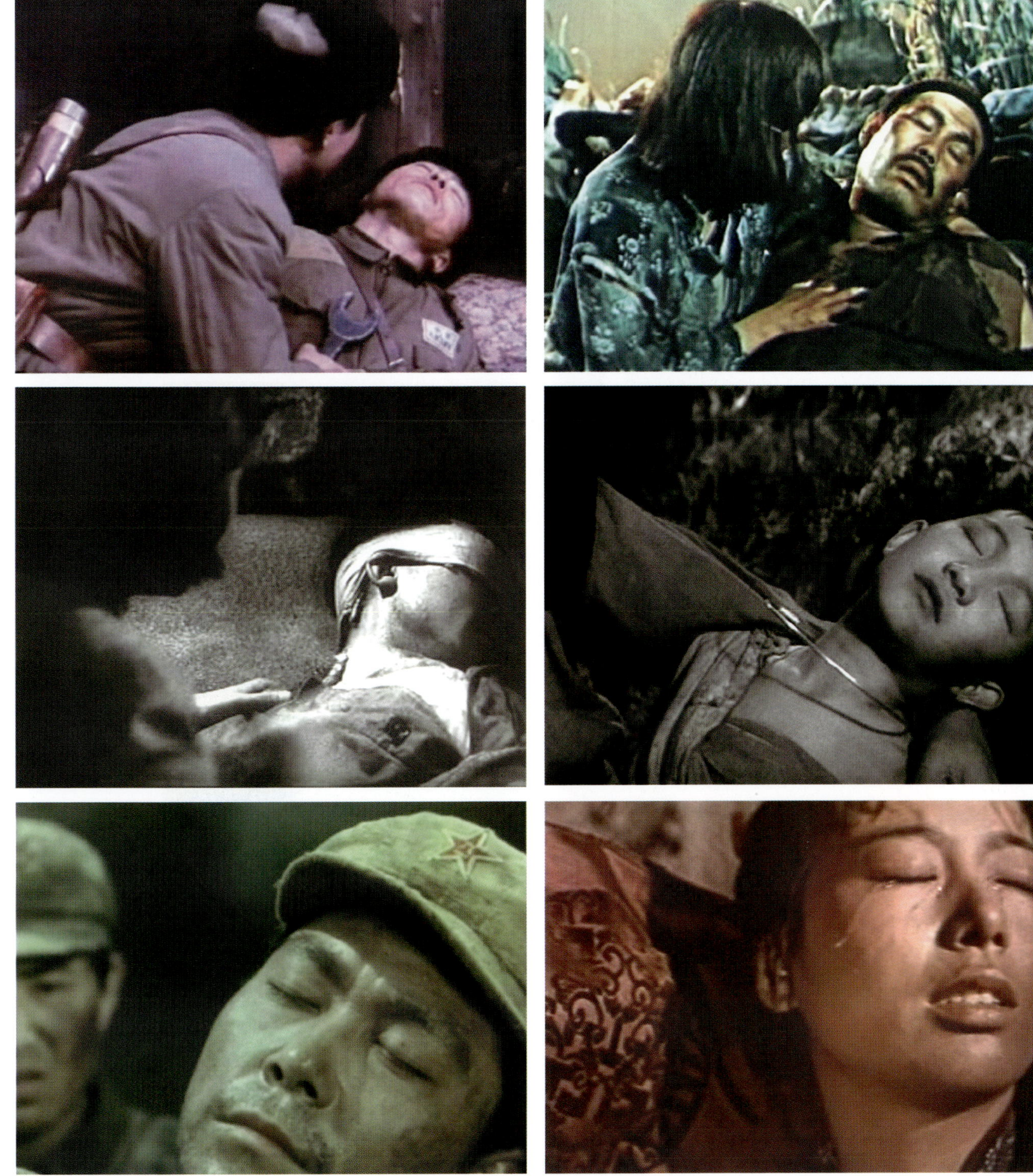

3

4

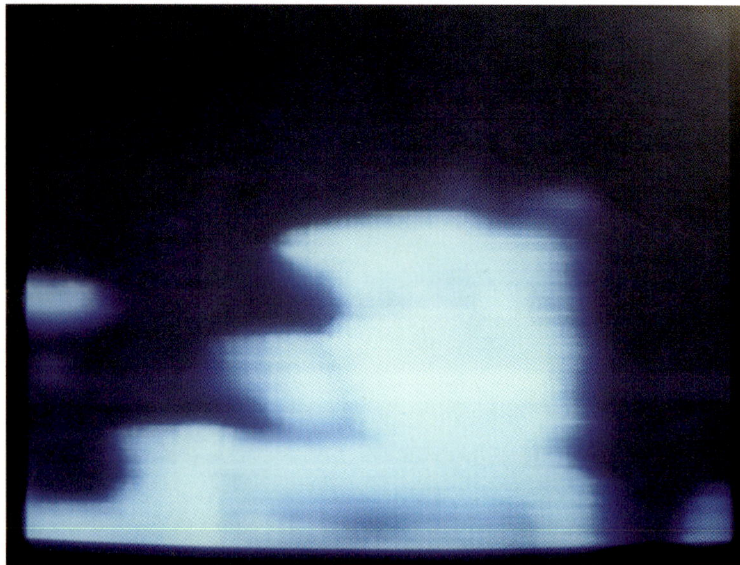

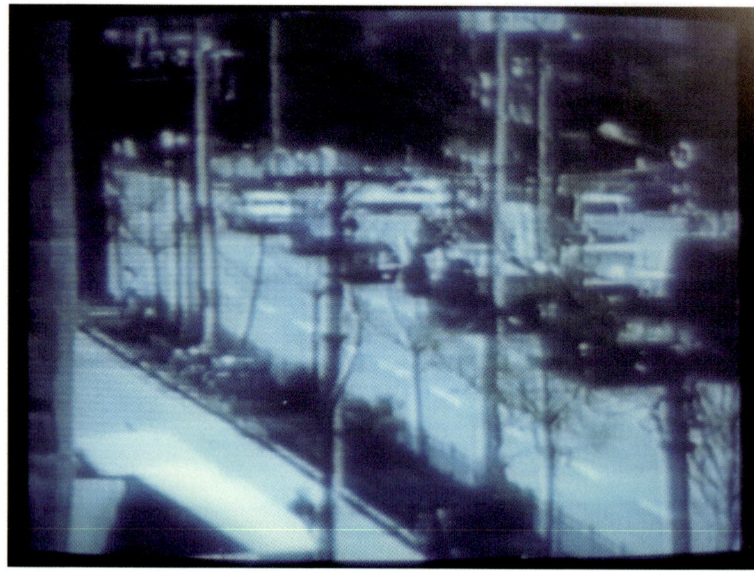

Zhang's attitude influences many young artists, although young people's narcissism bears contrarily artistic colours.

Zhang Peili's achievement is the surpassing of China's cultural identity by individual experience, becoming a typical model of universal strength. In his video works like "Children playground" (1993) and "Uncertain pleasure" (1996) he looks down at the simple use of Chinese cultural symbols, seeking to surpass the cultural differences with effort and ponders human character directly in universal subjects of body and space limits, body and mechanical movement.

Zhang Peili's recent creations turned again towards a rereading of historical images, and remakes of old movies, the absurdity of feelings being still his main subject of his deep rooted artistic style.

wirtschaftlichen ersetzt werden, da der Leib empfindlich, zerbrechlich und leicht zu verletzen ist. Zhangs Haltung beeinflusste viele junge Künstler, auch wenn der Narzissmus der jüngeren ganz andere künstlerische Farben trägt.

Zhang Peilis Leistung besteht darin, in gewisser Weise die kulturelle Identität Chinas hinter der eigenen Erfahrung verblassen zu lassen und daraus eine neue universale Stärke zu gewinnen. In seinen Videoarbeiten wie „Children playground" (1993) oder „Uncertain pleasure" (1996) dokumentiert er die überaus schlichte Verwendung der gängigen chinesischen Kultursymbole und versucht zugleich, die kulturellen Unterschiede zu überwinden sowie den menschlichen Charakter direkt im universalen Thema des Körpers und der Begrenzung seines Raums zu ergründen.

Zhang Peilis jüngste Arbeiten widmen sich einer neuen Deutung historischer Bilder und dem Remake von alten Kinofilmen. Nach wie vor ist aber die Absurdität der Gefühle das Hauptthema seines künstlerischen Schaffens.

张培力的近期创作转向对历史图像的重新解读，在对老电影画面的重新剪辑中，荒诞感依然是其根深蒂固的风格。

Qiu Zhijie

5

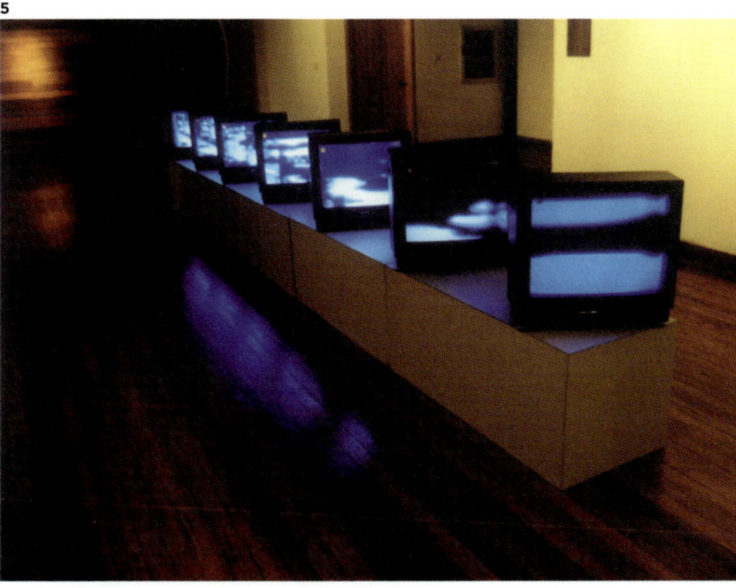

1 ***Happiness***, *2006*
Video, 6 min 39 sec; Video, 6 Min. 39 Sek.
《幸福》2006年，录像, 6分 39秒

2 ***Broadcast at the same time***, *2003*
Video, 10 min 30 sec; Video, 10 Min. 30 Sek.
《同时播放》2003年，录像, 10分 30秒

3 ***Last Words***, *2003*
Video, 20 min 28 sec; Video, 20 Min. 28 Sek.
《遗言》2003年，录像, 20分 28秒

4 ***Focal Distance***, *1996*
Video, 15 min; Video, 15 Min.
《焦距》1996年, 录像, 15分钟

5 ***Focal Distance***, *1996*
Video, installation view; Video, Installationsansicht
《焦距》1996年, 录像, 装置实景

6 ***Report on 1988 Hepatitis***, *1988*
Glass, rubber gloves, plaster, varnish, 48 x 170 x 7.5 cm (detail)
Glas, Gummihandschuhe, Gips, Lack, 48 x 170 x 7,5 cm (Detail)
《1988年甲肝情况的报告》1988年, 玻璃、橡胶、手套、石膏、清漆 48 x 170 x 7.5 cm（详细）

7 ***Report on 1988 Hepatitis***, *1988*
Glass, rubber gloves, plaster, varnish, 48 x 170 x 7.5 cm; Glas, Gummihandschuhe, Gips, Lack, 48 x 170 x 7,5 cm
《1988年甲肝情况的报告》1988年, 玻璃、橡胶、手套、石膏 、清漆 48 x 170 x 7.5 cm

6

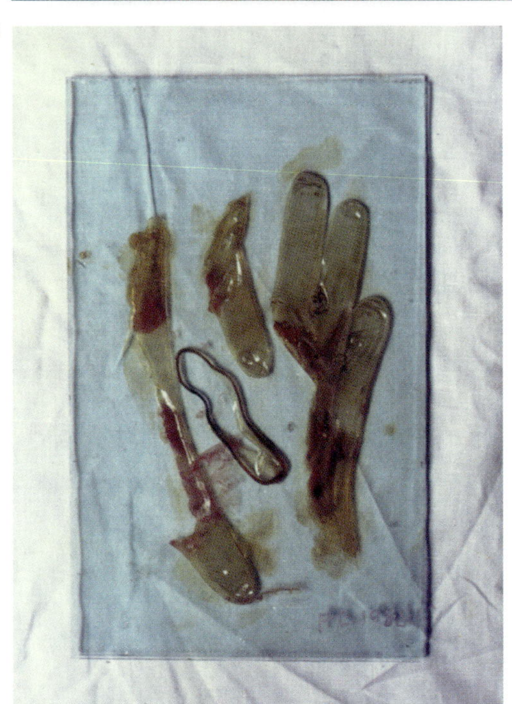

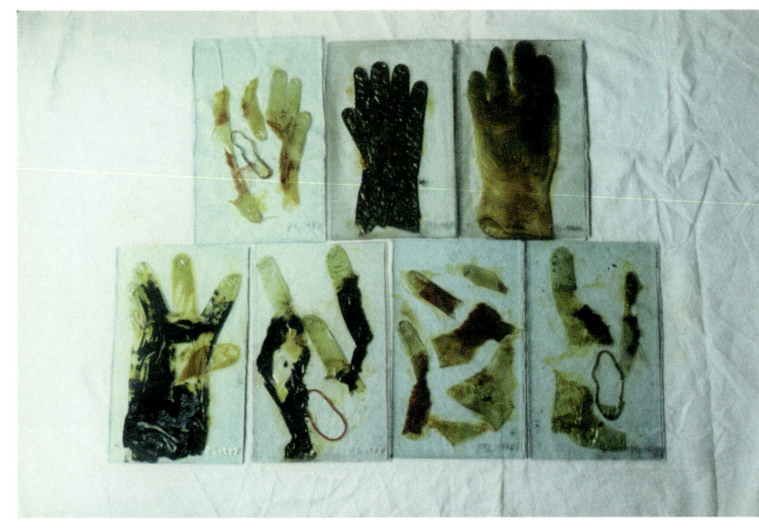

● 张培力 ●

褐皮书一号通告

《褐皮书一号》于 1988 年 4 月20 日至 6 月21 日完成。

一、《褐皮书一号》全部内容包括：①乳胶手套，或被支解的乳胶手套 ②说明书。

二、《褐皮书一号》以邮寄方式"展示"。

三、邮寄对象：国内各美术学院各系本科生研究生(本科一年级除外)。

四、在邮寄对象范围内以抽签方式选定具体接受人。

五、抽签由助手（甲、乙）代理。

六、邮寄相继进行四次。

七、每次邮寄均寄给每位接受者邮件一份，内容相同。

八、第一次邮寄 时间：4月20日 内容：乳胶手套一只，说明书一份（油印品） 邮寄地点：杭州市邮政局朝晖支局 邮政编码：310014 第二次邮寄 时间：5月28日 内容：一只被支解为20块的乳胶手套碎片一份(即1／20只乳胶手套)，说明书一份(油印品) 邮寄地点：杭州市邮政局中山中路支局 邮政编码：31001 第三次邮寄 时间：6月4日 内容：一只被支解为30块的乳胶手套碎片一份(即1／30只乳胶手套)，说明书一份(油印品) 邮寄地点、邮政编码：(同第一次邮寄) 第四次邮寄 时间：6月21日 内容：说明书第八条(油印品) 邮寄地点：杭州市邮政局延安路支局 邮政编码：310006

九、第一批邮件接受者共18人；第二批共20人；第三批共30人；第四批共89人。

十、邮件封皮均呈淡褐色。本人今后将不定期地针对不同对象采取不同内容的邮寄行动。

附件一：说明书 本人受命向你寄赠本品，并作说明如下：①依照有关规则，确认你为赠品接受人(以下称接受人)。②其余接受人均在你周围。③本品与你过去之德行、过错无关。③不要将本品转赠他人。⑤不要查找其他接受人。⑥不要查找本品寄赠人。⑦不要查找本品寄赠人之授命人。

附件二：接受人名单（略）

7

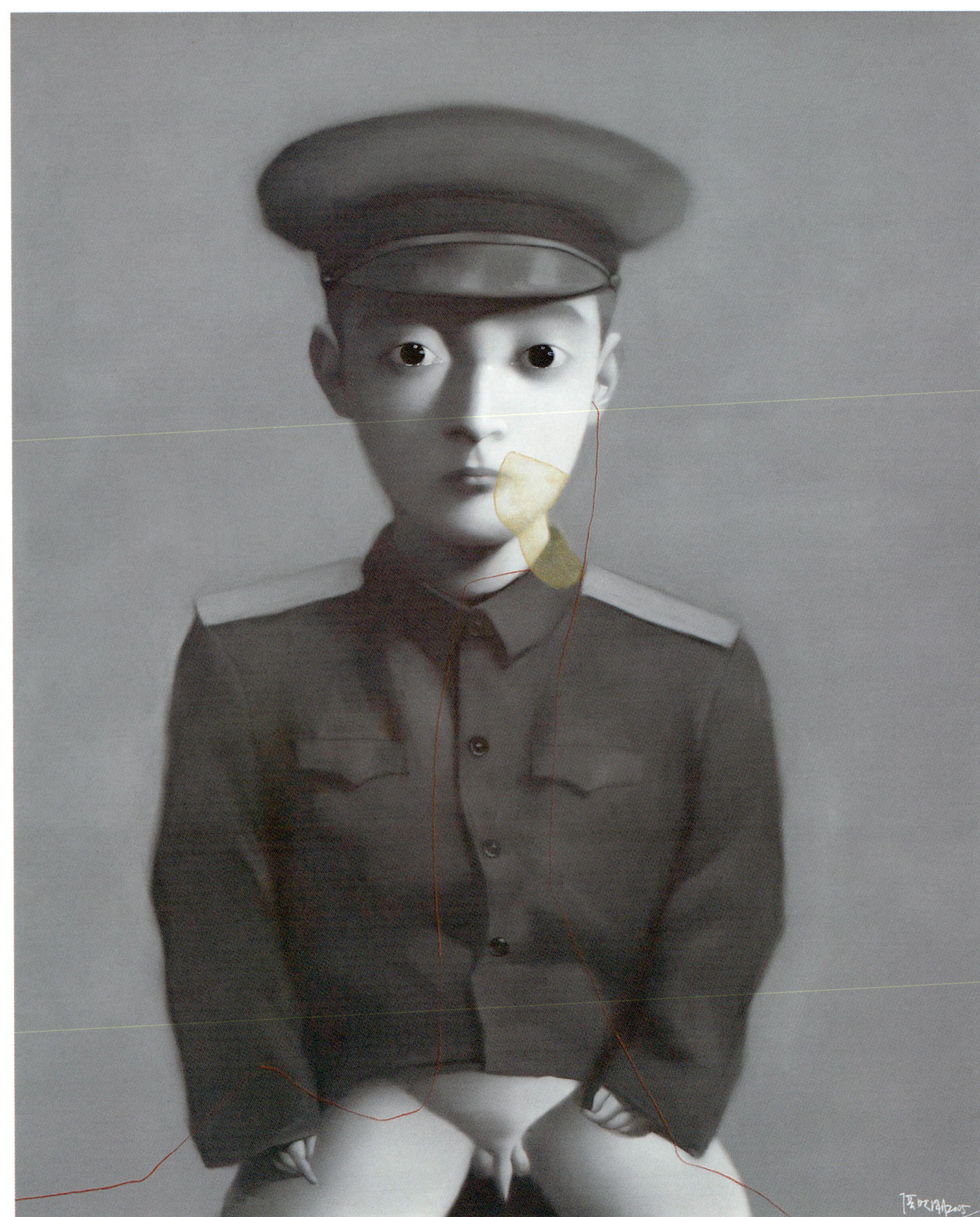

1

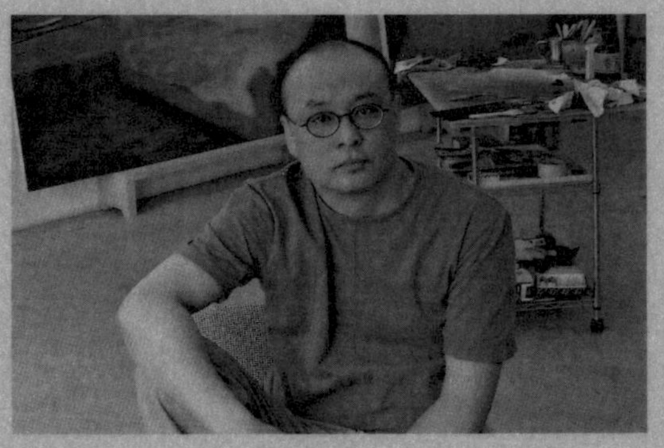

"We all live 'in a big family'. The first lesson we have to learn is how to protect ourselves and keep our experiences locked up in an inner chamber away from the prying eyes of others, while living in harmony as a member of this big family."

„Wir alle sind Teil einer ‚großen Familie'. Und die erste Lektion, die wir lernen müssen, ist, uns zu schützen und unsere Erfahrungen in einer inneren Kammer vor den neugierigen Augen der anderen zu verschließen, während wir gleichzeitig in Harmonie mit dieser Familie zu leben haben."

"我们都生活在一个大家庭里，我们必须学习的第一课 就是如何保护我们自己以及把自己的经验锁在内心的深处，远离别人的偷窥，而与此同时作为大家庭的一员和谐生活着。"

Born in 1958 in Kunming, China. Lives and works in Beijing
Geboren 1958 in Kunming, China. Lebt und arbeitet in Peking
1958 年出生于中国云南省昆明。居住工作在北京

***Selected exhibitions* / Ausgewählte Ausstellungen / 所选展览**

1994	21. Bienal de São Paulo, São Paulo, Brazil
1997	"Bloodline: The Big Family", Gallery of the Central Academy of Fine Arts, Beijing, China
1998	"Zhang Xiaogang", Hanart TZ Gallery, Hong Kong, China
1999	"Les Camarades", Galerie de France, Paris, France
2000	"Zhang Xiaogang 2000", Max Protetch, New York, NY, USA
2004	"Umbilical Cord of History: Paintings by Zhang Xiaogang", Hong Kong Arts Centre, Hong Kong, China
2007/08	"Zhang Xiaogang", Sara Hidén Museum, Tampere, Finland

1994年	第21届圣保罗双年展，圣保罗，巴西
1997年	《血缘：大家庭1997》中央美院画廊，北京中国
1998年	《张晓刚》汉雅轩画廊，香港
1999年	《同志》法兰西画廊，巴黎，法国
2000年	《张晓刚2000》Max Protetch 画廊，纽约
2004年	《时代的脐带 -- 张晓刚绘画》香港艺术中心，香港
2007/08年	《张晓刚》Sara Hidén 博物馆，坦佩雷，芬兰

***Selected publications* / Ausgewählte Publikationen / 所选著作**

Li Xiangyang (ed.): "Ost + West. Ausstellung für die zeitgenössische Kunst aus China", Vienna 2002
Chang Tsong-zung: "Between Reality and Illusion", Hong Kong 2004
Li Xiangyang, Shanghai Art Museum (eds.): "Dreaming of the Dragon's Nation", Shanghai 2005
Edward Lucie-Smith: "Zhang Xiaogang", Pittsburgh 2006

Li Xiangyang（编者）:《东+西。中国当代艺术展》维也纳 2002 年
Chang Tsong-zung（著）:《现实和幻觉之间》，汉雅轩画廊，香港2004年
Li Xiangyang 上海美术馆（编者）:《龙族之梦。中国当代艺术展》，现代艺术爱尔兰博物馆，都伯林2005年
Lucie-Smith, Edward（著）:《张晓刚》，匹兹堡2006年

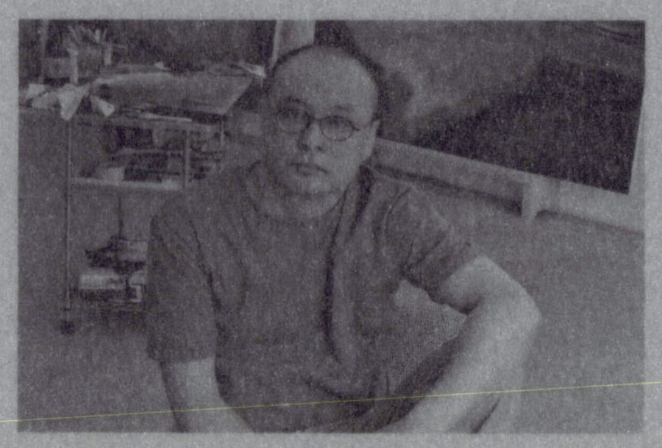

"We all live 'in a big family'. The first lesson we have to learn is how to protect ourselves and keep our experiences locked up in an inner chamber away from the prying eyes of others, while living in harmony as a member of this big family."

„Wir alle sind Teil einer ‚großen Familie'. Und die erste Lektion, die wir lernen müssen, ist, uns zu schützen und unsere Erfahrungen in einer inneren Kammer vor den neugierigen Augen der anderen zu verschließen, während wir gleichzeitig in Harmonie mit dieser Familie zu leben haben."

"我们都生活在一个大家庭里，我们必须学习的第一课 就是如何保护我们自己以及把自己的经验锁在内心的深处，远离别人的偷窥，而与此同时作为大家庭的一员和谐生活着。"

Born in 1958 in Kunming, China. Lives and works in Beijing
Geboren 1958 in Kunming, China. Lebt und arbeitet in Peking
1958 年出生于中国云南省昆明。居住工作在北京

Selected exhibitions / Ausgewählte Ausstellungen / 所选展览

1994 21. Bienal de São Paulo, São Paulo, Brazil
1997 "Bloodline: The Big Family", Gallery of the Central Academy of Fine Arts, Beijing, China
1998 "Zhang Xiaogang", Hanart TZ Gallery, Hong Kong, China
1999 "Les Camarades", Galerie de France, Paris, France
2000 "Zhang Xiaogang 2000", Max Protetch, New York, NY, USA
2004 "Umbilical Cord of History: Paintings by Zhang Xiaogang", Hong Kong Arts Centre, Hong Kong, China
2007/08 "Zhang Xiaogang", Sara Hidén Museum, Tampere, Finland

1994年 第21届圣保罗双年展，圣保罗，巴西
1997年 《血缘：大家庭1997》中央美院画廊，北京中国
1998年 《张晓刚》汉雅轩画廊，香港
1999年 《同志》法兰西画廊，巴黎，法国
2000年 《张晓刚2000》Max Protetch 画廊，纽约
2004年 《时代的脐带 — 张晓刚绘画》香港艺术中心，香港
2007/08年 《张晓刚》Sara Hidén 博物馆，坦佩雷，芬兰

Selected publications / Ausgewählte Publikationen / 所选著作

Li Xiangyang (ed.): "Ost + West. Ausstellung für die zeitgenössische Kunst aus China", Vienna 2002
Chang Tsong-zung: "Between Reality and Illusion", Hong Kong 2004
Li Xiangyang, Shanghai Art Museum (eds.): "Dreaming of the Dragon's Nation", Shanghai 2005
Edward Lucie-Smith: "Zhang Xiaogang", Pittsburgh 2006

Li Xiangyang（编著）：《东+西。中国当代艺术展》维也纳 2002 年
Chang Tsong-zung（著）：《现实和幻觉之间》，汉雅轩画廊，香港2004年
Li Xiangyang 上海美术馆（编著）：《龙族之梦。中国当代艺术展》，现代艺术爱尔兰博物馆，都伯林2005年
Lucie-Smith, Edward（著）：《张晓刚》，匹兹堡2006年

ZHANG XIAOGANG 张晓刚

[tʂaŋ ɕiaʊ kaŋ]

Born in 1958 in Kunming, under the full force of the Cultural Revolution, Zhang Xiaogang has seen his work soar to the top of the international art market in the past few years. He is undoubtedly the best known and most collected artist of his generation. But, underlying this work is a somber, almost pessimistic view of life in contemporary China, quite the opposite of the ebullient market this artist is now experiencing.

Graduating from the Sichuan Academy of Fine Arts in 1982, Zhang Xiaogang remained in Yunnan Province until moving to Beijing in 1999. Early in his career, he floundered, unsure of how to incorporate western realistic painting taught in the academy with his more personal concerns. But, by 1989, when he was included in the landmark "China/ Avant-Garde" exhibition at the National Gallery of Art in Beijing, he had begun developing his own vocabulary based on family photographs, traditional Chinese portrait painting and the surrealistic works of René Magritte. His "Bloodline" series, begun in 1993 and continuing to the present, depict nearly emotionless nuclear families, painted monochromatically, except for a splash of color across the face of a single child or a bright red line accenting the surface of the canvas. These works have been interpreted from multiple perspectives, ranging from a commentary on China's one child policy to a more generalized perspective of societal conformism. A more recent series, "Amnesia and Memory", also features these dead-pan faces, but frequently includes surrealistic still life's of light bulbs, a writing desk, an empty room, often with a disembodied hand floating into the frame.

In contrast to Political Pop and Cynical Realism movements that emerged in Beijing during this same time period, Zhang Xiaogang's imagery is emblematic of the Sichuan School with its predilection for psychological tension and personal stories. As iconographic and identifiable as these paintings seem, they are often based on Zhang Xiaogang's personal experiences and his own family members. His daughter, now twelve years old, is often the model for the various school

Zhang Xiaogang, der als Kind in Kunming das Wüten der Kulturrevolution erlebte, konnte in den letzten Jahren beobachten, wie sein Werk einen Spitzenplatz auf dem internationalen Kunstmarkt eroberte. Er ist zweifellos der bekannteste und meistgesammelte Künstler seiner Generation. Dabei liegt seinen Arbeiten eine düstere, fast pessimistische Sicht des Lebens im heutigen China zugrunde, die ziemlich genau das Gegenteil jenes Marktbooms verkörpert, den der Künstler zurzeit erlebt.

Nach seinem Abschluss an der Sichuan Academy of Fine Arts 1982 blieb Zhang Xiaogang zunächst in der Provinz Yunnan; erst 1999 zog er nach Peking um. Zu Beginn seiner Laufbahn tat er sich schwer, denn er war sich unschlüssig, wie sich die westlich-realistische Malweise, die an der Akademie gelehrt wurde, mit seinem persönlichen Ansatz vereinbaren lassen sollte. Doch schon 1989, als er in die epochale Ausstellung der „China/Avant-Garde" in der National Gallery of Art in Peking aufgenommen wurde, hatte er begonnen, seine eigene Sprache zu entwickeln, die auf Familienfotografien, traditioneller chinesischer Porträtmalerei und den surrealistischen Werken René Magrittes basiert. Seine Serie „Bloodline", die er seit 1993 bis auf den heutigen Tag fortsetzt, zeigt nahezu emotionslose Kernfamilien, monochrom gemalt – bis auf vereinzelte Farbflecken im Gesicht eines Einzelkinds oder grellrote Linien, die die Oberfläche der Leinwand akzentuieren. Diese Werke sind aus vielerlei Sicht interpretiert worden: Man sprach von einem Kommentar zur chinesischen Ein-Kind-Politik ebenso wie von einer Ausleuchtung gesellschaftlicher Gleichmacherei. In einer neueren Serie, „Amnesia and Memory", erscheinen wieder die gleichen unbewegten Gesichter, häufig in Kombination etwa mit Glühbirnen, einem Schreibtisch oder einem leeren Raum, und oft schwebt eine körperlose Hand in den Rahmen.

Im Kontrast zu Polit-Pop und Zynischem Realismus, die zur gleichen Zeit in Peking entstanden, ist Zhang Xiaogangs Bildsprache beispielhaft für die Sichuan-Schule mit ihrer Vorliebe für psychologische Spannung und persönliche

张晓刚1958年出生于云南省，经历了文化大革命的全部过程。最近几年，张目睹着其作品飙升到全球艺术市场的高端。他无疑是其这一代中最杰出的收藏艺术家。然而，隐藏作品下面的是位泣者，几乎以悲观的眼光看待着当代中国的生活，而兴旺的市场也与这位艺术家的经历完全相反。

1982年从四川美院毕业以后，张晓刚依然呆在云南省直到1999年移居北京，在其事业早期，他抽出着，不能确定怎样把 院校里的西方现实主义画法同其个人关注融为一体。然而直到1989年，其入选中国现代艺术展（中国美术馆，北京）的作品才刚刚开始显示出其自己的语言，作品以家庭照为基础，融合了中国传统肖像画画法和雷尼・马格利特作品的超现实手法。其从1993年开始创作，一直到现在的《血缘》系列作品，描述了几乎没有感情的基本家庭，采用单一纯色着色，偶尔在独生小孩脸上，溅上一抹颜色或是为突出画面而流出大红的线条。这些作品说明了作者的许多观点，从中国当代的独生政策到更多 另类与社会因循守旧的观点。最近的一组作品《失忆与记忆》也同样 刻画了这样呆板的脸庞，画面中频繁的出现超现实的静物，如灯泡，写字桌和空荡的房间，常常一只没有身体的手伸进环面中。

与同一时期出现在北京的政治运动，流行音乐以及愤世嫉俗的现实主义相比，张晓刚成为四川院校的标志，由于其心理压力和个人故事的偏好。从这些油画的肖像似乎可以确定，这些作品取材于张德亲身经历或其家庭成员。张的女儿，现在12岁，常常是油画中多个校童的原型，或是男孩或是女孩。家庭成员的穿着，从一度毫无例外的中山装或公务服，逐渐的演变为更加模糊奇迹的流行服饰。正如艺术家其自己所言，"虽然家庭破碎了，但血缘将延续永久"。对高速现代化的中国时局而言，这种感情既普遍而又具体。这应归咎于普遍适用的关心去权衡地方和高度的个体 的能力，正是因此使这部作品走向世界。

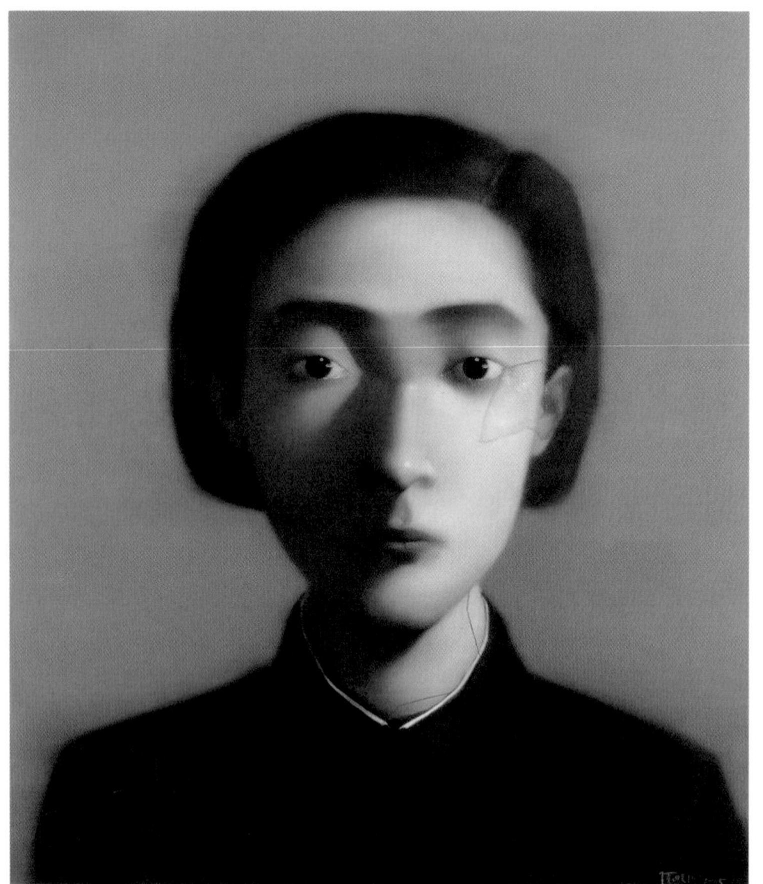

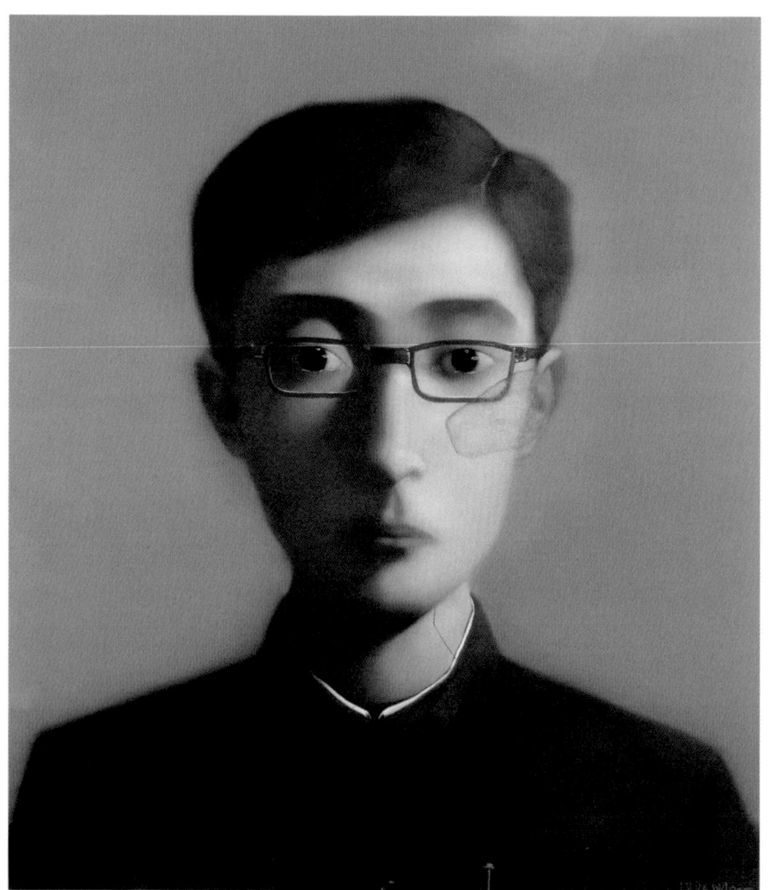

2

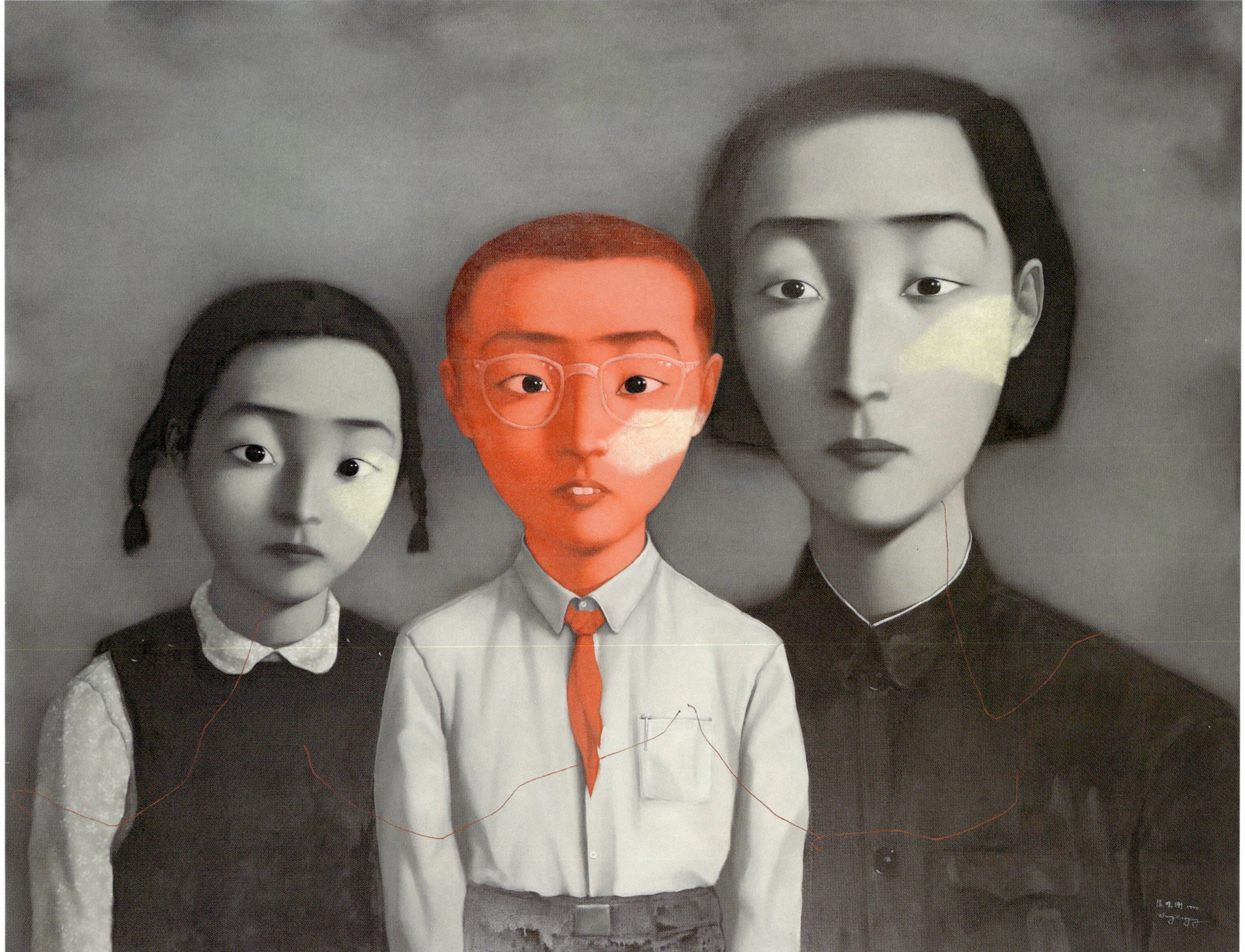

3

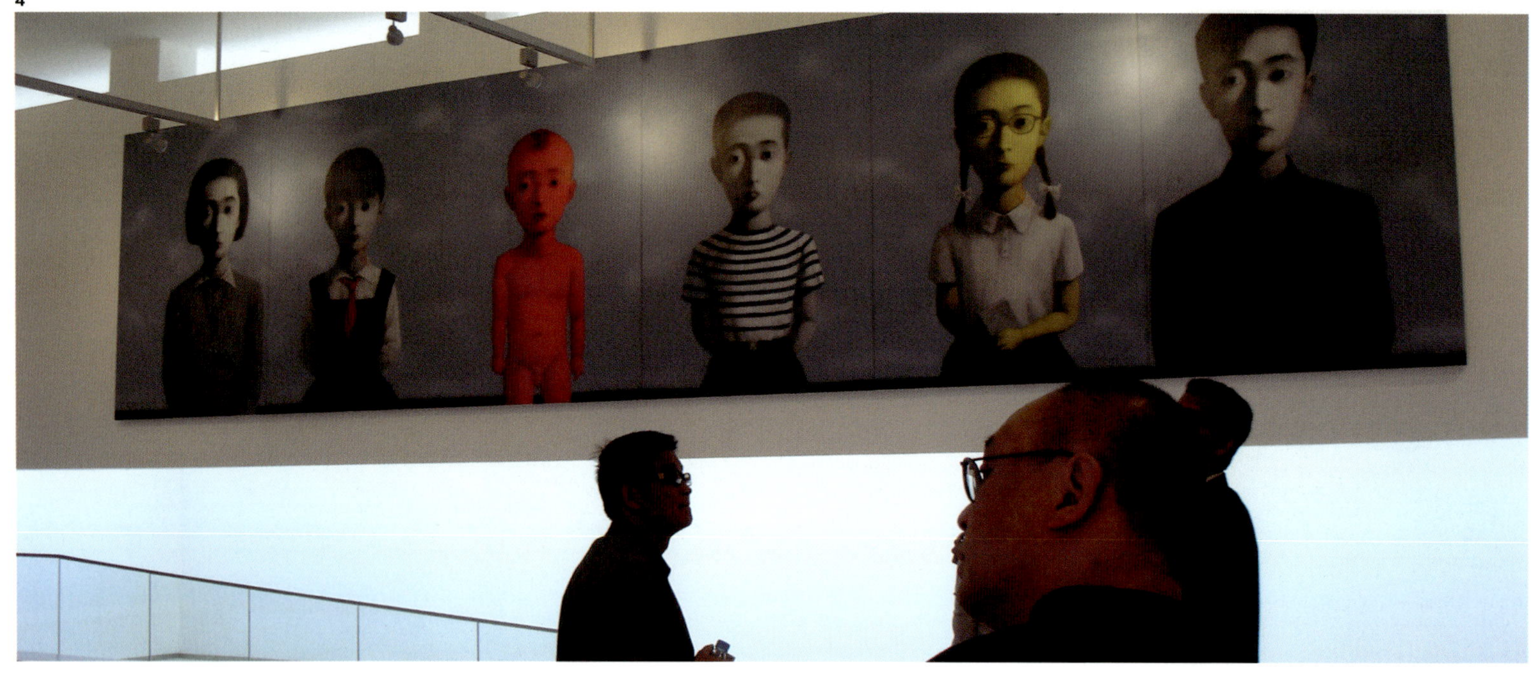

children in the pictures, both male and female. The clothes that the family members wear, once exclusively Mao jackets and official garb of his youth, have evolved into more vague, yet strangely contemporary outfits. As the artist himself has said, "Families disintegrate, but blood lines last forever," a sentiment that is as universal as it is specific to the current situation in a rapidly modernizing China. It is due to this ability to balance the local and highly personal, with more universally applicable concerns, that has lead this work to be embraced internationally.

While continuing these earlier series, in the past two years, Zhang Xiaogang has also developed far more mysterious paintings in what he calls the "In-Out" series. These are depictions of his personal living quarters or recreations of vintage Cultural Revolution propaganda scenes painted in a blurry, almost through a soft-focus lens, in the style of Gerhard Richter. Though his first full-scale retrospective took place at the Hong Kong Arts Centre in 1994, Zhang Xiaogang's work has been prominently featured in every major show of Chinese contemporary art since the mid-1990s, including "Inside Out" at Asia Society and P.S.1 in 1998. He won the top prize at the 1994 São Paulo Biennial and was included in the 46th Venice Biennial in 1995.

Geschichten. So hoch der ikonographische Wiedererkennungswert seiner Gemälde ist, so basieren sie doch meist auf Zhang Xiaogangs persönlichen Erfahrungen und denen seiner eigenen Familie. Seine inzwischen zwölfjährige Tochter diente ihm immer wieder als Modell für die verschiedenen Schulkinder auf den Bildern, ob Jungen oder Mädchen. Die Kleidung der Familienmitglieder, einst ausschließlich Mao-Jacken und die offizielle Tracht seiner Jugend, hat sich zu schwer definierbaren und doch seltsam modernen Outfits weiterentwickelt. Der Künstler sagt: „Familien lösen sich auf, aber Ahnenreihen währen ewig" – eine Position, die einerseits universell, andererseits spezifisch für die aktuelle Situation Chinas im Strudel der Modernisierung ist. Und genau diese Begabung, das Lokalspezifische und ganz Persönliche mit allgemeingültigeren Anliegen zu vereinbaren, hat Zhangs Werk internationale Akzeptanz eingebracht.

Während er seine früheren Serien fortführt, hat Zhang Xiaogang in den beiden letzten Jahren auch wesentlich mysteriösere Gemälde geschaffen: die „In-Out"-Serie. Dabei handelt es sich um Darstellungen seiner Privatwohnung oder um Reproduktionen altmodischer Propagandaszenen aus der Kulturrevolution, die in verschwommener Maltechnik, fast wie mit Weichzeichner, ausgeführt sind – im Stile eines Gerhard Richter. Obwohl seine erste große Retrospektive schon 1994 im Hong Kong Arts Centre gezeigt wurde, nimmt Zhang Xiaogang seit Mitte der 1990er Jahre in jeder wichtigen Ausstellung der chinesischen Gegenwartskunst nach wie vor einen bedeutenden Platz ein, so auch bei „Inside Out" in der Asia Society und im P.S.1, beide 1998. 1994 erhielt er den Hauptpreis der Biennale São Paulo und war 1995 auf der 46. Biennale von Venedig zu sehen.

在过去的两年中，虽然继续着早期的系列作品，张也创作了更加神秘他叫做《蜕变与突破》系列。作品或是描写了其个人住宅或者对过时的文革宣传场面的调侃，模仿格哈特·里希特的风格在短焦距的照片上上模糊的添补。虽然张的全面回顾展在1994年的香港艺术中心举行，但自20世纪90年代中期开始，张的作品就在中国当代艺术的所有主题中声名显赫，包括在1998年的《蜕变与突破：中国新艺术》纽约PS1当代艺术中心。1994年张荣获圣保罗双年展铜奖，1995年作品入选第46届威尼斯双年展。

Barbara Pollack

5

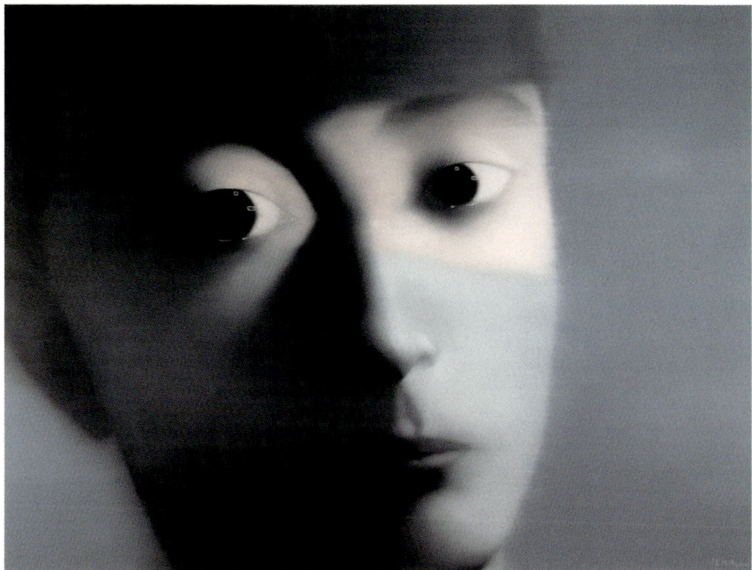

6

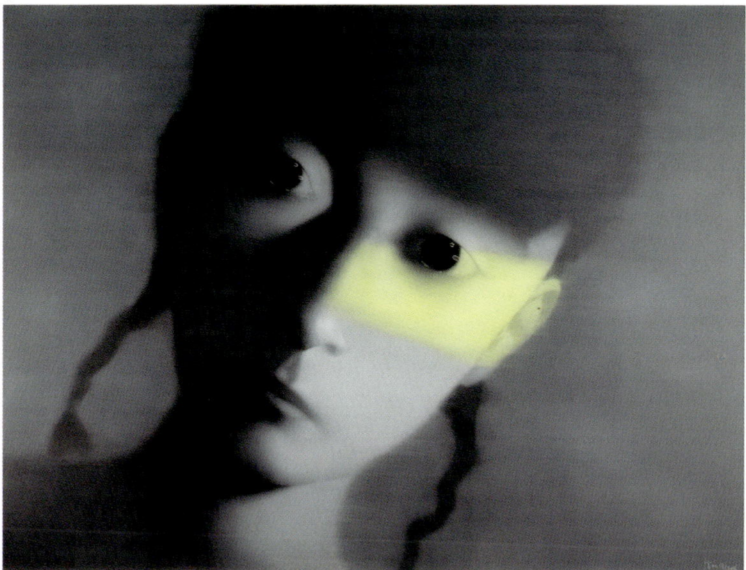

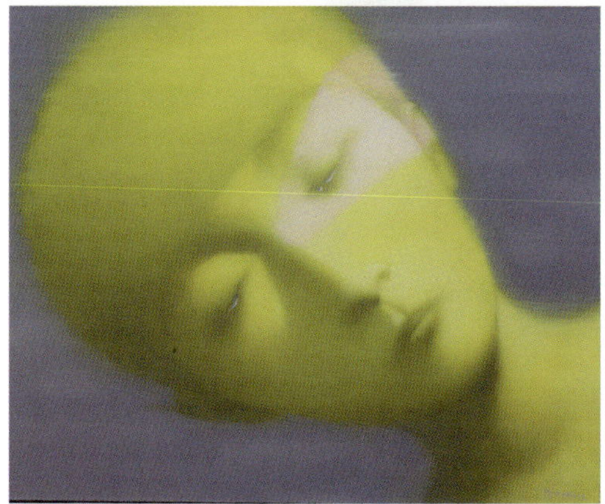

7

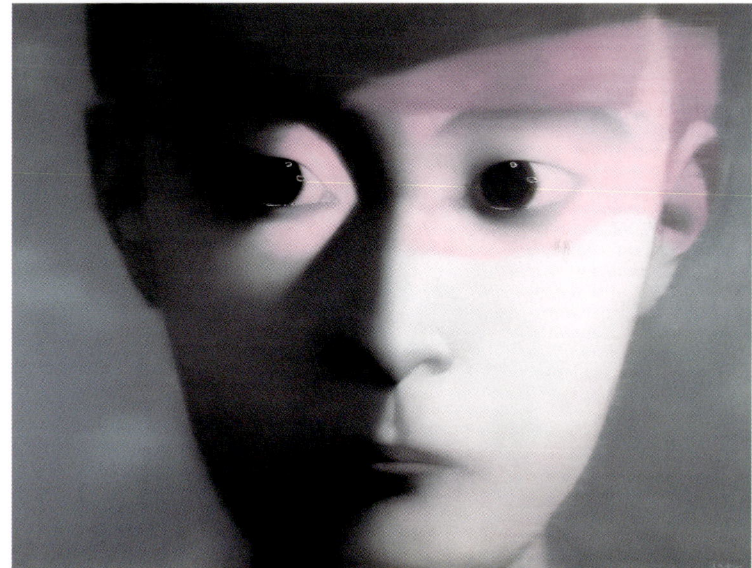

8

1 ***My Dream: Little General***, *2005*
Oil on canvas, 200 x 160 cm; Öl auf Leinwand, 200 x 160 cm
《我的梦想:小将军》2005年, 布面油画，200 x 160 cm

2 ***Comrade***, *2005*
Oil on canvas, diptych, 130 x 110 cm each; Öl auf Leinwand, Diptychon, je 130 x 110 cm
《同志》2005年, 布面油画, 双折, 每幅130 x 110 cm

3 ***A Big Family***, *1995*
Oil on canvas, 179 x 229 cm; Öl auf Leinwand, 179 x 229 cm
《大家庭》1995年, 布面油画, 179 x 229 cm

4 *Exhibition view "Umbilical Cord of History. Paintings by Zhang Xiaogang", Hong Kong Arts Centre, Hong Kong, 2004*
Ausstellungsansicht „Umbilical Cord of History. Paintings by Zhang Xiaogang", Hong Kong Arts Centre, Hongkong, 2004
《香港艺术中心展览实景》2004年

5 ***Untitled***, *2006*
Oil on canvas, 200 x 260 cm; Öl auf Leinwand, 200 x 260 cm
《无题》, 2006年, 布面油画, 200 x 260 cm

6 ***Untitled***, *2006*
Oil on canvas, 200 x 260 cm; Öl auf Leinwand, 200 x 260 cm
《无题》2006年, 布面油画, 200 x 260 cm

7 ***Yellow Memory Girl***, *2007*
Oil on canvas, 110 x 130 cm; Öl auf Leinwand, 110 x 130 cm
《黄色记忆女孩》2007年, 布面油画, 110 x 130 cm

8 ***Untitled***, *2006*
Oil on canvas, 200 x 260 cm; Öl auf Leinwand, 200 x 260 cm
《无题》2006年, 布面油画, 200 x 260 cm

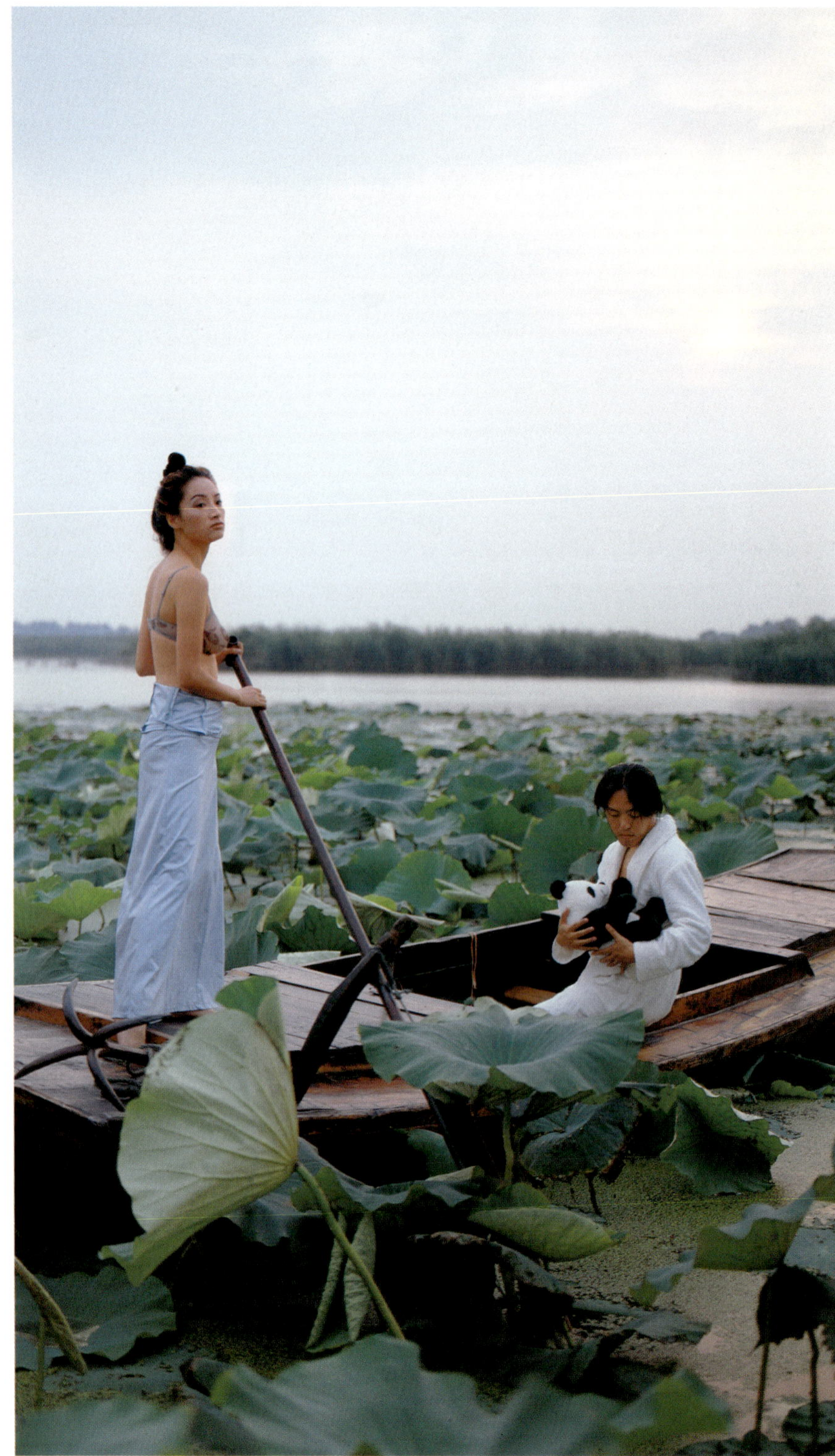

1

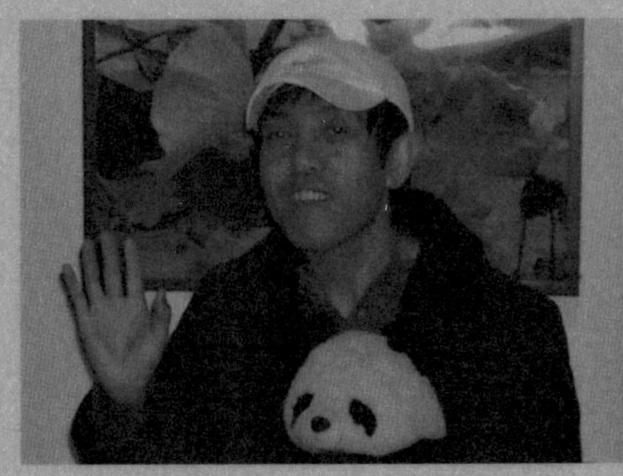

"I am not responsible for art."

„Ich bin nicht für die Kunst verantwortlich."

"我对艺术没有责任。"

Born in 1966 in Beijing, China. Lives and works in Beijing
Geboren 1966 in Peking, China. Lebt und arbeitet in Peking
1966 年出生于中国北京。居住工作在北京

***Selected exhibitions* / Ausgewählte Ausstellungen / 所选展览**

1999	48. Biennale di Venezia, Venice, Italy
2000	Shanghai Biennial, Shanghai Art Museum, Shanghai, China
2002	First Guangzhou Triennial, Guandong Museum of Art, Guangzhou, China
2004–07	"Between Past and Future, New Photography and Video from China", International Center of Photography, New York, NY, USA (travelling exhibition)
2005	"Reshaping the Wall: Contemporary Chinese Art", Millennium Art Museum, Beijing, China
2006	"MoCA Envisage 2006", Museum of Contemporary Art, Shanghai, China

1999年	《威尼斯双年展。48. 艺术国际展》威尼斯
2000年	上海双年展 上海美术馆 上海
2002年	《重新解读—中国当代艺术十年（1990-2000》首届广州三年展 广东美术馆 广州
2004-07年	《过去与未来之间—中国新影像展》国际摄影中心，纽约，美国（巡回展）
2005年	《墙 -- 中国当代艺术二十年》中华世纪坛，北京
2006年	《入境:中国美学》上海当代艺术馆,上海,中国

***Selected publications* / Ausgewählte Publikationen / 所选著作**

Wu Hung: "Exhibiting Experimental Art in China", Chicago 2000
Wu Hung (ed.): "The First Triennial: Reinterpretation: A Decade of Experimental Chinese Art (1990-2000)", Wuhan 2002
Gao Qianhui: "After Origin: Topic on Contemporary Chinese Art in New Age", Taipei 2004
Christopher Philipps, Wu Hung (eds.): "Between Past and Future: New Photography and Video from China", Göttingen 2004
Gao Minglu: "Reshaping the Wall: Contemporary Chinese Art", New York 2005

巫鸿（著）： 《中国二十世纪末实验艺术展》芝加哥 2000年
巫鸿（编者）：《首届中国艺术三年展》武汉 2002年
高千惠（著）：《艺术不原始：当代华人艺术跨领域阅读》台北2004年
Philipps, Christopher/巫鸿(编者)：《过去与未来之间一来自中国的新摄影及录像》2004年
高明潞（著）：《墙—中国当代艺术的历史与变节》纽约 2005年

"I am not responsible for art."

„Ich bin nicht für die Kunst verantwortlich."

"我对艺术没有责任。"

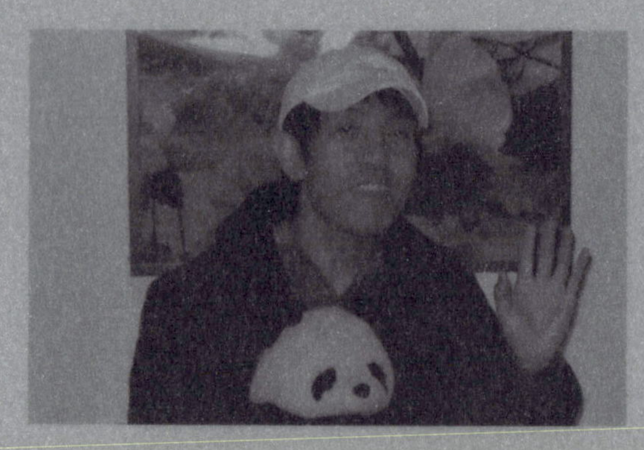

Born in 1966 in Beijing, China. Lives and works in Beijing
Geboren 1966 in Peking, China. Lebt und arbeitet in Peking
1966 年出生于中国北京。居住工作在北京

Selected exhibitions / Ausgewählte Ausstellungen / 所选展览

1999 48. Biennale di Venezia, Venice, Italy
2000 Shanghai Biennial, Shanghai Art Museum, Shanghai, China
2002 First Guangzhou Triennial, Guandong Museum of Art, Guangzhou, China
2004-07 "Between Past and Future, New Photography and Video from China", International Center of Photography, New York, NY, USA (travelling exhibition)
2005 "Reshaping the Wall: Contemporary Chinese Art", Millennium Art Museum, Beijing, China
2006 "MoCA Envisage 2006", Museum of Contemporary Art, Shanghai, China

1999年 《威尼斯双年展。48. 艺术国际展》威尼斯
2000年 上海双年展 上海美术馆 上海
2002年 《重新解读—中国当代艺术十年（1990-2000）》首届广州三年展 广东美术馆 广州
2004-07年 《过去与未来之间—中国新影像展》国际摄影中心，纽约，美国（巡回展）
2005年 《墙 — 中国当代艺术二十年》中华世纪坛，北京
2006年 《人境：中国美学》上海当代艺术馆，上海，中国

Selected publications / Ausgewählte Publikationen / 所选著作

Wu Hung: "Exhibiting Experimental Art in China", Chicago 2000
Wu Hung (ed.): "The First Triennial: Reinterpretation: A Decade of Experimental Chinese Art (1990-2000)", Wuhan 2002
Gao Qianhui: "After Origin: Topic on Contemporary Chinese Art in New Age", Taipei 2004
Christopher Philipps, Wu Hung (eds.): "Between Past and Future: New Photography and Video from China", Göttingen 2004
Gao Minglu: "Reshaping the Wall: Contemporary Chinese Art", New York 2005

巫鸿（著）：《中国二十世纪末实验艺术展》芝加哥 2000年
巫鸿（编著）：《首届中国艺术三年展》武汉 2002年
高千惠（著）：《艺术不原罪：当代华人艺术跨领域阅读》台北2004年
Philipps, Christopher/巫鸿(编著)：《过去与未来之间—来自中国的新摄影及录像》2004年
高明潞（著）：《墙—中国当代艺术的历史与变革》纽约 2005年

ZHAO BANDI 赵半狄

[tʂɑʊ panti]

Zhao Bandi's work resides comfortably in two worlds, the space of fantasy and that of reality, the art world and the public realm. Conscious of searching for an art form that can speak to the public, Zhao gave up painting in 1994. Subsequently, he spent two years, in his own words, "squandering ideas" before he eventually found his own voice while photographing himself clad in a sexy blue female nightgown, standing next to pop singer Zhang Qianqian and holding a panda in his arms. It was a kitschy oval shaped color photograph that he turned into a calendar poster intended for mass distribution beyond the contemporary art system ("Zhao Bandi and Zhang Qianqian", 1996). While originally posing with a piglet, Zhao decided to replace it at the last minute with an image of a panda, which he painted by hand and he believed to be more recognizable and appealing thanks to its status as a national treasure of China. The calendar didn't fare well in the mass market Zhao was targeting, but his concept of popularizing an artistic expression using techniques and network of mass media and distribution and the routine of appearing with a stuffed panda in made-up scenarios have become the core of his practice and against his will, an instant hit with the art circle.

While persistently pursuing what the artist considered the ideal audience, the non-art public, he struck again in 1999 with a series of subway advertising posters for public welfare in Beijing. To legitimise their appearance in a public space, Zhao appeared in conversations with a stuffed panda sending out messages about safe sex, smoking prohibition, no trespassing on lawns and many more issues related to public interests and welfare. This series was widely considered as an effective advertising campaign appreciated for its humor and critical undertone by the general public and thus Zhao was able to duplicate the same format on billboard ads in the Beijing airport, on a busy street intersection of Huaihai Road in Shanghai and on national TV. It was really a triumph in turning public communication channels into vehicles for a self-made publicist to have his individual voice heard despite the overwhelming volume of a collective way of speaking in China.

Zhao Bandis Werk ist gleichermaßen in den Sphären der Fantasie und der Realität zu Hause, in der Kunstwelt und in der Öffentlichkeit. Auf seiner Suche nach einer Kunstform, die die Öffentlichkeit erreicht, gab Zhao die Malerei 1994 auf. Die nächsten zwei Jahre verbrachte er damit, wie er selbst sagt, „Ideen zu verschleudern" – bevor er endlich zu seiner eigenen Ausdrucksweise fand, als er sich selbst im sexy blauen Damennachthemd neben Popsängerin Zhang Qianqian fotografierte, mit einem Panda auf dem Arm. Diese Farbfotografie im kitschigen ovalen Rahmen verwendete er für ein Kalenderblatt, das zur massenhaften Verbreitung außerhalb des Kunstmarkts bestimmt war („Zhao Bandi and Zhang Qianqian", 1996). Ursprünglich hatte Zhao mit einem Ferkel posieren wollen, bevor er sich in letzter Minute für das von ihm gemalte Bild eines Pandas entschied, der durch seinen Status als chinesisches Nationalsymbol einen höheren Wiedererkennungswert und größere Attraktivität besaß. Der Kalender war übrigens auf dem von Zhao anvisierten Massenmarkt kein großer Erfolg, aber seine Idee, den künstlerischen Ausdruck zu popularisieren, indem er sich Techniken und Strukturen der Massenmedien zunutze machte, sowie seine regelmäßigen Auftritte mit Plüschpandas in frei erfundenen Szenarien wurden zum Kern seines Schaffens und hatten – gegen seinen Willen – sofort Erfolg in der Kunstszene.

Beim Werben um das in seinen Augen ideale Publikum, die künstlerisch unverbildete Masse, schlug der Künstler 1999 wieder zu – mit einer Serie von „Werbeplakaten für das Allgemeinwohl" in der Pekinger U-Bahn. Zhao zeigte sich darauf mit einem Plüschpanda bei Gesprächen, die verschiedenste Botschaften vermittelten: „Sicherer Sex ist gut", „Rauchen ist schlecht", „Das Betreten des Rasens ist verboten" usw. Die Serie wurde weithin als wirkungsvolle Werbekampagne begrüßt und kam beim breiteren Publikum dank ihres Humors und ihrer kritischen Untertöne gut an. Das erlaubte es Zhao, seine Botschaften auch auf Plakatwänden am Flughafen von Peking und an einer verkehrsreichen Straßenkreuzung der Huaihai-Straße in Shanghai sowie im nationalen Fernsehen unterzubringen – seine

赵半狄的作品舒适地驻留在两个世界里：幻想空间和现实空间，艺术世界和公众领域。为了主动寻求一种能够面向公众的艺术形式，他于1994年放弃了绘画。随后，他花费了两年时间“挥霍灵感”（用他自己的话来说）。直到当他身着性感的蓝色女性睡衣，站在流行歌手张浅潜身旁，抱着一只熊猫拍照时，他才终于找到了他自己的心声。这是一张椭圆形的朦胧彩色照片，为了在当代艺术圈子以外大量发行，他将照片做成了日历海报。（《赵半狄和张浅潜》，1996年）赵半狄起初采用一只小猪造型，但在最后一分钟他决定使用熊猫的形象并手绘了这只熊猫，因为他相信，作为中国国宝的熊猫将更容易被认知，也更具吸引力。这本日历在他所面向的销售市场销量不佳，然而他却从此确定了自己艺术实践的核心，那就是使用技术、大众传媒网络及发行渠道将艺术性的表达大众化，以及在人为的情节中抱着一只熊猫咪出场的惯例。而事以愿违的是，他的这些做法立即对艺术圈子带来了冲击。

在不断努力追赶他心目中理想观众（非艺术公众）的对象过程中，赵半狄于 1999 年在北京再次打造了一个地铁公益广告海报系列。为使这些海报能够合法地在公共场所出现，赵半狄与熊猫咪以对话的方式出现，传达着关于安全性行为、禁止吸烟、不要践踏草坪以及更多的以公共利益和福利相关的信息。该系列被公众广泛认为是有效的广告活动，其中的幽默和批评的潜台词得到了公众的欣赏。赵半狄也因此得以在各种公众场所复制相同的形式，如北京机场的广告牌、上海淮海路繁华街道的十字路口以及国家电视等等。在将公共传播渠道变成自创宣传者的手段方面，这的确算得上是一场胜利。在中国，尽管集体方式的论调仍具有压倒性的优势，但他的个体声音却得以被大众听到。

赵半狄始终对任何圈子或体制保持怀疑和警惕，然而通过不断地挪用和模仿这样一个神话制造机制，却使他继续广受关注。他以各种方式频繁地出现在头条上，参加马拉松长跑、将两家当地报纸告上法

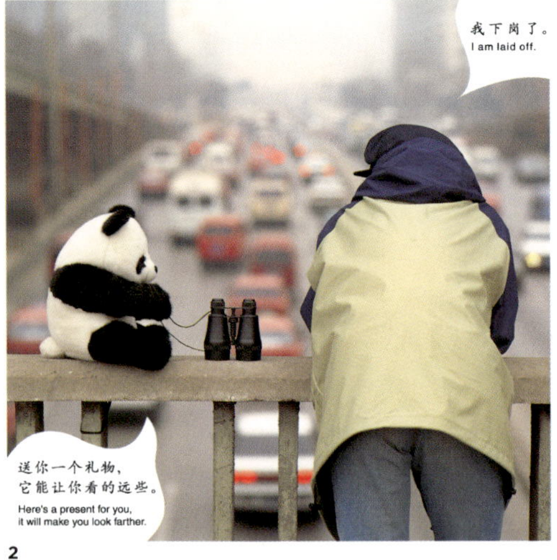
我下岗了。
I am laid off.
送你一个礼物，
它能让你看的远些。
Here's a present for you,
it will make you look farther.

2

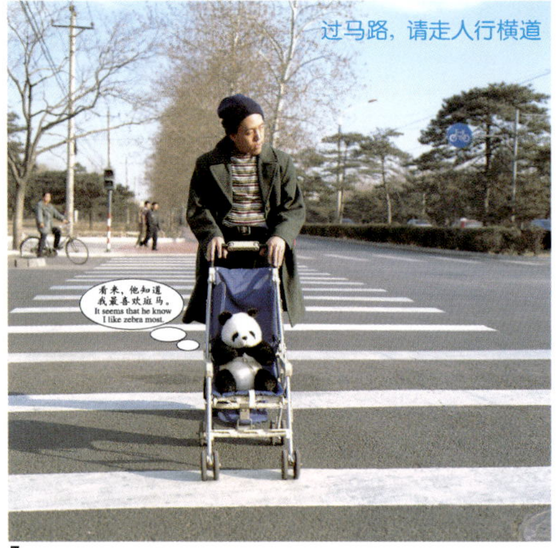
过马路，请走人行横道
看来，他知道
我最喜欢斑马。
It seems that he know
I like zebra most.

3

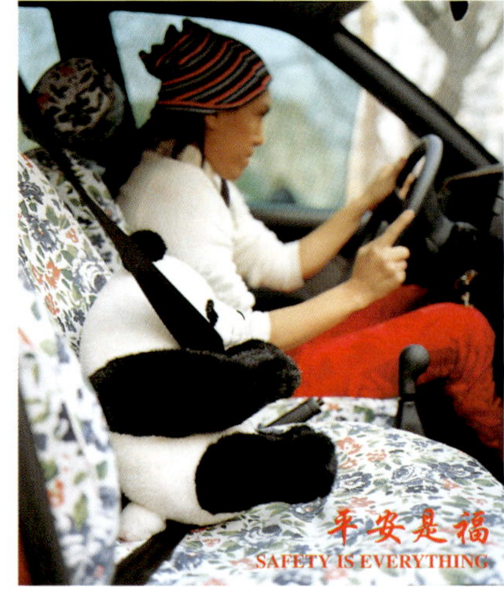
平安是福
SAFETY IS EVERYTHING

4

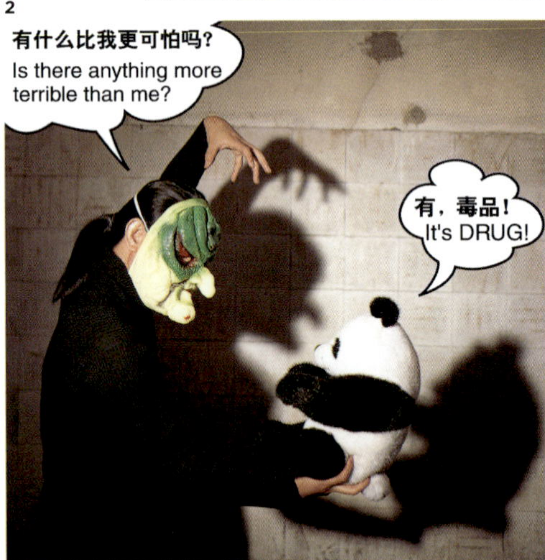
有什么比我更可怕吗？
Is there anything more terrible than me?
有，毒品！
It's DRUG!

5

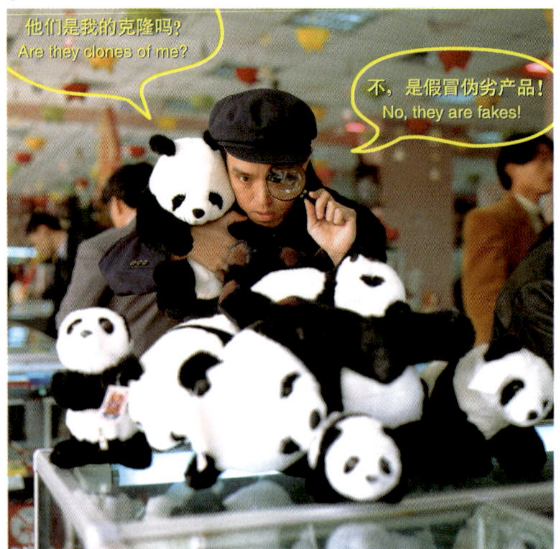
他们是我的克隆吗？
Are they clones of me?
不，是假冒伪劣产品！
No, they are fakes!

6

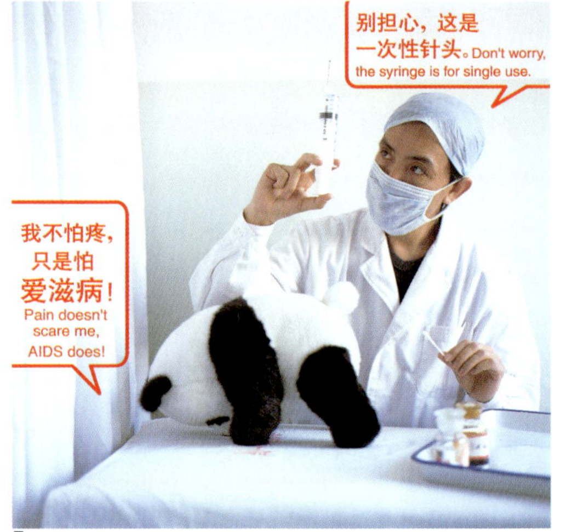
别担心，这是
一次性针头。Don't worry,
the syringe is for single use.
我不怕疼，
只是怕
爱滋病！
Pain doesn't
scare me,
AIDS does!

7

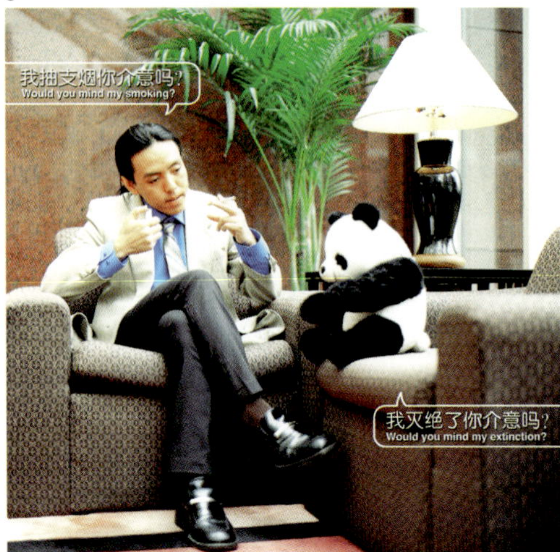
我抽支烟你介意吗？
Would you mind my smoking?
我灭绝了你介意吗？
Would you mind my extinction?

8

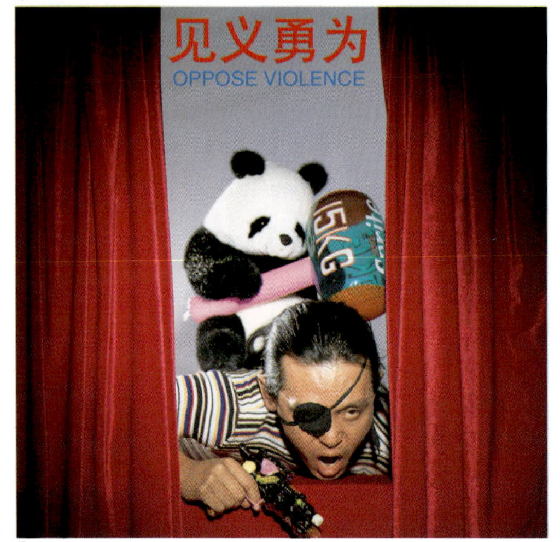
见义勇为
OPPOSE VIOLENCE
15KG

9

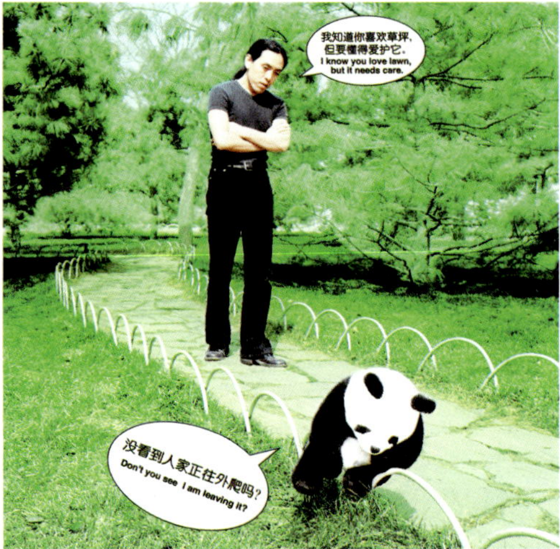
我知道你喜欢草坪，
但要懂得爱护它。
I know you love lawn,
but it needs care.
没看到人家正往外爬吗？
Don't you see I am leaving it?

10

阻击非典 保卫家园

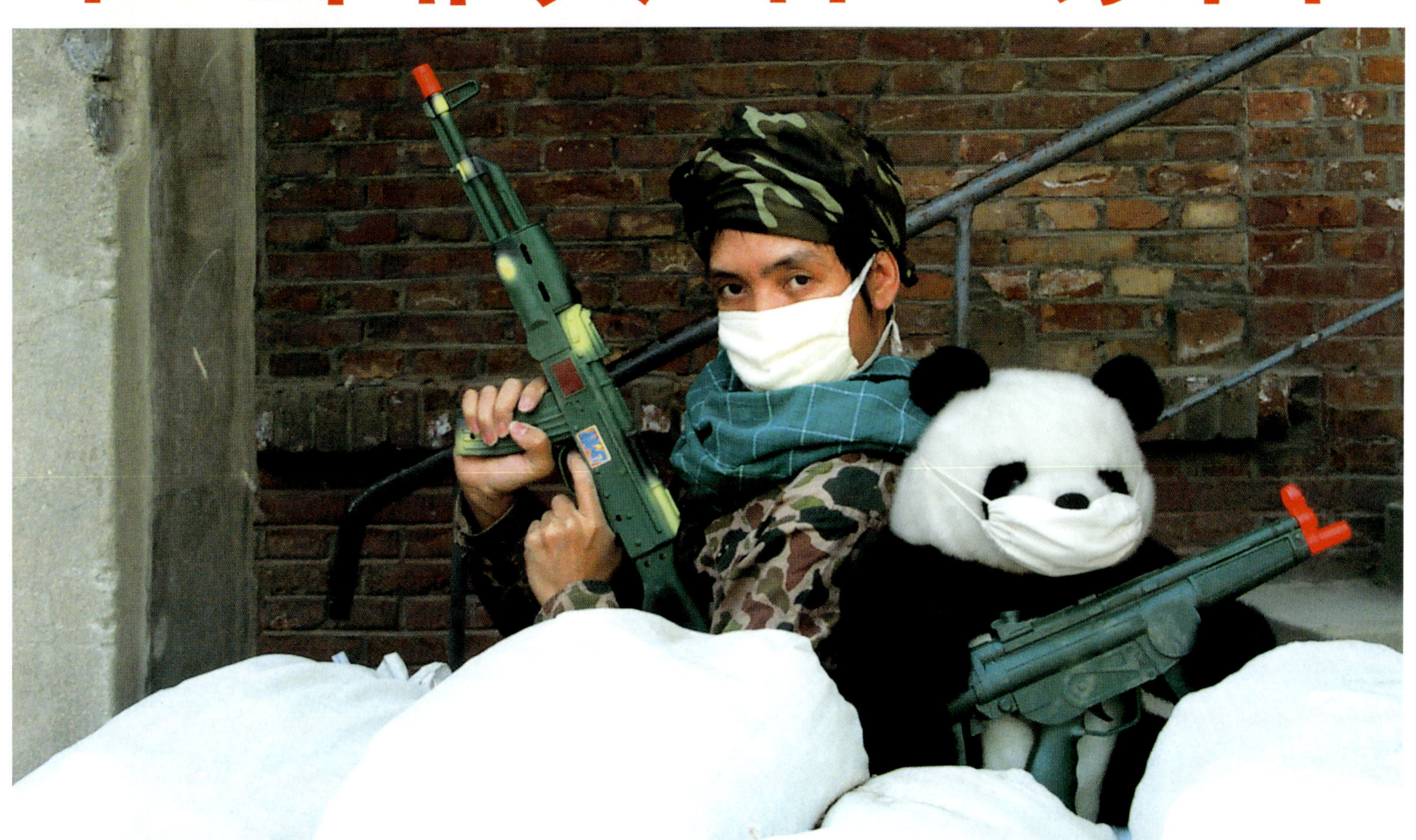

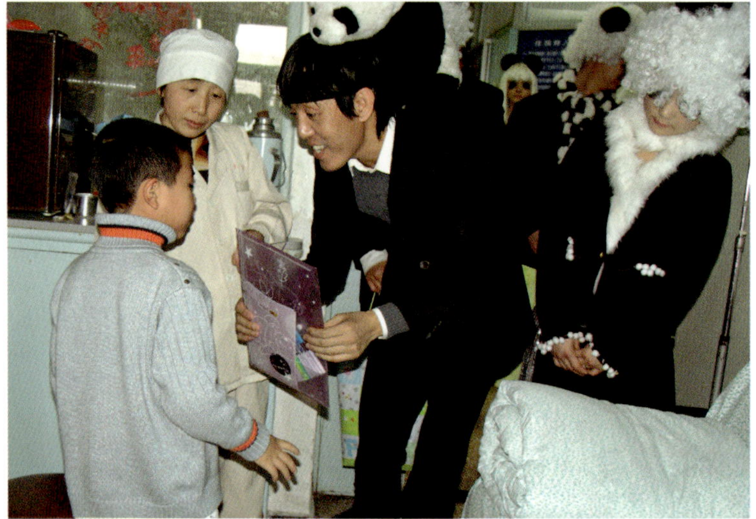

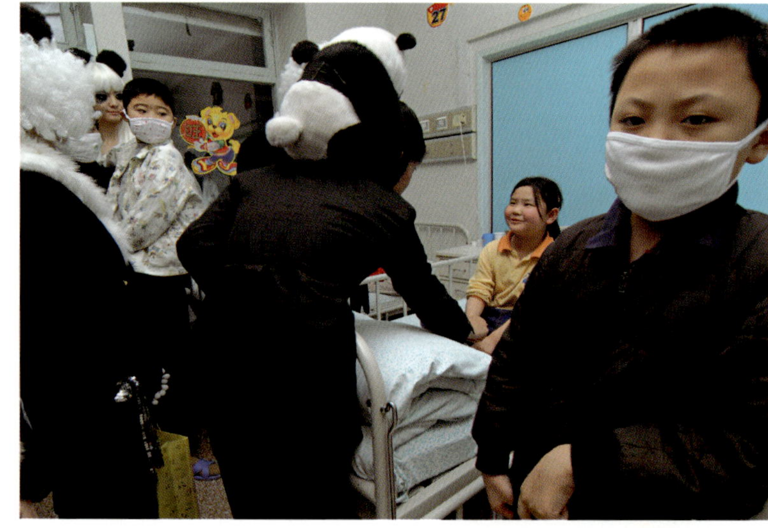

Zhao has always remained suspicious and vigilant of any circle or system, and yet continued to remain in the spotlight by constantly appropriating and imitating the myth making mechanisms of such a system. He has frequently made headlines by running in a marathon, taking two local newspapers to court for violating his copyright by using one of his images without permission, starring in a movie and orchestrating Zhao Bandi's version of Beijing's 2008 Olympics opening ceremony in the national stadium in Bern, Switzerland in 2005. For that purpose, replacing the local street names with familiar road names in Beijing and even placing an inflatable miniature Tian'anmen Square in the city of Bern. In all of these events, the constant presence of the stuffed panda by the artist's side or over the artist's head or shoulders further complicates the boundary between the real and the surreal, the reasonable and the absurd while feeding perfectly to the canon of the media.

In 2006, inspired by the political manœuver between Mainland China and Taiwan behind Taiwan's refusal to accept two pandas from Mainland China, Zhao has launched a nation-wide campaign to search for a selection of panda-looking or panda-spirited people to go as a delegation to visit Taiwan. The social resonance that such a campaign has generated so far testifies that Zhao Bandi is fighting a winning battle in his artistic conspiracy to interact and interfere with the society.

Strategie, öffentliche Kommunikationskanäle als Vehikel zu nutzen, um als selbsternannter Publicity-Manager seiner persönlichen Stimme Gehör zu verschaffen (trotz des ohrenbetäubenden Lärms der alltäglichen Kommunikation in China), erwies sich also als wahrer Triumph.

Zhao begegnet allen etablierten Szenen und Systemen mit Misstrauen. Gleichzeitig sucht er das Rampenlicht, um die mythenschaffenden Mechanismen solcher Systeme immer wieder zu annektieren und bloßzustellen. Er machte häufig Schlagzeilen: etwa mit seiner Teilnahme an einem Marathon, oder als er zwei Lokalzeitungen wegen Copyright-Verletzung verklagte, weil sie eins seiner Bilder ohne Genehmigung abgedruckt hatten, oder als er seine persönliche Version der Eröffnungszeremonie für die Pekinger Olympiade 2008 schon 2005 im Nationalstadion des schweizerischen Bern präsentierte – er ersetzte dabei örtliche Straßennamen durch bekannte Straßennamen aus Peking und baute sogar eine aufblasbare Miniaturausgabe des Platzes des Himmlischen Friedens in der Innenstadt von Bern auf. Bei all diesen Aktionen verwischt die Allgegenwart des Plüschpandas, der dem Künstler stets zur Seite steht oder auch nur über seinen Kopf oder seine Schulter lugt, immer wieder die Grenze zwischen Realität und Surrealität, Rationalität und Absurdität, während sie zugleich die Medienbedürfnisse perfekt bedient.

Im Gefolge des Dauerkonflikts zwischen Festland-China und Taiwan weigerte Taiwan sich 2006, zwei Pandas als Geschenk von Festland-China anzunehmen. Zhao startete daraufhin eine landesweite Kampagne, um eine Gruppe von Panda-ähnlichen oder Panda-seelenverwandten Menschen zusammenzubringen und als Delegation nach Taiwan zu entsenden. Die gesellschaftliche Resonanz, die diese Kampagne bisher gefunden hat, beweist, dass Zhao Bandi mit seinen künstlerischen Interaktionen und Interventionen auf der Gewinnerstraße ist.

庭（未经许可使用其肖像从而侵犯版权）、出演一部电影、编排赵半狄版北京　2008年的奥运会开幕式（2005年在瑞士伯尔尼国家体育馆）等等，不一而足。为此，他将伯尔尼市当地的街道名用熟悉的北京街道名替代，甚至还在伯尔尼市内放置了一个小型的充气式天安门模型。而在所有这些活动中，熊猫咪永远出现在他的身侧、头顶或肩膀上，这进一步模糊了现实与超现实、合理与荒谬之间的界限，并且深合媒体的胃口。2006年，在台湾拒绝接受中国大陆两只大熊猫的背景下，从中国大陆和台湾的政治策略中找到灵感的赵半狄，展开了一个全国范围的活动，搜寻长得像熊猫或神态像熊猫的人作为代表团访问台湾。这次活动所引发的社会共鸣之深远，证明了赵半狄用艺术谋略影响和干涉社会的战斗正在取得胜利。

Carol Lu

13

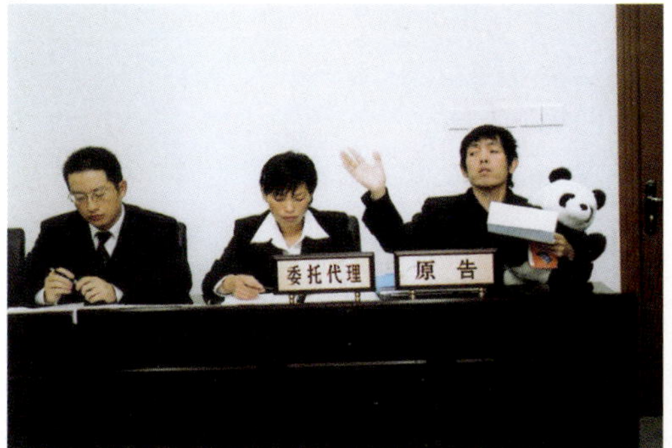

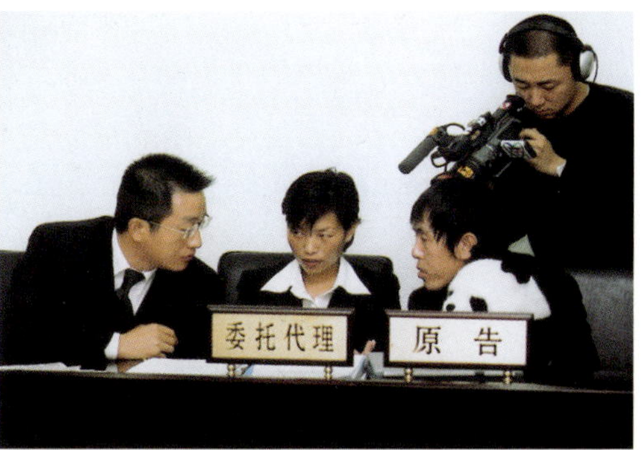

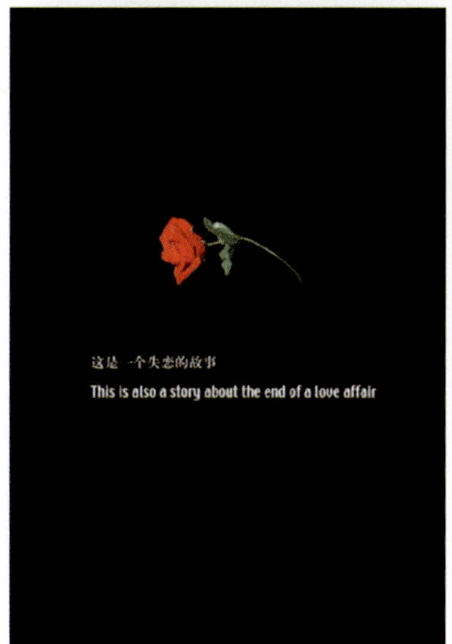

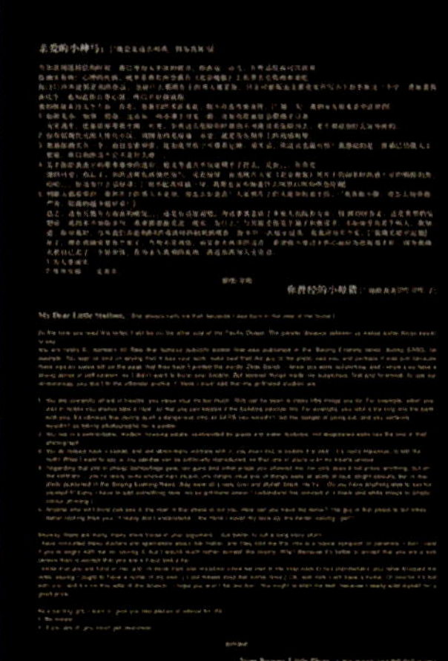

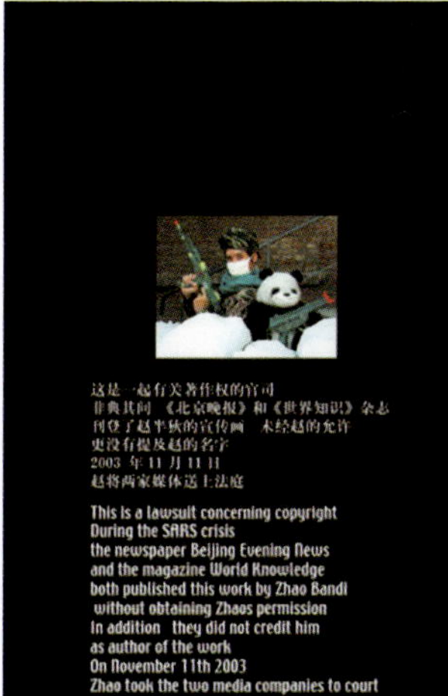

1 ***Chinese Story***, *1998*
C-print, 126 x 72 cm; C-print, 126 x 72 cm
《中国故事》1998年，C-印刷品，126 x 72 cm

2 ***"I am laid off" – "Here is a present for you, it will make you see further"***, *1999*
C-print, 125 x 125 cm; C-print, 125 x 125 cm
《我下病了》1999年，C-印刷品125 x 125 cm

3 ***It seems that he know I like Zebras most***, *1999*
C-print, 125 x 125 cm; C-print, 125 x 125 cm
《看起来他知道我最喜欢斑马》1999年，C-印刷品，125 x 125 cm

4 ***Safety is Everything***, *1999*
C-print, 125 x 125 cm; C-print, 125 x 125 cm
《平安是福》1999年，C-印刷品，125 x 125 cm

5 ***Zhao Bandi & panda (Drug)***, *1999*
C-print, 125 x 125 cm; C-print, 125 x 125 cm
《赵半狄和熊猫咪（毒）》1999年，C-印刷品，125 x 125 cm

6 ***"Are they clones of me?" – "No they are fakes!"***, *1999*
C-print, 125 x 125 cm; C-print, 125 x 125 cm
《他们是我的克隆吗?- 不，是假冒伪劣产品!》1999年，C-印刷品，125 x 125 cm

7 ***Zhao Bandi & panda (Aids)***, *1999*
C-print, 125 x 125 cm; C-print, 125 x 125 cm
《赵半狄和熊猫咪（爱滋病）》1999年，C-印刷品，125 x 125 cm

8 ***Zhao Bandi & panda (Extinction)***, *1999*
C-print, 125 x 125 cm; C-print, 125 x 125 cm
《赵半狄和熊猫咪（杀死）》1999年，C-印刷品，125 x 125 cm

9 ***Zhao Bandi & panda (Oppose)***, *1999*
C-print, 125 x 125 cm; C-print, 125 x 125 cm
《赵半狄和熊猫咪 （见义勇为）》1999年，C-印刷品，125 x 125 cm

10 ***Zhao Bandi & panda (Leaving)***, *1999*
C-print, 125 x 125 cm; C-print, 125 x 125 cm
《赵半狄和熊猫咪》1999年，C-印刷品，125 x 125 cm

11 ***Block SARS, defend the homeland***, *2003*
C-print, 96 x 119 cm; C-print, 96 x 119 cm
《阻击非典，保卫家园》2003年，C-印刷品，96 x 119 cm

12 ***Zhao Bandi pays a series of visits to varied people***, *2007*
Video, 12 min; Video, 12 Min.
《赵半狄付一系列的参观到各种各样的人民》2007年，录像，12分

13 ***A Court Case Nov. 11th, 2003 And also a Story about the End of a Love Story***, *2003*
C-prints, 120 x 82/82 x 120 cm each; C-prints, je 120 x 82/82 x 120 cm
《法案2003年11月11日》2003年，C-印刷品，120 x 82/82 x 120 cm 每幅

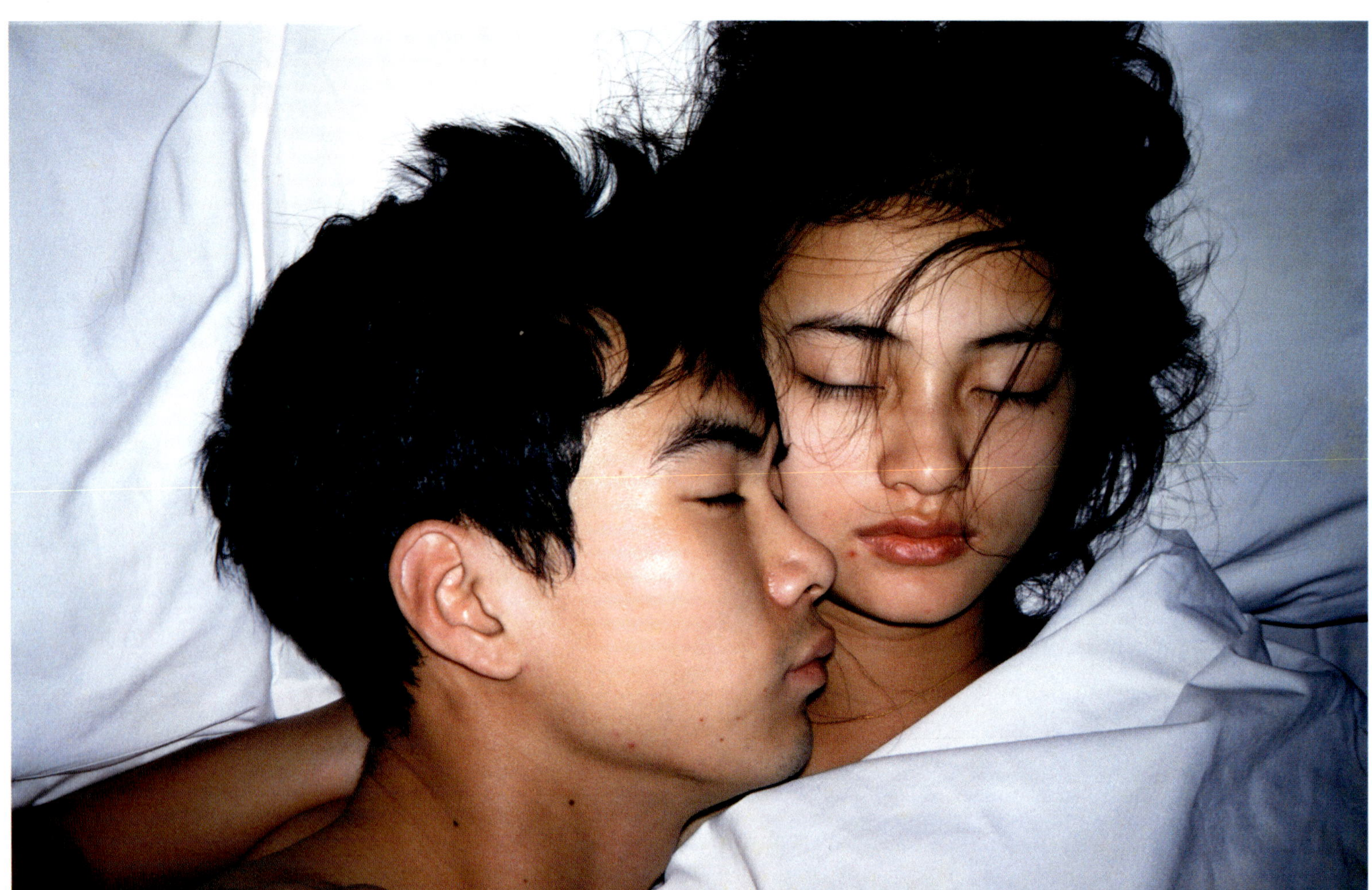

1

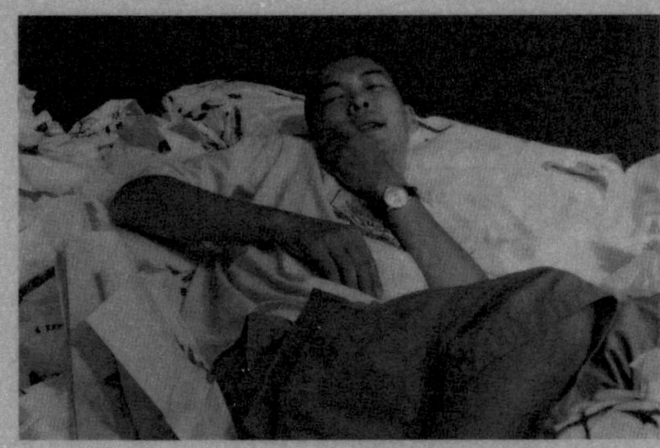

"Everything can be provided, everything is acceptable."

„Alles kann vorausgesetzt werden, alles ist annehmbar."

"一切都可能出现，一切都可能被世界接受。"

Born in 1970 in Yangjiang, China. Lives and works in Yangjiang
Geboren 1970 in Yangjiang, China. Lebt und arbeitet in Yangjiang
1970年出生于中国广东阳江，现在居住工作于阳江

***Selected exhibitions* / Ausgewählte Ausstellungen / 所选展览**

2000 "Zheng Guogu – More Dimensional", China Art Archives & Warehouse (CAAW), Beijing, China
2002 Gwangju Biennial, Gwangju, Korea
2003 50. Biennale di Venezia, Venice, Italy
"My Home is Your Museum", Vitamin Creative Space, Guangzhou, China
"The Fifth System: Public Art In The Age Of 'Post-Planning' " – Fourth Shenzhen Contemporary Sculpture Exhibition, Shenzhen, China
2005 Second Guangzhou Triennale, Guangzhou, China
2007 documenta 12, Kassel, Germany

2000年 《郑国谷-多维》艺术文件仓库，中国北京
2002年 光洲双年展，光洲，韩国
2003年 第50届威尼斯双年展，威尼斯, 意大利
《我家是你的博物馆》维他命创造空间 广州 中国
《第五系统:后规划时代的公共艺术》第五届深圳国际当代雕塑展，深圳
2005年 《第二届广州三年展》广州，中国
2007年 第十二届德国文件展，卡塞尔，德国

***Selected publications* / Ausgewählte Publikationen / 所选著作**

Zheng Guogu: "Cross Back and Forth Quickly", Hong Kong 2003
Jean-Marc Decrop (ed.): "Zheng Guogu", Hong Kong 2007
"The Real Thing. Contemporary Art from China", Liverpool 2007

《郑国谷》香港 2003年
Decrop, Jean-Marc（编者）:《郑国谷》香港2007年
《真实事件: 中国当代艺术》利物浦 2007年

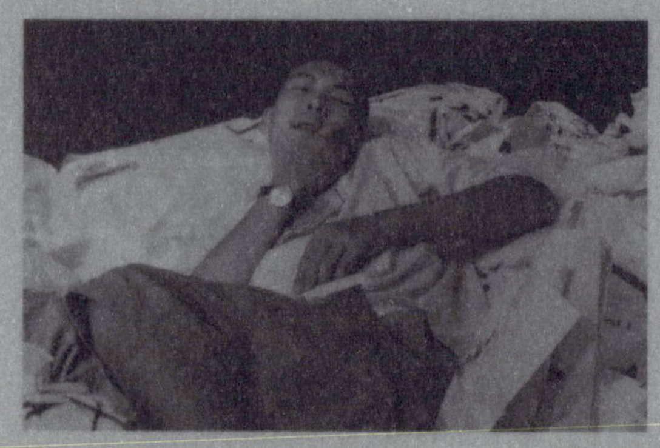

"Everything can be provided, everything is acceptable."

„Alles kann vorausgesetzt werden, alles ist annehmbar."

"一切都可能出现，一切都可能被世界接受。"

Born in 1970 in Yangjiang, China. Lives and works in Yangjiang
Geboren 1970 in Yangjiang, China. Lebt und arbeitet in Yangjiang
1970年出生于中国广东阳江，现在居住工作于阳江

Selected exhibitions / Ausgewählte Ausstellungen / 所选展览

2000 "Zheng Guogu - More Dimensional", China Art Archives & Warehouse (CAAW), Beijing, China
2002 Gwangju Biennial, Gwangju, Korea
2003 50. Biennale di Venezia, Venice, Italy
"My Home is Your Museum", Vitamin Creative Space, Guangzhou, China
"The Fifth System: Public Art In The Age Of 'Post-Planning' " - Fourth Shenzhen Contemporary Sculpture Exhibition, Shenzhen, China
2005 Second Guangzhou Triennale, Guangzhou, China
2007 documenta 12, Kassel, Germany

2000年 《郑国谷-多维》艺术文件仓库，中国北京
2002年 光州双年展，光州，韩国
2003年 第50届威尼斯双年展，威尼斯，意大利
《我家是你的博物馆》维他命创造空间 广州 中国
《第五系统：后规划时代的公共艺术》第五届深圳国际当代雕塑展，深圳
2005年 《第二届广州三年展》广州，中国
2007年 第十二届德国文件展，卡塞尔，德国

Selected publications / Ausgewählte Publikationen / 所选著作

Zheng Guogu: "Cross Back and Forth Quickly", Hong Kong 2003
Jean-Marc Decrop (ed.): "Zheng Guogu", Hong Kong 2007
"The Real Thing. Contemporary Art from China", Liverpool 2007

《郑国谷》香港 2003年
Decrop, Jean-Marc（编者）：《郑国谷》香港2007年
《真实事件：中国当代艺术》利物浦 2007年

ZHENG GUOGU 郑国谷

[tʂɤŋ kuɔku]

Zheng Guogu is a conceptual artist of globalisation, staging the world as opportunity in the endless universe of the acceptable. His functioning comparable to the work of a stage director surprises the spectator of his artistic works with a reality permeated by the ficticious. In cooperation with other artists and friends he often experiments with different media and materials to resolve the frontier between art and everyday life in another dimension.

Zheng is fond of the game and the challenge of the spectator by representations of the hitherto unthought of and astonishing. At the beginning of his artistic creations he made a name for himself with performances like "Planting Geese" (1994), the "planting" of geese dipped head first in black ink at one of the numerous construction site pits in his hometown Yangjiang or the deep frying of toy tanks ("Add Oil and March Forward Consumer", 1999) and he provokes with playful and humorous informality. Besides the quality of material the referential as well as symbolic features thereof attract his interest with his ongoing material experiments. The action on the material and his personal encounter with it build the centre and display his ravenous will for creation, the process being the utmost dictum.

Since the mid 1990s Zheng Guogu uses the media photography which due to its direct quality seems for him ideal to meet the abundance of life. For him "Nothing can compare with the directness of a 35mm shot. Photographs are easy to carry, easy to mail, easy to exhibit, easy for personal collection, easy to contact and dispose of at any time." The enthusiasm for the performance character is communicated by his photographs, true scenes of life. The work "My Teacher" (1997) is the photographic documentation of a cheerful meeting with a mentally disabled man, whose "different" view free of social restraints Zheng wants to integrate into the artistic cosmos.

The photographic works "My Bride" (1995) or "The Vagarious Life of Yangjiang Youth" (1996) are documentations of

Zheng Guogu, konzeptueller Künstler der Entgrenzung, inszeniert die Welt als Möglichkeit im unendlichen Kosmos des Annehmbaren. Mit einer Arbeitsweise, die der eines Regisseurs vergleichbar ist, überrascht er den Betrachter seiner Arbeiten mit einer vom Imaginären durchdrungenen Wirklichkeit. Oftmals in Zusammenarbeit mit anderen Künstlern und Freunden experimentiert er mit verschiedenen Medien und Materialien, um die Grenze zwischen Kunst und Alltag in einer anderen Dimension aufzulösen.

Zheng liebt das Spiel und die Herausforderung. Zu Beginn seines künstlerischen Schaffens machte er mit performativen Aktionen wie „Planting Geese" (1994) – dem „Einpflanzen" von zuvor kopfüber in schwarze Tusche getauchten Gänsen in einer der zahlreichen Baustellengruben in seiner Heimatstadt Yangjiang – oder dem Frittieren von Spielzeugpanzern – „Add Oil and March Forward Consumer" (1999) – von sich reden und provozierte mit spielerischer und humorvoller Zwanglosigkeit. Bei seinen sich bis heute fortsetzenden Experimenten interessieren ihn neben der Qualität des Materials stets auch dessen referenzielle und symbolische Eigenschaften. Die Aktion am Material und seine persönliche Begegnung mit ihm stehen im Mittelpunkt und zeigen seinen unbändigen Gestaltungswillen, dessen oberste Maxime das Prozesshafte ist.

Seit Mitte der 1990er Jahre arbeitet Zheng Guogu mit dem Medium der Fotografie, das ihm aufgrund seiner unmittelbaren Qualität ideal erscheint, um der Fülle des Lebens zu begegnen. Er selbst sagt: „Nichts ist zu vergleichen mit der Direktheit eines 35-mm-Schnappschusses. Fotografien kann man problemlos mit sich herumtragen, problemlos versenden, problemlos ausstellen, problemlos sammeln, sie stehen jederzeit problemlos zur Verfügung." So teilt sich seine Begeisterung für das Performative auch in seinen Fotografien mit. Die Arbeit „My Teacher" (1997) ist die fotografische Dokumentation einer fröhlichen Begegnung mit einem geistig behinderten Mann, dessen „anderen", von sozialen Zwängen unverstellten Blick Zheng in den künstlerischen Kosmos integrieren möchte.

郑国谷是全球化进程中的观念艺术家，在广大的人们可接受的世界中，他把整个世界作为自己的舞台。他象舞台导演一样创作着，他的艺术作品现实而虚幻，这让观众很惊异。与其他艺术家和朋友一起，他试验用不同的媒介和材料在另一种维度中去消除艺术和日常生活之间的界限。

郑国谷喜欢用人们不知道的东西和另人惊讶的东西，来嬉耍和挑战观众。在其创作初期，就因为运用象《栽鹅》（其过程是在他家乡阳江的一处建筑工地上把鹅的下半身分别栽在设计好的"陷井"内，然后强迫穿上湿淋淋的黑色"外衣"；鹅发出焦虑，和难以适应的叫声）的方式而出名，或是用油炸玩具坦克（《油炸玩具坦克》1999年）或是用游戏幽默的非正式方式挑衅社会传统。除材料的特性之外，其中的符号特征吸引他继续进行材料试验。材料试验活动和其个人与材料的碰撞，坚定了他的的创作决心，不可动摇。

从上世纪 90年代中期开始，郑国谷就用摄影创作，因为摄影的直接性能满足他在丰富多彩生活中创意的要求。对他来讲，没有其他东西能象35mm镜头更具直接性了。照片携带方便，易于邮递，展览简单，收藏简便，交流容易，在任何时候丢弃。他的照片和生活的真谛传递了热忱的行为性。作品《我的老师》（1997年）是摄影文件，记录了他与一位精神病人的欢乐相遇。郑国谷在把此人的不受社会局限的独特视角总结入其艺术体系中。

摄影作品《我的新娘》（1995年）和《阳江青年的越轨行为》"（1996年）既是记录文件，同时也是阳江生活的见证。阳江，郑国谷的家乡是他的创作空间也是他灵感的来源。《我的新娘》记录了他和一位阳江女子的虚拟婚礼，《阳江青年的越轨行为》展现了当地青年的生活方式；暴力和挥霍，照片中角色由他的朋友扮演。这幅作品的中心不是批评社会统治状况，而是对审美的和想像能力的质疑。摄影系列《一万个顾客》的主题是中国当前的消费主义

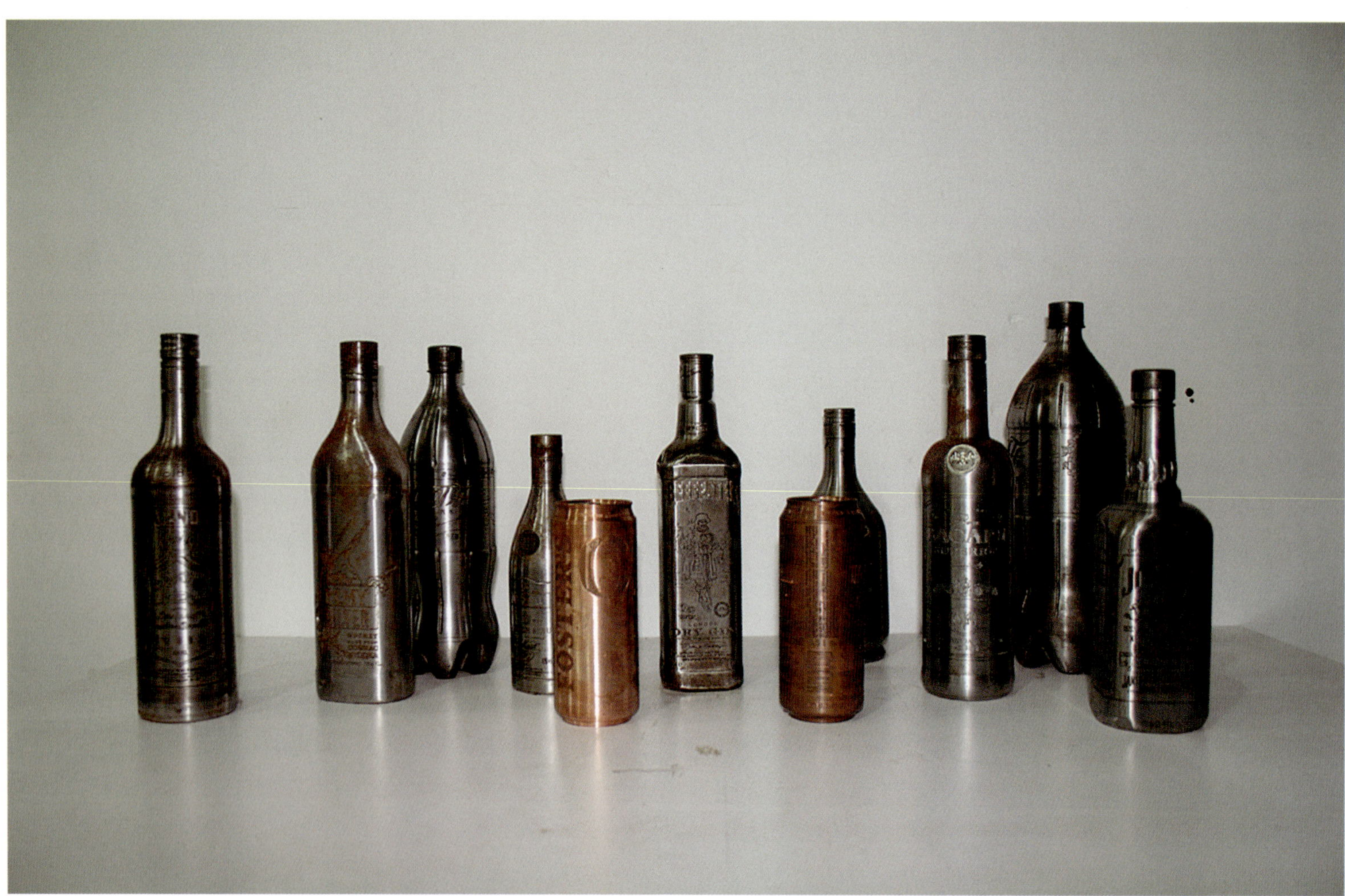

2

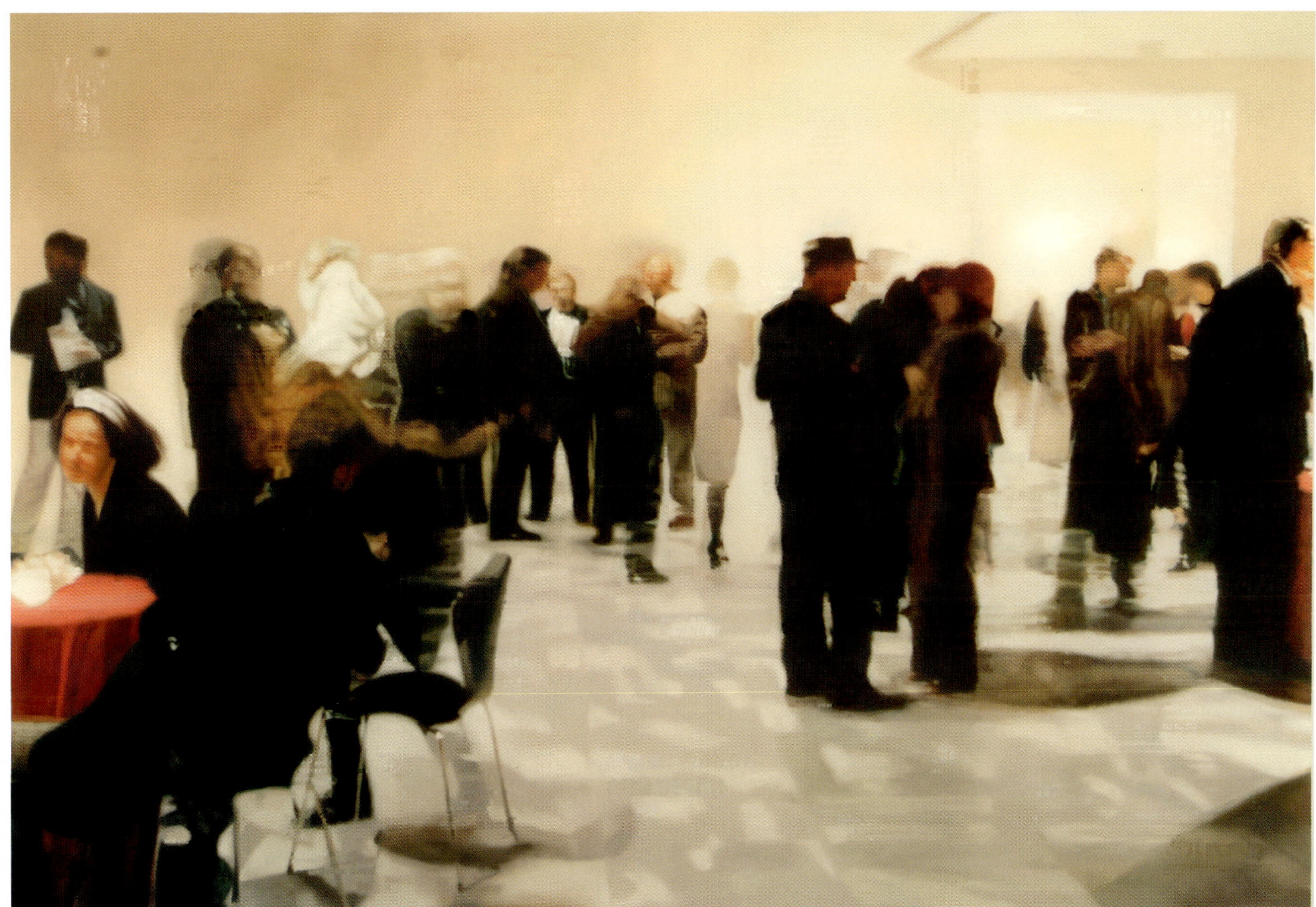

3

4

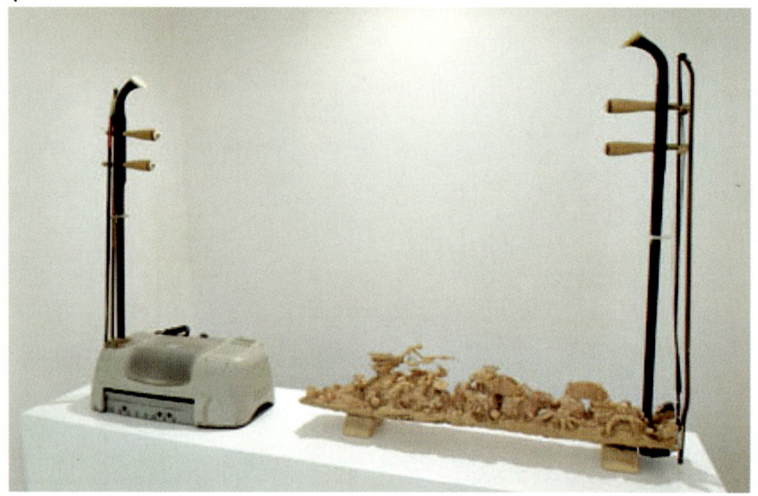

5

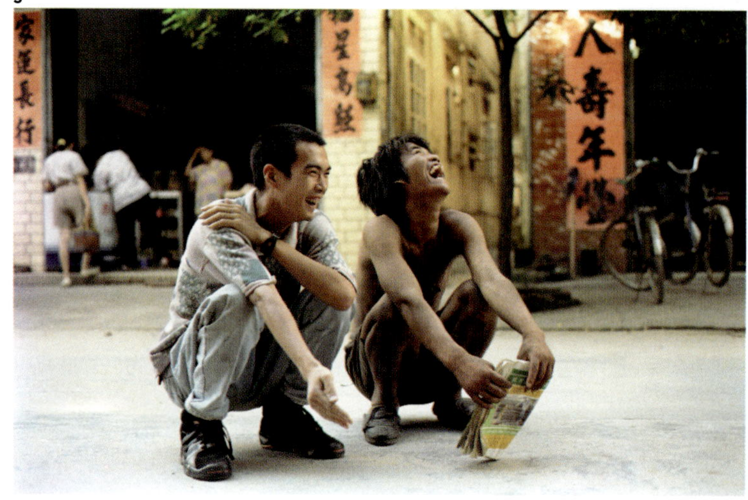

performances and referring at the same time to the life in Yangjiang, Zheng Guogu's hometown being action space as well as a source of inspiration. While "My Bride" documents his fictive wedding with a young girl of Yangjiang, the photograph series "The Vagarious Life of Yangjiang Youth" stages the life of the local youth, featured by violence and consumation, he had re-enacted by friends. The centre of this work is not the adversion on the ruling conditions, but the question of authenticity and the capability of the ficticious. The main subject of the photograph series "10000 Customers" (since 1997) is the current Chinese ideology of consumerism, drafts of individuality are expressed by spending capacity.

Zheng Guogu is an utmost multi-faceted artist. Besides performance and photography the bandwidth of his works reaches from painting, embroidery, and sculpture to calligraphy and installation. Together with his friends Chen Zaiyan, Sha Yeya and Sun Qinglin he initiated the "Yangjiang Group" in 2002, who make it their task to join traditional calligraphy with contemporary art practice in an innovative way. "Are You Going to Enjoy Calligraphy or Measure Blood Pressure?" (2002) is an interpreting installation of a traditional Chinese garden – composed of plants, a garden rock of crumpled up and dipped in wax calligraphies and an arch bridge over a "surface of water" of written rice paper being animated in wave like movements by a hidden "Qi-massage apparatus". The spectator can stroll through the garden, regard the calligraphy or may have his blood pressure measured to make in this way a new kind of aesthetic experience.

Die fotografischen Arbeiten „My Bride" (1995) oder „The Vagarious Life of Yangjiang Youth" (1996) sind Dokumentationen von Performances und nehmen zugleich Bezug auf das Leben in Yangjiang, der Heimatstadt Zheng Guogus, die für ihn sowohl Aktionsraum als auch Inspirationsquelle ist. Während er in „My Bride" seine fiktive Hochzeit mit einem jungen Yangjianger Mädchen dokumentiert, inszeniert er in der Serie „The Vagarious Life of Yangjiang Youth" das durch Gewalt und Konsum geprägte Leben der lokalen Jugend, das er von Freunden nachspielen lässt. Im Mittelpunkt steht nicht etwa die Kritik an den herrschenden Verhältnissen, sondern die Frage nach der Authentizität und dem Potenzial des Fiktiven. Thema von Zhengs Fotoserie „10 000 Customers" (seit 1997) ist die zeitgenössische chinesische Ideologie des Konsumismus, in der sich Individualitätsentwürfe in erster Linie in Kaufkraft ausdrücken.

Zheng Guogu ist ein äußerst vielseitiger Künstler. Neben Performance und Fotografie reicht die Bandbreite seiner Arbeiten von Malerei über Stickerei und Skulptur bis zu Kalligraphie und Installation. Mit seinen Freunden Chen Zaiyan, Sha Yeya und Sun Qinglin rief er im Jahr 2002 die „Yangjiang Group" ins Leben, die es sich zur Aufgabe gemacht hat, die traditionelle Schriftkunst mit zeitgenössischer Kunstpraxis auf innovative Art zu verbinden. „Are You Going to Enjoy Calligraphy or Measure Blood Pressure?" (2002) ist eine installative Interpretation eines traditionellen chinesischen Gartens – sie setzt sich aus Pflanzen, einem Gartenfelsen aus zerknüllten und in Wachs getauchten Kalligraphien sowie einer Bogenbrücke über einer „Wasseroberfläche" aus beschriebenem Reispapier zusammen, das durch eine darunter versteckte „Qi-Massage-Maschine" in wellenhafte Bewegungen versetzt wird. Der Betrachter kann durch den Garten schlendern, die Schriftkunst betrachten oder sich den Blutdruck messen lassen, um vielleicht auf diese Weise eine neuartige ästhetische Erfahrung zu machen.

观念，以及过度花钱，这种风气自1970年他出生以来就深深影响了他。

郑国谷是个多才多艺艺术家，除表演之和摄影之外，他还创作了油画、刺绣、雕塑、书法和装置作品。2002年，他与朋友陈再炎、沙业亚、孙庆麟一起创建了阳江小组，他们致力于用创新的手法将传统书法和当代艺术实践结合起来。《你去看书法还是量血压?》是中国传统园林的解释装置—园子里有花花草草，倒塌的岩石浸在蜡水中，一座拱桥跨在起伏的宣纸，宣纸在隐藏的加湿器的作用下，给人一种水波的感觉。观众在园子里溜达，浏览一幕幕现实与虚构的景色时，也许不禁心跳加速、血压增高。

Birgit Hopfener

6

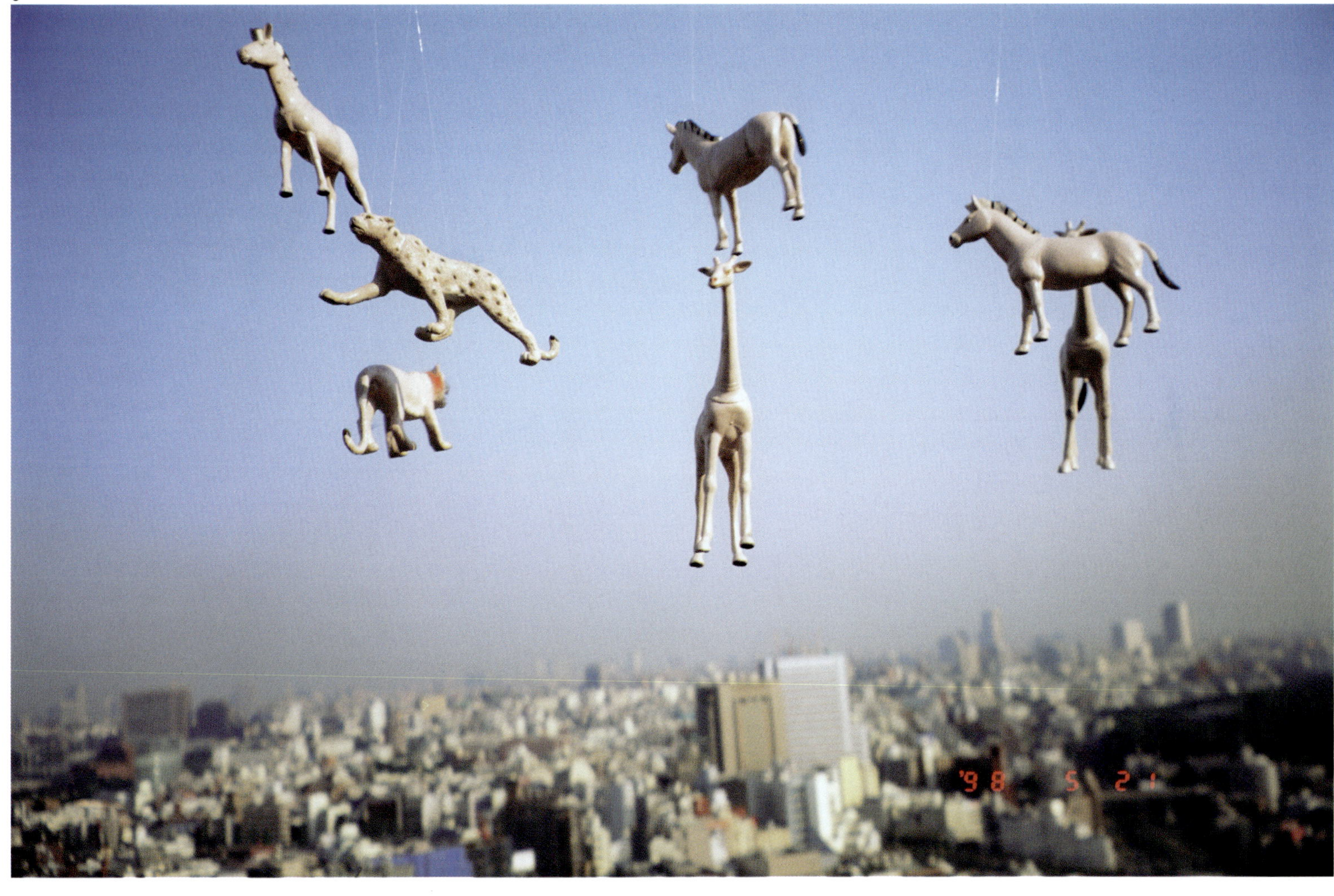

1 ***Honeymoon**, 1996*
Photograph, 60 x 100 cm
Fotografie, 60 x 100 cm
《蜜月》1996 年, 摄影, 60 x 100 cm

2 ***Year Two Thousand Another Two Thousand Years to Rust**, 2000*
23 hand made and etched life-size wine and beer bottles
23 handgefertigte und geätzte Bier- und Weinflaschen in Originalgröße
《公元两千年，再锈两千年》2000年, 23个手工雕刻实物大小酒瓶和啤酒罐

3 ***MoMA Party No. 1**, 2006/07*
Oil on canvas, 209 x 316 cm
Öl auf Leinwand, 209 x 316 cm
《MoMA 衆会 No. 1》2006/07年，布面油画和丙烯, 209 x 316 cm

4 ***Epson Printer with Erhu**, 2006*
Mixed media, 42 x 22 x 80 cm
Mixed Media, 42 x 22 x 80 cm
《带二胡的爱普生打印机》2006年, 42 x 22 x 80 cm

5 ***My Teacher**, 1997*
Photograph, 60 x 100 cm
Fotografie, 60 x 100 cm
《我的老师》1997 年, 摄影, 60 x 100 cm

6 ***Tokyo Sky Story 10**, 1998*
Photograph, 61 x 94.5 cm
Fotografie, 61 x 94,5 cm
《东京天空故事10》1998年, 摄影, 61 x 94.5 cm

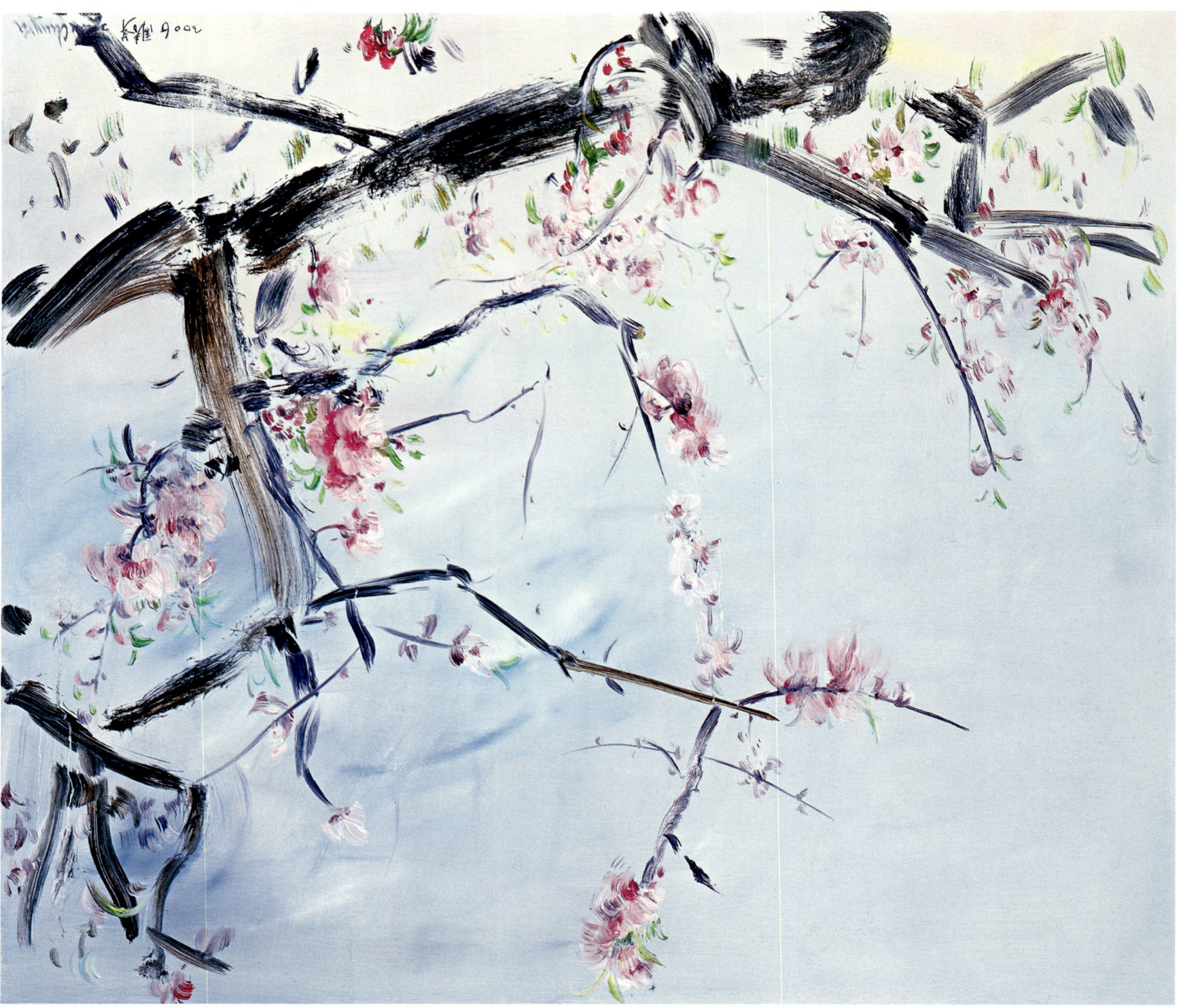

1

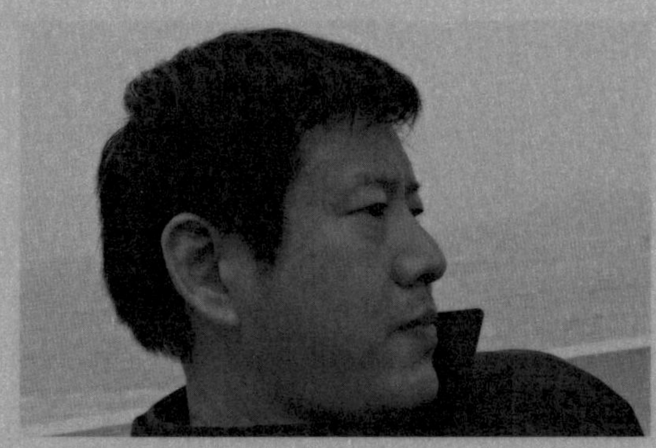

"Chinese people's minds are always complicated and contradictory, and I cherish this. Complexity of this kind is hardly to be found in modern Western pragmatic societies."

„Die Denkweise der Chinesen ist immer kompliziert und widersprüchlich, und das schätze ich sehr. Eine solche Komplexität ist in den modernen, pragmatischen Gesellschaften des Westens kaum zu finden."

"中国人的思想是复杂且自相矛盾的，但我对此而高兴。因为在现代西方的实用社会下，这种复杂性几乎难以寻觅。"

Born in 1955 in Chongqing, China. Lives and works in Chengdu
Geboren 1955 in Chongqing, China. Lebt und arbeitet in Chengdu
1955年出生于中国四川成都，现在成都居住工作

***Selected exhibitions* / Ausgewählte Ausstellungen / 所选展览**

1987 "Zhou Chunya Invitational Exhibition", Kulturzentrum Dornach-Anhof, Linz, Austria
1994 "The Works of Zhou Chunya", Xiaoya Gallery, Taipei, Taiwan
1997 "The Works of Zhou Chunya", Taipei Nothern Banker Art & Culture Art Gallery, Taipei, Taiwan
2002 "Zhou Chun Ya", Museo di Arte Moderna e Contemporanea, Trento, Italy
"Green Dogs", 314 International Art Center, Bergen, Norway
2004 "Dreaming of Dragon's Nation – Contemporary Art Exhibition from China", Irish Museum of Modern Art, Dublin, Ireland
2007 "Blooming Stories", Today Art Museum, Beijing, China

1987年 《周春芽作品邀请展》林茨，奥地利
1994年 《周春芽作品展》台北台湾
1997年 《周春芽作品展》北庄画廊, 台北, 台湾
2002年 《周春芽作品展》当代艺术博物馆，特仑托，意大利
《绿狗》, 314国际艺术中心，卑尔根 挪威
2004年 《龙之梦－中国当代艺术》爱尔兰现代艺术博物馆，都柏林，爱尔兰
2007年 《花间记》今天艺术馆，北京，中国

***Selected publications* / Ausgewählte Publikationen / 所选著作**

Lu Hong: "A Process of 'SELF' Discovery – Chinese Contemporary Oil Painting in the 1990s", in: "The First Academic Exhibition of Chinese Contemporary Art", Beijing 1996
Reena Jana: "East Meets East in the West at Limn Gallery", in: "Asian Art News", vol. 8, no. 3, May/June 1998
Yi Ying: "Bad Painting – 'Chinese Type' Contemporary Art", in: "Online Magazine", vol. 1, issue 3, March 1998

Lu Hong（著）:《 '自己' 的过程 发现– 中国当代油画在90 年代》于：《中国当代艺术的第一学术展览》, 北京 1996 年
Jana, Reena（著）:《东部见面东部在西方在Limn 画廊》于: Asian Art News, 第8卷，号3(1998年五月六月)
Yi Ying（著）:《坏的绘画 – "中国型，当代艺术》于: Online Magazine, 第1卷，号3（1998年三月）

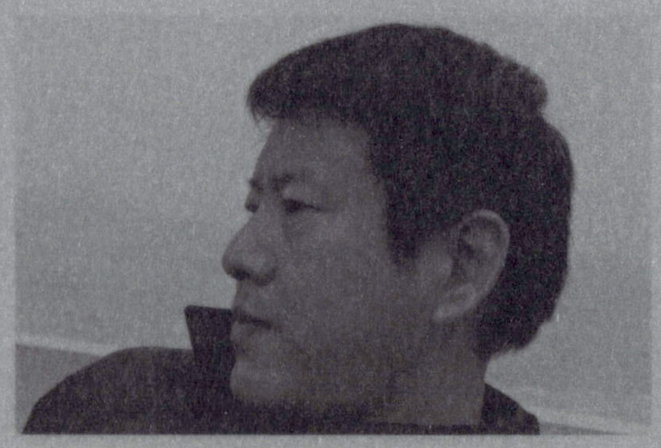

"Chinese people's minds are always complicated and contradictory, and I cherish this. Complexity of this kind is hardly to be found in modern Western pragmatic societies."

„Die Denkweise der Chinesen ist immer kompliziert und widersprüchlich, und das schätze ich sehr. Eine solche Komplexität ist in den modernen, pragmatischen Gesellschaften des Westens kaum zu finden."

"中国人的思想是复杂且自相矛盾的，但我对此而高兴。因为在现代西方的实用社会下，这种复杂性几乎难以寻觅。"

Born in 1955 in Chongqing, China. Lives and works in Chengdu
Geboren 1955 in Chongqing, China. Lebt und arbeitet in Chengdu
1955年出生于中国四川成都，现在成都居住工作

Selected exhibitions / Ausgewählte Ausstellungen / 所选展览

1987	"Zhou Chunya Invitational Exhibition", Kulturzentrum Dornach-Anhof, Linz, Austria
1994	"The Works of Zhou Chunya", Xiaoya Gallery, Taipei, Taiwan
1997	"The Works of Zhou Chunya", Taipei Nothern Banker Art & Culture Art Gallery, Taipei, Taiwan
2002	"Zhou Chun Ya", Museo di Arte Moderna e Contemporanea, Trento, Italy
	"Green Dogs", 314 International Art Center, Bergen, Norway
2004	"Dreaming of Dragon's Nation – Contemporary Art Exhibition from China", Irish Museum of Modern Art, Dublin, Ireland
2007	"Blooming Stories", Today Art Museum, Beijing, China

1987年	《周春芽作品邀请展》林茨，奥地利
1994年	《周春芽作品展》台北台湾
1997年	《周春芽作品展》北庄画廊，台北，台湾
2002年	《周春芽作品展》当代艺术博物馆，特仑托，意大利
	《绿狗》，314国际艺术中心，卑尔根，挪威
2004年	《龙之梦一中国当代艺术》爱尔兰现代艺术博物馆，都柏林，爱尔兰
2007年	《花间记》今天艺术馆，北京，中国

Selected publications / Ausgewählte Publikationen / 所选著作

Lu Hong: "A Process of 'SELF' Discovery – Chinese Contemporary Oil Painting in the 1990s", in: "The First Academic Exhibition of Chinese Contemporary Art", Beijing 1996
Reena Jana: "East Meets East in the West at Limn Gallery", in: "Asian Art News", vol. 8, no. 3, May/June 1998
Yi Ying: "Bad Painting – 'Chinese Type' Contemporary Art", in: "Online Magazine", vol. 1, issue 3, March 1998

Lu Hong（著）：《'自己'的过程 发现- 中国当代油画在90年代》于：《中国当代艺术的第一学术展览》，北京 1996 年
Jana, Reena（著）：《东部见面东部在西方在Limn 画廊》于：Asian Art News，第8卷，号3（1998年五月六月）
Yi Ying（著）：《坏的绘画 - "中国型，当代艺术》于：Online Magazine，第1卷，号3（1998年三月）

ZHOU CHUNYA 周春芽

[tʂʰou tʂuənja]

Zhou Chunya is one of a generation of Chinese painters from the inland regions whose careers read as sophisticated, knowing transitions from Socialist Realism to more contemporary, Western-influenced idioms. Born in Chongqing, he was actually trained as a painter during the Cultural Revolution, at one of the rare remaining open art schools named after Mao's famed July 5th 1940 speech arguing for "unity to the end". His parents were in fact intellectuals counted among the party faithful. After studying there between 1971 and 1974, Zhou spent two years as a propaganda painter, eventually entering the Sichuan Academy of Fine Arts in 1977, in the same class as Zhang Xiaogang, Ye Yongqing, Mao Xuhui, Wang Chuan, and a number of others who would go on to become major painters. As the first group to enter after years of political closure, the "Class of '77" was extraordinarily talented.

It was in the fervent environment of a group just getting back to work that Zhou re-made his painterly persona. In the long tradition of academic "painting from life" (xiesheng), he set off for nearby Tibet as he neared the end of his training, moving there in 1980 to complete a series of works about the locals and their customs, inflecting the Socialist Realism in which he had been trained with Impressionist devices. Having just begun to encounter a Western art history that formerly ended with Impressionism, Zhou was also eager to incorporate motifs and conventions from later post-Impressionist and Fauvist schools into these early-1980s works. He admired Giorgio de Chirico above all.

In 1986, he went to Germany, entering the master's program at the University of Kassel and visiting museums across the continent. It was then that he encountered the work of the Neo-Expressionists who would influence him so deeply: Georg Baselitz, Anselm Kiefer, A. R. Penck.

Toward the end of his time in Kassel, Zhou Chunya's interest in Chinese tradition surged, as he realized that he had never received a thorough grounding in the painting of his own nation. He returned from Germany just in time to witness

Zhou Chunya gehört zu einer Generation chinesischer Maler aus dem Landesinneren, deren Karrieren sich als differenzierte, bewusste Übergänge vom Sozialistischen Realismus zu einer zeitgemäßeren, westlich beeinflussten Bildsprache deuten lassen. Zhou wurde noch während der Kulturrevolution zum Maler ausgebildet, und zwar an einer der wenigen noch geöffneten Kunstschulen, die nach Maos berühmter Rede vom 5. Juli 1940 benannt war, in der er die „Einheit bis zum Ende" beschworen hatte. Zhous Eltern hätten als Intellektuelle eigentlich mit Repressionen rechnen müssen, wurden aber als parteikonform eingestuft. Nach seinem Studium von 1971 bis 1974 war Zhou Chunya zwei Jahre als Propagandamaler tätig und ging dann 1977 an die Sichuan Academy of Fine Arts, wo er dieselbe Klasse besuchte wie Zhang Xiaogang, Ye Yongqing, Mao Xuhui, Wang Chuan und andere heute bekannte Maler. Diese „Klasse von 1977", mit der nach Jahren der Schließung der Lehrbetrieb an der Akademie wieder aufgenommen wurde, strotzte geradezu von außergewöhnlichen Talenten.

In dem leidenschaftlichen Umfeld dieser Gruppe erfand Zhou seine Künstlerpersönlichkeit neu. In der langen Tradition des akademischen „Malens nach dem Leben" (xiesheng) brach er 1980, gegen Ende seiner Ausbildung, ins nahe Tibet auf, um eine Serie über die Tibeter und ihre Lebensweise zu schaffen, wobei er den erlernten Sozialistischen Realismus mit Mitteln des Impressionismus modifizierte, mit dem damals in China die westliche Kunstgeschichte endete. Anschließend war Zhou bemüht, auch Errungenschaften der post-impressionistischen und fauvistischen Schulen in seine frühen Arbeiten zu integrieren – mehr als jeden anderen bewunderte er allerdings den Italiener Giorgio de Chirico. 1986 ging Zhou nach Deutschland, absolvierte den Meister-Studiengang der Universität Kassel und besuchte Museen in ganz Europa, wobei er dem Werk jener Neo-Expressionisten begegnete, die ihn nachhaltig beeinflussen sollten: Georg Baselitz, Anselm Kiefer, A. R. Penck.

Gegen Ende seines Aufenthalts in Kassel entstand bei Zhou ein Interesse an der chinesischen Tradition, als ihm klar

在中国内陆地区中，周春芽是经历最为复杂的艺术家之一，其风格从社会主义现实主义转向更有当代的、受西方影响的绘画技巧。1955年出生于成都，在文化大革命期间成长为一位艺术家，当时他所就读的“五七艺校”是文化大革命时期仅存的几所院校之一。（“五七”这个名称来源于毛泽东的一份指示的日期），1971-1974年他在这里学习，毕业之后，做了两年的宣传画家，1977年考入四川美院，他所在的班上还有张晓刚，叶永青，毛旭辉，王川以及其他许多著名画家。（作为文化大革命结束后的首批学生，77班的学生出类拔萃。）

就是在这热情似火的学习环境中，周春芽改变了其艺术风格。在长期的传统写生中，周在临毕业前，到附近的西藏地区去体验生活，并在1980年完成一部系列作品。内容涉及当地风土人情，作品中融合印象主义和社会主义现实风格。印象主义是西方艺术史的终点，而周春芽在刚刚开始接触西方艺术史时，他也渴望将后印象主义和野兽派的主题和特点融入80年代早期的作品中。他最为欣赏德・基里科。1986年，他远赴德国，到德国卡塞尔综合大学攻读硕士学位，期间参观了许多博物馆。也正是那时他接触新表现主义艺术家的作品：巴泽利茨、彭克和基弗，他们周春芽的艺术生涯产生了深远的影响。

80 年代末期是其事业发展的重要时期。在即将结束卡塞尔综合大学留学时，周春芽意识到祖国的绘画缺乏深刻的了解，于是对中国传统文化产生了浓厚的兴趣并开始了研究。从德国返回中国时，正赶上1989年的学生运动，也结束自己的第一次婚姻。周春芽随后回到西藏，故地重访早年的足迹，也为其成熟系列油画作品《石头和花》奠定了基础，作品在形式和色彩上运用了在德国的所学手法。90年代初期，周回到四川，并与同行一起参展中国经验展，展览由评论家王林所策展，影响力较大。1994年，朋友赠送他一只德国牧羊犬，不久他就着手著名的系列油画，饱受争议的《绿狗》系列，作品以那只

2

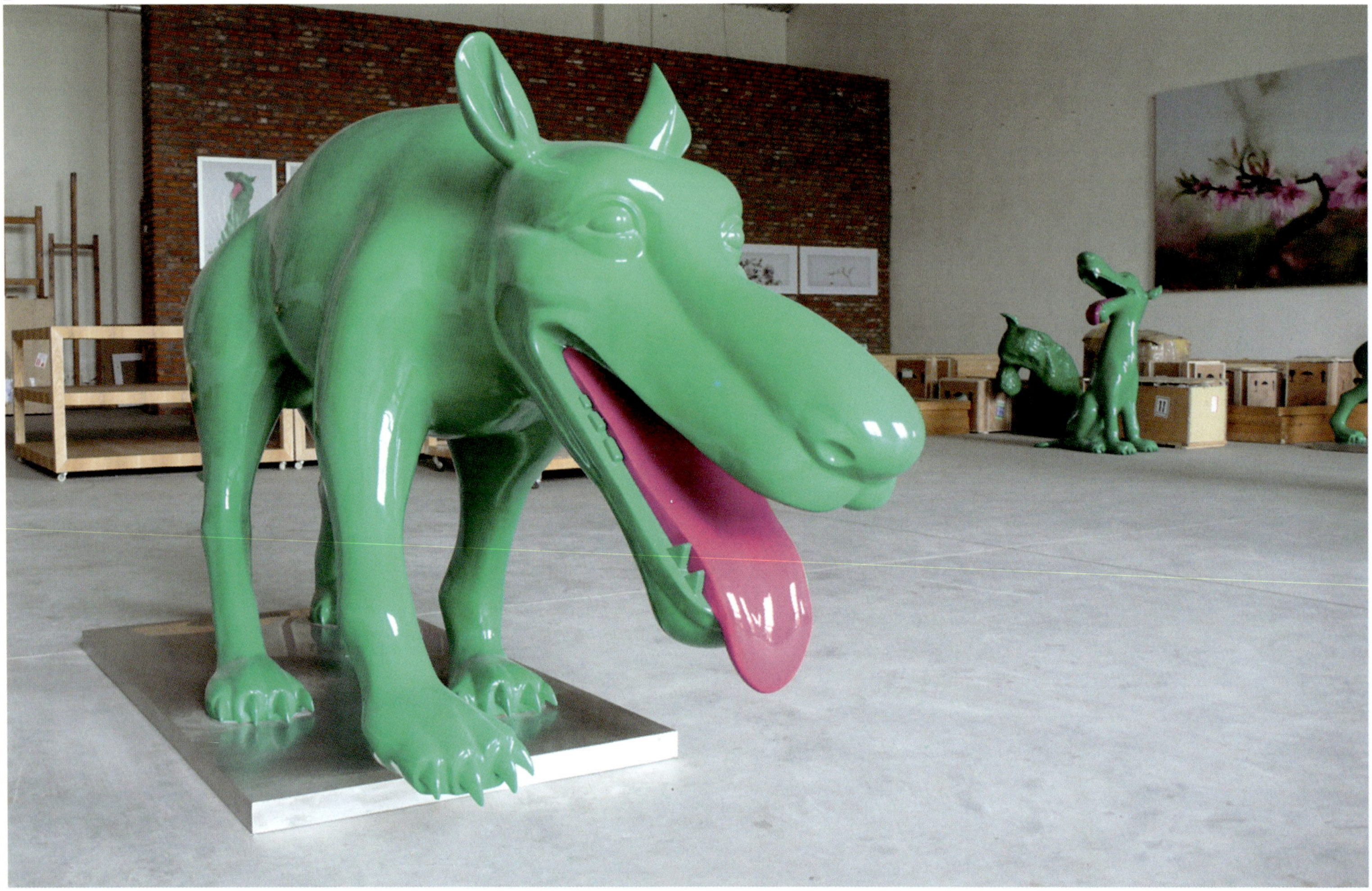

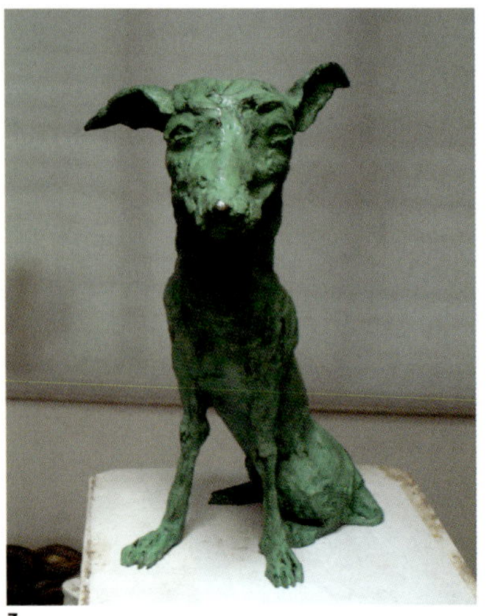

3

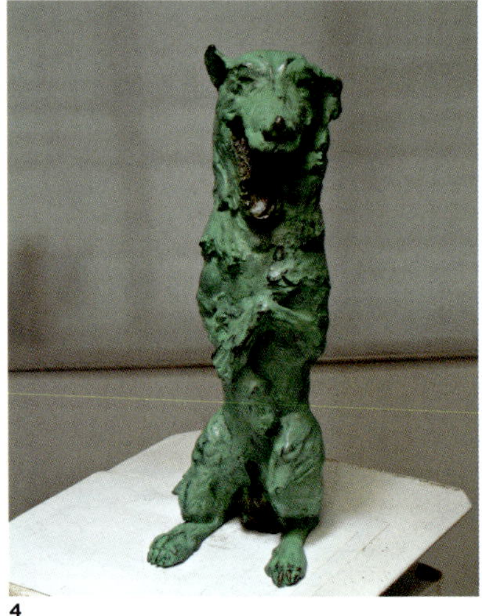

4

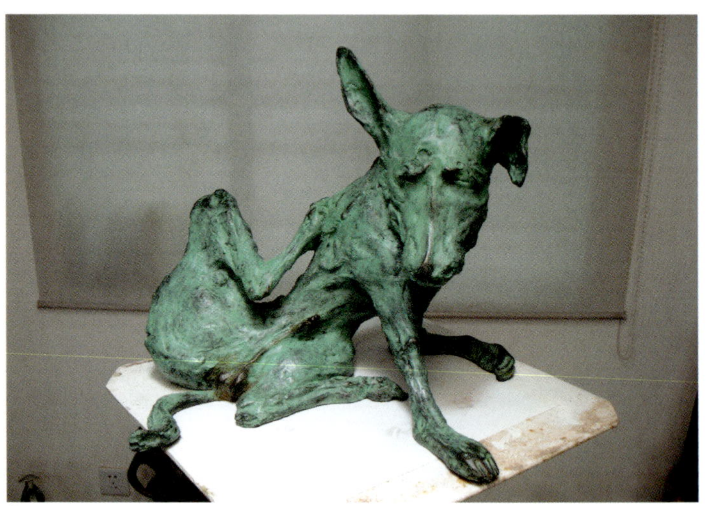

5

6

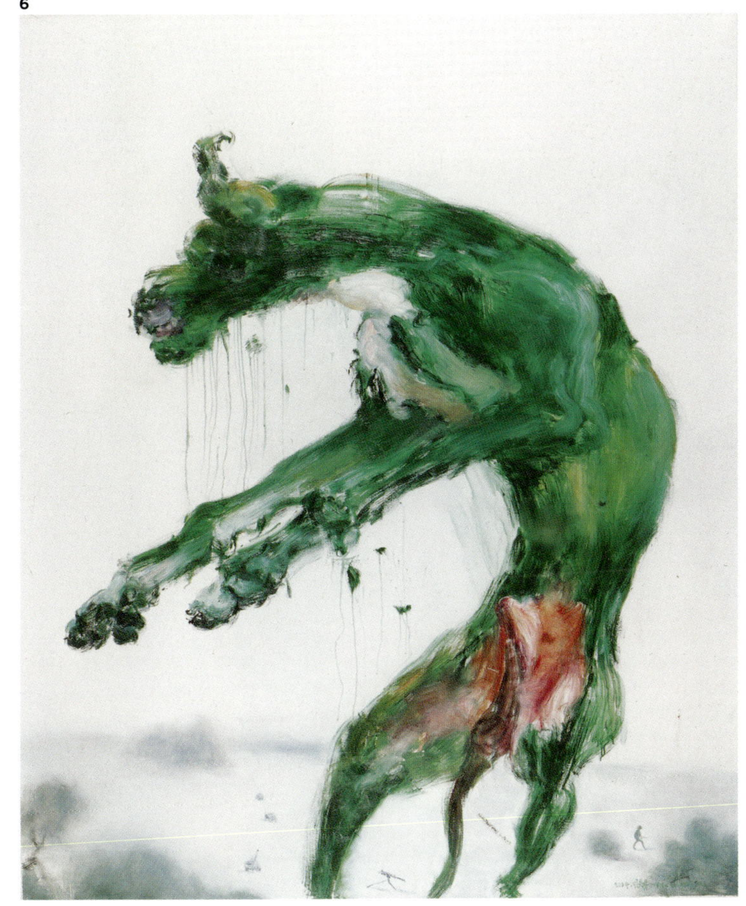

7

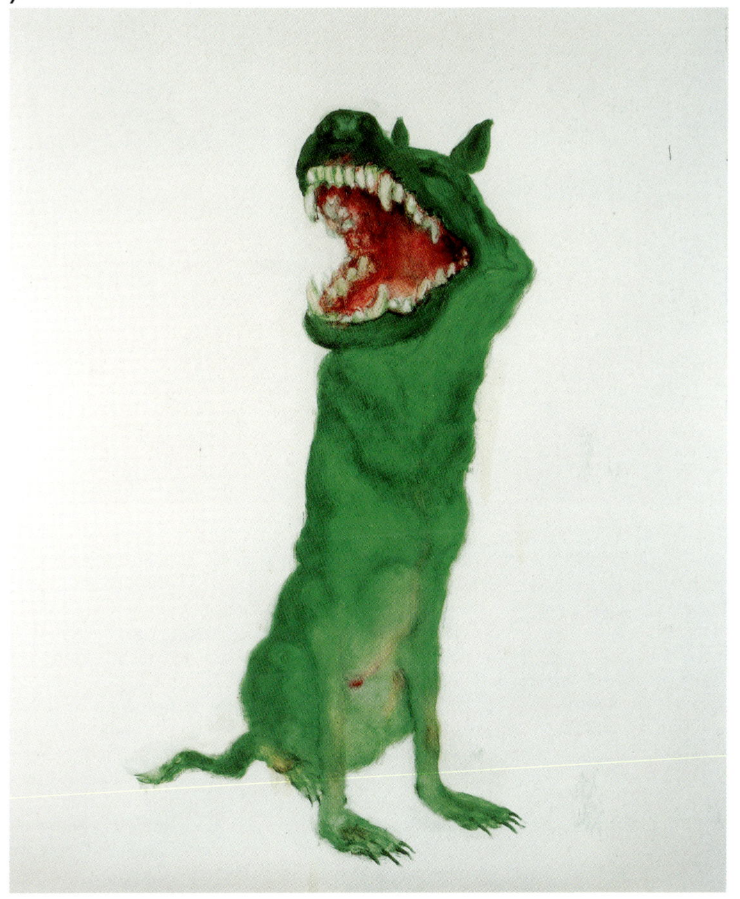

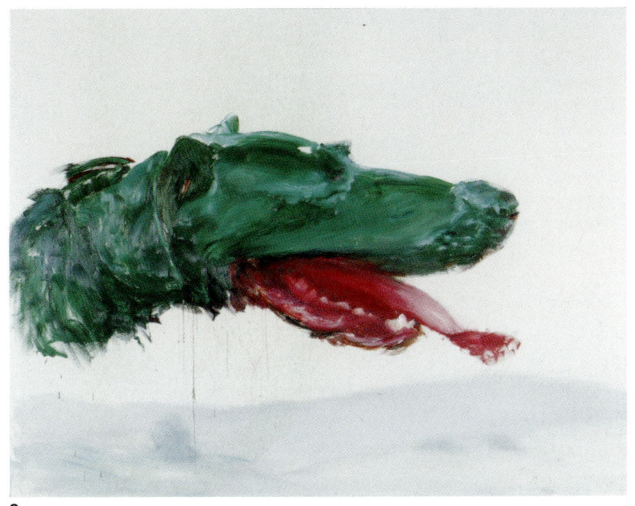

8

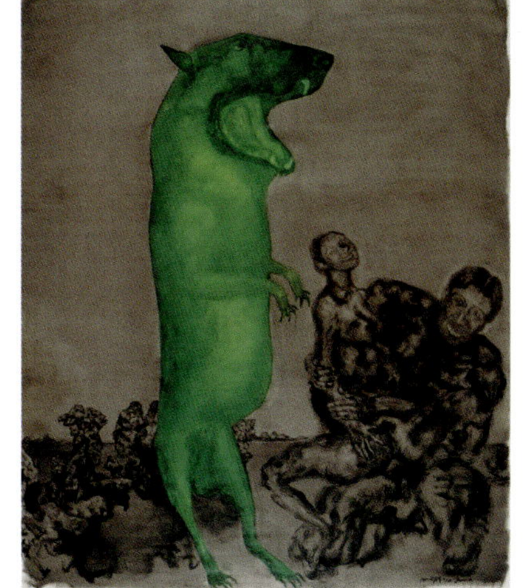

9

10

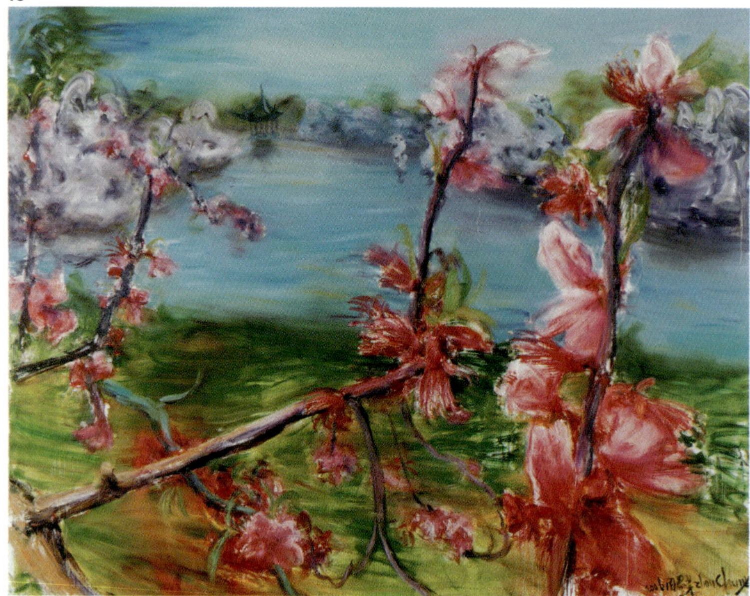

11

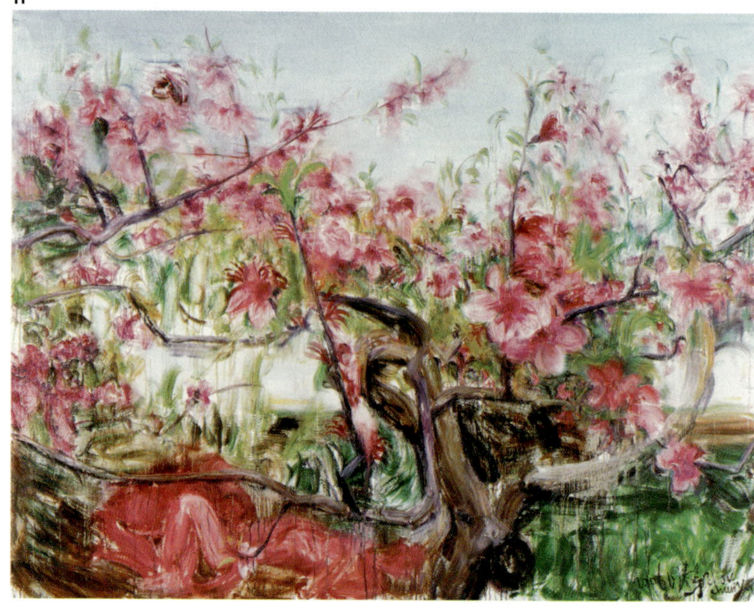

the events of 1989, which for him also included a divorce from his first wife.

Zhou soon returned to Tibet, revisiting his earlier roots and laying the foundations for his first mature series of "Stone and Floral paintings", experiments with form and colour that brought his German training back to China. In the early 1990s, back in Sichuan, he and his academy confreres mounted an influential exhibition under the curatorship of critic Wang Lin entitled "Chinese Experience."

In 1994, a friend gave him a German Shepherd puppy, and his best-known series soon began: the explosive green paintings of his faithful model, Hei Gen the dog. Hei Gen would live only until 1999, but managed to thoroughly transform Zhou Chunya's style into a direct reduction of Expressionist principles. Later series such as "Taihu Rocks" (2000), another round of Flowers, and most recently "Peach Blossoms" (2006), show a thoroughly confident Zhou, at home in a number of styles and languages. If the green dog is his signature, it never became his limit; Zhou's explorations and evolutions continue today.

wurde, dass er nie eine fundierte Grundausbildung in der Malerei seines eigenen Landes erhalten hatte. Er kehrte gerade rechtzeitig aus Deutschland zurück, um noch Zeuge der dramatischen Ereignisse von 1989 zu werden; dazu kam privat noch die Scheidung von seiner ersten Frau.

Wenig später ging Zhou erneut nach Tibet, wo er den Grundstein für seine erste ausgereifte Serie von Fels- und Blumengemälden legte, Experimente mit Form und Farbe, mittels derer er seine deutsche Ausbildung endgültig in seine chinesischen Wurzeln integrierte. In den frühen 1990er Jahren organisierten er und seine ehemaligen Kommilitonen von der Akademie in Sichuan die folgenreiche Ausstellung „Chinese Experience" unter kuratorischer Leitung des Kritikers Wang Lin.

Als 1994 ein Freund Zhou Chunya einen Schäferhundwelpen schenkte, gab er den Anstoß für Zhous bekannteste Serie: die aufsehenerregenden grünen Gemälde des Hundes Hei Gen. Obwohl das Tier schon 1999 starb, verwandelte es Zhous Stil grundlegend, der nun in direkter Reduktion expressionistischer Prinzipien arbeitete. Spätere Serien wie „Taihu Rocks" (2000), ein weiterer Blumen-Zyklus und zuletzt „Peach Blossoms" (2006) zeigen einen ausgesprochen selbstbewussten Zhou, der sich in den verschiedensten Stilen und Bildsprachen zu Hause fühlt. Der grüne Hund mag sein definitives Logo sein, bedeutete aber nie eine endgültige Ankunft: Zhous persönliche Erkundungs- und Entwicklungsreise setzt sich bis heute fort.

忠诚的狗黑根为模型。黑根在1999年死去，但却将表现主义原则直接地浓缩与周的风格中。后来的系列作品如《太湖石》，《花边人》以及近期的《桃花》，完成于这个十年的早期阶段，以多种风格和视觉语言全面展示了周的自信与实力。如果《绿狗》是他的形象，但并不是他奋斗的终点，周春芽的探索和发展至今仍在不断继续着。

Philip Tinari

12

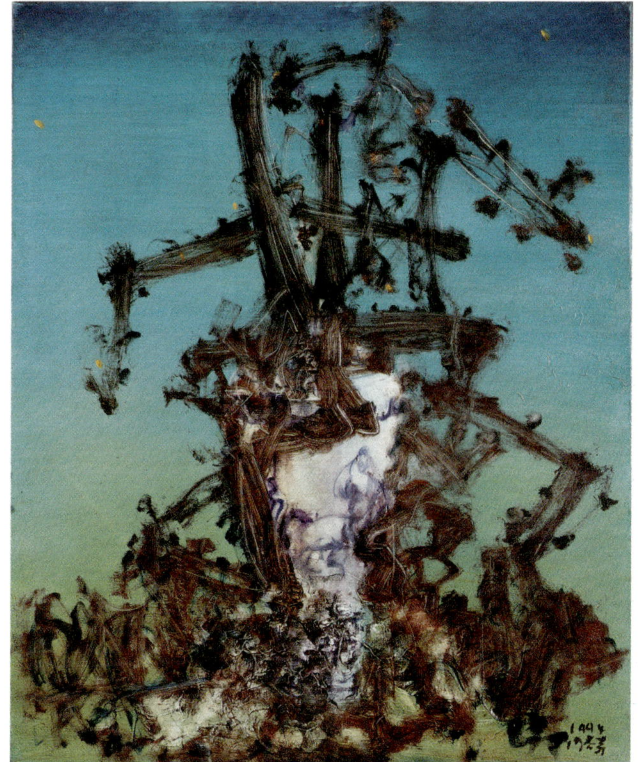

13

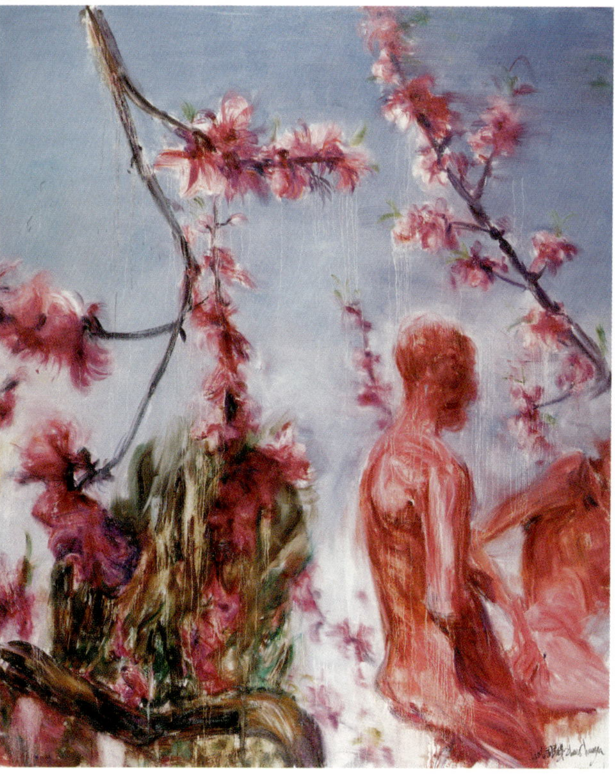

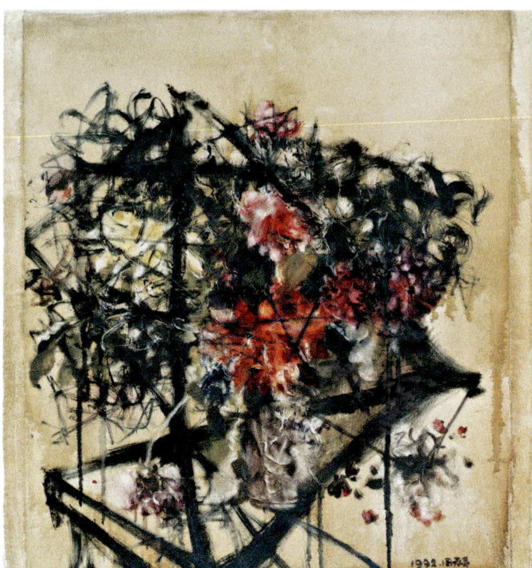

14

1 ***Meeting the Monk Huichong**, 2006*
Oil on canvas, 120 x 100 cm; Öl auf Leinwand, 120 x 100 cm
《和惠崇和尚交谈》2006, 布面油画, 120 x 100 cm

2 ***Green Dog**, 2006*
Metal, fibreglass, industrial paint, 80 x 200 x 40 cm
Metall, Fiberglas, Industriefarbe, 80 x 200 x 40 cm
《绿狗》2006年，金属，纤维玻璃，工业颜料，
80 x 200 x 40 cm

3 ***Smiling Hei Gen**, 2006*
Bronze, 46 x 30 x 24 cm; Bronze, 46 x 30 x 24 cm
《微笑的黑根》2006年, 青铜， 46 x 30 x 24 cm

4 ***Saluting Hei Gen**, 2006*
Bronze, 43 x 19 x 11 cm; Bronze, 43 x 19 x 11 cm
《作揖的黑根》2006年, 青铜， 43 x 19 x 11 cm

5 ***Scratching Hei Gen**, 2006*
Bronze, 31 x 37 x 32 cm; Bronze, 31 x 37 x 32 cm
《挠痒的黑根》2006年, 青铜， 31 x 37 x 32 cm

6 ***Green Dog No. 9**, 2004*
Oil on canvas, 250 x 200 cm; Öl auf Leinwand, 250 x 200 cm
《绿狗》No. 9, 2004年, 布面油画, 250 x 200 cm

7 ***Green Dog No. 10**, 2004*
Oil on canvas, 250 x 200 cm; Öl auf Leinwand, 250 x 200 cm
《绿狗》No. 10, 2004年, 布面油画, 250 x 200 cm

8 ***Green Dog No. 9**, 2004*
Oil on canvas, 250 x 200 cm; Öl auf Leinwand, 250 x 200 cm
《绿狗》No. 9, 2004年, 布面油画, 250 x 200 cm

9 ***Green Dog**, 2001*
Oil on canvas, 200 x 250 cm; Öl auf Leinwand, 200 x 250 cm
《绿狗》 2001年, 布面油画, 200 x 250 cm

10 ***Spring of Suzhou**, 2006*
Oil on canvas, 200 x 250 cm; Öl auf Leinwand, 200 x 250 cm
《苏州的春天》2006年, 布面油画， 200 x 250 cm

11 ***Life in Blooming Season**, 2006*
Oil on canvas, 200 x 250 cm; Öl auf Leinwand, 200 x 250 cm
《三月桃花》2006年, 布面油画, 200 x 250 cm

12 ***Flowers**, 1994*
Oil on canvas, 100 x 80 cm; Öl auf Leinwand, 100 x 80 cm
《花》1994年, 布面油画, 100 x 80 cm

13 ***Loving Stories**, 2006*
Oil on canvas, 250 x 200 cm; Öl auf Leinwand, 250 x 200 cm
《花间记》2006年, 布面油画， 250 x 200 cm

14 ***Flowers**, 1992*
Oil on canvas, 100 x 80 cm; Öl auf Leinwand, 100 x 80 cm
《花》1992年, 布面油画, 100 x 80 cm

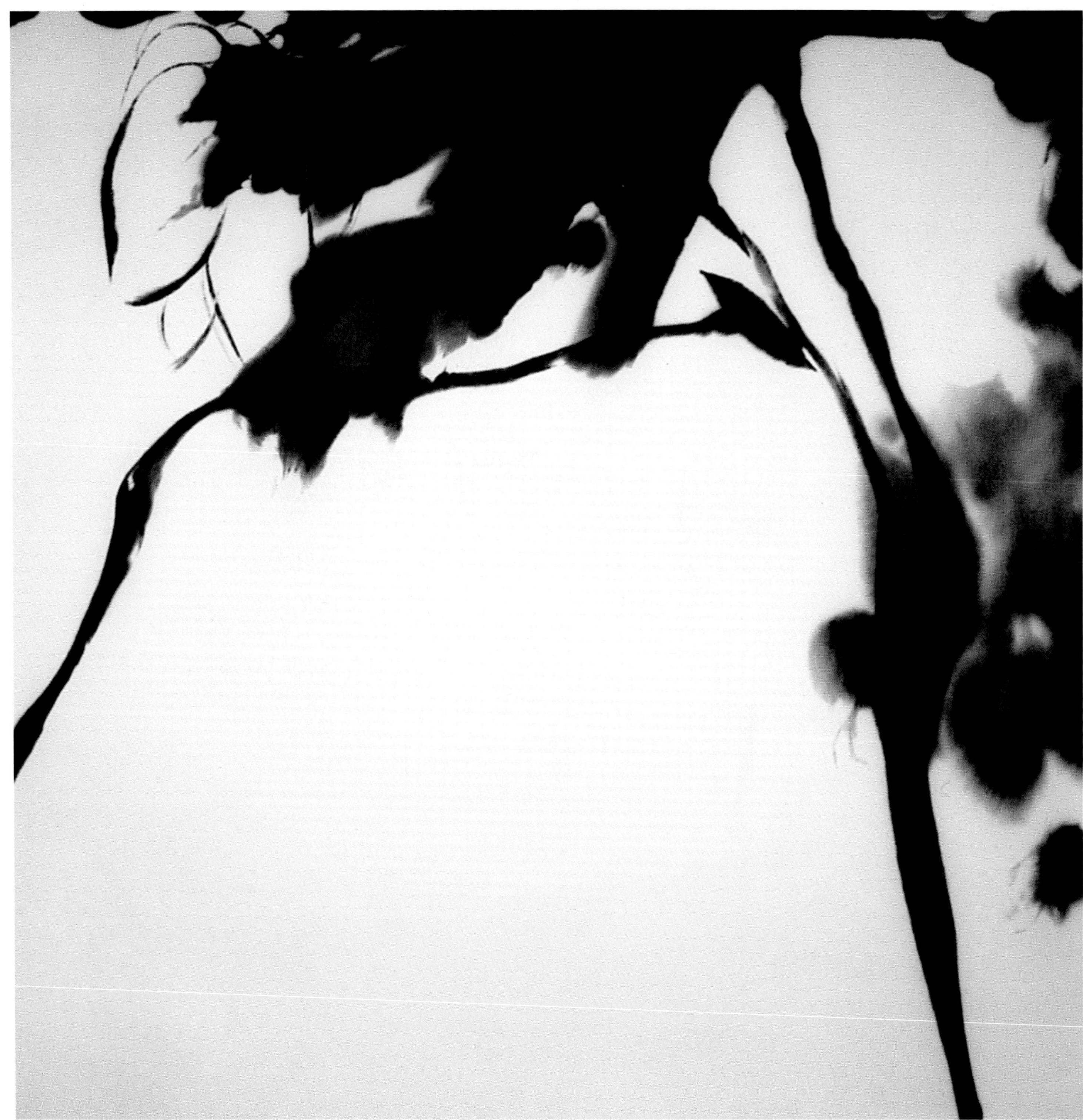

1

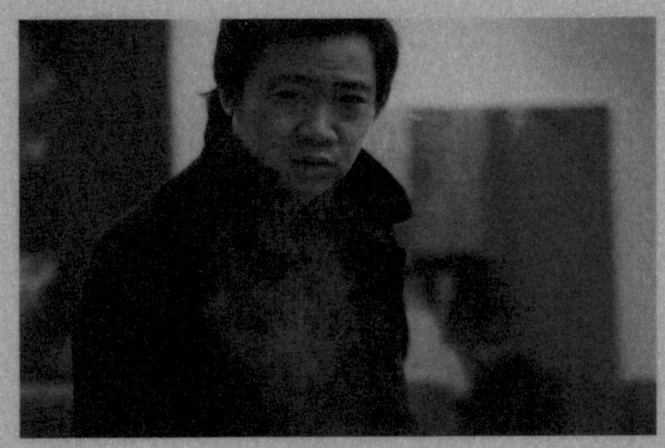

"I once wanted, like Duchamp, to open a window. But now I want to say no window is always closed and no window is always open."

„Einst wollte ich, wie Duchamp, ein Fenster öffnen. Aber jetzt würde ich sagen, dass kein Fenster immer geschlossen und kein Fenster immer geöffnet ist."

"我曾经想如Duchamp一样打开一扇窗户，但是现在想说，窗子不会永远关闭，窗子也不会永远 敞开。"

Born in 1966 in Shanghai, China. Lives and works in Shanghai
Geboren 1966 in Shanghai, China. Lebt und arbeitet in Shanghai
1966年出生于中国上海，居住工作在上海

***Selected exhibitions* / Ausgewählte Ausstellungen / 所选展览**

2004 "Zhou Tiehai: Works 1989–2003", ShanghART Gallery, Shanghai, China
5th Shanghai Biennial, Shanghai Art Museum, Shanghai, China
2005 "Follow Me! Chinese Contemporary Art at the Threshold of the Millennium", Mori Art Museum, Tokyo, Japan
2005–07 "Mahjong – Chinesische Gegenwartskunst aus der Sammlung Sigg", Kunstmuseum Bern, Berne, Switzerland; Hamburger Kunsthalle, Hamburg, Germany; Museum der Moderne, Salzburg, Austria
2006 "Zhou Tiehai: An Other History", Shanghai Art Museum, Shanghai, China
The 5th AsiaPacific Triennial of Contemporary Art, Gallery of Modern Art, Queensland Art Gallery, Melbourne, Australia

2004年 《周铁海：作品 1989-2003年》上海香格纳画廊，上海
影像生存-第五届上海双年展, 上海美术馆, 上海
2005年 《跟我来！新千年之际的中国艺术》森美 术馆，东京，日本
2005-07年 《麻将》西克中国当代艺术收藏展 伯尔尼美术馆 瑞士；汉堡美术馆 汉堡 德国；萨尔茨保现代美术馆 奥地利
2006年 《周铁海：另一种历史》周铁海艺术展, 上海美术馆，上海
《第五届亚太地区当代艺术三年展》澳大利亚墨尔本，昆士兰美术 馆

***Selected publications* / Ausgewählte Publikationen / 所选著作**

ShanghART Gallery (ed.): "Zhou Tiehai, ShanghART Gallery", Shanghai 2004
Harald Szeemann: "Zhou Tiehai: Placebo", Tokyo 2006
Uta Grosenick, Sine Bepler (eds.): "ShanghART Gallery 10 Years", Cologne 2006

ShanghART Gallery（著）:《周铁海》上海香格纳画廊，上海2004年
Szeemann, Harald（著）:《周铁海: 安慰药》日本，东京，原美术馆2006年
Grosenick, Uta/Bepler, Sine（编者）:《上海香格纳画廊10年》 科隆2006

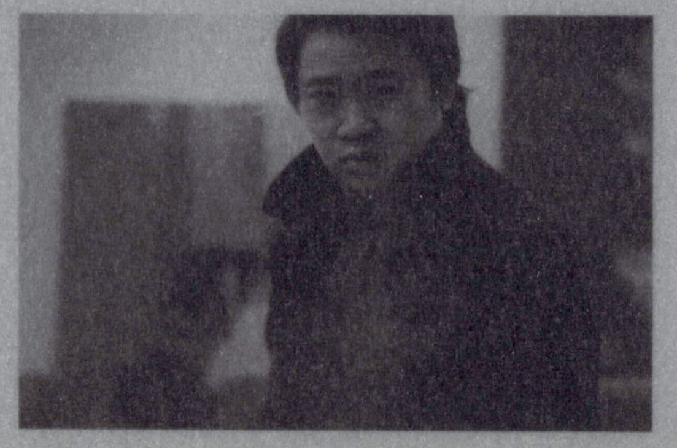

"I once wanted, like Duchamp, to open a window. But now I want to say no window is always closed and no window is always open."

„Einst wollte ich, wie Duchamp, ein Fenster öffnen. Aber jetzt würde ich sagen, dass kein Fenster immer geschlossen und kein Fenster immer geöffnet ist."

"我曾经想如Duchamp一样打开一扇窗户，但是现在想说，窗子不会永远关闭，窗子也不会永远 敞开。"

Born in 1966 in Shanghai, China. Lives and works in Shanghai
Geboren 1966 in Shanghai, China. Lebt und arbeitet in Shanghai
1966年出生于中国上海，居住工作在上海

Selected exhibitions / Ausgewählte Ausstellungen / 所选展览

2004 "Zhou Tiehai: Works 1989-2003", ShanghART Gallery, Shanghai, China
5th Shanghai Biennial, Shanghai Art Museum, Shanghai, China
2005 "Follow Me! Chinese Contemporary Art at the Threshold of the Millennium", Mori Art Museum, Tokyo, Japan
2005-07 "Mahjong - Chinesische Gegenwartskunst aus der Sammlung Sigg", Kunstmuseum Bern, Berne, Switzerland; Hamburger Kunsthalle, Hamburg, Germany; Museum der Moderne, Salzburg, Austria
2006 "Zhou Tiehai: An Other History", Shanghai Art Museum, Shanghai, China
The 5th AsiaPacific Triennial of Contemporary Art, Gallery of Modern Art, Queensland Art Gallery, Melbourne, Australia

2004年 《周铁海：作品 1989-2003年》上海香格纳画廊，上海
影像生存-第五届上海双年展，上海美术馆，上海
2005年 《跟我来！新千年之际的中国艺术》森美 术馆，东京，日本
2005-07年 《麻将》西克中国当代艺术收藏展 伯尔尼美术馆 瑞士：汉堡美术馆 汉堡 德国；萨尔茨堡现代美术馆 奥地利
2006年 《周铁海：另一种历史》周铁海艺术展，上海美术馆，上海
《第五届亚太地区当代艺术三年展》澳大利亚墨尔本，昆士兰美术 馆

Selected publications / Ausgewählte Publikationen / 所选著作

ShanghART Gallery (ed.): "Zhou Tiehai, ShanghART Gallery", Shanghai 2004
Harald Szeemann: "Zhou Tiehai: Placebo", Tokyo 2006
Uta Grosenick, Sine Bepler (eds.): "ShanghART Gallery 10 Years", Cologne 2006

ShanghART Gallery（著）：《周铁海》上海香格纳画廊，上海2004年
Szeemann, Harald（著）：《周铁海：安慰药》日本，东京，原美术馆2006年
Grosenick, Uta/Bepler, Sine（编著）：《上海香格纳画廊10年》 科隆2006

ZHOU TIEHAI 周铁海

[tʂou tʰiɛxaɪ]

Zhou Tiehai is the self-appointed critic of the Chinese art scene, creating works that lampoon the art market, collectors and artists alike, both from the East and the West. At the same time, he has embraced many of the tactics that he criticizes and by doing so has become one of the most high profile artists in China. He is a self-promoter while condemning narcissism, a painter who would never touch a paint brush, a copyist who celebrates originality.

His first projects, created in the late 1990s, pointedly satirized western attitudes towards Chinese artists. His film, "Will" (or "We must", 1997), showed a group of Chinese artists trying to reach out to an international audience by building an airport, but when the western critics and curators arrived, they made little effort to understand the art work on view. In "Press Conference" (1998), a photo-painting with text, Zhou Tiehai is seen standing at a podium and announcing, "The relations in the art world are the same as the relations between states in the post Cold War era." From this and other works, it is clear that this artist wants to expose the difficulties of making and exhibiting art in a global context, even as this phenomenon creates many new possibilities for Chinese artists.

Though many Chinese artists have used advertising logos and brand names to comment on commercialism, Zhou Tiehai thoroughly embraced this technique yet personalized it and made it his own. He is identified with his use of Joe Camel, the kid-friendly face of Camel cigarettes, whom the artist employs as an irreverent commentary on contemporary art. In this series, on-going since 2001, Joe Camel replaces the faces of famous figures from art history or he is found posing as collectors and artists known in contemporary art circles.

At the same time, Zhou Tiehai has also examined the workings of Chinese traditional painting, making imitations of well-known brush paintings, transposed into bright colors on canvas. He calls these two series "Placebo" (since 1999) and "Tonic" (since 2001), two antidotes to ills that are not

Zhou Tiehai ist der selbsternannte Kritiker der chinesischen Kunstszene. Seine Werke machen sich über den Kunstmarkt lustig, über Sammler und Künstler, ob aus Ost oder West. Gleichzeitig hat er sich viele der Methoden zu eigen gemacht, die er kritisiert, und ist dadurch zu einem der meistbeachteten Künstler Chinas geworden. Als Werbetreibender in eigener Sache prangert er gnadenlos den Narzissmus seiner Kollegen an – ein Maler, der niemals einen Pinsel anrühren würde, und ein Kopist, der die Originalität preist.

Seine ersten Projekte entstanden in den späten 1990er Jahren – treffende Satiren auf die Haltung des Westens gegenüber chinesischen Künstlern. Sein Film „Will" (oder „We must", 1997) zeigt eine Gruppe chinesischer Künstler, die ein internationales Publikum zu erreichen versuchen, indem sie einen Flughafen bauen. Als aber die westlichen Kritiker und Kuratoren dort eintreffen, geben diese sich kaum Mühe, die präsentierten Kunstwerke zu verstehen. In „Press Conference" (1998), einem Fotogemälde mit Text, sieht man Zhou Tiehai an einem Rednerpult verkünden: „Die Beziehungen in der heutigen Kunstwelt entsprechen haargenau den zwischenstaatlichen Beziehungen nach dem Kalten Krieg." Zhous Intention bei diesen und anderen Arbeiten ist es, aufzudecken, wie kompliziert es ist, Kunst im globalen Kontext zu schaffen und an die Öffentlichkeit zu bringen, auch wenn gerade dieser Kontext den chinesischen Künstlern zahlreiche neue Möglichkeiten eröffnet.

Viele chinesische Künstler haben Werbelogos und Markenzeichen verwendet, um die allgemeine Kommerzialisierung im Land zu kommentieren. Zhou Tiehai hat diese Taktik übernommen, sie personalisiert und etwas ganz Eigenes daraus gemacht: Man identifiziert ihn heute mit Joe Camel, dem kinderfreundlichen Gesicht der Camel-Werbung, das der Künstler für respektlose Kommentare zur zeitgenössischen Kunst instrumentalisiert. In dieser seit 2001 laufenden Serie setzt Zhou etwa an die Stelle der Gesichter berühmter Modelle aus der Kunstgeschichte das Antlitz Joe Camels, oder Joe Camel tritt in Gestalt von Sammlern und Künstlern auf, die in Kunstkreisen wohlbekannt sind.

周铁海自封为中国艺术批评家，他创作的一些作品讽刺了艺术市场，收藏家和艺术家，包括从东方到西方。在同一时期，他信奉许多他所批评的策略，因而成为中国最有鲜明姿态的艺术家之一。他是一位谴责自恋的自我促进者，一位从来没有碰过画刷的画家，一位赞美创新的模仿者。

他的首部作品，创作于20世纪90年代末期，作品尖锐地讽刺了西方对待中国艺术家的态度。他的影片《意愿》1997年，展示了一群中国艺术家通过建造一座机场来试图接近国际观众，但是当西方的评论家和艺术馆长抵达以后，他们却不努力去挖掘艺术作品所蕴含的观点。1998年的一张含有文本的照片绘画，《在记者招待会上》，周铁海站在指挥台上宣布：艺术领域的关系雷同于后冷战时期国与国之间的关系。从这部作品和其他作品，很明显地看出周铁海在试图揭露全球关系下创作和展示作品的艰难，即使这种现象可能为中国艺术家创造了许多新的机会。

虽然许多中国艺术家过去也常常用广告标志和品牌名称去评论商业主义，但周完全地拥抱这种手法并把其个人化，成为自己特有风格。周铁海因为使用Joe Camel，而著称，Joe Camel是Camel 香烟的孩子友好的面孔代言人。他用其作为对当代艺术的不尊重的注释，在这组作品到从2001年以来，Joe Camel 或是代替了艺术史上著名的人物，或是以当代艺术圈中著名的收藏家和艺术家的姿态出现。在同时，周也考察了中国传统国画的风格，模仿众所周知的毛笔画法，把鲜艳的色彩涂到到帆布上。他称作《安慰剂》和《补剂》，两部作品为绝症的解毒剂。同样地，在他许多作品中，周力求当代艺术放弃浅薄性而在作品中强调更重要的人性一面。

然而，周铁海没有遵循他自己的戒条，转而突出人造作品高于其他任何价值，如他在最近作品中的80年代的电影明星的肖像画. 类似于Andy Warhol, 周铁海的油画是由其助手团队运用油漆喷雾技术完成，

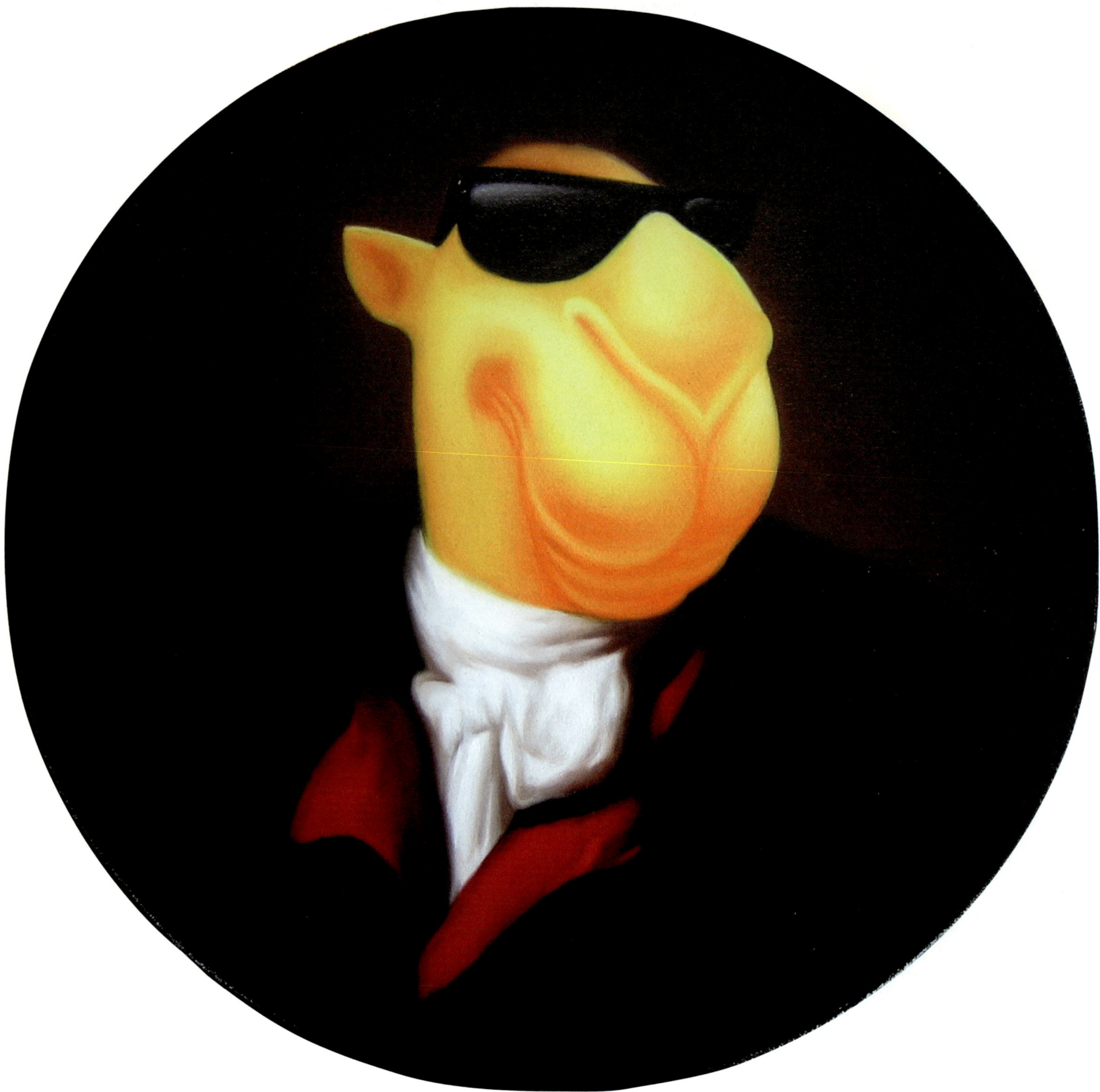

2

3

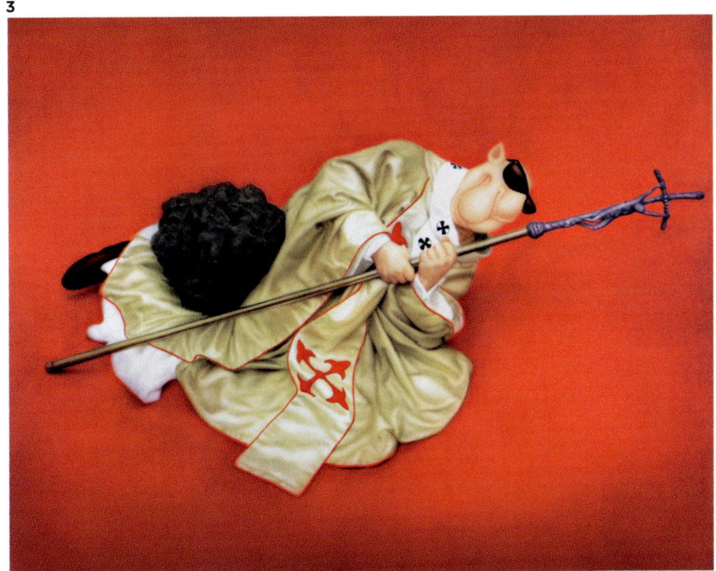

4

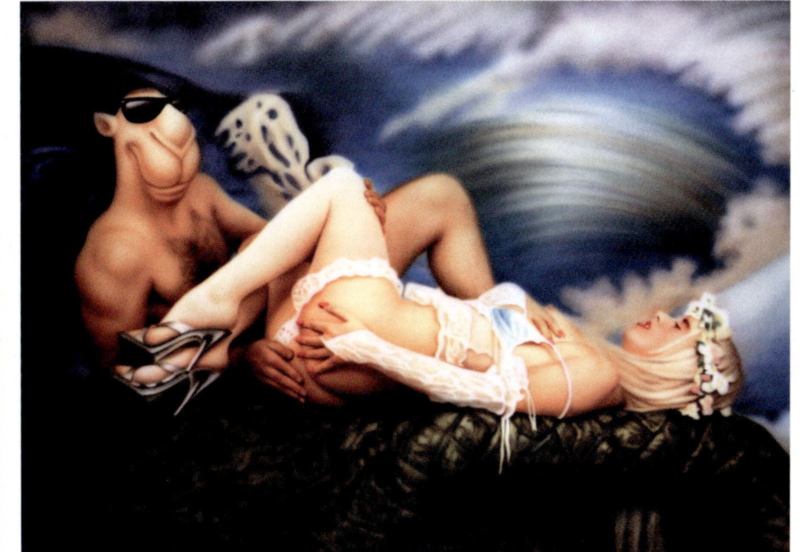

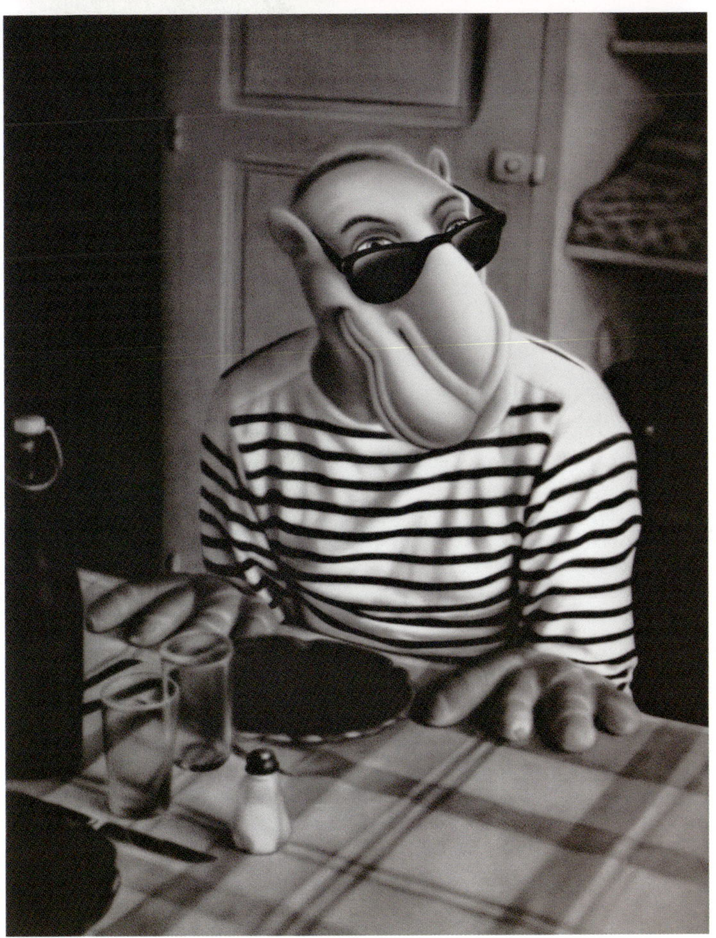

5

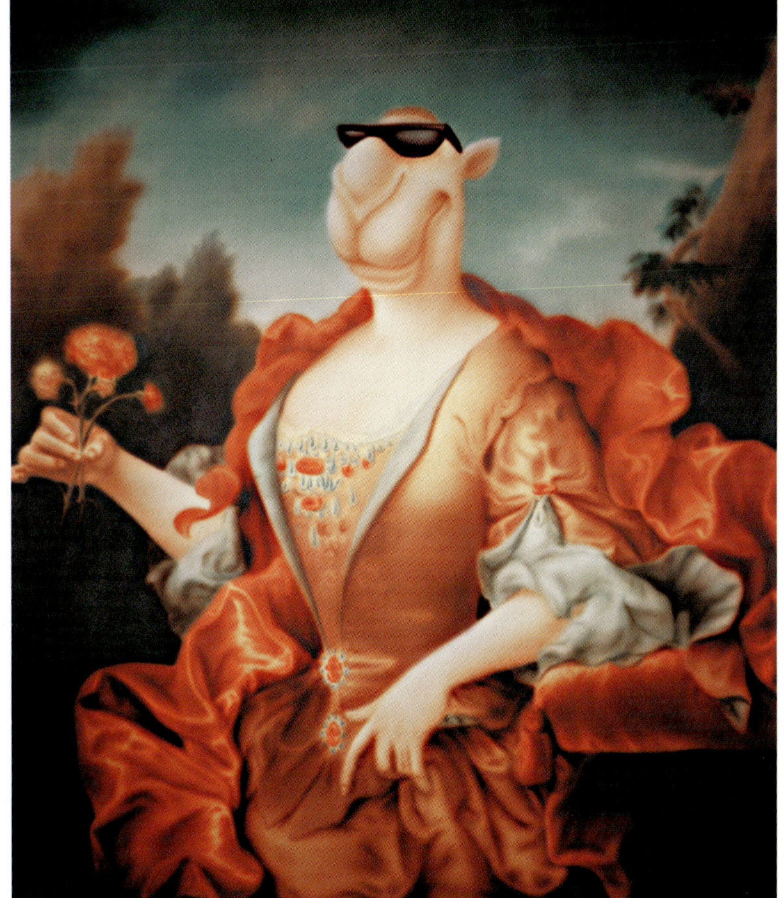

6

7

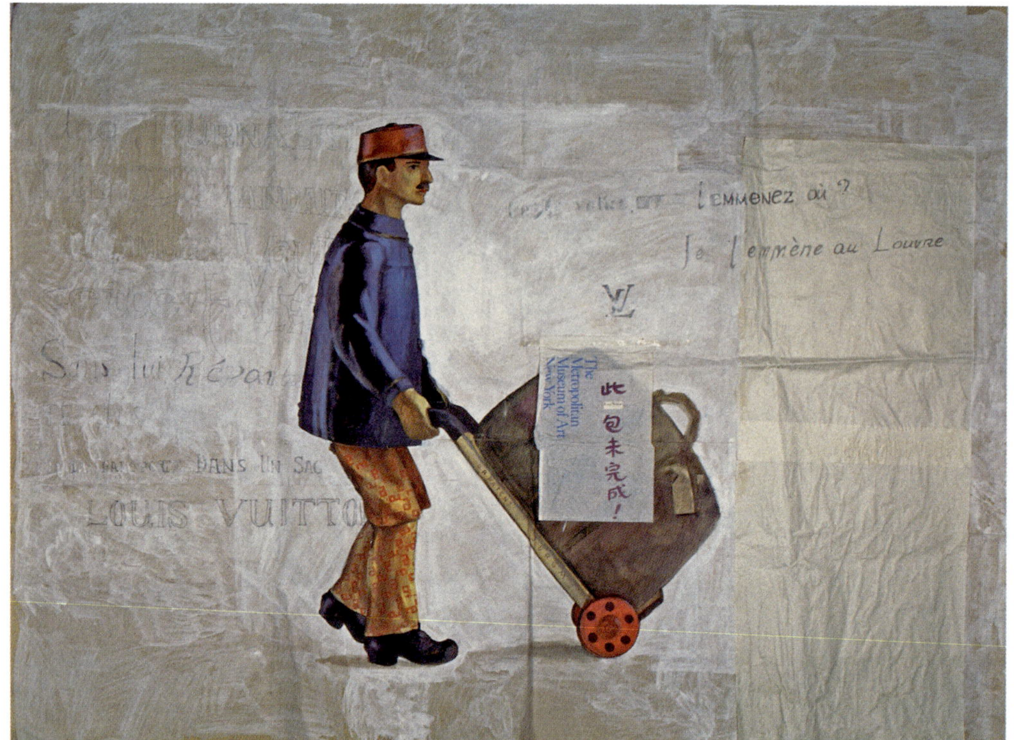

8

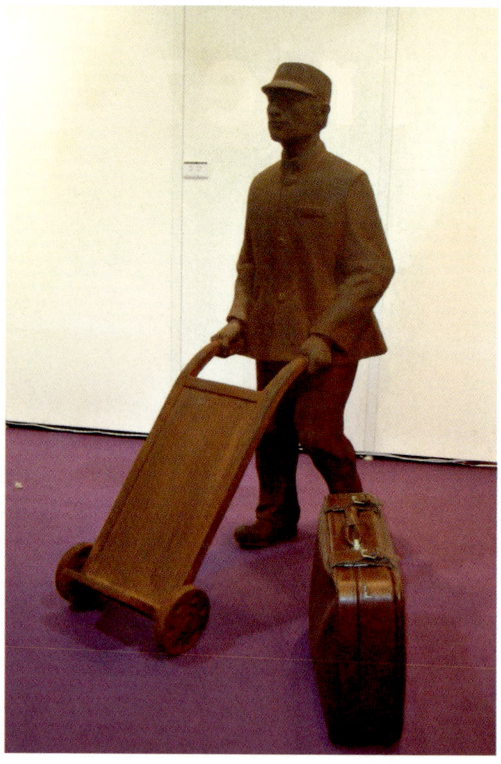

really cures. Likewise, in his many writings, this artist urges contemporary art to abandon superficiality and address more important aspects of the human condition.

Yet, Zhou Tiehai does not follow his own admonition, instead choosing to highlight artificiality above all other values, as in his more recent series of portraits of 1980s Chinese movie stars. Like Andy Warhol, his canvases are made by teams of assistants, using airbrush techniques employed by graphic designers and graffiti artists. The resulting effect is the complete consistency of mass production; the canvases could easily be billboards or posters which is, indeed, precisely the artist's point.

Parallel dazu untersuchte Zhou Tiehai die Funktion der traditionellen chinesischen Malerei, indem er Kopien bekannter Gemälde teils in Leuchtfarben auf die Leinwand übertrug. Er nannte die dabei entstandenen Serien „Placebo" (seit 1999) und „Tonic" (seit 2001) – beides als Mittel gegen bestimmte Leiden empfohlen, ohne echte Heilung zu bringen. Zugleich mahnt der Künstler in seinen vielen Schriften die zeitgenössische Kunst, der Oberflächlichkeit zu entsagen und sich wichtigeren Aspekten der menschlichen Existenz zuzuwenden.

Zhou Tiehai folgt dieser Mahnung selbst nicht unbedingt. Vielmehr konzentriert er sich darauf, die Künstlichkeit als höchsten aller herrschenden Werte zu entlarven, wie in seiner unlängst entstandenen Porträtserie chinesischer Kinostars aus den 1980er Jahren. Wie Andy Warhol lässt Zhou seine Leinwände durch ganze Teams von Gehilfen mit Airbrushtechniken bearbeiten, wie sie von Grafikdesignern und Graffitikünstlern eingesetzt werden. Das Resultat vermittelt die völlige Einheitlichkeit von Massenprodukten: Diese Gemälde könnten ebenso gut Werbewände oder Plakate sein – und eben darauf will der Künstler hinaus.

这些助理团队一般是美术设计师和街道画艺术家所雇用。所产生的效果是完全是规模生产的连贯性，这些帆布可以很容易的作为广告牌或海报使用，而这正是周的指向。

Barbara Pollack

9

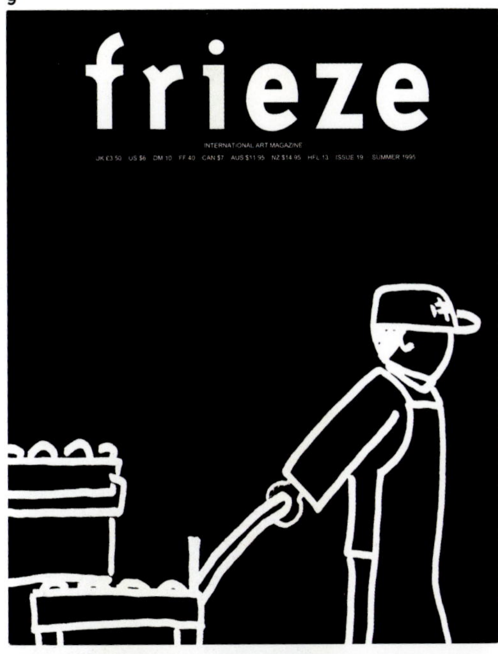

10

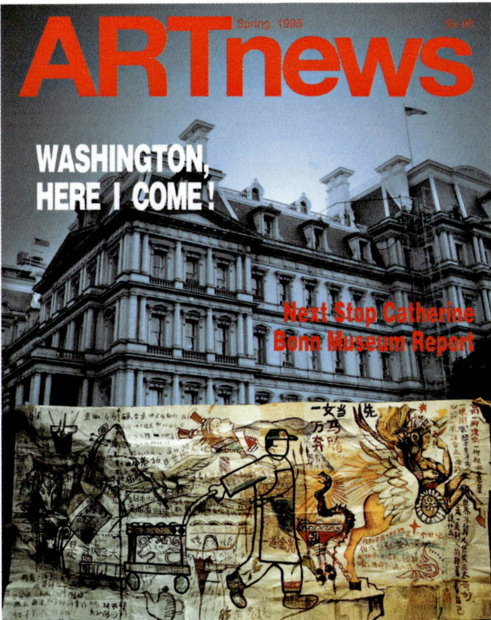

11

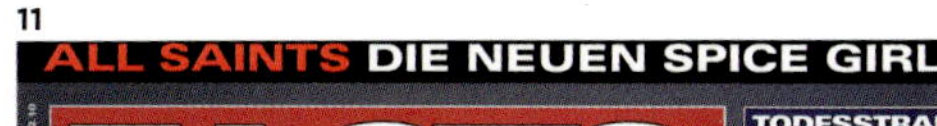

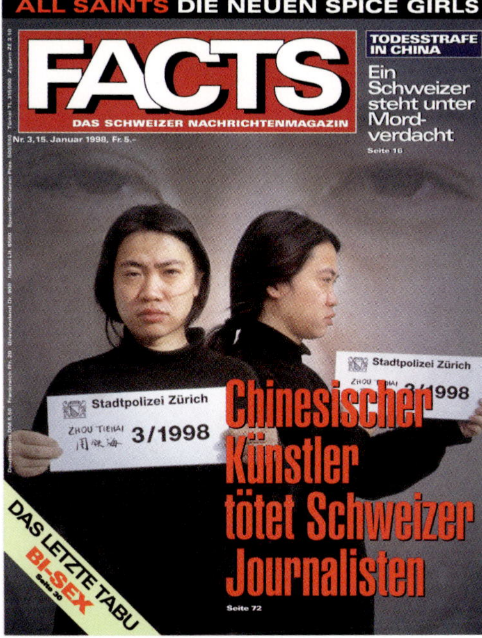

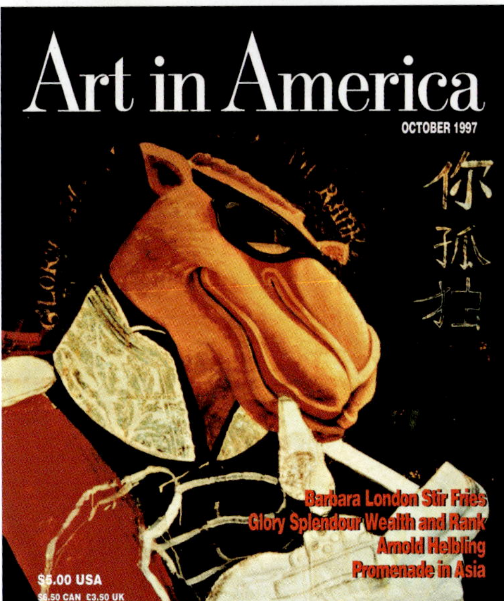

12

1 ***Lotus***, *2004*
Acrylic (airbrush) on canvas, 175 x 170 cm
Acryl (Airbrush) auf Leinwand, 175 x 170 cm
《莲》2004年，布面丙烯酸（气刷）175 x 170 cm

2 ***Untitled***, *2006*
Oil on canvas, 46 cm diameter
Untitled, 2006, Öl auf Leinwand, Durchmesser 46 cm
《无题》2006年，布面油画，直径 46 cm

3 ***Maurizio Cattelan I***, *2006*
Acrylic (airbrush) on canvas, 240 x 300 cm
Acryl (Airbrush) auf Leinwand, 240 x 300 cm
《Maurizio Cattelan I》2006年，布面丙烯酸（气刷）240 x 300 cm

4 ***Jeff Koons II***, *2006*
Acrylic (airbrush) on canvas, 175 x 240 cm
Acryl (Airbrush) auf Leinwand, 175 x 240 cm
《Jeff Koons II》2006年，布面丙烯酸（气刷）175 x 240 cm

5 ***Pablo Picasso***, *2006*
Acrylic (airbrush) on canvas, 240 x 180 cm
Acryl (Airbrush) auf Leinwand, 240 x 180 cm
《Pablo Picasso》2006年，布面丙烯酸（气刷）240 x 180 cm

6 ***Liberatas, Dei Te Servent***, *2002*
Acrylic (airbrush) on canvas, 350 x 250 cm
Acryl (Airbrush) auf Leinwand, 350 x 250 cm
《Liberatas, Dei Te Servent》2002年，布面丙烯酸（气刷）350 x 250 cm

7 ***Je la transporte dans un sac de Louis Vuitton***, *1994*
Mixed media on paper, 250 x 400 cm
Mixed media auf Papier, 250 x 400 cm
《我携带它于Louis Vuitton袋子》1994年，纸上综合材料，250 x 400 cm

8 ***Easy***, *2005*
Resin, Louis Vuitton suitcase, 175 x 60 x 130 cm
Kunstharz, Louis-Vuitton-Koffer, 175 x 60 x 130 cm
《容易》2005年，人造树脂，Louis Vuitton箱子，175 x 60 x 130 cm:

9 ***Fake Cover: Frieze***, *1995*
Print, 30 x 23 cm
Druck, 30 x 23 cm
封面:《Frieze》1995年，印刷品，30 × 23 cm

10 ***Fake Cover: ARTnews***, *1995*
Print, 28 x 21 cm
Druck, 28 x 21 cm
封面:《ARTnews》1995年，印刷品，28 x 21 cm

11 ***Fake Cover: Facts***, *1998*
Print, 28 x 21 cm
Druck, 28 x 21 cm
封面:《Facts》1998年，印刷品，28 x 21 cm

12 ***Fake Cover: Art in America***, *1997*
Print, 27 x 23 cm
Druck, 27 x 23 cm
封面:《Art in America》1997年，印刷品，27 x 23 cm

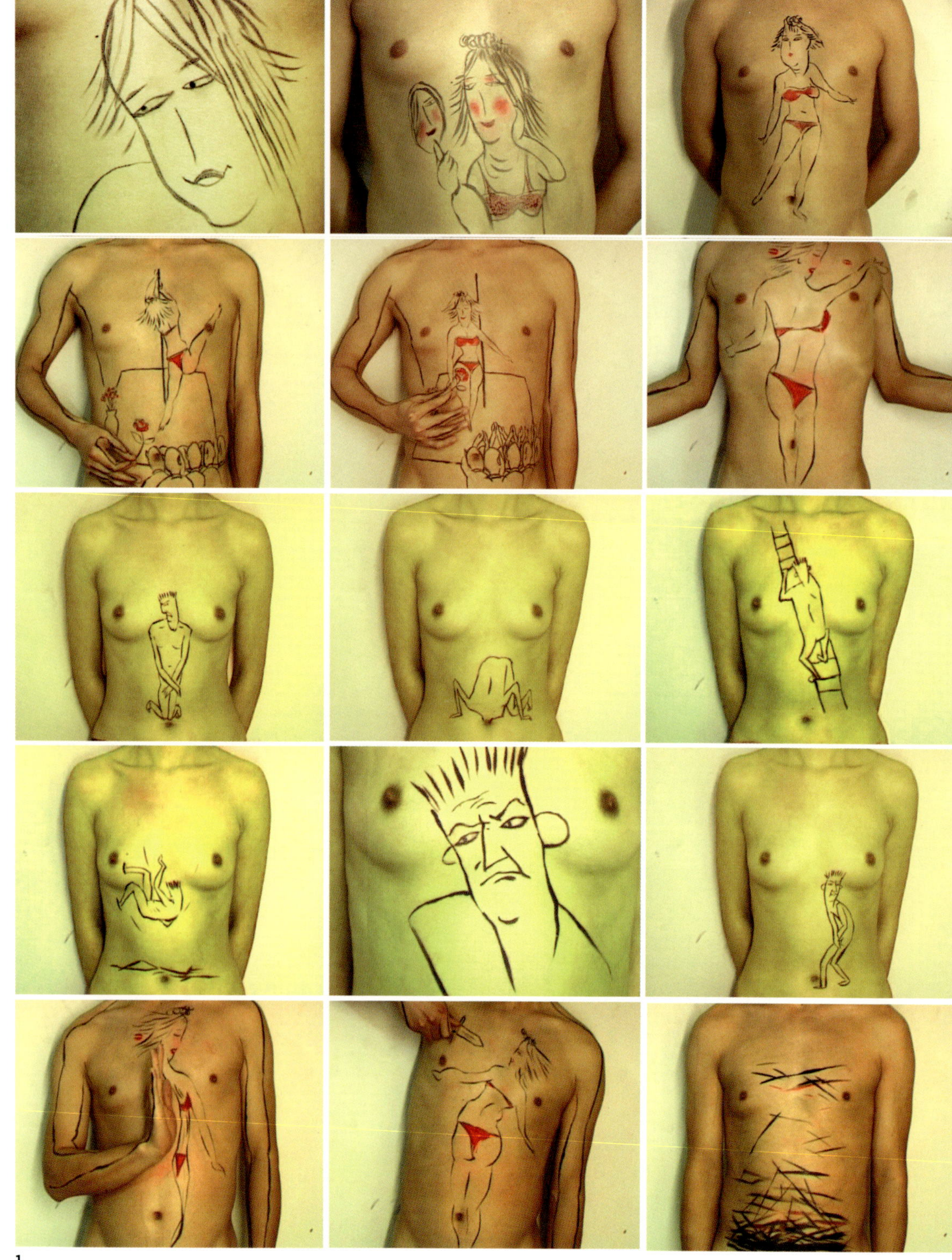

1

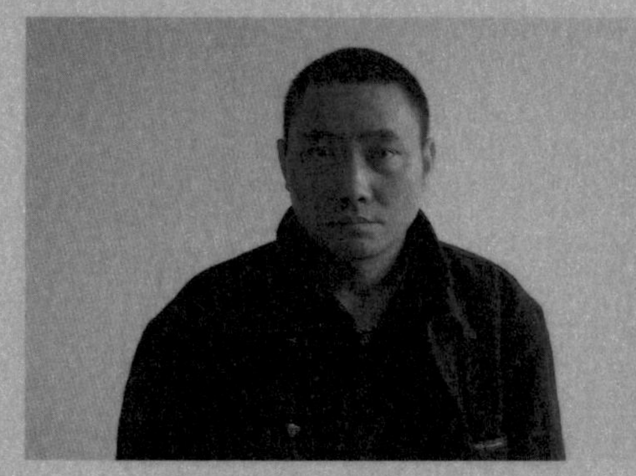

"No matter how much we can achieve with computers, and in spite of the perfect images they allow us to attain, I have always been conscious of injecting a 'hand-made' touch in my work that locates it in the sphere of fine art. Art can never be made by machine alone."

„Ganz egal, wie viel wir mit Computern erreichen können, und trotz der perfekten Bilder, die sie uns ermöglichen, habe ich meinen Werken immer bewusst einen ‚handgemachten' Touch gegeben, der sie der Sphäre der schönen Künste zuordnet. Kunst kann niemals von Maschinen allein gemacht werden."

"不论我们通过使用计算机能取得多少成就，也不管用计算机我们可以得到多么完美的图像，我总是有意识地在我的美术作品里加入"手工"的痕迹以使其进入完美艺术的范畴。机器本身是不会产生艺术的。"

Born in 1968 in Changzhou, China. Lives and works in Changzhou
Geboren 1968 in Changzhou, China. Lebt und arbeitet in Changzhou
1968 年出生于中国常州，居住工作在常州

Selected exhibitions **/ Ausgewählte Ausstellungen /** 所选展览

2000 Shanghai Biennial, Shanghai Art Museum, Shanghai, China
2001 "Excess Asia-Pacific", New Media Art Festival, Brisbane, Australia
2002 "Zhou Xiaohu's Photography", Moscow Central House of Artists, Moscow, Russia
2003 "Second Hand Reality", Today Art Museum, Beijing, China
2004 "Out the window – Spaces of distraction", The Japan Foundation Forum, Tokyo, Japan
2006 The 5th Asia-Pacific Triennial of Contemporary Art, Queensland Art Gallery, Melbourne, Australia
"New Urban Realities", Museum Boijmans Van Beuningen, Rotterdam, The Netherlands

2000年 《上海双年展》上海美术馆，中国上海
2001年 《过度亚洲和平》新媒介艺术节，布里斯班
2002年 《周啸虎的摄影》莫斯科艺术家中央议院，莫斯科
2003年 《第二只手现实》今日美术馆, 北京
2004年 《アウト・ザ・ウインドウ》国際交流基金, 东京
2006年 《第五届亚太地区当代艺术三年展》澳大利亚墨尔本，昆士兰美术馆
《新城市的现实》荷兰鹿特丹，波宁根美术馆

Selected publications **/ Ausgewählte Publikationen /** 所选著作

Pi Li: "Conspiracy in Contemporary Art", in: "Xiandai Yishu", Beijing May 2002
Li Xianting: "DV Puppet Show", in: "Art China" ("Yishu Dangdai"), Shanghai March 2003
Karen Smith: "Die Chinesen: Fotografie und Video aus China", Wolfsburg 2004
Harald Szeemann: "Zhou Xiao Hu", in: catalogue of 1. Bienal de Sevilla, Seville 2004
Jonathan Goodman: "Zhou Xiaohu Solo Exhibition", in: "Art in America", New York December 2005

Pi Li 皮力（著）：《阴谋》，《现代艺术Pi Li 皮力（著）：《阴谋》，《现代艺术》北京 2002年5月
Li Xianting 栗宪庭（著）：《DV"玩偶戏"》《艺术当代》上海 2003年3月
Smith, Karen（著）：《周啸虎》，《中国人》展册，沃尔夫斯堡 2004 年11月
Szeemann, Harald（著）：《关于周啸虎》《第一届塞维利亚双年展目录》塞维利亚 2004年
Goodman, Jonathan（著）：《周啸虎个展》《美术在美国》纽约 2005年12月

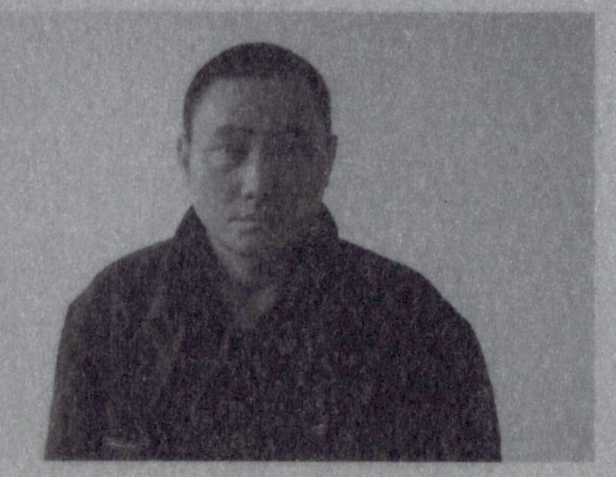

"No matter how much we can achieve with computers, and in spite of the perfect images they allow us to attain, I have always been conscious of injecting a 'hand-made' touch in my work that locates it in the sphere of fine art. Art can never be made by machine alone."

„Ganz egal, wie viel wir mit Computern erreichen können, und trotz der perfekten Bilder, die sie uns ermöglichen, habe ich meinen Werken immer bewusst einen ‚handgemachten' Touch gegeben, der sie der Sphäre der schönen Künste zuordnet. Kunst kann niemals von Maschinen allein gemacht werden."

"不论我们通过使用计算机能取得多少成就，也不管用计算机我们可以得到多么完美的图像，我总是有意识地在我的美术作品里加入"手工"的痕迹以使其进入完美艺术的范畴。机器本身是不会产生艺术的。"

Born in 1968 in Changzhou, China. Lives and works in Changzhou
Geboren 1968 in Changzhou, China. Lebt und arbeitet in Changzhou
1968 年出生于中国常州，居住工作在常州

Selected exhibitions / Ausgewählte Ausstellungen / 所选展览

2000	Shanghai Biennial, Shanghai Art Museum, Shanghai, China
2001	"Excess Asia-Pacific", New Media Art Festival, Brisbane, Australia
2002	"Zhou Xiaohu's Photography", Moscow Central House of Artists, Moscow, Russia
2003	"Second Hand Reality", Today Art Museum, Beijing, China
2004	"Out the window – Spaces of distraction", The Japan Foundation Forum, Tokyo, Japan
2006	The 5th Asia-Pacific Triennial of Contemporary Art, Queensland Art Gallery, Melbourne, Australia
	"New Urban Realities", Museum Boijmans Van Beuningen, Rotterdam, The Netherlands

2000年	《上海双年展》上海美术馆，中国上海
2001年	《过度亚洲和平》新媒介艺术节，布里斯班
2002年	《周啸虎的摄影》莫斯科艺术家中央议院，莫斯科
2003年	《第二只手现实》今日美术馆，北京
2004年	《アウト・ザ・ウインドウ》国際交流基金，东京
2006年	《第五届亚太地区当代艺术三年展》澳大利亚墨尔本，昆士兰美术馆
	《新城市的现实》荷兰鹿特丹，波宁根美术馆

Selected publications / Ausgewählte Publikationen / 所选著作

Pi Li: "Conspiracy in Contemporary Art", in: "Xiandai Yishu", Beijing May 2002
Li Xianting: "DV Puppet Show", in: "Art China" ("Yishu Dangdai"), Shanghai March 2003
Karen Smith: "Die Chinesen: Fotografie und Video aus China", Wolfsburg 2004
Harald Szeemann: "Zhou Xiao Hu", in: catalogue of 1. Bienal de Sevilla, Seville 2004
Jonathan Goodman: "Zhou Xiaohu Solo Exhibition", in: "Art in America", New York December 2005

Pi Li 皮力（著）：《阴谋》，《现代艺术Pi Li 皮力（著）：《阴谋》，《现代艺术》北京 2002年5月
Li Xianting 栗宪庭（著）：《DV"玩偶戏"》《艺术当代》上海 2003年3月
Smith, Karen（著）：《周啸虎》，《中国人》展册，沃尔夫斯堡 2004 年11月
Szeemann, Harald（著）：《关于周啸虎》《第一届塞维利亚双年展目录》塞维利亚 2004年
Goodman, Jonathan（著）：《周啸虎个展》《美术在美国》纽约 2005年12月

ZHOU XIAOHU 周啸虎

[tʂou ɕiaʊxu]

Zhou Xiaohu is known for animation works that successfully blend traditional and contemporary techniques. He began using computers as an artistic tool in 1997. Initial formats were CD-ROMs ("Maze", 1998), and the Internet ("B's Diary", 2000) – easily transportable means of interacting with an audience. Upon acquiring an analogue video camera, he began experimenting with film, incorporating video sequences into installations. For example, "No Malice Intended" (1999), includes two monitors each representing a male figure, engaged in a discussion about women.

The first video work was "Swimming in a Vase" (Shanghai Biennial, 2000). The technique was simple: videoed footage of a swimmer, played back on a television screen, refilmed through the filter of a tinted glass vase. Next, Zhou Xiaohu looked at stop-frame animation. His first attempts to breathe life into inanimate objects made articles of clothing crawl, walk, and dance. New digital technology then made it possible to expand his range. The first work to be realised was "The Gooey Gentleman" (2002), a humourous fantasy that remains one of his most accomplished pieces. Playing with the theme of fatal attraction between the sexes, Zhou Xiaohu tells a coy tale of sexual chemistry in an animated drawing inscribed across his own chest and that of a female counterpart. We see his hand drawing a nubile young woman, clothing her, and watching as she combines coquettish tricks with feminine wiles to tease and bait her man, all to the tune of a warbling Shanghainese songstress.

Zhou Xiaohu employed the technique for "Conspiracy" (2004), which points to the post-9/11 climate. The action unfolds across two screens in a medley of hand-drawn animation and live footage. The activities on the screens are synchronizsed to achieve the illusion of an interactive interplay between the two, and cleverly underscore the relationship between cause and effect. As always, serious subject matter is infused with humour: weighty, abstract issues are thus articulated in terms of a common experience that is both familiar and easily understood.

Zhou Xiaohu ist für seine Animationskunst bekannt, in der er auf besondere Weise traditionelle mit modernen Techniken verbindet. 1997 begann er, den Computer als künstlerisches Werkzeug einzusetzen. Seine anfänglichen Formate waren CD-ROM („Maze", 1998) und das Internet („B's Diary", 2000) – mobile Medien für die Interaktion mit einem mobilen Publikum. Dann legte er sich eine analoge Videokamera zu und begann mit Film zu experimentieren, indem er Videosequenzen in Installationen integrierte. So zeigt „No Malice Intended" (1999) zwei Monitore mit je einer männlichen Figur, die in eine Diskussion über Frauen verwickelt sind.

Seine erste reine Videoarbeit war „Swimming in a Vase" (Shanghai Biennale, 2000). Die Technik war simpel: Die Videoaufnahme eines Schwimmenden wurde auf einem Bildschirm abgespielt und durch den Filter einer getönten Glasvase von diesem wieder abgefilmt. Als nächstes wandte sich Zhou Xiaohu der Stop-Motion-Animation zu. Bei seinen ersten Versuchen, leblosen Objekten Leben einzuhauchen, ließ er Kleidungsstücke kriechen, laufen und tanzen. Bald bot ihm die neue Digitaltechnik erheblich erweiterte Spielräume. Das erste Werk, das er auf diese Weise umsetzte, war „The Gooey Gentleman" (2002), ein witziges Fantasiestück, das immer noch zu seinen gelungensten Arbeiten gehört. Zhou Xiaohu spielt hier mit dem Thema der fatalen Anziehung der Geschlechter und erzählt in Form eines Zeichentrickfilms eine neckische Geschichte rund um Sexualität, die sich auf seiner eigenen Brust sowie der eines weiblichen Gegenübers vollzieht: Seine Hand zeichnet und bekleidet eine attraktive junge Frau, und dann sehen wir zu, wie sie kokett weibliche Tricks einsetzt, um ihren Auserwählten zu becircen und zu ködern, alles begleitet vom Geträller einer Shanghaier Schnulzensängerin.

Bei „Conspiracy" (2004), das sich mit der Atmosphäre nach dem 11. September befasst, entfaltet sich das Geschehen wieder auf zwei Bildschirmen, allerdings in einer Mixtur aus handgezeichneter Animation und Live-Filmmaterial. Die Aktionen auf den Bildschirmen sind so synchronisiert, dass die Illusion eines interaktiven Zusammenspiels der beiden

周啸虎以融入传统和当代技巧的动画作品出名。早在 1997年他便开始使用计算机作为艺术创作工具。刚开始使用的格式是　CD-ROM《曲径迷宫》1998年），然后是互联网《阿 B 日记》2000年）-- 可以和观众互动的更易交流的方式。在得到一个模拟视频摄像头后，他开始尝试制作电影，将视频片段并入装置中。例如，《不怀恶意 1999 年》中，两个各自代表一个男性的监视器正在展开一场关于女人的讨论。

周啸虎的第一部视频作品是《在瓶中游泳》《上海双年展》，2000年）。技法很简单，一个游泳者的视频镜头在电视机上播放，然后透过有色玻璃瓶录制为电影。接着，周啸虎着眼于静帧动画。在他的第一次赋予单调物体以生命力的尝试中，衣服在爬行、步行和跳舞。而新的数码技术则使他得以进一步拓展自己的视野，第一个借助此技术实现的作品《蜜糖先生》是部幽默的幻想剧，如今依然是他最成功的作品之一。为了表现两性间致命吸引的主题，周啸虎通过在自己胸前绘制的动画讲述了一个两性间化学反应的爱情故事。我们可以看到他的手画出一个性感的年轻女子，给她穿衣服，我们接着看到她用女性的伎俩卖弄风情戏弄男人，全然一副莺昵的上海女歌手的腔调。

周啸虎在《阴谋》（2004年）里也采用了这种技法，这个作品指出了9月11日后的　风潮。动作将两个屏幕在混杂的手绘动画和动态镜头中展开。屏幕上的动作是同步的，以达到两个影像间交互作用的效果，巧妙地点出原因和结果间的关系。与以往一样，严肃的主题在幽默中得到体现：严肃性和抽性通过人们熟悉和易懂的共通体验连接在了一起。

周啸虎最主要的成果是 （2002 年） 的《乌托邦机器》。该作品耗时两年，作品中的陶土人物们滑稽地模仿电视新闻广播。我们可以看到中国在国外的访问团，而同时外国元首又到达北京机场。这里面有本地新闻：关于经济持续发展，关于政府防治腐

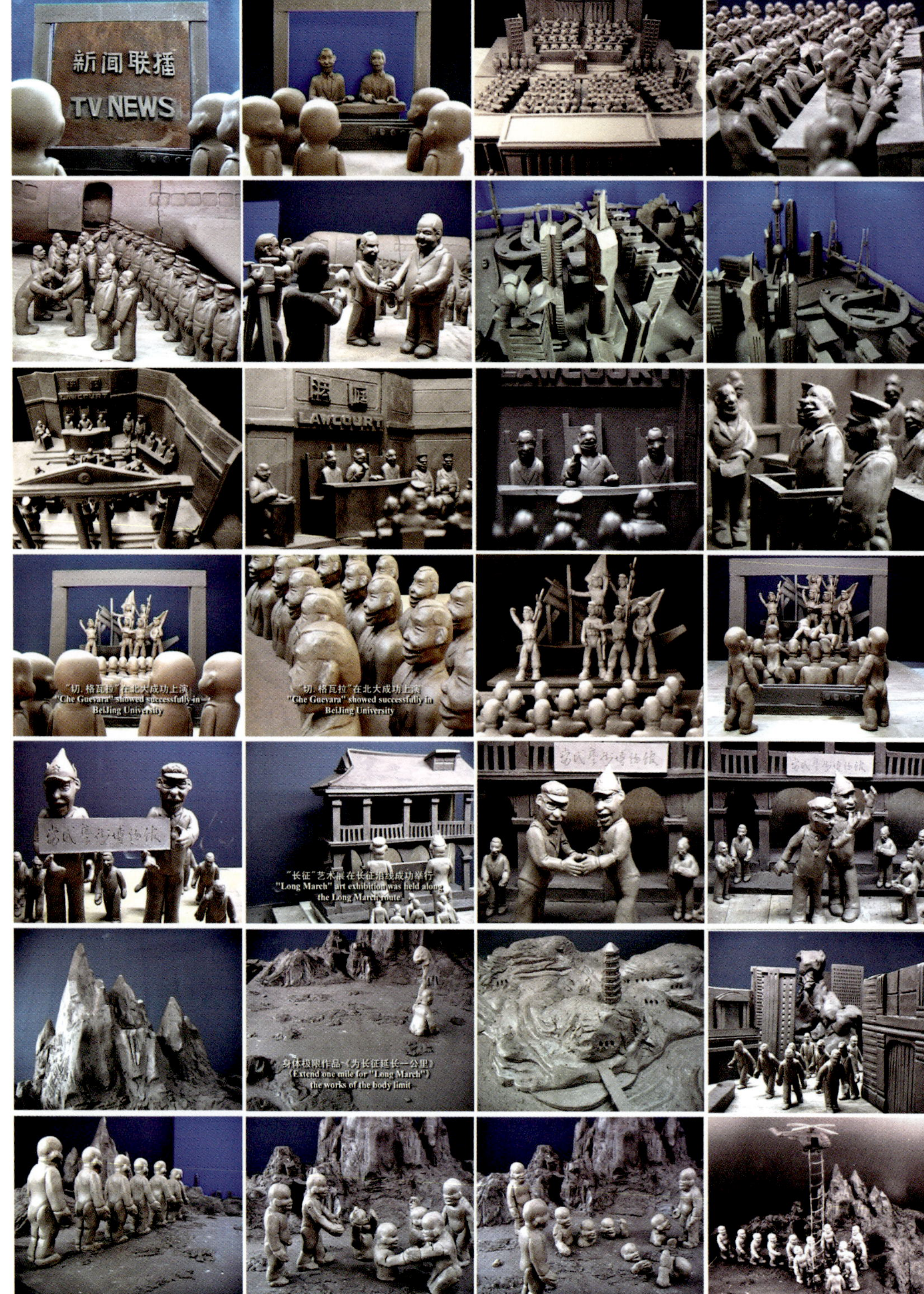
新闻联播
TV NEWS
LAWCOURT
"切. 格瓦拉"在北大成功上演
"Che Guevara" showed successfully in
BeiJing University
"切. 格瓦拉"在北大成功上演
"Che Guevara" showed successfully in
BeiJing University
"长征"艺术展在长征沿线成功举行
"Long March" art exhibition was held along
the Long March route
身体极限作品《为长征延长一公里》
(Extend one mile for "Long March")
the works of the body limit

2

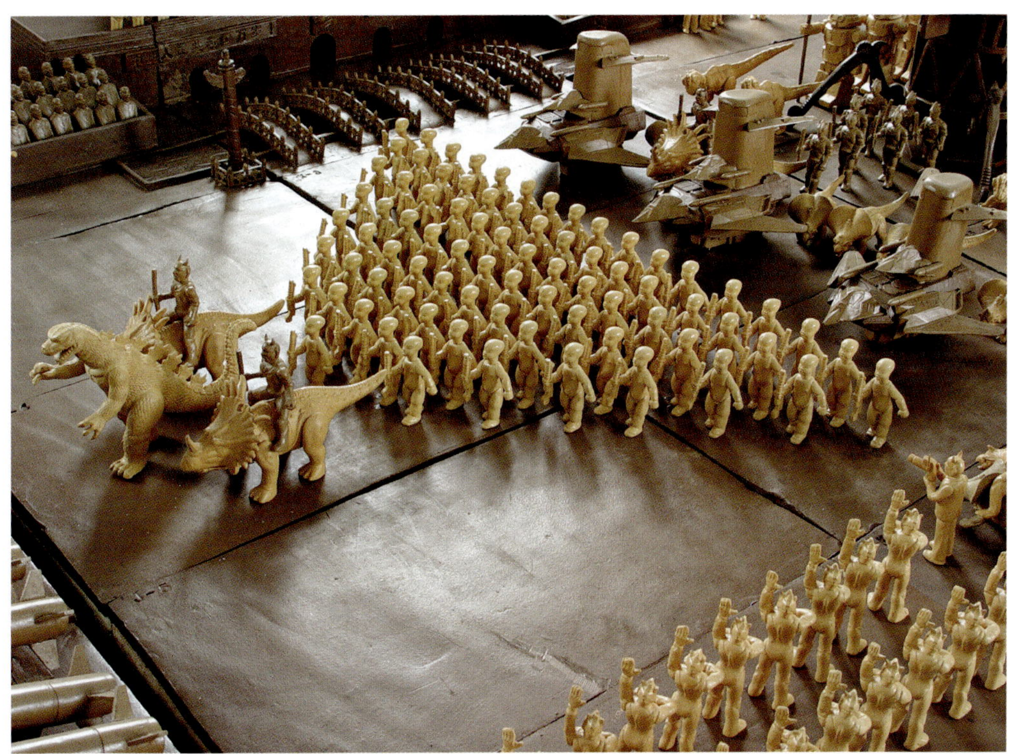

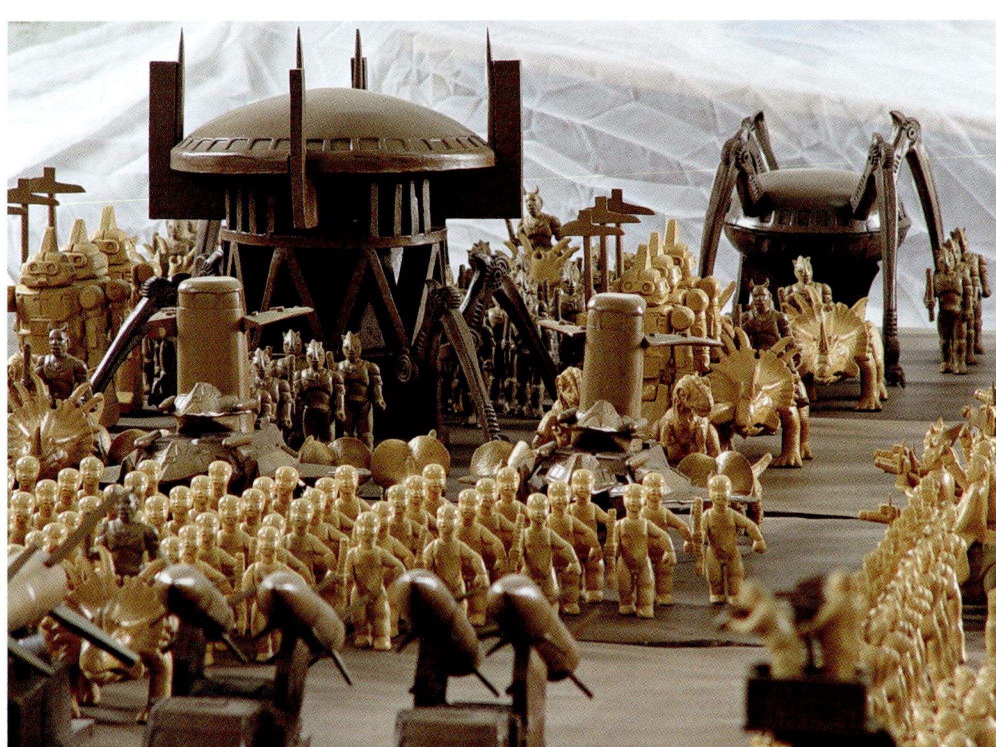

3

4

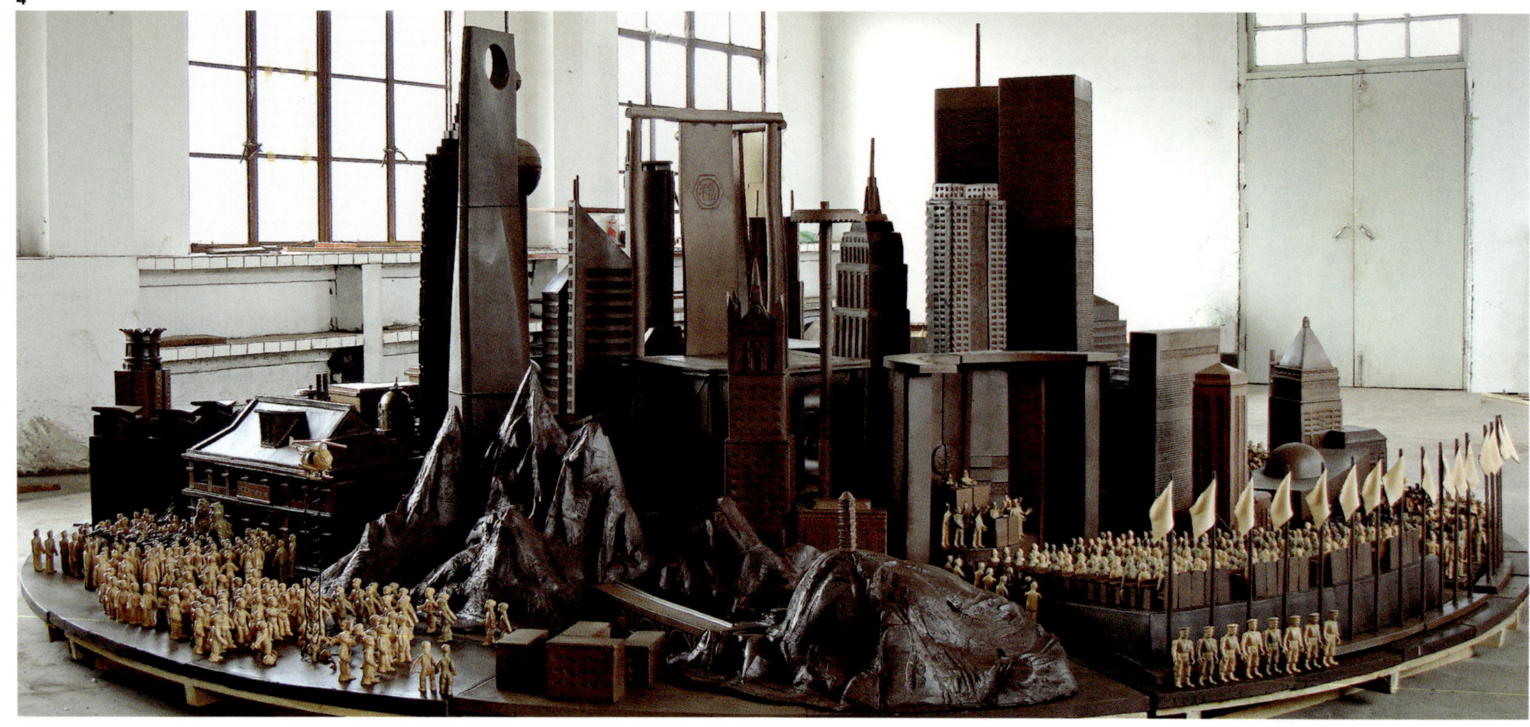

Zhou Xiaohu's most major undertaking remains "Utopian Machine" (2002). Two years in the making, it features a cast of clay figures that enact a parody of a television news broadcast. We see Chinese delegations on missions abroad, whilst foreign heads of state arrive at Beijing airport. There is local news: stories of redevelopment, of the government's fight against corruption and crime, and of natural disasters in the provinces. This is rounded off by a cultural section: a report on the musical "Che Guevara in Beijing", whilst in Zhunyi, China's new "Long Marchers" are joined by international cultural workers in a round of talks on the state of art and literature today. Finally, the programme is interrupted with a breaking story on the 9/11 terrorist attack in New York.

"Utopian Machine" is a powerful comment on the socio-political framework of present-day China. The approach has been reworked in various ways such as "Obsession – Century Celebration" (2003); "Summit Meeting" (2003), and "Crowd Around" (2003–2005), which combine animations with sets and props used in one giant installation. Zhou Xiaohu is now at work on a new series of "live" animations, and exploring the world of interactive technology.

entsteht, was auf raffinierte Weise die Beziehung zwischen Ursache und Wirkung unterstreicht. Wie stets bei Zhou wird der ernste Gegenstand mit Humor versüßt, und gewichtige abstrakte Themen werden als konkrete Erfahrungen artikuliert, die ebenso vertraut wie eingängig sind.

Zhou Xiaohus bislang größtes Unternehmen ist seine „Utopian Machine" (2002), deren Herstellung zwei Jahre dauerte. Eine Reihe Knetfiguren führt die Parodie einer Fernseh-Nachrichtensendung auf: Chinesische Delegationen gehen auf Auslandsmission, während fremde Staatsoberhäupter am Flughafen von Peking eintreffen. Lokalnachrichten bringen Berichte über Sanierungsprojekte, staatliche Kampagnen gegen Korruption und Kriminalität sowie Naturkatastrophen in den Provinzen. Als gefällige Abrundung fehlt auch ein Kulturteil nicht, in Form einer Reportage über das Musical „Che Guevara in Peking", während Chinas Teilnehmer des neuen „Langen Marsches" in Zhunyi mit internationalen „Kulturarbeitern" über die aktuelle Situation der modernen Kunst und Literatur debattieren. Schließlich wird das Programm durch eine Eilmeldung über die Terroranschläge des 11. September in New York unterbrochen.

„Utopian Machine" ist ein kraftvoller Kommentar zu den gesellschaftspolitischen Verhältnissen im heutigen China. Diesen Ansatz wandelte Zhou Xiaohu danach noch auf verschiedene Weise ab, z. B. in „Obsession – Century Celebration" (2003), in „Summit Meeting" (2003) und „Crowd Around" (2003–2005), wobei er Animationen mit Kulissen und Requisiten zu riesigen Installationen verbindet. Zurzeit arbeitet Zhou an einer neuen Serie von „Live"-Animationen und erkundet neugierig die Welt der interaktiven Technik.

败和犯罪，以及关于部分省市的自然灾害。文化部分使之更趋完美：一个关于北京举行的切·格瓦拉“音乐会”的报导，同时在遵义，国际文化工作者加入中国“新长征者”们当中一起讨论今天的艺术和文学。最后整个节目被纽约遭受 9月11日恐怖袭击的重大新闻中断。

《乌托邦机器》是对当前中国社会政治体制的一个有力评价。该表现方式曾经多次以不同的方式进行修改，例如 2003年《意乱情迷百年庆典》（装置/动画）；2003 年《峰会》以及 2003-2005 年集动画和布景道具为一体的大型装置作品《大群拥挤》。周啸虎现正在创作新系列的“生动”动画，并探索互动技艺的世界。

Karen Smith

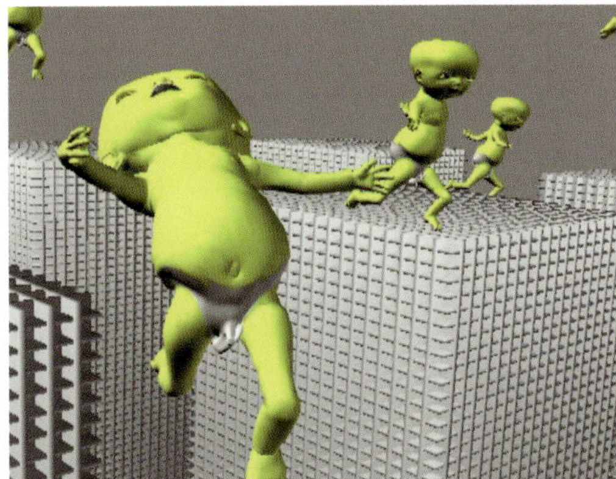
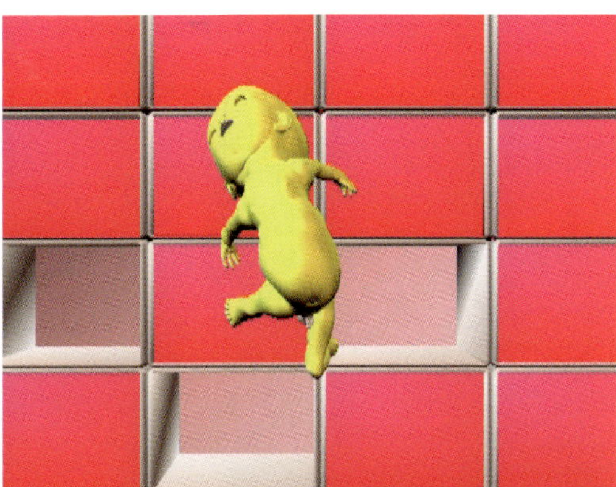
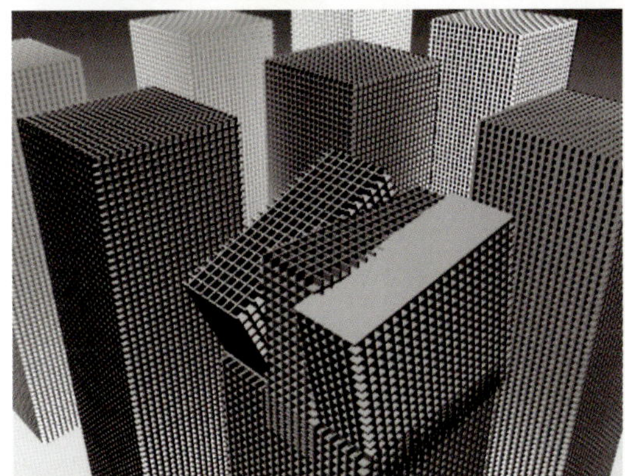
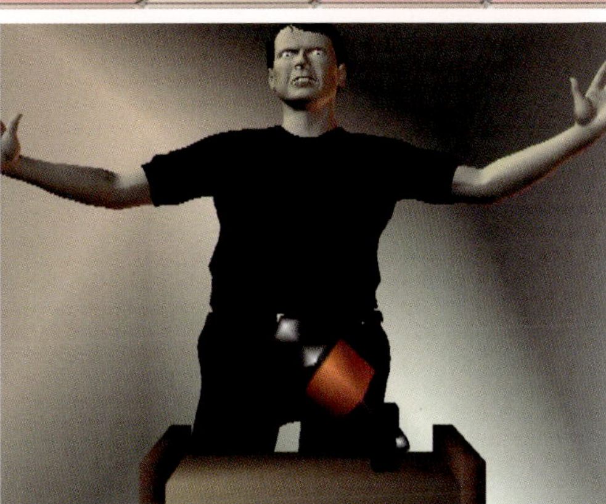
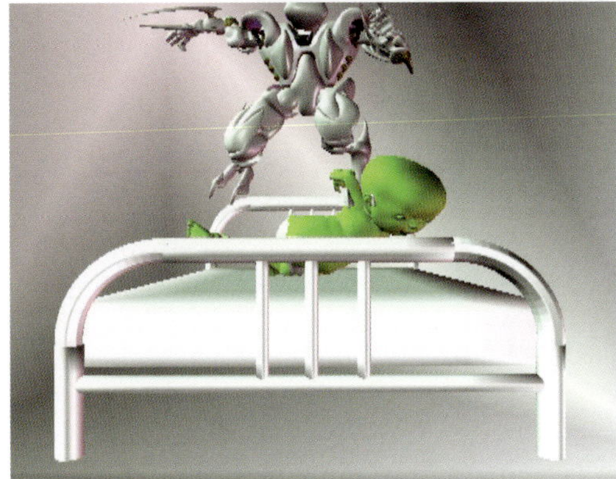
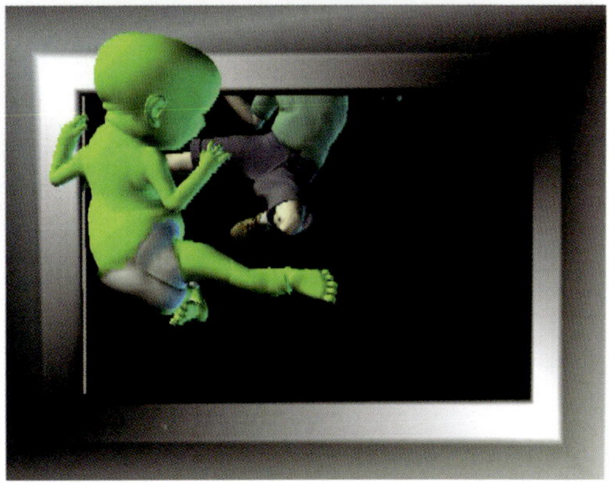

5

1 ***The Gooey Gentleman***, *2002*
Video, 4 min 40 sec
Video, 4 Min. 40 Sek.
《蜜糖先生》2002年, 录像, 4分 40秒

2 ***Utopian Machine***, *2002*
Video, 8 min 35 sec
Video, 8 Min. 35 Sek.
《乌托邦机器》2002年, 录像, 8分 35秒

3 ***Parade***, *2003*
Installation with ceramic figures and video, 882 x 222 cm (details)
Installation mit Tonfiguren und Video, 882 x 222 cm (Details)
《游行》2003年，黏土形象装置和录影，882 x 222 cm（详细）

4 ***Utopian Theatre***, *2006*
Installation
Installation
《乌托邦剧院》2006年, 装置

5 ***Channel of Socket Live***, *2003*
Video, 5 min
Video, 5 Min.
《穴居频道》2003年, 录像, 5分

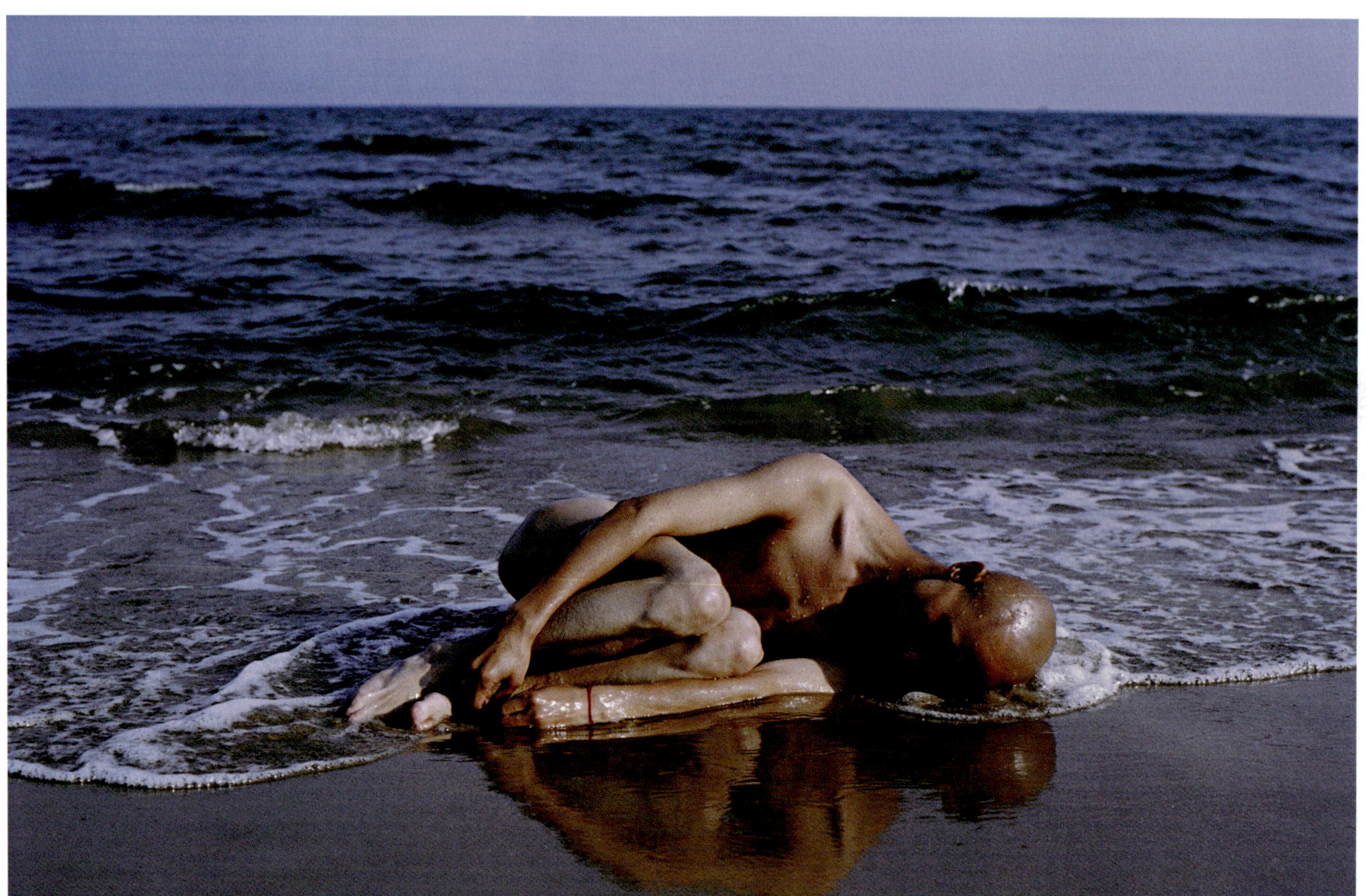

1

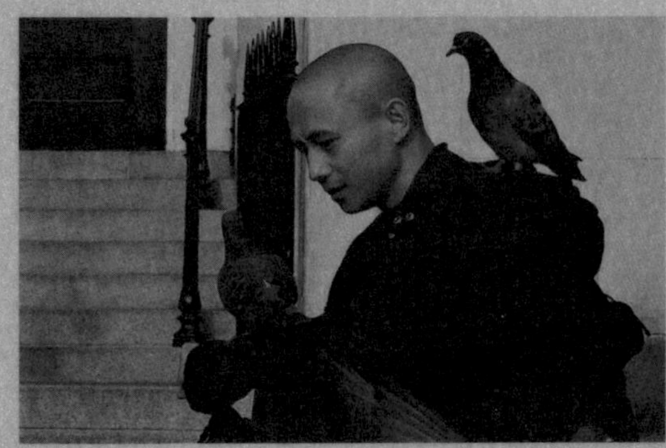

"The air inside the bubble and outside is the same."

„Die Luft innerhalb und außerhalb der Blase ist die gleiche."

"气泡内外的空气都是相同的。"

Born in 1972 in Changsha, China. Lives and works in Beijing
Geboren 1972 in Changsha, China. Lebt und arbeitet in Peking
1972年出生于中国湖南省长沙，现在北京居住工作

***Selected exhibitions* / Ausgewählte Ausstellungen / 所选展览**

1993 "Zhu Ming Art Exhibition", National Art Museum of China, Beijing, China
1995 "Anonymous Mountain", performance, Beijing, China
2000 "Fuck Off!", Eastlink Gallery, Shanghai, China
2003 "Liquid Sea", performance, Contemporary Art Museum of Sydney, Sydney, Australia
2006 Performance at Victoria & Albert Museum, London, UK
2007 Chinese Contemporary Gallery, Beijing, China

1993年 《朱冥现代艺术展》中国美术馆，北京，中国
1995年 《为无名山增高一米》行为表演，北京，中国
2000年 《不合作方式》东廊画廊，上海，中国
2003年 《清晰的海》行为表演，悉尼当代美术馆，澳大利亚
2006年 行为表演，维多利亚&阿尔贝特博物馆，伦敦，英国
2007年 中国现代画廊，北京，中国

***Selected publications* / Ausgewählte Publikationen / 所选著作**

"Contemporary Art Series, No 3: Transformism–Genesis and Displacement", Changsha 1992
Zeng Xiaojun, Ai Weiwei (eds.): "The Grey Cover Book", Beijing 1997
"Zhu Ming", in: "Yishu", vol. 1, no. 2, August 2002
"Zhu Ming – Artworks 1994–2006", Beijing 2007

当代艺术系列，第三刊：《变换主义--创世纪和位移》长沙 1992年
增小俊，艾未未(编者)：《灰皮书》北京1997 年
《朱冥》与：艺术：中国当代艺术杂志，卷1, 刊2, (2002年8月)
《朱冥 -- 艺术作品1994-2006年》北京2007年

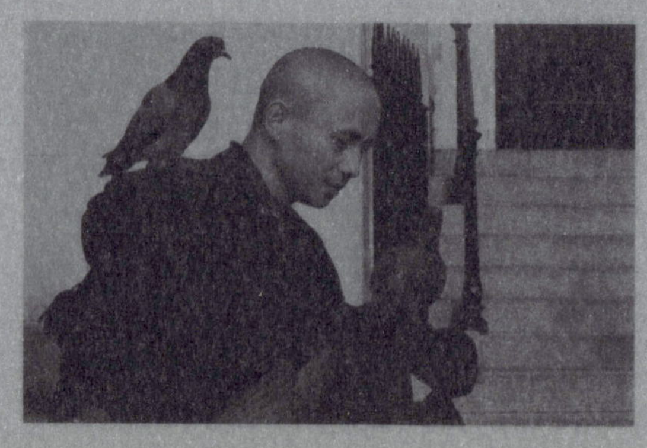

"The air inside the bubble and outside is the same."

„Die Luft innerhalb und außerhalb der Blase ist die gleiche."

"气泡内外的空气都是相同的。"

Born in 1972 in Changsha, China. Lives and works in Beijing
Geboren 1972 in Changsha, China. Lebt und arbeitet in Peking
1972年出生于中国湖南省长沙，现在北京居住工作

Selected exhibitions / Ausgewählte Ausstellungen / 所选展览

1993 "Zhu Ming Art Exhibition", National Art Museum of China, Beijing, China
1995 "Anonymous Mountain", performance, Beijing, China
2000 "Fuck Off!", Eastlink Gallery, Shanghai, China
2003 "Liquid Sea", performance, Contemporary Art Museum of Sydney, Sydney, Australia
2006 Performance at Victoria & Albert Museum, London, UK
2007 Chinese Contemporary Gallery, Beijing, China

1993年 《朱冥现代艺术展》中国美术馆，北京，中国
1995年 《为无名山增高一米》行为表演，北京，中国
2000年 《不合作方式》东廊画廊，上海，中国
2003年 《清晰的海》行为表演，悉尼当代美术馆，澳大利亚
2006年 行为表演，维多利亚&阿尔贝特博物馆，伦敦，英国
2007年 中国现代画廊，北京，中国

Selected publications / Ausgewählte Publikationen / 所选著作

"Contemporary Art Series, No 3: Transformism-Genesis and Displacement", Changsha 1992
Zeng Xiaojun, Ai Weiwei (eds.): "The Grey Cover Book", Beijing 1997
"Zhu Ming", in: "Yishu", vol. 1, no. 2, August 2002
"Zhu Ming - Artworks 1994-2006", Beijing 2007

当代艺术系列，第三刊：《变换主义--创世纪和位移》长沙 1992年
曾小俊，艾未未(编者)：《灰皮书》北京1997 年
《朱冥》与：艺术：中国当代艺术杂志，卷1，刊2，(2002年8月)
《朱冥 — 艺术作品1994-2006年》北京2007年

ZHU MING 朱冥

[tʂu miŋ]

At the top of one of perhaps the most iconic image in the history of contemporary performance art in China lies the diminutive body of Zhu Ming. That image – "The Anonymous Mountain Raised by a Meter" – comes from a performance executed by the core group of East Village performance artists in May of 1995. Zhu Ming was among that group, witness to and participant in the radical experimentation with the human body for which the short-lived East Village remains so famous. Where other artists who made their names and established their practices in that tight-knit community – Zhang Huan and Ma Liuming, for example – have moved on to media including sculpture and painting, Zhu Ming has remained a performer.

Newly arrived from his native Hunan to the East Village in 1992, without an academic training or a viable means of supporting himself, Zhu Ming made his name among his fellow artists with a performance involving laundry detergent, water, a fish tank, and a long tube, with which he blew a roomful of bubbles. Artist Xing Danwen, whom Zhu Ming asked to document this early performance, recalls how "Zhu Ming squatted on the ground, and with all his might and within the limits of his small fragile trunk he blew air into the fish tank. Little by little, bubbles inflated." And yet in this, as in the numerous similar performances that would follow, "You could hear the faint but cruel sound of the bubbles shattering. Here there was no death, only eternal existence, as if between Zhu Ming and the bubbles there was shrouded a sort of spiritual mysterious color, an intolerance for reality."

In 1997 Zhu Ming embarked upon the "Bubble" series performances, in which he traps himself, naked, inside an inflated plastic balloon with just a single tube by which to breathe. These bubbles have occupied public spaces ranging from the promenade outside the Hong Kong Museum of Art in Kowloon to the harbor beyond the Sydney Opera House to the waters off of Miami Beach during the first instantiation of the Art Basel fair there in 2002. The life-threatening daringness of such interventions however never comes off

Eines der ikonographisch vielleicht wichtigsten Bilder in der Geschichte der modernen chinesischen Performancekunst zeigt den zierlichen Körper von Zhu Ming. Dieses Bild – „The Anonymous Mountain Raised by a Metre" – entstand aus einer Performance, die die Kerngruppe der East-Village-Künstler im Mai 1995 veranstaltete. Zhu Ming war Augenzeuge und Mitwirkender bei jenen radikalen Experimenten mit dem menschlichen Körper, für die das kurzlebige East Village so berühmt wurde. Doch während andere Künstler, die sich durch diese verschworene Gemeinschaft einen Namen machten – wie Zhang Huan und Ma Liuming –, inzwischen zur Bildhauerei und Malerei abgewandert sind, ist Zhu Ming in erster Linie Performancekünstler geblieben.

Zhu kam 1992 aus seiner Heimatprovinz Hunan ins East Village – ohne jede akademische oder sonstige Ausbildung, um seinen Lebensunterhalt bestreiten zu können. Die Aufmerksamkeit seiner Künstlerkollegen erregte er mit einer Performance unter Einsatz von Waschmittel, Wasser, einem Aquarium und einem langen Schlauch, mit dem er ein ganzes Zimmer mit Seifenblasen füllte. Xing Danwen, den Zhu Ming bat, diese frühe Performance zu dokumentieren, erinnert sich: „Zhu Ming hockte auf dem Boden und blies mit aller Kraft und soweit es sein kleiner, zerbrechlicher Körper zuließ, Luft in das Aquarium. Nach und nach blähten sich die Blasen auf. Man konnte das schwache, aber grausame Geräusch hören, mit dem die Blasen zerplatzten. Hier gab es keinen Tod, nur ewige Existenz, als ob zwischen Zhu Ming und den Blasen eine Art spirituelle, mysteriöse, unsichtbare Farbigkeit sei, eine Intoleranz gegenüber der Realität."

1997 begann Zhu Ming eine ganze Serie von „Bubble"-Performances, bei denen er sich nackt in einen aufgeblasenen Plastikballon sperrte, mit der Außenwelt nur über einen Atemschlauch verbunden. Diese „Bubbles" waren an vielen öffentlichen Plätzen zu sehen – von der Promenade vor dem Hong Kong Museum of Art in Kowloon über das Hafenbecken am Opernhaus von Sydney bis zum Golf vor Miami Beach, als dort 2002 der Ableger der Art Basel erstmals stattfand. Die atemberaubende Kühnheit seiner Auftritte vermittelt

在一幅中国当代艺术表演史上最具标志性的照片上，躺着瘦小朱冥的身体。照片《为无名山增高一米》，来源于东村艺术家的一次集体表演，完成于1995年五月。朱冥是他们中的一员，参与并见证了这场具有重大意义的试验表演，这场表演也让东村声名鹊起，虽然东村存在的时间不长。在那个组织严密的村社里，那些艺术家已经成名并完成创作实践，并已经用雕塑和油画等去创作，如马六明和张洹，但朱冥却依然在继续进行艺术表演。

1992年，朱冥离开湖南老家来到北京，成为东村的一个新成员，当时他未接受过专业教育而且生活着落。朱冥和其他艺术家共同完成了一场表演，在这个表演中，他以洗洁精，鱼缸和一只长长的管子为道具，吹了满满一缸的泡泡。艺术家邢丹文（朱曾向她要过这个早期表演的资料），回忆：他蹲在地上，竭尽全力把空气吹进鱼缸里，渐渐地，泡泡膨胀了，越来越多。接着，在其它众多类似的表演中，他都这样，“甚至能听到泡泡破碎时的无力但痛苦的声音。那里没有死亡，只有永生，似乎在朱河泡泡之间隐藏着一种神秘的精神色彩，还有一种对现实的偏执。”

在1997朱冥又进行了泡泡系列表演，表演中，他裸着身体，站在一只膨胀的塑料气球中，用一只塑料管维持着呼吸。这些泡泡曾在许多公共空间展登场过，从九龙的香港美术馆外的舞会、悉尼剧院旁边的港口到2002年巴塞尔艺术节上迈阿密海滩。这种危险的尝试从虚张声势，而感觉象沉浸于出生与死亡的节奏中。在他的许多表演中，朱冥在气泡中幻想着子宫的位置，通过他的行为呼唤着回归生命之源。有些评论家甚至将这种子宫的幻想与朱冥和其母亲的关系联系起来，因为他的母亲在文化大革命艰难的时代中在长沙孤身一人抚养他成人。

在最近的作品《荧光人》中，朱将自己的脸涂上有毒的荧光粉，然后一个黑暗的房间里进行表演，并将其拍摄下来。他的表演中贯穿着自虐、宽容，存

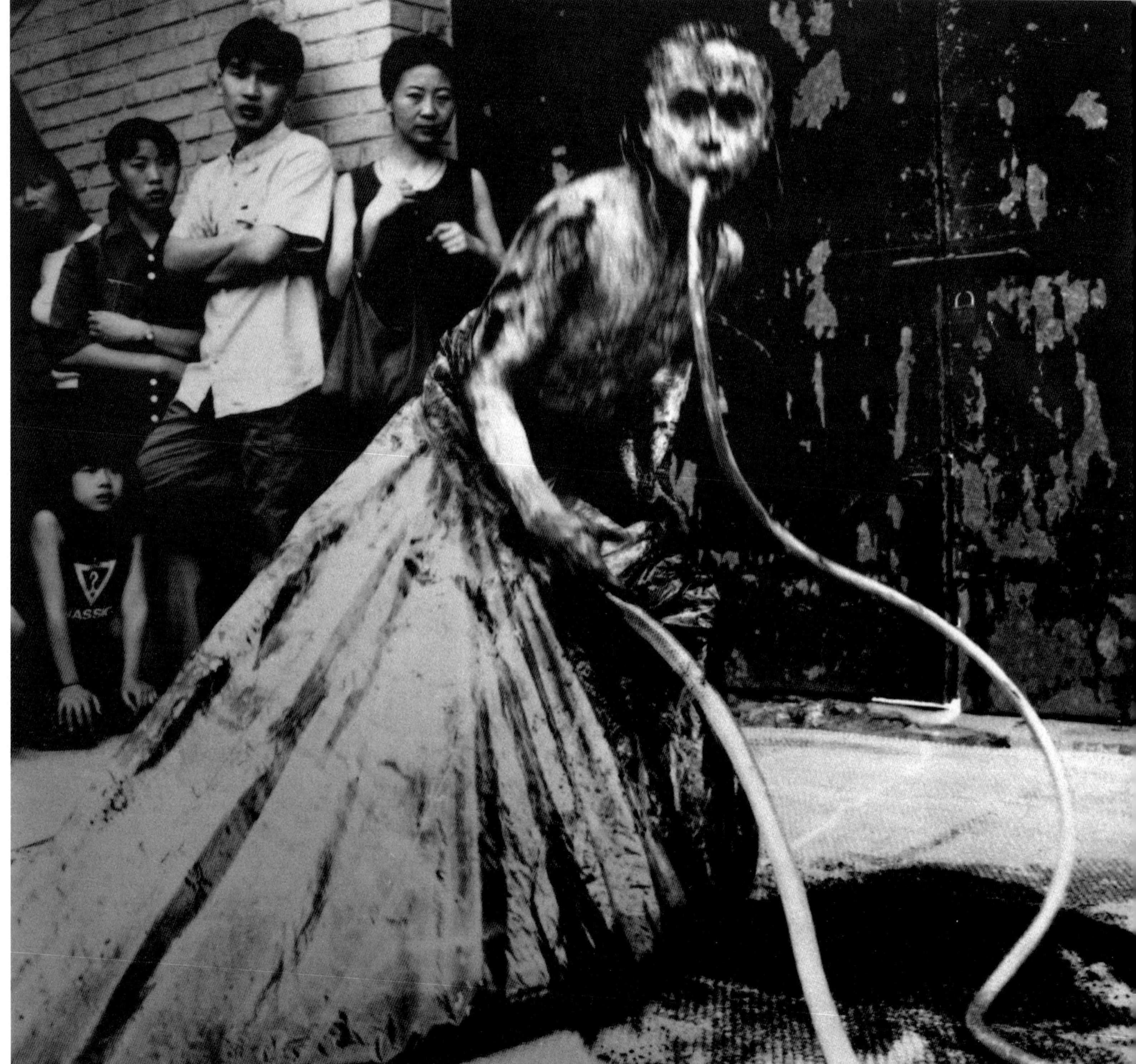

2

3

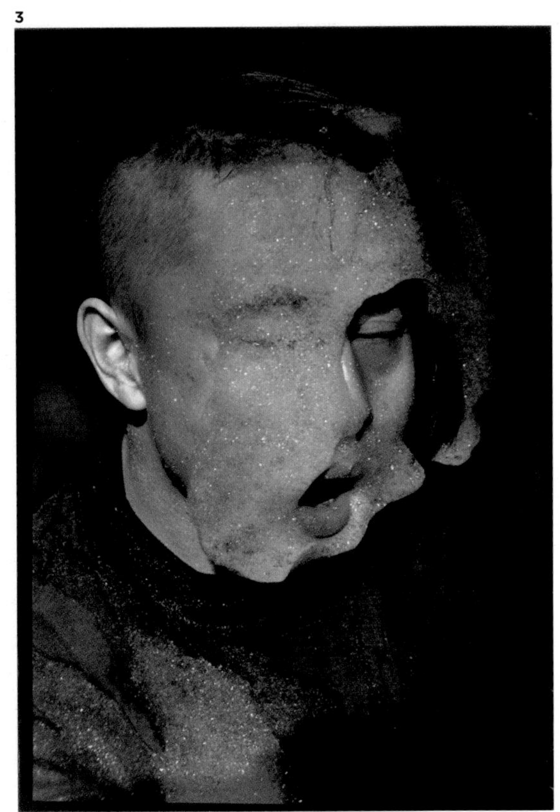

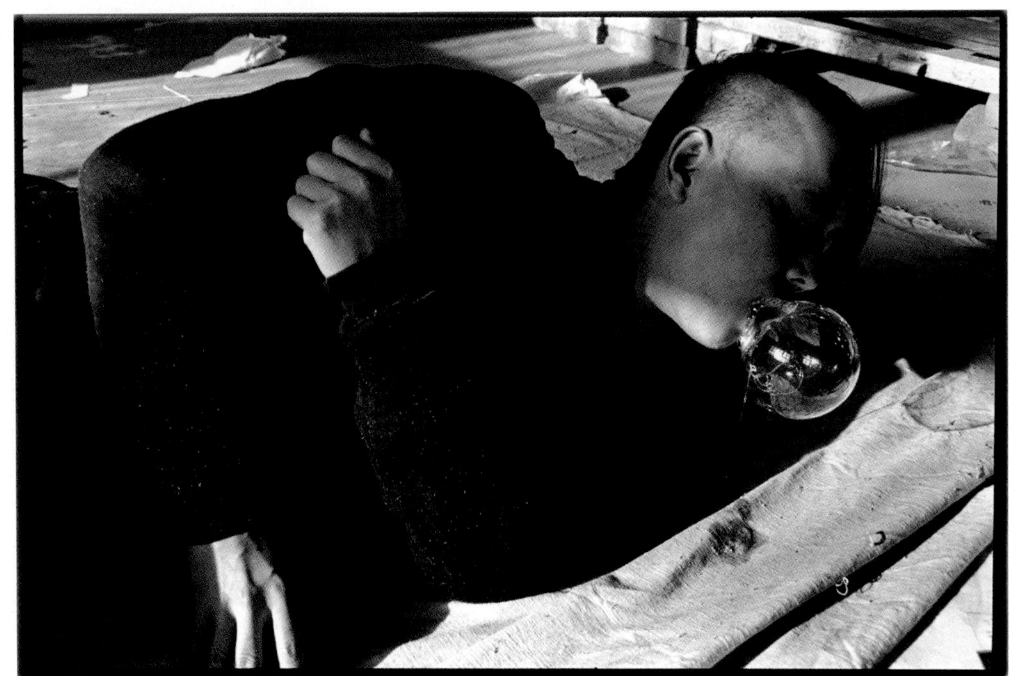

4

5

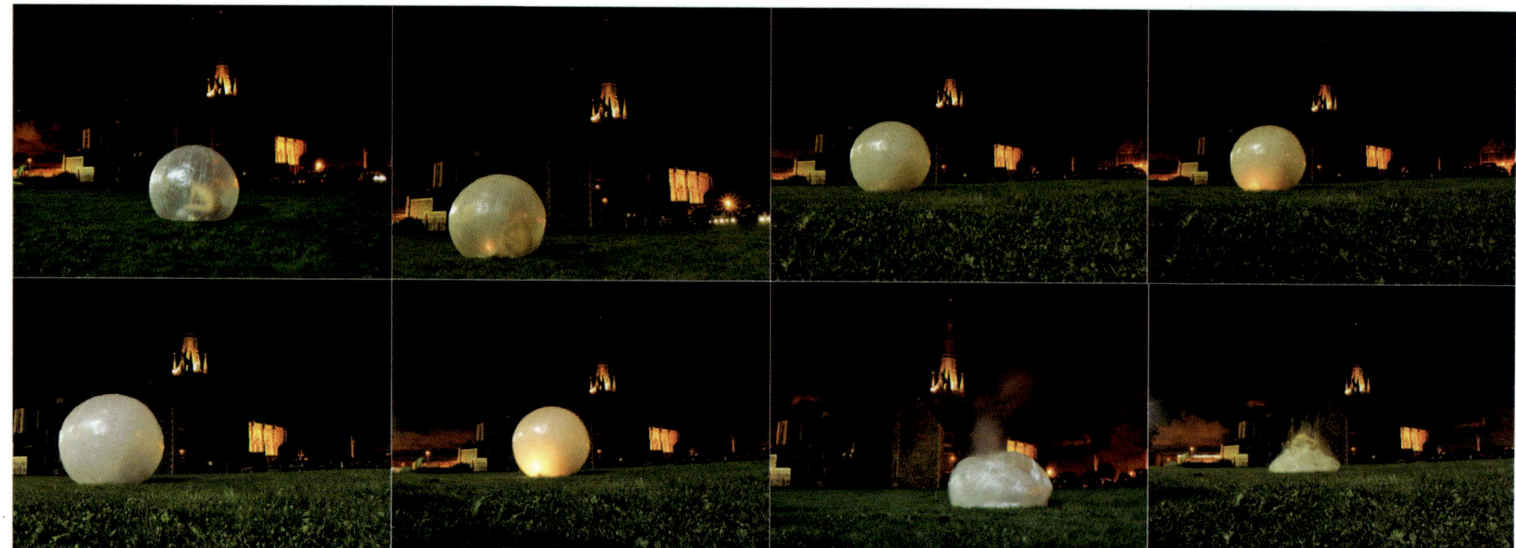

as bravado, but feels instead like a knowing surrender to the rhythms of birth and death. In these, as in many of his performances, Zhu Ming assumes the fetal position, crying through his actions for a return to the womb. Some critics have even pegged this fetal obsession to the artist's botched relationship with his mother, who raised him alone in Changsha during the waning years of the Cultural Revolution.

In a more recent series entitled "Luminescent Man" (2006), the artist paint his face with toxic, fluorescent powder, then photographs himself lurking eerily in dark spaces. Themes of masochism, tolerance, presence and absence run through these performances, as through his entire oeuvre. As the artist himself has said, "Things have a material existence in the world, but in my consciousness the world is actually a combination of illusion and reality. The two worlds interact: illusion is reflected by reality and reality exists through illusion."

nie den Eindruck von Leichtsinn, vielmehr scheint sich der Künstler dabei bewusst in die Rhythmen von Geburt und Tod zu ergeben. Wie auch in vielen anderen seiner Performances nimmt Zhu Ming hier eine embryonale Haltung ein, die einer Art Sehnsucht nach Rückkehr in den Mutterleib Ausdruck zu verleihen scheint. Einige Kritiker haben diese Fötalobsession an Zhus gestörter Beziehung zu seiner Mutter festmachen wollen, die ihn in Changsha während der letzten Phase der Kulturrevolution allein aufzog.

In einer neueren Serie mit dem Titel „Luminescent Man" (2006) bemalte der Künstler sein Gesicht mit toxischem, fluoreszierendem Puder und fotografiert sich dann selbst als ein bedrohlich lauerndes Wesen in düsterem Ambiente. Themen wie Masochismus, Toleranz, An- und Abwesenheit ziehen sich durch Zhus gesamtes Œuvre, oder wie Zhu Ming einmal selbst erläuterte: „Die Dinge haben eine materielle Existenz in der Welt, aber in meiner Wahrnehmung ist die Welt eine Kombination aus Illusion und Realität. Die beiden Welten interagieren: Die Illusion spiegelt sich in der Realität, und die Realität existiert durch die Illusion."

在和死亡的主题，同时也是他全部作品的主题。就如艺术家自己所言：任何东西在世间都有一个物质存在，而在我的意识里，世界时实际上是虚幻和现实的组合体。两个世界相互联系相互影响：实现影响了虚幻，而现实通过虚幻而存在。"

Philip Tinari

6

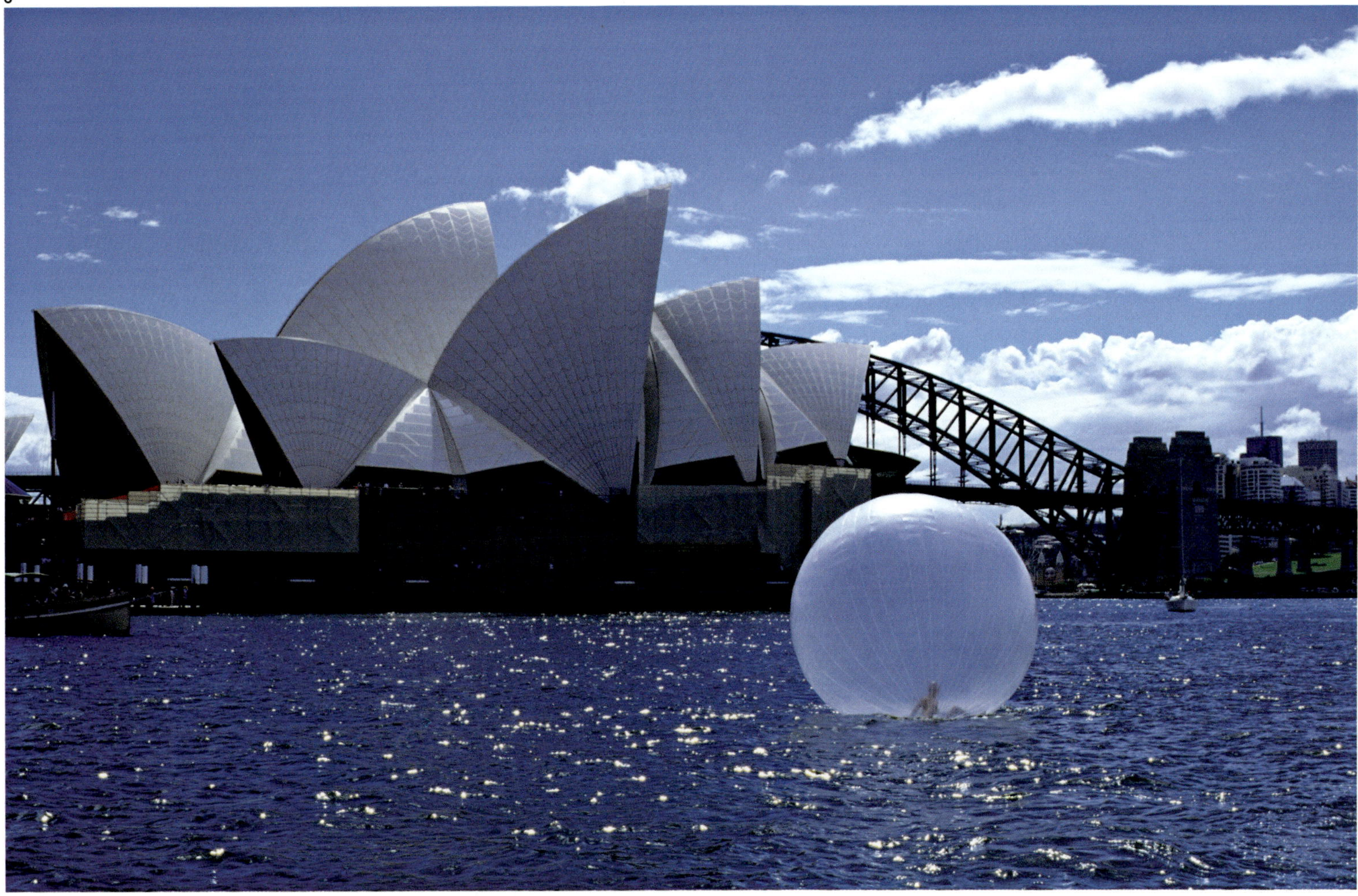

1 ***Improvisation absolute***, *2000*
Photograph, 116 x 174 cm; Fotografie, 116 x 174 cm
《绝对的即兴创作》2000年，摄影, 116 x 174 cm

2 ***May 8, 1999***, *1999*
Photograph, 170 x 217 cm; Fotografie, 170 x 217 cm
1999年5月8日, 1999年, 摄影, 170 x 217 cm

3 ***14 o'clock December 27, 1994***, *1994*
Photograph, 116 x 80 cm; Fotografie, 116 x 80 cm
1994年12月27日14点, 1994年, 摄影, 116 x 80 cm

4 ***12 o'clock December 27, 1994***, *1994*
Photograph, 80 x 116 cm; Fotografie, 80 x 116 cm
1994年12月27日12点, 1994年, 摄影, 80 x 116 cm

5 ***October 20, 2005***, *2005*
Photograph, 116 x 298 cm; Fotografie, 116 x 298 cm
2005年10月20日, 2005年, 摄影, 116 x 298 cm

6 ***March 9, 2003***, *2003*
Photograph, 116 x 176 cm; Fotografie, 116 x 176 cm
2003年3月9日, 2003年, 摄影, 116 x 176 cm

WRITERS & EDITORS
AUTOREN & HERAUSGEBER
作者和主编者

Biljana Ciric
has an M.A from East China Normal University, Shanghai. She was director of the Curatorial Department of Shanghai Duolun Museum of Modern Art and networking curator (China) for the Singapore Biannual. Her ongoing project "Migration Addicts" was presented at the Venice Biennale 2007 Collateral Events and she co-curated "Transit Forces–Exhibition of Asian Contemporary Art" that opened recently in Poland. She worked on major retrospectives of Basquiat and other shows around China and on "Electroscape," opening exhibition of Zendai MoMA. Biljana Ciric is a regular contributing writer for many Chinese art publications and "Yi Shu Journal." Currently she works as an independent curator based in Shanghai.

Biljana Ciric
erwarb ihren Master an der East China Normal University, Shanghai. Sie war Leiterin der kuratorischen Abteilung des Shanghaier Duolun Museum of Modern Art und Networking-Kuratorin für China für die Biennale Singapore. Ihr laufendes Projekt „Migration Addicts" fand als Nebenveranstaltung der Biennale Venedig 2007 statt; außerdem war Ciric Co-Kuratorin der Ausstellung „Asian Attitudes – Transit Forces" in Poznán. Sie hat an der Jean-Michel-Basquiat-Retrospektive, Ausstellungen in ganz China sowie an „Electroscape", der Eröffnungsausstellung des Zendai-MoMA, mitgearbeitet. Biljana Ciric schreibt regelmäßig für zahlreiche chinesische Kunstpublikationen und das „Yi Shu Journal". Zurzeit arbeitet sie als freie Kuratorin mit Hauptwohnsitz Shanghai.

Biljana Ciric, 系上海华东师范大学硕士研究生。曾为上海多伦美术馆策划部总监、新加坡双年展连网策展人。项目《迁移嗜好者》已在2007威尼斯双年展平行展展出。参与策展的《转变力-当代亚洲艺术展》最近在波兰展出。她另外策划了巴斯奎特回顾展和其他以中国和电子园林为主题的其他展出，展览都在上海证大现代艺术馆举行。Biljana Ciric 是许多中国艺术刊物和《艺术月刊》的专栏作家，现居上海，为独立策展人。

Feng Boyi
graduated in 1984 from the Department of History of Capital Normal University in Beijing. Currently he lives and works in Beijing. Feng devotes himself to comments and editions of the present Chinese experimental art. His main exhibitions are: "Trace of Existence: A Private Show of Contemporary Chinese Art," "First Triennial – Exhibition of Contemporary Art in Guangzhou," "The Left Hand and the Right Hand – a Sino-German Exhibition of Contemporary Art," "Convergence at E 116°/N40°" at Chengdu Biennial and International Contemporary Art Exhibition. Feng Boyi is one of the most active and independent curators and art critics in China.

Feng Boyi
machte 1984 seinen Abschluss in Geschichte an der Universität Peking und lebt und arbeitet augenblicklich in der Hauptstadt. Er konzipiert Ausstellungen zeitgenössischer experimenteller Kunst in China, außerdem ist er Kritiker und Herausgeber. Zu seinen wichtigsten Ausstellungen gehören „Trace of Existence: A Private Show of Contemporary Chinese Art" (1998), „First Triennial – Exhibition of Contemporary Art in Guangzhou" (2002), „The Left Hand and the Right Hand – a Sino-German Exhibition of Contemporary Art" (2005) und „Convergence at E 116°/N40°" bei der Chengdu Biennale und International Contemporary Art Exhibition. Feng Boyi zählt heute zu den renommiertesten unabhängigen Kuratoren und Kunstkritikern Chinas.

Feng Boyi, 出生于北京 1984年毕业于首都师范大学历史系 现生活工作于北京。致力于中国当代实验艺术的策划、评论、编辑等工作。撰写有几十万字的论文、评论文章。策划的重要展览有："生存痕迹——98中国当代艺术内部观摩展"、"不合作方式"展、"首届广州当代艺术三年展"、"左手与右手——中、德当代艺术展"、"进与出，或之间——空间位移的N种方式"当代艺术展、成都双年展、"东经116 与北纬40 的聚落"国际当代艺术展、"今日中国－中国当代艺术的转世魅影展"等。是为中国目前最活跃的独立策展人和评论家之一

Uta Grosenick
studied Art History, German Language and Literature and Dramatics at Cologne and Paris. She has worked as exhibition manager at the Deichtorhallen Hamburg and the Bundeskunsthalle in Bonn, and was curator at the Kunstmuseum Wolfsburg. She has edited "Art at the Turn of the Millennium" (1999), "Women Artists" (2001), "Art Now" (2002), and "Art Now Vol 2" (2005). Since 2006 she is working as Managing Editor at DuMont publishers in Cologne, for whom she co-authored "International Art Galleries: Post-war to Post-millennium" (2005). Her latest publications are "China Art Book", and "Photo-Art," a survey of 112 young photo artists.

Uta Grosenick
studierte Kunstgeschichte, Germanistik und Theaterwissenschaften in Köln und Paris. Sie hat als Ausstellungsorganisatorin an den Hamburger Deichtorhallen und der Bundeskunsthalle in Bonn gearbeitet und war Kuratorin am Kunstmuseum Wolfsburg. Sie hat „Art at the Turn of the Millennium" (1999), „Women Artists" (2001), „Art Now" (2002) sowie „Art Now Vol 2" (2005) herausgegeben. Seit 2006 ist sie programmverantwortliche Lektorin beim Kölner DuMont Verlag, für den sie „Insight Inside – Galerien 1945 bis heute" (2005) mitverfasst hat. Ihre neuesten Publikationen sind „China Art Book" und „Photo Art – Fotokunst im 21. Jahrhundert", ein Überblick über 112 junge Foto-Künstler.

Uta Grosenick, 学习艺术史，德语，文学和戏剧在巴黎和科隆。她曾担任过德国汉堡Deichtorhallen的策展人，波恩的德国联邦共和国艺术中心任项目经理，沃尔夫斯堡艺术博物馆的馆长。曾编辑《艺术在世纪千年转折时》(1999)，《女性艺术家》(2001年)，《艺术现在时》(2002年)，《艺术现在时 2》(2005年). 自2006年起，任科隆DuMont出版社总编辑，与人合著《国际画廊：从战后到新千年后》(2005年). 最新出版物有《CHINA ART BOOK》和 《PHOTO ART》，该书介绍了112位年轻摄影艺术家。

Birgit Hopfener
reads Art History and Chinese studies in Berlin and Nanjing and works as a freelance curator and cultural correspondent in China and Germany. In recent years this included working as a project consultant in the "Beijing Case" project initiated by the German Federal Cultural Foundation in cooperation with the Beijing Goethe-Institut, as scientific and curatorial assistant at the Center of Art and Media Karlsruhe (ZKM) Museum of Contemporary Art as well as curator of the exhibition "Great Expectations" at the OCAT Center for Contemporary Art in Shenzhen. Currently she is working on a dissertation on the subject of "Chinese installation art."

Birgit Hopfener
studierte Kunstgeschichte und Sinologie in Berlin und Nanjing und ist heute in China und Deutschland als freie Kuratorin und Kulturvermittlerin tätig. Zuletzt war sie Projektreferentin bei dem von der Kulturstiftung des Bundes in Zusammenarbeit mit dem Goethe-Institut Peking organisierten Projekt „Beijing Case" und wissenschaftliche Mitarbeiterin und kuratorische Assistentin im ZKM | Museum für Neue Kunst in Karlsruhe sowie Kuratorin der Ausstellung „Great Expectations" im OCAT Center for Contemporary Art in Shenzhen. Zurzeit arbeitet Birgit Hopfener an ihrer Dissertation zum Thema „Chinesische Installationskunst".

Birgit Hopfener，何波娜 在柏林和中国南京学习历史学和汉学，现在她是独立策展人以及为中德文化交流人。最近几年，何波娜在由德国联邦文化基金会和北京歌德学院合作项目《北京案件》中担任项目经理，是德国艺术与媒体中心的研究学者和项目经理，策划了深圳当代艺术中心举办的《大世界》展览。如今她在完成一项名为《中国装置艺术的》的学术研究.

Gregor Jansen
has a PhD in fine arts and is currently director of ZKM | Museum of Contemporary Art. He has worked as a curator, tutor, art critic and journalist since 1991. He was curator of numerous exhibitions on contemporary and Asian art, and project manager for the exhibition "Iconoclash" at the ZKM in 2002 organised by Bruno Latour and Peter Weibel. Jansen was also curator for "Beijing Case," a scholarship program initiated by the German Federal Cultural Foundation for exploring international urban development in mega-cities. The results were incorporated into an exhibition "totalstadt. beijing case" at the ZKM in autumn 2006.

Gregor Jansen
ist promovierter Kunstwissenschaftler und Leiter des ZKM | Museum für Neue Kunst Karlsruhe. Er arbeitet seit 1991 als Kurator, Dozent, Kunstkritiker und Publizist. Er war Kurator zahlreicher Ausstellungen zur Kunst der Gegenwart und zur asiatischen Kunst sowie Projektleiter der von Bruno Latour und Peter Weibel ausgerichteten Ausstellung „Iconoclash" am ZKM 2002. Für das von der Kulturstiftung des Bundes initiierte Stipendienprogramm zur Erforschung internationaler urbaner Entwicklungen in Megacities war er Kurator der Ausstellung „totalstadt. beijing case", 2006, am ZKM.

Gregor Jansen，格里格•杨森拥有美术学博士学位，现在是德国艺术与媒体中心的总监。从1991年起他以策展人、导师、艺术评论家和记者的身份工作着。格里格•杨森策划了众多关于当代艺术和亚洲艺术的展览，并在2002年在德国艺术与媒体中心由布鲁诺•拉图尔、彼得•魏贝尔策划的展览《Iconoclash》中担任项目经理。他还是德国联邦文化基金会和北京歌德学院合作项目《北京现场》的策展人。此项目的目的在探索大城市的国际化发展。北京常常是城市爆炸性增长的一个例子。城市过快增长使城市文化面临着传统与现代化发展冲突的考验。2006年秋期　最终的结果被融合入在德国艺术与媒体中心举行的展览《整体城市：北京案件》中。

Carol Yinghua Lu
Curator and art writer based in Beijing. Executive Editor of "Contemporary Art & Investment," a monthly Chinese language art magazine. As a graduate of the "Critical Studies" programme at the Malmö Art Academy, Lund University in Sweden, she was the China researcher for the Asia Art Archive from 2005 to 2007. She was curator for a number of exhibitions, like, "Image Beyond Image" (2004) in the Rooseum Center for Contemporary Art in Malmö, "Made in China" (2004) in the Asian Art Museum in Stockholm, two independent projects in ARCO'06 and ARCO'07 in Madrid and so on. She is currently working on an ongoing exhibition series under the theme of "People's Park." Carol Lu continuously writes and contributes to various international art magazines such as "Contemporary," "Tema Celeste," "Art AsiaPacific," "Yishu" among others.

Carol Yinghua Lu
ist Kuratorin und Autorin für Kunstthemen mit Hauptwohnsitz in Peking und Herausgeberin von „Contemporary Art & Investment", einem monatlich erscheinenden Kunstmagazin in chinesischer Sprache. Zunächst Absolventin des Programms „Critical Studies" der Malmö Art Academy, Universität Lund, Schweden, war Carol Lu von 2005 bis 2007 als China-Rechercheurin für das Asia Art Archive tätig. Sie hat eine Reihe von Ausstellungen als Kuratorin betreut, u. a. „Image Beyond Image" (2004) für das Rooseum Center for Contemporary Art in Malmö, „Made in China" (2004) für das Asian Art Museum in Stockholm, zwei unabhängige Projekte im Rahmen der ARCO'06 und ARCO'07 in Madrid. Zurzeit arbeitet sie an einer laufenden Ausstellungsreihe zum Thema „People's Park", außerdem schreibt sie regelmäßig für verschiedene internationale Kunstmagazine, wie „Contemporary", „Tema Celeste", „Art AsiaPacific", „Yishu".

Carol Lu，　卢迎华　北京的独立策展人和艺术作家，中文艺术杂志《当代艺术与投资》的执行编辑，毕业于瑞典隆德大学马尔默美术学院批评研究专业。卢迎华策划了许多展览，如在瑞典马尔默Rooseum美术馆的《象外之象》，斯德哥尔摩亚洲艺术美术馆《中国制造》2006和2007年马德里艺术博览会的两个独立项目以及《捕捉器》等等。她是2005年到2007年亚洲艺术文献库中国研究员。她现在正在策划组织主题为《人民公园》的一系列展出。卢迎华不断地为《当代》，《天堂的主题》，《亚太艺术》和《艺术》等多家媒体撰写投稿，并为许多艺术展会编写展册和出版物

Victoria Yung-Chih Lu
was born into a Shanghainese literati family in Taiwan. She emigrated to the U.S. in the early 1970s. She attended both the College of Chinese Culture in Taipei and the Académie Royale des Beaux-Arts in Brussels but received her B.A. and M.A. degrees from California State University, majoring in painting. She started writing art criticism in the mid 1970s for some Taiwanese newspapers and magazines. She began her curatorial career at the end of 1978 as the director/curator of the alternative space Stage One Gallery in southern California, showing mainly conceptual and installation art. Later, she returned to Taiwan, helping the government to establish policies regarding public art and the promotion of art education to the general public. Victoria Lu is the first female art critic and curator in the Chinese contemporary art world, and currently a professor at the Fashion and Media Design Graduate School of Shih-Chien University in Taipei and Art History Department of Shanghai University. She also serves as the Creative Director of the Museum of Contemporary Art in Shanghai to build a private contemporary art exhibition in China.

Victoria Yung-Chih Lu
kam in Taiwan als Kind einer Shanghaier Literatenfamilie zur Welt. Anfang der 1970er Jahre wanderte sie in die USA aus. Sie hat das College of Chinese Culture in Taipei und die Académie Royale des Beaux-Arts in Brüssel besucht; ihre Bachelor- und Master-Abschlüsse machte sie an der California State University, wo sie im Hauptfach Malerei studierte. Mitte der 1970er Jahre begann sie, Kunstkritiken für verschiedene taiwanesische Zeitungen und Magazine zu schreiben. Ihre Laufbahn als Kuratorin startete sie Ende 1978 als Leiterin der alternativen Stage One Gallery in Südkalifornien, die vorwiegend Konzept- und Installationskunst zeigte. Später kehrte Lu nach Taiwan zurück und unterstützte die Regierung bei der Vermittlung zeitgenössischer Kunst. Victoria Lu ist die erste Kunstkritikerin und Kuratorin der zeitgenössischen chinesischen Kunstszene. Sie ist Dozentin an der Fashion and Media Design Graduate School der Shih-Chien University in Taipei sowie am Fachbereich Kunstgeschichte der Shanghai University. Außerdem wirkt sie als Kreativdirektorin des Museum of Contemporary Art in Shanghai daran mit, eine private Sammlung von Gegenwartskunst in China aufzubauen.

Victoria Yung-Chih Lu，　陆蓉之　祖籍上海，出生于台湾，1970年代初期移民美国。曾就学于台湾中国文化大学、比利时布鲁塞尔皇家艺术学院，在美国加卅卅立大学获得艺术学士与硕士，主攻绘画。1970年代中期开始为台湾的艺术杂志、报纸撰写艺术评述文章，1978年底在美国南加卅创办以观念装置艺术为主的替代空间画廊，担任策展人的工作，日后在台湾推动公共艺术立法和当代艺术的教育推广而活跃于台湾艺坛，是中国当代艺术圈内中文书写最早的女性艺评家及策展人。陆蓉之目前是台北实践大学时尚与媒体研究所教授、上海大学史论系客座教授，同时担任上海当代艺术馆创意总监，打造中国第一家私营的当代艺术馆。

Barbara Pollack
is an artist and writer based in New York, engaged in contemporary art since 1988. She was the editor of the "ARTnewsletter" from 1994 to 1997. Since then, as contributing editor to "ARTnews" magazine and as a freelance journalist, she has written extensively on the art market and issues in contemporary art for an extensive range of publications, including the "Village Voice," "Art in America," the "New York Times," "Art & Auction," "Modern Painters" and "Art Review." Specifically, she provided coverage of the developing art scene in China for these and other publications since 1998 and is currently researching a book on developing art centers in China funded by a grant from the Asian Cultural Council. Barbara Pollack has written catalogue essays for Chi Peng, Luo Xu, and Lin Tianmiao, among many other artists. She is also a professor of contemporary theory and photography at the New York School of Visual Arts.

Qiu Zhijie
completed in 1992 his BFA at the Zhejiang Academy of Fine Arts, Hangzhou and is now teaching as a professor at China Academy of Art, Hangzhou. As an experimental artist, Qiu explores a vast array of media. He is also a curator, art critic, and professor at the Zhejiang Academy of Fine Arts. Qiu has worked as performer, photographer, video-artist, painter and print maker. Among his works, the photographic series "Tattoo I" and "Tattoo II" (1997) are especially well known. Qiu has exhibited his works at the 1992 exhibition "Concern to the New Life," Museum of National Academy of Fine Art, Huangzhou, China, and at group exhibitions as "Between Past and Future: New Photography and Video from China," International Center of Photography, New York, USA (2004), and the 50th Venice Biennial, Italy, in 2003.

Caspar H. Schübbe
Studied law and art history. Active as construction developer and start-up financier. Initiator of a sculpture park and museum in canton Wallis, Switzerland. Lives in Verbier, Switzerland, and is active worldwide.

Karen Smith
a British citizen, lives and works in Beijing since 1992. She is specialized in contemporary Chinese art. Her curatorial work encloses exhibitions like "The Chinese: Photography and Video from China," 2004, Kunstmuseum Wolfsburg, Germany, and "The Real Thing: Contemporary Art from China," 2007, Tate Liverpool, UK. Her work as art critic and writer comprises essays, research and analysis of contemporary Chinese art for magazines and exhibition catalogues. Smith is contributing critic for "Beijing Time Out," and published "Nine Lives: The Birth of Avant-Garde Art in New China" at Scalo publishers, Zurich, in 2006. A second book is in progress, "From Bang to Boom: Chinese Art in the 1990s," which explores this formative decade of contemporary art practice that is the foundation of the entire China art world today.

David Spalding
graduated 1994 with the bachelor's degree with the subject classical and critical theory from Saint Mary's College of California in Los Angeles. For a short time he is curator at the Ullens Centre for Contemporary Art in Beijing, which will be opened in autumn 2007. Spalding is China correspondent for magazines like "Artforum", "Contemporary", and "Art Papers".

Barbara Pollack
lebt als Künstlerin und Autorin in New York und ist seit 1988 in der Kunstszene aktiv. Von 1994 bis 1997 war sie Herausgeberin des „ARTnewsletter". Seitdem hat sie als Redakteurin des Magazins „ARTnews" und als freie Journalistin zahlreiche Beiträge über den Kunstmarkt und Themen der Gegenwartskunst für verschiedenste Publikationen verfasst, darunter „Village Voice", „Art in America", die „New York Times", „Art & Auction", „Modern Painters" und „Art Review". Insbesondere berichtet sie schon seit 1998 über die Entwicklung der chinesischen Kunstszene. Zurzeit recherchiert sie mit finanzieller Unterstützung des Asian Cultural Council für ein Buch über sich neu entwickelnde Kunstzentren in China. Sie hat für Kataloge Essays über Chi Peng, Luo Xu, Lin Tianmiao und zahlreiche andere Künstler verfasst. Außerdem ist Barbara Pollack Dozentin für zeitgenössische Theorie und Fotografie an der School of Visual Arts in New York.

Qiu Zhijie
machte 1992 seinen BFA-Abschluss an der Zhejiang Academy of Fine Arts, Hangzhou. Heute ist er Dozent an der China Academy of Art, ebenfalls in Hangzhou. Als experimenteller Künstler arbeitet Qiu mit verschiedenen Medien. Er ist außerdem als Kurator und Kunstkritiker sowie als Dozent an der Zhejiang Academy of Fine Arts tätig. Qiu hat als Performancekünstler, Fotograf, Videokünstler, Maler und Grafiker gewirkt. Seine bekanntesten Werke sind die Fotoserien „Tattoo I" und „Tattoo II" (1997). Seine Arbeiten waren 1992 in der Ausstellung „Concern to the New Life", Museum of National Academy of Fine Art, Huangzhou, China, sowie auf Gruppenausstellungen wie „Between Past and Future: New Photography and Video from China", im International Center of Photography, New York, USA (2004), und auf der 50. Biennale von Venedig 2003 zu sehen.

Caspar H. Schübbe
studierte Jura und Kunstgeschichte. Er ist als Bauentwickler und Start-up-Finanzierer tätig und ist Initiator eines Skulpturenparks und Museums im Kanton Wallis. Caspar H. Schübbe lebt in Verbier, Schweiz, und arbeitet weltweit.

Karen Smith
ist geborene Britin und lebt und arbeitet seit 1992 in Peking. Die chinesische Gegenwartskunst ist ihr Spezialgebiet. Als Kuratorin hat sie u. a. Ausstellungen wie „Die Chinesen: Fotografie und Video aus China" (2004), Kunstmuseum Wolfsburg, und „The Real Thing: Contemporary Art from China" (2007), Tate Liverpool, Großbritannien, betreut. Ihr Werk als Kunstkritikerin und Autorin umfasst Artikel, Recherchen und Analysen zur chinesischen Gegenwartskunst für Magazine und Ausstellungskataloge. Smith ist als Kritikerin für „Beijing Time Out" tätig und veröffentlichte 2006 die Untersuchung „Nine Lives: The Birth of Avant-Garde Art in New China". Ein zweites Buch – „From Bang to Boom: Chinese Art in the 1990s" – ist in Arbeit und beleuchtet jenes prägende Jahrzehnt, das den Grundstein für die aktuelle chinesische Kunstszene legte.

David Spalding
machte 1994 seinen Bachelor in klassischer und kritischer Theorie am Saint Mary's College of California in Los Angeles. Seit kurzem ist er Kurator am Ullens Center for Contemporary Art in Peking, das im Herbst 2007 eröffnet wird. Spalding schreibt als China-Korrespondent für die Magazine „Artforum", „Contemporary" und „Art Papers".

Barbara Pollack, 巴巴拉 • 波洛克 巴巴拉 • 波洛克来自纽约，艺术家，作家。自1988年起投身于当代艺术。1994年到1997年她是《艺术通讯》的编辑，从那时起作为《艺术通讯》的特约编辑和自由记者，为许多出版物撰写了大量艺术市场和当代艺术主题的文章，包括《村声周报》、《美国艺术》、《纽约时代杂志》、《艺术与拍卖》、《现代画家》和《艺术评论》尤其是，自1998起就为上述的杂志和其他出版物报道了发展中的中国艺术界。如今在亚洲文化协会的大力资助下，她正在调查撰写一本关于发展中的中国艺术中心的书。她已经为迟鹏，罗旭、林天苗等许多艺术家撰写了目录文章。巴巴拉还是视觉艺术学院的当代理论和摄影教授。巴巴拉还是视觉艺术学院的当代理论和摄影教授。

Qiu Zhijie, 出生于福建省。1992年从浙江美院毕业，获取美术学士学位，现为中国美院教授。作为试验艺术家，邱志杰探索了许多材料的创作。也是策展人，评论家和中国美院教授。邱志杰曾为行为艺术家，摄影师，视频艺术家，画家和版画复制师。其作品中，尤以摄影系列作品《纹身I》和《纹身 2》(1997年) 著名。邱展出了许多展览，如个展（Ethan Cohen 画廊，纽约美国），《关于新生活》（中国美院美术馆，杭州，中国（1992年）；群展有：《过去和未来之间： 中国新影展》（国际摄影中心，纽约，美国 （2004年） 和第50届威尼斯双年展意大利（2003年）。

Caspar H. Schübbe, 研究法律和艺术史。曾为房产开发商和启动资金筹集人。在瑞士瓦莱创建了一座雕塑公园和博物馆。现居瓦莱，在全球范围内活动。

Karen Smith, 英国人，自1992年在北京居住工作。. 她专门致力于中国当代艺术的研究。其展览的评论作品有：《国人—当代摄影摄像艺术展》(2004年沃尔夫斯堡美术馆 德国)、《真实事件：中国当代艺术》(2007年 泰特美术馆 利物浦 英国)。她的作品有艺术评论，以及为杂志和展会展册撰写了以中国当代艺术为主题的文章，研究和分析研究等。Smith 现为《乐-北京》杂志撰写评论文章，2006年出版了《当代艺术的九个文化英雄》（Scalo出版社，苏黎世）第二部著作《From Bang to Boom: Chinese Art in the 1990s》正在筹划之中，该书探索了当代艺术实践发展的十年，为整个中国艺术世界奠定了基础。

David Spalding, 丁达韦 1994年 获洛杉矶加州大学圣玛丽学院古典评论理学士学位，为北京尤伦斯当代艺术中心策展人，该馆将于2007年秋天开馆。丁达韦还是《艺术论坛》，《当代》，《美术论文》等杂志的中国通讯作者。

Philip Tinari
is a writer and curator based in Beijing. Tinari holds an M.A. in East Asian studies from Harvard (2005) and was Fulbright fellow at Peking University (2001/02). He is a frequent contributor to "Artforum," and his texts on contemporary art in China have appeared in publications including "The New York Times Magazine," "The Wall Street Journal," "Art AsiaPacific," and the Chinese journal "Dushu." He is China Advisor to Art Basel and academic consultant to Sotheby's Hong Kong. He was founding curator of Long March Space in Beijing and an editor of the English catalogue accompanying the First Guangzhou Triennial (2002). Tinari holds an M.A. in East Asian studies from Harvard (2005) and was Fulbright fellow at Peking University (2001-02). In 2007, he founded Office for Discourse Engineering, an editorial studio focused on research, publishing, and translation, which is currently editing "U-TURN," a periodical presenting the major movements and moments of the last thirty years of contemporary art in China.

Philip Tinari
lebt als Autor und Kurator in Peking. Er hat einen Master in East Asian Studies von der Harvard University (2005) und war als Fulbright-Stipendiat an der Peking University (2001/02). Er schreibt regelmäßig für „Artforum", und seine Texte über die chinesische Gegenwartskunst sind in zahlreichen Publikationen erschienen, u. a. im „New York Times Magazine", im „Wall Street Journal", in „Art AsiaPacific" und im chinesischen Journal „Dushu". Tinari ist China-Berater der Art Basel und akademischer Berater von Sotheby's Hong Kong. Außerdem war er mitbegründender Kurator des Long March Space in Peking und Redakteur des englischen Katalogs zur First Guangzhou Triennial (2002). 2007 gründete Tinari das Office for Discourse Engineering, ein Redaktionsbüro für Recherche, redaktionelle Betreuung und Übersetzungen, das „U-TURN" herausgibt, ein Magazin, das die großen Bewegungen und Momente der vergangenen 30 Jahre der chinesischen Gegenwartskunst präsentiert.

Philip Tinari, 现居北京，作家、策展人。他常为《艺术论坛》撰稿，其关于中国艺术文章曾发表于《纽约时报》，《华尔街日报》，《亚太艺术》以及中国《读书》杂志上。现为巴塞尔艺术节中国顾问，香港索思比的学术顾问。曾任北京 长征空间的创始策展人的创始策展人，2002年是首届广州三年展展册英文版编辑。硕士毕业于哈佛大学东亚文化研究专业，在2001-2002年是北京大学富布来特项目的参与者。2007年，成立 话坊，以研究、出版和翻译为主的编辑室。该机构现正编辑《U-TURN》，作品展示过去三十年间 中国当代艺术的长期趋势和运动。

Wu Hung
is the founder and director of the Center for the Art of East Asia at the University of Chicago, the Consulting Curator at the Smart Museum, and the Harrie A. Vanderstappen Distinguished Service Professor in Chinese Art History at the Department of Art History and the Department of East Asian Languages and Civilizations at that university. In 1998 and 2000 Wu Hung was curator of "Transience: Chinese Experimental Art at the End of the Twentieth Century," and "Canceled: Exhibiting Experimental Art in China". He was the chief curator of the First Guangzhou Triennial (2002). His more recent curatorial projects include "Between Past and Future: New Photography and Video from China" (International Center of Photography, New York, 2004), and "About Beauty" (2005) in Berlin's Haus der Kulturen der Welt. Wu Hungs publications on contemporary art include "Chinese Art at the Crossroads: Between Past and Future, Between East and West" (Hong Kong 2001), and "Remaking Beijing: Tiananmen Square and the Creation of Political Space" (London and Chicago 2005).

Wu Hung
ist Gründer und Direktor des Center for the Art of East Asia an der University of Chicago, beratender Kurator des Smart Museums und Inhaber des Harrie A. Vanderstappen-Ehrenlehrstuhls für chinesische Kunstgeschichte der Fachbereiche Kunstgeschichte und Ostasiatische Sprachen und Kulturen an der University of Chigaco. 1998 und 2000 kuratierte Wu Hung „Transience: Chinese Experimental Art at the End of the Twentieth Century" und „Canceled: Exhibiting Experimental Art in China". Wu war Chefkurator der First Guangzhou Triennial (2002). Zu seinen kuratorischen Projekten der jüngeren Zeit gehörten „Between Past and Future: New Photography and Video from China" (International Center of Photography, New York, 2004) und „About Beauty" (2005) im Berliner Haus der Kulturen der Welt. Wu Hung hat zahlreiche Katalogbeiträge geschrieben, u. a.: „Chinese Art at the Crossroads: Between Past and Future, Between East and West" (Hongkong 2001) und „Remaking Beijing: Tiananmen Square and the Creation of Political Space" (London und Chicago 2005).

Wu Hung, 巫鸿为芝加哥大学东亚艺术中心创始人、主任，美国芝加哥大学亚洲艺术系讲座教授、芝加哥大学斯马特美术馆顾问策展人. 他也是美国艺术与科学学院当选委员。1998 年到 2000年间，巫鸿策展了《瞬间：中国二十世纪末实验艺术展》和《被取缔：实验美术展览在中国》。他曾为首届广州三年展《重新解读：中国实验艺术十年（1990——2000年）》的首席策展人。近期的策展项目有《过去和将来之间：中国新摄影新录像艺术展》(国际摄影中心和 Smart美术馆)，《‘美’的协商》(世界文化宫, 柏林）和一系列重要中国当代艺术的新作展。巫鸿当代艺术的著作有《字路口的中国艺术：在过去和未来之间，在东方和西方之间》(香港： New Art Media, 2001年)，《荣荣的东村》(纽约，Chambers Fine Arts, 2003年)，《徐冰的烟草计划》(北京 2006年) 和《重建北京：天安门和一个政治空间的开创》(伦敦和芝加哥：Reaktion Books出版社和芝加哥大学出版社, 2005年)。

PICTURE CREDITS/ACKNOWLEDGEMENT
BILDNACHWEIS/DANKSAGUNG
摄影/感谢

We would like to thank all artists, individual people and galleries who placed photographs and information at our disposal for CHINA ART BOOK.
Unser Dank gilt allen Künstlern, Personen und Galerien, die uns Bildmaterial und Informationen zur Verfügung gestellt haben.
我们在《中国当代艺术》一书中使用了许多照片和相关信息，我们在此向所有相关艺术家，个人和画廊表示感谢。

Ai Weiwei – 1–3 Courtesy Galerie Urs Meile, Beijing/Lucerne, 4 + 6 Courtesy the artist, 5 Courtesy Sigg Collection, 7 Courtesy melchior art, Canada
Cai Guo-Qiang – 1, 3 + 4 Courtesy Caspar H. Schübbe, Switzerland, 2 + 5 Courtesy the artist and Deutsche Deutsche Bank AG, 6 Courtesy the artist, 2 + 5 Photos: Hiro Ihara
Cang Xin – 1–3, 5–9 Courtesy the artist, 4 Courtesy The Saatchi Gallery, London
Cao Fei – 1–3 Courtesy melchior art, Canada, 4–8 Courtesy Vitamin Creative Space, Guangzhou
Chen Shaoxiong – 1–9 Courtesy the artist
Chen Zhen – © VG Bild-Kunst, Bonn 2007, 1–3, 5–8 Courtesy the estate of the artist and Galleria Continua, San Gimignano/Beijing, 4 Courtesy melchior art, Canada, 1 Photo: Wolfgang Günzel, 2 Photo: Eric Angels, 3 + 4 Photos: Ela Bialkowska, 5 Photo: Chen Zhen, 6 Photo: Wang An Ping, 7 Photo: Chen Zhen and Guang Huai Bing
Cui Xiuwen – 1–8 Courtesy the artist
Fang Lijun – 1–5 Courtesy The Saatchi Gallery, London, 6 + 7 Courtesy Alexander Ochs Galleries, Berlin/Beijing and the artist, 8 Courtesy melchior art, Canada
Feng Mengbo – 1–4 Courtesy the artist and ShanghART, Shanghai
Feng Zhengjie – 1, 7–9 Courtesy The Saatchi Gallery, London, 2, 3–6, 10 Courtesy Wedel Fine Art, London
Geng Jianyi – 1–5 Courtesy ShanghART, Shanghai
Gu Dexin – 1 Courtesy melchior art, Canada, 2–5 Courtesy the artist and Galleria Continua, San Gimignano/Beijing
Gu Wenda – 1–7 Courtesy the artist
Hong Hao – 1–6 Courtesy the artist
Hu Xiaoyuan – 1–8 Courtesy the artist
Huang Yan – 1–9 Courtesy the artist
Huang Yong Ping – © VG Bild-Kunst, Bonn 2007, 1 Courtesy Caspar H. Schübbe, Switzerland, 2 + 3 Courtesy the artist, 4–6 Courtesy Gladstone Gallery, New York, 7 Courtesy Walker Art Center, Minneapolis, and Gladstone Gallery, New York, 4–6 Photos: David Regen, 7 Photo: Gene Pittman
Ji Dachun – 1–9 Courtesy Wedel Fine Art, London
Ji Wenyu – 1–8 Courtesy ShanghART, Shanghai
Kan Xuan – 1–5 Courtesy the artist
Li Songsong – 1–3, 8 Courtesy The Saatchi Gallery, London, 4 Courtesy Sigg Collection, 5–7 Courtesy Galerie Urs Meile, Beijing/Lucerne
Lin Tianmiao – 1–8 Courtesy the artist
Liu Ding – 1–6 Courtesy the artist and 1, 5 + 6 Courtesy UniversalStudios, Beijing, 2 Courtesy Grace Li Gallery, Zurich, 3 + 4 Courtesy L. A. Galerie Lothar Albrecht, Frankfurt a. M.
Liu Jianhua – 1 Caspar H. Schübbe, Switzerland, 2–7 Courtesy Wedel Fine Art, London
Liu Wei – 1–4 Courtesy Sigg Collection
Liu Wei – 1 + 2 The Saatchi Gallery, London, 3 Courtesy Long March Space, Beijing, 4 + 5 Courtesy the artist

Liu Xiaodong – 1–7 Courtesy the artist
Liu Ye – 1, 2, 4 + 6 Courtesy the artist, 3, 5, 7–9 Courtesy Sperone Westwater, New York, Portrait photo: Cao Yong
Liu Zheng – 1–8 Courtesy the artist and Pékin Fine Arts, Beijing
Lu Chunsheng – 1–7 Courtesy ShanghART, Shanghai
Ma Liuming – 1–5, 7–9 Courtesy the artist, 6 Courtesy Chinese Contemporary, Beijing/London/New York
Miao Xiaochun – 1–3 Courtesy The Saatchi Gallery, London, 4–7 Courtesy Alexander Ochs Galleries, Berlin/Beijing and the artist
Qiu Anxiong – 1–5 Courtesy the artist
Qiu Jie – 1, 3–6 Courtesy Wedel Fine Art, London, 2 Courtesy The Saatchi Gallery, London
Qiu Shihua – 1 + 2, 4 Courtesy Galerie Luis Campaña, Cologne, 3 Courtesy Galerie Urs Meile, Beijing/Lucerne, 5 + 6 Courtesy Sigg Collection, 1 + 2, 4 Photos: Achim Kukulies
Qiu Xiaofei – 1–6 Courtesy Wedel Fine Art, London
Qiu Zhijie – 1–8 Courtesy the artist
RongRong & Inri – 1–12 Courtesy Alexander Ochs Galleries, Berlin/Beijing and the artists
Shen Shaomin – 1, 3 + 4 Courtesy The Saatchi Gallery, London, 2 Courtesy melchior art, Canada, 5 + 6 Courtesy Wedel Fine Art, London
Shi Jinsong – 1, 4–9 Courtesy the artist and Chambers Fine Art, New York, 2 + 3 Courtesy The Saatchi Gallery, London
Shi Xinning – 1, 6 + 8 Courtesy Wedel Fine Art, London, 2–5 Courtesy The Saatchi Gallery, London, 7 Courtesy Sigg Collection
Shi Yong – 1–7 Courtesy the artist and ShanghART, Shanghai
Song Dong – 1 Courtesy Sigg Collection, 2, 5 + 6 Courtesy the artist, 3 Courtesy Wedel Fine Art London, 4 Courtesy Chambers Fine Art, New York
Song Kun – 1–8 Courtesy the artist and UniversalStudios, Beijing
Song Tao – 1–5 Courtesy ShanghART, Shanghai
Sui Jianguo – 1–9 Courtesy the artist
Sun Xun – 1–7 Courtesy Wedel Fine Art, London
Wang Du – © VG Bild-Kunst, Bonn 2007, 1, 3–5 Courtesy the artist, 2 Sigg Collection, 6 Galerie Laurent Godin, Paris
Wang Gongxin – 1–13 Courtesy the artist and Pékin Fine Arts, Beijing
Wang Guangyi – 1, 3, 4 + 6 Courtesy The Saatchi Gallery, London, 2 + 5 Courtesy the artist, 7 + 8 Courtesy Caspar H. Schübbe, Switzerland, 9 Courtesy Sigg Collection
Wang Jianwei – 1–6 Courtesy the artist
Wang Qingsong – 1 Pékin Fine Arts, Beijing, 2–9 Courtesy the artist
Wang Xingwei – 1 + 2 Courtesy Sigg Collection, 3–8 Courtesy Galerie Urs Meile, Beijing/Lucerne
Weng Fen – 1–11 Courtesy the artist
Wu Shanzhuan – 1–11 Courtesy Hanart, Hong Kong, 9 Photo: Maike Klein
Xie Nanxing – 1, 3–5, 7, 8 Courtesy Galerie Urs Meile, Beijing/Lucerne, 2 + 6 Courtesy Sigg Collection
Xing Danwen – 1–6 Courtesy the artist
Xu Bing – 1–7 Courtesy the artist
Xu Tan – 1–7 Courtesy Vitamin Creative Space, Guangzhou
Xu Zhen – 1–5 Courtesy ShanghART, Shanghai
Yan Pei-Ming – Portrait Courtesy David Zwirner, New York, 1 Courtesy Galleria Massimo de Carlo, Milan, 2 + 6 Courtesy the artist, 3–5, 7 Courtesy Galleria Massimo de Carlo, Milan, and David Zwirner, New York, Portrait, 1–5, 7 Photos: André Morin, 6 Photo: Masahiro Handa
Yang Fudong – 1–5 Courtesy ShanghART, Shanghai
Yang Maoyuan – 1–9 Courtesy Alexander Ochs Galerie, Berlin, White Space, Beijing and the artist, 10 – 15 Courtesy White Space, Beijing, and the artist
Yang Shaobin – 1, 3, 8 + 9 Courtesy Alexander Ochs Galleries, Berlin/Beijing and the artist, 2 melchior art, Canada, 4–6 Courtesy Schoeni Art Gallery, Hong Kong, 7 Long March Space, Beijing
Yang Zhenzhong – 1–6 Courtesy the artist and ShanghART, Shanghai
Yin Xiuzhen – 1 – 4, 7 Courtesy Alexander Ochs Galleries, Berlin/Beijing and the artist, 5 Courtesy Earl Lu Gallery, Singapore, Fukuoka Art Musuem, Japan, Alexander Ochs Galleries Berlin/Beijing, 6 Courtesy Beijing Commune and Alexander Ochs Galleries Berlin | Beijing, 8 Courtesy Beijing Commune, Beijing
Yu Hong – 1–6 Courtesy Wedel Fine Art, London
Yue Minjun – 1 + 4 Courtesy The Saatchi Collection, London, 2 Courtesy Sigg Collection, 3, 5–7 Courtesy the artist
Zeng Fanzhi – 1–3, 5 Courtesy The Saatchi Collection, London, 4, 6 + 7 Courtesy Wedel Fine Art, London, 8 Courtesy Sigg Collection
Zhan Wang – 1, 3–7 Courtesy the artist, 2 Courtesy The Red Mansion Foundation, London
Zhang Dali – 1, 6 + 7 Courtesy The Saatchi Collection, London, 2–5, 8 Courtesy the artist
Zhang Huan – 1, 6, 8 + 9 Courtesy The Saatchi Collection, London, 2 + 4 Courtesy Caspar H. Schübbe, Switzerland, 3, 5, 7, 10 Courtesy the artist
Zhang Peili – 1 – 7 Courtesy the artist
Zhang Xiaogang – 1–3, 5, 6, 8 Courtesy The Saatchi Collection, London, 4 + 7 Courtesy the artist
Zhao Bandi – 1–13 Courtesy the artist and ShanghART, Shanghai
Zheng Guogu – 1, 4–6 Courtesy Vitamin Creative Space, Guangzhou, 2 Courtesy The Saatchi Collection, London, 3 Courtesy melchior art, Canada
Zhou Chunya – 1–13 Courtesy the artist and Chinese Contemporary, Beijing, London, New York
Zhou Tiehai – 1–12 Courtesy ShanghART, Shanghai
Zhou Xiaohu – 1 + 2, 4 + 5 Courtesy the artist, 3 Courtesy Sigg Collection
Zhu Ming – 1–6 Courtesy the artist

Editors/Herausgeber
Uta Grosenick, Caspar H. Schübbe

Art Consultant/Beratung
Amelie von Wedel, London

Assistance/Assistenz
Pei-fen Sung, Xiaolan Bi

Authors/Texte
Feng Boyi, Biljana Ciric, Uta Grosenick, Birgit Hopfener, Wu Hung, Gregor Jansen, Carol Yinghua Lu, Victoria Yung-Chih Lu, Barbara Pollack, Karen Smith, David Spalding, Philip Tinari, Qiu Zhijie

External editorial office and editorial coordination/Externes Lektorat und redaktionelle Koordination
Ralph Henry Fischer, Köln

Internal editorial office/Internes Lektorat
Sabine Bleßmann

Assistance/Assistenz
Ina Bierwagen

Translations from Chinese into German and English,
from German into English and Chinese as well as from English into Chinese
Übersetzung aus dem Chinesischen ins Deutsche und Englische,
aus dem Deutschen ins Englische und Chinesische sowie aus dem Englischen ins Chinesische
Hannelore Eisenhofer-Halim, Wei Xue

Translations from English into German/Übersetzung aus dem Englischen ins Deutsche
Inga-Brita Thiele

Editorial office for Chinese and English/Chinesische und englische Redaktion
Hannelore Eisenhofer-Halim, Stephen Manson

Design/Design
Jonas Lundin, SoulSupply, Stockholm

Layout/Layout
Birgit Haermeyer

Typesetting/Satz
Birgit Beyer, Köln

Production/Produktion
Marcus Muraro

Reproduction, print an binding/Reproduktion, Druck und Bindung
GZD Grafisches Zentrum Drucktechnik, Ditzingen

www.dumont-buchverlag.de

ISBN 978-3-8321-7769-0
Printed in Germany

出版人
Uta Grosenick, Caspar H. Schübbe

咨询顾问
Amelie von Wedel，伦敦

协助
Pei-fen Sung, Xiaolan Bi

撰稿
冯博一，Biljana Ciric，Uta Grosenick，Birgit Hopfener，巫鸿，Gregor Jansen，卢迎华（Carol Lu），Victoria Yung-Chih Lu，Barbara Pollack，Karen Smith，丁达韦（David Spalding），Philip Tinari，邱志杰

外部校对和编辑协调
Ralph Henry Fischer，科隆
内部校对
Sabine Bleßmann
协助
Ina Bierwagen

中德、中英、德英、德中及英中翻译
Hannelore Eisenhofer-Halim，薛巍
英德翻译
Inga-Brita Thiele

中文和英文编辑
Hannelore Eisenhofer-Halim, Stephen Manson

设计
Jonas Lundin, SoulSupply，斯德哥尔摩

内部图像
Birgit Haermeyer

外部图像
Birgit Beyer，科隆

制作
Marcus Muraro
图片影印
GZD Grafisches Zentrum Drucktechnik，迪琴根
印刷装订
GZD Grafisches Zentrum Drucktechnik，迪琴根

www.dumont-buchverlag.de

书号
ISBN 978-3-8321-7769-0

德国印刷

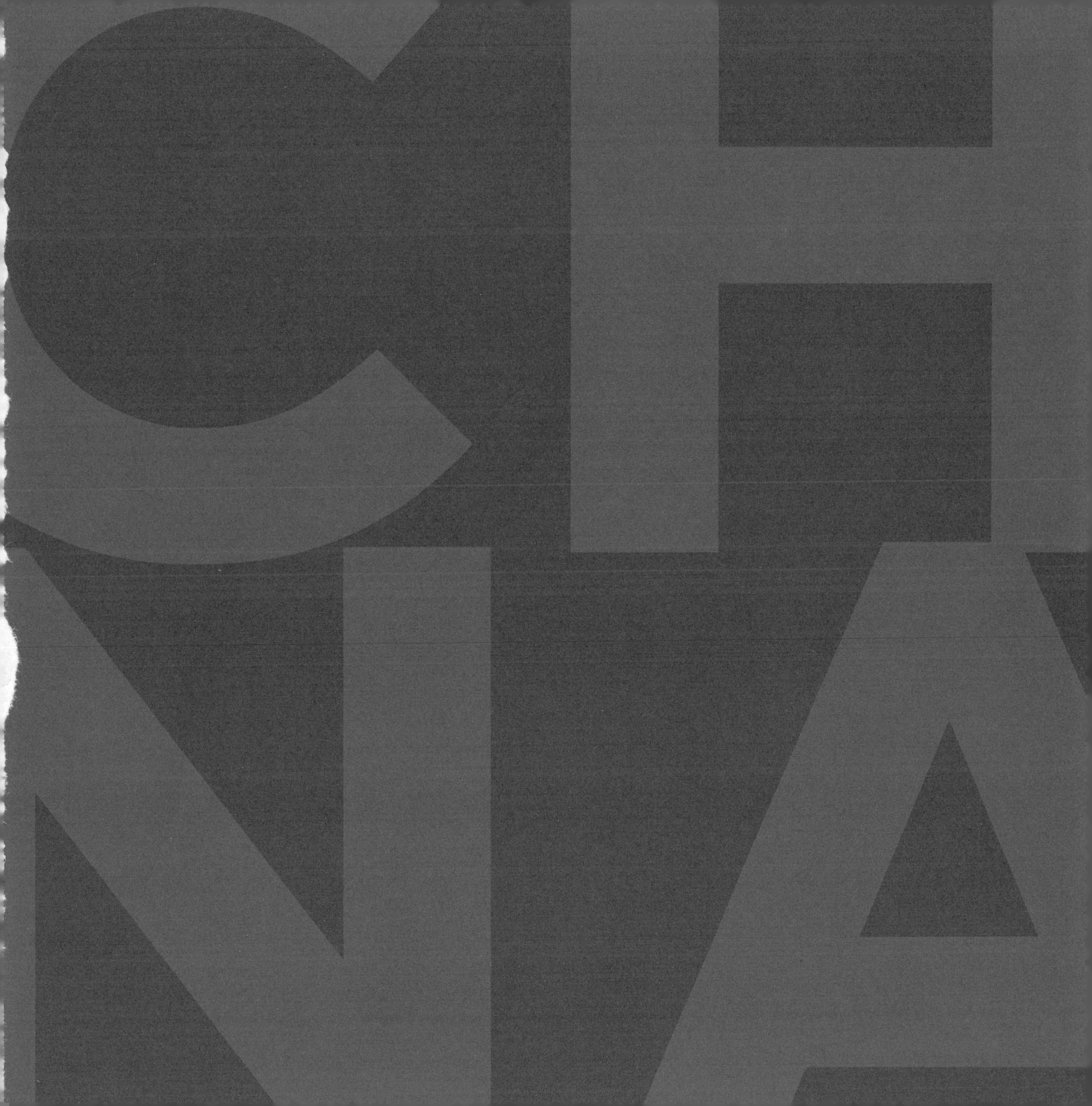

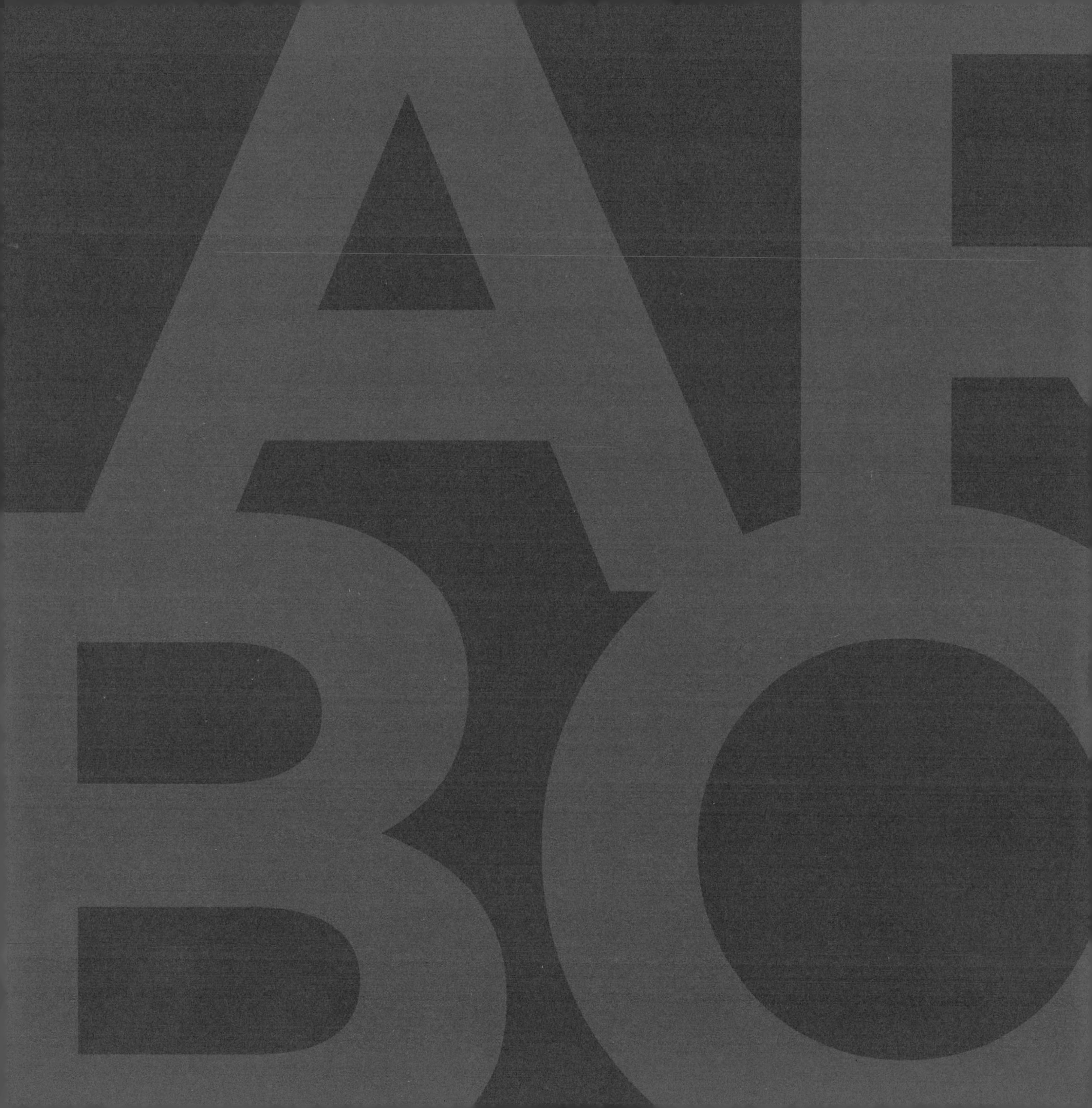